Brigitte Moore

Kristin Herzog

Sandra Boynton

1986 Artist's Market

1986 ARTIST'S MARKET®

WHERE TO SELL YOUR GRAPHIC ART

Edited by Diana Martin-Hoffman

Writer's
Digest
Books
Cincinnati, Ohio

Please Note:
If you are 1) a user of freelance design and illustration and would like to be considered for a listing in *Artist's Market 1987* or 2) a participating market or an artist interested in submitting freelance artwork for possible publication, material should be received by May 1, 1986. Contact: Editor, *Artist's Market*, 9933 Alliance Rd., Cincinnati OH 45242.

Distributed in Canada by Prentice-Hall of Canada Ltd., 1870 Birchmount Road, Scarborough, Ontario M1P 2J7 and in Australia and New Zealand by Bookwise (Aust.) Pty. Ltd., Box 296, Welland, S.A. 5007, Australia

Managing Editor, Market Books Department: Constance J. Achabal

International Standard Serial Number 0161-0546
International Standard Book Number 0-89879-200-2

Contents

The Profession

The Markets

Appendix

Glossary

Index

The Profession

Introduction

In today's art market you must possess one important key to unlock the door to freelance opportunities. *You must be an entrepreneur.* Whether you are a beginner or an established professional, an illustrator, cartoonist or designer, you must be as innovative and creative at finding assignments as you are at the drawing board.

In this twelfth edition of *Artist's Market*, with more than 2,500 listings of freelance art buyers, you will find the freelance assignment opportunities you seek! As the most comprehensive directory of graphic art information, *Artist's Market* offers you *more* than just a company name and address. Here you can learn the names of contact persons, art needs, payment methods, submission requirements and even "inside" tips from the markets you plan to approach.

And the 1986 *Artist's Market* is the biggest yet, containing 568 new listings, an increase of more than 25% over the 450 anticipated. All the new listings are marked with an *asterisk so you can locate them easily. Changes occur each year in freelance markets. In the returning listings there have been 87 company name changes, 287 address/phone changes, 434 contact person changes, 256 listings whose art needs are different and 214 changes in pay rates.

And there's more! Two fulltime, successful freelance artists authored the upfront articles, "Cartooning—Today's Marketplace" and "Breaking into Specialty Art Markets." These artists introduce you to the hot markets, the undiscovered markets and the growing markets—and they tell you how to approach them.

Well-known artists Mike Peters and Sandra Boynton are two of the ten Close-up artists featured throughout the book. These artists share with you their wisdom, humor and downright good sense learned from years of climbing the ladder of success.

And because the pictorial aspect of *Artist's Market* is so very important to you we have increased the number of illustrations from 35 to more than 65. You will find as much information as possible in each cutline about the specific assignment, what attracted the buyer to a particular art style or why the artwork was successful.

Near the end of the directory is the Glossary which defines unfamiliar words or phrases used within the book. The Appendix, titled "The Business of Freelancing," is your guide to contracts, samples, record keeping and other vital business knowhow. A valuable addition to this year's book is the Artist's Resource List located at the end of the Appendix. Listed there are 57 resources which give information on thousands of art buyers. To determine the market for which each publication is suited refer to the individual section introductions.

The book you hold in your hands *is* opportunity. It represents hopes, ideas and creations . . . and eventually dream-come-true publication and sales. Armed with talent and a heavy dose of determination and persistence, all you—the entrepreneur—have to do now is turn the page.

—*Diana Martin-Hoffman*

Using Your Artist's Market

The listings in this book are more than names and addresses. Included is information on whom to contact, what type of work the listing needs, how they utilize artists, and payment method and amount. Here are some tips to help you interpret these listings.

How To Read a Market Listing

- The asterisk (*) in front of a listing means that listing is new to this edition.
- The name and title of the person you should contact are given in most listings. If not, address your work to the art director or art-related person most appropriate for that field. For example, in performing arts a person commonly addressed is the Public Relations Director. Read through other listings in the section for the most commonly used title if you are unsure what it might be. When you are unable to tell from a given contact name whether the person is male or female, for example Lee Smith, it is appropriate to write your greeting as Dear Lee Smith.
- Established dates are listed only if they are 1983, 1984, 1985. This is to indicate the firm or publication is new and possibly more open to freelance artists.
- Be aware that reporting time and payment rates may vary from the listing in this directory. This may happen if a change in management occurs after our publication date and new policies are established.
- The number or percentage of jobs assigned to freelance artists or the number of artists a listing uses gives you an idea of the size of the market.
- Editorial descriptions and client lists appear in listings to help you slant your work toward that specific business.
- If a market does not return samples or original art, we have specified such. It is always professionally wise whenever corresponding, to include a self-addressed, stamped envelope (SASE) for a reply. If you are expecting the return of samples, especially slides or a portfolio, be sure that sufficient postage and proper packaging are included. If you live in the United States and are soliciting foreign listings, purchase International Reply Coupons (IRC) at your local post office to cover your postage. Investigate foreign sales regulations.
- Markets that accept previously published work (especially in publications) state it in their listings. Otherwise they do not accept these submissions.
- If a listing requests samples, we have tried to specify what types of samples it prefers. If the listing states it will keep material on file for possible future assignments, make sure your material easily fits the average 8½x11'' file.
- If a listing instructs you to query, please query. Do not send samples unless that is what they want you to do. Some listings tell you to query and then list what type of samples they prefer. This does *not* mean to send samples. It is simply added information so that when you have further contact with them, you will have an idea of what type of samples to submit if they do ask to see them.
- Note what rights the listing prefers to purchase. If several types of rights are listed, it usually means the firm will negotiate. But not always. Be certain you and the art buyer understand exactly what rights you are selling.
- Many firms work on assignment only. Do not expect them to buy the art you send as samples. When your style fills a current art need, they will contact you.
- Read the tips added to many of the listings. They give you handy personalized advice or a view of general market area information.
- Take advantage of the Artist's Resource List at the end of the Appendix. Listed are 57 publications with publishers' names and addresses which will help you find buyers and learn about specific markets.

Important

- When looking for a specific market, check the index. If you don't find it listed, it might be for one of these reasons: 1) It is not interested in reviewing new freelance work; 2) It requests not to be listed; 3) It has gone out of business; 4) It did not respond to our questionnaire; 5) It was not solicited for this edition for listing information; 6) It doesn't pay for art (we have, however, included some nonpaying listings because we feel the final printed artwork could be valuable to the artist's portfolio); 7) We have received complaints about it and it hasn't answered our inquiries satisfactorily.
- Listings are based on editorial questionnaires and interviews. They are *not* advertisements, nor are markets reported on endorsed by the *Artist's Market* editor.
- Remember, information in the listings is as current as possible, but art directors come and go; companies and publications move, and art needs fluctuate between the publication of this directory and when you buy it.
- *Artist's Market* reserves the right to exclude any listing that does not meet its requirements.

Breaking into Specialty Art Markets

BY CAROL ANN MORLEY

Today's illustration market covers a broad spectrum of visuals and offers lucrative assignment opportunities for nearly every freelance artist. Freelancers can utilize their artistic talents, skills and knowledge in dozens of areas—science fiction/fantasy, scientific, historical, technical, humor and romance illustration to name only a few. Moreover these visuals are rendered on posters, packages, puzzles, greeting cards, porcelain, toys, games, clothes, giftware, stationery, utensils, furniture, buildings and virtually any imaginable surface for every conceivable purpose.

Contemplating all this opportunity can be overwhelming. There is great potential, but in which direction do you go? And when it comes to selling your art, you *must* know where you are in this vast illustration field.

The most important decision you can ever make is to specialize—either by subject matter or medium, or a combination of these two. Why do you specialize? Because your competition—the thousands of other freelancers—forces you to do so. Today's art buyer looks among the myriad of artists for specialists—landscape painters, science fiction illustrators, artists who stand out from the freelance crowd. In order to stand out, you need something to set yourself apart, so you specialize.

To determine your area of specialization stop and take a look at both yourself and your artwork. What are your interests and hobbies? Are you a horse fanatic or a gardening buff? What are your strongest art skills—do you prefer rendering people or animals, cars or landscapes? Are you most adept with watercolor, pen & ink or airbrush? Study other artists' work; how does yours compare?

Once you have pinpointed your personal and artistic interests, think "style." You must create a style or "look" which can be identified as yours. By developing this look you are on your way towards achieving consistency in your artwork. And if your look is what the art buyer wants, your samples will show you can regularly provide it.

Determining *where* to market your artwork and skills is the next step. Illustrators serve thousands of art markets located throughout the U.S. and overseas. Geographic location does not limit a freelancer's opportunity since a large percentage of work is assigned by mail. The key point to remember as you begin to submit work is that this is a commercial world; your art—its style and content—*must be salable*. And it must be needed by the art buyer.

Freelance artists are needed by local, regional and national advertising agencies; corporations; art/design studios; trade and consumer magazines; newspapers; company publications; greeting card manufacturers; art publishers; architecture and interior design firms; book publishers; and record companies—to name only a few!

Four exciting areas of highly specialized illustration, still unfamiliar to many artists, are scientific illustration, art publishing, science fiction/fantasy illustration and collectibles art. These growing markets are diverse and offer freelancers creative satisfaction, numerous assignment possibilities, and the potential for good exposure and income. The collectibles market, in particular, waits to be discovered by many artists.

Carol Ann Morley *is a scientific and medical illustrator, art instructor and former art director residing in the New York City area.*

Collectibles

The collectibles industry is part of an ongoing cultural explosion. The increase in the popularity and sale of fine art prints and posters are evidence of this boom. Perhaps less known, but equally impressive, is the growth within the collectibles market where the buyers collect figurines, stamps, music boxes, coins and plates.

©1984 Reco

The trade magazine *Plate World* reports a remarkable jump in the amount of money spent each year by plate collectors, resulting primarily from the fact that it is affordable art with higher investment return potential. The Bradford Exchange, located in Niles/Chicago, is the "Stock Exchange" of collector's plates, handling 13,598 primary and secondary transactions every day. The Exchange estimates there are eight million collectors throughout the world with six million of them in the U.S.

"The Surrey Ride" is the eighth and final issue in Reco International Corp.'s nostalgic "Days Gone By" plate collection. The eight acrylic paintings by Brooklyn, New York artist Sandra Kuck took two years to complete from creation of the original artworks to their marketing. The artist worked with Vice President of Collectibles and Fine Gifts Brigitte Moore in the development of the series' original concept. The original pieces were 21 inches in diameter; the finished plate measures 9¼ inches. Kuck has worked exclusively with Reco since 1978.

The collectibles market is probably more familiar to you than you realize. You've seen plates, figurines and other collectibles in fine giftware shops, specialty and department stores. Ads for companies such as Knowles and Reco appear in trade and consumer magazines. What you may not realize is that much of the artwork appearing on these fine art products is created by freelance artists, and that collectible producers are *always* searching for new and exciting talents.

Collectible producers attend gallery exhibitions, look through magazines and visit trade shows in their search for new artists with an art style or theme that has never before appeared in the collectibles industry. Debbie Keller, manager/limited editions, Pickard, Inc. in Antioch, Illinois explains, "We look for artists who can render beautiful paintings of children which are our best sellers. Our buyers are mostly women and grandparents looking for a likeness of their own children. The paintings must be realistic, classical and show the 'cuteness' of children, such as their playing with dolls or dressing up. The cuter the child the better."

There is specific subject matter that sells best. Children are the most popular subjects; dogs, cats, wildlife, mother and child themes, Norman Rockwell themes and nostalgia are close behind. Movie stars such as James Dean and Elvis Presley are collectible hits, while themes related to Mother's Day and Christmas always sell.

You don't have to wait to be "discovered" in this field—take the initiative and submit your art samples or request a portfolio review. Increase your chances of being accepted by first determining each producer's areas of specialization. If a producer's plates feature children, and your speciality is animals, don't waste your time and money. Instead find the company that *wants* animal artwork.

To determine the art needs of collectible manufacturers, invest in the latest edition of *The Bradford Book of Collector's Plates* (The Bradford Exchange, 9333 Milwaukee, Niles/Chicago IL 60648) which is a pictorial guide to more than 1,250 plates. Read the trade magazines *Plate World*, *Gifts and Decorative Accessories*, *Collectors Mart* and *Figurine Magazine*. Study the ads and read the articles to learn more about the market. The Businesses section of this directory lists collectible manufacturers and extensive information about their needs and how to contact them. Read the Close-up interview with Brigitte Moore, vice president with Reco International Corp., to find out what she looks for in a collectibles artist. Attend trade shows where you meet artists, collectors and producers. The opportunity to see your artwork reproduced on 10,000 collector's plates is there.

Painting in the Round

Few artists know about the peculiarities of plate art as a medium. Working within a circle has constraints; a curved surface creates a certain motion and depth that's hard to achieve on a flat canvas. Manufacturers find it difficult to find artists who paint in the round or who even want to try.

Painting in the round is not a simple thing like cropping a square—that seldom works. Rather, the artist must change his whole approach—technique, sense of composition and use of light and shadow. He must learn how to put the subject matter into a circle. Figurative, not abstract, art sells to the collectors of plates because this medium has to tell a story.

Producers generally commit to a series format—that is, contract with artists to do two, four, six or more plates with a central theme or concept—because it takes a long time for a company to make an artist known in the industry. Collectors often identify with certain artists and follow their activities and output religiously.

An artist's personality is also considered by the plate producer. A plate artist should be personable, outgoing, promotable and capable of selling his own work because competition in the marketplace is extremely heavy.

If artists understand the time and money that go into the production and marketing of a plate series, the producer's job becomes easier. The initial investment required to produce a single proof plate with a 10,000 limited edition run, may cost between $50,000 and $70,000. And that's just for openers. Lead time in the industry, from art assignment to finished proof, can be from nine to eighteen months. By the time the plate is packaged, marketed, advertised and delivered to dealers, the producer's investment on a high quality product can be as much as $250,000!

—*Barbara M. Dawson*

Art Publishing

The art publishing market is definitely worthy of consideration by fine and graphic artists due to a dramatic increase the past two years in the popularity (and ultimately production) of wall graphics. Rising employment figures, lower interest rates and mortgage payments, more new houses and businesses and an increase in the number of bare walls needing graphics are motivators behind this art publishing boom. And as the boom continues, so will the art publishers' search for freelance artists to satisfy both consumer and corporate art needs.

Of the various types of art graphics—handpulled original prints, unlimited edition prints, limited edition prints and posters—the latter two, produced by photomechanical means, have experienced the greatest increases and present good opportunities for today's freelance artists.

The limited edition print is traditionally of a more timeless, and thus higher, quality than the poster which always incorporates some form of typography, perhaps an announcement of an art exhibit or an arts festival. Poster art is characteristically trendier and glitzier than prints, however many posters such as those published by Art Beats in Salt Lake City use typography in conjunction with very fine and unique artwork. Posters are reproduced in limitless quantities. Fine art prints, which tend to depict traditional, classic images, are printed in limited editions which are often signed and numbered by the artist.

Color is fast becoming a major influence in the purchase of offset reproductions and consequently in their design and illustration. As interior designers assume the responsibility for selecting wall graphics for private and corporate clientele, the coordination of an interior color scheme with the artwork is a primary concern. To increase the salability of your work to art publishers, be aware of the color predictions that are made at the beginning of each new year.

Two groups, the Color Marketing Group (CMG) and the Color Association of the United States (CAUS), develop palettes predicting the colors that will dominate during the year. While 1985 charts depicted pastels—particularly blue as a primary color—CAUS believes that 1986 will see interior design colors going brighter, lighter, clearer and truer with green and red becoming important. Keep on top of colors (styles and trends) by reading the trade magazine *Decor* and its annual color forecast in the January issue. Visit carpeting stores to note the colors of carpet being sold.

A poster or print's image is a factor in its sale. Copycatting is the major complaint voiced by publishers as certain images are becoming cliché and more innovative and original works are sought. According to Michael Markowicz, co-owner of Artistworks in Brookline, Massachusetts, "An artist comes out with a look that sells—whether it's style or subject matter—and once it's proven successful by the buying public, it tends to become a target for copycatting. Brian Davis' 'Calla Lily' is an example of an imitated poster."

For corporate clientele seeking ways to improve the work environment, traditional, representational artwork is popular. Corporations seek unobjectionable images which will not interfere with an employee's job. Many art publishers feel that consumer buyers, too, prefer graphics that are simple, clean and uncluttered, yet beautiful.

Historically, certain subject matter sells well. Ever popular poster images are landscapes, abstract and commemorative (such as art exhibits) artwork. Limited edition prints frequently depict wildlife, Western art, nostalgia, primitive art, Americana and landscape.

Most successful poster or print artists have one thing in common. Each specializes in a particular subject matter and/or art style. Peter Keating, a Bucks County, Pennsylvania artist, is well-known for his limited edition pastoral scenes. According to his publisher George Knight of Primrose Press, Keating's style combines the "vitality of pen and ink with the subtlety of watercolor washes, capturing a romantic view of the countryside." Keating's limited edition prints, such as "The Corner Flock" shown here, always sell well.

"It is important that an artist has a distinctive style," stresses Knight, "and to some extent concentrates on a particular subject matter. Publishers are attracted to artists showing proficiency in one subject matter. It's a given that a good artist can do a variety of subjects, but can he do one or two consistently well? When we receive samples showing a variety of images we don't know what to do with the artist."

Young artists lacking in direction should talk with different art publishers, suggests Knight. Request catalogs and study them. "While it doesn't mean there isn't room for something new, publishers tend to follow their own formula for what has worked in the past.''

Art publishers and artists join forces in two primary ways. The artist submits samples either in person or by mail, or the publisher regularly visits galleries and exhibitions, which is how Keating and Primrose Press began their relationship.

"It's a symbiotic relationship between the artist and the publisher," explains Patricia Knight, also of Primrose Press. "The publisher must be open with the artist, and the artist must be able to step back and be critical of his work. Artists get almost maternal and don't want to hear anything negative. Our role is not to make judgments about artwork, but to look for something that will be successful."

George Knight estimates that it costs $30,000 to develop two prints by a single artist; this price tag includes printing, trade show promotion, advertising and producing catalogs—the figure does not take into account royalties paid to the artist.

Artists are generally paid on a royalty basis of ten to fifteen percent, although the percentage can go up or down depending upon the artist's reputation and his track record. Many publishers buy rights to the artwork for reproduction as wall decorations, while others prefer exclusive (all) rights to the work. Some publishers pay artists an advance which is then taken out of the royalties. In all cases, negotiate your contract with a publisher so that the terms are agreeable to both of you.

When approaching an art publisher, be knowledgeable about the style and type—poster or print—of artwork he publishes. Request catalogs and read *Decor* regularly at your public library or by subscription—study the advertisements *and* the articles. Visit department stores, galleries, frame shops and other retail outlets; talk with the owners or store buyers and learn what sells and what doesn't.

Publishers prefer to receive color slides or photographs as samples, and it is vital that these samples be the *best* possible representation of your work. Poorly cropped, out-of-focus and under- or overexposed samples *will not sell* your artwork to a publisher. Include with your samples some biographical material, either a resumé or brochure, and a brief cover letter explaining your interest. Read the Close-up with Art Beats president Kelly Omana to learn how this publisher prefers to be contacted and what art style she seeks.

The main thing to remember as you approach this market is that art publishing is a gamble and the publisher is only going to be willing to gamble on *you* if you can produce *salable* artwork repeatedly. You can, in part, satisfy this requirement by doing your homework—study the market and learn what *does* sell and what each publisher in particular sells—and by presenting yourself as a professional, a businessperson *and* an artist.

Science Fiction/Fantasy Illustration

Today, as technological advances grow ordinary, the human imagination searches for something new, something to stimulate excitement and romance. Illustrators of science fiction (spaceships and characters) and fantasy (sorcerers and dragons) artwork play an important role in providing this "something new" by creating monsters, spaceships or even a universe that doesn't exist and that may *never* exist . . . except in the world of science fiction/fantasy illustration.

Advertising agencies, book publishers, magazines, newspapers, software and comic book publishers are major users of this specialty art style. Each of these art buyers entertains one common purpose—to in some way alter the common perception of reality.

In the advertising field, science fiction/fantasy artwork is used increasingly to enliven a product's image or to add a futuristic touch to ads. Magazine and newspaper ads, posters, catalogs and billboards use extraterrestrials and future technology to sell industrial components, cars, computers, video equipment, copy machines, automatic tellers, toys, games, movies, candy and even soft drinks.

Book, magazine, newspaper and comic book publishers use science fiction/fantasy artwork to illustrate covers and jackets, short stories, comic stories, articles

This fantasy-style advertising illustration, above, by Beau Daniels, Newbury Park, California, was assigned by the Foote, Cone & Belding ad agency for its client First Interstate Bank in Los Angeles. The artwork's Olympic theme was designed to encourage personnel at the games to bank with First Interstate during their stay in California. The original 20x16" airbrush piece was used as a magazine ad and a poster.

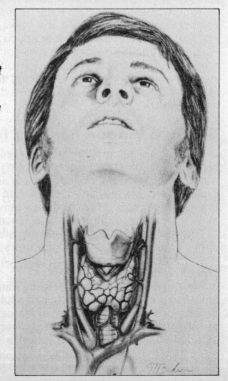

Valley Stream, New York artist Manuel Bekier created this throat illustration originally as a learning project while a student at the Medical College of Georgia. The image was later used by the school's surgery department in a teaching slide program and in a medical journal.

Upfront author and artist Carol Ann Morley of Garrison, New York, created this illustration of a skunk cabbage for exhibition purposes and to build up her portfolio. Originally a medical illustrator, Morley's love of nature led her into the natural science field which required a new portfolio. Although she sold the original piece, the artist's portfolio includes photographs of this and seven other similar "self-initiated" illustrations.

George and Patricia Knight, owners of Primrose Press art publishing company in Pennsylvania, first viewed artist Peter Keating's work in a gallery in New Hope, Pennsylvania. The first limited edition print by the artist was released in 1980, and Primrose Press has since published 12 Keating prints and two posters. "The Corner Flock," shown above, was printed in a signed and numbered edition of 950. The publisher bought rights to the original artwork for reproduction as wall decorations.

and sell copy. Software package design and illustration are the primary assignments from producers of videogames, such as Broderbund's "Lode Runner" or the interactive fiction program "King's Quest" by Roberta Williams. Freelance artist Carl Lundgren of Philadelphia talks in-depth about science fiction/fantasy assignments in his Close-up in the Book Publishers section of this directory.

The science fiction/fantasy art market is extremely strong and remains stable, report professionals in the field. In book publishing, "There's always a new generation of readers that enjoy this thing," explains Don Puckey, art director for Warner Books's Questar line. "The writing, and ultimately the artwork, tend to be more sophisticated today than in its earlier periods."

"The science fiction/fantasy software publishing market really blossomed around 1980," says Robert Sirotek, vice president of Sir-tech, a software publisher in Ogdensburg, New York. "I have seen terrific growth in this market and expect it to remain strong."

Science fiction/fantasy artists must possess certain *specific* qualities to succeed in any of these markets. In software packaging, where the artist's task is to reflect the character of the program, "Artists must have a bizarre mind," Sirotek explains frankly. "They have to be eccentric and think on a different plane than other graphic artists."

"You must have a good imagination and a scientific mentality," says California illustrator Beau Daniels. "People who draw the best science fiction read science fiction. You *have* to read it to get a feel for the story."

Technical skills are a must. The ability to accurately render the human figure, to paint realistically and to paint details are important. "Artists must be able to paint hardware, such as spaceships, *and* figures," explains Puckey. "I constantly run into the problem where an artist can do one or the other but not both. And you have to *like* this kind of painting." Art buyers agree that a science fiction/fantasy artist must put his heart and soul into a painting. "If you don't, it shows in your work," stresses Sirotek.

Brian Thomsen, an editor with the Questar line, believes that exposure is a key way to break into this art market. "Galleries, exhibits and conventions are great ways to get exposure. It's not a matter of hard sell, it's a question of being there at the right time. You have to catch an art director or editor's eye." Thomsen attends up to nine science fiction/fantasy conventions each year in search of artists and writers.

Software publishers prefer having art samples on file for future needs. Sirotek suggests artists submit full-color samples such as a single sheet printed with a number of illustrations. "Do a mass mailing to all the science fiction software publishers; send your samples and a cover letter focusing on what specifically you can do for that publisher. Also in the letter show clearly the cost of reproduction rights to the work you have submitted and quote rates for doing original work. You may never get a second chance at this, so spell it out."

To approach an advertising agency, Daniels advises artists to "put together a portfolio or direct-mail package of six to seven pieces that are science fiction-oriented. The pieces can be published or unpublished; the important thing is that they are evidence of a vivid imagination and strong conceptual ability, as well as skillful artistic techniques. If you have no published advertising samples, select a product and do original paintings or sketches."

Payment in most markets is by the project. Paperback book covers pay $2,000 and up, usually for first rights. Depending upon the artist's reputation, a software package illustration can range from $750-2,500. Fees in all science fiction/fantasy markets will vary, depending not only upon your reputation and experience, but upon the difficulty of the assignment, the size of the company you are working for and even the part of the country you live in.

In the science fiction/fantasy art market, the artist who is able to fulfill the very specific requirements of having a "bizarre mind," being "eccentric" and imaginative (not to mention being at the peak of your artistic and technical capabilities) will find himself in great demand. The top science fiction/fantasy artists often schedule assignments months in advance because they are so much in demand. Remember that this success did not come to these artists overnight, nor will it to you. But with talent, the *right* personality, fortitude and a professional, business-like approach good things can happen!

Scientific Illustration

Complex scientific ideas and data are often more easily understood when presented visually. This specialty art area—scientific illustration—is unique in its diversity and its strict requirements for the artists who work in it.

Scientific illustrators generally work in one of two areas—medical or natural science illustration. Artwork in both areas is used for teaching, research, advertising, legal, magazine cover and editorial illustration.

Artists in medical or natural science illustration must, by necessity, be knowledgeable in many scientific areas. Technical art skills must be sharp because there is little, if any, room for inaccuracies in the renderings this market requires. A medical illustrator must be capable of rendering a stomach as well as a hair follicle. Natural science artists must be able to illustrate from life or photograph a skunk cabbage as well as hundreds of other plant species. And besides technical accuracy, aesthetics dictates that the artwork be pleasing and imaginative.

Medical and natural science illustration are, although relatives in the world of scientific illustration, distinctly different. Courses of study vary as do the types of assignments, clientele and the commercial applications of the artwork.

Medical illustration specifically involves the depiction of anatomical subjects, microanatomical and surgical procedures. What this means in laymen's terms is that artists render any part of the human body including that which is microscopic, as well as any conceivable surgical operation. To pull off this feat, illustrators study gross anatomy (the body), pathology (disease), physiology (bodily functions), histology (animal tissue) and microanatomy (cells). Medical illustrators usually possess some form of science degree, but many are successful by taking individual courses on a non-degree basis.

Medical illustrator Manuel Bekier of Long Island, New York holds a master of science degree and has worked in the field for fifteen years. The constant increase in scientific research and its publication, according to Bekier, makes the medical illustration market a steady and solid one.

In medical illustration "the artist's objective is to understand what the client wants to convey," explains Bekier, "then find the most effective way to communicate it graphically and execute a visual not producible by a camera or any other method.

"The most common mistake artists make is to concentrate on creating a beautiful picture, missing the *point* of the illustration. The artist's intent is to create a work of art that is scientifically accurate, yet aesthetically attractive."

Artists in this market often work in teaching hospitals, in close contact with physicians, or as freelancers out of their own studios where they must maintain their own medical reference library. Medical and surgical suppliers, book and magazine publishers, advertising agencies, pharmaceutical companies and universities are good sources of assignments. Medical illustrations are reproduced in over 100 medical-related journals, textbooks and magazines in the United States and Canada. They are used for medical conference exhibits and audiovisual presentations, in advertisements and by law firms in malpractice and personal injury lawsuits.

The field of medical illustration is highly competitive, yet skilled illustrators are kept busy. Bekier advises aspiring medical illustrators to persevere but be realistic about their abilities. Have work appraised by other artists and art directors to learn strengths and weaknesses.

Canadian medical illustrator Jean Miller is a top medical illustrator in both her native country and in the U.S. Her Close-up interview in the Magazines section of this book tells how Miller entered this lucrative field and what it takes to remain successful.

For further information about courses pertinent to this field contact the Association of Medical Illustrators (Route 5, Box 311F, Midlothian, Virginia 23113). For listings of medical advertisers consult the December issue of *Medical Marketing & Media*; medical trade journals are listed in *Standard Rate and Data Services*.

One obvious element differentiates between medical and **natural science illustration**—the subject matter. Natural science illustration covers zoology (animals), botany (plants), paleontology (primitive man), anthropology (peoples) and geography (earth). Artists need not only to be knowledgeable of the subject matter, but possess a *high* degree of technical skill when rendering it.

It helps to have a degree or some coursework from the areas within this field. However, it is not always essential. The bottom line in this market is to create an accurate rendering and by working closely with reference materials, specimens and science professionals an artist can produce effective artwork.

The degree of skill and accuracy required varies, depending upon the assignment. An assignment from a science publication must show the highest degree of skill, while a *Ranger Rick* illustration allows the artist to create looser, less serious artwork. The wildlife illustrator, while creating aesthetically beautiful pieces of art, must draw his subjects with a high degree of accuracy.

Illustrations in this field are used to clarify articles in scientific publications, assist reader comparison between species, and enhance textbooks and exhibits. Buyers of natural science illustration include museums, universities and research institutes.

The commercial applications of natural science illustration are many. Artists render botanical and zoological subjects such as flowers, birds, fish and country scenes on porcelain, stamps, coins, greeting cards, prints and posters. Pharmaceutical advertising and package design often utilize botanical illustration while zoological subjects appear frequently in veterinary publications.

To learn more about natural science illustration attend the annual convention organized by the Guild of Natural Science Illustrators (Box 652, Ben Franklin Station, Washington DC 20044). There you can see new techniques and innovations, meet professional artists in the field, attend workshops and view exhibits of the best natural science illustration.

Expanding Your Opportunities

The old saying, "The sky is the limit," is not that far off in the world of freelance illustration. There are always new markets to explore, new techniques to learn and new heights to reach. We've opened some doors to possible assignments by introducing you to the art markets of collectibles, art publishing, science fiction/fantasy and scientific illustration. You now have an "insider's" knowledge of these markets and are steps ahead of your competition—other freelance artists. The next step, however, is yours. Take advantage of your new knowledge, and even if *these* markets aren't exactly what is *right* for you they may help you determine what is. You are limited only by the amount of research you do and the effort you want to put into your career. Be as creative about looking for freelance assignments as you are at the drawing board—there are hundreds of markets that need you!

Cartooning—Today's Marketplace

BY MORT GERBERG

In the 1950s a cartoonist was rigidly defined either as a magazine cartoonist, syndicated comic strip artist or humorous illustrator, working virtually full-time only within his field. But today's influences of television, the economy, higher production costs and the growth of special interest audiences have combined to change that picture.

The traditional cartoon markets in the '80s are tighter, which means fewer artistic and financial rewards for the artist. On the other hand, many different markets are opening up and expanding, offering additional possibilities for creativity and income. The key to success lies in the cartoonist's ability to adapt his or her talents to many areas and to pursue an inventive and aggressive marketing plan.

Contemporary young cartoonists comprise a new breed. "They must be entrepreneurs," says Lee Lorenz, a cartoonist and the art director of *The New Yorker*. "They must be more flexible, develop more business skills and create opportunities for themselves which may not have existed before. They must be clear-eyed about their own capabilities, know what their skills are and constantly reevaluate them."

Today's cartoonists work not only inside "the box"—magazine cartoons and syndicated newspaper comic strips, panels and political cartoons—but in markets outside the box as well, including humorous illustration of editorial and advertising copy for books and magazines, greeting cards, animation, comic books and children's books. Three popular markets in this group are children's books, magazines and syndicates.

Children's Books

Children's book publishers are always interested in cartoon illustrators. In this medium, cartoonists utilize their natural talents for communicating ideas simply, through funny drawings. They may illustrate another's story, write and illustrate their own story or even write a story which someone else illustrates. Standard book types in this market are picture books, joke/riddle books, light nonfiction, sticker, counting and ABC books.

Judith Whipple, publisher of children's books at MacMillan, estimates that of the more than 75 picture books MacMillan publishes every year, approximately fifteen are illustrated with cartoons. She adds that more books are now created for very young readers as parents press to start their children reading at an earlier age. These books are very simple and suit the natural talents of cartoonists—making this a rapidly expanding market.

Jean Feiwal is editor-in-chief of the Scholastic Book Group and estimates that

---

Mort Gerberg, *author of* The Arbor House Book of Cartooning, *contributes cartoons regularly to* The New Yorker *and* Playboy, *has written and illustrated numerous children's books, adult humor books and comic strips, and teaches cartooning at New York City's Parsons School of Design.*

cartoonists illustrate ten percent of the 300 books this company publishes. A "cartoonist's work has great vitality," she explains. It adds a "narrative flow" to any book and "lightens up nonfiction."

In picture books, there is typically a fifty-fifty split of the payment between the artist and the author. The common advance for a book is $5,000 and the standard royalty rate is ten percent for hardcovers and six percent for paperbacks. Some illustrators of juvenile titles work for flat fees which average $2,000 for approximately fifteen drawings, overlays and cover art.

There are many publishing houses and they all produce different types of books such as Greenwillow's picture books and Troubadour Press's activity, maze and puzzle books. A list of children's book publishers is obtainable from the Children's Book Council (67 Irving Place, New York City 10003). Read through

© 1985 Scholastic Inc.

In 1963 artist/writer Norman Bridwell walked into the offices of Scholastic Inc. bearing a single dummy book that featured a dog named Clifford. On that day Bridwell began a relationship with Scholastic and Clifford that remains strong to this day—18 million books sold! Clifford appears in 19 original picture, activity, ABC, sticker and counting books, all written and illustrated by Bridwell. In 1983 the books were changed from a 6x8" format to an 8" square. Colors went from red and black to four-color, and the page count was set at 32.

the listings in the Book Publishers section of this directory for additional names of children's publishers. It is important to research each company's book line before submitting your artwork. Don't overlook your local library, specifically the area devoted strictly to children's books. Read through the books, study the artwork and make notes on the publishers, art styles and the books' formats—size and color.

The samples or portfolio you submit to a publisher should feature your unique cartoon style, display a range of skills including drawings of people and animals. Provide published cartoons, some original color work and perhaps a drawing or two illustrating a popular classic. Make your initial inperson call with your portfolio to either the art director or editor, and if you have written a book, certainly see the editor. Call in advance to learn the editor or art director's name and to make an appointment. For submission by mail, include with your samples a typed cover letter briefly explaining why you are writing and describing your samples; include a self-addressed, stamped envelope (SASE) for return of your materials. Use the resources mentioned above to determine the name of the person you should submit your work to.

Magazines

The majority of magazines slant their editorial content to special interest audiences ranging from publications such as *Fantasy Book*, which emphasizes the world of science fiction and fantasy, to *Le Bureau*, whose audience includes corporate and financial executives and systems analysts. Selling your cartoons to consumer or trade magazines requires research—reading at least six recent issues—to determine what type cartoons are purchased.

Many cartoonists submit first to the top markets and work their way down, although chances are better for acceptance at smaller markets where the competition is not as tough. Submit your work on a regular basis, sending off a new batch of cartoons immediately after the previous group is returned. It is important to impress editors with your determination to sell.

A second way to impress an editor is to be yourself. Lorenz, who reviews over 3,000 cartoon roughs a week at *The New Yorker* and buys about 15, looks for "someone with a very clearly articulated voice of his own, rather than someone who can just do a gag." Michelle Urry, cartoon editor at *Playboy*, looks for suitable material and "something distinctive."

Submit only original roughs, not photocopies. This way you don't send the same drawings to different magazines which is generally not a good practice. Your batch of roughs can number as few as five. If the magazine is unfamiliar with your work, include a previously published cartoon or one finished drawing. Attach a cover letter explaining your submission and addressed to the current art director or cartoon editor, whose name is listed in the magazine's masthead or in the listings found in the Magazines section of this

"*Lately I've begun to dabble in quality.*"

© 1977, The New Yorker Magazine, Inc.

Lee Lorenz, art director at The New Yorker, receives 3,000 freelance cartoons per week and published this cartoon by New York-based artist Mort Gerberg. The 500,000 circulation magazine does not accept previously published cartoons and diligently checks submissions for duplications. The magazine buys all rights, but assigns secondary income to the cartoonist.

book. Keep your cover letter brief; it's your work that does the *real* talking. With mailed submissions an SASE is mandatory, along with heavy cardboard to protect against in-transit mutilation. Be sure to use correct postage on the outside of the return envelope.

A magazine may withhold drawings from your batch for publication or for final consideration later; if you then receive an "okay" you may be asked to do a "finish" which is a drawing that fits the publication's technical specifications.

Magazines normally buy first reproduction or reprint rights to cartoons, paying on acceptance of the drawing rather than on publication (which could be a long time). Rates of payment vary from publication to publication depending upon its circulation, advertising and art budget. The listings in this book indicate the general range for black-and-white cartoons to be from $10 in a small circulation quarterly to over $500 in *The New Yorker. Playboy* pays up to $600 for full-page color cartoons. For resources listing additional names and addresses of consumer, trade and specialty publications consult the Artist's Resource List at the end of this directory.

Syndicates

Creating and submitting comic strips, humor panels or political cartoons for syndication means a greater investment of time and creative energies than submitting to magazines. Theoretically, however, the payoff is greater. As with magazines, syndicate submissions are on speculation, meaning there is no guarantee that the work will be purchased.

A comic strip consists of ongoing characters and themes. The syndicate you submit to wants to see at least three weeks of finished samples—eighteen daily strips or panels and three Sunday panels without color—to judge your consistency. You can include another two weeks of roughs and a short description of the long-range aim of the strip, its characters and target audience. Unlike submitting to magazines, you may send several syndicates photocopies of your work and it is not uncommon for a cartoonist to mail off his first strip efforts to several syndicates simultaneously. However, it's good form to let each know.

©1983 United Feature Syndicate, Inc.

The Peanuts gang was created in 1950 by cartoonist Charles Schulz. That same year "Peanuts" was syndicated by United Feature Syndicate, Inc., and began a love affair with its readers that would eventually make it the most widely read syndicated comic strip. "Peanuts" appears in 2,033 newspapers in 26 languages, and its characters star in over 1,000 publications, four feature films and 33 TV specials. They are merchandised on clothing, toys, children's furniture, linens, telephones, pet products and cookies.

A syndicate interested in your strip will ask you to create more material. A period of development could continue for many months before a decision is made. Should the syndicate agree to accept your strip you will receive a contract which is usually a fifty-fifty split; negotiate your contract with the assistance of an attorney or a professional, established cartoonist familiar with syndication. It is not unusual that even after months of development the syndicate will scrap the strip due to a lack of response from newspapers.

Sarah Gillespie, comics editor at United Feature Syndicate, reports that a strip needs to appear in 100 papers today to do well. Bill Yates, Gillespie's counterpart at King Features agrees. "Many strips get stuck at 60 papers," he explains. "It's tough to get 100." At this level a cartoonist can earn between $500-600 a week, not including licensing or merchandising income.

Humor panels, such as "Herman" by Jim Unger, should have a wide audience appeal with a theme that has an on-going narrative structure and characters with strong, easily recognizable personality traits. For details on editorial requirements, read the listings in the Syndicates & Clip Art Firms section or write directly to the syndicate; some will send you printed artists' guidelines.

Artists interested in political/editorial cartooning face steep roads. The work is demanding—you must create unique caricatures, be politically knowledgeable on past and current affairs, and maintain a continuous outrage—and the field is small.

For more detailed information read the Close-up with Pulitzer Prize winner Mike Peters in the Newspapers/Newsletters section of this book. Peters offers inside information—especially about how he got started—on his editorial cartooning and syndication experiences.

Expanding Your Market

The area of humorous illustration—"outside the box"—is a giant, multi-faceted market offering a variety of opportunities to cartoonists. Don't wait for assignments to come to you; go out and get them yourself, with the aid of portfolio/samples and promotional pieces mailed to art directors in all fields. Create your own prospect list from the market listings and bibliography in this book. When your drawings are established in one area, you can use their "professional acceptability" to solicit jobs in other areas, assuming your work is appropriate to that field. Take the time to study the different markets and tailor your portfolio or samples for each field's specific needs.

Some of the areas in which cartoon-style illustrations are used include books, record album covers, in-house publications, sales brochures, direct-mail packages, logos, filmstrips, slide shows and annual reports. Major users of humorous illustration are newspapers, magazines and advertising agencies. Some cartoonists' styles are more suited for animation that others, so they get assignments to design and illustrate for TV commercials. Cartoonists with a following, those with well-known characters in syndication such as "Garfield" by Jim Davis, are more attractive to greeting card companies.

In editorial and advertising illustration the cartoonist creates drawings which enhance some form of writing. The artist works on assignment, generally responding to an art director's ideas. Art directors constantly seek artists who think well conceptually and communicate ideas in unique graphic solutions. Steve Heller, art director of *The New York Times Book Review*, feels that the successful illustrator "must establish a distinctive style and point of view."

As a cartoonist you should seek assignments which give good exposure and establish a reputation for reliability. The art director must feel secure with his artists since his own reputation is built on how his projects look.

The opportunities in today's humor market are measured only by the individual cartoonist's own view. Those seeing only fewer magazines buying fewer cartoons perceive a rapidly shrinking cartoon universe. The entrepreneurs willing to put their talents to work *out* of the box as well as *in* it can expand their careers and earn a living.

Most important, these cartoonists will continue to work at what they enjoy most, which is really the only reason anybody is a cartoonist. That, plus freedom of choice, is the attractiveness of freelance cartooning—you get to make up your own games, and play them until it's time to create new ones.

The Markets

Advertising, Audiovisual & Public Relations Firms

In the advertising, audiovisual and public relations markets, freelance artists are used either on a regular basis or only when the workload is too heavy for inhouse staff to handle. For economic reasons many of these companies have reduced or eliminated their staff artists and rely to a greater extent on freelancers. More and more seek the artist/designer knowledgeable enough to "project manage" his work with the firm from concept to finished product. Past experience is an asset in proving to an art director that you can handle the job.

Sharp presentation skills are necessary as you strive to land one of these firms as your client. Since you will most likely meet in person with an art director, your professionalism—from the manner of your dress to your portfolio—is taken into account. Gear your portfolio as much as possible to the advertising or PR firm's clients or types of clients. The most common complaint from art directors is that artists waste their time showing totally inappropriate work.

While audiovisual firms are open to working long-distance with artists, most advertising and PR firms prefer working with local artists (within a reasonable commuting distance) due to strict deadlines and last-minute revisions. To help locate firms nearest you, we've separated the listings by state and pulled out four major cities—Los Angeles, San Francisco, Chicago, New York—from their states. We've also included information to tell you the type of firm, its specialty and its client areas. Put this information to work when you tailor your portfolio.

Read the Close-up in this section featuring established artist David Smiton. He shares with you what he has learned from seven years' experience as an art director and his nineteen years of freelancing.

Additional names and addresses can be obtained from the *Standard Directory of Advertising Agencies*, *Audio Video Market Place* and *O'Dwyer's Directory of Public Relations Firms*. Read the weeklies *Advertising Age* and *Adweek* to keep current on the changes and trends in the advertising field.

This oil paint and ink illustration by Ken Maryanski of Boston was one of three he created for a series of ads for Allendale Insurance. The advertising agency of Cosmopulos, Crowley & Daly, Inc. assigned the job to this artist because of his "unusual and distinctive style." Maryanski sold all rights to the art.

Alabama

J.H. LEWIS ADVERTISING AGENCY INC., Box 3202, Mobile AL 36652. (205)438-2507. Senior Vice President/Creative Director: Larry D. Norris. Ad agency. Clients: retail, manufacturers, health care and direct mail. Buys 15 illustrations/year.
Needs: Works with illustrators and designers. Uses artists for mechanicals and layout for ads, annual reports, billboards, catalogs, letterheads, packaging, P-O-P displays, posters, TV and trademarks.
First Contact & Terms: Prefers southern artists. Query. SASE. Reports in 5 days. No originals returned to artist at job's completion. Payment by hour: $40-80, layout; $30-50, mechanicals. Pays promised fee for unused assigned work.

SPOTTSWOOD VIDEO/FILM STUDIO, 2524 Old Shell Rd., Mobile AL 36607. (205)478-9387. Contact: Manning W. Spottswood. AV/film/TV producer. Clients: industry, education, government and advertising. Produces mainly public relations and industrial films and tapes.
Needs: Assigns 5-15 jobs/year. Uses approximately 1 illustrator/month. Uses artists for illustrations, maps, charts, decorations, set design, etc.
First Contact & Terms: Artists "must live close by and have experience." Send resume or arrange interview by mail. Reports only if interested. Works on assignment only. Pays by the project. Method and amount of payment are negotiated with the individual artist. Considers complexity of project, client's budget, skill and experience of artist, geographic scope of finished project, turnaround time, rights purchased and quality of work when establishing payment.

Arizona

EVANS & MOTTA, INC., Suite 400, 2122 E. Highland, Phoenix AZ 85016. (602)957-6636. Art Director: Mike Smith. Ad agency. Clients: food store, retail, restaurants, homebuilders and industrial firms.
Needs: Works with 1-2 illustrators/month. Uses freelance artists for billboards, consumer and trade magazines, brochures, posters and newspapers.
First Contact & Terms: Send resume or promotional piece by mail; follow up with phone call for interview. Works on assignment basis only. Payment is by the project; negotiates according to client's budget.

FARNAM COMPANIES, INC., Box 34820, Phoenix AZ 85067-4820. (602)285-1660. Creative Director: Trish Spencer. Inhouse advertising agency—Charles Duff Agency—for animal health products firm. Clients which sell through distributors to feed stores, tack shops, co-ops, pet stores, horse and cattle industry.
Needs: Works with 3-10 freelance artists/year. Uses artists for illustrations for brochures, labels and ads. Especially looks for realism, skill in drawing animals and quick turnaround.
First Contact & Terms: Works on assignment only. Send query letter with brochure, business card and samples to be kept on file. Prefers any type of samples "which clearly show quality and detail of work." Samples not filed are returned only if requested. Reports back only if interested. Pays by the project, $100-500 average. Considers client's budget, skill and experience of artist, and geographic scope for the finished product when establishing payment. Rights purchased vary according to project.
Tips: "Mail us samples of work. They should be of animals (horses, dogs, cats, cattle, small animals) with rates and time estimates if possible."

*FILMS FOR CHRIST ASSOCIATION, Suite 1327, 2432 W. Peoria Ave., Phoenix AZ 85029. Contact: Paul S. Taylor. Motion picture producer. Audience: educational, religious and media. Produces motion pictures and videos.
Needs: Works with 1-5 illustrators/year. Uses artists for books, catalogs, and motion pictures. Also uses artists for animation, slide illustrations and ads.
First Contact & Terms: Query with resume and samples (photocopies, slides, tear sheets or snapshots). Prefers slides as samples. Samples returned by SASE. Reports in 4 weeks. Works on assignment only. Provide brochure/flyer, resume and tear sheets to be kept on file for future assignments. No originals returned to artist at job's completion. Considers complexity of project, and skill and experience of artist when establishing payment.

GILBERT ADVERTISING, LTD., Suite 102, 3216 N. 3rd St., Box 15710, Phoenix AZ 85060. Creative Director: T.R. Gilbert. Specializes in corporate identity; newspaper and magazine ads; brochures, catalogs and catalog sheets; and direct mail programs. Clients: primarily small firms in manufacturing and commercial services.

Needs: Works with 10-20 freelance artists/year. Uses artists for advertising, brochures, catalogs, mechanicals, retouching, direct mail packages, charts/graphs, AV presentations, lettering and logos.
First Contact & Terms: Artists "must be willing to sell all rights to reproduction of artwork for established or agreed-upon fee. We do not deal through artist's agents." Send query letter with brochure, resume, business card, copies of samples, and/or tear sheets to be kept on file. Prefers photostats, photocopies, photographic prints or slides as samples. Do *not* send original work. Samples not kept on file are returned by SASE. Reports only if interested. Works on assignment only. Pays for design by the project, $100-500 average; for b&w illustration by the project, $50-400 average; for color illustration by the project, $200-1,500 average. Considers complexity of project and client's budget when establishing payment.
Tips: Artists should "be professional in their presentations. Show only your best quality pieces; keep materials sharp and clean. Computer-assisted artwork creation will become more and more prevalent. As a tool for artists, we expect computers to save a great deal of time and to generate new avenues for design."

PAUL S. KARR PRODUCTIONS, 2949 W. Indian School Rd., Box 11711, Phoenix AZ 85017. (602)266-4198. Contact: Paul Karr. Utah Division: 1024 N. 250 East, Box 1254, Orem UT 84057. (801)226-8209. Contact: Micheal Karr. Film producer. Clients: industrial, business, educational, TV and cable.
Needs: Occasionally works with freelance filmmakers in motion picture projects.
First Contact & Terms: Advise of experience and abilities. Works on assignment only.
Tips: "If you know about motion pictures and are serious about breaking into the field, there are three avenues: 1) have relatives in the business; 2) be at the right place at the right time; or, 3) take upon yourself the marketing of your idea, or develop a film idea for a sponsor who will finance the project. Go to a film production company and tell them you have a client and the money. See if they will work with you on making the film. Work, watch and approve the various phases that involve you as it is being made. With the knowledge you have gained you will be able to present yourself and your abilities to others in the film business and to sponsors."

PHILLIPS-RAMSEY, 829 N. 1st Ave., Phoenix AZ 85003. (602)252-2565. Senior Art Director: Chris Poisson. Ad agency. Clients: savings and loan, racetrack, hotel, restaurant, high tech, public utility, consumer goods, medical, home builders. Client list provided for SASE.
Needs: Uses artists for illustration, photography and production.
First Contact & Terms: Works on assignment only. Send brochure to be kept on file. Reports only if interested. Pays by the project. Considers complexity of the project, client's budget, geographic scope for the finished product, turnaround time and rights purchased when establishing payment. Buys all rights; "our agency only works on a buy-out basis."

*THE PRODUCERS, INC., 1095 E. Indian School Rd., Phoenix AZ 85014. (602)279-7767. President: Judi Victor. Ad agency and audiovisual firm. Clients: developers, financial industry, computer industry, retailers, restaurants, builders and government.
Needs: Works with 20-25 freelance artists/year. Uses artists for layout and design, illustration, photography, videography, air brush, cartooning, animation and calligraphy. "Expediency, accuracy, creativity and ability to work with type and design simultaneously are especially important."
First Contact & Terms: Send query letter with brochure and samples to be kept on file; write for appointment to show portfolio. Prefers tear sheets, comps, photostats or actual material (brochures, etc.) as samples. Samples not filed are returned. Reports within 2 weeks. Pays by the hour, $10-30 average. Considers complexity of the project, client's budget, skill and experience of artist and turnaround time when establishing payment. Buys all rights.
Tips: "Always write first, then follow up with a call for an appointment. Send samples if you feel it will help give you the edge over the many other artists we interview constantly."

JOANNE RALSTON & ASSOCIATES, INC., 3003 N. Central, Phoenix AZ 85012. (602)264-2930. Vice President: Gail Dudley. PR firm. Clients: financial institutions; real estate developers/home-builders; industrial, electronics, manufacturing firms, hospital; resort hotels; major sports events (Phoenix Open PGA tourney, etc.).
Needs: Works with freelance illustrators and designers. Uses artists for brochures/flyers.
First Contact & Terms: Request personal interview to show portfolio and/or send resume. Selects freelancers based on needs, cost, quality and ability to meet deadlines. Provide flyers/brochures and ads to be kept on file for future assignments. No originals returned to artist at job's completion. Negotiates payment based on client's budget, amount of creativity required from artist, where work will appear, artist's previous experience/reputation and ability to meet deadlines.

Freelance artist Asa B. Douglas wanted to create an "electric effect" when designing this logo for Answer Fort Smith, an answering service. Douglas selected a contemporary, chrome-like typeface to assimilate metal and achieve the desired effect.
The logo, part of the company's identity package, appears on its letterhead, business card, envelopes, and in print and television advertising. Douglas was assigned the project by Asa C. Douglas, president of ADI Advertising/Public Relations
in Fort Smith, Arkansas. The artist was paid $300 for all rights.

Arkansas

ADI ADVERTISING/PUBLIC RELATIONS, Box 2299, Ft. Smith AR 72902. President: Asa
Douglas. Ad agency/PR. Clients: retail, personal service, small manufacturing, political.
Needs: Assigns 150-200 freelance jobs/year. Works with 2-3 freelance illustrators and 5-10 freelance
designers/month. Uses artists for consumer and trade magazines, billboards, brochures, catalogs,
newspapers, stationery, signage and posters.
First Contact & Terms: Regional artists only, within two-days mail time. Send query letter with
resume, business card and samples to be kept on file; write for appointment to show portfolio. Prefers
slides and/or photographs as samples. Samples not kept on file are returned by SASE. Reports only if
interested. Works on assignment only. Pays by the project, $25 minimum. Considers complexity of
project, client's budget, skill and experience of artist and rights purchased when establishing payment.
Buys all rights.
Tips: "Present a variety of work to show scope of skill."

MANGAN RAINS GINNAVEN HOLCOMB, 911 Savers Federal Bldg., Little Rock AR 72201.
Contact: Steve Mangan. Ad agency. Clients: recreation, financial, consumer, industrial, real estate.
Needs: Works with 5 designers and 5 illustrators/month. Assigns 50 jobs and buys 50 illustrations/year.
Uses artists for consumer magazines, stationery design, direct mail, brochures/flyers, trade magazines
and newspapers. Also uses artists for illustrations for print materials.
First Contact & Terms: Query with brochure and samples. SASE. Reports in 2 weeks. Provide
brochure, flyer and business card to be kept on file for possible future assignments. No originals returned
to artist at job's completion. Negotiates pay.

California

BARR FILMS, 3490 E. Foothill Blvd., Pasadena CA 91107. (213)681-6978. Advertising Director:
Ken Statleman. Film/AV producer. Clients: schools, libraries, universities, colleges and businesses.
Needs: Works with 1 designer/month. Uses artists for print ads and ad flyers (conception and execution).
First Contact & Terms: Call for appointment to show portfolio of published work. Works on
assignment only. Provide resume, flyer and samples of work to be kept on file for possible future
assignments. Samples not kept on file returned by SASE. Negotiates payment based on budget and
amount of creativity required.

BATTENBURG, FILLHARDT & WRIGHT, INC., 70 N. Second St., San Jose CA 95113.
(408)287-8500. Creative Director: Charles Fillhardt. Ad agency. Clients: highly technical electronics
and some consumer firms.

Needs: Works with 5-10 illustrators/year. Uses freelance artists for billboards, consumer and trade magazines, direct mail, P-O-P displays, brochures, posters, newspapers and AV presentations.
First Contact & Terms: Arrange interview to show portfolio. Prefers actual works, tear sheets or slides as samples. Samples returned. Works on assignment basis only. Payment is by the project; negotiates according to where work will appear and client's budget.
Tips: "Clients are becoming more aware of good photography and illustration. Artists interested in working for us should keep us up-to-date, via mail, on work being done."

BEAR ADVERTISING, 1424 N. Highland, Hollywood CA 90028. (213)466-6464. Vice President: Bruce Bear. Clients: fast food enterprises, sporting goods firms and industrial. Assigns 50-100 jobs/year.
Needs: Works with 1-2 illustrators and 2 designers/month. Uses artists for illustrations for annual reports, design of direct mail brochures, mechanicals and sign design.
First Contact & Terms: Local artists only. Call for interview. No originals returned. Negotiates pay.

RALPH BING ADVERTISING CO., 16109 Selva Dr., San Diego CA 92128. (619)487-7444. President: Ralph S. Bing. Ad agency. Clients: industrial (metals, steel warehousing, mechanical devices, glass, packaging, stamping tags and labels), political, automotive, food and entertainment.
Needs: Uses artists for consumer and trade magazines, brochures, layouts, keylines, illustrations and finished art for newspapers, magazines, direct mail and TV.
First Contact & Terms: Local artists only. "Call first; arrange an appointment if there is an existing need; bring easy-to-present portfolio. Provide portfolio of photocopies and tear sheets, and client reference as evidence of quality and/or versatility." Reports only if interested. Works on assignment only. No original work returned to artist at job's completion. Pays by the hour, $5-50 average; by the project, $10 minimum. Considers complexity of project and client's budget when establishing payment.

CANTOR ADVERTISING, Suite 101, 7894 Dagget, San Diego CA 92111. (619)268-8422. Contact: David Evans, senior art director for design, illustration and photography; April LoVecchio, production manager, for production. Ad agency. Clients: credit unions, fast food, retail, direct mail, technical. Client list provided for SASE with accompanying request explanation.
Needs: Works with 30-40 freelance artists/year. Uses artists for design, production, photography, calligraphy, illustration, airbrush. Especially looks for professionalism in handling a project.
First Contact & Terms: Artists must be able to meet terms, deadlines and be able to negotiate. Works on assignment only. Send information (brochure, resume and samples to be kept on file) then call for appointment to show portfolio. Accepts "any professional-looking medium" as samples. Samples not filed are returned by SASE only if requested. Reports only if interested. Pays by project according to negotiation with each artist or along budget lines. Considers client's budget, complexity of the project and turnaround time when establishing payment. Rights are negotiable.
Tips: "Have your act together. Exhibit good presentation skills and a positive personality."

*COPY GROUP ADVERTISING, Box 315, Encino CA 91316. Contact: Len Miller. Clients: resorts, travel spots, vacation areas and direct mail.
Needs: Uses artists for cartoons, illustrations, spot drawings and humorous sketches. "Artists with experience in book publishing, advertising and greeting cards would probably have the skills we're looking for."
First Contact & Terms: Send a small sampling of material for review. Prefers photocopies as samples; *do not send original work*. Reports in 3 days.

CUNDALL/WHITEHEAD/ADVERTISING INC., 3000 Bridgeway, Sausalito CA 94965. (415)332-3625. Contact: Alan Cundall. Ad agency.
Needs: Works with 6 designers/month. Uses artists for consumer magazines, stationery design, direct mail, slide shows, brochures/flyers, trade magazines and newspapers. Also uses artists for layout, paste-up and type spec.
First Contact & Terms: Call for appointment. Reports in 1 day. Seldom requests samples. Provide brochures, flyers, business card and resume to be kept on file for future assignments. No originals returned to artist at job's completion. Payment depends upon the budget and complexity of the job.
Tips: "Seek the counsel of a top agency art director as to the merits of your portfolio before seeing other agencies."

DIMON & ASSOCIATES, 3001 N. San Fernando Blvd., Burbank CA 91505. (213)849-7777. Art Director: Bobby Smith. Ad agency/printing firm. Serves clients in industry, finance, computers, electronics, health care and pharmaceuticals.
First Contact & Terms: Query with samples (tear sheets, original art, photocopies, etc.). SASE. Provide brochure, flyer, business card, resume and tear sheets to be kept on file for future assignments.

Considers complexity of project, turnaround time, client's budget, and skill and experience of artist when establishing payment.

DJC & ASSOCIATES, 6117 Florin Rd., Sacramento CA 95823. (916)421-6310. Contact: Donna Cicogni. Ad agency. Assigns 120 jobs/year.
Needs: Works with 1 illustrator/month. Uses artists for consumer and trade magazines, stationery design, direct mail, TV, brochures/flyers and newspapers.
First Contact & Terms: Local artists only. Query with samples or arrange interview to show portfolio. Prefers photographs, photostats, b&w line drawings and printed work as samples. Reports in 1 week. Works on assignment only. Provide business card, brochure/flyer, samples and tear sheets to be kept on file for possible future assignments. Samples not kept on file are returned by SASE. No originals returned to artist at job's completion. Negotiates pay.

ESTEY, HOOVER ADVERTISING AND P.R., INC., Suite 225, 3300 Irvine Ave., Newport Beach CA 92660. (714)549-8651. Creative Director: Art Silver. Clients: consumer, financial, real estate, industrial and medical.
Needs: Wants highly talented professional illustrators, but will consider serious "up and coming" talent. Uses freelance artists for ads, magazine, newspaper, TV, AV, brochures, catalogs, posters, annual reports, story boards. Likes "thinking, contributing illustration."
First Contact & Terms: Call for appointment or send "head sheet"—not originals. Reports only if interested. Prefers to see original material and published samples; will expect costs and price at time of viewing. Works on assignment only. Pays $50-5,000/project, net 30 days, or ongoing. Considers complexity of project, client's budget, skill and experience of artist, geographic scope of finished project and deadline when establishing payment.

*EXPANDING IMAGES, A-143, 14252 Culver Dr., Irvine CA 92714. (714)720-0864. President: Robert Denison. Estab. 1985. Audiovisual firm. Clients: mixed.
Needs: Works with 6 freelance artists/year. Uses artists for graphics, photography, illustration and design.
First Contact & Terms: Works on assignment only. Send samples to be kept on file. Prefers tear sheets as samples. Samples not filed are returned by SASE only if requested. Reports only if interested. Pays by the day, $100-600 average. Considers client's budget and skill and experience of artist when establishing payment. Buys all rights.

*FILM COMMUNICATORS, 11136 Weddington St., North Hollywood CA 91601. Produces educational and training motion pictures, slides, study prints, brochures, books, pamphlets, filmstrips, mailing pieces and advertisements.
Needs: Assigns 20-25 jobs/year. Works with 1 illustrator and 3 designers/month. Uses freelancers for catalogs, brochures, other promotional materials, ad illustrations and forms.
First Contact & Terms: Prefers local artists with at least 2 years experience in putting together brochures and ads. Send resume and samples in care of advertising department or call same department to set up appointment. Interested in "any samples similar to the type of promotional materials we use (i.e., brochures, catalogs, etc.)." Samples returned. Works on assignment only. Provide resume, samples and brochure/flyer to be kept on file for possible future assignments. Reports in 2 weeks. Pays by the project. Amount of payment is negotiated with the individual artist. No originals returned to artist following publication. Buys all rights.
Tips: "The business market is catching up with the consumer market in its need for clever and interesting designs. However, we still need to emphasize clear, simple designs that don't take away from the selling point."

F/M FILM GROUP, INC.,(formerly Paterson Productions, Ltd.), Suite 179, 8033 Sunset Blvd., West Hollywood CA 90046. Vice President/Creative Director: Chip Miller. Production Director: Travis Walker. AV producer. Clients: entertainment, motion picture, music, television and cable video. "Client list provided for SASE."
Needs: Assigns 10-20 freelance jobs/year. Works with 2-3 illustrators and 2-4 designers/month. Uses artists for trade magazines, billboards, brochures, filmstrips, movies, AV presentations and posters.
First Contact & Terms: Send query letter with brochure and resume to production director to be kept on

---

 The asterisk before a listing indicates that the listing is new in this edition. New markets are often the most receptive to freelance contributions.

"We are building a 'look' for our company, and Steve has a good sense of what we want," says Lisa Waggoner, marketing director of Film Communicators, an audiovisual producer in North Hollywood, California. Local artist Steve Wilson designed this "clean and appealing" logo which Waggoner feels "has enough appeal to make customers open the brochure" it was printed on. The brochure was used as a marketing tool for audiovisual materials depicting the management of various disasters from floods to fires. Waggoner bought the original artwork plus all rights.

file; contact through artist's agent. Works on assignment only. Prefers slides as samples; returned by SASE. Must have experience working with similar firms. Reports only if interested. Pays by the hour, $35-75 average. Considers complexity of project, client's budget, skill and experience of artist and turnaround time when establishing payment. Negotiates rights purchased.

DON FRANK & ASSOCIATES, #133C, 4316 Mariner City Dr., Marina Del Rey CA 90292. Art Director: Laurel Shoemaker. Ad agency. Clients: real estate. Client list provided upon request.
Needs: Works with 5-10 freelance artists/year. Uses artists for illustration, production, art direction and some copy. Especially looks for clean, fast production; intelligent communication, and well-targeted creative concept.
First Contact & Terms: Works on assignment only. Send query letter with samples to be kept on file. Prefers photostats or tear sheets as samples; photocopies okay. Samples not filed are returned only if requested. Reports back only if interested. Pays by the hour, $15-35 average. Considers skill and experience of artist and turnaround time when establishing payment. Rights purchased vary according to project.
Tips: "We are a small agency. The volume of freelance work available comes in waves and stages."

FRANKLIN & ASSOC., 600 B St., San Diego CA 92101. (619)231-6168. Art Director: Scott Mayeda. Ad agency. Clients: banks, paint manufacturer, radio stations, auto dealers, real estate, dental clinics.
Needs: Works with 12-15 freelance artists/year. Uses artists for production, art direction, illustration, comp work and photography. Especially looks for good hand skills and good production knowledge.
First Contact & Terms: Experienced, available artists only. Send resume and samples to be kept on file; call for appointment to show portfolio. Prefers tear sheets or photostats as samples. Samples are filed, not returned. Reports only if interested. Pays by the hour. Considers client's budget, skill and experience of artist and turnaround time when establishing payment. Buys all rights.
Tips: "Write/call first, samples requested. Experience relevant to quality level of work we do."

HANNA-BARBERA PRODUCTIONS INC., 3400 Cahuenga Blvd., Hollywood CA 90068. (213)851-5000. Producer: Harry Love. TV/motion picture producer. Clients: TV networks. Produces animation and motion pictures.
Needs: Works with designers and illustrators on animated motion pictures. Also uses artists for animation and related artwork.
First Contact & Terms: Uses mostly local artists. Query and arrange interview to show portfolio. Reports "as soon as possible." Provide resume to be kept on file for future assignments. No originals returned to artist at job's completion. Negotiates pay.

*ED MARZOLA AND ASSOCIATES, 11846 Ventura Blvd., Studio City CA 91604. (818)506-7788.
President: Ed Marzola. Ad agency. Clients: automotive, aerospace, industrial, publishing and entertainment.
Needs: Works with 8-10 freelance artists/year. Uses artists for paste-up, photography, make-up, styling, model making and illustration. "Be cost conscious and know enough about printing process to be able to save us money when job is printed."
First Contact & Terms: "Only real requirements are that artist deliver on-time, on-budget, and that we feel good on assigning the job." Works on assignment only. Send query letter with brochure and business card to be kept on file; call or write for appointment to show portfolio. Accepts photostats, photographs, slides, tear sheets, etc. as samples. Samples not filed are returned by SASE. Reports within 10 days. Pays by the project, $100 minimum. Considers complexity of the project, client's budget, skill and experience of artist and turnaround time when establishing payment. Rights purchased vary according to project.
Tips: Send professionally finished, clean material. Even if it is a photocopy, we can tell the professional artists from the marginal ones."

WARREN MILLER PRODUCTIONS, 505 Pier Ave., Hermosa Beach CA 90254. (213)376-2494.
Owner: Warren Miller. Produces sports documentaries, commercials, television format films and video cassettes for home use.
Needs: Works with 1 ad illustrator and 1 advertising designer/year. Uses artists for direct mail brochures, magazine ads and posters.
First Contact & Terms: Query with samples (original sports illustration—skiing, sailing, windsurfing, etc.) or write for interview. Reports within 2 weeks. Buys nonexclusive rights. Works on assignment only. Samples returned by SASE. Provide resume to be kept on file for future assignments. "We pay by the project and since they range from brochures to full color film posters, it is impossible to give a fair range. Some of these are complicated; some already laid out and need only finished art." Considers complexity of project and skill and experience of artist when establishing payment.
Tips: There is "less 'standard' work and a trend toward contemporary, avant-garde art in our area of business. We prefer to work with artists who have done sports illustrations and recreation-oriented art, but we respond to great talent. Please send some kinds of samples and background information on assignments."

PALKO ADVERTISING, INC., Suite 207, 2075 Palos Verdes Dr. N., Lomita CA 90717. (213)530-6800. Account Services: Judy Kolosvary. Ad agency. Clients: business to business.
Needs: Uses artists for layout, illustration, paste-up, mechanicals, copywriting and P-O-P displays. Produces ads, brochures and collateral material.
First Contact & Terms: Prefers local artists. Send query letter with brochure, resume, business card and samples to be kept on file. Write for appointment to show portfolio. Accepts tear sheets, photographs, photocopies, printed material or slides as samples. Samples not filed returned only if requested. Reports back only if interested. Pay is "discussed and negotiated." Negotiates rights purchased.

*PANORAMA PRODUCTIONS, 2353 De La Cruz Blvd., Santa Clara CA 95050. Graphics Manager: Debbie Moore. Audiovisual firm. Clients: industrial and commercial.
Needs: Works with a varying number of freelance artists/year. Uses artists for computer graphics, paste-up, layout, technical drawings, illustrations, medical illustrating, cartooning, storyboards, and boardwork.
First Contact & Terms: Send query letter with resume to be kept on file. Reports back only if interested. Pays by the hour, $5-10 average. Considers skill and experience of artist when establishing payment. Buys all rights.
Tips: "We interview only after receiving and reviewing resumes. From the resumes we match skills and experience to the potential job requirements."

PETTLER, deGRASSI & HILL, 5236 Claremont Ave., Oakland CA 94618. (415)653-5990.
President: A.H. deGrassi. Ad agency. Clients: industrial, financial, agricultural and some consumer firms; client list provided upon request.
Needs: Works with 4-5 illustrators/month. Uses freelance artists for billboards, consumer and trade magazines, direct mail, P-O-P displays, brochures, catalogs, posters, signage, newspapers and AV presentations.
First Contact & Terms: Local artists only. Arrange interview to show portfolio. Prefers photostats or slides as samples. Samples returned. Reports only if interested. Works on assignment only. Payment is by the project or by the hour, $30 minimum. Considers complexity of project and client's budget when establishing payment.

THE RUSS REID CO., Suite 600, 2 N. Lake Ave., Pasadena CA 91101. (818)449-6100. Contact: Art Director. Ad agency. Clients: religious and cause-related organizations; client list provided upon request.
Needs: Works with "very few" freelance artists. Uses freelance artists for trade magazines, direct mail, brochures, posters and newspapers.
First Contact & Terms: Local artists only. Arrange interview to show portfolio. Works on assignment basis only. Negotiates payment according to client's budget; "whether by the hour, project or day depends on job."

JIM SANT'ANDREA WEST, INC., 855 W. Victoria, Compton CA 90220. (213)979-9100. General Manager: Guy Hence. AV producer. Serves various types of clients. Produces slides, filmstrips, video tapes and materials for live performances.
Needs: Assigns approximately 20 jobs/year. Works with 2 illustrators and 2-4 designers/month. Uses artists for beauty sketches and storyboards.
First Contact & Terms: Send resume, query letter and samples (photocopies of storyboards preferred); arrange interview by phone or mail. Samples not returned. Provide resume, samples and business card to be kept on file for possible future assignments. Reports only if interested. Method of payment is negotiated with the individual artist; pays by the project or by the day. Considers complexity of project, client's budget and turnaround time when establishing payment. No originals returned to artist after publication.
Tips: Artists interested in working for us "must have storyboard experience and must be good with magic markers and ink."

RICHARD SIEDLECKI DIRECT MARKETING,(formerly Market-Direct Advertising), Box 817, El Toro CA 92630. (714)768-5830. Direct Marketing Consultant: Richard Siedlecki. Consulting agency. Clients: industrial, publishers, associations, air freight, consumer mail order firms, financial. Client list provided for SASE.
Needs: Assigns 15 freelance jobs/year. Works with 2 freelance designers/month. Uses artists for consumer and trade magazines, direct mail packages, brochures, catalogs and newspapers.
First Contact & Terms: Artists should be "experienced in direct response marketing." Send query letter with brochure, resume and business card to be kept on file. Reports only if interested. Works on assignment only. Pays by the hour, $25 minimum; by the project, $250 minimum. Considers complexity of project and client's budget when establishing payment. "All work automatically becomes the property of our client."
Tips: Artists "must understand (and be able to apply) direct mail/direct response marketing methods to all projects: space ads, direct mail, brochures, catalogs."

ROGER TILTON FILMS INC., 315 6th Ave., San Diego CA 92101. (619)233-6513. Film producer. Clients: industrial and corporate. Produces filmstrips, motion pictures and videotapes.
Needs: Uses artists for filmstrip, animation, retouching, catalog design, slide illustration and advertising.
First Contact & Terms: Query with resume and samples or arrange interview to show portfolio. Prefers photostats or slides as samples. Reports only if interested. Works on assignment only. Provide resume to be kept on file for future assignments. Originals become client's property. Negotiates pay. Considers complexity of project, client's budget, and skill and experience of artist when establishing payment.

***VIDEO IMAGERY**, 204 Calle De Anza, San Clemente CA 92672. (714)492-5082. Contact: Bob Fisher. Audiovisual firm. Clients: industrial and manufacturing. Client list available for SASE.
Needs: Works with 2 freelance artists/year. Uses artists for art work for videos.
First Contact & Terms: Seeks local artists only. Works on assignment only. Send brochure to be kept on file; call for appointment to show portfolio. Prefers photostats or tear sheets as samples. Samples not filed are returned only if requested. Reports only if interested. Pays by the day, $100-150 average. Considers complexity of the project, client's budget and rights purchased when establishing payment. Rights purchased vary according to project.

***VIDEO RESOURCES**, Suite 307, 1805 E. Dyer Rd., Santa Ana CA 92705. (714)261-7266. Producer: Brad Hagen. Audiovisual firm. Clients: automotive, banks, restaurants, computer, transportation and energy.
Needs: Works with 8 freelance artists/year. Uses artists for graphics, package comps, animation, etc.
First Contact & Terms: Southern California artists only with minimum 5 years' experience. Works on assignment only. Send query letter with brochure, resume, business card and samples (after contract) to be kept on file. Prefers photostats and tear sheets as samples. Samples not filed are returned by SASE. Considers complexity of the project and client's budget when establishing payment. Buys all rights.

*VIDEOVISION CORPORATION, Suite 130, 27285 Las Ramblas, Mission Viejo CA 92691. (714)831-7700. Vice President/Production & Marketing: Bob Nash. Audiovisual firm. Clients: large corporations, cable and broadcast.
Needs: Works with 6 freelance artists/year. Uses artists for logos, graphs, etc. Especially important is a strong commercial art background.
First Contact & Terms: Prefers local artists. Works on assignment only. Send resume and samples to be kept on file; write for appointment to show portfolio. Accepts photostats, photographs, slides, tear sheets, etc. as samples. Samples not filed are returned only if requested. Pays by the hour, $5 minimum; by the project or by the day, $100 minimum. Considers complexity of the project and client's budget when establishing payment. Buys all rights or variable rights according to project.
Tips: Prefers video background or experience.

WANK, WILLIAMS & NEYLAN, 401 Burgess Dr., Menlo Park CA 94025. (415)323-3183. Art Director: Alvin Joe. Ad agency. Clients: restaurants, public transit, financial and industrial accounts, including electronics.
Needs: Works with 10 illustrators/month. Uses freelance artists for billboards, trade magazines, direct mail, P-O-P displays, brochures, catalogs, posters, signage, newspapers and AV presentations.
First Contact & Terms: Local artists primarily. Query with resume of credits. Works on assignment only. Payment depends on individual job.

WEST COAST ADVERTISING, Suite 108, 31316 Via Colinas, Westlake Village CA 91361. (213)991-1779. President: Cherie A. Tippett. Ad agency. Clients: industrial, automotive, medical and consumer.
Needs: Assigns "many" jobs/year. Works with 2 freelance illustrators/month. Uses artists for consumer and trade magazines, direct mail packages, brochures, catalogs, newspapers, P-O-P displays and press releases.
First Contact & Terms: Local artists only. Works on assignment only. Pay is by the project. "Estimate is usually submitted; however we do not ask artist to break down his costs."
Tips: "At this time agency needs are satisfied with inhouse art direction and local freelance artists. This position changes with account acquisitions."

GLORIA ZIGNER & ASSOCIATES INC., 328 N. Newport Blvd., Newport Beach CA 92663. (714)645-6300. President: Gloria Zigner. PR firm. Clients: hotels, insurance companies, hospitals, restaurants, financial institutions, manufacturers, electronic companies, builders and developers. Buys 12-24 illustrations/year.
Needs: Works with 2-3 illustrators and 2-3 designers/month. Uses artists for billboards, P-O-P displays, consumer magazines, stationery design, multimedia kits, direct mail, brochures/flyers, trade magazines and newspapers. Also uses artists for design, color separations, layout, lettering, paste-up and type spec.
First Contact & Terms: Local artists only. Write for interview. Reports only if interested. Provide brochure, flyer, business card, resume and tear sheets to be kept on file for future assignments. No originals returned at job's completion. Pays promised fee for unused assigned work.

Los Angeles

N.W. AYER, INC.,707 Wilshire Blvd, Los Angeles CA 90017. (213)621-1400. Creative Director: John Littlewood. Associate Creative Director: Steve Garber. Executive Art Director: Bob Bowen. Senior Art Director: Lionel Banks. Graphics Buyer: Gayle Davis-Nanini. Ad agency. Serves clients in finance, food and government.
Needs: Uses 1-2 illustrators/month. Uses artists for billboards, P-O-P displays, filmstrips, consumer magazines, direct mail, television, slide sets, brochures/flyers, trade magazines, album covers and newspapers.
First Contact & Terms: Call for personal appointment to show portfolio. "People interested should research what type of clients N.W. Ayer has in such references as *Advertising Agency Register* and in the Red Book." Provide tear sheets, original art or photocopies to be kept on file for future assignments. Negotiates payment based on client's budget and amount of creativity required from artist. No originals returned at job's completion.

BANNING CO., Suite 210, 11818 Wilshire Blvd., Los Angeles CA 90025. (213)477-8517. Art Director: Bill Reynolds. Ad agency. Serves a variety of clients.
Needs: Works with 2 comp artists and 2-3 designers per month. Uses designers for P-O-P displays, consumer and trade magazines, stationery design, direct mail, brochures/flyers and newspapers.
First Contact & Terms: Call for interview. Prefers slides as samples. Samples returned by SASE.

Reports within 2-3 weeks. Works on assignment only. Provide business card and brochure to be kept on file for future assignments. No originals returned at job's completion. All pay is based on job. Considers complexity of project, client's budget, turnaround time and rights purchased when establishing payment.
Tips: "This is a business first; art folks need some business skills—not just artistic ones. Have patience and confidence."

*BOSUSTOW VIDEO, 2207 Colby Ave., West Los Angeles CA 90064. Contact: Tee Bosustow. Video production firm. Clients: broadcast series, feature films, corporate, etc.
Needs: Works with varying number of freelance artists depending on projects. Uses artists for titles, maps, graphs and other information illustrations.
First Contact & Terms: Local artists only. Hires per job; no staff artists. Works on assignment only. Send brochure and resume only to be kept on file. Do not send samples; required only for interview. Samples not filed are returned by SASE. Reports only if interested. Pays by the project, $50-500 average. Considers complexity of the project, client's budget and turnaround time when establishing payment. Usually buys all rights; varies according to project.
Tips: "Please, don't call me. I'll call you if I need your services."

BOZELL & JACOBS, INC., Suite 900, 10850 Wilshire Blvd., Los Angeles CA 90024. (213)879-1800. Senior Art Director: Mike Phillips. Ad agency. Clients: consumer/industrial. Media used include billboards, consumer and trade magazines, direct mail, newspapers, radio and TV.
First Contact & Terms: Call for personal appointment to show portfolio. Prefers photocopies, b&w/color or printed samples. Works on assignment only; reports only if interested. Provide business card, resume and samples to be kept on file for possible future assignments. Pays by the project, $150-2,500 average. Considers complexity of project, turnaround time, client's budget, rights purchased, and skill and experience of artist when establishing payment.
Tips: Show current work.

DYR, INC., 4751 Wilshire Blvd., Los Angeles CA 90010. (213)930-5000. Art Buyer: Robert Chandler. Ad agency. Clients: food and beverage, financial.
Needs: Works with about 3 freelance illustrators/month. Uses freelancers primarily for TV storyboards and comps to clients.
First Contact & Terms: Call for appointment to show portfolio. Selection based on portfolio review. Negotiates payment based on amount of creativity required from artist.
Tips: Wants to see versatility, new concepts and most importantly, indication that storyboards can be executed quickly while maintaining quality.

EVANS/WEINBERG ADVERTISING, 6380 Wilshire Blvd., Los Angeles CA 90048. (213)653-2300. Creative Director: Paul Waddel. Ad agency. Clients: "wide variety" of accounts; client list provided upon request.
Needs: Number of freelance artists used varies.
First Contact & Terms: Local artists only. Arrange interview to show portfolio. Payment varies according to job.

GARIN AGENCY, #614, 6253 Hollywood Blvd., Los Angeles CA 90028. (213)465-6249. Manager: P. Bogart. Ad agency/public relations firm. Clients: real estate, banks.
Needs: Works with 1-2 freelance artists/year. Uses artists for "creative work and TV commercials."
First Contact & Terms: Local artists only. Works on assignment only. Send query letter with samples to be kept on file for one year. Prefers photostats or tear sheets as samples. Samples not filed are not returned. Does not report back. Negotiates pay; by the hour. Considers client's budget and turnaround time when establishing payment. Buys all rights.
Tips: "Don't be too pushy and don't overprice yourself."

GUMPERTZ/BENTLEY/FRIED, 5900 Wilshire Blvd., Los Angeles CA 90036. (213)931-6301. Executive Art Director: Steve Hallingsworth. Ad agency. Clients: stockbrokers, banks, food companies and visitors' bureaus. Call to arrange interview to show portfolio.
Needs: Works with 3-4 illustrators/month; 2-3 designers/year. Uses artists for illustration and paste-up. Negotiates pay.

IMAGE STREAM, 5450 W. Washington Blvd., Los Angeles CA 90016. (213)933-9196. Art Director: Ben Paris. Design Director: Brad Hood. Producer of AV materials for various live formats, film and video. Clients: industry, government and advertising. Produces "usually the larger multi-image shows (12-18 projectors), but some smaller (3-6 projectors) are also produced."
Needs: Professional artists with 3-5 years' experience only. Assigns 10-15 jobs/year. Works with 2-6

designers/year. Uses artists for "overload situations, sometimes for presentation boards for proposals." Looking for stage designers.

First Contact & Terms: Arrange interview by phone, then send resume and samples (slides preferred). "Don't send original art—prefer to see it in portfolio." Samples returned by SASE. Provide resume, brochure/flyer, business card and slide sheet to be kept on file for possible future assignments. Works on assignment only. Reporting time is discussed at portfolio review. Method of payment is negotiated with the individual artist. Payment varies with each client's budget. No originals returned following publication. Negotiates rights purchased.

Tips: "I look for a steady hand, clean work, good design sense and technical expertise of the graphic arts. Working knowledge of photography is very helpful. Our work is a hybrid of design, graphics, photography and special effects, and animation. AV is a very fast growing, fairly young industry. Good qualified artists are hard to find. A technical aptitude is helpful in developing the potential in this field."

PAUL MUCHNICK CO., 5818 Venice Blvd., Los Angeles CA 90019. (213)934-7986. Art/Creative Director: Paul Muchnick. Ad agency. Serves clients in mail order, giftwares, publishing, housewares and general consumer products.

Needs: Uses artists for layout, paste-up, brochures/flyers and retouching for newspapers, magazines and direct mail.

First Contact & Terms: Local artists only. Call for interview. No originals returned to artist at job's completion.

MULTI-MEDIA WORKS, 7227 Beverly Blvd., Los Angeles CA 90036. (213)939-1185. Owner: Art Ganung. AV producer. Clients: industrial. Audience: salespeople. Produces filmstrips, multimedia kits, slide sets and sound-slide sets.

Needs: Works with 1 illustrator and 1 designer/every other month for filmstrips. Also uses artists for slide illustration, paste-up and assembly.

First Contact & Terms: Local artists only. Arrange interview to show portfolio. SASE. Reports only if interested. Works on assignment only. Provide resume and tear sheet to be kept on file. No originals returned after job's completion. Pays by the hour, $10-20 average. Considers client's budget, and skill and experience of artist when establishing payment.

Tips: "Understand and be aware of audiovisual needs for legibility and format."

NEEDHAM, HARPER & STEERS, INC., Suite 900, 11601 Wilshire Blvd., Los Angeles CA 90025. (213)208-5000. Manager, Art Services: Annie Ross. Ad agency. Serves clients in automobile, heavy equipment and baking.

Needs: Works with about 4 freelance illustrators/month. Uses freelancers for all media.

First Contact & Terms: Call art buyer for appointment to show portfolio. Selection based on portfolio review. Negotiates payment.

Tips: Wants to see variety of techniques.

OGILVY & MATHER SPECIAL MARKETS.(formerly Ogilvy & Mather Recruitment Advertising), 7th Floor, 5757 Wilshire Blvd., Los Angeles CA 90036. (213)930-6600. Branch Manager: Lorraine Rausch. Vice President/Creative Director: Morris Hertz. Recruitment and special project advertising agency. Clients: finance, banking, insurance, medical, universities; high technology - computer, data processing, telecommunications, aerospace.

Needs: Assigns 75-100 freelance jobs/year. Works with 4 freelance illustrators and 4 freelance designers/month. Uses artists for trade magazines, billboards, brochures and newspapers.

First Contact & Terms: Local artists only. Send business card and samples to be kept on file. Call for appointment to show portfolio. Photostats acceptable as samples. Samples returned only if requested. Reports only if interested. Works on assignment only. Pays by the hour, negotiable. Considers client's budget, skill and experience of artist, turnaround time and rights purchased when establishing payment. Buys all rights.

Tips: "Best days to set up appointments are Mondays and Tuesdays."

*RAPP & COLLINS/WEST ADVERTISING, 5900 Wilshire Blvd., Los Angeles CA 90036. (213)936-9600. Senior Art Director: Daniel Villefort. Ad agency. Clients: banking, food, fashion, etc. Client list provided upon request.

Needs: Works with 30-40 freelance artists/year. Uses artists for photography, illustration and art-mechanicals.

First Contact & Terms: Send samples to be kept on file; call for appointment to show portfolio. Prefers photographs or tear sheets as samples. Samples not filed are returned only if requested. Reports only if interested. Considers complexity of the project, client's budget, skill and experience of artist, geographic scope for the finished product, turnaround time and rights purchased when establishing payment. Buys first rights.

SCOTT LANCASTER MILLS ATHA, Suite 860, 2049 Century Park E., Los Angeles CA 90067. (213)552-6050. Creative Director: Peggy Lancaster. Ad agency. Clients: toys, wall coverings, hair care products and vitamins. Assigns 250 jobs and buys 40 illustrations/year.
Needs: Uses artists for animation, catalogs, magazines, packaging, P-O-P displays, posters, TV, newspapers, color separations, layout, mechanicals, lettering and retouching.
First Contact & Terms: Query with samples or arrange interview by letter. Calls are not preferable. Prefers slides, actual renderings and proofs, etc., as samples. Samples returned by SASE. Reports within 1 week. Works on assignment only. Provide business card, resume and samples to be kept on file for possible future assignments. Pay depends on client's budget.

*SLIDEMAKERS WEST, INC., Suite 1215, 3325 Wilshire Blvd., Los Angeles CA 90010. Vice President Production: Stacy Shramm. Computer graphics firm. Clients: professional and corporate.
Needs: Works with 2-5 freelance artists/year. Uses artists for computer graphics. Especially important is experience on the Genigraphics equipment.
First Contact & Terms: Minimum 1 year experience on equipment. Works on assignment only. Send query letter with samples (slides only) to be kept on file. Samples are returned only if requested. Reports within 2 weeks. Pays by the hour, $15 minimum. Considers skill and experience of artist and turnaround time when establishing payment. Buys all rights.

San Francisco

ARNOLD & ASSOCIATES PRODUCTIONS, 2159 Powell St., San Francisco CA 94133. (415)989-3490. President: John Arnold. Audiovisual firm. Clients: general.
Needs: Works with 30 freelance artists/year. Uses artists for multi-media, slide show and staging production.
First Contact & Terms: Prefers local artists, award-winning and experienced. "We're an established, national firm." Works on assignment only. Send resume to be kept on file. Considers complexity of the project, client's budget and skill and experience of artist when establishing payment.

FOOTE, CONE, & BELDING/HONIG, 1255 Battery St., Box 3183, San Francisco CA 94119. (415)398-5200. Executive Art Director: Mike Koelker. Ad agency. Clients: apparel, food, utilities, household cleaner.
First Contact & Terms: Send samples of work (slides) and follow up by phone. Negotiates payment based on client's budget. No originals returned at job's completion.

*FURMAN FILMS, 3466 21st St., San Francisco CA 94110. (415)824-8500. Producer: Jan Davis. Audiovisual and motion picture production firm. Clients: variety of corporate clients, and agricultural co-ops.
Needs: Works with 5 freelance artists/year. Uses artists for paste-up, design, maps, illustrations, signs and type spec. Especially important are speed, accuracy, knowledge of film/video media, and flexibility in working hours.
First Contact & Terms: Works on assignment only. Send query letter with resume and business card to be kept on file; write for appointment to show portfolio. "Information is kept on file and interviews done when need arises for freelance assistance." Prefers photostats, photographs or tear sheets as samples. Samples returned by SASE. Reports only if interested. Pays by the hour, $8-20 average; pays by the project, $100-250 average. Considers complexity of the project, client's budget, skill and experience of artist, turnaround time and rights purchased when establishing payment. Buys all rights or variable rights according to project; negotiates rights purchased.

KETCHUM COMMUNICATIONS, 55 Union St., San Francisco CA 94111. (415)781-9480. Executive Creative Director: Kenneth Dudwick. Ad agency. Serves clients in food and medicine.
Needs: Uses freelancers for consumer and trade magazines, newspapers, print ads and TV.
First Contact & Terms: Call for appointment to show portfolio. Selection based on portfolio review, mailers from freelancers and contact by reps. Negotiates payment based on client's budget, amount of creativity required from artist and where work will appear.
Tips: Wants to see in portfolio whatever best illustrates freelancer's style. Include past work used by other ad agencies and tear sheets of published art.

MARSCHALK, (formerly Dailey & Associates), 574 Pacific, San Francisco CA 94133. (415)981-2250. Executive Art Director: Alan Lefkort. Ad agency. Clients: primarily travel, wine and food.
Needs: Works with 3-4 freelance illustrators and 2 freelance designers/month. Uses freelancers for billboards, consumer and trade magazines, direct mail, brochures/flyers, newspapers, P-O-P displays, stationery design and TV.

First Contact & Terms: Call for appointment to show portfolio. Selection based on past association and review of portfolios. Negotiates payment based on usage and where work will appear.
Tips: Wants to see features that demonstrate freelancer's originality and competency.

MERCHANDISING FACTORY, 222 Front St., San Francisco CA 94111. (415)956-4990. Production Manager: Shauna Gladstone. Ad agency. Clients: real estate, airlines, restaurants, banks, sporting goods, retail paper products, food services and grocery store products.
Needs: Works with 2 illustrators and 2 designers/month. Uses artists for filmstrips, slide sets and brochures/flyers; also for color separations, layout, lettering, paste-up, retouching and comps.
First Contact & Terms: Mostly local artists. Query with samples (tear sheets, photocopies) or arrange interview. SASE. Reports within 1 week. Provide business card and tear sheets to be kept on file for future assignments. No originals returned to artist at job's completion.

O'KEEFFE'S INC., 75 Williams Ave., San Francisco CA 94124. (415)822-4222. Marketing Manager: Abby Lipman. Manufacturer of skylights, aluminum building products and fire-rated glass door, window and wall systems for architects, contractors and builders.
Needs: Works with 1-5 freelance artists/year. Uses artists for advertising, brochure and catalog design, illustration and layout.
First Contact & Terms: Works on assignment only. Call or write for appointment to show portfolio. Reports back only if interested. Pays by the hour, $25-50 average. Considers complexity of the project, skill and experience of artist, and turnaround time when establishing payment.
Tips: "Work more on planning, not necessarily on the finished piece—that's the printer's art."

EDGAR S. SPIZEL ADVERTISING INC., 1782 Pacific Ave., San Francisco CA 94109. (415)474-5735. President: Edgar S. Spizel. AV producer. Clients: "Consumer-oriented from department stores to symphony orchestras, supermarkets, financial institutions, radio, TV stations, political organizations, hotels and real estate firms." Works a great deal with major sports stars and TV personalities.
Needs: Uses artists for posters, ad illustrations, brochures and mechanicals.
First Contact & Terms: Query with samples (tear sheets). SASE. Reports within 3 weeks. Provide materials to be kept on file for future assignments. No originals returned at job's completion. Negotiates pay.

WILTON, COOMBS AND COLNETT, INC., 855 Front St., San Francisco CA 94111. (415)981-6250. Contact: Art Director. Ad agency. Clients: consumer, electronic, computers and high-tech products; client list provided upon request.
Needs: Works with 10-20 illustrators/year. Uses freelance artists for billboards, consumer and trade magazines, P-O-P displays, brochures, posters, newspapers and AV presentations.
First Contact & Terms: Arrange interview to show portfolio. Prefers to see ad proofs for real clients—also some original work in the area of experimentation as samples. Samples returned. Reports in 1-2 weeks. Works on assignment basis only. Provide materials to be kept on file for possible future assignments. Payment is by the project; negotiates according to client's budget, amount of creativity required, artist's previous experience and where work will appear. Usually pays going project rate, $500-3,000 average, but sometimes has to negotiate.

Colorado

*CINE DESIGN FILMS, 255 Washington St., Denver CO 80203. (303)777-4222. Producer/Director: Jon Husband. Audiovisual firm. Clients: automotive firms, banks, restaurants, etc.
Needs: Works with 3-7 freelance artists/year. Uses artists for layout, titles, animation and still photography. Clear concept ideas that relate to the client in question are important.
First Contact & Terms: Works on assignment only. Send query letter to be kept on file; write for appointment to show portfolio. Reports only if interested. Pays by the hour, $20-50 average; by the project, $300-1,000 average; by the day, $75-100 average. Considers complexity of the project, client's budget and rights purchased when establishing payment. Rights purchased vary according to project.

COMPUTER IMAGE PRODUCTIONS, INC., 2475 W. 2nd Ave., Denver CO 80223. (303)934-5801. Art Director: John Wood. Computer video animation producer. Clients: international broadcasters; advertising agencies; industrial, corporate and medical institutions; filmmakers and numerous independent clients who utilize broadcasting in their advertising.
Needs: Works with 1 illustrator and 1-2 graphic artists/month. Especially needs 1 illustrator, 1-2 graphic artists and camera people. Uses artists for storyboards, background illustration, print ads and production art. Artwork done daily.

First Contact & Terms: Send resume and samples (animated graphics on video cassette, samples of illustration, storyboards, graphic design and printed pieces). Samples not returned. Provide resume and business card to be kept on file one year for possible future assignments. Pays by the hour, $5 minimum; "Due to the nature of daily inhouse work, I pay freelance people hourly. Frequently art has to be changed or redone; by paying hourly no one loses out financially."
Tips: "Be aware of who is doing what with what and how they did it. Critically judge what you did a year ago with what you are doing now to advance yourself technically and graphically. Make sure you have some skill/talent before you try to sell it."

EVANS & BARTHOLOMEW, INC., Suite 309, 2128 15th St., Denver CO 80202. (303)534-2343. Creative Director: Chuck Bennett. Ad agency. Clients: consumer, public service, institutional and financial.
Needs: Works with about 6 freelance illustrators/month. Uses freelancers for consumer and trade magazines, brochures/flyers, newspapers and TV.
First Contact & Terms: Call for appointment to show portfolio. Negotiates payment based on client's budget and where work will appear.
Tips: Wants to see "great illustrations," past work used by other ad agencies and tear sheets of published art in portfolio.

SAM LUSKY ASSOCIATES, 633 17th St., Denver CO 80202. (303)292-4141. Senior Art Director: Bob Corneley. Ad agency. Clients: financial and consumer firms.
Needs: Works with 10 illustrators/month; rarely uses freelance designers. Uses freelance artists for billboards, consumer and trade magazines, direct mail, P-O-P displays, brochures, catalogs, posters, signage, newspapers and AV presentations.
First Contact & Terms: Works primarily with local artists but considers others. Arrange interview to show portfolio. Works on assignment basis only. Payment is by the project; negotiates according to client's budget.

STARWEST PRODUCTIONS, 1391 N. Speer Blvd., Denver CO 80204. (303)623-0636. Creative Director: Steve Pettit. Ad agency/audiovisual firm. Clients list provided upon request with SASE.
Needs: Works with 2-4 freelance artists/year. Uses artists for full concept to paste-up. Especially seeks paste-up skills.
First Contact & Terms: Local artists only, experienced in audiovisual, print, storyboard. Works on assignment only. Send resume and samples to be kept on file; write for appointment to show portfolio. Prefers slides, tear sheets, photostats as samples. Samples not filed are returned. Reports within 30 days. Pays by the project, $1,000. Considers client's budget, and skill and experience of artist when establishing payment. Negotiates rights purchased.
Tips: "Always looking for someone with 'new' ideas."

Connecticut

THE BERNI CORP., 666 Steamboat Rd., Greenwich CT 06830. (203)661-4747. Contact: Stuart Berni. Clients: manufacturers and retailers of consumer products. Buys 25 illustrations/year. Write or call for interview; local professionals only.
Needs: Uses artists for illustration, layout, lettering, paste-up, retouching and type spec for annual reports, catalogs, letterheads, P-O-P displays, packaging, design, production and trademarks. Pays $10-25. Pays promised fee for unused assigned work.

***EAGLEVISION, INC.**, Box 3347, Stamford CT 06905. (203)359-8777. Principal/Creative Director: Michael Macari, Jr. Estab. 1983. Audiovisual firm. Clients: corporate/industrial, music and arts and consumer home video programmer.
Needs: Works with 25-50 freelance artists/year. Uses artists for computer and digital graphics and animation footage.
First Contact & Terms: "Good quality and creativity" are especially important. Works on assignment only. Send query letter and samples to be kept on file; call or write for appointment to show portfolio. Prefers $3/4$" or $1/2$" VHS or BETA Hi-Fi videotapes as samples. Samples not filed are returned by SASE. Reports within 1 week only if interested. Pays by the project or by amount of material/footage. Considers complexity of the project, skill and experience of artist, and rights purchased when establishing payment. Buys one-time rights, all rights or variable rights according to project.

EDUCATIONAL DIMENSIONS GROUP, Box 126, Stamford CT 06904. (203)327-4612. Visual Editors: Marguerite Mead and Greg Byrnes. AV producer. Audience: businesses, schools and libraries.

Produces filmstrips, motion pictures, slide sets and videotapes.
Needs: Works with illustrators and designers. Uses designers and mechanical artists for catalogs, filmstrips, direct mail flyers and brochures, etc.
First Contact & Terms: Query with resume and photocopied samples and photostats. Samples returned only if requested. Reports in 2 weeks. Provide resume to be kept on file for future assignments. Works on assignment only. Originals only returned at job's completion when return has been negotiated earlier. Pays by job for filmstrip, slide and film illustrations, charts, graphics and diagrams. "Payment depends totally on type of project."
Tips: Looks for neatness, organization, fresh ideas and versatility.

JACOBY/STORM PRODUCTIONS INC., 22 Crescent Rd., Westport CT 06880. (203)227-2220. President: Doris Storm. AV/TV/film producer. Clients: schools, corporations and publishers. Produces filmstrips, motion pictures, slide sets, sound-slide sets and videotapes.
Needs: Assigns 6-8 jobs/year. Uses artists for lettering, illustrations for filmstrips and to design slide show graphics.
First Contact & Terms: Prefers local artists with filmstrip and graphics experience. Query with resume and arrange interview. SASE. Reports in 2 weeks. Usually buys all rights. Pays $20-30/frame, lettering; $50-100/frame, illustrations. Pays on acceptance.

THE McMANUS COMPANY, Box 446, Greens Farms CT 06436. (203)255-3301. President: John F. McManus. National advertising/marketing/PR agency. Serves clients in data processing, corporate, consumer, industrial, social agencies, automotives and other industries.
Needs: Works with 4 illustrators/month. Uses artists for art direction (TV commercials), graphic design (print ads and collateral pieces), illustration, publications, filmstrips, multimedia kits, storyboards and packaging.
First Contact & Terms: Send resume (to be kept on file for future assignments) and/or write for interview to show portfolio. Works on assignment only. Samples returned by SASE; reports back on future assignment possibilities. "Payment is determined on use of creative work, whether it will appear in national or regional media."

MARKETING EAST INC., 520 West Ave., Norwalk CT 06850. (203)866-2234. Contact: W. Greene. Ad agency.
Needs: Works with 2-3 freelance artists/year. Uses artists for mechanicals, etc.
First Contact & Terms: Experienced artists only. Send samples to be kept on file; call for appointment to show portfolio. Accepts photostats, photographs, slides or tear sheets as samples. Samples not filed are returned only if requested. Reports back only if interested. Pays by the job. Buys all rights

THE MERRILL ANDERSON CO. INC., 1166 Barnum Ave., Stratford CT 06497-5402. (203)377-4996. Art Director: Ellen Fairfield. Clients: financial.
Needs: Works with 2 illustrators/month. Uses artists for direct mail and brochures/flyers. Also uses artists for cartoons and realistic illustrations. Assigns 25 illustrations/year.
First Contact & Terms: Arrange interview to show portfolio. Prefers photographs, b&w line drawings or color art as samples. Reports in 2 weeks. Works on an assignment basis only. Provide brochure to be kept on file for future assignments. No originals returned to artist at job's completion. Pays $50/job.

STANLEY H. MURRAY ADVERTISING, 45 E. Putman Ave., Greenwich CT 06830. (203)869-8803. President: Stan Murray. Ad agency/PR firm. Assigns 250 jobs/year.
Needs: Works with 5-10 illustrators and 5-10 designers/month. Uses artists for billboards, P-O-P displays, filmstrips, consumer magazines, stationery design, multimedia kits, direct mail, slide sets, brochures/flyers, trade magazines and newspapers.
First Contact & Terms: Query with resume and samples or arrange interview to show portfolio. SASE. Reports within 1 week. Provide materials to be kept on file for future assignments. No originals returned at job's completion. Pays $30/hour.

PALM, DEBOMIS, RUSSO, INC., 800 Cottage Grove Rd., Bloomfield CT 06002. (203)242-6258. Art Director: Lynn Schultz. Ad agency. Clients: consumer and industrial products and services.
Needs: Works with 2-3 illustrators/month. Uses illustrators for consumer magazines, trade magazines and technical illustration. Also uses artists for layout, illustration, technical art, paste-up, retouching, lettering and storyboards for TV, newspapers, magazines, radio, billboards, direct mail and collateral.
First Contact & Terms: Submit samples or call for interview. Prefers slides, photographs, photostats, b&w line drawings and originals as samples. Samples returned by SASE "if requested." Reports within 4 weeks. Works on assignment only. Provide business card, resume, samples and tear sheets of work to be kept on file for future assignments. No originals returned at job's completion. Pays by the project,

$100-1,000 average. Considers complexity of project, client's budget, skill and experience of artist and turnaround time when establishing payment.
Tips: "Try not to submit too many styles of work—only what one is best at."

VIDEOWORKSHOP, 17¹/₂ S. Main St., Norwalk CT 06854. (203)838-1135. Media Coordinator: Frank Knize. Audiovisual firm. Clients: "anyone who needs commercials, documentories or video file tapes done."
Needs: Works with 10 freelance artists/year. "We are looking only for freelance people who can make a contribution in equipment (³/₄" video production, such as camera, editing and such) as well as having good production skills. We would like to team up with freelance people with the arrangement that he can be hired out as a package."
First Contact & Terms: Works on assignment only. Send resume to be kept on file. Reports only if interested. Pays by the day, $50-100 average, "plus what they get for their equipment." Considers complexity of project and client's budget when establishing payment. Rights purchased vary according to project.

*BERNARD WEISS & ASSOCIATES, 51 Regent Court, Stamford CT 06907. President: Bernard Weiss. Clients: health care industry and professions. Produces multimedia materials.
Needs: Works with 1 + illustrators and 1 + designers/month. Uses artists for magazine covers/illustrations, direct mail brochures, layout, multimedia kits, paste-up, anatomical drawings and type spec.
First Contact & Terms: Query or arrange interview. SASE. Reports in 1 week. Buys one-time and reprint rights. Provide name, address, phone number on 3x5 card to be kept on file for future assignments. Originals returned to artist at job's completion. Pays $500-1,200, brochure layout, design, type spec and paste-up; $50-500, anatomical illustrations.

THE WESTPORT COMMUNICATIONS GROUP INC., 155 Post Rd. E., Westport CT 06880. (203)226-3525. Art Director: H. Lindsay. AV producer. Clients: educational and corporate. Produces filmstrips, multimedia kits, slide sets, sound-slide sets and booklets.
Needs: Works with 10-15 illustrators/year. Uses artists for filmstrip, slide, booklet, brochure and trade magazine illustrations.
First Contact & Terms: Query or arrange interview to show portfolio. Reports within 1 month. Provide tear sheets to be kept on file for future assignments. Pays $35/educational filmstrip frame; negotiates pay on other assignments.

Delaware

ALOYSIUS, BUTLER, & CLARK, Bancroft Mills, 30 Hill Rd., Wilmington DE 19806. (302)655-1552. Creative Director: Scott Stooker. Ad agency. Clients: banks, industry, restaurants, real estate, hotels, small, local businesses, transit system, government offices.
Needs: Assigns "many" freelance jobs/year. Works with 3-4 freelance illustrators and 3-4 freelance designers/month. Uses artists for trade magazines, billboards, direct mail packages, brochures, newspapers, stationery, signage and posters.
First Contact & Terms: Local artists only "within reason (Philadelphia, Baltimore)." Send query letter with resume, business card and sample to be kept on file all except work that is "not worthy of consideration." Call for appointment to show portfolio. Prefers slides, photos, stats, photocopies as samples. Samples not kept on file returned only if requested. Reports only if interested. Works on assignment only. Pays by the project. Considers complexity of project, client's budget, and skill and experience of artist when establishing payment. Buys all rights.

CUSTOM CRAFT STUDIO, (formerly Bennett Studios), 310 Edgewood St., Bridgeville DE 19933. AV producer.
Needs: Works with 1 illustrator and 1 designer/month. Uses artists for filmstrips, slide sets, trade magazine and newspapers. Also uses artists for print finishing, color negative retouching and airbrush work.
First Contact & Terms: Write. Prefers slides or photographs as samples. Samples returned by SASE. Reports in 2 weeks. Works with freelance artists on an assignment basis only. Provide brochure/flyer, resume, samples and tear sheets to be kept on file for possible future assignments. No originals returned to artist at job's completion. Pay varies.

LYONS, INC., 715 Orange St., Wilmington DE 19801. (302)654-6146. Vice President: P. Coleman DuPont. AV/video/literature/display design producer. Clients: corporate and industrial.
Needs: Has need for storyboard artists and multi-image designers. Uses artists for multimedia

presentations, collateral, literature, advertising and displays.

First Contact & Terms: Send resume. Prefers printed pieces, original art, storyboards, slides and/or video and multi-image samples—screening facilities available. Samples returned by SASE. Reports only if interested. Provide flyer or slides to be kept on file for future assignments. Works on assignment only. Pays by the hour, $6-14 average. Considers complexity of project, client's budget, and skill and experience of artist when establishing payment.

MALCOLM L. MACKENZIE & ASSOCIATES, Box 25123, Wilmington DE 19899. (302)364-6755. President: Malcolm Mackenzie. Ad agency. Clients: "all types."

Needs: Assigns 15 freelance jobs/year. Works with 2 freelance illustrators and 1 freelance designer/month. Uses artists for billboards, direct mail packages, brochures, newspapers, filmstrips, movies, stationery, P-O-P displays, AV presentations, posters and press releases.

First Contact & Terms: Send query letter with resume to be kept on file. Does not report back. Works on assignment only. Pay rate "depends on the job." Considers complexity of project and client's budget when establishing payment. Buys all rights.

Tips: "We are well supplied now—little open opportunities."

SHIPLEY ASSOCIATES INC., Suite 214, 3844 Kennett Pike, Powder Mill Square, Wilmington DE 19807. (302)652-3051. Creative Director: Jack Parry. Ad/PR firm. Serves clients in harness racing, insurance, real estate and entertainment.

Needs: Works with 2 illustrators and 1 designer/month. Assigns 9 jobs/year. Uses artists for annual report illustrations, mechanicals, brochure and sign design.

First Contact & Terms: Query with previously published work. Prefers layouts (magazine & newspaper), mechanicals, line drawings and finished pieces as samples. Samples not returned. Reports within 2 weeks. Works with freelance artists on assignment only. Provide resume, samples and tear sheets to be kept on file for possible future assignments. No originals returned at job's completion. Negotiates payment.

District of Columbia

DANIEL J. EDELMAN, INC., 1730 Pennsylvania Ave. NW, Washington DC 20006. (202)393-1300. Office Manager: Betty LuLong. PR firm. Clients: trade association and foreign government.

Needs: Works with about 3 illustrators and designers/month. Uses artists for stationery design, brochures and press kit covers.

First Contact & Terms: Send letter of introduction to Kathy Baumann. Call for appointment to show portfolio. Negotiates pay based on freelancer's rate and client's budget.

Tips: Wants to see work already done for trade associations.

JAFFE ASSOCIATES, Suite 200, 2000 L St. NW, Washington DC 20036. (202)783-4848. Account Executive: Suzanne Wegman. PR and marketing firm. Clients: commercial real estate, banks, national associations, architectural and engineering, health care and accounting. Places advertising only to limited extent.

Needs: Works with several designers. Uses artists for stationery design, multimedia kits, direct mail, television, slide sets and brochures/flyers.

First Contact & Terms: Send resume and portfolio for review. "Freelancers are employed on basis of past experience, personal knowledge or special expertise." Provide brochures, flyers, business cards, resumes and tear sheets to be kept on file for future assignments. Originals returned only if prearranged. Negotiates payment based on client's budget, amount of creativity required from artist and artist's previous experience/reputation.

Tips: "Interested in samples of produced work and details regarding availability and ability to produce work on short time schedules. *Do not* deluge account executives with calls."

*HENRY J. KAUFMAN & ASSOCIATES, PR Division, 2233 Wisconsin Ave., Washington DC 20007. Senior Vice President/Creative Director: Roger Vilsack. Ad agency. Clients: electronics firms, trade associations, government contracts, financial, consumer services and products.

Needs: Works with 50 illustrators and photographers/year. Uses freelance artists for billboards, consumer and trade magazines, direct mail, P-O-P displays, brochures, posters, newspapers and AV presentations.

First Contact & Terms: Send mailer or brochure. Works on assignment basis only. Payment is by the project; negotiates according to client's budget.

KROLOFF, MARSHALL & ASSOCIATES, Suite 500, 1730 Rhode Island Ave. NW, Washington DC 20036. Vice President: Susanne Roschwalb. PR firm. Clients: major corporate, public interest and governmental; client list provided upon request.
Needs: Works with 12 illustrators/year. Uses freelance artists for advertising layouts.
First Contact & Terms: Query with resume of credits to be kept on file. Prefers photocopies or photographs as samples. Samples returned by SASE "if necessary." Reports only if interested. Works on assignment. Provide business card, brochure/flyer, resume, samples and tear sheets to be kept on file for possible future assignments. Pays by the hour, $40 minimum. Considers complexity of project, client's budget and turnaround time when establishing payment.
Tips: "It helps to pick up and deliver work; it helps to speak directly to the person giving the assignment. We receive many inquiries. Be patient. Frequently decisions are based on availability, turnaround time and always the suitability of the artist to the task."

MANNING, SELVAGE & LEE, INC., Suite 300, 1250 Eye St. NW, Washington DC 20005. (202)682-1660. Contact: Creative Director. PR firm. Clients: pharmaccutical firms, nonprofit associations, real estate developers, corporations and high-tech firms.
Needs: Uses artists for illustration and paste-up.

*SCREENSCOPE, INC., 3600 M St. NW, Washington DC 20016. President: Marilyn Weiner. Chairman: Harold M. Weiner. Audiovisual firm. Clients: large industrial corporations, PBS and trade associations.
Needs: Works with 10 freelance artists/year. Uses artists for graphic design, promotional materials and technical assistance in making films. Especially important is a sense of design and promotion.
First Contact & Terms: Artist must have a minimum of 3 years' experience. Works on assignment only. Send query letter with brochure and samples to be kept on file for 1 year. Prefers photostats, photographs or slides as samples. Samples not filed are returned by SASE only if requested. Does not report back. Pays negotiable rate, but not less than $150. Considers complexity of the project when establishing payment. Buys all rights.

Florida

COVALT ADVERTISING AGENCY, 730 NE 130th St., North Miami FL 33161. (305)891-1543. Creative Director: Fernando Vasquez. Ad agency. Clients: automotive, cosmetics, industrial banks, restaurants, financial, consumer products.
Needs: Uses artists for illustration (all kinds and styles), photography, mechanicals, copywriting, retouching (important), rendering and lettering.
First Contact & Terms: Prefers local artists; very seldom uses out of town artists. Artists must have minimum of 5 years' experience; accepts less experience only if artist is extremely talented. Works on assignment only. Send query letter with brochure, resume, business card and samples to be kept on file. Call for appointment to show portfolio. Accepts photostats, photographs, slides or tear sheets as samples. Samples not filed not returned. Reports only if interested. Payment varies according to assignment. Considers complexity of project, client's budget, skill and experience of artist, and turnaround time when establishing payment. Buys all rights or reprint rights.
Tips: "If at first you don't succeed, keep in touch. Eventually something will come up due to our diversity of accounts. If I have the person, I might design something with his particular skill in mind."

*CREATIVE DIRECTORS INC., 1320 S. Dixie Hwy., Coral Gables FL 33146. Creative Director: Thomas W. Ferguson. Ad agency. Clients: real estate builders and developers.
Needs: Works with 6 freelance artists/year. Uses artists for architectural renderings, illustrations and photo retouching.
First Contact & Terms: Works on assignment only. Send samples to be kept on file; write for appointment to show portfolio. Pays by the project relative to going rates in the Miami marketplace. Considers complexity of the project and client's budget when establishing payment. Rights purchased vary according to project.
Tips: "We look for professional level talent and dependability."

CREATIVE RESOURCES INC., 2000 S. Dixie Hwy., Miami FL 33133. (305)856-3474. President: Mac Seligman. Ad agency/PR firm. Clients: travel, hotels, airlines and resorts.
Needs: Works with 6 illustrators/designers/year. Uses artists for layout, type spec and design for brochures, ads, posters and renderings.
First Contact & Terms: Local artists only. Query or arrange interview to show portfolio. No file kept on artists. Original work returned after completion of job. Pays $20-30/hour or negotiates pay by job.

Considers complexity of project, client's budget, and skill and experience of artist when establishing payment.

HERB DIETZ ENTERPRISES INC., 1995 NE 150 St., N. Miami FL 33181. (305)945-1103. President: Herb Dietz. Produces motion pictures, TV spots, AV presentations and filmstrips.
Needs: Buys 10 designs/year. Uses artists for animation, multimedia kits and technical charts/illustrations.
First Contact & Terms: Query. SASE. Reports within 3 weeks. Buys all rights. Pays $200-6,500, animation; $15-100/job, charts/illustrations.

GASKILL-OERTEL ADVERTISING INC., Box 206, Boynton Beach FL 33425. (305)732-9433. President: Alice Gaskill. Ad agency. Clients: a variety of industries, especially manufacturing.
Needs: Assigns 10-12 jobs/year. Works with 1 or 2 illustrators/month. Uses illustrators for brochures/flyers and trade magazines.
First Contact & Terms: Local artists only. Arrange interview to show portfolio. SASE. Samples returned. Reports in 2 weeks. Works on assignment only. Provide business card to be kept on file for possible future assignments. Negotiates pay; pays by the hour, $10 minimum. Considers complexity of project, client's budget, skill and experience of artist and geographic scope of finished project when establishing payment.
Tips: "Understand reproduction, so you can produce art that can be reproduced as easily and inexpensively as possible."

G/D ADVERTISING, INC., 99 NW 183rd St., Miami FL 33169. (305)652-6100. President: Irwin Dushkin. Ad agency. Clients: resorts, industrial parks, land sales, condominium sales, restaurants.
Needs: Works with 6-8 freelance artists/year. Uses artists for layout, design and mechanical paste-ups. "Very rarely do we use major illustrations. What's important to us is creativity and fast delivery of magic marker, crisp layouts, neatness of paste-ups."
First Contact & Terms: Works on assignment only. Send query letter with resume to be kept on file; write for appointment to show portfolio. Reports back only if interested. Pays by the hour, $15-25 average. Considers skill and experience of artist, turnaround time and rights purchased when establishing payment. Buys all rights.
Tips: "Show layouts and finished art with samples."

GOUCHENOUR, INC., 385 Whooping Loop, Altamonte Springs FL 32701. (305)834-3232. Creative Director: Vicki Stewart. Ad agency. Clients: attractions, car dealers, real estate, dairy products, airlines.
Needs: Assigns 50-60 freelance jobs/year. Works with 4-5 freelance illustrators and 3-4 freelance designers/month. Uses artists for consumer magazines, billboards, direct mail packages, brochures, newspapers and posters.
First Contact & Terms: Send query letter with resume to be kept on file. Call for appointment to show portfolio. Reports only if interested. Works on assignment only. Pays by the hour, $25-65 average. Considers complexity of project, client's budget, skill and experience of artist and turnaround time when establishing payment. Buys all rights.
Tips: "Call us."

*THE HILTON AGENCY, 607 S. Magnolia, Tampa FL 33606. (813)254-5511. Art Director: Patty Pollizi. Marketing research, public relations and advertising agency. Clients: engineering and industrial firms; business to business.
Needs: Works with 12 freelance artists/year. Uses artists for illustration, design, photography and copywriting.
First Contact & Terms: Prefers local artists with at least 3 years' experience. Works on assignment only. Send query letter with business card and samples to be kept on file; call or write for appointment to show portfolio. Accepts photographs, slides, tear sheets as samples. Samples returned only if requested. Reports only if interested. Pays by the hour, $6.50-20 average. Considers client's budget when establishing payment. Buys all rights.
Tips: "More illustration rather than photography is being used in our field. This change creates a demand for freelance illustrators with airbrush ability, but there is a very limited supply of this in our area."

IMAGES, INCORPORATED, 1662 Stockton St., Jacksonville FL 32204. (904)388-3300. Production Coordinator: Anne Morgan. Audiovisual firm. Clients: insurance companies, hospitals, educational institutions, manufacturers.
Needs: Works with 6-10 freelance artists/year. Uses artists for typesetting, film processing, audio tape,

editing and mixing, design, drawing, paste-up, script writing and photography. Especially important is an understanding of AV art (animation).
First Contact & Terms: Professional artists only. Send query letter with brochure, resume, business card and samples to be kept on file, "except those we wouldn't be able to use." Prefers related actual work as samples. Samples not filed returned only if requested. Reports within 2 weeks. Pays by the hour. Considers complexity of project, client's budget, skill and experience of artist and turnaround time when establishing payment. Rights purchased vary according to project.
Tips: "We value a person who pays attention to detail both in presenting himself and his work."

IMAGEWORKS INC., 900 6th Ave. S., Naples FL 33940. (813)261-1545. AV producer. Serves clients in business, education and industry. Produces 35mm custom slides, slide/tape productions and other AV materials.
Needs: Assigns 150 jobs/year. Works with 3 designers/month. Uses artists for slide/tape presentations.
First Contact & Terms: Send resume, query letter and samples (prefers slides) and arrange interview by mail. Samples returned by SASE. Works on assignment only. Reports in 2 weeks. Method and amount of payment are negotiated with the individual artist. No originals returned to artist following publication. Negotiates rights purchased.

MICHAELJAY INC., 10383 Oak St. NE, St. Petersburg FL 33702. (813)577-2993. President: Michael Anderson. Audiovisual firm. Clients: developers, medical lab equipment, insurance firms, boating industry.
Needs: Works with 4 freelance artists/year. Uses artists for mechanical art and paste-up for slides, illustrations, line art for slides. Especially important are mechanical art skills, animation of art and slide design.
First Contact & Terms: Prefers local artists. Send query letter. Set up an appointment for interview. Pays by the hour, $12.50-30 average. Considers complexity of project and turnaround time when establishing payment. Buys all rights.
Tips: "Present clean mechanical work and show skills in slide design."

MULTIVISION PRODUCTIONS, 7000 SW 59th Place, S. Miami FL 33143. (305)662-6011. President: Robert Berkowitz. AV/film producer. Serves clients in industry and advertising. Produces multi-image sound-slide materials.
Needs: Assigns 50 jobs/year. Works with 2 animators and 3 designers/month. Uses artists for multi-image, AV/film projects.
First Contact & Terms: Prefers "in-camera slide art specialists." Send samples (prefers slides) and arrange interview by mail. Provide resume, samples and business card to be kept on file for possible future assignments. Samples not kept on file returned. Reports within 1 week. Pays by the project. Method of payment is negotiated with the individual artist. No originals returned following publication. Buys all rights.
Tips: "Forox and animation specialists are needed for slides."

PRUITT HUMPHRESS POWERS & MUNROE ADVERTISING AGENCY, INC., 516 N. Adams St., Tallahassee FL 32301. (904)222-1212. Ad agency. Clients: business to business, consumer. Media used includes: billboards, consumer and trade magazines, direct mail, newspapers, P-O-P displays, radio and TV.
Needs: Uses artists for direct mail, brochures/flyers, trade magazines and newspapers. "Freelancers used in every aspect of business and given as much freedom as their skill warrants."
First Contact & Terms: Send resume and portfolio for review. Provide brochure, flyer, business card, resume and tear sheets to be kept on file for future assignments. Negotiates payment based on client's budget and amount of creativity required from artist. Pays set fee/job.
Tips: In portfolio, "submit examples of past agency work in clean, orderly, businesslike fashion including written explanations of each work. Ten illustrations or less."

RESOURCE, INC., 14007 North Dale Mabry, Tampa FL 33618. (813)961-4290. General Manager: Stuart Freides. Audiovisual firm. Clients: utility, general industry.
Needs: Works with 3 freelance artists/year. Uses artists for brochure design. Especially important is creativity.
First Contact & Terms: Works on assignment only. Send query letter with resume to be kept on file. Call for appointment to show portfolio. Reports back. Considers complexity of project and turnaround time when establishing payment. Buys all rights.

SAGER ASSOCIATES OF FLORIDA, INC., 739 S. Orange Ave., Sarasota FL 33577. (813)366-4192. President: Coral Sager. Ad agency/AV/PR firm. Clients: financial, real estate development, resorts, tourism and hospitality, retail/mechanical, sports, international firms, automotive, restaurants, etc.

Needs: Uses artists for b&w/color roughs, layouts, ads, consumer magazines, billboards, brochures, catalogs, newspapers, movies, stationery, signage, AV presentations, posters and storyboards.

First Contact & Terms: Send query letter with resume and business card to be kept on file. Call for appointment to show portfolio. Prefers slides and actual rough layouts as samples. Samples returned only if requested. Reports within 2 weeks. Works on assignment only. Pays by the hour, $10-35 average; also by the project. Considers complexity of project, client's budget, skill and experience of artist, geographic scope of finished projects, turnaround time, rights purchased and importance of project when establishing payment. Buys one-time or all rights.

Tips: There is a trend toward "more freelance use and less staff build up, both for diversity and an increase of quality of work." Artists should "build exclusive arrangements with agencies in several markets rather than solicit work from general agencies in one market."

GERALD SCHWARTZ AGENCY, Suite 285, 420 Lincoln Road Bldg., Miami Beach FL 33139. (305)531-1174. Executive Vice President: Felice P. Schwartz. Ad/PR/fund-raising firm. Clients: banks, savings and loan associations, hospitals, universities, philanthropic agencies, political party campaigns and nursing homes. Assigns 100 jobs and buys 25 illustrations/year.

Needs: Works with 2 illustrators/month. Uses artists for billboards, filmstrips, slide sets, brochures/flyers and newspapers.

First Contact & Terms: Query with samples (photocopies). SASE. Reports within 2 weeks. No file kept on artists. Originals returned at job's completion. Payment by job: $25-300, annual reports; $50-1,000, catalogs; $50-250, letterheads; $25-500, newspapers; $25-75, trademarks; $15-75, layout and lettering. Pays promised fee for unused assigned work.

*J.J. SPECTOR & ASSOCIATES, 4250 Galt Ocean Dr., Ft. Lauderdale FL 33308. (305)561-3603. Vice President: Susan Roye Rosen. Direct mail marketing consultants/ad agency. Clients: publishers, manufacturers, insurance companies, banks, commercial/industrial firms and others who use direct mail heavily. Buys 10-15 illustrations/year.

Needs: Uses artists for color separations, layout, lettering, paste-up, retouching and type spec for ads, annual reports, catalogs, letterheads, packages and direct mail package components.

First Contact & Terms: Query. SASE. Reports in 1 week. Provide brochures, flyers, business card, resume and tear sheets. Originals returned to artist at job's completion. Pays $200-350, package design; $50-175, paste-up/mechanicals; $20-50/page, catalog layout. Pays original fee as agreed for unused assigned illustrations.

Tips: "Collect direct mail packages received at home and redesign them more forcefully into alternative dummies for submission as samples."

STARR/ROSS PHOTO CORPORATE COMMUNICATIONS, 2727 Ponce de Leon Blvd., Coral Gables FL 33134. (305)446-3300. Production Coordinator: Melinda Smith. AV producer. Clients: industry (80%) and advertising (20%). Produces "sales and marketing primarily, with some financial reporting and a little training."

Needs: Assigns approximately 100 jobs/year. Works with 2-3 illustrators and 1-2 designers/month. Uses artists for overall show design, cartoon work, paste up and board work.

First Contact & Terms: "We prefer AV experience and demand a high energy level." Send resume, then arrange interview by phone. Provide resume and business card to be kept on file for possible future assignments. Works on assignment only. Pays $50-5,000/project. No originals returned after publication. Buys all rights.

Tips: "We are more interested in high energy and willingness to work long and hard than anything in education or portfolio."

Georgia

ATLANTA AUDIO-VISUALS, 66 12th St., Atlanta GA 30303. Telex: 6501072756 MCI. Director: Robert Foah. AV producer. Serves clients in corporations. Produces multi-image materials.

Needs: Works with 3 illustrators/month.

First Contact & Terms: Send resume. Provide business card to be kept on file for possible future assignments only. Works on assignment only. Reports within 3 months. Pays by the project. Amount of payment is negotiated with the individual artist and varies with each client's budget. No originals returned after publication. Negotiates rights purchased.

BURST/GOSA PRODUCTIONS, INC., 1190 Euclid Ave. NE, Box 5354, Atlanta GA 30307. (404)523-8023. Office Manager: Karen Gibbs. Audiovisual firm. Clients: major corporations, religious organizations, nonprofit groups. Client list provided on request with SASE.

Needs: Works with 5 freelance artists/year. Uses artists for design and layout of graphics for 16mm film, slides and printed material, and some conceptual design for slide art. Artists should have a "good handle on graphic design and layout."

First Contact & Terms: Artists in Atlanta area only; minimum two years' experience. Works on assignment only. Send query letter with resume to be kept on file. Reports only if interested. Pays by the hour, $15 minimum or by the project, $50 minimum. Considers client's budget, skill and experience of artist, turnaround time and rights purchased when establishing payment. Rights purchased vary according to project.

Tips: "Write and send resume first *before* trying to talk to someone on phone."

*CHANNEL ONE INC., 1727 Clifton Rd., Atlanta GA 30329. Contact: W. Horlock. AV producer. Clients: educational, nonprofit, religious.

Needs: Works with 3-4 illustrators/month. Uses artists for album covers, motion pictures and graphic and set design.

First Contact & Terms: Prefers slides, photographs, photostats and b&w line drawings as samples. Samples returned by SASE. Reports in 2 months. Works on assignment only. Provide business card, brochure/flyer, resume and samples to be kept on file for possible future assignments. Originals returned to artist at job's completion if part of job contract. Payment depends on project.

DAVID W. EVANS/ATLANTA, INC., 550 Pharr Rd. NE, Atlanta GA 30305. (404)261-7000. Creative Director: Michael Jones-Kelly. Ad agency. Clients: all types but primarily industrial and consumer.

Needs: Works with 3 freelance illustrators/month. Uses freelancers for billboards, consumer and trade magazines, direct mail, brochures/flyers, newspapers, P-O-P displays, stationery design and TV.

First Contact & Terms: Send samples. Prefers work "that has been produced—rather than daydreams." Samples are filed and not returned. Negotiates payment based on individual needs of job.

Tips: Especially interested in realistic illustrators. "Show me work that accomplishes objectives. I'll go to museums and galleries for fine art shows."

FILMAMERICA, INC., Suite 209, 3177 Peachtree Rd. NE, Atlanta GA 30305. (404)261-3718. President: Avrum M. Fine. Audiovisual firm. Clients: advertising agencies.

Needs: Works with 2 freelance artists/year. Uses artists for film campaigns. Especially important are illustration and layout skills.

First Contact & Terms: Works on assignment only. Send query letter with resume and samples to be kept on file. Write for appointment to show portfolio. Prefers photographs or tear sheets as samples. Samples not filed are returned only if requested. Reports back only if interested. Pays by the project, $500 minimum. Considers complexity of the project and rights purchased when establishing payment. Rights purchased vary according to project.

Tips: "Be very patient!"

FLUKER & ASSOCIATES ADVERTISING AGENCY, 379 Rogers Ave., Macon GA 31204. (912)742-7551. Graphic Department Head: De Stephenson. Ad agency/AV/marketing/PR firm. Clients: commercial and industrial firms.

Needs: Assigns 40-50 freelance jobs/year. Uses artists for billboards, direct mail packages, catalogs, filmstrips, movies, signage and P-O-P displays.

First Contact & Terms: Send query letter with brochure and samples to be kept on file. Write for appointment to show portfolio. Prefers slides and photographs as samples. Samples not kept on file returned only if requested. Reports only if interested. Works on assignment only. Pays by quotations only. Considers client's budget, and skill and experience of artists when establishing payment. Buys all rights.

PAUL FRENCH AND PARTNERS, INC., Rt. 5, Box 285, LaGrange GA 30240. (404)882-5581. Contact: Ms. Gene Byrd. Audiovisual firm. Client list provided upon request.

Needs: Works with 3 freelance artists/year. Uses artists for illustration.

First Contact & Terms: Works on assignment only. Send query letter with samples to be kept on file; write for appointment to show portfolio. Prefers slides as samples. Samples not filed are returned by SASE. Reports back only if interested. Pays by the hour, $25-100 average. Considers client's budget when establishing payment. Buys all rights.

GARRETT COMMUNICATIONS, Box 53, Atlanta GA 30301. (404)755-2513. President: Ruby Grant Garrett. Production and placement firm for print media. Clients: banks, organizations, products-service consumer. Client list provided for SASE.

Needs: Assigns 24 freelance jobs/year. Works with 1 freelance illustrator and 1 freelance designer/month. Uses artists for billboards, brochures, signage and posters.
First Contact & Terms: Experienced, talented artists only. Send query letter with resume and samples to be kept on file. Samples returned by SASE if not kept on file. Reports within 10 days. Works on assignment only. Pays by the project, $100 minimum. Considers client's budget, skill and experience of artist and turnaround time when establishing payment. Negotiates rights purchased.

THE GORDON GROUP, INC., Suite A, 6350 McDonough Dr., Norcross GA 30093. (404)448-4431. President: M.J. Gordon. Art Director: A. Werth. Creative Director: Marilyn E. Murphy. Ad agency/AV and PR firm; "full service communications management." Clients: business to business, industry, service, non-retail, non-foods.
Needs: Assigns 30-50 freelance jobs/year. Uses artists for trade magazines, direct mail packages, brochures, catalogs, filmstrips, stationery, signage, P-O-P displays, AV presentations and posters. Artists should make contact "any way they can." Works on assignment only. Pays by the hour, $15 minimum. Pay "depends on the job and the budget. We pay hourly or on a project basis." Considers complexity of project, client's budget, skill and experience of artist, turnaround time and rights purchased when establishing payment. Buys all rights, material not copyrighted.
Tips: "Don't spend a lot of money on materials. Turn us on with a creative letter instead."

GREEN & PARTNERS, Suite 1717, 100 Colony Square, Atlanta GA 30361. (404)874-8100. Associate Creative Director: Chris Wright. Ad agency. Clients: hotel, package, retail.
Needs: Works with 10-15 freelance artists/year. Uses artists for illustration, storyboards, comprehensives, art direction and more.
First Contact & Terms: Works on assignment only. Send samples to be kept on file; call for appointment to show portfolio. Accepts photostats, photographs, slides or tear sheets as samples. Samples not filed are returned only if requested. Reports only if interested. Pays by the hour or by the day. Considers complexity of project, client's budget, skill and experience of artist, geographic scope for the finished product, turnaround time and rights purchased when establishing payment. Negotiates rights purchased.

HAYNES ADVERTISING, 90 Fifth St., Macon GA 31201. (912)742-5266. Contact: Phil Haynes. Ad agency. Clients: financial, industrial, automobile, professional.
Needs: Assigns 10 freelance jobs/year. Uses artists for brochures, newspapers and AV presentations.
First Contact & Terms: Send query letter with samples to be kept on file. Call or write for appointment to show portfolio. Prefers photocopies and press proofs as samples. Samples not kept on file returned by SASE. Reports only if interested. Works on assignment only. Pays by the project, $50-200 average. Considers complexity of project when establishing payment. Negotiate rights purchased.
Tips: "Feel free to call."

KAUFMANN ASSOCIATES, One Willow Sq., St. Simons Island GA 31522. (912)638-8678. Creative Director: S.C. Kaufmann. Ad agency. Clients: resort, food processor, bank.
Needs: Assigns "very few" freelance jobs/year. Works with 1 freelance illustrator/month. Uses artists for brochures.
First Contact & Terms: Send samples to be kept on file. Reports only if interested. Works on assignment only. Considers complexity of project, client's budget, and skill and experience of artist when establishing payment. Buys all rights.

LEWIS BROADCASTING CORP., Box 13646, Savannah GA 31406. Public Relations Director: C.A. Barbieri. TV producer.
Needs: Uses artists for direct mail brochures, billboards, posters, public service TV spots and motion picture work.
First Contact & Terms: Query with resume and printed photocopied samples. Samples returned by SASE. Reports in 2 weeks. Works on assignment only. Provide business card and resume to be kept on file. Originals returned to artist at job's completion. Pay "depends on job."
Tips: "Be willing to flesh out others' ideas."

PRINGLE DIXON PRINGLE, 3340 Peachtree Rd. NE, Atlanta GA 30326. (404)261-9542. Creative Director: Dan Scarlotto. Ad agency. Clients: fashion, financial, fast food and industrial firms; client list provided upon request.
Needs: Works with 2 illustrators/month. Uses freelance artists for billboards, consumer and trade magazines, direct mail, P-O-P displays, brochures, catalogs, posters, signage, newspapers and AV presentations.
First Contact & Terms: Local artists only. Arrange interview to show portfolio. Works on assignment basis only. Payment varies according to job and freelancer.

J. WALTER THOMPSON COMPANY, 2828 Tower Pl., 3340 Peachtree Rd. NE, Atlanta GA 30326. (404)266-2828. Executive Art Director: Bill Thomassi. Creative Art Director: Bruce Levitt. Ad agency. Clients: mainly financial, industrial and consumer. This office does creative work for Atlanta and the southeastern US.
Needs: Works with freelance illustrators. Uses artists for billboards, consumer magazines, trade magazines and newspapers.
First Contact & Terms: Call for appointment to show portfolio. Prefers slides, original work or stats as samples. Samples returned by SASE. Reports only if interested. Works on assignment only. Provide business card and samples to be kept on file for future assignments. No originals returned at job's completion. Pays by the hour, $20-35 average; by the project, $100-6,000 average; by the day, $150-3,500 average. Considers complexity of project, client's budget, skill and experience of artist and rights purchased when establishing payment.
Tips: Wants to see samples of work done for different clients. Likes to see work done in different mediums. Likes variety and versatility. Artists interested in working here should "be *professional* and do top grade work." Deals with artists' reps only.

TUCKER WAYNE & CO., Suite 2700, 230 Peachtree St. NW, Atlanta GA 30303. (404)522-2383. Creative Department Business Manager: Rita Morris. Ad agency. Serves a variety of clients including packaged products, food, utilities, transportation, agriculture and pesticide manufacturing.
Needs: A total of 6 art directors work with about 6 freelance illustrators/month. Uses freelancers for consumer and trade magazines, newspapers and TV.
First Contact & Terms: Call creative secretary for appointment. Selection based on portfolio review. Negotiates payment based on budget, where work will appear, travel expenses, etc.
Tips: Each art director has individual preference.

Hawaii

THE INNOVATION ORGANIZATION, Box 30162, Honolulu HI 96820. (808)395-3117. Producer: Ron Lewis. Publicity firm.
Needs: Works with 2-3 illustrators and 2-3 designers/month. Uses artists for billboards, P-O-P displays, consumer magazines, multimedia kits, direct mail, TV, brochure/flyer, trade magazines, album covers and newspaper.
First Contact & Terms: Query with resume and samples. SASE. Reports within 2-4 weeks. Provide business card, resume and tear sheet to be kept on file for possible future assignments. No originals returned to artists at job's completion. Negotiates pay.

MILICI/VALENTI ADVERTISING INC., Amfac Bldg., 700 Bishop St., Honolulu HI 96813. (808)536-0881. Contact: Creative Director. Ad agency. Serves clients in food, finance, utilities, entertainment, chemicals and personal care products.
Needs: Works with 3-4 illustrators/month. Uses artists for illustration, retouching and lettering for newspapers, multimedia kits, magazines, radio, TV and direct mail.
First Contact & Terms: Artists must be familiar with advertising demands; used to working long distance through the mail; and be familiar with Hawaii. Provide brochure, flyer and tear sheets to be kept on file for future assignments. No originals returned to artist at job's completion. Pays $200-2,000.

Idaho

I/D/E/A INC., 401 Main St., Caldwell ID 83605. (208)459-6357. Creative Director: Harold Brown. Ad agency. Clients: direct mail.
Needs: Assigns 12-15 freelance jobs/year. Uses artists for direct mail packages, brochures, airbrush and photographs.
First Contact & Terms: Call before sending query letter with brochure, resume and samples to be kept on file. Write for artists' guidelines. Prefers the "most convenient samples for the artist." Samples not kept on file returned only if requested. Reports only if interested. Works on assignment only. Pays by the

Market conditions are constantly changing! If this is 1987 or later, buy the newest edition of *Artist's Market* at your favorite bookstore or order directly from Writer's Digest Books.

project, amount varies. Considers complexity of project, client's budget, and skill and experience of artist when establishing payment. Rights purchased vary with project.
Tips: "Most work goes into catalogs or brochures."

Illinois

WILLIAM HART ADLER, INC., 5 Revere Dr., Northbrook IL 60062. (312)291-1730. President: Bill Adler. Ad agency. Clients: housewares, electronics/hi-fi—"wide variety" of firms.
Needs: Works with 4-5 illustrators/year. Uses freelance artists for billboards, consumer and trade magazines, direct mail, P-O-P displays, brochures, catalogs, posters, signage, newspapers and AV presentations.
First Contact & Terms: Works primarily with local freelancers. Chooses freelancers on a referral basis or phone for appointment. Works on assignment only. Negotiates payment; varies according to job and freelancer.

BRACKER COMMUNICATION, 330 W. Frontage Rd., Northfield IL 60093. (312)441-5534. President: Richard W. Bracker. Ad agency/public relations/publishing firm. Clients: construction, financial, acoustical, contractors, equipment manufacturers, trade associations, household fixtures, pest control products.
Needs: Works with 4-6 freelance artists/year. Uses artists for graphic design/key line. Especially important are type specing, design/layout and photo handling.
First Contact & Terms: "Use only artists based in the Chicago area for the most part. We look for ability and have used recent graduates." Works on assignment only. Phone or send resume to be kept on file; write for appointment to show portfolio. Reviews any type of sample. Reports within 2 weeks. Negotiates and/or accepts quotations on specific projects. Considers complexity of project, skill and experience of artist, and turnaround time when establishing payment. Buys all rights.
Tips: "Don't make assumptions about anything."

BRAGAW PUBLIC RELATIONS SERVICES, 800 E. Northwest Hwy., Palatine IL 60067. (312)934-5580. Principal: Richard S. Bragaw. PR firm. Clients: professional service firms, associations, industry.
Needs: Assigns 12 freelance jobs/year. Works with 1 freelance illustrator and 1 freelance designer/month. Uses artists for direct mail packages, brochures, signage, AV presentations and press releases.
First Contact & Terms: Local artists only. Send query letter with brochure and business card to be kept on file. Reports only if interested. Works on assignment only. Pays by the hour, $25-75 average. Considers complexity of project, skill and experience of artist and turnaround time when establishing payment. Buys all rights.
Tips: "Be honest."

JOHN CROWE ADVERTISING AGENCY, 1104 S. 2nd St., Springfield IL 62704. (217)528-1076. Contact: John Crowe. Ad/art agency. Clients: industries, manufacturers, retailers, banks, publishers, insurance firms, packaging firms, state agencies, aviation and law enforcement agencies.
Needs: Buys 3,000 illustrations/year. Works with 4 illustrators and 3 designers/month. Uses artists for color separations, animation, lettering, paste-up and type spec for work with consumer magazines, stationery design, direct mail, slide sets, brochures/flyers, trade magazines and newspapers. Especially needs layout, camera-ready art and photo retouching.
First Contact & Terms: "Send a letter to us regarding available work at agency. Tell us about yourself. We will reply if work is needed and request samples of work." Prefers tear sheets, original art, photocopies, etc. as samples. Samples returned by SASE. Works on assignment only. Provide brochure, samples, business card, resume and/or tear sheets to be kept on file. Reports in 2 weeks. Pays $25/hour illustration/camera-ready art; $4-10 per sketch. No originals returned to artist at job's completion. No payment for unused assigned illustrations.
Tips: Seeks neat, organized samples or portfolio. "Disorganized sloppy work in presenting talent," is the biggest mistake artists make. Foresees a trend toward computer art.

*DOREMUS AND COMPANY (ROCKFORD), 850 N. Church St., Rockford IL 61103. (815)963-1321. Manager, Graphic Services: Randall E. Klein. Ad agency/PR firm. Clients: financial, industrial, retail.
Needs: Assigns 6 freelance jobs/year. Uses artists for consumer and trade magazines, billboards, direct mail packages, brochures, catalogs, newspapers, filmstrips, movies, stationery, signage, P-O-P displays, AV presentations, posters and press releases "to some degree."
First Contact & Terms: Send query letter with brochure, resume, business card, samples and tear sheets

to be kept on file. Call or write for appointment to show portfolio. Send samples that show best one medium in which work is produced. Samples not kept on file are not returned. Reports only if interested. Works on assignment only. "Rates depend on talent and speed; could be anywhere from $5 to $30 an hour." Considers skill and experience of artist and turnaround time when establishing payment. Buys all rights.
Tips: "Have a good presentation, not just graphics."

ENGEL ADVERTISING, INC., 1212 S. Kaspar, Arlington Heights IL 60005. (312)255-4815. President: Joseph F. Engel. Specializes in publications, signage, technical illustration, printed materials, packaging, ads and collateral. Clients: manufacturers of business to business products, direct response, mail order.
Needs: Uses artists for advertising, brochure and catalog design, illustration and layout; retouching, poster and direct mail, illustration, lettering and logo design.
First Contact & Terms: Call for appointment to show portfolio in a review. Prefers actual art, photostats, b&w photos or color washes as samples. Works on assignment only; reports whether to expect future assignment. Negotiates rates; considers complexity of project, client's budget, and skill and experience of artist. Payment terms: 46-60 days.
Tips: Artists should "make themselves available to us and stay in contact. Out of sight-out of mind. Be specific in what you do best." Especially looks for "creativity and good quality, technical correctness in drawings."

FILLMAN ADVERTISING INC., 304 W. Hill St., Champaign IL 61820. (217)352-0002. Art/Creative Director: Mary Auth. Ad agency. Serves clients in industry. Assigns 60 jobs and buys 10 illustrations/year.
Needs: Works with 1-2 illustrators and 2-3 designers/month. Uses artists for stationery design, direct mail, brochures/flyers, trade magazines.
First Contact & Terms: Uses mostly local artists. Query with samples. Prefers originals, photographs, b&w line drawings, photocopies of inputs or finished printed pieces as samples. Samples returned by SASE. Reports in 2 weeks. Works on assignment only. Provide business card and resume to be kept on file for possible future assignments. No originals returned to artist at job's completion. Pays $35-600/project; by the hour, $15-25 average. Pays promised fee for unused assigned illustrations. Considers skill and experience of artist when establishing payment.

*FOLEY ADVERTISING INC., 17W715 Butterfield Rd., Oakbrook Terrace IL 60181. (312)782-1791. Ad agency. President: J.E. Foley. Industrial agency. Serves clients in equipment for science and manufacturing. Assigns 200 jobs/year.
Needs: Works with 3 designers/month. Uses artists for layout and mechanicals.
First Contact & Terms: Local, industrial artists only. Query with samples and arrange interview to show portfolio. Works on assignment only. Provide materials to be kept on file for future assignments. Considers complexity of project and client's budget when establishing payment.

HUGHES, MARTINDALE & ASSOCIATES, INC., Suite 119, 2045 S. Arlington Heights Rd., Arlington Heights IL 60005. (312)437-6400. President: R. Martindale. Communications consultants. Clients: financial. Media used include billboards, consumer and trade magazines, direct mail, newspapers, radio and TV.
Needs: "Work load varies; usually our extra assignments (beyond what our regular staff can service efficiently) bunch up in active months such as January, May, September and October. Those extra assignments might be 5 or 6 newspaper ad layouts, 2 or 3 brochures, and perhaps a special design assignment." Uses artists for work in direct mail, brochures/flyers and newspapers.
First Contact & Terms: Write and request personal interview to show portfolio. Provide resume to be kept on file for future assignments. Reports within 10 days. Works on assignment only. Pays by the hour or by the project. Considers complexity of project, client's budget, skill and experience of artist, and turnaround time when establishing payment.
Tips: "We prefer to let the individual decide what he or she wants to show. If they can't show a strong portfolio, we can't expect them to be strong enough for our purposes." Artist should "stay within the *guidelines* of the assigned project."

IMPERIAL INTERNATIONAL LEARNING CORP., Box 548, Kankakee IL 60901. (815)933-7735. President: Spencer Barnard. AV producer. Serves clients in education. Produces filmstrips, illustrated workbooks and microcomputer software.
Needs: Assigns 12 jobs/year. Works with 6 designers/year. Uses artists for original line art, color illustrations and graphic design.
First Contact & Terms: Send query letter and samples to be kept on file. Prefers tear sheets as samples.

Samples returned only if requested. Works on assignment only. Reports back only if interested. Method and amount of payment are negotiated with the individual artist. No originals returned to artist following publication. Considers skill and experience of artist when establishing payment. Buys all rights.
Tips: "More computer graphics are being used in our field."

ELVING JOHNSON ADVERTISING INC., 7800 W. College Dr., Palos Heights IL 60463. (312)361-2850. Art/Creative Director: Michael McNicholas. Ad agency. Serves clients in industrial machinery, construction materials, material handling, finance, etc.
Needs: Works with 2 illustrators/month. Uses artists for direct mail, brochures/flyers, trade magazines and newspapers. Also uses artists for layout, illustration, technical art, paste-up and retouching.
First Contact & Terms: Local artists only. Call for interview.

LERNER SCOTT CORP., 1000 Skokie Blvd., Wilmette IL 60091. (312)251-2447. Vice President/ Managing Art Director: Mark Bryzinski. Direct marketing/ad agency. Clients: insurance and communications companies, banks, wholesale distributors, entertainment (Playboy Clubs), home and commercial security, trade schools, nurseries.
Needs: Works with 8 freelance artists/year. Uses artists for advertising, brochure and catalog design, illustration and layout; P-O-P displays, and signage.
First Contact & Terms: Chicago area artists only. Works on assignment only. Send query letter with business card and samples to be kept on file; call for appointment to show portfolio. Prefers photocopies or tear sheets as samples. Samples not filed returned only if requested. Reports only if interested. Pays by the project. Considers complexity of project when establishing payment.

MEDIA DEPARTMENT, INC., Box 1006, St. Charles IL 60174. (312)377-0005. General Manager: Bruce Meisner. Clients: business and industry. Produces filmstrips, multimedia kits, overhead transparencies, slide sets and sound-slide sets.
Needs: Assigns 6-10 jobs/year. Works with 3 freelance artists/year. Uses artists for cartoons and technical illustration.
First Contact & Terms: Query with resume, brochure/flyer and samples to be kept on file for possible future assignments. Prefers slides as samples. Samples not kept on file are returned by SASE. Reports only if interested. Works on assignment only. Buys all rights. Pays $10-40/project per piece of art (more for detailed technical illustration); $10-18/hour. Considers complexity of project, client's budget, skill and experience of artist, turnaround time and rights purchased when establishing payment.

*ARTHUR MERIWETHER, INC., 1529 Brook Dr., Downers Grove IL 60515. (312)495-0600. Production Coordinator: Jeanne Bodor. Audiovisual firm, design studio and communications services. Clients: mainly industrial corporations (electronics, chemical, etc.) plus a few consumer clients.
Needs: Works with 10-20 freelance artists/year. Uses artists for keyline/pasteup, illustration and design. Especially important are knowledge of audiovisual and print production techniques.
First Contact & Terms: Artists should have minimum 2 years' experience; prefers local artists, will occasionally work with out-of-state illustrators. Send query letter with resume, business card and samples. Prefers slides and tear sheets as samples. Samples returned by SASE. Reports only if interested. Payment varies per project and artist's experience. Also considers client's budget, skill of artist and turnaround time when establishing payment. Rights purchased vary according to project; usually buys all rights.
Tips: "Call to find out what type of samples we may be looking for."

TOM MORRIS INC., 621 Devon, Park Ridge IL 60068. Contact: Tom Morris. AV producer/art studio/ industrial advertising agency. Clients: industrial marketers. Produces print media, charts, filmstrips, motion pictures and slides.
Needs: Works with 10 freelance illustrators and 12 designers/year.
First Contact & Terms: Prefers photographs and b&w or color line drawings as samples. Samples returned by SASE. Reports in 2 weeks. Works on assignment only. Provide resume and tear sheets to be kept on file for possible future assignments. Pay depends on project. Buys all rights.

MOTIVATION MEDIA INC., 1245 Milwaukee Ave., Glenview IL 60025. (312)297-4740. Creative Graphics Manager: Carol DeFabio. Clients: industrial. Produces multi-image slide programs, slide sets, sound-slide sets, filmstrips, and motion picture and videotape productions.
Needs: Works with 10 production artists and 5 designers/month. Uses artists for multi-image slide programs. Assigns 675 jobs/year.
First Contact & Terms: Local artists only. Query with resume and nonreturnable samples (photocopies, duplicates, etc.). SASE. Reports in 2 weeks if interested. Works on assignment only. Provide resume to be kept on file for future assignments. Pays $7-15/hour, animation, charts/graphs and

advertising; $10-30/hour, illustrations; also pays by the job. Considers complexity of project, client's budget, skill and experience of artist and turnaround time when establishing payment. Pays 30 days after receipt of invoice.
Tips: "Send resume and copies of work. Our schedule does not allow us extensive time for interviewing. Though I need people who know slide production, I'm most interested in people who know all areas of art production. Be able to see a project through from input to completion."

NEW ORIENT MEDIA, Communications Building, Second and Main Sts., West Dundee IL 60118. (312)428-6000. President: Bob Sandidge. AV producer. Clients: corporate, educational and industrial. Produces filmstrips, multimedia kits, sound-slide sets and computer slides.
Needs: Assigns 200 jobs/year. Uses artists for realistic illustrations, b&w line art and paste-up.
First Contact & Terms: Prefers Chicago area artists. Query with previously used work and arrange interview to show portfolio. SASE. Reports within 1-2 weeks. Negotiates pay.

TRANSLIGHT MEDIA ASSOCIATES, INC., 931 W. Liberty Dr., Wheaton IL 60187. Art Manager: Scott Davis. Audiovisual firm. Clients: office products industry, telecommunications, religious organizations, colleges.
Needs: Works with 10 freelance artists/year. Uses artists for logo development, design of AVs, layout, charts and graphs, special requirements, cartoons, "and more." Especially wants artists to have "an understanding of audiovisual and multi-image presentations and know how their art translates and fits into that medium."
First Contact & Terms: Works on assignment only. Send query letter with brochure, resume and samples (if available) to be kept on file. Samples not filed are returned only if requested. Reports back only if interested. Pays by the hour, $10-50 average. Considers client's budget, skill and experience of artist and turnaround time when establishing payment. Rights purchased vary according to project.

H. WILSON CO., 555 Taft Dr., South Holland IL 60473. (312)339-5111. Contact: Advertising Manager.
Needs: Assigns 20 jobs/year. Works with 2 illustrators and 2 designers/month. Uses artists for sales and marketing presentations, catalogs, direct mail, convention exhibits and promotion.
First Contact & Terms: Query with resume and samples (ads, brochures, etc.), then arrange interview to show portfolio. SASE. Reports within 2 weeks. No originals returned at job's completion. Provide resume, business card and brochure to be kept on file for future assignments. Pays "for creative work on a job basis, final art on an hourly basis."

Chicago

AUDITIONS BY SOUNDMASTERS, Box 8135, Chicago IL 60680. (312)787-8220. Executive Vice President: R.C. Hillsman. Produces radio/TV programs, commercials, jingles and records.
Needs: Buys 125-300 designs/year. Uses artists for animation, catalog covers/illustrations, layout, paste-up, multimedia kits and record album design.
First Contact & Terms: Mail 8x10" art. SASE. Reports in 3 weeks. Material copyrighted. Pays $500 minimum, animation; $100-350, record jackets; $50-225, layout; $35-165, paste-up.

N.W. AYER, INC., One Illinois Center, 111 E. Wacker Dr., Chicago IL 60601. (312)645-8800. Contact: Ken Ameral. Ad agency. "We cover a very wide range of clients."
First Contact & Terms: Call for personal appointment to show portfolio. Negotiates payment based on client's budget and the amount of creativity required from artist.
Tips: Portfolio should consist of past work used by ad agencies and commercial art.

BETZER PRODUCTIONS INC., 450 E. Ohio St., Chicago IL 60611. President: Joseph G. Betzer. Produces slide films and motion pictures.
Needs: Uses artists for motion picture animation and slide film art.
First Contact & Terms: Query with resume.

CLEARVUE, INC., 5711 N. Milwaukee, Chicago IL 60646. (312)775-9433. Contact: Editor. Audiovisual firm.
Needs: Works with 10-12 freelance artists/year. Uses artists for art for filmstrip programs.
First Contact & Terms: Works on assignment only. Send query letter to be kept on file; write for appointment to show portfolio. Prefers to review art boards or samples of actual filmstrips. Reports back within 10 days. Pays $30-40 per frame—average program is 35-50 frames. Considers complexity of the

project and budget when establishing payment. Buys all rights.
Tips: "Have some knowledge of filmstrip production requirements."

FRANK J. CORBETT, INC., 211 E. Chicago Ave., Chicago IL 60611. (312)664-5310. Associate Creative Director: Bill Reinwald. Ad agency. Serves clients in pharmaceuticals.
Needs: Works with 2-3 freelance illustrators/month. Uses freelancers primarily for direct mail and some trade magazines.
First Contact & Terms: Call for appointment to show portfolio or make contact through artist's agent. Selection based on portfolio review. Negotiates payment based on client's budget.
Tips: Wants to see the best of artist's work including that used by ad agencies, and tear sheets of published art. Especially interested in good medical illustration, but also uses a wide variety of photography and illustration.

THE CREATIVE ESTABLISHMENT, 1421 N. Wells, Chicago IL 60610. (312)943-6700. President: Joan Beugen. Also: 115 W. 31st St., New York NY 10001. (212)563-3337. Chairman: Ira Kerns. AV/multimedia/motion picture producer. Clients: Fortune 500 and other major U.S. corporations. Audience: top level executives, managers, salesmen, distributors and/or suppliers of the specific client. "We produce slides, films and multimedia presentations primarily for industry. Our specialty is large sales and management meetings, using multiscreen slide projection. The slides we use range over every conceivable type and format, since we produce in the neighborhood of 30,000 slides a month."
Needs: Works with 8-10 illustrators and 1-5 designers/month. Uses artists for motion pictures and slides. "We use illustrators, cartoonists, designers, costume and set designers, sculptors, model-makers . . . you name it."
First Contact & Terms: "I am most interested in hearing from artists and art directors who have experience in slides as opposed to print work. However, we do use illustrators occasionally and show them how to prepare their work for reproduction into slides." Local artists only. Works on assignment only. Send resume, brochure/flyer, business card, tear sheets and sample slides to be kept on file. Samples not filed returned by SASE. Reports within 2 weeks. Originals returned at job's completion if special arrangements are made. Pays by the hour and week; varies with assignment and function. Considers client's budget and turnaround time when establishing payment.

DANIEL J. EDELMAN, INC., 211 E. Ontario, Chicago IL 60611-3219. (312)280-7000. AV Manager: Raul Perez. PR firm.
Needs: Works with 1 illustrator/month. Uses artists for local projects including daily newspapers and trade publications.
First Contact & Terms: Call for appointment to show portfolio. Prefers slides or photos as samples. Samples returned. Works with freelance artists on an assignment basis only. Provide business card to be kept on file for possible future assignments.
Tips: Especially looks for "unique design and a variety of work that shows all of an artist's talents; also a list of past clients."

EISAMAN, JOHNS & LAWS ADVERTISING, Suite 2400, 333 N. Michigan Ave., Chicago IL 60601. (312)263-3474. Creative Director: Mike Waterkotte. Ad agency. Clients: Chicago office—automotive, TV station, radio station.
Needs: Assigns 12-20 freelance jobs/year. Uses artists for mainly illustration and design, some photography.
First Contact & Terms: Works on assignment only. Call or write for appointment to show portfolio. Prefers to review "printed pieces; reprints of Black Book ad, etc." Samples not filed returned only if requested. Reports only if interested. Pays by project, amount depends entirely on budget for project. Considers complexity of the project, client's budget, skill and experience of artist, geographic scope for the finished product, turnaround time and rights purchased when establishing payment. Rights purchased vary according to project.

HILL AND KNOWLTON, INC., 1 Illinois Center, 111 E. Wacker Dr., Chicago IL 60601. (312)565-1200. Creative Director: Jacqueline Kohn. PR firm. Clients: corporate, financial, industrial products, medical, pharmaceutical, and public utilities.
Needs: Works with 1-2 illustrators/month. Uses artists for annual reports, brochures, employee publications and associated print and collateral.
First Contact & Terms: Call for appointment to show portfolio. Prefers printed samples, slides or original photos and art as samples. Works on assignment only; reports back whether to expect possible future assignments. Provide business card, brochure/flyer, samples and tear sheets to be kept on file.
Tips: Has very broad needs of highest quality. Will discuss these and particular needs during initial call. Artists interested in working here should be "punctual on appointments; arrange portfolio to pertain to our needs only."

IMAGINE THAT!, Suite 3403, 405 N. Wabash Ave., Chicago IL 60611. (312)670-0234. President: John Beele. Ad agency. Clients: broadcast, insurance firm, University of Illinois sports program, Northwestern University athletics, retail furniture stores, real estate and professional rodeo.
Needs: Assigns 25-50 jobs and buys 10-12 illustrations/year. Uses artists for layout, illustration, mechanicals, cartoons and photography.
First Contact & Terms: Arrange interview to show portfolio with Sheila Dunbar. Pay is negotiable.

INTERAND CORPORATION, 3200 W. Peterson Ave., Chicago IL 60659. (312)943-1200. Director, Corporate Communications: Linda Thomas-Phillips. AV producer. Clients: national organizations, government and military, school and corporate. Audience: educators, students, business and government personnel. Produces instructional and training filmstrips, video tapes, multi-image shows. Assigns 3 jobs/year; mainly local artists.
Needs: Has irregular art needs. Uses artists for video tapes and electronic art via Telestrator™ Systems, charts/graphs, filmstrips, storyboards, packaging and print ads.
First Contact & Terms: Query with resume, brochure and previously published work to be kept on file. Prefers copies of art samples, brochures, etc. as samples. Especially looks for variety and the artist's ability to evaluate an assignment and come to a conclusion. Samples returned by SASE only if requested. Reports in 2 weeks. Works on assignment only. Buys all rights. Client retains original after job. Pays by the project; on acceptance. Considers complexity of project and client's budget when establishing payment.
Tips: There is a "trend toward videotape and electronics graphics capabilities, although we are still working in filmstrip and slide production. We have developed videotapes using computer-generated art for at least 85% of the visuals within a 20-minute tape. Thrust in the field of broadcasting is toward computer-generated art." Artists interested in working here should remember that "often proposals to clients take months to finalize. Artists' resumes are kept on file indefinitely."

ISKER & ADAJIAN INC., 435 N. Michigan Ave., Chicago IL 60611. (312)222-1646. Contact: K. Bird. Ad agency/PR firm/art agency/AV producer/art studio. Clients: tourism and manufacturing. Assigns 100 jobs/year.
Needs: Works with artists on billboards, P-O-P displays, filmstrips, stationery design, multimedia kits, direct mail, TV, slide sets, brochures/flyers, trade magazines, album covers, newspapers and books. Also uses artists for layout, illustration, retouching and mechanicals.
First Contact & Terms: Query with resume, business card, brochure/flyer and samples to be kept on file or arrange interview to show portfolio. SASE. Prefers photostats, slides or original work as samples. Reports only if interested. Works on assignment only and sometimes, *but rarely*, on a speculative basis. No originals returned at job's completion. Pays "going rates." Considers client's budget, and skill and experience of artist when establishing payment.
Tips: Artists should "be very competent (or very reasonable in pricing); have samples that show originality and have samples rendered in media usually used: ink, wash, felt pens, etc. Oils are not too common. Show best work only. No more than 10-12 samples."

KEROFF & ROSENBERG ADVERTISING, 444 N. Wabash, Chicago IL 60611. (312)321-9000. Creative Supervisor: Dan Oditt. Ad and design agency. Clients: realty, financing, hotels.
Needs: Works with 10-12 freelance artists/year. Uses artists for advertising illustration and layout, brochure illustration, model making and signage.
First Contact & Terms: Local, experienced artists only. Send query letter with resume and samples to be kept on file; write for appointment to show portfolio. Prefers photostats, photographs, slides or tear sheets as samples. Samples not filed returned by SASE only if requested. Reports only if interested. Considers complexity of project and turnaround time when establishing payment.
Tips: "Freelancers usually get the overflow, so it's frequently under a tight deadline. So be prepared."

MANDABACH & SIMS, Suite 3620, 20 N. Wacker Dr., Chicago IL 60606. (312)236-5333. Creative Director: B. Bentkover. Ad agency. Clients: food services, financial, graphic arts and real estate.
Needs: Works with 5-10 freelance illustrators/month. Uses freelancers for print advertising and collateral material.
First Contact & Terms: Samples not returned. Works on assignment only; reports back whether to expect possible future assignments. Provide business card and tear sheets to be kept on file. Negotiates payment based on client's budget.
Tips: Wants to see work relating to their clients' needs. Artists interested in working here should be "creative, businesslike, and remember the objective."

MANNING, SELVAGE & LEE/MID-AMERICA, Suite 1713, 2 Illinois Center, 233 N. Michigan Ave., Chicago IL 60601. (312)565-0927. PR firm. Account Supervisor: Nancy B. Newman. Clients:

medical, industry, food, beverage and corporate.
Needs: Assigns 2-3 jobs/year. Uses artists for brochures/flyers, and company magazines.
First Contact & Terms: Local artists only. Query with samples (include prices on samples) and arrange interview to show portfolio. Wants only samples of finished work: "depending on your specialty—the best, most recent (within 2 years) work you have done for the largest clients you have." Samples returned by SASE within 2 weeks. Works on assignment only. Provide brochure/flyer to be kept on file for possible future assignments. Pays $300-5,000/project; $50-150/hour—"we ask for estimate in advance." Considers complexity of project, client's budget, skill and experience of artist, and turnaround time when establishing payment.
Tips: "Artists interested in working with us should have good selection of brochures, mailers, annual reports, as well as a list of clients. Usually we ask freelance artists to send us a background letter telling us about work done and specialty if any. If interested, we will set up an appointment to view work, ask for a card, brochure, or something to be left behind for our files. We already have a number of artists we work with, so new ones are most likely to be kept on file."

MARKETING SUPPORT INC., 303 E. Wacker Dr., Chicago IL 60601. Executive Art Director: Robert Becker. Clients: plumbing, heating/cooling equipment, chemicals, hardware, ski equipment, home appliances, crafts and window covering.
Needs: Assigns 300 jobs/year. Works with 2-3 illustrators/month. Uses artists for filmstrips, slide sets, brochures/flyers and trade magazines. Also uses artists for layout, illustration, lettering, type spec, paste-up and retouching for trade magazines and direct mail.
First Contact & Terms: Local artists only. Arrange interview to show portfolio. Samples returned by SASE. Reports back only if interested. Works on assignment only. Provide business card to be kept on file for future assignments. No originals returned to artist at job's completion. Pays $15/hour and up. Considers complexity of project, client's budget, and skill and experience of artist when establishing payment.

O.M.A.R. INC., 5525 N. Broadway, Chicago IL 60640. (312)271-2720. Creative Director: Paul Sierra. Spanish language ad agency. Clients: consumer food, telephone communication, TV station and public utilities.
Needs: Number of freelance artists used varies. Uses artists for consumer magazines, posters, newspapers and TV graphics.
First Contact & Terms: Local artists only. Query with resume of credits and samples; follow with phone call. Prefers slides or originals (color), photostats (b&w) as samples. Samples returned by SASE. Reports within 3 weeks. Provide resume and samples to be kept on file for possible future assignments. Works on assignment only. Payment is by the project; negotiates according to client's budget. Buys all rights.
Tips: Three trends in this field are: "messages aimed at young audiences, bilingual TV commercials and more sophisticated Spanish language commercials." Artists interested in working here "must have sensitivity to the Hispanic culture. An artist should never sacrifice pride in his/her work for the sake of a deadline, yet must nevertheless meet the specified time of completion. Show only your best work during an interview, and don't take too much time."

POLYCOM TELEPRODUCTIONS, (formerly The Poly Com Group Inc.), 201 E. Erie, Chicago IL 60611. (312)337-6000. Executive Producer/Director: Mr. Carmen V. Trombetta. Producer: Debbie Heagy. Videotape teleproducer. Clients: 40% are major Chicago advertising and PR firms and educational/industrial enterprises and 60% are corporate enterprises. Produces filmstrips, motion pictures, multimedia kits, overhead transparencies, slide sets, sound-slide sets, videotapes and films.
Needs: Works with 2-3 illustrators/month. Assigns 150-200 jobs/year. Uses artists for motion pictures, videotape teleproduction, television copy art, storyboard animation and computer animation.
First Contact & Terms: Query with resume, business card and samples which may be kept on file for possible future assignments. Prefers slides as samples. Samples not kept on file are returned by SASE. Works on assignment only. Reports in 2-3 weeks. Original art returned to artist at job's completion. Negotiates pay by project.
Tips: "Artists must be familiar with film and videotape. We need more videotape graphics artists."

JIM SANT'ANDREA MIDWEST INC., 666 N. Lake Shore Dr., Chicago IL 60611. (312)787-2156. Production Manager: Barbara Picard. AV producer. Clients: Fortune 500 companies. Produces sales meetings, motion pictures, multi-image slide modules, sound-slide sets and videotapes.
Needs: Uses artists for proposal sketches, slides, filmstrips, storyboards, illustrations for slides, films, animation and video, and collateral print materials.
First Contact & Terms: Assigns 30 jobs/year; local artists only. Arrange interview to show portfolio. Prefers original artwork as samples. SASE. Works on assignment only. Pays $3/frame for storyboards.

Reports in 2 weeks. Pays $50-250, sketches; $50-1,000, illustrations. Considers client's budget and skill and experience of artist when establishing payment.

SIEBER & McINTYRE, INC., 625 N. Michigan Ave., Chicago IL 60611. (312)266-9200. Contact: Creative Services Manager. Ad agency. Clients: pharmaceutical and health care fields.
Needs: Work load varies. Uses freelancers for medical trade magazines, journal ads, brochures/flyers and direct mail to physicians. Especially needs sources for tight marker renderings and comp layouts.
First Contact & Terms: Call for appointment to show portfolio. Reports within 2 weeks. Works on assignment only. Pays by the hour, $10 minimum. Negotiates payment based on client's budget, where work will appear, complexity of project, skill and experience of artist and turnaround time.
Tips: Prefers to see original "terrific work" rather than reproductions, but will review past work used by other ad agencies. Needs good medical illustrators but is looking for the best person—one who can accomplish executions other than anatomical. Artists should send resume or letter for files.

*SOCIETY FOR VISUAL EDUCATION, INC., 1345 W. Diversey Pkwy., Chicago IL 60614. Graphic Arts Manager: Cathy Mijou. Audiovisual and microcomputer firm. No outside clients; all work done for SVE products and services. Produces filmstrips, micro software, video disks and some print materials (but not books) for education market—schools, libraries, etc.
Needs: Works with 10+ freelance artists/year. Uses artists for keyline/paste-up, illustration, design, photography, and computer graphics for filmstrips, micro software and print materials. Artist must have demonstrated ability in these areas.
First Contact & Terms: Works on assignment only. Send query letter and samples to be kept on file. Prefers photostats, tear sheets, etc. as samples—nonreturnable samples only. Reports only if interested. Payment varies according to scope and requirements of project. Considers complexity of the project, budget, skill and experience of artist, turnaround time and rights purchased when establishing payment. Buys all rights.

STONE & ADLER, INCORPORATED, division of Young & Rubicam, Inc., 1 S. Wacker Dr., Chicago IL 60606. (312)346-6100. Art Buyer: Connal Small. Ad agency/direct marketing firm. Clients: industrial, publishing, consumer.
Needs: Uses freelancers for billboards, consumer and trade magazines, brochures/flyers, newspapers, P-O-P displays, stationery design, TV and especially direct marketing.
First Contact & Terms: Call for appointment to show portfolio. Selection based on portfolio review. Negotiates payment based on client's budget and particular job.
Tips: Wants to see anything in portfolio which indicates individual's style (original and printed samples). Uses all styles of work.

WILK & BRICHTA ADVERTISING, 875 N. Michigan, Chicago IL 60611. (312)280-2807. Art Director: Pauline Bielski. Ad agency. Clients: medical, dental, and home and consumer products.
Needs: Uses artists for billboards, direct mail, brochures/flyers, trade magazines, newspapers and TV.
First Contact & Terms: Call for appointment to show portfolio. Negotiates pay based on client's budget.
Tips: Especially likes 4-color work.

Indiana

C.R.E. INC., 400 Victoria Centre, 22 E. Washington St., Indianapolis IN 46204. Creative Director: C.H. Dragoo. Ad agency. Clients: industrial, banks, agriculture and consumer.
Needs: Works with 15 freelance artists/year. Uses artists for line art, color illustrations and airbrushing.
First Contact & Terms: Works on assignment only. Send query letter with resume, business card and samples to be kept on file. Accepts photostats, photographs, slides or tear sheets as samples. Samples not filed are returned. Reports back only if interested. Pays by the project. Considers complexity of the project, client's budget, skill and experience of artist and rights purchased when establishing payment. Buys all rights.
Tips: "Show samples of good creative talent."

CALDWELL-VAN RIPER, INC. ADVERTISING-PUBLIC RELATIONS, 1314 N. Meridian St., Indianapolis IN 46202. (317)632-6501. Associate Creative Director: John Nagy. Ad agency/PR firm. Clients are a "good mix of consumer (banks, furniture, food, etc.) and industrial (chemicals, real estate, insurance, heavy industry)."
Needs: Assigns 100-200 freelance jobs/year. Works with 10-15 freelance illustrators/month. Uses artists

for consumer and magazine ads, billboards, direct mail packages, brochures, catalogs, newspaper ads, P-O-P displays, AV presentations and posters.
First Contact & Terms: Send query letter with brochure, samples and tear sheets to be kept on file. Call for appointment to show portfolio. Accepts any available samples. Samples not kept on file are returned by SASE only if requested. Reports only if interested. Works on assignment only. Pay is negotiated. Considers complexity of project, client's budget, skill and experience of artist and rights purchased when establishing payment. Buys all rights.
Tips: "Send 5 samples of best work (copies acceptable) followed by a phone call."

HANDLEY & MILLER, INC., 1712 N. Meridian, Indianapolis IN 46202. (317)927-5545. Art Director/Vice President: Irvin Showalter. Ad agency. Clients: package goods, sales promotion, retail, direct response, institutional and financial.
Needs: Works with 2 freelance illustrators/month. Uses freelancers for consumer and trade magazines, brochures/flyers, newspapers and P-O-P displays.
First Contact & Terms: Call for appointment to show portfolio. Selection based on portfolio review. Prefers photostats, slides and original work as samples. Reports within 5 days if interested. Works on assignment only. Provide business card and brochure/flyer to be kept on file for possible future assignments. Pays standard day rate; by the hour, $30-75 average; by the project, $200-2,000 average; also by contract. Considers complexity of project, client's budget, skill and experience of artist, and turnaround time when establishing payment.
Tips: Likes to see a variety of techniques.

MARTIN A. LAVE MARKETING, 3400 W. 86th St., Indianapolis IN 46268. (317)872-0971. Production Managers: Amy Feldman, George Wilson. Ad agency. Clients: schools, retailers and industrials.
Needs: Works with 5-6 freelance artists/year. Uses artists for layout and mechanicals. Especially looks for design capability.
First Contact & Terms: Local artists only. Works on assignment only. Send query letter; call for appointment to show portfolio. Pays by the hour, $20-40 average; by project, $35-300 average. Considers complexity of the project and client's budget when establishing payment. Buys all rights.

OUR SUNDAY VISITOR INC., Department of Religious Education, 200 Noll Plaza, Huntington IN 46750. Religious education audience. Produces sound filmstrips and multimedia kits.
Needs: Subjects range from the miracles and parables of Jesus to modern church history, liturgy, stories and doctrine.
First Contact & Terms: Send samples. Prefers slides as samples. Prefers to keep samples but will return upon request. Provide resume, tear sheets, brochures/flyers and samples to be kept on file for possible future assignments. Works on assignment only; reports back whether to expect possible future assignments. No originals returned to artist at job's completion.

QUINLAN KEENE PECK & McSHAY, INC., 5435 Emerson Way N., Indianapolis IN 46226. Executive Art Director: David Stahl. Ad agency. Client list provided for SASE.
Needs: Assigns 60 freelance jobs/year. Works with 4 freelance illustrators and 1-2 freelance designers/month. Uses artists for trade magazines, billboards, direct mail packages, brochures, catalogs, newspapers, filmstrips, movies, stationery, signage and posters.
First Contact & Terms: Send query letter with resume to be kept on file. Call for appointment to show portfolio. Reports only if interested. Works on assignment only. Pays by the project. Considers complexity of project, client's budget, geographic scope of finished project and turnaround time when establishing payment. Negotiates rights purchased.

Iowa

EBEL ADVERTISING AGENCY, (formerly Griffith & Somers Advertising Agency), 770 Orpheum Bldg., Sioux City IA 51101. (712)277-3343. President: Elmer Ebel. Ad agency. Clients: industrial, financial, agricultural and business.
Needs: Works with 1 illustrator/month. Uses artists for illustrations, cartoons, multimedia kits, brochures, direct mail, catalogs and multipage flyers.
First Contact & Terms: Query with samples (tear sheets). Artist should have previous agency experience. Reports in 3 weeks. Provide brochure and resume to be kept on file for possible future assignments. No originals returned to artist at job's completion. Pay negotiated.

LA GRAVE KLIPFEL INC., 1707 High St., Des Moines IA 50309. (515)283-2297. Art Director: Max Rauler. Ad agency. Clients: "wide range" of accounts—financial, industrial and retail; client list provided upon request.
Needs: Works with 3-4 illustrators or designers/month. Uses freelance artists for billboards, consumer and trade magazines, direct mail, P-O-P displays, brochures, catalogs, posters, signage, newspapers, TV art direction and AV presentations.
First Contact & Terms: Local artists only. Phone first and follow with mailed information. Works on assignment only. Negotiates payment by the project and on freelancer's previous experience.
Tips: "Present resume or self-promotion piece. Have a portfolio of no more than 20 pieces. Be neat and clean with presented pieces. Be brief and concise in talking about work; avoid speeches."

MOHAWK ADVERTISING CO., 1307 6th St. SW, Box 1608, Mason City IA 50401. (515)423-1354. Vice President/Executive Art Director: Phil Means. Senior Art Director: Steve Erikson. Art Director: Gary Gamble. Ad agency. Clients: industrial, agricultural, financial, consumer.
Needs: Assigns 15-25 jobs/year. Works with 1-3 illustrators/month. Uses artists for consumer and trade magazines, billboards, brochures and posters.
First Contact & Terms: Send query letter with brochure, business card, samples and tear sheets to be kept on file. Write for appointment to show portfolio. Prefers photostats or "a form we can keep on file" as samples. Samples returned by SASE if not kept on file. Reports within 10 days. Works on assignment only. Pays by project on bid. Considers complexity of project, client's budget, turnaround time and rights purchased when establishing payment. Buys reprint rights or all rights; negotiates rights. No originals returned at job's completion.

Kansas

BRYANT, LAHEY & BARNES, INC., Suite 309, 6400 Glenwood, Overland Park KS 66202. (913)677-3494 or 677-4711. Art Director: Terry Pritchett. Ad agency. Clients: agricultural and veterinary.
Needs: Uses artists for illustration and production, including keyline and paste-up, consumer and trade magazines and brochures/flyers.
First Contact & Terms: Local artists only. Query by phone. Send business card and resume to be kept on file for future assignments. Negotiates pay. No originals returned to artist at job's completion.

HARMON TRUE PRUITT, 4220 Johnson Dr., Shawnee Mission KS 66205. (913)362-5566. Art Directors: Steve Folen, Mike Peterson. Ad/PR firm. Clients: banks, fashion, lab equipment, pro football team, sporting goods, hospital and hotel.
Needs: Works with 3 illustrators/month. Uses artists for illustration.
First Contact & Terms: Local artists only. Arrange interview to show portfolio. SASE. "Letter kept on file; will call artist if needed." No originals returned at job's completion. Negotiates pay by job.

LANE & LESLIE ADVERTISING AGENCY INC., Petroleum Bldg., Box 578, Wichita KS 67201. President: David W. Lane. Ad agency. Clients: banks, savings and loans, consumer products and fast food.
Needs: Works with 1 illustrator and 6 designers/month. Uses artists for storyboards, billboards, P-O-P displays, filmstrips, multimedia kits, direct mail, slide sets, brochures/flyers, trade magazines and newspapers. Also uses artists for photography and retouching.
First Contact & Terms: Provide business card, brochure and resume to be kept on file for possible future assignments. No originals returned to artist at job's completion. "We prefer to buy all rights."

MARKETAIDE, INC., Box 600, Salina KS 67402-0600. (913)825-7161. Production Manager: Dennis Katzenmeier. Full-service advertising/marketing/direct mail firm. Clients: financial, agricultural machinery, industrial, some educational, and fast food.
Needs: Uses freelance artists for illustrations, retouching, signage.
First Contact & Terms: Prefers artists within one-state distance and possessing professional expertise. Send query letter with resume, business card and samples to be kept on file. Write for appointment to show portfolio. Accepts any kind of accurate representation as samples, depending upon medium. Samples not kept on file are returned only if requested. Reports only if interested. Works on assignment only. Pays by the hour, $15-75 average; "since projects vary in size we are forced to estimate according to each job's parameters." Considers complexity of project, skill and experience of artist, how work will be used, turnaround time and rights purchased when establishing payment.
Tips: Artists interested in working here "should be highly-polished in technical ability, have a good eye for design and be able to meet all deadline commitments."

*MARSHFILM ENTERPRISES, INC., Box 8082, Shawnee Mission KS 66208. (816)523-1059. President: Joan K. Marsh. Audiovisual firm. Clients: schools.
Needs: Works with 1-2 freelance artists/year. Uses artists for illustrating filmstrips. Artists must have experience and imagination.
First Contact & Terms: Works on assignment only. Send query letter, resume and samples to be kept on file "if it is potentially the type of art we would use"; write for appointment to show portfolio. Prefes slides or actual illustrations as samples. Samples not filed are returned. Reports within 1 month. Considers client's budget when establishing payment. Buys all rights.

NATIONAL PAGEANT ASSOCIATION INC., 6036 Metcalf, Overland Park KS 66202. (913)262-2624. President: Bob Myers. Promotion firm. Clients: producers of pageants and shows. Assigns 12 jobs/year.
Needs: Uses artists for illustration, paste-up and "all areas really, depending on the job being done." Work is done in the areas of direct mail and slide sets.
First Contact & Terms: Query with business card, resume, brochure and samples to be kept on file, or arrange interview to show portfolio. Prefers photostats, slides or tear sheets as samples. Samples not filed are returned. Works on assignment only. Contacts artists as needs arise. No originals returned to artist at job's completion. Pays an agreed contract price for each job. Considers complexity of project, client's budget, skill and experience of artist, geographic scope of finished project, turnaround time and rights purchased when establishing payment.

TRAVIS-WALZ AND ASSOCIATES, INC., 8500 W. 63rd. St., Shawnee Mission KS 66202. Contact: Gary Otteson. Ad agency. Serves clients in food, finance, broadcasting, utilities, pets, gardening and real estate.
Needs: Works with 2-4 illustrators/month. Uses illustrators for billboards, P-O-P displays, consumer magazines, direct mail, brochures/flyers, trade magazines and newspapers. Also uses artists for retouching. Does not buy design or layout. Agency has its own design staff.
First Contact & Terms: "We generally work with in-town talent because of tight deadlines." Prefers "anything *but* original work" as samples. Samples returned by SASE. Reports only if interested. Commissioned work only. Provide business card, brochure/flyer and samples to be kept on file for possible future assignments. No originals returned to artist at job's completion. Pays $50-1,200/project, "depending on job—b&w or color." Considers complexity of project, client's budget and turnaround time when establishing payment.
Tips: "We must see your work to buy. The best way to sell yourself is by your samples shown in person or brochure mailed to us."

Kentucky

*DAN BURCH ASSOCIATES, 2338 Frankfort Ave., Louisville KY 40206. (502)895-4881. Art Director: Joe Burch. Specializes in business-to-business and packaged goods advertising; brand and corporate identity, P-O-P displays, trade show exhibits, brochures, catalogs, direct mail, AV, packaging and signage. Clients: industrial, technical and consumer goods manufacturers and services.
Needs: Uses freelance artists for illustration and photo retouching on advertising and collateral materials.
First Contact & Terms: Send query letter with samples of work to be kept on file for future assignments. Negotiates payment.

DE BORD & OWEN, INC., 1027 Broadway Ave., Box 9640, Bowling Green KY 42101. (502)782-1774. Contact: Judith Byrd. Ad agency/PR firm. Clients: industry, restaurants and professionals.
Needs: Assigns 20-30 freelance jobs/year. Uses artists for brochures, catalogs, P-O-P displays and posters.
First Contact & Terms: Send query letter with samples and tear sheets to be kept on file. Call for appointment to show portfolio. Considers any type of samples. Samples not kept on file are returned only if requested. Reports only if interested. Works on assignment only. Pays by the hour, $7.50-10 average. "We like for the artist to quote each job in advance if possible." Considers complexity of project, skill and experience of artist and rights purchased when establishing payment. Buys reprint rights or all rights.

FESSEL, SIEGFRIEDT & MOELLER ADVERTISING, 1500 Heyburn Building, Box 1031, Louisville KY 40201. (502)585-5154. Vice President/Executive Art Director: James A. Berry. Ad agency. Clients: mostly consumer firms, some industrial.
Needs: Works with 3 illustrators/year. Uses freelance artists for billboards, consumer and trade

magazines, direct mail, P-O-P displays, brochures, catalogs, posters, signage, newspapers and AV presentations.
First Contact & Terms: Works primarily with local freelancers. Arrange interview to show portfolio. Works on assignment only. Payment varies according to project estimates.

McCANN-ERICKSON, LOUISVILLE, 1469 S. 4th, Louisville KY 40208. (502)636-0441. Creative Director: Todd Hoon. Ad agency. Serves clients in banking, retailing, manufacturing and quick-service food.
Needs: Freelance needs vary. Uses artists for billboards, P-O-P displays, consumer and trade magazines, direct mail, TV, brochures/flyers and newspapers; occasionally humorous or cartoon-style illustrations.
First Contact & Terms: Call for appointment to show portfolio or make contact through artist's rep. Prefers to review actual art (original) or slides. Samples returned by SASE if they are slides. Reports in 1 week. Works on assignment only. Provide brochure/flyer, samples and tear sheets to be kept on file for possible future assignments. Negotiates pay; pays by the project, $200-3,500 average. Considers client's budget, skill and experience of artist, turnaround time and rights purchased when establishing payment.
Tips: "We have a renewed interest in use of illustration. There is a market for more sophisticated illustration interpretation—clients are more receptive to a greater degree of abstraction, even when representating product. This allows us as an art broker to make greater use of illustration. Keep us informed of your current workstyles as they evolve."

Louisiana

HERBERT S. BENJAMIN ASSOCIATES, 2736 Florida St., Box 2151. Baton Rouge LA 70821. (504)387-0611. Associate Creative Director: Mr. Aubrey Shamburger. Clients: food, financial, industrial, retail fashion/furniture, etc.
Needs: Works with 2-3 illustrators/month. Uses artists for industrial, trade and business journals; newspapers, TV, brochures/flyers, newsletters.
First Contact & Terms: Call for appointment to show portfolio. Works with freelance artists on assignment only. Provide resume and samples to be kept on file for possible future assignments. Especially needs good retail illustrator in advertising areas such as furniture, fashion, etc. Illustrators must conform to area rates.
Tips: When reviewing an artist's work, particularly looks for "competence in drawing and lettering and knowledge of type, originality in ideas, simplicity and strength of design, and technique."

CARTER ADVERTISING INC., 800 American Tower, Shreveport LA 71101. (318)227-1920. President: Bill Bailey Carter. Ad agency. Clients: hotels, motor vehicles and manufacturing. Assigns 500 jobs and buys 50 illustrations/year.
Needs: Works with 2-3 illustrators and 2-3 designers/month. Uses artists for billboards, P-O-P displays, filmstrips, consumer magazines, stationery design, multimedia kits, direct mail, television, slide sets, brochures/flyers, trade magazines, album covers, newspapers, books and mechanicals.
First Contact & Terms: Prefers local artists. "Must have heavy production experience." Query with resume or arrange interview to show portfolio. SASE. Reports within 2 weeks. Provide brochure, flyer, business card, resume, tear sheets, etc., to be kept on file for future assignments. No originals returned at job's completion unless otherwise agreed upon. Pay negotiated by project. Considers complexity of project, client's budget, skill and experience of artist, geographic scope of finished project, turnaround time and rights purchased when establishing payment.

CUNNINGHAM, SLY & ASSOCIATES, INC., Box 4503, Shreveport LA 71134. Creative Director: Harold J. Sly. Ad agency. Clients: industrial/financial.
Needs: Works with 6-10 freelance artists/year. Uses artists for layout/design, illustrations, photo retouching, mechanical art and airbrushing. Especially looks for mechanical skills.
First Contact & Terms: Works on assignment only. Send query letter with brochure, resume, business card and samples to be kept on file. Samples not filed are returned only by request. Reports back only if interested. Pays by the hour, $20-50 average. Considers complexity of the project, client's budget and turnaround time when establishing payment. Rights purchased vary according to project.

DUKE UNLIMITED, INC., Suite 205, 1940 I-10 Service Road, Kenner LA 70065. (504)464-1891. President: Lana Duke. Ad agency. Clients: industrial, investment, medical, restaurants, entertainment, fashion and tourism.
Needs: Assigns 50 freelance jobs/year. Works with 2 freelance illustrators and 1 freelance designer/

This is one of a series of six illustrations created by Mike Fisher of New Orleans for Duke Unlimited, an advertising agency in Kenner, Louisiana. The illustration was part of an advertising campaign for a locally owned steak house. Fisher received $400 for all reproduction rights to each illustration. "Mike's style works very well for this account," says Art Director Anne Esposite. "It has a bold quality and reproduces extremely well in newspapers, the main source of print advertising for this client."

month. Uses artists for consumer and trade magazines, billboards, direct mail packages, brochures, catalogs, newspapers, filmstrips, movies, stationery, signage, P-O-P displays, AV presentations, posters and press releases.
First Contact & Terms: Send query letter with brochure, resume, business card, samples and tear sheets to be kept on file. Contact only through artist's agent. "We review all portfolios on Fridays, 9 am-noon." Prefers photostats as samples. Samples returned only if requested. Reports only if interested. Works on assignment. Pays by the project, $150-1,000 average. The artist must provide a firm quotation in writing. Considers complexity of project, client's budget, skill and experience of artist, turnaround time and rights purchased when establishing payment. Buys all rights.
Tips: "We use more computer graphics, mixing photography and illustration, resulting in surreal effect. This has created *less* need for photo retouching and special effects, and has put greater emphasis on designer working more closely with the printer or photographer."

THE RUB GROUP ADVERTISING, INC., 628 North Blvd., Baton Rouge LA 70802. (504)383-6169. Creative Director: Bill Wempren. Ad agency. Clients: banks, industry, travel/tourism. Client list provided for SASE.
Needs: Assigns 7 freelance illustration jobs/year. Uses artists for consumer and trade magazines, billboards, brochures and posters.
First Contact & Terms: Send business card and samples to be kept on file. Call or write for appointment to show portfolio. Prefers photographs or 35mm slides as samples. Reports only if interested. Works on assignment only. Pays by the project, $500-2,000 average. Considers complexity of project, client's budget and rights purchased when establishing payment. Negotiates rights purchased.
Tips: "We must see evidence of ability and versatility."

Maryland

*ADVERTISERS' INC., #2N, 10 Post Office Rd., Silver Spring MD 20910. (301)565-5223. President: Keith Krause. Ad agency/PR firm. Clients: various types. Clients list provided for SASE.
First Contact & Terms: Send query letter with resume and samples to be kept on file. Call for appointment to show portfolio. "Photocopy samples of work are sufficient." Reports only if interested. Works

on assignment only. Pays by the hour. Considers skill and experience of artist and turnaround time when establishing payment.

Tips: Artists should "make up an 8¹/₂x11 package with short resume plus montage of work samples that show type of work they feel most comfortable doing. If an expert in technical airbrush—say so. If architectural rendering is a specialty, voice that fact."

*SAMUEL R. BLATE ASSOCIATES, 10331 Watkins Mill Dr., Gaithersburg MD 20879-2935. (301)840-2248. President: Samuel R. Blate. Audiovisual firm. Clients: business/professional, US government, some private.

Needs: Works with 5 freelance artists/year. Uses artists for cartoons (especially for certain types of audiovisual presentations), illustrations (graphs, etc.) for 35mm slides, pamphlet and book design. Especially important are "technical and aesthetic excellence and ability to meet deadlines."

First Contact & Terms: "We prefer to work with artists in the Washington-Baltimore-Richmond metro area." Works on assignment only. Send query letter with resume and samples to be kept on file; call or write for appointment to show portfolio. Send slides, tear sheets or photographs as samples; "no original art, please!" Samples are returned by SASE. Reports only if interested. Pays by the hour, $20 minimum. "Payment varies as a function of experience, skills needed, size of project, and anticipated competition, if any." Also considers complexity of the project, client's budget, turnaround time and rights purchased when establishing payment. Rights purchased vary according to project, "but we prefer to purchase first rights only. This is sometimes not possible due to client demand, in which case we attempt to negotiate a financial adjustment for the artist."

Tips: "The demand for technically-oriented artwork has increased. At the same time, some clients who used artists have been satisfied with computer-generated art."

*COE COMMUNICATIONS, INC., 5813 Wicomico Ave., Rockville MD 20852. (301)881-2820. Executive Vice President: Janice V. Long. Audiovisual firm. Clients: associations, corporations and nonprofits.

Needs: Works with 25-30 freelance artists/year. Uses artists for photography, artwork and editing.

First Contact & Terms: Works on assignment only. Send resume to be kept on file. Samples not filed are returned by SASE. Reports only if interested. Pays by the project, $500-15,000 average. Buys all rights.

FOSTER AND GREEN ADVERTISING INC., 16 E. Chase St., Baltimore MD 21202. (301)837-5103. Art Director: Dan Townsend. Ad agency. Clients: industrial, financial, automotive.

Needs: Works with 3-4 freelance artists/year. Uses artists for busy periods, vacation relief and special projects.

First Contact & Terms: Send resume to be kept on file; call or write for appointment to show portfolio. Reports only if interested. Pays by the hour, $5-15 average. Considers complexity of project, client's budget, skill and experience of artist and turnaround time when establishing payment. Buys all rights.

HOLECHEK COMMUNICATIONS, Suite 305, 204 N. Liberty St., Baltimore MD 21201. (301)837-4200. President: Mark Holechek. Executive Vice President: James T. Holechek. Ad agency. Clients: publishers, cosmetic, fragrance, manufacturers, clothing manufacturers, computer services, housewares manufacturers. Client list provided "only if it is applicable to the work the freelancer is doing for us."

Needs: Assigns 50-100 freelance jobs/year. Works with 2-4 freelance illustrators and 2-4 freelance designers/month. Uses artists for consumer and trade magazines, billboards, brochures, catalogs and stationery.

First Contact & Terms: "Fast delivery time *usually* requires that the artist live in the Baltimore area, but depending on the scope of the project, we sometimes go to New York for freelancers." Send query letter with business card and samples to be kept on file. Write for appointment to show portfolio. "We take a large number of freelance calls, but we do request that no one call before contacting us in writing first. Photocopies are fine; we don't need an extensive presentation to determine the usefulness of a talent." Samples not kept on file are not returned. Reports if interested. Works on assignment depending on the particular situation. Pays by the project, $25-500 average. "Each project must be considered independent of others and prices vary accordingly." Considers complexity of project and turnaround time when establishing payment. Negotiates rights purchased.

Tips: "Walk softly but carry a good portfolio." Especially looks for a "variety of samples of talent, cost, turnaround, personality—although some of these don't come in the portfolio, they're just as important."

IMAGE DYNAMICS, INC., Suite 1400, 1101 N. Calvert St., Baltimore MD 21202. (301)539-7730. Art Director: Erin Ries. Ad agency/PR firm. Clients: wide mix, specializing in restaurants and hotels,

associations, colleges, hospitals and land developers.
Needs: Uses artists for illustration, design and paste-up; frequently buys humorous and cartoon-style illustrations.
First Contact & Terms: Local artists only. Call to arrange interview to show portfolio; "please do not drop in or write. Bring lots of b&w and 2-color samples; have printed or produced work to show." Samples are returned. Reports only if interested. Works on assignment only. Provide business card and samples to be kept on file for possible future assignments. Pays flat fee or by the hour, depending on project and budget. Considers complexity of project, client's budget, skill and experience of artist and turnaround time when establishing payment.
Tips: "We are able to use freelance illustrators more towards a more creative product."

*RECORDED BOOKS INC., Box 79, Charlotte Hall MD 20622. Contact: Sandy Spencer. Audiovisual publisher. "The company produces 24 original recordings each year for the general public."
Needs: Graphics to illustrate 24 titles/year. Looks for "imaginative and striking graphic illustration."
First Contact & Terms: Works on assignment only. Send query letter and samples to be kept on file. Photocopies acceptable as samples. Samples not filed are returned by SASE. Reports only if interested. Pays by the project, $20 minimum. Considers rights purchased when establishing payment. Buys reprint rights.

GILBERT SANDLER & ASSOCIATES, INC., 501 St. Paul Pl., Baltimore MD 21202. (301)837-7100. Senior Art Director: Loren Patten. Ad agency. Clients: institutional advertising (financial, industrial) and PR.
First Contact & Terms: Call for personal appointment to show portfolio. Negotiates payment based on client's budget and particular job. "Prefer to get an estimate from the freelancer and negotiate payment based on the budget."
Tips: Wants to see a little bit of all freelancer can do in portfolio but especially specific style and best work. Uses many types of art and prefers to see artist's speciality.

SHECTER & LEVIN ADVERTISING/PUBLIC RELATIONS, 1800 N. Charles St., Baltimore MD 21201. (301)752-4088. Production Executives: Virginia Lindler and David J. Levin. Ad agency/PR firm. Serves clients in real estate, finance, professional associations, social agencies, retailing, apartments and manufacturing.
Needs: Works with 3-4 illustrators/month. Uses designers for billboards, consumer magazines, stationery design, direct mail, television, brochures/flyers, trade magazines and newspapers. Also uses artists for layouts and mechanicals for brochures, newspaper and magazine ads.
First Contact & Terms: Query or arrange interview to show portfolio. SASE "but prefer no samples be sent unless arranged." No file kept on artists. No originals returned to artist at job's completion. Negotiates pay.

MARC SMITH CO., Box A, Severna Park MD 21146. (301)647-2606. Art/Creative Director: Marc Smith. Advertising agency. Clients: consumer and industrial products, sales services and public relations firms.
Needs: Works with 6 illustrators/month. Uses artists for layout, illustration, lettering, technical art, type spec, paste-up and retouching; illustrators and designers for direct mail, slide sets, brochures/flyers, trade magazines and newspapers; designers for billboards, P-O-P displays, film strips, consumer magazines, stationery, multimedia kits and TV; occasionally buys humorous and cartoon-style illustrations.
First Contact & Terms: Local artists only. Mail tear sheets or original art or call for interview. Keeps file on artists; does not return original artwork to artist after completion of assignment.
Tips: "More sophisticated techniques and equipment are being used in art and design. Our use of freelance material has intensified."

VAN SANT, DUGDALE & COMPANY, INC., The World Trade Center, Baltimore MD 21202. (301)539-5400. Creative Director: Stan Paulus. Ad agency. Clients: consumer, corporate, associations, financial, and industrial; "very wide range" of accounts; client list provided upon request.
Needs: Number of freelance artists used varies. Uses freelance artists for consumer and trade magazines, brochures, catalogs, newspapers and AV presentations.
First Contact & Terms: Works on assignment basis only. Negotiates payment according to client's budget, amount of creativity required, where work will appear and freelancer's previous experience.
Tips: Current trends include stronger colors, bolder designs and more innovative concepts. Many of these designs and illustrations are being used to convey high technology and state-of-the-art operations.

THE WOLFF COMPANY, 100 E. 23rd St., Baltimore MD 21218. (301)243-1421. Creative Director: Robert Canale. Ad agency. Clients: industrial, fashion and financial firms—"from furs to petroleum,

autos, savings and loans, etc."; client list provided upon request.
Needs: Works with "many, many illustrators and are in the process of building file of artists." Uses freelance artists for billboards, consumer and trade magazines, direct mail, P-O-P displays, brochures, catalogs, posters, signage and newspapers.
First Contact & Terms: Local artists only. Call to set up appointment for portfolio review. Works on assignment basis only. Negotiates payment according to client's budget.

Massachusetts

ARNOLD & COMPANY, 1111 Park Sq. Bldg., Boston MA 02116. (617)357-1900. Senior Vice President: Len Karsakov. Executive Creative Director: Wilson Siebert. Ad agency. Clients: fast food, financial and computer firms, retail.
Needs: Works with 10-12 illustrators/month. Uses freelance artists for billboards, consumer and trade magazines, direct mail, P-O-P displays, brochures, catalogs, posters, signage, newspapers, TV and AV presentations.
First Contact & Terms: Arrange interview to show portfolio; query with "good" samples. Samples returned by SASE. Reports within 1 week. Works on assignment only. Provide business card, brochure/flyer and samples to be kept on file for possible future assignments. Pays by the project. Negotiates payment according to client's budget and where work will appear.
Tips: "Show your best work—a distinctive style and full range."

*ASTRA COMMUNICATIONS, 581 Riverside Ave., Medford MA 02155. (617)391-0441. President: Charlotte B. Berman. Ad agency. Clients: computer and real estate firms, restaurants and retail women's clothing stores.
Needs: Works with 1-4 freelance artists/year. Uses artists for pen & ink sketches, ad layouts and design, and pasteup of mechanicals. "We need art that will reproduce well. We also look for speed of completion; good type selection, specifying; good knowledge of how to prepare complicated mechanicals for magazines and brochures; and generic product sketching."
First Contact & Terms: "If the artist is doing paste-up work we would like him/her to be willing to do it at our office." Works on assignment only. Send query letter, business card, samples and prices to be kept on file. Samples not filed are returned by SASE only if requested. Reports only if interested. Pays by the hour, $7-25 average; by the project, $25 minimum. Considers complexity of the project, client's budget, skill and experience of artist and turnaround time when establishing payment. Rights purchased vary according to project. "If the artwork is something we specifically ask to have drawn and give specifics for, we consider we own the rights."
Tips: "Please keep in mind we are usually a low-budget operation. But we are willing to try new people."

ROBERT BATOR AND ASSOCIATES, 40 Marion St., Chicopee MA 01013. Art Director: Robert Bator. Ad agency. Clients: newspapers, restaurants, small businesses and recording companies.
Needs: Uses artists for illustration, lettering, record jacket design, books, brochures/flyers, album covers, fashions—women's garments, casual and bathing wear.
First Contact & Terms: Send cover letter along with samples of work, printed or photostats—*no slides*. Provide brochure, flyer, business card, resume and tear sheets to be kept on file for future assignments. Samples returned only if requested. Reports within 10 days. No originals returned to artist at job's completion. Pays $250-395, comprehensive layout; $10-12/hour, lettering. Considers complexity of project when establishing payment.

BLACK & MUSEN, INC., Box 465, East Longmeadow MA 01028. (413)567-0361. Art Director: Victor Brisebois. Ad agency. Clients: consumer and industrial companies.
Needs: Works with 6 freelance artists/year. Uses artists for mechanicals and paste-ups and layouts for special projects (ads and collateral material). Especially looks for accuracy and crispness for paste-ups; creativity for layouts.
First Contact & Terms: Artists must live within local area for paste-up and mechanicals; within 75-mile radius for layouts and designs. Works on assignment only. Send resume to be kept on file; call for appointment to show portfolio. Prefers to review tear sheets or actual layouts. Reports back. Pays by the hour for paste-up, $10-15 minimum; by project for layout. Considers complexity of the project, client's budget, skill and experience of artist and turnaround time when establishing payment. Buys all rights.
Tips: "We are looking for new approaches and ideas that are salable."

BOUCHARD, WALTON PRODUCTIONS, Bishop's Rd., Kingston MA 02364. (617)585-6893. Executive Producer: Rene J. Bouchard, Jr. Clients: industry and business. Produces sales, training and technical information filmstrips and videotapes.

Ed Parker of Andover, Massachusetts, received this "charging rhino" assignment from Stavros Cosmopulos, creative director of Cosmopulos, Crowley & Daly, Inc. in Boston. The artwork was one in a series of trade magazine ads for a software company; "The ads were designed to be attention getting and intrusive," says Cosmopulos. "We liked Parker's crisp, contemporary style. The agency dictated the idea and direction."

Needs: Assigns 12-15 jobs/year. Works with 5+ illustrators and 4+ animators/year. Uses artists for "various jobs, depending on specific skill required."

First Contact & Terms: Send resume. "If there is interest we will request samples." Samples returned by SASE. Provide resume, samples and brochure/flyer to be kept on file for possible future assignments. Works on assignment only. Reports within 3 weeks. Pays by the project. Method and amount of payment are negotiated with the individual artist. Negotiates rights purchased.

COSMOPULOS, CROWLEY & DALY, INC., 250 Boylston St., Boston MA 02116. Chairman of the Board/Creative Director: Stavros Cosmopulos. Advertising and marketing agency. Clients: banking, restaurants, industrial, package goods, food and electronics.

Needs: Works with 6 illustrators and 1 animator/month. Uses artists for billboards, P-O-P displays, filmstrips, consumer magazines, stationery design, multimedia kits, direct mail, television, slide sets, brochures/flyers, trade magazines and newspapers.

First Contact & Terms: Make an appointment to show portfolio. Prefers photostats or slides as samples. Samples returned by SASE if not kept on file. Reports only if interested. Works on assignment only. Provide business card, flyer or examples of work to be kept on file for future assignments. No originals returned to artist at job's completion. Pays by the project, $50-10,000 average. Considers complexity of project, client's budget, geographic scope of finished project, turnaround time and rights purchased when establishing payment.

Tips: "Give a simple presentation of the range of work you can do including printed samples of actual jobs—but not a lot of samples."

*DETRICK LAWRENCE CORP., Box 1722, Duxbury MA 02331. (617)934-6561. Art Director: Jane Christopher. Audiovisual firm. Clients: nonprofit, hotel industry, television.

Needs: Works with 4 freelance artists/year. Uses artists for creating mechanicals for box covers, flat art

© 1984 Bob Barner

"We needed a clever, whimsical, yet sophisticated piece of artwork," explains Sheri Flagler, president/creative director of Flagler Advertising/Graphic Design in Brookline, Massachusetts. This illustration by Bob Barner of Boston is one of three he did for a print ad campaign. The artist was paid $600 for blanket rights to the three illustrations. "Bob Barner is an illustrator we have used before. He understands and grasps the situation or job, and his work is very professional," says Flagler.

for transfer to slides, creating logos, artwork for animation and artwork for advertising.
First Contact & Terms: Artists should have experience with audiovisual projects. Works on assignment only. Send query letter with brochure, resume, business card and samples to be kept on file; call or write for appointment to show portfolio. Accepts photostats, photographs, slides or tear sheets as samples. Samples not filed are returned by SASE. Reports only if interested. Pays by the project, $50-2,500 average. Considers complexity of the project, client's budget and skill and experience of artist when establishing payment. Negotiates rights purchased.

*FLAGLER ADVERTISING/GRAPHIC DESIGN, Box 1317, Brookline MA 02146. (617)566-6971. President/Creative Director: Sheri Flagler. Specializes in corporate identity, direct mail, fashion, publications and technical illustration. Clients: cable television, finance, real estate, fashion and direct mail agencies.
Needs: Works with 10-20 freelance artists/year. Uses artists for illustration, mechanicals, retouching, airbrushing, charts/graphs and lettering.
First Contact & Terms: Works on assignment only. Send resume, business card and samples to be kept on file. Call or write for appointment to show portfolio. Prefers brochures, photocopies or tear sheets. Samples not filed are not returned. Reports back only if interested. Pays for design by the project, $100-1,500 average; for illustration by the project, $150-1,200 average. Considers complexity of project, client's budget and turnaround time when establishing payment.
Tips: "Send a range and variety of style showing clean, crisp and professional work."

HBM/CREAMER, INC., (formerly Humphrey, Browning, MacDougall, Inc.), 1 Beacon St., Boston MA 02108. (617)723-7770. Art Buyer: Mary Pat Curran. Ad agency. Clients: consumer, financial, hi-tech and fashion.

Needs: Will look at storyboard artists and illustrators, but prefers to work with illustrators who have advertising experience.
First Contact & Terms: Send samples; follow up with phone call. Works on assignment only. Payment is contingent upon work involved.

*HILL HOLLIDAY CONNORS COSMOPULOS INC., John Hancock Tower, 200 Clarendon St., Boston MA 02116. (617)437-1600, ext. 4147. Art Buyer: Lowry Maclean. Ad agency. Clients: computer firm, banks, consumer products, *Globe* newspaper, lottery, etc.
Needs: Works with 750 freelance artists (illustrators, designers; photographers)/year. Uses artists for illustration and photography. Fast turn-around time is important.
First Contact & Terms: Works on assignment only. Send nonreturnable samples to be kept on file; write for appointment to show portfolio. Samples not filed are not returned. Does not report back. Pays by the project. Considers complexity of the project, client's budget, turnaround time and rights purchased when establishing payment. Rights purchased vary according to project.

LAYMAN ASSOCIATES, INC., 280 Bridge St., Dedham MA 02026. (617)329-7030. Contact: L.A. Layman. Ad agency. Clients: industrial, commercial and services, especially capital equipment manufacturers.
Needs: Works with 2 designers/month. Uses designers for direct mail, slide sets and trade magazines. Also needs artists for technical illustration, type spec, layouts, retouching, paste-up and lettering for newspapers, trade magazines, direct mail, P-O-P displays, collateral and exhibits.
First Contact & Terms: Prefers local artists. Arrange interview or mail art. Provide materials to be kept on file for future assignments. No originals returned to artist at job's completion. Pays $25-75, layout; $10-15/hour, paste-up.

*ROB MACINTOSH COMMUNICATIONS, INC., 288 Newbury St., Boston MA 02115. (617)267-4912. President: Rob MacIntosh. Ad agency. Clients: graphic arts industry—printers, paper manufacturers and computer software.
Needs: Works with 20 freelance artists/year. Uses artists for various assignments from primary illustration to spot work. "We need a total range of skills; that's why we use freelancers."
First Contact & Terms: Works on assignment only. Send brochure, resume, business card and samples to be kept on file. Accepts photostats, photographs, slides or tear sheets as samples. Samples not filed are returned by SASE only if requested. Reports only if interested. Pays by the project, $200 minimum. Considers complexity of project, client's budget, skill and experience of artist and turnaround time when establishing payment. Rights purchased vary according to project.

McKINNEY/NEW ENGLAND, 58 Commercial Wharf, Boston MA 02110. (617)227-5090. Creative Director: Joe Toomey. Ad agency. Clients: industrial and high tech.
Needs: Occasionally uses freelancers for print collateral—ads and brochures.
First Contact & Terms: Usually works by recommendation but does occasionally set up appointments by phone to review portfolio. Negotiates payment based on client's budget, amount of creativity required from artist, where work will appear and freelancer's expertise in area.
Tips: Wants to see illustrator's best work and "a lot of it." Work must be professional, with style, even if it's just a simple line drawing.

PHOTOGRAPHERS' COLOR SERVICE, 10 Harvard St., Worcester MA 01608. (617)752-1921. President: M. Richmond. Photographic studio. Clients: educational, industrial and business. Produces filmstrips, slide sets and color prints.
Needs: Assigns 30 jobs/year. Uses artists for slide and ad illustrations.
First Contact & Terms: Query with resume and samples. Samples returned with SASE. Reports in 2 weeks. Provide business card to be kept on file for possible future assignments. Negotiates pay by the project.

PETER SIMMONS PRODUCTIONS, 660 Main St., Woburn MA 01801. President: Peter Simmons. AV/film producer. Clients: corporations.
Needs: Works with 2 illustrators/month. Uses artists for filmstrips, motion pictures and storyboards.
First Contact & Terms: Write for interview to show portfolio, or send resume, business card or brochure/flyer to be kept on file for future assignments. SASE. Works on assignment only. Pays going rates. Negotiates pay based on amount of creativity required and artist's previous experience/reputation.

*JAMIL SIMON ASSOCIATES, 2 Tyler Ct., Cambridge MA 02140. (617)491-4300. Associate Producer: Lisa Podoloff. Audiovisual firm. Clients: hotels, computer companies, government and nonprofit agencies.

Needs: Works with 5-8 freelance artists/year. Uses artists for drawings for slide presentations, printed materials, layouts and presentations.
First Contact & Terms; Local artists only. Works on assignment only. Send query letter with brochure and samples to be kept on file. Prefers tear sheets as samples. Samples not filed are returned only if requested. Does not report back. Pays by the project, $75-250 average. Considers complexity of the project and skill and experience of artist when establishing payment. Rights purchased vary according to project.

*TR PRODUCTIONS, 1031 Commonweath Ave., Boston MA 02215. (617)783-0200. Production Manager: Tom Cramer. Audiovisual firm. Clients: industrial and high-tech.
Needs: Works with 5-10 freelance artists/year. Uses artists for slide graphics, layout, mechanical, computer graphics, and 2-color and 4-color collateral design. Especially important is clean, accurate board work.
First Contact & Terms: For slide work, artist must have experience in design and mechanicals for slides/multi-image. Works on assignment only. Send query letter with brochure (if any), resume and nonreturnable samples to be kept on file. Prefers slides or brochures as samples. Samples not filed are not returned. Reports only if interested. Pays by the hour, $8-25 average. Considers complexity of project, client's budget, skill and experience of artist and turnaround time when establishing payment. Buys all audiovisual rights.

Michigan

COMMON SENSE COMMUNICATIONS, INC., 225 W. Morley Dr., Saginaw MI 48605-5074. (517)755-8171. Executive Art Director: Bob Lauka. Art Director: James Kinnaman. Serves clients in machinery, automobiles, insurance, building supplies and banking.
Needs: Buys 25 full-color illustrations/year. Uses artists for illustrations, color separations, layout, lettering, paste-up, retouching and type spec for ads, annual reports, billboards, catalogs, letterheads, packaging, P-O-P displays, posters, TV and trademarks.
First Contact & Terms: Mail slides or printed samples. SASE. Reports within 4 weeks. Works on assignment only. Provide business card, brochure/flyer, resume, samples, tear sheets or "all the information an artist has available for analyzing assignments" to be kept on file for possible future assignments. Artist quotes his price. Considers client's budget when establishing payment. Agency pays for unused completed work ("assignments usually approved or disapproved at tissue stage").
Tips: "Have a complete portfolio of work showing how you developed a project right through the finished product. That way I can determine whether or not I need to work more closely with artists or I can feel confident that they can work on their own to achieve the result we need."

CREATIVE HOUSE ADVERTISING INC., Suite 200, 24472 Northwestern Hwy., Southfield MI 48075. (313)355-3344. Executive Vice President/Creative Director: Robert G. Washburn. Advertising/graphics/display/art firm. Clients: residential and commercial construction, land development, consumer, retail, finance and manufacturing. Assigns 20-30 jobs and buys 10-20 illustrations/year.
Needs: Works with 3 illustrators and 2 designers/month. Uses artists for filmstrips, consumer magazines, multimedia kits, direct mail, television, slide sets, brochures/flyers, trade magazines and newspapers. Also uses artists for illustration, design and comp layouts of ads, brochures, catalogs, annual reports and displays.
First Contact & Terms: Local artists only. Query with resume and samples and arrange interview to show portfolio. Prefers originals, reproduced, and published pieces as samples. Samples returned by SASE. Reports in 2 weeks. Provide review and presentation of samples, business card, brochure/flyer and resume to be kept on file for possible future assignments. No originals returned to artist at job's completion. Pays $50-5,000/project; $10-60/hour. Considers complexity of project, client's budget and rights purchased when establishing payment. Reproduction rights are purchased as a buy-out.
Tips: There is a trend toward "computerization to expedite research, reference and techniques. Maintain the basics of art, illustration and medium. Be flexible in pricing/budgeting."

GLOBE ADVERTISING, 35075 Automation, Mt. Clemens MI 48043. (313)791-2801. Vice President: Craig Tarbeck. Clients: publishing, wholesaling and retailing (especially novelties).
Needs: Buys "several hundred" illustrations/year. Uses artists for color separations, retouching and type spec. Especially needs layout, catalog and magazine illustration and lettering.
First Contact & Terms: Local artists preferred. Query or write for interview. SASE. Reports in 1 week. Minimum payment: $10, layout; $5, illustration. Pays promised fee for unused assigned work.

HENRY HOOK ADVERTISING, 38 W. Bethune, Detroit MI 48202. (313)871-5333. Art/Creative Director: Henry Hook. Ad agency. Clients: premium manufacturers.

Needs: Works with 1 illustrator and 1 designer/month. Uses artists for direct mail, brochures/flyers and trade magazines and cartoons.
First Contact & Terms: Mail art (photocopies) to be kept on file. Samples not kept on file returned by SASE. Reports in 2 weeks. Pays $100-500/project; $10-15/hour.
Tips: "Less emphasis on resume, more on portfolio."

JACOBY & CO., 8469 E. Jefferson St., Detroit MI 48214 and 505 S. Grand, Leland MI 49654. President: Albert K. Jacoby. Ad/PR agency. Clients: manufacturers, publisher, professional association, auction services, real estate and race tracks (horse).
Needs: Works with 3 illustrators and 6 designers/month. Uses artists for layout, illustration, technical art, type spec, paste-up, retouching and lettering for newspapers, magazines, TV, billboards, sales meetings, conventions and seminars.
First Contact & Terms: Arrange appointment or mail samples (tear sheets and photocopies). Provide materials to be kept on file for future assignments. No originals returned to artist at job's completion. Reports only if interested. Works on assignment only. Considers complexity of project and client's budget when establishing payment.

LAMPE COMMUNICATIONS, INC., Box 5339, West Bloomsfield MI 48033. (313)682-8834. Production Manager: A.M. Lampe. PR firm. Clients: industry.
Needs: Assigns 100 freelance jobs/year. Works with 1 freelance illustrator and 2 freelance designers/month. Uses artists for trade magazine ads, brochures, stationery, signage and press releases.
First Contact & Terms: Send query letter with business card to be kept on file. Samples not kept on file are returned by SASE. Reports only if interested. Works on assignment only. Considers complexity of project, client's budget, and skill and experience of artist when establishing payment. Buys all rights.

MOLNER & CO., ADVERTISING, 21500 Greenfield Rd., Oak Park MI 48237. (313)968-2770. President: Monroe "Bob" Molner. Serves clients in a variety of industries.
Needs: Buys 100-150 illustrations/year. Uses artists for print ads, TV storyboards, layouts, and fashion and furniture illustrations.
First Contact & Terms: Local artists only. Query. SASE. Reports in 1 week. Works on assignment only. Pays $10-50, fashion or furniture illustration; $10-15/hour, layout. Pays original fee as agreed for unused assigned illustrations. No originals returned to artist at job's completion.

PHOTO COMMUNICATION SERVICES, INC., 6410 Knapp NE, Ada MI 49301. (616)676-2429. President: Michael Jackson. Audiovisual firm. Clients: commercial and industrial; "local to international, large variety."
Needs: Works with 10 freelance artists/year. Uses artists for multi-image slide presentations, film and video. Especially important is knowledge of animation and pin registration.
First Contact & Terms: Works on assignment only. Send query letter with brochure, resume, business card and samples to be kept on file. Call or write for appointment to show portfolio. Prefers photographs or slides as samples. Samples not filed are returned by SASE only if requested. Reports back only if interested. Negotiates payment by the project. Considers complexity of the project, client's budget, skill and experience of artist, geographic scope for the finished product, turnaround time and rights purchased when establishing payment. Negotiates rights purchased.

SYNCHRONOUS MEDIA INTERNATIONAL, 1217 Turner, Lansing MI 48906. Contact: Sam Mills. Audiovisual firm. Clients: industrial, commercial, government. Client list provided for SASE.
Needs: Works with 20-30 freelance artists/year. Uses artists for voice and camera talent, and graphics. Especially looks for communication skills and professional attitude.
First Contact & Terms: Works on assignment only. Send query letter with resume and samples to be kept on file. Prefers slides as samples. Samples not filed are returned by SASE. Reports back only if interested. Pays by the hour, $8-20 average; by the project, $500-5,000 average; or by the day, $100-300 average. Considers complexity of the project, client's budget, and skill and experience of artist when establishing payment. Rights purchased vary according to project.

J. WALTER THOMPSON COMPANY, 600 Renaissance Center, Detroit MI 48243. (313)568-3800. Assistant Art Administrator: Maryann Inson. Ad agency. Clients: automotive, consumer, industrial, media related.
Needs: Usually does not use freelancers; deals primarily with established artists' representatives and art/design studios.
First Contact & Terms: Call for appointment to show portfolio. Brochures, flyers, posters kept on file for reference. Assignments awarded on lowest bid. Payment net 30 days.
Tips: Agency deals with proven illustrators from an "approved vendor's list." New vendors are considered for list periodically.

Minnesota

*ART & COPY OVERLOAD, Suite 2, 2010 Marshall Ave., St. Paul MN 55104. (612)644-3443. Contact: John Borden. Ad agency. Clients: food, ice, medical, financial, industrial, manufacturing.
Needs: Works with 8 freelance artists/year. Uses artists for layout, paste-up, drawing and illustration. Especially important is an understanding of layout.
First Contact & Terms: Requires 2 years' commercial experience, prefers local artists. Works on assignment only. Send brochure, resume, business card and samples to be kept on file up to 1 year. Call for appointment to show portfolio. Prefers photostats or photocopies as samples. Samples not filed are returned by SASE. Does not report back. Pays by the hour, $15-45 average or by the day, $40-180 average. Considers complexity of the project, client's budget, skill and experience of artist and rights purchased when establishing payment. Rights purchased vary according to project.

BATTEN, BARTON, DURSTINE, & OSBORN, INC., 900 Brotherhood Bldg., 625 4th Ave. S., Minneapolis MN 55415. (612)338-8401. Art Buyer: Pam Schmidt. Ad agency. Clients: industrial, food, financial and corporate.
Needs: Uses artists for consumer and trade magazines, newspaper, billboard, P-O-P/collateral.
First Contact & Terms: Call for personal appointment to show portfolio. Prefers slides, photographs or photostats as samples. Works with freelance artists on an assignment basis only. Helpful to provide samples that can be kept on file for future reference. No originals returned at job's completion. Pays by the project; negotiates payment based on time/work involved, skill and experience of artist, and sometimes where the work will appear. Also asks for estimates and reviews them with client's budget in mind.
Tips: "When we're considering someone for a job, samples they've sent or left behind are a great help in remembering that person's work."

JOHN BORDEN & ASSOCIATES, Suite 2, 2010 Marshall Ave., St. Paul MN 55104. (612)644-3443. Contact: John Borden. Ad agency. Clients: business, industrial, financial, food and food related and advertising. Specialists in recruitment advertising and PR. Assigns 15 jobs and buys 50 illustrations/year.
Needs: Works with 4 illustrators/month. Uses artists for layouts, finished art, type spec, consumer and trade magazines, stationery design, direct mail, brochures/flyers and newspapers.
First Contact & Terms: Local professionals only. Query with samples or call to arrange interview to show portfolio. Prefers photographs, photostats and b&w line drawings as samples. Especially looks for layout ability, styles of art, and calligraphy. Prefers to review 12-24 samples. Samples returned by SASE. Reports in 2 weeks. Provide brochure/flyer, photostats or reprints of samples to be kept on file for possible future assignments. Works by assignment only. Originals become client's property at job's completion. Reports in 2 weeks. Pays $12-35/hour; $300-10,000/project.
Tips: Also owns Art and Copy Overload Service supplying freelancers to other companies that need them (for annual reports, etc.).

FABER SHERVEY ADVERTISING, 160 W. 79th St., Minneapolis MN 55420. (612)881-5111. Creative Director: Paul D. Shervey. Ad agency. Clients: business to business, industrial and farm.
Needs: Works with 25 freelance artists/year. Uses artists for retouching, line art, keyline, illustration.
First Contact & Terms: Prefers local artists. Send brochure and business card; call or write for appointment to show portfolio. Do *not* send samples. Does not report back. Pays by the hour, $20-80 average. Considers complexity of the project when establishing payment. Buys all rights.

IMAGE MEDIA INC., 1362 LaSalle Ave., Minneapolis MN 55403. (612)872-0578. President: Michael Rifkin. AV/TV/film producer. Clients: ad agencies, industrial and educational.
Needs: Works with 4 freelance illustrators and 1-3 designers/year. Uses artists for filmstrips, motion pictures, storyboards, print ads, slide illustrations, animation and titles.
First Contact & Terms: Send resume. SASE. Works on assignment only. Reports back. Provide resume and some samples of materials to be kept on file. Negotiates pay based on client's budget and amount of creativity required.

*LINHOFF PRODUCTIONS, 4400 France Ave. S, Box 24005, Minneapolis MN 55424. (612)927-7333. Art Director: LuAnne Speeter-Belden. Audiovisual firm. Clients: banks, computer companies and financial services companies.
Needs: Works with 8-15 freelance artists/year. Uses artists for keylining, artwork and typesetting. Especially important are ruling; an eye for layout; good word skills for proofreading; copy camera capabilities; graphic arts computer; typesetting knowledge a plus (Comp-Edit 5810).
First Contact & Terms: Local artists only; must work in-house. Works on assignment only. Send query letter with resume and samples to be kept on file, or call for appointment to show portfolio. Prefers pho-

tostats or photocopies as samples. Samples not filed are returned by SASE. Reports within 2 weeks. Pays by the hour, $7 minimum. Considers skill and experience of artist when establishing payment. Buys all rights.
Tips: "Speed and accuracy are essential."

PEDERSON HERZOG & NEE INC., 6401 University Ave. NE, Minneapolis MN 55401. (612)333-1234. Art Director: Luke Pegoraro. Ad agency. Serves clients in automotive, sporting equipment, farming equipment and industrial supplies. Assigns 12 illustrations/year.
Needs: Works with 2 illustrators and 1 designer/month. Uses artists for billboards, P-O-P displays, consumer magazines, television, trade magazines, newspapers and brochures.
First Contact & Terms: Local artists only. Query with samples to be kept on file for future assignments. No originals returned at job's completion. Pays $50-2,000/job.

CHUCK RUHR ADVERTISING, INC., 1221 Nicollet Mall, Minneapolis MN 55403. (612)332-4565. Art Director: Doug Lew. Ad agency. Clients: consumer and industrial firms; client list provided upon request.
Needs: Works with 30 illustrators/year; very seldom uses freelance designers. Uses freelance artists for billboards, consumer and trade magazines, direct mail, P-O-P displays, brochures, catalogs, posters, signage, newspapers, AV presentations and sometimes TV.
First Contact & Terms: Send samples to be kept on file. Works on assignment only. Negotiates payment according to client's budget; then the amount of creativity, where work will appear and previous experience are taken into consideration.

ROY WALLACE AND ASSOCIATES, INC., 1200 Foshay Tower, 821 Marquette Ave., Minneapolis MN 55402. (612)340-9620. Account Executive & Manager, Graphic Design and Production: Betsy Massie. PR firm. Clients: transportation companies, manufacturing companies, high technology companies, agribusiness, etc.
Needs: Number of jobs assigned to freelance artists varies. Uses artists for brochures, AV presentations and annual reports.
First Contact & Terms: Send query letter with brochure, resume and business card to be kept on file. Write for appointment to show portfolio. Reports within 30 days. Works on assignment only. Pays by the hour or by the project. Considers complexity of project, client's budget, skill and experience of artist and turnaround time when establishing payment.

Missouri

FRANK BLOCK ASSOCIATES, Chase Park Plaza, St. Louis MO 63108. (314)367-9600. Art Directors: Ray Muskopf and Dave Meinecke. Ad agency. Clients: primarily industrial firms; client list provided upon request.
Needs: Works with 6 illustrators/month. Uses freelance artists for billboards, consumer and trade magazines, direct mail, brochures, catalogs, posters, signage, newspapers, TV and AV presentations.
First Contact & Terms: Arrange interview to show portfolio. Works on assignment only. Negotiates payment by the project and on freelancer's ability.

BRYAN DONALD ADVERTISING, 2345 Grand, Suite 2712, Kansas City MO 64108. (816)471-4866. President/Creative Director: Don Funk.
Needs: Works with 1 illustrator/month. Uses artists to do complete layouts "from start to finish."
First Contact & Terms: Local artists only. Call to arrange interview. No originals returned at job's completion. Negotiates pay.

D'ARCY MacMANUS MASIUS, Gateway Tower, 1 Memorial Dr., St. Louis MO 63102. (314)342-8600. Senior Vice President/Director of Creative Services: Carl Klinghammer. Ad agency. Clients: all types including brewery.
Needs: Works with 20-30 freelance illustrators and 10 freelance designers/month. Uses freelancers for billboards, consumer and trade magazines, direct mail, brochures/flyers, newspapers, P-O-P displays, stationery design and TV.
First Contact & Terms: Call for appointment to show portfolio. Reporting time varies. Works with freelance artists on assignment only. Provide brochure/flyer, resume and tear sheets to be kept on file for possible future assignments. Negotiates payment based on client's budget, amount of creativity required from artist and where work will appear.
Tips: Likes to see latest styles and techniques (anything from realism to abstract) in portfolio.

FREMERMAN, ROSENFIELD & LANE, Suite 2102, 106 W. 14th St., Kansas City MO 64105. (816)474-8120. Art Directors: Bob Coldwell and Leanne Zembrunner. Ad agency. Clients: retail, consumer and trade accounts; client list provided upon request.
Needs: Works with 10-15 illustrators/month. Uses freelance artists for billboards, consumer and trade magazines, direct mail, P-O-P displays, brochures, catalogs, posters, signage, newspapers and AV presentations.
First Contact & Terms: Works primarily with local artists. Arrange interview to show portfolio; query with resume of credits and samples. Payment is by the project or by the day; negotiates according to client's budget and where work will appear.

GARDNER ADVERTISING, 10 S. Broadway, St. Louis MO 63102. (314)444-2000. Director of Creative Services: Bob Fanter. Ad agency. Clients: primarily consumer food and dog food; also industrial, financial, recreation and services.
Needs: Works with about 15 illustrators/month and occasionally uses designers for packaging. Uses artists for consumer print and TV.
First Contact & Terms: Call for appointment to show portfolio or make contact through artist's rep. Negotiates pay based on budget and where work will appear, whether color or b&w, etc.

GEORGE JOHNSON, ADVERTISING, 763 New Ballas Rd. S., St. Louis MO 63141. (314)569-3440. Art Director: Lisa Riley. Ad agency. Serves clients in real estate, financial and social agencies.
Needs: Works with 1-2 illustrators/month. Uses artists for illustrations, animation, layout, lettering, paste-up, retouching, type spec and design for annual reports, billboards, catalogs, print ads, letterheads, packaging, P-O-P displays, posters, TV and trademarks.
First Contact & Terms: Local artists only. Write or call for appointment to show agency samples of work (tear sheets, roughs and work done for other ad agencies). SASE. Reports within 1 week. Originals returned at job's completion.

KENRICK ADVERTISING INC., 7711 Carondelet, St. Louis MO 63105. (314)726-6020. Creative Director: Jeff Miller. Full service advertising firm. Serves clients in automotives, animal care products, agriculture, retail and business to business.
Needs: Uses illustrators and designers for ad design layout, direct mail brochures, signs, sets, slide shows, P-O-P displays and packages, billboards, filmstrips, letterhead, TV, newspapers, books, flip-charts, illustrative lettering and retouching.
First Contact & Terms: Query with samples (tear sheets or photocopies) and arrange interview to show portfolio. Reports within 4 weeks. Provide business card and tear sheets to be kept on file for future assignments. Returns original art only when "arrangements have been made prior to assignment."

BEVERLY NORMAN PUBLIC RELATIONS, Suite 411, 800 W. 47th St, Kansas City MO 66212. (816)531-3577. President: Beverly Norman. PR firm. Clients: real estate, associations, nonprofit, special events.
Needs: Assigns 15-30 freelance jobs/year. Works with 2-3 freelance illustrators and 1-2 freelance designers/month. Uses artists for consumer and trade magazines, billboards, brochures, newspapers, stationery, signage and posters.
First Contact & Terms: Send query letter with brochure and samples to be kept on file. Prefers reproductions, copies, PMT's of actual artwork as samples. Works on assignment only. Pays by the hour. Considers client's budget and skill and experience of artist when establishing payment.

PREMIER FILM VIDEO & RECORDING, 3033 Locust St., St. Louis MO 63103. (314)531-3555. Secretary/Treasurer: Grace Dalzell. AV/film/animation/TV producer. Serves clients in business, religion, education and advertising. Produces videotape, motion 35mm, 16mm and Super 8mm, strip films, cassette dupes 8 tracks, TV and radio spots.
Needs: Assigns 50-60 jobs/year. Works with 8-10 illustrators, "a few" designers/month. Uses artists for strip film and slide presentations, TV commercials and motion picture productions.
First Contact & Terms: Send resume to be kept on file. "We do not accept samples; we review them during interviews only." Works on assignment only. Reporting time varies with available work. Pays by the project; method and amount of payment are negotiated with the individual artist. Pay varies with each client's budget. No originals returned to artist following publication; "copies supplied when possible." Buys all rights, but sometimes negotiates.
Tips: "In developing a brochure, begin by simply stating work capability and area of work most capable of producing, i.e., animation, cartoons, production, direction or editing—whatever you want to do for a living. Be specific."

STOLZ ADVERTISING CO., Suite 500, 7701 Forsyth Blvd., St. Louis MO 63105. (314)863-0005. Contact: Executive Creative Director. Ad agency. Clients: consumer firms.

Needs: Works with 2 illustrators/month; occasionally uses freelance designers. Uses freelance artists for billboards, consumer and trade magazines, direct mail, P-O-P displays, brochures, posters, newspapers and AV presentations.
First Contact & Terms: Arrange interview to show portfolio or query with samples. Works on assignment only. Negotiates payment according to particular job.

Montana

SAGE ADVERTISING/BILLINGS, Box 20977, Billings MT 59104. (406)652-3232. Art Director: Lori Richards-Burda. Ad agency/AV/PR firm/radio and TV; "a full service agency." Clients: financial, utilities, industry, hotel/motel, real estate.
Needs: Assigns 24 freelance jobs/year. Works with 2 freelance illustrators/month. Uses artists for filmstrips, AV presentations, photography and illustration.
First Contact & Terms: Send query letter with resume and samples to be kept on file. Call or write for appointment to show portfolio. Prefers slides or printed samples. Samples not kept on file are returned only if requested. Reports within 2 weeks. Works on assignment only. Pays by the project. Considers complexity of project, client's budget, skill and experience of artist, geographic scope of finished project, turnaround time and rights purchased when establishing payment. Negotiates rights purchased.

Nebraska

MILLER FRIENDT LUDEMANN INC., 801 S. 48th St., Lincoln NE 68510. Senior Art Director: Phillip R. Voyles. Art Director: Kathy Guiducci. Ad agency/PR firm. Clients: bank, industry, restaurants, tourism and retail.
Needs: Assigns 400 freelance jobs/year. Works with 4-5 freelance illustrators and 6-10 freelance designers/month. Uses artists for consumer and trade magazines, billboards, direct mail packages, brochures, newspapers, stationery, signage, P-O-P displays, AV presentations, posters, press releases, trade show displays and TV graphics.
First Contact & Terms: Send query letter with brochure or resume, business card and samples to be kept on file. Write for appointment to show portfolio, "if regional/national; call if local." Prefers slides as samples. Samples not kept on file are returned by SASE. Reports within 10 days. Works on assignment only. Pays by the project, $100-1,500 average. Considers complexity of project, client's budget, skill and experience of artist, turnaround time and rights purchased when establishing payment. Buys all rights.

J. GREG SMITH, Suite 102, Burlington Place, 1004 Farnam St., Omaha NE 68102. (402)444-1600. Art Director: Shelly Bartek. Ad agency. Clients: financial, banking institutions, associations, agricultural, travel and tourism.
Needs: Works with 3 illustrators/year. Uses freelance artists for consumer and trade magazines, brochures, catalogs and AV presentations.
First Contact & Terms: Send query with samples. Works on assignment only. Reports only if interested. Payment is by the project; negotiates according to client's budget.
Tips: Current trends include a certain "flexibility." Agencies are now able "to use any style or method that best fits the job."

Nevada

STUDIOS KAMINSKI PHOTOGRAPHY LTD., 1040 Matley Lane, Reno NV 89502. (702)786-2615. President: T.J. Kaminski. AV/TV/film producer. Clients: educational, industrial and corporate. Produces filmstrips, motion pictures, multimedia kits, overhead transparencies, slide sets, sound-slide sets and videotapes.
Needs: Works with about 3 illustrators/year. Has need of illustrators to paint portraits from photos once in a while. Uses artists for slide illustration and retouching, catalog design and ad illustration.
First Contact & Terms: Arrange interview to show portfolio. Samples returned by SASE. Reports within 1 week. Works on assignment only. Provide brochure/flyer, resume or tear sheet to be kept on file for possible future assignments. Pays $20-50/hour; $150-400/day.
Tips: Have good samples and be qualified.

New Jersey

SOL ABRAMS ASSOCIATES INC., 331 Webster Dr., New Milford NJ 07646. (201)262-4111. President: Sol Abrams. Public relations firm. Clients: real estate, food, fashion, beauty, entertainment, government, retailing, sports, nonprofit organizations, etc. Media used include billboards, consumer magazines, trade magazines, direct mail, newspapers, P-O-P displays, radio and TV.
Needs: Assigns 6 freelance jobs/year. Uses artists for consumer magazines, billboards, brochures, catalogs, newspapers, stationery, signage, AV presentations and press releases.
First Contact & Terms: "We prefer working with artists in a 50-mile radius of New York City." Send query letter with samples which may be kept on file. Prefers photographs and photostats as samples. Samples not kept on file returned by SASE. Reports only if interested. Works on assignment only. Pay varies according to client and job. Considers client's budget, and skill and experience of artist when establishing payment. Buys all rights.
Tips: "As one who started his career as an artist before deciding to become a public relations consultant, I empathize with young artists. If material interests me and I cannot use it, I might develop leads or refer it to people and firms which may use it. Artists should be honest and sincere. Dedication and integrity are as important as talent."

ADLER, SCHWARTZ INC., 140 Sylvan Ave., Englewood Cliffs NJ 07632. Executive Vice President: Peter Adler. Ad agency. Clients: automotive, shipping and high fidelity firms.
Needs: Buys 50 illustrations/year. Uses artists for billboards, P-O-P displays, consumer magazines, trade magazines, newspapers, direct mail, slide presentations, brochures/flyers. Also uses artists for layout, lettering, color separations, paste-up, retouching and type spec for brochures, annual reports, print ads, letterheads, packaging, posters and trademarks. Especially needs line drawings and washes of people, cars and interiors.
First Contact & Terms: Query with samples, tear sheets or call for interview. SASE. Reports in 2 weeks. Provide business card or tear sheets to be kept on file for possible future assignments.

ALBERTSSON DIRECT RESPONSE ADVERTISING/MARKETING, Box 400, River Edge NJ 07661. President: Maurice J. Weiss. Ad agency. Clients: "new and growing businesses of various kinds."
Needs: Works with 2-4 freelance artists/year. Uses artists for advertising and brochure design, illustration and layout; and illustration on product.
First Contact & Terms: Works on assignment only. Send query letter with brochure and business card to be kept on file; write for appointment to show portfolio. Prefers to review photocopies. Material not filed is returned by SASE. Reports within 1 month. Negotiates pay by the project. Considers complexity of the project, turnaround time, skill and experience of artist, how work will be used and the rights purchased when establishing payment.

DAVID H. BLOCK ADVERTISING, INC., 33 S. Fullerton Ave., Montclair NJ 07042 (201)744-6900. Executive Art Director: Karen Deluca. Clients: finance, industrial and consumer. Buys 100-200 illustrations/year.
Needs: Uses artists for illustrations, layout, lettering, type spec, mechanicals and retouching for ads, annual reports, billboards, catalogs, letterheads, brochures and trademarks.
First Contact & Terms: Prefers to work with "artists with at least 3-5 years experience in paste-up and 'on premises' work for mechanicals and design." Arrange interview. Contact: Kevin Moore, studio manager. SASE. Reports within 2 weeks. No originals returned at job's completion unless agreed upon. Pays $50 + , retouching; $100-250, spot illustration; $20/hour, comps/layout; $15-18/hour, mechanicals. Full pay for unused assigned work.
Tips: "Please send some kind of sample of work. If mechanical artist; line art printed sample. If layout artist; composition of some type and photographs or illustrations."

*CABSCOTT BROADCAST PRODUCTION, INC., 517 7th Ave., Lindenwold NJ 08021. (609)346-3400. President: Anne Foster. Audiovisual firm, production company. Clients: retail, broadcasters (radio and TV), ad agencies and industrial users.
Needs: Works with 5 freelance artists/year. Uses artist for art, layout and storyboard creation. Especially important are freehand skills.
First Contact & Terms: Prefers local artists experienced in television storyboarding. Works on assignment only. Send query letter with resume and samples to be kept on file. Prefers any type sample that gives an idea of artist's style. Samples are returned by SASE if requested. Reports only if interested. Negotiates payment by the project. Considers complexity of project, client's budget, skill and experience of artist and turnaround time when establishing payment. Negotiates rights purchased.

CREATIVE PRODUCTIONS, INC., 200 Main St., Orange NJ 07050. (201)676-4422. Partner: Gus J. Nichols. Audiovisual firm. Clients: pharmaceutical firms, paper manufacturers, chemical, financial, construction firms.
Needs: Works with 30 freelance artists/year. Uses artists for mechanicals, paste-ups, charts and graphs. Especially important is "accuracy, neat work and the ability to take direction."
First Contact & Terms: Artists must be within 1 hour travel time to studio with 1 year's experience. Send resume to be kept on file; call for appointment to show portfolio. Reports back only if interested. Pays by the hour, $7-10 average. Considers skill and experience of artist when establishing payment.

*DAVIS, HAYS & COMPANY, 426 Hudson St., Hackensack NJ 07601. (201)641-4910. Contact: Art Director. Estab. 1984. Ad agency, public relations firm. Clients: medical, healthcare, marketing research, service industries and beauty.
Needs: Works with 3-5 freelance artists/year. Uses artists for design, layout, mechanicals, illustration and production. "Professionalism and deadline and budget restrictions awareness are important."
First Contact & Terms: Artist must have experience working with agencies. Send query letter with brochure, business card and samples to be kept on file; write for appointment to show portfolio. Accepts photostats as samples. Samples not filed are returned only if requested. Reports within 1 month. Pays by the hour, $15-50 average. Considers complexity of the project, client's budget and turnaround time when establishing payment. Buys all rights.
Tips: "We are looking for positive thinkers: those who say 'we'll find a way to do it' even when there are no easy answers."

PAUL A. DE JESSE, INC., ADVERTISING, 34 E. Main St., Freehold NJ 07728. (201)780-6909. Vice President/Creative Director: Phyllis DeJesse. Ad agency. Clients: pharmaceutical/health care industry.
Needs: Uses artists for trade magazines, direct mail packages, brochures, P-O-P displays and AV presentations.
First Contact & Terms: Artists must be available to work with staff in agency. Send query letter with resume to be kept on file. Write for appointment to show portfolio. Reports only if interested. Works on assignment only. Pays by the hour, $10-25 average; by the project, $100 minimum; by the day, $100-250 average. Considers complexity of project, client's budget, skill and experience of artist and turnaround time when establishing payment. Buys all rights.
Tips: "We are interested only in dedicated, skilled professionals."

DE MARTINI ASSOCIATES, INC., 414 4th Ave., Haddon Heights NJ 08035. (609)547-2800. Creative Director: Alfred De Martini. Art studio/AV producer. Clients: industrial corporations, universities, marine service organizations and frozen and fast-food firms.
Needs: Works with 3 illustrators and 3 designers/month. Uses artists for audiovisual, filmstrips and slide programs as well as humorous illustration for newspapers, TV, billboards, direct mail, catalogs, and magazines.
First Contact & Terms: Mail samples; do not send original work, only photocopies. Samples not returned. Artist should be versed in contemporary layout and humorous illustrations. Prefers to work by mail, rather than in person. Provide brochure/flyer, resume and tear sheets to be kept on file for possible future assignments. No originals returned to artist at job's completion. Pays $15-50/hour, layout; $10/ hour, paste-up; $100/job, graphic design; $50, layout conceptuals; and $25, quantity spot illustration. Considers skill and experience of artist when establishing payment.

DIEGNAN & ASSOCIATES, Box 298, Oldwick NJ 08858. (201)832-7951. President: Norman Diegnan. PR firm. Clients: commercial.
Needs: Assigns 25 freelance jobs/year. Uses artists for catalogs and AV presentations.
First Contact & Terms: Send brochure to be kept on file; write for appointment to show portfolio; may also send portfolio. Reports only if interested. Works on assignment only. Pays artist's rate. Considers client's budget when establishing payment. Buys all rights.

ABNER J. GELULA & ASSOCIATES, 29 E. West Jersey Ave., Pleasantville NJ 08232. (609)645-1200. Ad agency/PR firm. Clients: cities, hotels and travel. Media used includes billboards, consumer magazines, trade magazines, direct mail, newspapers, P-O-P displays, radio and TV.
First Contact & Terms: Negotiates payment based on client's budget.

GRAPHIC WORKSHOP INC., 466 Old Hook Rd., Emerson NJ 07630. (201)967-8500. Creative Director: Al Nudelman. Sales promotion agency. Clients: AV, computer accounts, industrial tools, men's wear, ladies' wear.
Needs: Works with 10-15 freelance artists/year. Uses artists for illustration, paste-up and mechanical,

design comps. Especially looks for knowledge of type and good design sense.
First Contact & Terms: Prefers local artists with a minimum of 3-5 years' experience; "retail layout and some design background helpful." Works on assignment only. Send query letter with business card and samples to be kept on file. Prefers slides or "whatever shows work off the best" as samples. Samples not filed are returned only if requested. Reports back only if interested. Pays by the hour, $10-15 average; by the day, $75-100 average. Considers client's budget, complexity of the project, and skill and experience of artist when establishing payment. Buys all rights.

JANUARY PRODUCTIONS, 249 Gaffle Rd., Hawthorne NJ 07506. (201)423-4666. Art Director: Paulete Cochet. AV producer. Serves clients in education. Produces sound filmstrips and read-along books and cassettes.
Needs: Assigns 5-10 jobs/year. Works with 5 illustrators/year. Uses artists for artwork for filmstrips, sketches for books and layout work.
First Contact & Terms: "While not a requirement, an artist living in the same geographic area is a plus." Send resume and arrange interview by phone. "If and when an interview is arranged, artist will bring samples." Prefers original work to review. Samples returned "if samples were specifically requested." Provide resume to be kept on file for possible future assignments. Works on assignment only, "although if someone had a project already put together, we would consider it." Pays by the project. Method and amount of payment are negotiated with the individual artist. Considers complexity of project, and skill and experience of artist when establishing payment. No originals returned following publication. Buys all rights.

J. M. KESSLINGER & ASSOCIATES, 37 Saybrook Place, Newark NJ 07102. (201)623-0007. Art Director: J. Dietz. Advertising agency. Serves clients in a variety of industries.
Needs: Uses 1-2 illustrators/month for illustrations, mechanicals, direct mail, brochures, flyers, trade magazines and newspapers.
First Contact & Terms: Prefers local artists. Phone for appointment. Prefers photostats, tear sheets, slides as samples. Samples returned by SASE only if requested. Reports only if interested. Works on assignment only. Does not return original artwork to artist unless contracted otherwise. Negotiates pay. Pays by the hour, $15-50 average. Pay range depends on the type of freelance work, i.e. mechanicals vs. creative. Considers complexity of project, client's budget, skill and experience of artist, and rights purchased when establishing payment.

KEYES, MARTIN & COMPANY, 841 Mountain Ave., Springfield NJ 07081. (201)376-7300. Ad agency. Art Director: Marvin Slatkin. Clients: manufacturing, retailing, banking, social agencies, communications and insurance. Media used include: billboards, consumer and trade magazines, direct mail, newspapers, P-O-P displays, radio, and TV.
First Contact & Terms: Send resume and portfolio for review. Negotiates payment based on client's budget and artist's rate.

LINDEN COLOR LABS, 1622 S. Wood Ave., Box 4115, Linden NJ 07036. (201)862-5800. Photographic labs. Clients: business, advertising and industry agencies.
Needs: Works with 17 freelance artists/year. Uses artists for artwork, board work, layout and creative slide designs. Especially important is creativity.
First Contact & Terms: Local artists only—"short deadline work." Works on assignment only. Send resume and business card to be kept on file; call or write for appointment to show portfolio. Prefers to review slides. Reports back. Considers client's budget when establishing payment. Rights purchased vary according to project.

MORVAY ADVERTISING AGENCY, 177 Valley St., South Orange NJ 07079. (201)762-3331. Art Director: Mrs. Tobia L. Meyers. Ad agency. Clients: electronic, restaurants, clothing, caterers, luggage, hardware, travel, auto rental.
Needs: Assigns 5 jobs/year. Uses artists for catalog covers, photo retouching and paste-up.
First Contact & Terms: Prefers local artists. Query with samples. Prefers photographs, photostats, previously published work and b&w line drawings as samples. Samples returned by SASE. Reports in 4 weeks. Works on assignment only. Provide business card, resume, brochure/flyer or tear sheets to be kept on file for future assignments. Pays $10 minimum; pay "depends on job required." Considers complexity of project, client's budget, and skill and experience of artist when establishing payment.
Tips: "Call first and set up an appointment." Especially looks for clean work and sharp pen line rendering. Current trends in the field include much more subtlety between art and copy requiring a greater depth of understanding subject matter.

SAI GROUP INC., SAI Building, 900 Dudley Ave., Cherry Hill NJ 08002. (609)665-8833. Advertising Manager: Ellen IuLiucci.

Needs: Works with 3 designers. Uses artists for consumer magazines, direct mail, brochures/flyers and newspapers.

First Contact & Terms: Local artists only. Call for interview. Artists must have experience in designing mailings and/or ads for major consumer direct mail business, preferably in insurance, financial services, etc. Provide brochure, flyer, business card, resume and tear sheets, etc. No originals returned at job's completion. "We generally work on a per job basis not an hourly one, and we find that we are paying the generally accepted fees in this area of the country."

SPOONER & CO., Box 126, Verona NJ 07044. (201)857-0053. President: William B. Spooner III. Industrial ad agency. Clients: mills, mixers, vacuum pumps, metals and ores, plastic blow molding machines and conveyor belts.

Needs: Works with 2 illustrators and 2 designers/month. Uses artists for stationery design, slide sets, brochures/flyers and trade magazines. Also uses artists for layout, illustration, technical art, type spec, paste-up, retouching and lettering for newspapers, trade magazines, direct mail, technical literature and trade shows.

First Contact & Terms: Call first or send letter with qualifications and experience. Provide brochure, flyer, business card and resume to be kept on file. Do not send original work. Samples returned by SASE. Reports back only if interested. Works on assignment basis only. Payment negotiated. Considers complexity of project, client's budget, and skill and experience of artist when establishing payment.

*STARBUCK CREATIVE SERVICES, 26 Steven Tr., West Orange NJ 07052. Senior Vice President: B. Siegel. Ad agency. Clients: health care. Client list provided for SASE.

Needs: Works with 2-5 freelance artists/year. Uses artists for special projects and back-up.

First Contact & Terms: Send query letter with brochure, resume, business card and samples to be kept on file; write for appointment to show portfolio. Accepts photostats, photographs, slides or tear sheets as samples. Samples not filed are returned by SASE only if requested. Reports within 3 weeks. Payment open. Considers complexity of the project, client's budget, skill and experience of artist, geographic scope for the finished product, turnaround time and rights purchased when establishing payment. Rights purchased vary according to project.

*TROLL ASSOCIATES, 320 Rt. 17, Mahwah NJ 07430. Vice President, Production: Marian Schecter. AV producer/book publisher. Audience: children. Produces books, records, filmstrips and multimedia.

Needs: Buys approximately 200 designs/year. Uses artists for catalog covers/illustrations, direct mail brochures, multimedia kits, record album designs and book illustrations.

First Contact & Terms: Local artists only. Query with resume and samples (slides preferred). SASE. Reports in 4 weeks. Provide resume, samples, brochure/flyer or business card to be kept on file for future assignments. No originals returned to artist at job's completion. Pays by the project. Buys all rights.

WREN ASSOCIATES, INC., Communications Park, 208 Bunn Dr., Princeton NJ 08540. (609)924-8085. Personnel Director: Karen Faller. Audiovisual firm. Clients: industrial, *Fortune 500* (automotive, pharmaceutical, financial, etc.).

Needs: Works with 10-25 freelance artists/year. Uses artists for mechanical preparation, photography, storyboard and design, video crew, typesetting, Forox photography, computer slide generation, project management. Especially important are design and mechanical preparation skills, slide preparation skills, multi-image training, Forox experience, computer slide experience, rendering and storyboarding.

First Contact & Terms: Artists must have minimum of 1½ years' experience. Send query letter with resume and samples. Letter and resume are filed; samples are returned if postage is paid by the artist. Call for appointment to show portfolio. Prefers slides and videocassettes of completed shows as samples. Reports back only if interested. Pays by the hour, $8-18 (board artist); design rates vary according to skill level and project; photography rates vary according to project. Considers client's budget, and skill and experience of artist when establishing payment. Rights purchased vary according to project.

Tips: "Wren Associates is very interested in attracting experienced multimedia designers and producers. We are most interested in seeing videotapes of completed projects which include photography direction, narration, soundtrack direction and strong conceptual skills. Freelance artists who are interested in our firm but do not fulfill this experience level should be able to show their level of expertise in the production of slides, computer graphics, Forox photography and/or video."

ZM SQUARED, 903 Edgewood Lane, Cinnaminson NJ 08077. (609)786-0612. Executive Director: Mr. Pete Zakroff. AV producer. Clients: industry, business, education and unions. Produces slides, filmstrips, overhead transparencies and handbooks.

Needs: Assigns 8 jobs/year. Works with 2 illustrators/month. Uses artists for cartoons, illustrations and technical art.
First Contact & Terms: Prefers artists with previous work experience who specialize. Send resume and samples (slides preferred). Samples returned by SASE. Provide samples and brochure/flyer to be kept on file for possible future assignments. Works on assignment only. Reports in 3 weeks. Pays by the project. Payment varies with each client's budget. No originals returned to artist following publication. Buys all rights.

New Mexico

AIRY ADVERTISING, INC., Box 70, Albuquerque NM 87103. (505)242-1120. Art Director: Joe McDonnell. Ad agency. Clients: industrial, land developer, clip art/editorial service, fast food chain and home builder.
Needs: Works with 5-7 freelance artists/year. Uses artists for illustrations, mechanicals/production and layouts. Especially looks for ability to draw and for clean/precise art production. "We buy realistic pen & ink-type illustrations."
First Contact & Terms: Works on assignment only. Send resume and samples; samples are returned by SASE. Resume is filed. Call or write for appointment to show portfolio. Samples not filed are not returned. Prefers slides, tear sheets, paste-ups or photostats as samples. Reports back only if interested. Pays by the hour, $12-15 average; sometimes by the project in advance by estimate. Considers complexity of the project, client's budget, and skill and experience of artist when establishing payment. Negotiates rights purchased; vary according to project.
Tips: "Call first."

New York

ACKERMAN ADVERTISING COMMUNICATIONS INC., 55 Northern Blvd., Greenvale NY 11548. (516)484-5150. Creative Director: Skip Ackerman. Art Director: Maxine Brenner. Serves clients in food, finance and tourism.
Needs: Works with 4 illustrators and 2 designers/month. Uses artists for layout, paste-up, illustration and retouching for newspapers, TV, magazines, transit signage, billboards, collateral, direct mail and P-O-P displays.
First Contact & Terms: Local artists only; arrange interview. No originals returned.

GENE BARTCZAK ASSOCIATES INC., Box E, North Bellmore NY 11710. (516)781-6230. Manager: Gordon Willson. PR firm. Clients: technical industrial companies and related organizations. Buys 10-15 illustrations/year.
Needs: Works with 1-2 illustrators/month. Uses artists for P-O-P displays, direct mail, brochures/flyers; and design and mechanicals for ads and catalogs.
First Contact & Terms: Query. No original work returned at job's completion. Works on assignment only; reports back whether to expect possible future assignments. Provide business card and resume to be kept on file for possible future assignments. Negotiates pay. Pays promised fee for unused assigned work.

JAMES BLOOM AGENCY, INC., 5 Bond St., Great Neck NY 11021. (516)482-4660. Art Director: A. Rosenthal. Ad agency. Clients: industrial.
Needs: Assigns 10-12 freelance jobs/year. Uses artists for trade magazines, direct mail packages, brochures and catalogs.
First Contact & Terms: Local artists only. Send query letter with resume to be kept on file. Call or write for appointment to show portfolio. Reports only if interested. Works on assignment only. Pays by the project. Considers complexity of project, client's budget and turnaround time when establishing payment. Buys all rights.

CASTAGNE COMMUNICATIONS, 63 Adams St., Bedford Hills NY 10507. (914)241-1965. Executive/Vice President: Bob Meshnick. Art Director: Joyce Trerotola. Ad agency. Clients: industry.
Needs: Assigns 12 freelance jobs/year. Works with 1 freelance designer/month. Uses artists for trade magazines and brochures.
First Contact & Terms: "Strongly prefer local artists." Send query letter with resume to be kept on file. Call or write for appointment to show portfolio. Reports only if interested. Works on assignment only. Pays by the project. Considers complexity of project, client's budget, and skill and experience of artist when establishing payment. Material not copyrighted.

COMMAND PRODUCTIONS INC., 62 Bowman Ave., Rye Brook NY 10573. (914)937-7000. Studio Manager: J. Meyerowitz. Clients: industrial and corporate. Produces video animation, multimedia, slide presentations, videotapes and print materials.
Needs: Assigns 25 jobs/year. Uses artists for slide graphics, layout of brochures, design catalogs, corporate brochures, annual reports, filmstrips, slide shows, layouts and mechanicals.
First Contact & Terms: Local artists only (New York City, Manhattan and Westchester). "Send note on availability and previous work." SASE. Reports in 2 weeks. Provide materials to be kept on file for future assignments. No originals returned at job's completion. Pays $10-20/hour.

DIDIK TV PRODUCTIONS, Box 133, Rego Park NY 11374. (212)843-6839. Art Director: Mike Dickson. Audiovisual firm. Clients: government, ad agencies and corporate.
Needs: Works with 10-15 freelance artists/year. Uses artists for certain animations, graphics and from time to time for posters and catalogs. "Artists must be good and have an eye for what art sells."
First Contact & Terms: Local artists only; "must be expert." Works on assignment only. Send query letter with brochure, resume and business card. Prefers tear sheets or photostats to review. Material not filed is returned by SASE. Reports back only if interested. Pay varies according to job. Considers complexity of the project and client's budget when establishing payment. Buys all rights.

ALAN G. EISEN CO. INC., 1188 Round Swamp Rd., Old Bethpage NY 11804. (516)752-1008. President: Alan G. Eisen. PR firm. Clients: consumer and individual product manufacturers, service organizations and financial firms.
Needs: Works with 1 illustrator/month average. Uses illustrators for jobs dealing with consumer magazines, direct mail, brochures/flyers, trade magazines, annual reports and newspapers.
First Contact & Terms: Local artists only. Query with resume. Prefers photographs as samples. Samples not returned. Reports within weeks. Works on assignment only. Provide business card, brochure/flyer and resume to be kept on file for possible future assignments. Pays by the project. Total rights purchased.

FILMS FIVE INC., 42 Overlook Rd., Great Neck NY 10020. (516)487-5865. Contact: Walter Bergman.
Needs: Uses artists for documentaries and industrial films.
First Contact & Terms: Query with resume. Does not report back. Works on assignment only. Considers client's budget when establishing payment.

GREENSTONE & RABASCA ADVERTISING, 1 Huntington Quadrangle, Melville NY 11747. (516)249-2121. Contact: Art Director. Ad agency. Clients: industrial and consumer firms; client list provided upon request.
Needs: Works with 10 illustrators/year. Uses freelance artists for billboards, consumer and trade magazines, brochures, catalogs, posters, newspapers and AV presentations.
First Contact & Terms: Query with resume of credits and samples. Works on assignment only. Payment is by the project; negotiates according to client's budget.

HEALY, SCHUTTE & COMSTOCK, 1207 Delaware Ave., Buffalo NY 14209. (716)884-2120. Associate Creative Director: Dennis Domkowski. Ad agency. Clients: food service, industrial, retail department stores, consumer food, financial and health-related accounts; client list provided upon request.
Needs: Works with 5 illustrators/month. Uses freelance artists for consumer and trade magazines, direct mail, P-O-P displays, brochures, catalogs, posters, signage, newspapers and AV presentations.
First Contact & Terms: Contact is usually through representative—illustrator or design group. Payment is by the project.

HUMAN RELATIONS MEDIA, 175 Tompkins Ave., Pleasantville NY 10570. (914)769-7496. Vice President: Peter Cochran. Audiovisual firm. Clients: junior and senior high schools, colleges, hospitals, personnel departments of business organizations.
Needs: Works with 5 freelance artists/year. Uses artists for illustrations for filmstrip and slide programs and software packaging. "It is helpful if artists have skills pertaining to science-related topics."
First Contact & Terms: Prefers local artists. Send query letter with resume and samples to be kept on file. Call for appointment to show portfolio. Prefers slides or tear sheets as samples. Samples not filed are returned by SASE. Reports back only if interested. Pays by the project, $65 minimum for audiovisu-

---

 The asterisk before a listing indicates that the listing is new in this edition. New markets are often the most receptive to freelance contributions.

al; $250 minimum for packaging. Considers complexity of the project, client's budget, skill and experience of artist and turnaround time when establishing payment. Rights purchased vary according to project.

KOPF & ISAACSON, 35 Pinelawn Rd., Melville NY 11747. Art Directors: Art Zimmermann or Evelyn Rysdyk. Ad agency. Clients: technical, i.e. telephones, computer firms etc.; some consumer, i.e. fast food, clothing manufacturing.
Needs: Uses artists for technical drawings/charts, etc.; mechanicals/design, some illustration and some layout/comp.
First Contact & Terms: Works on assignment only. Send query letter with resume and samples to be kept on file. No phone queries. Write for appointment to show portfolio. Prefers photostats, slides or tear sheets as samples. Samples not filed are returned by SASE only if requested. Reports back only if interested. Pays by the hour, $6-30 average; by the project, $100 minimum. Considers complexity of the project, client's budget, skill and experience of artist, and geographic scope for the finished product when establishing payment. Rights purchased vary according to project.

LDA COMMUNICATIONS, INC., (formerly Lester Dinoff Associates, Inc.), 984 N. Broadway, Yonkers NY 10701. (914)968-1008. President: L. Dinoff. PR firm. Clients: real estate, computers, motion picture, transportation.
Needs: Assigns 25 + freelance jobs/year. Works with 2 freelance illustrators and 2 freelance designers/month. Uses artists for consumer and trade magazines, brochures, catalogs, stationery, signage, AV presentations and posters.
First Contact & Terms: Send resume and samples to be kept on file. Write for appointment to show portfolio. Reports only if interested. Pays by the project. Considers complexity of project and client's budget when establishing payment. Buys all rights.

McANDREW ADVERTISING, 2125 St. Raymond Ave., Bronx NY 10462. (212)892-8660. Art/Creative Director: Robert McAndrew. Ad agency. Clients: industrial and technical firms. Assigns 200 jobs and buys 120 illustrations/year.
Needs: Works with 2 illustrators and 4 designers/month. Uses artists for stationery design, direct mail, brochures/flyers and trade magazines.
First Contact & Terms: Uses mostly local artists. Query with resume. Prefers photocopies as samples. Samples not returned. Reports in 1 month. Provide business card and brochure/flyer to be kept on file for future assignments. No originals returned to artist at job's completion. Pays $20-40/hour for annual reports, catalogs, trade magazines, letterheads, trademarks, layout and paste-up. Considers complexity of project, client's budget, and skill and experience of artist when establishing payment.

McCUE ADVERTISING & PUBLIC RELATIONS, Press Bldg., 19 Chenango St., Binghamton NY 13901. Contact: Donna McCue. Ad/PR firm. Clients: retailers, nonprofit and industrial.
Needs: Uses artists for direct mail, television, brochures/flyers, trade magazines, newspapers, mechanicals and logo design.
First Contact & Terms: Artists with at least 2 professional assignments only. Query with resume, brochure, flyer, business card and tear sheets to be kept on file. SASE. Reports in 3-4 weeks. No originals returned at job's completion. Negotiates pay.

LLOYD MANSFIELD CO. INC., Suite 900, 237 Main St., Buffalo NY 14203. (716)854-2762. Executive Art Director: Richard Alan Baxter. Ad/PR firm, marketing communications. Serves clients in a variety of industries.
Needs: Assigns a minimum of 3 jobs and buys 25 illustrations/year. Uses artists for illustrations, mechanicals, layout and retouching.
First Contact & Terms: Local artists primarily. Works on assignment only. Query with resume and arrange interview to show portfolio. Especially looks for "neatness and creativity of presentation." SASE. Reports in 3 weeks. Provide business card, brochure/flyer or resume to be kept on file for possible future assignments. Pays $12-50/hour.
Tips: " 'New Wave' influence dictates use of artists who are leaders of this style."

ERIC MOWER & ASSOCIATES, INC., 101 S. Salina St., Syracuse NY 13202. (315)472-4703. Executive Art Director: Thomas C. Hite. Ad agency/PR firm. Clients: industry, fast food, banks, agriculture, insurance, wines/beverages, jewelry, clothing, sportswear and horse racing.
Needs: Works with 100-150 freelance artists/year. Uses artists for advertising, brochure and catalog illustration, display fixture design, P-O-P displays, model making and signage.
First Contact & Terms: "We are open to any artist who is good, professional, works within the budget and is on time with due dates." Send query letter with brochure, resume, business card, samples and tear

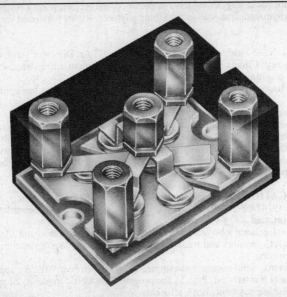

"Technical understanding and airbrush technique" were the two important ingredients Robert McAndrew, art/creative director of McAndrew Advertising Co., Bronx, New York, sought when he assigned this illustration to local artist Ben Valdiveso. The artist received $75 for all rights to the illustration which was used in ads, catalog sheets and for publicity.

sheets to be kept on file. Prefers photostats, slides, photographs or original work as samples. Samples not kept on file are returned by SASE only if requested by artist. Reports only if interested. Works on assignment only. Pays by the hour or by the project. Considers complexity of project, skill and experience of artist, how work will be used, turnaround time, rights purchased and client's budget when establishing payment.

Tips: "Artists should be professional and experienced. Not interested in beginners just out of school."

NATIONAL TEACHING AIDS INC., 120 Fulton Ave., Garden City Park NY 11040. (516)248-5590. Contact: Aaron Becker. Publisher. Produces educational silent filmstrips, models and slides.
Needs: Uses artists for books and catalogs. Also uses artists for technical illustration.
First Contact & Terms: Local artists only. Arrange interview. Provide brochures/flyers to be kept on file for future assignments. No originals returned at job's completion. Negotiates pay.

RICHARD-LEWIS CORP., 455 Central Park Ave., Scarsdale NY 10583. President: R. Byer. Clients: machinery, tool, publishers, office supplies, chemical, detergent, film and printing supplies.
Needs: Uses artists for illustrations, retouching and some ad layout and mechanicals.
First Contact & Terms: Query with resume or arrange interview to show portfolio; local artists only. SASE. Reports in 2-3 weeks. Negotiates pay.

RONAN, HOWARD, ASSOCIATES, INC., 11 Buena Vista Ave., Spring Valley NY 10977-3040. (914)356-6668. President: Muriel Brown. Ad/PR firm. Clients: still and motion picture (cine) photography products and services; video production products; lighting products; electronic components.
Needs: Works with 2-3 freelance artists/year. Uses artists for mechanicals, retouching, charts/graphs and AV presentations.
First Contact & Terms: Query. "Samples and/or other material will not be returned. Please do not send unordered material with a demand for return. It is an unwarranted burden on our shipping department." SASE. Reports immediately. Pays $25 minimum for illustrations, layout, lettering, paste-up, retouching and mechanicals for newspapers, magazines, catalogs and P-O-P displays. Pays promised fee for unused assigned illustrations.

HORACE SADOWSKY & ASSOCIATES, 20 Jerusalem Ave., Hicksville, Long Island NY 11801. (516)681-6550. President/Creative Director: Horace Sadowsky. Clients: industrial, medical, electronics, housewares, giftwares, building contractors.
Needs: Uses designers for brochures/flyers and trade magazines. Uses artists for layout, illustration, technical art, paste-up and retouching for magazines, direct mail, brochures, annual reports and corporate promotions.
First Contact & Terms: Local artists only. Arrange interview. Works on assignment only. Reports only if interested. Provide brochures, flyers, tear sheets, business card or resume to be kept on file for future assignments. Pays by the day, $40-150 average. Considers client's budget, and skill and experience of artist when establishing payment. No originals returned to artist at job's completion.
Tips: "Call for appointment. Do *not drop in.*"

*SPITZ ADVERTISING AGENCY, 530 Oak St., Syracuse NY 13203. Contact: William Spitz, Nick Bibko or Chris Slater. Serves clients in plastic products, hotels, finance and electronics.
Needs: Uses artists for illustration, design, animated cartoons, technical art layout and retouching for catalogs, direct mail, graphics, trademarks, letterheads, newspapers, trade magazines, radio, TV and billboards.
First Contact & Terms: Mail samples. Payment varies with job.

*WALLACK & WALLACK ADVERTISING, INC., 33 Great Neck Rd., Great Neck NY 11021. Art Director: John Napolitano. Ad agency. Clients: fashion eyewear, entertainment, computer and industrial.
Needs: Works with 10-15 artists/year. Uses artists for mechanicals, layout and design, illustration, photography and retouching. Mechanical and print production skills are important.
First Contact & Terms: Send query letter with brochure, resume, business card and samples to be kept on file; call or write for appointment to show portfolio. Prefers photostats or photocopies as samples. Samples returned only if requested. Reports only if interested. Pays by the hour, $8-15 average; by the project, $150-750 average. Considers complexity of the project, client's budget, skill and experience of artist, turnaround time, geographic scope for the finished product, and rights purchased when establishing payment. Rights purchased vary according to project.
Tips: "Only present that work at which you are most proficient."

WINTERKORN LILLIS INC., Hiram Sibley Bldg., 311 Alexander at East Ave., Rochester NY 14604. (716)454-1010. Creative Director: Wendy Nelson. Ad agency. Clients: consumer packaged goods and industrial firms; national and international level only—no regional accounts.
Needs: Works with 8-10 new illustrators/year; 6-10 new designers/year. Uses freelance artists for trade and consumer magazines, direct mail, P-O-P displays, brochures, posters, AV presentations and literature, and coverage for sales promotions and sales meetings.
First Contact & Terms: Query with samples to be kept on file. Prefers slide carousel or laminated tear sheets as samples. Samples returned only if requested. Reports only if interested. Works on assignment only. Pays by the project, $700-8,000 average. Considers complexity of project, client's budget, skill and experience of artist, turnaround time and rights purchased when establishing payment.
Tips: "Present only top professional work, 18 pieces maximum, in a very organized manner."

WOLKCAS ADVERTISING INC., 8 Wade Rd., Latham NY 12110. (518)783-5151. Creative Director: Stewart Sacklow. Clients: retail, industrial and leisure time.
Needs: Works with 6 illustrators and 4 designers/month. All jobs are freelance and buys 100-135 illustrations/year. Uses artists for billboards, P-O-P displays, consumer magazines, stationery design, direct mail, television and newspapers.
First Contact & Terms: Query with samples or arrange interview to show portfolio. Prefers photostats and b&w line drawings as samples. Samples not returned. Reports within 1 week. Works on assignment only. Provide business card, brochure/flyer, resume, samples, tear sheets—anything that will help—to be kept on file for possible future assignments. No originals returned at job's completion. Negotiates pay, by the project or by the hour. Considers complexity of project, client's budget, and skill and experience of artist when establishing payment.
Tips: "We see more use of freelance art. Show a professional portfolio."

ZELMAN STUDIOS LTD., 623 Cortelyou Rd., Brooklyn NY 11218. (718)941-5500. General Manager: Jerry Krone. AV producer. Serves clients in industry, education, government and advertising. Produces slides, videotape and film (Super 8 and 16mm).
Needs: Assigns 30 jobs/year. Works with 3 designers/year. Uses artists for art design and cel preparation.
First Contact & Terms: Local artists only (25-mile radius). Send samples (slides preferred). Samples

returned with SASE. Provide samples, brochure/flyer and tear sheets to be kept on file for possible future assignments. Works on assignment only. Reports in 2 weeks. Pays by the project. Payment varies with each client's budget. No originals returned to artist after publication. Buys all rights.

New York City

A.V. MEDIA CRAFTSMAN, INC., Room 600, 110 E. 23rd St., New York NY 10010. (212)228-6644. President: Carolyn Clark. AV firm. Clients: public relations firms, publishers, banks, security firm, ad agencies, educational publishers and internal corporate communications departments. Produces filmstrips, multiscreen slide shows, multimedia kits, overhead transparencies, cassettes, sound-slide sets and videotapes. Assigns approximately 20 jobs/year.
Needs: Works with audiovisual illustrators and designers only and mechanical artists on a project basis. "Artists must have total knowledge of graphic slide production and kodalith pin registration techniques. Others please do not apply."
First Contact & Terms: Local, experienced audiovisual artists only. Provide resume and tear sheets or a photocopy of art to be kept on file. Samples not filed are not returned. Reports only if interested. "You may be called to bid on projects. Jobs on *freelance* basis only. Educational and training budgeting on the lower side, generally."

*****ADELANTE ADVERTISING, INC.**, 386 Park Ave. S, New York NY 10016. (212)696-0855. Vice President: Ted Amber. Ad agency. Clients: national consumer. Client list available.
Needs: Works with a varying number of freelance artists/year. Uses artists for a variety of jobs.
First Contact & Terms: Seeks experienced professionals. Sometimes works on assignment only. Send query letter with brochure, resume and samples to be kept on file. Call for appointment to show portfolio. Prefers photographs, slides or tear sheets as samples. Samples not filed are not returned. Reports only if interested. Pays by the hour, $15 minimum. Considers complexity of the project, client's budget, skill and experience of artist, geographic scope for finished product and turnaround time when establishing payment. Rights purchased vary according to project.

ADMASTER INC., 95 Madison Ave., New York NY 10016. (212)679-1134. Director of Visual Services: Andrew Corn. Clients: businesses. Produces slide sets, multimedia kits, multiple images, video cassettes and brochures. Assigns 300 jobs/year.
Needs: Works with 5 illustrators and 1 designer/month. Uses artists for slides, motion pictures and TV.
First Contact & Terms: Local artists only. Query and arrange interview. Prefers slides as samples. Reports in 1 week. Provide materials to be kept on file for future assignment. Samples returned by SASE if not kept on file. No originals returned to artist at job's completion. Buys all rights. Pays $8-20/hour, charts/graphs and technical art; $10-20/hour, illustrations; $8-20/hour, mechanicals; on acceptance. Considers skill and experience of artist when establishing payment.
Tips: Artists should have "good clean corporate samples."

AHREND ASSOCIATES INC., 80 5th Ave., New York NY 10011. (212)620-0015. Vice President/Production: Beth Lippman. Ad agency. Clients: publishers, industrial, direct response and mail order firms, financial institutions and nonprofit organizations.
Needs: Works with a few illustrators and 3-5 designers/month. Uses designers for consumer magazines, direct mail, catalogs and brochures/flyers. Also uses artists for design, layout, lettering, paste-up and type spec.
First Contact & Terms: Works with local illustrators and designers only. Query or write for interview. Reports in 1 week. Provide business card, resume or tear sheets to be kept on file for future assignments. No originals returned to artist at job's completion. "In each instance, cost is agreed upon (specifically or within a range) before work is assigned." No payment for unsatisfactory assigned work; "if because of client's change of mind, full payment."
Tips: "Should have advertising, preferably direct response, experience. Must know basic requirements for submission to printers, platemakers and others involved in production of promotional material (except for illustrations or spots which will be used as elements of a mechanical and are not the mechanicals themselves)." Especially looks for an "awareness of the product that is being sold and of the audience the product is aimed at" in samples.

ASH/LEDONNE INC., 1500 Broadway, New York NY 10036. (212)221-0140. Vice President/Associate Creative Director: Don Gordon. Clients: Broadway theatre, motion picture producers and entertainment arenas (Madison Square Gardens, Radio City Music Hall).
Needs: Uses artists for posters, TV, letterheads, newspapers, trademarks, lettering and comps. Espe-

cially needs poster and graphic illustrators and "super fast" mechanical people.
First Contact & Terms: Local artists only. Mail samples and submissions, and arrange portfolio drop-off. Reports within 1 week. Pays $12-15/hour, layout; $12/hour, paste-up and mechanicals.

AVRETT, FREE AND GINSBERG, INC., 800 3rd Ave., New York NY 10022. (212)832-3800. Art/Creative Director: Frank C. Ginsberg. Serves clients in food, publishing, drug manufacturing, toiletries and clothing.
Needs: Uses artists for storyboards, concept, animation, illustrations and print ads.
First Contact & Terms: Assigns numerous illustrations/year. Mail resume, art or previously published work. SASE. Reports within 2 weeks.

***BIRD & FALBORN**, 220 E. 23rd St., New York NY 10010. Production Manager: Leonard Grow. Ad agency. Clients: travel, insurance and publishers.
Needs: Works with several freelance artists/year. Uses artists for design, illustration and paste-up.
First Contact & Terms: Send query letter with resume to be kept on file. Reports only if interested. Pays by the hour, $10-30 average. Considers skill and experience of artist when establishing payment.

BOZELL & JACOBS INTERNATIONAL, 1 Dag Hammarskjold Plaza, New York NY 10017. (212)705-6000. VP/Creative Director: Marce Mayhew. Ad agency. Clients: industrial and packaged goods.
Needs: Works with illustrators on regular basis as needs arise. Uses artists for consumer magazines, newspapers and brochures/flyers.
First Contact & Terms: Make contact only through artist's rep. Works on assignment only. Provide brochure, resume and business card to be kept on file for future assignments. Negotiates payment based on client's budget.

***JOHN BRANSBY PRODUCTIONS, LTD.**, 221 W. 57th St., New York NY 10019. Vice President: W. Comcowich. Film, video, videodisc producer. Clients: "federal government and *Fortune 500*; we concentrate in the fields of science, medicine and technology." Produces filmstrips, videotapes and interactive videodisc programs and print materials. Assigns 40 jobs/year.
Needs: Works with 2-3 illustrators and 1-2 designers/month. Uses artists for motion pictures and professional monographs. Also uses artists for 16mm film animation design and graphics, 35mm slide illustration and graphics, and medical illustrations.
First Contact & Terms: Query with resume and samples (no originals). Prefers slides, photographs and color prints as samples. Works on assignment only. SASE. Reports in 4 weeks. Provide brochure/flyer and resume to be kept on file for future assignments. Negotiates pay by the project.
Tips: "There is greater need for medical artists and animators."

ANITA HELEN BROOKS ASSOCIATES, 155 E. 55th St., New York NY 10022. (212)755-4498. President: Anita Helen Brooks. PR firm. Clients: fashion, "society," travel, restaurants, politics and diplomats, books.
Needs: Number of freelance jobs assigned/year varies. Uses artists for consumer magazines, newspapers and press releases. "We're currently using more abstract designs."
First Contact & Terms: Call for appointment to show portfolio. Reports only if interested. Works on assignment only. Payment determined by client's needs. Considers client's budget and skill and experience of artist when establishing payment.
Tips: Artists interested in working with us must provide "rate schedule, partial list of clients and media outlets. We look for graphic appeal when reviewing samples."

CALVILLO, SHEVACK, GOLDBERG, & PARTNERS, (formerly LCF&S), 1350 Ave. of the Americas, New York NY 10019. (212)245-7300. President/Chief Executive: Brett Shevack. Ad agency. Serves clients in personal care products, apparel and liquor.
Needs: Works with 5-10 illustrators and 1 or less designer/month. Uses artists for animation, billboards, magazines, packaging, posters and newspapers. "We are in constant need of fast, talented sketch people to do storyboard renderings. Finished ad illustration is also greatly needed."
First Contact & Terms: Query with samples (original art or photocopies). Provide brochure, flyer and/or business card to be kept on file for future assignments. No originals returned at job's completion. Pay is negotiable.
Tips: "Storyboard artists should be fast, cooperative and be able to give a feeling of environment and action with a nice loose style."

CANAAN COMMUNICATIONS INC., 310 E. 44th St., New York NY 10017. (212)682-4030. President: Lee Canaan. PR firm. Clients: restaurants, celebrities, corporate accounts, advertising agencies, political, art museums and galleries. Client list provided for SASE.

Needs: Assigns 12 freelance jobs/year. Uses artists for consumer and trade magazines, brochures, catalogs, newspapers, filmstrips and stationery.
First Contact & Terms: Send query letter with brochure, resume, business card, samples and tear sheets to be kept on file. Works on assignment only.

CANON & SHEA ASSOCIATES, INC., 875 Ave. of Americas, New York NY 10001. (212)564-8822. Art Director: Richard Long. Ad/PR/marketing firm. Clients: business to business with emphasis in the industrial marketplace.
Needs: Assigns 20-40 jobs and buys 50-60 illustrations/year.
First Contact & Terms: Mostly local artists. Query with nonreturnable samples. Payment by hour: $20-35, animation, annual reports, catalogs, trade and consumer magazines; $25-50, packaging; $50-250, corporate identification/graphics; $8-28, layout, lettering and paste-up.
Tips: "Artists should have industrial or consumer materials as samples and should understand the marketplace."

*CINETUDES FILM PRODUCTIONS, LTD., 293-295 W. 4th St., New York NY 10014. (212)966-4600. Office Manager: Jacqueline Graf. Film/TV producer. Serves clients in industry and advertising. Produces motion pictures.
Needs: Assigns more than 20 jobs/year. Works with 1 animator and 1 designer/month and 6 illustrators/year. Uses artists for motion pictures.
First Contact & Terms: Send samples and arrange interview by mail. Prefers slides as samples. Samples returned by SASE. Provide resume and tear sheets to be kept on file for possible future assignments. Works on assignment only. Reports in 2 weeks. Pays by the project. Considers complexity of project when establishing payment. No originals returned to artist following publication. Buys all rights.

*THE CREATIVE ESTABLISHMENT, 115 W. 31st St., New York NY 10001. (212)563-3337. Producer: Diana Davis. AV/film/multi-image producer. Serves clients in industry. Produces materials for businesss meetings, product introductions, corporate image and P-O-P.
Needs: Assigns 20 jobs/year. Works with 5 board artists, 1 animator and 2 designers/month. Uses artists for most projects.
First Contact & Terms: New York metropolitan area artists only. "Artists must have at least 3 years' experience in work applied for." Send resume and samples (12 or more slides preferred). Samples not kept on file are returned with SASE. Provide resume, samples, brochure/flyer, business card or tear sheets to be kept on file for possible future assignments. Reporting time depends on current needs. Method and amount of payment are negotiated with the individual artist and vary with each client's budget. No originals returned to artist after publication. Negotiates rights purchased.
Tips: "With more use of computer art, freelancers now need a more technical background."

CRYSTAL PICTURES INC., 1560 Broadway, New York NY 10036. (212)757-5130. Contact: S. Tager. Motion picture/TV producer/distributor. General audience.
Needs: Works with 1 illustrator/month. Uses artists for film posters, press books, motion pictures, catalogs, paste-ups and mechanicals.
First Contact & Terms: New York City artists only. Send nonreturnable samples (nonreturnable copies) and describe skills relevant to requirements. No file kept on artists. No originals returned to artist at job's completion.

RAUL DA SILVA & OTHER FILMMAKERS, 311 E. 85h St., New York NY 10028. (212)535-5760. Creative Director: Raul da Silva. TV/film/animation/AV producer and limited publishing firm. Clients: business, industrial, institutional, educational and entertainment.
Needs: Works with 3-4 illustrators and 1 designer/month. "Seeking several artists with experience in slide/multimedia production, layout and materials. Also seeking designers, plus illustrators capable of rendering sci-fi/fantasy art in the *Heavy Metal* style—see the magazine for the years '77-'79." Uses artists for filmstrips, motion pictures, record jackets, multimedia kits, storyboards and titles.
First Contact & Terms: Send resume including references with phone numbers and addresses, and electrostatic copies which will *not* be returned. Samples returned by SASE only if requested; samples "always kept on file if they merit space. Do not send any original work without obtaining our request for it." Returns only solicited work. Reports within 2 weeks only if interested. Works on assignment only. Payment for illustrations and layout "depends completely on end use." Storyboards, $15-50/frame; continuity design, $300 and up/program. Considers complexity of project, client's budget, skill and experience of artist, turnaround time and rights purchased when establishing payment.
Tips: "We are a small, highly professional studio using only committed, *skilled* professionals who enjoy having their good work appreciated and rewarded. Hobbyists, dabblers usually do not make the grade for us."

DANCER-FITZGERALD-SAMPLE INC., 405 Lexington Ave., New York NY 10174. Vice President/Director of Art Services: Warren C. Krey. Ad agency. Serves clients in food, household products, beauty products, publishing, hosiery, and automobiles.
Needs: Works with 25 illustrators and 3 designers/month. Uses artists for billboards, P-O-P displays, filmstrips, consumer and trade magazines, TV, slide sets, brochures/flyers and newspapers; cartoons and humorous and cartoon-style illustrations (4-5 each/year). also uses artists for layout, retouching and lettering.
First Contact & Terms: Mail samples. Prefers printed pieces or slides as samples. Samples returned by SASE. Works on assignment only. Provide flyers to be kept on file for future assignments. No originals returned to artist at job's completion. Pays $200-5,000, depending upon use and degree of difficulty. Considers complexity of project, client's budget and rights purchased when establishing payment.

DARINO FILMS, 222 Park Ave. S, New York NY 10003. (212)228-4024. Mailing Address: Box 1496, New York NY 10017. Creative Director: Ed Darino. Film/animation producer. Clients: educational, some industrial, TV station and corporate.
Needs: Works with 5-8 illustrators, 2-3 animators/month, plus airbrush artists and lettering artists. Also works with freelance designers. Uses artists for motion pictures.
First Contact & Terms: "No visits and no calls." Works on assignment only. Provide business card, brochure/flyer to be kept on file for future assignments. Reports back on future assignment possibilities. Payment to illustrators by illustration or by week; animators, within union salary; background artist, per background only (union scale). 3-6 month internship program.
Tips: Especially looks for "flexible communication of the graphic message in mailed submissions."

DITTMAN INCENTIVE MARKETING, 22 W. 23rd St., New York NY 10010. (212)741-8040. Art Director: W. Whetsel. AV producer/print sales promotion agency. Serves clients in corporations. Produces multimedia motivational materials and single-projector individual selling presentations.
Needs: Assigns 18 jobs/year. Works with 4 designers/year. Uses artists for multimedia, motivational materials and single-project individual selling presentations.
First Contact & Terms: Provide resume and samples to be kept on file for possible future assignments. Prefers slides, original publications as samples. Works on assignment only. Reports within weeks. Pays by the project or by the hour, "depending on task." Considers complexity of project, client's budget, turnaround time and sometimes skill and experience of artist and rights purchased when establishing payment. No originals returned to artist following publication. Negotiates rights purchased.
Tips: "We maintain extremely high standards, and only those artists who feel that their work is extraordinary in creation and execution should contact us. We work only with artists who have a high level of imagination and intense pride in the finished product—supported, of course, by samples that prove it."

CHRISTOPHER DIXON, INC., 116 E. 63rd St., New York NY 10021 (212)838-9069. President: Christopher Dixon. Motion picture/television production firm. Clients: entertainment industry.
Needs: Works with 10 freelance artists/year. Uses artists for storyboarding, promotional materials, design title sequence, computer animation and posters.
First Contact & Terms: Works on assignment only. Send resume to be kept on file. Call for appointment to show portfolio. Reports back only if interested. Pays by the project, $200-5,000 average. Considers complexity of the project, skill and experience of artist and rights purchased when establishing payment. Buys all rights.
Tips: "Send resume, follow up with a phone call."

***DOLPHIN PRODUCTIONS**, 140 E. 80th St., New York NY 10021. (212)628-5930. Contact: Allan Stanley. TV producers.
Needs: Uses artists for animation and graphic design.
First Contact & Terms: Submit cassette (video). Provide resume to be kept on file for future assignments. Reports within 3 weeks. Considers complexity of project, client's budget, and skill and experience of artist when establishing payment.

JODY DONOHUE ASSOC., INC., 32 E. 57th St., New York NY 10022. (212)688-8653. Contact: Interview, Review Portfolios Department. PR firm. Clients: fashion and beauty. Media used includes direct mail and P-O-P displays.
Needs: Works with 1-5 illustrators and 1-5 designers/month. Uses artists for P-O-P displays, stationery design, multimedia kits, direct mail, slide sets and brochures/flyers.
First Contact & Terms: Call for personal appointment to show portfolio. Provide brochure or flyer to be kept on file for future assignments. No originals returned to artist at job's completion. Negotiates payment based on client's budget, amount of creativity required from artist, and where work will appear.
Tips: Wants to see recent work that has been used (printed piece, etc.) and strength in an area (i.e., still life, children, etc.).

MICHAEL FAIN ADVERTISING, 156 5th Ave., New York NY 10010. (212)243-6825. Art/Creative Director: Mike Fain. Ad agency. Clients: industrial and surgical firms.
Needs: Uses designers for P-O-P displays, consumer magazines, direct mail, brochures/flyers, trade magazines and newspapers. Also uses artists for layout, paste-up and retouching.
First Contact & Terms: Local artists only. Call for interview. Provide business card or resume to be kept on file for future assignments. Original artwork "paid for by our agency, becomes possession of agency."
Tips: "One of the many qualities required of professional artists with whom we deal is a good understanding of copyfitting. An artist designs a layout and indicates space for text. Some artists are inclined to 'fake' it instead of actually making sure the required type will fit the space."

RICHARD FALK ASSOC., 1472 Broadway, New York NY 10036. (212)221-0043. PR firm. Clients: industry, entertainment and Broadway shows.
Needs: Uses 4 artists/year. Uses artists for consumer magazines, brochures/flyers and newspapers; occasionally buys cartoon-style illustrations.
First Contact & Terms: Send resume. Provide flyer and business card to be kept on file for future assignments. No originals returned to artist at job's completion. Negotiates payment based on client's budget.
Tips: "Don't get too complex—make it really simple."

TONI FICALORA PRODUCTIONS, 28 E. 29th St., New York NY 10016. (212)679-7700. Film/TV commercial producer. Serves clients in advertising. Produces TV commercials.
Needs: Assigns 50 jobs/year. Uses artists for "elaborate sets requiring freelance stylist and prop persons."
First Contact & Terms: Prefers artists who specialize. Send resume only (no samples). Works on assignment only. Reports within weeks. Pays by the project. Amount of payment is negotiated with the individual artist and varies with each client's budget. No originals returned to artist after publication. Buys all rights.

*****FLAX ADVERTISING**, 1500 Broadway, New York NY 10036. (212)944-9797. Contact: Elliot Flax. Clients: women's fashions, menswear and fabrics. Assigns 100 jobs and buys 100-200 illustrations/year.
Needs: Uses artists for mechanicals, illustrations, technical art, retouching and lettering for newspapers, magazines, fashion illustration, P-O-P displays, some cartooning and direct mail.
First Contact & Terms: Local artists only. Arrange interview to show portfolio. Reports in 1 week. Provide materials to be kept on file for future assignments. No originals returned to artist at job's completion. Pay varies.

*****ALBERT FRANK-GUENTHER LAW**, 71 Broadway, New York NY 10006. (212)248-5200. Senior Art Director: D. Algieri. Ad agency. Clients: financial, general consumer.
Needs: Works with varying number of illustrators and designers/month. Uses artists for trade papers, consumer papers, and magazines.
First Contact & Terms: Call for appointment to show portfolio.

*****LARRY FREDERICKS ASSOCIATES**, 845 3rd Ave., 15th Floor, New York NY 10022. Contact: Larry Fredericks. Clients: book publishers, firms with quarterly house organs and retailers.
Needs: Uses artists for layout, illustration, type spec, paste-up and retouching for consumer and trade magazines.
First Contact & Terms: Prefers local artists. Call for interview.

GHA COMMUNICATIONS, 1133 Broadway, New York NY 10010. (212)929-3853. President: George Hudak. Audiovisual firm. Clients: corporate.
Needs: Works with 5 freelance artists/year. Uses artists for design of promotion brochures, AV shows, etc. Artists must be "creative and dependable."
First Contact & Terms: Local artists only. Works on assignment only. Send brochure, resume, business card and samples to be kept on file; call for appointment to show portfolio. Accepts photostats, photographs, slides or tear sheets as samples. Samples not filed returned only if requested. Reports only if interested. Pay negotiated by the project. Considers complexity of project, client's budget, and skill and experience of artist when establishing payment. Negotiates rights purchased.

GRAPHIC MEDIA, INC., 12 W. 27th St., New York NY 10001. (212)696-0880. Director of Marketing: Marco Cardamone. Audiovisual firm. Clients: corporate.
Needs: Works with 8-10 freelance artists/year. Uses artists to design graphic slides and print collateral

and to prepare camera-ready art. Especially important are strong graphic design and color sense and meticulous neatness in art preparation.

First Contact & Terms: Works on assignment only. Send query letter with resume to be kept on file. Write for appointment to show portfolio. Prefers to review slides. Reports back only if interested. Pays by the hour, $14-25 average. Considers client's budget and artist's skill and experience when establishing payment. Buys all rights on a work-for-hire basis.

GREY ADVERTISING INC., 777 3rd Ave., New York NY 10017. Print Business Manager: Gerda Henge. Needs ad illustrations.

First Contact & Terms: Works on assignment only. Call for an appointment. Prefers original artwork as samples. Provide flyer to be kept on file for possible future assignments. Pays by the project; amount varies. Considers client's budget and rights purchased when establishing payment.

Tips: "Most of our advertising is done with photography. We use illustrations on a very limited basis."

*GREY FALCON HOUSE, 124 Waverly Pl., New York NY 10011. (212)777-9042. Art Director: Ann Grifalconi. General agency—audiovisual, public relations, market research and design firm. Clients: public service, corporate and research.

Needs: Occasionally uses outside artists for paste-up, lettering, occasional specialized art and illustration. Especially important are animation and layout, and specialized skill, such as medical, cartoon, storyboard, etc.

First Contact & Terms: Local artists only, minimum 3 years' experience. Works on assignment only. Call and outline special skills and background; send simple resume and 1 sample only to be kept on file for 1 year. Prefers photostat or tear sheet as sample. Sample not filed is not returned. Reports only if interested. Pays by the hour, $15-30 average; by the project, $250-1,000 average; by the day, $50-200 average. Considers complexity of the project, client's budget, skill and experience of artist, geographic scope for the finished product, turnaround time and rights purchased when establishing payment. Negotiates rights purchased according to project.

CHARLES HANS FILM PRODUCTIONS INC., 25 W. 38th St., New York NY 10018. (212)382-1280. Art Director: Evelyn Simon. AV producer. Clients: industrial and corporate. Produces filmstrips, motion pictures, multimedia kits, overhead transparencies, slide sets, sound-slide sets, slide-a-motion and videotapes.

Needs: Works with 10-15 illustrators/year. Uses artists for "all phases of artwork," including chart work, paste-ups, mechanicals and some illustration and design as in animation or spot illustrations. The majority of the work is for slides.

First Contact & Terms: Arrange interview to show portfolio. SASE. Reports within 2 weeks. Pay varies. Works on assignment only. Provide business card to be kept on file for possible future assignment.

*HERMAN & ASSOCIATES INC., 488 Madison Ave., New York NY 10022. President: Paula Herman. Serves clients in insurance, retailing (cameras, carpet), travel and tourism.

Needs: Uses artists for mechanicals, illustrations and retouching for newspapers, magazines and direct mail.

First Contact & Terms: Mail samples or write for interview; prefers local artists who have worked on at least 2-3 professional assignments previously. Prefers whatever best represents artist's work as samples. Samples returned by SASE. Reporting time "depends on clients." Works on assignment only; reports back whether to expect possible future assignments. Provide brochure/flyer (file card style helps) to be kept on file for possible future assignments. Pays by the project.

Tips: "There is a trend toward more illustration. Artists interested in working with us should be persistent—keep following up."

JIM JOHNSTON ADVERTISING INC., 551 5th Ave., New York NY 10176. (212)490-2121. Art/Creative Director: Doug Johnston. Serves clients in publishing, corporate and business-to-business.

Needs: Works with 3-4 illustrators/month. Uses artists for consumer magazines, trade magazines and newspapers.

First Contact & Terms: Query with previously published work or samples, or arrange interview. SASE. Reports in 2 weeks. Provide tear sheets to be kept on file for possible future assignments. Payment by job: $250-6,500, annual reports; $250-2,000, billboards; $125-2,500, consumer magazines; $150-5,000, packaging; $250-1,000, P-O-P displays; $150-1,500, posters; $125-600, trade magazines; $100-1,000, letterheads; $200-1,500, trademarks; $300-2,500, newspapers. Payment by hour: $20 minimum, catalogs; $5-20, paste-up. Pays 25% of promised fee for unused assigned illustrations.

JORDAN, CASE & McGRATH, 445 Park Ave., New York NY 10022. (212)906-3600. Art Director: Dolois Bennett.Clients: toiletries and drugs manufacturers, food companies, food product firms, liquor

and wine, hosiery, insurance and bank. Assigns 50 jobs/year.
Needs: Works with 3 illustrators/month. Uses artists for billboards, consumer magazines and TV storyboards.
First Contact & Terms: Arrange interview. Provide example of work along with name, phone number, etc. to be kept on file for future assignments. Originals returned only upon request.

CHRISTOPHER LARDAS ADVERTISING, Box 1440, Radio City Station, New York NY 10101. (212)688-5199. President: Christopher Lardas. Ad agency. Clients: paper products, safety equipment, chocolate-confectionery, real estate, writing instruments/art materials.
Needs: Works with 6 freelance artists/year. Uses artists for illustration, layout, mechanicals.
First Contact & Terms: Local artists only; must have heavy experience. Works on assignment only. Send query letter with brochure, resume, business card and samples to be kept on file. Write for appointment to show portfolio. Accepts photostats, photographs, slides or tear sheets as samples. Samples not filed are returned only if requested. Reports back only if interested. Pays by the project. Considers client's budget when establishing payment. Buys all rights.

WILLIAM V. LEVINE ASSOCIATES, 31 E. 28th St., New York NY 10016. (212)683-7177. Vice President: Mark Netski. AV producer. Serves clients in industry and consumer products. Produces sales meeting modules and slides for speaker support.
Needs: Assigns 20 jobs/year. Works with 2-3 artists/month. Uses artists primarily for illustration, cartoons, etc.
First Contact & Terms: Send resume. Works on assignment only. Reports in 2 weeks. Pays by the project. No originals returned to artist after publication. Negotiates rights purchased.

H. ALLEN LIGHTMAN, 515 Madison Ave., New York NY 10022. (212)355-6717. Vice President: Susan Sona. Ad agency. Clients: cosmetic. Client list provided upon request.
Needs: Works with 1-2 freelance artists/year. Uses artists for drawings and mechanicals. Especially looks for creativity and accuracy.
First Contact & Terms: Works on assignment only. Send brochure and samples to be kept on file; call for appointment to show portfolio. Prefers tear sheets as samples. Samples not filed returned only if requested. Reports only if interested. Pays by the project, $50-100 average minimum. Considers client's budget when establishing payment. Rights purchased vary according to project.
Tips: "Have all credits, samples and portfolio ready upon request."

MALLORY FACTOR INC., 1500 Broadway, New York NY 10036. PR firm. Clients: *Fortune* 500 companies, hotels. Client list provided for SASE.
Needs: Assigns 25 freelance jobs/year. Works with 4 freelance illustrators and 2 freelance designers/month. Uses artists for brochures, stationery, posters and advertising.
First Contact & Terms: Artists must be local. Call or write for appointment to show portfolio. Samples not kept on file are not returned. Reports only if interested. Works on assignment only. Pay is on a project basis. Considers client's budget and turnaround time when establishing payment. Buys all rights.

MARTIN/ARNOLD COLOR SYSTEMS, 150 5th Ave., New York NY 10011. (212)675-7270. President: Martin Block. Vice President Marketing: A.D. Gewirtz. AV producer. Clients: industry, education, government and advertising. Produces slides, filmstrips and Vu Graphs.
Needs: Assigns 20 jobs/year. Works with 2 illustrators and 2 designers/month.
First Contact & Terms: Send resume and arrange interview bymail. Provide resume to be kept on file for possible future assignments. Works on assignment only. Payment varies with each client's budget. Original artwork returned to artist after publication. Negotiates rights purchased.

MEDICAL MULTIMEDIA CORP., 211 E. 43rd St., New York NY 10017. (212)986-0180. AV/motion picture/TV producer. Clients: pharmaceutical manufacturers and manufacturers of diagnostic equipment (e.g. x-ray, ultrasound, CAT scanning, nuclear imaging). Audiences: health care industry—sellers and/or users. Produces educational programs in health sciences. Buys 150-200 designs/year.
Needs: Works with 1-2 illustrators/month and infrequently with designers. Uses artists for album covers, books, catalogs, filmstrips and motion pictures. Also uses artists for layout, multimedia kits, paste-up, technical charts and medical illustrations.
First Contact & Terms: New York artists only. Call for interview. Provide brochure/flyer, resume and tear sheets to be kept on file for future assignments. No originals returned to artist at job's completion. Buys all rights. Pays $8-15/hour, mechanicals; $25-40/hour, design.

MARCELO MONTEALEGRE INC., 3rd Floor, 512 Broadway, New York NY 10012. (212)226-2796. President: Marcelo Montealegre. AV producer. Serves clients in industry, education, institutions and advertising. Produces slide presentations, slide shows, filmstrips and film titles.

Needs: Assigns 30-40 jobs/year. Works with 10 illustrators and 2 animators/year. Uses artists for commercial and educational projects.

First Contact & Terms: Prefers previous AV experience. Arrange interview by phone. Samples and tear sheets kept on file for possible future assignments. Prefers slides, flyers, or photostats as samples. Reports only if interested. Works on assignment only. Amount of payment is negotiated with the individual artist. Pays by the hour, $15 minimum. Considers client's budget, skill and experience of artist and rights purchased when establishing payment. Originals returned to artist after publication. Negotiates rights purchased.

Tips: "Call first, come prepared, show only your best work, slanted towards client's need. And don't explain your work."

RUTH MORRISON ASSOC., 509 Madison Ave., New York NY 10022. (212)838-9221. Contact: Deidre Rockmaker. PR firm. Clients: food, home furnishings, liquor, travel and general. Media used include consumer and trade magazines, direct mail, newspapers and P-O-P.

Needs: Works with 2-3 illustrators and 2-3 designers/year. Uses artists for brochures/flyers, P-O-P displays, stationery design and trade magazines.

First Contact & Terms: Send a note and photocopies of samples with SASE. When reviewing samples, looks for "impact first, freshness second, and total craftsmanship third." Provide flyer and tear sheet to be kept on file for future assignments. No originals returned to artist at job's completion. Negotiates payment based on client's budget and amount of creativity required from artist.

Tips: "We are looking for highest professional standards plus fresh creativity."

MUIR CORNELIUS MOORE, INC., 750 Third Ave., New York NY 10017. Creative Resources Administrator: Virginia Martin. Specializes in business to business advertising, sales promotion, corporate identity, displays, direct mail and exhibits. Clients: financial, high technology, industrial and medical accounts.

Needs: Works with 15-25 freelance artists/year. Uses artists for design, illustration, mechanicals and lettering; brochures, catalogs, books, P-O-P displays, posters, direct mail packages, charts/graphs, AV materials, logos, exhibits and advertisements.

First Contact & Terms: Works on assignment only. Do not call. Send query letter with brochure, resume and samples to be kept on file. Prefers samples that do not have to be returned, but will return unfiled material by SASE. Reports back only if interested. Pays by the hour or by the project. Considers complexity of the project, client's budget, skill and experience of artist, how the work will be used, turnaround time and rights purchased when establishing payment.

MULLER, JORDAN, WEISS, INC., 666 5th Ave., New York NY 10019. (212)399-2700. Contact: Art Director. Ad agency. Clients: fashion, agricultural, plastics, food firms, financial, corporate— "wide variety of accounts."

Needs: Works with 25 illustrators/year. Uses freelance artists for consumer and trade magazines, direct mail, P-O-P displays, brochures, posters, newspapers and AV presentations.

First Contact & Terms: Phone for appointment. Works on assignment basis only. Payment varies according to job.

NEWMARK'S ADVERTISING AGENCY INC., 253 W. 26th St., New York NY 10001. Art/Creative Director: Al Wasserman. Art/ad agency. Clients: manufacturing, industrial, banking, leisure activities, consumer, real estate, and construction firms.

Needs: Works with 1 designer/every 2 months. Uses artists for billboards, P-O-P displays, consumer magazines, slide sets, brochures/flyers and trade magazines. Also uses artists for figure illustration, cartoons, technical art, paste-up and retouching.

First Contact & Terms: Provide stat samples to be kept on file for future assignments. No originals returned to artist at job's completion. Pays $8-15/hour, paste-up and $75-3,000/job.

NOSTRADAMUS ADVERTISING, Suite 1128-A, 250 W. 57th St., New York NY 10107. Creative Director: B.N. Sher. Specializes in annual reports, corporate identity, publications, signage, flyers, posters, advertising, logos. Clients: ad agencies, book publishers, nonprofit organizations and politicians.

Needs: Works with 5 freelance artists/year. Uses artists for advertising design, illustration and layout; brochure design, mechanicals, posters, direct mail packages, charts/graphs, logos, catalogs, books and magazines.

First Contact & Terms: Send query letter with brochure, resume, business card, samples and tear sheets to be kept on file; call for appointment to show portfolio. Do *not* send slides as samples; will accept "anything else that doesn't have to be returned." Samples not kept on file are not returned. Reports only if interested. Pays for design and illustration by the hour, $15-25 average. Considers skill and experience of artist when establishing payment.

OGILVY & MATHER ADVERTISING, 2 E. 48th St., New York NY 10017. (212)907-3498. Contact: Dick Chandler. Ad agency. Serves clients in cosmetics, food, clothing, tourism, pharmaceuticals, airlines, automobiles, insurance, banking, toys, hotels, wines, beer.
Needs: Selection of freelancers based on drawing ability. Wants artists to be able to emote expression and attitude of people. "The artist has to be like an actor himself. His personality should spill over into his work." Especially interested in "people artists." Also artists who can express *mood* in storyboards and comps.
First Contact & Terms: Call Dick Chandler for appointment to show portfolio. Wants to see samples—no art director's roughs. Looking strictly for the *sketch artist*, marker renderings for storyboards and comps. Samples not kept on file are returned by SASE. Works on assignment only. Provide samples to be kept on file for possible future assignments. Payment varies.

OVATION FILMS INC., 15 W. 26th St., New York NY 10010. (212)686-4540. Contact: Art Petricone.
Needs: Uses artists for exhibit/set design and animation.
First Contact & Terms: Arrange interview. Works on assignment only. Prefers "original art where possible" as samples. Samples returned by SASE. Provide samples and tear sheets to be kept on file for possible future assignments.

*PACE ADVERTISING AGENCY, 485 5th Ave., New York NY 10017. Senior Art Director: Sid Nemiron. Ad agency. Clients: real estate, schools and food.
Needs: Works with 6 freelance artists/year. Uses artists for illustration and mechanicals.
First Contact & Terms: Send query letter with brochure and resume to be kept on file; write for appointment to show portfolio. Samples not filed are returned by SASE. Reports only if interested. Pays for mechanicals by the hour, $20-25 average; for illustrations by the project. Considers skill and experience of artist when establishing payment. Buys all rights.
Tips: "Artists must be experienced in our type of clientele."

*PERPETUAL MOTION PICTURES, INC., 17 W. 45th St., New York NY 10036. (212)953-9110. Producer: Hal Hoffer. Animation/TV/film producer. Clients: industrial, corporate, ad agencies and TV networks.
Needs: Uses artists for comps and animatics, and animation design. "Use very little freelance work."
First Contact & Terms: Local artists only. Query with resume and samples. SASE. Reports in 2 weeks. Pays $30-100/panel or going rate by day. Pays $150 minimum.

PHOENIX FILMS INC., 468 Park Ave. S., New York NY 10016. (212)684-5910. President: Heinz Gelles. Vice President: Barbara Bryant. Clients: libraries, museums, religious institutions, U.S. government, schools, universities, film societies and businesses. Produces and distributes motion pictures. Assigns 20-30 jobs/year.
Needs: Uses artists for motion picture catalog sheets, direct mail brochures, posters and study guides.
First Contact & Terms: Local artists only. Query with samples (tear sheets and photocopies). SASE. Reports in 3 weeks. Buys all rights. Originals returned to artist at job's request. Pays on production. Free catalog.

PM GROUP, LTD., 770 Lexington Ave., New York NY 10021. Account Group Director/Vice President: Jill Shaw. PR firm/AV/ad agency. Clients: travel, wine and spirits, consumer and food.
Needs: Uses artists for posters, direct mail packages, brochures, signage, P-O-P displays and invitations.
First Contact & Terms: Send query letter with brochure, resume, business card, samples and tear sheets to be kept on file except for "those that do not interest us." Write for appointment to show portfolio. Prefers photostats as samples. Samples not kept on file are returned by SASE if requested. Reports within 2 weeks. Works on assignment only. Payment depends upon job, but conforms to artists' usual scales." Considers complexity of project, client's budget and turnaround time when establishing payment. Buys all rights.
Tips: "We seek bold, imaginative work. Show us only your best and not a lot of that either."

REEVES CORPORATE SERVICES, a division of Reeves Communications Corp., 11th Floor, 708 3rd Ave., New York NY 10017. (212)573-8634. Art Director: Bob Gary. Produces TV, film, AV, multimedia presentations, collateral print and display material.
Needs: For general production needs print and AV/film mechanical artists, repro and AV production

generalists. For specialized production needs AV designers, editorial and print designers, film/video art and animation designers.

First Contact & Terms: Call for interview. Produced material is copyrighted by RCC. Job or hourly rates are dependent upon situation.

RICHARD H. ROFFMAN ASSOCIATES, Suite 6A, 697 West End Ave., New York NY 10025. (212)749-3647. Vice President: John Bowman. PR firm. Clients: restaurants, art galleries, boutiques, hotels and cabarets, nonprofit organizations, publishers and all professional and business fields.
Needs: Assigns 24 freelance jobs/year. Works with 2 freelance illustrators and 2 freelance designers/month. Uses artists for consumer and trade magazines, brochures, newspapers, stationery, posters and press releases.
First Contact & Terms: Send query letter and resume to be kept on file; call or write for appointment to show portfolio. Prefers photographs and photostats as samples. Reports only if interested. Pays by the hour, $10-25 average; by the project, $75-250 average; by the day, $150-250 average. Considers complexity of project, client's budget, and skill and experience of artist when establishing payment. Buys first rights or one-time rights. Returns material only if SASE enclosed.
Tips: "Realize that affirmative answers cannot always be immediate—do have patience."

ALBERT JAY ROSENTHAL & CO., 545 Madison Ave., New York NY 10022. (212)826-6610. Executive Art Director: Jack McKie. Clients: consumer and trade, packaged goods, travel and service.
Needs: Uses artists for advertising layout and design, illustration, lettering and storyboards.
First Contact & Terms: Local artists only. Query with samples and explain interests or call for an appointment. SASE. Provide business card, flyer, brochure and tear sheets. No originals returned at job's completion. Pay is negotiable.

PETER ROTHHOLZ ASSOCIATES INC., 380 Lexington Ave., New York NY 10017. (212)687-6565. President: Peter Rothholz. PR firm. Clients: government (tourism and industrial development), publishing, pharmaceuticals (health and beauty products).
Needs: Works with 2 illustrators, 2 designers/month.
First Contact & Terms: Call for appointment to show portfolio. Samples returned by SASE. Reports in 2 weeks. Works on assignment only. Provide resume or brochure/flyer to be kept on file for future assignments. Assignments made based on freelancer's experience, cost, style and whether he/she is local. No originals returned to artist at job's completion. Negotiates payment based on client's budget.

*JASPER SAMUEL ADVERTISING, 406 W. 31st St., New York NY 10001. (212)239-9544. Art Director: Joseph Samuel. Ad agency. Clients: health centers, travel agency, hair salons, etc.
Needs: Works with 5-10 freelance artists/year. Uses artists for advertising, brochure and catalog design, illustration and layout; product design and illustration on product.
First Contact & Terms: Works on assignment only. Send query letter with brochure, resume, business card and samples to be kept on file; call or write for appointment to show portfolio. Prefers photographs and tear sheets as samples. Samples not filed are returned. Reports within 1 month. Pays by the project. Considers complexity of the project and skill and experience of the artist when establishing payment.

JIM SANT'ANDREA INC., 320 W. 57th, New York NY 10019. (212)974-5400. Corporate Creative Director: Gerry Ranson. Multimedia Producer/Director. Clients: "top companies." Produces motion pictures, design exhibits, multimedia, sound-slide modules and videotapes.
Needs: Assigns approximately 200 jobs/year. Uses artists for design, storyboards, and comprehensive stage renderings.
First Contact & Terms: Prefers local artists. Call for appointment to show samples. Provide resume to be kept on file for future assignments. "Payment varies depending on the complexity. An 80-frame storyboard would pay around $400-500. We pay by the job; $250 minimum." Also considers client's budget, skill and experience of artist, geographic scope of finished project, turnaround time and rights purchased when establishing payment.

PHOEBE T. SNOW PRODUCTIONS, INC., 240 Madison Ave., New York NY 10016. (212)679-8756. Vice President: Lisbeth Bagnold. AV production company. Serves clients in industry. Produces slides, film and video materials.
Needs: Assigns 250 jobs/year. Works with 6 illustrators and 2 designers/month. Uses artists for slides, film and video materials.
First Contact & Terms: Send resume to the attention of Barbara Bagnold, Production Coordinator; arrange interview by phone. Provide resume and business card to be kept on file for possible future assignments. Works on assignment only. Reports within 1 week. Pays by the project or by the hour. No originals returned following publication. Buys all rights.

THE SOFTNESS GROUP INC., 3 E. 54th St., New York NY 10022. Executive Vice President: Carol Blades. PR firm. Clients: corporations and manufacturers.
Needs: Works with 3 illustrators, 1 designer/month. Uses artists to work with filmstrips, consumer magazines, stationery design, multimedia kits, slide sets, brochures/flyers, trade magazines and newspapers.
First Contact & Terms: Query with resume and samples. SASE. Reports in 2 weeks. Provide brochure or flyer to be kept on file for future assignments. No originals returned to artist at job's completion. Negotiates pay.

*SPINDLER PRODUCTIONS, 1501 Broadway at 44th St., New York NY 10036. (212)730-1255. Contact: Art Director. Audiovisual firm.
Needs: Works with 30-40 freelance artists/year. Uses artists for everything from board work to illustrations. "Artists should be able to interpret difficult-to-understand concepts and translate them into clear, concise graphics."
First Contact & Terms: Send samples to be kept on file; write for appointment to show portfolio. Prefers slides as samples. Samples not filed are returned by SASE only if requested. Reports only if interested. Pays by the hour, $10 minimum. Considers skill and experience of artist when establishing payment. Buys all rights.
Tips: "Unless strictly freelance, all work is by client-dictated project. No library, style catalog, or preconceived approach is considered."

LEE EDWARD STERN ASSOCIATES, 1 Park Ave., New York NY 10016. (212)689-2376. President: Lee Stern. Communications planning/editorial services. Clients: businesses of all kinds. Client list provided for SASE.
Needs: Assigns 6-10 freelance jobs/year. Uses artists for direct mail packages, brochures, annual reports, video-cassette bridges, titles.
First Contact & Terms: Send query letter with resume and samples. Material usually kept on file; write for appointment to show portfolio. Prefers expendable printed material as samples. Samples not kept on file are returned only if requested. Reports only if interested. Works on assignment only. Pays by the hour, $20-25 average. Considers complexity of project, client's budget, skill and experience of artist when establishing payment. Rights purchased varies.
Tips: "Few assignments here, but fun and creativity are encouraged."

SULLIVAN & BRUGNATELLI ADV., INC., 740 Broadway, New York NY 10003. (212)505-1110. Executive Art Director: John Benetos. Ad agency. Serves clients in packaged goods; consumer foods and drinks, ie., fruit juices; banking and over-the-counter drugs.
Needs: Works with 4 illustrators/year, mostly line artwork. Uses artists for consumer and trade magazines and newspapers.
First Contact & Terms: Drop off book or send query letter, then call for appointment to show portfolio or make contact through artist's rep. Prefers 8x10" chromes, original artwork if possible, tear sheets and photos as samples. Samples returned. Reports within 1 week. Works on assignment only. Provide brochure/flyer to be kept on file for future assignments. Pays $300-1,500/project.
Tips: There is a trend toward "more competition, but moving away from conventional executions can create more opportunities. I prefer to get a card in the mail, as opposed to a phone call to arrange appointments. After I've seen a sample I'll welcome a call."

TALCO PRODUCTIONS, 279 E. 44th St., New York NY 10017. (212)697-4015. President: Alan Lawrence. TV/film producer. Clients: nonprofit organizations, industry, associations and public relations firms. Produces motion pictures, videotapes and some filmstrips and sound-slide sets.
Needs: Assigns 4-10 jobs/year. Works with an average of 1 illustrator/month for filmstrips, motion pictures, animation and charts/graphs.
First Contact & Terms: Prefers local artists with professional experience. Query with resume. SASE. Reports only if interested. Pay varies according to assignment. Negotiates fees. Provide resume to be kept on file for future assignments. On some jobs originals returned to artist after completion. Buys all rights. Pays on production. Considers complexity of project, client's budget and rights purchased when establishing payment.
Tips: "Do not send anything but a resume!"

THE TARRAGANO COMPANY, 230 Park Ave., New York NY 10169. (212)972-1250. President: Morris Tarragano. Ad agency and PR firm. Clients: manufacturers of products and services of all types. Media used include consumer and trade magazine, direct mail and newspapers.
First Contact & Terms: Write and request personal interview to show portfolio and/or send resume. Selection based on review of portfolio and references. Negotiates payment based on amount of creativity required from artist and previous experience/reputation.

TELECONCEPTS INTERNATIONAL, (formerly Teleconcepts in Communications, Inc.), Suite 6B, 145 E. 49th St., New York NY 10017. (212)355-7113. TV producer. Serves clients in industry, education and government. Produces films, videotape, teleconferences and multi-city closed-circuit satellite telecasts.
Needs: Assigns 6-12 jobs/year. Works with 2 illustrators and 2 designers/month. Uses artists for film and videotape.
First Contact & Terms: Send query letter. Works on assignment only. Provide samples, business card and tear sheets to be kept on file for possible future assignments. Reports in 2 weeks. Method and amount of payment are negotiated with the individual artist. No originals returned to artist following publication. Negotiates rights purchased.

TELEMATED MOTION PICTURES, Box 176, New York NY 10012. (212)475-8050. Producer/Director: Saul Taffet. AV/TV/film producer. Clients: industry, ad agencies, film producers and business. Produces filmstrips, motion pictures, slide sets and sound-slide sets.
First Contact & Terms: Local artists only. Call to arrange interview. Do not submit art. Buys all rights. Pays on production. Pays $5-10 minimum/hour for animation, charts/graphs, storyboards, lettering, illustrations, retouching and technical art.

TOGG FILMS, INC., 630 9th Ave., New York NY 10036. (212)974-9507. Producer/Director: Grania Gurievitch. AV/film producer. Serves clients in industry, education and government. Produces educational documentaries.
Needs: Uses artists for opticals and credits design.
First Contact & Terms: Experienced New York City area artists only. Send query letter. Reports only if interested. Works on assignment only. Pays by the project. Amount of payment is negotiated with the individual artist. Considers complexity of project, client's budget, skill and experience of artist, turnaround time and rights purchased when establishing payment. Original artwork not returned after publication. Buys all rights, but will negotiate.

*DON TREVOR ASSOCIATES INC., 20 E. 9th St., New York NY 10003. (212)473-0868. Producer/Director: Don Trevor. Produces documentaries, commercials and sales training/industrial films.
Needs: Uses artists for animation and set design.
First Contact & Terms: Query with resume.

VAN BRUNT & COMPANY, ADVERTISING MARKETING, INC., 300 E. 42nd St., New York NY 10017. (212)949-1300. Art Directors: Joseph Amarah, Walter Winchurch, Lisa Salay, Carl Van Brunt. Ad agency. Clients: general consumer firms; client list provided upon request.
Needs: Uses freelance artists for consumer and trade magazines, direct mail, P-O-P displays, brochures, catalogs, posters, newspapers and AV presentations.
First Contact & Terms: Arrange interview to show portfolio. Works on assignment only. Payment is by the project; negotiates according to client's budget and where work will appear.

VAN VECHTEN & ASSOCIATES PUBLIC RELATIONS, 427 E. 74th St., New York NY 10021. (212)570-6510. President: Jay Van Vechten. PR firm. Clients: medical, tourism, industry. Client list provided for SASE.
Needs: Assigns 20 + freelance jobs/year. Works with 2 freelance illustrators and 2 freelance designers/month. Uses artists for consumer and trade magazines, brochures, newspapers, stationery, signage, AV presentations and press releases.
First Contact & Terms: Send query letter with brochure, resume, business card and samples to be kept on file; write for appointment to show portfolio. Prefers photographs or photostats as samples. Samples not kept on file are returned by SASE. Reports only if interested. Works on assignment only. Pays by the hour, $10-15 average. Considers client's budget when establishing payment. Buys all rights.

MORTON DENNIS WAX & ASSOCIATES INC., Suite 301, 200 W. 51st St., New York NY 10019. (212)247-2159. President: Morton Wax. Public relations firm. Clients: entertainment, communication arts and corporate.
Needs: Uses artists for trade magazine ads, brochures and other relevant artwork.
First Contact & Terms: Artists must have references and minimum 3 years of experience. Works on assignment only. Send query letter with resume and samples to be kept on file; write for appointment to show portfolio. Prefers photostats or tear sheets as samples. Samples not filed are returned by SASE. Reports only if interested. "We select and use freelancers on a per project basis, based on specific requirements of clients. Each project is unique." Considers complexity of project, client's budget, turnaround time and rights purchased when establishing payment. Rights vary according to project.

Close-up

David Smiton
Freelance Artist
Hartsdale, New York

Artist: David R. Smiton

David Smiton held his first public art exhibition when he was only four years old. The medium was chalk on concrete, the setting a New York City apartment building and the critic his parent's landlord. The youthful exhibition covered not only the building's sidewalk, but continued up its brick walls and into the structure, only stopping at his family's apartment door.

Smiton has been drawing ever since this first unabashed display of love for art. After graduation from Parsons School of Design he worked as an artist in the Air Force and then returned to the private sector to do advertising illustration. For seven years, the "Big Apple" native worked as an art director. When he began freelancing exclusively in 1967, he used his experiences as an art director to satisfy the needs of art studios, advertising agencies, public relations firms, television stations, ship lines, collector plate manufacturers and others.

"I learned that most art directors, who are trained more in type and the concept of the printed page, aren't good draftsmen. My ability to draw well has given me many opportunities to do layouts and comprehensives."

Throughout his twenty-six-year art career Smiton has been active in both fine and graphic art, frequently incorporating both into his freelance jobs. A series of collector plates designed for Creative World displayed not only his fine art skills, but also his sense of design. "They were worked carefully in pencil first, and as I did them I was more conscious of design patterns and shapes, contrary to my earlier, more spontaneous approach to creating and painting."

Two basic supports aid Smiton in his work with fine and graphic art. One is a complete reference library built up throughout his career and encompassing books and magazines on a variety of subjects.

The second is the artist's sketchbook. "I draw from life and the environment every day. This practice keeps my tools sharp, my skills honed, and I see my talent developing and growing constantly as a result of observing life."

However, simply possessing a reference library and a sketchbook does not ensure success as a freelance artist. "I advise young artists to be tenacious. When you write an art director, ask in your letter if you can call. After a portfolio review send a thank you note. Call back. Send another thank you. You want people to remember you."

Smiton advises artists to always submit non-returnable samples. "Only send things that won't hurt you financially or emotionally. Be prepared to not get your material back.

"Remember too that criticism from an art director is invaluable. Don't be afraid to accept criticism. Most artists are sensitive, creative, and easily hurt and discouraged. The key is to understand that you are up against a competitive market.

"It is vital to keep working even during the lulls, even when you aren't on assignment. Keep making new samples. Constantly experiment with your medium and with different media. Get comfortable with one which best expresses your talent. Look at as much contemporary professional design and illustration as you can find.

"Stay alert. Keep your head, eyes and mind open to new things. Do not become cloistered in your thinking. You will make an imprint eventually."

Smiton used full-color gouache for this first in a series of paintings depicting children of the world in native ceremonial costumes. Creative World purchased the rights to reproduce the artwork on collector's plates only.

The charcoal pencil drawing below was commissioned by the public relations firm Corey Nadell Inc. for use on a concert program cover. Due to the fund raising nature of the concert, Smiton granted his client unlimited use of the artwork.

Smiton created this colored crayon sketch of attorney F. Lee Bailey, left, during the trial of Captain Ernest Medina. ABC-TV assigned the artist to cover the six-month-long trial and televised six of his sketches daily.

WELLS, RICH, GREENE, INC., 767 5th Ave., New York NY 10153. (212)758-4300. Contact: "Write for list of Art Directors." Ad agency. Clients: cosmetic, fashion, airline accounts and package goods.
Needs: Works with up to 2 illustrators/month. Uses freelance artists for storyboards.
First Contact & Terms: Arrange interview with one of the art directors to show portfolio. Pay varies according to skill and talent.

North Carolina

CAROLINA BIOLOGICAL SUPPLY, 2700 York Rd., Burlington NC 27215. (919)584-0381. Art Director: Dr. Kenneth Perkins. AV producer. Serves clients in education. Produces filmstrips, charts and booklets, educational games.
Needs: Assigns 20 jobs/year. Works with 2 illustrators/month. Uses artists for illustration work, both biological and medical. "We buy some cartoons for our pamphlets, filmstrips and advertising and some cartoon-style illustrations."
First Contact & Terms: Prefers artists located in the southeast who do good line work and use watercolor, acrylic or airbrush. Send resume and samples (prefers photostats or slides) to be kept on file. Samples are returned by SASE if not kept on file. Works on assignment only. Reports within 1 month. Amount of payment is negotiated with the individual artist; by the hour, $12 minimum. Considers complexity of project, skill and experience of artist and rights purchased when establishing payment. No originals returned to artist following publication. Buys all rights.

EDGECOMBE MARKETING INC., Box 1406, Tarboro NC 27886: (919)823-4151. Media Coordinator: Marty Smith. Ad agency. Serves clients in agriculture and industry.
Needs: Limited freelance needs. Uses illustrators for consumer magazines, brochures/flyers and trade magazines. Also uses artists for layout, technical art, type spec, paste-up and retouching.
First Contact & Terms: Query with samples of original art. No originals returned at job's completion. Payment varies.
Tips: "I find it very interesting to see finished art (illustrations, mechanicals, etc.) and the final billing for the job."

GARNER & ASSOCIATES, INC., Suite 350, 3721 Latrobe Dr., Charlotte NC 28211. (704)365-3455. Art Directors: Arkon Stewart, Cathy Morris. Ad agency. Clients: "wide range" of accounts; client list provided upon request.
Needs: Works with 2 illustrators/month. Uses freelance artists for billboards, consumer and trade magazines, direct mail, P-O-P displays, brochures, catalogs, posters, signage, newspapers and AV presentations.
First Contact & Terms: Send printed samples or phone for appointment. Works on assignment only. Payment is by the project; negotiates according to client's budget.

LEWIS ADVERTISING, INC., 2309 Sunset Ave., Rocky Mount NC 27801. (919)443-5131. Senior Art Director: Scott Brandt. Ad agency. Clients: fast food, communications, convenience stores, financials. Client list provided upon request with SASE.
Needs: Works with 20-25 freelance artists/year. Uses artists for illustration and part-time paste-up. Especially looks for "consistently excellent results, on time and on budget."
First Contact & Terms: Works on assignment only. Send query letter with resume, business card and samples to be kept on file. Call for appointment to show portfolio. "Any type of sample is acceptable; however returnable items must be cleary marked. Artists should show examples of previous work, price range requirements and previous employers." Samples not filed returned by SASE only if requested. Reports only if interested. Pays by project. Considers complexity of the project, client's budget, turnaround time and ability of artist when establishing payment. Buys all rights.

MORPHIS & FRIENDS, INC., 230 Oakwood Dr., Drawer 5096, Winston-Salem NC 27103. (919)723-2901. Art Director: Joe Nemoseck. Ad agency. Clients: banks, restaurants, clothing, cable, industry and furniture.
Needs: Assigns 20-30 freelance jobs/year. Works with approximately 2 freelance illustrators/month. Uses artists for consumer and trade magazines, billboards, direct mail packages, brochures and newspapers.
First Contact & Terms: Send query letter with business card and samples to be kept on file. Call for appointment to show portfolio. Prefers photos or photostats as samples. Samples not kept on file are returned only if requested. Reports only if interested. Works on assignment only. Pays by the hour, $25-50 average. "Negotiate on job basis." Considers complexity of project, client's budget, skill and experi-

ence of artist, geographic scope of finished project, turnaround time and rights purchased when establishing payment. Buys all rights.
Tips: "Send a letter of introduction with a few samples to be followed up by phone call."

SSF ADVERTISING, (formerly Short Shepler Fogleman Advertising), Division of Inform Inc., Drawer 1708, Hickory NC 28603. (704)328-5618 or 322-7766. President: James B. Fry. Ad agency. Clients: association management, public relations, industrial relations and advertising.
Needs: Assigns 50 freelance jobs/year. Works with 1 freelance illustrator and 1-3 freelance designers/month. Uses artists for consumer and trade magazines, billboards, direct mail packages, brochures, catalogs, newspapers, P-O-P displays and posters.
First Contact & Terms: Prefers artists in the southeast. Send query letter with brochure to be kept on file. Call or write for appointment to show portfolio. Accepts any type of samples. Samples not kept on file are returned. Reports only if interested. Pays by the hour or by the project. Considers complexity of project, client's budget, and skill and experience of artist when establishing payment. Buys all rights.

THOMPSON AGENCY, Suite 200, 1 Tyron Centre, 112 S. Tyron St., Charlotte NC 28284. (704)333-8821. Managing Art Director: Gordon Smith. Ad agency. Clients: banks, fast food, soft drink, TV station, resort, utility, automotive services.
Needs: Assigns approximately 200 freelance jobs/year. Works with 5 freelance illustrators/month. Uses artists for consumer and trade magazines, billboards, direct mail packages, brochures, newspapers, signage, P-O-P displays and posters.
First Contact & Terms: Send business card and samples to be kept on file. Call or write for appointment to show portfolio. Printed work accepted as samples. Samples returned by SASE if requested by the artist. Reports only if interested. Works on assignment only. Pays according to job. Considers complexity of project, client's budget, skill and experience of artist, turnaround time and rights purchased when establishing payment. Buys all rights.

Ohio

CORBETT ADVERTISING, INC., 40 S. 3rd St., Columbus OH 43215. (614)221-2395. Creative Director: Steve Beskid. 4-A agency. Clients: hospitals, insurance, colleges, industries, financial institutions—"variety of accounts."
Needs: Number of freelance artists used varies. Uses freelance artists for billboards, consumer and trade magazines, brochures, posters, newspapers and AV presentations.
First Contact & Terms: Arrange interview to show portfolio; *will not see walk-ins*. Works on assignment only. Payment is by the hour, by the day, or by the project; negotiates according to client's budget.
Tips: "Do some research on clients and present portfolio in accordance."

FAHLGREN & FERRISS, INC., 136 N. Summit, Toledo OH 43604. (419)241-5201. Creative Director: Bob Molnar. Ad agency. Serves clients in industrial equipment services and finance.
Needs: Works with 5-6 freelance illustrators/month. Uses freelancers for consumer and trade magazines, direct mail, brochures/flyers, newspapers and P-O-P displays.
First Contact & Terms: Call for appointment to show portfolio or make contact through artist's rep. Selection is usually based on reviewing portfolios through reps but will see individual freelancers. Negotiates payment based on client's budget, amount of creativity required from artist and where work will appear.
Tips: Pieces that are produced are best in portfolio. "Printed pieces have a lot more credibility."

FARRAGHER MARKETING SERVICES, 7 Court St., Canfield OH 44406. (216)533-3347. Creative Director: John Druga. Marketing service firm. Serves clients in industry and technical science. Assigns 20+ jobs/year.
Needs: Uses artists for P-O-P displays, stationery design, direct mail, brochures/flyers and trade magazines. Also uses artists for annual reports, catalogs, brochures, corporate identity, newsletters and promotional materials.
First Contact & Terms: Query with resume and samples. Prefers photographs and originals as samples. Samples returned by SASE. Reports as soon as possible. Works on assignment only. Provide resume, brochure/flyer and business card to be kept on file. Originals returned to artist at job's completion if requested. Negotiates pay.
Tips: "Be practical and businesslike."

THE FILM HOUSE INC., 6058 Montgomery Rd., Cincinnati OH 45213. (513)631-0035. President: Ken Williamson. TV/film producer. Clients: industrial and corporate. Produces filmstrips, motion pictures, sound-slide sets and videotapes.
Needs: Assigns 30 jobs/year. Uses artists for filmstrip animation and ad illustrations.

First Contact & Terms: Query with resume. Samples returned by SASE. Reports in 1 week. Works on assignment only. Provide business card and resume to be kept on file. Negotiates pay; pays by the project.
Tips: "Maintain contact every 45 days."

GERBIG, SNELL/WEISHEIMER & ASSOC., Suite 600, 425 Metro Pl. N., Dublin OH 43017. (614)764-3838. Vice President, Creative Director: Christopher J. Snell. Art Director: Diane Hay. Ad agency. Clients: business to business, financial and medical.
Needs: Works with 30 freelance artists/year. Uses artists for illustration, design, keyline and photography.
First Contact & Terms: Works on assignment only. Send query letter with brochure, resume, business card and samples to be kept on file. Write for appointment to show portfolio. Accepts photostats, photographs, slides or tear sheets as samples. Samples not filed returned only if requested. Reports only if interested. Pays by the project, $500-1,500 average. Considers complexity of the project, client's budget, skill and experience of artist, geographic scope for the finished product and turnaround time when establishing payment. Rights purchased vary according to project.

GRISWOLD INC., 55 Public Sq., Cleveland OH 44114. (216)696-3400. Executive Art Director: Tom Gilday. Ad agency. Clients: consumer and industrial firms; client list provided upon request.
Needs: Works with 30-40 illustrators/year. Uses freelance artists for billboards, consumer and trade magazines, direct mail, P-O-P displays, brochures, catalogs, posters, newspapers and AV presentations.
First Contact & Terms: Works primarily with local artists, but occasionally uses others. Arrange interview to show portfolio. Works on assignment only. Provide materials to be kept on file for possible future assignments. Payment is by the project; negotiates according to client's budget.

HAMEROFF/MILENTHAL, INC., Suite 450, 1 Capital South, 175 S. 3rd St., Columbus OH 43215. (614)221-7667. Vice President/Creative Services: Bill Gallagher. Ad Agency. Clients: "wide variety" of accounts; client list provided upon request.
Needs: Number of freelance artists used varies. Uses freelance artists for billboards, consumer and trade magazines, direct mail, P-O-P displays, brochures, catalogs, posters, signage, newspapers and AV presentations.
First Contact & Terms: Make initial contact by letter with resume. Works on assignment only. Payment varies according to job. Considers complexity of project, client's budget, turnaround time and rights purchased when establishing payment.

HAYES PUBLISHING CO. INC., 6304 Hamilton Ave., Cincinnati OH 45224. (513)681-7559. Office Manager: Marge Lammers. AV producer/book publisher. Produces educational books, brochures and audiovisuals on human sexuality and abortion. Free catalog.
Needs: Uses artists for direct mail brochures and books.
First Contact & Terms: Mail samples. Prefers slides and photographs as samples. Samples returned by SASE. Reports in 2 weeks. Provide business card to be kept on file for possible future assignments. Pays by job.

IMAGEMATRIX, 2 Garfield Pl., Cincinnati OH 45202. (513)381-1380. Vice President: Peter Schwartz. Audiovisual firm.
Needs: Works with 25 freelance artists/year. Uses artists for paste-up, mechanicals, airbrushing, storyboards, photography, lab work, illustration for AV; buys cartoons 4-5 times/year. Especially important is AV knowledge and animation understanding.
First Contact & Terms: Local artists only; must have portfolio of work. Artwork buy-out. Works on assignment only. Send business card and samples to be kept on file. Write for appointment to show portfolio. Prefers slides as samples. Samples not filed are returned by SASE. Reports within 2 months. Pays by the hour, $9-35 average; by the project, $150 minimum. Considers complexity of the project, client's budget, skill and experience of artist and turnaround time when establishing payment. Buys all rights.
Tips: "Specialize your portfolio; show an understanding of working for a 35mm final product. We are using more design for video graphics and computer graphics."

GEORGE C. INNES & ASSOCIATES, 132 Middle Ave., Elyria OH 44036. (216)323-4526. President: George C. Innes. Ad/art agency. Clients: industrial and consumer. Assigns 25-50 jobs/year.
Needs: Works with 3-4 illustrators/month. Uses illustrators for filmstrips, stationery design, technical illustrations, airbrush, multimedia kits, direct mail, slide sets, brochures/flyers, trade magazines, newspapers and books. Also uses artists for layout and design for reports, catalogs, print ads, direct mail/publicity, brochures, displays, employee handbooks, exhibits, products, technical charts/illustrations,

trademarks, logos and company publications.

First Contact & Terms: Query with samples of work. Prefers photocopies, tear sheets or slides as samples. Samples not filed are not returned. Reports in 2 weeks. Works on assignment only. No originals returned to artist at job's completion. Pays $4-12/hour, keyline/line illustrations; $4-12/hour, continuous-tone illustrations; $5-300/project.

THE JONETHIS ORGANIZATION, Suite 401, 159 S. Main St., Akron OH 44308. (216)375-5122. Project Manager: Doug Fritz. Marketing services firm. Clients: industrial, consumer and retail. Client list provided upon request.

Needs: Works with 6-8 freelance artists/year. Uses artists for design and production. Especially important are design sense, language understanding and production sense.

First Contact & Terms: Send query letter with resume to be kept on file. Call for appointment to show portfolio. Reports only if interested. Pays by the project, $100-200 average. Considers complexity of project, client's budget, skill and experience of artist, and turnaround time when establishing payment. Buys all rights.

MERVIN N. LEVEY CO., 316 N. Michigan, Toledo OH 43624. (419)242-1122. President: M.N. Levey. Advertising agency and marketing consultant to manufacturers of consumer products in the U.S., Canada, Europe and the Far East. Clients: manufacturers, distributors, land developers, real estate, insurance, machinery, home furnishings, major appliances, floor coverings, foods, automotive, pet foods, health and beauty aids, department stores, supermarket and drug store chains.

Needs: Original art, layout and paste-up for newspapers, magazines, TV, direct mail and P-O-P.

First Contact & Terms: Local artists only. Prefers photostats as samples. Samples returned. Reports within 4 weeks. Pays by the hour, $12-20 average. Considers client's budget, and skill and experience of artist when establishing payment.

Tips: "We'd like to have a group located in nearby cities to do keyline and lettering (full page newspaper ads) once monthly."

LOHRE & ASSOCIATES, 1420 E. McMillan St., Cincinnati OH 45206. (513)961-1174. Art Director: Charles R. Lohre. Ad agency. Clients: industrial firms.

Needs: Works with 2 illustrators/month. Uses freelance artists for trade magazines, direct mail, P-O-P displays, brochures and catalogs.

First Contact & Terms: Local artists only. Arrange interview to show portfolio. Especially looks for "excellent line control and realistic people or products." Works on assignment basis only. Payment is by the job.

MCKINNEY/GREAT LAKES ADVERTISING, 1166 Hanna Bldg., Cleveland OH 44115. (216)621-0648. Contact: Art Directors. Clients: mainly industrial and a few consumer accounts; client list provided upon request.

Needs: Uses freelance artists for consumer and trade magazines, direct mail, brochures, catalogs, newspapers and AV presentations.

First Contact & Terms: Works primarily with local freelancers but uses others. Arrange interview to show portfolio. Payment is by the project or by the day; negotiates according to client's budget and where work will appear.

Tips: "We primarily use photography; using more retouchers who are also illustrators."

THE MARSCHALK COMPANY, 601 Rockwell Ave., Cleveland OH 44114. (216)687-8800. Creative Director: Patrick Arbour. Ad agency. Clients: utilities, broadcasting, oil, national fast food chain.

Needs: Uses artists for consumer and trade magazines and newspapers.

First Contact & Terms: Call for appointment to show portfolio. Negotiates pay based on job complexity.

Tips: Wants to see current work and "imaginative ideas, either published or unpublished."

CHARLES MAYER STUDIOS INC., 168 E. Market St., Akron OH 44308. (216)535-6121. President: C.W. Mayer, Jr. AV producer since 1934. Clients: mostly industrial. Produces film and manufactures visual aids for trade show exhibits.

Needs: Works with 1-2 illustrators/month. Uses illustrators for catalogs, filmstrips, brochures and slides. Also uses artists for brochures/layout, photo retouching and cartooning for charts/visuals.

First Contact & Terms: Send samples or arrange interview to show portfolio. Prefers slides, photographs, photostats or b&w line drawings as samples. Samples not kept on file are returned. Reports in 1 week. Provide resume and a sample or tear sheet to be kept on file for future assignments. Originals returned to artist at job's completion. Negotiates pay.

ART MERIMS COMMUNICATIONS, 700 Bulkley Building, Cleveland OH 44115. (216)621-6683. President: Arthur M. Merims. PR firm. Clients: industry.
Needs: Assigns 10 freelance jobs/year. Works with 1-2 freelance illustrators and 1-2 freelance designers/month. Uses artists for trade magazines, brochures, catalogs, signage and AV presentations.
First Contact & Terms: Prefers local artists. Send query letter with samples to be kept on file. Call or write for appointment to show portfolio. Accepts "copies of any kind" as samples. Works on assignment only. Pays by the hour, $10-20 average or by the project. Considers complexity of project, client's budget, and skill and experience of artist when establishing payment.
Tips: When reviewing samples, looks for "creativity and reasonableness of cost."

PENNY/OHLMANN/NEIMAN INC., 1605 N. Main St., Dayton OH 45405. (513)278-0681. Creative Director: Karen Ingle. Art Directors: Jim Rupp, Jim Sichman. Ad agency.
Needs: Works with 3 illustrators and 3 designers/month. Uses artists for P-O-P displays, album covers, TV, renderings of building interiors, audiovisuals, billboards, calligraphy, cartoons, catalog illustrations/covers, convention exhibits, magazine editorial decorative spots, direct mail brochures, letterheads, layout, posters and trademarks.
First Contact & Terms: "Only pros who have had work published. Proximity is important." Call or write for interview. Prefers slides, photographs, photostats and b&w line drawings as samples. Samples not returned. Reports within 1 week. Works on assignment only. Provide a brochure and/or business card to be kept on file for future assignments. No originals returned to artist at job's completion. Pays $25-40/hour.

JEROME H. SCHMELZER & ASSOCIATES, 750 Prospect Ave., Cleveland OH 44115. (216)696-5550. Vice-President: Michael Prunty. Ad agency and public relations firm. Clients: retail, industrial, institutional. Client list provided on request.
Needs: Assigns 15-20 freelance jobs/year. Works with 1 freelance illustrator/month. Uses artists for consumer and trade magazines, brochures, catalogs, filmstrips, P-O-P displays and AV presentations.
First Contact & Terms: Local artists only. Send query letter with resume, business card and samples to be kept on file. Write for appointment to show portfolio. Prefers photographs and photostats as samples. Samples returned only if requested. Reports only if interested. Works on assignment only. Pays by the hour, $7-20; by the project, $500-1,500. "We keep originals at completion of job." Considers complexity of project, skill and experience of artist, and turnaround time when establishing payment. Buys all rights.
Tips: "Be professional, business-like and able to handle pressure of time."

*****TRIAD**, (Terry Robie Industrial Advertising, Inc.), 124 N. Ontario St., Toledo OH 43624. (419)241-5110. Vice President/Creative Director: Janice Robie. Ad agency/graphics/promotions. Clients: industrial, consumer, medical.
Needs: Assigns 30 freelance jobs/year. Works with 1-2 freelance illustrators/month and 2-3 freelance designers/month. Uses artists for consumer and trade magazines, brochures, catalogs, newspapers, filmstrips, stationery, signage, P-O-P displays, AV presentations, posters and illustrations (technial and/or creative).
First Contact & Terms: Send query letter with resume and samples to be kept on file. Prefers slides, photographs, photostats or printed samples. Samples returned by SASE if not kept on file. Reports only if interested. Works on assignment only. Pays by the hour, $10-60; by the project, $25-2,500. Considers client's budget, and skill and experience of artist when establishing payment. Negotiates rights purchased.
Tips: "We are interested in knowing your specialty."

Oklahoma

ADVERTISING INCORPORATED, Box 707626, Tulsa OK 74170. (918)747-8871. Director of Illustration: David Butterfield. Ad agency. Clients: industrial, financial, retail.
Needs: Works with 12 + freelance artists/year. Uses artists primarily for finished illustration; also design and layout. Especially important are the ability to take direction, quick turnaround and prompt delivery, and tight, clean illustration.
First Contact & Terms: Works on assignment only. Send query letter with brochure and samples to be kept on file; call or write for appointment to show portfolio. Prefers photostats, photographs or slides as samples. Samples not filed are returned by SASE. Reports back only if interested. Pays by the project, $100 minimum. Considers complexity of the project, client's budget, skill and experience of artist, turnaround time and rights purchased when establishing payment. Buys all rights.
Tips: "We expect quick turnaround time."

ANDERSON BAKER BEAM, Box 4114, Tulsa OK 74159. (918)587-8883. Art Director: Anne Evans. Ad agency. Clients: primarily financial institutions. Client list provided upon request with SASE.
Needs: Works with 12-15 freelance artists/year. Uses artists for everything from illustration and design to paste-up. Especially looks for the ability to translate written or verbal instructions into effective art.
First Contact & Terms: Local artists get first consideration only because of time factors. Works on assignment only. Send query letter with samples. Samples not filed returned by SASE. Reports only if interested. Pay varies. Considers complexity of project, client's budget, skill and experience of artists, geographic scope for the finished product, turnaround time and rights purchased when establishing payment. Buys all rights.
Tips: "Show us how versatile you can be. If you're good in more than one aspect of art (i.e., cartooning, airbrushing, illustration, pen & ink sketches—whatever), we'd like to know that."

HOOD, HOPE & ASSOCIATES, Box 35408, Tulsa OK 74153. (918)250-9511. Executive Art Director: Karl Tani. Ad agency. Clients: sporting goods, financial, industrial and retail firms; client list provided upon request.
Needs: Works with 3-4 illustrators/year. Uses freelance artists for billboards, consumer and trade magazines, direct mail, P-O-P displays, brochures, catalogs, posters, newspapers and AV presentations.
First Contact & Terms: Local artists only. Telephone or stop by office. Prefers slides as samples. Samples returned. Reports within 1 week. Works on assignment only. Provide business card and tear sheet to be kept on file for possible future assignments. Pays by the project.

Oregon

WILLIAM CAIN INC., 1500 SW 1st Ave., Portland OR 97201. (503)222-5940. Art Director: Jack Allen. Ad agency. Clients: industry, port authority.
Needs: Assigns 340 freelance jobs/year including photographers. Works with 2 freelance illustrators and 4 freelance designers/month. Uses artists for consumer and trade magazines, direct mail packages, brochures, newspapers and P-O-P displays.
First Contact & Terms: Prefers artists with "quality work, dependability and a firm understanding of price before beginning job." Send brochure to be kept on file. Call or write for appointment to show portfolio. Prefers photostats or printed brochures as samples. Samples not kept on file are returned. Reports only if interested. Works on assignment only. Pays by the project, $150-2,000 average. Considers complexity of project, client's budget, and skill and experience of artists when establishing payment. Buys all rights.
Tips: "Make sure your work is competitive with the top people in your field. Deliver on time. Be extremely neat in your presentation. Don't talk too much."

***CREATIVE COMPANY, INC.**, 345 Court St. NE, Salem OR 97301. (503)363-4433. President/Owner: Jennifer Larsen. Specializes in corporate identity and packaging. Clients: local consumer-oriented clients, professionals, and trade accounts on a regional and national level, all in the Salem/Valley area.
Needs: Works with 3-4 freelance artists/year. Uses artists for design, illustration, retouching, airbrushing, posters and lettering. "Clean, fresh designs!"
First Contact & Terms: Prefers local artists. "We also require a portfolio review. Years of experience not important if portfolio is good." Works on assignment only. Send query letter with brochure, resume, business card and samples to be kept on file; call for appointment to show portfolio. Accepts photocopies or tear sheets as samples. "We prefer one-on-one review of portfolio to discuss individual projects/time/approach." Samples returned only if requested. Reports only if interested. Pays for design by the hour, $10-30 average. Pays for illustration by the hour, $25-40 average. Considers complexity of project and skill and experience of artist when establishing payment.
Tips: "Don't drop in, always call and make an appointment. Have a clean and well-organized portfolio, and a resume or something to keep on file."

GREEN/ASSOCIATES ADVERTISING, INC., 1176 W. 7th St., Box 2565, Eugene OR 97402. (503)343-2548. Art Director: Bob Smith. AV/film/animation/TV producer; full-service ad agency with marketing and PR services.
Needs: Assigns 50-150 jobs/year. Works with 1 illustrator and 1 designer/month; 10 illustrators/year. Uses animators rarely. Uses artists for "all kinds of projects. We use freelancers when our staff is overloaded."
First Contact & Terms: Prefers experienced local artists, "unless the talent is rare, i.e., animation."

Send samples and query letter. ("Photostats (6) will do if they adequately show artist's work.") Arrange interview by mail, "phone only following negotiation by mail." Samples returned by SASE. Provide resume, samples, business card, tear sheet or other materials "if applicable and appropriate" to be kept on file for possible future assignments. Works on assignment only. Reports within weeks. "If we are talking a specific project—as we usually are—we report in a matter of days." Pays by the project. Method and amount of payment are negotiated with the individual artist. Pay "depends totally on project and artist's capability. This small market does not pay as well as larger ones." No originals returned to artist following publication "unless agreed to in advance." Negotiates rights purchased. "We usually reserve rights for clients."

Pennsylvania

*AMERICAN ADVERTISING SERVICE, 121 Chestnut, Philadelphia PA 19106. Creative Director: Joseph Ball. Ad agency. Prefers personal contact, but mailed art or photocopies OK. Not responsible for art after submission.
Needs: Advertising, billboards, package design, graphic design, commercials, cover design, exhibits and art renderings.

ANIMATION ARTS ASSOCIATES INC., Lee Park, Suite 301, 1100 E. Hector St., Conshohocken PA 19428. President: Harry E. Ziegler. AV/motion picture/TV producer. Clients: government, industry, education and TV. Audience: engineers, doctors, military, general public. Produces 35/16mm films, sound/slide programs and filmstrips.
Needs: Works with designers and illustrators. Uses artists for filmstrips, motion pictures and animation.
First Contact & Terms: Call for interview. Provide resume to be kept on file for possible future assignments. No work returned at job's completion. Pays $5-10/hour, cartoon and technical animation.

BAKER PRODUCTIONS INC., 1501 Walnut St., Philadelphia PA 19102. (215)988-0434. President: Alan Baker. Produces TV film and videotape commercials, documentaries, industrial films, and computer graphics.
Needs: Buys approximately 100 designs/year. Uses artists for logo designs for TV commercials, storyboards, title cards and titles. Uses very few freelancers.
First Contact & Terms: Local artists only. Prefers artists with broadcast art or ad agency experience. Write for interview. Prefers photographs as samples. Samples not returned. Reports within 1 week "if prospect is pending"; otherwise, in 3 weeks. Works on assignment only. Provide resume to be kept on file for possible future assignments. Buys all rights. Pays $9/panel, storyboards; $12/title card, titles.
Tips: Most graphics used are computer generated.

TED BARKUS CO. INC., 225 S. 15th St., Philadelphia PA 19102. President/Creative Director: Ted Barkus. Ad agency/PR firm. Serves clients in finance and in manufacturing of various products.
Needs: Works with 2 illustrators and 1 designer/month. Uses designers for billboards, P-O-P displays, consumer and trade magazines, stationery design, multimedia kits, direct mail, TV, slide sets and newspapers. Uses illustrators for brochures/flyers.
First Contact & Terms: Local artists with experience working with similar firms only. Prefers slides, photographs and b&w line drawings as samples. Samples returned by SASE. Reports in 2 weeks. Works on assignment only. Send business card to be kept on file. No original work returned after job completed. Pay is by the project or by the hour, $10-25 average. Considers complexity of project and skill and experience of artist when establishing payment.

*COLOR FILM SERVICE, INC., 46 Garrett Rd., Upper Darby PA 19082. (215)352-2350. Vice President: Gary N. Gruerio. Audivisual firm. Clients: commercial and industrial.
Needs: Uses artists for line work, paste-up type and mechanicals, concept, design for 35mm slides. "Artist must have the ability to work efficiently with our own staff, and have experience working with 35mm slides."
First Contact & Terms: Local artists only who can work anytime, day, night, weekend. Send query letter with resume and samples to be kept on file; call or write for appointment to show portfolio. Prefers photostats or slides as samples. Samples not filed are returned by SASE. Reports only if interested. Pays by the hour, according to experience. Considers complexity of project and skill and experience of artist when establishing payment. Buys all rights.

EDUCATIONAL COMMUNICATIONS INC., 761 Fifth Ave., King of Prussia PA 19406. Contact: Art Director. Audiovisual firm. Clients: automotive, pharmaceutical.

Needs: Works with 2-3 freelance artists/year. Uses artists for overload—cartoons and technical illustrations. Especially important are cartoon or technical illustration skills.
First Contact & Terms: Works on assignment only. Send query letter with resume to be kept on file. Samples are not returned. Does not report back. Considers complexity of the project, and skill and experience of artist when establishing payment. Buys all rights.

MARTIN EZRA & ASSOCIATES, 48 Garrett Rd., Upper Darby PA 19082. (215)352-9595. President: Martin Ezra. AV/film producer. Producer of special projects in communications. Serves clients in industry, education, ad agencies and associations. Produces films, filmstrips, slide/tape and multimedia productions for sales, training and education.
Needs: Assigns 50 + jobs/year. Works with 2 illustrators, 1 animator and 2 designers/month. Uses artists for AV, film and print work, including design, illustration and mechanics.
First Contact & Terms: Prefers artists from the Philadelphia, Washington DC and New York City areas. Send representative samples, including slides, that do not need to be returned. Arrange interview by phone or by mail. Provide samples, brochure/flyer, business card and tear sheets to be kept on file for possible future assignments. Works on assignment only. Method and amount of payment are negotiated with the individual artist. Original artwork sometimes returned following publication, "depending on assignment and client requirements." Negotiates rights purchased; type of rights purchased "depends on assignment."

HOOD LIGHT & GEISE, 509 N. 2nd St., Harrisburg PA 17101. (717)234-8091. Art Director: Paul Gallo. Advertising/public relations firm. Serves clients in banking, commercial attractions and associations.
Needs: Uses artists for illustrations and brochure paste-up.
First Contact & Terms: Query with samples. SASE. Reports within 1 week. Pays hourly for paste-up; pays by job for illustrations.

JERRYEND COMMUNICATIONS, INC., Rt. #2, Box 356H, Birdsboro PA 19508. (215)689-9118. Vice President: Gerard E. End, Jr. Advertising/PR firm. Clients: industry, banks, technical services, professional societies and automotive aftermarket.
Needs: Assigns 3-5 freelance jobs/year. Uses 1-2 freelance illustrators/month. Uses artists for trade magazines, brochures, signage, AV presentations, posters and press releases.
First Contact & Terms: Works "primarily with local artists for time, convenience and accessibility." Send query letter with tear sheets to be kept on file. Samples not kept on file returned only if requested. Reports within 2 weeks. Works on assignment only. Pays by the hour, $25-50 average. Considers complexity of project, client's budget, turnaround time and rights purchased when establishing payment. Buys all rights.
Tips: Have a "realistic approach to art; clients are conservative and not inclined to impressionistic or surrealistic techniques."

J.B. LIPPINCOTT CO., Media Development/Health Sciences Division, E. Washington Square, Philadelphia PA 19105. (215)238-4200. Editor-in-Chief, Media Department: H. Michael Eisler. AV producer. Audiences: nursing and medical professions. Produces self-instructional and other educational multi-frame audiovisual presentations in the health sciences (16mm, ¾" videocassettes and 35mm sound filmstrips).
Needs: Assigns 3 jobs/year. Uses artists for full-color artboards for 35mm strips; illustrations for 16mm filming with background, sized and colored for filming and projection; and line drawings for workbooks.
First Contact & Terms: Artists should have previous experience with slides, filmstrips and motion pictures, also with anatomy, biology and medical illustrations for projectables. Prefers, but is not restricted to, local artists (Boston-Washington corridor). Query with brochure/flyer and resume to be kept on file for future assignments. Reports in 1 month. Works on assignment only. Material copyrighted. Free catalog. No originals returned to artist at job's completion. Pays $30-50/frame; negotiable. Also pays by the project; "payment varies depending on media format." Buys all rights.

MARC AND COMPANY, 3600 U.S. Steel Bldg., Pittsburgh PA 15219. (412)562-2000. Art Director: Bob Griffing. Ad agency. Clients: retailers, fast food, office furniture; no industrial accounts.
Needs: Works with 4-5 illustrators/month. Uses freelance artists for direct mail, P-O-P displays, brochures, catalogs, posters, signage, newspapers, storyboards and AV presentations.
First Contact & Terms: Works primarily with local artists. Query with resume first and then arrange interview to show portfolio. Works on assignment only. Negotiates payment according to client's budget.

B.C. NEWTON MARKETING & ADVERTISING, 178 N. Madison Ave., Highland Park PA 19082. Art/Creative Director: B.C. Newton. Ad agency. Clients: retail, consumer and industrial.

Needs: Buys 200 illustrations/year. Uses artists for billboards, consumer magazines, stationery design, direct mail, television, slide sets, brochures/flyers, trade magazines, newspapers and books; lettering, layout, paste-up and mechanicals. Especially needs storyboards, slide presentation for audiovisuals and illustration.
First Contact & Terms: Local artists only. Provide business card and brochure/flyer. Prefers photostats and slides as samples. SASE. Reports back only if interested. No originals returned to artist at job's completion. Works on assignment only. Pays $5-10/hour for layout, paste-up and mechanicals. Considers complexity of project and client's budget when establishing payment.

NYCOM, (formerly New York Communications, Inc.), Suite 300, 101 Bryn Mawr Ave., Bryn Mawr PA 19010. (215)527-5100. Creative Supervisor: Howard Mermel. Motion picture/TV/marketing consulting firm. Clients: radio & TV stations.
Needs: Uses artists for motion pictures and storyboards. Works with 2 illustrators and 1 designer/month.
First Contact & Terms: Query with resume. Reports within 1 week. Works on assignment only. Provide resume, sample storyboards, business card, brochure/flyer to be kept on file for future assignments. Prefers "anything demonstrating talent for color storyboards" (original work/photostats) as samples. Samples not kept on file returned by SASE. No originals returned to artist at job's completion. "Average pay is $10 per panel on a storyboard. Most storyboards are comprised of 8 to 12 frames. It really depends on the artist's talent." Considers skill and experience of artist and turnaround time when establishing payment.
Tips: "Pay attention to composition in TV commercials. Look at how the shots in the best commercials are set up (placement of actors, background details, etc)."

*PERCEPTIVE MARKETERS AGENCY LTD., Suite 903, 1920 Chestnut St., Philadelphia PA 19103. (215)665-8736. Art Director: Marci Mansfield-Fickes. Ad agency. Clients: retail furniture, contract furniture, commuter airline, lighting distribution company; several nonprofit organizations for the arts, and a publishing firm.
Needs: Works with 15-20 freelance artists/year. In order of priority, uses artists for mechanicals, photography, illustration, comps/layout, photo retouching and design/art direction. Concepts, ability to follow instructions/layouts and precision/accuracy are important.
First Contact & Terms: Uses mostly local talent. Send resume and samples to be kept on file; call for appointment to show portfolio. Accepts photostats, photographs and tear sheets as samples—"whatever best represents artist's work—but preferably not slides." Samples not filed are returned by SASE only. Reports only if interested. Pays by the hour, $10 minimum; by the project, $50 minimum. Considers complexity of the project, client's budget and turnaround time when establishing payment. Buys all rights.
Tips: "Freelance artists should approach us with unique, creative and professional work. And it's especially helpful to follow-up interviews with new samples of work, (i.e., to send a month later a 'reminder' card or sample of current work to keep on file.)"

THE REICH GROUP, INC., 230 S. Broad St., Philadelphia PA 19102. (215)546-1636. Art Director: Yvonne Mucci. Ad agency. Specializes in print media and direct mail/collateral material. Clients: banks, insurance companies, business to business services, associations, religious groups.
Needs: Works with 15-20 freelance artists/year. Uses artists for advertising and brochure design and illustration, design of direct mail kits and illustrations for association magazines. Rarely uses unusual techniques; prefers primarily realistic styles. No cartoons.
First Contact & Terms: Send query letter with samples to be kept on file; write for appointment to show portfolio. Prefers to review photocopies or other types of samples which are nonreturnable. Reports only if interested. Works on assignment only. Pays by the hour, $12-25 average; by the project, $125-400 average. Considers skill and experience of artist, turnaround time and rights purchased when establishing payment.
Tips: "Show commercial work that has been used in print. No school samples or experimentals."

LIZ SCOTT ENTERPRISES, 3514 5th Ave., Pittsburgh PA 15213. (412)661-5429. Manager: Liz Scott. Ad/PR firm. Clients: social service agencies, small businesses and individuals.
Needs: Assigns 3-5 jobs/year. Uses artists for illustration and mechanicals for annual reports, ads and brochures.
First Contact & Terms: Local artists only. "Send letter, follow up with call and arrange interview to show work." SASE. Reports in 2-3 weeks. No originals returned to artist at job's completion. Negotiates pay; $15 minimum/hour. Considers skill and experience of artist when establising payment.
Tips: "Don't label yourself as 'fashion' or 'graphic'; this makes you look limited to us." Experience in commercial work preferred.

*E.J. STEWART, INC., 525 Mildred Ave., Primos PA 19018. (215)626-6500. Production Coordinator: Karen Brooks. TV producer. Serves clients in industry, education, government, interactive video and advertising. Produces videotape programs and commercials.
Needs: Assigns 50 + jobs/year. Works with 2 illustrators and 2 designers/month. Uses artists for set design and storyboards.
First Contact & Terms: Philadelphia area artists only. Send resume. Provide resume, brochure/flyer and business card to be kept on file for possible future assignments. Works on assignment only. Reports in 3 weeks. Method and amount of payment are negotitated with the individual artist. No originals returned to artists following publication. Buys all rights.
Tips: "There is more interest in computer generated animation in our field. 10% of work is cartoon-style illustrations."

THOMAS R. SUNDHEIM INC., The Benson East, Jenkintown PA 19046. Vice President/Creative Director: John F. Tucker, Jr. Serves clients in industrial and scientific products and services.
Needs: Works with 3 illustrators, 3 designers/year. Uses artists for illustration, technical art, retouching, trade magazines, direct mail and collateral; also work on P-O-P displays, stationery design and newspapers.
First Contact & Terms: Prefers local artists. Works on assignment only. Call for interview. Provide business card, brochure/flyer and samples to be kept on file for possible future assignments. Prefers roughs through final as samples. Samples returned by SASE. No originals returned to artist at job's completion.
Tips: "Imitation is all I'm finding—and imitation of pretty bad stuff. Learn about our clients' products before coming in—don't expect me to brief you." Looks for the artist's *style* in samples or a portfolio.

Rhode Island

BUDEK FILMS & SLIDES, 73 Pelham St., Newport RI 02840. (401)846-6580. Director: Elizabeth Allen. AV producer. Serves clients in education. Produces 35mm slides of architecture, painting and sculpture.
Needs: Assigns 1-4 jobs/year. "Purchases slides of architecture, painting or sculpture, textiles, decorative arts." Send resume, query letter and samples (original 35mm color slides preferred). Arrange interview by mail. Samples returned by SASE if not kept on file. Provide resume and samples to be kept on file for possible future assignments. Reports within 3 weeks. Method and amount of payment are negotiated with the individual artist. Considers complexity of project, client's budget, skill and experience of artist and rights purchased when establishing payment.

South Carolina

BRADHAM-HAMILTON ADVERTISING, INC., Box 729, Charleston SC 29402. (803)884-6445. Art Director: Mike Schumpert. Ad agency. Clients: savings and loan, regional shopping mall, hotels, dairy, managers and service industries. Clients: financial institutions, hotel, resort, mall, dairy, restaurants, fast food, contractor, manufacturer.
Needs: Assigns 100 freelance jobs/year. Works with a total of 2-3 freelance illustrators and 2-3 freelance designers. Uses artists for consumer and trade magazines, billboards, direct mail packages, brochures, newspapers, filmstrips, P-O-P displays, AV presentations and posters. Needs pen & ink, pencil, wash, acrylic and airbrush.
First Contact & Terms: Send query letter with brochure and samples to be kept on file. Call for appointment to show portfolio. Prefers photostats or tear sheets as samples. Samples not kept on file returned by SASE. Reports within 2 weeks. Works on assignment only. Pays $50-500 average. Considers complexity of project, client's budget, skill and experience of artist and turnaround time when establishing payment. All rights purchased.
Tips: "Approach us in a business-like, professional way: write a letter and follow-up with a phone call. Submit samples of specific type of work requested."

SHOREY & WALTER INC., 1617 E. North St., Greenville SC 29607. (803)242-5407. Senior Art Director: Lance C. Bell. Full service ad agency specializing in industrial clients.
Needs: Uses illustrators.
First Contact & Terms: Query with samples. Provide materials to be kept on file for future assignments. Samples not returned. Does not report back. Works on assignment only. No originals returned at job's completion. Pays by the project. Considers complexity of project, client's budget, and skill and experience of artist when establishing payment.

Tennessee

WARD ARCHER & ASSOCIATES, INC., 65 Union at Front, Box 3300, Memphis TN 38173-0300. (901)526-8700. Ad agency/PR firm. Clients: industrial, agricultural, consumer goods. Media used include billboards, consumer magazines, trade magazines, direct mail, newspapers, P-O-P displays, radio and TV.
Needs: Works with 4 illustrators/month. May be assigned as many as 4 jobs in 1 month. Uses artists for P-O-P displays, stationery design, direct mail and brochures/flyers.
First Contact & Terms: Write with resume requesting an interview to show portfolio. Reports in 4 weeks. Works on assignment only. Provide business card and brochure/flyer to be kept on file for future assignments. "Many variables determine price."
Portfolio Tips: "Be professional. Pride in work is expected, but ego can't get in the way. Twenty samples are usually sufficient, unless there are some pieces involving experimental processes. I like to see versatility in subject matter. I look for style and techniques, then determine which is best for the particular job at hand. Then, time and cost become important factors in determining who gets the assignment. Clients are becoming very price conscious."

BUNTIN ADVERTISING INC., 1001 Hawkins St., Nashville TN 37203. Director of Operations: Jack Pentzer. Clients: manufacturers, banks, shoes, fast foods and retail. Call for appointment. Must bring portfolio and be from the general area.
Needs: Uses artists for layout, mechanicals, illustration, paste-up, retouching and commercials for newspapers, radio, TV, magazines and direct mail.

METCALFE-COOK & SMITH, INC., 4701 Fronsdale Dr., Nashville TN 37220. (615)834-6323. President/Creative Director: Betty Cook. Ad agency. Clients: banks, fast food restaurants, industry and retail stores.
Needs: Assigns 26 freelance jobs/year. Works with 2 freelance illustrators and 2-5 freelance designers/month. Uses artists for trade magazines, billboards, brochures, catalogs, newspapers and filmstrips.
First Contact & Terms: Local artists only. Send business card and samples to be kept on file. Write for appointment to show portfolio. Prefers slides, photographs or photostats as samples. Samples not kept on file are returned by SASE. Reports within 8-10 days. Works on assignment only. Pays by the hour or by the project. Considers complexity of project and client's budget when establishing payment. Negotiates rights purchased.

***MUSICAL IMAGE DESIGNS**, 1212 Ardee Ave., Nashville TN 37216. (615)226-1509. Creative Director: Stacy Slocum. Estab. 1984. Ad agency serving the music industry.
Needs: Works with an unlimited number of freelance artists/year. Uses artists for trademarks, letterheads, and T-shirts.
First Contact & Terms: Send resume and samples to be kept on file. Write for artists' guidelines. Prefers samples showing clear b&w designs on 8½x11 paper. Samples not filed are returned by SASE. Reports within 1 month. Considers complexity of the project and skill of artist when establishing payment. Buys first rights or all rights.
Tips: "Send sample of your idea involving musical instruments, stars, etc. If we accept your ideas and designs we will send a purchase agreement. All work must be original and unpublished."

Texas

ALAMO AD CENTER INC., 217 Arden Grove, San Antonio TX 78215. (512)225-6294. Art Director: Elias San Miguel. Ad agency/PR firm. Serves clients in medical supplies, animal breeding, food, retailing (especially jewelry), real estate and manufacturing.
Needs: Works with 6 illustrators and 4 designers/month. Uses artists for work in consumer magazines, brochures/flyers, trade magazines, album covers and architectural renderings and "overflow work."
First Contact & Terms: Local artists only. Arrange interview to show portfolio of tear sheets. Provide brochure, flyer, business card, resume and tear sheets to be kept on file for possible future assignments. SASE. Reports within 4 weeks if interested. No originals returned at job's completion. Works on assignment only. Pay is negotiable. Considers skill and experience of artist when establishing payment.

ATKINS & ASSOCIATES, Suite 500, 1802 NE Loop 410, San Antonio TX 78217. (512)828-0611. Creative Director: David Parker. Ad agency. Clients: "full-range"—retail, industrial, financial, retaurants, etc.
Needs: Assigns 150 freelance jobs/year. Works with 4 freelance illustrators and 2 freelance designers/month. Uses artists for consumer and trade magazines, billboards, direct mail packages, brochures,

newspapers, signage, P-O-P displays and posters.
First Contact & Terms: Send query letter with brochure, business card and samples to be kept on file. Write for appointment to show portfolio. Prefers photographs, chromes gevas, original art or tear sheets to be kept on file. Reports only if interested. Works on assignment only. Pay is negotiated by the project. Considers complexity of project, client's budget, skill and experience of artist, geographic scope of finished project, turnaround time and rights purchased when establishing payment. Buys all rights or negotiates rights.
Tips: "Keep portfolio as brief as possible."

AVW PRODUCTIONS, 2241 Irving Blvd., Dallas TX 75207. (214)634-9060. Vice President: Bob Walker. AV/film/animation producer. Serves clients in industry and advertising. Produces multi-image materials, multiple-exposure slides, etc.
Needs: Works with 1-2 illustrators, 1-2 animators and 1-2 designers/year. Uses artist for "any projects that the inhouse staff can't handle."
First Contact & Terms: Artists must work at the company's facility in Dallas. Send resume, samples (slides preferred) and arrange interview by phone. Samples not kept on file are returned. Provide resume, samples, brochure/flyer and business card to be kept on file for possible future assignments. Works on assignment only. Reports within weeks. Pays by the project or by the hour. Method and amount of payment are negotiated with the individual artist. Payment varies with each client's budget. No originals returned to artist following publication. Negotiates rights purchased.

BOZELL & JACOBS, Box 61200, Dallas-Ft. Worth Airport TX 75261. (214)556-1100. Creative Director: Ron Fisher. Ad agency. Clients: all types.
Needs: Works with 4-5 freelance illustrators/month. Uses freelancers for billboards, newspapers, P-O-P displays, TV and trade magazines.
First Contact & Terms: Call for appointment to show portfolio. Reports within 3 weeks. Works on assignment only. Provide business card, brochure/flyer, resume and samples to be kept on file for possible future assignments. Samples not kept on file are returned. Payment is negotiated.
Tips: Wants to see a wide variety including past work used by ad agencies and tear sheets of published art.

DORSEY AGENCY, Box 64951, Dallas TX 75206. President: Mr. Lon Dorsey. Ad agency/PR firm/magazine publishers. Clients: corporate, industrial and retail.
Needs: Assigns 10-50 freelance jobs/year. Works with varied number of freelance illustrators and designers/month. Uses artists for consumer and trade magazines, billboards, direct mail packages, brochures, cartooning, catalogs, newspapers, stationery, signage, P-O-P displays, AV presentations and posters. New division in firm called "Cartooninks" seeks single-panel cartoons with gaglines; b&w line drawings, b&w or color washes. Themes include business, sports, oil; clean humor.
First Contact & Terms: Send query letter with brochure, resume, business card and samples to be kept on file. Write for appointment to show portfolio. "First contact *must* be made by mail. An example of work should be sent (photocopy or photocopy paste-up—no originals); no phone calls." Samples returned by SASE if requested by the artist; "we file if interested for later use." Especially looks for "a classy, clean style which is void of subversion and sexual overtones and which excels in strength, agility and good subject matter." Reports within 30 days. Pays by the project, $30-5,000. Considers complexity of project, client's budget, skill and experience of artist, turnaround time and rights purchased when establishing payment. Buys reprint rights, all rights or material not copyrighted.
Tips: There is a trend toward "detail in corporate artwork and corporate cartooning, food art, magazine art for covers, etc." Artists should "be brief, to the point, thorough and professional."

DYKEMAN ASSOCIATES INC., 4205 Herschel Rd., Dallas TX 75219. (214)528-2991. Contact: Alice Dykeman or Carolyn Whetzel. PR firm. Clients: business, industry, sports, environmental, energy, health. Assigns 150 jobs/year.
Needs: Works with 5 illustrators/designers per month. "We prefer artists who can both design and illustrate." Uses artists for design of brochures, exhibits, corporate identification, signs, posters, ads, title slides, slide artwork and all design and finished artwork for graphics and printed materials.
First Contact & Terms: Local artists only. Arrange interview to show portfolio. Provide business card and brochures. No originals returned to artist at job's completion. Pays by the project, $40-1,500 average; "artist makes an estimate; we approve or negotiate." Considers complexity of project, client's budget, skill and experience of artist and turnaround time when establishing payment.
Tips: "Be enthusiastic. Present an organized portfolio with a variety of work. Have a price structure but be willing to negotiate per project."

EMERY ADVERTISING, 1519 Montana, El Paso TX 79902. (915)532-3636. Art Director: Henry Martinez. Ad agency. Clients: automotive firms, banks, restaurants.

Needs: Works with 5-6 freelance artists/year. Uses artists for design, illustration, production.
First Contact & Terms: Works on assignment only. Send query letter with resume and samples to be kept on file; call for appointment to show portfolio. Prefers tear sheets as samples. Samples not filed returned by SASE. Reports back. Considers complexity of project, client's budget and turnaround time when establishing payment. Rights purchased vary according to project.
Tips: Especially looks for "consistency and dependability."

EVANS WYATT ADVERTISING, Gilbralter Savings Bldg., 5151 Flynn Pkwy., Corpus Christi TX 78411. (512)854-1661. Contact: Mr. E. Wyatt. Ad/exhibit/display/producer.
Needs: Assigns 500 freelance illustrations/year; uses some cartoons and humorous and cartoon-style illustrations.
First Contact & Terms: Query with samples or previously published work or arrange interview to show portfolio. Prefers scrapbook, slides or stats as samples. "No originals, please." Samples not kept on file are returned. Reports in 1 week. Works on assignment only. Provide business card, brochure/flyer, resume, samples, tear sheets and photocopies to be kept on file for possible future assignments. Pays by the project, by the day or by the hour, $50-90 average. Considers client's budget, and skill and experience of artist when establishing payment. "We pay flat for all rights."
Tips: More "by the project" assignments at negotiated charge. "Send 6-12 samples of general scope of work plus best specialty and price expected."

HEPWORTH ADVERTISING CO., 3403 McKinney Ave., Dallas TX 75204. (214)525-7785. Manager: S.W. Hepworth. Ad agency. Clients: finance, food, machinery and insurance.
Needs: Works with 2 illustrators and 2 designers/month. Uses artists for billboards, consumer magazines, direct mail, slide sets, brochures/flyers and trade magazines.
First Contact & Terms: Local artists only. Query with samples (tear sheets). Provide materials to be kept on file for future assignments. No originals returned to artist at job's completion.
Tips: Looks for variety in samples or portfolio.

INFORMEDIA, Box 13287, Austin TX 78711. (512)327-3227. President: Michael Sidoric. AV producer. Serves clients in industry, advertising, government and education. Produces new product introductions, marketing presentations, historical and educational slide multimedia presentations; single to 125 projector; single or multi-screen format; presentations both fixed and touring.
Needs: Assigns 60+ jobs/year. Works with 2 illustrators and 2 animators/month. Uses artists for specialized areas (historical, industrial) shows.
First Contact & Terms: Prefers "Southwestern artists who have backgrounds in strong graphics (line work) and who are familiar with 35mm slides as a medium. To be considered, one must have an unbounded imagination." Send query letter and a "representative sample of photostats or slides." Arrange interview by mail. Samples not returned. Provide samples, brochure/flyer and business card to be kept on file for possible future assignments. Works on assignment only. Reports in 1 month. Method and amount of payment are negotiated with individual artist. Payment varies according to client's budget. No originals returned to artist after publication. Negotiates rights purchased.
Tips: "AV demands rigid time and mechanical restrictions (i.e., pin registration). Artist must know capabilites and limitations of AV and be willing to experiment in this exciting new medium!"

KNOX PUBLIC RELATIONS, Suite A, Guthrie Creek Park, 708 Glencrest, Longview TX 75601. (214)758-6439. President: Donna Mayo Knox. PR firm. Clients: civic, social organizations, private schools and businesses.
Needs: Works with 2 illustrators/month. Uses artists for billboards, stationery design, multimedia kits, direct mail and brochures/flyers.
First Contact & Terms: Query. Prefers line drawings as samples. Samples returned by SASE. Works on assignment only. Reports in 3 weeks. Provide resume and portfolio to be kept on file for possible future assignments. Originals returned to artist at job's completion. Pays by the hour.
Tips: "Please query first."

McCANN-ERICKSON WORLDWIDE, Briar Hollow Bldg., 520 S. Post Oak Rd., Houston TX 77027. (713)965-0303. Senior Vice President/Creative Director: Jesse Caesar. Ad agency. Clients: all types including industrial, fashion, entertainment, computers and high tech.
Needs: Works with about 20 freelance illustrators/month. Uses freelancers in all media.
First Contact & Terms: Call for appointment to show portfolio. Selection based on portfolio review. Negotiates payment based on client's budget and where work will appear.
Tips: Wants to see full range of work including past work used by other ad agencies and tear sheets of published art in portfolio.

McNEE PHOTO COMMUNICATIONS INC., 1622 W. Alabama, Houston TX 77006. (713)526-5110. President: Jim McNee. AV/film producer. Serves clients in industry and advertising. Produces slide presentations, video tapes, brochures and films.
Needs: Assigns 20 jobs/year. Works with 4 illustrators/month. Uses artists for brochures, annual reports and artwork for slides, film and tape.
First Contact & Terms: Prefers local artists with previous work experience. "Will review samples by appointment only." Provide resume, brochure/flyer and business card to be kept on file for possible future assignments. Works on assignment only. Reports within 1 month. Method of payment is negotiated with the individual artist. Pays by the hour, $30-60 average. Considers client's budget when establishing payment. No originals returned after publication. Buys all rights, but will negotiate.

MEDIA COMMUNICATIONS, INC., 1001 MoPac Circle, Austin TX 78746. (512)327-7890. Production Manager: Nancy Hargis. Ad agency. Clients: "wide variety" of accounts, financial institutions, fast food, real estate and high tech.
Needs: Freelance artists used on all accounts. Uses freelance artists for consumer and trade magazines, direct mail, P-O-P displays, brochures, catalogs, posters, signage, newspapers and AV presentations.
First Contact & Terms: Arrange interview to show portfolio. Reports within 1 week. Works on assignment only. Pays by the hour, $30-45 average; by the project, $200 minimum. Considers complexity of project, client's budget, skill and experience of artist, geographic scope of finished project and turnaround time when establishing payment.

METZDORF-MARSCHALK, 3040 Postoak, Houston TX 77056. (713)840-0491. Art Director: Ellie Malivis. Ad agency. Clients: consumer, food, financial and some industrial firms.
Needs: Works with 12 illustrators/year. Uses freelance artists for billboards, consumer and trade magazines, direct mail, catalogs, posters, newspapers and advertising.
First Contact & Terms: Send slides, tear sheets, photostats or cards showing style used, or contact through artist representative. Reports only if interested. Works on assignment only. Usually deals with artist representative about payment for illustrators. Pays by the project, $125-4,000 average. Considers complexity of project and rights purchased when establishing payment.
Tips: "We are looking for artists with specific styles or specialties or unusual treatments to otherwise mundane subjects. Send examples of your work before attempting to make an appointment. Postcard mailings have been successful."

*MULTI-IMAGE RESOURCES, 14832 Venture Dr., Dallas TX 75234. Art Director: Janet Wrzesinski. Audiovisual firm. Clients: ad agencies, banks, restaurants and major corporations.
Needs: Works with 2 freelance artists/year. "When our work load is too much we use artists to produce art used in multi-media productions, some cartoons, stage set renderings. Especially important is knowledge of paste-up, pens and other tools, and colors in light; darkroom skills very helpful.
First Contact & Terms: Must have experience in audiovisual. Send resume to be kept on file; call for appointment to show portfolio. Prefers slides or tear sheets as samples. Samples not filed are returned only if requested. Reports only if interested. Pays by the hour, $8-20 average. Considers complexity of the project, client's budget and turnaround time when establishing payment. Buys all rights.

PHOTO-SYNTHESIS INC., Suite 190, 3160 Commonwealth, Dallas TX 75247. Producer: John Kindervag. AV producer. Clients: mostly corporate. Produces slide sets and audiovisual shows. Assigns 15 jobs/year minimum.
Needs: Uses artists for slide illustrations and freelance production people.
First Contact & Terms: Local artists only. Query with resume and samples and arrange interview to show portfolio. Prefers photostats, slides or printed material as samples. Samples returned by SASE. Reports only if interested. Works on assignment only. Provide portfolio with resume, business card, tear sheet, brochure and/or flyers to be kept on file for future assignments. Pays by the project; or pays $5-30/hour. Considers skill and experience of artist when establishing payment.
Tips: There is a trend toward "expansion to all forms of business communications." Artists interested in working for us should be "neat, clean and dependable."

NEAL SPELCE COMMUNICATIONS, Suite 15, Inter-First Tower, Austin TX 78701. (512)476-4644. Creative Director: D. Childress. Ad agency. Serves clients in finance, hospitals, professional associations and real estate.
Needs: Works with 3 illustrators and 4 designers/month. Uses artists for consumer and trade magazines, direct mail, newspapers, P-O-P displays, brochures/flyers and TV.
First Contact & Terms: Write requesting interview to show portfolio (illustrations and printed pieces incorporating the illustrations), send resume or make contact through artist's rep. Prefers slides or photostats as samples. Samples returned by SASE. Reports within 2 weeks. Works on assignment only. Pro-

vide resume, brochure or promotional materials showing work and/or samples to be kept on file for future assignments. Pay is negotiable.
Tips: "We tend to use illustrators, rather than designers, for freelance work."

*TEXAS PACIFIC FILM VIDEO, INC., 501 N. I35, Austin TX 78702. (512)478-8585. Producer: Laura Kooris. Film/video production firm. Clients: ad agencies, music companies, etc. Client list provided for SASE.
Needs: Works with 5 freelance artists/year. Uses artists for set design, logos and signs, and costumes and makeup.
First Contact & Terms: Works on assignment only. Send query letter with samples to be kept on file; write for appointment to show portfolio. Prefers reels as samples. Samples not filed are returned by SASE. Reports only if interested. Pays by the project or by the day. Considers client's budget and skill and experience of artist when establishing payment. Rights purchased vary according to project.

WOMACK/CLAYPOOLE, Suite 501, 8585 N. Stemmons Fwy., Dallas TX 75247-3805. Senior Art Director: Bob Hult. Ad agency. Clients: petroleum, aviation, financial, insurance and retail firms.
Needs: Works with 2-3 illustrators/month. Uses freelance artists for billboards, brochures, AV presentations, print and collateral pieces.
First Contact & Terms: Arrange interview to show portfolio. Payment is by the project; negotiates according to client's budget or where work will appear.

*ZACHRY ASSOCIATES, INC., 709 N. 2nd, Box 1739, Abilene TX 79604. (915)677-1342. Art Director: T. Rigsby. Ad agency, audiovisual and printing firm. Clients: industrial, institutional and religious service. Client list provided for SASE.
Needs: Works with 6 freelance artists/year. Uses artists for illustration, calligraphy and mechanical preparation.
First Contact & Terms: Works on assignment only. Send query letter with samples, if available, to be kept on file; call or write for appointment to show portfolio. Samples not filed are returned by SASE. Negotiates payment. Considers complexity of the project, client's budget and turnaround time when establishing payment. Rights purchased vary according to project.

Utah

FRANCOM ADVERTISING, INC., Suite D-100, 5282 S. 320 West, Salt Lake City UT 84107. (801)263-3125. President: A. Sterling Francom. Ad agency. Clients: banks, car dealers, restaurants, industrial, video rental. Client list provided upon request.
Needs: Assigns 120 freelance jobs/year. Works with 3 freelance illustrators and 2 freelance designers/month. Uses artists for billboards, direct mail packages, brochures, catalogs, newspapers and signage.
First Contact & Terms: Local artists only. Send query letter with resume, business card and samples to be kept on file. Call for appointment to show portfolio; "portfolio and resume required." Prefers photographs as samples. Samples returned by SASE if not kept on file. Reports within 2 weeks. Works on assignment only. Pays by the project, $25-1,500; amount of payment negotiated with artist in advance. Considers complexity of project, client's budget and turnaround time when establishing payment. Material not copyrighted.
Tips: Artists should possess "creativity and professionalism, and full service capability from design concept to printer. Portfolio must include current commercial work similar to or complimentary to advertising agency's regular types of art work. Artwork submitted must be *commercial* art, not portraits, scenes, etc., either the original or published art of sample brochures, ads from newspapers, magazines, etc." Current trends include contemporary and computer generated design using high tech colors.

ALAN FRANK & ASSOCIATES INC., 1524 S. 11th E., Salt Lake City UT 84105. (801)486-7455. Art Director: Kazuo Shiotani. Serves clients in travel, fast food chains and retailing. Mail art. SASE. Reports within 2 weeks.
Needs: Illustrations, animation and retouching for annual reports, billboards, ads, letterheads, TV and packaging. Minimum payment: $500, animation; $100, illustrations; $200, brochure layout.

Vermont

IMAGE, 138 S. Willard St., Burlington VT 05401. (802)862-8261. President: Linda Kelliher. Ad agency. Clients: restaurants, automotive, ski resorts, banks, universities. Client list provided upon request.

Needs: Works with 3 freelance artists/year. Uses artists for illustrations and mechanical preparation when busy.
First Contact & Terms: Works on assignment only. Send query letter with resume and samples to be kept on file. Write for appointment to show portfolio. Accepts photostats, photographs, slides or tear sheets as samples. Samples not filed returned only if requested. Reports within 2-3 weeks. Considers complexity of project, client's budget, skill and experience of artist, geographic scope for the finished product, turnaround time and rights purchased when establishing payment. Rights purchased vary according to project.

NEW ENGLAND SLIDE SERVICE, (formerly Logoptics A-V), Box 231, Rutland VT 05701. (802)773-2581. President: David Fracht. AV producer. Serves clients in industry, government and advertising. Produces slide/tape presentations, single-projector and multi-screen shows, and graphic and effects slides.
Needs: Needs vary. Presently using artists for work overload.
First Contact & Terms: Prefers artists who live "within 1-1½ hours' driving time of Rutland, Vermont." Send resume and samples (slides preferred). Arrange interview by phone or mail. Samples returned. Provide resume and samples to be kept on file for possible future assignments. Works on assignment only. Reports within 1 month. Method and amount of payment are negotiated with the individual artist. Payment varies with each client's budget. No originals returned after publication. Negotiates rights purchased.

Virginia

DAN ADVERTISING & PUBLIC RELATIONS, 408 W. Bute St., Norfolk VA 23510. (804)625-2518. Art Director: Oliver Raoust. Ad/PR firm.
Needs: Uses artists for work in building and mechanical renderings, airbrushing, animation, TV animation, TV/film production, P-O-P displays, filmstrips, consumer magazines, multimedia kits, slide sets, brochures/flyers and finished work. Negotiates pay.
First Contact & Terms: Query with samples of previously published work. SASE. Reports within 3-4 weeks "if interested." Provide brochures, flyers, resume, tearsheets, samples and 3/4" video tape when possible to be kept on file for future assignments. Originals returned at completion on some jobs.

DEADY ADVERTISING, 17 E. Cary St., Richmond VA 23236. (804)643-4011. President: Jim Deady. Specializes in corporate identity, displays and publications. Clients: tobacco and porcelain accounts, and projects.
Needs: Works with 10-15 freelance artists/year. Uses artists for design, illustration, mechanicals, retouching and airbrushing; brochures, magazine, newspaper and advertisements.
First Contact & Terms: Local or regional artists only with minimum of 2 years' experience with an agency. Works on assignment only. Send query letter with resume to be kept on file; also send samples. Call or write for appointment to show portfolio. Prefers photographs as samples. Samples are returned. Reports back only if interested. Pays for design by the hour, $35-75 average, or by the project, $250-2,500 average; for illustration by the project, $275-1,500 average. Considers client's budget, skill and experience of artist and turnaround time when establishing payment.
Tips: "Be on time with all projects."

HAYCOX PHOTORAMIC INC., Box 12190, Norfolk VA 23502. (804)855-1911. Art Director: Betty Credle. AV/TV/film producer. Produces filmstrips, motion pictures, overhead transparencies, slide sets, sound-slide sets and videotapes.
Needs: Uses artists for slide illustrations, displays, mechanicals and schematics, on freelance/part-time basis.
First Contact & Terms: Prefers local artists. Query with resume and arrange interview to show portfolio. Prefers slides and photostats as samples. Samples returned by SASE. Reports in 2 weeks. Works on assignment only. Provide business card, resume, AV materials and graphic designs to be kept on file. Pays $5-10/hour.
Tips: Artists interested in working with us should "get experience in preparing art panels for slide shows."

*KSK COMMUNICATIONS, LTD., Suite 100, 1485 Chain Bridge Rd., McLean VA 22101. Art Directors: Gwynn Fuchs and Carol Meade. Ad agency. Clients: high-tech business.
Needs: Works with 6 freelance artists/year. Uses artists for illustration and production. Especially important are inking and mechanical skills and experience with stat camera.

First Contact & Terms: Local and regional artists only. Works on assignment only. Send query letter with business card and samples to be kept on file. Accepts photostats, photographs, slides, tear sheets, etc. as samples. Samples not filed are returned by SASE. Reports only if interested. Pays by the hour, $12 minimum. Considers complexity of the project, client's budget, skill and experience of artist, geographic scope for the finished product, turnaround time and rights purchased when establishing payment. Buys all rights.

PAYNE ROSS & DEVINS ADVERTISING, INC., 206 E. Jefferson St., Charlottesville VA 22901. (804)977-7607. Creative Director: Lisa Ross. Ad agency. Clients: resorts, thoroughbred farms, manufacturing plants, former President's home, bank.
Needs: Works with 12-20 freelance artists/year. Uses artists for photography, illustration and copy-writing; occasionally for paste-up. Especially looks for "experience, so that there is minimum supervision needed, but neatness and clarity are important."
First Contact & Terms: Send query letter with resume to be kept on file; call or write for appointment to show portfolio. Prefers to review slides or any good reproduction. Reports back only if interested. Pay varies according to "experience, type of work, etc." Considers skill and experience of artist and turnaround time when establishing payment. Rights purchased vary according to project.
Tips: "Please limit your portfolio to advertising and design, showing your best pieces only. Do not bring a lot of 'free sketches' and personal paintings. Don't show too many pieces (15 is plenty)."

WILLIAM C. PFLAUM CO. INC., Reston International Center, Reston VA 22091. (703)620-3773. Art Director: John Cuddahy. PR firm.
Needs: Works with 1-2 designers/month. Uses artists for stationery design, direct mail, television, slide sets, brochures/flyers, trade magazines and newspapers.
First Contact & Terms: Local artists only. Query with samples. No originals returned at job's completion.

SIDDALL, MATUS AND COUGHTER, Fidelity Bldg., 9th & Main Sts., Richmond VA 23219. Art Directors: Jessica Welton, Tom Hale. Ad agency/PR firm. Clients: industrial, travel, land development, bank, chemical.
Needs: Assigns 50 freelance jobs/year. Works with 4 freelance illustrators/month. Uses artists for consumer and trade magazines, billboards, direct mail packages, brochures, newspapers and posters.
First Contact & Terms: Send query letter with samples and tear sheets to be kept on file. Call or write for appointment to show portfolio. Prefers printed samples that can be kept. Samples returned only if requested. Reports only if interested. Works on assignment only. Considers complexity of project, client's budget, skill and experience of artist, geographic scope of fnished project, turnaround time and rights purchased when establishing payment. Buys all rights.

WEBB AND ATHEY, INC., 1703 Parham Rd., Richmond VA 23229. (804)285-8691. Executive Art Director: Robert Riffe. Full service ad agency. Clients: variety of accounts—real estate development, drug chain, elderly wellcare facility, financial, insurance and small business cooperative advertising.
Needs: Uses freelance artists to help provide a full range of collateral advertising and broadcasting for a wide range of clients.
First Contact & Terms: Make initial contact by phone and schedule interview to see portfolio.

Washington

A.L. SKAAR & COMPANY INC., Suite 209, South 104 Freya, Spokane WA 99202. (509)535-9702. Creative Director: Al Skaar. Ad agency. Clients: furniture manufacturers, retailers and distributors.
Needs: Works with 2 illustrators and 2 designers/month. Assigns 150 jobs and buys 50 illustrations/year. Uses artist for consumer magazines, stationery design, direct mail, television, brochures/flyers, trade magazines and newspapers. Also uses artists for poster design and illustration, spot illustrations and mechanicals.
First Contact & Terms: Query with resume and previously published work; "follow-up with phone call." SASE. Reports within 2 weeks. Fees negotiated.

SODERBERG AND ASSOCIATES, INC., Suite 500, 220 W. Mercer, Seattle WA 98119. Creative Director: Stan Soderberg. Ad agency. Serves clients in entertainment, manufacturing, finance, restaurants, automobile retailing, airplane kit manufacturing and sportswear manufacturing.
Needs: Works with 5-10 illustrators, 10-15 designers/month. Uses artists for layout, illustration, type

spec, paste-up, retouching and lettering for newspapers, magazines, TV, billboards, P-O-P displays, filmstrips and direct mail.
First Contact & Terms: Mail samples. Provide business card and flyer to be kept on file for possible future assignments. Originals sometimes returned to artist at job's completion.

WATTS-SILVERSTEIN, 1921 2nd Ave., Seattle WA 98101. (206)625-1875. Contact: R. Lindberg. AV producer. Serves clients in industry and advertising. Produces multi-image slide shows and print collateral.
Needs: Assigns 25 jobs/year. Works with 2 illustrators and 2 animators/month. Uses artists for "all our slide shows."
First Contact & Terms: Send resume and samples (slides preferred). Samples returned with SASE. Provide resume, samples and business card to be kept on file for possible future assignments. Works on assignment only. Reports within 2 weeks. Method and amount of payment are negotiated with the individual artist. Original art returned after publication. Negotiates rights purchased.

West Virginia

GUTMAN ADVERTISING AGENCY, 600 Board of Trade Building, Wheeling WV 26003. (304)233-4700. President: Milton Gutman. Ad agency. Clients: finance, glass, fast food, media, industrial supplies (tools, pipes) and furniture.
Needs: Works with 3-4 illustrators/month. Uses artists for billboards, stationery design, television, brochures/flyers, trade magazines and newspapers. Also uses artists for retouching work.
First Contact & Terms: Local artists only except for infrequent and special needs. Call for interview. Mail materials to be kept on file for possible future assignments. No originals returned at job's completion. Negotiates payment.

Wisconsin

BARKIN, HERMAN, SOLOCHECK & PAULSEN, INC., 777 E. Wisconsin Ave., Milwaukee WI 53202. (414)271-7434. Account Executive: Kathleen Sieja. Wisconsin's oldest PR firm. Clients: educational organization, financial, manufacturing, hospital, insurance, brewery, leisure time and real estate development.
Needs: Works with freelance illustrators and designers according to individual needs. Uses artists for all communications media.
First Contact & Terms: Call account executive for appointment to show portfolio. Negotiates payment depending on job requirements.

THE CRAMER-KRASSELT CO., 733 N. Van Buren, Milwaukee WI 53202. (414)276-3500. Executive Art Director: Robert Hagen. Ad agency. Clients: consumer, financial , industrial and service account.
Needs: Uses artists for consumer and trade magazines and newspapers.
First Contact & Terms: Call for names of individual art directors to contact. Sometimes shows are set up for portfolio review by all art directors and interested persons. Negotiates payment based on quotes from freelancers and available budget.
Tips: Likes to see artist's best work in color.

HOFFMAN YORK & COMPTON, 330 E. Kilbourne Ave., Milwaukee WI 53202. (414)289-9700. Contact: Art Director. Ad agency. Serves clients in machinery, food service.
Needs: Works with "many" illustrators/month. Needs vary. Uses freelancers and studios for all print media.
First Contact & Terms: Call for appointment to show portfolio. Negotiates payment.
Tips: Wants to see best work. Will probably use freelancer's area of specialty.

L. QUILLIN & ASSOCIATES, INC., V.I.P. Bldg., 2101 Victory St., La Crosse WI 54601. (608)788-8292. Vice President: Wayne Krause. Ad agency. Clients: manufacturing, business to business.
Needs: Works with 6-8 freelance artists/year. Especially important are skills, creativity and understanding needs.
First Contact & Terms: Works on assignment only. Send query letter with resume and samples to be kept on file. Call for appointment to show portfolio. Samples not filed are returned only if requested. Reports back only if interested. Pay varies. Considers complexity of the project, client's budget and turnaround time when establishing payment. Buys all rights.

SORGEL-STUDIOS, INC., 205 W. Highland Ave., Milwaukee WI 53203. (414)224-9600. Contact: Art Director. AV producer. Clients: business, corporate, multi-image and videotapes. Assigns 5 jobs/year.
Needs: Works with 1 illustrator/month. Uses artists for stylized illustrations, human figures and animation.
First Contact & Terms: Query with resume and samples (slides). SASE. Reports in 3 weeks. Provide resume and brochures/flyers to be kept on file for possible future assignments. No originals returned to artist at job's completion. Negotiates pay.
Tips: "Most of our artwork is now computer generated and that limits our use of freelancers."

ZIGMAN-JOSEPH-SKEEN, 700 North Water St., Milwaukee WI 53202. (414)273-4680. Office Manager: Barbara Andrietsch. PR firm. Clients: consumer, finance, investor, medical, health care, marketing and opinion research.
Needs: Freelance needs vary. Uses artists for annual reports, brochures, catalogs, posters, exhibits, layout, paste-up, newsletters and trade magazines. Negotiates pay based on client's budget.
First Contact & Terms: Call an account executive for appointment to show portfolio, send resume or samples. Prefers photographs, b&w line drawings, mock-ups of client's suggestions and examples of previous work as samples. Samples returned. Reporting time "depends on client's acceptance." Works on assignment only. Provide business card, samples, tear sheets, past work to be kept on file. Pays by the project.

Canada

*ATKINSON FILM-ARTS LTD., 19 Fairmont Ave., Ottawa, Ontario K1Y 1X4 Canada. (613)728-3513. Personnel Manager: Cathy Morriscey. Audiovisual firm. Produces animated motion pictures—cartoon and technical, series, features. Clients: corporate interests, government, small business, all areas.
Needs: Works with 150 freelance artists/year. Uses artists for animation, background and layout art. Artists must have "a graduate diploma from a classical animation program or a minimum of 3 years' experience in an animation studio and a demo reel of sample materials."
First Contact & Terms: Local artists perferred. Works on assignment only. Send query letter with resume and samples to be kept on file. Call or write for appointment to show portfolio. Prefers demo reels from animators and photographs from background and layout artists. Samples not filed are returned only by request with an SASE. Reports only if interested. Pays by the footage or per piece of artwork. Considers complexity of the project, client's budget, skill and experience of artist, geographic scope for the finished product, turnaround time and rights purchased when establishing payment. Buys all rights.

DOYLE DANE BERNBACH ADVERTISING LTD., Suite 1902, 77 Bloor St. W, Toronto, Ontario M5S 2Z8 Canada. (416)925-8911. Ad agency. Serves clients in automotives, consumer and personal products, entertainment and travel.
Needs: Use of freelance designers varies. Works with artists in all media.
First Contact & Terms: Call for appointment to show portfolio. Negotiates pay based on client's budget, amount of creativity required and where work will appear.

*DYNACOM COMMUNICATIONS, Box 702, Snowdon Station, Montreal, Quebec H3X 3X8 Canada. Director: David P. Leonard. Audiovisual/TV/film producer. Clients: large industries, government, education and health institutions.
Needs: Produces motion pictures, multimedia kits, overhead transparencies, slide sets, sound-slide sets, color videotapes and multiscreen mixed media "for training, motivation, sales, orientation and entertainment." Uses artists for album covers.
First Contact & Terms: Query with resume. Reports "only if we have a requirement." Buys all rights. Negotiates time of payment. Pays $20-40/frame, animated cartoons; $15-60, charts/graphs and technical art. Payment by hour: $5-15, advertising and illustrations; $5-10, lettering and mechanicals.

INSIGHT COMMUNICATIONS, 1850 Champlain Ave., Box 363, Whitby, Ontario L1N 5S4 Canada. (416)686-1144. Art Director: Garnet McPherson. AV firm. Clients: corporate, industry and travel industry.
Needs: Assigns 45 freelance jobs/year. Works with 2 freelance illustrators and 3 freelance designers/month. Uses artists for brochures, filmstrips, P-O-P displays, AV presentations, posters and graphics.
First Contact & Terms: Prefers "local artists for assignment; any artist for stock art or photography." Send query letter with business card and samples to be kept on file. Call for appointment to show portfolio. Prefers slides as samples, tear sheets will be accepted. Samples not kept on file are returned by SASE only if requested. Reports within 3 weeks. Pays by the project, $25-2,500 average. Considers

complexity of project, client's budget, skill and experience of artist and rights purchased when establishing payment. Negotiates rights purchased.

Tips: "In contacting us, artists should send query with samples, then call 2 weeks later for an appointment."

McCANN-ERICKSON ADVERTISING OF CANADA, Britannica House, 151 Bloor W, Toronto, Ontario MS5 1S8 Canada. (416)925-3231. Contact: Art Directors. Ad agency. Clients: consumer food, service industry and financial accounts.

Needs: Uses freelance artists and photographers on all accounts.

First Contact & Terms: Local artists only. Arrange a personal interview to show portfolio with individual art directors. Especially looks for a "unique style" in a portfolio—also "enthusiasm and dedication." Works on assignment only. Payment is by the project; negotiates according to client's budget and freelancer's previous experience.

Tips: "Artists should be more selective in the work they show. One poor piece of work lets down the whole portfolio."

Architectural, Interior & Landscape Design Firms

The ability to draw well is only one requisite for working with architectural, interior and landscape design firms. Artists must be able to render a building that is yet to be built, complete an interior according to someone else's taste or pictorially cultivate a landscape where only mud now collects. An understanding of architects' and designers' language and the ability to interpret blueprints are absolutes. A good sense of perspective, color and style (old and new) are musts. You will generally visualize the ideas of a client, architect, designer or staff personnel and since your assignment may not be a totally creative one, cooperation and flexibility are assets.

In this litigation-conscious society, realism and accuracy are high priorities among designers and architects. So as not to mislead a client, buildings, interiors and surroundings must be portrayed as they will actually appear.

Research the firm you're considering. Some projects require on-site construction visits, working closely with the designer and/or client from beginning to end. Others require executing renderings in the office or at home for presentations, while still others may mean a commission for fine art to complement the architecture and design. If it's within your interests and capabilities to provide one-of-a-kind artwork, sculpture, wall hangings—any type of fine art—remember that more and more collaboration is occurring among architect, landscape designer, interior designer and artist in order to create a total environment for the client.

Professionalism in face-to-face interviewing, a quality portfolio and a businesslike attitude are needed to land jobs with these firms. Designers and architects are often very busy people, so always make an appointment for a portfolio review. Gear your portfolio samples specifically to the reason you are approaching that firm; show your strongest skill so the firm can judge how well you fit into their plan. Have as much information as possible available with the sample of your work—the name of the client for whom you did the job, your involvement in the project, the length of time it took for completion and how much you were paid. All of this information at the fingertips of the reviewer saves time and energy for both of you.

To keep up on changes and trends in these fields refer to the *AIA Journal*, *Architectural Digest*, *Architectural Record* and *Interior Design* as well as *House & Garden*, *House Beautiful* and *Better Homes and Gardens*.

© Theresa Hart

Local artist Theresa Hart created this architectural rendering on commission for display in the office of Margot Siegel, AIA, Architect, Los Angeles. The art was also used in the firm's brochure and marketing pieces. Hart's "clean line style, good composition and values won her this assignment," says Margot Siegel.

ABEND SINGLETON ASSOCIATES INC., 20 W. 9th, Kansas City MO 64105. (816)221-5011. Contact: Steve Abend. Clients: corporate, government, institutional, commercial and residential. Services: architectural, interior design, engineering, planning and landscape architecture.
Needs: Works with 8 freelance artists for architectural renderings; 1, interior design; 2, graphic design; 2, model making; 1, landscape design; and 1, stained glass.

ARCHITECTURE +, 3rd Floor, 1220 N. 18th St., Monroe LA 71201. (318)387-2800. Chief Designer: William R. Acheson. Architectural planning firm providing all types of architectural design, working drawings and job supervision. Clients: commercial.
Needs: Works with 3-4 freelance artists/year. Uses artists for brochure design and layout, interior design, and interior and architectural renderings.
First Contact & Terms: Send query letter with brochure, resume and samples to be kept on file. Call for appointment to show portfolio. Prefers slides or photographs as samples. Samples not kept on file returned. Reports within 1 week. Works on assignment only. Pays by the hour, $30-35 average, for design; by the project for illustration, varies depending on complexity. Considers complexity of project, skill and experience of artist and turnaround time when establishing payment.

MILLARD ARCHULETA ASSOCIATES, 7440 N. Figueroa St., Los Angeles CA 90041. (213)254-9121. Director of Design: Frank J. Wong/AIA. Architectural firm providing original prints and limited editions. Clients: financial institutions, shopping centers, corporate office buildings.
Needs: Works with 12 freelance artists/year. Uses artists for interior and architectural renderings, landscape design, and model making.
First Contact & Terms: Send brochure to be kept on file; call for appointment to show portfolio. Prefers slides or photographs as samples. Reports only if interested. Pays for illustration by the project, $700-1,500 average. Considers client's budget when establishing payment.
Tips: "A very popular current trend is abstract design."

ARNOLD & STACKS ARCHITECTS, 527 W. Washington, Box 69, Jonesboro AR 72403. (501)932-5530; Box 1560, 901 Central Ave., Hot Springs AR 71902. (501)624-4678. Contact: Doug Arnold. Architectural/interior and landscape design firm providing planning, design, architecture, landscape design, graphic design, interior design and construction administration. Clients: private, public residential, governmental, educational, industrial.
Needs: Works with 1-2 freelance artists/year. Uses artists for advertising design, brochure design, illustration and layout; landscape and interior design, architectural and interior renderings, design consulting and furnishings.
First Contact & Terms: Send query letter with brochure, resume, business card, samples and tear sheets to be kept on file. Call for appointment to show portfolio. Prefers slides or photographs as samples. Reports within 2 weeks. Pay rate "depends on work, circumstances, etc." Considers complexity of project, client's budget, skill and experience of artist and turnaround time when establishing payment.

ART-IN-ARCHITECTURE PROGRAM, U.S. General Services Administration, 18th and F Sts. NW, Washington DC 20405. (202)566-0629. Director: Donald Thalacker. Clients: federal agencies.
Needs: Works with varying number of artists for murals, wall hangings, sculpture and stained glass. Uses artists to create works as an integral part of federal architecture. Recent commissions include interior sculpture by Robert Irwin, mural by Jennifer Bartlett and plaza sculpture by Richard Serra.
First Contact & Terms: Reports in 4 weeks. Provide resume and nonreturnable labeled 35mm color slides of existing work in plastic sheet to be kept on file for future assignments. Pays $750-250,000 for original art.
Tips: "Getting exposure is usually the key to getting more exposure. Even if you're not selected for a commission, your work has at least been seen and studied. And once your work has been seen, somebody may remember it. Don't waste time and money creating a design to submit to the panel. Send quality slides of completed work. Even if your work is great, a poor slide won't sell it. Though many commissioned works have been done by big names like Louise Nevelson and George Segal, there is plenty of room for locally and regionally-known artists. Of the approximately 20 artists accepted annually from about 1,000 applications, there are as many local and regional artists as there are nationally-known people." Looks for originality and a track record of good work. There is a trend towards "collaboration among artists, architects, landscape architects, designers, etc."

ASHWORTH SNYDER CORP., 2549 E. Brown, Phoenix AZ 85028. (602)992-6560. Contact: Dean Ashworth or Diane Blair. Architecture/commercial/apartments/golf course/resort hotels/landscape/interior design firm. Clients: commercial, industrial and residential.
Needs: Assigns 40 jobs/year. Uses artists for architectural renderings, art renderings, interior design, ar-

chitectural models, murals, ceramics, fiber arts and stained glass.
First Contact & Terms: Mail designs. SASE. Reports within 3 weeks. Pays $8-14/hour or $400-1,000 + /job or negotiates. Considers complexity of project, client's budget, skill and experience of artist, how work will be used, turnaround time and rights purchased when establishing payment.
Tips: Artists must show "very professional work." Artists should also go more into their personal background when selling themselves. "It would be great to know more details about how work was done."

ATELIER DESIGN GROUP, INC., (formerly Briel Rhame Poynter & Houser), 1437 Highland Ave., Melbourne FL 32935. (305)259-7005. Architect: William Doan AIA/ASID. Architecture/interior design firm providing architecture, interior architecture, space planning, interior furnishing selection. Clients: residential, commercial and industrial.
Needs: Works with 3 freelance artists/year. Uses artists for brochure design, illustration and layout; interior and landscape design; interior and architectural renderings; design consulting; furnishings and model making.
First Contact & Terms: Florida artists only; "geographic location is important for interfacing." Send query letter with brochure, resume and business card to be kept on file. Write for appointment to show portfolio. Prefers photostats or photographs as samples. Samples are returned. Reports only if interested. Works on assignment only. Pays by the project, $800-2,000 average. Considers complexity of project, client's budget, how work will be used and turnaround time when establishing payment.

LEON BARMACHE DESIGN ASSOCIATES LTD., 225 E. 57th St., New York NY 10022. (212)759-3840. Executive Designer: Leon Barmache F.A.S.I.D. Interior space planners and designer. Clients: private.
Needs: Needs artists to render interiors, furniture, rugs, etc., from rough sketches; b&w or color, for presentations. Also uses artists for design, illustration, displays and model making.
First Contact & Terms: Send query letter with brochure, resume and samples to be kept on file; call or write for appointment to show portfolio. Prefers photostats, copies or tear sheets as samples. Samples not filed returned by SASE only if requested. Reports within 2 weeks if interested. Pays by the project, $250-500 average for design and illustration. Considers the skill and experience of artist when establishing payment.
Tips: Artist should have "a portfolio of renderings showing his drawing capabilities using the means available—pencil, ink, marker, gouache, airbrush, etc."

BARNOUW & VASI, INC., Box 364, Katonah NY 10536. President: Alan A. Barnouw. Interior design firm. Clients: shopping centers, department stores, shops, showrooms, offices, banks, restaurants.
Needs: Works with 2-3 freelance artists/year. Uses artists for design and illustration.
First Contact & Terms: "Working with local artists is easier" and some experience is preferred because "we can't run a training program." Send query letter with resume and samples to be kept on file; "if representative samples of the artist's work are sent, we will contact the artist whose work and rates best suit our needs for a given project." Accepts "any medium" as samples, but "work will be filed. Photographs, if clear, are fine." Samples not filed are not returned. Reports within 2-3 weeks. Payment varies "based on the work to be performed, the type of project and the contractual arrangements." Considers the complexity of the project, skill and experience of the artist, turnaround time and "our 'budgeted' amount for artwork for any given project" when establishing payment.
Tips: "Give as much information as possible with your submitted sample—what the fee was, how long it took to complete, what information you were given. The more information we have to use in making a decision, the happier everyone will be in the end."

DWIGHT E. BENNETT & ASSOCIATES, 3929 Long Beach Blvd., Long Beach CA 90807. (213)595-1691. Contact: Dwight Bennett. Architecture firm. Clients: industrial, residential and commercial.
Needs: Assigns 6 jobs/year. Uses artists for architectural renderings.
First Contact & Terms: Local artists only. Query with brochure or samples. Reports within 1 week. Pays $400-2,500.

ALEXANDER BRAILAS ASSOCIATES, 8722 Ferris, Houston TX 77096. (713)668-2848. Architect: Alexander Brailas AIA. Architectural firm providing architecture and related services. Clients: institutional, commercial, industrial, health facilities, educational.
Needs: Uses artists for architectural renderings and model making.
First Contact & Terms: Send query letter with brochure to be kept on file. Call for appointment to show portfolio. Reports only if interested. Works on assignment only. Pays according to specific project requirements. Considers complexity of project, client's budget, skill and experience of artist, how work will be used and turnaround time when establishing payment.

Tips: Especially looks at color, composition and draftsmanship in samples or portfolio. Does not like artists "pushing trendy fads with color and composition."

BRENDLER-DOVE ASSOCIATES, INC., Suite 900, 300 Convent, San Antonio TX 78205. (512)271-7999. Marketing Director: Marcia Mattingly. Architectural, interior design, landscape design and promotional service firm. Clients: developers.
Needs: Works with 30 or more freelance artists/year. Uses artists for advertising and brochure design, illustration and layout; signage, charts and model making.
First Contact & Terms: Artists are "subcontracted under BDA corporate name." Send query letter with resume, business card and samples to be kept on file. Call or write for appointment to show portfolio. Prefers finished pieces or photographs as samples. Samples not filed not returned. Reports within 30 days. Payment varies according to project. Considers complexity of project, client's budget, skill and experience of artist, how work will be used, turnaround time and rights purchased when establishing payment.

LYNWOOD BROWN AIA AND ASSOCIATES, INC., 1220 Prince St., Alexandria VA 22314. (703)836-5523. President: L. Brown. Architectural firm providing architecture and engineering. Clients: commercial, industrial, institutional.
Needs: Works with 2-3 freelance artists/year. Uses artists for interior design, architectural renderings and model making.
First Contact & Terms: Works on assignment only. Send query letter with brochure; call for appointment to show portfolio. Prefers "photos or prints" as samples. Samples not filed are returned by SASE only if requested. Reports within 30 days. Pays for design by the hour, $9-20 average; for illustration by the hour, $8-18 average. Considers client's budget, skill and experience of artist and turnaround time when establishing payment.

BROWN, BROWN & ASSOCIATES, AIA, Suite 202, 1202 Richardson Dr., Richardson TX 75080. (214)235-8379. Contact: John Hall Brown, Sr. Architectural firm. Clients: churches, industrial, residential and commercial.
Needs: Assigns 12 jobs/year. Uses artists for architectural renderings, interior design and illustrations.
First Contact & Terms: Prefers artists who have worked with other firms of this type or have had work published. Arrange interview to show portfolio. SASE. Reports within 1 week. Pays $300-1,500/job. Considers complexity of project, client's budget, skill and experience of artist, and turnaround time when establishing payment.

BRUEGGEMAN & CAULDER, ARCHITECTS P.A., 1510 S. Broadway, Little Rock AR 72202. (501)375-0222. Administrative Assistant: Velma Caulder. Architectural firm providing design of commercial, residential structures, hospitals, churches, schools, high rise apartments, single family housing projects.
Needs: Uses artists for architectural renderings.
First Contact & Terms: Local artists only. Send query letter with brochure, business card and samples to be kept on file. Call or write for appointment to show portfolio. Prefers to see original works in watercolor as samples. Works on assignment only. Pays for design by the project, $400 minimum. Considers client's budget, and skill and experience of artist when establishing payment.

L.M. BRUINIER & ASSOC. INC., 1304 SW Bertha Blvd., Portland OR 97219. (503)246-7412. President: Lou Bruinier. Architectural design/residential planner/publisher of plan books. Clients: contractors and individuals.
Needs: Works with 1-3 freelance artists/year. Uses artists for design and illustration, brochures, catalogs and books. Especially needs 3-dimensional perspectives (basically residential).
First Contact & Terms: Send resume and samples to be kept on file. Perfers photostats or photocopies as samples. Material not filed not returned. Reports only if interested. Pays for design by the hour, $6-15 average; for illustration by project, $40-500 average. Considers the complexity of project and skill and experience of the artist when establishing payment.

BRUNNER & BRUNNER, ARCHITECTS & ENGINEERS, INC.,, Blue Valley Building, 106 S. 7th St., St. Joseph MO 64501. (816)279-0809. President: William A. Brunner. Architectural firm providing architectural and engineering services. Clients: airport hangar analysis, commercial, industrial, institutional, governmental, residential and multifamily construction.
Needs: Uses artists for interior design and interior/architectural renderings.
First Contact & Terms: Artists with three years' experience only. Send brochure to be kept on file; write for appointment to show portfolio. Considers complexity of project, client's budget, skill and experience of artist, turnaround time and rights purchased when establishing payment.

ALLEN R. CARNEY, A.I.A. & ASSOCIATES, 6000 Grand Central Ave., Box 5146, Vienna WV 26105. (304)295-9410. AIA, Architect: Allen R. Carney. Architectural/interior design firm offering architectural, engineering and interior design. Clients: residential, churches, banks, commercial, instituional.
Needs: Works with 2 freelance artists/year. Uses artists for brochure design, illustration and layout; interior and landscape design and renderings; architectural renderings, charts and model making.
First Contact & Terms: Prefers local artists. Works on assignment only. Send query letter with brochure, resume and business card to be kept on file. Prefers to review slides or tear sheets. Material not filed returned by SASE only if requested. Reports within 2 weeks. Pays for design by the hour, $5-15 average; by project, $300-1,600 average; or by the day, $40-120 average. Considers complexity of the project, client's budget, skill and experience of artist, and turnaround time when establishing payment.

CBT/CHILDS BERTMAN TSECKARES & CASENDINO INC., 306 Dartmouth St., Boston MA 02116. (617)262-4354. Architectural/interior and landscape design/urban design planning firm. Clients: developers and owners of offices and multifamily housing projects; institutions (schools and universities, churches, hospitals); government (municipal, state and federal).
Needs: Works with 3 freelance artists/year. Uses artists for brochure design, illustration and layout; landscape, interior and architectural renderings; and model making.
First Contact & Terms: Experienced artists in the greater Boston area only. Send query letter with brochure, resume, business card, samples and tear sheets to be kept on file. Prefers photostats, slides, photographs as samples; nothing that has to be returned (2-3 samples maximum). Samples not kept on file not returned. Does not report back. Works on assignment only. Pays for design by the project, $100-1,000 average; for illustration by the project, $50-600 average. Considers complexity of project, skill and experience of artist, and turnaround time when establishing payment.

CHAMPLIN/HAUPT INC. ARCHITECTS, 424 E. 4th St., Cincinnati OH 45202. (513)241-4474. Designer: Joan Tepe. Architecture/interior design firm providing complete architectural services, planning, interior design for commercial, institutional and business clients.
Needs: Works with 2 freelance artists/year. Uses artists for interior and architectural renderings and occasionally custom artwork.
First Contact & Terms: Desires artists who can deliver work on time, have a good portfolio and references. Send query letter with brochure to be kept on file; call for appointment to show portfolio. Prefers photographs or good quality photocopies as samples. Does not report back; "artist should follow up." Works on assignment only. Pays for illustrations by the project, $300-500 average; pay rate depends on size and difficulty. Considers complexity of project and how work will be used when establishing payment.

THE CHERVENAK ARCHITECTS, P.S., Market Place One, Suite 200, 2001 Western Ave., Seattle WA 98121. (206)223-1020. Principal (Architect): Robert A. Chervenak. Architectural firm providing architectural services for commercial and institutional buildings. Clients: government (federal and state) and private.
Needs: Works with 3 freelance artists/year. Uses artists for brochure design, landscape design, architectural renderings, art glass design and religious artwork. Especially needs artists whose art can be integrated in building design and construction.
First Contact & Terms: Works on assignment only. Send query letter with brochure, resume, business card and samples to be kept on file. Call or write for appointment to show portfolio. Prefers photocopies as samples. Samples not kept on file are returned only if requested. Reports back when artist is needed for project. Pays by the project. Considers client's budget, and skill and experience of artist when establishing payment.

CHRISMAN, MILLER, WOODFORD, INC., 326 S. Broadway, Lexington KY 40508. (606)254-6623. Contact: Karen A. Jones, ASID. Architectural, interior and landscape design and planning engineering firm. Clients: corporate (commerical, industrial); private (residential—large commissioning only); local, state and federal government agencies; and institutional (educational, health care, religious).
Needs: Works with varied number of freelance artists/year. Uses artists for architectural renderings.
First Contact & Terms: "Artist must be able to come into our offices or to visit job site per project demands. More than 90% of our work is conducted in Kentucky." Send query letter with brochure/flyer or resume; write for appointment. Samples returned by SASE. Reporting time depends on circumstances of individual projects. Works on assignment only; reports back whether to expect possible future assignments. Provide business card, brochure, flyer, samples and tear sheets to be kept on file for possible future assignments. Amount and method of payment vary according to client's budget and contractual agreement.

Tips: "We'll work with anyone, regardless of location. Persons we work with must make themselves readily available to our clients and staff. We will appreciate good art without regard to reputation of artist, etc."

WILLIAM A. CIOTTI & ASSOCIATES/ARCHITECTS, 309 S. 13th St., Philadelphia PA 19107. Contact: William A. Ciotti. Architecture firm. Clients: industrial.
Needs: Uses artists for architectural renderings occasionally.
First Contact & Terms: Call or visit. Reports immediately. Negotiates pay.

FJ CLARK INCORPORATED, 126 N. McDuffie St., Anderson SC 29621. (803)261-3902. President: Frank J. Clark, AIA. Architectural/interior/urban design firm. Clients: institutional, governmental, college and university, industrial and residential.
Needs: Works with approximately 4 freelance artists/year. Uses artists for brochure design and layout, interior and landscape design, interior and architectural renderings, and model making.
First Contact & Terms: Works on assignment only. Send query letter with brochure, resume and samples to be kept on file. Accepts a brochure, photographs, tear sheets or photocopies as samples. Samples are not returned. Reports back only if interested. Pays by the project for design and illustration. Considers complexity of the project, skill and experience of artist and how work will be used when establishing payment.

***CONNELLY ABBOTT TRULL P.A.**, 222 N. Pine, Magnolia AR 71753. (501)234-7008. President: T.G. Connelly. Architectural firm providing complete architectural-engineering services. Clients: residential, institutional, commercial and industrial.
Needs: Works with 4-6 freelance artists/year. Uses artists for interior, landscape and architectural renderings; interior design consulting; furnishings; and model making.
First Contact & Terms: Requires 5+ years' experience in artist's area of specialty. Works on assignment only. Send brochure and samples to be kept on file; write for appointment to show portfolio. Prefers color photographs or photocopies as samples. Samples not filed are returned by SASE only if requested. Reports back to artist. Pays by the hour or by the project for design and illustration. Pay is negotiated. Considers complexity of the project, client's budget, skill and experience of artist, how work will be used, turnaround time and rights purchased when establishing payment.

MAURICE COURLAND & SON/ARCHITECTS-ENGINEERS-PLANNERS, Central Savings Bank Building, 2112 Broadway, New York NY 10023. (212)362-7018. Contact: R.H. Courland or N.M. Courland. Architecture/engineering/space planning/design firm. Clients: industrial, banks, residential, commercial, corporate, financial institutions, government, public and semi-public, institutional and educational.
Needs: Buys 2-6 renderings of new buildings/year. Uses artists for architectural and interior renderings, murals/graphics and scale models.
First Contact & Terms: Query with brochure. Would like to see portfolio with color photos. SASE. Reports within "weeks." Works on assignment only. Provide resume, business card, brochure and tear sheets to be kept on file for possible future assignments. Negotiates pay/project. Certain projects require design and execution; murals; sculpture; paintings; graphics; logos; presentation (color) renderings; exteriors and interiors. Considers complexity of project, client's budget, skill and experience of artist and how work will be used when establishing payment.

THE CRAYCROFT ARCHITECTS, INC., Suite 400, 2602 McKinney Ave., Dallas TX 75204-2520. (214)871-0401. Vice President: Don H. Price. Architectural firm providing programming, design, construction documents, project administration. Clients: multifamily housing, hotels, country club facilities, commercial office buildings, retail shopping centers.
Needs: Works with 2-3 freelance artists/year. Uses artists for architectural renderings and model making; more presentation type material is needed for neighborhood opposition meetings, planning and zoning meetings, public hearings, governmental approvals, etc.
First Contact & Terms: Local artists mainly; credentials necessary. Call for appointment to show portfolio. Works on assignment only. Pay rate varies according to project. Considers complexity of project, client's budget, skill and experience of artist, how work will be used and turnaround time when establishing payment.

CREATIVE RETAILING, INC., Suite 265, 2222 Martin St., Irvine CA 92715. (714)476-8611. President: Clark Richey. Store planning and design firm. Plans, designs and installs retail speciality chain stores including space planning, fixturing, decor design, visual merchandise presentation and establishment of image.
Needs: Uses artists for advertising and brochure design and illustration, brochure layout, interior de-

sign, interior and architectural renderings, design consulting, furnishings, charts and model making. **First Contact & Terms:** Call or write for appointment to show portfolio. Reports within 30 days. Works on assignment only. Pays for illustration or design by the project, $250-1,500 average. "All creative work becomes the property of Creative Retailing." Considers complexity of project, client's budget, and skill and experience of artist when establishing payment.

CROOKS & GEORGE-ARCHITECTS, INC., 1515 W. Lane Ave., Columbus OH 43221. (614)488-8322 or 488-8377. Contact: P.W. George. Architectural firm. Clients: institutional.
Needs: Uses artists for architectural renderings.
First Contact & Terms: Send query letter with brochure and samples to be kept on file. Call for appointment to show portfolio. Prefers photographs as samples. Samples returned if not kept on file. Considers complexity of project, client's budget, and skill and experience of artist when establishing payment.

JERRY CUMMINGS ASSOCIATES INC., Suite 301, 420 Boyd St., Los Angeles CA 90013. (213)621-2756. Contact: Jerry Cummings. Landscape architecture firm. Clients: commercial and residential. Assigns 20-30 freelance renderings/year.
Needs: Works with artists for architectural and landscape renderings.
First Contact & Terms: Query and arrange interview. Reports within 2 weeks. Works on assignment only. Samples returned by SASE; reports back on future possibilities. Provide resume, business card, brochure, flyer and tear sheet to be kept on file for future assignments.

DAT CONSULTANTS LTD., SFA, 118 W. 16th St., New York NY 10011. (212)741-2121. Architect: S. Fernandez. Architecture and interior design firms. Clients: industrial, residential, commercial and institutional.
Needs: Assigns 10 jobs and buys 10 renderings/year. Uses artists for renderings, interior design, sculptures, graphics and scale models.
First Contact & Terms: Prefers local artists. Query with resume or arrange interview to show portfolio. Reports in 1 week. Pays $200-400/job or $15-25/hour.

JOHN LAWRENCE DAW & ASSOCIATES, 912 Baltimore Ave., Kansas City MO 64105. (816)474-9410. Architect: J.L. Daw. Architectural/interior design firm. Clients: commercial, institutional.
Needs: Uses artists for brochure design and layout, interior design, architectural renderings and model making.
First Contact & Terms: Send query letter with brochure and resume to be kept on file. Call or write for appointment to show portfolio. Accepts "whatever artist feels is expendable" as samples. Samples not returned. Reports back to artist.

DEL CAMPO & MARU ARCHITECTS, (formerly Del Campo Associates), 45 Lansing St., San Francisco CA 94105. (415)777-4025. Contact: Martin Del Campo. Architecture firm. Provides architectural, planning and engineering services. Clients: residential, commercial and institutional. Assigns 6 jobs/year.
Needs: Works with 1 artist for architectural renderings; 1, advertising art; 1, wall hangings; and 1, landscape design.
First Contact & Terms: Local artists only. Query with resume. Reports within 2 weeks. Works on assignment only. Samples returned by SASE; reports on future assignment possibilities. Provide resume and flyer to be kept on file for future assignments. Pays for illustration by the project, $2,000-3,000 average. Considers complexity of project, and skill and experience of artist when establishing payment. payment.
Tips: "We don't like drawings that are 'stiff' or commercial-looking."

ROBERT E. DES LAURIERS, A.I.A., ARCHITECT & ASSOCIATES, 9349 El Cajon Blvd., La Mesa CA 92041. (619)469-0135. President: Robert E. Des Lauriers, A.I.A. Architectural firm providing architectural services for churches, schools, commercial and residential interior design.
Needs: Works with 6-10 freelance artists/year. Uses artists for brochure illustration; interior and landscape design and renderings; architectural renderings, design consulting, furnishings and model making.
First Contact & Terms: Local artists only with strong background. Send query letter with brochure, resume, business card and samples to be kept on file. Write for appointment to show portfolio. Prefers photographs as samples. Samples returned only if requested. Reports within 10 days. Works on assignment only. Pays for design and for illustration in lump sum. Considers complexity of project, client's budget, skill and experience of artist and how work will be used when establishing payment.

THE DESIGNPOINT, 307 Laurel St., San Diego CA 92101. (619)234-2565. President: R. Milberg. Art Director: Kerry Summers. Interior and graphic design firm also providing space planning, corporate identity, package design. Clients: commercial.
Needs: Works with 10 freelance artists/year. Uses artists for brochure illustration, interior and architectural renderings, and model making.
First Contact & Terms: Local, qualified artists only. Send brochure and tear sheets to be kept on file; call for appointment to show portfolio. Reports only if interested. Works on assignment only. Pays for design and illustration by the hour. Considers complexity of project, client's budget, and skill and experience of artist when establishing payment.

WILLIAM DORSKY ASSOCIATES, 23200 Chagrin Blvd., Cleveland OH 44122. (216)464-8600. Designers: Curt Johnson, Doug Anderson. Architecture firm. Clients: commercial, residential, institutional.
Needs: Works with 3-4 artists for architectural renderings; 2, interior design; 2, graphic design; 2, signage design; 1, model making; 2-3, sculpture; and 4-5 landscape design.
First Contact & Terms: Call for interview to show photos or transparencies. Works on assignment only. Samples returned by SASE; reports back on future assignment possibilities. Provide resume and brochure to be kept on file.
Tips: "Prepare reproducible examples of work that can be kept on file for ready reference."

THE EGGERS GROUP, P.C., 2 Park Ave., New York NY 10016. (212)725-2100. Director of Interior Design: Robert H. Welz, A.I.A. Architectural/interior design firm providing full architectural and interior design services. Clients: institutional, corporate, residential, academic.
Needs: Works with 10 freelance artists/year. Uses artists for interior and architectural renderings, and model making.
First Contact & Terms: Send query letter with resume and samples to be kept on file. Call or write for appointment to show portfolio. Prefers that artists show portfolio in person. Reports only if interested. Works on assignment only. Pay is negotiable. Considers client's budget, and skill and experience of artist when establishing payment.

HENRY ELDEN & ASSOCIATES, ARCHITECTS, Box 3201, Charleston WV 25332. Architect: Ted Elden. Architectural/interior design firm providing full range of services. Clients: residential, industrial, commercial, government.
Needs: Works with 4-6 freelance artists/year. Uses artists for advertising and brochure design and illustration, brochure layout, interior and landscape design and renderings, architectural renderings, furnishings and maps.
First Contact & Terms: Send brochure and samples to be kept on file. Prefers slides as samples. Samples not kept on file are returned by SASE. Reports within 10 days. Works on assignment only. Pays for design and illustration by the hour, $5-50 average. Considers skill and experience of artist when establishing payment.

FALICK/KLEIN PARTNERSHIP, INC., Suite 1900, 5847 San Felipe, Houston TX 77057-3005. (713)782-9000. Contact: David G. Puckett. Architectural/interior design firm providing full services. Clients: institutional (hospitals), developers, governmental, financial, professional office buildings.
Needs: Works with 10-30 freelance artists/year. Uses artists for advertising illustration and layout, brochure design; interior, landscape and architectural renderings and model making.
First Contact & Terms: "Experienced, innovative" artists only. Send query letter with brochure to be kept on file. Write for appointment to show portfolio. Reports only if interested.

FEICK ASSOCIATES, 224 E. Water St., Sandusky OH 44870. (419)625-2554. Architect: John A. Feick. Architectural firm providing complete architectural services. Clients: residential, commercial and industrial.
Needs: Works with 1 freelance artist/year. Uses artists for architectural renderings.
First Contact & Terms: Send query letter with brochure and business card to be kept on file. Reports only if interested. Works on assignment only. Pays for design by the project, $200 minimum. Considers complexity of project and client's budget when establishing payment.
Tips: "Be brief and concise in contact."

FEREBEE, WALTERS AND ASSOCIATES, Box 2029, Charlotte NC 28211. (704)542-5586. Architectural/interior and landscape design firm providing complete environmental design and planning services. Clients: residential, commercial, industrial, institutional.
Needs: Works with 2-3 freelance artists/year. Uses artists for advertising design and layout, brochure design, and interior and architectural renderings.

First Contact & Terms: Send query letter with brochure, resume and tear sheets; also send samples and business cards. Prefers to see samples that are best illustration of talent. Samples not returned. Does not report back. Considers complexity of project, client's budget, skill and experience of artist, how work will be used, turnaround time and rights purchased when establishing payment.

ROBERT P. GERSIN ASSOCIATES, 11 E. 22nd St., New York NY 10010. President: Robert P. Gersin. Industrial design firm providing interiors, architecture, graphics, packaging, products and exhibits.
Needs: Works with 15 freelance artists/year. Uses artists for interior, graphic and brochure design, brochure illustration and layout; package and product design and illustration on products.
First Contact & Terms: Send query letter with resume; write for appointment. Prefers slides as samples. Samples returned by SASE. Reports in 2-3 weeks. Provide resume, business card, brochure and flyer to be kept on file for possible future assignments. Negotiates payment. Considers client's budget, skill and experience of artist and how work will be used when establishing payment.
Tips: "Be professional and pay attention to details."

VINOD M. GHOTING, AIA, 8501 Potomac Ave., College Park MD 20740. (301)474-3719. Contact: Vinod M. Ghoting, AIA. Architectural/interior design/urban design firm providing complete architectural and interior design services, from schematic design through construction documents and management. Clients: residential, institutional, medical, commercial and industrial.
Needs: Works with 1 freelance artist/year. Uses artists for interior design and renderings.
First Contact & Terms: Local artists only at this time. Send query letter with business card and samples to be kept on file. Prefers photostats as samples. Reports within 15 days. Works on assignment only. Amount of payment varies according to client's budget and complexity of project.

*GREEN & ASSOCIATES, Suite C-26, 915 King St., Alexandria VA 22314. (703)548-7010. Contact: James F. Green. Interior design firm providing residential and contract interior design and space planning plus custom furniture design. Clients: residential, corporate offices and retail design.
Needs: Number of freelance artists used/year varies. Uses artists for interior design and interior and architectural renderings.
First Contact & Terms: Prefers local artists; "sometimes we require on-site inspections." Send query letter with brochure, resume and samples to be kept on file. Prefers photostats or photographs as samples only; color preferred. Reports only if interested. Works on assignment only. Pays for design and illustration by the project, $250 minimum. "Persons we work with must be able to make themselves available to our clients and staff. We will appreciate good art without regard to reputation of artist, etc." Considers complexity of project, client's budget and skill and experience of artist when establishing payment.

GUNN LEVINE ASSOC. ARCH. PLANNERS, 15 E. Kirby, Detroit MI 48202. (313)873-3280. President: Tom Gunn. Architectural design and planning/medical facility planning firm providing complete architectural and engineering services, hospital consulting and interior design. Clients: medical, commercial, educational.
Needs: Works with 1-3 freelance artists/year. Uses artists for advertising design and layout, architectural renderings and sculpture.
First Contact & Terms: "Established" artists only. Send query letter with resume and tear sheets to be kept on file. Prefers nonreturnable samples only. Reports within weeks. Works on assignment only. Negotiates pay. Considers client's budget when establishing payment.

H.K.S. & PARTNERS, 1111 Plaza of Americas, Dallas TX 75201. (214)969-5599. Vice President: Ron Brame. Architecture/interior design firm also providing artworks for architectures and interiors. Clients: corporate, commercial, institutional, residential, industrial and health care.
Needs: Works with 20-30 freelance artists/year. Uses artists for advertising and brochure design, brochure layout, interior design and renderings, architectural renderings, design consulting and model making.
First Contact & Terms: Send query letter with brochure and samples to be kept on file; call or write for appointment to show portfolio. Prefers slides, tear sheets, photographs or original work as samples. Samples not kept on file returned by SASE only if requested. Reports only if interested. Pays for design and illustration by the project. Considers skill and experience of artist and turnaround time when establishing payment.

JOHN D. HAINES, ARCHITECTS AND PLANNERS, INC., Main St., Box 403, Manchester VT 05254-0403. (802)362-3776. Contact: Marian Louise. Architectural firm providing total design/planning services. Clients: commercial, governmental, residential, educational, cultural.
Needs: Works with 5-6 freelance artists/year. Uses artists for brochure illustration, landscape design and renderings, architectural renderings, furnishings and model making. Especially needs artists for renderings.

First Contact & Terms: Works on assignment only. Send resume and business card to be kept on file. Reports back only if interested. Considers complexity of the project, skill and experience of artist and turnaround time when establishing payment.

HARDWICKE JOHNSON INC., (formerly Hardwicke, Ekstrom and Associates, Ltd.), Suite 103, 2601 Willard Rd., Richmond VA 23229. Director of Architecture: Gilbert O. Nicholson. Architectural/ engineering/interior design planning firm providing full service architecture. Clients: commercial and institutional, primarily multistory office, hotel and library work.
Needs: Works with 7 freelance artists/year. Uses artists for landscape design and custom reproduction furnishings.
First Contact & Terms: Virginia-based artists only. Send query letter with brochure, business card and samples to be kept on file. Contact only through artist's agent. Prefers slides or photographs as samples. Samples not kept on file are returned by SASE. Reports only if interested. Works on assignment only. Pays for design by the hour, $10-50 average; for illustration by the hour, $5-25 average. Considers complexity of project, client's budget, and skill and experience of artist when establishing payment.
Tips: Current trends include "a greater use of color in general and a return to the use of traditional motifs."

DAVID B. HILL & ASSOCIATES, INC., Box 178, Seymour IN 47274. President-Architect: David W. Correll. Vice President-Architect: Donald H. Bradley. Architectural firm offering all ranges of architectural services. Clients: all types.
Needs: Works with 2-3 freelance artists/year. Uses artists for advertising, brochure, interior and landscape design and architectural renderings.
First Contact & Terms: Send query letter with brochure to be kept on file; write for appointment to show portfolio. Material not filed is returned by SASE only if requested. Reports back only if interested. Pays by contract negotiation. Considers complexity of the project, client's budget, and skill and experience of artist when establishing payment.

HOLSHOUSER & ASSOCIATES, 219 N. Clark Ave., Cape Girardeau MO 63701. (314)334-6422. Architect: Thomas C. Holshouser, AIA. Architectural firm providing architectural design services. Clients: commercial (90%), residential (10%).
Needs: Uses artists for architectural renderings.
First Contact & Terms: Send brochure to be kept on file. Reports only if interested. Works on assignment only. Pays for design and illustration by the project, $400-1,000 average. Considers complexity of project and skill and experience of artist when establishing payment.

HUNTER/MILLER & ASSOCIATES, 110 S. Lee St., Alexandria VA 22314. (703)548-0600. President: Jeffrey Miller. Architectural/interior design/landscape design firm offering comprehensive services. Clients: commercial, institutional, government.
Needs: Works with 1-2 freelance artists/year. Uses artists for brochure design, illustration and layout; interior design and renderings; architectural renderings, design consulting, furnishings, charts, maps and model making.
First Contact & Terms: "Experienced, quality artists" only. Works on assignment only. Send query letter with brochure, resume, business card and samples to be kept on file. Reports back only if interested. Pays for design and illustration by the hour, $20 minimum. Considers skill and experience of artist when establishing payment.

IDENTITIA INCORPORATED, Suite 515, 1000 N. Ashley Dr., Tampa FL 33602. (813)221-3326. Interior and graphic design firm providing consultative services to health care facilities. Clients: institutional, hospitals, courthouses and parking garages.
Needs: Works with 3 freelance artists/year. Uses artists for architectural renderings, interior and graphic design and signage.
First Contact & Terms: Send query letter. Samples returned. Reports within 2 weeks. Works on assignment only. Payment varies according to job.

THE IMAGE GROUP, 398 S. Grant Ave., Columbus OH 43215. (614)221-1016. Contact: Richard Henry Eiselt. Architecture/interior design firm. Clients: commercial.
Needs: Uses artists for restaurant design, architectural and full-color renderings, graphic and interior design, paintings, sculpture, signs and wall art.
First Contact & Terms: Mail photos or transparencies. Pay varies according to client's budget, and skill and experience of artist.

*INTERNATIONAL DESIGN COLLABORATIVE, INC., Box 5846, Santa Monica CA 90405-0846. (213)454-0203. President: Ralph Iredale. Architectural/interior design/city planning firm. Cli-

ents: public and private—residential/commercial/institutional.
Needs: Uses artists for brochure design, interior and architectural renderings and model making.
First Contact & Terms: Send brochure, resume and business card to be kept on file. Reports only if interested. Pays for illustration by the project. Considers complexity of project, client's budget and skill and experience of artist when establishing payment.

INTRAPRO/ATLANTA, Box 7962, Atlanta GA 30357. Executive Director: James J. Bachteler. Architectural/interior and landscape design/photography/graphics firm. Clients: residential, commercial. Specializes in greeting cards, displays, automobile racing promotion and photography, package design and point-of-purchase.
Needs: Works with 10 freelance artists/year. Uses artists for advertising and brochure design, landscape and interior design, architectural and interior renderings, design consulting and furnishings.
First Contact & Terms: Send query letter with brochure, resume and business card to be kept on file. Write for appointment to show portfolio; write for artists' guidelines. Reports within days. Pay varies according to assignment. Considers complexity of project, client's budget, skill and experience of artist, how work will be used, turnaround time and rights purchased when establishing payment.

JAMES, DURANT, MATTHEWS & SHELLEY A.I.A., 128 E. Liberty St., Sumter SC 29150. (803)773-3318. Architects: J.E. Matthews/W.D. Shelley. Architectural firm. Clients: educational, commercial.
Needs: Works with 1 freelance artist/year. Uses artists for architectural renderings.
First Contact & Terms: Seeks "good, imaginative work." Works on assignment only. Send query letter with brochure to be kept on file; call or write for appointment to show portfolio. Material not filed returned by SASE. Reports only if interested. Pays for illustration by the project, $250-800 average. Considers complexity of project, client's budget, and skill of artist when establishing payment.

JENSEN-HASLEM ASSOCIATES, 135 N. Main, Logan UT 84321. (801)753-2141. Contact: Thomas C. Jensen. Architectural firm providing architectural design and engineering. Clients: commercial, institutional, residential.
Needs: Works with 4-5 freelance artists/year. Uses artists for brochure/design, illustration and layout; interior design, architectural renderings and model making.
First Contact & Terms: Artists with two years experience only. Send query letter with resume, business card and samples to be kept on file. Write for appointment to show portfolio. Prefers photostats as samples. Samples not kept on file returned only if requested. SASE. Reports only if interested. Works on assignment only. Negotiates pay by the job.

BEN H. JOHNSON & ASSOCIATES, Suite 123, Executive Plaza, 12835 Bellevue-Redmond Rd., Bellevue WA 98005. (206)455-5502. Principal: Ben H. Johnson, A.I.A. Architectural/interior design firm providing architecture, planning and interior design. Clients: single family and multi-family residential, retail, offices, churches, libraries; yacht and corporate aircraft interiors.
Needs: Works with 6 freelance artists/year. Uses artists for brochure illustration, interior and architectural renderings, landscape design and model making.
First Contact & Terms: Artists must exhibit "a willingness to meet time and/or cost deadline (or not accept the commission)." Works on assignment only. Send query letter with resume, business card and samples to be kept on file; call for appointment to show portfolio. Accepts photostats, slides, photographs, photocopies or tear sheets as samples. Reports within 1 week. Pays by the hour, $8-22 average for design, $6-18 average for illustration. Considers complexity of the project, client's budget, skill and experience of artist and rights purchased when establishing payment.
Tips: "There is a tremendous hesitancy to use artistic graphics except in the largest projects. It is only after a design and contract drawings are nearly complete that graphic art is required for sales and/or publicity presentations."

LAWRENCE KASSER ASSOCIATES, ARCHITECTS AND PLANNERS, Box 772, Saxtons River VT 05154. (802)463-9576. Principal: Lawrence Kasser. Architectural/interior design/landscape design firm providing design, construction documents and promotional material. Clients: commercial, residential, institutional, developers.
Needs: Works with 3 freelance artists/year. Uses artists for brochure design, illustration and layout; interior and landscape design and renderings; architectural renderings, design consulting, furnishings and model making.
First Contact & Terms: New England area artists only, with 3 years' experience. Works on assignment basis. Send query letter with brochure and samples to be kept on file; write for appointment to show portfolio. Prefers slides as samples. Reports within 3 weeks. Pays for design and illustration by the hour, $10-15 average. Considers client's budget when establishing payment.

ARLAN KAY & ASSOCIATES, 110 King St., Madison WI 53703. (608)251-7515. Architect: Arlan Kay. Architectural firm offering architecture and construction management. Clients: commercial, residential, and institutional with 70% of work in recycling/restoration of existing buildings.
Needs: Works with 1-2 freelance artists/year. Uses artists for brochure design and architectural renderings.
First Contact & Terms: Prefers local artists. Works on assignment only. Send query letter with brochure to be kept on file. Reports only if interested. Pays for illustration by the hour, $7-25 average; by the project, $100-500 average; or by the day, $50-150 average. Considers complexity of the project, client's budget, and skill and experience of artist when establishing payment.

GEROLD F. KESSLER & ASSOCIATES INC., 2101 S. Clermont, Denver CO 80222. (303)756-1536. Contact: Gerold Kessler. Landscape/architecture/project planning firm providing consulting services as project planners/land planners/landscape designers. Clients: residential and industrial.
Needs: Works with 1 artist for architectural renderings; 1, graphic design; 1, model making; and 1, landscape design. Also uses artists for site plans and subdivision development layout.
First Contact & Terms: Works on assignment only. Query with photos or brochures; local artists only. Reports within 1 week. Samples returned by SASE. Pays $500-700, landscape and general site renderings; $600-1,000, subdivision land plan; $20-50/hour for design and illustration.

KIRKHAM, MICHAEL AND ASSOCIATES, 9110 W. Dodge Rd., Omaha NE 68114. (402)393-5630. Architectural designer: David Scott Nordstrom. Full service architecture, interior design, landscape design, engineering and planning firm. Clients: commercial, industrial, institutional, governmental, healthcare, housing.
Needs: Works with 5 freelance artists/year. Uses artists for advertising and brochure design, illustration and layout; landscape design, architectural renderings and design consulting.
First Contact & Terms: Send query letter with brochure, business card and samples to be kept on file. Write for appointment to show portfolio. Prefers photos and slides as samples. Reports only if interested. Works on assignment only. Pays according to variable contracts. Considers complexity of project, client's budget, skill and experience of artist, how work will be used, turnaround time and rights purchased when establishing payment.

KNAPP ASSOCIATES LTD., ARCHITECT-MARKET ANALYST, 2801 Fish Hatchery Rd., Madison WI 53713. (608)271-0140. President: E. John Knapp AIA. Architectural and market analysis firm providing full service architectural services, market analysis and demographic studies for site locations, nationwide. Clients: professional, retail.
Needs: Works with 3 freelance artists/year. Uses artists for architectural renderings, design consulting and model making.
First Contact & Terms: Works on assignment only. Send query letter with brochure and resume to be kept on file. Reports only if interested. Pay is negotiated by the project. Considers client's budget, and skill and experience of artist when establishing payment.

KNODT/MADDOX, INC., ARCHITECTS-PLANNERS, Suite F, 1455 S. Fourth St., Columbus OH 43207. (614)443-0579. President: Jerry E. Maddox. Architectural firm providing full scope architectural services for both new construction and rehabilitation projects; land planning. Clients: well-elderly retirement centers, medical office buildings, nursing homes, multi-family housing, commercial development.
Needs: Works with 3 freelance artists/year. Uses artists for architectural renderings.
First Contact & Terms: Prefers local artists, five years' experience. Send brochure, resume, business card and samples to be kept on file. Prefers "photostats and/or photographs as samples to be furnished in initial contact via mail. Original artwork required at interview." Samples returned by SASE if not kept on file. Reports only if interested. Works on assignment only. Considers complexity of project, client's budget, skill and experience of artist and turnaround time when establishing payment.

FRANCES KOO & ASSOCIATES, INC., Suite 105, 601 University Ave., Sacramento CA 95825. (916)924-1375. Chief Architect: Francis Koo. Clients: commercial, industrial, military, institutional and residential.
Needs: Assigns 20 jobs/year. Works with 3 artists for architectural renderings; 3, interior design; 1, graphic design; 1, advertising art; 2 signage design; 2, model making; 2, murals; 1, wall hangings; 2, landscape design; and 1, charts/graphs.
First Contact & Terms: Query. SASE. Reports in 1 week. Works on assignment only. Samples returned by SASE; reports back on future assignment possibilities. Provide resume, business card and brochure to be kept on file for future assignments. Maximum payment: $1,600, architectural renderings; $1,500, art renderings; $3,000, graphic design; $15,000, scale models; $5,000, signs; $250,000, mu-

rals and sculpture. Pays minimum $500. Negotiates payment for paintings and wall art. Considers complexity of project, skill and experience of artist and turnaround time when establishing payment.
Tips: "We like to have a name list in different type of service artists provide, then we can contact them when we need that kind of service."

KRESSCOX ASSOCIATES, P.C., 2909 M St. NW, Washington DC 20007. Contact: Jerrily Kress. Clients: commercial and governmental.
Needs: Works with artists for architectural renderings, graphic design, signage design, model making, wall hangings, sculpture and landscape design.
First Contact & Terms: Query with resume or arrange interview. Reports in 1 week. Works on assignment only. Samples returned by SASE; reports back on future assignment possibilities. Provide resume, brochure or flyer to be kept on file. Pays by job.

LABUNSKI ASSOCIATES ARCHITECTS, 115 W. Van Buren, Harlingen TX 78550. (512)428-4334. President: R.A. Labunski. Architectural firm providing architecture, construction, design, space planning, interiors, advertising. Clients: commercial, retail, residential, corporate, banks, hotel/motel/restaurant.
Needs: Works with 5 freelance artists/year. Uses artists for advertising design, illustration and layout; brochure design, interior and architectural renderings, design consulting, furnishings and model making.
First Contact & Terms: Desires "affordable, practical" artists with referrals/references. Send query letter with brochure, resume and business cards to be kept on file; also send samples. Call or write for appointment to show portfolio. Samples returned by SASE. Reports within 2 weeks. Works on assignment only. Pays by the project. Considers complexity of project, client's budget, and skill and experience of artist when establishing payment.

JOSEPH LADD & ASSOCIATES, P.C., 2405 Westwood Ave., Richmond VA 23230. (804)355-0849. President: Joseph N. Ladd, AIA, CCS. Architectural firm providing architecture, interior design and space planning. Clients: private sector; federal, state and local governments.
Needs: Works with 1 freelance artist/year. Uses artists for architectural renderings, interior, landscape and graphic design, furnishings, design consulting, model making and signage.
First Contact & Terms: Artist must have work experience. Send brochure/flyer, business card and resume to be kept on file. Reports in 1 week. Works on assignment only. Payment varies according to the job.
Tips: Artists "must maintain quality workmanship."

LANDOW AND LANDOW ARCHITECTS, PC, 3000 Marcus Ave., Lake Success NY 11042. (516)326-1111. President, AIA: Lloyd J. Landow. Architectural/interior design firm providing complete architectural, space planning and interior design services. Clients: corporate and institutional.
Needs: Uses artists for architectural renderings and model making. Also commissions for buildings.
First Contact & Terms: Send query letter with brochure, resume, business card, samples and tear sheets to be kept on file. Prefers photostats and photographs as samples. Samples returned by SASE if not kept on file. Reports only if interested. Considers complexity of project, client's budget, skill and experience of artist and turnaround time when establishing payment.

ERNEST LUTHER LANE, AIA, 1040 Elbon Rd., Cleveland Heights OH 44121. Contact: Ernest Luther Lane. Architectural/construction management firm.
Needs: Currently works with 0 freelance artists. Uses artists for architectural renderings.
First Contact & Terms: Send query letter with brochure to be kept on file. Reports within 4 weeks. Works on assignment basis only. Negotiates pay per service. Considers client's budget; "prefer owner to select artist."

LANE & ASSOCIATES, ARCHITECTS, 1318 N. "B", Box 3929, Fort Smith AR 72913. (501)782-4277. Contact: John E. Lane, AIA-ASID. Architectural and interior design firm providing architecture and interiors for remodeling and new construction; also art consultant. Clients: residential, multi-family, commercial and industrial.
Needs: Works with 10-12 freelance artists/year. Uses artists occasionally for architectural renderings, charts, graphic design and advertising illustration; selects or commissions art pieces for clients; paintings, drawings, sculpture, photographs, macrame, tapestry (all mediums). Arranges art exhibits for large local bank—"would like sources of talent for various mediums, painting, sculptures, photography, drawings, etc."
First Contact & Terms: Prefers to be able to meet in person with artist. Send query letter with resume. Samples returned by SASE, but "would prefer to retain." Provide resume, business card, slides or pho-

tos of work and brochure to be kept on file for possible future assignments. Payment varies. Considers complexity of project, client's budget, skill and experience of artist and how work will be used when establishing payment.

JOHN D. LEACH, ARCHITECT, 111 First St., Hartsville SC 29550. (803)332-7812. Contact: John D. Leach. Architectural/interior design/landscape design firm providing complete architectural services (turnkey), landscape design and supervision, and interior design (fixed items primarily). Clients: commercial, residential, institutional, industrial.
Needs: Works with 3-4 freelance artists/year. Uses artists for advertising and brochure illustration, interior and architectural renderings, landscape design and furnishings.
First Contact & Terms: Prefers experienced artists. Works on assignment only. Send query letter with brochure and resume to be kept on file; write for appointment to show portfolio. Prefers slides or photocopies as samples. Samples not filed returned only if requested. Reports only if interested or if return card is enclosed. Payment negotiated according to project requirements. Considers complexity of project, client's budget and turnaround time when establishing payment.

*PETER A. LENDRUM ASSOCIATES, 2920 E. Camelback Rd., Phoenix AZ 85016. (602)955-2100. Director, Public Relations: Pat Lynn. Architectural/interior design/landscape design firm providing planning, architecture, interiors, landscape architecture, and civil, mechanical and electrical engineering services. Clients: corporate, industrial, commercial and institutional.
Needs: Works with 20 freelance artists/year. Uses artists for advertising and brochure illustration; interior, landscape and architectural renderings; charts, maps and model making.
First Contact & Terms: Prefers local/regional artists. "We use only experienced, specialized (i.e., model making, architectural rendering) artists with great portfolios." Works on assignment only. Send query letter with brochure, business card and samples to be kept on file; write for appointment to show portfolio. Samples not filed are returned by SASE only if requested. Reports only if interested. Pays for design by the project, $1,500-12,000 average; for illustration by the project, $1,500-5,000 average. Considers complexity of the project, client's budget, skill and experience of artist, how work will be used, turnaround time and rights purchased when establishing payment.

LOUISVILLE ART GLASS STUDIO, 1110 Baxter Ave., Louisville KY 40204. (502)585-5421. Specializes in art glass and design fabrication. President: Gary D. Meeker. Clients: commercial, residential, churches and related liturgical.
Needs: Works with 2 artists for interior design; 3, graphic design; 2, sculpture; and 4, stained glass. Also uses artists for leaded glass design.
First Contact & Terms: Prefers artists with previous glass experience. Works on assignment only. Query with resume and samples to be kept on file. Reports within 4 weeks. Samples not filed returned by SASE. Prefers slides or photos as samples. Pays by the job, based on square footage and size of work; or by the hour.
Tips: There are "more good freelance artists availiable now than at any other time but not enough good, qualified craftsmen to execute the work." Artists approaching this firm should have "confidence that our execution will be of the very best quality and the newest techniques."

LUDEROWSKI PLANNING & DESIGN, 66 W. Broadway, New York NY 10007. (212)962-0015. Contact: Nils Luderowski. Architectural/interior/landscape design firm. Clients: corporations and individuals.
Needs: Works with 1-3 freelance artists/year. Uses artists for drafting.
First Contact & Terms: Local, professional artists only with minimum of 3 years' experience. Works on assignment only. Send query letter with resume and business card to be kept on file; write for appointment to show portfolio. Samples not filed are returned by SASE. Pays for drafting by the hour, $10-30 average or negotiates. Considers client's budget, and skill and experience of the artist when establishing payment.

DON L. MCKEE, ARCHITECT, A.I.A. & ASSOCIATES, 807 Fourth St., Anacortes WA 98221. (206)293-6012. Principal: Don L. McKee. Architectural firm offering building design and construction coordination. Clients: residential, commercial, industrial, governmental, institutional.
Needs: Works with 1-2 freelance artists/year. Uses artists for advertising illustration, brochure design and illustration, and interior and architectural renderings.

Market conditions are constantly changing! If this is 1987 or later, buy the newest edition of *Artist's Market* at your favorite bookstore or order directly from Writer's Digest Books.

First Contact & Terms: Local artists only (greater Seattle area). Works on assignment only. Send query letter with brochure and resume to be kept on file; call or write for appointment to show portfolio. Material not filed returned by SASE only if requested. Considers complexity of project, client's budget, and skill and experience of artist when establishing payment.

MAHER & ASSOC. ARCHITECTS SC., 810 N. Plankinton Ave., Milwaukee WI 53203. (414)276-0811. President: J. Thomas Maher A.I.A. Architectural firm providing total architectural and interior design. Clients: industrial, commercial, hotel and medical.
Needs: Works with several freelance artists/year. Uses artists for interior and landscape design, interior and architectural renderings, design consulting, furnishings and model making.
First Contact & Terms: Works on assignment only. Send query letter with brochure, resume and business card to be kept on file. Accepts photostats, photographs or any samples that can be retained. Samples not filed are returned only if requested. Reports back within 5 days. Pays by the project. Considers client's budget, and skill and experience of artist when establishing payment.

MANIKTALA ASSOCIATES, P.C., 100 Metropolitan Dr., Box 4753, Syracuse NY 13221. (315)457-1210. Managing Architect: Alan D. Nock. Architectural and engineering firm providing architectural, structural, civil, electrical, mechanical, geotechnical engineering disciplines; construction inspection, interior design, construction cost estimating. Clients: industrial, commercial, municipal, governmental, private.
Needs: Works with 4 freelance artists/year. Uses artists for advertising and brochure design and illustration, and brochure layout.
First Contact & Terms: Artists must "provide high-quality, professional services and be willing to work as diligently as their client." Send query letter with brochure and business card to be kept on file. Reports within 2-3 weeks. Works on assignment only. Pays for design by the hour, $15-25 average; for illustration by the hour, $13-22 average. Considers complexity of project, client's budget, skill and experience of artist, how work will be used, turnaround time and rights purchased when establishing payment.

MARTIN & DETHOFF REGISTERED ARCHITECTS, 422 Franklin St., Reading PA 19602. Contact: Robert S. Martin. Architectural/interior design firm providing architectural, engineering and interior design. Clients: commercial.
Needs: Works with 4 freelance artists/year. Uses artists for architectural renderings and furnishings.
First Contact & Terms: Works on assignment only. Send query letter with resume to be kept on file. Reports back only if interested. Pays by the project, $250 minimum. Considers complexity and size of project when establishing payment.

THE MATHES GROUP, 929 Howard Ave., New Orleans LA 70113. (504)586-9303. President: Edward C. Mathes. Architectural/interior design/landscape design firm providing all services associated with architecture, landscape architecture and interior design. Clients: commercial (90%) and residential (10%).
Needs: Works with 10 freelance artists/year. Uses artists for interior design, architectural renderings, design consulting, furnishings, model making and as sources for artwork.
First Contact & Terms: Send query letter with brochure, resume, samples and tear sheets to be kept on file unless unsuitable; write for appointment to show portfolio. Prefers slides, photographs, clear photocopies as samples. Samples not kept on file returned only if requested. Reports only if interested. Works on assignment only. Pays by the project for design and illustration. Considers complexity of project, client's budget, and skill and experience of artist when establishing payment.

MESSINA ASSOCIATES-ARCHITECT, (formerly Frank Jon Messina, AIA), Box 1125, San Carlos CA 94070. (415)364-6405. Contact: Frank Jon Messina. Architecture/interior design firm. Clients: industrial, residential and commercial. Assigns 10-12 jobs/year.
Needs: Works with 1 artist for architectural renderings; 5, interior design; 1, mural; 1, wall hangings; and 10, landscape design.
First Contact & Terms: Query with samples. Reports within 1 week. Works on assignment only. Samples returned by SASE; reports back on future assignment possibilities. Provide business card and flyer to be kept on file for future assignments. Pays $200 minimum/job.

METCALF HAEFNER ARCHITECTS, 1052 Main St., Stevens Point WI 54481. (715)344-7205. Partner: Michael Metcalf. Achitectural firm providing building design, planning, energy design, interior design and rendering. Clients: residential, commercial, industrial, medical and religious.
Needs: Works with 2-3 freelance artists/year. Uses artists for advertising, interior and landscape design; landscape and architectural renderings, furnishings and model making.

First Contact & Terms: Send brochure, resume, business card and samples to be kept on file. Call or write for appointment to show portfolio. Pays by the project. Considers complexity of the project, client's budget, and skill and experience of artist when establishing payment.

MITCHELL & JENSEN, AIA, ARCHITECT & ENGINEER, 4247 Philadelphia Dr., Dayton OH 45405. (513)277-9338. Architect: Stan Mitchell. Architectural firm providing architectural engineering, landscape, planning, interiors and energy management design.
Needs: Works with 1-4 freelance artists/year. Uses artists for interior and architectural renderings, design consulting and furnishings.
First Contact & Terms: Send query letter to be kept on file. Call for appointment to show portfolio. Prefers quality slides as samples. Samples returned only if requested. Reports back only if requested. Pays for design by the hour, project or day; for illustration by the project, $250-1,000 average. Considers complexity of project, client's budget, skill and experience of artist and how work will be used when establishing payment.

NAUTILUS ARCHITECTURE AND PLANNING, 168 North 100 East, St. George UT 34770. (801)628-3655. Architect: W. David Varga. Architectural firm offering architecture consulting plus complete turn-key development services as management coordinator. Clients: developers, financial institutions, investors, public institutions.
Needs: Works with 3 freelance artists/year. Uses artists for advertising and brochure design, illustration and layout; interior design and renderings; landscape design, architectural renderings, furnishings and model making; consults with interior designers on special design features and architectural effects.
First Contact & Terms: High-quality, experienced artists only; local artists preferred, but not mandatory. Works on assignment only. Send query letter with brochure, resume and samples to be kept on file. Write for appointment to show portfolio. Accepts "artist's preference" or 8 ½x11" glossy photographs as samples. Samples not filed returned only by SASE. Reports only if interested. Pays according to bid; "artists establish their own terms and submit them for comparison with other qualifications. For each commission, contenders are evaluated together on typical scope of service needed. Cost is not always the prime determinant." Considers complexity of project, client's budget, skill and experience of artist, how work will be used, turnaround time and rights purchased when establishing payment.

CHARLES E. NOLAN JR & ASSOCIATES, Box 1788, Alamogordo NM 88310. (505)437-1405. President: Charles E. Nolan Jr. Architectural firm providing architectural design, interior design, feasibility studies and master planning. Clients: commercial, institutional, educational, government.
Needs: Works with 2-3 freelance artists/year. Uses artists for architectural renderings, furnishings, murals and sculpture in building design.
First Contact & Terms: Send query letter with brochure and samples to be kept on file. Prefers slides and photos (color or b&w). Samples returned if not kept on file. Reports within 14 days. Pays for design by the hour, $10-40 average; by the day, $100-300 average. Pays for illustration by the hour, $10-15 average. Considers complexity of project, skill and experience of artist and how work will be used when establishing payment.

THE OSBORNE ASSOCIATES, 161 W. Wisconsin Ave., Milwaukee WI 53203. (414)271-0123. Principal: Edward Osborne. Architectural firm offering full architectural and engineering services for any type of project. Clients: residential developers, commercial and cemetery owners (mausoleums).
Needs: Works with freelance artists 6 times/year. Uses artists for landscape design and architectural renderings.
First Contact & Terms: Works on assignment only. Send query letter with brochure and resume to be kept on file. Call for appointment to show portfolio. Accepts any type of samples. Samples not filed are returned. Reports within 10 days. Pays for illustration by the project, $300-700 average. Considers complexity of the project, and skill and experience of artist when establishing payment.
Tips: Especially looks for "accuracy, life-like quality and detail" in samples or portfolio.

PACIFIC DESIGN GROUP, (formerly Ressa/Zeck & Company, P.S.), W815 7th Ave., Spokane WA 99204. (509)624-1186. Project Architect: Jerry Ressa. Architectural/planning firm offering standard full service or partial service, as requested. Clients: residential, commercial, institutional, military.
Needs: Uses artists for interior and architectural renderings. Especially needs interior building graphics.
First Contact & Terms: Seeks artists in locale of office or project. Works on assignment only. Send query letter with brochure, resume and business card to be kept on file; call or write for appointment to show portfolio. Material not filed returned by SASE only if requested. Reports only if interested. Negotiates pay.

PARKEY & PARTNERS Architects, Suite 833, 3333 Lee Pkwy., Dallas TX 75219. (214)522-4321. Architectural firm providing complete range of architectural services. Clients: commercial, governmental and some residential.
Needs: Works with 6 freelance artists/year. Uses artists for landscape and interior design renderings, architectural renderings, design consulting, furnishings and model making.
First Contact & Terms: Desires artists who are "able to respond quickly to our needs within a reasonable fee." Send query letter with brochure, resume, business card and tear sheets to be kept on file. Call for appointment to show portfolio. Reports only if interested. Works on assignment only. Pay rate depends on artist and project. Considers complexity of project, client's budget, skill and experience of artist and turnaround time when establishing payment.
Tips: Sees artists/designers operating "in a more business-like manner."

PDT & COMPANY ARCHITECTS/PLANNERS, 7434 Montgomery Rd., Cincinnati OH 45236. (513)891-4605. Contact: John Bammerlin.
Needs: Works with 2 artists for architectural renderings; 5, interior design; 1, model making; and 3, landscape design. Uses artists for architectural renderings.
First Contact & Terms: Mail samples (examples of finished work). Works on assignment only. Samples returned by SASE; reports back on future possibilities. Provide business card and brochure to be kept on file. Pays by job.

RALPH PEDERSEN A.I.A. ARCHITECT, Box 1885, Clarksburg WV 26302. (304)624-9298. Contact: Ralph Pedersen. Architectural firm providing full architectural services. Clients: residential, commercial.
Needs: Works with 4 freelance artists/year. Uses artists for interior and architectural renderings, and interior design.
First Contact & Terms: Works on assignment only. Send brochure, resume, business card and samples to be kept on file; write for appointment to show portfolio. Prefers to receive copies of similar material that need not be returned. Samples not kept on file returned by SASE. Reports only if interested. Pays for design by the hour, $10 minimum, or by the project, $200 minimum with $400 average; for illustration by the project, $150 minimum with $325 average. Considers skill and experience of artist, turnaround time and rights purchased when establishing payment.

PFLUM, KLAUSMEIER & WAGNER CONSULTANTS, 7125 Reading Rd., Cincinnati OH 45237. (513)631-2690. Contact: Peter Wagner. Architecture/landscape/planning firm. Clients: residential, commercial and industrial.
Needs: Assigns 12 jobs/year. Uses artists for architectural renderings, graphic design, landscape design, model buildings and urban planning materials.
First Contact & Terms: Local artists only. Query with photos. Reports in 1 month. Pays $1,000-2,500, graphic design.

PLUMB, TUCKETT & ASSOCIATES, Architects, Engineers & Surveyors, 6481 Taft St., Merrillville IN 46410. (219)980-0500 or (312)731-6175. Chief Architect: Robert C. Book. Architectural firm providing full services—"financing through to construction." Clients: commercial, medical.
Needs: Works with 1-2 freelance artists/year. Uses artists for advertising and brochure design, interior design, architectural renderings and model making.
First Contact & Terms: Artists with minimum of three years' experience only. Works on assignment only. Send query letter with brochure to be kept on file. Pays for design and illustration by the hour, $40 minimum. Considers complexity of project, client's budget, and skill and experience of artist when establishing payment.

QUINN ASSOCIATES INC. - ARCHITECTS AIA, Avon Park North, Avon CT 06001. (203)678-1319. President: Richard W. Quinn AIA. Architectural firm providing architectural design, interior design and planning. Clients: commercial, institutional, residential.
Needs: Works with various numbers of freelance artists/year. Uses artists for brochure design, interior and architectural renderings, and furnishings.
First Contact & Terms: Send query letter with brochure, resume and samples to be kept on file. Call or write for appointment to show portfolio. Prefers slides or photographs as samples. Samples returned by SASE only if requested. Reports within 30 days. Works on assignment only. Payment varies with assignment. Considers complexity of project, client's budget, and skill and experience of artist when establishing payment.

*DAVID C. RACKER ASLA & ASSOCIATES, 3120 S. 950 E., Bountiful UT 84010. (801)295-5335. Contact: Dave Racker. Architecture/landscape/land planning firm, providing consulting services.

Clients: commercial, residential and some industrial.
Needs: Assigns 20-30 jobs/year. Works with artists for architectural renderings, graphic design and scale models.
First Contact & Terms: Query. SASE. Reports in 2 weeks. Pays $50-500.

RESEARCH PLANNING ASSOCIATES, 1831 Chestnut St., Philadelphia PA 19103. (215)561-9700. Contact: R. Lindsay Volkening. Architectural and interior design firm providing architectural interior design, feasibility studies and architecture. Clients: commercial.
Needs: Works with 4-10 freelance artists/year. Uses artists for architectural renderings, interior, graphic and brochure design; interior and landscape art renderings; furnishings, design consulting, charts, model making and signage.
First Contact & Terms: Send query letter. Samples returned by SASE. Works on assignment only. Provide resume, business card, brochure, flyer, samples and tear sheets to be kept on file for possible future assignments. Negotiates payment. Pays for design and illustration by the hour, $10-25 average. Considers complexity of project, client's budget, skill and experience of artist and turnaround time when establishing payment.
Tips: The architectural field is becoming more energy conscious. "There is more use of specialized artists. Present your work in a concise, clear manner."

REUS & SPEEGLE, ARCHITECTS & PLANNERS, Suite 3, 306 N. Presa, San Antonio TX 78205. (512)228-9921. President: John J. Speegle. Architectural firm offering residential, commercial and multi-family design and construction document, and construction building and observation services.
Needs: Works with 5 freelance artists/year. Uses artists for advertising and brochure design, architectural renderings and model making.
First Contact & Terms: Prefers local and regional artists with experience and examples. Works on assignment only. Send query letter with brochure and resume samples. Prefers photostats and tear sheets as samples. Samples not filed are not returned. Reports only if interested. Pays for design by the hour, $25-90 average; for illustration by the project, $200-500 average. Considers complexity of the project, client's budget, skill and experience of artist, how work will be used and turnaround time when establishing payment.

ROBERT AND COMPANY, 96 Poplar St. NW, Atlanta GA 30335. (404)577-4000. Art Director: Peter Lyon. Architecture/engineering/planning firm providing marketing and support graphics for company and clients. Clients: industrial, governmental/municpal, educational, military, medical, multi-residential.
Needs: Works with 5-6 freelance artists/year. Uses artists for advertising and brochure illustration; landscape, interior and architectural renderings; charts, maps and model makings; also uses photographers.
First Contact & Terms: Local artists preferred. Send query letter with resume, samples and tear sheets to be kept on file; write for appointment to show portfolio. Prefers photostats, slides, photographs as samples; original work only necessary for interview. Samples not kept on file returned by SASE only if requested. Reports only if interested. Pays by the project; requests artist's estimate/bid. Considers complexity of project, skill and experience of artist, and turnaround time when establishing payment.

ROE/ELISEO, INC., 576 5th Ave., New York NY 10036. (212)398-1078. Director, Project Development: Phyllis R. Ghougasian. Architecture/interior design firm providing architectural planning, design, interior design and construction services. Clients: health, commercial, industrial, government.
Needs: Uses artists for brochure design, illustration and layout; interior and landscape design; interior, landscape and architectural renderings; model making.
First Contact & Terms: Send query letter with resume to be kept on file. Prefers slides, photographs or original work as samples. Samples not kept on file are returned by SASE. Reports only if interested. Works on assignment only. Pays by the project; rate depends on scope of project, fee, structure, etc. Considers client's budget when establishing payment.

GEORGE RUSCITTO-ASSOCIATES, 1515 E. Carson St., Box 4251, Pittsburgh PA 15203. (412)381-2933. Contact: George Ruscitto. Architectural firm providing building space planning, design and financial planning. Clients: institutional, commercial.
Needs: Works with 1 freelance artist/year. Uses artists for interior design and interior/architectural renderings.
First Contact & Terms: Local artists only. Works on assignment only. Send query letter with brochure and samples to be kept on file. Call or write for appointment to show portfolio. Prefers actual work or photographs as samples. Samples not filed are returned. Reports only if interested. Payment varies according to project. Considers complexity of project and client's budget when establishing payment.

SACKVILLE-WEST/CORNTER, P.S., W815 7th Ave., Spokane WA 99204. (509)747-3103. Administrator: Kathleen Titus. Architectural firm. Clients: commercial, industrial, educational.
Needs: Works with 1-2 freelance artists/year. Uses artists for interior and architectural renderings.
First Contact & Terms: Works on assignment only. Send query letter with resume, samples to be kept on file. Prefers photocopies as samples. Reports only if interested. Pays for illustration by the hour, $6-125 average, or by project, $600 minimum. Considers complexity of the project, client's budget, skill and experience of artist and how work will be used when establishing payment.

*THE SCHEMMER ASSOCIATES INC., Suite 110, 3165 McCrory Place, Orlando FL 32803. Architecture/engineering firm. Clients: commercial and industrial.
Needs: Works with 4 artists for architectural renderings and 2 for interior design.
First Contact & Terms: Query with photos. SASE. Reports in 1 week. Works on assignment only. Samples returned by SASE; reports back on future assignment possibilities. Provide brochure and flyer to be kept on file for future assignments. Pays $150-550, renderings; $500-750, model buildings.

JANET SCHIRN INTERIORS, 919 N. Michigan Ave., Chicago IL 60611. President: Janet Schirn. Interior design firm providing contract and residential interior design. Clients: business, restaurant and mercantile (wholesale).
Needs: Uses artists for graphics and fine art.
First Contact & Terms: Send letter with resume and samples. Pays by the project. Considers client's budget, and skill and experience of artist when establishing payment.
Tips: "Better quality work is necessary; there is greater client sophistication. Just show your work—no sales pitch."

JEAN SEDOR DESIGNS, (formerly Potter Lawson & Pawlowsky), 305 S. Main St., Janesville, WI 53545. Interior Designer: Jean Sedor. Interior design firm. "We function as interior designers doing everything from finish schedules to supervising and contracting for entire art programs for various installations." Clients: contract, i.e., banks, insurance companies, utilites, etc.
Needs: Works with freelance artists. Uses artists for art furnishings.
First Contact & Terms: Send query letter with brochure, resume, business card, samples and tear sheets to be kept on file. Call or write for appointment to show portfolio. Prefers slides, photographs, original work as samples. Samples returned only if requested. Reports only if interested. Works on assignment only. Pays for design and illustration by the project, $100-12,000 average. Considers complexity of project, client's budget, skill and experience of artist and how work will be used when establishing payment.

RICHARD SEIDEN INTERIORS, 238 N. Allen St., Albany NY 12206. (518)482-8600. President: Richard Seiden. Interior design firm. Provides residential and contract interior design. Clients: residential.
Needs: Works with 4 artists for graphic design; 3, signage design; 2, model making; 3, murals; 4, wall hangings; 3, landscape design; 2, charts/graphs; and 2, stained glass.
First Contact & Terms: Query with resume. SASE. Reports in 3 weeks. Works on assignment only. Provide materials to be kept on file for future assignments. Pays $150-1,800, original wall decor; also according to project. Considers complexity of project and client's budget when establishing payment.
Tips: Prefers to see photos rather than slides, if possible.

SEMPARTNERS, INC., 100 E. Prince St., Drawer Q, Beckley WV 25802. (304)255-6181. Contact: J. Blair Frier. Architectural firm offering architectural, planning, engineering, programming, construction administration, consulting. Clients: commercial, residential, education, state and federal, health care.
Needs: Uses artists for interior design, design consulting and model making.
First Contact & Terms: Works on assignment only. Send brochure and samples to be kept on file. Call for appointment to show portfolio. Samples not filed are returned only if requested. Reports within 1 month. Pays for design by the project. Considers complexity of the project and client's budget when establishing payment.

SFS INTERIORS, 14 W. Kirk Ave., Roanoke VA 24011. (703)345-5220. Interior Designer: Debbie Voss. Interior design firm providing specifiers, consultants, purchasing agents. Clients: contract commercial (some residential).
Needs: Works with 2-6 freelance artists/year. Uses artists for brochure and landscape design, and interior renderings.
First Contact & Terms: Send query letter with brochure and samples to be kept on file. Prefers slides, photographs as samples. Samples not kept on file are returned only if requested. Reports within 15 days.

Works on assignment only. Pays for design by the hour, $7-40 average; for illustration by the project, $100-1,000 average. Considers complexity of project and client's budget when establishing payment.

ROGER SHERMAN ASSOCIATES, R.S. INTERIORS, Suite 300, 13530 Michigan Ave., Dearborn MI 48126. (313)582-8844. Contact: Joy Noteboom. Interior design and contract purchasing firms providing architectural and interior design for commercial restaurants, stores, hotels and shopping centers and complete furnishing purchasing. Clients: commercial.
Needs: Uses artists for architectural renderings, furnishings, landscape and graphic design, model making and signage; also for special decor items as focal points for commercial installations, such as paintings, wood carvings, etc.
First Contact & Terms: Artists with past work experience only, able to provide photos of work and references. Send query letter with brochure/flyer or resume and samples to be kept on file. Call or write for appointment. Prefers slides and examples of original work as samples. Samples not returned. Reporting time depends on scope of project. Works on assignment only. Negotiates payment; varies according to client's budget.

MARGOT SIEGEL, AIA, ARCHITECT INC., Penthouse Suite, 5858 Wilshire Blvd., Los Angeles CA 90036. (213)930-1750. Architecture firm providing planning and limited interior design services. Clients: commercial and residential. Buys 3 renderings/year.
Needs: Works with 3 artists for architectural renderings; 3, graphic design; and 2, landscape design.
First Contact & Terms: Local artists only. Query with samples and arrange interview to show portfolio; no calls. Works on assignment only. Samples returned by SASE; reports back on future assignment possibilities. Work must be reproducible in b&w, i.e. line drawing with color added. Provide resume and business card to be kept on file for future assignments. Pays by the project for design and illustration.

SPACE DESIGN INTERNATIONAL, INC., Suite 445, 309 Vine St., Cincinnati OH 45202. (513)241-3000. Director of Communications: Cecily Hudson. Interior and graphic design firm providing programming, space planning, interior architecture, store planning, interior and graphic design. Clients: corporate, commercial, institutional.
Needs: Uses freelance artists for architectural and interior design renderings, graphic design and model making.
First Contact & Terms: Prefers artists with some experience; it helps if artists are near by. Send query letter with samples and brochure/flyer or resume to be kept on file; write for appointment. Prefers original work in portfolio if reviewed in person; if mailed in, prefers reproductions. Samples returned by SASE. Works on assignment only. Negotiates payment by the project or by the hour; varies according to client's budget.

GEORGE STATEN & ASSOCIATES INC., ARCHITECTS & PLANNERS, Suite 101, 4849 N. Mesa, El Paso TX 79912. (915)544-7000. Contact: George Staten AIA. Architecture/interior design firm. Clients: residential, institutional, hotel, medical and commercial.
Needs: Works with 3 artists for architectural renderings; 1, interior design; 2, graphic design; 2, signage design; 1, model making; 2, sculpture; 2, landscape design; and 2, stained glass.
First Contact & Terms: Query or write for interview. SASE. Reports in 1 week. Works on assignment only. Provide resume, business card and brochure to be kept on file for future assignments. Pays $200-2,500, architectural renderings; $50-1,000, building interiors; $300-3,000, full-color renderings; $100 minimum, landscape design.

SUNDESIGNS ARCHITECTS, 901 Blake Ave., Glenwood Springs CO 81601. Architects: D.K. Moffatt and C.F. Brenner. Architectural/interior and landscape design/land planning firm providing commercial and residential architectural design and land planning of residential P.U.D.'s and resorts. Clients: bank buildings, office buildings, resorts and housing developers.
Needs: Works with 6 freelance artists/year. Uses artists for advertising illustration, brochure and interior design, landscape, interior and architectural renderings.
First Contact & Terms: Local, experienced and innovative artists only. Send query letter with brochure to be kept on file. Reports within 1 month. Pay rate varies; pay is negotiated after scope of work is defined. Considers complexity of project, client's budget, and skill and experience of artists when establishing payment.

THE TARQUINI ORGANIZATION, A Professional Association of Architects and Planners, 1812 Federal St., Camden NJ 08105. (609)365-7270. Vice President: Robert Giacomelli AIA. Architectural firm. Clients: commercial, residential, municipal.
Needs: Works with 2 freelance artists/year. Uses artists for advertising, brochure and interior design; ar-

chitectural renderings and model making.
First Contact & Terms: Send query letter with brochure, business card and samples to be kept on file. Prefers photostats as samples. Samples returned by SASE if requested by artist. Reports only if interested. Works on assignment only. Pays per job basis. Considers client's budget, and skill and experience of artist when establishing payment.

THOMAS-CAMPBELL-PRIDGEON, INC., 735 E. Main St., Box 3028, Spartanburg SC 29304. (803)583-1456. Vice President: Richard Campbell. Architectural firm offering design services with interior and landscape design. Clients: commercial, education, governmental, industrial, residential, religious.
Needs: Works with 1-2 freelance artists/year. Uses artists for brochure design and architectural renderings.
First Contact & Terms: Works on assignment only. Send query letter with brochure to be kept on file. Prefers to review photocopies. Reports only if interested. Pays for illustration by project. Considers complexity of the project, client's budget, and skill and experience of artist when establishing payment.

RONALD W. THURBER, AIA, 1523 Hays, Boise ID 83702. (208)345-4698. Contact: Ronald Thurber. Clients: commercial.
Needs: Works with 1 artist for architectural renderings; 1, signage design; and 1, stained glass.
First Contact & Terms: Western US artists only. Query. SASE. Reports in 1 week. Provide brochure to be kept on file for future assignments. Pays $100-300/job, renderings; by the hour, $5-8 average, and by the project, $150-300 average, for design.

TUGGLE & GRAVES, INC.-ARCHITECTS, Suite 755, 711 Navarro, San Antonio TX 78205. (512)222-0194. Contact: Tuggle or Graves. Architectural/interior design firm offering architectural and space planning. Clients: school districts, commercial, government, industrial, residential.
Needs: Works with 3 freelance artists/year. Uses artists for brochure and interior design, architectural renderings, maps and model making.
First Contact & Terms: Artists with three years' experience only. Works on assignment only. Call or write for appointment to show portfolio. Reports within 1 day if interested. Pays for design by the project, $200-1,000 average. Considers complexity of project, client's budget, skill and experience of artist and how work will be used when establishing payment.

TURN KEY CONCEPTS CORP., 21 E. Shore Rd., Manhasset NY 11030. (516)365-7700. Designer: Gita Rose. Specializes in interior design. Clients: hotels and restaurants.
Needs: Works with 5 freelance artists/year. Uses artists for wall displays.
First Contact & Terms: Send query letter with brochure, resume, business card and samples to be kept on file. Call for appointment to show portfolio. Reports back only if interested. Pays for design by the project. Considers complexity of project and client's budget when establishing payment.

PHILIP TUSA DESIGN INC., Box 14, Roosevelt Island Station, New York NY 10044. (212)753-2810. President: Philip M. Tusa. Specializes in interior design. Clients: commercial firms, corporations and residential.
Needs: Uses artists for illustration, model making, interior rendering and drafting.
First Contact & Terms: Works on assignment only. Send query letter with brochure, resume, business card and samples to be kept on file. Prefers slides and/or tear sheets as samples. Reports back only if interested. Considers complexity of project, client's budget, skill and experience of artist, how work will be used, turnaround time and rights purchased when establishing payment.

URBAN DESIGN ASSOCIATES, 258 Church St., New Haven CT 06510. (203)865-3381. Architect: George Conklin. Specializes in architectural design and solar design. Clients: commercial, residential, housing project.
Needs: Works with 3 artists for architectural renderings; 1, interior design; 1, graphic design; 1, signage design; 1, model making; and 1, landscape design.
First Contact & Terms: New England-New York area artists only. Query with samples. SASE. Reports in 2 weeks. Works on assignment only. No samples returned. Provide resume and brochure to be kept on file. Payment by job: $250 minimum, architectural renderings; $300 minimum, scale models; $150-350, graphic design; $100-300, signs.

VALENTOUR ENGLISH AND ASSOCIATES, Registered Architects, 470 Washington Rd., Pittsburgh PA 15228. Interior Designer: Denise L. Lostetter. Architectural firm providing architectural and interior design, working drawings, etc. Clients: primarily institutional and some commercial.
Needs: Works with 1 freelance artist/year. Uses artist for advertising illustration and interior renderings.

First Contact & Terms: Local artists only. Write for appointment to show portfolio; enclose resume to be kept on file. Reports within 2 weeks. Works on assignment only. Pays for design by the project, $20 minimum. Considers complexity of project, client's budget, skill and experience of artist, how work will be used, turnaround time and rights purchased when establishing payment.

*VBN CORPORATION, 363 13th St., Oakland CA 94612. (415)763-1313. Principal: Dean Aron Tatsuno. Architectural/interior design/urban planning firm providing full-service architectural design, interior design and urban planning. Clients: commercial, residential, governmental and corporate.
Needs: Works with 5-10 freelance artists/year. Uses artists for interior and landscape design, interior and architectural renderings, furnishings and model making.
First Contact & Terms: Prefers local artists. Works on assignment only. Send query letter with brochure and business card to be kept on file. Accepts photostats, slides, photocopies, tear sheets, etc. as samples—"whatever best shows artist's work." Reports only if interested. Pays for design and illustration by the hour, $5-50 average. Considers complexity of the project, client's budget, skill and experience of artist and turnaround time when establishing payment.

*VERCESI & SCHARFSPITZ, ARCHITECTS, 353 Broad Ave., Leonia NJ 07605. Contact: Tony Vercesi. Architectural firm providing full architectural services. Clients: residential (custom homes and apartment houses); commercial (space improvements, office and industrial buildings).
Needs: Works with several freelance artists/year. Uses artists for interior design, architectural renderings, design consultation, furnishings and model making.
First Contact & Terms: Artists "must be talented and productive." Send business card to be kept on file; write for appointment to show portfolio. Reports only if interested. Works on assignment only. Pays by the hour, $15-50 average. Considers complexity of project, client's budget, and skill and experience of artist when establishing payment.

VICKREY/OVRESAT/AWSUMB ASSOCIATES, INC., 500 S. Magnolia Ave., Orlando FL 32801. (305)425-2500. Senior Vice President: John K. Awsumb, AIA. Coordinator-Project Development: Sandra Moore. Architectural/interior design firm providing architecture, planning, interior design, space planning and construction administration. Clients: industrial, residential, religious, military, hotel and restaurant, educational and medical facilities.
Needs: Works with 1-5 freelance artists/year. Uses artists for interior and architectural renderings, and model making.
First Contact & Terms: Send query letter with resume and samples to be kept on file; call for appointment to show portfolio. Prefers slides as samples. Samples not kept on file are returned only if requested. Reports back only if artist requests. Works on assignment only. Pays by the project. Considers client's budget when establishing payment.

BERNARD VINICK ASSOCIATES, INC., 211 Wethersfield Ave., Hartford CT 06114. (203)525-4293. Vice President: Barbara Ebstein. Interior design firm providing office, restaurant, bank, store, institutional and residential design.
Needs: Uses 4 freelance artists/year. Uses artists for architectural renderings and interior and graphic design.
First Contact & Terms: Send query letter, resume and business card to be kept on file; also send samples. Prefers slides as samples. Samples returned. Reports within 1 week. Works on assignment only. Provide resume and business card to be kept on file for possible future assignments. Payment is by the project; $200-500 average.

LORRIN L. WARD, ARCHITECT INC., 341 W. 4th St., Chico CA 95928. (916)342-4265. President: Lorrin Ward. Architecture firm. Provides architectural design, planning, project administration. Clients: governmental, industrial and commercial. Buys 2-5 renderings/year.
Needs: Works with 2 artists for architectural renderings; 1, model making; and 1, landscape design.
First Contact & Terms: Prefers artists who have worked with other firms of this type. Query with brochure. SASE. Reports within 1-2 weeks. Provide resume, business card and brochure to be kept on file for future assignments. Pays for design by the hour, $15-35 average; by the project, $100-900 average; by the day, $120-280 average. Pays for illustration by the hour, $20-40 average; by the project, $200-900 average; by the day, $150-400 average. Considers complexity of project, skill and experience of artist, turnaround time and rights purchased when establishing payment.

CHRIS WEBER & ASSOC., 530 Chestnut St., W. Reading PA 19611. (215)374-4178. Contact: Chris Weber. Architectural firm providing full architectural and engineering services. Clients: "all types."
Needs: Works with "several" freelance artists/year. Uses artists for landscape design, interior and architectural renderings, furnishings and model making.

First Contact & Terms: Send brochure, business card and samples. Prefers photostats, slides or photocopies as samples. Samples not filed are returned only if requested. Reports back only if interested. Pays according to quote. Considers complexity of the project, client's budget, skill and experience of artist and turnaround time when establishing payment.

HENRY P. WILHELMI, LANDSCAPE ARCHITECT/COMMUNITY PLANNER, 420 E. Genesee, Syracuse NY 13202. (315)474-7567. Contact: Henry P. Wilhelmi. Clients: government and institutions.
Needs: Works with 3-4 artists for architectural renderings; 1-2, graphic design; occasional, signage design; occasional, model making; 1-2, murals; and 1-2, sculpture.
First Contact & Terms: Local artists only. Mail photos or transparencies. Works on assignment only. Samples returned by SASE; and reports back on future possibilities. Provide resume, business card, brochure, flyer and tear sheet or any combination which will provide basic data to be kept on file for future assignments. Pays by job.
Tips: "Because of budget considerations, clients appear to be less receptive to including sculpture, murals, etc. as site features."

CLIFFORD N. WRIGHT ASSOC. ARCHITECTS, 4066 W. Maple, Birmingham MI 48010. (313)647-2022. President: William L. Baldner A.I.A. Vice President: William D. Shiels. Architectural firm providing total architectural services. Clients: residential, commercial, light industrial.
Needs: Works with 10 freelance artists/year. Uses artists for landscape and interior design, interior and architectural renderings, design consulting and furnishings.
First Contact & Terms: Send brochure and resume to be kept on file; call for appointment to show portfolio. Reports only if interested. Works on assignment only. Pays by the project for design and illustration. Considers complexity of project, client's budget, and skill and experience of artist when establishing payment.

Art/Design Studios

Art/design studios, which can be as small as a one-man operation or as large as a big-name advertising agency, continue to offer artists a wide range of freelance assignments. No longer are these studios all things to all people; instead, they are concentrating on supplying the art needs of a select number of clients. Even with a limited clientele, art/design studios must offer a range of services from design, illustration and layout to mechanicals, paste-up and retouching. Many studios report their clients contract with them for shorter periods than in the past; this trend requires the studios to continually find new artists to fill the specific needs of their new clients.

Tight deadlines are an inherent aspect of working with art/design studios; for this reason many studios must work with nearby artists. In addition to consulting the listings given here, check the Yellow Pages and Business to Business Directory for studios within commuting distance. *The Design Directory*, available in most libraries, provides names of studios by state plus their areas of professional service.

Key to getting jobs with a studio is selling yourself and articulating what you can do for that studio and its clientele. Included in the listings is information to help you gear your samples to a studio's services and client needs. Increase the odds of successfully selling yourself by doing the necessary research and then approaching only those studios seeking your particular artistic skills.

Once you decide to contact a studio, edit your portfolio and samples to suit its needs. Be prepared during a review to explain your total involvement in each project you show the studio director. Thumbnails, roughs, comprehensives and finished pieces are vital in explaining your design process for each project.

In addition to looking at your art work, directors look for professionalism in your manner; well-designed and illustrated promotional pieces; and the ability to take directions and to communicate with printers, studio personnel and clients.

Read the Close-up with Arthur Ritter, president of Arthur Ritter Inc., New York City. Twenty-five years as a graphic designer, art director and teacher have taught Ritter what it takes to succeed as a designer in a field where competition is keen.

This technical pen illustration created by Taylor Oughton, Bucks County, Pennsylvania, was used as a spot illustration in a promotional booklet designed and produced by Alan Gorelick & Associates Inc. The art was printed on a separate sheet of paper for insertion into the booklet.

AARON, SAUTER, GAINES & ASSOCIATES/DIRECT MARKETING, Suite 110, 5229 7th Ave., Phoenix AZ 85013. (602)265-1933. President: Cameron G. Sauter. Specializes in brand identity, direct marketing, direct response ads, catalogs and P-O-P displays for retail stores, banks, industrial, mail order and service companies.
Needs: Works with 5-10 freelance artists/year. Uses artists for advertising, brochure and catalog design and illustration, mechanicals, retouching and direct mail packages.
First Contact and Terms: Seeks artists with professionalism, speed and experience only. Send query letter with brochure, resume and business card to be kept on file. Prefers original work, photos or slides as samples. Samples returned by SASE if not kept on file. Reports only if interested. Works on assignment basis. Pays for design, by the hour, $15-50 average; by the project, $100-1,000 average; by the day, $50-100 average. Pays for illustration, by the hour, $25-75 average; by the project, $100-2,000 average; by the day, $100-150 average. Considers complexity of project, client's budget, skill and experience of artist and turnaround time when establishing payment. "All art is purchased with full rights and no limitations."

*ADAM, FILIPPO & MORAN DESIGN CONSULTANTS, 1206 5th Ave., Pittsburgh PA 15219. (412)261-3720. Contact: Robert Adam, Lewis Filippo, Dennis Moran. Specializes in annual reports, brand identity, corporate identity, displays, interior design, packaging, publications and signage. Clients: major corporations and facilities.
Needs: Uses artists for mechanicals, retouching and model making.
First Contact & Terms: Send query letter with brochure, resume, business card and samples to be kept on file for 6 months. Prefers slides as samples. Samples returned only by SASE. Reports only if interested. Pays for design by the hour, $10-25 average. Considers client's budget, skill and experience of artist and turnaround time when establishing payment.

LEE AMES & ZAK, LTD., 6500 Jericho Turnpike, Commack NY 11725. President: Lee J. Ames. Specializes in publications, technical illustration, general illustration, science illustration and cartoons. Clients: Major book publishers.
Needs: Works with 15 freelance artists/year. Uses artists for science illustration, book design and illustration, mechanicals and charts/graphics.
First Contact & Terms: Send query letter with resume and tear sheets to be kept on file unless "unsuitable." Prefers disposable photocopies as samples. Samples not kept on file are not returned. Reports only if interested. Works on assignment only. Pays "as much as possible." Considers complexity of project, client's budget, skill and experience of artist, how work will be used, turnaround time and rights purchased when establishing payment.

ANCO/BOSTON, 441 Stuart St., Boston MA 02116. (617)267-9700. Graphic Director: Julie Gallagher. Art agency. Clients: educational publishers, commercial and industrial.
Needs: Works with 10 illustrators. Uses artists for books, charts, graphs, technical art and paste-up. Most of the artwork required is one-color line art.
First Contact & Terms: Local artists only. Arrange interview. Provide business card, resume, tear sheets and brochure to be kept on file for future assignments. All art becomes the property of Anco/Boston.

ANDREN & ASSOCIATES INC., 6400 N. Keating Ave., Lincolnwood IL 60646. (312)267-8500. Contact: Kenneth E. Andren. Clients: beauty products and tool manufacturers, clothing retailers, laboratories, banks, cameras and paper products.
Needs: Assigns 6-7 jobs/month. Uses artists for catalogs, direct mail brochures, flyers, packages, P-O-P displays and print media advertising.
First Contact & Terms: Local artists only. Query with samples or arrange interview. SASE. Reports in 1-2 weeks. Pays $15 minimum/hour for animation, design, illustrations, layout, lettering, mechanicals, paste-up, retouching and type spec.

ANTISDEL IMAGE GROUP, INC., 3242 De La Cruz Blvd., Santa Clara CA 95054. (408)988-1010. President: G.C. Antisdel. Specializes in annual reports, corporate identity, displays, interior design, packaging, publications, signage and photo illustration. Clients: high technology 80%, energy 10%, and banking 10%.
Needs: Uses artists for illustration, mechanicals, retouching, airbrushing, direct mail packages, model making, charts/graphs, AV materials and lettering.
First Contact & Terms: Works on assignment only. Send query letter with brochure, business card and samples to be kept on file. Write for appointment to show portfolio or contact through agent. Reports back only if interested. Pays for design and illustration by the project. Considers complexity of project,

Close-up

Arthur Ritter, President
Arthur Ritter, Inc.
New York, New York

Not all New York City graphic design studios are big, and not all are located in the mid-town Manhattan area. One small but thriving graphic design studio, situated just north of Greenwich Village on West Tenth Street, is Arthur Ritter, Inc.

Artist: David R. Smiton

A production manager, art director, sales manager and freelance artists comprise this studio whose clientele run the gamut from media and publishing to hospitals and other non-profit public service organizations.

The head of this seventeen-year-old creative group is Arthur Ritter—graphic designer, art director and teacher. Twenty-five years of experience have taught Ritter the difference between a graphic designer and an illustrator or painter.

"As a graphic designer you start a project with very little information. You then must imagine the various ways to put together the package. You must enjoy not only the illustrating and designing, but the challenge of solving a given problem."

A freelance designer must possess certain basic skills before approaching a design studio. "You should understand abstract concepts, be able to handle type in all phases and know production methods. You must be exacting in what you do, be able to fit layout to copy and be comfortable with composition of the printed page."

The bottom line for success as a designer is the ability to sell yourself and to articulate what you can do for a particular client. "Research the market to find the firms you should approach. Study directories in your area to learn who does what, then ask yourself if your work fits into these markets. My studio, for example, needs artists primarily for technical work. We work a lot with typography and seek people whose skills are in line with that need."

Once you focus on a particular design studio, gear your portfolio and samples to suit its art needs. Ritter advises including with mailed samples a typed cover letter on your own letterhead. In the letter indicate that you plan to call and then *call*. Follow-up, according to Ritter, is essential in your selling process.

The follow-up telephone call can indicate your professionalism. "It is important to communicate well in order to sell yourself to a studio or later to a studio's clients. Your ability to talk with me by phone can indicate your ability to talk with printers and a studio's designers, and to communicate ideas and explain your design processes."

Once you begin working as a freelancer don't expect to climb the rungs of success right away. "Expect to work your way up in this field. It is necessary that you do mechanicals to gain experience. Consider working in related areas such as typography or printing for further experience.

"Be curious about and aware of the world and your environment. You never know where along the way you will see a particular art form which will help you to interpret your client's needs in the future."

client's budget, skill and experience of artist, how work will be used, turnaround time and rights purchased when establishing payment.

Tips: "Our top grade clients are not subject to 'trendy' fads."

THE ART WORKS, 4409 Maple Ave., Dallas TX 75219. (214)521-2121. Creative Director: Fred Henley. Specializes in annual reports, brand identity, corporate identity, displays, packaging, publications, signage, illustration and photography.

Needs: Works with 15-20 freelance artists/year. Uses artists for advertising, brochure, catalog and book design and illustration; advertising, brochure and catalog layout; P-O-P displays, mechanicals, retouching, posters, direct mail packages, lettering and logos.

First Contact and Terms: Send brochure, business card and samples to be kept on file. Call or write for appointment to show portfolio. Prefers slides, original work as samples. Samples returned by SASE only if requested by artist. Reports within 7 days. Pays for design and illustration by the project. Considers complexity of project, client's budget, skill and experience of artist and turnaround time when establishing payment.

ARTHUR RITTER, INC., 45 W. 10th St., New York NY 10011. (212)505-0241. Administrative Art Director: Valerie Ritter. Specializes in annual reports, corporate identity, brochures, catalogs and promotion for publishers, corporations, public service organizations and hospitals.

Needs: Works with 5 freelance artists/year according to firm's needs. Uses artists for advertising design and illustration, brochure design, mechanicals, charts and graphs.

First Contact & Terms: Prefers experienced artists, although "talented 'self-starters' with design expertise/education are also considered." Send query letter with brochure, resume and samples to be kept on file. "Follow up within a week of the query letter about the possibility of arranging an appointment for a portfolio review." Prefers printed pieces as samples. Samples not filed are returned by SASE. Does not always work on assignment only; "sometimes we need a freelancer on a day-to-day basis at the studio." Pays for design by the hour, $10-20 average; by the project, $100-500 average; or by the day, $65-120 average. Pays for illustration by the project, $50-500 average. Considers complexity of the project, client's budget, skill and experience of the artist and turnaround time when establishing payment.

JEREMIAH AUSTIN GRAPHIC DESIGN, Suite 309, 1770 Broadway, Oakland CA 94612. (415)452-0313. Creative Director: Jeremiah Austin. Specializes in annual reports, corporate indentity, packaging, publications and signage. Clients: corporations and companies in the fields of high technology, real estate, banking and financial services.

Needs: Works with 4-6 freelance artist/year. Uses artists for illustration, mechanicals, retouching and lettering.

First Contact & Terms: Artists for mechanicals and retouching must be local; artists for illustration and lettering may be national. All must have minimum of 3 years' experience and be capable of fast turnaround. Works on assignment only. Send query letter with brochure, business card and samples to be kept on file. Call or write for appointment to show portfolio. Prefers slides as samples; tear sheets or clean photocopies OK. Samples not filed are returned by SASE only if requested. Reports back only if interested. Pays by the hour for illustration, $25-50 average. Considers complexity of project, client's budget, skill and experience of artist, turnaround time and rights purchased when establishing payment.

Tips: "We are a busy, professional design office and prefer to work with professional freelancers. Know what you can and cannot do, how much time and money it will take to do and stick to your promises."

*CAROL BANCROFT & FRIENDS, 185 Goodhill Rd., Weston CT 06883. (203)226-7674. President: Carol Bancroft. Specializes in publications. Clients: publishing companies, ad agencies, studios and major corporations.

Needs: Works with 40 freelance artists/year. Uses artists for advertising, brochure, catalog and book illustration, and charts/graphics.

First Contact & Terms: Send resume, samples and tear sheets to be kept on file. Call for appointment to show portfolio; contact through artist's agent. Prefers slides, tear sheets and photos as samples. Samples not kept on file are returned. Reports within 1 day. Considers complexity of project, client's budget, turnaround time and rights purchased when establishing payment.

BANKA-MANGO, Room 274, Merchandise Mart, Chicago IL 60654. (312)467-0059. Director of Graphic Design: Joseph R. Mango. Specializes in brand and corporate identity, displays, exhibits and shows, interior design and signage. Clients: retail stores and manufacturers of retail products.

Needs: Works with 1-2 freelance artists/year. Uses artists for packaging design and illustration, brochure design, mechanicals, retouching, poster illustration, model making, charts/graphs, lettering and logo design.

First Contact & Terms: Send query letter with brochure/flyer or resume; call or write for appointment.

Prefers slides or originals as samples. Samples returned by SASE. Reports within 1 week. Works on assignment only. Provide brochure/flyer and tear sheets to be kept on file for possible future assignments. Pays by the project on completion for design and illustration
Tips: "Have good, current samples."

BARNSTORM STUDIOS, Suite 301, 2502½ W. Colorado Ave., Colorado Springs CO 80904. (303)630-7200. Art Director: Douglas D. Blough. Specializes in corporate identity, brochure design, multi-image slide presentations and publications. Clients: ad agencies, high-technology corporations.
Needs: Works with 2-4 freelance artists/year. Uses artists for design, illustration, brochures, mechanicals, retouching, AV materials and lettering.
First Contact & Terms: Works with local, experienced (clean, fast and accurate) artists on assignment. Send query letter with resume and samples to be kept on file. Call or write for appointment to show portfolio. Prefers "good originals or reproductions, professionally presented in any form" as samples. Samples not kept on file are returned by SASE. Reports back only if interested. Pays for design by the hour, $15-25 average. Pays for illustration by the project, $50 minimum, b&w; $100, color. Considers client's budget, skill and experience of artist, and turnaround time when establishing payment.

BASIC/BEDELL ADVERTISING SELLING IMPROVEMENT CORP., 2040 Alameda Padre Serra, Santa Barbara CA 93103. President: C. Barrie Bedell. Specializes in publications, advertisements and direct mail. Clients: national and international newspapers, publishers, direct response marketers, retail stores, hard lines manufacturers and trade associations plus extensive self-promotion.
Needs: Uses artists for publication design, book covers and dust jackets, direct mail layout and pasteup. Especially wants to hear from publishing and "direct response" pros. Negotiates payment by the project. Considers client's budget, and skill and experience of artist when establishing payment.
Tips: "Substantial increase in use of freelance talent and increasing need for true professionals with exceptional skills and responsible performance (delivery as promised and 'on target'). It is very difficult to locate freelance talent with expertise in design of advertising and direct mail with heavy use of type. If work is truly professional and freelancer is business-like, contact with personal letter and photocopy of one or more samples of work that needn't be returned." Artists shouldn't "show only the finished, printed work, making it all but impossible to determine what the artist truly did, and the process that led to the final result. We prefer to see thumbnails and roughs in addition to the finished piece."

LAWRENCE BENDER & ASSOCIATES, 512 Hamilton Ave., Palo Alto CA 94301. (415)327-3821. President: Lawrence Bender. Specializes in annual reports. Clients: electronic manufacturers.
Needs: Works with 12 freelance artists/year. Uses artists for design, illustration, mechanicals, retouching and airbrushing.
First Contact & Terms: Send query letter with resume, business card and samples to be kept on file. Call or write for appointment to show portfolio. Samples not kept on file returned only if requested. Reports only if interested. Pays for design by the hour, project or day. Pays for illustration by the project. Considers complexity of project, client's budget, skill and experience of artist and rights purchased when establishing payment.

J.H. BERMAN AND ASSOCIATES, Suite 621, 2025 I St. NW, Washington DC 20006. (202)775-0892. General Manager: Jackie Deitch. Specializes in annual reports, corporate identity, publications and signage. Clients: real estate developers, architects, high-technology corporations and financial-oriented firms (banks, investment firms, etc.).
Needs: Works with 10-15 (6 consistently) freelance artists/year. Uses artists for design, illustration, brochures, magazines, books, P-O-P displays, mechanicals, retouching, airbrushing, posters, model making, charts/graphs, AV materials, lettering and advertisements. Especially needs designers, illustrators, technical illustrators, architectural renderers and mechanical/production artists.
First Contact & Terms: "Artists should be highly professional, with at least 2 years' experience. Highest quality work required. Restricted to local artists for mechanicals only." Send query letter with brochure, resume, business card and samples to be kept on file. Call or write for appointment to show portfolio or contact through agent. "Samples should be as compact as possible; slides not suggested." Samples not kept on file returned by SASE. Reports only if interested. Pays for design by the hour, $12-50 average. Pays for illustration by the project, $200 minimum. Considers complexity of project, skill and experience of artist, how work will be used, turnaround time and rights purchased when establishing payment.
Tips: Artists should have a "totally professional approach."

JOHN BLAIR & CO., 1290 Avenue of the Americas, New York NY 10104. Vice President, Corporate Relations: Josef B. Rosenberg. Marketing: Ira Ginsberg. Blair Television: Kenn Donnellon. Blair Radio: Dorothy Lancaster. Blair Entertainment: Dorothy Hamilton. Uses local artists for technical charts, annual reports, sales literature, booklets, illustrations and exhibit designs.

BOB BOEBERITZ DESIGN, (formerly Kelso Associates Ltd.), 247 Charlotte St., Asheville NC 28801. (704)258-0316. Owner: Bob Boeberitz. Graphic design studio. Clients: malls, hotels, restaurants, car dealers, resorts, land developers and furniture manufacturers.
Needs: Works with freelance artists on occasion. Uses artists primarily for illustration; occasionally buys humorous or cartoon-style illustrations.
First Contact & Terms: Send query letter with brochure, resume, business card, samples and tear sheets to be kept on file. Call for appointment to show portfolio. Prefers slides as samples. "Anything too large to fit in file" is discarded. Reports only if interested. Pays by the job. Considers complexity of project, client's budget, skill and experience of artist and turnaround time when establishing payment. Buys all rights.

BOWYER ASSOCIATES, INC., 43 Eglinton Ave. E, Toronto, Ontario M4P 1A2 Canada. (416)484-8848. President: Robert Bowyer. Studio. Clients: retail, industrial, commercial.
Needs: Assigns approximately 150 jobs/year to freelance artists. Works with 2 freelance illustrators/month. Uses artists for illustrations and finished artwork.
First Contact & Terms: Send resume; will be kept on file if interested. Reports only if interested. Sometimes works on assignment. Pays by the project. Considers complexity of project, client's budget, and skill and experience of artist when establishing payment. Buys all rights.
Tips: Especially looks for "originality, self-expression and neatness." Artists should "show only top quality work and finished artwork, anything artist thinks is good, in a range from illustration to packaging. Do not show artwork that you did in school—this lacks diversity."

BRANDYWINE ART, LTD., Box 1299, Boston MA 02205. President: M.L. Conklin. Specializes in product design and illustration. Clients: producers of consumer goods products.
Needs: Works with 40 freelance artists/year. Uses artists for "all aspects and types of creative design and illustration."
First Contact & Terms: "Artists should be experienced and professional in their work, be able to take direction and meet deadlines." Send query letter with brochure, resume, samples and tear sheets to be kept on file. Prefers photographs, photostats, actual samples, slides (no original artwork) as samples. Samples returned only if requested. Reports only if interested. Works on assignment only. Pays for design and illustration by the project, $50-1,000 average. Considers complexity of project, client's budget, skill and experience of artist, how work will be used, turnaround time and rights purchased when establishing payment.

BRODSKY GRAPHICS INC., 270 Madison Ave., New York NY 10016. (212)684-2600. Art Director: Ed Brodsky. Specializes in corporate identity, direct mail, promotion and packaging. Clients: ad agencies and corporations.
Needs: Works with 10 freelance artists/year. Uses artists for illustration, mechanicals, retouching, airbrushing, charts/graphs, AV materials and lettering.
First Contact & Terms: Works on assignment only. Send business card to be kept on file. Prefers tear sheets as samples. Reports back only if interested. Considers complexity of project, client's budget, skill and experience of artist and turnaround time when establishing payment.

THE CHESTNUT HOUSE GROUP INC., 540 N. Lakeshore Dr., Chicago IL 60611. (312)222-9090. Creative Directors: Norman Baugher and Miles Zimmerman. Clients: major educational publishers. Arrange interview.
Needs: Illustration, layout and assembly. Pays by job.

A. CHRISTIE DESIGN, 207 Pontiac St., Lester PA 19113. (215)521-2569. President: Alice P. Christie. Specializes in corporate identity, displays, interior design, packaging, publications, technical illustration, human factors and product design. Clients: corporations including industry, engineering, technical publishing, printing services and electronics.
Needs: Works with 5-10 freelance artists/year. Uses artists for design, illustration, brochures, mechanicals, retouching, posters, model making, charts/graphs, AV materials, lettering, logos and advertisements.
First Contact & Terms: Local artists only. Send query letter with samples to be kept on file. Write for appointment to show portfolio. Prefers photostats, slides and tear sheets as samples. Samples not kept on file are returned by SASE. Reports back within 2 weeks. Pays for design and illustration by the hour, $3.55 first use. "Pay higher when satisfied with performance." Considers complexity of project, client's budget, skill of artist and turnaround time when establishing payment.
Tips: "Be able to do what you claim."

COLLINS DESIGN, 9090 N. 51st St., Milwaukee WI 53223. (414)354-2200. President: Scott Collins. Specializes in corporate identity, displays, packaging, technical illustration, industrial design and

product development. Clients: manufacturers and corporations, medium and large.
Needs: Works with 3 freelance artists/year. Uses artists for design, illustration, P-O-P displays, mechanicals, model making and product development and styling.
First Contact & Terms: Artists should have "industrial design background with experience in rendering, mechanical drawing and model making." Send query letter with resume to be kept on file. Write for appointment to show portfolio. Prefers slides or flat work in portfolio form as samples. Samples not kept on file are returned only if interested. Payment is "based on experience, capability and direct negotiation with artist." Considers complexity of project, client's budget and turnaround time when establishing payment.
Tips: There is the "potential for full-time employment based on performance."

CONTOURS CONSULTING DESIGN GROUP, INC., 864 Stearns Rd., Bartlett IL 60103. (312)837-4100. Director, Graphics Group: Richard Wittosch. Specializes in annual reports, brand identity, corporate identity, displays, direct mail, packaging and signage. Clients: various corporations.
Needs: Uses artists for illustration, mechanicals and retouching.
First Contact & Terms: Works on assignment only. Call or write for appointment to show portfolio. Pays for design and illustration by the hour or by the job. Considers client's budget when establishing payment.

THE CORPORATE COMMUNICATIONS GROUP, 413 City Island Ave., New York NY 10464. Director: Barry L.S. Mirenburg. Specializes in annual reports, brand identity, corporate identity, packaging, publications, image development, advertising, graphic design and marketing. Clients: industrial and commercial manufacturers, and publishers.
Needs: Works with 6-10 freelance artists/year. Uses artists for illustration, brochures, catalogs, mechanicals, retouching, airbrushing, charts/graphs, lettering, advertisements and paste-up.
First Contact & Terms: Professional artists only. Works on assignment only. Send brochure, resume and samples to be kept on file. "Do not call. All information/samples will be reviewed and kept on file for future needs." Wants samples that give the best presentation and best clarity. Samples not filed are not returned. Pay varies. Considers complexity of project, client's budget, skill and experience of artist, how work will be used, turnaround time and rights purchased when establishing payment.

CORPORATE GRAPHICS, 1447 Lombard St., San Francisco CA 94123. (415)474-2888. President: Edward de St. Maurice. Specializes in annual reports, corporate identity, direct mail, publications and advertising. Clients: include high tech firms, banks, real estate firms; diversified clients.
Needs: Uses artists for illustration, mechanicals, charts/graphs and lettering.
First Contact & Terms: Send query letter with resume and samples to be kept on file. Call for an appointment to show portfolio. Accepts photostats, slides or tear sheets as samples. Reports within 1 month. Considers client's budget, and skill and experience of artist when establishing payment.

CREATIVE DESIGN CENTER, INC., 23141-K La Cadena Dr., Laguna Hills CA 92653. President: Robert Greene. Vice President: Clair Samhammer. Specializes in corporate identity, displays, interior design, packaging, technical illustration and product design and development. Clients: manufacturing and marketing groups (medical, data processing/office equipment and consumer products).
Needs: Works with 15 freelance designers/year. Uses designers for design, illustration, brochures, P-O-P displays, mechanicals, model making and logos.
First Contact & Terms: Prefers designers with "minimum 3-5 years' experience, except in exceptional cases, and proven ability." Works on assignment only. Send query letter with brochure, resume, business card and samples to be kept on file. Write for appointment to show portfolio. Samples not kept on file are returned only if requested. Pays for design and illustration by the hour, $13-20 average. Considers client's budget, skill and experience of designers and turnaround time when establishing payment.
Tips: Especially looks for "poetic, knowledgeable and intelligent solutions" as samples. Not interested in designers with "their heart on their sleeve and an ego chip on their shoulder."

CREATIVE WORKS, 300 Prosperity Farms Rd., North Palm Beach FL 33408. (305)844-8222. Interior Designer (Drafting): Suzi Addessa. Art Director (Mechanicals): Ken Roscoe. Specializes in corporate identity, displays, interior design, packaging, signage, product and sales offices. Clients: ad agencies, public relations firms, real estate developers, manufacturers and promoters.
Needs: Works with 50 freelance artists/year. Uses artists for design, illustration, mechanicals, airbrushing, model making and drafting. Especially needs drafting/mechanical people.
First Contact & Terms: Uses local (work in house), experienced artists. Send query letter with brochure and resume to be kept on file. Call or write for appointment to show portfolio. Prefers slides or finished work as samples. Samples not kept on file are returned by SASE only if requested. Reports back in 1 week. Pays by the hour for drafting and mechanicals. Considers complexity of project, client's budget,

skill and experience of artist and turnaround time when establishing payment.
Tips: "Send resume for interest and follow by appointment."

CSOKA/BENATO/FLEURANT INC., 134 W. 26th St., New York NY 10001. (212)242-6777. President: Robert Fleurant. Clients: insurance, national retail chains and communications.
Needs: Uses artists for record jacket covers and sales promotion projects.
First Contact & Terms: Assigns 10-20 jobs/year. Arrange interview. Pays $15-25/hour, layout; $8-15/hour, paste-up and mechanicals; $500 maximum/job, record jacket covers. Negotiates payment by job for annual reports, catalogs, packaging, posters and P-O-P displays.
Tips: Professional presentation of work is a *must*.

CUERDEN ADVERTISING DESIGN, 1730 Gaylord St., Denver CO 80206. (303)321-4163. Contact: Glenn Cuerden. Specializes in annual reports, corporate identity, direct mail, publications and signage. Clients: industrial companies, manufacturers, financial institutions, schools, government and high technology firms.
Needs: Works with 10 freelance artists/year. Uses artists for illustration, retouching and airbrushing.
First Contact & Terms: Artists should be "experienced, professional and dependable." Works on assignment only. Send query letter with resume and samples to be kept on file. Call or write for appointment to show portfolio. Prefers photocopies and tear sheets as samples. Samples not kept on file are returned by SASE. Reports back only if interested. Considers complexity of project, client's budget, skill and experience of artist, how work will be used and rights purchased when establishing payment.

CWI INC., 255 Glenville Rd., Greenwich CT 06830. (202)531-0300. Contact: Geoffrey Chaite. Design studio. Specializes in annual reports, brand identity, corporate identity, displays, exhibits and shows. Clients: packaged goods, foods, tools, publishing, drugs, tobacco, banks and sports.
Needs: Works with up to 10 illustrators and 2-3 designers/month. Uses artists for P-O-P displays, stationery design, multimedia kits, direct mail, slide sets, brochures/flyers, trade magazines, newspapers, layout, technical art, type spec, paste-up, retouching and lettering. Especially needs photography, illustration and paste-up.
First Contact & Terms: Minimum 5 years' experience. Prefers b&w line drawings, roughs, previously published work, comps, mechanicals as samples. Provide flyers, business card and tear sheets to be kept on file for future assignments. May return originals to artist at job's completion. Payment is negotiated.

*DESIGN & PRODUCTION INCORPORATED, 6001 Farrington Ave., Alexandria VA 22304. (703)751-5150. Design Director: Lothar P. Witteborg. Specializes in displays, interior design, signage and exhibition design. Clients: ad agencies, PR firms, architectural firms, institutions and major corporations.
Needs: Works with 10-20 freelance artists/year. Uses artists for design, illustration, brochures, catalogs, mechanicals, model making and exhibit design.
First Contact & Terms: Prefers local artists who are established professionals. Works on assignment only. Send query letter with brochure, resume and samples to be kept on file; call for appointment to show portfolio. Prefers slides or tear sheets as samples. Samples not filed are returned by SASE. Reports within 2 weeks. Pays for design by the hour, $25-50 average; by the project, $1,000-15,000 average. Pays for illustration by the hour, $20-45 average; by the project, $1,000-3,000 average. Considers complexity of project, client's budget, and skill and experience of artist when establishing payment.
Tips: "Only experienced freelancers need apply."

DESIGN COMMUNICATION, INC., Suite 1009, 1346 Connecticut Ave. NW, Washington DC 20036. (202)833-9087. Art Director: Beth Singer. Specializes in annual reports, corporate identity, publication, audio visual presentation and programs and communication consultation. Clients: corporations, government agencies, architects and developers, and associations.
Needs: Works with 12 freelance artists/year. Uses artists for design, illustration, brochures, magazines, mechanicals, retouching, airbrushing, charts/graphs, AV materials and logos.
First Contact & Terms: Prefers local artists. Works on assignment only. Send query letter with resume, business card and samples to be kept on file. Call for appointment to show portfolio. Samples not kept on file returned by SASE only if requested. Reports only if interested. Pays for design by the hour, $9-20 average; by the project, $100-2,000 average. Pays for illustration by the project, $1,000-2,500 average. Considers complexity of project, client's budget, skill and experience of artist, how work will be used, turnaround time and rights purchased when establishing payment.
Tips: "Be persistent and show enthusiasm."

DESIGN NORTH, INC., 8007 Douglas Ave., Racine WI 53402. (414)639-2080. Design Directors: Dennis Wolken (corporate), Jim Neill (promotional). Specializes in annual reports, brand identity, cor-

porate identity, displays, all internal and external collateral. Clients: direct accounts—consumer/industrial products.
Needs: Works with 10 freelance artists/year. Uses artists for illustration, P-O-P displays, mechanicals, retouching, airbrushing, lettering and logos.
First Contact & Terms: "Freelancer must not call directly or be in competition with us on accounts." Works on assignment only. Send query letter with brochure and samples to be kept on file. Prefers photostats, slides, photocopies and tear sheets as samples. Samples not kept on file are returned by SASE. Reports back in 2 weeks. Pays by the project. Considers client's budget, skill and experience of artist, and turnaround time when establishing payment.
Tips: "Don't waste time submitting non-professional samples."

THE DESIGN OFFICE OF STEVE NEUMANN & FRIENDS, Suite 103, 3000 Richmond Ave., Houston TX 77098. (713)629-7501. Contact: Cynthia J. Whitney. Specializes in corporate identity and signage. Clients: architects, interior designers, developers, hospitals, universities, etc.
Needs: Works with 2-4 freelance artists/year. Uses artists for design, illustration, retouching, model making, drafting and signage. Especially needs full-time architecture student/draftsperson.
First Contact & Terms: Artists must be local with "good background." Send query letter with brochure, resume, references, business card and samples to be kept on file. Write for appointment to show portfolio. Prefers slides as samples. Reports back within 15 days. Pays for design by the hour based on job contract. Considers complexity of project, client's budget, skill and experience of artist, and how work will be used when establishing payment.
Tips: "We have acquired a computer which utilizes graphics, and we have less need of freelance artists."

THE DESIGN QUARTER, 2900 4th Ave., San Diego CA 92103. (619)297-7900. Administrative Assistant: Jean Haight. Specializes in annual reports, corporate identity, direct mail and publications. Clients: corporations and publishers.
Needs: Works with 6 freelance artists/year. Uses artists for catalogs, books, mechanicals, retouching, airbrushing, model making and charts/graphs.
First Contact & Terms: Send business card to be kept on file. Call for appointment to show portfolio. Prefers photostats, photocopies and tear sheets as samples. Samples not kept on file are returned only if requested. Reports back only if interested. Pays for design by the hour, $10-30 average; by the project, $25-1,800 average. Pays for illustration by the hour, $25-50 average; by the project, $100-5,000 average. Considers complexity of project, client's budget, and skill and experience of artist when establishing payment.

DESIGN TRAIN, 434 Hidden Valley Ln., Cincinnati OH 45215. (513)761-7099. Contact: Joseph Pagliaro. Specializes in annual reports, brand identity, corporate identity, direct mail, packaging, publications, AV educational programs and book covers. Clients: book publishers and industrial manufacturers.
Needs: Works with 4-5 freelance artists/year. Uses artists for design, illustration, airbrushing and AV materials.
First Contact & Terms: Artists must be experienced, usually local. Works on assignment only. Send query letter with brochure, resume, business card and samples to be kept on file. Call for appointment to show portfolio. Samples not kept on file are returned. Reports back only if interested. Pays for design by the hour, $15-35 average. Pays for illustration by the project, $100-1,000 average. Considers complexity of project, client's budget, and skill and experience of artist when establishing payment.

DESIGN TRANSLATIONS, 1 Tracy Ln., Milford OH 45150. (513)248-0629. Contact: Richard Riggs. Specializes in graphic design. Clients: engineering and technical firms, hospitals and medical firms, and miscellaneous businesses.
Needs: Works with 2-3 freelance artists/year. Uses artists for mechanicals, airbrushing and AV materials.
First Contact & Terms: "Artist must have superb craft and meticulous attention to detail; must have enough experience to not need hand-holding; must be able to understand directions." Send query letter with resume and samples to be kept on file. Prefers stats and/or slides as samples. Samples not kept on file are returned by SASE only if requested. Reports back only if interested. Pays on a per job basis. Considers complexity of project, client's budget, skill and experience of artist, and turnaround time when establishing payment.

DESIGN VECTORS, #2, 408 Columbus Ave., San Francisco CA 94133. Contact: Tony Williams or Jim Tetzlaff. Specializes in brand identity, corporate identity, displays, direct mail, packaging, magazine design, publications and signage. Clients: public relation firms, banks, ad agencies and other corporations.

Needs: Works with 12 freelance artists/year. Uses artists for design, illustration, brochures, magazines, mechanicals, airbrushing, charts/graphs and advertisements.
First Contact & Terms: Local artists only. Send query letter with brochure and resume or samples to be kept on file. "Send only resume or samples that we can keep." Reports back only if interested. Pays for design and illustration by the hour, $10 minimum. Considers complexity of project, client's budget, skill and experience of artist and turnaround time when establishing payment.

*DESIGN WORKS, INC., 521 W. Ormsby Ave., Louisville KY 40203. (502)636-9101. Chief Designer: Ron Patterson. Specializes in corporate identity, displays and packaging. Clients: advertisers and ad agencies.
Needs: Works with 3-5 freelance artists/year. Uses artists for design, illustration, mechanicals and retouching.
First Contact & Terms: Artist must work in-house. Works on assignment only. Call or write for appointment to show portfolio. Accepts photostats, slides, photocopies or tear sheets as samples. Samples not filed are returned only if requested. Reports back only if interested. Pays for design by the hour, $15-25 average. Considers complexity of project, client's budget, and skill and experience of artist when establishing payment.

DESIGNS FOR MEDICINE, INC., 301 Cherry St., Philadelphia PA 19106. (215)925-7100. President: Peter W. Bressler. Specializes in annual reports, corporate identity, packaging, technical illustrations, product design and graphic design. Clients: ad agencies, manufacturers and inventors.
Needs: Works with 8 freelance artists/year. Uses artists for design, illustration, brochures, mechanicals, airbrushing, model making, lettering, logos and advertisements.
First Contact & Terms: "Local artists only to work in our office primarily; experience required varies." Works on assignment only. Send query letter with brochure, resume, business card and samples to be kept on file, except for slides which will be returned to sender. Write for appointment to show portfolio. Prefers slides and tear sheets as samples. Samples not filed returned. Reports within 3 weeks. Pays for design by the hour, $5-20 average (quotation basis). Considers complexity of project, client's budget, and skill and experience of artist when establishing payment.
Tips: "Be aggressive, very talented and creative."

DESIGNWORKS, INC., 5 Bridge St., Watertown MA 02172. (617)926-6286. Art Directors: S. Bindari, J.R. Bush. Provides design for publishing industry. Specializes in educational publications. Clients: book publishers.
Needs: Works with 10 freelance artists/year. Uses artists for book illustration, charts/graphs. Prefers styles "appropriate for educational materials."
First Contact & Terms: Send brochure/flyer and samples; "Photocopies are OK (color and b&w)." Works on assignment only. Provide brochure/flyer, tear sheets and samples to be kept on file ("unless we feel it is inappropriate") for possible future assignments. Prefers photostats, photographs and photocopies as samples. Payment by the project; also negotiates "according to the budget given to us by the publisher." Considers complexity of project, client's budget, and skill and experience of artist when establishing payment.
Tips: "We like samples for our files but we do not have a lot of office time for reviewing portfolios as we are producing during work hours ourselves."

DESKEY ASSOCIATES, INC., 15 W. 39th St., New York NY 10018. Director of Graphic Operations: Emmitt B. Sears. Specializes in brand and/or corporate identity, displays, packaging, illustration and mechanical art. Clients: corporations.
Needs: Works with approximately 10 freelance artists/year. Uses artists for design, illustration, P-O-P displays, mechanicals, retouching, airbrushing, model making, charts/graphs, lettering and logos.
First Contact & Terms: "Artists should present their resume, hourly wages and make a written request to present their work. Send resume to be kept on file. Prefers to see "best samples of areas in which artist may be of help—design/mechanicals/photos of models designed and very rough conceptual sketches." Samples are not returned. Reports back within days. Pays for design by the hour or by the project. Pays for illustration by the project. Considers complexity of project, client's budget, skill and experience of artist, and turnaround time when establishing payment.
Tips: "Too often artists present work that is a finished product—one wonders what efforts or contributions were made to develop the final product."

DI FRANZA-WILLIAMSON INC., 1414 Avenue of the Americas, New York NY 10019. (212)832-2343. Contact: Jack Williamson. Clients: businesses and advertising agencies.
Needs: Uses artists for layout, comps, illustration, cartoons, lettering and retouching for catalogs, direct mail brochures, flyers, packaging, P-O-P displays and slides.

First Contact & Terms: Assigns 250 jobs/year; local artists with 2-3 years minimum experience only. Query with resume and request interview. No work returned. Payment by hour: $12-20, design and layout; $15-50, illustrations; $15-20, mechanicals and paste-up; $15-22, type spec. Considers complexity of project, client's budget, skill and experience of artist, and how work will be used when establishing payment.
Tips: "Show me good work." There is a "need for designers who can draw. Show me roughs and layouts, not just finished pieces. Illustration is coming back."

ANTHONY DI MARCO, ADVERTISING AND DESIGN AGENCY, 2948 Grand Route St. John, New Orleans LA 70119. (504)948-3128. Creative Director: Anthony Di Marco. Specializes in brand identity, packaging, publications, and technical illustration. Clients: individuals and major corporations.
Needs: Works with 5-10 freelance artists/year. Uses artists for design, illustration, mechanicals, retouching, airbrushing, posters, model making, charts/graphs. Computer-generated graphics are a current interest.
First Contact & Terms: Seeks "local artists with ambition. Artists should have substantial portfolios and an understanding of business requirements." Send query letter with resume, business card and samples to be kept on file. Call or write for appointment to show portfolio. Prefers slides and tear sheets as samples. Samples not kept on file are returned by SASE. Reports back within 1 week if interested. Pays for design and illustration by the project, $50-500 average. Considers complexity of project, skill and experience of artist, turnaround time and rights purchased when establishing payment.
Tips: "Keep professionalism in mind at all times. Artists should put forth their best effort."

DIAMOND ART STUDIO LTD., 11 E. 36th St., New York NY 10016. (212)685-6622. Creative Directors: Gary and Douglas Diamond. Vice President: John Taylor. Art studio. Clients: advertising agencies, corporations, manufacturers and publishers. Assigns 500 jobs/year.
Needs: Works with 10 illustrators/month. Uses artists for cartoons, charts, graphs, illustrations, layout, lettering, logo design, paste-up, retouching, technical art and type spec.
First Contact & Terms: Write for interview. SASE. Provide resume and tear sheets to be kept on file for future assignments. Pays for design by the hour. Pays for illustration by the project. Considers complexity of project, client's budget, skill and experience of artist, and turnaround time when establishing payment.
Tips: "Leave behind something memorable and well thought out."

DIMENSIONAL DESIGN, 11046 McCormick, North Hollywood CA 91601. (213)769-5694. Contact: Design Director. Specializes in brand and corporate identity, displays, exhibits and shows, packaging, publications, signage and technical illustration, direct mail marketing, movie titles and film production. Clients: multi-field corporations, manufacturers, shopping centers and advertising agencies.
Needs: Works with 20-30 freelance artists/year. Uses artists for advertising, brochure and catalog design, illustration and layout; P-O-P displays, mechanicals, retouching; poster, book and direct mail package design and illustration; model making, charts/graphs, lettering and logo design.
First Contact & Terms: Send query letter with brochure/flyer and samples "as one unit to us;" call or write for appointment. Samples returned by SASE, "but would like to keep samples, resume/brochure, etc. on file." Reports in 2 months. Works on assignment only. Pays $8-17 average/hour or $100 average/project for design; $50-3,000 average/project for illustration; also negotiates.
Tips: "Become as professional as possible, not only in art, but also in art reproduction."

DONATO & BERKLEY INC., 386 Park Ave. S, New York NY 10016. (212)532-3884. Contact: Sy Berkley or Steve Sherman. Advertising art studio. Specializes in direct mail response advertising, annual reports, brand identity, corporate identity and publications. Clients: ad agencies, public relations firms, direct response advertisers and publishers.
Needs: Works with 1-2 illustrators and 1-2 designers/month. Uses artists for consumer magazines, direct mail, brochures/flyers, newspapers, layout, technical art, type spec, paste-up, lettering and retouching. Especially needs illustrations, retouching and mechanical paste-up.
First Contact & Terms: Local experienced artists only. Call for interview. Prefers photostats, b&w line drawings, roughs and previously published work as samples. Provide flyers, business card, resume to be kept on file for future assignments. No originals returned to artist at job's completion. Pays for design and illustration by the hour and by the project. Considers complexity of project and client's budget when establishing payment.
Tips: "We foresee a need for direct response art directors and the mushrooming of computer graphics. Clients are much more careful as to price and quality of work."

DAVE ELLIES INDUSTRIAL DESIGN, INC., 2015 W. Fifth Ave., Columbus OH 43212. (614)488-7995. Creative Manager: Ron Bushman. Specializes in corporate identity, displays, interior design, packaging and signage.

Needs: Works with 10 freelance artists/year. Uses artists for design, illustration, mechanicals, model making, AV materials and logos.

First Contact & Terms: Prefers regional freelance artists with 3-5 years' experience. Works on assignment only. Send query letter with resume, business card and samples to be kept on file. Call or write for appointment to show portfolio. Prefers slides as samples. Samples not kept on file returned by SASE. Reports within 2 weeks. Considers complexity of project, client's budget, skill and experience of artist, and turnaround time when establishing payment.

Tips: Especially looks for "quality not quantity, professionalism, variety and effective problem solving" in samples.

RAY ENGLE & ASSOCIATES, 626 S. Kenmore, Los Angeles CA 90005. (213)381-5001. President: Ray Engle. Specializes in annual reports, brand identity, corporate identity, displays, packaging, publications and signage. Clients: ad agencies, public relation agencies and corporations.

Needs: Works with 2-3 freelance artists/year. Uses artists for illustration, retouching and model making.

First Contact & Terms: Local artists only. Works on assignment only. Send query letter with brochure, business card and samples to be kept on file. Prefers photocopies, slides and photostats as samples. Samples are not kept on file are returned by SASE. Reports back only if interested. Pays for illustration by the hour $25 minimum. Considers complexity of project, client's budget, skill and experience of artist, how work will be used and turnaround time when establishing payment.

ENSIGN DESIGN INC., 201 College Ave., Salem VA 24153. (703)389-0482. President: Jim Edgell. Specializes in corporate identity, displays, packaging, publications, signage, technical illustrations, product design prototypes and models. Clients: industry, communications, consumer products.

Needs: Works with "a few" freelance artists/year. Uses artists for illustration, airbrushing and model making. Especially needs a good airbrush artist.

First Contact & Terms: Prefers local artists and that they work on premises. Send query letter with brochure, resume, business card and samples to be kept on file. Call or write for appointment to show portfolio. Samples not filed returned by SASE. Reports only if interested. Pays by the hour, $6-20 average. Considers complexity of project, clients's budget, and skill and experience of artist when establishing payment.

MEL ERIKSON/ART SERVICES, 31 Meadow Rd., Kings Park NY 11754-3812. (516)544-9191. Art Director: Toniann Manfredi. Specializes in publications and technical illustration. Clients: book publishers.

Needs: Works with 8-10 freelance artists/year. Uses artists for advertising illustration, book design and illustration, mechanicals, retouching and charts/graphs.

First Contact & Terms: Local artists only. Send samples to be kept on file. Prefers photocopies as samples. Samples not kept on file are not returned. Does not report back. Pays by the project, $75-200 average for design, $15-100 average for illustration. Considers complexity of project and client's budget when establishing payment.

*ETC GRAPHICS, INC., Suite 308, 386 Park Ave. S, New York NY 10016. (212)889-8777. President: Edwart T. Chin. Specializes in direct mail and marketing-oriented corporate graphics. Clients: Fortune 500 corporations, ad agencies, PR firms, magazine publishers, small- and medium-size companies.

Needs: Works with 17 freelance artists/year. Uses artists for design, illustration, catalogs, mechanicals, retouching, airbrushing and lettering.

First Contact & Terms: Minimum 2-3 years' experience. Works on assignment only. Send query letter with brochure, resume, business card and samples to be kept on file. Write for appointment to show portfolio. Prefers tear sheets or photocopies as samples. Samples not filed are returned by SASE. Reports within 2 weeks. Pays for design by the hour, $10-20 average; for illustration by the hour, $10-20 average, or by the project, $25-300 average. Considers complexity of project, client's budget, skill and experience of artist, how work will be used, turnaround time and rights purchased when establishing payment.

FINN STUDIO LIMITED, 154 E. 64th St., New York NY 10021. (212)838-1212. Creative Director: Finn. Clients: theaters, boutiques and magazines, fashion, ad agencies. Mail slides. SASE. Reports in 4 weeks.

Needs: Uses artists for T-shirt designs, illustrations, calligraphy; creative concepts in art for fashion and promotional T-shirts. Pays $50-500; sometimes also offers royalty.

THE FLACK STUDIO, 288 Lexington St., Watertown MA 02172. Production Manager: Joseph F. Weiler. Specializes in book publishing. Clients: book publishers.

Needs: Works with 1-2 freelance artists/year. Uses artists for book illustration.
First Contact & Terms: "Experienced, professional artists only, 5 years' experience, graduates of art school." Send query letter with tear sheets to be kept on file. Samples not kept on file are returned by SASE. Reports only if interested. Works on assignment only. Pays for illustration by the project. Pay "varies with medium, size. We work within the book publisher's budget." Considers complexity of project, client's budget, skill and experience of artist, how work will be used, turnaround time and rights purchased when establishing payment.

HANS FLINK DESIGN INC., 222 Mamaroneck Ave., White Plains NY 10605. (914)328-0888. President: Hans D. Flink. Specializes in brand identity, corporate identity, packaging and signage. Clients: corporate, packaged products.
Needs: Works with 10-20 freelance artists/year. Uses artists for design, illustration, P-0-P displays, mechanicals, retouching, airbrushing, model making, lettering, logos and package related services.
First Contact & Terms: Send query letter with brochure and resume to be kept on file; call or write for appointment to show portfolio. Reports back only if interested. Pays for design by the hour, $10-35 average; by the project, $500-3,000 average; by the day, $100-250 average. Pays for illustration by the project, $250-2,000 average. Considers complexity of project, client's budget, skill and experience of artist, how work will be used, turnaround time and rights purchased when establishing payment.

*FORSYTHE FRENCH, INC., 4115 Broadway, Kansas City MO 64111. (816)561-6678. Director/Design Services: Alan Hickman. Specializes in architectural graphics. Clients: hospitals and universities.
Needs: Works with 10-20 freelance artists/year. Uses artists for design, brochures, mechanicals and model making.
First Contact & Terms: Local artists only. Works on assignment only. Send query letter with resume to be kept on file; call or write for appointment to show portfolio. Prefers slides as samples. Samples returned by SASE. Reports only if interested. Pays by the project. Considers complexity of project, and skill and experience of artist when establishing payment.

FREELANCE EXCHANGE, INC., 150 Fifth Ave., New York NY 10011. (212)741-8020. Multiservice company.
Needs: Uses artists for cartoons, charts, graphs, illustrations, layout, lettering, logo design and mechanicals.
First Contact & Terms: Mail resume and photocopied samples. "Say you saw the listing in *Artist's Market*." Provide materials to be kept on file for future assignments. No originals returned to artist at job's completion.

FREEMAN DESIGN GROUP, 415 Farms Rd., Greenwich CT 06830. (203)968-0026. President: Bill Freeman. Specializes in annual reports, corporate identity, packaging, publications and signage. Clients: corporations.
Needs: Works with 5-10 freelance artists/year. Uses artists for illustration, mechanicals, retouching and airbrushing.
First Contact & Terms: New York City/Fairfield County artists only. Works on assignment only. Send query letter with brochure and business card to be kept on file; call for appointment to show portfolio. Prefers to review slides, tear sheets or original work at time of interview *only*. Material not filed is returned by SASE only if requested. Reports back only if interested. Pays for design by the hour, $10-15 average, or by the project, $50-2,500 average; for illustration by the project, $50-500 average. Considers complexity of project, client's budget, how work will be used and rights purchased when establishing payment.
Tips: "Present a clean portfolio of your best work, not necessarily printed samples."

FREEMAN DESIGN INCORPORATED, 2555 M Street NW, Washington DC 20037. (202)296-7272. Creative Director/President: Sheila Freeman. Specializes in corporate identity, displays, direct mail, publications, image development, brochures (capability, selling), newsletters and AV presentations. Clients: corporations, associations and public relation firms.
Needs: Works with 20 freelance artists/year. Uses artists for illustration, mechanicals, retouching, airbrushing, charts/graphs and lettering.
First Contact & Terms: Prefers artists with "one year experience at least, to work in our office." Send query letter with resume, business card and samples to be kept on file. Write for appointment to show portfolio. Prefers tear sheets and slides as samples. Reports back only if interested. Pays for design by the hour, $15 average; for illustration by the project; for mechanicals, $12. Considers complexity of project, client's budget, and skill and experience of artist when establishing payment.

STEPHANIE FURNISS DESIGN, 1327 Via Sessi, San Rafael CA 94901. (415)459-4730. Contact: Stephanie Furniss. Specializes in corporate identity, architectural and environmental graphics, super-graphics, interior design, packaging, sculpture and signage.
Needs: Works with 5 freelance artists/year. Uses artists for lettering and production work. Send query letter with brochure, resume and business card. Call for appointment to show portfolio. Prefers slides or tear sheets as samples. Considers complexity of project, skill and experience of artist and turnaround time when establishing payment.

GAILEN ASSOCIATES, INC., 584-A Roger Williams, Highland Park IL 60035. (312)432-7390. President: Bob Gailen. Specializes in annual reports, brand identity, corporate identity, packaging, publications and signage. Clients: direct mail, ad agencies, marketing firms.
Needs: Works with 5 freelance artists/year. Uses artists for illustration, photography, airbrushing and model making.
First Contact & Terms: Works on assignment basis. Send query letter with resume and samples to be kept on file. Does not report back. Pays for design, by the hour $25 minimum; for illustration, per illustrator's quote. Considers complexity of project, client's budget, and skill and experience of artist when establishing payment.

*ROBERT A. GALE, INC., 970 Park Ave., New York NY 10028. President: Robert A. Gale. Specializes in annual reports, brand identity, corporate identity, displays, packaging, publications and signage. Clients: corporations.
Needs: Uses artists for illustration, mechanicals, retouching, airbrushing, model making, charts/graphs and lettering.
First Contact & Terms: Send brochure, resume, business card and samples to be kept on file. Write for appointment to show portfolio. Considers skill and experience of artist when establishing payment.

GARRETT COMMUNICATIONS, INC., Box 53, Atlanta GA 30301. (404)755-2513. President: Ruby Grant Garrett. Specializes in brand identity, corporate identity and packaging. Clients: manufacturers, public relation firms and ad agencies.
Needs: Works with 6 freelance artists/year. Uses artists for illustration, mechanicals, retouching, airbrushing, P-O-P displays, model making and lettering. Buys 3 cartoons, 6 cartoon-style and 6 humorous illustrations/year.
First Contact & Terms: Works on assignment only. Send resume, business card and samples to be kept on file. Prefers photocopies as samples. Samples not kept on file are returned only if requested. Reports back within 10 days. Pays for design by the hour, $35-40 average; by the project, $210-500 average. Pays for illustration by the hour, $35-40 average; by the project, $210-800. Considers client's budget, turnaround time and rights purchased when establishing payment.

GIOVANNI DESIGN ASSOCIATES, 137 E. 36th St., New York NY 10016. (212)725-8536. Contact: John E. Frontino. Specializes in packaging. Clients: industry and fragrance/cosmetic firms.
Needs: Uses artists for advertising, brochure and catalog design, illustration and layout; P-O-P displays, mechanicals; poster, book and direct mail package design and illustration; AV presentations, lettering and logo design "as needed."
First Contact & Terms: Send brochure/flyer and samples; submit portfolio for review. Prefers slides as samples. Samples returned by SASE if not kept on file. Reports "as soon as possible." Works on assignment only. Provide brochure/flyer, resume, business card, tear sheets and samples to be kept on file for possible future assignments. Negotiates payment method and payment.

ERIC GLUCKMAN COMMUNICATIONS, INC., 60 E. 42nd St., New York NY 10165. (212)697-3670. President: Eric Gluckman. Specializes in corporate identity, direct mail, publications, industrial advertising and promotion, corporate capability brochures and sales promotion (trade). "We usually deal directly with client."
Needs: Works with 20 freelance artists/year. Uses artists for design, illustration, brochures, mechanicals, retouching, airbrushing, direct mail packages, posters, charts/graphs, lettering, logos and advertisements.
First Contact & Terms: Artists should have 3 years' experience minimum. "All rights to art and photography revert to client." Works on assignment only. Send query letter with resume and samples to be kept on file. Call or write to Art Director: Clare Ultimo for appointment to show portfolio. No slides as samples. Samples not kept on file returned by SASE. Reports only if interested. Pay is negotiable. Considers complexity of project, client's budget, skill and experience of artist, and turnaround time when establishing payment. Buys all rights.
Tips: "Be professional, make deadlines."

Freelance illustrator Taylor Oughton created this technical pen art, in addition to the spot illustration reproduced in this section's introduction, for the graphic design firm of Alan Gorelick & Associates, Clark, New Jersey. The artwork was used on a double-page spread in a marketing booklet that promoted the conservation and preservation of old buildings. Oughton, who has been a general illustrator for 35 years, created both pieces from photographs.

GOLDSMITH YAMASAKI SPECHT INC, 504, 840 N. Michigan Ave., Chicago IL 60611. (312)266-8404. Industrial Designer: William M. Goldsmith. Specializes in corporate identity, packaging, product design and graphics. Clients: industrial firms, institutions, service organizations, ad agencies, government agencies, etc.

Needs: Works with 6-10 freelance artists/year. Uses artists for design (especially graphics), illustration, retouching, model making, lettering and production art.

First Contact & Terms: "We generally use local artists, simply for convenience." Works on assignment only. Send query letter with brochure and resume to be kept on file. Samples not kept on file are returned only if requested. Reports back only if interested. Considers complexity of project, client's budget, skill and experience of artist, how work will be used, turnaround time and rights purchased when establishing payment.

Tips: "If we receive many inquiries, obviously our time commitment may be short, necessarily. Please understand."

*ALAN GORELICK & ASSOCIATES INC., Graphic Designers, 999 Raritan Rd., Clark NJ 07066. President/Creative Director: Alan Gorelick. Specializes in corporate identity, displays, direct mail, signage, technical illustration and company and product literature. Clients: health care and pharmaceutical corporations, industrial, manufacturing.

Needs: Works with 6-10 freelance artists/year. Uses artists for design, illustration, brochures, mechanicals, retouching, airbrushing, posters, direct mail packages, posters, charts/graphs, logos and advertisements.

First Contact & Terms: Works with "seasoned professional or extremely talented entry-level" artists only. Send query letter with brochure, resume, business card and samples to be kept on file; call or write for appointment to show portfolio. Accepts photostats, slides, photocopies, tear sheets as samples. Samples not filed are returned by SASE only if requested. Reports only if interested. Pays for design by the hour, $15-35 average. Pays for illustration by the hour, $15-50 average. Considers complexity of

project, client's budget, and skill and experience of artist when establishing payment.
Tips: Requires "straight talk, professional work ethic and commitment to assignment."

*GRAPHIC MARKETING SPECIALISTS, Suite 850, 2600 Southwest Freeway, Houston TX 77098. (713)526-5790. President: Linda Carol Griffith. Graphic/marketing firm providing design/production/consulting services. Clients: petro-chemical, professional services firms, institutional, industrial, corporations, engineering and construction, high tech/computer, developers.
Needs: Works with 20 freelance artists/year. Uses artists for advertising and brochure design, illustration and layout; interior and architectural renderings; design consulting, charts, maps and model making.
First Contact & Terms: Prefers artists with 4-5 years' experience. Send resume to be kept on file. Call for appointment to show portfolio. Reports only if interested. Works on assignment only. Pays for design by the hour, negotiable. Also works on bid basis. Considers complexity of project, client's budget, and skill and experience of artist when establishing payment.

*GRAPHICS HOUSE, 2605 N. 32nd St., Phoenix AZ 85008. (602)955-7310. Manager: Chuck Posenauer. Specializes in technical illustration (including patent drawings), publications, corporate identity, packaging, displays, brand identity, annual reports, exhibits and shows.
Needs: Works with 4-6 freelance artists/year. Uses artists for P-O-P displays, mechanicals, retouching, posters, direct mail packages, model making, charts/graphs, AV presentations, lettering, logos and most types of technical art, 35mm and overhead slide art.
First Contact & Terms: Experienced artists only. Send query letter with resume and/or business card to be kept on file. Write for appointment to show portfolio. Prefers original work as samples; will accept photographs. Samples returned by SASE. Reports only if interested. Pays for design and illustration by the hour, $6-20 average; by the project, $100-1,500 average. Considers complexity of project, client's budget, skill and experience of artist, how work will be used, turnaround time and rights purchased when establishing payment.

*GRAPHICUS, 11046 McCormick, North Hollywood CA 91601. (818)877-5694. President: Wayne Hallowell. Specializes in annual reports, brand and corporate identity, displays, exhibits and shows, packaging, publications, signage and technical illustration. Clients: advertising agencies, corporations, manufacturers (in all fields); "we supply all areas of corporate communications."
Needs: Works with 20 freelance artists/year. Uses artists for advertising, brochure and catalog design and illustration, advertising layout, P-O-P displays, mechanicals; poster, book and direct mail package design and illustration; model making, AV presentations, lettering, and logo and package design. Especially needs "good, clean, knowledgeable artists who are true professionals and know what happens to their work after it leaves the drawing boards."
First Contact & Terms: Prefers at least 5 years' experience. Send query letter with brochure/flyer, resume and samples; call or write for appointment. Ther eis no preference in samples but "the way they present them tells a lot about their work and themselves." Samples returned by SASE "only when requested; it is far better to have samples available in our offices." Reports in 4 weeks. Works on assignment only; reports back on whether to expect possible future assignments. Pays $50-2,000 average/project for design; $50-4,000 average/project for illustration; payment is negotiable.
Tips: "An artist should know the profession, become more business-like and train as an athlete does."

GRAPHICUS ART STUDIO, 2025 Maryland Ave., Baltimore MD 21218. (301)727-5553. Art Director: Charles Piccirilli. Specializes in annual reports, brand and corporate identity, displays, packaging, publications and signage. Clients: recreational sport industries, fleet leasing companies, technical product manufacturers, commercial packaging corporations, direct mail advertising firms, realty companies and home heating oil companies.
Needs: Uses artist for advertising, brochure, catalog and poster illustration, retouching and AV presentations. Especially needs high quality illustration.
First Contact & Terms: Send samples of actual work; call for appointment. Prefers originals as samples. Samples returned by SASE. Works on assignment only; reports on whether to expect possible future assignments. Provide business card and tear sheets to be kept on file. Payment is by the project.
Tips: Artists should have "flexibility."

GRIMALDI DESIGN INC., Box 864, Murray Hill Station, New York NY 10016. (212)532-3773. Assistants to Director: John Tassi, Ann Thornley and Joseph Grimaldi. Specializes in displays, interior design, packaging and signage.
Needs: Works with 6-8 freelance artists/year. Uses artists for illustration, mechanicals and model making.
First Contact & Terms: Prefers 3 years' experience. Works on assignment only. Send resume and sam-

·ples to be kept on file. Write for appointment to show portfolio. Prefers slides as samples. Samples not kept on file returned. Reports within 2 weeks. Pays for design by the hour, $10 maximum. Illustration rates on request. Considers complexity of project and client's budget when establishing payment.

STEPHEN HALL DESIGN INC., 555 Louisville Galleria, Louisville KY 40202. (502)584-5030. Art Director: Stephen Hall. Specializes in publications. Clients: publishers and corporate communications.
Needs: Works with 20-25 freelance artists/year. Uses artists for advertising, brochure and catalog illustration, mechanicals and charts/graphs. Especially needs illustrators who can handle editorial assignments.
First Contact & Terms: Send brochure/flyer and samples. Prefers slides as samples. Samples not kept on file returned by SASE. Works on assignment only. Provide brochure/flyer, tear sheets and samples to be kept on file for possible future assignments. Pays for design by the hour, $10-25 average. Pays for illustration by the project, $15-500 average. Considers complexity of project, client's budget, skill and experience of artist, how work will be used and rights purchased when establishing payment.
Tips: "Show only your best work. We would prefer to give assignments to artists who are willing to brainstorm with us and to reach an agreement on an idea."

HALSTED & MURAMATSU, 1762 N. Neville St., Orange CA 92665. (714)974-9410. Contact: Art Director. Specializes in displays, packaging, trade show exhibits and product design. Clients: various manufacturers.
Needs: Works with 10-15 freelance artists/year. Uses artists for exhibit and product design, illustration, P-O-P displays, mechanicals, posters and model making.
First Contact & Terms: Local artists preferred. Works on assignment. Send query letter with brochure, resume and business card to be kept on file. Call for appointment to show portfolio. Samples not kept on file are returned by SASE only if requested. Reports back only if interested. Considers complexity of project, client's budget, skill and experience of artist, how work will be used, turnaround time and rights purchased when establishing payment.
Tips: Contemporary design philosophy.

HAMILTON DESIGN, INC., (formerly Hamilton Design & Associates), 2130 Stella Ct., Columbus OH 43215. (614)481-8016. Contact: Bill Hamilton or Joan Etter. Specializes in brand identity, displays, packaging, publications and direct mail—merchandising and selling ads. Clients: publications and manufacturers.
Needs: Uses artists for advertising and brochure layout; catalog design and layout, P-O-P displays, mechanicals, retouching, direct response packages.
First Contact & Terms: Works on assignment only. Send query letter with resume and samples. Call for appointment to show portfolio. Prefers slides as samples. Samples not kept on file are returned. Reports in 2 weeks. Pays for design and illustration by the hour, $10-70 average. Considers how work will be used and rights purchased when establishing payment.

PAIGE HARDY & ASSOCIATES, 1731 Kettner Blvd., San Diego CA 92101. (619)233-7238. Contact: Paige Hardy or Lorie Kennedy. Specializes in corporate identity, publications, technical illustration and advertising art. Clients: retail firms and publications.
Needs: Works with 25 freelance artists/year. Uses artists for advertising, brochure and catalog design, illustration and layout; mechanicals, retouching and logo design. Especially needs production artist/paste-up with heavy experience.
First Contact & Terms: Send query letter with resume; call or write for appointment to submit portfolio for review. Samples not returned. Reports in 1 week. Usually works on assignment only. Provide resume and business card to be kept on file. Pays by the hour and project; negotiates payment.

HARPER & ASSOCIATES, INC., 2285 116th Ave. NE, Bellevue WA 98004. (206)462-0405. Creative Director: Randi Harper Jorgenson. Office Manager: Kelley Wood. Specializes in brand and corporate identity. Clients: high tech, manufacturers professional services, (i.e., architects, doctors, attorneys, yacht brokers, stockbrokers, etc.), food, fashion, etc.
Needs: Works with 10-12 freelance artists/year. Uses artists for illustration and airbrush.
First Contact & Terms: Send resume and samples. Prefers slides as samples. Samples returned by SASE. Reports only if interested. Works on assignment only. Pays for design by the hour, $8-20; for illustration by the hour, $10-30, or by the project. Considers complexity of project, client's budget, skill and experience of artist, how work will be used, turnaround time and rights purchased when establishing payment.
Tips: "Be honest about your abilities and do no be afraid to turn down an assignment if it is not appropriate for you."

Harper & Associates, Inc. Bellevue, Washington, commissioned this illustration for use on a small folder promoting infant and maternal care at Overlake Hospital Medical Center in Seattle. The firm had used the work of artist Wendy Edelson of Seattle for related illustrations, and "it was important to us that the style remain consistent," explains Randi Harper Jorgenson, president. Edelson received $900 for unlimited use of the illustration.

Overlake Hospital Medical Center

*HARRINGTON-JACKSON, INC., 10 Newbury St., Boston MA 02116. (617)536-6164. Art Director: Jenny Levy. Specializes in collateral materials—brochures, flyers, posters and other sales/promotional pieces. Clients: manufacturers and trade (industrial).
Needs: Works with 3-4 freelance artists/year. Uses artists for illustration, brochures, mechancials, retouching and airbrushing. "We especially need experienced (2-3 years) mechanical artists who can work in our studio."
First Contact & Terms: Local artists only with 2-3 years' experience. Works on assignment only. Send query letter with resume to be kept on file for 6 months; call for appointment to show portfolio. Reports only if interested. Pays for illustration by the hour, $6-10; for mechanical art, $5-8. Considers skill and experience of artist when establishing payment.
Tips: "Call 2-3 hours in advance to make sure someone is available to review portfolio."

LEE HELMER DESIGN, 54 John St., Charleston SC 29403. (803)723-4570. President: Lee Helmer. Specializes in corporate identity, direct mail and publications. Clients: ad agencies, theatre and fine arts organizations, retail businesses and corporations.
Needs: Works with approximately 6 freelance artists/year. Uses artists for illustrations, charts/graphs, lettering and map making.
First Contact & Terms: No restrictions "other than price." Works on assignment only. Send query letter with samples to be kept on file. Call for appointment to show portfolio. Reports back only if interested. Pays for illustration by job quotation; by the project, $50-500 average. Considers complexity of project, client's budget, skill and experience of artist, how work will be used, turnaround time and rights purchased when establishing payment.
Tips: "Charleston has a very limited market for illustrators demanding high fees."

HERBST, LAZAR, ROGERS & BELL, INC., Suite 406, 10 N. Market St., Lancaster PA 17603. Office Manager: Sarah Preston. Specializes in brand identity, corporate identity, displays, interior design, packaging, publications, signage, technical illustration, product design and cost reduction. Clients: manufacturers, ad agencies and retailers.
Needs: Works with 10 freelance artists/year. Uses artists for illustration, brochures, catalogs, mechanicals, model making, charts/graphs, lettering, logos and advertisements.
First Contact & Terms: Artists should be within driving distance; "prefer freelancers to work in-house." Works on assignment only. Send query letter with brochure, resume, business card and samples to be kept on file. Prefers slides as samples. Samples not kept on file are returned. Reports back within 15 days. Considers complexity of project, and skill and experience of artist when establishing payment.

GRANT HOEKSTRA GRAPHICS, INC., 333 N. Michigan Ave., Chicago IL 60601. (312)641-6940. President: Grant Hoekstra. Specializes in publications. Clients: publishers, ad agencies and corporations.
Needs: Works with 15 freelance artists/year. Uses artists for design, illustration, brochures, retouching and lettering. Especially needs "illustrator who understands 'fundamental Christian' market."
First Contact & Terms: Local artists with experience only. Works on assignment only. Send samples and prices to be kept on file. Call for appointment to show portfolio. Prefers photocopies as samples. Pays for design by the hour, $15-50 average. Pays for illustration by the project $10-1,000 average. Considers complexity of project, client's budget and how work will be used when establishing payment.

THE HOLM GROUP, 3rd Floor, 405 Sansome, San Francisco CA 94111. (415)397-7272. Specializes in corporate identity and collateral. Clients: corporations.
Needs: Works with 5-10 freelance artists/year. Uses artists for illustration, mechanicals, retouching, airbrushing, lettering and logos.
First Contact & Terms: "Artist must send 'leave behind' first; then, we'll call to see portfolio." Send query letter with brochure, resume, business card and samples to be kept on file (except for bulky items or items requested returned). "Photocopies of samples are fine if they demonstrate the quality of work." Samples not kept on file are returned by SASE. Reports back only if interested (may be much later). Pays for design by the hour, $20 average; by the project, $300-900 average. Pays for illustration by the project, $350-800+ average. Pays $10-15 in production. Considers complexity of project, client's budget and turnaround time when establishing payment.
Tips: "Put together an eye-catching resume to leave behind."

*KAREN HOLUM DESIGN, 911 Western Ave., Seattle WA 98104. (206)623-8349. Owner: Karen Holum. Specializes in annual reports and corporate identity. Clients: all levels governmental agencies, high tech corporations, retailers and travel industry.
Needs: Works with 5-10 freelance artists/year. Uses artists for design, illustration, mechanicals, retouching, airbrushing, charts/graphs, AV materials and lettering.
First Contact & Terms: Send query letter with samples. Write for appointment to show portfolio. Accepts photostats, slides, photocopies or tear sheets as samples. Samples returned by SASE. Reports only if interested. Pays for design by the hour, $20-50 average; by the project, $50 minimum. Pays for illustration by the hour, $35 minimum; by the project, $50 minimum. Considers complexity of project, client's budget, skill and experience of artist, how work will be used, turnaround time and rights purchased when establishing payment.
Tips: Freelancers should present "clean, neat work and a professionally-typed cover letter addressed to the proper person—not 'to whom it may concern'."

MEL HOLZSAGER/ASSOCIATES, INC., 275 Seventh Ave., New York NY 10001. (212)741-7373. President/Art Director: Mel Holzsager. Specializes in corporate identity, packaging and general graphic design. Clients: publisher and manufacturers.
Needs: Works with occasional freelance artists according to the work load. Uses artists for advertising and brochure illustration, mechanicals and retouching.
First Contact & Terms: Prefers local artists. Write or phone first or send brochure/flyer. Will request sample viewing if required. Samples returned if requested. Provide brochure/flyer and tear sheets to be kept on file for possible future assignments. Negotiates payment.
Tips: A mistake artists make is "trying to be too versatile. Great specialization would be stronger."

FRANK HOSICK DESIGN, Box H, Vashon Island WA 98070. (206)463-5454. Contact: Frank Hosick. Specializes in brand identity, corporate identity, packaging, product design and model building. Clients: manufacturers.
Needs: Uses artists for illustration, mechanicals, retouching, airbrushing and model making.
First Contact & Terms: Works on assignment only. Send query letter with brochure, resume, business

card and samples to be kept on file. Call for appointment to show portfolio. Samples not kept on file are returned only if requested. Reports back only if interested. Pays for design by the hour, $15-50 average; by the project, $100 minimum; or by the day, $75-350 average. Pays for illustration by the hour, $15-50 average; by the project, $100-1,500 average; or by the day, $75-350 average. Considers complexity of project, client's budget, skill and experience of artist and how work will be used when establishing payment.

Tips: Especially looks for "creativity, craftsmanship and quality of presentation" when reviewing a portfolio. Changes in the field include "big influence by computers, both in concept work and execution. Computer knowledge is helpful."

*THE HOYT GROUP, INC., 5 Harrison Ave., Waldwick NJ 07463. President: Earl Hoyt. Specializes in corporate identity and packaging. Clients: *Fortune* 500 firms.

Needs: Works with 10-15 freelance artists/year. Uses artists for design, mechanicals, airbrushing, model making, lettering and logos.

First Contact & Terms: Seeks experienced professionals. Works on assignment only. Send brochure to be kept on file; write for appointment to show portfolio. Send reproductions only as samples—no original art. Reports only if interested. Considers client's budget, and skill and experience of artist when establishing payment.

*IDENTITY CENTER, 955G N. Plum Grove Rd., Schaumburg IL 60195. (312)843-2378. President: Wayne Kosterman. Specializes in brand identity, corporate identity, publications, signage and brochures. Clients: hospitals and corporations.

Needs: Works with up to 12 freelance artists/year. Uses artists for illustration, mechanicals, retouching, airbrushing, model making, keyline and paste-up.

First Contact & Terms: Artist must have at least 3 years' experience. Send query letter with samples to be kept on file. Prefers photocopies as samples. Samples not filed are returned only if requested. Reports within 2 weeks. Pays for illustration by the hour, $12 minimum; by the project, $100 minimum. Considers complexity of project, client's budget, skill and experience of artist, how work will be used and turnaround time when establishing payment.

IMAGES, 1835 Hampden Ct., Louisville KY 40205. (502)459-0804. Creative Director: Julius Freedman. Specializes in annual reports, corporate identity, poster design and publications. Clients: corporate.

Needs: Works with approximately 100 freelance artists/year. Uses artists for advertising illustration and layout, brochure and catalog design and illustration, brochure layout, mechanicals, retouching, poster design, book design and illustration, charts/graphs, lettering and logo design.

First Contact & Terms: Prefers experienced artists only. Send brochure/flyer or resume and business card as samples to be kept on file. Samples not filed returned by SASE. Works on assignment only; reports whether to expect possible future assignments. Pays by the project for design and illustration.

INDIANA DESIGN CONSORTIUM, INC., 300 River City Market Bldg., Box 180, Lafayette IN 47902. Vice President: Kendall Smith. Specializes in corporate identity, displays, exhibits and shows, packaging, publications, signage and technical illustration. Clients: industry, agriculture, banks and professionals.

Needs: Works with 4-5 freelance artists/year. Uses artists for advertising illustration, brochure and catalog design and illustration, mechanicals, retouching, model making and AV presentations.

First Contact & Terms: Send brochure/flyer or resume and samples; write for appointment. Samples returned. Reports in 2 weeks. Works on assignment only; reports back whether to expect possible future assignments. Provide brochure/flyer, resume, business card, tear sheets and samples to be kept on file. Pays according to project quote for design and illustration.

INNOVATIVE DESIGN & GRAPHICS, Suite 252, 708 Church St., Evanston IL 60201. (312)475-7772. Contact: Tim Sonder and Maret Thorpe. Specializes in publications. Clients: magazine publishers, corporate communication departments, associations.

Needs: Works with 3-15 freelance artists/year. Uses artists for illustration and airbrushing. Also seeks "accurate paste-up artist who is willing to learn some typesetting and to work on a regular, part-time basis."

First Contact & Terms: Local artists only. Send query letter with resume and samples to be kept on file. Call for appointment to show portfolio. Prefers photostats or tear sheets as samples. Reports back only if interested. Pays for illustration by the project, $50-500 average; for keyline by the hour according to speed. Considers complexity of project, client's budget and turnaround time when establishing payment.

Tips: "Interested in meeting new illustrators, but have a tight schedule. Looking for people who can grasp complex ideas and turn them into high-quality illustrations. Ability to draw people well is a must."

JMH CORPORATION, Suite 300, 247 S. Meridian, Indianapolis IN 46225. (317)639-2535. President: Michael Hayes. Specializes in corporate identity, packaging and publications. Clients: publishing, consumer products, corporate and institutional.
Needs: Works with 10 freelance artists/year. Uses artists for advertising, brochure, catalog design, illustration and design, P-O-P displays, mechanicals, retouching, charts/graphs and lettering.
First Contact & Terms: Prefers experienced, talented and responsible artists only. Works on assignment only. Send query letter with brochure/flyer, resume and samples; write for appointment. Prefers slides as samples. Samples returned by SASE, "but we prefer to keep them." Reporting time "depends entirely on our needs." Pay is by the project for design and illustration. Pays $100-1,000/project average; also negotiates. Considers complexity of project, client's budget, skill and experience of artist, how work will be used, turnaround time and rights purchased when establishing payment.
Tips: "Prepare an outstanding mailing piece and 'leave-behind' that allows work to remain on file."

JOHNSON DESIGN GROUP, INC., 3426 N. Washington Blvd., Arlington VA 22201. (703)525-0808. Art Director: Leonard A. Johnson. Specializes in publications. Clients: corporations, associations and public relations firms.
Needs: Works with 12 freelance artists/year. Uses artists for brochure and book illustration, mechanicals, retouching and lettering. Especially needs line illustration and a realistic handling of human figure in real life situations.
First Contact & Terms: Works on assignment only. Send query letter with samples of style. Samples not returned. Provide brochure/flyer and samples (photocopies OK) to be kept on file. Negotiates payment by the project.

JONES MEDINGER KINDSCHI INC., Fields Ln., RFD 2, North Salem NY 10560. Contact: Wynn Medinger. Specializes in annual reports, corporate identity and publications. Clients: corporations.
Needs: Works with 15 freelance artists/year. Uses artists for illustration.
First Contact & Terms: "*No* phone calls!" Works on assignment only. Send query letter with samples to be kept on file. Prefers tear sheets or slides for color, photostats or photocopies for b&w. Samples not kept on file are returned by SASE only. Reports back only if interested. Pays for illustration by the project $250-2,000 average. Considers client's budget, skill and experience of artist and how work will be used when establishing payment.
Tips: "We mainly use editorial-style illustration for corporate house organs."

JONSON PEDERSEN HINRICHS & SHAKERY, 141 Lexington Ave., New York NY 10016. Clients: corporations and publishers.
Needs: Uses artists and photographers for annual reports, publications, catalogs, etc. Pays $15-20, mechanicals and paste-up. Negotiates pay for color separations, illustrations, lettering, retouching and technical art.
First Contact & Terms: Query; prefers local artists. SASE.

GEORGE JOSEPH & ASSOCIATES, 425 N. Michigan, Chicago IL 60611. (312)245-0003. Contact: George J. Goldberg, Leonard La Bonar or Steven Azuma. Art and design studio; promotions, graphics and typesetting. Clients: businesses, advertising agencies and industries.
Needs: Works with 2-4 illustrators/month. Uses artists for designs, illustrations and cartoons for annual reports, billboards, bumper stickers, catalogs, charts/graphs, direct mail brochures, exhibits, flyers, packaging, P-O-P displays, print media and TV.
First Contact & Terms: Query with samples or arrange interview. Professional artists with a minimum of 5 years' experience only. SASE. Provide materials to be kept on file for future assignments. No originals returned at job's completion. Pays for design and illustration by the project. Considers client's budget and turnaround time when establishing payment.

*FREDERICK JUNGCLAUS, Designer/Illustrator, 145 E. 14th St., Indianapolis IN 46202. (317)636-4891. Owner: Fred Jungclaus. Specializes in annual reports, corporate identity, displays, architectural renderings and 3-D photo props. Clients: ad agencies and architects.
Needs: Works with 3-5 freelance artists/year. Uses artists for retouching and airbrushing. Seeks artists capable of illustrating Indy-type race cars or antique cars.
First Contact & Terms: Works on assignment only. Send samples to be kept on file; call for appointment to show portfolio. Prefers slides or tear sheets as samples. Samples not filed are returned only if requested. Reports only if interested. Pays by the project. Considers skill and experience of artist and turnaround time when establishing payment.

DAVID KAGEYAMA, DESIGNER, 2119 Smith Tower, Seattle WA 98104. Contact: David Kageyama. Specializes in annual reports, brand and corporate identity, displays, packaging, publications and signage. Clients: advertising agencies, public service agencies, corporations, banking and insurance, attorneys and other professionals.

Needs: Works with 12 freelance artists/year. Uses artists for advertising, brochure, poster, direct mail package, book and catalog illustration; mechanicals, retouching, AV presentations and lettering. Especially needs good, quick line/wash, humorous illustrator.

First Contact & Terms: Send brochure/flyer or resume, business card and samples to be kept on file for possible future assignments; call for appointment. Prefers photos (prints), actual illustrations and printed pieces as samples. Works on assignment only. Pays $100-300 average/project for illustration. Considers client's budget, skill and experience of artist and turnaround time when establishing payment.

Tips: "We are much more apt to respond to the artist with a specific style or who specializes in a particular topic rather than the generalist. Keep in touch with your latest work. I like to see rough sketches as well as finished work. My firm buys all photography and virtually all illustration used for our clients."

AL KAHN GROUP, 221 W. 82nd St., New York NY 10024. (212)580-3517. Contact: Al Kahn. Specializes in annual reports, corporate identity, packaging and publications. Clients: industrial, high tech, entertainment, fashion and beauty.

Needs: Works with 36 freelance artists/year. Uses artists for advertising design and layout, brochure and catalog design, illustration and layout; poster design and illustration, model making, charts/graphs, lettering and logo design. Prefers 3-dimensional construction style.

First Contact & Terms: Send brochure/flyer or resume; write or call first for appointment. Prefers slides, b&w photos and color washes for samples. Samples returned by SASE. Reports in 1 week. Works on assignment only. Provide business card to be kept on file for possible future assignments. Pays $20-25 average/hour for design; $200-500 average/project for illustration.

Tips: "We specialize in 'emotional response' advertising and image building."

KEITHLEY & ASSOCIATES, INC., 32 W. 22nd St., New York NY 10010. (212)807-8388. Studio Manager/Art Director: Nancy P. Danahy. Specializes in publications. Primary clients: publishing (book and promotion departments); secondary clients: small advertising agencies.

Needs: Works with 3-6 freelance artists/year. Uses artists for design, brochures, catalogs, books (design and dummy), mechanicals, retouching and charts/graphs.

First Contact & Terms: "Except for artists doing retouching and some design work, all work must be done in our studio. We prefer experienced artists (2 years minimum)." Call for appointment to show portfolio. Do not send samples. Reports only if interested. Pays for design by the hour $10-15 average. Pays for mechanicals by the hour, $6-15 average. Considers client's budget, and skill and experience of artist when establishing payment.

Tips: "We will be most likely to use you if you can handle the assignment completely—concept, presentation comps, type specs, mechanicals—or efficiently pick up a project in mid-course." A mistake artists make in presenting their portfolio is "not pointing out the obstacles they had to overcome during the course of a job."

LARRY KERBS STUDIOS INC., 419 Park Ave. S., New York NY 10016. (212)686-0420. Contact: Larry Kerbs or Jim Lincoln. Specializes in sales promotion design, some ad work and placement, annual reports, corporate identity, publications and technical illustration. Clients: industrial, chemical, insurance and public relations.

Needs: Works with 3 illustrators and 1 designer/month. Uses artists for direct mail, layout, illustration, slide sets, technical art, paste-up and retouching for annual reports, trade magazines, product brochures and direct mail. Especially needs freelance comps through mechanicals; type specification.

First Contact & Terms: New York, New Jersey and Connecticut artists only. Mail samples or call for interview. Prefers b&w line drawings, roughs, previously published work as samples. Provide brochures, business card and resume to be kept on file for future assignments. No originals returned to artist at job's completion. Pays $14-18/hour, paste-up; $18-20/hour, comprehensive layout; $18-22/hour average, design; negotiates payment by the project for illustration.

Tips: "Improve hand lettering for comps; strengthen typographic knowledge and application."

ARVID KNUDSEN AND ASSOCIATES, 592 A Main St., Hackensack NJ 07601. (201)488-7857. Contact: Arvid Knudsen. Specializes in publications. Clients: publishing companies.

Needs: Works with 12 freelance artists/year. Uses artists for catalog design, illustration and layout; book and magazine design and illustration, mechanicals.

First Contact & Terms: Artists with "creativity, technical skills, experience and dependability" only. Send photocopied samples and tear sheets to be kept on file. Prefers tear sheets of full color work, photocopies of b&w work, as samples. Samples not kept on file are returned only if requested. Reports only if interested. Works on assignment only. Pay for all work "is negotiated and related to client's budget," also complexity of project.

Tips: "First, find out precisely what kind of work we are interested in. Then, if possible, send in tear sheets or photocopies of work that comes close to that need."

*BARBARA KOELLING DESIGN, 1615 Parkway Dr., Port Washington WI 53074. (414)284-6004. Owner/Designer: Barbara Koelling. Specializes in packaging, publications, technical illustration and industrial design. Clients: manufacturers mainly.
Needs: Uses artists for retouching, airbrushing, model making and AV materials.
First Contact & Terms: Local artists only. Send query letter with brochure to be kept on file. Accepts photostats, slides, photocopies or tear sheets as samples. Samples are returned only if requested. Reports only if interested. Considers complexity of project, client's budget, skill and experience of artist, how work will be used, turnaround time and rights purchased when establishing payment.

KOVACH ASSOCIATES INC., (formerly Ronald Kovach Design), 719 S. Dearborn, Chicago IL 60605. (312)461-9888. President: Ronald Kovach. Specializes in annual reports, corporate identity, packaging, publications and signage. Clients: real estate, industrial manufacturers, public relations and retail manufacturers.
Needs: Uses artists for advertising, brochure, poster and direct mail package illustration. Prefers a classic look for annual reports and packaging; "probably includes illustration for logotype or company mark when appropriate."
First Contact & Terms: Send query letter with brochure/flyer or resume; call or write for appointment. Prefers finished art or finished products as samples. Samples returned by SASE. Reports within 2 weeks. Provide resume, business card and brochure/flyer to be kept on file for possible future assignments. Pays $100-3,000 average/project for design or illustration; also negotiates.
Tips: "Most good work relationships center on the personal relationship between parties. Although direct mail solicitation is effective, if you see a company you like, visit with them personally as often as possible."

F. PATRICK LA SALLE DESIGN/GRAPHICS, 225 Sheridan St., Rockford IL 61103. (815)963-2089. Contact: F. Patrick La Salle. Specializes in corporate identity, displays, direct mail, packaging, publications and signage. Clients: small corporations, ad agencies, book publishers and hospitals.
Needs: Works with 10-15 freelance artists/year. Uses artists for design, illustration, brochures, catalogs, books, magazines, newspapers, P-O-P displays, mechanicals, photography (studio and on-location), retouching, airbrushing, posters, direct mail packages, model making and AV materials.
First Contact & Terms: Experienced artists only. Send query letter with brochure and samples to be kept on file. Call for appointment to show portfolio. "Photocopies as samples okay if technique is clear." Samples not kept on file are not returned. Reports back only if interested. Pays for design by the hour, $10-25 average. Pays for illustration by the hour, $20-35 average. Considers complexity of project, client's budget and turnaround time when establishing payment. "Artist will be paid after client has paid invoice."
Tips: "Most freelancers work here at the studio with provided supplies. Payment schedules set up with client *before* work is begun. Frequently, there is a 45-60 day wait for payment after billing has been completed. Recently, our clients have depended a great deal on our co-ordination and consultation with small to elaborate audiovisual presentations. Some have included live actors with slide support for demonstrations. Many artists, in the form of freelance support and production companies, have been involved."

LEGAL ARTS, 711 Twelfth Ave., San Diego CA 92101. (619)231-1551. Contact: James Gripp. Specializes in displays; technical illustration; and forensic exhibits including: medical illustration, scale diagrams and models; and charts and graphs. Clients: law firms.
Needs: Works with 3-5 freelance artists/year. Uses artists for illustration, airbrushing, model making, charts/graphs and AV materials. Especially needs medical illustrator and model maker.
First Contact & Terms: Prefers "degreed artists (AA or BA); local to San Diego County." Works on assignment only. Send query letter with resume and samples to be kept on file. Write for appointment to show portfolio. "Samples may be shown by appointment in lieu of portfolio. Artist must send at least 5 photocopy samples with query letter." Reports back within 5 days. Pays for design and illustration by the hour, $7.50 minimum. Considers skill and experience of artist and turnaround time when establishing payment. "Always 'work for hire' due to legal application of original art."
Tips: Especially looks for "diversity of media, specific applications towards my needs and superior craftsmanship" in samples for portfolio. "If you are a 'generalist', good! We do work that will be used as evidence in court—it must be accurate *every* time. In the legal field, the background of the artist (i.e. degrees), is of great importance to the courts. One must qualify as being educationally capable rather than just physically capable of preparing exhibits for trial use. Hence, the freelancer must have some documented background that a non-artist (judge or juror), will deem as being necessary before the artist can truthfully, accurately and honestly portray whatever is in the exhibit."

THE LEPREVOST CORPORATION, Suite #6, 29350 Pacific Coast Hwy., Malibu CA 90265. (213)457-3742. President: John LePrevost. Specializes in corporate identity, record covers, television and film design. Clients: corporations—CBS television, Metromedia Producers Corporation, P.M. Magazine/Westinghouse Broadcasting.
Needs: Works with 10 freelance artists/year. Uses artists for animation and film design and illustration; lettering and logo design. Animation and design becoming more sophisticated.
First Contact & Terms: Prefers "talented and professional" artists only. Call for appointment. Samples not returned. Works on assignment only. Provide information to be kept on file for possible future assignments; reports back. Payment by the project for both design and illustration. Considers complexity of project, client's budget, skill and experience of artist, how work will be used, turnaround time and rights purchased when establishing payment.

LESLEY-HILLE, INC., 32 E. 21st St., New York NY 10010. (212)677-7570. President: Valrie Lesley. Specializes in annual reports, corporate identity, publications, advertising and sales promotion. Clients: financial, fashion, nonprofit organizations, hotels, restaurants, investment firms, oil and real estate firms.
Needs: Works with "many" freelance artists/year. Uses artists for illustration, mechanicals, airbrushing, model making, charts/graphs, AV materials and lettering.
First Contact & Terms: "Experienced and competent" artists only. Send query letter with resume, business card and samples to be kept on file. Call or write for appointment to show portfolio. Accepts "whatever best shows work capability" as samples. Samples not filed are returned by SASE. Reports back only if interested. Pay varies according to project. Considers complexity of project, client's budget, skill and experience of artist, and turnaround time before establishing payment.
Tips: Artists must "be *able to do* what they say they can and agree to do . . . professionally and on time!"

*****TOM LEWIS & THE DESIGN QUARTER**, 2900 4th Ave., San Diego CA 92103. (619)297-7900. Senior Art Directors: Tom Lewis and Don Young. Specializes in annual reports, corporate identity, packaging, publications, signage, collateral material or sales brochures. Clients: manufacturers, service, publishers, financial.
Needs: Works with 10 freelance artists/year. Uses artists for advertising, brochure, catalog and book illustration; mechanicals, retouching, model making and lettering.
First Contact & Terms: Send resume and phone number to be kept on file. Call or write for appointment to show portfolio. Prefers photostats and photographs as samples. Reports only if interested. Pays for design by the hour, $10-50 average. Pays for illustration by the hour, $20-60 average; varies according to project. Considers complexity of project, client's budget, skill and experience of artist, and rights purchased when establishing payment.

*****LIGATURE INC.**, 165 N. Canal St., Chicago IL 60606. (312)648-1233. Design Director: Josef Godlewski. Specializes in annual reports, corporate identity, displays, publications, signage and technical illustration. Clients: educational publishers, general book and magazine publishers, financial institutions and corporations.
Needs: Works with 100 freelance artists/year. Uses artists for advertising, brochure and book illustration; mechanicals and lettering.
First Contact & Terms: "All publishing work is rented as work-for-hire and upon acceptance becomes the property of the publisher." Send query letter with resume, samples and/or tear sheets to be kept on file except original samples. Write for appointment to show portfolio. Any form of samples are acceptable. Samples not kept on file are returned. Reports only if interested. Works on assignment only. Pay based on project. Considers complexity of project, client's budget, skill and experience of artist, how work will be used, turnaround time and rights purchased.

LIKA ASSOCIATES INC., 160 E. 38th St., New York NY 10016. (212)490-3660. President: Art Lika. Specializes in annual reports, brand identity, corporate identity, displays, direct mail, packaging, publications, signage and technical illustration. Clients: corporations, banks, public relation firms, ad agencies and publishers.
Needs: Works with 1-6 freelance artists/year. Uses artists for design, illustration, brochures, catalogs, books, magazines, newspapers, P-O-P displays, mechanicals, retouching, airbrushing, posters, direct mail packages, model making, charts/graphs, AV materials, lettering, logos and advertisements. Especially needs designers and mechanical artist.
First Contact & Terms: Works on assignment only. Send query letter with resume and business card to be kept on file. Call for appointment to show portfolio. Prefers roughs, comps, finished art and final printed materials as samples. Samples not kept on file returned by SASE. Reports within 1 week. Pays for design by the hour, $20-100 average. Considers complexity of project, client's budget and how work will be used when establishing payment.

JAN LORENC DESIGN, INC., #460, 3475 Lenox Rd., Atlanta GA 30326. (404)266-2711. President: Mr. Jan Lorenc. Specializes in corporate identity, displays, packaging, publications, architectural signage design and industrial design. Clients: developers, product manufacturers, architects and institutions.
Needs: Works with 10 freelance artists/year. Uses artists for design, illustration, brochures, catalogs, books, P-O-P displays, mechanicals, retouching, airbrushing, posters, direct mail packages, model making, charts/graphs, AV materials, lettering and logos. Especially needs architectural signage designers.
First Contact & Terms: Local artists only—senior designers. Send brochure, resume and samples to be kept on file. Call or write for appointment to show portfolio. Prefers slides as samples. Samples not kept on file are returned. Pays for design by the hour $10-25 average; by the project, $100-3,000 average. Considers complexity of project, client's budget, and skill and experience of artist when establishing payment.

JACK LUCEY/ART & DESIGN, 84 Crestwood Dr., San Rafael CA 94901. (415)453-3172. Contact: Jack Lucey. Art agency. Specializes in annual reports, brand identity, corporate identity, publications, signage, technical illustration and illustrations/cover designs. Clients: businesses, agencies and freelancers.
Needs: Works with 1 illustrator/month. Uses artists for illustration and lettering for newspaper work. Especially needs agricultural painting and corporation illustrations.
First Contact & Terms: Uses mostly local artists. Query. Prefers photostats and published work as samples. Provide brochures, business card and resume to be kept on file for future assignments. No originals returned to artist at job's completion. Payment is negotiated by the project.
Tips: "We would like to see an upgrade of portfolios."

MCGRAPHICS DESIGN, Suite 206, 1010A W. Magnolia Blvd., Burbank CA 91506. (213)841-1266. Owner: Kathleen McGuinness. Specializes in brand identity, corporate identity, direct mail, packaging and publications. Clients: corporations (manufacturers and distributors), some public relation firms and printers.
Needs: Works with 10 freelance artists/year. Uses artists for illustration, catalogs, mechanicals, retouching, airbrushing and newsletters. Especially needs b&w line illustration.
First Contact & Terms: "Local artists only, personable and presentable in the corporate environment." Works on assignment only. Send brochure, business card and samples to be kept on file. Call or write for appointment to show portfolio. Prefers brochures with some information about artist and samples of work. Samples not kept on file are not returned. Reports back "only if the artist calls and follows up." Pays for design by the hour, $20-30 average. Pays for illustration by the project, $100-250 average. Considers complexity of project, client's budget, and skill and experience of artist when establishing payment.
Tips: "Send samples first then make an appointment. Show up on time and *follow up* if we say we are interested."

*MCGUIRE WILLIS & ASSOCIATES, 249 E. Cook Rd., Columbus OH 43214. (614)262-8124. Contact: Sue Willis. Specializes in annual reports, audiovisual and publications. Clients: schools, training departments of companies, sales and banking.
Needs: Works with 20 freelance artists/year. Uses artists for advertising, brochure, catalog, poster, direct mail package and book design and illustration, and mechanicals.
First Contact & Terms: Send query letter with samples. Prefers photostats and slides as samples. Samples returned by SASE if not kept on file. Reports in 2 weeks. Works on assignment only; reports back on whether to expect possible future assignments. Provide brochure/flyer and samples to be kept on file for possible future assignments. Negotiates payment.

ROB MacINTOSH COMMUNICATIONS, INC., 288 Newbury St., Boston MA 02115. President: Rob MacIntosh. Specializes in annual reports, advertising design and collateral. Clients: manufacturers, graphic arts industry, nonprofit/public service agencies.
Needs: Works with 12 freelance artists/year. Uses artists for advertising and brochure design, illustration and layout; mechanicals, retouching and charts/graphs. Occasionally uses humorous and cartoonstyle illustrations.
First Contact & Terms: Portfolio and work experience required. Send samples to be kept on file. Irregular sizes or abundant material will not be filed. Write for appointment to show portfolio. "Never send original work unless it's a printed sample. A simple, compact presentation is best. Often photostats are adequate." Reports only if interested and "generally only when we require more information and/or services." Pays for design by the day, $100 minimum. Pays for illustration by the project, $100 minimum. Considers complexity of project, client's budget, skill and experience of artist and turnaround time when establishing payment.

MCS, 600 Valley Rd., Wayne NJ 07470. (201)628-9630. Director: Pamela K. Johnson. Specializes in brand identity, corporate identity, displays and packaging. Clients: consumer product companies.
Needs: Works with 10 freelance artists/year. Uses artists for illustration, retouching, airbrushing and AV materials.
First Contact & Terms: Prefers local artists. Works on assignment only. Call or write for appointment to show portfolio. Prefers slides and printed material as samples. Samples not kept on file returned by SASE. Reports only if interested. Pays for design and illustration by the hour. Considers complexity of project, client's budget and turnaround time when establishing payment.
Tips: "The cool-fine artist approach is a turn-off. Professionalism, clean work, originality and a cooperative attitude is a plus. If excessive verbal explanation of work is necessary then obviously the visual doesn't communicate on its own."

DONYA MELANSON ASSOCIATES, 437 Main St., Boston MA 02129. Contact: Donya Melanson. Art agency. Clients: industries, associations, publishers, financial and government.
Needs: Most work is handled by staff, but may occasionally use illustrators and designers. Uses artists for stationery design, direct mail, brochures/flyers, annual reports, charts/graphs and book illustrations.
First Contact & Terms: Local artists only. Query with photocopies. Reports in 1-2 months. Provide materials (no originals) to be kept on file for future assignments. Originals returned to artist after use only when specified in advance. Pays $10-25/hour, cartoons, design, illustrations, lettering, retouching, technical art and logo design. Pays $10-20/hour, mechanicals. Considers complexity of project, client's budget, skill and experience of artist and how work will be used when establishing payment.

MG DESIGN ASSOCIATES INC., 824 W. Superior, Chicago IL 60622. (312)243-3661. Contact: Michael Grivas. Specializes in trade show exhibits, museum exhibits, expositions and commercial interiors. Clients: industrial manufacturers, consumer-oriented product manufacturers, pharmaceutical firms, state and federal government, automotive parts manufacturers, etc.
Needs: Works with 4-6 freelance artists/year. Uses artists for design, illustration, detail drawings and model making.
First Contact & Terms: Artists must be local exhibit designers with minimum of 5 years' experience. Works on assignment only. Send resume to be evaluated. Write for appointment to show portfolio. Prefers slides and photocopies as samples. Samples not kept on file are returned only if requested. Considers complexity of project, client's budget, and skill and experience of artist when establishing payment.

E.M. MITCHELL, INC., 820 2nd Ave., New York NY 10017. (212)986-5595. Vice President: Steven E. Mitchell. Specializes in brand identity, corporate identity, displays, direct mail and packaging. Clients: major corporations.
Needs: Works with 20-25 freelance artists/year. Uses artists for design, illustration, mechanicals, retouching, airbrushing, model making, lettering and logos.
First Contact & Terms: "Most work is done in our studio." Send query letter with brochure, resume, business card and samples to be kept on file. Call or write for appointment to show portfolio. Prefers photostats and slides as samples. Reports back only if interested. Pays for design by the hour, $20 minimum; by the project, $250 minimum. Pays for illustration by the project, $150 minimum. Considers complexity of project, client's budget, skill and experience of artist, how work will be used, turnaround time and rights purchased when establishing payment.
Tips: "Call first."

MIZEREK ADVERTISING, 48 E. 43rd St., New York NY 10017. (212)986-5702. President: Leonard Mizerek. Specializes in catalogs, fashion and technical illustration. Clients: corporations— various service-oriented clientele.
Needs: Works with 25-30 freelance artists/year. Uses artists for design, illustration, brochures, retouching, airbrushing and logos.
First Contact & Terms: Experienced artists only. Works on assignment only. Send business card to be kept on file. "Slides can be mailed, viewed and returned easily; we have no time for interview." Reports back only if interested. Pays for design by the project, $100-500 average. Pays for illustration by the project, $25-500 average. Considers client's budget and turnaround time when establishing payment.
Tips: "Contact by mail; don't press for interview. Let the work speak for itself."

MOODY GRAPHICS, 639 Howard St., San Francisco CA 94105. (415)495-5186. President: Carol Moody. Specializes in annual reports, corporate identity, direct mail, publications and technical illustration. Clients: executives, printers and printing brokers.
Needs: Works with 3-5 freelance artists/year. Uses artists for design, illustration, brochures, catalogs, mechanicals, retouching, airbrushing, direct mail packages, charts/graphs, lettering, logos and advertisements.

ment only. Send query letter with brochure, resume, business card and samples to be kept on file; call or write for appointment to show portfolio. Prefers slides, tear sheets or photographs as samples. Samples not filed are returned by SASE. Reports within 2 weeks. Pays for design by the hour, $8-20 average. Pays for illustration by the hour, $8-15 average. "Speed and quality are the determining factors regarding pay." Considers complexity of project, and skill and experience of artist when establishing payment.
Tips: "Our firm likes to use the work of artists who can take direction and meet short deadlines with quality work."

PROFESSIONAL GRAPHICS, 80 A Belvedere St., San Rafael CA 94901. (415)459-5300. Contact: Zai Zatoon. Design studio providing camera ready illustration and graphic design. Clients: corporate and private businesses of all sizes.
Needs: Number of freelance artists used/year varies. Uses artists for advertising, brochure and catalog design, illustration and layout, signage and copywriting.
First Contact & Terms: Send query letter with resume and samples to be kept on file; call or write for appointment to show portfolio. Prefers printed sample pieces only (no originals). Samples not kept on file are returned by SASE only if requested. Reports only if interested. Works on assignment only. Pays by the hour, $8-10; "volunteers welcome for nonprofit, tax-exempt projects." Considers complexity of project, skill and experience of artist, client's budget and turnaround time when establishing payment.

PULSE COMMUNICATIONS, (formerly Pulse Visual Communications), 2445 N. Sayre Ave., Chicago IL 60635. (312)622-7066. Creative Director: Frank G. Konrath. Specializes in annual reports, corporate identity, displays, landscape design, interior design, packaging, publications, signage and technical illustration. Clients include corporations.
Needs: Works with 5-15 freelance artists/year. Uses artists for projects involving many different specialities.
First Contact & Terms: "Local artists preferred. I will always consider talent over experience." Works on assignment only. Send query letter with resume and business card to be kept on file. "Please don't call. Send your business card and give me an idea of what you're best at; I'll call you to arrange an interview when something comes up in your area. Save your samples until I ask to see them." Reports back only if interested. Considers complexity of project, client's budget, turnaround time and rights purchased when establishing payment.
Tips: "Know what area you want to work in. We hire freelance artists for their talent in specific areas of discipline and for what they can produce consistently. I've notice that many artists seem overly occupied with primary colors; I like design that's not locked in or trendy."

QUALLY & COMPANY INC., A2502, 30 E. Huron, Chicago IL 60611. (312)944-0237. Creative Director: Robert Qually. Specializes in advertising, graphic design and new product development. Clients: major corporations.
Needs: Works with 20-25 freelance artists/year. Uses artists for design, illustration, mechanicals, retouching and lettering.
First Contact & Terms: "Artists must be good and have the right attitude." Works on assignment only. Send query letter with brochure, resume, business card and samples to be kept on file. Call or write for appointment to show portfolio. Samples not kept on file are returned by SASE. Reports back within several days. Considers complexity of project, client's budget, skill and experience of artist, how work will be used, turnaround time and rights purchased when establishing payment.
Tips: Looks for talent, point of view, style, craftsmanship, depth and innovation in portfolio or samples. Sees "too many look-a-likes. Very little innovation. Few people who understand how to create an image, who know how to conceptualize, who can think." Artists often "don't know how to sell or what's involved in selling."

THE QUARASAN GROUP, INC., Suites 7 and 14, 1845 Oak St., Northfield IL 60093. (312)446-4777. Director of Creative Services: Randi S. Brill. Design Supervisor: Marcia Vecchione. Specializes in books. Clients: book publishers.
Needs: Works with 10-35 freelance artists/year. Uses artists for illustration, books, mechanicals, charts/graphs, lettering and production.
First Contact & Terms: Artists with publishing experience only. Send query letter with brochure or resume and samples to design supervisor to be kept on file. Prefers "anything that we can retain for our files; photostats, photocopies, tear sheets or dupe slides that do not have to be returned" as samples. Reports only if interested. Pays for production by the hour, $8-15 average; for illustration by the project, $75-200 average. Considers complexity of project, client's budget, how work will be used and turnaround time when establishing payment. "For illustration, size is also a factor; complexity is the key factor."
Tips: "It's very difficult to get approval for unknown/untried work. If artists are interested in illustrat-

ing for publishers, they must learn the market and understand why certain styles, ethnic balances and media work better than others. Look and learn and ask yourself how you can do it better.''

QUARSON ASSOCIATES, 160 S. Arrowhead Ave., San Bernardino CA 92408. (714)885-4442. Art Director: Joel Pilcher. Specializes in corporate identity, advertising design, brochures, data sheets and catalogs. Clients: book publishers, educational institutions, health maintenance organizations, hospitals and industrial firms.
Needs: Works with about 10 freelance artists/year. Uses artists for illustration, brochures, catalogs, retouching, airbrushing, lettering and advertisements.
First Contact & Terms: Works on assignment only. Send query letter with resume and samples to be kept on file. Call for appointment to show portfolio. Prefers slides, photocopies and tear sheets as samples. Samples not filed are returned by SASE only if requested. Reports back only if interested. Pays for design and illustration by the project, $50-1,500 average. Considers client's budget when establishing payment.
Tips: "I look for freelance work that keeps pace with our changing field—high technology. Clients are very aware of changes in the field. Plan to come in and show your portfolio and talk for about 30 minutes (not 60 or 90).'' When reviewing work, looks for "quality, the details. Is it creative or just a spin off?'' Artists shouldn't show too much; stick to only the best. Projects they liked 10 years ago are often included; they're not important to me. I can tell with about ten items if the artist is the one I want or not.''

JOHN RACILA ASSOCIATES, 2820 Oak Brook Rd., Oak Brook IL 60521. (312)655-1444. Design Director: John Neher. Specializes in brand identity, corporate identity, displays, interior design, direct mail, packaging, publications and signage. Clients: manufacturer of consumer and industrial products.
Needs: Works with 0-8 freelance artists/year. Uses artists for design, illustration, brochures, catalogs, books, P-O-P displays, mechanicals, retouching, airbrushing, model making, lettering, logos and advertisements.
First Contact & Terms: Works on assignment only. Send query letter with brochure, resume and business card to be kept on file; also send samples. Call or write for appointment to show portfolio. Prefers slides as samples. Samples returned by SASE only if requested. Reports only if interested. Considers complexity of project, client's budget, skill and experience of artist, and how work will be used when establishing payment.

COCO RAYNES GRAPHICS, INC., 11 Remington St., Cambridge MA 02138. President: Coco Raynes. Specializes in brand identity, corporate identity, displays, direct mail, packaging, publications and signage. Clients: corporations, institutions (private and public) and architects.
First Contact & Terms: Send query letter with brochure, resume and samples to be kept on file. Call or write for appointment to show portfolio. Reports back only if interested. Considers client's budget, and skill and experience of artist when establishing payment.

*RENAISSANCE COMMUNICATIONS, INC., 7835 Eastern Ave., Silver Spring MD 20910. (301)587-1505. Production Manager: Janice Mesich. Specializes in corporate identity, publications, technical illustration, general illustrations and audio visual presentations. Clients: government design and graphic departments, high tech firms.
Needs: Works with 30-40 freelance artists/year. Uses artists for design, illustration, mechanicals, retouching, airbrushing, charts/graphs, AV materials and lettering.
First Contact & Terms: Send query letter with resume to be kept on file. Reports back only if interested. Pays for design and illustration by the hour, $10-20 average; for art production by the hour, $6-15 average. Considers complexity of project, skill and experience of artist and turnaround time when establishing payment.

RICHARDS GRAPHIC DESIGN, 4722 Old Kingston Pk., Knoxville TN 37919. (615)588-9707. Contact: Stephanie Dixon. Specializes in corporate identity. Clients: ad agencies, magazine publisher, industrial and consumer business.
Needs: Uses artists for illustration, mechanicals, retouching and lettering.
First Contact & Terms: Works on assignment only. Send query letter with samples to be kept on file. Call for appointment to show portfolio. Prefers tear sheets as samples. Samples not kept on file are returned only if requested. Reports back only if interested. Pays for design by the hour, $10-25 average. Considers complexity of project, how work will be used, turnaround time and rights purchased when establishing payment.

THE ANDREW ROSS STUDIO INC., 148 W. 28th St., New York NY 10001. (212)807-6699. Contact: Andrew Ross. Graphic design studio. Clients: magazines, AV, sales presentations, sales promotions and direct mail.

Needs: Works with 1 or 2 illustrators/month. Uses artists for direct mail, slides, brochures/flyers, trade magazines, illustration, paste-up, lettering and retouching.
First Contact & Terms: Local artists only. Call for interview. Provide brochures and tear sheets to be kept on file for future assignments. Originals returned to artist upon request. Pays for illustration by the project, $100-1,000 average. Pays for mechanicals and paste-up approximately $10-15/hour. Doesn't buy design.

BEDA ROSS DESIGN LTD., 310 W. Chicago Ave., Chicago IL 60610. Creative Director: Philip Ross. Specializes in brand identity, corporate identity, displays, posters, direct mail, fashion, packaging, publications and signage. Clients: ad agencies, public relation firms, corporations and poster publishers.
Needs: Works with 10 freelance artists/year. Uses artists for design, illustration, brochures, catalogs, P-O-P displays, mechanicals, retouching, airbrushing, posters, direct mail packages, lettering, logos and advertisements. Especially needs experienced artists for graphic design and art production.
First Contact & Terms: Prefers artists with 3 years' experience. Send query letter with resume and samples to be kept on file. Call for appointment to show portfolio. Prefers photostats and slides as samples. Reports back within 30 days. Pays for design by the hour, $10-20 average. Considers complexity of project and client's budget when establishing payment.
Tips: "Especially looks for "visual impact, simplicity, sensitivity to typography and color, and clean line when reviewing work."

*RUBICK & FUNK GRAPHIC COMMUNICATIONS, #1, 1234 Pearl St., Eugene OR 97401. (503)485-1932. Creative Director: Mari Carmin. Specializes in brand identity, corporate identity, displays, direct mail, packaging, publications, signage and technical illustration. Clients: high tech, tourism and economic development.
Needs: Works with a varying number of freelance artists/year. Uses artists for design, illustration, mechanicals and lettering.
First Contact & Terms: Works on assignment only. Send query letter with resume, business card and samples to be kept on file. Call or write for appointment to show portfolio. Accepts any type sample. Samples not kept on file are returned by SASE. Reports back only if interested. Payment varies. Considers complexity of project, client's budget, skill and experience of artist, how work will be used, turnaround time and rights purchased when establishing payment.

JOHN RYAN & COMPANY, 12400 Whitewater Dr., Minnetonka MN 55343. (612)936-9900. Creative Director: Stevan L. Olson. Specializes in brand identity, corporate identity, displays, interior design, fashion, packaging and signage. Clients: major national retail chains, book publishers and retailers, food, clothing and hi-tech manufacturers and retailers.
Needs: Works with 30-50 freelance artists/year. Uses artists for illustration, brochures, books, P-O-P displays, mechanicals, retouching, airbrushing, posters, direct mail packages, AV materials, lettering, logos and advertisements. Especially looking for "fresh new talent in black-and-white, graphic, airbrush and classic painterly styles, plus people working in new media such as 3.0 and paper sculpture."
First Contact & Terms: "Local and regional artists are preferred, but I will work with talented people anywhere. Professionalism is more important than experience; quality must be of the highest. Artists much be fast and priced within normal market rates." Send query letter with brochure, resume, business card and samples to be kept on file. Call for appointment to show portfolio. Accepts color stats, slides, photocopies, photostats or printed samples, "preferably in 8½x11" format so that they are filable." Samples not filed are returned by SASE only if requested. Reports within 1 month. Pays for design by the hour, $20-50 average; by the project, $50-300 average. Pays for illustration by the project, $50-2,000 average. Considers complexity of project, client's budget, skill and experience of artist, turnaround time and rights purchased when establishing payment.
Tips: "Artist's work should be fresh in approach, superlative in execution, turned around in reasonable deadline, priced along normal rate guidelines. Creative problem solving and dazzling execution are premiums here."

SANTORO DESIGN CONSULTANTS LTD., 503 W. 27th St., New York NY 10001. (212)714-9207. President: Joseph L. Santoro. Specializes in annual reports, corporate identity, direct mail, packaging, publications and signage. Clients: major corporations, public relation firms, book publishers, not-for-profit institutions, real estate developers and architects.
Needs: Works with 2 freelance artists/year. Uses artists for mechanicals and charts/graphs.
First Contact & Terms: "Artists must be local, willing to perform services that support a small business, open-minded and have strong drawing ability." Send query letter with resume to be kept on file. Call for appointment to show portfolio. "Save your samples. I'd prefer to meet artists as I review work." Samples not kept on file are not returned. Considers client's budget, and skill and experience of artist when establishing payment.

JACK SCHECTERSON ASSOCIATES INC., 6 E. 39th St., New York NY 10016. (212)889-3950. Contact: Jack Schecterson. Art/ad agency. Specializes in packaging, product design, annual reports, brand identity, corporate identity, displays, exhibits and shows, publications and signage. Clients: manufacturers of consumer/industrial products.
Needs: Uses artists for annual reports, catalogs, direct mail brochures, exhibits, flyers, packaging, industrial design, slide sets, album covers, corporate design, graphics, trademark, logotype design, sales promotion, audiovisuals, P-O-P displays and print media advertising. Especially needs package and product designers.
First Contact & Terms: Uses local artists. Query with resume and samples, or write for appointment. Samples returned by SASE. Reports "as soon as possible." Works on assignment only. Provide brochures, flyers, samples and tear sheets to be kept on file for future assignments. Pays by the project for design and illustration; negotiates payment. Reproduction rights purchased.

SHAREFF DESIGNS, 81 Irving Place, New York NY 10003. (212)475-3963. Designer: Ira Shareff. Specializes in brand identity, corporate identity, displays, packaging, publications, signage, technical illustration, hand lettering, off-the-loom tapestries, financial graphics and murals. Clients: publishers, ad agencies and independent clients.
Needs: Works with 3-4 freelance artists/year. Uses artists for illustration, catalogs, mechanicals, retouching, airbrushing, model making, charts/graphs and AV materials.
First Contact & Terms: Artists must have 3 years' experience in the required areas. Works on assignment only. Send resume and samples. Prefers photocopies or tear sheets as samples. Samples are returned only if requested. Considers complexity of project, client's budget and turnaround time when establishing payment.

SHERIN & MATEJKA, INC., 400 Park Ave. S, New York NY 10016. (212)686-8410. President: Jack Sherin. Specializes in corporate communications, publications and sales promotion. Clients: banks, consumer magazines and insurance companies.
Needs: Works with 25 freelance artists/year. Uses artists for advertising and brochure design and illustration, mechanicals, retouching, model making, charts/graphs and lettering.
First Contact & Terms: Prefers artists located nearby with solid professional experience. Call for appointment to submit portfolio for review. Prefers printed samples, actual art or reproductions of art as samples. Samples returned by SASE. Reports in 1 week. Works on assignment only. Provide brochure/flyer to be kept on file for possible future assignments. Pays $15-40/hour for design; negotiates illustration payment method. Considers complexity of project, client's budget, skill and experience of artist, and how work will be used when establishing payment.
Tips: "We buy many humorous illustrations for use in corporate publications."

SMALLKAPS ASSOCIATES, INC., 40 E. 34th St., New York NY 10016. (212)683-0339. Creative Directors: Marla Kaplan and Guy Smalley. Specializes in brand identity, corporate identity, brochures and posters. Clients: publishers, major corporations and large ad agencies.
Needs: Works with 5 freelance artists/year. Uses artists for mechanicals, retouching, charts/graphs and AV materials.
First Contact & Terms: "Artists must do accurate, clean work and have great mechanical skills." Works on assignment only. Send query letter with resume, business card and samples to be kept on file. Call for appointment to show portfolio. Samples not kept on file are returned by SASE only. Reports back only if interested. Pays for illustration by the project, $50-300 average; mechanicals, $8-15. Considers complexity of project, client's budget, skill and experience of artist, how work will be used and turnaround time when establishing payment.
Tips: "Artist must do fast, *clean* mechanicals and have good work habits."

SMITH & DRESS, (formerly Industrial Artists), 202 E. Main St., Huntington NY 11743. (516)427-9333. Contact: A. Dress. Specializes in annual reports, corporate identity, displays, direct mail, packaging, publications and signage. Clients: corporations.
Needs: Works with 3-4 freelance artists/year. Uses artists for illustration, retouching, airbrushing and lettering.
First Contact & Terms: Local artists only. Works on assignment only. Send query letter with brochure and samples to be kept on file (except for works larger than 8½x11). Prefers tear sheets as samples. Pays for illustration by the project. Considers client's budget and turnaround time when establishing payment.

SMYTHE GRAPHICS, 1125 Camino Del Mar, Del Mar CA 92014. (619)755-0842. Specializes in annual reports, corporate identity, brochures and publications. Clients: industrial, research and development, medical products and hospitals, consulting firms, high technology firms.

Needs: Works with 10-12 freelance artists/year. Uses artists for advertising layout, brochure and catalog illustration and layout; mechanicals, retouching, posters, direct mail packages and charts/graphics. **First Contact & Terms:** Artists must be "conveniently located since they pick up and deliver to/from us. They must do neat, clean work." Works on assignment only. Send query letter with resume, samples and tear sheets to be kept on file. Call or write for appointment to show portfolio. Photocopies are acceptable as samples. Samples returned by SASE only if requested. Reports only if interested. Pays for design by the hour, $20-30 average. Pays for illustration by the hour, $5-15 average. Considers complexity of project, and skill and experience of artist when establishing payment. Estimated completion time required from artist. Reproduction rights are purchased with payment for work done.

SPLANE DESIGN ASSOCIATES, 10850 White Oaks Ave., Granada Hills CA 91344. (818)366-2069. Contact: Robson Lindsay Splane. Specializes in product design, corporate identity, displays, packaging, exhibitry and furniture design.
Needs: Uses artists for illustration, mechanicals, and model making.
First Contact & Terms: Local artists only. Works on assignment only. Send query letter to be kept on file. Reports back only if interested. Considers complexity of project, client's budget, skill and experience of artist, and turnaround time when establishing payment.

THOMAS STARR & ASSOCIATES, 23 E. 37th St., New York NY 10016. President: Thomas Starr. Specializes in corporate identity, direct mail and publications. Clients: ad agencies, film and video publishers, eyewear manufacturers, retail stores, computer software firms, restaurants and real estate developers.
Needs: Works with 8 freelance artists/year. Uses artists for illustration, mechanicals, retouching, airbrushing, model making, charts/graphs and logos.
First Contact & Terms: Works on assignment only. Send query letter with brochure, resume and samples to be kept on file. Prefers tear sheets as samples. Reports back only if interested. Pays for design by the hour, $15-30 average. Pays for illustration by the project, $250-1,500 average. Considers complexity of project, client's budget, skill and experience of artist, how work will be used, turnaround time and rights purchased when establishing payment.

*STEPAN DESIGN, 317 S. Prairie Ave., Mt. Prospect IL 60056. (312)364-4121. Designer: J. Stepan. Specializes in annual reports, brand identity, corporate identity, direct mail, packaging, publications and signage. Clients: corporations, ad agencies, arts organizations and hospitals.
Needs: Works with 4 freelance artists/year. Uses artists for illustration, P-O-P displays, mechanicals, retouching, model making, lettering and gift items. Currently seeks production-oriented designers.
First Contact & Terms: "Must see folio or examples of art for reproduction as well as finished product." Works on assignment only. Send query letter with brochure, resume and samples to be kept on file. Call for appointment to show portfolio. Samples not filed are returned by SASE. Reports back within 2 months. Pays for design by the hour, $10-25, average; for illustration by the project, $50-500, average. Considers complexity of project, client's budget, skill and experience of artist, how work will be used, turnaround time and rights purchased when establishing payment.

LINDA STILLMAN INC., 114 E. 91st St., New York NY 10128. (212)410-3225. Art Director: Linda Stillman. Specializes in promotion, brochures and publications. Clients: cultural and art organizations, publishers, insurance companies and financial companies.
Needs: Works with numerous freelance artists. Uses artists for design, illustration, mechanicals and retouching. "We mostly need mechanical artists."
First Contact & Terms: Local artists only. Send query letter, resume or samples to be kept on file. Prefers tear sheets or photocopies as samples. Considers complexity of project, client's budget, skill and experience of artist, how work will be used, turnaround time, and rights purchased when establishing payment. Payment varies.

*GORDON STROMBERG DESIGN, 5423 N. Artesian, Chicago IL 60625. (312)275-9449. President: Gordon Stromberg. Specializes in corporate identity, interior design, direct mail, publications and signage. Clients: advertising agencies, book publishing, small businesses, manufacturers, public relations firms, nonprofit organizations, religious groups/charities and magazine publishers.
Needs: Works with variable number of artists/year. Uses artists for illustration, brochures, catalogs, books, calligraphy, retouching and charts/graphs.
First Contact & Terms: Looks for "quality, price and appropriateness in artists' work." Works on assignment only. Send query letter with brochure, resume and samples—"anything that will give me insight into your ability"—to be kept on file; write for appointment to show portfolio. "A phone call will only delay the process until you send brochure or samples or photocopies of samples." Prefers slides; accepts photocopies. Samples are returned by SASE only if requested. Considers complexity of project,

This artwork was created by Steve Björkmann of Irvine, California, for use on a poster, brochure, book cover and as text illustration by MAP International Inc., a Christian medical support organization to missions worldwide. Gordon Stromberg of Gordon Stromberg Design, Chicago, assigned the job to Björkmann "because I knew Steve would do a super job in a tight deadline situation with just the right amount of humor to appeal to teens and adults."

client's budget, skill and experience of artist, how work will be used, turnaround time and rights purchased when establishing payment.

SYNTHEGRAPHICS CORPORATION, 940 Pleasant Ave., Highland Park IL 60035. (312)432-7774. President: Richard Young. Specializes in publications. Clients: PR agencies, ad agencies and book publishers.
Needs: Works with 4-5 freelance artists/year. Uses artists for advertising and brochure design, illustration and layout; book design and illustration, mechanicals and charts/graphs.
First Contact & Terms: "Prefer local artists, particularly ones good at juvenile, multi-ethnic illustrations." Works on assignment only. Send brochure, resume, business card, samples and tear sheets to be kept on file. Call for appointment to show portfolio. No preference for kind of sample. Reports only if interested. Pays for design by the hour, $15-25 average. Pays for illustration by the hour, $10-15 average. Considers complexity of project, client's budget, and skill and experience of artist when establishing payment.

DOUGLAS R. TERCOUICH ASSOC. INC., 575 Madison Ave., New York NY 10022. (212)838-4800. President: Douglas Tercouich. Specializes in packaging, brand identity, displays, sales promotion and fashion. Clients: cosmetic companies, industry and corporations.
Needs: Works with 15 freelance artists/year. Uses artists for design, illustration, brochures, P-O-P displays, mechanicals, retouching, airbrushing, posters, lettering and logos.
First Contact & Terms: Works on assignment only. Send resume and samples to be kept on file. Write

for appointment to show portfolio. Prefers photostats or tear sheets as samples. Reports back only if interested. Pays by the project: design $75 minimum; illustration $150-1,100 average. Considers complexity of project and client's budget when establishing payment.
Tips: "Mechanicals should be of packaging quality."

TESA DESIGN INC., 7015 Carroll Rd., San Diego CA 92121. (619)453-2490. President: Thomas E. Stephenson. Specializes in brand identity, corporate identity, packaging, signage and technical illustration. Clients: original equipment manufacturers.
Needs: Works with 4 freelance artists/year. Uses artists for design, illustration, brochures, catalogs, P-O-P displays, mechanicals, airbrushing, model making and logos.
First Contact & Terms: Works on assignment only. Send brochure and resume to be kept on file. Call for appointment to show portfolio. Samples not kept on file are returned by SASE. Reports back only if interested. Pays for design and illustration by the project. Considers complexity of project, skill and experience of artist, and how work will be used when establishing payment.
Tips: "Portfolio should include industrial or mechanical subject matter."

TOKYO DESIGN CENTER, Suite 928, 548 S. Spring St., Los Angeles CA 90013. (213)680-1294. Creative Art Director: Mac Watanabe. Specializes in corporate identity, advertising and packaging. Clients: fashion, cosmetic, architectural and industrial firms.
Needs: Works with 4 freelance artists/year. Uses artists for design, illustration, brochures, catalogs, books, P-O-P displays, mechanicals, airbrushing, charts/graphs and advertisements.
First Contact & Terms: Send samples to be kept on file. Samples not kept on file not returned. Reports only if interested. Pays for design and illustration by the project. Considers client's budget when establishing payment.

TOKYO DESIGN CENTER, Suite 252, 703 Market St., San Francisco CA 94103. Contact: Curtis Tsukano. Specializes in annual reports, brand identity, corporate identity, packaging and publications. Clients: consumer products, travel agencies and retailers.
Needs: Uses artists for design and illustration.
First Contact & Terms: Send business card and samples to be kept on file. Prefers slides, tear sheets and printed material as samples. Samples not kept on file are returned by SASE only if requested. Reports back only if interested. Pays for design by the project, $50-1,000 average. Pays for illustration by the project, $100-1,500 average. Considers client's budget, skill and experience of artist, turnaround time and rights purchased when establishing payment.

TOTAL DESIGNERS, B3, 3511 Pinemont, Houston TX 77018. (713)688-7766. President: Ed Lorts. Specializes in annual reports, brand identity, corporate identity, displays, interior design, packaging, signage and technical illustration. Clients: ad agencies, public relation firms and corporate public relations persons.
Needs: Works with 7-10 freelance artists/year. Uses artists for design, illustration, brochures, catalogs, P-O-P displays, mechanicals, retouching, airbrushing, posters, model making, charts/graphs, lettering, logos and advertisements. Especially needs sign and graphics installations.
First Contact & Terms: Experienced artists preferred. Works on assignment only. Send query letter with business card and samples to be kept on file. Call for appointment to show portfolio. Prefers photostats and slides as samples. Samples not kept on file are returned by SASE if requested. Reports back only if interested. Pays for design by the hour, $10-25 average; by the project, $100-250 average; by the day, $100-300 average. Pays for illustration by the hour, $25-75 average; by the project, $250-500 average; by the day, $300-500 average. Considers complexity of project, skill and experience of artist, turnaround time and rights purchased when establishing payment.
Tips: "Be willing to diversify."

UNICOM, 4100 W. River Ln., Milwaukee WI 53209. (414)354-5440. Art Director: Paul Young. Specializes in annual reports, brand identity, corporate identity, packaging, publications and signage. Clients: retailers, industrial firms, fashion and professionals.
Needs: Works with 3-4 freelance artists/year. Uses artist for design, illustration, brochures, catalogs, mechanicals, retouching and airbrushing.
First Contact & Terms: Works on assignment only. Send samples to be kept on file. Call or write for appointment to show portfolio. Samples not kept on file returned by SASE. Reports only if interested. Considers complexity of project, client's budget, skill and experience of artist, how work will be used and turnaround time when establishing payment.

UNIT 1, INC., 1556 Williams St., Denver CO 80218. (303)320-1116. President: Chuck Danford. Specializes in annual reports, brand identity, corporate identity, direct mail, packaging, publications and signage.

Needs: Uses artists for design, brochures, catalogs, P-O-P displays, mechanicals, posters, direct mail packages, charts/graphs, logos and advertisements.
First Contact & Terms: Send resume and samples to be kept on file. Call or write for appointment to show portfolio. Prefers to receive slides and actual samples. Samples not kept on file are returned. Reports back only if interested. Pays for design by the hour. Considers skill and experience of artist when establishing payment.

UNIVERSAL EXHIBITS, 9517 E. Rush St., South El Monte CA 91733. (213)686-0562. Director of Design: John Perez. Specializes in displays and interior design. Clients: ad agencies and companies.
Needs: Works with 5 freelance artists/year. Uses artists for design and model making.
First Contact & Terms: Prefers local artists, up to 40 miles, with excellent sketching abilities. Works on assignment only. Send resume and samples to be kept on file. Call for appointment to show portfolio. Prefers slides as samples; reviews original art. Samples not kept on file are returned only if requested. Reports back within 5 days. Pays for design by the hour, $10-25 average. Considers client's budget and turnaround time when establishing payment.

WALTER VAN ENCK DESIGN LTD., 3830 N. Marshfield, Chicago IL 60613. (312)935-9438. President: Walter Van Enck. Specializes in annual reports, brand identity, corporate identity, displays, direct mail, packaging, publications and signage. Clients: book publishers, financial associations, health care institutions, investment advisory corporations and medium-sized corporations.
Needs: Works with 2-3 freelance artists/year. Uses artists for design, illustration, mechanicals, retouching, model making and lettering.
First Contact & Terms: Prefers local artists. Works on assignment only. Send query letter with business card and samples to be kept on file. Call or write for appointment to show portfolio. Prefers "slides or photostats that do justice to line art." Samples not kept on file are returned only if requested. Reports back within 1 week. Pays for design by the hour, $8-15 average. Pays for illustration by the project, $500-2,500 average. Considers client's budget, and skill and experience of artist when establishing payment.

VIE DESIGN STUDIOS, INC., 830 Xenia Ave., Yellow Springs OH 45387. (513)767-7293. President: Read Viemeister. Specializes in corporate identity, packaging, publications and signage.
Needs: Works with 2 freelance illustrators/photographers per year. Uses keyliners for mechanicals and charts/graphs.
First Contact & Terms: Artists must be local, or have a "very special style." Works on assignment only. Send query letter with resume to be kept on file. Write for appointment to show portfolio. Prefers to review photostats and prints. Samples not kept on file are returned by SASE. Reports back only if interested. Pays for illustration by the hour, $20-30 average; or by the project. Considers turnaround time when establishing payment.
Tips: "Smaller budgets require that design solutions be designed around existing resources, thus freelancer must be a known quantity."

WHITE FLEET, INE WIJTVLIET DESIGN, 386 Park Ave. S, New York NY 10016. (212)684-4575. Contact: Design Production. Specializes in annual reports, brand and corporate identity, displays, exhibits and shows, packaging, publications, signage and slide shows. Clients: large corporation in computers, software computer, retail stores, hospitals, banks, architects and industry.
Needs: Works with 8 freelance artists/year. Uses artists for brochure and catalog layout, mechanicals, retouching, model making, charts/graphs, AV presentations, lettering and logo design. Especially needs good artists for mechanicals for brochures and other print. Prefers Swiss graphic style.
First Contact & Terms: Send brochure/flyer and resume; submit portfolio for review. Prefers actual printed samples or color slides. Samples returned by SASE. Reports within 1 week. Provide brochure/flyer, resume and tear sheets to be kept on file for possible future assignments. Pays $10-15 average/hour for mechanicals; pays/project for illustration.
Tips: Artists should "not start so high if unknown; give a break on the first 2 days to work in."

WISNER ASSOCIATES, Advertising, Marketing & Design, (formerly Brown/Wisner Advertising & Creative Services), 1991 Garden Ave., Eugene OR 97403. (503)683-3235. Creative Director: Linda Wisner. Specializes in brand identity, corporate identity, direct mail, packaging and publications. Clients: small businesses, manufacturers, public relation firms and book publishers.
Needs: Works with 7-10 freelance artists/year. Uses artists for illustration, books, mechanicals, airbrushing and lettering.
First Contact & Terms: Prefers experienced artists and "fast clean work." Works on assignment only. Send query letter with brochure, resume, business card and samples to be kept on file. Call or write for appointment to show portfolio. Prefers "examples of completed pieces, which show the abilities of the

artist to his/her fullest." Samples not kept on file are returned by SASE only if requested. Reports back only if interested. Pays for illustration by the hour, $10-20 average. Pays for paste-up/production by the hour, $8.50-10. Considers complexity of project, client's budget, skill and experience of artist, how work will be used and turnaround time when establishing payment.
Tips: "Bring a complete portfolio with up-to-date pieces."

BENEDICT NORBERT WONG MARKETING DESIGN, 55 Osgood Pl., San Francisco CA 94133. (415)781-7590. President/Creative Director: Ben Wong. Specializes in annual reports, corporate identity, direct mail and marketing design for financial services. Clients: financial services companies (banks, savings and loans, insurance companies, stock brokerage houses) and direct mail marketing firms (ad agencies, mail houses).
Needs: Works with 15 freelance artists/year. Uses artists for design, illustration, brochures, catalogs, P-O-P displays, mechanicals, retouching, posters, direct mail packages, charts/graphs, lettering, logos and advertisements. Especially needs "experienced mechanical artists in area of direct mail production."
First Contact & Terms: Send query letter with resume, business card and samples to be kept on file. Call for appointment to show portfolio. Prefers tear sheets as samples. Reports back only if interested. "Payment depends on experience and portfolio." Considers complexity of project, client's budget, skill and experience of artist, how work will be used, turnaround time and rights purchased when establishing payment.
Tips: "Please show imaginative problem solving skills which can be applied to clients in the financial services industry."

THE WORKSHOP INC., 735 Bismark Rd., Atlanta GA 30324. (404)875-0141. President: David Dobra. Specializes in corporate identity, fashion and publications. Clients: ad agencies, retail stores and manufacturing companies.
Needs: Uses artists for advertising, brochure, catalog and book illustration; retouching and lettering.
First Contact & Terms: Requires several years experience. Send samples to be kept on file. Prefers photographs or printed samples. Reports only if interested. Works on assignment only. Pays for design and illustration by the hour, $15-20 average. Considers client's budget, and skill and experience of artist when establishing payment.

*X-GROUP, INC., 636 Avenue of the Americas, New York NY 10011. (212)255-5900. Art Directors: Frank DeMarco or Ernie Bellico. Specializes in marketing communications, brand identity, corporate identity, displays, audiovisual slide presentations and video and film animation. Clients: advertising agencies, public relation firms and corporations.
Needs: Works with 20 freelance artists/year. Uses artists for illustration, mechanicals, retouching, airbrushing, model making, charts/graphs, AV materials and animation.
First Contact & Terms: Send query letter with brochure, resume, business card and samples to be kept on file. Prefers slides and tear sheets as samples. Reports back only if interested. Pays for design by the hour, $5-15 average. Pays for illustration by the project, $75-3,000 average. Considers complexity of project, client's budget, skill and experience of artist, how work will be used, turnaround time and rights purchased when establishing payment.
Tips: "Be professional, direct and to the point. No fluff."

ZIM-LERNER INC., Industrial and Residential Design Group, 123 University Pl., New York NY 10003. (212)777-1907. Principals: Larry Zim, Mel Lerner. Specializes in corporate identity, displays, interior design, packaging and signage. Clients: department stores, shopping malls, boutiques.
Needs: Uses artists for design, P-O-P displays, mechanicals, retouching and model making. Especially needs interior rendering.
First Contact & Terms: Experienced artists only. Works on assignment only. Send resume to be kept on file; write for appointment to show portfolio. Do not send samples until requested. Reports back only if interested. Considers complexity of project when establishing payment.

Associations & Institutions

Freelance artists continue to be a major source of design and artwork for associations and institutions unable to support full-time staff artists and designers. These markets offer artists opportunities for both inperson and long-distance assignments with needs ranging from occasional spot art to complex, high-budget campaigns. Some projects require a local artist when constant communication is necessary. Others, such as magazine illustration or spot art, can be discussed, assigned and submitted by mail.

This field with its variety of themes, needs and pay rates particularly seeks artists who *listen* when the group "image" is explained to them and then adapt their work to fit that image rather than working from their own preconceptions. Flexibility is an asset since you may be used for several different jobs, each requiring a different approach.

Although these groups inform, promote and solicit via print *and* film media, it's print that dominates the demand for artwork. Many associations/institutions use a modern, graphic approach to their publications coupled with a direct, simple message to communicate with their public. One piece of artwork, or selected portions of it, often is used to thematically unite several printed pieces, such as posters, invitations, catalogs and flyers.

When approaching this market, present samples that show your area of specialization so that an art director (or communications/public relations director) can best judge how your talent fits his needs. Keep in mind that your samples should reproduce well in print, exhibit low-cost design solutions and be flexible enough for application to several uses. Demand for artwork from any one association or institution can fluctuate, so keep samples on file at as many places as you feel are suitable for your skills.

Some of the listings here do not pay for artwork, but request that it be donated instead. Is this a good idea for an artist? If you don't have a strong interest in supporting an organization's cause, remember that contributing work means exposure through publication which might lead to referrals and paying jobs.

For additional information, consult the *Encyclopedia of Associations*, *Barron's Profiles of American Colleges* and *Comparative Guide to American Colleges*.

Deborah Derr McClintock's pen & ink artwork for this genocide symposium mailer/poster "caused the right amount of shock value needed to get people to attend the conference," says Richard McClintock, director of publications, Hampden-Sydney College, Hampden-Sydney, Virginia. The artist, from Farmville, Virginia, received $50 for all rights to the art. The logo was also used on programs and in ads.

ADRENAL METABOLIC RESEARCH SOCIETY OF THE HYPOGLYCEMIA FOUNDA-TION, INC., 153 Pawling Ave., Troy NY 12180. (518)272-7154. President: Marilyn Hamilton Light. Nonprofit association providing information and research on functional hypoglycemia and related endocrine disorders for lay and professional persons.
Needs: Works with 1 freelance artist/year. Prefers design representative of content of material—medical designs, etc.
First Contact & Terms: Send query letter with samples and resume; write for appointment. "Photostats are acceptable as samples." Samples returned by SASE if not kept on file. Reports in 2 weeks. Works on assignment basis only. Provide brochure and samples to be kept on file for possible future assignments. Payment is negotiable; varies according to client's budget.

AESTHETICIANS INTERNATIONAL ASSOCIATION, INC., Suite A-II, 339 Medallion Ctr., Dallas TX 75229. (214)987-4466. Chairman of the Board: Ron Renee. Promotes education and public awareness of skin care, make-up and body therapy. Produces seminars and holds an annual congress; produces a magazine, *Dermascope*, published bimonthly.
Needs: Works with 6 freelance artists/year. Uses artists for advertising design, illustration and layout, brochure and magazine/newspaper design, exhibits, displays and posters.
First Contact & Terms: Send query letter with brochure, samples and tear sheets to be kept on file; write for appointment to show portfolio. Considers photostats, original work, slides or photographs as samples. Samples not kept on file are returned by SASE. Reports only if interested. Works on assignment only. Pays by the hour, $3.75-6 average. Considers available budget when establishing payment.
Tips: "Have something that is creative that reflects our profession."

*AFFILIATE ARTISTS INC., 155 W. 68th St., New York NY 10023. Director, Communications: Katharine Hoblitzelle. A national not-for-profit organization, producing residencies for performing artists of all disciplines. "Through residencies, Affiliate Artists supports the professional development of exceptionally talented performers and builds audiences for live performance. Residencies are sponsored by corporations and corporate foundations, and presented locally by arts institutions and community organizations. Roster represents every discipline."
Needs: Works with 3 freelance artists/year. Uses artists for advertising and brochure design, illustration and layout.
First Contact & Terms: Send query letter with resume and samples. Prefers photostats as samples. Samples returned only if requested. Reports only if interested. Works on assignment only. Pays by the project. Considers available budget when establishing payment.

AMERICAN BONSAI SOCIETY, INC., Box 358, Keene NH 03431. (603)352-9034. Executive Secretary: Anne D. Moyle. Nonprofit educational corporation and organization of individuals interested in the art of miniature trees; a journal and newsletter published quarterly.
Needs: Works with 2-3 freelance artists/year.
First Contact & Terms: Send query letter to be kept on file.

AMERICAN CHEMICAL SOCIETY, 1155 16th St. NW, Washington DC 20036. Art Director: Alan Kahan. Works on various publications including 5 magazines and 22 journals, direct mail packages and marketing books, and serves chemists.
Needs: Works with 20 freelance artists/year. Uses artists primarily for technical illustration including charts and graphs, but also for brochure and magazine design, illustration and layout; and AV presentations.
First Contact & Terms: Local artists only. Send query letter with brochure, resume and samples to be kept on file. Write for appointment to show portfolio. Accepts any type of sample, but original work preferred. Samples not filed returned by SASE only if requested. Reports only if interested. Pays by the hour, $10-15 average; by the project, $75-300 average; or by the day, $70-100 average. Considers complexity of project, available budget, skill and experience of artist, how work will be used, turnaround time, and rights purchased when establishing payment.

AMERICAN CORRECTIONAL ASSOCIATION, Suite L-208, 4321 Hartwick Rd., College Park MD 20740. (301)699-7627. Publications Manager/Art Director: Martin J. Pociask. 14,000-member nonprofit association dealing primarily with correctional personnel and services to improve the correctional field.
Needs: Works with 3-5 freelance artists/year. Uses artists for advertising, brochure, catalog and magazine/newspaper layout and pasteup. Prefers themes on corrections.
First Contact & Terms: Prefers primarily local artists; "however, there may be infrequent exceptions." Send query letter with resume to be kept on file; call for appointment to show portfolio. Reports only if interested. Works on assignment only. Pays by the hour, $6 minimum. Considers complexity of

project, available budget, skill and experience of artist and turnaround time when establishing payment.
Tips: "Artists' work should be clean, concise, with quick turnaround." Abilities should not be too specialized. "Most clients are not interested in dividing their work among several artists. They prefer to work closely with only one or two artists."

AMERICAN INDIAN ARCHAEOLOGICAL INSTITUTE, Box 260, Washington CT 06793. (203)868-0518. President: Susan F. Payne. Nonprofit museum center for the study of prehistoric and historic man in Connecticut, New England and the Northeast. Serves 1,400 memberships, 12,000 visitors and 12,000 students annually.
Needs: Works with 1-3 freelance artists/year. Uses artists for magazine/newspaper design; advertising, brochure and catalog design, illustration and layout; exhibits, displays, posters and photography.
First Contact & Terms: Send query letter with brochure, resume, business card, samples and tear sheets to be kept on file. Prefers photographs and slides as samples. Samples not kept on file returned only if requested. Reports only if interested. Works on assignment basis only. Negotiates pay/project. Considers available budget, skill and experience of artist and rights purchased when establishing payment.

AMERICAN SOCIETY FOR THE PREVENTION OF CRUELTY TO ANIMALS, 441 E. 92nd St., New York NY 10128. (212)876-7700. Head of Publications: Louise Spirer. A nonprofit humane society which cares for 200,000 animals annually. Its members are animal lovers and those concerned about humane issues.
Needs: Often uses illustrations for posters, booklets and newsletters. "We prefer realistic depictions of animals rather than cartoons."
First Contact & Terms: Write with samples. Samples returned by SASE. Provide resume, brochure/flyer and tear sheet samples to be kept on file for future assignments. Reports within 3 weeks. Pays $25/small illustration for a pamphlet. Pay for product design and illustration depends on job required and funds available.

AMUSEMENT AND MUSIC OPERATORS ASSOCIATION, Suite 220, 2000 Spring Rd., Oak Brook IL 60521. (312)654-2662. Director Communications & Research: J.D. Meacham. Represents the coin-operated entertainment industry (primarily jukeboxes and videogames) with 3,000 member companies, operators, distributors, suppliers and manufacturers.
Needs: Works with 4 freelance artists/year. Uses artists for magazine/newspaper design, illustration and layout; exhibits, signage and posters. Prefers themes revolving around the coin-op entertainment industry.
First Contact & Terms: Local artists only. Send query letter with brochure, resume, business card, samples and tear sheets to be kept on file; do not call. Accepts photostats, original work, slides or photographs as samples. Reports only if interested. Works on assignment basis only. Negotiates pay by the project. Considers complexity of project, available budget, turnaround time and rights purchased when establishing payment.

BIKECENTENNIAL, INC., Box 8308, Missoula MT 59807. (406)721-1776. Art Director: Greg Siple. Service organization for touring bicyclists; 18,000 members.
Needs: Uses artists for illustration. Prefers bicycle themes; considers various styles.
First Contact & Terms: Send query letter with samples to be kept on file. Call or write for appointment to show portfolio. Prefers slides as samples. Samples not kept on file returned. Reports within 4 weeks. Works on assignment only. Pays by the project, $25-65. Considers complexity of project, available budget, skill and experience of artist and how work will be used when establishing payment.
Tips: "We only assign specific illustrations. Our reproduction quality is good—you'll like the results."

BROWARD COMMUNITY COLLEGE, 225 E. Las Olas Blvd., Ft. Lauderdale FL 33301. (305)761-7490. Director of Cultural Affairs: Dr. Ellen Chandler. Assigns 2 jobs/year.
Needs: Works with 1 illustrator and 1 designer/year. Seasonal illustration needs during concert season: October-March. Uses artists for exhibits/displays. Especially needs season brochure and/or poster.
First Contact & Terms: Mostly local artists. Query with samples (photographs) or call for interview. Looks for "imaginative design and clean, clear work." Reports in 1 month. Works on assignment only. Samples returned by SASE. Pay varies. Considers complexity of project and available budget when establishing payment.

 The asterisk before a listing indicates that the listing is new in this edition. New markets are often the most receptive to freelance contributions.

Tips: "Our own college art students and printing department have become more actively involved in our projects."

BUCKNELL UNIVERSITY, Lewisburg PA 17837. (717)523-3200. Contact: Director of Public Relations and Publications. 3,400-student university; public relations department serves students, alumni (31,000), donors and students' parents.
Needs: Works with 3-4 freelance artists/year. Uses artists for brochure, catalog and magazine/newspaper design, illustration and layout; graphic design and posters. Especially needs brochure design.
First Contact & Terms: Prefers freelancers with strong experience in college/university graphics and located within a 3-hour drive from campus. Send query letter with samples, brochure/flyer and resume; call or write for appointment to show portfolio. Accepts any type samples. Looks for innovation, appropriateness of design concept to target audience and "sensitivity to our particular 'look'—rather classic and dignified, but not boring" when reviewing artist's work. Samples returned by SASE. Reports in 1 month. Payment is by the project, $50-3,000 average or by the hour, $10-20 average; method is negotiable. Considers complexity of project, available budget and turnaround time when establishing payment.
Tips: "Artists should "be able to help me produce graphically strong and cost-effective pieces."

CALIFORNIA BAPTIST COLLEGE, 8432 Magnolia Ave., Riverside CA 92504. (714)689-5771. Vice President for Public Affairs: Dr. Jay P. Chance.
Needs: Uses artists for annual reports, catalog covers/layouts, direct mail/publicity brochures, displays, newspaper ad layouts, lettering, recruitment literature and company publications.
First Contact & Terms: Assigns 3-5 jobs/year; local artists only. Query with samples. SASE. Reports in 3 weeks. Pays by hour.

CCCO/An Agency for Military and Draft Counseling, 2208 South St., Philadelphia PA 19146. (215)545-4626. Publications Director: Robert A. Seeley. "The largest national draft and military counseling organization in the country; publishes an extensive line of literature, a quarterly newsletter reaching 45,000 people, and one other special-interest newsletter." Serves CCCO contributors and conscientious objectors registered with CCCO. "All are peace-oriented and interested in issues surrounding the draft and military."
Needs: Uses artists for brochure and magazine/newspaper illustration, and possibly for brochure design. Interested in war and peace themes particularly as they affect individuals; open to any style. Graphics and illustrations considered on a case by case basis; especially interested in cartoons.
First Contact & Terms: Send query letter with samples to be kept on file. Reviews any type of sample; finished artwork must be camera-ready. Samples not kept on file returned by SASE. Reports within 3 weeks. "We pay only in contributors' copies, but since our material reaches 45,000 people nationwide, including a number of magazines, we also offer exposure."
Tips: "Send several samples if possible."

CENTRE COLLEGE, 111 Maple St., Alumni House, Danville KY 40422. Publications Director: Mike Norris. Small liberal arts college with high academic standards serving students from every part of the US.
Needs: Works with 1 freelance artist/year. May use artists for advertising, brochure and catalog illustration; brochure, catalog, graphic and magazine/newspaper design. Prefers mainly realistic line drawings. Especially needs line drawings of students in typical campus settings.
First Contact & Terms: Send query letter with business card and samples to be kept on file. Prefers "work as it appeared when printed, if possible," as samples. Looks for "an effective style suitable for print reproduction" when reviewing artist's work. Samples not returned. Reports in 1 month. Works on assignment basis only. Payment varies according to job.
Tips: "As the need for artwork becomes more specialized, artists will have to be willing to learn about the institution/client they are working for. Send samples of work which relate specifically to the type of institution you are querying."

CHAPMAN COLLEGE, 333 N. Glassell, Orange CA 92666. Director of Publications: Annie P. Long. A 4-year private liberal arts college producing publications for use by donors and approximately 1,800 students enrolled on the home campus and the surrounding community.
Needs: Works with 2 fulltime and 2 part-time artists and occasionally freelancers. Uses artists for catalog design, illustration and layout; exhibits, displays, signage and AV presentations. Especially needs freelance editorial illustrations, and production artists/designers.
First Contact & Terms: Prefers artists who "live in the surrounding area to be available for meetings." Send query letter, resume and business card with samples to be kept on file; write for appointment. Prefers photos or photocopies as samples. Looks for "quality, creative, clean and cost-conscious design" when reviewing artist's work. Samples not filed are returned by SASE. Works on assignment basis only.

Payment varies according to job; considers complexity of project, available budget, and skill and experience of artist when establishing payment.

Tips: CASE, The Council for the Advancement of Secondary Education, and UCDA, The University & College Designers Association, and local community organizations such as public relations societies or business associations are helpful organizations to join for education art contacts. "The ability to communicate clearly is important. Administrators at institutions are involved in so many meetings and other tasks that the opportunity to catch them anytime with questions is not always there. Artists need to be versatile and able to illustrate, design and have a working knowledge of production and printing processes." Artists should avoid "underselling themselves by asking for less than they deserve, or overselling by asking for much more than their experience shows."

CHILD AND FAMILY SERVICES OF NEW HAMPSHIRE, 99 Hanover St., Box 448, Manchester NH 03105. (603)668-1920. Contact: Public Relations Director. "Our purposes are to reduce social problems, promote and conserve wholesome family life, serve children's needs and guard children's rights."

Needs: Works with 1 illustrator and designer/year; February-May only. Uses artists for annual reports, direct mail brochures, exhibits/displays, posters, publicity brochures and trademarks/logotypes. Especially needs illustrations of children and/or families.

First Contact & Terms: Query with business card and tear sheets to be kept on file or arrange interview. Looks for human interest appeal when reviewing artist's work. Reports in 2 weeks. Works on assignment only. Samples returned by SASE. Considers complexity of project and available budget when establishing payment.

CLUB WORLD PUBLICATIONS, Division of National Allied Services, Inc., Box 4105, Pensacola FL 32507. Vice President: David A. Matheny. Provides support services to family recreation clubs and social organizations.

Needs: Works with 4-10 freelance artists/year. Uses artists for advertising, brochure and catalog design, magazine/newspaper illustration, signage and posters.

First Contact & Terms: Send query letter with samples and tear sheets to be kept on file; write for appointment to show portfolio. Prefers original work or photographs as samples. Samples not kept on file are returned. Reports within 30 days. Pay varies. Considers available budget, skill and experience of artist and how work will be used when establishing payment.

Tips: "We are happy to hear from artists. We realize that their time is important also; therefore, we treat their inquiries with respect."

COACHING ASSOCIATION OF CANADA, 333 River Rd., Ottawa, Ontario, Canada K1L 8B9. (613)741-0036. Editor: Vic Mackenzie. National nonprofit organization dedicated to coaching development and the profession of coaching.

Needs: Works with 18 freelance artists/year. Uses artists for advertising, brochure, catalog and magazine illustration. Prefers coaching (sport) themes in realistic styles.

First Contact & Terms: Send brochure and samples to be kept on file. Prefers slides or photographs as samples. Samples not kept on file are returned. Reports within 3 weeks. Works on assignment only. Pays by the project, $50-500 average. Considers complexity of project, available budget, skill and experience of artist, how work will be used and rights purchased when establishing payment.

Tips: "Artists must have a good understanding of sport."

COLLEGE OF THE SOUTHWEST, Lovington Highway, Hobbs NM 88240. (505)392-6561. Contact: Public Information Officer. Privately supported, independently governed 4-year college offering professional studies on a foundation of arts and sciences, emphasizing Christian principles and the private enterprise system.

Needs: Works with varying number of freelance artists/year. Uses artists for advertising, brochure and graphic design; advertising and brochure illustration; and posters. Especially needs artwork "relating to Southwestern heritage."

First Contact & Terms: Prefers to work with artists in the Southwest. Send query letter; submit portfolio for review. Prefers 5-10 photostats or slides as samples. Samples returned by SASE. Reports within 2 weeks. Works on assignment only. Provide resume and samples to be kept on file for possible future assignments. Negotiates payment.

THE CONTEMPORARY ARTS CENTER, 115 E. 5th St., Cincinnati OH 45202. (513)721-0390. Publications Coordinator: Carolyn Krause. The Center is a small organization (8-10 fulltime positions) with changing exhibitions of contemporary art surveying individuals, movements, regional artists, etc., in all media. "We have a growing membership which is geared toward contemporary art and design."

Needs: Works with 2-5 freelance artists/year. Uses artists for advertising, brochure and catalog design,

illustration and layout; magazine/newspaper design and layout; signage and posters. Prefers contemporary styles.
First Contact & Terms: Send query letter with brochure and resume to be kept on file. Reports only if interested. Works on assignment only. Pays by the project; "other payment arrangements can be devised as needed." Considers complexity of project, available budget, skill and experience of artist, and turnaround time when establishing payment.

CORE PUBLICATIONS, 236 W. 116th St., New York NY 10026. (212)316-1577. Communications Coordinator: George Holmes. Nonprofit association providing civil rights publications.
Needs: Works with 20-30 freelance artists/year. Uses artists for advertising and magazine/newspaper design, illustration and layout.
First Contact & Terms: Send query letter with samples and resume. Especially looks for artistic skill, imagination, reproduction ability and originality when reviewing work. Samples not filed returned by SASE. Reports within 6 weeks. Works on assignment only. Negotiates payment by the project.

CULTURAL ENRICHMENT COMMITTEE/COMMUNITY DEVELOPMENT FOUNDATION, Drawer A, Tupelo MS 38802. (601)842-4521. Division Manager: Mitch Stennett. Nonprofit association with a $284,860 annual operating budget serving as the Chamber of Commerce, art council and industrial development office for 800 business, professional, industrial and individual members.
Needs: Works with 2-3 freelance artists/year. Uses artists for advertising, brochure, catalog and graphic design; advertising and catalog layout; brochure illustration and displays, ad layout, logo design.
First Contact & Terms: Send query letter; call or write for appointment. Prefers photostats as samples. Looks for professionalism, image depth in artist's work. Samples not returned. Reports within 2 months. Works on assignment only. Provide resume and brochure to be kept on file. Payment varies according to job.

DISCOVERY: THE ARTS WITH YOUTH IN THERAPY, 3977 2nd Ave., Detroit MI 48201. (313)832-4357. Director: Fr. Russ Kohler. "We fund self-employed artists to work for 15 weekly house calls to youth with cancer and long-term illnesses."
Needs: Works with "artists as we need them upon referral of patients by physicians and medical social workers. We prefer artists who are somewhat isolated in their medium and willing to enter the isolation of the child overly identified with his disease. Prefer a minimum of psychological and medical jargon; emphasis on the language of art and visual expression and experience."
First Contact & Terms: Write with resume to be kept on file for future assignments.

DREXEL UNIVERSITY, Dept. of Publications and Communications, 32nd and Chestnut Sts., Philadelphia PA 19104. (215)895-2613. Director: Philip Terranova. Assigns 20 jobs and buys 10 illustrations/year.
Needs: Works with 3 illustrators and 6 designers/year. Seasonal needs: September-June. Uses designers for books, pamphlets and posters; illustrators for covers, jacket covers, spot art, etc. Also uses artists for advertising, annual reports, charts, direct mail brochures, exhibits/displays, handbooks, publicity, recruitment literature, magazines, newsletters and trademarks/logos.
First Contact & Terms: Query with samples (b&w tearsheets; no slides) or arrange interview. Looks for originality and sound production skills. SASE. Reports in 1 week. Provide resume, business card and tear sheet to be kept on file for future assignments. Considers available budget and skill and experience of artist when establishing payment.

EDUCATIONAL FILM LIBRARY ASSOCIATION, INC., Suite 301, 45 John St., New York NY 10038. (212)227-5599. Executive Director: Marilyn Levin. "The leading professional association concentrating on 16mm films, video and other nonprint media for education and community use." Members include: public libraries, universities/colleges, museums, community groups, film programmers, filmmakers, film teachers, etc.
Needs: Works with 1 artist/year for all illustrations; 1 for ad design. "Artists must work within strict guidelines."
First Contact & Terms: Query by mail or write with samples. Works on assignment only. Samples returned by SASE. Reports back on future assignment possibilities. Provide resume, business card, brochure/flyer, tear sheet samples or "anything that gives a good idea of work experience" to be kept on file for future assignments. Pay is negotiable.
Tips: "Send samples that apply to film/video technology, film librarians, independent video and filmmakers."

EMPIRE STATE VETERANS ASSOCIATION, INC., Suite 5-D, 20 Cliff St., Staten Island NY 10305. (212)448-6094. Executive Director: Frank Johnson. New York state military veterans association serving 4,000 members.

180 Artist's Market '86

Needs: "We purchase letterhead designs and logos at present."
First Contact & Terms: Send query letter to be kept on file. Reports within 1 month. Works on assignment only. Considers skill and experience of artist when establishing payment.

EPILEPSY FOUNDATION OF AMERICA, Suite 406, 4351 Garden City Dr., Landover MD 20785. (301)459-3700. Director of Administrative Services: Hugh S. Gage. Nonprofit association providing direct and indirect programs of advocacy, public health education and information, research, government liaison and fundraising to persons with epilepsy, their families and professionals concerned with the disorder.
Needs: Works with 3-4 freelance artists/year. Uses artists for advertising layout, brochure design, illustration and layout; graphic design, exhibits, displays, signage, AV presentations, annual reports, illustrations and layouts for fundraising materials. Themes must be suitable to a publicly funded, charitable organization. Especially needs slide presentations, exhibit panels and brochure covers.
First Contact & Terms: Prefers local artists "because of tight deadlines. Sometimes this is not a problem. However it depends on the job." Call for appointment. Looks for "diversity, taste, 'non-cute' approaches." Samples returned by SASE. Works on assignment basis only; reports back on whether to expect possible future assignments. Provide business card to be kept on file. Payment is by the project. Considers complexity of project and available budget when establishing payment.
Tips: "We're looking for the most value for our money. Don't bring banged up, poorly printed samples."

*FAIRLEIGH DICKINSON UNIVERSITY, 171 Montross Ave., Rutherford NJ 07070. (201)460-5194. Director of Public Relations: Bill Carey. New Jersey's largest private university.
Needs: Works with 6-12 freelance artists/year. Uses artists for advertisting design and layout; brochure design, illustration and layout; catalog design and layout; magazine/newspaper design, illustration and layout; AV presentations and posters.
First Contact & Terms: Send query letter with brochure and samples to be kept on file. Call or write for appointment to show portfolio. Prefers original work or slides as samples. Samples not kept on file are returned only if requested. Reports within 10 days. Works on assignment only. Range of payment is "very broad." Considers complexity of project and turnaround time when establishing payment.

THE FINE ARTS CENTER, CHEEKWOOD, Forrest Park Dr., Nashville TN 37205. (615)352-8632. Director: Kevin Grogan. Art musuem; fulltime staff of 7; collects, preserves, exhibits and interprets art with special emphasis on American painting. The Tennessee Botanical Gardens and Fine Arts Center, Inc., has a membership in excess of 8,000 drawn primarily from Nashville (Davidson County) and neighboring counties in the middle-Tennessee, southern Kentucky region.
Needs: Works with 1-3 freelance artists/year. Uses artists for advertising, brochure and catalog design and layout; signage and posters.
First Contact & Terms: Prefers local artists. Send query letter with resume, business card and samples to be kept on file; "slides, if any, will be returned." Write for appointment to show portfolio and for artists' guidelines. Prefers slides and photographs as samples. Reports within 4 weeks. Pays by the hour, $5-20 average. Considers complexity of project, available budget, skill and experience of artist, how work will be used and turnaround time when establishing payment.

FLORIDA MEMORIAL COLLEGE, 15800 NW 42nd Ave., Miami FL 33054. (305)625-4141. Public Affairs Director: Nadine Drew. Baptist-related, 4-year, accredited liberal arts college located on a 50-acre site with enrollment of 1,800 multi-racial students.
Needs: Works with 2-3 freelance artists/year. Uses artists for advertising, brochure and catalog design, illustration and layout.
First Contact & Terms: Send brochure/flyer with samples and actual work. Prefers actual printed material as samples. Samples returned upon request only with SASE. Reports immediately. Works on assignment basis only. Provide business card, brochure, flyer, samples and tear sheets to be kept on file for possible future assignments.

FRANKLIN PIERCE COLLEGE, Public Relations Office, Rindge NH 03461. Director/Public Relations: Richard W. Kipperman.
Needs: Uses artists for cover illustrations for brochure and catalog covers, occasionally for brochure design and logo/institutional identity designs.
First Contact & Terms: Regional artists only. Query with previously published work. Looks for "quality, artistic ability" when reviewing samples. Works on assignment only. Samples returned by SASE; and reports back on future possibilities. Provide resume and business card to be kept on file for future assignments. Pays per completed assignment (includes concept/roughs/comps/mechanicals).

*GEORGIA INSTITUTE OF TECHNOLOGY, Office of Publications, Alumni/Faculty House, Atlanta GA 30332. (404)894-2450. Director: Thomas Vitale. University with 11,000 students; publications serving alumni, graduate and undergraduate students and faculty.
Needs: Works with 5 freelance artists/year. Uses artists for brochure design and illustration, magazine/newspaper illustration and posters. Themes and styles vary with each project.
First Contact & Terms: Send query letter with brochure and samples to be kept on file; call or write for appointment to show portfolio. Samples not filed are returned only if requested. Reports only if interested. Works on assignment only. Pays by the hour, $25-100 average. Considers complexity of project, available budget, skill and experience of artist, how work will be used, turnaround time and rights purchased when establishing payment.
Tips: "We are a state school—budgets are tight, but the work is very high-quality."

THE GRACE BRETHREN HOME MISSIONS COUNCIL, INC., Box 587, Winona Lake IN 46590. (219)267-5161. Promotional Secretary: Liz Cutler. Church planting ministry that works with "the Fellowship of Grace Brethren Churches in establishing new churches in North America. Our promotional activity is geared for fundraising for this work."
Needs: Works with 3 freelance artists/year. Uses artists for advertising and brochure, illustration and layout; fold-up display design and execution; and for illustration for the *Brethren Missionary Herald* magazine.
First Contact & Terms: Local, experienced Christian artists only. Works on assignment only. Send query letter with brochure, resume, business card and samples to be kept on file. Write for appointment to show portfolio. Prefers photocopies or slides as samples. Samples not filed are returned by SASE. Reports back only if interested. Pays for design by the hour, $8 minimum; for illustration by the project, $35 minimum. Considers the complexity of the project when establishing payment.

HAMPDEN-SYDNEY COLLEGE, Hampden-Sydney VA 23943. (804)223-4382. Director of Publications: Dr. Richard McClintock. Nonprofit all-male liberal arts college of 750 students in a historic zone campus.
Needs: Works with 5-6 freelance artists/year. Uses artists for advertising, brochure, catalog and graphic design; brochure and magazine/newspaper illustration; brochure, catalog and magazine/newspaper layout; AV presentations and posters. Especially needs illustrations and mechanical preparations.
First Contact & Terms: Send query letter with actual work; write for appointment; submit portfolio for review. Prefers original work, both in raw state (artwork) and in reproduced state, as samples. Samples returned by SASE. Reports in 1 week. Works on assignment basis only. Provide resume and samples to be kept on file for possible future assignments. Negotiates payment.
Tips: "Changes in art and design include more formality, careful design and quality of 'look.' "

INTERNATIONAL ASSOCIATION OF INDEPENDENT PRODUCERS, Box 2801, Washington DC 20013. (202)638-5595. Executive Director/Editor: Dr. Edward VonRothkirch. Associate Director: Ted Edwards.
Needs: Works with 15-25 illustrators and 3-4 designers/year. Uses graphic designers for art which pertains to motion pictures, TV, records, tapes, advertising and book/record cover illustrations. Specific needs include layouts, logos and column heads.
First Contact & Terms: Send resume, brochure and tear sheet to be kept on file; also send samples. Prefers tear sheets, photocopies or transparencies as samples. Usually buys all rights. Works on assignment only. Samples returned by SASE; reports back on future assignment possibilities. Pays by job.

INTERNATIONAL FABRICARE INSTITUTE, 12251 Tech Rd., Silver Spring MD 20904. (301)622-1900. Director of Communications: Karen Graber. Trade association for drycleaners and launderers serving 10,000 members.
Needs: Works with 2-3 freelance artists/year. Uses artists for brochure and catalog design, illustration and layout; and posters.
First Contact & Terms: Local artists only; "must have references, be reachable by phone, reliable and honor schedules." Call or write for appointment to show portfolio. Especially looks for "neatness, appeal to my own esthetics and suitability to our company image." Reports only if interested. Works on assignment only. Pay varies according to project; "typical #10 brochure, $500-800." Considers complexity of project, available budget, and skill and experience of artist when establishing payment.
Tips: "Call for an appointment; don't 'drop in.' Have your portfolio ready and references available. Follow up if necessary; I'm busy and may forget by the time a suitable project comes up."

INVITATIONAL PROMOTIONS, INC., 6930 Owensmouth Ave., Canoga Park CA 91303. (818)999-6515. Vice President, Creative: John A. Buchanan. National agency serving over 2,500 financial institutions, and 2,500 auto dealers in over 120 cities. Works in areas of auto, furniture, travel

promotion; also deals in incentives and sales promotion, credit card systems, insurance, grocery chains.
Needs: Uses artists for advertising, brochure, magazine/newspaper and catalog design, illustration and layout; exhibits, displays, signage and posters.
First Contact & Terms: Send query letter with resume, business card, samples and tear sheets to be kept on file; write for appointment to show portfolio. Prefers photostats, original layouts and printed samples of those layouts as samples. Samples not kept on file are returned. Reports within 1 week. Works on assignment only. Pays by the hour, $3.85 minimum; by the project, rate varies. "Projects are generally quoted as a result of the scale; artists must work in a do-not-exceed price structure." Considers complexity of project, available budget, skill and experience of artist and turnaround time when establishing payment.
Tips: Artists should "make sure their books are concise and self-explanatory, and show as wide a range of work as possible. We will work with artists on a national basis because we use printing facilities in over 120 cities."

LANE COLLEGE, 545 Lane Ave., Jackson TN 38301. (901)424-4600, ext. 241. Public Relations Director: Ms. Martha Robinson. Predominantly black church-affiliated institution.
Needs: Assigns 5-10 jobs/year. Uses artists for advertising, exhibits/displays, publicity brochures, recruitment literature and trademarks/logos.
First Contact & Terms: Local artists only. Mail art or query with samples. SASE. Reports within 2 weeks. Provide resume, business card and brochure to be kept on file for future assignments. Payment by job: $10-75, design; $30-80, illustration; $40-100, layout; $40-80, production.

LONG BEACH STATE UNIVERSITY SPORTS INFORMATION BUREAU, 1250 Bellflower Blvd., Long Beach CA 90840. (213)498-4667. Sports Information Director: Shayne Schroeder. Emphasizes sports publicity and publications for the men's and women's sports programs at Long Beach University.
Needs: Uses 2 local artists/year for product illustrations. "We don't have a huge art budget and we like artists to be local."
First Contact & Terms: Write with samples. Provide business card, brochure and tear sheets to be kept on file for future assignments. Works on assignment only. Samples returned by SASE. Reports back on future assignment possibilities. Interest in sports drawings involving people. Pays $50 for cover design. Product design and illustration is negotiated with artist. Contact S.Schroeder for information regarding 1 year internship program.

LOYOLA UNIVERSITY OF CHICAGO, 820 N. Michigan Ave., Chicago IL 60611. (312)670-2974. Assistant Vice President/University Public Relations: James Reilly. One of the largest private universities in Illinois providing higher education to 15,000 students on 3 Chicago area campuses and one in Rome, Italy.
Needs: Works with 6-7 freelance artists/year. Uses artists for brochure and catalog design and layout; graphic design, exhibits, displays, signage, AV presentations and posters.
First Contact & Terms: Send query letter; write for appointment to show portfolio. Prefers original work as samples. Samples returned. Reports in 6 weeks. Works on assignment basis only. Payment varies according to job.
Tips: "Keep up with the latest trends."

MACALESTER COLLEGE, Office of Public Relations & Publications, 1600 Grand Ave., St. Paul MN 55105. (612)696-6203. Director: Nancy A. Peterson. Designer: Mary M. Wiseman. Four-year liberal arts college "with reputation as one of nation's finest." Produces materials for student recruitment, academic use, alumni relations, fundraising, etc.
Needs: Works with a few freelance artists/year. Uses artists for advertising, brochure and catalog design, illustration and layout; graphic design, magazine/newspaper design and illustration; and posters. Prefers variety of themes and styles.
First Contact & Terms: Call or write for appointment to show portfolio. Samples not kept on file are returned. Works on assignment basis only; reports back on whether to expect possible future assignments. Provide business card and samples to be kept on file. Payment varies according to job and client's budget.

MARCH OF DIMES BIRTH DEFECTS FOUNDATION, 1275 Mamroneck Ave., White Plains NY 10605. (914)428-7100. Print Production Supervisor: Susan Lynn. Nonprofit organization dedicated to the prevention of birth defects.
Needs: Works with 12 freelance artists/year. Uses artists for advertising, brochure, catalog and magazine/newspaper design, illustration and layout; AV presentations, exhibits, displays and posters.
First Contact & Terms: Send query letter with business card and samples to be kept on file; call for ap-

pointment to show portfolio. Prefers "current jobs completed by the artist pertaining to brochures, ads, newsletters, etc." as samples. Samples not kept on file are not returned. Works on assignment only.

METHODIST COLLEGE, Raleigh Rd., Fayetteville NC 28301. (919)488-7110. Director of Publications: Gwen Sykes. Nonprofit, small liberal arts college of 1,000 students.
Needs: Works with 2 freelance artists/year. Uses artists for advertising, brochure and catalog design, illustration and layout; regularly buys cartoons for college newspaper and humorous illustrations; occasionally buys cartoon-style illustrations. Especially needs cover design for admissions material; pen & inks of campus buildings, and graphics to accompany news and feature stories. Looks for clarity, style and reproduction quality when reviewing samples.
First Contact & Terms: Send query letter with samples, brochure/flyer and resume; call for appointment to show portfolio. Prefers photostats as samples. Samples returned by SASE. Reports in 2 weeks. Works on assignment basis only. Provide resume and business card to be kept on file for possible future assignments. Negotiates payment. Considers complexity of project, available budget and how work will be used when establishing payment.
Tips: "Bring fresh perspective. You will be paid as much for your perception as your performance."

***MID-AMERICA BIBLE COLLEGE**, 3500 S.W. 119th, Oklahoma City OK 73170-9797. (405)691-3881. Director of College Relations: Bill Cissna. A single purpose institution that prepares leadership for Christian service; serves approximately 350 students (55% male, 45% female and 32% married).
Needs: Works with 2-3 freelance artists/year. Uses artists for advertising, brochure, catalog and magazine/newspaper design; advertising, brochure, catalog and magazine/newspaper illustration; brochure and catalog layout; signage and posters. Prefers religious themes; "lots of people." Especially needs posters for distribution to local churches nationwide; brochures and response card for each degree program.
First Contact & Terms: Artists must be sympathetic with the Christian philosophy of life and have a well-balanced portfolio. Send query letter with samples, brochure/flyer and resume; submit portfolio for review. Prefers "whatever is most convenient and economical for the artist" as samples. "Appeal to Christian high school student; work in sympathy with a conservative college." Samples returned. Reports in 5 weeks. Works on assignment basis only. Provide business card, brochure, flyer and samples to be kept on file for possible future assignments. Negotiates payment. Considers available budget and how work will be used when establishing payment.
Tips: "We like one artistic concept to do a multiple number of things." There has been "addition of new degree programs" here.

***MODERN LANGUAGE ASSOCIATION**, 62 5th Ave., New York NY 10011. Production Manager: Judith Altreuter. Not-for-profit professional organization; membership consists of 25,000 professors of English and foreign languages in universities.
Needs: Works with 2-5 freelance artists/year. Uses artists for brochure design. Prefers 2-color graphics; classic; "interesting, but not flashy."
First Contact & Terms: Send query letter with brochure, resume and business card to be kept on file; write for appointment to show portfolio. Reports only if interested. Works on assignment only. Pays by the project, $150-500 average. Considers complexity of project, available budget, skill and experience of artist, how work will be used and turnaround time when establishing payment.
Tips: Artists should be "reliable and patient."

NATIONAL AESTHETICIAN AND NAIL ARTISTS ASSOCIATION, 16 N. Wabash, Chicago IL 60602. (312)782-1329. Executive Director: Phyllis Monier. Association for manicure, pedicure, skin care cosmetics.
Needs: Works with 3 freelance artists/year. Uses artists for advertising design and illustration, displays, signage and posters. Prefers line drawings.
First Contact & Terms: Send brochure and samples to be kept on file; write for appointment to show portfolio. Prefers photostats or original work as samples. Samples not filed returned by SASE. Reports only if interested. Works on assignment only. Considers available budget when establishing payment.

NATIONAL ASSOCIATION OF CHRISTIANS IN THE ARTS, Box 2995, Boston MA 02101. (617)574-0668. National Director: Roberta J. Ramzy. Estab. 1983. Support association for Christians involved in creative endeavors.
Needs: Uses artists for advertising, brochure and magazine/newspaper design, illustration and layout; exhibits and displays.
First Contact & Terms: Prefers artists who subscribe to the principles of the organization. Send query letter with brochure, resume, business card and samples to be kept on file. Prefers photostats or tear

sheets as samples. Samples not filed are returned by SASE. Reports within 1 month. Negotiates pay. Considers complexity of project, available budget, and skill and experience of artist when establishing payment.
Tips: "Be professional in presentations."

NATIONAL ASSOCIATION OF EVANGELICALS, Box 28, Wheaton IL 60189. (312)665-0500. Director of Information: Donald R. Brown. Voluntary fellowship of evangelical denominations, churches, schools, organizations and individuals; seeks to be a means of cooperative effort between its various members; provides evangelical identification for 43,000 churches and 4 million Christians.
Needs: Works with 1-5 freelance artists/year. Uses artists for advertising illustrations and layout, and brochure design. Themes are specified per project.
First Contact & Terms: Send query letter with brochure, resume, business card, samples and tear sheets; call or write for appointment to show portfolio. Prefers photostats as samples. Samples are returned by SASE. Reports within 2 months. Pay varies according to assignment. Considers complexity of project, available budget, skill and experience of artist, how work will be used, turnaround time and rights purchased when establishing payment.
Tips: Artists should have "an understanding of the National Association of Evangelicals: its history, current projects and ministries; and its objectives and purpose."

THE NATIONAL ASSOCIATION OF LIFE UNDERWRITERS, 1922 F St. NW, Washington DC 20006. (202)331-6070. Editor: Edward Keenan. Publishes *Life Association News*, the monthly official association magazine with a circulation of 135,000. Subscriptions are limited to members and affiliated organizations. Also publishes numerous brochures and catalogs. Serves life underwriters (life insurance agents), financial brokers and consultants, and businesspersons associated with finance in general.
Needs: Works with 5-10 freelance artists/year. Uses artists for brochure, catalog and magazine illustration. Prefers pen & ink, washes, drybrush and airbrush.
First Contact & Terms: DC metropolitan area artists only. Works on assignment only. Send query letter with resume and samples to be kept on file. Write for appointment to show portfolio. Prefers original work, photostats or tear sheets as samples. Material not filed returned by SASE only if requested. Reports only if interested. Pays by the project, $50-75 average for spot art. Considers complexity of project and turnaround time when establishing payment.

NATIONAL ASSOCIATION OF TOWNS & TOWNSHIPS, Suite 730, 1522 K St. NW, Washington DC 20005. Director of Communications: Bruce G. Rosenthal. Professional association providing educational materials and representation for local elected officials from small communities.
Needs: Works with several freelance artists/year. Uses artists for brochure and magazine/newspaper design and illustration, brochure layout and signage.
First Contact & Terms: Prefers local artists with "references from similar associations and creative style/ideas for a relatively limited budget." Send query letter with brochure to be kept on file. Reports only if interested. Works on assignment only. Considers complexity of project, available budget, and skill and experience of artist when establishing payment.

NATIONAL BUFFALO ASSOCIATION, Box 706, Custer SD 57730. (605)673-2073. Executive Director-Editor: Judi Hebbring. Breed organization representing commercial producers of buffalo (bison); also caters to collectors, historians, etc. Publishes bimonthly magazine of interest to buffalo enthusiasts, collectors and producers; circulation 1,400. Membership: 1,000.
Needs: Works with 4-5 freelance artists/year. "We feature artists in the magazine (must paint, sketch, sculpt, etc., buffalo); also feature artwork on cover."
First Contact & Terms: Send query letter with brochure and samples; material is kept on file until used, then it is returned to artist. Prefers photographs as samples. Samples not kept on file are returned. Reports within 2-3 weeks. No pay; "we trade magazine exposure for use of photos and story about the artist in *Buffalo!* magazine.
Tips: Especially looks for "a good representation of the American buffalo, as well as a well-rounded subject portfolio. Awards and credentials are also looked at but not as primary criteria—talent and salability of the work is number one." Current trends include "a back-to-basics movement where artists are doing native animals rather than the exotics that were the vogue a few years ago."

NATIONAL COMMITTEE FOR CITIZENS IN EDUCATION, 410 Wilde Lake Village Green, Columbia MD 21044. (301)997-9300. Editor: Chrissie Bamber. Purpose is to improve the education of children by mobilizing and assisting citizens, including parents, to strengthen public schools; an advocate for citizens helping them gain and use information and skills to influence the quality of public education.
Needs: Works with 3-4 freelance artists/year. Uses artists for advertising, brochure and catalog design

and layout; brochure illustration, magazine/newspaper design and illustration, and AV presentations.
First Contact & Terms: Local artists preferred except for newspaper illustration. Send query letter with samples and tear sheets to be kept on file. Write for artists' guidelines. Prefers photostats as samples. Samples not kept on file returned by SASE. Reports within 2 weeks. Works on assignment only. Pays by the project, $25-50 average for single illustration for newspaper; rates for "design of bookcover, brochure, AV aids, etc, are higher." Considers complexity of project, available budget, skill and experience of artist, how work will be used, turnaround time and rights purchased when establishing payment.
Tips: Artists should exhibit an "understanding of current education issues" in their work.

NATIONAL COUNCIL ON ART IN JEWISH LIFE INC., 15 E. 84th St., New York NY 10028. (212)877-4500. President: Julius Schatz. Provides education, exhibits, publications, books and information.
Needs: Uses artists for exhibits/displays, promotions and mailings.
First Contact & Terms: Mail art, or query with samples or previously used work. SASE. Reports in 2 weeks.

NATIONAL GALLERY OF ART, DEPARTMENT OF EXTENSION PROGRAMS, National Gallery Plaza, Washington DC 20565. (202)737-4215. Curator: Ruth R. Perlin. Clients: schools, museums and libraries.
Needs: Works with 3-4 designers/year. Uses artists for design of text brochures, programs, catalogs and posters.
First Contact & Terms: Local artists only. Query with resume and samples (brochures, pamphlets, posters) and arrange interview to show portfolio. Works on assignment only. Samples returned by SASE; reports back on future assignment possibilities. Provide resume, business card and brochure to be kept on file.

NATIONAL SHOE RETAILERS ASSOCIATION, 1414 Avenue of the Americas, New York NY 10019. (212)752-2555. Editor: Anisa Mycak. Provides information and services to 4,500 members nationwide; has monthly newsletter and bimonthly magazine, also direct mail pieces. Serves shoe retailers.
Needs: Works with 1-2 freelance artists/year. Prefers fine, high-fashion illustrations of footwear items (shoes, boots, bags) or crisp, clean cartoons of business situations; b&w line drawings or b&w with color or washes.
First Contact & Terms: Prefers local artists but not exclusively. Send query letter with samples to be kept on file; write for appointment to show portfolio and for artists' guidelines. Accepts photocopies only as samples. Samples not kept on file are returned by SASE. Reports within 1 month. Works on assignment only. Pays $30-40/cartoon. Considers complexity of project, available budget, turnaround time and rights purchased when establishing payment.

NATIONAL SKEET SHOOTING ASSOCIATION, Box 28188, San Antonio TX 78228. (512)688-3371. Editor, *Skeet Shooting Review* Magazine: Paula J. Long. Emphasizes shotgun target shooting, particularly "skeet" shooting; approximately 15,000 members.
Needs: Works with 3-6 freelance artists/year. Uses artists for brochure and magazine illustration. Prefers shooting sports themes; primarily b&w illustrations (pen & ink, charcoal, etc.).
First Contact & Terms: Send query letter. Write for appointment to show portfolio. Reports within 1 week. Pays by the project, $50-200 average. Considers available budget and skill and experience of artist when establishing payment.
Tips: "This is an excellent opportunity for inexperienced artists to get published in a national publication."

NORML, National Organization for the Reform of Marijuana Laws, Suite 640, 2035 S St. NW, Washington DC 20009. (202)483-5500. National Director: Kevin Zeese. Nonprofit consumer lobby working for reform of marijuana laws.
Needs: Works with 4-6 freelance artists/year. Uses artists for advertising, brochure, catalog and magazine/newspaper design, graphic design, public service announcements, original artwork for auction, AV presentations and posters. Especially needs magazine ads. Prefers marijuana theme.
First Contact & Terms: Send query letter. Reports within 1 week. Works on assignment only. "Work should relate to issue of marijuana law reform." Provide business card and tear sheets to be kept on file for possible future assignments. Payment varies according to job and available budget.
Tips: "Opportunity for major national coverage at initial public interest group rate of pay."

OCCIDENTAL COLLEGE, 1600 Campus Rd., Los Angeles CA 90041. (213)259-2677. Contact: Director of Public Information and Publications. Educational institution with approximately 1,600 students providing a liberal arts education and serving current students, alumni, faculty, administration, trustees, staff and the community.

Needs: Publishes a quarterly magazine, currently ranked as one of the "Top Five College Magazines" in the country. Magazine often showcases a single illustrator, who provides artwork for cover and four feature articles related by a common theme. Excellent exposure for aspiring illustrators in need of impressive portfolio piece. Occasionally uses illustrators for other publications, such as catalogs and fund-raising brochures.

First Contact & Terms: Magazine showcase illustrators are paid $400 for the series of cover and feature illustrations. For other publications, artists must be willing to furnish high-quality illustrations or photographs at very modest cost. Send query letter with business card and samples; submit portfolio for review. Prefers original work or photocopies as samples. Looks for "originality, nice clean layout and realistic renderings, as opposed to fantasy pieces" when reviewing artist's work. Samples not returned. Reports in 2 weeks. Works on assignment only. Payment varies according to job and client's budget.

Tips: "Tight financial picture demands development of one comprehensive illustration/publication that has components which can be reproduced on their own throughout the publication."

OPTICIANS ASSOCIATION OF AMERICA, 10341 Democracy Lane, Box 10110, Fairfax VA 22030. Editor: James H. McCormick. Associate Editor: Robert Rathbone. Nonprofit association to advance the objectives of the retail dispensing optician and to serve 10,000 opticians.

Needs: "Not a major user or buyer of art or artist's work." Works with 8-9 freelance artists/year. Uses artists for brochure and magazine/newspaper design, illustration (b&w and full-color art) and layout (roughs; nonmechanical). Especially needs work relating to retail dispensing opticians at work.

First Contact & Terms: Send query letter with samples or brochure/flyer to be kept on file. Looks for the ideas the artwork communicates. Prefers several representative, nonreturnable photostats as samples. Samples not returned. Reports in 1 month. Payment is by the project; $20-250 average—"covers for magazine usually are more." Considers complexity of project, available budget, skill and experience of artist, how work will be used and rights purchased ("we usually buy only optical industry rights") when establishing payment.

Tips: "Always query before doing any work for us. There is a trend toward greater use of semi-abstract art."

PGA OF AMERICA, 100 Avenue of the Champions, Box 12458, Palm Beach Gardens, FL 33410. (305)626-3600. Editor/Advertising Sales Director: William A. Burbaum. Represents 13,000 golf club professionals and apprentices nationwide.

Needs: Works with 2 artists/year for magazine illustrations. Artists "should know something about golf and golf tournaments." Interested in title page art and golf tip illustrations for magazine that circulates to professionals and 20,000 amateur golfers nationwide.

First Contact & Terms: Write with samples. Works on assignment most of the time. Samples returned by SASE. Reports back on future assignment possibilities. Provide tear sheet samples to be kept on file. Reports in 2 weeks. Negotiates pay by prior agreement.

Tips: "Read our magazine, and read and check the artwork in golf's two major national publications: *Golf Magazine* and *Golf Digest*."

RIPON COLLEGE, Box 248, Ripon WI 54971. (414)748-8115. Director of College Relations: Andrew G. Miller. Four-year, coeducational, liberal arts college serving 950 students, alumni and prospective students.

Needs: Works with 3-4 freelance artists/year. Uses artists for advertising, brochure and magazine/newspaper illustration; graphic design and AV presentations; photography. Buys 1-2 cartoon-style illustrations/year.

First Contact & Terms: Send query letter; call for appointment to show portfolio. Prefers original work as samples. Samples returned by SASE. Works on assignment basis only; reports back on whether to expect possible future assignments. Provide resume and samples to be kept on file for possible future assignments. Negotiates payment.

ROWAN COUNTY HISTORICAL SOCIETY, Rt. 6, Box 498, Morehead KY 40351. (606)784-9145. Public Relations Director: Lloyd Dean. "A society that studies the history of Rowan County and Morehead and collects pictures, prints, histories, diaries and items of historical interest."

Needs: "We might need artists to draw pictures of historical places in Rowan County and Morehead."

First Contact & Terms: Query by mail or write with resume. SASE. Provide business card, brochure and flyer to be kept on file for possible future assignments. Reports in 5 weeks.

Tips: There is a trend toward "more concern for the historical past."

ST. VINCENT COLLEGE, Latrobe PA 15650. (412)539-9761. Director/Publications and Publicity: Don Orlando.

Needs: Assigns 25 jobs/year. Uses artists for advertising, annual reports, direct mail brochures, exhibits, flyers, graphics, posters and programs.
First Contact & Terms: Query with samples. SASE. Reports in 1 month. Pays $10 minimum/hour, design, illustration and layout.

SAN FRANCISCO AFRICAN AMERICAN HISTORICAL AND CULTURAL SOCIETY, Fort Mason Center, Building C-165, San Francisco CA 94123. (415)441-0640. Executive Director: Jule C. Anderson. Membership organization established to promote an accurate account of the contributions to world development by people of African descent. Gallery, museum and library are open to the public. Publications and lectures/class workshops are available. Serves "people of all ages and ethnic backgrounds who are interested in acquiring knowledge on culture and contributions of people of African descent."
Needs: Works with 20 freelance artists/year. Uses artists for brochure design and layout; AV presentations, exhibits, displays, posters, invitations and designs. Prefers African or African-American themes.
First Contact & Terms: Send query letter with brochure, resume and samples to be kept on file. Prefers photographs as samples. Samples returned only if requested. Reports within 30 days. Works on assignment only. Considers complexity of project, available budget, skill and experience of artist and references, how work will be used, turnaround time and rights purchased when establishing payment.
Tips: "Write a letter and send photos of work. Request return of photos if so desired."

*SLOCUMB GALLERY, East Tennessee State University, Department of Art, Box 23740A, Johnson City TN 37614-0002. (615)929-4247. Gallery Director: M. Wayne Dyer. Nonprofit university gallery.
Needs: Works with 0-2 freelance artists/year. Uses artists for advertising design, illustration and layout; brochure and catalog design; exhibits, signage and posters.
First Contact & Terms: Send query letter with samples to be kept on file. Prefers slides as samples. Samples not filed are returned only if requested. Reports within 1 month. Works on assignment only. Negotiates payment. Considers complexity of project and available budget when establishing payment.

SOCIETY FOR INTERNATIONAL DEVELOPMENT, Room 510-M, 1889 F St. NW, Washington DC 20006. Send *all* correspondence to: Kim Winnard, Visual Media Specialist, 107 N. Jackson St., Arlington VA 22201. Organization focusing on international development issues.
Needs: Works with 3 freelance artists/year. Uses artists for design and illustration of brochures, reports and magazines.
First Contact & Terms: Works on assignment only. Send query letter with samples to be kept on file. Prefers tear sheets or photocopies as samples. Samples not filed are returned by SASE. Reports within 1 month. Returns original artwork after job's completion. Pays by the project, $150-450 average for design; $50 average/drawing for illustration. Considers project's budget when establishing payment. Rights purchased vary according to project.

SOROPTIMIST INTERNATIONAL OF THE AMERICAS, 1616 Walnut St., Philadelphia PA 19103. (215)732-0512. Editor: Joan Mintz Ulmer. 40,000-member classified service organization for professional and executive business women.
Needs: Uses artists for brochure and magazine/newspaper illustration.
First Contact & Terms: Send query letter with brochure, resume, business card and samples to be kept on file. Prefers copies of brochures, publications in which artwork has appeared as samples. Reports only if interested. Works on assignment only. Pays by the project, $50-300 average. Consider complexity of project and available budget when establishing payment.
Tips: "My needs vary with each publication. I may need original art for 6 magazines in a row then none for 6 months. I prefer to have resumes/samples on file to call upon artist when I have a need."

SPIRIT OF THE FUTURE CREATIVE INSTITUTE, Box 40296, San Francisco CA 94110. (415)821-7800. Creative Director: Gary Marchi. Provides information on future science and technology/space innovations, free enterprise system (new business ventures development, vital growth industries), mental development (applied logic, creativity, learning improvement systems), conservation, survival and self-reliance planning, and natural health. Operates central library archive, information clearinghouse, creative innovation center and media network systems to serve innovators, pioneers, inventors, futurists, investigative researchers, research and development groups, selected media, educators, and all creative, self-reliant, future consumers—applied thinkers.
Needs: Uses freelance artists for brochure design, illustration and layout; AV presentations, displays, posters and television computer graphics. Themes of institute image design (letters structure and logos), celestial/space, nature, futuristic designs.
First Contact & Terms: San Francisco Bay area artists only. Send query letter with brochure, resume, business card and samples to be kept on file; write for appointment to show portfolio. Prefers color pho-

tographs, photostats or slides as samples. Samples not kept on file are returned by SASE. Reports within 3 weeks. Works on assignment only. Payment is "mutual exchange trading (barter)—advisory service on marketing and promoting their work, skills, for albums, cassette covers, book covers, acquiring an agent." Considers complexity of project, skill and experience of artist, how work will be used, rights purchased, available budget and "a strong interest in our institute, goals, purpose, future plans. Artists should clearly state their purpose, objectives and interests in writing."

SUNDAY SCHOOL BOARD OF THE SOUTHERN BAPTIST CONVENTION, 127 9th Ave. N., Nashville TN 37234. (615)251-2365. Supervisor, Curriculum Design Section: Mrs. Doris Mae Adams. Religious publisher of periodicals, books, Bibles, records, kits, visual aids, posters, etc. for churches.
Needs: Works with 45-50 freelance artists/year. Uses artists for illustration.
First Contact & Terms: Artists must be "people with experience that meet our quality requirements." Works on assignment only. Send query letter with samples; call or write for appointment to show portfolio. Originals are preferred, tear sheets are acceptable; do not send slides. Samples are returned. Reports within 2 weeks. Pays by the illustration, $80-150 average. "For the price range quoted here, we buy all rights and retain the work." Considers complexity of project, skill and experience of the artist and how the work will be used when establishing payment.

THE TEXTILE MUSEUM, 2320 S St. NW, Washington DC 20008. (202)667-0441. Public Relations Manager: Joan Wessel. Private, nonprofit museum dedicated to preservation, education and exhibition of textiles.
Needs: Works with 1-2 freelance artists/year. Uses artists for brochure illustration and layout, catalog design and layout, exhibits, displays and posters.
First Contact & Terms: Local artists only. Send query letter with samples to be kept on file. Prefers original work as samples. Reports only if interested. Works on assignment only. Negotiates pay according to project.
Tips: "Send samples of newsletters, invitations, catalogs or posters as these are items most often used by the institution; keep in mind the low budget of client."

UNITED HOSPITALS, 333 N. Smith Ave., St. Paul MN 55102. (612)292-5531. Assistant Public Relations Director: Sandra Hansen.
Needs: Works with 5 illustrators and designers/year. Uses artists for brochure and newsletter design, programs and general publications artwork. Especially needs logo design, publication and brochure design and keyline.
First Contact & Terms: Local artists only. Query with resume. SASE. Looks for "fast service, reasonable price, and creative and well thought-out approaches to project goals" when reviewing artist's work. Reports in 2 weeks. Works on assignment only. Samples returned by SASE. Provide resume and business card to be kept on file for possible future assignments. Pays by hour. Considers complexity of project, available budget and turnaround time when establishing payment.
Tips: Especially likes "clean, uncluttered, simple, striking design."

*UNIVERSITY OF LOWELL, ART DEPARTMENT, 1 University Dr., Lowell MA 01854. (617)452-5000. Chairperson Art Department: Dr. Liana Cheney. Teaching institution, granting a BA degree and BFA in commercial art and drawing/painting degrees.
Needs: Works with 2 freelance artists/year. Uses artists for advertising, brochure and catalog design, illustration and layout. Prefers college-related themes, single style.
First Contact & Terms: Local artists only. Send resume to be kept on file for 1 year; mail slides. Slides are returned. Reports within 1 month. Works on assignment only. Pays by the hour, $9 minimum. Considers available budget when establishing payment.
Tips: "Be patient."

UNIVERSITY OF NEW HAVEN, West Haven CT 06516. (203)932-7000. Public Relations Director: Sally Devaney.
Needs: Works with illustrators for catalogs, magazines, newsletters, direct mail brochures, schedules, booklets, exhibits/displays, handbooks, publicity brochures and recruitment literature. Looks for "simplicity of reproduction. Prefers b&w line art for illustrations. Contemporary style that would appeal to students (18-34)."
First Contact & Terms: Query with samples (brochures and other publications, especially those for educational or service organizations; cover designs; illustrations). SASE. Works on assignment only. No samples returned. Provide resume if available, business card, fee structure, and samples of work to be kept on file for future assignments. Considers complexity of project, available budget, skill and experience of artist and turnaround time when establishing payment.
Tips: "Our budget is modest. Most pieces are one or two colors. We'd like to see work that would appeal to younger and older students. We're interested in variety of styles. Also interested in area talent."

*UNIVERSITY OF SAN FRANCISCO, 2130 Fulton St., San Francisco CA 94117. Contact: Publications Editor. Largest private university in San Francisco with eight colleges and professional schools providing the principles of humanistic Jesuit education to 6,500 students, alumni, parents and the general public.

Needs: Works with 10 freelance artists/year. Uses artists for advertising, brochure and catalog design and layout; graphic design, displays and posters. Prefers designs that can be coordinated under a university integrated design concept, using Times Roman type, certain standard formats, university logo, etc.

First Contact & Terms: Local artists only. Send query letter with samples; write for appointment. Prefers portfolio of original work during interview; photostats acceptable by mail "to show us style" before interview. Looks for "professionalism, that is, ability to work within established budgets and editorial guidelines; ability to meet deadlines; accuracy and creativity in solving design problems." Samples returned by SASE. Reports in 2 weeks. Works on assignment basis only; reports back on whether to expect possible future assignments. Provide resume, business card, brochure, flyer, samples and tear sheets to be kept on file for possible future assignments. Payment varies according to job.

Tips: "Smaller colleges may provide better creative opportunities than large universities committed to a particular design concept, although there are large institutions which have varied-design publications. We have had personnel cuts on our staff, so we must buy more art and design from freelancers."

VERIFICATION GALLERY, MAYNARD LISTENER LIBRARY, 171 Washington, Taunton MA 02780. (617)823-3783. Executive Director: Merrill A. Maynard. Nonprofit free service organization for the blind and physically handicapped, served through The Maynard Listener Library.

Needs: Works with 90 freelance artists/year. Uses artists for graphic design, exhibits and displays. Especially needs calendar material. Prefers mobility information theme.

First Contact & Terms: Prefers artist with "motivation." Send query letter with samples. Prefers photostats or slides as samples. Samples returned by SASE. Reports within 2 months. Provide samples to be kept on file for possible future assignments. Negotiates payment.

Tips: "We are creating a demand for our product; therefore artists should realize its potential."

*WASHINGTON UNIVERSITY IN ST. LOUIS, Campus Box 1070, St. Louis MO 63110. Art Director: John Howze. Educational institution publication office serving alumni development (alumni magazines) and various schools' recruiting and promotional needs.

Needs: Works with 20 freelance artists/year. Uses artists for advertising, brochure, catalog, and magazine/newspaper illustration.

First Contact & Terms: Send brochure, business card, samples and tear sheets to be kept on file; call or write for appointment to show portfolio. Prefers photostats, slides or photographs as samples. Samples not filed are returned by SASE only if requested. Reports only if interested. Works on assignment only. Pays by the project, $50 minimum. Considers complexity of project, available budget, skill and experience of artist, how work will be used, turnaround time and rights purchased when establishing payment.

Tips: "Show variety of work if possible and be patient."

WISCONSIN CONSERVATORY OF MUSIC, 1584 N. Prospect Ave., Milwaukee WI 53202. (414)276-4350. Contact: PR Director. Educational institution.

Needs: Works with 5 freelance artists/year. Uses artists for advertising and brochure design. Prefers music theme.

First Contact & Terms: Local artists only. Send query letter with samples. Samples returned by SASE. Reports within 1 month. Works on assignment basis only. Provide resume and samples to be kept on file for possible future assignments. Payment is by the project: $100-500 average.

*WORCESTER POLYTECHNIC INSTITUTE, 100 Institute Rd., Worcester MA 01609. (617)793-5609. Director of Publications: Kenneth McDonnell. Third oldest college of engineering and science in US with 3,500 students in undergraduate and graduate programs.

Needs: Works with 2-6 freelance artists/year. Uses artists for advertising illustration; brochure design, illustration and layout; catalog illustration and layout; AV presentations, exhibits, displays, signage and posters.

First Contact & Terms: Prefers local artists. Send query letter with resume and samples. Write for appointment to show portfolio. Prefers photostats, slides, photographs and tearsheets as samples. Samples are returned by SASE. Reports within 2 weeks. Works on assignment only. Negotiates payment. Considers complexity of project, available budget, skill and experience of artist, turnaround time and rights purchased when establishing payment.

WORLD WILDLIFE FUND, 1601 Connecticut Ave. NW, Washington DC 20009. Publications Editor: Pamela S. Cubberly. Private international conservation organization dedicated to saving endangered wildlife and habitats around the world and to protecting biological diversity upon which human well-being depends.

Needs: Works with 3-4 freelance artists/year. Uses artists for brochure and magazine/newspaper design, illustration and layout; AV presentations, and exhibits. Prefers "pen & ink for our b&w publications. Illustrations must be scientifically accurate. We avoid illustrations which anthropomorphize animals. We are always on the lookout for illustrators of tropical forest species. Other themes are marine ecosystems (whales, sea turtles, etc.), Africa (especially African elephant, rhinoceros, mountain gorillas); Nepal (tiger, snow leopard, greater one-horned rhinoceros, gharial crocodile, among others); primates; wetlands, endangered and migratory species; plants. Would appreciate finding cartoonist with a good sense of humor who could draw cartoon at spur of moment."
First Contact & Terms: Send query letter with brochure, resume, business card, samples and tear sheets to be kept on file. Prefers photostats of high quality to show detail or slides as samples. Samples not kept on file are returned by SASE. Reports within 1 month. Pays by the hour, $5-7 average, or by the project; "as a nonprofit organization, we have limited funds. Usually our freelancers work for no or a low fee depending on the project. We always give credit and try to pass other potential customers on to our freelancers."
Tips: "Primarily, we are looking for persons interested in contributing to the conservation of wildlife willing to donate their time and work. We do, however, contract for low fee work for layout, illustrations, etc., on occasion. We do look primarily for highly talented artists." Artwork must be "highly accurate and beautiful; something that grabs the reader's attention and elicits a positive emotional response to wildlife. Should be easily reproduced in black and white. We especially need someone who could draw something up within a very short time period, relating to a specific story we are developing."

YOUTH LAW NEWS/NATIONAL CENTER FOR YOUTH LAW, 5th Floor, 1663 Mission St., San Francisco CA 94103. (415)543-3307. Editor, *Youth Law News*: Nicky Gonzalez.
Needs: Works with 8 freelance artists and photographers/year. Uses artists and photographers for brochure design and magazine/newspaper illustrations and layout. Prefers themes involving children's issues.
First Contact & Terms: Artists "must have lower price rate for nonprofit organization." Send query letter with resume and samples to be kept on file; write for artists' guidelines. Open to any type of sample; "artist's preference." Reports back as soon as possible. Works on assignment only. Pays by the project. Considers complexity of project, available budget, skill and experience of artist, how work will be used and turnaround time when establishing payment.

Book Publishers

The 50+ new listings in this section are evidence that the book publishing industry is continuing its upward climb. As the market strengthens, certain publishing areas boast the greatest increases in production and sales. Religion, young adult fiction, how-to and instructional titles, and educational materials are the areas experiencing the most growth. A significant increase in the production of calendars, story tapes, bookmarks and other non-book lines indicates a need by publishers for freelancers to design and illustrate these products.

Additional good news for graphic artists is that textbook publishers are seeking more professional and sophisticated illustrations than was the norm five years ago. The publishing of these educational materials is expanding quickly in order to match increasing school enrollment, particularly on the elementary level.

Freelance artists are used within the book publishing industry primarily for book design, jacket/cover design and illustration, and text illustration. Most of this section's listings offer a breakdown of these areas and give specific information as to needs, payment and more. Collateral materials needed by publishers—posters, advertisements and P-O-P displays—should not be overlooked by freelancers. And as the publishing houses compete for sales, more of these products are displaying innovative illustration and design combined with full-color to attract consumers.

In this section, artist Carl Lundgren of Philadelphia, Pennsylvania, provides an inside look at the magical world of science fiction/fantasy illustration, an integral part of the book publishing industry.

For additional information on this market, refer to *Writer's Market 1986*, *Literary Market Place*, *Books in Print* (vol. 4) and *International Directory of Little Magazines and Small Presses*. The trade magazine *Publishers Weekly* provides updates on books currently being published.

This illustration—"a vaguely anarchistic medieval romp filled with a melange of strange characters"—was "perfect" for Lyonesse, *according to Underwood-Miller publisher Chuck Miller. Jack Christiansen of Orem, Utah, received $2,500 for first rights for this acrylic painting. Christiansen is primarily a fine artist working in oils and acrylics, but does some books and science fiction/fantasy illustrations.*

A.D. BOOK CO., 10 E. 39th St., New York NY 10016. (212)889-6500. Art Director: Amy S. Heit. Publishes hardcover and paperback originals on advertising design and photography. Publishes 12-15 titles/year; 4-5 of which require designers, 1-2 use illustrators.
First Contact & Terms: Send letter of inquiry which can be kept on file and arrange to show portfolio (4-10 tear sheets). Samples returned by SASE. Buys first rights. Originals returned to artist at job's completion. Free catalog. Advertising design must be contemporary. Pays $100 minimum/book design.
Jackets/Covers: Pays $100 minimum.

ACROPOLIS BOOKS LTD., 2400 17th St. NW, Washington DC 20009. Production Manager: Lloyd Greene. Publishes how-to, self help, educational, political and Americana.
First Contact & Terms: Local artists only. Query with information on your background and specialties.
Needs: Uses artists for jacket design and illustration and advertising layouts.

BOB ADAMS, INC., 840 Summer St., Boston MA 02127. (617)782-5707. Managing Editor: J. Michel Fiedler. Specializes in career guide publications. Publishes 10 titles/year plus annual magazine.
First Contact & Terms: Works with 1 freelance artist/year. Local artists only. Send query letter with samples to be kept on file. Prefers line drawings as samples. Samples returned only by SASE. Reporting time varies. Works on assignment only. No originals returned after job's completion. Buys all rights and may negotiate.
Book Design: Assigns 1-2 freelance jobs/year. Pays by the project, $500-750 average. "A royalty payment would be considered if the artist submits essentially a complete book ready to be published."
Jackets/Covers: Assigns 1-2 design and 5 illustration jobs/year. Prefers cartoons. Pays for illustration by the job.

ADDISON-WESLEY, Jacob Way, Reading MA 01867. (617)944-3700. Art Director: Marshall Henrichs. Publishes adult trade books. Publishes 100 titles/year; 50% require freelance designers. Handles higher educational books.
First Contact & Terms: Send proofs. Buys all rights. Works on assignment only. Reports back on future assignment possibilities. Provide resume, business card and tear sheet to be kept on file for future assignments. Check for most recent titles in bookstores.
Jackets/Covers: Needs trade cover designers. Pays $300-800.

*AEOLUS PUBLISHING LTD., Box 2643, Vista CA 92083. (619)724-5703. President: Chuck Banks. Estab. 1984. Specializes in hardcover and paperback originals and reprints on militaria. Publishes 12 titles/year.
First Contact & Terms: Works with 3 freelance artists/year. Send query letter. "No calls from artist or artist's agent." Samples returned only if requested. Reports within 1 month. Return of original work after job's completion depends on contract. Considers complexity of the project, skill and experience of artist, project's budget, turnaround time and rights purchased when establishing payment. Rights purchased vary according to project.
Book Design: Assigns 3 freelance jobs/year. Negotiates payment.
Jackets/Covers: Assigns 3 freelance illustration jobs/year. Negotiates payment.
Text Illustration: Assigns 2 freelance jobs/year. Negotiates payment.

AERO PUBLISHERS INC., 329 W. Aviation Rd., Fallbrook CA 92028. (714)728-8456. President: E. J. Gentle. Publishes hardcover and paperback originals on aviation and space. Produces 15-20 titles/year.
First Contact & Terms: Send query letter with resume and samples; arrange interview to show portfolio. Samples should include "four-color creative art centering around aviation subjects." Samples returned by SASE. All work on assignment only. Provide resume, business card, inquiry letter and/or brochure to be kept on file for future assignments. Reports in 3-4 weeks. Buys all rights; keeps originals. Artist should supply overlays for cover artwork (but not necessary). Free catalog.
Jackets/Covers: Assigns 3-5 jobs/year. Art should pertain to aviation subjects. Pays $100-500, 4-color finished art.
Tips: Especially seeks "accurate drawings to indicate authentic aircraft presentations" in samples or a portfolio.

AIR-PLUS ENTERPRISES, Box 367, Glassboro NJ 08028. (609)881-0724. Director: Ann Saltenberger. Specializes in hardcover and paperback originals on women's interest (particularly case histories of abortion complications—physical or other) and human sexuality. Publishes 2 titles/year.
First Contact & Terms: Works with 2 freelance artists/year. "We give anybody a chance." Send query letter with samples to be kept on file "unless unsuitable." Prefers original sketches or photographs as

samples. Samples not kept on file are returned by SASE. Reports within 2 months. No originals returned to artist at job's completion. Considers project's budget when establishing payment. Buys all rights.
Jackets/Covers: Assigns 2 freelance illustration jobs/year. Pays by the project, $35-100 average.
Text Illustration: Assigns 2 freelance jobs/year. Pays by the project, $25-250 average.
Tips: Uses medical illustrations. "We see an increased need for technical work and have found that our best people in this field don't do cartoons well at all, so we now seek cartoon makers."

*ALADDIN PRESS, #10, 318 Harvard St., Brookline MA 02146. Co-Owner: Carolyn Heidenry. Estab. 1984. Specializes in paperback originals on natural foods/diet health. Publishes 2-3 titles/year.
First Contact & Terms: Works with 2-3 freelance artists/year. Works on assignment only. Send query letter with samples to be kept on file. Interested in b&w samples only; no color; photostats and photocopies OK. Samples not filed are not returned. Reports only if interested. Original work returned after job's completion if desired. Considers skill and experience of artist and project's budget when establishing payment. Buys first rights or reprint rights.
Book Design: Assigns 2-3 freelance jobs/year. Pays on individual basis.
Jackets/Covers: Assigns 2-3 freelance design jobs/year. Pays by the project, $300-500 average.
Text Illustration: Assigns 2-3 freelance jobs/year. Pays according to quality.

ALLYN AND BACON INC., College Division, 7 Wells Ave., Newton MA 02159. (617)964-5530. Cover Administrator: Linda Knowles Dickinson. Publishes hardcover and paperback textbooks. Publishes 75 titles/year; 75% require freelance cover designers.
First Contact & Terms: Needs artists/designers experienced in preparing mechanicals for print production; designers must be experienced at college textbook cover design and specification.
Jackets/Covers: Pays $250-600, 2-color and 4-color.
Tips: "Keep stylistically and technically up to date. Learn *not* to over-design: read instructions, and ask questions. Introductory letter must state experience and include at least photocopies of samples of your work. We prefer designers/artists based in the Boston area."

ALPINE PUBLICATIONS, INC., 214 19th St. SE, Loveland Co 80537. Publisher: Betty Jo McKinney. Specializes in hardcover and paperback breed books on dogs (purebred), cats and horses. Also some training and other nonfiction subjects related to dogs and horses. Publishes 5 titles/year; 50% require freelance designers, 50% require freelance illustrators. Frequently needs high quality pen & ink illustrations of specific purebred dog breeds.
First Contact & Terms: Works with 2 freelance artists/year. "Designers or illustrators must be in Colorado area within driving distance." Send query letter with resume, business card and samples to be kept on file. Prefers slides, photostats, printed samples or photocopies of line illustrations as samples. Samples not kept on file returned by SASE. Reports within 6 weeks. Works on assignment only. No originals returned at job's completion. Considers complexity of project, skill and experience of artist, project's budget and rights purchased when establishing payment. Negotiates rights purchased.
Book Design: Pays by the hour, $10 average.
Jackets/Covers: Assigns 4-6 freelance design jobs/year.
Text Illustration: Assigns 3 freelance jobs/year. Prefers ink line illustrations, usually technical, often structure of animal. Pays by the project, $10 minimum.

ANTIOCH PUBLISHING COMPANY, Box 28, Yellow Springs OH 45387. Art Director: Marty Roelandt. Publishes calendars, bookmarks, bookplates, greeting cards and children's books. Also has separate religious/inspirational line.
First Contact & Terms: Do not send original art. Send SASE, attention Creative Guidelines, for copy of Antioch Artist's Guidelines before sending samples of any kind. Works on assignment only. Buys 100 or more illustrations/year. Buys various rights. Pays $100-200/illustration, depending on use and in-house preparation time.
Text Illustration: Uses artists for illustrations. "Most of our needs are of the full color, magical-unicorn-rainbow-charming-whimsical-humorous variety. I want art from people who know how to use color for good reproduction. I want to work with professionals who know the importance of deadlines, flexibility and marketability. Because of this I prefer working with experienced, previously published artists, although I've also worked with relative newcomers who have a high degree of professionalism." Buys occasional science fiction/fantasy artwork.
Tips: "Airbrush, patterns, minimal yet more sophisticated type of humor are still important in this market. A sketchy, more spontaneous-seeming style sometimes with outrageous coloration is becoming more prevalent—probably owing to punk and New Wave. So far, it has not significantly affected our use of freelance work."

*APPLEZABA PRESS, Box 4134, Long Beach CA 90804. (213)591-0015. Publisher: D.H. Lloyd. Specializes in paperbacks on poetry and fiction. Publishes 2-4 titles/year.

First Contact & Terms: Works on assignment only. Send query letter with brochure and samples to be kept on file. Prefers tear sheets and photographs as samples. Samples not filed are returned by SASE. Reports only if interested. Originals returned to artist at job's completion. Considers project's budget and rights purchased when establishing payment. Rights purchased vary according to project.
Jackets/Covers: Assigns 1 freelance design job/year. Pays by the project, $30-100 average.

*APRIL PUBLICATIONS, INC., Box 1000, Staten Island NY 10314. Art Director: Verna Hart. Specializes in paperback nonfiction. Publishes 20 titles/year.
First Contact & Terms: Works with 10 freelance artists/year. Works on assignment only. Send query letter with samples to be kept on file. Prefers photostats as samples. Samples not filed are returned by SASE. Reports only if interested. Originals returned to artist at job's completion. Considers project's budget and rights purchased when establishing payment. Buys all rights.

ARCO PUBLISHING INC., 215 Park Ave. S., New York NY 10003. Editorial Director: William Mlawer. Art Director: Wolfgang H. Reimann. Publishes hardcover and paperback trade and reference originals and reprints.
First Contact & Terms: Will keep on file submitted art samples. Will return samples if return postage is provided. Relevant resumes will be kept on file.
Tips: "We request our authors to supply needed artwork or photographs, and rarely use freelance illustrative materials."

*ARCUS PUBLISHING COMPANY, Box 228, Sonoma CA 95476. (707)996-9529. Owner: Betty Gordon. Estab. 1983. Specializes in hardcover and paperback originals. "We are not confining our publishing efforts to any one category of subject matter. We expect to do some children's books, non-fiction books on various subjects, humor and, when meeting our standards, some fiction."
First Contact & Terms: Works on assignment only. Send query letter with brochure and resume to be kept on file. Call or write for appointment to show portfolio. Prefers photographs, tear sheets or photocopies as samples. Samples returned by SASE only if requested. Reports only if interested. Originals returned to artist at job's completion. Consider complexity of the project, skill and experience of artist and project's budget when establishing payment. Buys variable rights according to project.

ART DIRECTION BOOK CO., 10 E. 39th St., New York NY 10016. (212)889-6500. Art Director: Amy S. Heit. Specializes in hardcover and paperback books on advertising art and design. Publishes 15 titles/year; 50% require freelance designers.
First Contact & Terms: Works with 5 freelance artists/year. Professional artists only. Call for appointment. Drop off portfolio. Samples returned by SASE. Originals returned to artist at job's completion. Buys one-time rights.
Book Design: Assigns 10 jobs/year. Uses artists for layout and mechanicals. Pays by the job, $100 minimum.
Jackets/Covers: Assigns 10 design jobs/year. Pays by the job, $100 minimum.

ARTIST'S MARKET, Writer's Digest Books, 9933 Alliance Rd., Cincinnati OH 45242. (513)984-0717. Contact: Editor. Annual hardcover directory of freelance markets for graphic artists. Send b&w samples—photographs, photostats or good quality photocopies—of artwork. "Since *Artist's Market* is published only once a year, submissions are kept on file for the next upcoming edition until selections are made. Material is then returned by SASE." Buys one-time rights.
Needs: Buys 30-40 illustrations/year. "I need examples of art that has sold to one of the listings in *Artist's Market*. Thumb through the book to see the type of art I'm seeking. The art must have been freelanced; it cannot have been done as staff work. Include the name of the listing that purchased the work, what the art was used for, and the payment you received." Pays $25 to holder of reproduction rights and free copy of *Artist's Market* when published.

*ARTS END BOOKS, Box 162, Newton MA 02168. (617)965-2478. Editor and Publisher: Marshall Brooks. Specializes in hardcover and paperback originals and reprints of contemporary literature. Publishes 2 titles/year.
First Contact & Terms: Works with 2-3 freelance artists/year. Send query letter with samples to be kept on file. Prefers photostats and tear sheets as samples. Samples not filed are returned by SASE. Reports within a few days. Return of original work depends on arrangement with artist. Considers complexity of the project, skill and experience of artist, project's budget, turnaround time and rights purchased when establishing payment. Rights purchased vary according to project.
Book Design: Pays by the project.
Jackets/Covers: Assigns 2 freelance jobs/year. Pays by the project.
Text Illustration: Prefers pen and ink work. Pays by the project.

ASHLEY BOOKS INC., 30 Main St., Port Washington NY 11050. (516)883-2221. President: Billie Young. Publishes hardcover originals; controversial, medical and timely, fiction and nonfiction. Publishes 50 titles/year; 40% require freelance designers or freelance illustrators. Also uses artists for promotional aids.
First Contact & Terms: Arrange interview to show portfolio. Metropolitan New York area residents only; experienced artists with book publisher or record album jacket experience. Buys first rights. Negotiates pay. Free catalog.
Book Design: Assigns 35 jobs/year. Uses artist for layout and paste-up.
Jackets/Covers: Assigns 35 jobs/year. "Covers are less busy; those that have a stark quality seem to be dominating."
Tips: "As a result of an upsurge in consumer interest in cooking, more cookbooks will be produced generating more illustrations and more artwork."

ATHENEUM PUBLISHERS, Juvenile Division, 115 Fifth Ave., New York NY 10003. (212)614-1300. Vice President/Juvenile Books: Jean Karl. Juveniles Art Director: Mary A. Ahern. Publishes hardcover original trade uvenile books for all ages from 4-14. Publishes 60-70 titles/year; all of which require freelance illustrators.
First Contact & Terms: Arrange to show portfolio (10-20 pieces, preferably printed but not absolutely necessary); no slides. Prefers realistic or completely fantasy, and science fiction. Provide business card and tear sheets to be kept on file for future assignments. Works on assignment only. Samples returned by SASE. Reports back on future assignment possibilities. Buys first rights. Originals returned to artist at job's completion.
Jackets/Covers: Realistic or fantasy including science fiction. Pays $650-750/color.
Text Illustrations: Realistic or fantasy including science fiction. Pays $500-2,000/b&w.
Tips: "Bring a good variety of things, but not so much that it is confusing. We do not use much in the way of cartoonish art for young children. We will be using less inside art on older books and more full-color jackets."

THE ATHLETIC PRESS, Box 80250, Pasadena CA 91108. Contact: Donald Duke. Publishes sports training and conditioning books.
First Contact & Terms: Query.
Needs: "We are looking for line art of sport movements, anatomical drawings, etc."

AUGSBURG PUBLISHING HOUSE, 426 S. 5th St., Box 1209, Minneapolis MN 55440. (612)330-3300. Manager, Editorial/Design Services: James Lipscomb. Publishes paperback Protestant/Lutheran books (45 titles/year); religious education materials; audiovisual resources; periodicals. Also uses artists for catalog cover design, advertising circulars; advertising layout, design and illustration. Negotiates pay, b&w and color.
First Contact & Terms: "We don't have a rule to only work locally, but the majority of the artists are close enough to meet here on assignments." Call, write, or send slides or photocopies. Reports in 5-8 weeks. Works on assignment only. Samples returned by SASE if not kept on file. Reports back on future assignment possibilities. Provide brochure, flyer, tear sheet, good photocopies and 35mm transparencies; if artist willing to have samples retained, they are kept on file for future assignments. Buys all rights on a work-for-hire basis except for cartoons. May require artist to supply overlays on color work.
Book Design: Assigns 45 jobs/year. Uses artists primarily for cover design; occasionally inside illustration, sample chapter openers. Pays $400-600 for cover design.
Text Illustrations: Negotiates pay, 1-, 2-, and 4-color.
Tips: Buys 20 cartoons/year. Uses material on family, church situation and social commentary. Pays $15-20 minimum for one-time use.

*AVALON COMMUNICATIONS INC., 1705 Broadway, Hewlett NY 11557. President: Sy Uslan. Specializes in hardcover and paperback originals. "We are also book packagers." Publishes 5-10 titles/year.
First Contact & Terms: Works with 1-2 freelance artists/year. Seeks artists with book layout and design and jacket design experience. Works on an assignment basis only. Send query letter with brochure, resume and business card to be kept on file. Original work returned to the artist only if requested. Considers skill and experience of artist, project's budget and rights purchased when establishing payment. Negotiates rights purchased.
Book Design: Assigns 5-10 jobs/year. Pays by the project, $500 minimum.
Jackets/Covers: Assigns 5-10 freelance design and 5-10 freelance illustration jobs/year. Pays by the project, $200-2,500 average.
Text Illustration: Assigns 5-10 jobs/year. Pays by the project, $50 minimum.

AVON BOOKS, Art Department, 1790 Broadway, New York NY 10019. (212)399-4500. Publisher: Walter Meade. Art Director: Matthew Tepper. Publishes paperback originals and reprints—mass market, trade and juvenile. Publishes 300 titles/year; 80% require freelance illustrators.
First Contact and Terms: Works with 100 freelance artists/year. Works on assignment only. Send query letter with resume and samples to be filed. Call or write for an appointment to show a portfolio. Accepts any type sample. Samples returned only by request. Reports within 1 month. Works on assignment only. Original work returned to the artist after job's completion. Considers complexity of the project, skill and experience of the artist and project's budget when establishing payment.
Book Design: Assigns 20 jobs/year. Uses artists for all aspects. Payment varies.
Jackets/Covers: Assigns 150 freelance design and 150 freelance illustration jobs/year.
Text Illustrations: Assigns 20 freelance jobs/year.
Tips: "Look at our books to see if work is appropriate for us before submitting."

AZTEX CORP., 1126 N. 6th Ave., Box 50046, Tucson AZ 85703. (602)882-4656. President: W. R. Haessner. Publishes hardcover and paperback originals on sports, mainstream and how-to. Publishes 9-12 titles/year.
First Contact & Terms: Query with samples. Especially looks for realism and detail when reviewing samples. Reports in 6 weeks. Works on assignment only. Samples returned by SASE. Provide resume and/or brochure to be kept on file for future assignments. Buys reprint or all rights. No originals returned to artist at job's completion. Free catalog.
Jackets/Covers: Assigns 4 jobs/year. "We need technical drawings and cutaways." Pays $50-150, opaque watercolors and oils.

BAKER STREET PRODUCTIONS LTD., 502 Range St., Mankato MN 56001. (507)625-2482. Contact: Karyne Jacobsen. Production firm providing artwork for juvenile book publishers.
First Contact & Terms: Artists must be able to meet exact deadlines. Seeks local artists in Minnesota, Wisconsin, South Dakota, North Dakota and Iowa. Works on assignment only. Send query letter with samples. Prefers photographs, slides or tear sheets as samples. Reports back within 3 months. Fee is determined by the size of the project involved. Considers complexity of the project and how work will be used when establishing payment.
Needs: Works with 2 freelance artists/year. Uses artists for book diagrams. Artists must work with color.

BARNWOOD PRESS COOPERATIVE, RR 2, Box 11C, Daleville IN 47334. (317)378-0921. Editor: Thomas Koontz. Specializes in paperback originals of poetry. Publishes 8 titles/year; 100% require freelance designers and illustrators.
First Contact & Terms: Works with 3 freelance artists/year. Send query letter with samples to be kept on file. Prefers samples which are the "least expensive but adequately represent the work." Reports in 1 month. Works on assignment only. Originals returned to artist at job's completion. Considers complexity of project and project's budget when establishing payment. Buys reprint rights.
Book Design: Assigns 8 freelance jobs/year. Pays by the project, $25-100 average.
Jackets/Covers: Assigns 8 freelance design and illustration jobs/year. Pays by the project, $25-300 average.
Text Illustration: Assigns 8 freelance jobs/year. Pays by the project, $50-300 average.

*THE BARRETT PRESS, Room 805, 32 Union Sq., New York NY 10003. (212)420-9639. Editor: John Barrett. Estab. 1984. Specializes in paperback fiction and nonfiction. Publishes 3-5 titles/year.
First Contact & Terms: Works with 3 freelance artists/year. Artist must have 3 years' experience in design, preferably a B.A. in art. Works on assignment only. Send samples to be kept on file. Prefers slides or photographs as samples. SASE. Samples not filed are returned only if requested. Reports only if interested. Originals not returned to artist at job's completion. Considers complexity of the project, skill and experience of artist, project's budget, turnaround time and rights purchased when establishing payment. Buys all rights.
Book Design: Assigns 1-3 freelance jobs/year. Pays by the hour, $15 minimum; by the project, $2,000-15,000 average.
Jackets/Covers: Assigns 1-3 freelance design and 1-3 freelance illustration jobs/year. Pays by the hour, $15 minimum; by the project, $2,000-15,000 average.

WILLIAM L. BAUHAN, PUBLISHER, Dublin NH 03444. Art Director: W.L. Bauhan. Publishes hardbound and paperback books on New England. Publishes 6-8 titles/year.
First Contact & Terms: Send query letter. SASE. Reports in 4 weeks. Purchases outright. Works on assignment only. Provide resume and sample or just samples of work to be kept on file for future assignments; do not send originals. Check for most recent titles in bookstores.
Needs: Uses artists for jackets, covers, text illustrations. Uses line drawings and block prints, all b&w.

*BEECHTREE PRESS, Box 15669, Long Beach CA 90815. Production Manager: JoAnn Beecher. Estab. 1984. Specializes in paperbacks on family life, juvenile nonfiction and self-help.
First Contact & Terms: Works with 3 freelance artists/year. Works on assignment only. Send query letter with business card and samples to be kept on file. "No initial phone calls." Prefers photocopies of b&w work; slides of color. Samples not filed are returned by SASE. Reports within 3 months. Original work not returned after job's completion. Considers complexity of the project, skill and experience of artist, project's budget and turnaround time when establishing payment. Rights purchased vary according to project.
Book Design: Assigns 1 freelance job/year. Negotiates payment by the project.
Jackets/Covers: Assigns 2 freelance design and 2 freelance illustration jobs/year. Negotiates payment by the project.
Text Illustration: Assigns 3 freelance jobs/year. Prefers b&w line illustrations. Negotiates payment by the project.
Tips: "We are a small press and are just starting out, but we plan to expand the number of books we publish each year."

BENGAL PRESS, INC., 1885 Spaulding SE, Grand Rapids MI 49506. (616)949-8895. President: John Ilich. Specializes in paperback and hardcover originals and reprints of nonfiction (business, history, law, how-to) and fiction (science fiction, religious, inspirational). Publishes 1-4 titles/year; 100% require freelance designers; 25% require freelance illustrators.
First Contact & Terms: Send query letter with samples to be kept on file. Accepts any samples the artist deems relevant to show quality and type of work. Reports only if interested. Works on assignment only. No originals returned to artist at job's completion. Considers complexity of project, skill and experience of artist and project's budget when establishing payment. Buys all rights.
Book Design: Assigns 1-3 freelance jobs/year. Pays by the project with fee negotiated at the time artist is hired.
Jackets/Covers: Assigns 1-3 freelance design and 1-4 freelance illustration jobs/year. Pays by the project with fee negotiated at the time artist is hired.
Text Illustration: Assigns 1-3 freelance jobs/year. Pays by the project with fee negotiated at the time artist is hired.

*BLACKTHORNE PUBLISHING INC., 786 Blackthorne Ave., El Cajon CA 92020. (619)463-9603. Art Director: Steven J. Schanes. Estab. 1983. Specializes in paperback originals and reprints, comic books, signed prints, and trade books. Publishes 48 titles/year.
First Contact & Terms: Works with 50 freelance artists/year. "We look for professional standards in artists we work with." Send query letter with brochure, resume, and samples to be kept on file; originals will be returned. Prefers slides and photostats as samples. Samples not filed are returned. Reports within 3 weeks. Originals returned to artist after job's completion. Considers complexity of the project, skill and experience of artist, project's budget and turnaround time when establishing payment. Rights purchased vary according to project.
Book Design: Assigns 50 jobs/year. Pays by the project, depending on the job, from $50 for a spot illustration to $15,000 for a complete comic book series.
Jackets/Covers: Assigns 15 freelance design and 30 freelance illustration jobs/year. Pays by the hour, $5-40 average; by the project, $50-10,000 average.
Text Illustration: Assigns 15 jobs/year. Prefers pen & ink. Pays by the hour, $5-40 average; by the project, $50-10,000 average.

BLACKWELL SCIENTIFIC PUBLICATIONS, INC., 52 Beacon St., Boston MA 02108. (617)720-0761. Production Manager: Elizabeth O'Neill McGuire. Specializes in hardcovers of medical and nursing books. Publishes 5 titles/year.
First Contact & Terms: Artists must have experience in specific field. Send query letter with brochure, resume and samples to be kept on file; call or write for appointment to show portfolio. Prefers photocopies and photostats as samples. Samples not kept on file are returned by SASE. Reports only if interested. Works on assignment only. No originals returned to artist at job's completion. Considers project budget and turnaround time when establishing payment. Buys all rights.
Jackets/Covers: Assigns 3 freelance design jobs/year.
Tips: Artists should "investigate the potential purchaser to see if their work is even appropriate."

*BLUEJAY BOOKS INC., Suite 514, 130 W. 42nd St., New York NY 10036. (212)221-1841. Publisher: James Frenkel. Specializes in hardcover and paperback originals and reprints of science fiction and fantasy. Publishes 35 titles/year.
First Contact & Terms: Works with 20 freelance artists/year. Works on assignment only. Send query letter with samples to be kept on file; call for appointment to show portfolio. Prefers Cibachromes as

samples. Samples not filed are returned by SASE. Reports only if interested. Original work returned after job's completion. Considers project's budget when establishing payment. Rights purchased vary according to project.

Jackets/Covers: Assigns 35 freelance illustration jobs/year. Pays by the project, $500 minimum.

Text Illustration: Assigns 5 freelance jobs/year. Prefers b&w illustrations. Pays by the project, $50 minimum.

BOWLING GREEN UNIVERSITY POPULAR PRESS, Bowling Green University, Bowling Green OH 43403. (419)372-2981. Managing Editor: Pat Browne. Publishes hardcover and paperback originals on popular culture, folklore, women studies, science fiction criticism, detective fiction criticism, music and drama. Publishes 15-20 titles and 8 journals/year.

First Contact & Terms: Send previously published work. SASE. Reports in 2 weeks. Buys all rights. Free catalog.

Jackets/Covers: Assigns 20 jobs/year. Pays $50 minimum, color washes, opaque watercolors, gray opaques, b&w line drawings and washes.

BRADY COMMUNICATIONS COMPANY, INC., a Prentice-Hall Company, 14999 Annapolis Rd., Bowie MD 20715. (301)262-6300. Executive Art Director/Chief Medical Illustrator: Don Sellers, AMI. Publishes medical, allied health, emergency care, nursing and home computer textbooks.

First Contact & Terms: Artists must be experienced cover designers (high-tech computer covers for home computer books) or experienced textbook illustrators. Works on assignment only. Send resume and samples to be kept on file. Prefers tear sheets of illustrations or printed flat sheets of covers, both computer and medical, as samples. Samples not filed are returned by SASE. Reports back only if interested. Pays by the project; cover designs, rough comprehensive full color to size, $250; text illustrations, rough and final inking, $50. Considers the complexity of the project, skill and experience of artist, turnaround time and rights purchased when establishing payment.

Needs: Works with 50 freelance artists/year. Uses artists for textbook illustration and cover design.

Tips: "Work must be of a high quality, neat, clean. We prefer previously published examples only; no school work."

GEORGE BRAZILLER INC., 1 Park Ave., New York NY 10016. (212)889-0909. Contact: Herman Figatner. Publishes hardcover and paperback originals on history of art and architecture; philosophy and religion. Publishes 20 titles/year. Also uses artists for advertising, paste-up, catalog layout and design, posters. Query with resume; local artists only. Works on assignment only. Provide resume and samples to be kept on file. Buys one-time rights.

Book Design: Assigns 25 jobs/year. Designer is responsible for type spec, composition arrangements, through finished mechanicals. Pays by the project, $2,000 maximum.

Jackets/Covers: Uses freelance designers and illustrators. Prefers line drawings, color wash, prints (wood blocks) as cover illustrations. Pays for design and illustration by the project, $150-300 average.

Tips: "Show work directly geared to a particular publisher."

BRIARCLIFF PRESS, 11 Wimbledon Court, Jericho NY 11753. (516)681-1505. Editorial/Art Director: Trudy Settel. Publishes hardcover and paperback cookbook, decorating, baby care, gardening, sewing, crafts and driving originals and reprints. Publishes 18 titles/year; 100% require freelance designers and illustrators. Uses artists for color separations, lettering and mechanicals; assigns 25 jobs/year, pays $5-10/hour. Also assigns 5 advertising jobs/year for catalogs and direct mail brochures; pays $5-10/hour.

First Contact & Terms: Query by mail; no samples until requested. Artists should have worked on a professional basis with other firms of this type. SASE. Reports in 3 weeks. Buys all rights. No advance. Pays promised fee for unused assigned work.

Book Design: Assigns 25/year. Pays $6 minimum/hour, layout and type spec.

Jackets/Covers: Buys 24/year. Pays $100-300, b&w; $250-500, color.

Text Illustrations: Uses artists for text illustrations and cartoons. Buys 250/year. Pays $10-30, b&w; $25-50, color.

BROADMAN PRESS, 127 9th Ave. N., Nashville TN 37234. (615)251-2630. Art Director: Jack Jewell. Religious publishing house.

First Contact & Terms: Artist must be experienced, professional illustrator or book cover designer. Works on assignment only. Send query letter with brochure and samples to be kept on file. Call or write for appointment to show portfolio. Send slides, tear sheets, photostats or photocopies; "samples *cannot* be returned." Reports back only if interested. Pays by the project, $50-600 average. Considers complexity of the project, client's budget and rights purchased when establishing payment. Buys all rights.

Needs: Works with 50 freelance artists/year. Uses artists for illustration and occasionally graphic de-

sign. "We publish for all ages in traditional and contemporary styles, thus our needs are quite varied."
Tips: "The quality of design in the Christian book publishing market has greatly improved in the last five years. We actively search for 'realist' illustrators who can work in a style that looks contemporary."

WILLIAM C. BROWN PUBLISHERS, 2460 Kerper Blvd., Dubuque IA 52001. (319)588-1451. Vice President and Director, Production Development and Design: David A. Corona. Design Director: Marilyn A. Phelps. Publishes hardbound and paperback college textbooks. Publishes 200 titles/year; 3% require freelance designers, 50% require freelance illustrators. Also uses artists for advertising. Pays $35-350, b&w and color promotional artwork.
First Contact & Terms: Query with finished 11x14" or smaller (transparencies if larger) art samples or call for interview. Reports in 4 weeks. Works on assignment only. Samples returned by SASE if requested. Reports back on future assignment possibilities. Provide resume, letter of inquiry, brochure, tear sheet or 8½x11" photocopies of samples to be kept on file for future assignments. Buys all rights. Pays half contract for unused assigned work.
Book Design: Assigns 10-20 jobs/year. Uses artists for all phases of process. Negotiates pay by the job; varies widely according to complexity. Pays by the hour, mechanicals.
Jackets/Covers: Assigns 15-25 freelance design jobs and 20-30 freelance illustration jobs/year. Pays $100-350 average and negotiates pay for special projects.
Text Illustrations: Assigns 40-50 freelance jobs/year. Uses b&w and color work. Pays $35-200. Artwork includes medical illustration.
Tips: "There is more emphasis on visuals—more color use in our field. Publishers of textbooks require more professional and sophisticated illustrations than they did three to five years ago. Production schedules are tighter requiring use of more freelancers."

CAREER PUBLISHING, INC., Box 5486, Orange CA 92667. (714)771-5155. Secretary/Treasurer: Sherry Robson. Specializes in paperback original textbooks on trucking, medical office management, medical insurance billing, motorcycle dictionary, real estate dictionary, micro computer courses and guidance for jobs. Also uses artists for advertising, direct mail and posters.
First Contact & Terms: Works with 3 freelance artists/year. Send query letter with brochure/flyer or resume and samples or actual work; submit portfolio for review. Guidelines given for each project. Prefers photostats and line drawings as samples. Samples returned by SASE. Reports in 2 months. Works on assignment only. Provide resume, business card, brochure/flyer, samples and tear sheets to be kept on file for possible future assignments. No originals returned to artist at job's completion. Buys all rights.
Book Design: Assigns 12 jobs/year. Negotiates payment by the job.
Jackets/Covers: Assigns 12 design and 150 illustration jobs/year. Prefers line drawings, paintings and cartoons for illustrations. Negotiates payment by the job.
Text Illustration: Assigns approximately 10 jobs/year. Negotiates payment by the job.
Tips: Uses some medical illustrations.

*CARNIVAL ENTERPRISES, Box 19087, Minneapolis MN 55419. (612)870-0169. Director of Operations: Gregory N. Lee. "Carnival is a book producer, not a publisher. The titles we create are for clients who market them in many outlets and editions. Produces juvenile fiction and nonfiction. Produces 25-45 titles/year.
First Contact & Terms: Works with 25-45 freelance artists/year. "Experience in children's literature is *crucial*, including past published children's books and experience in picturebook design." Works on an assignment basis only. Send query letter with brochure, resume and samples to be kept on file. Prefers photocopies, slides, printed excerpts—anything except original work. "Carnival uses a file system and only contacts artists on an assignment basis. No specific submissions will be accepted; no queries are followed upon by Carnival due to the volume of our mail. We literally match up artists with appropriate styles. All samples are welcome, but bulk should be kept to a minimum for easy filing. Samples not filed are returned *only* by request with an SASE. Does not report back to the artist. Considers complexity of the project, skill and experience of artist, project's budget, (vital) turnaround time, rights purchased and going rates when establishing payment. Rights purchased vary from client to client.
Text Illustration: Assigns 25-45 titles/year. Considers watercolor, markers, colored pencil and gouache—any "flexible" medium for laser separation. Pays by the project, $2,000-6,000 for color. B&w line art pays less.

CATHOLIC BOOK PUBLISHING CO., 257 W. 17th St., New York NY 10011. (212)243-4515. Manager: Robert W. Cavalero. Specializes in hardcover and paperback originals. Publishes 10 titles/year; 50% require freelance illustrators.
First Contact & Terms: Works with 6 freelance artists/year. Send samples and tear sheets to be kept on file; call or write for appointment to show portfolio. Reports within 1 week. Works on assignment only.

No originals returned to artist at job's completion. Considers skill and experience of artist when establishing payment. Buys all rights.
Text Illustration: Assigns 10 freelance jobs/year.

THE CHILD'S WORLD, INC., Box 989, Elgin IL 60120. Editor: Diane Dow Suire. Specializes in hardcover originals on early childhood education. Publishes 40 titles/year; 60% require freelance designers; 100% require freelance illustrators.
First Contact & Terms: Works with 20 freelance artists/year. Prefers artists who have experience illustrating for children. Send samples and tear sheets to be kept on file except for original work. "Correspond please. Don't call." Reports only if interested. Works on assignment only. No originals returned to artist at job's completion. Considers complexity of project, skill and experience of artist and project's budget when establishing payment. Buys all rights.
Book Design: Assigns 4-6 (by series) freelance jobs/year. Pays by the project for design and illustration.
Jackets/Covers: Assigns 4-6 (by series) freelance design jobs/year. Pays by the project for design and illustration.
Text Illustration: "We do about 40 books in series format. We publish in full color and use very little black-and-white art." Pays by the project.
Tips: Looks for "art geared for the very young child—there's a big demand for more quality books for preschool children."

CHILTON BOOK CO., 201 King of Prussia Rd., Radnor PA 19089. (215)964-4711. Art Director: Edna H. Jones. Publishes hardbound and paperback arts and crafts, business, computer, technical, trade and automotive books. Publishes 80 titles/year; 50% require freelance designers, fewer than 5% require freelance illustrators.
First Contact & Terms: Query. "I prefer to deal in person rather than through the mail." Reports within 3 weeks. Buys world rights. No originals returned at job's completion. Works on assignment only. Samples returned by SASE. Provide resume, business card, flyer and tear sheet to be kept on file for future assignments. Check for most recent titles in bookstores. Artist sometimes supplies overlays for color work. Full payment for unused assigned work. Pays on acceptance.
Book Design: Assigns 40 jobs/year. Uses artists for layout, type spec and scaling art, castoffs. Pays upon completion and acceptance. Price is discussed at beginning of the job with the designer.
Jackets/Covers: Pays $300-400, b&w; $400-700, color.
Text Illustrations: Pays $50-150, b&w.

CHRISTIAN BOARD OF PUBLICATION, Box 179, St. Louis MO 63166. Director of Product Development, Design and Promotion: Guin Tuckett. Publishes several paperbacks annually. Also publishes magazines, curriculum, catalogs and advertising pieces. Uses artists for design and illustration of curriculum, books, direct mail brochures and display pieces.
First Contact & Terms: Query with resume and samples. SASE. Reports in 6-8 weeks. Buys all rights. No originals returned to artist at job's completion. Works on assignment only. Samples returned by SASE. Provide resume and brochure or copies of work to be kept on file for future assignments.
Jackets/Covers: Assigns a few jobs/year. Pays $100 minimum, 2-color and 4-color.
Text Illustrations: Assigns many jobs/year. Pays $40 minimum, 2-color; $55 minimum, 4-color. "In a teen-age monthly magazine we use about 8-10 cartoons/issue."

CHRONICLE BOOKS, Suite 806, One Hallidie Plaza, San Francisco CA 94102. (415)777-7240. Production and Art Director: David Barich. Publishes hardcover and paperback originals on California and the West Coast, how-to, architecture, California history, urban living, guidebooks, art and photography; some paperback reprints. Publishes 25-35 titles/year; 75% require freelance designers, 10% require freelance illustrators.
First Contact & Terms: Personal contact required. Query with resume or arrange interview to show portfolio. SASE. Reports within 2 weeks. Buys various rights. Free catalog.
Book Design: Assigns 25 jobs/year. Uses artists for layout, type spec and design. Pays by the project, $225-550 average. Payment upon completion of project.
Jackets/Covers: Assigns 40 jobs/year. Pays by the project, $225-550 average for design; by the project, $125-400 average for illustrations, b&w line drawings, washes and gray opaques; $400-650, color washes and opaque watercolors.
Text Illustration: Pays by the project, $200 minimum.

CLIFFS NOTES INC., Box 80728, Lincoln NE 68501. Contact: Michele Spence. Publishes educational and trade (Centennial Press) books.
First Contact & Terms: Works on assignment only. Samples returned by SASE. Reports back on future assignment possibilities. Provide brochure, flyer and/or resume. No originals returned to artist at job's

completion. Buys all rights. Artist supplies overlays for color art.
Jackets/Covers: Uses artists for covers and jackets.
Text Illustrations: Uses technical illustrators for mathematics, science, miscellaneous.

COASTAL PLAINS PUBLISHING CO., Box 1101, Danville VA 24543. (919)379-8778. Publisher: Margaret Kale. Specializes in paperback originals, fiction and nonfiction. Publishes 1 title/year.
First Contact & Terms: Works with 2 freelance artists/year. Send query letter with samples to be kept on file. Any form of samples accepted. Samples not kept on file are returned by SASE. Reports within 2 months. Works on assignment only. No originals returned to artist at job's completion. Considers complexity of project, skill and experience of artist and project's budget when establishing payment. Negotiates rights purchased.
Book Design: Assigns 1 freelance job/year. Pay depends on job.
Jackets/Covers: Assigns 1 freelance design and 1 freelance illustration job/year. Pay depends on project.
Text Illustration: Assigns 1 freelance job/year.

*COASTAR PUBLISHING, Subsidiary of Newtek Industries, Box 46116, Los Angeles CA 90046. (213)874-6669. Publisher: Jules Brenner. Estab. 1984. Publishes 1 original paperback—the *Brenner Restaurant Index*—each year. Also publishes a software program for home and office computers.
First Contact & Terms: "We are not yet working with artists, but would consider doing so." Send query letter with resume and samples to be kept on file. Accepts any type sample. Samples not filed are returned by SASE. Reports back to artist within 3 weeks. Original work returned to artist "if artist insists." Rights purchased vary according to project.
Jackets/Covers: Will probably assign 1 freelance illustration job/year. Pays 3 copies of book.
Text Illustration: Will consider using text illustration.

*COLOR-A-STORY, Box 99, Burley WA 98322. Art Director: J. Scott. Specializes in paperback originals, juvenile fiction and nonfiction. Publishes 12 titles/year.
First Contact & Terms: Works with 7 freelance artists/year. Artist "must be capable of producing illustrations compatible with the Color-A-Story series." Works on assignment only. Send resume and samples to be kept on file, except for "those which do not interest us." Prefers photocopies as samples, although slides and/or photographs are acceptable. Samples not filed are returned by SASE. Reports only if interested. Original work may be returned to the artist. Considers complexity of the project, skill and experience of artist, project's budget, turnaround time and rights purchased when establishing payment. Rights purchased vary according to project.
Jackets/Covers: Assigns 12 freelance illustration jobs/year.
Text Illustration: Assigns 12 jobs/year. Prefers pen & ink illustrations. "Artist is assigned text and cover." Pays royalty up to 15%.
Tips: "We are happy to assign work to new artists provided they produce quality work, on time, and follow outlines provided with assignments."

COMPCARE PUBLICATIONS, 2415 Annapolis Ln., Minneapolis MN 55441. (800)328-3330. Publisher: Margaret Marsh. Specializes in personal growth books including alcohol/chemical dependency, stress management, parenting and weight control. Publishes 10-15 titles/year. Uses artists for text illustrations and cover art.
First Contact & Terms: Works with 4 freelance artists/year. "We only consider artists who have illustrated for trade books." Send query letter with tear sheets. Works on assignment only. Negotiates payment arrangement with artist.

COMPUTER SCIENCE PRESS INC., 1803 Research Blvd., Rockville MD 20850. (301)251-9050. Publishes hardcover and paperback computer science, engineering, computers and math textbooks. Publishes 14 titles/year; 100% require freelance illustrators. Also uses artists for technical drawings using templates and form letters or Leroy lettering.
First Contact & Terms: Send query letter with samples (template work); call. Samples should include an illustration or line drawing as well as an upper and lower case alphabet and some words in Leroy or Berol lettering. Photocopy of work is OK. Samples not returned. Buys all rights. No originals returned to artist at job's completion. Works on assignment only. Provide business card, letter of inquiry and sample of work to be kept on file for future assignments. Check for most recent titles in bookstores. Artist supplies overlays for cover artwork.
Needs: Send artwork to the attention of Ilene Hammer. Buys text illustrations (artist "reproduces our rough art"), jacket designs and cover designs. Assigns 12 freelance text illustration jobs/year; prefers pen & ink drawings.
Tips: "We would like to develop a file of freelance technical draftsmen familiar with Leroy or Berol lettering. Local artists preferred. We provide rough art to copy."

Close-up

Carl Lundgren
Science Fiction Illustrator
Philadelphia, Pennsylvania

Artist: David R. Smiton

"Science fiction illustration differs from any other kind of illustration because in most cases you have to create a picture of something that in fact cannot happen." This definition of the science fiction illustration field comes from Carl Lundgren who for eleven years has been a top illustrator in this area.

Lundgren's career began at age twenty-seven with the first of what would prove to be hundreds of book covers. Four years later, in 1978, a major break came with the opportunity to illustrate twelve of Robert A. Heinlein's science fiction novels, including *Stranger in a Strange Land*, one of the eminent writer's most popular novels.

Many changes have occurred in the science fiction market since Lundgren's first book cover. "When I started working in this field there was barely a handful of professional science fiction artists; now there are nearly fifty. Also, back then I worked primarily with the art director, while today the book's editor plays a big part in deciding what goes on the cover and who paints it. The importance of science fiction in the art world is increasing and the competition is continuing to grow. This in turn increases the value and appreciation of science fiction art."

Lundgren, who today receives a minimum of $2,000 per job, approaches science fiction projects with a basic philosophy. "You change the common perception of reality while still making it believable. You take something imaginary and put it into a real context or vice versa. I tell my students that something

should happen in their pictures; it should be something unexpected or unusual.

"In science fiction art any situation is possible, and I consider it a challenge to depict them. Most of my cover illustration ideas are based on the books themselves, but some come from my own imagination. I then find a pattern to work from—color schemes or compositions. For example, pastels are universally used for dreamy fantasyscapes and hot colors for dramatic scenes."

In today's science fiction industry, Lundgren is considered "established" which, according to the artist, means "art directors trust you to not ruin a job, from sketch to deadline," and this time span is usually only four weeks. But according to the 38-year-old artist, "even though I am established I must continually keep in touch with the publishing field. Art directors are always changing, moving to different companies. My agent, who is my wife Michelle, is constantly on the phone. I advertise in various illustrators' books and still go out of my way to do promotional mailings.

"My mailing package includes a full-color folder with my photograph, biography and seven paintings printed on the folder. I also send out an updated resume and other promotional pieces. I try to get my name and face publicized as often as possible. I make myself visible, and I do more self-promotion now than ever."

Merchandising is a major aspect of Lundgren's career. By reproducing his artwork on puzzles, posters and greeting cards the artist's work reaches people who normally do not buy a science fiction book. Lundgren also points out that "you must remember that all merchandising stems from second reproduction rights, which I own. This means that from one book cover I can generate dozens of extra sales."

Lundgren's future seems wide open. "I hope to do some collector plate designs and am assembling a presentation for a book on my work. My wife and I have opened The Gallery of Illustration and Fine Art in Philadelphia. We hope to promote interest in collecting and investing in all forms of contemporary illustration."

Pocket Books commissioned this oil painting for $1,800. Lundgren merchandises many of his illustrations for use on puzzles, posters and greeting cards. The artist sells only first rights to publishers so that he is able to generate additional sales from each illustration.

Most of Lundgren's cover illustrations, such as this one for Tor Books, are based on the book itself, although many originate from the artist's own imagination.

Lundgren created this oil painting for use by Warner Books as a science fiction paperback cover. The artist received $1,800 for first North American rights.

CONCH MAGAZINE LTD., PUBLISHERS, 102 Normal Ave., Buffalo NY 14213. (716)885-3686. Creative Director: Jeannine Zoto. Specializes in hardcover and paperback originals, scholarly and educational. Publishes 10-20 titles/year 99% require freelance designers and illustrators.
First Contact & Terms: Send query letter with brochure, business card, samples and tear sheets to be kept on file. Samples should be whatever is convenient and available. Reports only if interested. Works on assignment only. Considers complexity of project, skill and experience of artist and turnaround time when establishing payment.
Book Design: Assigns 10 freelance jobs/year. Pays by the project, $25-50 average.
Jackets/Covers: Assigns 10 freelance design and 10 freelance illustration jobs/year. Pays by the project, $25-50 average. Artwork includes medical illustration.

DAVID C. COOK PUBLISHING COMPANY, Book Division, 850 N. Grove Ave., Elgin IL 60120. (312)741-2400. Managing Editor: Catherine L. Davis. Publishes religious books spanning ages infant-junior high. Publishes 50 titles/year; 60% require freelance illustrators.
First Contact & Terms: Prefers artists with publishing experience. Send photocopies of work or 35mm slides with return package and postage. Samples returned by SASE. Provide "anything that can be kept or photocopied" to be kept on file for future assignments. Check for most recent titles in bookstores. Artist sometimes supplies overlays on inside illustrations.
Book Design: Assigns 20-35/year. Buys realistic illustrations. Uses artists for layout and full-color art. Illustrated books usually have an advance and royalty.
Jackets/Covers: Assigns 20-35/year. Buys realistic illustrations; prefers b&w and full color. Uses artists for layout and full-color art. Pays by the job.

CORNERSTONE PRESS image magazine, Box 28048, St. Louis MO 63119. (314)296-9662. Art-Graphics Editor: Bob Bangert. Specializes in paperbacks of poetry, fiction, fantasy and science fiction.
First Contact & Terms: Works with 5-10 freelance artists/year. Send query letter with samples; write for artists' guidelines. Samples not kept on file are returned by SASE. Reports in 8 weeks. Occasionally works on assignment. Originals returned to artist at job's completion. Considers complexity of project, project's budget and turnaround time when establishing payment. Negotiates rights purchased.
Book Design: Assigns 1-4 freelance jobs/year. Pays by the project $5-100 average.
Jackets/Covers: Assigns 3-5 freelance design and 10-60 freelance illustration jobs/year. Pays by the project, $5-100 average.
Text Illustration: Prefers pen and ink, collage and prints. Pays by the project, $5-100 average.

CORTINA LEARNING INTERNATIONAL, INC., 17 Riverside Ave., Westport CT 06880. Publishes language teaching materials, art courses in commercial art, oil and watercolor painting, young people's arts, writing (fiction and nonfiction) and photography
First Contact & Terms: Send "outline of proposed project or photocopies only of table of contents and sample chapters." No originals returned to artist at job's completion. Works on assignment only. Samples returned by SASE; reports back on future assignment possibilities. Provide resume and samples of style to be kept on file for future assignments. Artist supplies overlays for cover artwork.
Jackets/Covers: Uses artists for jacket design.
Text Illustrations: Uses artists for text illustrations. Negotiates pay.
Tips: Also uses artists for direct mail promotion and advertising art.

CPI, 223 E. 48th St., New York NY 10017. (212)753-3800. Contact: Sherry Olan. Publishes hardcover originals, workbooks and textbooks for ages 4-14. Publishes 40 titles/year; 100% require freelance illustrators. Also uses artists for instructional materials, workbooks, textbook and scientific illustration.
First Contact & Terms: Local artists only. Query with samples. Reports in 2 weeks. Works on assignment only. Samples returned by SASE; and reports back on future assignment possibilities. Provide flyer, tear sheet and photocopies of work to be kept on file for future assignments. No originals returned to artist at job's completion. Buys all rights. Free artist's guidelines.
Text Illustrations: "Submit color samples of action subjects. In general, realistic and representational art is required." Pays $50-120, opaque watercolors or any strong color medium. Also buys b&w line drawings.

CRAFTSMAN BOOK COMPANY, 6058 Corte del Cedro, Carlsbad CA 92008. (714)438-7828. Art Director: Bill Grote. Specializes in paperback technical construction books. Publishes 10 titles/year; 50% require freelance illustrators.
First Contact & Terms: Works with 6 freelance artists/year. Send query letter with brochure/flyer or resume. Reports back whether to expect future assignments. Provide resume, business card, brochure/flyer, samples, photocopies or tear sheets to be kept on file. Originals returned to artist at job's completion. Buys all rights.

Jackets/Covers: Assigns 6 design and 10 illustration jobs/year. Prefers color comps for illustrations. Pays by the job, $50-350 average.
Text Illustration: Assigns 5 jobs/year. Prefers b&w pen & ink, light wash and screens. Pays by the hour, $4-6 average.
Tips: "List prices up front. We are using more 4-color. We need artists with full-color background and experience."

THE CROSSING PRESS, Box 640, Trumansburg NY 14886. (607)387-6217. Publishers: John and Elaine Gill. Publishes hardcover and paperback cookbooks, how-to, feminist/gay literature, and greeting cards and calendars. Publishes 15 titles/year.
First Contact & Terms: Query. SASE. Reports within 4 weeks. Free catalog.
Jackets/Covers: Assigns 6 jobs/year. Pay varies up to $200, b&w line drawings and washes.
Text Illustration: Assigns 3-4 jobs/year. Pays $20 and up/illustration or $300-1,000/book for b&w line drawings and washes.

*CUBE PUBLICATIONS, INC., 1 Buena Vista Rd., Box 66, Port Jefferson NY 11777. (516)331-4990. Editor: Katherine B. Glean. Specializes in original hardcover, paperback, text and nonfiction books. Past topics are drug abuse, juvenile delinquency and wife abuse. Publishes 4 titles/year.
First Contact & Terms: Works with 2-4 freelance artists/year. Prefers local (Long Island) artists but "We are open to anyone—newcomer or established artists." Works on assignment only. Send query letter with brochure, resume and samples to be kept on file. Write for appointment to show portfolio. Prefers tear sheets as samples. Samples not filed returned by SASE. Reports back to the artist within 30 days. Original work is not returned to the artist. Considers complexity of the project, skill and experience of artist and project's budget when establishing payment. Rights purchased vary according to project.
Book Design: Assigns 1-3 jobs/year. Pays by the project.
Jackets/Covers: Assigns 4 freelance design and 4 freelance illustration jobs/year. Pays by the project.
Text Illustration: Assigns 1-2 jobs/year. Pays by the project.
Tips: "We're using more line drawings."

CURRICULUM ASSOCIATES, INC., 5 Esquire Rd., North Billerica MA 01862. (617)667-8000. Production Manager: Kerry Donovan. Educational publisher of el/hi materials (textbooks).
First Contact & Terms: Works on assignment only. Send query letter with resume and samples to be kept on file; call for appointment to show portfolio. Samples not filed returned by SASE.
Needs: Uses artists for advertising, brochure and catalog illustration and layout.

*CUSTOM COMIC SERVICES, Box 50028, Austin TX 78763. Art Director: Scott Deschaine. Estab. 1985. Specializes in cartoon booklets for promotion and advertising for use by business, education, and government. "Our main product is four-color newsprint booklets, with stories reaching 16 pages long." Publishes 6 titles/year.
First Contact & Terms: Works with 6 freelance artists/year. "We are looking for artists who can produce finished artwork for sequential storytelling from layouts provided by the publisher. They should be able to produce consistently high quality cartoons for mutually agreeable deadlines, with no exceptions." Works on assignment only. Send query letter with business card and nonreturnable samples to be kept on file. Samples should be of finished comic book pages; prefers photostats. Reports within 6 weeks. No originals returned to artist at job's completion. Considers complexity of project and skill and experience of artist when establishing payment. Buys all rights.
Text Illustration: "Finished artwork will be black-and-white, clean, and uncluttered. Artists can have styles ranging from the highly cartoony to the highly realistic."

DAWNWOOD PRESS, Suite 2650, 2 Park Ave., New York NY 10016. (212)532-7160. President: Ms. Kathryn Drayton. Estab. 1983. Specializes in hardcover originals of fiction with contemporary themes of social significance. Publishes 1-2 titles/year.
First Contact & Terms: Works with 1 freelance artist/year. Highly experienced, local artists only. Works on assignment only. Send query letter with brochure to be kept on file; write for appointment to show portfolio. Contact through artist's agent preferred. Prefers to review photographs as samples. Reports within 10 days. No original work returned after job's completion. Considers complexity of the project and project's budget when establishing payment. Buys all rights.
Jackets/Covers: Assigns 1 freelance job/year. Pays by the project, $400-700 average.

DILITHIUM PRESS, 921 SW Washington St., Portland OR 97205. (800)547-1842 or (503)646-2713. Art Director: Becky Bradshaw. Specializes in paperback originals and reprints on general computer science. Publishes 90-100 titles/year.

First Contact & Terms: Works with 15 artists/year. Experienced artists only. Send query letter with samples, brochure and tear sheets to be kept on file; write for appointment to show portfolio. Prefers photographs or photostats as samples. Especially looks for "a good sense of color relationships, good use of typography integrated with illustration and consistent high quality throughout" when reviewing samples. Samples not kept on file returned by SASE only if requested. Works on assignment only; reports only if interested. No originals returned at job's completion. Considers complexity of project when establishing payment.
Book Design: Assigns 10 freelance jobs/year. Pays by the project, $500 average minimum.
Jackets/Covers: Assigns 20 freelance design and 60 freelance illustration jobs/year. Pays by the project, $500 average minimm.
Text Illustrations: Assigns 10 freelance jobs/year. Pays by the project, $300 average minimum.
Tips: "We look for colorful, friendly approaches to illustration. We don't use high-tech, space-age art. Any medium may be applicable."

*DILLON PRESS, 242 Portland Ave. S, Minneapolis MN 55415. (612)333-2691. Publisher: Uva Dillon. Specializes in hardcovers of juvenile fiction (Gemstone Books) and nonfiction for school library and trade markets. Publishes 30 titles/year.
First Contact & Terms: Works with 5 freelance artists/year. Works on assignment only. Send query letter with resume and samples to be kept on file. Call or write for appointment to show portfolio. Prefers slides and tear sheets as samples. Samples not filed are returned by SASE. Reports within 6 weeks. Originals not returned to artist. Considers complexity of the project, skill and experience of artist and project's budget when establishing payment. Rights purchased vary according to project.
Book Design: Assigns 10 jobs/year. Pays by the hour or by the project, negotiated so as competitive with other publishers in area.
Jackets/Covers: Assigns 10 freelance design and 10 freelance illustration jobs/year. Pays by the hour or by the project, negotiated so as competitive with other publishers in area.
Text Illustration: Assigns 10 jobs/year. Seeks a variety of media and styles. Pays by the hour or by the project, negotiated so as competitive with other publishers in area.

THE DONNING COMPANY/PUBLISHERS, 5659 Virginia Beach Blvd., Norfolk VA 23502. Publishes hardcover and paperback originals on pictorial histories, science fiction, fantasy and horror, illustrated cookbooks, general and regional. Publishes 30-35 titles/year.
First Contact & Terms: Send letter of inquiry to be kept on file for future assignments. Works on assignment only. Samples returned by SASE. Reports in 4 weeks. Buys first rights. Originals returned to artist at job's completion. Artist supplies overlays for cover artwork. Free catalog.

DOUBLEDAY AND CO. INC., 245 Park Ave., New York NY 10167. (212)953-4561. Contact: Art Director. Publishes general adult, juvenile, western, science fiction, mystery, religious and special interest titles. Call for interview.
Needs: Uses artists for jackets, inside illustrations.

*DOWN THERE PRESS/YES PRESS, Box 2086, Burlingame CA 94010. Contact: Joani Blank. Specializes in paperback originals on sexuality, for adults and children. Publishes 1-2 titles/year.
First Contact & Terms: Works with 1 freelance artist/year. Local artists strongly preferred. Works on assignment only. Send brochure and samples. Brochure will be kept on file; samples may be. Prefers tear sheets or photocopies as samples. Samples not filed are returned by SASE. Original work is returned to the artist. Purchases one-time rights.
Jackets/Covers: Assigns 1 freelance design and 1 freelance illustration job/year. Pays by the project.
Text Illustration: Prefers b&w line drawings, no color work. Pays $200 minimum, plus royalties. Small advance sometimes given.

DRAMA BOOK PUBLISHERS, 821 Broadway, New York NY 10003. (212)228-3400. Editor-in-Chief: Ralph Pine. Contact: Judith Holmes. Publishes hardcover and paperback originals and reprints on performing arts. Publishes 20 titles/year; 80% require freelance designers, 20% require freelance illustrators. Also uses artists for direct mail brochures and advertising layouts.
First Contact & Terms: Query with brochure/flyer or mail photocopies or transparencies. "Nonreturnable copies, no matter how primitive, preferred to returnable copies, no matter how slick." Buys various rights. Works on assignment only. Reports back to artist on future assignment possibilities. Provide samples of work—particularly samples showing type treatments with or without illustration for use on jackets or covers, whether or not the designs were actually used; samples are kept on file and reviewed when future assignments come in. Check for most recent titles in bookstores. Artist supplies overlays for cover artwork. Free catalog.
Book Design: Assigns 20 freelance jobs/year. Pays by the project.

Jackets/Covers: Assigns 20 freelance design jobs/year. Pays by the project.
Text Illustrations: Pays by the project.

*EASTVIEW EDITIONS, INC., Box 783, Westfield NJ 07091. (201)964-9485. Manager: Mr. N. Glenn. Specializes in hardcover and paperback books on "all the arts"—fine arts, architecture, design, music, dance, antiques, hobbies, nature, history. Publishes 12 titles/year. Uses artists for book design, jacket/cover design and text illustrations. Also "looking for people who want cooperative publication."
First Contact & Terms: Send outline and description of work; "no samples that must be returned, only 'second generation' illustrations." Pays in royalties, fees.

THE ECONOMY COMPANY, 1200 N.W. 63rd St., Oklahoma City OK 73116. (405)840-1444. Art Director: William Mathison. Specializes in hardcover and paperback original and reprint textbooks in the language arts (K-8th grade). Publishes 2,000 titles; 75% require freelance illustrators. Also uses artists for occasional posters and other teaching aids.
First Contact & Terms: Works with 100 artists/year. Works only with published artists experienced in book illustration. Send brochure/flyer and samples or actual work; submit portfolio for review. Prefers color illustrations, either originals or tear sheets, as samples. Samples returned by SASE. Reports in 2 weeks. Works on assignment only. Provide brochure/flyer, samples and tear sheets to be kept on file for possible future assignments. No originals returned to artist at job's completion. Buys all rights.

EDC PUBLISHING, a division of Educational Development Corp., 8141 E. 44th St., Tulsa OK 74145. Vice President Marketing: Rich Howard. Specializes in highly colorful, quality books for children, preschool-12 years, on a variety of subjects. Publishes 50 titles/year. Uses artists for book design, jacket/cover design and illustration, and text illustration.
First Contact & Terms: Works with 7 freelance artists/year. Send samples to be kept on file. Prefers photostats as samples. Works on assignment only.

EFFECTIVE LEARNING INC., Box 2212, Mount Vernon NY 10550. (914)664-7944. Art Director: Rosemary Campion. Publishes paperback educational materials. Publishes 10 titles/year. Also uses artists for posters, direct mail brochure illustration, catalog and letterhead design. Negotiates pay.
First Contact & Terms: Send resume and samples; local and experienced artists only. SASE. Reports within 1 month. Works on assignment only. Reports back on whether to expect future assignments. Provide business card, flyer and tear sheet to be kept on file for possible future assignments. Originals not returned after completing assignment. "Samples supplied to artists we wish to consider." Buys all rights unless negotiated.
Book Design: Assigns 5-10 jobs/year. Uses artists for layout and type spec. Negotiates pay.
Jackets/Covers: Assigns 2 jobs/year. Buys color washes, opaque watercolors, gray opaques, b&w line drawings and washes. Negotiates pay.
Text Illustrations: Assigns 5 jobs/year. Buys opaque watercolors, color washes, gray opaques, b&w line drawings and washes. Negotiates pay.
Tips: Buys small number of cartoons for use as cover art in educational material. Negotiates pay.

EMC PUBLISHING, 300 York Ave., St. Paul MN 55101. (612)771-1555. Editor: Rosie Barry. Specializes in educational books and workbooks for schools and libraries. Uses artists for book design and illustration.
First Contact & Terms: Works with 1-2 freelance artists/year. Prefers local artists with book experience. Send query letter with resume; call for appointment. Do not send samples. Reports in 3 weeks. Works on assignment only. Provide resume, business card and samples to be kept on file for possible future assignments. Buys all rights. Negotiates payment by the project.

ENTELEK, Ward-Whidden House/The Hill, Box 1303, Portsmouth NH 03801. Editorial Director: Albert E. Hickey. Publishes paperback education originals; specializing in computer books and software. Clients: business, schools, colleges and individuals.
First Contact & Terms: Query with samples. Prefers previously published work as samples. SASE. Reports in 1 week. Free catalog. Works on assignment only. Provide brochure, flyer and tear sheets to be kept on file for possible future assignments. Pays $300, catalogs and direct mail brochures.
Needs: Works with 1 artist for ad illustrations; 1, advertising design; and 1, illustration, for use on 6 products/year. Especially needs cover designs/brochure designs.

ESPress, Inc., Box 55482, Washington DC 20011. (202)723-4578. President: Rev. Henry J. Nagorka. Specializes in nonfiction in the area of parapsychology, frontiers of science and holistic inner development. Publishes 4-8 titles/year; 5% require freelance designers, 10% require freelance illustrators.
First Contact & Terms: Works with 1-2 freelance artists/year. Send query letter with resume, samples

and tear sheets to be kept on file. Prefers slides or photographs as samples. Especially looks for clarity of concept, effective technique in realizing it and maturity/experience/authority when reviewing samples. Reports within 2 weeks. Works on assignment only. No originals returned to artist at job's completion. Considers project's budget when establishing payment. Buys first rights or reprint rights.

Jackets/Covers: Assigns 3-4 freelance design and 1-2 freelance illustration jobs/year. Pays by the project, $50-100 average.

Text Illustration: Assigns 1-2 freelance jobs/year. "Guidelines set for each book."

EXECUTIVE EDUCATION PRESS, Suite 204, 114 Liberty St., New York NY 10006. (212)620-4060. Publisher: Sally O. Smyth. Specializes in paperback originals on international trade. Publishes 1 title/year; requires freelance designers and illustrators; "over 100 illustrations in our most recent book."

First Contact & Terms: Works with 1 freelance artist/year. The artist must be able to meet in New York City. Send query letter with samples and tear sheets to be kept on file; call or write for appointment to show portfolio. Prefers "samples first we are too small to see many artists." Prefers photostats or photographs as samples. Samples not kept on file are returned only if requested. Reports only if interested. Works on assignment only. No originals returned to artist at job's completion. Considers complexity of project, project's budget, turnaround time and accurate fulfillment of requested assignment when establishing payment. Negotiates rights purchased.

Book Design: Works with 1 freelance artist/year. Pay must be negotiated according to complexity.

Jackets/Covers: Assigns 1 freelance design and 1 freelance illustration job/year. Pays by the project according to complexity.

Text Illustration: Assigns 1 book/year to freelancer. Prefers illustrations on plain paper suitable for opticopy camera mounting. Pays by the project according to complexity.

*THE FAMILY WORKSHOP INC., Box 1000, Bixby OK 74008. (918)366-6532. Art Director: Dale Crain. Book publisher of 14-15 titles/year plus 2 how-to columns weekly on woodworking, fabric work, crafts, etc.

First Contact & Terms: Works on assignment only. Send query letter with brochure, resume, business card and samples to be kept on file; call or write for appointment to show portfolio. Samples not filed are returned only if requested. Reports only if interested. Pays on acceptance and publication. Considers skill and experience of artist, salability of artwork, clients' preferences and rights purchased when establishing payment. Buys all rights.

Text Illustration: Assigns 5 freelance jobs/year for b&w and color cartoons (single, double and multi-panel), illustrations and spot drawings. Payment open.

FARRAR, STRAUS & GIROUX INC., 19 Union Square W., New York NY 10003. Contact: Dorris Janowitz. Publishes general fiction, nonfiction, biography and juveniles. Publishes 90 titles/year; 75% require freelance designers, 20% require freelance illustrators. Send samples.

Needs: Uses artists for jacket designs and inside illustrations. Pays $550, pre-separated 3-color jacket, and $600-750 full-color illustration, with type.

Book Design: Assigns 65 jobs/year. Requires castoff from mss, layouts, type spec sheets and follow through on proofs.

Tips: "Learn how to do the jacket typography as well as illustrate."

FATHOM PUBLISHING COMPANY, Box 821, Cordova AK 99574. (907)424-3116. President/Manager: Connie Taylor. Specializes in paperback originals, newsletters, flyers, and cards on commercial fishing, poetry and Alaska. Publishes 2 + titles/year; 100% require freelance illustrators.

First Contact & Terms: Works with 3 freelance artists/year. Prefers local artists. Send query letter with samples to be kept on file. Prefers photocopies as samples; no originals. Reports within 2 weeks. Works on assignment only. No originals returned at job's completion. Considers complexity of project and rights purchased when establishing payment. Negotiates rights purchased.

Text Illustration: Assigns 5-10 freelance jobs/year. Prefers pen & ink. Pays by the hour, $15 minimum; by the project, $10-65 average.

Tips: "Bring me an idea that I can sell to the public."

FOREIGN SERVICES RESEARCH INSTITUTE/WHEAT FORDERS, Box 6317, Washington DC 20015. (202)362-1588. Director: John E. Whiteford Boyle. Specializes in paperback originals of modern thought; nonfiction and philosophical poetry.

First Contact & Terms: Works with 2 freelance artists/year. Artist should understand the principles of book jacket design. Send query letter to be kept on file. Reports within 15 days. Works on assignment only. No originals returned, "they're needed for repeats. Artists should make their own copies." Considers project's budget when establishing payment. Buys first rights or reprint rights.

Book Design: Assigns 1-2 freelance jobs/year. Pays by hour, $25-35 average.

Jackets/Covers: Assigns 1-2 freelance design jobs/year. Pays by the project, $250 minimum.
Tips: "Submit samples of book jackets designed for and accepted by other clients. SASE, please."

C.J. FROMPOVICH PUBLICATIONS, RD 1, Chestnut Rd., Coopersburg PA 18036. (215)346-8461. Publisher: Catherine Frompovich. Specializes in self-help and technical books on nutrition, especially natural nutrition. Publishes 3 titles/year. Uses artists for jacket/cover design and illustration, text illustrations, games, cards, pamphlets.
First Contact & Terms: Works with 3 freelance artists/year. Send query letter with samples and tear sheets. Prefers finished work as samples; no sketches. Samples returned by SASE. Pays by the project.
Tips: "Do not solicit via telephone. Send a written resume and photocopies of some recently completed work."

FUNKY PUNKY AND CHIC, Box 601, Cooper Sta., New York NY 10276. (212)533-1772. Creative Director: R. Eugene Watlington. Specializes in paperback originals on poetry, celebrity photos and topics dealing with new wave, high fashion. Publishes 4 titles/year; 50% require freelance designers; 75% require freelance illustrators.
First Contact & Terms: Works with 20 freelance artists/year. Send query letter with business card and samples; write for appointment to show portfolio. Prefers photographs and slides as samples. Samples not kept on file are returned by SASE. Reports only if interested. No originals returned to artist at job's completion. Considers complexity of project and project's budget when establishing payment. Buys all rights.
Book Design: Assigns 1 freelance job/year. Pays by the project, $100-300 average.
Jackets/Covers: Assigns 3 freelance illustration jobs/year. Pays by the project, $50-75 average.
Text Illustration: Assigns 2 freelance jobs/year. Pays by the project, $50-75 average.

GEMINI SMITH INC., 5858 Desert View Dr., La Jolla CA 92037. (619)454-4321. Manager: Darlene La Madrid. Publishes oversize hardcover mainstream and visual books on art, history, animals and erotica. Publishes 2 books/year.
First Contact & Terms: Send resume; "local artists only, although New York references preferred." SASE. Reports within 2 weeks.
Book Design: Assigns 1-2 jobs/year. Uses artists for layout, paste-up and type spec. Pays $100-3,000/job.
Jackets/Covers: Assigns 2 jobs/year. Negotiates pay.
Tips: "Artists must have solid background in book design and production."

GENERAL HALL INC., 23-45 Corporal Kennedy St., Bayside NY 11360. Editor, for editorial and advertising work: Ravi Mehra. Publishes hardcover and paperback originals; college texts and supplementary materials. Publishes 4-6 titles/year; 100% require freelance designers, 10% require freelance illustrators.
First Contact & Terms: Local artists only. Query. SASE. Reports in 1-2 weeks. No originals returned to artist at job's completion. Works on assignment only. Provide brochure/flyer to be kept on file for future assignment. Artist provides overlays for color artwork. Buys all rights. Free catalog and artist's guidelines.
Book Design: Assigns 4-6 jobs/year. Uses artists for layout. Pays on job basis.
Jackets/Covers: Assigns 3-5 jobs/year. Pays by the project, $50-100 for design; $25-50 for illustration, b&w line drawings, washes, gray opaques and color washes.
Text Illustrations: Assigns 1-2 jobs/year. Pays by the project, $10-25, b&w line drawings, washes and gray opaques.

GENEVA DIVINITY SCHOOL PRESS, 708 Hamvasy Ln., Tyler TX 75701. (214)592-0620. Publisher: Michael R. Gilstrap. Specializes in hardcovers dealing with theological, Biblical, ecclesiological, and sociological topics from a Christian perspective. Publishes 4-6 titles/year; 100% require freelance designers.
First Contact & Terms: Artists should have 5 years of experience. Send query letter with brochure, business card, samples, tear sheets and references of other publishers for whom artist has worked to be kept on file. Prefers photographs and examples of designed covers as samples. Reports within 2 months. Works on assignment only. Considers complexity of project, skill and experience of artist, project's budget and turnaround time when establishing payment.
Jackets/Covers: Pays by the project, $250-1,500 average.

GMG PUBLISHING, 25 W. 43rd St., New York NY 10036. (212)354-8840. President: Gerald Galison. Specializes in hardcover and paperback originals on soft science and the arts. Publishes 5-10 titles/year.

First Contact & Terms: Local artists only. Send query letter with resume to be kept on file; call or write for appointment to show portfolio. Reports only if interested. Works on assignment only. Originals returned to artist at job's completion. Considers complexity of project, skill and experience of artist, project's budget, turnaround time and rights purchased when establishing payment. Negotiates rights purchased.
Book Design: Assigns 10 freelance jobs/year. Pays by the project, $500 average minimum.
Jackets/Covers: Assigns 10 freelance design jobs/year. Pays by the project, $500 average minimum.

GOLDEN WEST BOOKS, Box 80250, San Marino CA 91108. Contact: Donald Duke. Publishes Americana railroad, steamship and transportation history books. Publishes 5 titles/year; 45% require freelance illustrators.
First Contact & Terms: Buys first rights. Catalog available.
Needs: Uses artists for jacket design. Pays $250 minimum.

*GRAPHIC IMAGE PUBLICATIONS, Box 1740, La Jolla CA 92038. Assistant Art Director: Ann Ross. Specializes in hardcover, paperback originals, mass market romance, calendars. Publishes 5-10 titles/year.
First Contact & Terms: Works with 5-10 freelance artists/year, on assignment only. Send query letter with brochure or resume, business card and samples to be kept on file; write for appointment to show portfolio. Prefers 2-5 slides, photostats or photographs as samples. Samples not filed are returned by SASE. Reports within 3 months. Original work returned to artist unless all rights purchased. Considers complexity of the project, project's budget and rights purchased when establishing payment. Rights purchased vary according to project.
Book Design: Assigns 5-10 jobs/year. Pays by the hour, $10-50; by the project, $35-5,000.
Jackets/Covers: Assigns 2-5 freelance design and 2-5 freelance illustration jobs/year. Pays by the hour, $10-50; by the project, $35-50.
Text Illustration: Assigns 20-30 jobs/year. Pays by the hour, $10-50; by the project, $35-5,000.
Tips: Seeks "innovative designs. Artist should accept constructive criticism."

GREAT COMMISSION PUBLICATIONS, 7401 Old York Rd., Philadelphia PA 19126. (215)635-6515. Art Director: John Tolsma. Publishes paperback original educational and promotional materials for two Presbyterian denominations and one seminary.
First Contact & Term: Works with 6 freelance artists/year. Seeks experienced illustrators, usually local artists, but some may be from out-of-state. Works on assignment only. Send query letter with brochure, resume, business card and tear sheets to be kept on file. Material not filed is returned only if requested. Reports only if interested. No originals returned at job's completion. Considers complexity of project, skill and experience of artist, and the project's budget when establishing payment. Buys all rights.
Text Illustration: Assigns "many" jobs per year. Prefers stylized and humorous illustration, primarily figure work with some Biblical art; 1-, 2- and 4-color art. Pays by the project.

*THE GREEN TIGER PRESS, 1061 India St., San Diego CA 92101. Art Director: Sandra Darling. Specializes in original paperback gift and children's books with "imaginative plus unusual themes and illustrations." Publishes 8-10 titles/year.
First Contact & Terms: Works with 3-4 freelance artists/year. Works on assignment only. Send query letter with samples to be kept on file "only if it's work we're interested in." Write for artists' guidelines. Prefers slides and photographs as samples. Never send originals. Samples not filed are returned by SASE. Reports back to the artist within 8 weeks. Originals returned at job's completion. Considers project's budget and rights purchased when establishing payment. Rights purchased vary according to project.
Text Illustration: Assigns 3-6 freelance jobs/year. Payment is usually on a royalty basis.
Tips:"We are looking for artists who have a subtle style and imagination that reflect our aesthetic views."

*GUERNICA EDITIONS, Box 633, Station N.D.G., Montreal, Quebec H4A 3R1 Canada. President: Antonio D'Alfonso. Specializes in hardcover and paperback originals of poetry, juvenile and essays. Publishes 8 titles/year.
First Contact & Terms: Works with 5 local freelance artists/year. Works on assignment only. Send query letter with brochure to be kept on file; write for appointment to show portfolio. Prefers photographs as samples. Samples not filed are returned by SASE. Reports only if interested. Originals returned to artist at job's completion depending on royalty agreement. Buys all rights.
Book Design: Assigns 3 freelance jobs/year. Pays by the project, $200-500 average.
Jackets/Covers: Assigns 3 freelance design and 3 freelance illustration jobs/year. Pays by the project, $200-500 average.
Text Illustration: Assigns 1-2 freelance jobs/year. Pays by the project, royalties, $200 maximum.

HAPPINESS PRESS, LTD., 14351 Wycliff Way, Box ADD, Magalia CA 95954. Executive Editor: Jacques deLangre. Book publisher/audiovisual firm.
First Contact & Terms: "We will work with artists living anywhere; looking for excellent workmanship and insist artists meet our deadlines." Works on assignment only. Send query letter with samples (may be unpublished work) to be kept on file; original work and portfolios are not filed. Write for appointment to show portfolio and/or for art guidelines (optional). Prefers good photocopies, photostats, photographs or slides as samples. Samples not filed returned by SASE. Reports within 1 month. Pays by project, $25/spot illustration to $125/full page, average. Considers complexity of the project, book's budget and medium used when establishing payment. Buys first rights and reprint rights (for the same book title).
Needs: Works with 12 freelance artists/year. Uses artists for specific book illustrations—technical, food, gourmet, natural, precise methodology how-to for mechanical instructions. Especially important skills for artist to have are traditional precision at following layout, accurate renderings, pen & ink, scratchboard, litho crayon, notan, silhouettes and cartouches.
Tips: "Though we seek traditional skills and precision, we are open to expressive book illustrations that catch the imagination while retaining factual delineation of the subject. Send no more than six samples showing *your* style and approach. Use full figures, clothed or not, containing expression and body language. Indicate your forte and the special field you *love* to work in."

HAYDEN BOOK CO. INC., 10 Mulholland Dr., Hasbruck Heights NJ 07604. Art Director: Jim Bernard. Publishes computer technology and theory, electronics books. Publishes 100 titles/year.
First Contact & Terms: NJ/NY area artists only. Prefers "mostly printed samples—a few original composite sketches." Buys all rights. Originals returned to artist at job's completion. Works on assignment only. Samples returned by SASE; and reports back on future assignment possibilities. Provide business card to be kept on file for future assignments. Check for most recent titles in bookstores and "compare to competitive material."
Needs: Buys cover designs, illustrations, text designs, and special effects photography. Pays $450 minimum, cover design, plus mechanicals and art costs.
Tips: "Prefer trade book experience. *Don't* like to see 'school projects.'"

D.C. HEATH AND CO., Division of Raytheon, 125 Spring St., Lexington MA 02173. (617)862-6650. Contact: School Division Design Dept. Publishes elementary and secondary textbooks. (Separate College Division at same address also buys illustrations and cover designs.)
First Contact & Terms: Submit samples. Prefers copies or tear sheets which can be kept on file. May show portfolio in person by appointment. Provide flyer, tear sheet or brochure to be kept on file for future assignments. (Photocopies OK.) Buys textbook rights. Originals usually returned.
Needs: Uses artists for inside illustrations and cover design. "Must be relevant to textbook subject and grade level." Occasionally uses freelance book designers. "Recent major el/hi series have used thousands of 4-color cartoon-type illustrations, as well as realistic scientific paintings, and a variety of 'story' pictures for reading books; also black line work for workbooks and duplicating masters." Payment is usually by project, and varies greatly, "but is competitive with other textbook publishers."

*HEMKUNT PRESS, A-78 Naraina Indl. Area Ph.I, New Delhi 110028 India. Phone: 505079. Director: Mr. G.P. Singh. Specializes in educational textbooks, illustrated general books for children and adults. Subjects include religion and history. Publishes 30-50 titles/year.
First Contact & Terms: Works with 7-8 freelance artists/year. Works on assignment only. Send query letter with resume and samples to be kept on file. Prefers photographs and tear sheets as samples. Samples not filed are not returned. Report only if interested. Original not returned to artist. Considers complexity of the project, skill and experience of artist and project's budget when establishing payment. Buys all rights.
Book Design: Assigns 40-50 titles/year. Payment varies from job to job.
Jackets/Covers: Assigns 30-40 freelance design jobs/year. Payment varies.
Text Illustration: Assigns 30-40 jobs/year. Pays by the project, $50-600.

T. EMMETT HENDERSON, PUBLISHER, 130 W. Main St., Middletown NY 10940. (914)343-1038. Contact: T. Emmett Henderson. Publishes hardcover and paperback local history, American Indian, archaeology, and genealogy originals and reprints. Publishes 2-3 titles/year; 100% require freelance designers, 100% require freelance illustrators. Also assigns 5 advertising jobs/year; pays $10 minimum.
First Contact & Terms: Query. No work returned. Reports in 4 weeks. Buys book rights. Originals returned to artist at job's completion. Works on assignment only. Provide resume to be kept on file for future assignments. Check for most recent titles in bookstores. Artist supplies overlays for cover artwork. No advance. No pay for unused assigned work.

Book Design: Assigns 2-4 jobs/year. Uses artists for cover art work, some text illustration. Prefers representational style.
Jackets/Covers: Buys 2-4/year. Uses representational art. Pays $20 minimum, b&w line drawings and color-separated work.
Text Illustrations: Pays $10 minimum, b&w. Buys 5-15 cartoons/year. Uses cartoons as chapter headings. Pays $5-12 minimum, b&w.

HOLDEN-DAY INC., 4432 Telegraph Ave., Oakland CA 94609. (415)428-9400. Production Coordinator: Lisa Curet. Publishes hardcover and paperback college and graduate level textbooks in mathematics, computers, statistics, business management, chemistry and physics. Publishes 10-12 titles/year. Query with resume and previously published work or arrange interview to show portfolio. SASE. Reports in 2 weeks. Buys all rights.
Book Design: Assigns 8 jobs/year. Uses artists for type spec. Negotiates pay.
Jackets/Covers: Assigns 8 jobs/year. Negotiates pay.
Text Illustrations: Assigns 8 jobs/year. Buys b&w line drawings. Negotiates pay.

HOLIDAY HOUSE, 18 E. 53rd St., New York NY 10022. (212)688-0085. Editor: Margery Cuyler. Publishes hardcover originals for juveniles; fiction, nature, nonfiction and picture books. Publishes 35 titles/year.
First Contact & Terms: Arrange interview to show portfolio to art director, David Rogers. Must have samples of color separations. SASE. Buys all rights. Originals returned at job's completion. Works on assignment only. Provide flyer and brochure to be kept on file for future assignments. Check for most recent titles in bookstores. Artist supplies overlays for cover artwork and inside illustrations. Negotiates pay. Free catalog.
Jackets/Covers: Assigns 5-10 jobs/year. Uses mostly "young adult-oriented themes (humor and problems)." Buys full-color and color-separated work.
Text Illustrations: Assigns 5-10 jobs/year. Uses illustrations for non-fiction and picture books. Buys color-separated work and b&w line drawings. Offers advance.

HOLLOWAY HOUSE PUBLISHING COMPANY, 8060 Melrose Ave., Los Angeles CA 90046. (213)653-8060. President: Ralph Weinstock. Specializes in paperbacks directed to the black reader, i.e., romance books, biographies, fiction, nonfiction, gambling-game books. Publishes 30-50 titles/year.
First Contact & Terms: Works with 6-10 freelance artists/year. Professional artists only. Works on assignment only. Send query letter with resume and samples to be kept on file. Call for appointment to show portfolio. Accepts slides, photostats, photographs or tear sheets as samples. Samples not filed are returned by SASE only if requested. Reports back only if interested. Considers project's budget when establishing payment. Rights purchased vary according to project.
Needs: Assigns 25-50 book design and jacket/cover illustration jobs/year.

HOMESTEAD PUBLISHING, Box 193, Moose WY 83012. Art Director: Carl Schreier. Specializes in hardcover and paperback originals of nonfiction, natural history, Western art and general Western regional literature. Publishes 3 + titles/year.
First Contact & Terms: Works with 16 freelance artists/year. Works on assignment only. Send query letter with samples to be kept on file or write for appointment to show portfolio. Prefers to receive as samples "examples of past work, if available (such as published books or illustrations used in magazines, etc.). For color work, slides are suitable; for b&w technical pen, photostats. And one piece of original artwork which can be returned." Samples not filed are returned by SASE only if requested. Reports within 10 days. No original work returned after job's completion. Considers complexity of the project, skill and experience of artist, project's budget and turnaround time when establishing payment. Rights purchased vary according to project.
Book Design: Assigns 6 freelance jobs/year. Pays by the project, $50-3,500 average.
Jackets/Covers: Assigns 2 freelance design and 4 freelance illustration jobs/year. Pays by the project, $50-3,500 average.
Text Illustration: Assigns 26 freelance jobs/year. Prefers technical pen illustrations, maps (using airbrush, overlays, etc.), watercolor illustrations for children's books, and calligraphy for titles. Pays by the hour, $5-20 average; by the project, $50-3,500 average.
Tips: "We are using more graphic, contemporary designs."

HUMAN KINETICS PUBLISHERS, Box 5076, Champaign IL 61820. Production Director: Sara Chilton. Hardcover and paperback originals; trade, scholarly, textbooks in sports and sports science. Imprints: Human Kinetics; Leisure Press; Life Enhancement Publications. Publisher of YMCA of the USA materials. Publishes 75 titles/year; 90% require freelance illustrators for covers; 15% for interior art.

First Contact & Terms: Works with 10 freelance artists/year. Looking for quality and reasonable cost. Send query letter with brochure on samples to be kept on file; write for appointment to show portfolio. Prefers photostats or photos as samples. Works on assignment only. Considers complexity of project, skill and experience of artist, project's budget and turnaround time when establishing payment. Buys all rights.
Jackets/Covers: Pays by the hour, $15-35 average.
Text Illustration: Prefers very graphic pen & ink. Pays by the hour, $15-35 average; by the project, $10 minimum/illustration. Artwork includes medical illustration.
Tips: "Don't call endlessly. First send a letter, then use a follow-up call. If we arrange to meet, come with a good variety of work that shows full range of talents."

HUMANICS LIMITED, Suite 201, 1389 W. Peachtree St., Atlanta GA 30309. (404)874-2176. Editor: Diane M. Campbell. Specializes in original paperback textbooks on early childhood education and development. Publishes 10 titles/year. Also uses artists for advertising, direct mail pieces, catalogs, posters.
First Contact & Terms: Works with 5 freelance artists/year. Prefers local artists. Send query letter with resume and business card to be kept on file. Call or write for appointment to show portfolio. Prefers line drawings, finished work, published ads and brochures as samples. Samples returned by SASE. Reports witin 1 week. Works on assignment only. No originals returnedafter job's completion. Buys all rights.
Book Design: Assigns 10 freelance jobs/year. Pays by the job; "we solicit bids on jobs and give the job to the lowest bidder."
Jackets/Covers: Assigns 10 design and 10 illustration jobs/year. Prefers b&w line drawings and mechanical designs suitable for PMS colors. Pays for illustration by the job.
Text Illustrations: Assigns 10 jobs/year. Prefers line illustrations. Pays by the job; "we negotiate a per illustration rate."

CARL HUNGNESS PUBLISHING, Box 24308, Speedway IN 46224. (317)244-4792. Editorial Director: Carl Hungness. Publishes hardcover automotive originals. Publishes 2-4 titles/year. Query with samples. SASE. Reports in 2 weeks. Offers $100 advance. Buys book, one-time or all rights. No pay for unused assigned work. Free catalog.

HURTIG PUBLISHERS LTD., 10560 105th St., Edmonton, Alberta T5H 2W7 Canada. (403)426-2359. Editor-in-Chief: Elizabeth Munroe. Specializes in hardcover and paperback originals of nonfiction, primarily on Canadian-oriented topics. Publishes 10-20 titles/year.
First Contact & Terms: Artists must have "considerable experience and be based in Canada." Send query letter to be kept on file; "almost all work is specially commissioned from current sources." Reports within 3 months. Considers complexity of the project, skill and experience of artist, project's budget, turnaround time and rights purchased when establishing payment. Rights purchased vary according to project.

ILLUMINATI, Suite 203, 8812 W. Pico Blvd., Los Angeles CA 90035. Art Director: P. Schneidre. Specializes in hardcover, paperbound and limited editions of literature and art. Publishes 25 titles/year.
First Contact & Terms: Works with 10 freelance artists/year. Send samples to be kept on file. Prefers photocopies as samples. Samples returned by SASE. Reports within 2 weeks. Originals returned to artist after job's completion. Buys first rights.
Jackets/Covers: Assigns 6 design and 6 illustration jobs/year. Prefers b&w artwork. Pays for illustration by the project, $50 minimum.

INSTITUTE FOR THE STUDY OF HUMAN ISSUES (ISHI PUBLICATIONS), 210 S. 13th St., Philadelphia PA 19107. (215)732-9729. Managing Editor: Brad Fisher. Marketing Director: Edward A. Jutkowitz. Publishes hardcover and paperback political science, anthropology, folklore, drug studies, and history—originals and paperback reprints. Publishes 20 titles/year. Uses artists for dust jackets, covers, maps, flowcharts, graphs, catalogs and advertising flyers. Assigns 20-30 freelance jobs/year.
First Contact & Terms: Prefers local artists. Especially likes artists with "directly related experience in needed areas and whose estimated charges are appropriate to the job in question. Most jobs involve jacket design and mechanicals; text art limited. Mostly black and white; some 2-color, little 4-color work." Query with samples. Reports in 2 weeks. Buys all rights. No originals returned to artist at job's completion. Works on assignment only. Samples returned by SASE. Provide resume and samples to be kept on file for future assignments. Artist supplies overlays for cover artwork and advertising art. Pays promised fee for unused assigned work. Free catalog.
Jackets/Covers: Assigns approximately 20 freelance design and illustration jobs/year. Prefers line drawings or mezzotint and screened photos for cover illustrations. Pays by the job, $100-200 average; $250-350 for jacket mechanicals.
Text Illustrations: Assigns approximately 10 freelance jobs/year. Prefers line art. Pays by the job, $50-

250 average. Includes "maps, charts, graphs, other simple line art and labeling."
Tips: "In the nonfiction area the new emphasis is on simplicity of design; the use of decorative typefaces and strong color combinations is very much in evidence."

JANUS BOOK PUBLISHERS, 2501 Industrial Pkwy. W., Hayward CA 94545. (415)785-9625 or (415)887-7070. Production Manager: Carol Gee. Publishes remedial reading materials and soft-cover workbooks for high school and basic adult education. Publishes 25 titles/year.
First Contact & Terms: Works on assignment only. Send samples or arrange interview to show portfolio; prefers local artists. SASE. Reports within 3 weeks. Buys various rights. Provide resume and "photocopies of samples" to be kept on file for future assignments. Artist supplies overlays for 2-color cover artwork; sometimes for advertising art. Free catalog. Also uses artists for catalog design. Pays $15-20/hour.
Book Design: Assigns 10 jobs/year. Layout done inhouse. Offers advance "upon completion of acceptable roughs."
Jackets/Covers: Uses "2-color, very direct and very simple designs" Pays for design and illustration by the project, $800-1,000 average.
Text Illustrations: Assigns 12-15 jobs/year. Especially seeks realistic drawings. Pays $40-50 for ¼ or ½-page spot drawings; also pays by the project, $50 (single drawing)-2,400 (entire book). Buys b&w line drawings and washes. Offers advance "upon completion of acceptable roughs." Also uses a realistic type of cartoon. "Our 'cartoons' are used to illustrate meaning of words and phrases, either line or halftone wash work. Artist is given specifications, and asked to supply rough, revised, rough and finished art." Pays $25, b&w.
Tips: "Clear, concise, figure work with emphasis on minority groups (black, Chicano, Asian). Simple and direct, no fussy detail. Beginners should show their work to anyone who will take the time to look at it. Keep trying."

JUDSON PRESS, American Baptist Churches USA, Board of Educational Ministries, Publishing Division, Valley Forge PA 19481. Assistant Production Manager: David E. Monyer. Specializes in paperbacks on religious themes (inspirational, Christian education, church administration, missions). Publishes 40 titles/year; 90% require freelance designers.
First Contact & Terms: Works with 6 or more freelance artists/year. Artists with book cover experience only. Send query letter, brochure/flyer, resume and samples to be kept on file. Prefers examples of book cover designs as samples. Samples not kept on file are returned by SASE. "We don't report on acceptance or rejection, but keep samples on file." Works on assignment only. No originals returned to artist at job's completion.
Jackets/Covers: Assigns 25-30 design jobs/year. Prefers 2-color, usual bold graphics, title dominant, for cover designs. Pays by the job, $300-400 average; "We pay for type and stats."
Tips: "Stay with bold graphics, up-to-date typography."

*KAR-BEN COPIES, INC., 6800 Tildenwood Ln., Rockville MD 20852. Editor: Madeline Wikler. Specializes in hardcovers and paperbacks on juvenile Judaica. Publishes 8 titles/year.
First Contact & Terms: Works with 3 freelance artists/year. Send query letter with samples to be kept on file or returned. Prefers photostats or tear sheets as samples. Samples not filed are returned by SASE. Reports within 2 weeks only by SASE. Originals returned after job's completion. Considers skill and experience of artist and turnaround time when establishing payment. Buys all rights.
Text Illustration: Assigns 3 jobs/year. Pays by the project, $500-1,500 average, or royalty.

*KIDS CAN PRESS, 585½ Bloor St. W, Toronto, Ontario M6G 1K5 Canada. (416)534-3141. Editor: Susan Cravit. Specializes in hardcover and paperback originals for juveniles. Publishes 8 titles/year.
First Contact & Terms: Works with 8 freelance arists/year. Toronto artists only. Works on assignment only. Send query letter with samples to be kept on file. Call or write for appointment to show portfolio. Prefers photographs or tear sheets as samples. Samples not filed are returned by SASE and only by request. Does not report back to artist. Original work returned at job's completion. Considers complexity of the project, skill and experience of artist, project's budget, turnaround time and rights purchased when establishing payment. Buys all rights.
Book Design: Assigns 8 jobs/year.

KNEES PAPERBACK PUBLISHING CO., 4115 Marshall St., Dallas TX 75210. (214)948-3613. Managing Editor: Dorothy J. Watkins. Specializes in paperback originals on poetry, children's and prose books. Publishes 2 titles/year; 15% require freelance designers; 15% require freelance illustrators.
First Contact & Terms: Works with 2 freelance artists/year. Local artists only. Send query letter with business card to be kept on file. Prefers slides as samples. Reports within 2 weeks. Works on assignment only. No originals returned to artist at job's completion. Considers complexity of project, and skill and

experience of artist when establishing payment. Buys one-time rights or negotiates.
Book Design: Assigns 7 freelance jobs/year. Pays by the hour, the project or negotiates.
Tips: Artists should "always adhere to the given schedule." Current trends in the field are toward "more abstract design." Especially looks for "creativity, form and projection" when reviewing samples.

*LACE PUBLICATIONS, INC., Box 10037, Denver CO 80210-0037. Managing Editor: Artemis OakGrove. Specializes in paperbacks of lesbian fiction. Publishes 5 titles/year.
First Contact & Terms: Works with 10-15 freelance artists/year. Lesbians or sexually sensitive women only. Works on assignment only. Send query letter with resume and samples to be kept on file except for "the ones I don't like." Prefers b&w photographs or photocopies as samples. Samples not filed are returned by SASE. Reports within 1 month. Original work returned after the job's completion; cover art returned only if requested. Considers complexity of the project, skill and experience of artist and project's budget when establishing payment. Rights purchased vary according to project; all rights purchased on cover art.
Jackets/Covers: Assigns 5 freelance design and varying number of freelance illustration jobs/year. Pays by the project, $75 minimum.

DAVID S. LAKE PUBLISHER INC., (formerly Fearon/Pitman Publishing Inc.,) 19 Davis Dr., Belmont CA 94002. Director of Design: Eleanor Mennick. Publishes special education, teacher-aid, professional and management training books. Query.
Covers and Text Illustrations: Uses artists for 1, 2 and 4-color work. Also needs experienced book designers and production people.

LAKE VIEW PRESS, Box 578279, Chicago IL 60657. Director: Paul Elitzik. Specializes in hardcover and paperback nonfiction originals on film and political science. Publishes 4-6 titles/year; 100% require freelance designers.
First Contact & Terms: Works with 3 freelance artists/year. Prefers artists with Chicago residence and experience in book design or printing. Send query letter with resume to be kept on file. Reports only if interested. Works on assignment only. Originals returned to artist at job's completion. Considers project's budget when establishing payment. Buys all rights.
Book Design: Assigns 4-6 freelance jobs/year. Pays by the project, $100-300 average.
Jackets/Covers: Assigns 4 freelance design jobs/year. Pays by the project, $100-300 average.

*LARANMARK PRESS, 220 Main St., Box 253, Neshkoro WI 54960. (414)293-4377. Art Director: Peggy Eagan. Specializes in hardcover, tradesize paperback (5½x8½) and leather-bound originals and reprints on adventure, mystery, occult, romance and horror fiction; also nonfiction. Published 14 titles in 1984, 24 in 1985; anticipates 36 in 1986.
First Contact & Terms: Works with 3 freelance artists/year. "Would like to work with more." Buys art solicited and unsolicited. Send query letter with brochure, resume and samples to be kept on file. Prefers slides or good quality photocopies as samples. Photos and tearsheets are acceptable. "Never send originals." Samples not filed are returned by SASE. Reports within 1 month. Originals not returned to artist, unless special arrangements are made in advance. Considers complexity of the project, skill and experience of artist, project's budget, turnaround time and rights purchased when establishing payment. Rights purchased vary according to project.
Jackets/Covers: Assigns 1 freelance design and 3 freelance illustration jobs/year. Pays by the project. $150-1,000.
Text Illustration: Assigns 1 job/year. Prefers pen & ink drawings. Pays by the project.
Tips: "I would be happy to look at anyone's portfolio. Graphic design and illustration experience is helpful, of course, but limiting. I would like to hear from artists with fresh ideas for calendars. We are thinking of expanding into this field. We are making a 'maiden voyage' into the calendar art field with a 'Dragon' calendar of pen & ink drawings with soft pastel coloring."

LITTLE, BROWN AND COMPANY ADULT TRADE DIVISION, 34 Beacon St., Boston MA 02106. (617)227-0730. Publishes mainstream hardcover originals. Publishes 125 titles/year.
First Contact & Terms: Send samples or arrange interview to show portfolio. Reports within 2-3 weeks. Buys first and reprint rights. "We have no artist's guidelines but will gladly answer questions."
Jackets/Covers: Assigns 100 jobs/year. Buys graphic design, color washes, opaque watercolors, gray opaques, oils, b&w line drawings and washes. Negotiates pay.

LLEWELLYN PUBLICATIONS, Box 64383, St. Paul MN 55164. Art Director: Terry Buske. Publishes metaphysical, astrology and New Age books. Works with at least 6 freelance artists/year. Uses artists for book cover designs and inside art, color and b&w.

First Contact & Terms: Send query letter with samples to be kept on file. No preference regarding types of samples, but "must be professionally submitted. No roughs, fragments or photocopies of other than excellent quality. Do not send actual artwork." Samples not kept on file are returned by SASE only if requested. Reports within 2 weeks after receipt of submission. Works on assigment only. Negotiates payment. Considers project's budget, skill and experience of artist and rights purchased when establishing payment. Negotiates rights purchased.

Tips: "People expect more of a high-tech, photo realistic or refined look for the product. Where amateurish covers were acceptable before on magic and astrology books, they are not acceptable to the public now. We are interested in artists who express our themes in more general terms reaching a broad audience. We are interested in realistic (photo-realism) art." Especially looks for "technique and professionalism" in artist's work. Uses many airbrush paintings.

LODESTAR BOOKS, division of E.P. Dutton, 2 Park Ave., New York NY 10016. (212)725-1818. Associate Editor: Rosemary Brosnan. Publishes young adult fiction (10-14 and 12-16 years) and nonfiction hardcovers, and fiction for ages 9-11 years. "No picture books." Publishes 20-25 titles/year.
First Contact & Terms: Query with samples or arrange interview. Especially looks for "knowledge of book requirements, previous jackets, good color, strong design and ability to draw people" when reviewing samples. SASE. Prefers to buy all rights.
Jackets/Covers: Assigns approximately 15 jackets/year. Pays $600 minimum, color.
Tips: In young adult fiction, there is a trend toward "covers that are more realistic with the focus on one or two characters. In nonfiction, strong, simple graphic design, often utilizing a photograph. Two color jackets are popular; occasionally full-color is used."

McGRAW HILL PUBLISHING, College Division, 1221 6th Ave., New York NY 10020. Art Director, College and University Division: Merrill Haber. Submit samples.
Needs: Uses artists for book and jacket design; technical, medical and biological illustrations.

McGRAW-HILL RYERSON LIMITED, 330 Progress Ave., Scarborough, Ontario M1P 2Z5 Canada. (416)293-1911. Art Supervisor: Dan Kewley. Publishes educational books for school and college levels, and professional and reference books. Works with 10 freelance artists/year. Uses artists for book production, paste-up, line illustrations (technical and interpretive); medical, biology and science text illustration; some cover designs.
First Contact & Terms: Local artists only with experience in publishing. Send resume, business card and samples to be kept on file; call for appointment to show portfolio. Prefers photostats or photocopies as samples. Especially looks for "flexibility of style, application to company needs, and quality of work and of presentation" when reviewing samples. Reports only if interested. Works on assignment only. Considers complexity and quantity of project, how work will be used, and turnaround time when establishing payment.
Tips: "We require accurate, high quality work which meets our company standards."

MACMILLAN PUBLISHING CO., School Division, 866 Third Ave., New York NY 10022. (212)702-7925. Design Director: Zlata Paces. Publishes hardcover and auxiliary originals and reprints for elementary and high schools. Publishes 250 titles/year; 30% of which require freelance designers; 80% use freelance illustrators.
First Contact & Terms: Send letter of inquiry, resume and samples. Prefers tear sheets, stats, color photocopies, etc. as samples or drop off portfolio (overnight). Samples will be kept on file for future reference unless accompanied by SASE. Works on assignment only. Buys one-time rights. Originals returned to artist at job's completion.
Book Design: Assigns 10 jobs/year. Uses freelance artists for layout and type specs. Pays by the hour, $10-15 average; also pays by the day.
Jackets/Covers: Assigns 30 jobs/year. Pays for illustration by the project; $200-400 average.
Text Illustrations: Assigns 800-1,500 jobs/year. Pays by the project, "depends on assignment."

*MERCURY PRINTING CO., 15126 Downey Ave., Paramount CA 90723. (213)531-4550. Vice President: Allen B. Hughes. Specializes in legal books. Publishes 4 titles/year.
First Contact & Terms: Works with 1 local freelance artist/year on assignment only. Send query letter with resume to be kept on file; call for appointment to show portfolio. Prefers tear sheets as samples. Samples not filed are returned by SASE. Reports only if interested. Originals returned to artist at job's completion. Considers project's budget when establishing payment. Buys all rights.

*METAMORPHOUS PRESS, Suite 67, 4 SW Touchstone, Box 1712, Lake Oswego OR 97034. (503)635-6709. Publisher: Victor Roberge. Specializes in hardcover and paperback originals, medical/science fiction. "We are a general book publisher for a general audience in North America." Publishes at least 12 titles/year.

First Contact & Terms: Works with a varying number of freelance artists/year. "We're interested in what an artist can do for us—not experience with others." Works on assignment only. Send query letter with brochure, business card and samples to be kept on file. Prefers photostats, photographs, and tear sheets as samples. Samples not filed are: returned by SASE. Reports within a few days usually. Originals returned to artist at job's completion if requested. Considers complexity of the project and project's budget when establishing payment. Rights purchased vary according to project.
Book Design: Rarely assigns freelance jobs. "We negotiate payment on an individual basis according to project."
Jackets/Covers: Will possibly assign 5-10 jobs in both freelance design and freelance illustration this year. Payment would vary as to project and budget.
Text Illustration: Assigns 5-10 freelance jobs/year. Payment varies as to project and budget.

MILADY PUBLISHING CORP., 3839 White Plains Rd., Bronx, New York NY 10467. (800)223-8055. Editor: Miriam Helbok. Publishes textbooks and audiovisual aids for vocational schools.
First Contact & Terms: Works on assignment only. Send query letter with samples to be kept on file; write for appointment to show portfolio. Prefers photostats as samples. Samples not filed are returned by SASE. Reports only if interested. Pays by the hour, $5 minimum; by the project depending on nature of project and length of time needed for completion. Considers complexity of the project, client's budget and skill and experience of artist when establishing payment. Buys all rights. Catalog costs $1.
Needs: Works with 3 freelance artists/year during overloads. Especially important are ability to produce accurate and neat mechanicals and clean line illustrations. Uses technical and "fashion features and hairstyles" illustrations.
Tips: "Build up skills in illustrating hands and hair."

MINNE HA! HA!, Box 14009, Minneapolis MN 55414. Editor/Publisher: Lance Anger. Specializes in paperback originals on political humor, cartoons and cartooning. Publishes 1-3 titles/year.
First Contact & Terms: Works with 3-10 freelance artists/year. Work must be of good quality. Send query letter with brochure, resume, business card, samples and tear sheets to be kept on file; write for appointment to show portfolio. Prefers photocopies as samples which do not have to be returned. Samples not kept on file are not returned. Reports only if interested. Originals returned to artist at job's completion. Considers project's budget and cooperative profit-sharing when establishing payment. Buys one-time rights.
Book Design: Assigns 1-3 freelance jobs/year. Pay is negotiable.
Jackets/Covers: Assigns 1-3 freelance design jobs/year.
Text Illustration: Assigns 1-3 freelance jobs/year.
Tips: "We are using more art integrated with words/text."

BARRY LEONARD STEFFAN MIRENBURG, DESIGN, 413 City Island Ave., New York NY 10064. Design Director: Barry L.S. Mirenburg. Specializes in hardcover and paperback nonfiction originals. Publishes 10 titles/year; 20% require freelance designers; 80% require freelance illustrators. Also uses artists for posters, annual reports, graphic design, trademarks, etc.
First Contact & Terms: Works with 12 freelance artists/year. Send brochure/flyer or resume and samples; samples not returned. Works on assignment only; sometimes reports back whether to expect possible future assignments. Provide resume, business card, brochure/flyer, samples and tear sheets to be kept on file for possible future assignments. Negotiates rights purchased.
Book Design: Assigns 12 jobs/year. Uses artists for layout, type spec and mechanicals. Pays "going rates."
Jackets/Covers: Assigns 20% to freelance designers and 80% of needs to freelance illustrators. Prefers b&w line drawings, paintings, color washes, gray opaques; no cartoon style. Payment varies.
Text Illustrations: Number of jobs assigned/year varies. Prefers b&w line drawings, paintings, color washes, gray opaques; no cartoon style. Payment varies.

MODERN CURRICULUM PRESS, 13900 Prospect Rd., Cleveland OH 44136. (216)238-2222. Art Director: John K. Crum. Specializes in supplemental text books. Publishes 100 titles/year. Also uses local artists for advertising and mechanicals.
First Contact & Terms: All freelance. Send resume and samples to be kept on file. Prefers drawings of various aged children and animals as samples. Samples not kept on file are returned by SASE. Reports within 2-3 weeks. Works on assignment only. Buys all rights.
Book Design: Assigns 2-3 freelance jobs/year. Uses artists for layout, mechanicals, type specs. Pays by the job.
Jackets/Covers: Pays by the job.
Text Illustrations: Prefers real life themes. Pays by the job. Artwork includes medical illustration.

*MOJAVE BOOKS, 7118 Canby, Reseda CA 91335. (213)342-3403. Editorial Director: Judith Bazol. Art Director: Zvi Erez. Publishes hardcover and paperback general, poetry and some juvenile originals. Publishes 35-40 titles/year.
First Contact & Terms: Query with resume and samples. SASE. Reports in 2 weeks. Buys all rights. No originals returned to artist at job's completion. Works on assignment only. Reports back to artist on future assignment possibilities. Provide resume and business card to be kept on file for future assignments. Artist supplies overlays for cover artwork. No advance. Pays promised fee for unused assigned work. Free catalog.
Jackets/Covers: Buys 10-15/year. Minimum payment: $100, b&w; $150, color.
Text Illustrations: Buys 6-10/year. Pays $25 minimum, b&w and color.

*MONUMENT PRESS, 513 S. Rosemont St., Dallas TX 75208. (214)948-7001. Editor: Dr. Aruthur Ide. Estab. 1984. Specializes in books on women—historical and scholarly. Publishes 5 titles/year.
First Contact & Terms: Works with 3 freelance artists/year. Send query letter with samples. Write for appointment to show portfolio. Prefers photos and tear sheets as samples. Samples not filed are returned by SASE. Reports within 3 weeks. Considers complexity of the project, skill and experience of artist, project's budget, turnaround time and rights purchased when establishing payment. Negotiates rights purchased.
Book Design: Assigns 5 jobs/year. Pays by the project, up to $5,000 maximum.
Jackets/Covers: Assigns 5 freelance design and 5 freelance illustration jobs/year. Pays by the project, up to $5,000 maximum.
Text Illustration: Assigns 5 titles/year. Pays by the project, up to $500 maximum.

*MOSAIC PRESS—PUBLISHERS, Box 1032, Oakville, Ontario Canada. Art Director: Douglas Frank. Specializes in hardcover, paperback and limited edition books on literature, arts, music, architecture, academics and international studies; also fiction. Publishes 25 titles/year.
First Contact & Terms: Works with 5 freelance artists/year. Seeks local, young artists. Works on assignment basis only. Send query letter with brochure and samples to be kept on file. Prefers slides and tear sheets as samples. Samples not filed are returned if accompanied by SASE. Reports only if interested. Original work not returned to artist. Considers project's budget when establishing payment. Purchases all rights.
Book Design: Assigns 5 job/year. Payment negotiable by the project.
Jackets/Covers: Assigns 5 freelance design and 1 freelance illustration jobs/year. Payment negotiated by the project.
Text Illustration: Assigns 2 jobs/year. Payment negotiated by the project.

MOTT MEDIA INC., PUBLISHERS, 1000 E. Huron, Milford MI 48042. Contact: Leonard G. Goss or Joyce Bohn. Publishes hardcover and paperback Christian books and textbooks. Publishes 20-25 titles/year. Also uses artists for posters and mailables.
First Contact & Terms: Query with samples or tear sheets (originals not necessary) or contact by agent. Reports in 1 month. SASE. Buys all rights. No originals returned to artist at job's completion. Works on assignment only. Reports back on future assignment possiblities. Provide resume, flyer, tear sheet and letter of inquiry to be kept on file for possible future assignments. Artist supplies all color overlays. Pays ½ on acceptance of sketch and ½ on submission of finished art. Free catalog.
Needs: Special need for book cover design, and internal illustration for children's books. Assigns 20-25 book design jobs/year. Minimum payment: $400 + for complete cover art and mechanicals; $150 for inside b&w sketch.

JOHN MUIR PUBLICATIONS, Box 613, Santa Fe NM 87501. (505)982-4078. President: Ken Luboff. Specializes in paperback how-to manuals. "We specialize in auto repair manuals and are always actively looking for new illustrations in that field." Publishes 6-8 titles/year.
First Contact & Terms: Works with 5-6 freelance artists/year. Send query letter with resume and samples to be kept on file; write for appointment to show portfolio. Accepts any type of sample "as long as it's professionally presented." Samples not filed are returned by SASE. Reports back within months; "it depends on how harried our schedule is at the time." Originals returned at job's completion. Considers complexity of the project, skill and experience of artist, project's budget, turnaround time and rights purchased when establishing payment. Buys all rights.
Jackets/Covers: Assigns 6-8 freelance design and freelance illustration jobs/year. Negotiates payment.
Text Illustration: Assigns 6-8 freelance jobs/year. Usually prefers pen & ink. Negotiates payment.

NELSON-HALL INC., 111 N. Canal St., Chicago IL 60606. Vice President: Stephen A. Ferrara. Publishes 85 titles/year; 100% require freelance designers, 50% require freelance illustrators. Also uses artists for technical illustration, advertising layout and catalog illustration.

First Contact & Terms: Submit resume and photocopies. Buys all rights. Pays on acceptance. Catalog available.
Book Design: Assigns 200 jobs/year.
Jacket/Covers: Pays $200, jacket design plus type.

*NEW SOCIETY PUBLISHERS, 4722 Baltimore Ave., Philadelphia PA 19143. (215)726-6543. Production Director: Nina Huizinga. Specializes in hardcover and paperback originals and reprints on nonviolent social change. Publishes 10 titles/year.
First Contact & Terms: Works with 4 freelance artists/year. Works on assignment only. Send query letter with samples to be kept on file. Call for appointment to show portfolio. Prefers photostats and photographs as samples. Samples not filed are returned only by SASE. Reports only if interested. Original work may or may not be returned to the artist. Considers complexity of the project, project's budget and rights purchased when establishing payment. Negotiates rights purchased.
Book Design: Usually "done in-house with occasional exceptions." Pays by the hour, $5-100.
Jackets/Covers: Assigns 4-5 freelance design jobs/year. Pays by the project, $50 for 3 sketches. "If one is accepted then $150 for completed mechanicals. Additional must be negotiated—normally on 2-color jobs only.
Text Illustration: Assigns 1-2 jobs/year. Prefers pen & ink line drawings. Pays by the hour, $5-10 or negotiated by the project.

NEWBURY HOUSE PUBLISHERS, 54 Warehouse Lane, Rowley MA 01969. (617)948-2704. Production Manager: Jacquelin Sanborn. Publishes linguistics, foreign languages and English as second language texts; paperback originals and reprints. Publishes 30 titles/year; 65% require freelance designers, 50% require freelance illustrators. Also uses artists for production. Assigns 20-25 jobs/year. Pays $35 minimum/job, paste-up.
First Contact & Terms: Prefers local artists "so inperson conferences are possible." Query with resume and samples. SASE. Reports in 4 weeks. No advance. Buys all rights. No originals returned to artist at job's completion. Provide resume, flyer, tearsheet, brochure and "inexpensive photocopies of artist's best work (in his opinion)" to be kept on file for future assignments. Write for free catalog, issued in

David Albert, marketing director at New Society Publishers, Philadelphia, wanted "something upbeat and showing motion" and designed to fit in a "window" for A Manual on Nonviolence and Children. John Gummere, a local freelance designer and painter, captured the feeling of motion as well as the concept of "support and unity" in this pen & ink illustration. He received $200 plus costs for the mechanicals.

Includes *For the Fun of It! Selected Cooperative Games for Children and Adults*

A Manual on Nonviolence and Children

Compiled and Edited by Stephanie Judson
Foreword by Paula J. Paul, Educators for Social Responsibility

September; usually not available between March and September.
Book Design: Assigns 20 jobs/year. Uses artists for design, typemark and manuscript. Prefers textbook style. Pays by contract.
Jacket/Covers: Buys 30/year. Pays $100 minimum, b&w line drawings, washes and color-separated work.
Text Illustrations: "Mostly charts." Pays $5 minimum/2x2", b&w line drawings, color-separated work and preliminary sketches. Publishes cartoons "occasionally." Interested in "stick figure cartoons illustrating specific actions (usually to demonstrate verbs)."
Tips: Especially looks for "realistic work because of our field of publication." Artists shouldn't be "too modest or too confident" in selling their work.

NICHOLS PUBLISHING COMPANY, Box 96, New York NY 10024. (212)580-8079. President: Linda Kahn. Specializes in hardcover professional and reference books in architecture, business, education, technology, energy and international relations. Publishes 30 titles/year.
First Contact & Terms: Works with 4 freelance artists/year. Works on promotion assignment only. Artists must be in New York area. Send query letter with brochure and resume; call or write for appointment to show portfolio. Prefers promotion brochures as samples. Samples not kept on file are returned only if requested. Reports only if interested. Considers complexity of project, skill and experience of artist and project's budget when establishing payment. Rights purchased vary.

*NORTHWOODS PRESS, Box 88, Thomaston ME 04861. Editor: Robert Olmsted. Specializes in hardcover and paperback originals of poetry; fiction in novelette form. Publishes approximately 20 titles/year.
First Contact & Terms: Works with 1-2 freelance artists/year. Send query letter to be kept on file. Reports within 10 days. Originals returned to artist at job's completion. Considers complexity of the project, skill and experience of artist, project's budget, turnaround time and rights purchased when establishing payment. Buys one-time rights and occasionally all rights.
Jackets/Covers: Assigns 4-5 freelance design jobs and 4-5 freelance illustration jobs/year. "The author provides the art work and payment."

NOYES PRESS, Noyes Building, Park Ridge NJ 07656. Contact: Robert Noyes. Publishes academic and technical books on chemistry, chemical engineering, food, environment, art, electronics, archaeology and classical studies.
Needs: Uses artists for jacket design. Pays $250 minimum, 2-color camera-ready art.

ODDO PUBLISHING, INC., 745 Beauregard Blvd., Fayetteville GA 30214. (404)461-7627. Vice President: Charles W. Oddo. Specializes in hardcovers on juvenile fiction. Publishes 6-10 titles/year; 100% require freelance illustration.
First Contact & Terms: Works with 3 freelance artists/year. Send query letter with brochure, resume, business card, samples or tear sheets to be kept on file; write for appointment to show portfolio. Accepts "whatever is best for artist to present" as samples. Samples not kept on file are returned by SASE only if requested. Reports only if interested. Works on assignment only. No originals returned to artist at job's completion. Pay is negotiated. Buys all rights.
Book Design: Assigns 3 freelance jobs/year. Pay is negotiated.
Text Illustration: Assigns 3 freelance jobs/year. Artwork purchased includes science fiction/fantasy.

ONCE UPON A PLANET, INC., 65-42 Fresh Meadow Lane, Fresh Meadows NY 11365. Art Director: Alis Jordan. Publishes trade paperback originals, greeting cards, pads and novelty books (humor). Uses artists for book design, cover and text illustration, mechanicals, displays, brochures and flyers.
First Contact & Terms: Prefers local artists. Send query letter with resume and samples. Works on assignment only. Provide brochure, flyer, tear sheet, photocopies and/or slides to be kept on file for future assignments. If originals are sent, SASE must be enclosed for return. Reports in 3-5 weeks. Prefers to buy all rights, but will negotiate. Payment is negotiated.
Book Design: Assigns 8-12 jobs/year. Uses artists for layout, type specifications.
Jackets/Covers: Assigns 6 jobs/year. Uses 2-color art, occasionally 4-color art.
Text Illustration: Assigns 8-12 jobs/year. Uses b&w line drawings and washes.

101 PRODUCTIONS, 834 Mission St., San Francisco CA 94103. Art Director: Lynne O'Neil. Specializes in paperback cookbooks, travel guides and restaurant guides. Publishes 10-12 titles/year; 40% require freelance illustrators.
First Contact & Terms: Works with 4 freelance artists/year. Send query letter with resume and samples to be kept on file. Prefers good-quality photocopies of b&w line drawings, etc., related to food and architecture; do not send original art. Samples returned with SASE only.

Jackets/Covers: Inhouse cover design done in cooperation with illustrator. Illustrator does both cover and text art on one book. Payment usually on royalty basis.
Tips: "Know your market—I look for food and architecture subjects and don't want to see portfolios that lack these."

*OTTENHEIMER PUBLISHERS, INC., 300 Reisterstown Rd., Baltimore MD 21208. (301)484-2100. Art Director: Diane Parameros. Specializes in mass market-oriented hardcover and paperback originals and reprints—encyclopedias, dictionaries, self-help books, cookbooks, children's coloring and activity books, story books and novelty books. Publishes 240 titles/year.
First Contact & Terms: Works with 15-20 freelance artists/year. Local artists only, preferably professional graphic designers and illustrators. Works on assignment only. Send query letter with resume and samples to be kept on file except for work style which is unsuitable for us. Call or write for appointment to show portfolio. Prefers slides, photostats, photocopies or tear sheets as samples. Samples not filed are returned by SASE. Reports only if interested. Original work not returned after job's completion. Considers complexity of the project, project's budget and turnaround time when establishing payment. Buys all rights.
Book Design: Assigns 20-40 jobs/year. Pays by the project, $75-300 average.
Jackets/Covers: Assigns 25 + freelance design and 25 + freelance illustration jobs/year. Pays by the project, $50-400 average, depending upon project, time spent and any changes.
Text Illustration: Assigns 30 + jobs/year. Prefers water-based color media and b&w line work. Prefers graphic approaches as well as very illustrative. Pays by the project, $50-2,000 average.

OUTDOOR EMPIRE PUBLISHING INC., 511 Eastlake Ave. E., Box C-19000, Seattle WA 98109. (206)624-3845. Vice President/General Manager: Alec Purcell. Publishes paperback outdoor and how-to books on all aspects of outdoor recreation. Publishes 40 titles/year: 10% require freelance designers, 50% require freelance illustrators. Also uses artists for advertising layout and illustration. Minimum payment: $10-15, b&w; $25-50, color.
First Contact & Terms: Arrange interview or mail art. Especially looks for style, accuracy in rendering figures and technical illustrations when reviewing samples. Reports within 3 weeks. Buys all rights. No originals returned at job's completion. Works on assignment only. Samples returned by SASE; and reports back on future assignment possiblities. Provide resume, flyer, business card, tear sheet, brochure and photocopies of samples that show style to be kept on file. Artist sometimes supplies overlays for color or artwork. Gives minimum payment for unused assigned work. Pays on publication.
Book Design: Uses artists for layout and type spec. Pays by the hour, $10-35 average; by the project, $10-1,500; "depends upon project."
Jacket/Covers: Pays for design by the hour, $10-35 average; by the project $50-1,000 average. Pays for illustration by the hour, $10-35 average; by the project, $10-500 average.
Text Illustrations: Pays by the hour, $10-35 average; by the project, $10-100 average. Occasionally uses cartoons; buys 6 cartoons/year. Pays $10, b&w.
Tips: "Assignments sometimes depend upon timing—right style for the right project. Availability is important, especially with 'rush' projects. The competition is getting tougher. More people are trying to break into the field."

OXFORD UNIVERSITY PRESS, ELT Department, 200 Madison Ave., New York NY 10016. (212)679-7300. Art Director: Cecilia Yung. Specializes in hardcover and paperback originals; educational materials for English as a second language. Publishes 15-20 titles/year: 25% require freelance designers; 100% require freelance illustrators.
First Contact & Terms: Works with 25 freelance artists/year. Prefers artists with experience in juvenile or educational publishing. Send query letter with resume, samples and tear sheets to be kept on file. Call to show portfolio. Prefers photostats, photocopies or printed samples. Samples not kept on file are returned by SASE. Reports only if interested. Works on assignment basis only. Considers complexity of project, skill and experience of artist and project's budget when establishing payment. Buys all rights.
Book Design: Assigns 5 freelance artists/year. Pays by the project.
Book Advertising and Promotion: Assigns 15-20 freelance projects/year. Pays by the project.
Text Illustration: Assigns 15-20 freelance projects/year. Pays by the project.
Tips: Looks for "a developed sense of style, a good understanding of the problem and its visual solution, creativity within a set of tight specs and good renderings of children and ethnic features" when reviewing samples.

OXMOOR HOUSE, Box 2262, Birmingham AL 35202. (205)877-6000. Editor-in-Chief: John Logue. Publishes hardcover art books, craft books and cookbooks. Produces approximately 13 titles/year.
First Contact & Terms: Query by mail with book idea. Reports within 1 week. No file kept on artists. Pay varies.
Needs: Southern artists only. "We are a buyer of artwork but on a limited basis."

PALADIN PRESS, Box 1307, Boulder CO 80306. (303)443-7250. Art Director: Fran Porter. Publishes hardcover and paperback originals and reprints; military-related (weaponry, self-defense, martial arts and survival) and titles of general interest. Publishes 30 titles/year. Also uses artists for subject-related illustrations for extensive use in catalogs (6 catalogs, trade and mail-order, published yearly) and in magazine ads.
First Contact & Terms: Local artists only for book design, etc; no restrictions for catalog and ad illustrations. Query with good quality photocopies of sample work to be kept on file. Reports in 1 month. Buys all rights. Works on assignment only. Samples returned by SASE; and reports back on future assignment possiblities. Artist supplies overlays for all color artwork. Free catalog for SASE.
Text Illustration: Assigns 8/year. Uses "99% pen & ink, b&w. Often tehnical." Buys b&w line drawings, washes and color washes. Negotiates pay.
Tips: "We prefer working with artists who have a strong background in mechanical and production skills (have they ever worked with a printer?). There is continued expansion into the martial arts market, financial survival, outdoor skills, etc. Also an increased demand for high caliber execution of how-to photo layouts."

PANJANDRUM BOOKS, Suite 1, 11321 Iowa Ave., Los Angeles CA 90025. (213)477-8771. Editor and Publisher: Dennis Koran. Publishes hardcover and paperback original nonfiction (cookbooks, philosophy, health, music, drama, herbs and vegetarianism), fiction (fantasy, European works), and poetry. Publishes 4-5 titles/year; 50% require freelance designers, 40% require freelance illustrators.
First Contact & Terms: Works with 3 freelance artists/year. Prefers local artists, but not mandatory. Works on assignment only. Send query letter with brochure or samples to be kept on file; call or write for an appointment to show portfolio. Accepts slides, photostats, tear sheets, photographs or original art as samples. Reports within 1 month. Sometimes returns original work after job's completion. Considers complexity of the project, skill and experience of the artist and project's budget when establishing payment. Buys all rights "for the book involved."
Book Design: Assigns 4-5 jobs/year. Pays by the project, $150-750 average.
Jacket/Covers: Assigns 4 freelance design jobs/year. Pays by the project, $150-750 average.
Text Illustration: Assigns 2-3 jobs/year. Prefers line drawings. Pay varies by the project.

PARTNER PRESS, Box 124, Livonia MI 48152. Vice President Sales/Marketing: John R. Faitel. Specializes in paperback preschool education materials. Publishes 3 titles/year.
First Contact & Terms: Works with 2 freelance artists/year. Artists must be good in drawing children's faces/bodies. Send query letter with samples to be kept on file. Prefers tear sheets as samples. Samples not filed returned by SASE. Reports only if interested. No originals returned after job's completion. Considers complexity of project and project's budget when establishing payment. Buys all rights.
Book Design: Assigns 2 freelance jobs/year. Pays by the project, $300 minimum.
Jackets/Covers: Assigns 2 freelance design jobs/year. Pays by the project, $100 minimum.
Text Illustration: Assigns 2 freelance jobs/year. Prefers b&w line drawings. Pays by the project, $300 minimum.

PELICAN PUBLISHING CO., 1101 Monroe St., Box 189, Gretna LA 70053. (504)368-1175. Production Manager: Sam Buddin. Publishes hardcover and paperback originals and reprints. Publishes 30 titles/year.
First Contact & Terms: Send letter of inquiry and 3-4 samples. SASE. Works on assignment only. No samples returned. Reports back on future assignment possibilities. Provide resume, letter of inquiry, tear sheets, samples or slides to be kept on file for future assignments. No originals returned at job's completion. Buys complete rights.

PENUMBRA PRESS, 920 S. 38th St., Omaha NE 68105. (319)455-2182. Contact: Bonnie O'Connell. Specializes in limited editions of hand printed books—generally contemporary poetry with graphics or original prints as illustration. Subjects include contemporary poetry, very short fiction, graphics and original prints. Publishes 1-3 titles/year.
First Contact & Terms: Works with 1 artist every 2 years. Send query letter with samples to be kept on file; material not suitable for letterpress book production will not be kept on file. Prefers good photocopies of line work, color slides which can be returned. Samples not kept on file are returned by SASE or adequate return postage. Reports within 4 weeks. Works on assignment only. Originals returned to artist at job's completion. Considers complexity of project and skill and experience of artist when establishing payment.
Text Illustration: Prefers line drawings, photographs, collage and mixed media work. Pays price requested by artist and/or royalty copies.

PERGAMON PRESS INC., Fairview Park, Elmsford NY 10523. (914)592-7700. Art Department Manager: Deborah Speed. Publishes scientific, technical, scholarly, educational, professional and business books. Publishes 120 titles/year: 5% require freelance designers, 5% require freelance illustrators. Also uses artists for promotion design.

First Contact & Terms: Prefers local artists. Call for interview. No originals returned at job's completion. Works on assignment only. Check for most recent titles in bookstores.

Book Design: Assigns 0-5 jobs/year. Uses artists for design and mechanicals, when necessary. Prefers "scholarly" style. Pays net 90 days.

Needs: Uses artists for jacket designs, cover designs, text illustrations, advertising design, advertising illustrations and direct mail brochures; 1 and 2-color.

Tips: There has been a formation of an internal art department. Rarely needs freelance work now.

*PINE MOUNTAIN PRESS, INC., Box 7553, Bradenton FL 33507. (813)755-2586. Publisher: Robert W. Pradt. Specializes in nonfiction paperbacks on the West, psychology, self-help and (some) inspirational. Publishes 20-30 titles/year.

First Contact & Terms: Works with 5 freelance artists/year. Works on assignment only. Send query letter with brochure and samples to be kept on file. Write for appointment to show portfolio. Prefers photographs and tear sheets as samples. Samples not filed are returned by SASE. Reports only if interested. Original work returned to artist. Considers complexity of the project and rights purchased when establishing payment. Purchases one-time rights, but can vary according to project.

Book Design: Assigns 10 jobs/year. Pays by the project, $75-150.

Jackets/Covers: Assigns 10 freelance illustration jobs/year. Pays by the project, $75-150.

Text Illustration: Pays by the project, $25-50, b&w.

PLYMOUTH MUSIC CO., INC., 170 NE 33rd St., Ft. Lauderdale FL 33334. (305)563-1844. General Manager: Bernard Fisher. Specializes in paperbacks dealing with all types of music. Publishes 60-75 titles/year; 100% require freelance designers, 100% require freelance illustrators.

First Contact & Terms: Works with 10 freelance artists/year. Artists "must be within our area." Send brochure, resume and samples to be kept on file; call for appointment to show portfolio. Samples not kept on file are returned. Reports within 1 week. Works on assignment only. No originals returned to artist at job's completion. Considers complexity of project when establishing payment. Buys all rights.

Jackets/Covers: Assigns 5 freelance design and 5 freelance illustration jobs/year. Pays by the project.

POCKET BOOKS, Art Department, Simon & Schuster Bldg., 1230 Avenue of the Americas, New York NY 10020. (212)246-2121, ext. 166. Art Director: Milton Charles. Publishes paperback romance, science fiction, Westerns, young adult, fiction, nonfiction and classics. Publishes 250 titles/year; 80% require freelance illustrators.

First Contact & Terms: Works with 30 freelance artists/year. "We prefer artists who live close enough that they are able to deliver and discuss their work in person. We judge them on their portfolio work. We prefer color illustration." Send brochure/flyer and samples; submit portfolio for review, no appointment necessary. Prefers color slides, transparencies and prints as samples. Samples not kept on file are returned by SASE. Reports in weeks. Works on assignment only. Provide brochure/flyer, samples, tear sheets to be kept on file for possible future assignments. Originals returned to artist at job's completion. Buys all rights.

Jackets/Covers: Assigns 220 freelance illustration jobs/year. Prefers paintings and color washes. Pays by the job, $800-4,000 average.

POLARIS PRESS, 16540 Camellia Terrace, Los Gatos CA 95030. (408)356-7795. Editor: Edward W. Ludwig. Publishes softcover science fiction and science fantasy, (weird and occult), some ethnic and bilingual, historical and scientific nonfiction for college audience. Publishes 2-3 titles/year; all use illustrators.

First Contact & Terms: "The work may be done in the artist's home." Send letter of inquiry, resume, samples (tear sheets or photocopies; *no* slides) and "inquire as to our current needs. Because our needs are small and varied, a query is essential." Provide resume and letter of inquiry to be kept on file for possible future assignments. Works on assignment only. Samples returned by SASE. Reports in 2 months. Buys first rights. Originals returned to artist at job's completion. Check for most recent titles in bookstores or "order 2 or 3 of our books directly." Artist supplies overlays for cover artwork if possible.

Jackets/Covers: Uses full-color art for covers. Also wants artist to include title lettering. Pays for illustration by the project, $30-400 average. Pays $50 minimum/b&w; $300 minimum/color.

Text Illustration: Pays by the project, $30-50 average; one-time payment.

Tips: "Query first; send samples for our files as we like to select the artist whose work seems most suitable for our current project. Artists sometimes are ill-informed as to needs. We receive too many stereotyped drawings of Super Heroes."

PORTER SARGENT PUBLISHERS, INC., 11 Beacon St., Boston MA 02108. (617)523-1670. Coordinating Editor: Peter Casey. Specializes in hardcover and paperback originals and reprints of college

texts in the social sciences, particularly political science, sociology and history. Publishes 4-5 titles/ year; 20% require freelance designers, 20% require freelance illustrators.
First Contact & Terms: Works with 2-4 freelance artists/year. Local artists only. Send query letter with resume, business card and tear sheets to be kept on file; write for appointment to show portfolio. "We are basically looking for samples of dust jacket cover designs." Samples not kept on file returned by SASE. Reports only if interested. Works on assignment only. No originals returned at job's completion. Considers complexity of project, and skill and experience of artist when establishing payment. Buys all rights.
Jackets/Covers: Assigns 1-2 freelance design jobs/year. Pays by the project, $200 minimum; negotiates.

CLARKSON N. POTTER INC., 1 Park Ave., New York NY 10016. (212)532-9200. Art Director: Gael Towery Dillon. Publishes hardbound and paperback books on Americana, fiction, fashion, interior decoration, satire, art, cooking, photographs, life style. Publishes 35 titles/year; 90% require freelance designers, 20% require freelance illustrators.
First Contact & Terms: Prefers minimum of 3 years experience, New York location. Query with photocopies or call for an appointment. SASE. Reports within 2 weeks "if we like samples." Buys all rights. Free sample catalog.
Book Design: Assigns 30 jobs/year. Uses artists for all aspects of the book as a package. Pays $300-400 for jacket design, $450 for text design, $50 full page illustration and $15-20 for spot illustration.
Tips: "Illustrations should try to create a book concept."

*PRENTICE-HALL, INC., Children's Book Division, Englewood Cliffs NJ 07632. (201)592-2618. Editor-in-Chief and Art Director: Barbara Francis. Specializes in hardcover juvenile trade books. "We specialize in high quality full-color picture books for children aged 4-8." Publishes 30 hardcovers and 15 paperback reprints/year.
First Contact & Terms: Works with 30 freelance artists/year. Send samples to be kept on file. "Follow up with a call or write for an appointment to show portfolio." Prefers tear sheets or photocopies of b&w art. Samples not filed are not returned. Reports only if interested. Original work returned after the job's completion. Considers complexity of the project, skill and experience of artist and project's budget when establishing payment. Buys all book rights.
Text Illustration: Assigns 30 jobs/year. Pays an advance against royalty.

G.P. PUTNAM'S SONS, (Philomel Books), 51 Madison Ave., New York NY 10010. (212)689-9200. Art Director, Children's Books: Nanette Stevenson. Publishes hardcover and paperback juvenile books. Publishes 100 titles/year.
First Contact & Terms: "We take drop-offs on Tuesday mornings. Please call Alice Groton in advance with the date you want to drop off your portfolio." Originals returned to artist at job's completion. Works on assignment only. Samples returned by SASE. Provide flyer, tear sheet, brochure and photocopy or stat to be kept on file for possible future assignments. Artist often supplies overlays for cover artwork and inside illustrations. Free catalog.
Book Design: Assigns 20 jobs/year. Novels, nonfiction, photo essay and picture books. Pays one-time fee.
Jacket/Covers: "Full-color paintings, tight style."
Text Illustrations: "A wide cross section of styles for story and picture books."

QUINTESSENCE PUBLICATIONS, 356 Bunker Hill Mine Rd., Amador City CA 95601. (209)267-5470. Proprietor: Marlan Beilke, aka Linomarl. Specializes in letter-press hardcover and paperback originals and reprints on literature, literary criticism, poetry and art history. Publishes 2 titles/year. "Largest linotype museum in the West; hot metal typography specialists."
First Contact & Terms: Works with 1-2 freelance artists/year. Send query letter with business card and samples. Prefers line drawings. Samples not kept on file are returned by SASE. Reports in 1 month. Originals returned to artist at job's completion. Considers project's budget when establishing payment. Negotiates rights purchased.
Book Design: Assigns 1-2 freelance jobs/year. Pays by the project.
Jackets/Covers: Assigns 1 freelance illustration job/year. Pays by the project.
Text Illustration: Assigns 1 freelance job/year. Prefers line drawings for letter-press reproduction. Pays by the project.
Tips: Artists should "seek a long-time, cooperative association with flexibility on a number of projects. Line drawings reproduce best in letter-press work." Especially looks for "clean line and crisp detail in samples or a portfolio. Do try to avoid the trendy. We prefer the old look—art nouveau and classic."

RAINTREE PUBLISHERS GROUP, 330 E. Kilbourn Ave., Milwaukee WI 53202. (414)273-0873. Art Director: Geri Strigenz. Specializes in hardcover informational books for children. Publishes 12 ti-

tles/year; 90% require freelance illustrators.
First Contact & Terms: Works with 12 freelance artists/year. Send samples or submit portfolio for review. Do not call in person. Prefers slides, tear sheets or photocopies as samples. Provide samples to be kept on file for possible future assignments. Samples not kept on file are returned by SASE. Reports in 2-3 weeks. Works on assignment only. Originals sometimes returned to artist at job's completion. Buys all rights.
Jackets/Covers: Assigns 12 illustration jobs/year. Pays by the job, $200-500 average.
Text Illustrations: Assigns 12 jobs/year. Pays by the job, $2,000-3,500 average.

REGENTS PUBLISHING COMPANY, INC., 2 Park Ave., New York NY 10016. (212)889-2780. ESL Editor: Louis Carrillo. Specializes in paperback language textbooks, primarily English as a Second Language. Publishes 24 titles/year; 100% require freelance designers and illustrators. Also uses artists for advertising.
First Contact & Terms: Works with 12 freelance artists/year. "Some experience necessary, but quality of work more important." Call for appointment. Prefers copies as samples. Samples not returned. Reports in 1 month "if a specific project is in production." Provide samples with name, address and phone number to be kept on file for possible future assignments. All work on assignment only. No originals returned to artist at job's completion. Buys all rights. Pay rates depend on quality of work and artist's experience.
Book Design: Assigns 12 jobs/year. Uses artists for original art. Negotiates payment.
Jackets/Covers: Assigns 12 design and 2 illustration jobs/year. Negotiates payment.
Text Illustrations: Assigns 12 jobs/year. Negotiates payment.
Tips: Especially looks for "humor or realistic humans in motion" in samples or a portfolio.

*ROSSEL BOOKS, 44 Dunbow Dr., Chappaqua NY 10514. (914)238-8954. President: Seymour Rossel. Specializes in hardcover and paperback originals, reprints and textbooks on Judaism and Jewish culture, adult and juvenile—juvenile fiction historical, mystery, romance and science fiction. Publishes 6-8 titles/year.
First Contact & Terms: Works with 10 freelance artists/year. Artists must have experience in graphic design (covers and illustrations) and book design (text and type design). Works on assignment only. Send query letter with resume and samples (no originals) to be kept on file. Call for appointment to show portfolio. Prefers tear sheets and photocopies (no originals) as samples. Samples not filed are returned by SASE. Reports only if interested. Original work not returned to artist. Considers skill and experience of artist, project's budget and turnaround time when establishing payment. Buys all rights.
Book Design: Assigns 4 jobs/year. Pays by the project, $250-1,000 maximum.
Jackets/Covers: Assigns 6-8 freelance design and 1 freelance illustration job/year. Pays by the project, $250 minimum.
Text Illustration: Assigns 1 job/year. Prefers pen & ink and line illustrations. Pays by the project, $250 minimum.

*ROWAN TREE PRESS, 124 Chestnut St., Boston MA 02108. (617)523-7627. Specializes in paperback originals and reprints on poetry, mystery, juvenile and memoir. Publishes 6 titles/year; 100% require freelance designers, 50% require freelance illustrators.
First Contact & Terms: Area artists only. Send query letter with brochure, resume and samples to be kept on file; call or write for appointment to show portfolio. Prefers photographs as samples. Samples not kept on file are returned by SASE. Reports within 2 months. Works on assignment only. Originals returned to artist at job's completion. Considers complexity of project, skill and experience of artist and project's budget when establishing payment. Negotiates rights purchased. Material not copyrighted.
Jackets/Covers: Assigns 6 freelance design and 2 freelance illustration jobs/year. Pays by the project, $200-300 average.
Text Illustration: Pays by the project, $100 maximum.

ROYAL HOUSE PUBLISHING CO., INC., Book Division of Recipes-of-the-Month Club, 9465 Wilshire Blvd., Box 5027, Beverly Hills CA 90210. (213)277-7220 or 550-7170. Director: Mrs. Harold Klein. Publishes paperbacks on entertaining and cooking. Publishes 3 titles/year. Also uses artists for brochures, ads, letterheads and business forms.
First Contact & Terms: Query with samples; local artists only. SASE. Reports in 4-6 weeks. Purchases outright. No originals returned to artist at job's completion. Works on assignment only. Provide brochure to be kept on file for future assignments. Check for most recent titles in bookstores. Negotiates pay.
Book Design: Assigns 8-12 jobs/year. Uses artists for layout and type spec.
Jackets/Covers: Assigns 8-12 jobs/year. Uses "4-color art; old-fashioned heirloom quality." Buys color washes, opaque watercolors and b&w line drawings.
Text Illustrations: Assigns 8-12 jobs/year. Buys b&w line drawings.

WILLIAM H. SADLIER INC., 11 Park Place, New York NY 10007. (212)227-2120. Art Director: Grace Kao. Publishes hardcover and paperback Catholic adult education, religious, mathematics, social studies and language arts books. Publishes 60 titles/year. Also uses artists for direct mail pieces and catalogs. Pays $12-15/hour or $175-350/job.
First Contact & Terms: Query with samples. SASE. Reports within 2 weeks. Buys all rights.
Book Design: Assigns 40 jobs/year. Uses artists for layout, type spec and mechanicals. Pays $10-15/hour.
Text Illustrations: Assigns 30 jobs/year. Pays $125-350, color washes and opaque watercolors; $75-200, gray opaques, b&w line drawings and washes.

*SANTILLANA PUBLISHING CO. INC., 257 Union St., Northvale NJ 07647. (201)767-6961. President: Sam Laredo. Specializes in hardcover and paperback juvenile, textbooks and workbooks. Publishes 20 titles/year.
First Contact & Terms: Works with 5 freelance artists/year. Works on assignment only. Send query letter with brochure to be kept on file. Call or write for appointment to show portfolio. Prefers tear sheets as samples or "anything we don't have to return." Samples not filed are returned by SASE. Reports only if interested. No originals returned to artist at job's completion. Considers skill and experience of artist, project's budget and rights purchased when establishing payment. Buys all rights or negotiates rights purchased.
Text Illustration: All jobs assigned to freelancers. Pays by the project, $200-5,000 average.

SCHOCKEN BOOKS INC., 62 Cooper square, New York NY 10003. (212)685-6500. Production/Art Director: Millicent Fairhurst. Trade and academic, paperback and hardcover publisher. Publishes 70-80 titles/year; 40% require freelance designers.
First Contact & Terms: Works with 30-40 freelance artists/year. Send query letter with samples to be kept on file; call or write for appointment to show portfolio. Prefers best reproductions possible as samples. Samples not kept on file are returned by SASE. Reports within 10 days. Works on assignment only. Originals returned to artist at job's completion. Considers complexity of project and project's budget when establishing payment. Buys one-time rights.
Book Design: Assigns 30-40 freelance jobs/year. Pays by the hour, $15 minimum; by the project, $350-500 average.
Jackets/Covers: Assigns 30-40 freelance design jobs/year. Pays by the project, $450 minimum.

SCHOLIUM INTERNATIONAL INC., 265 Great Neck Rd., Great Neck NY 11021. (516)466-5181. President: A. L. Candido. Publishes scientific and technical books. Send photocopies or transparencies.
Needs: Uses artists for jacket design, direct mail brochures and advertising layouts/art.

CHARLES SCRIBNER'S SONS, 115 Fifth Ave., New York NY 10003. (212)614-1300. Art Director for children's books: Vikki Sheatsley. Art Director for adult books: Ruth Kolbert. "Send in nonreturnable samples of work (machine copies OK) before calling for appointment."
Needs: Uses illustrators for jacket designs and inside illustrations. Pays $600 + for "mainly full-color jacket illustration. Artists must be able to handle color separations."

SERVANT PUBLICATIONS, Box 8617, Ann Arbor MI 48107. (313)761-8505. Creative Director: Michael Andaloro. Specializes in hardcover and paperback originals on Christian living, perspective, inspiration and Bible study. Publishes 20-25 titles/year; 30% require freelance illustrators.
First Contact & Terms: Works with 5 freelance artists/year. Send query letter with samples or tear sheets to be kept on file except for "work from artists we do not think we will use." Accepts any type of sample; color desired where applicable. Samples not kept on file returned by SASE only if requested. Reports only if interested. Works on assignment only. Considers complexity of project, skill and experience of artist, project's budget and rights purchased when establishing payment. Negotiates rights purchased.
Jackets/Covers: Assigns 7 freelance illustration jobs/year. Pays by the project, $300-600 average.
Text Illustration: Assigns 2 freelance jobs/year. Prefers b&w. Pays by the project, $100-300 average.
Tips: "The main thing I look at to give me a clue to the artist's competence is naturalness of form and movement in depicting the human body."

SEVEN SEAS PRESS, 524 Thames St., Newport RI 02840. (401)847-1588. Editor: Jim Gilbert. Specializes in hardcover originals of nautical subject matter. Publishes 12 titles/year; 25% require freelance illustrators.
First Contact & Terms: Works with 7-10 freelance artists/year. "Marine illustrating experience necessary. Our requirements generally are for technical illustrations." Send resume, samples and/or tear

sheets to be kept on file; write for appointment to show portfolio. Prefers photostats as samples. Samples not kept on file are returned only if requested. Reports only if interested. Originals returned to artist at job's completion. Considers complexity of project, skill and experience of artist, project's budget, turn-around time and rights purchased when establishing payment. Negotiates rights purchased.

Book Design: "All book design done inhouse."

Jackets/Covers: Assigns 12 freelance design and 12 + freelance illustration jobs/year. Pays by the project, $300-600 average.

Text Illustration: Assigns 12 + freelance jobs/year. Prefers line drawings, mechanical. Pays $35 minimum/illustration.

Tips: "A superb technical illustration, to me, is one that presents the complex clearly and at the same time does not threaten those who may be inclined to be put off by technical subject matter. Besides ability, the next most important criterion for an artist is setting and meeting deadlines."

SHARON PUBLICATIONS, EDREI COMMUNICATIONS, 105 Union Ave., Cresskill NJ 07626. (201)569-5055. Art Director in Chief: Paul Castori. Publishes Star books, Sharon Romances for teens, Bambi Classic series for 10-12 year olds, board books for toddlers, coloring books and more. Also publishes music entertainment and teen oriented magazines (see D.S. Magazines listing in Magazines section).

First Contact & Terms: Send query letter with brochure, resume, business card and samples to be kept on file; call for appointment to show portfolio. Accepts photostats, photographs, photocopies, slides or tear sheets as samples. Samples not filed returned only by SASE. Reports only if interested. Payment varies according to project; "we have a wide range." Considers the complexity of project, how work will be used and turnaround time. Pays on publication.

Needs: Works with 5 freelance artists/year. Uses artists for brochure layout, product illustrations, paste-up and mechanicals.

HAROLD SHAW PUBLISHERS, Box 567, 388 Gundersen Dr., Wheaton IL 60189. (312)665-6700. Managing Editor: Megs Singer for editorial work. Production Manager: Joyce Schram. Publishes original cloth and paperback Christian literature for adults, Bible study guides for adults and teens and literary criticism series. Publishes 20-25 titles/year; 10% require freelance designers; 10% require freelance illustrators.

First Contact & Terms: Local artists only; must be experienced. Query with samples. Reports in 3-4 weeks. Usually buys one-time rights. Works on assignment only. Samples returned by SASE. Provide resume, brochure and one or two samples to be kept on file for future assignments. Check for most recent titles in bookstores. Negotiates pay.

Book Design: Assigns 2-3 jobs/year. Uses artists for layout, type spec and covers. Pays by the project.

Jackets/Covers: Assigns 2-3 jobs/year. Buys photographs and b&w line drawings. Pays for design and illustration by the project.

Text Illustrations: Assigns 2 jobs/year. Buys b&w line drawings. Pays by the project.

Tips: "Be acquainted with our full line of books; show samples already published."

SIERRA CLUB BOOKS, 2034 Fillmore St., San Francisco CA 94115. Publisher: Jon Beckmann. Editorial Director: Daniel Moses. Design Director: Eileen Max. Publishes books on natural history, science, ecology, conservation issues and related themes, and calendars and guides.

First Contact & Terms: Query with resume. Provide resume, tear sheet and/or business card to be kept on file.

Needs: Uses artists for book design and illustration (maps, juvenile art) and jacket design. Pays by the project, $450-700 for book design. Pays by the project, $450-1,000 for jacket/cover design; $175-500 for jacket/cover illustration; $1,000-2,000 average for text illustration. Buys US or world rights.

SINGER COMMUNICATIONS, INC., 3164 Tyler Ave., Anaheim CA 92801. (714)527-5650. Contact: Natalie Carlton. Publishes paperback originals and reprints; mass market, Western, romance, doctor/nurse, mystery, science fiction, nonfiction and biographies. Publishes 200 titles/year through affiliates, 95% require freelance designers for book covers. Also buys 3,000 cartoons/year to be internationally syndicated to newspaper and magazine publishers—also used for topical books. Pays minimum $10/b&w cartoon, $25/color.

First Contact & Terms: Send query letter with business card, brochure and samples to be kept on file. Prefers tear sheets as samples; do not send original work. Material not filed is returned by SASE. Reports in 2 weeks. Buys first and reprint rights. Originals returned to artist at job's completion. Artist's guidelines $1.

Book Design: Assigns "many" jobs/year. Uses artists for reprints for world market. Prefers clean, clear uncluttered style.

Jackets/Covers: Assigns 400 jobs/year. Popular styles include Western, romance, mystery, science fic-

tion/fantasy, war and gothic. "We are only interested in color transparencies for paperbacks." Pays $100-250, color. Offers advance.
Tips: "Study the market. Study first the best seller list, the current magazines, the current paperbacks and then come up with something better if possible or something new. We now utilize old sales for reprint." Looking for "new ideas, imagination, uniqueness. Every artist is in daily competition with the best artists in the field. A search for excellence helps."

SOUTHERN HISTORICAL PRESS, INC., 103 N. A St., Box 738, Easley SC 29641-0738. (803)859-2346. President: The Rev. Silas Emmett Lucas, Jr. Specializes in hardcover and paperback originals and reprints on genealogy and history. Publishes 40 titles/year.
First Contact & Terms: Works with 1 freelance artist/year. Works on assignment only. Send query letter and samples to be kept on file. Call or write for appointment to show portfolio. Prefers tear sheets or photographs as samples. Samples not filed are returned by SASE if requested. Reports back only if interested. Original work not returned after job's completion. Considers complexity of the project, skill and experience of artist, project's budget and turnaround time when establishing payment. Buys all rights.
Needs: Assigns 5 freelance book design, cover design and illustration, and text illustration jobs/year.

STANDARD PUBLISHING, 8121 Hamilton Ave., Cincinnati OH 45231. Advertising Manager: John Weidner. Art Director: Frank Sutton. Publishes religious, self-help and children's books.
First Contact & Terms: Artists with at least 4 year's experience. Query with samples. Provide business card to be kept on file for future assignments. SASE. Reports in 2 weeks. Buys all rights. Free catalog.
Needs: Art director uses artists for illustrations only. Advertising manager uses artists for advertising, books, catalogs, convention exhibits, decorative spots, direct mail brochures, letterheads, magazines, packages and posters.

STEIN AND DAY, Scarborough House, Briarcliff Manor NY 10510. Art Director: Janice Rossi. Publishes hardcover, paperback and mass market fiction and nonfiction. Publishes 105 titles/year; 10% require freelance designers, 20% require freelance cover illustrators.
First Contact & Terms: Prefers local artists with experience with other publishers, but young unpublished artists are welcome to submit. Query with nonreturnable samples. Especially looks for clean, smooth art, good color design and layout; also a variety of technical skills. SASE. Works on assignment only. Reports back on future assignment possibilities. Portfolios accepted at Westchester office for review. Provide resume, brochure and/or flyer to be kept on file for future assignments. Artist provides overlays for color covers. Buys all rights. Negotiates pay for unused assigned work. Pays on publication. Free catalog.
Jackets/Covers: Assigns 10-15 jackets for illustration/season. Pays for design by the project, $400-800 average; pays for illustration by the project, $400-800 average; mass market cover illustration, $700-1,500 average.
Text Illustrations: Uses artists for line work—how-to books. Pays by the project. Rarely buys b&w line drawings.
Tips: "Art today seems to reflect the style of today. Bold colors, bizarre subject matter, futuristic at times. In publishing, books are selling by covers. The most enticing and interesting jackets are selling the books. I see more of a mass market treatment being given to hardcover jackets."

STEMMER HOUSE PUBLISHERS, INC., 2627 Caves Rd., Owings Mills MD 21117. (301)363-3690. President: Barbara Holdridge. Specializes in hardcover and paperback fiction, nonfiction, art books, juvenile and design resource originals. Publishes 15 titles/year; 50% require freelance designers, 75% require freelance illustrators.
First Contact & Terms: Works with 10 freelance artists/year. Works on assignment only. Send brochure/flyer and samples to be kept on file; submission must include SASE. Prefers tear sheets, photocopies or color slides as samples; do not send original work. Material not filed is returned by SASE. Call or write for appointment to show portfolio. Reports in 6 weeks. Works on assignment only. Provide brochure/flyer, samples and tear sheets to be kept on file for possible future assignments. Originals returned to artist at job's completion on request. Negotiates rights purchased.
Book Design: Assigns 5 jobs/year. Uses artists for design. Pays by the job, flat fee.
Jackets/Covers: Assigns 2 design jobs/year. Prefers paintings. Pays by the job, $300 average.
Text Illustrations: Assigns 10 jobs/year. Prefers full-color artwork for text illustrations. Pays royalty.

STONE WALL PRESS INC., 1241 30th St. NW, Washington DC 20007. Publisher: Henry Wheelwright. Publishes paperback and hardcover environmental, backpacking, fishing, beginning and advanced outdoor originals, also medical. Publishes 2-4 titles/year; 10% require freelance illustrators.
First Contact & Terms: Prefers artists who are accessible. Works on assignment only. Query with re-

sume and brochure to be kept on file. Samples returned by SASE. Reports in 2 weeks. Buys one-time rights. Originals returned to artist at job's completion.
Book Design: Assigns 1 job/year. Uses artists for composition, layout, jacket design. Prefers generally realistic style—photo, color or b&w. Artist supplies overlays for cover artwork. Pays cash upon accepted art.
Text Illustrations: Buys b&w line drawings.

*STONEYDALE PRESS PUBLISHING COMPANY, Drawer B, Stevensville MT 59870. (406)777-2729. Publisher: Dale Burk. Specializes in hardcover and paperback originals on outdoor recreation, nature, history and western art. Publishes 4-6 titles/year.
First Contact & Terms: Works with 3-4 freelance artists/year. Works on assignment only. Send query letter with samples to be kept on file. Samples not filed are returned by SASE. Reports within 2-3 weeks. Original work not returned to artist. Considers complexity of the project, project's budget and rights purchased when establishing payment. Negotiates rights purchased.
Book Design: Assigns 2-3 jobs/year. Pays on the basis of artist's bid.
Jackets/Covers: Assigns 4-6 freelance design and 2-3 freelance illustration jobs/year. Pays on the basis of artist's bid.

TEN SPEED PRESS, Box 7123, Berkeley CA 94707. (415)845-8414. Editorial Director: Phil Wood. Publishes hardcover and paperback cookbook, history, sports, gardening, career and life planning originals and reprints. Publishes 15-20 titles/year. Assigns 15 advertising jobs/year. Pays $1,500 maximum/job, catalogs; $1,000 maximum/job, direct mail brochures.
First Contact & Terms: Submit query. Reports within 4 weeks. Works on assignment only. Samples returned by SASE. Provide resume, flyer and/or sample art which may be kept on file for future assignments. Buys all rights, but may reassign rights to artist after publication. Pays flat fee. Offers advance. Pays promised fee for unused assigned work. Free catalog.
Book Design: Assigns 20 jobs/year. Pays $1,000 minimum.
Jackets/Covers: Buys 20/year. Pays $1,000-3,000.
Text Illustrations: Buys 500/year. Pay varies.

*THEOSOPHICAL PUBLISHING HOUSE, Box 270, Wheaton IL 60189-0270. Senior Editor: Shirley Nicholson. Specializes in paperback originals and reprints on meditation, yoga, comparative religion, mysticism, transpersonal psychology, holistic philosophy and health and healing. Publishes 12 titles/year.
First Contact & Terms: Works with 2-3 freelance artists/year. Works on assignment only. Send query letter with samples to be kept on file; write for appointment to show portfolio. Prefers photostats or tear sheets as samples. Samples not filed are returned only if requested. Reports only if interested. No originals returned to artist at job's completion. Considers complexity of the project and project's budget when establishing payment. Negotiates rights purchased.
Jackets/Covers: Assigns 12 freelance design and 12 freelance illustration jobs/year. Pays by the project.
Text Illustration: Assigns 2-3 freelance jobs/year. Prefers line drawings. Pays by the project.

THUNDER'S MOUTH PRESS, Box 780, New York NY 10025. (212)866-4329. President: Neil Ortenberg. Specializes in hardcovers and paperbacks of poetry, plays and translations; fiction—ethnic, science fiction, historical and humorous. Publishes 6 titles/year; 100% require freelance designers, 25% require freelance illustrators.
First Contact & Terms: Works with 10 freelance artists/year. Send query letter with brochure and resume to be kept on file; write for appointment to show portfolio. Samples not kept on file are returned by SASE. Reports within 2 months. Works on assignment only. Originals returned to artist at job's completion. Considers complexity of project, skill and experience of artist and project's budget when establishing payment. Buys one-time rights.
Book Design: Assigns 6 freelance jobs/year. Pays by the hour.

*TOR BOOKS, 49 W. 24th St., New York NY 10018. Senior Editor: Beth Meacham. Specializes in hardcover and paperback originals and reprints: espionage, thrillers, horror, mysteries and science fiction. Publishes 180 titles/year; heavy on science fiction.
First Contact & Terms: All covers are freelance. Works on assignment only. Send query letter with samples to be kept on file "unless unsuitable"; call for appointment to show portfolio. Prefers color photographs, slides or tearsheets as samples. Samples not filed are returned by SASE. Reports only if interested. Original wrok returned after job's completion. Considers skill and experience of artist and project's budget when establishing payment. "We buy the right to use art on all editions of book it is commissioned for and in promotion of book."
Jackets/Covers: Assigns 180 freelance illustration jobs/year. Pays by the project, $500 minimum.

TRADO-MEDIC BOOKS, division of Conch Magazine Ltd., Publishers, 102 Normal Ave. Buffalo NY 14213. (716)885-3686. Managing Editor: Lynda S. Anozie. Publishes hardcover and paperback originals on health, medicine and culture in the Third World, Africa in particular. Publishes 10 titles/year. Also uses artists for catalog, letterhead and envelope design and brochure illustrations. Themes include Africa, traditional medicine of all kinds, botany, etc. Pays $25-50/job, b&w or color.
First Contact & Terms: Query with samples. Prefers "as wide a variety of samples as the artist has; tear sheets preferred to originals." Artist should be professional, with a feel for African local color. Reports within 2 weeks. Buys all rights. No originals returned at job's completion. Works on assignment only. Samples returned by SASE. Reports back on future assignment possibilities. Provide resume, flyer, tear sheet and brochure to be kept on file for future assignments. Artist supplies overlays for all color artwork. Free catalog if available.
Book Design: Assigns 4/year. Themes include Africa, traditional medicine of all kinds, botany, etc. Pays $25-50/job, layout.
Jackets/Covers: Assigns 4/year. Pays $25-50, b&w line drawings, gray opaques and 2-color designs.
Text Illustrations: Pays $25-50, b&w line drawings, gray opaques and 2-color designs. Buys over 1,000/year. Also uses cartoons. Number cartoons bought/year varies. Themes include Africa, traditional medicine of all kinds, botany, etc. Minimum payment: b&w, $25.

*TRIBECA COMMUNICATIONS, INC., 401 Broadway, New York NY 10013. Publisher: Jim Mann. Specializes in hardcover and paperback originals and reprints on general nonfiction. Publishes 20 titles/year.
First Contact & Terms: Works with 10 freelance artists/year. Works on assignment only. Send query letter with resume and samples to be kept on file. Accepts any type sample. Samples not filed are not returned. Reports only if interested. Original work not returned at job's completion. Considers project's budget when establishing payment. Rights purchased vary according to project.
Book Design: Assigns 20 jobs/year. Pays by the project, $200 minimum.
Jackets/Covers: Assigns 20 freelance design and 20 freelance illustration jobs/year. Pays by the project, $200 minimum.
Text Illustration: Assigns 5 jobs/year. Pays by the project, $10 minimum.

TROLL ASSOCIATES, Book Division, 320 Rt. 17, Mahwah NJ 07430. Vice President: Marian Schecter. Specializes in hardcover and paperbacks for juveniles 5 to 15 years. Publishes 100 + titles/year; 30% require freelance designers and illustrators.
First Contact & Terms: Works with 30 freelance artists/year. Send query letter with brochure/flyer or resume and samples. Prefers photostats or photocopies as samples. Samples "usually" returned by SASE. Reports in 3 weeks. Works on assignment only. Provide resume, business card and brochure/flyer to be kept on file for possible future assignments. Originals "usually not" returned to artist at job's completion. Negotiates all rights.

TROUBADOR PRESS INC., Suite 205, 1 Sutter St., San Francisco CA 94104. (415)397-3716. Editorial Director: Malcolm K. Whyte. Publishes mostly children's paperback project and activity books (coloring, cut-out, maze, puzzle and paperdoll books), also science fiction/fantasy. Publishes 4-6 titles/year.
First Contact & Terms: Query with copies of b&w art outline of work. SASE must accompany submissions. Reports in 4 weeks. Originals returned to artist at job's completion, upon request. Provide resume and tear sheet to be kept on file for future assignments. Check most recent titles in toy, art supply and bookstores for current style. All rights may be purchased or royalty contract arranged. Pays 4-6% royalty. Offers advance. Pays promised fee for unused assigned work. Catalog and artist's guidelines for SASE with 39¢ postage.
Needs: Uses artists for design and illustrations for coloring, game, cut-out books and some art books. Pays $25-100/illustration.
Tips: "Study our existing books in print for style, quality and interest range before sending material. See that it *fits* the publisher." Current trends in children's publishing include "more and more emphasis on educational titles (how to read, add, write, etc.)."

TUFFY BOOKS, INC., 84 Calvert St., Harrison NY 10528. President: Phillip Mann. Publishes 20 titles/year. Uses artists for book and jacket/cover design and text illustrations.
First Contact & Terms: Works with 4 freelance artists/year. Local artists only. Call for appointment to show portfolio. Works on assignment only.

TYNDALE HOUSE PUBLISHERS, 336 Gundersen Dr., Wheaton IL 60189. (312)668-8300. Art Director: Tim Botts. Publishes hardcover and paperback originals and reprints on Christian beliefs, the Christian way of life, family, Bible study, missions, contemporary issues for adult and juveniles; also

"Elizabeth Miles' artwork was perfect for the detailed but open work we require for our coloring book line," says Malcolm K. Whyte, editorial director of Troubador Press Inc., San Francisco. *"Although we have never met face to face we worked out the rough compositions, the comprehensive pencils and the final inking and cover painting without a hitch by mail and phone."* This artwork was one of fifteen full-page illustrations for the Mother Goose Coloring Album. Whyte purchased all rights to the artwork. *"Elizabeth has a unique point of view and a vitality we found irresistible for re-telling some of the Mother Goose stories and rhymes,"* says Whyte.

Bible products. Publishes 100 titles/year; 3% require freelance designers, 25% require freelance illustrators. Uses artists for *The Christian Reader* magazine, and *Have a Good Day* leaflet. Also buys 10 cartoons/year. Minimum payment: $35, b&w; $75, color.

First Contact & Terms: Works with 20-30 freelance illustrators/year. Artists must be able to meet deadlines. Send brochure/flyer and samples, preferably 8½x11", to be kept on file. "We only want to see an illustrator's best work, so quality is more important than quantity." Samples not returned. Reports only if interested. Publisher retains original art unless otherwise negotiated.

Book Design: Assigns 2-5 freelance jobs/year; "most of this work is done inhouse." Uses artists for total design by special agreement with some authors.

Jackets/Covers: Assigns 2-5 freelance design and 25 freelance illustration jobs/year. Various media used; style is according to subject matter of book. Pays by the job, $100 minimum, b&w; $400 average, full-color cover illustration.

Text Illustrations: Assigns 25-30 jobs/year. Medium and style vary according to subject matter and budget available for reproduction. Pays by the job, $35-100 average, b&w; $100 minimum, color.

Tips: "We are using more illustration and less photography on book covers than five years ago." Especially looks for "an artist's ability to tell a story visually. I would rather see three or four samples than one to give me a better sense of the artist's consistency."

*UNDERWOOD-MILLER, 651 Chestnut St., Columbia PA 17512. (717)684-7335. Publisher: Chuck Miller. Specializes in hardcover originals and reprints on science fiction, fantasy, romance and popular literature. Publishes 12-20 titles/year.

First Contact & Terms: Works with 5 freelance artists/year. Works on assignment only. Send query letter with samples (not original art) to be kept on file. Prefers photostats, photos, tearsheets as samples. Samples not filed are returned by SASE. Reports only if interested. Original work returned to artist. Considers complexity of the project, project's budget and rights when establishing payment. Usually buys one-time rights, but can vary according to project.

Book Design: Assigns 2 jobs/year. Pays by the project, $250 minimum.

Jackets/Covers: Assigns 15 freelance illustration jobs/year. Pays by the project, $250 minimum.

Text Illustration: Assigns 4 jobs/year. Prefers b&w line drawings. Pays by the project, $250 minimum.

Leo and Diane Dillon of Brooklyn, New York, worked as a team on this jacket artwork for Floating Dragon, *a horror/suspense novel published by Underwood-Miller, Columbia, Pennsylvania. "The Dillons have been active in science fiction/fantasy since the early sixties," says publisher Chuck Miller, "and we felt they were best for the job." The original illustration was acrylic on acetate for which the Dillons received $2,000. "We do primarily children's books and our style varies from heavy to light," says Leo Dillon. "We are very flexible and can meet many different art style needs." Layout and typography are by Jeff and Andrea Levin.*

UNION OF AMERICAN HEBREW CONGREGATIONS, 838 5th Ave., New York NY 10021. (212)249-0100. Director of Publications: Stuart L. Benick. Produces books, filmstrips and magazines for Jewish school children and adult education.
First Contact & Terms: Mail samples or write for interview. SASE. Reports within 3 weeks. Free catalog. Pays $50-200, illustrations.
Needs: Buys book covers and illustrations.

UNIQUEST CORPORATION, (formerly Questron Corporation), Suite 100, Staples Mill Professional Bldg., 2120 Staples Mill Rd., Richmond VA 23230-2918. Chief Executive Officer: Craig Chilton. Estab. 1983. Specializes in paperback originals on general nonfiction with emphasis on marketing and science. Publishes 5-10 titles/year.
First Contact & Terms: Works with 4-7 freelance artists/year. Works on assignment only. Send query letter with resume, business card, brochure, if available, and samples to be kept on file. Write for appointment to show portfolio. Prefers photographs in color as samples, "when appropriate. Good, clear photostats are acceptable as second choice for b&w, but b&w photographic prints are preferred." All samples are filed, "unless work clearly does not meet our needs. In that event, samples are returned by SASE." Reports within 3 weeks. Original work usually not returned after job's completion, "but exceptions to this are possible, upon occasion." Considers complexity of the project, skill and experience of artist, project's budget, turnaround time and rights purchased when establishing payment. Rights purchased vary according to project.
Book Design: Assigns 5-10 jobs/year. Pays by the project, $30 minimum; "minimum generally applies to one rendition. Complex projects pay substantially more."
Jackets/Covers: Assigns 3-4 freelance design and 2-3 freelance illustration jobs/year. Pays by the project, $100 minimum.
Text Illustration: Assigns 4-8 freelance jobs/year. Prefers pen & ink, "but other media may be employ-

ed.'' Pays by the project, $30 minimum.
Tips: ''All minimum pay figures here are rock bottom, for absolutely minimal work.''

UNIVELT INC., Box 28130, San Diego CA 92128. (619)746-4005. Manager: H. Jacobs. Publishes hardcover and paperback originals on astronautics and related fields; occasionally publishes science fiction/fantasy. Publishes 10 titles/year; all have illustrations.
First Contact & Terms: Prefers local artists. Send letter of inquiry, resume, business card and/or flyer to be kept on file. Works on assignment only. Samples not filed are returned by SASE. Reports in 4 weeks on unsolicited submissions. Buys one-time rights. Originals returned to artist at job's completion. Artist supplies overlays for cover artwork. Free catalog.
Book Design: Assigns 10 jobs/year. Uses artists for covers, title sheets, dividers, occasionally a few illustrations. Pays $50-100/book design; also per assignment.
Tips: ''Designs have to be space-related.''

UNIVERSITY OF IOWA PRESS, Old Public Library Bldg., University of Iowa, Iowa City IA 52242. Director: Paul Zimmer. Publishes scholarly works and short fiction series. Publishes 20 titles/year; 7 require freelance book designers, 1 requires freelance illustrator.
First Contact & Terms: ''We use freelance book designers.'' Query with ''two or three samples; originals not required.'' Works on assignment only. Samples returned by SASE. Check for most recent titles in bookstores. Free catalog and artist's guidelines.
Book Design: Assigns 12 freelance jobs/year. Uses artists to draw specifications and prepare layouts. Pays $300 minimum, book design; $100, jacket.

UNIVERSITY OF NEBRASKA PRESS, 901 N. 17th St., Lincoln NE 68588-0520. (402)472-3581. Production Manager: Debra K. Turner. Publishes hardcover and paperback books on Western and literary history. Buys 5 designs/year.
First Contact & Terms: Query with samples (4-5 tear sheets). Buys various rights. Originals returned to artist at job's completion. Works on assignment only. No samples returned. Provide tear sheet and brochure to be kept on file. Check for most recent titles in bookstores. Negotiates pay for unused assigned work. Pays on acceptance.
Book Design: Pays by the project, $200-500 average.
Jackets/Covers: Pays for design by the project, $100-200 average; pays for illustration by the project, $100-250 average.
Text Illustrations: Pays by the project, $30-60; ''varies widely.''
Tips: ''Be familiar with the best of university press publishing by examining catalogs of the American Association of University Press Book Show, an annual event.''

UNIVERSITY OF PENNSYLVANIA PRESS, Blockley Hall, 13th Fl., 418 Service Dr., Philadelphia PA 19104. Director: Thomas M. Rotell. Design & Production Manager: Carl E. Gross. Publishes scholarly books and texts; hardcover and paperback originals and reprints. Publishes 35-40 titles/year. Also uses artists for advertising layout, catalog illustration, direct mail design, book design and cover design. Assigns 10-15 advertising jobs/year. Minimum payment: $400, catalogs or direct mail brochures. Assigns 15-20 production jobs/year. Pays $9/hour maximum, mechanicals and paste-ups. Arrange interview; local artists only. SASE. Buys all rights. No advance. Negotiates payment for unused assigned work. Free catalog.
Book Design: Assigns 35-40 jobs/year. Uses artists for layout, type spec; all design shipped out-of-house. Pays $250-300/job, text layout; $75/job, type spec.
Jackets/Covers: Assigns 35-40 jobs/year. Pays for design by the job, $250-300 average; $300-350 b&w line drawings and washes, gray opaques and color-separated work.
Text Illustration: Pays $10-15/hour for maps, charts.
Tips: Production of books has doubled. Artists should have some experience in book and jacket design.

THE UNIVERSITY OF WISCONSIN PRESS, 114 N. Murray St., Madison WI 53715. (608)262-4978. Production Manager: Gardner R. Wills. Publishes scholarly hardcover and paperback books. Publishes 30-40 titles/year; 85% require freelance designers.
First Contact & Terms: Query first. Reports in 2 weeks. Buys all rights. No originals returned to artist at job's completion. Works on assignment only. Samples returned by SASE. Reports back on future assignment possibilities. Provide letter of inquiry and samples as agreed upon to be kept on file. Check for most recent titles in bookstores. Designer supplies overlays for cover artwork. No advance.
Book Design: Assigns 20-25/year. Prefers a style ''toward the conservative end.'' Pays upon completion of design. Pays by the project, $200-300 average.
Jackets/Covers: Buys 30-40/year. Pays for design by the project, $175-250; b&w line drawings, washes, halftones and color-separated work ''only if part of the jacket/cover design package. We do not purchase individual items of art.''

VITACHART, INC., 3446 Fort Independent St., Bronx NY 10463. (212)796-7413. President: Carolyn West. Specializes in nutrition and health charts. Publishes 1 title/year. Uses artists for layout and design plus spot drawings of herbs, foods.
First Contact & Terms: Works with 1 freelance artist/year. Greater New York City area artists only. Send samples and tear sheets. Prefers photostats as samples. Negotiates payment arrangement with artist. Especially needs mechanical artists.

VONGRUTNORV OG PRESS, Box 411, Troy ID 83871. (208)835-4902. Publisher: Steve E. Erickson. Specializes in paperback originals on philosophy, metaphysics, poetry, creative fiction.
First Contact & Terms: Works with 1-2 freelance artists/year. Works on assignment only. Send query letter with samples to be kept on file. Prefers photostats or copies as samples. Samples not filed not returned. Reports within 6 weeks. Whether original work is returned after the job's completion "depends on the type of assignment and agreement or cotract with the artist." Considers complexity of project, project's budget and rights purchased when establishing payment. Rights purchased vary according to project.

*W.I.M. PUBLICATIONS, Box 367, College Corner OH 45003. (513)523-5994. Publisher: Dr. SDiane Bogus. Specializes in hardcover and paperbacks on poetry—feminist, lesbian, black and gay. Publishes 2-6 titles/year.
First Contact & Terms: Works with 2-6 freelance artists/year. Works on assignment only. Send query letter with samples to be kept on file except for large samples. Call for appointment to show portfolio. Prefers nonreturnable photocopies, tearsheets or photographs. Samples not filed are returned by SASE. Reports within 1 week. Original work not returned to artist. "We buy the material outright and we give the artist credit on title page of book." Considers project's budget when establishing payments. Purchases all rights. "The artist may be allowed to reprint broadside or small lithos of work which appear in any one of our poetry books, but notice must be given that the work appeared in the book and by our press." Artist is asked to supply paste-up, camera-ready mechanical when work is accepted.
Book Design: Assigns 1-6 jobs/year. Pays by the project, $10-100 average. "We can negotiate payments. That may include promotional consideration, i.e., a listing in our yearly catalog or a mention in our promotion of a project."
Jackets/Covers: Assigns 1-6 freelance illustration jobs/year. Pays by the project, $10-100 average.
Text Illustration: Assigns 1-6 jobs/year. Prefers b&w line drawings—figures and scenes—artistic interpretations of poems. Pays by the project, $10-100 average.
Tips: "We accept work from any artist who is not biased toward gays or Blacks. We welcome a sample of any artist's work. We usually like realistic illustrations as opposed to abstract representation." Sometimes buys science fiction/fantasy themes. "We keep a file of all freelance artists we've worked with and draw from it."

*J. WESTON WALCH, PUBLISHER, Box 658, Portland ME 04104-0658. (207)772-2846. Managing Editor: Richard Kimball. Specializes in supplemental secondary school materials including books, poster sets, filmstrips and computer software. Publishes 120 titles/year.
First Contact & Terms: Works with 20 freelance artists/year. Works on assignment only. Send query letter with resume and samples to be kept on file. Write for artists' guidelines. Prefers photostats as samples. Samples not filed are returned only by request. Reports within 6 weeks. Original work not returned to the artist after job's completion. Considers project's budget when establishing payment. Rights purchased vary according to project.
Jackets/Covers: Assigns 20 freelance design and 20 freelance illustration jobs/year. Pays by the project, $100 minimum.
Text Illustration: Assigns 10 freelance jobs/year. Prefers b&w pen & ink. Pays by the project, $100 minimum.

WALKER & COMPANY, 720 Fifth Ave., New York NY 10019. (212)265-3632. Cable address: REKLAWSAM. Art Director: Laurie McBarnette. Publishes hardcover originals and reprints of mysteries, regency romance, children's science, adult trade, etc. Publishes 200 titles/year; 50% require freelance designers, 80% require freelance illustrators. Also uses artists for catalog design and layout (educational).
First Contact & Terms: Works with 20-30 freelance artists/year. Illustrators must be within 2 hours of New York; book designers must have textbook experience. Send business card and samples to be filed. Prefers any sample except slides. Samples are returned by SASE. Reports only if interested. Works on assignment only. Buys all rights. Originals returned to artist at job's completion (except in special instances).
Book Design: Assigns 7 jobs/year. Uses freelance artists for complete follow-through on job, layout, type spec. Prefers classic style—modern conservative. Pays by the hour, $7.50-15 average, or by the

This cartoon by Aaron Bacall of Staten Island, appeared in Life Extension Companion *published by Warner Books, New York City. "I sent a promo sheet to Warner," says Bacall, "and the authors contacted me and then sent a computer printout of the book asking me to submit sketches for some chapters. They eventually purchased twenty-three drawings." Payment was $100 per drawing for North American hardcover and softcover book rights.*

© 1983 A. Bacall

"Air quality is unacceptable today ... without antioxidants."

project $200-600 average; 60 days upon completion.
Jackets/Covers: Assigns 40 freelance illustration jobs/year. Pays by the project, $100 minimum.
Text Illustration: Assigns 3 freelance jobs/year. Prefers b&w line drawings or pencil. Pays by the project $500 minimum.

WARNER BOOKS INC., 666 Fifth Ave., New York NY 10103. (212)484-3151. Art Director: Jackie Meyer. Publishes 400 titles/year; 50% require freelance designers, 80% require freelance illustrators.
First Contact & Terms: Works on assignment only. Query or call. Buys first rights. Originals returned at job's completion (artist must pick up). Provide tear sheets to be kept on file for future assignments. Check for most recent titles in bookstores.
Jackets/Covers: Uses realistic jacket illustrations. Payment subject to negotiation.
Tips: Industry trends include "more graphics and stylized art; computer graphics are increasing in popularity." Especially looks for "photorealistic style with imaginative and original design and use of eyecatching color variations." Artists shouldn't "talk too much. Good design and art should speak for themselves."

SAMUEL WEISER INC., Box 612, York Beach ME 03910. (207)363-4393. President: Donald Weiser. Specializes in occult and Oriental philosophy. Publishes 12-14 titles/year. Uses artists for jacket/cover design.
First Contact & Terms: Works with 2-3 freelance artists/year. Send query letter with samples and tear sheets to Alden Cole, art director. Prefers actual copies of book cover work done for other publishers as samples. Samples are filed; not returned.
Tips: Current trends include "sleek, sophisticated, subtle and simplified" artwork. A mistake artists make is "pricing themselves out of the competition."

WESTBURG ASSOC., PUBLISHERS, 1745 Madison St., Fennimore WI 53809. (608)822-6237. Editor/Publisher: John Westburg. Specializes in paperback originals of essays, criticism, short fiction, poetry, in the fields of literature and humanities. Publishes 1-3 titles/year.
First Contact & Terms: Works with 3-5 freelance artists/year. Send query letter with brochure and business card to be kept on file. Do not send samples until requested; do not send original work. Samples not filed are returned by SASE. No original work returned after job's completion. Considers project's budget when establishing payment. Buys all rights or negotiates rights purchased.

Jackets/Covers: Assigns 1-3 freelance design and illustration jobs/year. Pays by the project, $25-50 average.
Text Illustration: Assigns 1 + freelance illustration jobs/year. Prefers b&w line drawings. Pays by the project, $25-50 average.

WHITCOULLS PUBLISHERS, Private Bag, Christchurch, New Zealand. 794580. Art Director: Grant Nelson. Specializes in hardcover, some paperback originals. Publishes 30-35 titles/year.
First Contact & Terms: Works with approximately 8 freelance artists/year. Works on assignment only. Send query letter with business card and samples to be kept on file. Call or write for appointment to show portfolio. Prefers photostats, photographs and tear sheets as samples. Samples not filed are returned only if requested. Reports back only if interested. Original work returned to artist at job's completion. Considers project's budget when establishing payment. Buys all rights.
Jackets/Covers: Assigns approximately 4 freelance illustration jobs/year. Pays by the project.
Text Illustration: Assigns 2-3 freelance jobs/year. Pays by the project.

WHITE EAGLE PUBLISHER, Dept. A-0111, Box 1332, Lowell MA 01853. President: Jack Loisel. Specializes in paperbacks on religion and poetry. Publishes 5 titles/year; 100% require freelance designers and illustrators.
First Contact & Terms: Works with 7 freelance artists/year. Artists should have experience. Send query letter with brochure and samples to be kept on file. Prefers photographs and photostats as samples. Reports only if interested. Works on assignment only. No originals returned to artist at job's completion. Considers complexity of project and project's budget when establishing payment. Buys one-time or all rights. Material not copyrighted.
Book Design: Assigns 5 freelance jobs/year. Pays by the project, $500 minimum.
Jackets/Covers: Assigns 5 freelance design and 10 freelance illustration jobs/year. Pays by the project, $400 minimum.
Text Illustration: Assigns 2 freelance jobs/year. Pays by the project, $300 minimum.

ALBERT WHITMAN & COMPANY, 5747 W. Howard St., Niles IL 60648. Editor: Kathleen Tucker. Specializes in hardcover original juvenile fiction and nonfiction—many picture books for young children. Publishes 21 titles/year; 100% require freelance illustrators.
First Contact & Terms: Works with 18 freelance artists/year. Prefers working with artists who have experience illustrating juvenile trade books. Works on assignment only. Send brochure/flyer or resume and "a few slides and photocopies of original art and tear sheets that we can keep in our files. Do *not* send original art through the mail." Samples not returned. Reports to an artist if "we have a project that seems right for him. We like to see evidence that an artist can show the same children in a variety of moods and poses." Original work returned to artist at job's completion "if artist holds the copyright." Rights purchased vary.
Cover/Text Illustrations: Cover assignment is usually part of illustration assignment. Assigns 18 jobs/year. Prefers realistic art. Pays by flat fee or royalties.
Tips: Especially looks for "an artist's ability to draw people, especially children."

WILSHIRE BOOK CO., 12015 Sherman Rd., North Hollywood CA 91605. (213)875-1711 or (818)983-1105. President: Melvin Powers. Publishes paperback reprints on psychology, self-help, inspirational and other types of nonfiction. Publishes 25 titles/year.
First Contact & Terms: Local artists only. Call. Buys first, reprint or one-time rights. Negotiates pay. Free catalog.
Jackets/Covers: Assigns 25 jobs/year. Buys b&w line drawings.

WINSTON PRESS, 430 Oak Grove, Minneapolis MN 55403. (612)871-7000. Contact Amy Rood with book jacket design and Art Department with illustrations. Works on assignment only. Send slides or samples of work and SASE.

WISCONSIN TALES & TRAILS, INC., Box 5650, Madison WI 53705. (608)231-2444. Publisher: Howard Mead. Publishes adult trade books; "only those that relate in some way to Wisconsin. 3 categories: Wisconsiana, guides, nature/environment. Publishes 1 title/year.
First Contact & Terms: Send letter of inquiry and samples to be kept on file for future assignments. Works on assignment only. Samples returned by SASE "if requested." Reports back on future assignment possibilities. Buys one-time rights. Return of original artwork "depends on individual contract or agreement negotiated."
Tips: Also publishes bimonthly magazine, *Wisconsin Trails*. "We have been using freelance artwork regularly in our magazine, all b&w."

WOMEN'S AGLOW FELLOWSHIP, Publications Division, Box I, Lynnwood WA 98036. (206)775-7282. Art Director: Kathy Boice. Specializes in Bible studies and Christian literature, and a bimonthly magazine offering Christian women's material. Publishes 20 titles/year; 75% require freelance illustrators and calligraphers.
First Contact & Terms: Works with 30 freelance artists/year. Send samples; call or write for appointment to show portfolio. Prefers slides, photostats, line drawings and reproduced art as samples. Samples returned by SASE. Reports in 6 weeks. Provide resume, business card, brochure/flyer, samples and tear sheets to be kept on file for possible future assignments. Originals returned to artist at job's completion. Buys one-time rights.
Book Design: Uses artists for cover design. Pays by the job, $80-200 average.
Jackets/Covers: Prefers b&w line drawings. Pays for design and illustration by the job, $80-250 average.
Magazine Illustration: Pays $80-175, b&w line drawings; $200-325, color, inside; $500-700, color, cover.
Text Illustration: Prefers b&w line drawings. Pays by the job, $80-200 average.
Tips: "Be aware of organization's emphasis. Be motivated to work for a women's organization."

WOODALL PUBLISHING COMPANY, 500 Hyacinth Pl., Highland Park IL 60035. (312)433-4550. Directory Manager: Debby Spriggs. Specializes in paperback annuals on camping. Publishes 2 titles/year.
First Contact & Terms: Works with 4 freelance artists/year. Works on assignment only. Call for appointment to show portfolio. Reports within 4 weeks. No original work returned after job's completion. Considers complexity of the project, skill and experience of artist, and project's budget when establishing payment. Rights purchased vary according to project.
Book Design: Assigns 3-4 jobs/year. Pays by the project.
Jackets/Covers: Assigns 2 freelance design and illustration jobs/year. Pays by the project.
Text Illustration: Pays by the project.

*WOODSONG GRAPHICS INC., Box 238, New Hope PA 18938. (215)794-8321. President: Ellen Bordner. Specializes in paperback originals covering a wide variety of subjects, "but no textbooks or technical material so far." Publishes 6-10 titles/year.
First Contact & Terms: Works with 1-5 freelance artists/year depending on projects and schedules. Works on assignment only. Send query letter with brochure and samples to be kept on file. Any format is acceptable for samples, except originals. Samples not filed are returned by SASE. Reports only if interested. Originals returned to artist at job's completion. Considers complexity of the assignment, skill and experience of artist, project's budget and turnaround time when establishing payment. Rights purchased vary according to project.
Book Design: Assigns 2-3 freelance jobs/year. Pays by the project, $400 minimum.
Jackets/Covers: Assigns 3-6 freelance illustration jobs/year. Pays by the project, $100 minimum.
Text Illustration: Assigns 2-3 freelance jobs/year. Medium and style vary according to job. Pays by the project, $250 minimum.

*THE WORDSHOP, Division of Slawson Communications, 3719 6th Ave., San Diego CA 92103. (619)291-9126. Art Director: Ed Roxburgh. Specializes in paperback computer books and childrens color books. Subjects include computers, childrens teaching books, and literary. Publishes 25 titles/year.
First Contact & Terms: Works with 20-25 freelance artists/year. Works on assignment only. Send query letter with resume and samples to be kept on file; call for appointment to show portfolio. Samples not filed are returned by SASE. Reports only if interested. Originals not returned to artist at job's completion. Considers complexity of the project and project's budget when establishing payment. Rights purchased vary according to project.
Jackets/Covers: Assigns 10-15 freelance design and 15-20 freelance illustration jobs/year. Pays by the project, $300-600 average.
Text Illustration: Assigns 20 jobs/year. Pays by the illustration, $15-50 average depending on complexity, color, etc.

WRITER'S DIGEST BOOKS/NORTH LIGHT, F&W Publishing, 9933 Alliance Rd., Cincinnati OH 45242. Art Director: Carol Buchanan. Publishes 25-30 books annually for writers, artists, photographers, plus selected trade titles. Query with samples or request appointment to show portfolio. "Prefer that artist has had work published in area of assignment." SASE. Reports in 3 weeks. Also uses artists for ad illustration and design. Assigns 25-50/year. Payment by job: $50-350, catalogs; $50 minimum, direct mail brochures; $25 minimum, magazines.
Jackets/Covers: Buys 8-10/year. Pays $350-500 for concept through mechanical art.
Text Illustration: Uses artists for text illustration and cartoons. Pays $5 minimum.

YANKEE PUBLISHING INCORPORATED, BOOK DIVISION, Main St., Dublin NH 03444. Art Director: Jill Shaffer. Specializes in hardcover and paperback originals on New England topics; cookbooks. Publishes 12 titles/year; 50% require freelance illustrators.
First Contact & Terms: Works with 10 freelance artists/year. Send query letter with resume and samples to be kept on file; write for appointment to show portfolio. Prefers slides or photocopies as samples. Samples not kept on file are returned by SASE. Works on assignment only. Originals returned to the artist at job's completion if stated in contract. Considers complexity of project, project's budget and rights purchased when establishing payment. Negotiates rights purchased.
Jackets/Covers: Pays by the project, $200-600 average, usually full color.
Text Illustration: Pays by the project, $50-500 average, usually b&w line art.

YE GALLEON PRESS, Box 25, Fairfield WA 99012. (509)283-2422. Editorial Director: Glen Adams. Publishes rare western history, Indian material, antiquarian shipwreck and old whaling accounts, and town and area histories; hardcover and paperback originals and reprints. Publishes 30 titles/year; 20% require freelance illustrators.
First Contact & Terms: Query with samples. SASE. No advance. Pays promised fee for unused assigned work. Buys book rights. Free catalog.
Text Illustrations: Buys b&w line drawings, some pen & ink drawings of a historical nature; prefers drawings of groups with facial expressions and some drawings of sailing and whaling vessels. Pays $5-35.
Tips: " 'Wild' artwork is hardly suited to book illustration for my purposes. Many correspondents wish to sell oil paintings which at this time we do not buy. It costs too much to print them for short edition work."

Businesses

If variety is the spice of life, then the listings in this Businesses section are the "special seasoning" of this directory. There is a wide assortment of business types whose art/design needs range from the known to the relatively unknown. Belt buckle and t-shirt manufacturers, sign makers, software producers and a radio/television station are only a few. This year's Businesses section also boasts the addition of collectible manufacturers which seek artists for the design and illustration of plates, figurines and more.

We've included in-depth information on the collectibles market both in this section's Close-up featuring Brigette Moore of Reco International Corp. and the upfront article "Breaking into Specialty Art Markets." Learn what collectibles art buyers look for in artwork *and* artists, what the requisites are for becoming a collectibles artist, how to approach a manufacturer and other tips to help you break into this new and growing field.

Fashion firms have been singled out at the end of this section so you can locate them more easily since their art needs revolve around a similar theme—clothing and the accessories that enhance it. Nothing is as changeable as fashion—being alert to trends is essential to the freelance artist who wants to work for manufacturers buying clothing design, companies needing textile or pattern design or stores using fashion illustration.

Stay current with economic and business trends by reading the newspaper financial pages and periodicals. If you're interested in a particular product area, check the Yellow Pages and ask at your local library for suggestions of trade periodicals dealing with that specific interest. Additional manufacturers can be obtained from *Thomas Register*, which lists companies alphabetically and according to product.

To increase your knowledge of the exhibit, display and sign field refer to the trade magazine *Visual Merchandising & Store Design* and consult the Yellow Pages for local firms.

Fashion demands you look months ahead in your designs, whether garment or pattern. To keep aware of trends, refer to *Women's Wear Daily*, a leading trade newspaper, or its "sister" magazine *W. Homesewing Trade News* keeps you current with the homesewing industry.

This pen & ink wildlife illustration was originally created by freelancer Larry Anderson of Des Moines, Iowa, for use on belt buckles. The work was commissioned by Mark H. West, vice president of West Supply in Appleton, Wisconsin. Anderson later redrew the artwork with more detail for reproduction by lithography onto a hardwood surface for use as a wall hanging.

© West Supply, Inc.

*ADELE'S II, INC., 17300 Ventura Blvd., Encino CA 91316. (818)990-5544. Contact: Shirley Margulis. Franchisor and retailer of personalized gifts including acrylic and oak desk accessories, novelty clocks, personalized gift items from any medium. Sells to "high-quality-conscious" customers.
Needs: Works with 100-150 freelance artists/year. Uses artists for product design, model making and lettering.
First Contact & Terms: Send query letter with samples or photos to be kept on file. Write for appointment to show portfolio. Prefers photos as samples. Samples not filed are returned by SASE. Reports only if interested. Negotiates payment. Considers rights purchased when establishing payment.
Tips: "Talk to us first. Get an idea of what we are looking for—then show us only items that are applicable."

ADVANCED R&D INC., Box 7600, Orlando FL 32804. Personnel Administrator: Ruth Byron. Contract engineering firm. Clients: electronics, aerospace, heavy industry.
Needs: Uses artists for illustrations for use on products. For product designs, submit natural themes, such as technical illustrations, schematic, exploded views, aerospace, avionics equipment related also to product. Also needs technical art for catalog covers, publications, charts, graphs, manuals and isometrics (exploded and cutaway views and schematics). Especially needs design, drafting, illustration and engineering.
First Contact & Terms: Prefers b&w line drawings and previously published work as samples. Provide resume to be kept on file for possible future assignments. Pays by the hour, $10-15 average. Considers complexity of project, and skill and experience of artist when establishing payment.

AERO PRODUCTS RESEARCH INC., 11201 Hindry Ave., Los Angeles CA 90045. Director of Public Relations: J. Parr. Aviation training materials producer. Produces line of plastic greeting cards, religious and inspirational cards, credit and business cards.
Needs: Works with about 2 illustrators/month. Uses artists for brochures, album covers, books, catalogs, filmstrips, advertisements, graphs and illustrations.
First Contact & Terms: Prefers local artists. Query with resume. Provide brochure/flyer, resume and tear sheets to be kept on file for future assignment. No originals returned to artist at job's completion. Negotiates pay according to experience and project.

AHPA ENTERPRISES, Box 506, Sheffield AL 35660. Marketing Manager: Allen Turner. Media products producer/marketer. Provides illustrations, fiction, layouts, video productions, computer-printed material, etc. Specializes in adult male, special-interest material. Clients: limited-press publishers, authors, private investors, etc.
Needs: Seeking illustrators for illustration of realistic original fiction or concepts.
First Contact & Terms: Wants only those artists "who are in a position to work with us on an intermittent but long-term basis." Works on assignment only. Send query letter with resume and samples to be kept on file. Prefers photocopies or tear sheets as samples. Samples not filed are returned by SASE only if requested. Reports back only if interested (within 3-7 days). Pays by the project, $50-300 average. Considers complexity of the project and number and type of illustrations ordered when establishing payment.
Tips: "Samples should indicate capability in realistic (if 'glamorized') face-and-figure illustration. Continuity-art experience is preferred. This is an excellent place for capable amateurs to 'turn pro' on a part-time, open-end basis."

AK INTERNATIONAL, 40 N. Water St., Lititz PA 17543. (717)626-0505. President: O. Ali Akincilar. Produces brass photo frames and ornaments. Clients: the gift industry.
Needs: Buys approximately 10 designs/year from freelance artists. Prefers line drawings for illustrations.
First Contact & Terms: Artists must have a knowledge of photo etching. Works on assignment only. Send query letter with brochure, resume and samples to be kept on file. Call for appointment to show portfolio. Prefers photographs as samples. Samples not filed are returned only if requested. Reports only if interested. Original art not returned after reproduction. Pays by the project, $50-500 average. Buys all rights.

ALBEE SIGN CO., 561 E. 3rd St., Mt. Vernon NY 10553. (914)668-0201. President: William Lieberman. Produces interior and exterior signs and graphics. Clients are commercial accounts, banks and real estate companies.
Needs: Works with 6 artists for sign design, 6 for display fixture design, 6 for P-O-P design and 6 for custom sign illustration. Pays by job.
First Contact & Terms: Local artists only. Query with samples (pictures of completed work). Previous experience with other firms preferred. SASE. Reports within 2-3 weeks. Works on assignment only. No

samples returned. Reports back as assignment occurs. Provide resume, business card and pictures of work to be kept on file for future assignments.

ALFA-LAVAL, INC., Box 1316, 2115 Linwood Ave., Fort Lee NJ 07024. (201)592-7800. Manager, Marketing Communications: David Closs. Assistant Manager, Marketing Communications: Rosemarie Bosi. Operations Assistant: Stefanie Gosse Batory. Manufacturer of industrial centrifuges and heat exchangers. Clients: chemical, dairy, food processing, heating, ventilating, air conditioning, petrochemical, offshore drilling, steel and power generation industries and marine.
Needs: Works with 4 freelance artists per year. Uses artists for brochure and catalog design, illustration and layout. Especially needs brochures and direct mail.
First Contact & Terms: Prefers artists within a 175-mile radius of Fort Lee NJ. Send query letter; prefers samples of brochures and direct mail pieces, roughs or published pieces. Samples returned by SASE. Reports within 2 weeks. Works on assignment only. Provide business card to be kept on file for possible future assignments. Payment determined by approved estimate of the project.
Tips: Artists "should be able to execute piece from thumbnails to mechanicals."

ALL-STATE LEGAL SUPPLY CO., One Commerce Dr., Cranford NJ 07016. (201)272-0800. Advertising Manager: Paul Ellman. Manufacturer and distributor of supplies, stationery, engraving, printing. Clients: lawyers.
Needs: Works with 6 freelance artists/year. Uses artists for advertising, brochure and catalog design, illustration and layout; display fixture design, and illustration on product.
First Contact & Terms: Experienced, local artists and designers only. Send query letter with samples to be kept on file. Call for appointment to show portfolio. Prefers photostats as samples. Reports only if interested. Works on assignment only. Pays by the project, $150-9,000 average. Considers complexity of project, skill and experience of artist and turnaround time when establishing payment.

ALMOST HEAVEN HOT TUBS, LTD, Attention: Art Dept., Route 5, Renick WV 24966. (304)497-3163. Art Director: Barry Glick. Manufacturer of hot water leisure products, i.e., hot tubs, spas, whirlpools, saunas. Clients: distributors, dealers, retailers, consumers.
Needs: Works with 5 freelance artists/year. Uses artists for advertising, brochure and catalog design, illustration and layout; product and display fixture design, illustration on product, P-O-P displays, posters, model making and signage.
First Contact & Terms: Send query letter with brochure, resume, business card, samples and tear sheets to be kept on file. Reports within 1 week. Pay varies. Considers complexity of project, skill and experience of artist, how work will be used, turnaround time and rights purchased when establishing payment.

*AMERICAN ARTISTS, Division of Graphics Buying Service, 225 W. Hubbard St., Chicago IL 60610. (312)828-0555. Advertising Coordinator: Lorraine Light. Manufacturer of limited edition plates and figurines. Specializes in horse, children and cat themes, but considers most others. Clients: wholesalers and retailers.
Needs: Works with 3 freelance artists/year. Uses artists for plate and figurine design and illustration; brochure design, illustration and layout. Open to most art styles.
First Contact & Terms: Does not work on assignment only. Send query letter with resume and samples to be kept on file unless return is requested or artwork is unsuitable. Call or write for appointment to show portfolio. Prefers transparencies or slides but will accept photos—color only. Samples not filed are returned only if requested or if unsuitable. Reports within 1 month. Payment varies and is negotiated. Rights purchased vary. Considers complexity of project, skill and experience of artist, how work will be used and rights purchased when establishing payment.

AMERICAN BOOKDEALERS EXCHANGE, Box 2525, La Mesa CA 92041. Editor: Al Galasso. Publisher of *Book Dealers World* targeted to self-publishers, writers and mail order book dealers. Clients: self-publishers, writers, business opportunity seekers.
Needs: Works with 3 freelance artists/year. Uses artists for advertising, brochure and catalog design and illustration.
First Contact & Terms: Prefers artists with at least a year's experience. Send query letter with samples to be kept on file. Prefers photostats as samples. Samples not kept on file are returned only if requested. Reports only if interested. Works on assignment only. Pays by the project, $25-200 average. Considers complexity of project, skill and experience of artist, turnaround time and rights purchased when establishing payment.

*AMERICAN MANAGEMENT ASSOCIATION, 135 W. 50th St., New York NY 10020. (212)903-8157. Art Director: Dolores Wesnak. Provides educational courses, conferences and topical briefings to

business managers and support staff. Clients: business executives, managers and supervisors.
Needs: works with 6-10 freelance artists/year. Uses artists for brochure design and layout, catalog design and layout, and posters.
First Contact & Terms: Prefers local artists experienced in 2-color brochures, full-time professionals. The ability to conceptionally develop ideas is important. Send query letter with tear sheets to be kept on file. Call or write for appointment to show portfolio. Reports only if interested. Works on assignment only. Pays by the project, $350 minimum. Considers complexity of project and skill and experience of artist when establishing payment.
Tips: Artists "must have a knowledge of design for direct mail and of postal regulations."

AMERICAN PRODUCTS DIVISION, 5550 N. Elston, Chicago IL 60630. (312)774-2020. Vice President Marketing: Robert Gore. Direct marketing firm. Provides catalogs of tabletop giftware and holloware, and direct mail general consumer items, such as, power tools, stereos, etc. Clients: oil companies and "our own mailing lists."
Needs: Works occasionally with freelance artists. Uses artists for advertising, brochure and catalog layout; and brochure illustration.
First Contact & Terms: Call for appointment to show portfolio. Works on assignment only. Pay depends on assignment and competition. Considers complexity of project and skill and experience of artist when establishing payment.
Tips: "Be honest and direct."

ANNIS-WAY SIGNS LTD., 595 West St. S., Orillia, Ontario Canada. Contact: Lloyd H. Annis.
Needs: Uses artists for exhibit, trademark and display design, sign redesign and lettering.
First Contact & Terms: Send resume.

ANTECH, INC., 788 Myrtle St., Roswell GA 30075. (404)993-7270. President: A.K. Nagrani. Contact: M.E. McKinnon, Marketing Manager. Publisher and distributor of software programs for the architectural and engineering industries. Clients: engineers, architects, technical community.
Needs: Works with 2 freelance artists/year. Uses artists for advertising, brochure and catalog design, illustration and layout; and illustration on product.
First Contact & Terms: Local artists only. Works on assignment only. Send query letter with samples to be kept on file; write for appointment to show portfolio. Samples not filed are returned only if requested. Reports back only if interested. Pays by the project. Considers complexity of the project, and skill and experience of the artist when establishing payment.

*****ARMSTRONG'S**, 150 E. 3rd St., Pomona CA 91766. (714)623-6464. President: David W. Armstrong. Wholesale and retail manufacturer/gallery of collector plates, figurines and lithographs. Clients: wholesale and retail customers of all age groups.
Needs: Uses professional artists for plate design; limited edition free art prints; advertising posters; advertising, brochure and catalog design, illustration and layout.
Contact & Terms: Works on assignment only. Send query letter with brochure, resume, business card and samples to be kept on file. Prefers photographs, transparencies and tear sheets as samples. Samples not filed are returned. Reports within 2 weeks. Payment is determined on a case-by-case basis. Considers skill and experience of the artist and rights purchased when establishing payment.
Tips: "Make your initial contact by letter and do not make excessive telephone calls to our offices."

AUTOMATIC MAIL SERVICES, INC., 30-02 48th Ave., Long Island City NY 11101. (212)361-3091. Contact: Michael Waskover. Manufacturer and service firm. Provides printing and direct mail advertising. Clients: publishers, banks, stores, clubs.
Needs: Works with 5-10 freelance artists/year. Uses artists for advertising, brochure and catalog design, illustration and layout.
First Contact & Terms: Send business card and samples to be kept on file. Call for appointment to show portfolio. Prefers photostats as samples. Samples not kept on file are returned only if requested. Works on assignment only. Pays by the project, $10-1,000 average. Considers skill and experience of artist and turnaround time when establishing payment.

*****AVALON INDUSTRIES**, 95 Lorimer St., Brooklyn NY 11206. R&D Director: Anne Pitrone. Manufacturer of toys.
Needs: Works with 4-5 freelance artists/year. Uses artists for advertising, brochure and catalog design.
First Contact & Terms: Seeks artists with "toy experience." Works on assignment only. Send query letter with brochure and samples to be kept on file. Call or write for appointment to show portfolio. Prefers photographs, slides or tear sheets as samples. Samples not filed are returned. Reports only if interested. Pays by the project. Considers complexity of the project and skill and experience of the artist when establishing payment.

BAKER STREET PRODUCTIONS LTD., Box 3610, Mankato MN 56001. (507)625-2482. Contact: Karyne Jacobsen. Service-related firm providing juvenile books to publishers.
Needs: Works with 2 freelance artists/year. Uses artists for advertising illustration, illustration on product and book illustration.
First Contact & Terms: Artists must be able to meet exact deadlines. Works on assignment only. Send query letter. Prefers photographs or photocopies to review. Reports back within 3 months. Fee is determined by the size of the project involved. Considers complexity of the project and how work will be used when establishing payment.

BANKERS LIFE & CASUALTY COMPANY, 1000 Sunset Ridge Rd., Northbrook IL 60062. (312)498-1500. Manager-Sales Media/Communications: Charles S. Pusateri. Insurance firm.
Needs: Works with 5-10 freelance artists/year. Uses artists for advertising and brochure displays, illustration and layout; posters and signage.
First Contact & Terms: Send query letter with business card and samples to be kept on file. Prefers printed pieces as samples. Samples returned only if requested. Reports within 2 weeks only if interested. Works on assignment only. Pays by the hour, $25-50 average. Considers complexity of project, skill and experience of artist, and turnaround time when establishing payment.

BAY AREA RAPID TRANSIT (BART), 800 Madison St., Oakland CA 94619. (415)465-4100. Manager Passenger Service: Kay Springer. Transportation service firm providing passenger brochures, flyers, signs, information, advertising.
Needs: Works with 6-10 freelance artists/year. Uses artists for advertising and brochure design, illustration and layout; posters and signage.
First Contact & Terms: Local artists only (San Francisco Bay area). Send query letter with brochure, resume, business card and samples to be kept on file. Prefers original work as samples. Reports only if interested. Works on assignment only. Pays by the hour or by the project. Considers complexity of project and turnaround time when establishing payment.

BERMAN LEATHERCRAFT INC., 25 Melcher St., Boston MA 02120. (617)426-0870. President: Robert S. Berman. Manufacturer/importer/mail order firm providing leathercraft kits and leather supplies, diaries and notepads. Clients: shops, hobbyists, schools and hospitals. "We mail to 5,000-25,000 people every six weeks."
Needs: Works with 2-4 freelance artists/year. Uses artists for brochure design, illustration and layout; "we produce two- to four-page fliers."
First Contact & Terms: Local artists only "for the convenience of both parties." Send query letter with samples; "follow up with a phone call three to five days later." Prefers printed brochures as samples. Samples not filed are returned by SASE only if requested. Pays by the project. Considers complexity of project, and skill and experience of artist when establishing payment.

BEROL, Berol Corp., Eagle Rd., Danbury CT 06810. (203)744-0000. Art Product Group Manager: Lance Hopkins. Manufactures writing instruments and drawing materials (Prismacolor art pencils and markers, Art Stix artist crayons).
Needs: Assigns 6 jobs/year. Uses artists for illustrations and layout for catalogs, ads, brochures, displays, packages and posters. Artists must use Prismacolor and/or Verithin products only.
First Contact & Terms: Query with samples to be kept on file. Prefers photographs and slides as samples. Samples returned only by request. Reports within 2 weeks. Pays by the project.

BEST WESTERN INTERNATIONAL INC., Best Western Way, Box 10203, Phoenix AZ 85064. (602)957-5763. Creative Director: Barbara Lanterman. Motel inn/hotel resort chain. Clients: motels, hotels, resorts.
Needs: Assigns 200 jobs/year. Especially needs photography, illustration, production art, design.
First Contact & Terms: Query with samples. Prefers samples of printed or published pieces, illustrations.

BLONDER-TONGUE LABORATORIES INC., 1 Jake Brown Rd., Old Bridge NJ 08857. (201)679-4000. Vice President: James Fitzpatrick. Manufactures TV signal distribution equipment for schools, hotels, hospitals and communities.
Needs: Uses artists for catalog cover designs, spec sheet layouts, P-O-P display designs and direct mail brochures.
First Contact & Terms: Submit resume. Reports within 2 weeks.

BLUE CROSS AND BLUE SHIELD OF MICHIGAN, 600 Lafayette E., Detroit MI 48226. (313)225-8115. Art/Production Manager: Robert H. Jones.

Needs: Uses 4 artists for product illustration/year. Also uses artists for designs for annual reports, brochures, posters, booklets, keylining and figure illustration.
First Contact & Terms: Local artists only. Query with printed samples. Artists must have at least 5 years in the field and a portfolio to back up professional experience. Payment negotiated.

*THE BRADFORD EXCHANGE, 9333 Milwaukee, Niles-Chicago IL 60648. (312)966-2770, ext. 300. Artist Liaison: Ed Bailey-Mershon. Manufacturer of collectible plates, "with possibilities of expanding into other collectibles." Clients: plate collectors in all age groups and income groups.
Needs: Works with 200 freelance artists/year. Uses artists for plate design, model making and collectibles design; interested in all media, 2-D, 3-D. Subject matter is predominately mothers, children; new areas: animals and movie themes. "Quality painting reproduced on plate."
First Contact & Terms: Works on assignment only. Send query letter with brochure, resume and samples to be kept on file, except for slides, which are duplicated and returned; call or write for appointment to show portfolio. Prefers slides, photographs, photocopies, tear hseets or photostats (in that order) as samples. Samples not filed are returned. Reports within 45 days. Pays for design "on spec"; $200 maximum. Contract negotiated for series. Considers complexity of the project, project's budget, skill and experience of the artist and rights purchased when establishing payment.

BULLETIN & DIRECTORY BOARD MFG. CO., 2317 W. Pico, Los Angeles CA 90006. (213)382-1147. Manager: John Curtis. Exhibit/sign firm. Also does wall graphics and murals. Assigns 30 jobs/year.
Needs: Works with 3-6 artists for sign design, 3-6 for exhibit design, 10 for print advertising and custom sign illustration. "Basically, we do only ink."
First Contact & Terms: Query or send samples. Reports in 1 week. Works on assignment only. Samples returned by SASE. Provide brochure, flyer and sample of print work if possible to be kept on file for future assignments. Pays $10/hour minimum.

*CANTERBURY DESIGNS, INC.. Box 4060, Martinez GA 30907. (800)241-2732 or (404)860-1674. President: Angie A. Newton. Publisher and distributor of charted design books; counted cross stitch mainly. Clients: needlework specialty shops, wholesale distributors (craft and needlework), department stores and chain stores.
Needs: Works with 12-20 freelance artists/year. Uses artists for product design.
First Contact & Terms: Send query letter with samples to be kept on file, or call for appointment to show portfolio. Prefers stitched needlework, paintings, photographs or charts as samples. Samples not filed are returned. Reports within 1 month. Payment varies. "Some designs purchased outright, some are paid on a royalty basis." Considers complexity of project, salability, customer appeal and rights purchased when establishing payment.
Tips: "When sending your work for our review, be sure to photocopy it first. This protects you. Also, you have a copy from which to reconstruct your design should it be lost in mail. Also, send your work by certified mail. You have proof it was actually received by someone."

*KEN CAPLAN PRODUCT DESIGN, 4651 Fitch Ave., Lincolnwood IL 60646. (312)674-2643. Art Director: Ken Caplan. Product development of hobbycrafts, activity toys, Christmas ornaments, leather crafts, clock kits and toys. "We create, invent, design the product, it's color and 'look' for child and adult shelf appeal." Clients: manufacturers.
Needs: Uses artists for advertising and catalog illustration and layout, brochure illustration, product design, illustration on product and model making. "We use whimsical illustrations that are conducive to game boards, cards and all children's products."
First Contact & Terms: Works on assignment only. Send query letter with brochure and business card to be kept on file; write for appointment to show portfolio. Prefers photocopies, photographs, tear sheets or proofs as samples. Samples not returned. Reports within 10 days. Pays by the project. Considers complexity of the project, how work will be used and rights purchased when establishing payment.
Tips: "Top creativity and hard work pays off."

CENIT LETTERS, INC., 7438 Varna Ave., North Hollywood CA 91605. (818)983-1234 or (213)875-0880. President: Don Kurtz. Sign firm producing custom cutout letters. Clients: building managers and their tenants (high rise), designers and architects. Assigns 25 jobs/year.
Needs: Works with artists for sign design, exhibit design, P-O-P design, and custom sign artwork. Also uses artists for layout and gold leaf work.
First Contact & Terms: Local artists only. Query or call. SASE. Reports in 1 week. Works on assignment only. Samples returned by SASE. Provide resume to be kept on file for future assignments. Pays $100 minimum gold leaf.
Tips: Especially looks for "proficiency in hand lettering and accurate full-scale layouts."

CHARLOTTE MOTOR SPEEDWAY, Box 600, Harrisburg NC 28075. (704)455-2121. Contact: Public Relations Director. Speedway for stock/sports cars and motorcycles. Assigns 6 jobs/year.
Needs: Uses artists for advertising, direct mail brochures, posters, publicity brochures, signage and souvenir program covers for races.
First Contact & Terms: Query with samples. SASE. Reports within 2 weeks. Pays $600 maximum/job, design/layout and illustration.

CLYMER'S OF BUCKS COUNTY, 141 Canal St., Nashua NH 03061. (603)882-2180. Vice President Divisional Manager: Joan B. Litle. Mail order catalog of gifts and collectibles, primarily American made. Clients: consumers.
Needs: Works with 12 freelance artists/year. Uses artists for advertising, brochure and catalog design, illustration and layout.
First Contact & Terms: Prefers local artists with experience in direct mail catalogs. Send query letter with brochure, references, samples and tear sheets to be kept on file. Prefers photostats as samples. Samples not kept on file are returned by SASE. Reports only if interested. Works on assignment only. Pay varies according to project. Considers skill and experience of artist and turnaround time when establishing payment.

CMA MICRO COMPUTER, 55722 Santa Fe Trail, Yucca Valley CA 92284. (619)365-9718. Director/Advertising: Phyllis Wattenbarger. Manufacturer/distributor of computer software. Clients: computer software manufacturers and distributors.
Needs: Works with 10 freelance artists/year. Uses artists for advertising and brochure design and illustration.
First Contact & Terms: Send query letter with samples to be kept on file. Accepts photostats, photographs, photocopies or tear sheets as samples. Samples not filed returned only if requested. Reports only if interested. Pays by the project, $50-2,000 average. Considers complexity of project, skill and experience of the artist, how work will be used and turnaround time ("very important") when establishing payment.

***COLORSCAN SERVICES, INC.**, 241 Stuyvesant Ave., Lyndhurst NJ 07071. (201)438-6729. President: J. Principato. Graphic services firm providing separations and printing services. Clients: ad agencies, printers, manufacturers and publishers.
Needs: Works with 3 freelance artists/year. Uses artists for advertising, brochure and catalog design, illustration and layout; product design; illustration on product; P-O-P displays; display fixture design; posters; model making; and signage.
First Contact & Terms: Works on assignment only. Send resume and samples to be kept on file; write for appointment to show portfolio. Prefers tear sheets as samples. Samples not filed are returned by SASE. Reports only if interested. Pays by the project. Considers complexity of the project and rights purchased when establishing payment.

COMMUNICATION SKILL BUILDERS, INC., Box 42050, Tucson AZ 85733. (602)323-7500. Production Manager: Sharon Walters. Publisher of education materials for special education (K-12), gifted education and microcomputer education. Clients: teachers, special education professionals, hospitals, clinics, etc.
Needs: Works with 10 freelance artists/year. Uses artists for advertising, brochure and catalog design, illustration and layout; product and display fixture design; illustration on product; and posters.
First Contact & Terms: Prefers local artists, but "can work with out-of-town artists as well. Must have experience." Send query letter with brochure and samples to be kept on file. Write for appointment to show portfolio. Prefers slides, photos, printed work as samples. Reports within 2 weeks. Works on assignment only. Considers complexity of project, turnaround time and rights purchased when establishing payment.
Tips: "Artists should have experience doing materials for educational publishers."

COMMUNICATIONS ELECTRONICS, Dept. AM, Box 1045, Ann Arbor MI 48106-1045. (313)973-8888. Editor: Ken Ascher. Manufacturer, distributor and ad agency (10 company divisions). Clients: electronics, computers.
Needs: Works with 150 freelance artists/year. Uses artists for advertising, brochure and catalog design, illustration and layout; product design, illustration on product, P-O-P displays, posters and renderings.
First Contact & Terms: Send query letter with brochure, resume, business card, samples and tear sheets to be kept on file. Call or write for appointment to show portfolio. Samples not kept on file returned by SASE. Reports within 1 month. Pays by the project, $25-350 average. Considers complexity of project, skill and experience of artist, how work will be used, turnaround time and rights purchased when establishing payment.

CONIMAR CORPORATION, Box 1509, Ocala FL 32678. (904)732-7235. Manufactures placemats, coasters, table hot pads, calendars, recipe cards, note cards, postcards.
Needs: Buys 10-15 designs/year. Designs range from floral to abstract and children's designs. Artist quotes price to be considered by Conimar. "Our designs are based a lot on designs of dinnerware, glassware and stationery items."
First Contact & Terms: Send letter, resume and samples of work. Reports in 1 week. Works on assignment only. Samples returned by SASE. Provide resume and brochure to be kept on file for future assignments. Past payment has ranged from $250-400.

CONSOLIDATED MOUNTING & FINISHING, 50-10 Kneeland St., Elmhurst NY 11373. Chief Designer: C. Sutnar. Display firm. Assigns 60-100 jobs/year.
Needs: Uses artists for exhibit design, display fixture design, model-making, P-O-P design, print advertising and scale models.
First Contact & Terms: Query with samples (cardboard, corrugated board, plastics and wood) or write for interview. Prefers b&w line drawings, photostats, roughs and previously published work as samples. SASE. Reports in 3 weeks. Works on assignment only. Provide resume, business card and flyer to be kept on file for future assignments. Pays $16/hour or considers complexity of project, and skill and experience of artist when establishing payment.

CONSOLIDATED STAMP MFG. CO., 7220 Wilson Ave., Harwood Heights IL 60656. (312)867-5800. Advertising/Marketing Manager: Edward C. Harris. Manufacturer and distributor of customized stationery embossers and notarial seals, marking devices of all types, security badges, advertising medallions, transportation tokens, premiums for banks, store chains, etc. Clients: office and stationery supply stores, department stores, direct mail chains, security outfits, transportation systems, consumer direct mail.
Needs: Works with 2-3 freelance artists/year. Uses artists for advertising design, illustration and layout; brochure, catalog and display fixture design; and P-O-P displays. There is a trend in the field toward "a simplification of overall design with the use of more open spaces."
First Contact & Terms: Local, experienced artists only; "must not work for our competition." Works on assignment only. Send query letter with resume, business card and samples to be kept on file. Call or write for appointment to show portfolio. Prefers "whatever artist has available, original art, printed brochures, etc." as samples. Samples not filed are returned by SASE. Reports only if interested. Pays by the project. "We prefer the artist to quote on the entire job." Considers complexity of project, and skill and experience of artist when establishing payment.
Tips: "At least be familiar with our product line. An artist who comes in and inquires as to what we do is given little consideration. Many artists make a fatal mistake of bringing dirty, worn-out samples, or poor examples of their work. Most come ill-prepared to explain their capabilities. An artist is a salesman. In a large firm like ours we can't gamble with the unknown factors." When reviewing samples, especially looks for "originality, certainly, but of more importance is an artist's ability to understand our specific art problems or our promotional communication problems. His flexibility is also important."

COVERDELL INSURANCE GROUP, 2015 Peachtree Rd. NE, Atlanta GA 30309. (404)355-8880. Director of Production: Ruth Lasky. Insurance marketing. Provides direct mail marketing of insurance plans. Clients: banks, savings and loans, finance companies, rural electric cooperatives.
Needs: Works with 6 freelance artists/year. Uses artists for advertising and brochure design, illustration and layout.
First Contact & Terms: Prefers local artists with direct mail materials experience. Call or write for appointment to show portfolio. Works on assignment only. Pays by the project, $50-2,000 average. Considers complexity of project, skill and experience of artist and how work will be used when establishing payment.
Tips: Artists "should have some design samples of direct mail materials or projects."

***CREATE YOUR OWN, INC.**, R.R. #2, Box 201A, Hickory Corner Rd., Milford NJ 08848. (201)479-4015. President: Catherine C. Knowles. Vice President: George S. Wetteland. Manufactures needlework and craft kits, including needlepoint, crewel, fabric, dolls, crochet, stamped cross stitch and counted cross stitch, plastic canvas, candlewicking and lace net darning. Clients: catalog houses, department store chains, needlework chains, retail stores, etc.
Needs: Works with 2-3 freelance artists/year. Uses artists for product design in needlework area only and model making.
First Contact & Terms: Prefers local artists with some experience in needleworking design, if possible. Works on assignment only. Send query letter with brochure, resume, business card and samples to be kept on file, except for original art work. Prefers photographs or tear sheets as samples. Samples returned only if requested. Reports only if interested. Pays by the hour, $8 average. Considers skill and ex-

perience of the artist, how work will be used, turnaround time and rights purchased when establishing payment.

CREATIVE AWARDS BY LANE, 1575 Elmhurst Rd., Elk Grove IL 60007. (312)593-7700. Contact: Don Thompson. Distributor of recognition incentive awards consisting of trophies, plaques, jewelry, crystal, ad specialties and personalized premiums. Clients: companies, clubs, associations, athletic organizations.
Needs: Works with 3-4 freelance artists/year. Uses artists for advertising, brochure and catalog design, illustration and layout; and signage.
First Contact & Terms: Local artists only. Send query letter to be kept on file; write for appointment to show portfolio. Prefers to review photostats, photographs or photocopies. Reports within 10 days. Pays by the project. Considers complexity of project when establishing payment.

*CUSTOM HOUSE OF NEEDLE ARTS, INC., 200 Stow Rd., Marlborough MA 01752. (617)485-6699. Owner/President: Carolyn Purcell. Manufacturer of traditional crewel embroidery kits. Clients: needlework shops and catalogs.
Needs: Uses artists for product design. "We hope that artist is a crewel stitcher and can produce sample model."
First Contact & Terms: Send query letter with samples and any pertinent information to be kept on file. Prefers colored drawings or photos (if good closeup) as samples. Samples not filed are returned by SASE only if requested. Reports within 1 month. Pays royalty on kits sold.
Tips: "We emphasize *traditional* designs; use *some* current 'cutsy' type designs, but only if exceptional, for pictures, pillows, bellpulls, chair seats and clock faces."

CUSTOM STUDIOS, 1337 W. Devon Ave., Chicago IL 60660. (312)761-1150. President: Gary Wing. Custom T-shirt manufacturer. "We specialize in designing and screen printing of custom T-shirts for schools, business promotions, fundraising and for our own line of stock."
Needs: Works with 4 illustrators and 4 designers/month. Assigns 50 jobs/year. Especially needs b&w illustrations (some original and some from customer's sketch). Uses artists for direct mail and brochures/flyers, but mostly for custom and stock T-shirts.
First Contact & Terms: Query with samples or arrange interview. Prefers photostats or photocopies as samples; "do not send originals as we will not return them." Reports in 3-4 weeks. Provide resume and business card to be kept on file for possible future assignments. Pays by the hour, $5-20 average. Considers turnaround time and rights purchased when establishing payment. On designs submitted to be used as stock T-shirt designs, pays 5-10% royalty.
Tips: "Send good copies of your best work."

GEORGE DELL, INC., 133 W. 25th St., New York NY 10001. (212)206-8460. President: George Dell. Manufacturer of display decorative materials, exclusively for use by stores in interior or window display. Clients: department stores, specialty stores, real estate.
Needs: Works with 2-3 freelance artists/year. Uses artists for advertising and brochure design, illustration and layout; product design and illustration on product.
First Contact & Terms: Prefers local artists with some experience. Send resume and tear sheets to be kept on file. Prefers photostats as samples. Reports within 2 weeks. Pays by the project, $300-600. Considers complexity of project, skill and experience of artist, and rights purchased when establishing payment.
Tips: Artists should be "neat in their presentation."

DISPLAYCO, 2055 McCarter Hwy., Newark NJ 07104. (201)485-0023. Contact: Art Director. Designers and producers of P-O-P displays in all materials. Clients: "any consumer products manufacturers."
Needs: Works with 12 freelance artists/year. Uses artists for advertising layout, brochure illustration and layout, display fixture and P-O-P design, and model making. Especially needs P-O-P designers with excellent sketching and rendering skills.
First Contact & Terms: Prefers artists experienced in P-O-P or display/exhibit. Send samples, brochure/flyer and resume; submit portfolio for review or call for appointment. Prefers renderings, models, produced work, photos of models, work, etc., as samples. Samples not returned. Works on assignment only; reports back on whether to expect possible future assignments. Provide resume, business card, brochure, flyer or tear sheets to be kept on file for possible future assignments. Payment is determined by the project; method is negotiable and varies according to job.
Tips: There is a "need for greater creativity and new solutions. Freelancers should have knowledge of P-O-P materials (plastics, wire, metal, wood) and how their designs can be produced."

*DMP HACKETT AMERICAN, Suite D, 12891 Western Ave., Garden Grove CA 92641. (714)895-2912. Manager: James R. Hackett. Manufacturer and art publisher of wholesale collector plates, lithographs, figurines and miniatures. Clients: wholesalers, dealers and consumers.
Needs: Works with 20-30 freelance artists/year. Uses freelance artists for plate design and illustration; figurine design; and limited edition fine art prints. Seeks illustrative, realistic style artwork.
First Contact & Terms: Works on assignment basis only. Send query letter with samples to be kept on file. Write for appointment to show portfolio. Prefers slides and photographs as samples. Samples not kept on file are returned only if requested. Reports within 30 days. Pays by the project, $500-2,000 or on a royalty basis. Considers skill and experience of artist when establishing payment.

DUKE'S CUSTOM SIGN CO., 601 2nd St. NE, Canton OH 44702. (216)456-2729. Clients: banks, merchants, architects, hospitals, schools and construction firms.
Needs: Assigns 5-10 jobs/year. Works with 5-10 artists/year for sign design. Especially needs sign shapes for outdoor and free-standing displays.
First Contact & Terms: Local artists preferred. Query with resume or call. SASE. Reports within 2 weeks. Works on assignment only. Samples returned by SASE; reports back on future possibilities. Provide resume and samples (photographs, etc.) to be kept on file for future assignments. Pays $5-20/hour; by the project, $10-500 average; by the day $60-500. Considers complexity of project, skill and experience of artist, and how work will be used when establishing payment.
Tips: "Please bring samples of what you think are quality sign displays."

EARTHWARE COMPUTER SERVICES, Box 30039, Eugene OR 97403. (503)344-3383. President: Donna J. Goles. Manufacturer of software for home and school. The educational products are geared for jr. high through college ages.
Needs: Works with 2-4 freelance artists/year. Uses artists for advertising design, illustration and layout; and product design.
First Contact & Terms: Prefers local or regional artists. Works on assignment only. Send query letter with brochure, resume, business card and samples to be kept on file. Accepts photostats, photographs, photocopies, slides or tear sheets as samples. Samples not filed are returned. Reports within 1 month. Pays by the project. Considers complexity of project when establishing payment.
Tips: "Do not over supply us with samples."

EDUCATIONAL PRODUCTS CO., Box 295, Hope NJ 07844. (201)459-4220. General Manager: H.R. Maier. Operates Land of Make Believe, children's theme park, and manufactures plastic cookie cutters. Clients: stores, jobbers, distributors, plus consumers (for cookie cutters), schools and general public.
Needs: Uses artists for illustration of direct mail pieces, catalogs and brochures. Will need new catalog for next year.
First Contact & Terms: Local artists only. Query with previously published work and arrange interview to show portfolio. SASE. Reports within 2-3 weeks. Negotiates pay.

EDUCATIONAL SUBSCRIPTION SERVICE, INC., 3308 South Cedar, South Pointe Plaza, Lansing MI 48910. Marketing Manager: Ted Simmons. Executive Secretary: Cindy Hartmann. Direct-mail firm. Offers educational courtesy rates for magazine subscriptions. Clients: college students and educators.
Needs: Works with 1-3 freelance artists/year. Uses artists for advertising, brochure and catalog design, illustration and layout. "We also do some promotional work, free of charge, for local nonprofit organizations requiring artwork."
First Contact & Terms: Send query letter with resume and samples to be kept on file. "We would like to see final printed brochures, layouts, catalogs, etc." as samples. Samples not kept on file are returned. Reports within 6 weeks. Works on assignment only. Negotiates pay. Considers complexity of project, skill and experience of artist, how work will be used and turnaround time when establishing payment.
Tips: "Most of our advertising has been conservative. Please plan presentations accordingly."

EMBOSOGRAPH DISPLAY MFG. CO., 1430 W. Wrightwood, Chicago IL 60614. (312)472-6660. Vice President/Personnel: Lee Frizane. Specializes in "complete creative art services and manufacturing in litho, silk screen, plastic molding of all kinds, spray, hot stamping, embossing, die cutting, metal work and assembly." Clients: brewery, beverage, food, automotive, hardware, cosmetics, service stations, appliances and clocks, plus consumer wall decor.
Needs: Assigns 50-100 jobs/year. Works with 15 artists for sign design, display fixture design, costume design, model-making, P-O-P design, print advertising and custom sign illustration. Especially needs P-O-P design.
First Contact & Terms: Query with resume or call. Prefers roughs and previously published work as

samples. Reports in 2 weeks. Works on assignment only. Samples returned by SASE. Provide resume and brochure to be kept on file for possible future assignments. Pays $25-45/hour.
Tips: "We have added consumer items, mostly wall decor." There is a trend toward "counter and wall cases and stands" in this business field.

EPSILON DATA MANAGEMENT, INC., 50 Cambridge St., Burlington MA 01803. Art Director: Thomas Flynn. Full-service direct response advertising and direct mail for commercial and not-for-profit organizations. Clients: 250 diversified clients nationwide, nonprofit and commercial.
Needs: Works with 20 freelance artists/year. Uses artists for direct mail packaging; advertising, brochure and catalog design, illustration and layout; and signage.
First Contact & Terms: Local artists only with three years' experience, plus "must work fast and accurately on very tight deadlines." Send query letter with brochure, resume, business card, samples and tear sheets to be kept on file. Considers photostats, slides, photographs or original work as samples. Samples not kept on file are not returned. Reports only if interested. Works on assignment only. Pays by the hour, $30-60 average; by the project, $150-3,000 average; by the day, $150-300 average. Considers complexity of project, skill and experience of artist and turnaround time when establishing payment.
Tips: "Be well experienced in direct response advertising."

EXHIBIT BUILDERS INC., 150 Wildwood Rd., Box 226, Deland FL 32720. (904)734-3196. Contact: J.C. Burkhalter. Produces custom exhibits, displays, scale models, dioramas, sales centers and character costumes. Clients: primarily manufacturers, ad agencies and tourist attractions.
Needs: Uses artists for exhibit/display design and scale models.
First Contact & Terms: Works on assignment only. Samples returned by SASE; reports back on future possibilities. Provide resume, business card and brochure to be kept on file for future assignments. Considers complexity of project, skill and experience of artist, how work will be used, turnaround time and rights purchased when establishing payment.
Tips: "Wants to see examples of previous design work for other clients; not interested in seeing school-developed portfolios."

GEORGE E. FERN CO., 1100 Gest St., Cincinnati OH 45203. (513)621-6111. General Manager: George J. Budig. Exposition service contractor/display firm.
Needs: Very limited art needs; "almost zero." Sometimes uses artists for backdrop displays, trade show exhibit/design, convention entrances and special room decorations.
First Contact & Terms: Query by phone. Reports in 1 week. Works on assignment only. Samples returned by SASE. Pays by the hour, $20-35 average; by the project, $100-500 average. Considers complexity of project, skill and experience of artist, how work will be used and turnaround time when establishing payment.
Tips: "We need some names, addresses and phone numbers so we can call."

*FRELINE, INC., Box 889, Hagerstown MD 21740. Art Director: Mark Kretzer. Manufacturer and developer of library promotional aids—posters, mobiles, bookmarks, reading motivators and other products to promote reading, library services and resources. Clients: school and public libraries, classroom teachers.
Needs: Works with 6 freelance artists/year. Uses artists for advertising design, illustration and layout; catalog design, illustration and layout; product design, illustration on product and posters.
First Contact & Terms: Experienced designers or illustrators only. Works on assignment only. Send query letter with brochure, resume and samples to be kept on file except for returned material. Prefers photographs, slides or tear sheets as samples. Samples not filed are returned. Reports within 15 days. Pays by the project, $250-800 average. Considers complexity of the project, skill and experience of the artist, turnaround time and rights purchased when establishing payment.
Tips: "We love good idea and concept artists."

G.A.I. AND ASSOCIATES, INC., Box 30309, Indianapolis IN 46230. (317)257-7100. President: William S. Gardiner. Licensing agents. "We represent artists to the collectibles industry, i.e., manufacturers of high-quality prints, collector's plates, figurines, bells, etc. There is no up-front fee for our services. We receive a commission for any payment the artist receives as a result of our efforts." Clients: manufacturers of high-quality prints and lithographs, porcelain products.
Needs: Works with 30-40 freelance artists/year.
First Contact & Terms: "We are not interested in landscapes, still lifes, or modern art. We are looking for 'people-oriented' art that will appeal to the average person." Send query letter with resume and samples. Prefers color photographs as samples; do *not* send original work. Samples not kept on file are returned by SASE. Reports in 1 month. Works on assignment only. Payment: "If we are successful in putting together a program for the artist with a manufacturer, the artist is usually paid a royalty on the sale of

the product using his art. This varies from 4%-10%." Considers complexity of project, skill and experience of artist, how work will be used and rights purchased when establishing payment; "payment is negotiated individually for each project."
Tips: "We are looking for art with broad emotional appeal."

GADSDEN COUNTY CHAMBER OF COMMERCE, Box 389, Quincy FL 32351. (904)627-9231. Executive Director: Ben Ellinor.
Needs: Assigns 2 jobs/year. Uses artists for direct mail/publicity brochures, newspaper ad layouts, trade magazine ads and publications.
First Contact & Terms: Arrange interview or mail art. SASE. Reports in 1 month. Negotiates payment.

GARDEN STATE MARKETING SERVICES, INC., (formerly Edu-tron), Box 343, Oakland NJ 07436. (201)337-3888. President: Jack Doherty. Service-related firm providing public relations and advertising services, mailing services and fulfillment. Clients: associations, publishers, manufacturers.
Needs: Works with 6 freelance artists/year. Uses artists for advertising and brochure design, illustration and layout; display fixture design, P-O-P displays and posters.
First Contact & Terms: Send query letter with brochure, resume, business card and samples to be kept on file. Prefers copies as samples. Samples not kept on file are returned. Reports only if interested. Works on assignment only. Open pay rate. Considers complexity of project, skill and experience of artist and how work will be used when establishing payment.
Tips: "We have noticed a movement toward one color with use of bendays."

GARON PRODUCTS INC., 1924 Highway 35, Wall NJ 07719. (201)449-1776. Marketing Manager: Christy Karl. Industrial direct marketers of maintenance products, i.e., concrete repair, roof repair. Clients: maintenance departments of corporations, government facilities, small businesses.
Needs: Works with 3 freelance artists/year. Uses artists for brochure and catalog design, illustration and layout. Seeks "local artists and ones who will work within the organization so that corrections and additions can be done on the spot." Send query letter with brochure, resume and business card to be kept on file. Prefers photographs or photostats as mailed samples. Reports only if interested. Pays by the page or by the project. Considers complexity of project, and skill and experience of artist when establishing payment.
Tips: "Professionalism is a must! Work should be camera-ready for commercial printing upon completion. I need experienced catalog artists with creative ideas."

GARTH PRODUCTS, INC., 32-4 Littell Rd., East Hanover NJ 07936. (201)887-8487. President: Garth Patterson. Manufacturer of silkscreened ceramic and glass souvenirs. Clients: banks, museums, amusement parks, restored villages, tourist attractions, resorts, hotels and retail stores.
Needs: Works with 5 artists per year. Uses artists for illustrations on products. Especially needs line drawings of buildings, statues, flowers and songbirds.
First Contact & Terms: Send query letter, samples, brochure/flyer or actual work. Prefers photostats as samples. Samples returned by SASE. Reports within 3-4 weeks. Provide business card, brochure and samples to be kept on file for possible future assignments. Payment is by the project; $25-100 average and varies according to complexity of job and skill and experience of artist.
Tips: "Understand the type of line work needed for silkscreening. We now also use pencil work. Better artwork is more appreciated."

GEORGIA-PACIFIC CORP., 133 Peachtree St., Atlanta GA 30303. (404)521-4758. Contact: Manager of Graphics Production. Manufactures building products, pulp, paper and chemicals.
Needs: Works with 5-10 artists/year for ad illustrations; 15-20, advertising design; 3, product design; and 4-5, illustrations for use on products. Also uses artists for direct mail brochures, annual reports, billboards, interior design, posters, catalogs, spec sheets and print collateral. Needs material for vinyl and leather products.
First Contact & Terms: Prefers local artists. Query with resume and printed samples. Provide resume, business card, brochure and flyer to be kept on file for future assignments. Pays $35-50/hour, design; $25-30/hour, finish. Fees on large projects are estimated by artist—"generally runs at $35-50/hour."

GOLDBERGS' MARINE, 202 Market St., Philadelphia PA 19106. (215)829-2200. Vice President Marketing: Richard Goldberg. Produces 9 mail order catalogs of pleasure boating equipment and watersport gear for the active family.
Needs: Works with 3 freelance artists/year. Uses artists for brochure and catalog design, illustration and layout; and signage.
First Contact & Terms: Artists must be "flexible with knowledge of 4-color printing, have a willing-

ness to work with paste-up and printing staff, and exhibit the ability to follow up and take charge." Send query letter with brochure, business card, samples and tear sheets to be kept on file. Call for appointment to show portfolio. Samples should be "printed material. Original work (mechanicals) may be required at portfolio showing." Reports only if interested. Pays by the project. Considers complexity of project, how work will be used and turnaround time when establishing payment.
Tips: "Boating experience is helpful and a willingness to do research is sometimes necessary. Long-term relationships usually exist with our company."

GOLDEN STATE ENVELOPE, INC., 1741 N. Ivar Ave., Los Angeles CA 90028. (213)461-3044. Distributor of Hard-To-Find envelopes. Clients: broad spectrum of businesses.
Needs: Works with 1 freelance artist/year. Uses artist for brochure design.
First Contact & Terms: Local artists only.

GUILFORD PUBLICATIONS INC., 200 Park Ave. S., New York NY 10003. (212)674-1900. Marketing Manager: Marian Robinson. Produces professional, educational and industrial audiovisuals and books.
Needs: Assigns 20 jobs/year. Uses artists for catalog design, book jackets and ads.
First Contact & Terms: Local artists only. Query. SASE. Reports within 4 weeks. Pays by job.

THE HAMILTON COLLECTION, Suite 1000, 9550 Regency Square Blvd., Jacksonville FL 32211. Vice President, Product Development: Melanie Hart; Art Director (for commercial art/advertising): Debra McKinney. Direct mail/marketing firm for collectibles and limited edition art, plates, sculpture. Clients: general public and specialized lists of collectible buyers.
Needs: Works with 5 freelance artists in creative department and 10 in product development/year. Uses artists for advertising mechanicals, brochure illustration and mechanicals, product design and illustration on product.
First Contact & Terms: Only local artists with three years' experience for mechanical work. For illustration and product design, "no restrictions on locality, but must have *quality* work and flexibility regarding changes which are sometimes necessary. Also, a 'name' and notoriety help." Send query letter with samples to be kept on file, except for fine art which is to be returned (must include a SASE or appropriate container with sufficient postage). Call or write for appointment to show portfolio. Samples not kept on file are returned only if requested by artist. Reports within 2-4 weeks. Pays by the hour for mechanicals, $20 average. Considers complexity of project, skill and experience of artist, how work will be used and rights purchased when establishing payment.
Tips: "Be prepared to offer sketches on speculation."

HARTMAN CARDS, 839 N. Woodstock St., Philadelphia PA 19130. (215)236-4944. Contact: Louis Hartman. Distributor of greeting cards, calendars, stationery, gifts and t-shirts.
Needs: Buys finished products from artists; prefers a "contemporary, trendy" look. "Artists sell me the product once it's produced."
First Contact & Terms: Call for appointment to show portfolio. Prefers to review photographs. Samples not filed are returned.
Tips: "Artists should have initiative, flexibility, and the ability to develop a product line."

HERFF JONES, Box 6500, Providence RI 02940-6500. (401)331-1240. Art Director: Fred Spinney. Manufacturer of class ring jewelry; motivation/recognition/emblematic awards—service pins, medals, medallions and trophies. Clients: high school and college level students; a variety of companies/firms establishing recognition programs.
Needs: Works with 6 freelance artists/year. Uses artists for illustration of product.
First Contact & Terms: Artists need not necessarily be local, "but should have three years previous experience in this particular field." Send query letter with brochure, resume, business card and samples (copies of original work) to be kept on file; originals will be returned if sent. Write for appointment to show portfolio. Prefers slides and photographs as samples. Samples not kept on file returned by SASE. Reports only if interested. Works on assignment only. Pays by the project, $15-50 average. Considers complexity of project, skill and experience of artist, and turnaround time when establishing payment.
Tips: Artists approaching this firm "should be of a professional level. The artist should have a good versatile background in illustrating as well as having some mechanical drawing abilities, such as hand lettering."

HOWARD JOHNSON CO., #1 Monarch Dr., North Quincy MA 02269-9102. Graphics/Design Director: Robert C. Downing. Services/Products: Food and lodging and specialty restaurant concepts, grocery products, ice cream and frozen foods and candy products.
Needs: Works with illustrators, advertising design shops, product designers and 2-3 freelancers/year.

Uses artists for product illustrations, sales promotion literature, menu design, catalog covers/illustrations, exhibit designs and displays.
First Contact & Terms: Prefers local artists. Must have professional experience in food and/or lodging industry. Query with samples. "Illustrators should submit samples which will be returned. Would especially like to see food illustration all styles, color and/or black and white." Provide resume, brochure and flyer to be kept on file for future assignments. "All copyrights on purchased material will be assigned to Howard Johnson's with original artist retaining the right to use designs for self-promotion only. Fees for assignments will be established prior to each job and an *itemized* bill should be submitted with completed job, coded to a purchase order number assigned to a particular job."

HUTCHESON DISPLAYS, INC., 517 S. 14th St., Omaha NE 68102. (402)341-0707. President: Wm. S. Hutcheson. Manufacturer of screen printed display materials. Clients: advertisers.
Needs: Works with 6 freelance artists/year. Uses artists for advertising layout. Especially needs graphic design.
First Contact & Terms: Send samples. Submit roughs or copies of work done for similar companies. Samples returned. Pays by the project. Negotiates payment. Considers complexity of project when establishing payment.

IDEAL SCHOOL SUPPLY CO., 11000 S. Lavergne, Oak Lawn IL 60453. Graphic Arts Coordinator: Charles A. Koch. Manufactures educational materials. Clients: distributors and dealers of educational materials.
Needs: Assigns 25-50 jobs and buys 25 illustrations/year. Uses artists for direct mail brochures, packaging, book illustrations and game designs. Especially needs illustrations, keyline and production. Looks for "crisp layout renderings, creative and colorful illustrations, and accurate production techniques to assure fidelity in reproduction."
First Contact & Terms: Primarily uses local artists. Send resume or letter. Follow up with samples (stats or photos to keep on file) and prices; "if original art is sent artist must provide return package complete with postage and insurance." Prefers artists who have had work published. Pays by the hour, $12-20 average, or flat rate based on complete project, graphic art.
Tips: "Artists must work promptly and stay within the budget allocated for art."

IGPC, 48 W. 48th St., New York NY 10036. (212)869-5588. Postage Stamp Art Director: Steve Fox. Agent to foreign governments; "we produce postage stamps and related items on behalf of thirty different foreign governments."
Needs: Works with 25-35 freelance artists/year. Uses artists primarily for postage stamp design; sometimes uses them for advertising, brochure and catalog design, illustration and layout.
First Contact & Terms: Artists should be within metropolitan (NY) or tri-state area. "No actual experience required except to have good tight art skills (4-color) and excellent design skills." Call for appointment to show portfolio. Reports immediately. Works on assignment only. Pays by the project, $750-3,000 average. Considers government allowance per project when establishing payment.
Tips: "Artists considering working with IGPC must have excellent 4-color abilities (in general or specific topics, i.e., flora, fauna, transport, famous people, etc.); sufficient design skills to arrange for and position type; the ability to create artwork that will reduce to postage stamp size and still hold up to clarity and perfection. 90% of the work we require is realistic art and 10% is graphic. In most cases, we supply the basic layout and reference material; however, we appreciate an artist who knows where to find references and can present new and interesting concepts."

*INCOLAY STUDIES INCORPORATED, 445 N. Fox St., Box 592, San Fernando CA 91340. (818)365-2521. Curator: Brenda Lynch-Silvestri. Manufacturer of wholesale Incolay stone bas-relief giftware. Clients: high-end jewelry and gift stores.
Needs: Works with 6 freelance artists/year. Uses freelance artists to sculpt bas-relief designs.
First Contact & Terms: "Artists must have experience in sculpture but more important they must have talent." Works on assignment only. Send query letter with samples to be kept on file. Prefers photographs or slides as samples. Reports back to the artist within 2 weeks. Payment is by the project on a royalty basis (% of wholesale). Considers complexity of the project and project budget when establishing payment.

INTERNATIONAL RESEARCH & EVALUATION, 21098 Ire Control Ctr., Eagan MN 55121. (612)888-9635. Art Director: Ronald Owon. Private, nonpartisan, interdisciplinary research firm that collects, stores and disseminates information on line, on demand to industry, labor and government on contract/subscription basis.
Needs: Works with 30-40 freelance artists/year. Uses artists for advertising, brochure and catalog design, illustration and layout; product design and P-O-P displays.

First Contact & Terms: Artists should request "Capabilities Analysis" form from firm. Reports only if interested. Works on assignment only. Pays by the hour, $50-250 average. Considers how work will be used when establishing payment.

JOULÉ INC., 54 Oakwood Ave., Orange NJ 07051. (201)672-2000. Marketing Manager: Carl Tuosto. Engineering firm.
Needs: Uses artists for advertising gimmicks, graphic sales promotion, audiovisual presentations and exhibit equipment.
First Contact & Terms: Works on assignment only. Send business card and brochure to be kept on file for possible future assignments. Reports back. Pays $500-1,000 average for camera-ready art.

KELLERMAN JEWEL CHEST COMPANY, 543 Mineral Spring Ave., Pawtucket RI 02860. (401)724-1600. Product Manager: David McLoughlin. Manufacturer and distributor of jewelry boxes, poker boxes, card boxes, assorted duck boxes and leather travel boxes. Clients: department stores, jewelry stores.
Needs: Works with 4-6 freelance artists/year. Uses artists for product design.
First Contact & Terms: Send query letter with brochure to be kept on file. Reports within 10 days. Negotiates pay. Considers skill and experience of the artist when establishing payment.
Tips: "Suggest innovations which will benefit my product when they're applied."

*KERN COLLECTIBLES, 1987 Industrial Blvd., Box 366, Stillwater MN 55082. (612)439-5544. Manager: Matthew Brummer. Art publisher of wholesale and retail collector plates and figurines featuring children, birds, wildlife, and fantasy art. Clinets: retail stores and consumers.
Needs: Works with 6 freelance artists/year. Uses artists for plate and figurine design and illustration. Prefers realistic styles.
First Contact & Terms: Send query letter with brochure and samples; brochure only is filed. Prefers slides and photographs as samples. Samples are returned. Reports back within 30 days. Negotiates payment. Considers skill and experience of the artist and rights purchased when establishing payment.

KLITZNER IND., INC., 44 Warren St., Providence RI 02901. (401)751-7500, ext. 242. Design Director: Louis Marini. Manufacturer; "four separate divisions that serve uniquely different markets: ad specialty, fraternal, direct mail and retail."
Needs: Works with "several" freelance artists/year. Uses artists for product design, illustration on product and model making.
First Contact & Terms: Artists must be "qualified to provide the desired quality of work within our time frame." Works on assignment only. Send query letter with resume to be kept on file; write for appointment to show portfolio. Reviews photostats, photographs, photocopies, slides or tear sheets; "they must clearly illustrate the quality, detail, etc. of artist's work." Materials not filed are returned by SASE. Reports back only if interested. Pays by the project; "a mutually agreed upon figure *before* the project is undertaken."
Tips: "Turn-around time on most projects has been virtually cut in half. More competitive market warrants quick, dependable service. This change has created a bigger need for outside assistance during heavy backlog periods."

KOPPEL COLOR, 153 Central Ave., Hawthorne NJ 07507. (201)427-3151. Administrative Coordinator: Marilyn Korona. Printer serving photographers, businesses and manufacturers.
Needs: Works with 2-3 artists/year for advertising design and 2-3 for illustrations on products. Uses artists for animation, cartoons, illustration, design, layout, lettering, technical art, mechanicals and retouching for catalogs, direct mail brochures, flyers and postcards. Especially needs line art, mechanical art and layout.
First Contact & Terms: Query with resume; always call or write in advance for an appointment. SASE. Reports within 2 weeks. Works on assignment only. Provide resume and copies of samples, reduced to fit a standard file, to be kept on file. Prefers roughs, comprehensive layouts and line drawings as samples. No samples returned. Pays by the job, "quoted in line with going fees paid this area; not hourly, but by value of work done," $75-150 average. Considers complexity of project and how work will be used when establishing payment.

KOZAK AUTO DRYWASH, INC., 6 S. Lyon St., Box 910, Batavia NY 14020. (716)343-8111. President: Ed Harding. Manufacturer and direct marketer of automotive cleaning and polishing cloths and related auto care products distributed by direct mail and retail. Clients: stores with car care lines, consumers and specialty groups.
Needs: Works with up to 2 freelance artists/year. Uses artists for advertising design and illustration, P-O-P displays, packaging design and direct response advertising.

First Contact & Terms: Prefers artist located within a convenient meeting distance with experience in desired areas (P-O-P, packaging, direct response). Works on assignment only. Send query letter with brochure, resume and business card to be kept on file. Material not filed returned only if requested. Reports within 2 weeks. Pays by the project. Considers complexity of project, skill and experience of artist, and how work will be used when establishing payment.

KRON-TV, NBC, 1001 Van Ness Ave., San Francisco CA 94119. (415)441-4444. Design Director: Judy Rosenfeld. TV/film producer. Produces videotapes and still photos.
Needs: Works with 1-2 artists/year for ad illustrations, 1-2 for advertising design and 1-5 for product design. Uses artists for design and production of all types of print advertising, direct mail brochures, promotion and sales pieces. Especially needs computer graphic art.
First Contact & Terms: Local artists only. Query. Provide resume and business card to be kept on file for future assignments.
Tips: "We're looking for experienced designers with heavy production knowledge that would enable them to handle a job from design concept through printing."

KVCR—TV/FM RADIO, 701 S. Mount Vernon Ave., San Bernardino CA 92410. (714)888-6511 or 825-3103. Program Director: Lew Warren. Specializes in public and educational radio/TV.
Needs: Works with 1 ad illustrator and 2 product illustrators/year. Assigns 1-10 jobs/year. Uses artists for graphic/set design, set design painters and camera-ready cards.
First Contact & Terms: Query and mail photos or slides. Reports in 2 weeks. Works on assignment only. Samples returned by SASE. Pays $20-30, camera-ready cards.

LEISURE AND RECREATION CONCEPTS INC., 2151 Fort Worth Ave., Dallas TX 75211. (214)942-4474. President: Michael Jenkins. Designs and builds amusement and theme parks.
Needs: Assigns 200 jobs/year. Uses artists for exhibits/displays and sketches of park building sections and bird's eye views of facilities.
First Contact & Terms: Query with samples or previously used work, or arrange interview. SASE. Reports in 1 week. Pay determined by job.

LEISURE LEARNING PRODUCTS INC., 16 Division St. W, Box 4869, Greenwich CT 06830. (203)531-8700. Advertising/Sales Promotion Manager: Richard Bendett. Manufactures children's games, activities, books and educational products.
Needs: Uses artists for illustration and design for sales literature, inhouse publications, recruitment literature, catalogs, exhibits and displays. Also needs cartoon-type color illustrations similar to the style of Walt Disney illustrations, Peanuts and Nancy strips. Must appeal to the 3-8 year old range.
First Contact & Terms: Query with photocopies or art. Pays $10-25 minimum, product illustration.

LEWIS PAPER PLACE, 220 Marquardt Dr., Wheeling IL 60090. (312)520-3355. General Manager: Steve Miller. Distributor of paper products, fine paper and graphics supply. Clients: retail businesses, churches, printers.
Needs: Works with 2 freelance artists/year. Uses artists for advertising and catalog design, illustration and layout; illustration on product and posters.
First Contact & Terms: Chicago or Denver area artists only; "knowledge of retail-type advertising through direct mail necessary." Works on assignment only. Call for appointment to show portfolio. Prefers to review rough draft art. Samples returned by SASE only if requested. Reports only if interested. Pays by project, $400-500 maximum. Considers complexity of project and turnaround time when establishing payment.

LILLIAN VERNON CORP., 510 S. Fulton Ave., Mount Vernon NY 10550. (914)699-4131. Vice President: David Hochberg. Direct mail giftware firm that produces greeting cards, giftwrap, calendars, stationery and paper tableware products. Also produces toiletries, housewares, textiles, dinnerware and toys. Two divisions: one serves general consumers, the other serves retail stores.
Needs: Buys 250 designs and 100 illustrations/year from freelance artists. Also uses artists for P-O-P displays. Considers all types of media for illustrations. "We are heavily oriented toward Christmas merchandise"; submit seasonal artwork in January or February.
First Contact & Terms: Artists within 250 miles "for ease in communication." Works on assignment only. Send query letter with brochure, resume and samples to be kept on file. Prefers photostats, photographs or tear sheets as samples. Samples not filed are returned only if requested. Reports within 2 weeks. Original art not returned after reproduction. Pays flat fee. Buys first rights.
Tips: "We are *always* on the lookout for good talent!"

LOON MOUNTAIN RECREATION CORP., Kancamagus Hwy., Lincoln NH 03251. (603)745-8111. Marketing Director: Rick Owen. Ski resort with inn, restaurants and lounges.

Needs: Works with 2 advertising designers/year. Assigns 6 jobs and buys 2 illustrations/year. Uses artists for design and illustration of brochures, signs, displays, mailings and other promotional materials. Especially needs renderings of future projects.
First Contact & Terms: Arrange interview. SASE. Reports within 2 weeks. Negotiates pay; pays by the hour, $10 average. Considers skill and experience of artist, and turnaround time when establishing payment.

MARIAN HELPERS CENTER, Eden Hill, Stockbridge MA 01263. (413)298-3691. Director: Fr. Donald Van Alstyne. Publishes *Marian Helpers Bulletin*, pamphlets, prayer cards and thought cards.
Needs: Works with 1-2 freelance artists/year. Uses artists for illustration to accompany articles, brochure covers, etc.
First Contact & Terms: Prefers artists experienced in religious subjects. Traditional preferred, but contemporary acceptable. Send resume, business card and samples to be kept on file. Call or write for appointment to show portfolio. Prefers slides as samples, photostats acceptable. Samples not kept on file are returned by SASE. Reports within 2 weeks. Pays by the project, $10-150 average. Considers skill and experience of artist and how work will be used when establishing payment.

*MARURI USA CORP., 15145 Califa St., Van Nuys CA 91411. Director/Sales and Marketing: Edward J. Purcell. Manufacturer of wholesale limited edition porcelain figurines and ceramic giftware. Clients: retailers.
Needs: Works with 3-5 freelance artists/year. Uses artists for figurine design and illustration; advertising, brochure and catalog design and illustration.
First Contact & Terms: Works on assignment only. Send query letter with brochure, resume and samples to be kept on file. Write for appointment to show portfolio. Prefers photographs and tear sheets as samples. Samples not filed are returned only if requested. Reports back only if interested. Pays for design by the project, $500 minimum; for illustration by the project, $100 minimum. Considers complexity of the project and how work will be used when establishing payment.

MILWAUKEE SIGNS CO., (formerly Communa-K, Inc.), 1964 Wisconsin Ave., Grafton WI 53024. (414)377-8920. Director of Marketing: Bob Aiken.
Needs: Works with 3 artists for sign design and P-O-P design. Also uses artists for custom sign faces, brochure and ad design.
First Contact & Terms: Local artists only. Arrange interview to show portfolio. Works on assignment only. Samples returned by SASE; reports back on future possibilities. Provide resume, business card and brochure to be kept on file. Considers complexity of project, skill and experience of artist, and how work will be used when establishing payment.

MODERN MASTERS LTD., Box 369, Frankfort IL 60423. Management Director: Paula Linstrot. Manufacturer/distributor of limited edition collectible plates, figurines, giftware and lithographs. Clients: wholesalers, retailers and consumers.
Needs: Works with 5 freelance artists/year for plate and figure design and illustration; and limited edition fine art prints. Considers oils, acrylics, watercolors, pastels, mixed media and scratchboard. Prefers themes of children, animals and wildlife.
First Contact & Terms: Works on assignment only. Send query letter with brochure, resume and samples to be kept on file. Prefers photographs or slides as samples. Samples not filed are returned by SASE. Reports back on submissions. Negotiates payment. Considers complexity of project, how work will be used and rights purchased when establishing payment.
Tips: "We are looking for attractive, appealing artwork that will lend itself to the collectible industry, especially limited edition plates."

MURPHY INTERNATIONAL SALES ORGANIZATION, 11444 Zelzah Ave., Granada Hills CA 91344. (818)363-1410. President: F.S. Murphy. Distributor and service-related firm providing retrofit, covering materials, new products and patents. Clients: building and home owners.
Needs: Works with 2 freelance artists/year. Uses artists for advertising, brochure and catalog design, and illustration on product.
First Contact & Terms: Send samples to be kept on file. Write for art guidelines. Prefers photocopies as samples. Samples not filed are not returned. Reports back only if interested. Pays by the project. Considers how work will be used when establishing payment.
Tips: "Design should be realistic. Art is becoming more simple and less dramatic."

MURRAY HILL PRESS, 43 N. Village Ave., Rockville Centre NY 11570. (516)764-6262. President: Ralph Ceisler. Printer. Clients: paint manufacturers, chemical manufacturers. Assigns 12 jobs/year; uses mostly local artists.

Needs: Uses artists for catalogs, direct mail brochures, flyers and P-O-P displays. Especially needs P-O-P displays in retail stores, paint and hardware stores in particular.
First Contact & Terms: Query with samples. SASE. Reports in 2 weeks. Pay depends strictly on job and is negotiable. Considers complexity of project, skill and experience of artist, and how work will be used when establishing payment.

NEIBAUER PRESS, INC., 20 Industrial Dr., Warminister PA 18974. (215)322-6200. Contact: Nathan Neibauer. Publishers and printers of religious publications.
Needs: Works with 12 freelance artists/year. Uses artists for advertising, brochure and catalog design, illustration and layout; illustration on product, and posters.
First Contact & Terms: Send query letter with samples. Write for appointment to show portfolio. Prefers photocopies as samples. Reports only if interested. Works on assignment only. Pays by the hour, $10 minimum; or by the project. Considers skill and experience of artist when establishing payment.

THE NORMAN ROCKWELL MUSEUM, INC., 2840 Maria Ave., Northbrook IL 60062. Creative Director: Donna Benson.
Needs: Uses artists for product illustration, advertising, design, direct mail and collateral materials. Needs realistic portraitists—artists specializing in children and animals, particularly birds and dogs.
First Contact & Terms: Call or write for appointment; Chicago and local artists only. Prefers mail order/trade layouts or actual sample pieces as samples. Solicited samples returned. Works on assignment only; reports back whether to expect possible future assignments. Provide business card to be kept on file for possible future assignments. Negotiates pay.

NORTON OUTDOOR ADVERTISING, 5280 Kennedy Ave., Cincinnati OH 45213. (513)631-4864. Contact: Tom Norton. Outdoor advertising firm.
Needs: Assigns 30-60 jobs/year. Uses artists for billboards.
First Contact & Terms: Local artists only. Call for interview. Pays $25 minimum, roughs; $75-100, finished sketch.

NOT-POLYOPTICS, 13721 Lynn St., Woodbridge VA 22191. (703)491-5543. General Partner: Michael Capobianco. Manufacturer/distributor of software and hardware for the Texas Instruments 99/4(A) home computer. Clients: individuals, distributors, software stores.
Needs: Works with 3-4 freelance artists/year. Uses artists for advertising design, illustration and layout; catalog design and illustration; illustration on product and art co-ordination for total effect.
First Contact & Terms: Works on assignment only. Send query letter with resume and samples to be kept on file. Accepts "whatever is appropriate" as samples. Samples not filed are returned by SASE. Reports within 1 month. Pays by the project, $100-500 average; terms of payment are negotiable. Considers complexity of the project, skill of the artist, turnaround time and rights purchased when establishing payment.
Tips: "We are particularly interested in high-quality color and b&w renditions of game situations. Airbrush skill is important."

*NUARC COMPANY, INC., 6200 W. Howard St., Niles IL 60648. (312)278-3300. Advertising Manager: Robert Goranson. Manufactures pre-press graphic arts equipment. Clients: printers, publishers, screen printers, in-plant printers, art departments, ad agencies, graphics studios, designers, schools, etc.
Needs: Works with 1-2 freelance artists/year. Uses artists for signage, technical drawings for instructional materials, and illustrations for news releases.
First Contact & Terms: Works with local, experienced freelance artists on assignment only. Send query letter with brochure to be kept on file; call for appointment to show portfolio. Accepts photocopies as samples. Samples not filed are returned only if requested with SASE. Reports back on query. Pays by the project. Considers complexity of the project and turnaround time when establishing payment.

O'DONNELL-USEN FISHERIES, 255 Northern Ave., Boston MA 02210. (617)542-2700. Executive Vice President: Arnold S. Wolf. Processes frozen seafoods.
Needs: Assigns 20-30 jobs and buys 15 illustrations/year. Uses artists for packaging, point of sale material and letterheads, etc. Especially needs new packaging design.
First Contact & Terms: Query with samples (rough sketches, mock up design). SASE. Reports in 3 weeks. Provide resume to be kept on file for possible future assignments. Pays compensation based on agreement by the project. Considers complexity of project and rights purchased when establishing payment.
Tips: "Present boxes are being redesigned and made more modern." Artists should "have past experience in design of packaging."

OMNIPROSE LIMITED, 94 Crockford Blvd., Scarborough, Ontario Canada. Vice President Marketing: K. McCarrol. Distributor by direct response for book clubs, record clubs, continuity programs. Clients: consumers.
Needs: Uses artists for advertising design, illustration and layout.
First Contact & Terms: Artists must have direct response experience. Works on assignment only. Send query letter with resume and samples to be kept on file. Write for appointment to show portfolio. Prefers photographs and tear sheets as samples. Samples not filed are returned by SASE only if requested (nonresidents include IRC). Reports back only if interested. Pays by the project. Considers skill and experience of the artist when establishing payment.

ORGANIC COMPUTING, 96 Caddo Peak, Joshua TX 76058. (817)295-3802. Contact: H.C. Joel. Service-related firm providing software products for small business computers. Clients: wholesalers, manufacturers, schools, banks.
First Contact & Terms: Works on assignment only. Send query letter with samples to be kept on file. Prefers photocopies or slides as samples. Samples not filed returned by SASE. Reports within 1 week. Pays by the hour, $30-40 average. Considers skill and experience of the artist when establishing payment.

PALMLOOM CO., Box 1541, New York NY 10017. (212)688-8797. Advertising Manager: N. Tyler. Direct response (mail order) marketer (magazines) and catalogs.
Needs: Works with 2-3 freelance artists/year. Uses artists for advertising design (mail order), brochure and catalog design and layout, and paste-up.
First Contact & Terms: Send query letter with samples to be kept on file. Prefers tear sheets (nonreturnable printed matter) as samples. Reports back only if interested. Pays $10/hour for paste-up; $20/hour for design and layout.

PERFECT PEN & STATIONERY CO. LTD., #42, 1241 Denison St., Markham, Ontario L3R 4B4 Canada. (416)474-1866. President: S. Szlrtes. Distributor of advertising specialties, office specialties and gifts. Clients: "all businesses across Canada."
Needs: Works with 6 freelance artists/year. Uses artists for advertising, brochure and catalog design and layout; photography and film work.
First Contact & Terms: Artists must have a minimum of 5 years' experience and references. Works on assignment only. Send query letter with brochure to be kept on file; write for appointment to show portfolio. Prefers tear sheets as samples. Samples not filed are not returned. Reports back only if interested. Pays by the project. Considers complexity of the project when establishing payment.
Tips: "Apply only if you're experienced in direct mail advertising or a closely related area."

*PICKARD, INC., 782 Corona Ave., Antioch IL 60002. Contact: Product Development Manager. Manufacturer of wholesale fine china dinnerware and collector plates. Clients: retailers.
Needs: Works with 3-4 freelance artists/year. Uses artists for patterns for dinnerware and fine art for collector plates. Prefers realistic and classical styles. Seeks "fine art as opposed to illustration for our limited edition plates."
First Contact & Terms: Works on assignment only. Send query letter with brochure, resume and samples. Prefers slides or printed brochure as samples. Samples not filed are returned only if requested. Reports back within 1 month. Negotiates payment; generally a flat fee and/or royalties. Considers complexity of the project, project's budget, skill and experience of the artist, how work will be used, turnaround time and rights purchased when establishing payment.

PICTURESQUE PRODUCTS, Box 41630, Tucson AZ 85717. President: B.B. Nelson. Mail order firm of general gift items. Clients: consumers.
Needs: Works with 2 freelance artists/year. Uses artists for advertising, brochure and catalog design, illustration and layout; and P-O-P displays.
First Contact & Terms: Send query letter to be kept on file. Reports only if interested. Pays by the project, $100-500 average. Considers skill and experience of artist, how work will be used and rights purchased when establishing payment.
Tips: "Originality in the presentation sells me."

*PITTSBURGH DISPLAY, 200 Federal St., Pittsburgh PA 15212. (412)322-5800. President: Art Pearlman. Distributes decorative material, fabrics, papers, plastics, and photographic arts. Clients: malls, shopping centers, banks, utilities and retail merchants.
Needs: Works with 8-12 freelance artists/year. Uses artists for brochure and catalog design, illustration and layout; P-O-P dislpays; display fixture design; posters; and signage.
First Contact & Terms: Send query letter with brochure and samples to be kept on file; call for appoint-

ment to show portfolio. Prefers photographs, photocopies and tear sheets as samples. Samples not filed are returned by SASE. Does not report back. Pays by the project, $60-200 average. Considers complexity of the project when establishing payment. Amount allowed within bid to customer.

PLANET-TRANS, INC., 5 Blake Ave., Brooklyn NY 11212. (718)773-3332. President: Marino Bonilla. Manufacturer of iron-on heat transfers in all types of designs—adults, children, souvenir, babies, with worldwide distribution.
Needs: Works with 10 freelance artists/year. Uses artists for advertising illustration.
First Contact & Terms: Send query letter with samples to be kept on file or call or write for appointment to show portfolio. Prefers original work, slides or photos as samples. Samples returned by SASE if not kept on file. Reports only if interested. Works on assignment only. Pays by the project, $125-200 average. Considers skill and experience of artist when establishing payment.
Tips: Prefers airbrush artwork on boards.

PRESTIGELINE INC., 5 Inez Dr., Brentwood NY 11717. (516)273-3636. Director of Marketing: Ken Golden. Manufacturer of lighting products.
Needs: Buys 35 illustrations from freelance artists/year. Uses artists for advertising and catalog design, illustrations and layout; and illustration on product. Prefers b&w line drawings. Produces seasonal material for Christmas, Mother's Day, Father's Day, Thanksgiving, Easter, back-to-school and graduations; submit work 3-4 months before season.
First Contact & Terms: Send resume, business card and samples; call for appointment. Prefers photostats as samples. Samples returned by SASE. Reports within 2 weeks. Buys all rights. Payment method is negotiable.
Tips: "There is an increased demand for b&w line art for newspaper advertisements."

PROFESSIONAL TRAINING AIDS, 38 W. Bethune, Detroit MI 48202. Contact: H. Hook. Produces direct mail sales and motivation programs. Clients: industrial accounts.
Needs: Works with 1 ad illustrator, 1 advertising designer and 1 illustrator for product illustration/year. Uses artists for line art, cartoons, posters, etc. Especially needs illustrations. Interested in line drawings and poster style.
First Contact & Terms: Submit tear sheets or photocopies. Reports in 10 days. Provide brochure, tear sheet and photocopy of samples to be kept on file for future assignments. Payment varies.
Tips: Especially looks for reproducibility in samples.

PUCCI MANIKINS, 578 Broadway, New York NY 10012. (212)219-0142. Manufacturer of manikins—art work on faces, clay for sculptures. Clients: department stores.
Needs: Uses artists for model making.

PULPDENT CORPORATION OF AMERICA, 75 Boylston St., Brookline MA 02147. (617)232-2380. Director of Product Information: Jane Hart Berk. Manufacturer/distributor of dental supplies including instruments, pharmaceuticals, X-ray supplies, sterilizers, needles, articulating paper, etc. Clients: dental supply dealers and dentists.
Needs: Works with 3-5 freelance artists/year. Uses artists for advertising, brochure and catalog design, illustration and layout; photography and technical illustration.
First Contact & Terms: Prefers local artists. Send query letter with business card, samples and tear sheets; call or write for appointment to show portfolio. Anything but original work may be sent as samples; prefers photostats or tear sheets. Samples returned by SASE if not kept on file. Reports within 6 weeks. Works on assignment only. Pays by the project, $40 minimum. Considers complexity of project, and skill and experience of artist when establishing payment; "how much our product is worth determines to some extent the amount we are willing to invest in designing, etc."
Tips: "We prefer simple, not-too-trendy designs aimed at the dental professional"; may consider cartoons and humorous and cartoon-style illustrations for upcoming promotions.

RECO INTERNATIONAL CORPORATION, Collector's Division, 138-150 Haven Ave., Box 951, Port Washington NY 11050. (516)767-2400. Manufacturer/distributor of limited editions collectors plates, lithographs and figurines. Clients: stores.
Needs: Works with 4 freelance artists/year. Uses artists for plate and figurine design, and limited edition fine art prints. Prefers romantic and realistic styles.
First Contact & Terms: Send query letter and brochure to be filed. Write for appointment to show a portfolio. Reports back within 3 weeks. Negotiates payment.

RECO INTERNATIONAL CORPORATION, Kitchen Gourmet Accessories Division, 138-150 Haven Ave., Port Washington NY 11050. (516)767-2400. President: Heio W. Reich. Publisher and manufacturer.

Close-up

Brigitte Moore, Vice President
Reco International Corp.
Port Washington, New York

Artist: David R. Smiton

The search for collector plate artists rivals Jason's quest for the Golden Fleece, Lancelot's for the Holy Grail and the shepherd's for his lost sheep.

Brigitte Moore, vice president of Collectibles and Fine Gifts, Reco International Corp., will tell you this search is an authentic "looking for a needle in a haystack." Finding a talented artist is one thing. But because of the intricacies involved in plate art, finding the *right* one is what counts. Subject matter, style, technique and color sense must all be combined and transferrable to the round plate format.

Perhaps five percent of the artists interviewed by plate producers possess the qualities needed for designing plates. Sometimes, an artist's style simply doesn't lend itself to a specific subject matter.

"We can talk to half a dozen artists before the right one walks through the door," says Moore. "If it happens that we don't have a concept, we'll ask for the artist's ideas. If we come up with one we think we can market, we ask for a few preliminary sketches. However, it may take several revisions before we get exactly what we think will sell."

Moore is encouraged by artists' increasing interest in collector plates, but despite the industry's growth there is still a dearth of artistic talent to call upon. "More and more artists are calling for interviews," states Moore. "They are beginning to recognize the value of plate art and the exposure it can offer. "We're looking for artists who can generate outstanding ideas. Subject matter should be nostalgic, sentimental, something that hits the heart strings. We're not irrevocably locked into these elements, but they are salable commodities. My own experience has been that just when I think every concept I've envisioned has already been done, or else I've rejected it, someone else comes out with it."

The best way for an artist to approach this plate producer is by letter. Enclose good photographs of sample artwork; save original art for a face-to-face interview. When Moore spots something promising, she usually spends time with the artist discussing and explaining the dos and don'ts of the industry. Moore, who is approached by four to six artists a month, explains simply "If the art has no emotional appeal, there's no sale."

Payment methods—flat fee, royalty or both—vary throughout the industry and are negotiated on an individual basis.

Collector plates, concludes Moore, require a very special kind of art, art that demands a great deal of patience coupled with a comprehensive knowledge of the field. "We in the industry know what we think will sell. Yet, nobody can be absolutely certain that it will. One thing we do know is that collector plates need the talent of creative, sensitive artists who can help make the producer's investment, in money and time, a rewarding one for everybody concerned."

—*Barbara M. Dawson*

Needs: Designers to design houseware and kitchen utensils on an exclusive basis for production according to designs.
First Contact & Terms: Send query letter and resume; submit portfolio for review. Prefers to see "anything that will show artist's ability." Reports "when needed." Works on assignment only. Provide resume, business card, brochure and samples to be kept on file. Negotiates payments.

***BOB ROBINSON MARKETING INC.**, 366 N. Broadway, Jericho NY 11753. (516)931-5900. President: Bob Robinson.
Needs: Assigns 100 jobs/year. Uses artists for display/P-O-P design and scale models.
First Contact & Terms: Arrange interview to show portfolio. SASE. Reports in 2 weeks. Pays $50-300/sketch or $100-1,000/job for design of permanent displays.

ROCKING HORSE, Box 306, Highland NY 12528. Convention center, ranch-resort. Clients: social vacationers—business meeting executives, senior citizens, couples, families.
Needs: Works with 2 ad illustrators, 2 ad designers, 2 or 3 product designers and 2 illustrators for products/year. Uses artists for descriptive brochures, exhibits, signs and meeting room decorations. Especially needs caricatures, brochures, rate schedule line work or design as samples.
First Contact & Terms: Send published samples (resort ads around a western scene). Prefers "bartering" as payment method.
Tips: "Foresees more use of artists" in the field. Artists should "make their abilities and offerings known to potential clients."

***ROCKY POINT PARK**, Warwick RI 02889. (401)737-8000. President/General Manager: Conrad Feria. Clients: general public.
Needs: Uses artists for direct mail brochures, programs, trade magazine ads, bumper stickers, and pennants.
First Contact & Terms: Submit photos, roughs or tear sheets of published work. Pays going rates.

***ROYCE ET KLAUDIUS**, Box 1840, Santa Monica CA 90406. (213)559-7735. President: L. Aravena. Manufactures custom work (furnishing/accesories/art work) in metals, glass, arcrylics, etc. Clients: residential and commercial.
Needs: Uses artists for catalog design, illustration and layout; product design; illustration on product; display fixture design; and model making.
First Contact & Terms: Works on assignment only. Send brochure, resume, business card and samples to be kept on file. Prefers photographs and tear sheets as samples. Samples not filed are returned only if requested. Reports only if interested. Pays by the hour, $15-30 average. Considers skill and experience of the artist when establishing payment.

RSVP MARKETING, Suite 5, 450 Plain St., Marshfield MA 02050. (617)837-2804. President: Edward C. Hicks. Direct marketing consultant services—catalogs, direct mail and telemarketing. Clients: primarily industry and distributors.
Needs: Works with 7-8 freelance artists/year. Uses artists for advertising, copy brochure and catalog design, illustration and layout.
First Contact & Terms: Desires "primarily local artists; must have direct marketing skills." Send query letter with resume and samples to be kept on file. Prefers finished, printed work as samples. Reports only if interested. Pays by the job, $250-500 minimum. Considers skill and experience of artist when establishing payment.

SANTA FE PARK SPEEDWAY, 9100 S. Wolf Rd., Hinsdale IL 60521. (312)839-1050. Public Relations: Mary Lou Tiedt. Stock car racetrack. Clients: "We are a public family entertainment establishment and service a wide variety of manufacturers, patrons and small businesses locally. A large portion of advertisers, which need the work of our artists, are auto shops, motorcycle shops and restaurants."
Needs: Works with 2 artists/year for advertising design. Uses artists for advertising, direct mail brochures, posters, publicity brochures, yearly programs, bumper stickers and road signs. "We are looking for new original layouts and designs for racing." Especially needs speedway logo to be used on t-shirts, mailings and the program cover.
First Contact & Terms: Mail art. Will review basic pencil sketches or photos; previously published work is preferred. SASE. Reports in 2-4 weeks. Provide business card to be kept on file for possible future assignments. Negotiates pay. Considers how work will be used, turnaround time and rights purchased when establishing payment.
Tips: "Artist must keep up to date on the car models on the market for designs as we run a 'late model stock car' division; also on trends in t-shirt design and what will work well for printing (silk screen). Keep in touch and be persistent, as we get very busy. Send samples with envelope to return work in-

...this allows a quick return and response to work. The best time to contact us for work is in November or late January. The spring season is much too late. By March, we are already set for the summer season."

*SCHMID BROS., INC., 55 Pacella Park Dr., Randolph MA 02368. (617)961-3000. Vice President Collectibles: Dennis Hurst. Manufacturer of wholesale figurines, dolls and collectible plates. Clients: retailers.
Needs: Works with a varying number of freelance artists/year. Uses artists for plate and figurine design.
First Contact & Terms: Works on assignment only. Send query letter with resume and samples to be kept on file. Write for appointment to show portfolio. Prefers photographs and models as samples. Samples not filed are returned only if requested by artist. Reports within 30 days.

THE J.H. SCHULER CO., 1649 Broadway, Hanover PA 17331. (717)632-5000. Director of Art and Advertising: Bruce N. Wolff. Distributor of giftware for fundraising. Clients: nonprofit groups.
Needs: Uses artists for advertising, brochure, catalog and product design.
First Contact & Terms: Send query letter with samples. Prefers printed pieces as samples. Samples returned by SASE only if requested.

SEVEN CONTINENTS ENTERPRISES, INC., 350 Wallace Ave., Toronto, Ontario M6P 3P2 Canada. (416)535-5101. Creative Director: Sinclair Russell. Manufacturer providing display products, silk yardage, accessories to home furnishings. Materials used: silk, teakwood, cotton, bamboo, brass. Clients: department stores—window display, store interiors, fashion coordinators, furnishings; hotels—upholstery, urns.
Needs: Works with 5 freelance artists/year. Uses artists for advertising, brochure and catalog design, illustration and layout; product and display fixture design, illustration on product, P-O-P displays, model making and signage.
First Contact & Terms: Artists must possess "unusual creativity using much color and wild sizes." Send query letter with brochure, resume and samples to be kept on file or write for appointment to show portfolio. Samples returned only by request. Prefers color photographs and drawings as samples. Reports only if interested. Pays by the project, $200 minimum; or by the hour, $8-30. Considers complexity of project, skill and experience of artist, how work will be used, turnaround time and rights purchased when establishing payment.
Tips: "If you are not creative and terribly energetic, forget it."

SITKA STORE FIXTURES, Box 392, Kansas City MO 64141. (816)221-4520. General Manager: Mary Williams. Manufacturer of wood store fixtures and merchandisers. Clients: pharmacies, hardware, paint and wallpaper stores, bakers, jewelers and department stores.
Needs: Works with artists for fixture design.
First Contact & Terms: Query. Reports within 3 weeks. Works on assignment only. Samples returned by SASE; and reports back on future possibilities. Provide resume to be kept on file for future assignments. Pay determined by job.

SLADE CREATIVE MARKETING, Suite 3, 26 W. Mission, Box 484, Santa Barbara CA 93102. (805)687-5331. President: S. Richard Slade. Service-related firm providing graphics, brochures, technical drawings, collateral material and general advertising. Clients: technical and consumer.
Needs: Works with 10-12 freelance artists/year. Uses artists for advertising, brochure and catalog design, illustration and layout; illustration on product, P-O-P displays, signage, photography and technical writing.
First Contact & Terms: Artists must be able to communicate directly with company. Works on assignment only. Send query letter with resume and samples to be kept on file. Write for appointment to show portfolio. Accepts photostats, photographs, photocopies, slides or tear sheets as samples. Samples not filed returned by SASE only if requested. Reports only if interested. Pays by project, $100-750 average. Considers complexity of project, how work will be used and rights purchased when establishing payment.
Tips: "Be flexible and open to any job within your range."

TOM SNYDER PRODUCTIONS, INC., 123 Mt. Auburn St., Cambridge MA 02138. Art Director: Peter Reynolds. Developer of educational computer software for ages 5-adult; develops software, documentation, ancillary materials (music, art, books). Clients: schools, department stores, program stores.
Needs: Works with 3 + freelance artists/year. Uses artists for brochure design, illustration and layout; illustration on product and package design.
First Contact & Terms: Works on assignment only. Send query letter with resume and samples to be kept on file. Prefers photocopies as samples. Samples not filed are returned by SASE only if requested. Reports back only if interested. Pays by the hour, $15-25 average. Considers complexity of the project,

skill and experience of the artist, how work will be used and turnaround time when establishing payments.
Tips: Let your work speak for itself. Just send photocopies and be patient. When an appropriate job comes up and your work is on file, we'll call you.''

SOFTSYNC, INC., 14 E. 34th St., New York NY 10016. (212)685-2080. Director of Creative Services: Linda Schupack. Manufacturer of software for a variety of home computers. Subject matter includes games, education, personal productivity. Clients: computer and mass market retail stores.
Needs: Works with 5 freelance artists/year. Uses artists for advertising and brochure design, illustration and layout; illustration on product, P-O-P displays and posters.
First Contact & Terms: Works on assignment only. Send query letter with brochure and samples to be kept on file. Call or write for appointment to show portfolio. Prefers photographs, slides or tear sheets as samples. Samples not filed are returned only if requested. Reports within days. Pays by the hour, $10-15 average, or by the project, $350-1,000 average. Considers complexity of the project, skill and experience of the artist and how work will be used when establishing payment.
Tips: "For mechanicals artists, we need people who are quick and accurate. For illustrators, bring us samples that are colorful, zippy and innovative."

SPENCER GIFTS, INC., 1050 Black Horse Pike, Pleasantville NJ 08232. (609)645-5526. Art Director: James Stevenson. Retail gift chain located in approximately 440 malls in 43 states; gifts range from posters to jewelry.
Needs: Assigns 150-200 jobs/year. Uses artists for package design illustration, hard line art, fashion illustration, newspaper ads and toy, poster, package and product design, T-shirt design and other soft goods.
First Contact & Terms: Query with samples, previously published work or arrange interview to show portfolio. With samples, enclose phone number where you can be reached during business hours. Prefers artists with professional experience in their field of advertising art. Reports within 2 weeks. Negotiates pay.

SPS INC., Suite C-34, 150 Shoreline Hwy., Mill Valley CA 94941. (415)331-3344. Account Executive: Cindy Thomas. Compilers specializing in national and California regional lists of executives, professionals, businesses, upper income and specialized wealth lists; also home owners and income property owners in a number of California counties by type and value of property. Clients: banks, savings and loans, finance companies, direct mail advertising services, commodity brokers, fundraising counselors, insurance companies, office supply stores, marketing consultants, auctioneers, real estate developers, building materials dealers.
Needs: Number of freelance artists used/year varies. Uses artists for advertising, brochure and catalog design, illustration and layout; signage, and copywriting.
First Contact & Terms: Send query letter with brochure, resume, business card and samples to be kept on file. Prefers samples of printed pieces. Samples not kept on file are returned by SASE only if requested. Reports only if interested. Works on assignment only. Pays by the hour, $5-20 average. Considers complexity of project and skill and experience of artist when establishing payment.

STAMP COLLECTORS SOCIETY OF AMERICA, Box 3, W. Redding CT 06896. Executive Vice President and Creative Director: Malcolm Decker. Philatelic marketing firm. Develops mail order/direct response buyers of stamps using publications and mailing lists.
Needs: Works with 6 freelance artists/year. Uses artists for advertising and brochure design, illustration and layout; product design, album and editorial design, and "full-dress" direct mail packages.
First Contact & Terms: Prefers local (Westchester, New Haven, Fairfield County and New York City) artists; "experience requirement is determined by the job complexity." Works on assignment only. Send a letter and a resume; "if interested, we'll call you. Show your portfolio and leave behind or send in samples or photocopies as requested." Pays by the hour, by the project, or offers a retainer. Considers the complexity of the project and the skill and experience of the artist when establishing payment.
Tips: "Send a comprehensive, detailed resume listing all the clients served, noting those for whom the most work was done."

SYSTEMS PLUS, INC., 500 Clyde Ave., Mountain View CA 94043. Media Relations: Norman Stephens. Software publisher of vertical and horizontal business software for microcomputers.
Needs: Works with less than 5 freelance artists/year. Uses artists for advertising design and illustration; brochure design, illustration and layout; product design, illustration on product and P-O-P displays.
First Contact & Terms: Prefers local artists with extensive experience in the computer field and marketing. Works on assignment only. Send query letter with brochure and business card to be kept on file; "samples should be sent only on request." Samples not filed returned *if* accompanied by SASE. Reports

only if interested, "usually." Pays by the project. Considers complexity of project, skill and experience of the artist, and turnaround time when establishing payment.

TEACH YOURSELF BY COMPUTER SOFTWARE, INC., 2128 W. Jefferson Rd., Pittsford NY 14534. (716)427-7065. Public Relations Director: Lois B. Bennett. Publisher of educational software for microcomputers. Clients: schools, individuals, stores.
Needs: Uses artists for advertising, brochure and catalog design, illustration and layout; and illustration on product.
First Contact & Terms: Local artists only. Works on assignment only. Send query letter with brochure, resume and samples to be kept on file. Call or write for appointment to show portfolio. Accepts photostats, photographs, photocopies, slides or tear sheets as samples. Samples not filed are returned by SASE. Reports within 6 weeks. Considers complexity of the project, skill and experience of the artist, how work will be used, turnaround time and rights purchased when establishing payment.

THOMAS NELSON PUBLISHERS, Nelson Place, Elm Hill Pike, Box 141000, Nashville TN 37214. (615)889-9000. Vice President Advertising and Marketing: Robert J. Schwalb. Manufacturer and distributor of religious materials, Bibles, Christian books; also secular markets from subsidiary companies. Clients: retailers, book stores.
Needs: Works with 60 freelance artists/year. Uses artists for advertising, brochure and catalog design, illustration and layout; product and display fixture design, illustration on product, P-O-P displays, posters, model making and signage.
First Contact & Terms: Firm reserves publishing rights. Send query letter with samples. Call for appointment to show portfolio. Samples not kept on file are returned. Reports only if interested. Works on assignment only. No set pay range; "project budget sets price." Payment terms of 10 days or 30-day turnaround.
Tips: Industry trends are toward "a clean-cut motif with simple design." When reviewing work, evaluates "presentation of work, cleaness and creative concept." Artists should "research the type of work or creative needs of the business they interview with."

TREASURE CRAFT/POTTERY CRAFT, 2320 N. Alameda, Compton CA 90222. President: Bruce Levin. Manufacturer of earthenware and stoneware housewares and gift items. Clients: department stores and gift shops.
Needs: Works with 3 freelance artists/year. Uses artists for advertising and product design, illustrations, layout and model making.
First Contact & Terms: Prefers local area artists. Send query letter. Reports in 3 weeks. Works on assignment basis only. Provide business card and flyer to be kept on file for possible future assignments. Payment determined by the project.

TRI-COMMUNITY AREA CHAMBER OF COMMERCE, 111 Main St., Southbridge MA 01550. (617)764-3283. Contact: Richardson K. Prouty Jr. The tri-community area consists of Southbridge, a primarily industrial community; Sturbridge, a restored historical village and tourist mecca; and Charlton, an agricultural community.
Needs: Works with 3 ad illustrators and 2 advertising designers/year. Uses artists for ad illustrations.
First Contact & Terms: Prefers local artists. Call for interview to show portfolio. Works on assignment only. Reports back on future assignment possibilities. Provide brochure to be kept on file for possible future assignments. Pays $500, brochure design.

TRIM CORPORATION OF AMERICA (TRIMCO), 459 W. 15th St., New York NY 10011. (212)989-1616. Advertising Director: Ray Caputo. Distributor providing display supply, store planning. Clients: retail, manufacturers.
Needs: Works with 2-3 freelance artists/year. Uses artists for advertising, product and display fixture design; and P-O-P displays.
First Contact & Terms: Send query letter with business card and tear sheets to be kept on file; write for appointment to show portfolio. Samples are returned. Reports within 3 weeks. Works on assignment only. Pays by the project, $200-250 average. Considers complexity of project and skill and experience of artist when establishing payment.

TURNROTH SIGN CO., 1207 E. Rock Falls Rd., Rock Falls IL 61071. (815)625-1155. Contact: R. Neil Turnroth. Clients: banks, business, retail and industry.
Needs: Works with artists for billboards ($25-50), neon signage ($20-75), sign redesign ($20-100). Assigns 15-20 jobs/year.
First Contact & Terms: Works primarily with out-of-town artists. Query with samples. SASE. Reports within 1 week. Payment by job.
Tips: Artists should have some nice photos of sketch work.

UMSI INCORPORATED, Box 450, Scotch Plains NJ 07076. (201)668-1313. President: Robert Bokor. Mail order firm with two divisions: Division #1 offers Colonial Country and Victorian items for the home directed to predominately female clients, ages 35-55; Division #2 offers magic tricks and novelties marketed to children, primarily boys, ages 8-15.

Needs: Works with 2 freelance artists/year. Uses artists for advertising and catalog design, illustration and layout.

First Contact & Terms: Local artists only "who have samples of similar product links (gifts or children's products)." Send query letter with brochure, resume and samples to be kept on file "unless the samples exhibit that the artist does not have closely related experience." Call for appointment to show portfolio. Prefers samples that need not be returned. Samples not kept on file are returned by SASE. Reports only if interested. Works on assignment only. Pays by the project, $1,000 minimum for catalog design, less for smaller projects (ads, etc.). Considers complexity of project and skill and experience of artist when establishing payment.

Tips: "We are aggressively marketing our Colonial line and do want to hear from artists who have had experience only with 4-color Colonial and Country catalogs; or at least gift-type items."

UNION PEN & PENCIL CO., 777 W. Putnam Ave., Greenwich CT 06830. Assistant Production Manager: Anne Perzeszty. Direct mail marketer of advertising specialties to businesses.

Needs: Works with 6 freelance artists/year. Uses artists for advertising, brochure and catalog design, illustration and layout.

First Contact & Terms: Seeks artists with "competence, quality work and awareness of cost efficiency." Send query letter with relevant samples to be kept on file. Write for appointment to show portfolio. Usually prefers printed sample of relative work. Samples not kept on file returned if requested. Reports only if interested. Works on assignment only. Pays by the project, $100-2,500 average. Considers complexity of project, skill and experience of artist, how work will be used, turnaround time, rights purchased and "our requirements" when establishing payment.

Tips: Artists need "an understanding of direct mail business requirements" to work here.

*THE VANESSA-ANN COLLECTION, Box 9113, Ogden UT 84409. (801)621-2777. President: Jo P. Buehler. Publishes needlework books, charts and designs. Clients: needlework and craft shops.

Needs: Works with 5 freelance artists/year. Considers pen & ink line drawings, oil and acrylic paintings, pastels, watercolors and mixed media—all to be converted into needlework charts/designs. Especially likes children, holiday and kitchen themes.

First Contact & Terms: Send query letter with samples to be kept on file. Samples not filed are returned. Reports within 1 month. Buys all rights. Negotiates payment; offers advance.

*VISUAL AID/VISAID MARKETING, Box 4502, Inglewood CA 90309. (213)473-0286. Manager: Lee Clapp. Distributes sales promotion (aids), marketing consultant (service)—involved in all phases. Clients: manufacturers, distributors, publishers and graphics firms (printing and promotion) in 23 zip code areas.

Needs: Works with 3-5 freelance artists/year. Uses artists for advertising, brochure and catalog design, illustration and layout; product design, illustration on product, P-O-P displays, display fixture design and posters. Buys some cartoons and humorous and cartoon-style illustrations.

First Contact & Terms: Works on assignment only. Send query letter with brochure, resume, business card and samples to be kept on file; write for appointment to show portfolio. Prefers photostats, duplicate photographs, photocopies and tear sheets as samples. Originals returned by SASE. Reports within 2 weeks. Negotiates payment by the project. Considers complexity of the project, skill and experience of the artist and turnaround time when establishing payment.

Tips: "Do not say 'I can do anything.' We want to know best media you work in (pen/ink, line, illustration, layout, etc.)."

WEBB DESIGN INC., 1155 N. Johnson Ave., El Cajon CA 92022. (619)442-0391. President/Sales Manager: Bob Webb. Manufactures many interior design products.

Needs: Uses artists for textile and product design as well as brochure and package design.

First Contact & Terms: Query with samples or arrange interview to show portfolio. Reports within 2-3 weeks. Negotiates pay.

*WEST SUPPLY, INC., 319 N. Appleton St., Appleton WI 54911. (414)734-2313. Vice President: Mark H. West. Manufactures wall hangings with pen and ink artwork reproduced on wood, and several lines of belt buckles. Clients: retail stores, distributors and wholesalers.

Needs: Works with 7 freelance artists/year. Uses artists for illustration on product; black on white pen & ink art to be reproduced on belt buckles and wall hangings.

First Contact & Terms: "We prefer to purchase reproduction rights." Send query letter with brochure

and samples to be kept on file, except for originals which will be returned if not used; write for art guidelines. Accepts photocopies as samples. Samples not filed are returned if requested. Reports within 2 weeks. Pays per piece by mutual agreement. Considers complexity of the project, how work will be used and rights purchased when establishing payment.
Tips: "We are price conscious, but easy to work with, and we are happy to review your work."

THE WILD SIDE INC., 7300 SW 42nd St., Miami FL 33155. (305)264-7320. Contact: Chris Fowler. Imprinted sportswear company.
Needs: Assigns 50+ jobs/year. Needs artists for t-shirt design.
First Contact & Terms: Query with resume and samples. "Don't call on the telephone. We must see samples of your work." Prefers samples of color work; slides or original art samples returned. Reports within 1 week. No original art returned at job's completion. Pays $100 for each design used.

*WINDOW DISPLAY SERVICE & DESIGN, 29-31 Leavenworth St., Waterbury CT 06702. (203)756-3083. Owner: Guy R. Livolsi. Manufactures custom furniture, signage and prop design; does window display design and consultation; sells new and used store fixtures (racks, mannequins). Clients: banks, stores, private firms, building managements, private clients, corporations, theaters and country clubs.
Needs: Works with 15 freelance artists/year. Uses artists for advertising design, illustration and layout; product design; P-O-P displays; display fixture design; model making; signage; and prop design.
First Contact & Terms: Send resume, business card and samples to be kept on file; write for art guidelines. Prefers slides as samples. Samples not filed are returned by SASE. Reports only if interested. Pays generally by the project. Considers skill and experience of the artist when establishing payment.

*WOODMERE CHINA INC., Box 5305, New Castle PA 16105. (412)658-1630. President: L.E. Tway. Manufacturer and importer of all types of collectible plate and porcelain figurines, dinnerware and giftware. Clients: wholesalers, retailers and corporations.
Needs: Works with 2-4 freelance artists/year. Uses artists for plate and figurine design; mechanicals; advertising, brochure and catalog design, illustration and layout.
First Contact & Terms: Works on assignment only. Send query letter with resume and samples to be filed unless returned requested. Accepts any type sample. Reports within 2 weeks. Pays by the project, $50-1,000 or on a royalty basis. Considers complexity of the project, skill and experience of the artist and reputation of artist in market when establishing payment.
Tips: Be professional. Seeks "only art styles that fit our markets and that are good, tight quality work."

YORK DISPLAY FINISHING CO., INC., 240 Kent Ave., Brooklyn NY 11211. (718)782-0710. President: Stanley Singer. Manufacturer and display firm providing P-O-P advertising displays in vacuum formed plastics, cardboard, corrugated and paper. Clients: display agencies, printers, artists, etc.
Needs: Works with 2 freelance artists/year. Uses artists for P-O-P design and model making.
First Contact & Terms: New York City metro area artists only, thoroughly experienced in P-O-P design. Send query letter. Reports in 3 weeks. Samples returned by SASE. Provide resume or business card to be kept on file for possible future assignments. Pays by the project, $100-1,500 average.

YUMA CIVIC CONVENTION CENTER, Box 6468, Yuma AZ 85364. (602)344-3800. Director: Suzanne Murray.
Needs: Works with 2-3 advertising illustrators and designers/year. Assigns 20 jobs/year. Uses artists for illustration, design, layout, lettering and production for ads, direct mail brochures, posters, publicity brochures and trademarks/logo.
First Contact & Terms: Works mostly with local artists. Works on assignment only. Mail art or query for advertising art with samples (¼ page in magazine). SASE. Reports in 2 weeks. No samples returned. Provide business card and brochure to be kept on file for future assignments.
Tips: Current trends include "clean ads—simple with a specific message being broadcast."

Fashion

*ACROPOLIS BOOKS LTD., 2400 17th St. NW, Washington DC 20009. Art Director: Robert Hickey. Specializes in hardcover and paperback originals on adult nonfiction, self help and general interest. Publishes 25 titles/year.
Needs: Assigns 1-2 jobs/year. Prefers b&w line art—fashion and food only. Pays by the project.
First Contact & Terms: Works with 1-2 freelance artists/year. "Local artist preferred for convenience." Send business card and samples of style to be kept on file except for those that are too bulky. Prefers photocopies as samples. SASE. Samples not filed are returned if accompanied by SASE. Does not report back to the artist. Original work is not returned to artist. Considers project's budget when establishing payment. Purchases all rights.

ACT YOUNG IMPORTS INC., 49 W. 37th St., New York NY 10018. (212)354-8894. Executive Vice President: Joe Hafif. Manufacturers and importers of printed totes, diaper bags, knapsacks, school bags, ladies handbags, clutches made of canvas, vinyl, oxford nylon, etc.
Needs: Buys 300-600 designs/year. Especially needs experienced designers.
First Contact & Terms: Local artists only. Query with samples. Designs on paper only, no sample manufacturing necessary.

AFRICAN FABRIC PRINTS/AFRICAN GARMENTS INC., Box 91, New York NY 10108. (212)725-1199. Contact: Vince Jordan.
Needs: Uses artists for fashion and textile design and ready-to-wear patterns.
First Contact & Terms: Mail tear sheets, original art or design ideas. Reports in 5-6 weeks. Pays $50 minimum.

LILLIAN ALBUS SHOPS INC., 139 Kings Hwy. E., Haddonfield NJ 08033. (609)429-1875. General Manager: Mr. S. Ross. Women's retail specialty chain. Sells better ready-to-wear, sportswear and gifts.
Needs: Works with 1 freelance illustrator or designer/year. Especially needs fashion illustrations.
First Contact & Terms: Local artists only. Arrange interview to show portfolio. Reports within 1 week. Works on assignment only. Samples returned by SASE; and reports back on future assignment possibilities. $30 minimum per design; $30 minimum per illustration.

*ARKANSAS GAZETTE, Box 1821, Little Rock AR 72203. (501)371-3723. Woman's Editor: Mardi Epes. Weekly newspaper woman's section featuring fashion and beauty. Circ. 130,000. Accepts previously published material. Returns original artwork to the artist after publication. Sample copy and art guidelines available.
Needs: Buys a varying number of fashion illustrations per issue. Seek styles "with a 'feel' rather than catalogue details." Color and b&w possibilities. Works on an assignment basis only.
First Contact & Terms: Send query letter with samples to be kept on file. Accepts any type sample. Samples not kept on file are returned if accompanied by an SASE. Reports back to the artist. Purchases first rights. Pays on publication.

BAIMS, 408 Main, Pine Bluff AR 71601. (501)534-0121. Contact: David A. Shapiro. Retailer. Carries Haggar, Van Heusen and other labels.
Needs: Works with 2-3 illustrators/designers/year. Assigns 25-100 jobs/year. Uses artists for ad illustrations.
First Contact & Terms: Query with resume and samples, and arrange interview to show portfolio. SASE. Reports in 2 weeks. Provide resume, business card and samples to be kept on file for possible future assignments. Pays $5-20/job.

BENO'S, 1515 Santee St., Los Angeles CA 90015. (213)748-2222. Director of Advertising and Sales Promotion: Gregg Seaman. Department and family apparel chain in California and Oregon.
Needs: Works with 4-5 freelance artists/year. Uses artists for illustrations of men's, women's and children's fashions, some hard lines and domestics (pillows, blankets, sheets) for newspapers ads and direct mail coupon books.
First Contact & Terms: Local artists only. Arrange interview to show portfolio. Prefers b&w line drawings, airbrush, charcoal, and previously published work as samples. SASE. Reports in 1-2 weeks. Pays by the project, $10-75 average; negotiates payment based on experience and skill of artist, and turnaround time.

BODY FASHIONS/INTIMATE APPAREL, 545 5th Ave., New York NY 10017. (212)503-2910. Editor/Associate Publisher: Jill Gerson. Information for merchandise managers, buyers, manufacturers and suppliers about men's and women's hosiery and underwear and women's intimate apparel and leisurewear. Monthly. Circ. 13,500.
Illustrations: Interested in fashion illustrations of intimate apparel. Do not mail artwork. Arrange interview to show portfolio. Works on assignment only. Keeps file consisting of editor's comments on portfolio review and samples of work. Reports in 4 weeks. Pays on publication.

*CATALINA/Division of Kayser Roth, 6040 Bandini Blvd., Los Angeles CA 90040. (213)726-1262, ext. 281. Art Director: Rhonda Gawthrop. Manufacturer of women's, men's, juniors, and girls' swimwear and sportswear; Catalina.
Needs: Works with 10 freelance artists/year. Uses artists for fashion illustration, paste-up and mechanicals. Seeks "contemporary but not 'high' fasion look" in art styles.
First Contact & Terms: Local artists only. Send samples to be kept on file. Call for appointment to show portfolio. Prefers photostats and photographs as samples. Reports to the artist only if interested. Pays by the hour, $18-25 for production; by the project, $125-250 for illustration/per figure. "For catalogs that are totally illustrated, we would like to make arrangements according to budget." Considers complexity of project, available budget and how work will be used when establishing payment.

EARNSHAW'S REVIEW, 393 7th Ave., New York NY 10001. (212)563-2742. Publisher: Thomas Hudson. Managing Editor: Christina Gruber. Editor/Fashion Coordinator: Jo Ann Furtak. Art Director: Bette Gallucci. For designers, manufacturers, buyers and retailers in the children's fashion industry. Monthly. Circ. 10,000.
Illustrations: Buys 180/year on fashion (infants to pre-teenagers). Arrange interview. SASE. Reports in 1 week. Buys all rights. Cover: Pays $150-250, color; $50 minimum, b&w. Inside: Pays $30, color; $15-20, b&w.
Advertising: Pays $35-50/figure, b&w, $45 and up color; on publication.
Tips: "Artist must have at least 4 child fashion illustrations in his portfolio. He must work quickly and accurately and know the difference between the figures of a 3-and 6-year old."

FOOTWEAR FOCUS, 1414 Avenue of the Americas, New York NY 10019. (212)752-2555. Editor: Anisa Mycak. Readers are shoe retailers (store owners, buyers and managers). Emphasizes new methods, creative ideas and reliable information on fashion and retail trends to help readers better operate their businesses. Published 6 times/year. Circ. 20,000. Free sample copy.
Illustrations: Uses 4 illustrations/issue; buys all from freelancers. Currently receives a few submissions from freelancers. Works on assignment only. Interested in fashion illustrations—ready-to-wear and shoes—and some cartoons to illustrate business features. Prefers b&w line drawings, and b&w or color washes. Arrange personal appointment to show portfolio or send samples of style. SASE. Reports in 2 weeks. Buys all rights. Pays $35 maximum for inside b&w and $75 for color inside; on acceptance.
Tips: When reviewing an artist's work, looks for art that "suits the style of our publication."

*GARLAND CORPORATION, 6th Floor, 1411 Broadway, New York NY 10018. Technical Coordinator: Tamara Lenkeit. Manufacuter of sweaters; updated classics; Garland and Yves Jennet.
Needs: Works with 1 freelance artist/year. Uses artists for brochure illustration.
First Contact & Terms: Seeks local artists only with previous experience. Send query letter with business card and samples to be kept on file. Write for appointment to show portfolio. Prefers photographs as samples. Reports to the artist only if interested. Pays by the project, $10-150 for illustration. Considers complexity of project when establishing payment.

GELMART INDUSTRIES, INC., 180 Madison Ave., New York NY 10016. (212)889-7225. Vice President and Head of Design: Ed Adler. Manufacturer of high fashion socks, gloves, headwear, scarves, and other knitted accessories. "We are prime manufacturers for many major brands and designer names."
Needs: Uses artists for fashion accessory design.
First Contact & Terms: Call for appointment to show portfolio.
Tips: "Keep the products in mind and show us how your ideas can adapt."

*JOHN PAUL GOEBEL, 10 Park Ave., New York NY 10016. Vice President: Suzette Lynch. Specializes in fashion. Clients: fibers, textiles and ready to wear.
Needs: Works with 2-6 freelance artists/year. Uses artists for illustrations, brochures, catalogs, newspapers and model making.
First Contact & Terms: Works on assignment only. Send query letter with brochure, business card and samples to be kept on file. Write for appointment to show portfolio. Prefers photostats, photocopies or

tear sheets as samples. Reports back only if interested. Pays for illustration by the project, $100-5,000 average. Considers complexity of project, client's budget and how work will be used when establishing payment.
Tips: "Submit examples of their fashion illustrations. We deal primarily with mens apparel."

GOLD MILLS INC., 1441 Broadway, New York NY 10018. (212)944-0700. Fashion Coordinator: Pat Diblasi. Mill providing warp knits for knitted fabrics.
Needs: Works with 2 freelance artists/year. Uses artists for advertising design and illustration; brochure, catalog and fashion design.
First Contact & Terms: Send query letter to be kept on file. Reports within 2 weeks. Considers complexity of project and available budget when establishing payment.

HOSIERY AND UNDERWEAR, 545 Third Ave., New York NY 10017. (212)503-2910. Managing Editor: Susan DeFetefuno. Emphasizes hosiery; directed to hosiery buyers (from department and specialty stores mass merchandisers, etc.) and hosiery manufacturers nationwide. Monthly. Circ. 10,000. Returns original artwork after publication if requested. Sample copy free for SASE; art guidelines available.
Illustrations: Considers illustrations of hosiery; "we look for a clean style that pays attention to detail, but has a fresh, '80s look." Works on assignment only. Send query letter with brochure, resume and samples to be kept on file; or write for appointment to show portfolio. Accepts photostats, tear sheets or photocopies as samples; no slides and photographs. Samples not filed are returned only if requested. Reports back. Buys all rights. Pays $8/b&w figure; $75-100 for color spread. Pays on acceptance.

JOSEPHS BROTHERS EMBROIDERY CORP., 6030 Monroe Pl., West New York NJ 07093. (201)861-2290. President: Bernard Josephs. Manufacturer of embroidery for apparel.
Needs: Works with 3 freelance artists/year. Uses artists for fashion accessory design.
First Contact & Terms: Negotiates payment. Considers how work will be used when establishing payment.

KOALA ARTS INC., 3450 Channel Way, San Diego CA 92110. (619)223-2555. President: Ken Klempan. Specializes in fashion, promotional sportswear (imprinted). Clients: corporations (directly), agencies and wholesale distributors.
Needs: Works with 6-10 freelance artists/year. Uses artists for design, mechanicals, lettering and logos.
First Contact & Terms: "Local southern California artists only with experience in imprinted sportswear design." Works on assignment only. Send query letter with brochure, resume and samples, if available, to be kept on file. "Screen printed samples preferred; if not available slides are acceptable." Reports back only if interested. Pays for design by the hour, $10-50 average; by the project, $25 minimum. Pays for illustration by the project, $25 minimum. Considers complexity of project, client's budget, and rights purchased when establishing payment.

LEE CO., Division of Lee Byron Corp., Suite 4619, Empire State Building, New York NY 10118. (212)244-4440. Contact: Dan L. Lieberfarb. Produces belts and personal leather goods. Mail samples or call for interview; prefers New York City artists.
Needs: Uses artists for fashion design of men's and boys' belts, sales promotion/ad layouts, package design and direct mail brochures.

MADEMOISELLE PROMOTIONS LTD., 350 7th Ave., New York NY 10001. Contact: Stuart Schwartz. Prefers local artists. Buys all rights. Pays on acceptance.
Needs: Uses line illustrations made from photos of women's sportswear and corporate logos made into textile patterns. Pays $10 minimum/figure, line illustration.

MS. LIZ, 61 W. 68th St., New York NY 10023. Design studio providing designs for apparel, gifts; television production, advertising (animation); Ms. Liz label.
Needs: Works with 10 freelance artists/year. Uses artists for advertising and brochure design, illustration, and layout; fashion design, fashion accessory design, package design, graphics, illustration on product and animation. Prefers "cartoon art—high fashion—adult appeal."
First Contact & Terms: Artists with heavy experience, New York City area only. Send query letter with brochure, resume, samples and tear sheets to be kept on file. Write for appointment to show portfolio. Accepts "anything but original work" as samples. Samples returned by SASE if not kept on file. Reports within 2-3 weeks. Pays for design by the hour, $12-25 average; by the project, $100-5,000 average; by the day, $75-200 average. Pays for illustration by the hour, $10-20 average; by the project, $75-1,000 average; by the day $75-150 average. Considers complexity of project, available budget, and skill and experience of artist when establishing payment.

NAZARETH/CENTURY MILLS, 350 5th Ave., New York NY 10118. (212)613-0500. Designers: Kathryn Harmes (girls'/ladies' sportswear); Eileen Kornbluh (boys'/mens' sportswear); Martha Deutsch (sleepwear). Manufactures children's sleepwear, men's, boys', girls' and ladies' sportswear and underwear; cotton and polyester/cotton; Nazareth Mills, Savage and Lady Nazareth labels.
Needs: Buys 50-100 illustrations/year.
First Contact & Terms: Works with 6 local freelance artists/year. Query with samples. Reports within 4 weeks. Works on assignment only. Samples returned by SASE; and reports back on future assignment possibilities. Provide flyer to be kept on file for future assignments. Pays $100-200/job, artwork for screen printing.

NEUVILLE INDUSTRIES INC., (formerly Neuville Mobil-Sox Inc.), 200 Madison Ave., New York NY 10016. (212)532-2510. Contact: Stephen Schwartz. Specializes in anklets and knee-hi socks for all ages.
Needs: Works with 3-4 freelance artists/year. Uses artists for sales promotion/ad layouts, package design and direct mail brochures.
First Contact & Terms: Query with brochure and tear sheets to be kept in file for possible future assignments. SASE. Reports within 2 weeks. Pays by the project for design and illustration.

THE PARIS, 618 Felix St., St. Joseph MO 64501. (816)232-8446. General Manager: Paul Yanuck. 16-store chains of women's and junior clothing store. Assigns 150 + jobs/year.
First Contact & Terms: Query with samples. Reports in 1 week. Pays $10-25, newspaper ad illustrations.

***PENDLETON WOOLEN MILLS**, 218 SW Jefferson, Portland OR 97201. Menswear Communications Manager: Carolyn A. Zelle; Womenswear Communications Manager: Pat McKevitt. Manufacturer of men's and women's sportswear, blankets and piece goods; all 100% pure virgin wool. Label: Pendleton Woolen Mills.
Needs: Works with 1 or 2 freelance artists/year directly, "through our agency more." Uses artists for advertising illustration.
First Contact & Terms: Seeks local artist for line art. Send query letter to be kept on file. Write for appointment to show portfolio. Reports to the artist within 3 weeks. Considers complexity of project, available budget and how work will be used when establishing payment.

PERSONAL LEATHER DESIGN, INC., 111 Charter Oak Ave., Hartford CT 06106. (203)722-1700. President: Larry Bell. Manufactures leather bags, clothing, etc.
Needs: Works with fashion illustrators in New York and the Northeast for advertising and promotional material. Buys 10-15 sketches/year. Especially needs illustrations for newspaper ads and direct mail.
First Contact & Terms: Needs unique fashion style. Prefers illustrators with a new approach. Query. SASE. Reports in 2 weeks. Works on assignment only. Prefers b&w line drawings as samples. Provide resume and samples of work to be kept on file for future assignment possibilities. Pays by the project.

PINEHURST TEXTILES INC., Box 1628, Asheboro NC 27204. (919)625-2153. Contact: Lloyd E. Milks Jr. Manufactures ladies' lingerie, sleepwear and leisurewear; nylon tricot, woven polyester/cotton, brushed tricot and fleece; Pinehurst Lingerie label.
Needs: Works with 2 illustrators/year. Seasonal needs: spring and summer due September 1; fall and winter due March 1.

***PLYMOUTH MILLS, INC.**, 330 Tompkins Ave., Staten Island NY 10304. (718)447-6707. President: Alan Elewson. Manufacturer of imprinted sportswear—t-shirts, sweatshirts, fashionwear, caps, aprons and bags. Clients: mass merchandisers/retailers.
Needs: Works with 6 freelance artists/year. Uses freelance artists for advertising and catalog design, illustration and layout; product design.
First Contact & Terms: Send brochure and resume. Reports back only if interested. Negotiates payment; pays by the project. Considers complexity of the project and how work will be used when establishing payment.

QUEEN CASUALS, INC., 1411 Broadway, New York NY 10018. (212)398-9977. Advertising Director: Tillie Smith. Manufacturer of misses and women's coordinated sportswear, misses sizes 8-20, womens sizes 38-46 in polyester knits; Queen Casuals, Lady Queen and Smith, Smith & Jones for Her, Smith & Jones Petites labels.
Needs: Works with a varied number of freelance artists/year. Uses artists for fashion illustration and mechanicals.
First Contact & Terms: Prefers artists in New York, New Jersey, Pennsylvania and Connecticut areas

primarily. Send samples then call for appointment. Prefers tear sheets as samples. Sample returned by SASE. Does not report on acceptance or rejection, "artist should call." Works on assigment only. Provide resume and tear sheets to be kept on file for possible future assignments. Pays by the hour for mechanicals; by the project, illustration.
Tips: "Fashion illustration is more realistic now."

ROTH INTERNATIONAL, Suites 110-113, 31368 Via Colinas, Westlake Village CA 91362. Contact: Art Director.
Needs: Uses freelance artists for graphics relating to home fashions, housewear, novelty gift items, fashion and novelty wearing apparel and textiles.
First Contact: Send resume and samples of work with SASE.
Tips: "There is a need for knowledge of what is currently happening in the market place in the above mentioned product areas, as well as a need for innovative and creative design concepts."

*R-TEX DECORATIVES CO., INC., 59 Sea Cliff Ave., Glen Cove NY 11542. (516)671-7600. Vice President: Lillian Sturm. Manufacturer of high-fashion decorative yard goods, posters, panels and banners. Clients: department stores.
Needs: Works with 3-4 freelance artists/year. Uses artists for product design and posters.
First Contact & Terms: Works on assignment only. Send query letter with brochure and samples to be kept on file. Call or write for appointment to show portfolio. Accepts any type sample. Samples not filed are returned only if requested. Reports back only if interested. Pays by the project. Considers complexity of the project and artist's bid when establishing payment.

*SEW NEWS, News Plaza, Box 1790, Peoria IL 61656. Art Director: Cathy Ford. Tabloid emphasizing home sewing and fashion for primarily women, average age 49. Monthly. Does not accept previously published material. Original artwork is not returned to the artist after publication. Sample copy and art guidelines are not available.
Needs: Buys up to 10 illustrations per issue. Works on an assignment basis only.
First Contact & Terms: Send query letter with resume. Write for appointment to show portfolio. Reports back to the artist only if interested. Purchases all rights. Pays on acceptance.

SHIREY COMPANY, 1917 Stanford St., Greenville TX 75401. (214)455-5235. Vice President, Merchandising: Michelle Jenkins. Manufacturer of children's sleepwear, infants through juniors, boys and girls, in a variety of fabrics; Shirey label.
Needs: Works with 5-8 freelance artists/year. Uses artists for advertising, brochure and catalog illustration, illustration on products and direct mail promotions.
First Contact & Terms: Prefers Dallas area artists only. Send resume and samples; write for appointment. Prefers actual work as samples. Samples returned. Works on assignment only. Pays for design and illustration by the hour, $5 minimum; by the project, $400-1,000 average. Provide resume, business card and brochure/flyer to be kept on file for possible future assignments.
Tips: "I need to see sketches of 'cute' kids."

SILVIL CORP., 34 W. 33rd St., New York NY 10001. Contact: Sy Silverberg. Produces boys' robes and pajamas. Mail samples.
Needs: Uses artists to design screen prints for pajamas.

*LES STEINHARDT INC., 15841 Stagg St., Van Nuys CA 91406. (213)988-8600. President: Les Steinhardt. Manufacturer of dance products: leotards, tights, jazz pants, skirts and related dance items; Les Steinhardt label.
Needs: Uses artists for advertising, brochure design and illustration, fashion design, ready-to-wear pattern design, package design and direct mail packages.
First Contact & Terms: Send query letter with photocopies of work or tear sheets to be kept on file. Reports within 10 days. "Artist should advise what his fee may be." Considers available budget and how work will be used when establishing payment.

STRETCH & SEW INC., Box 185, Eugene OR 97401. (503)726-9000. Contact: Katie Nyland. Publishes patterns and books, and teaches sewing methods.
Needs: Assigns 50 jobs/year. Works with 3 freelance artists/year on a regular basis. Uses artists for pattern envelopes/instructions, catalog covers/layouts, direct mail/publicity brochures, newspaper ad layouts, packaging, posters and company publications. Especially needs technical illustrations for sewing instructions; also some paste-up.
First Contact & Terms: Seeks artists with fashion illustration experience and technical art inking experience. Query with samples. Prefers b&w line drawings, roughs, photostats and previously published

work—technical art illustration in particular—as samples. SASE. Reports in 2 weeks. Payment depends on complexity of project.
Tips: "Please don't waste your time or ours by sending bad photocopies."

PRESTON STUART ART SERVICES, 12 E. 97 St., New York NY 10029. (212)722-6637. Director: Preston Stuart. Specializes in fashion. Clients: fashion manufacturers, retail stores, magazines, ad agencies and videogame software.
Needs: Works with 10 freelance artists/year. Uses artists for advertising design and illustration, mechanicals and retouching.
First Contact & Terms: Desires "a professional relationship and good work." Send query letter with samples and tear sheets to be kept on file. Call for appointment to show portfolio. "Photocopied samples are best." Reports only if interested. Works on assignment only. Pays for illustration by the project, $150-800 average. Considers client's budget, skill and experience of artist, how work will be used, turnaround time and rights purchased when establishing payment.

TRIBORO QUILT MFG. CORP., 172 S. Broadway, White Plains NY 10605. (914)428-7551. Sales Manager: Alvin Kaplan. Produces infants' wear and bedding under the Triboro label; for chain and department stores.
Needs: Works with 3 designers, 3 textile designers and 3 illustrator/designers/year. Uses artists for advertising/catalog layouts, direct mail brochures, fabric and fashion design, hang tags, inserts, iron-ons and package design for infant items.
First Contact & Terms: Call for interview or provide resume, business card and brochure to be kept on file for future assignments. Reports in 1 week. Works on assignment only. Samples returned by SASE; and reports back on future assignment possibilities.

UNIFORMS MANUFACTURING INC., Box 5336, W. Bloomfield MI 48033. (313)851-6744. President: L.P. Tucker. Manufacturer of all types of wearing apparel—smocks, lab coats, shirts, trousers, coveralls, dresses, aprons, gloves in cotton, polyester and knits; Uniform label.
Needs: Works with 3 freelance artists/year. Uses artists for advertising, brochure and catalog design; advertising illustration and direct mail promotions.
First Contact & Terms: Send brochure/flyer. Prefers slides as samples. Samples returned by SASE. Reports as soon as possible. Works on assignment only; reports back whether to expect possible future assignments. Negotiates payment.

*U.S. SHOE CORPORATION, One Eastwood Dr., Cincinnati OH 45227. (513)527-7000. Promotion Services Director: Philip Gleeson. Manufacturer of shoes featuring current fashion trends. Red Cross, Socialites, Cobbies, Joyce, Selby, Pappagallo and Capezio labels.
Needs: Works with 3 freelance artists/year. Uses artists for advertising, brochure and catalog design, illustration and layout; fashion design and illustration; paste-up and mechanicals.
First Contact & Terms: "Experience is normally necessary." Send query letter with samples to be kept on file. Call or write for appointment to show portfolio. Accepts any type sample. Samples not kept on file are returned only if requested by artist. Reports to the artist only if interested. Pays by the hour, $25-30 for design; $30-35 for illustration. Considers complexity of project, available budget and turnaround time when establishing payment.

WESTERN ART MFG. CO. INC., 1990 S. Broadway, Denver CO 80210. (303)778-1885. Vice President: Gary Hilb. Specializes in children's wear, juniorwear and men's wear.
Needs: Works with 2-3 designers/year. Uses artists for t-shirt and sweatshirt art and children's wear. Especially interested in cartoons and styled art for t-shirts.
First Contact & Terms: Mail samples (slides or sketches showing artist's ability). Works on assignment only. Samples returned by SASE; and reports back on future assignment possibilities. Provide resume, brochure and flyer to be kept on file for future assignments.

*WHITE STAG MFG. CO., 5100 SE Harney Dr., Portland OR 97206. Vice President Advertising: Robert Zwald. Manufacturer of women's sportswear, men's and women's warmups and ski-wear; White Stag, Mountain Goat labels.
Needs: Works with 8-10 freelance artists/year. Uses artists for advertising and brochure design and illustration; catalog illustration; fashion illustration; and direct mail.
First Contact & Terms: "Most pieces require quick-turnaround and/or daily coordination." Send query letter with resume and samples to be kept on file. Call for appointment to show portfolio after mail contact. Prefers transparencies, photographs or printed work as samples. Samples not kept on file are returned only if requested by artist. Reports to the artist only if interested. Pays by the hour, $25-60 for design and illustration. Considers complexity of project, available budget, skill and experience of artist, how work will be used, turnaround time and rights purchased when establishing payment.

WILROY INC., 530 7th Ave., New York NY 10018. (212)221-2200. Women's apparel manufacturer specializing in sportswear and dresses sizes 6 through 20 of fine fabrics; Setiage and Wilroy sport labels.
Needs: Works with 6 freelance artists/year. Uses artists for advertising illustrations. Prefers soft, sophisticated, elegant illustrations, color only.
First Contact & Terms: Artists should be in New York City limits. Send query letter with brochure/flyer or resume; all artists should present a portfolio at appointment. Samples returned. Works on assignment only. Provide information to be kept on file for possible future assignment. Negotiates payment.

Greeting Cards & Paper Products___

Thanks to Christmas, Easter, Valentine's Day and cardshops full of other holiday greetings, the demand for and sale of greeting cards makes this $3.2 billion-a-year industry one of the best markets open to freelance artists. Not only does this market need a lot of artwork and design, but long lead times mean you can handle greeting card work easily through the mail, often without assignment, while receiving high visibility for your work and the potential for royalties.

The key to successfully marketing your art to the more than 300 greeting card firms nationwide is to know the market and a particular firm's line of cards. Different card companies specialize in different styles, themes, types of illustrations and media. So "study before the exam" to save time (yours), money (yours) and face (yours).

Greeting card formats have evolved greatly since the tradition first began. In addition to the standard folded card with sentimental verse inside, today's consumers select from musical, pop-up, jigsaw puzzle, die-cut, holograph, paper sculpture, embossed and foil-stamped greeting cards. Special occasion cards now cover divorce, the death of a family pet, weight loss and new cars.

As the market expands, the need for new images and new styles increases. Multi-color calligraphy, mixed media and text combined with illustration are recent innovations.

Greetings Magazine updates trends and new products in the greeting card industry. Read books such as Ron Lister's *Designing Greeting* 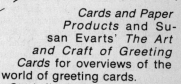 *Cards and Paper Products* and Susan Evarts' *The Art and Craft of Greeting Cards* for overviews of the world of greeting cards.

Study firsthand the card lines in stationery and card shops, book stores and novelty shops. Character licensing is on the upswing so note the peripheral products from the various companies. Look at what's available, the different lines and styles, and how the illustration relates to the occasion and to the sentiment of the card.

Most art directors feel that greeting card artists need to understand the content of the cards they're designing and the motivation urging people to buy them. Product Manager John C.W. Carrol of C.R. Gibson stresses that the artists should possess a strong "empathy for what drives people to give cards— love, caring and a desire to share those emotions . . . the imagery must also be appropriate, especially on occasion and holiday cards."

The following listings indicate how the art directors at over 100 companies prefer to be contacted and what samples artists should send. A query letter and résumé with samples and SASE (although the return of unsolicited samples is not guaranteed) are standard. Or you can write or call and request art guidelines and/or a catalog before you submit.

You can read first-hand advice on the business, design and illustration of greeting cards, paper products and peripheral products in this section's Close-up interviews with greeting card artists Sandra Boynton of Lakeville, Connecticut, and Riva Greenberg of New York City.

Boynton

AFRICA CARD CO. INC., Box 91, New York NY 10108. (212)725-1199. President: Vince Jordan. Publishes greeting cards and posters. Mail art, or arrange interview. SASE. Reports in 6 weeks. Buys all rights.
Needs: Buys 25 designs/year. Pays $50 minimum, greeting cards and posters.

*ALBION CARDS, Box 102, Albion MI 49224. Owner: Maggie LaNoue. Produces greeting cards, prints, note cards, postcards, catalogues and brochures. Uses b&w, line art, realistic, detailed, old fashioned, clear; must hold line quality when reduced—to "jump out"—high contrast. Directs products to women, older people, tourists, nostalgia buffs and sports enthusiasts.
Needs: Buys approximately 200 designs from freelance artists/year. Uses artists for calligraphy and mechanicals. Considers pen & ink and watercolors. Size of originals 9x12" or proportionate; important elements of design and artist's signature should be one inch from all edges of the drawing. Produces material for Christmas and summer (skiing, golfing, boating); other subjects: animals (cats & ducks especially), landscapes, wild flowers and herbs. Also buys cartoons as needed for use by corporations. "We act as agents representing several cartoonists. Humorous and cartoon-type illustrations are considered for card designs and for use by corporations; theme must be "upbeat" and positive.
First Contact & Terms: Send query letter with brochure, resume, business card and samples to be kept on file; catalog $2; art guidelines for SASE. Prefers photographs, photocopies and tear sheets as samples. Samples not filed are not returned. Reports back within 2 months. Originals returned to the artist at job's completion. Pays royalties of 5% and free cards of accepted works. Buys rights for cards only; artist retains rights for other items; negotiates rights for prints.
Tips: "We are interested in producing series of cards relating to scenic tourist areas, sea scapes, street scenes and landmarks. We can help promote other artists' works in their own locale. The card market is expanding; nostalgia is gaining in popularity. Our needs for freelance work have increased dramatically.

*ALLEYCARDS INC., 110 W. 17th St., New York NY 10011. Vice-President: Howard Parker. Produces greeting cards.
Needs: Buys 60 designs from freelance artists/year. Uses artists for mechanicals. No b&w media. Final art size 10½x14½" or 5¼x7¼". Produces material for all seasons and holidays; submit 9 months in advance.
First Contact & Terms: Send query letter and samples to be kept on file; write for appointment to show portfolio. Prefers slides, photographs, photocopies and original art as samples. Samples not filed are returned by SASE only if requested. Reports only if interested. Originals can be returned to artist at job's completion. Pays on case-by-case basis. Buys first rights, one-time rights or negotiates rights purchased on case-by-case basis.
Tips: "Artists should have professional presentation."

AMBERLEY GREETING CARD CO., Box 36159, Cincinnati OH 45236. Art Director: Ned Stern. Publishes studio and humorous greeting cards.
Needs: Assigns 200 jobs/year. Uses local freelance artists for product illustration. Especially needs humorous cards.
First Contact & Terms: Local artists only. Call first. Buys all rights. No original work returned at job's completion. Pays $60, color illustrations; on acceptance.
Tips: Visit greeting card shops to get a better idea of the types of cards published by Amberley. When reviewing an artist's work, "the first thing I look for is the professionalism of the presentation, i.e. samples neatly displayed (no loose drawings, scraps of paper, etc.); creativity—what has the artist done differently and effectively; use of color, and lettering." An artist's biggest mistake is having a sloppy portfolio; "I'd rather see 5 good examples of work than 25 poorly done."

AMCAL INC., 1050 Shary Ct., Concord CA 94518. (415)689-9930. Publishes and imports calendars and greeting cards. Markets to all major gift, book and department stores throughout US, Europe and Japan. Rapidly expanding company looking for distinctive card and gift ideas for growing market demand. "All subjects considered that fit our quality image."
First Contact & Terms: Send samples in any form or call for appointment. Responds within 2 weeks. Payment and terms negotiable. No portfolios, please.
Tips: "Artwork must be suitable for an expandable line of greeting cards for a multitude of occasions and holidays. The minimum number of cards in a greeting card line is around 24. We find that any less than that number doesn't make a significant enough impact with buyers to make a line successful. New card ideas using embossing, hot stamping and die-cuts are of particular interest to us. Know the market. Go to gift shows and visit lots of stationery stores. Read all the trade magazines. Talk to store owners to find out what's selling and what isn't."

AMERICAN GREETINGS CORP., 10500 American Rd., Cleveland OH 44102. (216)252-7300. Director Creative Personnel: Kathy McConaughy. Publishes humorous, studio and conventional greeting

Maggie LaNoue, owner of Albion Cards in Albion, Michigan, chose this artwork by P.L. Klein of Grand Rapids for use as a design for notecards and postcards. "We have arranged to pay 5% royalties on all card sales, 30% for all print sales," says LaNoue. Klein's artwork was chosen because the subject matter is "old-fashioned but not trite or over-simplified. I like the artist's study of the subjects, the layout and texture," adds LaNoue.

cards, calendars, giftwrap, posters, stationery and paper tableware products. Manufactures candles and ceramic figurines.

First Contact & Terms: Query with resume. Forms for submitting portfolio will be mailed. Portfolios received without necessary paperwork will be returned unreviewed.

Tips: "We are staffed to generate our own ideas internally, but we will review portfolios for full-time or freelance employment."

ANTIOCH PUBLISHING COMPANY, Box 28, Yellow Springs OH 45387. Art Director: Marty Roelandt. Publishes calendars, bookmarks, bookplates, greeting cards and children's books. Also has separate religious/inspirational line.

Needs: Uses artists for illustrations. "Most of our needs are of the full color, magical-unicorn-rainbow-charming-whimsical-humorous variety. I want art from people who know how to use color for good reproduction. I want to work with professionals who know the importance of deadlines, flexibility and marketability. Because of this I prefer working with experienced, previously published artists, although I've also worked with relative newcomers who have a high degree of professionalism."

First Contact & Terms: Do not send original art. Send SASE, attention Creative Guidelines, for copy of Antioch artist's guidelines before sending samples of any kind. Works on assignment only. Buys 100 or more illustrations per year. Buys various rights. Pays $100-200/illustration, depending on use and in-house preparation time.

Tips: "We appreciate a professional presentation of work by an artist who is creative, familiar with our products and responsive to ideas of marketability and will work with us to achieve desired results on time."

APPARENT COMPANY, 702 E. Arbutus Lake Rd., Traverse City MI 49684. (616)947-4888. Director, Product Development: Marilyn Kopp. Produces greeting cards, games, memo pads and coffee mugs. Specializes in "heavy use of word play, jokes about professionals, such as attorneys, doctors. Also interested in clean, feeling, or spiritual art for greeting cards."

Needs: Buys 96 designs and 60 illustrations/year from freelance artists. Also uses artists for paste-up and mechanicals. Considers all media for product illustration. Produces seasonal material for Christmas; submit art work 6-9 months in advance.

First Contact & Terms: Send query letter with resume and samples to be kept on file. Prefers photographs, photocopies or tear sheets as samples. Samples not filed are returned by SASE only if requested. Reports within 4 weeks. Sometimes returns original art after reproduction; "depends on contract." Pays flat fee of $50/design or illustration, pays by the project (payment varies) or pays royalty of 5%; negotiates. Buys all rights or negotiates rights purchased.

Tips "Please send samples of art first before telephoning, etc. If we are interested, we typically contract for an entire line. We are interested in individual designs and illustrations as well."

*ARACON CARDS, 1370 Johnston Dr., Watchung NJ 07060. Designer/Sales Manager: Jane Saltzman. Produces greeting cards. "85% of all card buyers are women—we want them to buy our cards."

Needs: Uses artists for paste-up and mechanicals. "We're open to new media—whatever is needed to get the card message across." No specific size for final art if it can be reduced to 4¾x6¾". Produces material for Christmas cards and Valentine's Day; submit 6 months before holiday.

First Contact & Terms: Send query letter with brochure, resume, business card and samples to be kept on file; write for appointment to show portfolio. Reports only if interested. Originals sometimes returned to artist at job's completion. Pays according to design. Negotiates rights purchased.

Tips: "We're new and just beginning to look for new designs."

*ARGUS COMMUNICATIONS, INC., Division of DLM, One DLM Park, Allen TX 75002. Product Director: Izzie Waller. Produces greeting cards, postcards, calendars, posters, etc.

Needs: Works with hundreds of freelance artists/year. Uses artists for roughs, layouts and final art.

First Contact & Terms: Must be professional artist. Works on assignment only. Send query letter with resume and samples to be kept on file; write for appointment to show portfolio. Prefers photostats, slides or tear sheets as samples; or ideas for new product. Samples not filed are returned by SASE. Reports only if interested. Payment depends on project. Considers complexity of the project, turnaround time and rights purchased when establishing payment. Negotiates rights purchased.

Tips: "Be familiar with our product line before contacting us."

BARNARD, ROBERTS & CO., INC., 305 Gun Rd., Baltimore MD 21227. Contact: Charles S. Roberts. Publishes greeting cards, certificates and stationery primarily for the Catholic religious field.

First Contact & Terms: SASE. Reports in 2-3 weeks. Buys all rights. Previously published work OK "only if exclusive in our field." No original work returned at job's completion. Write for artist's guidelines. Pays $75, design idea; $100, color transparency; $150-200, full-color art. Considers complexity of project, and skill and experience of artist when establishing payment.

Tips: "Send *something* to indicate skill level."

BARTON-COTTON INC., 1405 Parker Rd., Baltimore MD 21227. (301)247-4800. Contact: Creative/Art Department. Produces religious greeting cards, wildlife Christmas cards and commercial Christmas cards. Free guidelines and sample cards; specify area of interest: religious, wildlife, general, etc.

Needs: Buys 150-200 illustrations each year. Submit seasonal work "any time of the year."

First Contact & Terms: Query with resume and samples or send roughs. Previously published work and simultaneous submissions accepted. Reports in 4 weeks. Submit full-color work only (watercolors, gouache, pastels, oils and acrylics); pays $200-600/illustration; on acceptance.

Tips: "Fresh approaches are needed for traditional Christmas card designs. Good draftsmanship is a must, particularly with figures and faces."

BEACH PRODUCTS, 1 Paper Pl., Kalamazoo MI 49001. (616)349-2626. Creative Director: Susan Turner. Publishes paper tableware products; general and seasonal, birthday, special occasion, invitations, announcements, stationery, wrappings and thank you notes for children and adults.

Needs: Buys 100 designs/year from freelance artists. Uses artists for product design and illustration. Sometimes buys humorous and cartoon-style illustrations. Prefers flat four-color designs; 5 1/4. wide x 5 1/2" high for luncheon napkins. Produces seasonal material for Christmas, Mother's Day, Thanksgiving, Easter, Valentine's Day, St. Patrick's Day, Halloween and New Year's Day. Submit seasonal material before June 1; everyday (not holidays) material before April.

First Contact & Terms: Send query letter with SASE (9x12" envelope) so catalog can be sent with response. Samples returned; prefers SASE. Reports in 6-8 weeks. Previously published work OK. Originals not returned to artist at job's completion; "all artwork purchased becomes the property of Beach Products. Items not purchased are returned." Buys all rights. Pays average flat fee of $100/design; on acceptance. Considers product use when establishing payment.

Tips: "When asking for specifications and catalog, the SASE should be large enough to accommodate the catalog, for example, a 9x12" envelope. Artwork should have a clean, professional appearance and be the specified size for submissions, as well as a maximum of four flat colors."

*BITTERSWEET CARDS, INC., 770 3rd Ave., Brooklyn NY 11232. (212)499-4172. Art Director: Barbara Davilman. Produces greeting cards, posters and memo pads. Themes are "mostly humorous." Directs products to 18-35-year-old group.

Needs: Buys 50-60 illustrations from freelance artists/year. Uses artists for mechanicals. Considers pen & ink, watercolors, acrylics—"anything, really." Final art size: 5x7 cards, 6x8" memo pads. Produces material for Christmas and Valentine's Day; submit year round.

First Contact & Terms: Send brochure, resume and samples to be kept on file. Accepts slides, photostats, photographs, photocopies, and tear sheets as samples. Samples not filed are returned by SASE only if requested. Reports only if interested. Originals returned to artist at job's completion. Pays average flat fee, $25/design; $50/illustration; or royalties of 5%. Buys reprint rights.

Tips: "Each illustration should be strong enough to jump off the shelf. The artist should consider each illustration to be an advertisement."

*BLOOMIN' IMAGES, 70 W. Cedar St., Box H, Poughkeepsie NY 12602. (914)471-3110. Administrative Services Manager: Vera Lawrence. Estab. 1983. Produces a unique variety of greeting cards and stationery sold primarily on the east coast.

Needs: Buys 20 designs and illustrations from freelance artists/year. Uses artists for calligraphy and paste-up. Prefers pen & ink.

First Contact & Terms: Works on assignment only. Send query letter with samples to be kept on file. Prefers tear sheet as samples. Samples not filed are returned. Reports within 2 months. Returns original artwork after reproduction. Negotiates payment and rights purchased.

BRETT-FORER GREETINGS, INC., 105 73rd St., New York NY 10021. Art Director: Barbara T. Schaffer. Publishes cute and whimsical greeting cards; Christmas and everyday.

Needs: Uses artists for design of 6x9" and 4 1/2x6" Christmas cards, and 4 3/4x6 1/2" everyday cards. Considers all media. Produces seasonal cards for Valentine's Day and Mother's Day.

First Contact & Terms: Send samples. Reports in 4 weeks. No originals returned to artist at job's completion. Buys all rights. Pays average flat fee of $125/design. Considers complexity of project when establishing payment.

BRILLIANT ENTERPRISES, 117 W. Valerio St., Santa Barbara CA 93101. Art Director: Ashleigh Brilliant. Publishes postcards.

Freelance artist Kliever DuBois of Chichester, New York, submitted this image to Bloomin' Images, Poughkeepsie, New York, on speculation. Not only did the company purchase the use of this artwork, they commissioned the artist to create seven additional animal and flower images. All eight illustrations were reproduced on stationery cards and distributed as a set. According to Administrative Services Manager Vera Lawrence, "Ms. DuBois's illustrations have a wonderful appeal. They are imaginative, subtle and full of life." The gorilla image "is clever and unique in its simplicity." DuBois sold Bloomin' Images the right to use this illustration on stationery cards only.

© Kliever DuBois

Needs: Uses up to 300 designs/year. Artists may submit designs for word-and-picture postcards, illustrated with line drawings.
First Contact & Terms: Submit 5¹/₂x3¹/₂" horizontal b&w line drawings. SASE. Reports in 2 weeks. Buys all rights. "Since our approach is very offbeat, it is essential that freelancers first study our line. Ashleigh Brilliant's books include *I May Not Be Totally Perfect, But Parts of Me Are Excellent* and *Appreciate Me Now and Avoid the Rush.* We supply a catalog and sample set of cards for $2." Pays $40 minimum, depending on "the going rate" for camera-ready word-and-picture design.

SIDNEY J. BURGOYNE & SONS INC., 2030 E. Byberry Rd., Philadelphia PA 19116. (215)677-8000. Art Director: Jon Harding. Publishes greeting cards and calendars; Christmas, winter and religious themes.
Needs: Buys 40-50 designs/year. Uses freelance artists for products design and illustration, and calligraphy. Will review any media; prefers art proportional to 5¹/₂x7³/₈". Produces seasonal material for Christmas; will review new work at any time.
First Contact & Terms: Prefers artists experienced in greeting card design. Send query letter with samples or actual work; call or write for appointment, submit portfolio for review. Prefers original art or published work as samples. Samples returned by SASE. Simultaneous submissions OK. Reports in 2 weeks. No originals returned to artist at job's completion. Provide resume and samples to be kept on file for possible future assignments. Buys all rights. Negotiates payment; on acceptance.
Tips: "Study cards of all publishers for style, subject matter and formats."

*CAPE SHORE PAPER PRODUCTS, INC., 42A N. Elm St., Box 537, Yarmouth ME 04096. Art Director: Anne W. Macleod. Produces notes, giftwrap and stationery predominantly nautical in theme. Directs products to gift and stationery stores/shops.
Needs: Buys 25-50 designs and illustrations/year from freelance artists. Prefers watercolor, acrylics, cut paper and gouache. Specific sizes for finalart listed in guideline letter. Produces material for Christmas cards; June deadline for finished artwork.

First Contact & Terms: Send query letter with brochure and resume to be kept on file. Reports within several weeks. Pays flat fee for design. Prefers to buy all rights. Originals returned to artist if not purchased.
Tips: "We do not use black-and-white artwork, nor do we use any greeting card prose."

CARD MASTERS, INC., 2990 Griffin Rd., Ft. Lauderdale FL 33312. (305)989-8877. Executive Art Director: Harry Horowitz. Produces greeting cards.
Needs: Uses artists with a minimum of 3 years' experience for greeting cards. Buys 100 designs/year. Interested in 5x7" everyday, masculine, floral and sympathy designs. Also needs studio designs including gags in birthday, get well, friendship and anniversary.
First Contact & Terms: Query with resume and samples. Prefers roughs as samples. Material is not filed. Send artwork. SASE. Reports in 10 days. No originals returned at job's completion. Pays on acceptance.
Tips: Particularly needs humorous studio cards.

CAROLYN BEAN PUBLISHING, LTD., 120 2nd St., San Francisco CA 94105. (415)957-9574. Art Director: Tom Drew. Publishes greeting cards and stationery; diverse themes.
Needs: Buys 200-300 designs/illustrations per year from freelance artists. Uses artists for product design. Produces greatly expanded occasions and holiday images; submit material 12-18 months in advance.
First Contact & Terms: Send query letter with samples; do not call or write to schedule an interview. Prefers slides or photocopies as samples. Samples returned by SASE. Reports in 4 weeks. Originals returned to artist at job's completion. Provide samples, business card and tear sheets to be kept on file for possible future assignments. Negotiates rights purchased; prefers royalty arrangement. "To date, we have offered small advances against royalties that range from 5% of wholesale." Payment is made according to time schedule established in contract.
Tips: "Think about *cards*. I see good work all the time, but rarely things that have been created with greeting cards in mind."

CAROUSEL DESIGNS, INC., 369 NE 59th St., Miami FL 33137. (305)751-1100. Marketing Director: Cynthia Huffling. Wallpaper and decorative fabrics firm. Products are "eclectic with emphasis on the more contemporary for residential and commercial customers furnishing homes and commercial buildings."
Needs: Buys 12-20 designs from freelance artists/year. Uses artists for product design and mechanicals. Prefers 27" wide by 25½" vertical repeat.
First Contact & Terms: Send query letter with brochure, samples and tear sheets to be kept on file; call or write for appointment to show portfolio. Prefers to see original work (color washes) as samples. Samples not filed are returned. Reports within 14 days. No originals returned to artist at job's completion. Pays $300-500 per design; will consider royalty agreement for full program. Buys all rights.

H. GEORGE CASPARI, INC., 225 Fifth Ave., New York NY 10010. (212)685-9726. President: Douglas H. Stevens. Publishes greeting cards, Christmas cards, invitations, giftwrap and paper napkins. The line maintains a very traditional theme.
Needs: Buys 80-100 illustrations/year from freelance artists. Prefers watercolors, color pencil, and other color media. Produces seasonal material for Christmas, Mother's Day, Father's Day, Easter and Valentine's Day.
First Contact & Terms: Arrange an appointment with Lisa Fingeret to review portfolio. Prefers unpublished original illustrations as samples. Reports within 4 weeks. Negotiates payment on acceptance.
Tips: "Caspari and many other small companies rely on freelance artists to give the line a fresh, overall style rather than relying on one artist. We feel this is a strong point of our company."

CLEARWATER GRAPHICS, 2222 S. Louisiana St., Little Rock AR 72206. (501)374-0040. Senior Designer: Sandy Gullikson. Produces greeting cards; humorous, whimsical, watercolor illustrated.
Needs: Buys 4 designs/year from freelance artists. Considers watercolors, and pen & ink for illustrations. Prefers 7x10" with vertical layout for final art. Produces seasonal material for Christmas and St. Valentine's Day; submit work 8 months in advance.
First Contact & Terms: Artists experienced in greeting card illustration only. Send query letter with brochure, resume, business card and samples to be kept on file. Prefers photographs or tear sheets as samples; do not send original art. Samples not filed returned by SASE. Reports within 2 months. Pays flat fee of $100/design. Buys all rights.
Tips: "I am interested only in humorous, lighthearted, clever work, done in watercolor or colored pencil. I encourage an artist to include copy to go with illustration."

CONTENOVA GIFTS, INC., 1239 Adanac St., Vancouver, British Columbia V6A 2C8 Canada. (604)253-4444. Creative Director: Jeff Sinclair. Produces greeting cards, novelty coffee mugs and plaques with mainly humorous themes. Art guidelines for SASE.
Needs: Buys 200 illustrations/year from freelance artists. Prefers local artists but will consider working with professionals via mail. We are interested in a variety of cartoon and illustration styles. We use freelancers for cartoons on mugs, plaques, keychains and greeting cards. Mugs are designed in black and white with color silk screened later. Submit off-the-wall ideas for series lines. (12 mugs per series). Considers any medium for product illustrations. Prefers 4x9" final art for studio greeting cards; 3x3 ½" for coffee mugs. Seasonal material includes Valentine's Day, Mother's Day, Father's Day, Christmas.
First Contact & Terms: Works on assignment only. Send query letter with samples to be kept on file; call for appointment to show portfolio. Prefers tear sheets as samples. Samples not filed are returned by SASE (nonresidents include IRC). Reports within 1 week. Original artwork not returned after reproduction. Pays flat fee, $70/illustration. Buys all rights. Payment for series designs negotiable.
Tips: "Research the humorous greeting card market and coffee mugs for format and reproduction. In the risque card business, there is now a trend, away from very risque to more subtle, cute risque. Drinking cards seem to be on the wane; play on words cards are likely to follow. Turning back to more friendship, positive cards. Cartoon-style illustrations are good for friendship style cards."

*CRABWALK, INC., 648 Broadway, New York NY 10012. (212)260-1901. Art Director: Alan Gabay. Produces greeting cards, calendars and novelty items with contemporary theme for all ages.
Needs: Purchases only complete lines. Also uses artists for P-O-P displays, paste-up and mechanicals. Considers all media. Finished greeting card 5½x7½". Produces material for Christmas and Valentine's Day; submit 6-9 months before holiday.
First Contact & Terms: Send query letter with samples to be kept on file; call or write for appointment to show portfolio; write for art guidelines. Prefers tear sheets and photocopies as samples. Samples not filed are returned by SASE. Reports within 2 months. Originals sometimes returned to artist at job's completion. Pays by the project. Negotiates rights purchased.
Tips: "We are only interested in card lines with 30-36 pieces in the line. All other ideas looked at."

CREATIVE PAPER PRODUCTS, INC., 1523 Prudential, Dallas TX 75235. (214)634-1283. President: David Hardenbergh. Publishes greeting cards, giftwrap, posters, pads, invitations, games, stationery and paper tableware products; everyday, current designer themes for women.
Needs: Buys "simplistic flat art that is very colorful" from freelance artists. Uses artists for product design and illustration. Produces seasonal material; submit art 6 months before holiday.
First Contact & Terms: Send samples. Prefers photostats and slides as samples. Samples returned on request. Reports within 3 weeks. Provide samples to be kept on file for possible future assignments. Material not copyrighted. Negotiates payment on acceptance.

CREATIVE PAPERS BY C.R. GIBSON, The C.R. Gibson Co., Knight St., Norwalk CT 06856. (203)847-4543. Vice President Creative Papers: Steven P. Mack. Publishes stationery, note paper, invitations and silk-screened giftwrap. Interested in material for lines of products. "Two to three designs are sufficient to get across a concept. We don't use too many regional designs. Stationery themes are up-to-date, fashion oriented. Designs should be somewhat sophisticated without being limiting. Classic designs and current material from the giftware business do well."
Needs: Buys 100-200 designs/year. Especially needs new 4-color art for note line and invitations; "we need designs that relate to current fashion trends as well as a wide variety of illustrations suitable for boxed note cards. We constantly update our invitation line and can use a diverse selection of ideas." Uses humorous illustrations especially for invitation line. Speculation art has no size limitations. Finished size of notes is 4x5½" and 3¾x5"; invitations, 3¾x5"; and giftwrap repeat, 8x8" minimum.
First Contact & Terms: Prefers 4-6 samples (slides or chromes of work or originals), published or unpublished. Previously published, photocopied and simultaneous submissions OK, if they have not been published as cards and the artist has previous publishers' permissions. SASE. Reports in 6 weeks. Pays $35 for rough sketch. Pays average flat fee of $175/design; $200/illustration; negotiates payment. Considers complexity of project, skill and experience of artist, reproduction expense and rights purchased. Usually buys all rights; sometimes buys limited rights.
Tips: "Almost all of the artists we work with or have worked with are professional in that they have a background of other professional assignments and exhibits as well as a good art education. We have been fortunate to make a few 'discoveries,' but even these people have been at it for a number of years and have a very distinctive style with complete understanding of printing specifications and mechanicals. Keep your presentation neat and don't send very large pieces of art. The world is becoming more design and color-oriented. Be aware of designs currently available on the market and how your designs relate. The home furnishings industry is more closely linked to the stationery and giftware business than ever before."

DESIGNERS STUDIO, 157 Centre St., Brockton MA 02403. (617)583-6775. General Manager: Martin H. Slobodkin. Produces Christmas cards only.
Needs: Buys 50 designs/year from freelance artists. Considers watercolors for illustrations. Submit seasonal material 15 months in advance.
First Contact & Terms: Send samples; prefers to receive original artwork. Samples are returned by SASE. Reports back only if interested. Does not return original art after reproduction. Pays flat fee of $75; buys all rights.

*DICKENS COMPANY, 61-12 Parsons Blvd., Flushing NY 11365. (718)762-6262, (800)445-4632. Vice President: James Chou. Art Director: David Podwal. Produces greeting cards including musical greetings.
Buys: Buys 100 designs from freelance artists/year; also buys illustrations. Prefers watercolors mainly. Final art size 5¾x8". Produces material for Valentine's Day, Mother's Day, Father's Day and Christmas; submit 9 months in advance.
First Contact & Terms: Prefers local artists with experience in greeting card design. Send resume and samples to be kept on file; call or write for appointment to show portfolio. Prefers photographs or slides as samples. Samples not filed are returned only if requested. Reports within 1 month. Originals returned to artist at job's completion. Pays average flat fee of $100-500/design; $20-100/illustration; or royalties. Negotiates rights purchased.
Tips: "We need experienced artist for greeting cards artwork badly."

THE DRAWING BOARD GREETING CARDS, INC., 8200 Carpenter Freeway, Dallas TX 75247. (214)638-4800. Design Director: Richard Hunt. Produces greeting cards, calendars, giftwrap, paper tableware products and stationery.
Needs: Number bought/year varies. Uses color washes, opaque watercolors and oil or acrylics.
First Contact & Terms: Submit seasonal work 6-12 months in advance. Interested in 10-20 of any kind of samples of style. SASE. Reports in 1 week. Buys all rights. Pays $125 minimum for color; on acceptance.
Tips: "Have prior greeting card experience and an unusual style or technique."

THE EVERGREEN PRESS, INC., 3380 Vincent Rd., Pleasant Hill CA 94523. (415)933-9700. Art Director: Malcolm K. Nielsen. Publishes greeting cards, giftwrap, and stationery; high quality art reproductions, Christmas cards and Christmas postcards.
Needs: Buys 200 designs/year from freelance artists. Uses artists for product design (any design that can be used to produce greeting cards, giftwrap, stationery and other products sold through book, stationery, card and gift stores). Uses only full-color artwork in any media in unusual designs, sophisticated art and humor or series with a common theme. No super-sentimental Christmas themes, single greeting card designs with no relation to each other, or single color pen or pencil sketches. Roughs may be in any size to get an idea of work; final art must meet size specifications. Produces seasonal material for Christmas, Easter and Valentine's Day; "we examine artwork at any time of the year to be published for the next following holiday."
First Contact & Terms: Send query letter with actual work; write for art guidelines. Prefers original work and roughs as samples. Samples returned by SASE. Reports within 2 weeks. Originals returned at job's completion. Negotiates rights purchased. "We usually make a cash down payment against royalties; royalty to be negotiated. Royalties depend upon the type of product that is submitted and the state of readiness for publication." Considers product use and reproduction expense when establishing payment. Pays on publication.

EXCLUSIVE HANDPRINTS INC., 96 NW 72nd St., Miami FL 33150. (305)751-0281. Vice President: Stanley Bercovitch. Wallpaper firm.
Needs: Buys 12 designs from freelance artists/year. Uses artists for wallpaper and fabric patterns. If design is repeated, accepts 18" repeat pattern; will also consider nonrepeated designs.
First Contact & Terms: Artists who are "well experienced in wallpaper and fabric designs" only. Call or write for appointment to show portfolio. No originals returned at job's completion. Pays flat fee/design. Buys all rights.

*FREEDOM GREETINGS, Box 715, Bristol PA 19007. (215)945-3300. Vice President: Jay Levitt. Produces greeting cards featuring flowers and scenery.
Needs: Buys 100 designs from freelance artists/year. Considers watercolors, acrylics, etc. Call for size specifications. Produces material for all seasons and holidays; submit 14 months in advance.
First Contact & Terms: Works on assignment only. Send query letter with resume and samples. Prefers slides and photographs as samples. Samples are returned by SASE. Reports within 10 days. Originals returned to artist at job's completion. Buys all rights.

Close-up

Riva Greenberg
Freelance Artist
New York, New York

Artist: David R. Smiton

In 1981 Riva Greenberg was a successful Madison Avenue copywriter. At the same time that she was writing advertising copy for Crisco Oil, Greenberg was defining her values and redefining her career goals via a self-awareness training group. One day, to show how the group members had impacted her life, she made original greeting cards for each person. The enthusiastic response to the cards convinced the soon-to-be artist to bid Madison Avenue adieu and establish her own greeting card company—Rivacakes.

Psychology is a vital part of everything Greenberg does, so logically it is important in what she communicates through her cards. "In my first group of cards I just had to say what I had to say, with little thought about how the cards were perceived—good or bad. It was purely a creative venture. Now, five years later, I have learned to effectively combine my creativity, art and words, so that their impact is salable."

Greenberg's million-dollar wisdom did not come easily. The first six months of 1981 were spent designing cards, studying card shop merchandise, attending stationery shows and talking—a lot—to shop owners, artists and manufacturers.

By the end of that year, Rivacakes' first card line consisted of 49 designs printed in b&w and handcolored by friends and family. By acting as her own sales representative the artist learned that consumers were interested more in occasion-oriented cards—birthday, anniversary, get well—not her purely inspirational designs.

Greenberg then designed 27 new cards, making them more occasion-oriented and thus more salable. She printed the designs on better paper stock, used more color and larger images and placed the art higher on the card's faces so it would show when displayed on a card rack. The Rivacakes characters also grew up changing not only physically, but growing more confident and certain, like the artist herself.

Greenberg's business also reflects an evolution. The selling and marketing aspect of running a business offered the artist invaluable insight into improving her product's salability. She learned the importance of having an image, presenting it professionally, sending out mailing pieces and keeping records.

She accepted the necessity of doing freelance illustration and writing to keep afloat as she learned. "I know that the only thing holding me back in this is me. Sure I've thought about going back and getting a 'real' job, but I would never give up my cards.

"I've come to know that I prefer designing rather than managing a business. Because of this I am now looking to design for a larger manufacturer, rather than being my own manufacturer and distributor."

Would Greenberg have decided to leave her 'real' job in 1981 had she known of the obstacles, the ups and downs she would face in the greeting card industry? "If I keep going on what I know I *want*, I will get there. No matter what."

Listen to the Mustn'ts child
Listen to the Don'ts
Listen to the Shouldn'ts
the Impossibles, the Won'ts
Listen to the Never Cans
Then listen close to me,
Anything can happen child
Anything can be.

Greenberg's writing is an integral
part of her card designs. This blank
verse inspirational pen & ink design,
one of the artist's early creations,
was printed and then hand-colored
with watercolor.

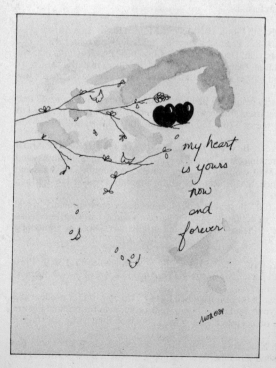

my heart
is yours
now
and
forever.

With this more recent design, the artist worked around a special occasion
theme—wedding anniversary. Occasion-oriented cards, such as for birth-
days and illness, are more salable
than non-occasion cards, says Greenberg.

THE C.R. GIBSON CO., 32 Knight St., Norwalk CT 06856. (203)847-4543. Director of Creative Services: Gary E. Carpenter. Publishes stationery, albums and gift products. SASE. Reports in 1 month. No finished art, paid for, is returned. Buys all rights.
Needs: Buys 200 designs/year. Uses artists for product design, illustration and calligraphy. Assigns specific art needs for individual projects. Does not usually buy unsolicited finished art. Query with samples to the attention of Creative Services Coordinator: Marilyn Schoenleber.

*THE C.R. GIBSON CO., Greeting Cards, 32 Knight St., Norwalk CT 06856. (203)847-4543. Product Manager: John C.W. Carroll. Produces greeting cards.
Needs: Buys 100-200 designs and illustrations from freelance artists/year. Considers most media except collage. Scale work to a minimum of 5x7". Prefers vertical image. Submit seasonal material 9-12 months before the holiday.
First Contact & Terms: Send query letter with samples to be kept on file except for "clearly inappropriate material." Call or write for appointment to show portfolio. Write for art guidelines. Prefers any sample. Do not send originals. Samples not filed are returned by SASE. Reports in 6-8 weeks. Original artwork returned at job's completion. Pays flat fee and/or royalties. Negotiates rights purchased.
Tips: "Women are our consumers."

GRAND RAPIDS CALENDAR CO., 906 S. Division Ave., Grand Rapids MI 49507. (616)243-1732. Art Director: Rob Van Sledright. Publishes calendars; pharmacy, medical and family themes.
Needs: Buys approximately 15 designs/year. Uses artists for advertising art and line drawings.
First Contact & Terms: Query; send SASE for information sheet. Reports in 2 weeks. Previously published, photocopied and simultaneous submissions OK. Pays $10 minimum.

GRAND SLAM GREETINGS, INC., 55 N. Moore St., New York NY 10013. President: Kent Wood. Produces t-shirts, sweatshirts and children's wear, and "we plan to add greeting cards in the near future."
Needs: Buys 6 designs/year from freelance artists. Also uses artists for paste-up and mechanicals. Considers pen & ink for illustrations.
First Contact & Terms: Local artists only. Send query letter with resume and samples to be kept on file; "I'll make contact when interview time is available." Prefers photographs as samples. Samples not filed are returned by SASE. Reports back only if interested. Pays by the hour, $7-15 average; by the project, $100-350 average. Negotiates rights purchased.

*GRANDMA JENNY GREETING CARDS, 5th Floor, 10100 Santa Monica Blvd., Los Angeles CA 90067. Vice President: Zahava Ofri. Estab. 1982. Produces greeting cards with cartoon theme.
Needs: Buys illustrations from freelance artists/year. Uses artists for calligraphy. Prefers pen & ink, watercolors, color pencils and acrylics. Prefers larger than 5x7" for final art. Produces material for Christmas, Hanukah, Valentine's Day, Mother's and Father's Day—"all in addition to everyday cards"; submit 9 months in advance.
First Contact & Terms: Send query letter with resume to be kept on file. Prefers photostats and tear sheets as samples. Samples not filed are not returned. Reports within 2 weeks. No originals returned to artist at job's completion. Pays average flat fee of $100-250/illustration. Buys all rights.

THE GRAPHIC ARTISAN, LTD., 3 Cross St., Box 388, Suffren NY 10901. (914)368-1700. Art Director: Peter A. Aron. Publishes stationery, greeting cards, invitations, calendars, posters, diplomas and certificates; general, romantic and Biblical. Mail samples or arrange interview; submit Christmas and Jewish New Year's designs 9 months in advance. SASE. Reports within 1 month. Previously published and simultaneous submissions OK. Buys all rights.
Needs: Buys 50-100 designs/year. Pays $10-100, illustrations. Present needs are predominantly in realistic/cartoon pen & ink sketches of people "in action"—playing games, sports, partying, etc. Also needs animal sketches—single, cartoon type. "Please do not submit original art; photo or photocopy will do."

*GREAT AMERICAN GIFT COMPANY, INC., 33 Portman Rd., New Rochelle NY 10801. President: Nina Joan Mattikow. Giftware and retail packaging; nostalgia personalities, era of the 40s themes; children's products, candy, games and novelties.
Needs: "We do not buy actual work. All artwork is commissioned by us." Uses artists for product and P-O-P design, advertising illustration and layout. Prefers full-color inks or tempera for product illustrations. "Art must be customized to suit us. We do not purchase any work, but look for a particular style of work."
First Contact & Terms: Artists must be in New York metropolitan area. Send query letter with brochure and resume to be kept on file. Do not send samples. Write for appointment to show portfolio. Fin-

ished original art seen by appointment only. Reports only if interested. Works on assignment only. No originals returned to artist at job's completion. Pays by the project, $200-500 average. Buys all rights.

*GREAT LAKES CONCEPTS DESIGNED, Box 2107, Traverse City MI 49685. (616)941-1372. General Manager: Ardana J. Titus. Estab. 1983. Produces greeting cards. Seeks "simple romantic and humorous designs with one or two subjects—no detailed designs. We need colorful and imaginative designs for all-occasion notecard line." No landscapes.
Needs: Buys 12 designs from freelance artists/year. Considers primarily watercolor—bright, distinct colors and designs—no washes. Final art size 8x11"; allow ¼" on all sides for trim. Prefers vertical designs but will consider horizontal.
First Contact & Terms: Prefers local artists. Send query letter with samples to be kept on file. Write for art guidelines with SASE. Prefers photographs or originals as samples. Samples not filed are returned by SASE. Reports back within 3 months. Original art returned after reproduction. Pays flat fee of $50 for design. Purchases first rights and/or reprint rights.
Tips: "When submitting material, send simple, bright designs using imaginative approaches. An example is a white lily on a bright yellow background. We will consider a series. We're looking for designs of one or two children as subjects. Designs must be of easily recognizable subjects. Customers want designs of distinct subject work, landscapes don't seem to do well on stationery cards. Occasionally uses cartoon-style illustrations."

*THE GREAT NORTHWESTERN GREETING SEED COMPANY, Box 776, Oregon City OR 97045. (503)631-3425. Assistant Art Director: Betty Barrett. Produces greeting cards. Uses pastel watercolor, black overlay; whimsical, botanical and natural themes.
Needs: Uses artists for calligraphy, P-O-P displays, paste-up and mechanicals. Prefers pen & ink and watercolor. Produces material for Christmas, Mother's Day, Father's Day and Valentine's Day.
First Contact & Terms: Prefers to work on assignment with local artists. Send query letter with samples to be kept on file. Accepts slides, photostats, photographs, photocopies and tear sheets as samples. Samples not filed are returned. Reports within several weeks. No originals returned to artist at job's completion. Buys all rights.

GREEN TIGER PRESS, 1061 India St., San Diego CA 92101. (619)238-1001. Art Director: Sandra Darling. Publishes greeting cards, giftwrap, calendars, posters, stationery and books; fantasy, nostalgia, The World of the Child themes.
Needs: Buys 50 designs and 100 illustrations/year from freelance artists. Uses artists for product, book and calendar illustration. Prefers b&w drawings and full-color painting. Produces seasonal material for Christmas, Easter and Valentine's Day; submit art 1 year before holiday.
First Contact & Terms: Send samples or actual work; submit portfolio for review. "For first contact any examples of work will serve." Provide samples to be kept on file for possible future assignments. Negotiates rights purchased. Samples not kept on file are returned by SASE. Reports in 2 months. Originals returned to artist at job's completion. Negotiates payment.
Tips: Artists should have a "good variety of samples; include human figures if available."

GREETWELL, D-23, M.I.D.C., Satpur, Nasik 422 007 India. Chief Executive: H.L. Sanghavi. Estab. 1983. Produces greeting cards, calendars and posters. Specializes in wildlife, flowers, landscapes; general purpose only.
Needs: Buys 100 designs from freelance artists/year. Will review any media; final art is acceptable any size. Accepts seasonal material "any time during the year, but preferably before April."
First Contact & Terms: Send resume and samples to be kept on file. Prefers printed proofs as samples; color photographs or photostats are acceptable. Samples not filed are returned only if requested. Reports within 4 weeks. Original art returned after reproduction. Pays flat fee of $60/design. Buys reprint rights.
Tips: "Submit printed proof of past work so that we can send guidelines and a sample of our requirements."

H & L ENTERPRISES, INC., 76 Dover Ave., Trenton NJ 08638. (609)882-3080. President: Jerry Wagner. Produces greeting cards and incense matches.
Needs: Buys 8 designs and illustrations/year from freelance artists. Also uses artists for mechanicals. Considers pen & ink and acrylics for illustrations.
First Contact & Terms: Works on assignment only. Call for appointment to show portfolio. Sometimes returns original work after reproduction. Pays by the project.

H.W.H. CREATIVE PRODUCTIONS, INC., 87-53 167th St., Jamaica NY 11432. (212)297-2208. President: Willis Hogans, Jr. Publishes greeting cards, stationery; humorous, designer, primitive art themes and high-tech designs.

Needs: Buys 5 designs and 10 illustrations/year from freelance artists. Uses artists for product illustrations, calligraphy plus advertising and catalog illustration and layout. Prefers b&w line drawings and watercolor for product illustrations; 8½x11" and 3 11/16x5¼". Produces seasonal material for Christmas, Thanksgiving, Valentine's Day and Halloween; submit art 6 months before holiday. Also mod humorist illustrations.
First Contact & Terms: Send query letter with samples and brochure/flyer; call for appointment. Prefers continuous tone photos and color slides as samples. Samples not kept on file are returned by SASE. Reports in 2 weeks. Originals returned to artist at job's completion. Provide resume, samples, business card and brochure/flyer to be kept on file for possible future assignments. Negotiates rights purchased but material not copyrighted sometimes. Pays by piece, up to $100 on publication.

HARPER HOUSES, 3562 Eastlam Dr., Culver City CA 90230. (213)837-6900. Contact: Art Director. Produces calendars and stationery. Designers of personal planning systems and accessories, i.e. organizers, personal management systems.
Needs: Number of designs bought from freelance artists is open. Also uses artists for paste-up and mechanicals. Considers pen & ink.
First Contact & Terms: Works on assignment only. Send query letter with samples to be kept on file. Call or write for appointment to show portfolio. Prefers photostats as samples (no original art). Samples not filed returned only if requested. Reports only if interested. Sometimes returns original art after reproduction. Negotiates rights purchased and payments.
Tips: "Look at our product—Day Runner Harper House stationery."

INTERCONTINENTAL GREETINGS LTD., 176 Madison Ave., New York NY 10016. (212)683-5830. Creative Marketing Director: Robin Lipner. Sells reproduction rights on a per country per product basis. Licenses and syndicates to 4,500-5,000 publishers and manufacturers in 50 different countries. Industries include greeting cards, calendars, prints, posters, stationery, books, textiles, heat transfers, giftware, china, plastics, toys and allied industries, scholastic items and giftwrap.
Needs: Assigns 400-500 jobs and 1,500 designs and illustrations/year. "The trend is to more graphic—clean, modern work." Uses some humorous and cartoon-style illustrations. Prefers full-color original artwork, C-prints or transparencies.
First Contact & Terms: Send query letter and/or resume with artwork samples and SASE. Pays by the project, design and illustration. "Royalties and/or commission; minimum advances." Pays royalties upon sale of reproduction rights on all selected designs. Contractual agreements made with artists and licensing representatives, will negotiate reasonable terms. Considers skill and experience of artist, product use, turnaround time and rights purchased when establishing payment. Provides promotion, color separation and portfolio samples, worldwide trade show display.
Tips: Should present "professional and concise presentations both on interview and mail. We have gone into a more licensing-oriented direction."

*INTRAPRO/ATLANTA, Box 7962, Atlanta GA 30357. Director: Mr. J. Bach. Produces greeting cards, calendars, posters and stationery with 1930's-40's look.
Needs: Buys 6 designs and 12 illustrations/year from freelance artists. Also uses artists for calligraphy, P-O-P displays, paste-up and mechanicals. Considers all media. Produces products for all seasons.
First Contact: Works on assignment only. Send query letter with brochure, business card and samples to be kept on file. Write for art guidelines. Accepts any type sample. Samples not filed are returned by SASE. Reports only if interested. Original artwork returned to the artist after reproduction.

JOLI GREETING CARD CO., 2520 W. Irving Park Rd., Chicago IL 60618. (312)588-3770. President: Joel Weil. Produces greeting cards and stationery.
Needs: Number of designs and illustrations bought/year varies. Also uses artists for P-O-P displays. Considers airbrush for product illustration. Prefers finished art of 4x9" for studio cards and 5x7" for 5x7" line. Publishes seasonal material for Christmas, St. Valentine's Day, Mother's Day, Father's Day.
First Contact & Terms: Artists must not have worked for Joli's immediate competition. Send query letter with samples to be kept on file. Accepts "whatever is available" as samples. Samples not filed are returned by SASE. Reports within 1 month. Sometimes returns original art after reproduction. Pays flat fee; "open, depending on project." Buys all rights.
Tips: "We are looking for a 'today-look' primarily in the medium of airbrushing."

LAFF MASTERS STUDIOS INC., 557 Oak St., Copiague NY 11726. (516)789-8361. Also: Robin Lane Art Studios (counter card division), same address and phone number. Creative Art Director: Sylvia Hacker. Publishes greeting cards: humorous, sophisticated, conventional and youth-oriented. "Robin Lane is concerned with all categories of everyday counter cards, from birth congratulations to formal sympathy cards. Its art standards are extremely high and its freelance work and inhouse requirements are handled by top professionals." In most cases, prefer artists who are nearby and can work with inhouse staff.

Needs: Buys 150-250 illustrations/year. Especially needs humorous and conventional art on assignment only.

First Contact & Terms: Artists must be well-versed in knowledge of latest greeting card printing and finishing techniques. Also requires artists who are skilled in juvenile style artwork for future juvenile lines. Submit published samples only. "Never send unsolicited unpublished material. All samples submitted must have SASE. We cannot return unsolicited samples which do not have SASE and correct postage." Reports within 1 week. No originals returned at job's completion. Pays $75 and up; on acceptance. Buys all rights.

Tips: "We assign work. We never buy unsolicited art. We require artists who are familiar with all phases of greeting card finishing and printing requirements. We see a trend toward more sophisticated and stylized art."

LENNON WALLPAPER CO., Box 8, Joliet IL 60434. (815)727-9245. Vice President Marketing: Dennis P. Maiotti. Wallpaper firm. Produces traditional wallcoverings directed to women, 25-45 years old.

Needs: Buys 30 designs from freelance artists/year.

First Contact & Terms: Send query letter with resume; call for appointment to show portfolio. Reports only if interested. No originals returned at job's completion. Pays flat fee. Buys all rights.

***PAUL LEVY-DESIGNER**, 2993 Lakewood Lane, Hollywood FL 33021. (305)989-8009. President: Paul Levy. Produces wallpaper and fabrics.

Needs: Buys 12 designs from freelance artists/year. Uses artists for original designs for wallcovering and fabric. Prefers gouache - watercolor designers colors for illustrations; side repeats divisible into 27" and down repeats 18" to 27".

LITTLE KENNY PUBLICATIONS, INC., 1315 W. Belmont Ave., Chicago IL 60657. (312)281-7633. President: Ken Dagdigian. Produces games, posters, stationery, and stickers.

First Contact & Terms: Works on assignment only. Send query letter with brochure and samples to be kept on file. Prefers tear sheets as samples. Samples not filed returned by SASE. Does not report back. Original art not returned after reproduction. Pays flat fee.

MAINE LINE COMPANY, Box 418, Rockport ME 04856. (207)236-8536. Contact: Elizabeth Stanley or Perri Ardman. Publishes greeting cards for contempory women from college age up, with primary concentration on women in their 30s. Most of the cards are humorous and deal with women's contemporary concerns.

Needs: Buys 300-400 illustrations a year from freelance artists; most work is commissioned. "We're looking for illustrators with a sense of humor, whose style is contemporary and colorful. Illustrators who can do hand-lettering and whose sense of graphic design is strong are good candidates for us. You need not write your own copy to illustrate cards for us, but we're also looking for illustrators who write as well as illustrate." Most often commissions a group or series of cards, rather than a single card. Also reviews artists or designers concepts for greeting card and postcard series. "As most artwork is commissioned, we rarely buy cartoons unless we buy a whole group of cartoons that are specifically created for greeting cards. However, we're actively seeking cartoonists who can create greeting cards for us." Pays advance against royalties for commissioned work.

First Contact & Terms: Send query letter with samples (photocopies OK), tearsheets, etc. or submit portfolio for review. SASE needed for return of samples. Sample card $1 each; creative guidelines for SASE with 60¢ postage.

Tips: "I think we offer illustrators a unique opportunity to have a greeting card series of their own, and we're looking for illustrators who want to establish themselves as greeting card artists."

MARCEL SCHURMAN CO. INC., 954 60th St., Oakland CA 94608. (415)428-0200. Art Director: Philip Schurman. Produces greeting cards, giftwrap and stationery. Specializes in "very fine art work with many different looks: classical, humorous, children's illustration."

Needs: Buys 50-75 designs/year from freelance artists. Considers watercolors and acrylics for product illustrations. Prefers final art sizes of 5x7", 4x6"; "all can be made 100%-150% larger and reduced." Produces seasonal material for Valentine's Day, Easter, Mother's Day, Father's Day, graduation, Halloween, Christmas, Hanukkah and Thanksgiving. Submit art by May for Valentine's Day and Easter, June for Mother's and Father's Day, graduation; November for Christmas, Halloween, Thanksgiving and Hanukkah.

First Contact & Terms: Send query letter with samples to be kept on file; call or write for appointment to show portfolio. Prefers slides or photographs as samples. Samples not filed returned by SASE. Re-

ports within 2 weeks. Returns original art after reproduction. Buys all rights.
Tips: "Please send work; we are very open to see new designs."

*MARK I INC., 1733 W. Irvine Park Rd., Chicago IL 60613. (312)281-1111. Produces calendars and posters directed to adults 18-35 years old.
Needs: Buys 200 designs from freelance artists/year. Uses artists for calligraphy. Considers all media. Produces material for Valentine's Day and Christmas; submit 1 year before holiday.
First Contact & Terms: Works on assignment only. Send query letter to be kept on file; write for appointment to show portfolio; write for art guidelines. Samples not filed are returned by SASE. Reports within 2 weeks. Originals returned to artist at job's completion. Pays by the hour, by the project, or royalties. Buys all rights.

MASTERPIECE STUDIOS, 5400 W. 35th St., Chicago IL 60650. (312)656-4000. Vice President/ Creative Director: George Major. Publishes Christmas cards, stationery and notes. Free artist's guidelines. Submit seasonal work "any time." Interested in original material for lines of cards and stationery. Prefers samples of unpublished Christmas cards and stationery. SASE. Reports in 3-4 weeks. No originals returned to artist at job's completion. Buys all rights.
Needs: "We are interested in reviewing any Christmas art on spec, regardless of experience." Pays flat fee of $60/design; $150-300/illustration; on acceptance. Considers complexity of project, and skill and experience of artist when establishing payment.
Tips: "Originate highly stylized, updated designs with plenty of emphasis on originality, color and design."

*MIDWEST ART PUBLISHERS, 1123 Washington Ave., St. Louis MO 63101. (314)241-1404. Contact: Sales Manager. Publishes calendars, combination of paper and vinyl products such as pad and pen sets, photo albums, pocket calendars and recipe books with mixed themes—cute children, animals, outdoor scenes, scenic for women.
Needs: Uses artists for product illustrations and catalog design, illustration and layout. Main product size approximately 3½"x6½" (checkbook size) and 3¾"x5¼".
First Contact & Terms: Send query letter with samples. Prefers photostats and original work showing artist's style as samples. Unsolicited samples returned only if requested by SASE. Provide resume and samples to be kept on file for possible future assignments. Pays an average flat fee; also negotiates.

*MILES KIMBALL COMPANY, 41 W. 8th Ave., Oshkosh WI 54901. Vice President-Christmas Card Design and Sales: Alfred F. Miyamoto. Produces greeting cards. "We sell cards by direct mail to people who are looking for a 'custom' look—cards designed around the personalized theme."
Needs: Buys 2-20 designs with copy from freelance artists/year. "We are looking for designers for personalized Christmas cards. Our look is more 'cozy' than high-tech or sophisticated. We want someone able to create a whole concept: design and copy." Considers idea roughs on vellum stock in almost any media. "We are looking for ideas more than technique." Standard greeting card sizes; "4¼x5½" is the most popular folded size." Produces material for Christmas only; "best time to submit material is early spring; but material is accepted year round."
First Contact & Terms: "We need experienced artists who can write the text for their cards, too." Send query letter with samples to be kept on file; write for art guidelines. "As we are looking for ideas mainly, roughs are accepted for preliminary evaluation. We prefer not to have slides or photographs sent. Samples not filed are returned by SASE only. Reports within 2 months. No originals returned to artist at job's completion. Pays flat fee. Buys all rights.
Tips: "Since our cards are sold imprinted with customer's name, we are looking for designers who can create a total card concept, that looks as if each was made especially for the buyer. Studio card humor and ultra-sophistication does not work for us. We will give guidelines after previewing samples."

MILLEN CARDS INC., 45 Ranick Dr. E., Amityville NY 11701. (516)842-2276. Art Director: Mrs. Lois Millner. Produces traditional greeting cards. Submit seasonal work 10 months in advance. SASE. Simultaneous submissions OK. Free artist's guidelines.
Needs: Assigns over 50/year. All artwork is freelanced.
First Contact & Terms: Query with samples of previously published work. Reports within 4 weeks. Samples returned by SASE. Provide business card and samples to be kept on file. Pays average flat fee of $85/design; average flat fee of $85/illustration. Considers complexity of project, skill and experience of artist, reproduction expense, turnaround time and rights purchased when establishing payment.

*MORNING STAR, INC., 6680 Shady Oak Rd., Eden Prairie MN 55344. (612)941-9080. Line Planner: Beth Tolaas. Produces greeting cards, giftwrap, calendars, posters, stationery, announcements, invitations, buttons, stickers, boxed Christmas cards and seasonal counter cards. "We publish Christian greeting cards and stationery products featuring the highest quality and fresh, contemporary colors/designs.'' Directs products primarily to the evangelical Christian and religious markets.

Needs: Buys designs and illustrations from freelance artists. Also uses artists for calligraphy. Prefers primarily watercolors (interested in full-color work), but have used some acrylic and some pen & ink. Wrapping paper repeats: 18''; average greeting card: $4^7/_8$x7'' vertical ("leave bleed room, please"). Produces material for Easter, Mother's Day, Father's Day, Graduation, Confirmation, First Communion, Grandparent's Day, Thanksgiving, Christmas and Valentine's Day; submit 9 months in advance.

First Contact & Terms: Send query letter with printed samples to be kept on file or original art; call for appointment to show portfolio. Original art and samples not filed are returned only if requested. Reports as soon as possible. No originals returned to artist at job's completion. Pays flat fee. Buys all rights.

Tips: "Work on flexible board, as white as possible. Do not draw outline around suggested cropping. Leave plenty of bleed room all the way around art. Send by registered mail."

*MUSICAL IMAGE DESIGNS, 1212 Ardee Ave., Nashville TN 37216. (615)226-1509. Creative Director: Stacy Slocum. Estab. 1985. Produces greeting cards, giftwrap, stationery and banners. "We cater to the music business. We want musical themes—piano, staff, banjo, any musical instrument."

Needs: Uses artists for designs, illustration, calligraphy and P-O-P displays. Considers pen & ink. Produces material for all holidays. "Music should be integrated into the holiday theme." Submit seasonal material 3 months in advance.

First Contact & Terms: Send resume and samples to be kept on file. Write or call for art guidelines. Prefers photocopies or tear sheets as samples. Samples not filed are returned only by request with SASE. Reports within 1 month. No originals returned at job's completion. Pays by the project. "If they are great ideas and followed through with care this will be a factor. Complexity does not necessarily make it more valuable to us." Buys all rights or first rights.

Tips: "I am most interested in what you can do now. Send me samples of musical designs. What you've done in the past is of no real interest to me. I would like all work in black ink on $8^1/_2$x$5^1/_2$'' white paper."

NEW APPROACHES, INC., Box 1265, New Canaan CT 06840. (203)966-7933. Publishes calendars.

Needs: Buys 0-3 designs/year from freelance artists.

First Contact & Terms: Send samples and brochure/flyer. Samples returned by SASE. Reports within 3 weeks. Buys all rights. Negotiates payment.

OATMEAL STUDIOS, Box 138, Rochester VT 05767. (802)767-3325. Art Director: Helene Lehrer. Publishes greeting cards; creative ideas for everyday cards and holidays.

Needs: Buys 100-150 designs/illustrations per year from freelance artists. Uses artists for greeting card design and illustration. Considers all media; prefers 5x7'', 6x$8^1/_2$'', vertical composition. Produces seasonal material for Christmas, Mother's Day, Father's Day, Easter, Valentine's Day and Hanukkah. Submit art in October for Christmas and Hanukkah, in March for other holidays.

First Contact & Terms: Send query letter with samples; write for artists' guidelines. Prefers slides, roughs or printed pieces as samples. Samples returned by SASE. Reports in 2-4 weeks. Provide brochure/flyer to be kept on file for possible future assignments. "If brochure/flyer is not available, we ask to keep one slide or printed piece." Negotiates payment arrangement with artist.

Tips: "We're looking for exciting and creative illustrations and graphic design for greeting cards. Also, light humor with appeal to college age and up."

PAPEL, INC., Box 9879, North Hollywood CA 91609. (818)765-1100. Art Coordinator: Helen Scheffler. Produces souvenir and seasonal ceramic giftware items: mugs, photo frames, greeting tiles.

Needs: Buys 500 illustrations from freelance artists/year. Uses artists for product and P-O-P design, illustrations on product, calligraphy, paste-up and mechanicals. Produces material for Christmas, Valentine's Day, Easter, St. Patrick's Day, Mother's and Father's Day; submit one year before holiday.

First Contact & Terms: Artists with minimum 3 years' experience in greeting cards only; "our product is ceramic but ceramic experience not necessary." Send query letter with brochure, resume, business card, samples and tear sheets to be kept on file. Samples not kept on file are returned by SASE if requested. Reports within 2 weeks. No originals returned to artist at job's completion. Pays by the project, $50-350 average. Buys all rights.

Tips: "We are using more graphic design and less illustration."

PECK INC., 3963 Vernal Pike, Box 1148, Bloomington IN 47402. Art Director: Trisha Vollmer. Manufactures Christmas tags; Christmas, Halloween, Valentine and Easter cutouts; and educational bulletin board aids.

Needs: Uses artists for product design and illustrations. Specific needs include juvenile characters, animals, traditional Christmas, Halloween and/or all occasion design.

ns: Query with color samples or slides. SASE. Reports in approximately 2 ~ject; negotiates payment according to complexity of project and product use. r "full-color work and emphasis on clarity of color and design."

⌐DUCTIONS, Box D, Ojai CA 93023. (805)646-4389. President: John Kirvan. ⌐eeting cards and stationery. "Look" is generally sophisticated, soft. "We emphasize good ⌐g as a component. We are looking to diversify look, but not to de-emphasize the words."
ɴeeds: Uses artists for creation of entire card lines. "We are not interested in one-shot designs; we look for style and substance that can be developed." Cards are generally 5x7", art proportionate. Produces material for Christmas and Valentine's Day.
First Contact & Terms: Works on assignment only. Send query letter with samples to be kept on file; call or write for appointment to show portfolio. Any samples that show technique, substance and color are acceptable. Samples not filed are returned. Reports back within 2 weeks. Originals sometimes returned to artist at job's completion. Pays flat fee of $115 minimum/illustration. Sometimes pays royalty depending on size and status of project. Buys all rights or negotiates rights purchased.
Tips: "We are looking for artists strong enough to have a product line built around their skills."

PICKHARDT & SIEBERT (USA) INC., 16201 Trade Zone Ave., Upper Marlboro MD 20772. (301)249-7900. Produces wallpaper, bed linens and accessories.
Needs: Uses artists for product design, illustration on product, calligraphy, paste-up and mechanicals. "Wallpaper manufacturing being done in Germany; some wallpaper textile designs are purchased in the US. We do find the need for *local* freelance artists to do paste-up."
First Contact & Terms: Send query letter with brochure and resume to keep on file; write for appointment to show portfolio. Reports only if interested. Negotiates pay.

POST-OP-PRODUCTIONS INC., Box 2178, Reston VA 22090. (703)860-2507. President: Phillip Corrigan. Produces greeting cards and posters.
Needs: Number of designs purchased from freelance artists varies. Also uses artists for P-O-P displays and mechanicals. Considers any medium; "we are interested in anything unusual or humorous." Produces seasonal material for Christmas, St. Valentine's Day and Mother's Day.
First Contact & Terms: Send query letter with business card and samples to be kept on file. Accepts any type of sample. Samples not filed returned by SASE. Reports within 2 weeks. Returns original art after reproduction if requested. Pays flat fee or royalty of 5%. Negotiates rights purchased.

*PREFERRED STOCK, INC., 1020 Turnpike St., Canton MA 02021. (617)244-7558. President: Ann C. Cohen. Produces greeting cards, stationery, bags, pads, pencils and invitations using graphics and illustrations.
Needs: Buys 200 designs and 150 illustrations from freelance artists/year. Also uses artists for calligraphy and mechanicals. Considers watercolors, acrylics, etc. Prefers 5x7" size for final art. Produces material for Christmas, Valentine's Day, Mother's Day, Father's Day, Graduation, Chanukah and Jewish New Year; submit 1 year in advance.
First Contact & Terms: Works on assignment only. Send query letter with brochure, resume, business card and samples to be kept on file. Prefers slides, colored photostats and printed pieces as samples. Samples not filed are returned by SASE. Reports only if interested. Originals sometimes returned to artist at job's completion. Pays average flat fee of $100/design or $100-150/illustration. Buys all rights.
Tips: Especially wants "humorous cards, *colorful* illustrations and professionalism."

THE PRINTERY HOUSE OF CONCEPTION ABBEY, Conception MO 64433. Art Director: Rev. Norbert Schappler. A publisher of religious greeting cards; religious Christmas and all occasion themes for people interested in religious yet contemporary expressions of faith. "Our card designs are meant to touch the heart, and feature strong graphics, classical calligraphy and other styles."
Needs: Works with 25 freelance artists/year. Uses artists for product illustrations. Prefers silk-screen, oil, watercolor, line drawings; classical and contemporary calligraphy. Produces seasonal material for Christmas and Easter.
First Contact & Terms: Send query letter, then samples. Prefers printed examples, slides or original work as samples; "representative sample of various styles from one artist is especially important." Samples returned by SASE. Reports in 3 weeks. Provide resume to be kept on file for possible future assignments. "In general, we continue to work with artists year after year once we have begun to accept work from them." Pays by the project; $100-250. Usually purchases complete reproduction rights; occasionally only greeting card rights.
Tips: "We are seeing a revival of interest in classically-clean designs, along with an interest in new colors, better graphics, mixed-media work, appropriate Biblical quotations, etc. Computerized graphics are beginning to have an impact in our field; multi-colored calligraphy is a new development."

*PRODUCT CENTRE-S.W. INC./THE TEXAS POSTCARD CO., Box 708, Plano TX 75074. (214)423-0411. Art Director: Susan Hudson. Produces greeting cards, calendars, posters, melamine trays, coasters and postcards. Themes range from nostalgia to art deco to pop/rock for contemporary buyers.
Needs: Buys 150 designs from freelance artists/year. Uses artists for calligraphy, P-O-P display, paste-up and mechanicals. Considers any media, "we do use a lot of acrylic/air brush designs." Final art must not be larger than 8x10. "Certain products require specific measurements; we will provide these when assigned. Produces Christmas material; submit 1 year in advance.
First Contact & Terms: "Artist should be able to submit camera-ready work and understand printer's requirements. The majority of our designs are assigned." Send resume, business card and samples to be kept on file; call or write for appointment to show portfolio. Accepts slides, photostats, photographs, photocopies and tear sheets as samples. Samples not filed are returned only by request with SASE including return insurance. Reports within 1 month. No originals returned to artist at job's completion. Pays average flat fee of $100/design maximum. Buys all rights.

RAINBOW ARTS, 488 Main St., Fitchburg MA 01420. (617)345-4476. Art Director: Ian Michaels. Assistant Art Director: Michael Schindler. Public Relations: Toby Michaels. Produces greeting cards, specializing in everyday, all occasion and Valentine's Day cards.
Needs: Buys 100-125 designs/illustrations from freelance artists/year. Uses artists for product design and illustration on product. Considers wide variety of media for illustrations; "we've used just about every medium—watercolor, acrylics, colored line work, markers, airbrush, gouache, silkscreen, batik, etc. The medium isn't as important to us as the proper use of color and composition." Prefers artwork "larger than our 5¼x6½" format, but in direct proportion; otherwise you have a card with disproportionate borders or have to crop part of the artwork." Produces seasonal material for Valentine's Day, Mother's Day, Father's Day, Easter and Christmas, but "each work should be able to relate to other occasions such as, blanks (cards with no verse), birthday, anniversary, etc." Submit seasonal material 6-12 months before holiday. "We also design and manufacture stickers."
First Contact & Terms: Send resume, samples and tear sheets, possibly to be kept on file; write for appointment to show portfolio and for artists' guidelines. Prefers slides and photographs as samples; "we can't be responsible for original art unless otherwise stated." Samples not kept on file are returned by SASE. Usually reports within 1 month, but may vary during the year. Originals returned to artist at job's completion. Pays royalties of 8% against an advance of $150-200. Buys reprint rights for greeting cards.
Tips: "With new freelance artists we look more for new looks. The market surge is in cartoon-style illustration, in both the cute category and the risque market. Send us your samples with an SASE and we'll include *The Artist's Guide to the Freelance Market* by Ian Michaels with our response."

RAINBOWORLD INC., 319 A St., Boston MA 02210. (617)350-0260. Contact: Sallie Horton, production department. Publishes greeting cards, giftwrap, calendars and stationery; general themes.
Needs: Buys 20 designs and 50 illustrations/year from freelance artists. Uses artists for advertising illustration. Considers any color media sized 10x14" or larger. Produces seasonal material for Christmas and Valentine's Day; submit art 6-12 months before holiday.
First Contact & Terms: Send samples and brochure/flyer *which do not need to be returned*. No originals or slides. "If work is suitable, we will arrange to review portfolio and other work." Works on assignment only. Reports as soon as possible. Originals returned to artist at job's completion. Buys first rights and reprint rights. Negotiates payment, $250 and up/project; on publication. Considers complexity of project, skill and experience of artist, product use and rights purchased when establishing payment.
Tips: "For initial contact, artists should submit copies of their work which we can *keep* on file—even photocopies. This allows us to keep a 'review' file to use as projects develop and allows us to quickly discover which artists are suitable for our market with a minimum of inconvenience to both parties. Do not send resumes without samples and do not bother to write asking for further information on firm. Send samples. This is a visual medium not verbal."

RECYCLED PAPER PRODUCTS INC., 3636 N. Broadway, Chicago IL 60613. Art Director: Audrey Christie. Publishes greeting cards, giftwrap, calendars, posters and stationery; unique subjects. Artist's guidelines available.
Needs: Buys 500 designs and 1,000-2,000 illustrations/year from freelance artists. Uses artists for product design and illustrations, calligraphy and P-O-P design. Considers b&w line and color—"no real restrictions." Prefers 5x7" for cards, 10-14" maximum. "Our primary concern is card design." Produces seasonal material for Christmas, Hanukkah, Mother's Day, Father's Day, Thanksgiving, Easter, Valentine's Day, St. Patrick's Day and Halloween. Submit seasonal material 12-18 months in advance for Christmas or send at holidays for following year.
First Contact & Terms: Send query letter with samples or actual work. Prefers slides, roughs and printed pieces as samples. Samples returned by SASE. Reports in 2 months. Original work usually not re-

Close-up

Sandra Boynton
Cartoonist
Lakeville, Connecticut

Artist: David R. Smiton

Every year over 100,000,000 people receive a "Boynton" greeting card. The popular beasty creations—hippos, birds, elephants and cats—which grace these cards also star on calendars, wallpaper, children's clothes, gift wrap, mugs, t-shirts, posters and even in their own books. What is less well-known than the Boynton animals, though, is the creator herself.

That familiar Boynton signature belongs to Sandra Boynton, a self-assured, well-spoken mother of three who has a degree in English from Yale and has studied drama at both Berkeley and Yale.

Boynton's entry into cartooning was, as she describes it, "a little bit through the back door. It's not something I started out to do." Her greeting card career began the summer she spent designing and marketing gift enclosure cards to earn additional college funds. Graduate school necessitated her turning the card selling over to Recycled Paper Products—eleven years later she and that same company are still going strong.

Education has played only a small part in her success. "I didn't have any technical art training, but the art program at my high school was wonderful. They took art very seriously.

"Where any cartoonist learns most, though, is from imitation of what he admires. George Booth and William Steig were major influences in my development, as were *The New Yorker* and children's picture books, particularly those having broad art styles rather than realistic drawings."

Boynton gradually developed her own "broad" art style which is evident in her infamous line of animal characters. The artist stresses that her greeting cards are more than mere vehicles for displaying artwork. For her there is a strong connection between design, words and relationships.

"Cards are inherently a communication between one person and another. When I do them I envision a type of relationship between these people. I prefer to celebrate the higher side of life on my cards, not promote false sentiments and illusory relationships of a saccharine nature."

Designing cards helps Boynton in other creative undertakings because "everything feeds into everything else. It affects the way I view and interpret things. I have found that working exclusively in cartooning the past ten years has made me a better fine artist. I have gotten better at summarizing what I am doing in a few strokes which is the skill of cartooning."

In her development as an artist, Boynton finds herself becoming increasingly critical of her work while witnessing a gradual evolution of her art and design.

"My characters are very different now than when I first began doing them. Although there is a certain continuity, there has been a gradual change, such as the animals are now on two legs rather than on four. I always work to make them better.

"Other design projects affect what

I do. A wallpaper collection was a challenge because I knew it could not depend upon words. It was going to sell or not sell based entirely upon design, color and layout. A collection of children's clothes carried over into my wrapping paper designs because both involved doing patterns with bright colors."

Boynton's being involved in so many projects and at the same time creating card designs leads one to question the artist's ability to maintain her energy and enthusiasm. But for Sandra Boynton this is not a problem because she likes what she does.

"Most kids do for fun what I do—coloring things, pasting things together, playing with piles of paper. I have the perfect job. People are amazed that I work weekends, saying that I have earned the right to get away. I laugh and answer that I have earned the right to do it!"

Boynton has earned the right to work weekends through a combination of her creative abilities and her business knowledge. "I learned a lot by selling my own cards the summer of my senior year in college. I learned the whole gamut—dealing with printers, talking with store buyers and understanding how to market my cards. I also learned how well my cards sold, and thus I didn't have to sell them short.

"If you want to be a graphic artist you must understand the commerce of it—what makes things sell, how they should be displayed, where the design has to be, how dirty the paper may get."

Boynton sees an incredible paranoia among artists who feel they are going to be taken advantage of in the business world—"that the books aren't going to be kept accurately. Artists become demanding and many companies then balk because they know they will always have trouble with those artists. There has to be a certain trust. Yes, sometimes your trust may be violated, but without it you will cut your own throat."

So far I've lost three pounds and eight friends.

for tomorrow we may diet.

turned at job's completion, but "negotiable." Provide samples and tear sheets to be kept on file for possible future assignments. Buys all rights. Pays average flat fee of $150/design or illustration; also negotiates payment "if we have major interest"; on acceptance.
Tips: "Sophisticated, light humor is our keynote. We're trend setters, not followers."

RED FARM STUDIO, 334 Pleasant St., Box 347, Pawtucket RI 02862. (401)728-9300. Creative Director: Mary M. Hood. Produces greeting cards, giftwrap, coloring books, paper dolls, story coloring books, placemats, Christmas cards, gift enclosures, notes, postcards and paintables. Specializing in country themes and fine watercolors.
Needs: Buys approximately 200 designs and illustrations/year from freelance artists. Considers watercolor artwork. Prefers final art of $6\frac{3}{4}x9\frac{9}{16}$" ($\frac{3}{16}$" bleed) for Christmas cards; $4\frac{3}{4}x6\frac{3}{4}$" ($\frac{1}{8}$" bleed) for everyday cards; and $6\frac{3}{16}x8\frac{13}{16}$" ($\frac{3}{16}$" bleed) for notes. Submit Christmas artwork 1 year in advance.
First Contact & Terms: Send query letter with samples to be kept on file. Call or write for appointment to show portfolio. Write for art guidelines. Accepts slides, photographs, photocopies or tear sheets as samples. Samples not filed are returned by SASE. Reports within 1-2 weeks. Original artwork not returned after reproduction. Pays flat fee of $150/design. Buys all rights.
Tips: "Look at our cards. Make sure the samples have our look. Ours is a rather conservative, traditional look."

C.A. REED, INC., 99 Chestnut St., Box 3128, Williamsport PA 17701-0128. Art Director: Bob Crain. Publishes paper tableware products; birthday, everyday, seasonal and holiday.
Needs: Buys 150-200 designs/year. Uses artists for product design and illustration. Interested in material for paper tableware, i.e. plates, napkins, cups, etc. No greeting cards.
First Contact & Terms: Query with samples. SASE. Reports in 6 weeks. Photocopied and simultaneous submissions OK. "Buys all rights within our field of publication." Pays $100-150, product design.
Tips: Artist should visit stationery shops and/or request artist's guidelines.

REED STARLINE CARD CO., Box 26247, Los Angeles CA 90026. Purchases humorous everyday and seasonal greeting card copy and art. Especially needs counter card promotions. Payment is negotiated.

REGENCY & CENTURY GREETINGS, (formerly Williamhouse-Regency, Inc. & Century Greetings), 1500 W. Monroe St., Chicago IL 60607. (312)666-8686. Art Director: David Cuthbertson. Publishes Christmas cards; traditional and some religious Christmas.
Needs: Buys 200 illustrations and designs/year.
First Contact & Terms: Query with samples. Submit seasonal art 8 months in advance. Reports in 4-6 weeks. Previously published work OK. Buys *exclusively Christmas* card reproduction rights. Originals returned to artist at job's completion. Pays $90 minimum, b&w; $125, color; $90-150, design. Pays on acceptance.
Tips: Artist should visit stationery shops for ideas, and request artist's guidelines to become familiar with the products. "Traditional still sells best in more expensive lines."

RENAISSANCE GREETING CARDS, Box 127, Springvale ME 04083. Creative Director: Robin Kleinrock. Publishes greeting cards; "current approaches" to all occasion cards, seasonal cards, Christmas cards and nostalgic Christmas themes.
Needs: Buys 600 illustrations/year from freelance artists. Full-color illustrations only. Prefers art proportional to $8\frac{1}{2}x11$". Produces seasonal material for Christmas, Valentine's Day, Mother's Day, Father's Day, Easter, graduation, St. Patrick's Day, Halloween, Thanksgiving, Passover, Jewish New Year and Hanukkah; submit art 15 months in advance for Christmas material; 1 year for other holidays.
First Contact & Terms: Send query letter with samples; write for artists' guidelines. Prefers slides as samples. Samples returned by SASE. Reports in 6 weeks. Originals returned to artist at job's completion. Negotiates rights purchased. Negotiates payment amount.
Tips: "Start by sending a small (10-12) sampling of 'best' work preferably in slide form (with SASE for return). This allows a preview for possible fit, saving time and expense."

ROCKSHOTS, INC., 8th Floor, 632 Broadway, New York NY 10012-2416. (212)420-1400. Art Director: Tolin Greene. Publishes greeting cards, calendars, posters and stationery; humorous, erotic and satirical themes for "anyone who loves well-designed, outrageous, humorous, sexy cards."
Needs: Buys 150 designs and 150 illustrations/year from freelance artists. Uses artists for card, calendar and catalog illustration layout and catalog design. No airbrush, prefer cartoon—bright, full-color artwork. Produces seasonal material for birthday, Christmas, Mother's Day, Father's Day, Easter, Valentine's Day and Halloween; submit art 10 months before holiday.
First Contact & Terms: Send resume and actual work; call for appointment, submit portfolio for re-

view. Prefers slides and examples of artist's style of original work as samples. Samples returned by SASE. Reports within 2 weeks. Originals returned to artist at job's completion. Provide tear sheets to be kept on file for possible future assignments. Buys all rights. Negotiates payment; on acceptance.

ROUSANA CARDS, 28 Sager Pl., Hillside NJ 07205. Art Director: Dorothy Chmielewski. Produces seasonal (all) and everyday greeting cards.
Needs: Established greeting card designers only.
First Contact & Terms: "Submit printed samples of your style."

THE ROYAL STATIONERY INC., Minneapolis Industrial Park, 13000 County Rd. 6 at Hwy. 55, Minneapolis MN 55441. (612)559-3671. Produces stationery, postcards, note cards, mugs, key chains and soaps; floral, scenic, animal, children and novelty. Interested in material for lines of products.
Needs: Buys 50 designs/year. Uses artists for product design, and b&w and color illustrations.
First Contact & Terms: Submit 4-5 illustrations. Prefers unpublished samples. SASE. Reports within 4 weeks. No originals returned at job's completion. Buys all rights. Pays by the project, $25 minimum, camera-ready designs. Considers complexity of project, skill and experience of artist, and reproduction expense when establishing payment.

ROYCE INTERNATIONAL, #106, 6924 Canby Ave., Reseda CA 91335. (818)342-8900. Production Co-ordinator: Barbara Levitan. Produces greeting cards, giftwrap, buttons, bumper stickers, multi paper and plastic goods, and key chains.
Needs: Buys designs from freelance artists. Also uses artists for P-O-P displays and mechanicals. Considers watercolors and acrylics for illustrations. Uses mostly animals, drawings of and about animals of all kinds. Produces seasonal material for Christmas, Easter and St. Valentine's Day; submit art a minimum of three months in advance.
First Contact & Terms: Works on assignment only. Send query letter with brochure, resume and samples to be kept on file. Call or write for appointment to show portfolio. Accepts photostats, photographs, photocopies or tear sheets as samples; "anything the artist wishes to submit as examples of his work." Samples not filed returned by SASE only if requested. Reports only if interested. Originals not returned after reproduction. Pays flat fee or by the project; negotiates. Buys all rights.

SACKBUT PRESS, 2513 E. Webster Place, Milwaukee WI 53211. Contact: Angela Peckenpaugh. Publishes poem postcards and notecards.
Needs: "A few line drawings for very specific themes."
First Contact and Terms: Query first. Samples returned. Reports in 1 month. Buys one-time rights. Pays in contributor's copies; on publication.
Tips: "I went from publishing a literary magazine to publishing poem postcards and notecards."

ST. CLAIR PAKWELL, 120 25th Ave., Bellwood IL 60104. (312)547-7500 ext. 262. Design Art Director: Elaine Brochocki. Publishes gift boxes, giftwrap and graphic packaging.
Needs: Buys 50-150 designs/year. Uses artists for giftwrap designs. Especially needs Christmas giftwrap designs. Prefers giftwrap pattern repeat in an even division or 24" from top to bottom.
First Contact & Terms: Query. SASE. Reports in 3 weeks. Buys all rights. Negotiates payment.

ST. CLAIR-PAKWELL PAPER PRODUCTS, Box 800, Wilsonville OR 97070. (503)638-9833. Art Director: Anna Mack. Publishes gift boxes, giftwrap and paper bags.
Needs: Buys 100 designs/year. Uses artists for product design and illustration. "For use in department stores as courtesy wrap or used for pre-wrapped box coverings."
First Contact & Terms: Mail slides/prints or original sketches. Prefers 15" repeat and even divisions thereof. SASE. Reports in 2 weeks. Buys all rights. No originals returned to artist at job's completion. Pays $50 minimum, giftwrap design.
Tips: To get an idea of the type of work sought, take notice of department store packaging. "Traditional Christmas motifs still very popular with us."

SMARTASS ENTERPRISES, 295 7th Ave., New York NY 10001. (212)691-9860. Art Director: Diane Williams. Produces greeting cards. Products are "bold, brash, sensual, shocking."
Needs: Buys 25 designs and 50 illustrations/year from freelance artists. Also uses artists for P-O-P displays. Considers photography, watercolors, acrylics, oils for illustrations. Prefers final art size of 5x6". Produces seasonal material for Christmas and Valentine's Day; submit art 5 months in advance.
First Contact & Terms: Send query letter with brochure, resume and samples to be kept on file. Call or write for appointment to show portfolio. Prefers photographs as samples. Samples not filed are returned by SASE. Reports within 1 week. Returns original art after reproduction.

CAROLE SMITH GALLERY, 456 Court St. NE, Salem OR 97301. (503)362-9185. Contact: Manager. Produces greeting cards; "very clean, colorful graphic images, floral and animal themes—nonmessage greeting cards carried mainly by bookstores, coffee shops and galleries."
Needs: Buys 120-150 designs/year from freelance artists. Considers "any form of color, especially watercolor, pastel" for illustrations. Prefers vertical rectangle for finished art, "but will consider anything."
First Contact & Terms: Send query letter with business card; accepts slides *only*. Samples are returned *only* if SASE is included. Reports back if SASE is included. Pays flat fee of $100/design plus 200 free cards for personal use. Buys reproduction right for card use only, editions of 10,000.
Tips: "Work must fit with images currently produced. Write and ask for color catalog to see if your work is complementary. Do *not* show up in person with samples."

STONEWAY LTD., 4th & Coates St., Bridgeport PA 19405. (215)272-4400. Contact: Art Director. Publishes coloring books and brochures, children cartoon themes for 2-8 year-olds.
Needs: Buys 10 designs and 125 illustrations/year from freelance artists. Uses artists for product design and illustrations plus advertising and catalog design, illustration and layout. Prefers b&w line drawings and color washes; 17x22" for coloring books, 11x17", 8½x11", 17x22" for brochures. Also produces seasonal material.
First Contact & Terms: Needs artists experienced in children's illustration line. Send query letter with samples and resume to be kept on file; write for appointment. Prefers roughs as samples. Samples not kept on file are returned by SASE. Reports in 3 weeks. No originals returned to artist at job's completion. Buys all rights. Payment varies per type of job or project. Pays on acceptance *only*.

SUNRISE PUBLICATIONS INC., Box 2699, Bloomington IN 47402. (812)336-9900. Manager of Creative Services: Lorraine Merriman. Publishes greeting cards. Art guidelines available.
Needs: Generally works on assignment, but picks up existing pieces from unsolicited submissions. Purchases 300-350 designs and illustrations/year. Considers any medium. Full-color illustrations scaled to 5x7" vertical, but these can vary. "We are interested in full range of styles for everyday and seasonal use, from highly illustrated to simple and/or humorous." Produces seasonal material for Christmas, Valentine's Day, St. Patrick's Day, Easter, Mother's Day, Father's Day, graduation, Halloween and Thanksgiving.
First Contact & Terms: Send query letter with brochure or resume, business card and samples to be kept on file. Prefers slides as samples, but any type is acceptable. Reports in 4-6 weeks. Call or write for appointment to show portfolio. Samples returned only by SASE. Originals returned to artist at job's completion. Offers a royalty program. Negotiates rights purchased.
Tips: "First, study our cards in your local card shops or send for our catalogs to get an idea of our look. To best fulfill the consumers' needs, we have begun to purchase rights to a much broader scope of contemporary subject matter and application with an emphasis on humor."

ARTHUR THOMPSON & COMPANY, 1260 S. 16th St., Omaha NE 68108. (402)342-2162. Executive Vice President: Nadine Seymour. Publishes greeting cards and letterheads; holiday and special occasion designs.
Needs: Uses 6 freelance artists/year for product illustrations. Prefers oils, acrylic paintings or mixed media; fall and winter scenes, Christmas and Thanksgiving background designs, birthday and special occasion designs.
First Contact & Terms: Write and send samples if possible. Prefers transparencies, slides of original art or original art as samples. Samples returned. Reports in 6 weeks. Provide sample and tear sheets to be kept on file for possible future assignments. Pays flat fee or negotiates payment. Considers product use and rights purchased when establishing payment.

*THOUGHT FACTORY, 6725 Valjean Ave., Van Nuys CA 91406. (818)786-2445. Creative Director: Paula M. Havey. Produces greeting cards, calendars, posters, stationery, notepads, self-adhesive stickers, stationery, lap-packs, books and mugs. "Promotional line—try to place designs/a look/across all product lines—trendy." Directs products to middle America.
Needs: Buys variable number of designs and illustrations from freelance artists/year. Uses artists for calligraphy, paste-up, mechanicals and design. Considers full-color art and photogrpahy. Produces material for Valentine's Day and Christmas.
First Contact & Terms: Prefers artists with background in the gift/stationery market. Send query letter with resume, business card and samples to be kept on file; call for appointment to show portfolio; write for art guidelines. Prefers slides and tear sheets as samples. Samples not filed are returned by SASE if requested. Originals sometimes returned to artist at job's completion. Negotiates payment and rights purchased.
Tips: "No students. Artists should have at least 1 year experience in the gift/stationery market."

WILDCARD, (formerly Cardesign, Inc.), Box 3960, Berkeley CA 94703-0960. Art Director: Leah Charonnat. Publishes greeting cards and stationery; current, avant-garde themes for 20-40 year olds— "young, upwardly mobile urbanites." Send $2 for sample cards and additonal information.
Needs: Buys 100 + illustrations/year from freelance artists. "We will be needing good, imaginative illustrations that fit the basic greeting card market themes (birthday, Christmas, Valentine's, friendship, etc.) must be very graphic as opposed to illustrated. Also looking for artists with new, innovative line ideas. Specializes in die-cut, 3-D cards."
First Contact & Terms: Best if artists have had commercial experience and been published but need not have been in cards before. Send samples, SASE, and brochure/flyer or resume to be kept on file. All materials 8½x11 only. Prefers brochure of work with nonreturnable pen & ink photostats or photocopies as samples; do not send original work. "If your project is accepted, we will contact you. But we cannot always promise to contact everyone who submits." Pays by the project, $50-250 average; average flat fee of $75/illustration. Considers complexity of project, product use and reproduction expense when establishing payment. "We will have all publishing rights for any work published. Artist may retain ownership of illustration, but this is to be negotiated." Pays on acceptance.
Tips: "Present only commercially potential examples of your work. *Do not* present work that is not of a professional nature or what one would expect to see published. Know what is already in the market and have a feeling for the subjects the market is interested in. Go out and look at *many* card stores before submitting. Ask the owner or buyer to 'review' your work prior to submitting."

*WILLITTS DESIGNS, 1327 Clegg St., Box 178, Petaluma CA 94953. (707)778-7211. Art Director: Ms. Mary Kern. Produces giftware in porcelain and earthware, "everything from figurines to mugs, cookie jars to night lights; some musical using Sankyo movements. We have a series of different 'looks'. Some of our lines are whimsical, some are quite detailed and serious. For example we have a line of accurate carousel reproductions done in porcelain. We also design musical/nonmusical plush." Directs products to 'cardshop buyer,' age 20-40, educated, professional.
Needs: Buys 60 + designs and illustrations from freelance artists/year. Also uses artists for calligraphy, paste-up, mechanicals, line drawings and slicks. Uses cartoons for porcelain decals on mugs, light switch plates, or for humorous porcelain giftware. "We prefer that color art be submitted using Dr. Martin's Water Based dyes on Vellum, but will look at almost any media. Designs should be done at 200% for mugs (limited to 3 colors preferred). Other submissions should not exceed 14x20" maximum." Produces material for all holidays, "but would like to see material for springtime most of all, i.e., Valentine's Day, Easter, Mother's and Father's Day, and wedding themes"; submit 1 year in advance. "If a design is accepted, it will take 6 months-1 year to produce and have on the market."
First Contact & Terms: "Conceptualize designs for sculpture, i.e., front view, side view and back view for figurines." Send query letter and samples to be kept on file; call or write for appointment to show portfolio. Prefers slides or photographs as samples. Samples not filed are returned by SASE. Reports within 1 month. Originals sometimes returned to artist at job's completion if requested. Pays average flat fee of $50/design or illustration; and royalties of 3-6%. "Special series concepts developed and designed by artists may allow for negotiation." Buys all rights or negotiates rights purchased.
Tips: "We compete with larger gift and novelty companies, but we do not produce cards . . . try to remember that concepts will be in three-dimensions, and that simplicity is sometimes preferred. Also, we like to balance our lines with whimsical, serious and nostalgic portrayals of subjects. Rapid growth in the better quality giftware business has increased our need for good designers and illustrators."

CAROL WILSON FINE ARTS, INC., Box 17394, Portland OR 97217. (503)283-2338 or 281-0780. Contact: Gary Spector. Produces greeting cards, postcards, posters and stationery that range from contemporary to nostalgic. "At the present time we are actively looking for unusual humor to expand our contemporary humor line. We want cards that will make peole laugh out loud!"
Needs: Uses artists for product design and illustration. Considers all media. Produces seasonal material for Christmas, Valentine's Day and Mother's Day; submit art preferably 1 year in advance.
First Contact & Terms: Send query letter with resume, business card and samples to be kept on file. Write for an appointment to show portfolio or for artists' guidelines. Prefers slides and photographs as samples; do *not* send original artwork. "All approaches are considered but, if possible, we prefer to see ideas that are applicable to specific occasions, such as birthday, anniversary, wedding, new baby, etc. We look for artists with creativity and ability." Samples not filed are returned by SASE. Reports within 2 months. Negotiates return of original art after reproduction. Negotiates pay; buys all rights.
Tips: "We have noticed an increased emphasis on humorous cards for specific occasions and, specifically, feminist humor."

WORLDLING DESIGNS, INC./NYC CARD CO., INC., Box 1935, Madison Square Station, New York NY 10159. (212)505-7732. Contact: Rick Siegel. Produces greeting cards, giftwrap, posters, postcards and jig saw puzzles with "very high tech illustration, New York City look; airbrush preferred." Product directed to 18-35 age groups—"young, affluent, primarily female or leaning to the gay type of design; communication-friendship-love-party."

Needs: Buys 25-50 designs and 75-100 illustrations/year from freelance artists; "art for publication is obtained exclusively through freelancers." Also uses artists for calligraphy, P-O-P displays, paste-up and mechanicals. Considers b&w media for postcards, ink for calligraphy, full color for greeting cards; "medium is not as important as quality." Prefers final art in repeat pattern for giftwrap only; greeting cards must be 5⅛x7⅛" gross size to be cropped to a 5x7" image. "Art may be larger but must shrink to conform." Produces seasonal material for Christmas; submit art 1 year in advance.

First Contact & Terms: Send query letter with brochure, resume and samples to be kept on file; original art is not filed. Call or write for appointment to show portfolio; write for art guidelines. Prefers slides as samples. Samples not filed are returned by SASE. Reports within 6 weeks. Returns original art after reproduction. Negotiates payment. Buys all rights on calligraphy; limited license agreement on cards negotiable.

Tips: "You must have artwork that is *unique* and of the highest quality, or do not waste your time with us."

Magazines

You don't have to live in New York City to work as a magazine illustrator or cartoonist. If you live within reasonable distance of a post office—and most people do today—you can submit your work to more than 700 magazine listings in this section. And for quick deadlines, express mail services can now guarantee your artwork will reach the art director within twenty-four hours or sooner.

One key to becoming a successful "at home" illustrator is to know the magazine market, particularly the specific magazines you are interested in. Study the topics, themes and styles of artwork published in magazines you plan to contact, just as you would study greeting card lines or a record company's album covers. Review at least four to six current issues of each publication before submitting your material. Always edit your illustrations or cartoons to fit the specific needs of the publication.

Many of the more specialized publications deviate very little from their usual issue-to-issue illustration or cartoon subject matter. But most magazines want even the "usual" artwork to be presented in new and varying ways. Read the Close-up with Kristin Herzog, Design/Production Director of *Phi Delta Kappan* for insightful advice on submitting cartoons and illustrations to a magazine.

"*Actually, I made straight A's, but, after taxes and deductions, I ended up with three C's and two B's.*"

Martha Campbell of Harrison, Arkansas, received $25 from Phi Delta Kappan *for one-time use of this cartoon.*

More and more magazines use freelance cartoons, not just as fillers but as unique parts of the editorial content. Cartoons are more frequently bought unsolicited; illustrations are more often done on an assignment basis when an artist's style fits the look the art director seeks.

Keep pace with the changes that occur in publications by making regular trips to your newsstand or library. Read the masthead for the names of any new art directors or editors.

If you're just now beginning as an artist, realize that acceptance from large-circulation publications is more difficult than from smaller, lower-paying magazines.

In addition to the listings offered in this section, check your local business or reference library for the *Gebbie Press All-In-One Directory*, *The Magazine Directory* and the *Internal Publications Directory*, *Ayer Directory of Publications*, *Ulrich's International Periodicals Directory* and *Writer's Market 1986*.

Artist: Andrea Eberbach

Artist: Bob Gale

Artist: David Fietze

Artist: Thierry Sauer

*ABYSS, 1402 21st St. NW, Washington DC 20036. Editor: David F. Nalle. Digest-sized magazine emphasizing fantasy and adventure games for adult game players with sophisticated and varied interests. Bimonthly. Circ. 1,300. Does not accept previously published material. Returns original artwork after publication. Sample copy for $2. Art guidelines free for SASE with 22¢ postage.
Cartoons: Buys up to 2/issue. Prefers humorous, game or fantasy-oriented themes. Prefers single, double or multiple panel with or without gagline; b&w line drawings. Send query letter with roughs. Write for appointment to show portfolio. Material not filed is returned by SASE. Reports within 3 weeks. Buys first rights. Pays $5-10, b&w; on publication.
Illustrations: Buys 8-12/issue. Prefers fantasy, dark fantasy, horror or mythology themes. Send query letter with samples. Write for appointment to show portfolio. Prefers photocopies or photographs as samples. Samples not filed are returned by SASE. Reports within 1 month. Buys first rights. Pays $20-30, b&w, and $30-50, color, cover; $3-8, b&w, inside; on publication.

ACCENT, 1720 Washington Blvd., Box 10010, Ogden UT 84409. (801)394-9446. Editor: Fern Porras. Concerns travel. Circ. 90,000. Monthly. Sample copy $1.
Cartoons: Buys 10-12/year on business, sports and everyday life, "in good taste." Samples returned by SASE. Reports in 3 weeks. Pays on acceptance.

ACCENT ON LIVING, Box 700, Bloomington IL 61702. Editor: Betty Garee. Emphasis on success and ideas for better living for the physically handicapped. Quarterly. Original artwork returned after publication, if requested. Sample copy $2.
Cartoons: Uses 18-20/issue; buys all from freelancers. Receives 5 submissions/week from freelancers. Interested in people with disabilities in different situations. Send finished cartoons. SASE. Reports in 2 weeks. Buys first-time rights (unless specified). Pays $20; on acceptance.
Illustrations: Uses 3-5 illustrations/issue. Interested in illustrations that "depict articles/topics we run." Works on assignment only. Provide samples of style to be kept on file for future assignments. Samples not kept on file are returned by SASE. Reports in 2 weeks. Buys all rights on a work-for-hire basis. Pays on acceptance.
Tips: "Send a sample and be sure to include various styles of artwork that you can do."

ACROSS THE BOARD, 845 Third Ave., New York NY 10022. (212)759-0900. Art Director: Josef Kozlakowski. Emphasizes business-related topics for Chief Executive Officers in the business field and industry. Monthly. Returns original artwork after publication. Sample copy free for SASE.
Cartoons: Cartoons are used to accompany articles, not as individual works. Assignments made per manuscript. Send roughs; call for appointment to show portfolio. Material not filed is returned by SASE. Reports back only if interested. Buys first rights. Pays $75 for b&w; on publication.
Illustrations: Buys 4-6 illustrations/issue from freelancers. Works on assignment only. Send brochure and samples to be kept on file; call for appointment to show portfolio. Prefers tear sheets or photocopies as samples. Samples not filed are returned by SASE. Reports back only if interested. Buys first rights. Pays $400 for color cover; $200 for b&w inside; on publication.

ACTION, 901 College Ave., Winona Lake IN 46590. (219)267-7656. Contact: Vera Bethel. For ages 9-11. Circ. 25,000. Weekly. SASE. Reports in 1 month. Pays on acceptance.
Cartoons: Buys 1/issue on school, pets and family. Pays $10, b&w. Send finished artwork.
Illustrations: Uses color illustrations on assignment. Send samples or slides. Pays $75 for full-color drawings (no overlays).

ADAM, 8060 Melrose Ave., Los Angeles CA 90046. Concerns "human sexuality in contemporary society." Monthly.
Cartoons: Buys no unsolicited cartoons.
Illustrations: Buys 1-2 illustrations/issue on assigned themes. Arrange interview to show portfolio. SASE. Reports in 2-3 weeks. Pays $25-100, b&w; $35-300, color.

ADIRONDAC, 172 Ridge St., Glens Falls NY 12801. Editor: Neal Burdick. Emphasizes the Adirondack Mountains and conservation for members of Adirondack Mountain Club, conservationists, and outdoor-oriented people in general. Published 10 times/year. Circ. 9,000. Accepts previously published material and simultaneous submissions. Original artwork returned after publication. Sample copy $1.75; art guidelines free for SASE.
Cartoons: Uses 1-2 cartoons/issue. Interested in environmental concerns, conservation, outdoor activities as themes. Prefers single panel with gagline; b&w line drawings. Send query letter to be kept on file. Reports within 2 weeks. Negotiates rights purchased. No payment.
Illustrations: Uses 3 illustrations/issue. Prefers maps, specific illustrations for articles. Works on assignment only. Send query letter to be kept on file. Reports within 2 weeks. No payment.

*AFTA-THE ALTERNATIVE MAGAZINE, Second Floor, 153 George St., New Brunswick NJ 08901. (201)828-5467. Editor: Bill-Dale Marcinko. Emphasizes rock music, films, TV and books for young (18-35) male readers who are regular consumers of books, records, films and magazines; and socially and politically aware. 60% are gay; 50% are college educated or attending college. Quarterly. Circ. 25,000. Receives 10 cartoons and 30 illustrations/week from freelance artists. Previously published material and simultaneous submissions OK. Original work returned after publication. Sample copy $3.50. Especially needs political satire; rock and film illustrations, surreal, erotic work.
Cartoons: Uses 50 cartoons/issue; buys all from freelancers. Interested in satires on social attitudes, current political events, films, TV, books, rock music world, sexuality; single and multi-panel with gagline, b&w line drawings. No color work accepted. Send query letter with samples of style. Samples returned. Buys one-time rights. Pays in contributor copies; on publication.
Illustrations: Uses 75 illustrations/issue; buys all from freelancers. Interested in illustrations from films, rock music stars, books and TV programs. No color work accepted. Send query letter with samples of style to be kept on file. Samples not kept on file are returned. Reports in 1 week. Buys one-time rights. Pays in contributor copies; on publication.
Tips: "Read a sample copy of *AFTA* before submitting work."

AGRI FINANCE, Century Communications, Inc., 5520-G Touhy Ave., Skokie IL 60077. (312)676-4060. Art Director: Judy Krajewski. Concerns financial management for "ag-bankers and agricultural-related professions." Published 10 times/year. Circ. 23,000. Simultaneous submissions and previously published work OK. Sample copy $3.
Illustrations: Cover: Buys color and b&w work. Inside: Buys b&w line drawings, washes and gray opaques. Arrange interview to show portfolio. SASE. Reports in 3 weeks. Negotiates pay; pays on publication.

AGRI MARKETING, Century Communications, Inc., 5520-G Touhy Ave., Skokie IL 60077. (312)676-4060. Art Director: Judy Krajewski. Serving agri-business professionals. Published 13 times/year; Simultaneous submissions and previously published work OK. Sample copy $3.
Illustrations: Cover: Buys color and b&w work. Inside: Buys gray opaques, b&w line drawings and washes. Arrange interview to show portfolio. SASE. Negotiates pay; pays on publication.

AIM, Box 20554, Chicago IL 60620. (312)874-6184. Editor-in-Chief: Ruth Apilado. Managing Editor: Dr. Myron Apilado. Art Director: Bill Jackson. Readers are those "wanting to eliminate bigotry and desiring a world without inequalities in education, housing, etc." Quarterly. Circ. 16,000. Sample copy $3; artist's guidelines for SASE. Reports in 3 weeks. Previously published, photocopied and simultaneous submissions OK. Receives 12 cartoons and 4 illustrations/week from freelance artists.
Cartoons: Uses 1-2 cartoons/issue; all from freelancers. Interested in education, environment, family life, humor through youth, politics and retirement; single panel with gagline. Especially needs "cartoons about the stupidity of bigotry." Mail finished art. SASE. Reports in 3 weeks. Buys all rights on a work-for-hire basis. Pays $5-15, b&w line drawings; on publication.
Illustrations: Uses 6 illustrations/issue; half from freelancers. Interested in current events, education, environment, humor through youth, politics and retirement. Provide brochure to be kept on file for future assignments. No samples returned. Reports in 4 weeks. Prefers b&w for cover and inside art. Buys all rights on a work-for-hire basis. Pays $5-15, b&w line drawings; on publication.
Tips: "Because of the possibility of nuclear war, people are seeking out ways for survival. They are feeling more alienated from society and are more conscious of the importance of getting together. Their submissions reflect their concern. For the most part, artists submit material omitting black characters. We would be able to use more illustrations and cartoons with people from all ethnic and racial backgrounds in them. We also use material of general interest."

*AIRBRUSH DIGEST, 521 S.W. 11th Ave., Portland OR 97205. (503)226-1608. Editor: William Urban. Emphasizes art. Annually. Original artwork returned after publication.
Illustrations: Buys 12-20 text illustrations/year; 6 designs and 2 illustrations for cover/year. Send query letter with samples (35mm color slides) to be kept on file; write for appointment to show portfolio; write for artists' guidelines. Samples not filed are returned. Reports within 6 weeks. Buys all rights. Pays by the project, $200-1,500 average, cover design and illustrations; by the hour, $15-45 average, text illustration.

ALFRED HITCHCOCK MYSTERY MAGAZINE, Davis Publications, 380 Lexington Ave., New York NY 10017. (212)557-9100. Art Director: Jerry Hawkins. Art Editor: Ron Kuliner. Emphasizes mystery fiction.
Needs: Line drawings, minimum payment: $100.
First Contact & Terms: Call for interview. Reports in 1 week. Pays on acceptance. Buys first rights.

This scratchboard artwork by H.E. Knickerbocker of Seattle, Washington, accompanied two poems in Amelia magazine and "seemed to validate the essence of the poetry and to heighten its impact," says editor Frederick A. Raborg, Jr. "The artist is philosophically perceptive beyond the norm for an artist. His work is clean, and his eye for detail, demanding. He senses and uses space especially well and works in enough techniques to give an editor wide choices." Amelia bought all rights to the work.

ALIVE!, Christian Board of Publication, Box 179, St. Louis MO 63166. Editor: Mike Dixon. For junior high students. Monthly. Sample copy $1.
Cartoons: Buys 8 cartoons/issue on life and teenage problems. Prefers to see finished cartoons. SASE. Reports in 2 weeks. Buys one-time rights. Pays $10.
Illustrations: Illustrations should appeal to junior high. Interested in inks, line drawings and washes. Prefers to see finished art and samples of style; samples returned by SASE. Provide business card, brochure and/or tear sheets to be kept on file. Reports in 2 weeks. Buys first North American serial rights. Pays $30-50; on acceptance.

*ALTERNATIVE HOUSING BUILDER MAGAZINE, 16 1st Ave., Corry PA 16407. Managing Editor: Marc Warren. Emphasizes alternative housing: log homes, domes, earth shelters, post & beam construction and any other type of non-conventional housing for kit package manufacturers and builder-dealers of these homes. Bimonthly. Circ. 11,000. Original artwork returned after publication if requested. Sample copy and art guidelines free for SASE.
Cartoons: Buys 1-2 cartoons/issue from freelancers. Considers anything pertaining to log homes, geodesics, earth shelters, post & beam construction or the problems faced by the men and women who are building these homes. Prefers single panel with or without gagline; b&w line drawings or b&w washes. Send query letter with finished cartoons to be kept on file. Material not filed is returned only if requested. Reports within 2 weeks. Buys all rights. Pays $10-15, b&w on publication.

*AMATEUR GOLF REGISTER, 2843 Pembroke Rd., Hollywood FL 33020. (305)921-0881. Managing Editor; Bernard Block. Estab. 1985. Emphasizes golf for golfers. Monthly. Circ. 7,000. Original artwork returned after publication. Sample copy and art guidelines free for SASE.
Cartoons: Buys 1 cartoon/issue from freelancers. Prefers single panel with gagline; b&w line drawings. Send finished cartoons to be kept on file for 3 months. If not used, returned by SASE. Buys first rights. Pays $5, b&w; on publication.
Illustrations: Buys 3-5 illustrations/issue from freelancers. Prefers golf-oriented theme. Send query letter. Prefers tear sheets, slides or photographs as samples. Samples not filed are returned by SASE. Reports within 1 month. Buys first rights.

*AMELIA, 329 "E" St., Bakersfield CA 93304. (805)323-4064. Editor: Frederick A. Raborg, Jr. Estab. 1983. Magazine; also publishes 2 supplements—*Cicada* (haiku) and *SPSM&H* (sonnets) and illustrated postcards. Emphasizes fiction and poetry for the general review. "Our readers are drawn from a cross-section of reading tastes and educational levels, though the majority tend to be college-educated."

Quarterly. Circ. 1,000. Accepts some previously published material from illustrators. Original artwork returned after publication if requested with SASE. Sample copy $4.75; art guidelines for SASE.

Cartoons: Buys 1-2 cartoons/issue from freelancers. Prefers sophicated or witty themes (see Wayne Hogan's work in April 1985 issue). Prefers single panel with or without gagline; b&w line drawings, b&w washes. Send query letter with finished cartoons to be kept on file. Material not filed is returned by SASE. Reports within 1 week. Buys first rights or one-time rights; prefers first rights. Pays $5-25, b&w; on acceptance.

Ilustrations: Buys 8-10 illustrations annually from freelancers for *Amelia;* 2-4 for *Cicada*; 2-4 for *SPSM&H*; and 50-60 for postcards. Considers all themes; "no taboos except no explicit sex; nude studies in taste are welcomed, however." Send query letter with samples to be kept on file; unaccepted material returned immediately by SASE. Prefers photostats and/or photocopies as samples. "See work by H. E. Knickerbocker, Wayne Hogan, Walt Phillips, Gregory Powell, Bott Beeson, Julie Ball, Hope Zimmerman, David Sheskin, L. John Gieslinski, Jean Youell Johnson in our October 1984 and April 1985 issues." Reports in 1 week. Buys first rights or one-time rights; prefers first rights; Pays $25, b&w, cover; $5-25, b&w, inside; on acceptance.

*AMERICAN AGRICULTURIST, Box 370, Ithaca NY 14851. (607)273-3507. Production Manager: Andrew Dellava. Emphasizes agriculture in the Northeast, specifically New York, New Jersey and New England. Monthly. Circ. 72,000. Original artwork not returned after publication. Art guidelines free for SASE.

Cartoons: Buys 3 cartoons/issue from freelancers. Prefers agriculture theme. Single panel, 2⅛" wide by 2¾-3¼" high or similar proportions, with gagline; b&w line drawings. Send query letter with finished cartoons. Material returned. Reports within 3 weeks. Buys first rights or one-time rights. Pays $10, b&w; on acceptance.

AMERICAN ARTIST, 1515 Broadway, New York NY 10036. (212)764-7300. Emphasizes the American artist—realistic, naturalistic and fine art for artists, students and teachers. Monthly. Circ. 162,000. Sample copy $2.50; art guidelines for SASE.

Needs: Does not assign or use freelancers. If an artist wants to be the subject of a feature article, he should contact the editor. Wants to see slides or b&w glossies of artist's work for possible feature articles.

THE AMERICAN ATHEIST, Box 2117, Austin TX 78768. (512)458-1244. Editor: R. Murray-O'Hair. For atheists, agnostics, materialists and realists. Monthly. Circ. 30,000. Previously published and simultaneous submissions OK. Free sample copy.

Needs: Buys b&w drawings, cover designs and cartoons. Especially needs 4-seasons art for covers and greeting cards. Send photocopies. "All illustrations must have bite from the atheist point of view and hit hard." Pays on publication. Cartoons, $15 each. Line drawings, $25. Four-color art and photos, $100.

Tips: *"The American Atheist* looks for clean lines, directness and originality. We are not interested in side-stepping cartoons and esoteric illustrations. Our writing is hard-punching and we want artwork to match."

AMERICAN BABY INC., 575 Lexington Ave., New York NY 10022. (212)752-0775. Art Director: Blair Davis. Four publications emphasizing babies, children and parents. Monthly, quarterly and annually. Circ. 1,000,000. Returns original artwork after publication. Sample copy free for SASE, art guidelines available.

Illustrations: Buys 3-5 illustrations/issue from freelancers. Works on assignment only. Send business card and samples to be kept on file. Samples not filed are not returned. Reports back only if interested. Buys one-time rights. Pays on publication.

AMERICAN BANKERS ASSOCIATION-BANKING JOURNAL, 345 Hudson St., New York NY 10014. (212)620-7256. Art Director: Rob Klein. Emphasizes banking for middle and upper level banking executives and managers. Monthly. Circ. 42,000. Accepts previously published material. Returns original artwork after publication.

Illustrations: Buys 2 illustrations/issue from freelancers. Themes relate to stories, primarily, financial; styles vary, realistic, cartoon, surreal. Works on assignment only. Send query letter with brochure and samples to be kept on file. Prefers tear sheets, slides or photographs as samples. Samples not filed are returned by SASE. Negotiates rights purchased. Pays $350-500 for color cover and $100-250 for b&w or color inside; on acceptance.

THE AMERICAN BAPTIST MAGAZINE, Box 851, Valley Forge PA 19482-0851. (215)768-2077. Manager of Print Media Services: Richard W. Schramm. National publication of American Baptist Churches in the USA. Reports religious and secular news of interest to the American Baptist constituen-

How American Families are Changing

by Paul C. Glick

After two decades of rapid growth in American households, moderation may be setting in. The Census Bureau reports that household growth between 1982 and 1983 was too slow to be statistically significant. The total number of households in the United States rose by only 391,000, the first time that the U.S. has gained fewer than one million households in one year since 1966—67, and the first statistically insignificant increase in two decades. Average household size increased from 2.72 to 2.73 persons per household.

The recession may explain this moderation. But the household formation trends of the past also may be changing, leading to slower household growth in the 1980s.

The household growth that does occur is likely to be unevenly distributed by type of household. While the number of households will continue to increase from 1981 to 1990, the magnitude of the increase is likely to be only two-thirds as great as in the years from 1970 to 1981.

If these assumptions hold, households will increase by 12.7 million between 1981 and 1990, a 15.4 percent gain to 95.1 million. Married-couple households will increase only 8 percent during these years, resulting in a continuing decline in the share of households headed by married-couples—from 60 percent of all households in 1981 to about 55 percent in 1990.

Households maintained by a woman with no husband present will increase by 26 percent, while those maintained by a man with no wife present will increase by 35 percent.

Paul C. Glick, professor of sociology at Arizona State University, was a Census Bureau demographer for many years and is an authority on the family.

American Demographics .21

Sally Kuhn, a freelance artist from Long Beach, California, received this long-distance assignment from Caroline Arthur, managing editor of American Demographics, a monthly magazine in Ithaca, New York. Kuhn received $100 for one-time rights to the editorial illustration. Michael Rider, the magazine's art director, designed the spread.

cy. Circ. 90,000. Monthly (except combined July-August issue). Sample and guidelines available.
Illustrations and Cartoons: May make occasional use of freelance work; one-color art and cartoons. All artwork on assignment for specific themes/subjects. Compensation negotiable. Portfolio samples and resumes welcomed; enclose SASE for material to be returned.
Tips: "Submissions considered for aesthetic appeal, promptness and accuracy. Artists should be accessible and willing to produce quickly."

AMERICAN BIRDS, National Audubon Society, 950 3rd Ave., New York NY 10022. (212)546-9193. Assistant Editor: Anne Wagner. Emphasizes ornithology — migration, distribution, breeding and behavior of North and South American birds, including Hawaii and the West Indies. Journal for the scientific community, serious birders. Bimonthly. Circ. 15,000, paid. Accepts simultaneous submissions. Sample copy $3; art guidelines for SASE.
Illustrations: Uses 1-2 illustrations/issue; buys all from freelancers. Prefers North and South American birds drawn with strict adherence to anatomical detail. Occasionally uses stylized drawings. Send query letter with samples to be kept on file. Write for appointment to show portfolio. Prefers sharp photostats or original pen & ink drawings; occasionally publishes color. Samples returned by SASE if not kept on file. Reports within 4 weeks. Buys first rights. Pays $20-35 b&w, inside; $100 color, cover.

AMERICAN BOOKSELLER, Booksellers Publishing Inc., Suite 1410, 122 E. 42nd St., New York NY 10168. (212)867-9060. Editor-in-Chief: Ginger Curwen. Art Director: Amy Bogert. For booksellers interested in trends, merchandising, recommendations, laws and industry news. Monthly. Circ. 8,700. Original artwork returned after publication. Sample copy $3.
Cartoons: Uses 4 cartoons/year; buys all from freelancers. Receives 5-10 submissions/week from freelancers. Interested in bookselling, authors and publishing; single panel with gagline. Send finished cartoons. SASE. Reports in 2 weeks. Buys first North American serial rights.
Illustrations: Uses 6 illustrations/issue; buys 6/issue from freelancers. Receives 10 submissions/week from freelancers. Looks for strong concepts and an original style. Interested in books, inventory or ma-

terial for specific assignments. Works on assignment only. Provide business card, flyer and tear sheet to be kept on file for future assignments. Prefers finished art, samples of style or portfolio. SASE. Reports in 2 days. Buys first North American serial rights. Pays $45 minimum for b&w line drawings, washes and gray opaques; on acceptance.

Tips: "Computers are entering the bookselling business. Illustrations are by assignment almost exclusively as articles are more specific in their subject matter. We would like to see idea-oriented pieces."

AMERICAN CLASSIC SCREEN MAGAZINE, Suite 106, 8340 Mission Rd., Shawnee Mission KS 66206. (913)341-1919. Editor/Cover Artist: Dr. John Tibbetts. Emphasizes the preservation of the motion picture industry for "readers from all 50 states and 29 foreign countries that are both movie fans and scholars of the industry, along with a great many people from the industry itself." Bimonthly. Circ. 19,900. Accepts previously published material and simultaneous submissions. Original artwork returned after publication. Sample copy free for SASE.

Cartoons: Prefers themes. Send query letter with samples of style to be kept on file. Material not kept on file is returned only if requested. Reports within 10 days. Buys reprint rights.

Illustrations: Uses 3 illustrations/issue. Prefers movie industry theme or tie-in. Send query letter with samples to be kept on file. Prefers photostats as samples. Samples not kept on file are returned only if requested. Reports within 10 days.

AMERICAN DEMOGRAPHICS, Box 68, Ithaca NY 14851. (607)273-6343. Managing Editor: Caroline Arthur. Emphasizes demographics and population trends. Readers are business decision makers, advertising agencies, market researchers, newspapers, banks and professional demographers and business analysts. Monthly. Circ. 10,000. Original artwork returned after publication. Sample copy $5.

Cartoons: Uses 1-3 cartoons/issue, all from freelancers. Receives 5-10 submissions/week from freelancers. Interested in population trends including moving, aging, families, birth rate, the census, surveys, changing neighborhoods, women working, data (use, computers, etc.), market research, business forecasting and demographers. Format: single panel b&w line drawings and b&w washes with gagline. Prefers to see finished cartoons. SASE. Reports in 2 weeks. Buys one-time rights. Pays $50-100 on publication.

Illustrations: Uses 5 illustrations/issue. Interested in demographic themes. Needs "styles that reproduce best in b&w. Spare statements with a light approach to the subject." Prefers to see portfolio; contact Caroline Arthur. SASE. Provide photocopies of work to be kept on file for future needs. Reports in 1 month. Buys one-time rights. Inside: pays $35, under 1/2 page; $65, 1/2 page; $100, full page. Cover: pay is negotiable ($100-300).

AMERICAN HERITAGE, 10 Rockefeller Plaza, New York NY 10020. (212)399-8900. Corporate Art Director: Murray Belsky. Concerns American history. Bimonthly. Circ. 150,000.

Illustrations: Assigns work for 1-2 articles/issue. Prefers b&w line, 2- and 4-color with historical ambiance. Drop off portfolio with receptionist; pick up following morning.

THE AMERICAN LEGION MAGAZINE, Box 1055, Indianapolis IN 46206. Contact: Cartoon Editor. Emphasizes the historical development of the world at present, and milestones of history; general interest magazine for veterans and their families. Monthly. Original artwork not returned after publication.

Cartoons: Uses 4 cartoons/issue, all from freelancers. Receives 100 submissions/week from freelancers. Especially needs general humor, in good taste. "Generally interested in cartoons with a broad, mass appeal. Prefer action in the drawing, rather than the illustrated joke-type gag. Those which have a beguiling character or ludicrous situation that attract the reader and lead him to read the caption rate the highest attention. No-caption gags purchased only occasionally. Because of the tight space problem, we're not in the market for the spread-type or multipanel cartoon, but use both vertical and horizontal format single-panel cartoons. Themes should be home life, business, sports and everyday Americana. Cartoons which pertain only to one branch of the service are too restricted for this magazine. The service-type gag should be recognized and appreciated by any ex-serviceman or woman. Cartoons in bad taste, off-color or which may offend the reader not accepted. Liquor, sex, religion and racial differences are taboo. Ink roughs not necessary, but are desirable. Finish should be line, Ben-Day." Prefers to review roughs. Reports immediately. Buys first rights; "pays on receipt of Ben-Day acceptance." Pays $75-125.

Tips: "Artists should submit their work as we are always seeking a new slant or more timely humor."

AMERICAN LIBRARIES, American Library Association, 50 E. Huron St., Chicago IL 60611. (312)944-6780. Editor-in-Chief: Arthur Plotnik. Assistant Managing Editor: Edith McCormick. For professional librarians, library employees and individuals in business-related fields. Published 11 times/year. Circ. 42,000. Sample copy $3. Free artist's guidelines.

Cartoons: Buys 4-10/year on libraries and library-patron interaction; single panel with gag line. Avoid stereotypes. Query with samples or with resume and portfolio. SASE. Reports only if interested. Buys first North American serial rights. Pays $30-75, b&w line drawings and washes, depending on assignments.

Illustrations: Buys 4-8/year on libraries, library-patron interaction and assigned themes. Query with samples or with resume and portfolio. SASE. Reports only if interested. Buys first North American serial rights. Cover: Pays $50-200, b&w; $300 maximum, color. Inside: Pays $15-200, color and b&w; on acceptance.

Tips: "Review a few issues of our magazine at your public library so you are familiar with the type of articles we illustrate. Avoid stereotypical images of librarians."

AMERICAN MOTORCYCLIST, American Motorcyclist Association, Box 6114, Westerville OH 43081-6114. (614)891-2425. Executive Editor: Greg Harrison. Associate Editors: Bill Wood and John Van Barriger. Monthly. Circ. 130,000. For "enthusiastic motorcyclists, investing considerable time and money in the sport." Sample copy $1.50.

Cartoons: Uses 2-3 cartoons/issue; all from freelancers. Receives 5-7 submissions/week from freelancers. Interested in motorcycling; "single panel gags." Prefers to receive finished cartoons. SASE. Reports in 2 weeks. Buys all rights on a work-for-hire basis. Pays $15 minimum, b&w washes; on publication.

Illustrations: Uses 1-2 illustrations/issue, almost all from freelancers. Receives 1-3 submissions/week from freelancers. Interested in motorcycling themes. Works on assignment only. Provide resume and tear sheets to be kept on file. Prefers to see samples of style and resume. Samples returned by SASE. Reports in 2 weeks. Buys first North American serial rights. Cover: Pays $75 minimum, color. Inside: $30-100, b&w and color; on publication.

AMERICAN PRINTER, 300 W. Adams St., Chicago IL 60606. (312)726-2802. Editor: Elizabeth G. Berglund. Printing, publishing and graphic arts industry monthly magazine. Receives 2-5 cartoons and 1-3 illustrations/week from freelance artists.

Illustrations: Uses illustrations frequently throughout the year, all from freelancers. Interested in "any style—some general, some specific to the industry." Works on assignment only. Prefers to see resume, portfolio and samples of style. SASE. Provide resume, business card or letter of inquiry to be kept on file for possible future assignments. Reports in 30-60 days. Buys all rights on a work-for-hire basis. Pays $100-400, sometimes higher.

Tips: "Read several issues of our magazine—our needs and preferences should be quite apparent."

AMERICAN SQUAREDANCE, Box 488, Huron OH 44839. Editors: Stan and Cathie Burdick. For squaredancers, callers and teachers. Emphasizes personalities, conventions and choreography. Monthly. Original artwork returned after publication if requested. Free sample copy.

Cartoons: Uses 1 cartoon/issue; buys 6/year from freelancers. Interested in dance theme; single panel. Send finished cartoons. SASE. Reports in 1 week. Buys all rights on a work-for-hire basis. Pays $5-15, halftones and washes; on publication.

Illustrations: Uses 5 illustrations/issue; buys 1/issue from freelancers. Interested in dance themes. Send finished art. SASE. Reports in 1 week. Buys all rights on a work-for-hire basis. Cover: Pays $10-25, b&w line drawings, washes and color-separated art. Inside: Pays $5-15, b&w line drawings and washes; on publication.

AMERICAN TRUCKER MAGAZINE, Box 6366, San Bernardino CA 92412. Editor: Steve Sturgess. Emphasizes trucks and trucking topics of interest to the single truck owner operator and the small truck fleet businessman. Monthly. Circ. 46,800. Accepts previously published material only in exceptional circumstances. Does not return original artwork after publication. Sample copy free for SASE.

Illustrations: Buys 1 illustration/issue from freelancers. Prefers realistic styles. Works on assignment only. Send query letter; write for appointment to show portfolio. Buys first rights. Pays $100/page for b&w; on publication.

*ANGLER & HUNTER MAGAZINE, 169 Charlotte St., Box 1541, Peterborough, Ontario Canada K9J 7H7. (705)748-3891. Art Director: David Golden. Emphasizes angling, hunting and conservation of natural resources. Monthly except November/December and January/February are published as single issues. Circ. 51,000. Accepts previously published material. Original artwork returned after publication. Sample copy and art guidelines free for SASE.

Cartoons: Prefers angling, hunting or conservation themes; single panel with gagline; b&w line drawings, b&w washes. Send query letter with samples of style or finished cartoons to be kept on file. Material not filed is returned if requested. Reports within 3 weeks. Buys one-time rights. Pays on publication.

Illustrations: Prefers angling, hunting and conservation themes; humorous and cartoon-style illustrations are presently a potential market. Works on assignment only. Send query letter with brochure, resume, business card and 3 samples to be kept on file. Prefers tear sheets, slides or photographs as samples. Samples not filed are returned if requested. Reports back within 3 weeks. Buys one-time rights. Pays on publication.
Tips: "Industry trends appear to be toward utilizing materials that enhance and clarify editorial stands. Our present search for illustrators and cartoonists reflects our desire to present our readership with a more attractive, more interesting, more comprehensively understandable package."

ANIMALS, 350 S. Huntington Ave., Boston MA 02130. Editor-in-Chief: Susan Burns. Art Director: Malcolm Mansfield. For members of 3 affiliated humane organizations in the Northeast. Bimonthly. Circ. 21,000. Simultaneous submissions OK. Buys one-time rights. Sample copy for $1.75 and SASE; artist's guidelines for SASE.
Illustrations: Buys 1-2/issues on animals. Receives 20 illustrations/week from freelance artists. Send query letter to be kept on file; also send samples. Samples returned by SASE. Buys first rights. Reports in 2 weeks. Cover: Pays $50-100, full-color. Inside: Pays $10-30, b&w line drawings; $30-60, color washes and full-color renderings.
Tips: "We are the publication of the *MSPCA* and thus emphasize humane issues."

THE ANTIQUARIAN, Box 798, Huntington NY 11743. (516)271-8990. Editors: Marguerite Cantine and Elizabeth Kilpatrick. Concerns antiques, arts, shows and news of the market; for dealers and collectors. Monthly. Circ. 15,000.
Illustrations: Receives 2 illustrations/week from freelance artists. "We are one magazine that hates the use of photography but it's more available to us than good illustrations. We ran a complete history of the teddy bear and would have used all drawings if we could have found an illustrator. Instead we had to use photos. We've also recently started using many illustrations of colonial and Victorian buildings." Buys b&w line drawings. Especially needs illustration for ad designs. Query with resume, samples and SASE. "No phone calls, please!" Include 8½x11" SASE with $1.25 if sample copy is requested. Reports in 4-8 weeks. Buys all rights. Pay "depends on the size of the article. We commission the entire article or issue if possible to one artist. I like for the artist to quote his/her rates." Pays $10 maximum, b&w; on acceptance.
Tips: "Our covers are us. They are children's illustrations from fine, usually German, books circa 1850-1875. If an artist can get the feel of what we're trying to convey with our covers, the rest is easy. We specialize in totally designed magazines. I think we're a leader in the antiques trade field and people will follow the trend. We are heavily illustrated—we use few photos. Send 5-10 illustrations *after* reviewing the publications. Suggest a price range. If the illustration is good, needed, usable, the price is never a problem. So suggest one. Only the artist knows the time involved. We buy *all rights only*. Please quote prices accordingly."

ANTIQUES DEALER, 1115 Clifton Ave., Clifton NJ 07013. (201)779-1600. Editor: Nancy Adams. For antiques dealers. Monthly. Circ. 7,500. Query first. Receives 4 cartoons/year from freelance artists.
Cartoons: Buys 4/year on antiques theme. Query or mail art. SASE. Reports in 4 weeks. Buys all rights. Pays $25, b&w line drawings, washes and half tones. "We're looking for sophisticated, sublime humor; avoid derogatory tone."

*AOPA PILOT, 421 Aviation Way, Frederick MD 21701. (301)695-2353. Emphasizes general aviation (no military or airline) for aircraft owners and pilots. Monthly. Circ. 270,000. Original artwork returned after publication. Sample copy $2.
Illustrations: Uses illustrations specifically for manuscripts. Works on assignment only. Send query letter with samples; write or call for appointment to show portfolio. Accepts any type of sample; no cartoons. Samples returned by SASE. Reports only if interested. Buys first rights. Pays on acceptance.

*APALACHEE QUARTERLY, Box 20106, Tallahassee FL 32304. Editor: Barbara Hamby. Literary magazine emphasizing fine arts for a well-educated, literary audience. Quarterly. Circ. 500. Accepts previously published material. Original artwork returned after publication. Sample copy $3.50; art guidelines available.
Illustrations: Buys 5-10 illustrations/issue from freelancers. "We're very open on themes and styles. We like playful, technically accomplished work." Send samples to be kept on file. Prefers photostats, photographs or photocopies as samples. Samples not filed are returned by SASE. Reports within 2 months. Buys one-time rights. Pays in 2 copies, b&w; cover and inside. "We pay as we receive grants."

APPALACHIAN TRAILWAY NEWS, Box 807, Harpers Ferry WV 25425. (304)535-6331. Editor: Judith Jenner. Emphasizes the Appalachian Trail for members of the Appalachian Trail Conference. Bi-

monthly. Circ. 22,000. Sometimes accepts previously published material. Returns original artwork after publication. Sample copy $1 for serious inquiries; art guidelines free for SASE with 22¢ postage.
Cartoons: Buys 0-1 cartoons/issue from freelancers. Prefers themes on hikers and trailworkers on Appalachian Trail. Open to all formats. Send query letter with roughs and finished cartoons. Only materials pertinent to Appalachian Trail are considered. Material not filed is returned by SASE. Reports within 1 month. Negotiates rights purchased. Pays $25-50 for b&w; on acceptance.
Illustrations: Buys 2-5 illustrations/issue from freelancers. Themes/styles are assigned to particular story ideas. Send query letter with samples to be kept on file. Write for appointment to show portfolio. Prefers photostats, photocopies or tear sheets as samples. Samples not filed are returned by SASE. Reports within 1 month. Negotiates rights purchased. Pays $75-150, b&w and $150 up, color (watercolor only) for covers; $25-100, b&w and color for inside; pays on acceptance.

APPLIED CARDIOLOGY—JOURNAL OF CARDIOVASCULAR AND PULMONARY TECHNIQUE, (formerly *CVP Journal of Cardiovascular and Pulmonary Technique*), 825 S. Barrington Ave., Los Angeles CA 90049. Publisher: Martin Waldman. Art Director: Tom Medsger. Emphasizes medical technological and professional news.
Illustrations: Submit brochure/flyer to be kept on file for possible future assignment. Reports only when assignment available. Buys all rights. Pays $60-up, spot art; $400, full-color cover; on acceptance.

ART DIRECTION, 10 E. 39th St., New York NY 10016. (212)889-6500. Editor: Loren Bliss. Emphasizes advertising for art directors. Monthly. Circ. 12,000. Original work returned after publication. Sample copy $2.50. Receives 7 illustrations/week from freelance artists.
Illustrations: Uses 2-3 illustrations/issue; all from freelancers. Interested in themes that relate to advertising. Send query letter. Provide information to be kept on file for possible future assignments. Samples not returned. Reports in 1 month. No payment for cover or editorial art.

*ART MATERIAL TRADE NEWS, 390 5th Ave., New York NY 10018. (212)613-9700. Editor: Jeff Abugel. Emphasizes art material business, merchandising and selling trends, products, store and manufacturer profiles for dealers, manufacturers, wholesalers of artist supplies. Monthly. Circ. 11,500. Accepts previously published material. Original artwork returned after publication. Sample copy available.
Cartoons: Themes and styles open. Send query letter with samples of style to be kept on file "if desired by artist." Write for appointment to show portfolio. Material not kept on file returned by SASE. Reports "as soon as possible." Negotiates rights purchased. Payment negotiable. Pays on publication.
Illustrations: Works on assignment only. Send brochure, resume, samples and tear sheets to be kept on file. Write for an appointment to show portfolio. Prefers "anything but originals" as samples. Samples returned by SASE if not kept on file. Reports "as soon as possible." Negotiates rights purchased. Pays on publication.

*ARTFUL DODGE, Box 1473, Bloomington IN 47402. (812)332-0310. Art Editor: Karen Kovacik. Emphasizes literature (all genres). "Our readers are interested in challenging poetry, fiction, and drama, both from the U.S. and abroad (particularly Eastern Europe)." Bianually/irregularly. Circ. 400. Original artwork returned after publication. Sample copy $2.75; art guidelines available.
Illustrations: Prefers pen & ink drawings, woodcuts—high contrast black-and-white work that reproduces well. "Please no science fiction or cat cartoons. We look for visually interesting work that can stand on its own apart from our literary offerings." Prefers good photocopies or samples. Samples cannot be returned. Reports within 2-3 months. Buys first rights or one-time rights. Pays in copies (2).

THE ARTIST'S MAGAZINE, 9933 Alliance Rd., Cincinnati OH 45242. (513)984-0717. Editor: Mike Ward. Estab. 1984. Emphasizes the techniques of working artists for the serious beginning and amateur artist. Published 12 times/year. Circ. 160,000. Occasionally accepts previously published material. Returns original artwork after publication. Sample copy $2 with SASE and $1.25 postage.
Cartoons: Buys 4-5 cartoons/issue from freelancers. Prefers single-panel finished cartoons with or without gagline; b&w line drawings, b&w washes. Cartoons should be artist-oriented, appealing to the working artist (versus the gallery-goer), and should not denigrate art or artists. Avoid cliché situations. Vertical-format cartoons are always welcome. Send query letter with preferably 4 or more cartoons; write for appointment to show portfolio. Material not filed is returned by SASE. Reports within 1 month. Pays $50 for b&w; on acceptance.
Illustrations: Contact Carol Buchanan, art director. Buys 3-4 illustrations/issue from freelancers. Themes depend on editorial copy being illustrated; "mostly humorous, but most important, well-composed art that appeals to artists." Works on assignment only. Send query letter with brochure, resume and samples to be kept on file. Write for appointment to show portfolio. Prefers photostats or tear sheets

as samples. Samples not filed are returned by SASE. Reports within 1 month. Buys first rights. Pays on acceptance.

ASSOCIATION AND SOCIETY MANAGER, Brentwood Publishing Corp., 825 S. Barrington Ave., Los Angeles CA 90049. Publishers: Martin H. Waldman and Hal Spector. Art Director: Tom Medsger. Devoted to the interests of managers of professional membership societies.
First Contact & Terms: Submit brochure/flyer to be kept on file for possible future assignment. Reports only when assignment available. Buys all rights. Pays $60 and up, spot art; $400, full-color cover; on acceptance.

ATLANTIC CITY MAGAZINE, 1637 Atlantic Ave., Atlantic City NJ 08401. (609)348-6886. Art Director: Drew Hires. Emphasizes the growth, people and entertainment of Atlantic City for residents and visitors. Monthly. Circ. 50,000.
Illustrations: Mainly b&w, some 4-color. Works on assignment only. Provide resume, business card and tear sheets to be kept on file for possible future assignments. Send samples of style. Samples returned by SASE. Reports in 3 weeks. Buys first rights. Pays $50-250 inside, b&w, $150-400, color.
Tips: "We are looking for intelligent, reliable artists who can work within the confines of our budget and time frame. Deliver good art and receive good tear sheets."

*ATLANTIC SALMON JOURNAL, 1435 St. Alexandre, Montreal, Quebec H3A 2G4 Canada (514)842-8059. Managing Editor: Joanne Eidinger. Emphasizes conservation and angling of Atlantic salmon; travel, biology and cuisine for educated, well-travelled, affluent and informed anglers and conservationists, biologists and professionals. Quarterly. Circ. 20,000. Does not accept previously published material. Returns original artwork after publication. Sample copy free for SASE. Art guidelines available.
Cartoons: Uses 2-4/issue. Prefers environmental or political themes, specific to salmon resource management, travel and tourism—light and whimsical. Prefers single panel with or without gagline; b&w line drawings. Send query letter with samples of style to be kept on file. Material not filed is returned. Reports within 8 weeks. Buys first rights and one-time rights. Pays $50-100, b&w; on publication.
Illustrations: Uses 4-6/issue. Prefers themes on angling, environmental scenes and biological drawings. Send query letter with samples to be kept on file. Prefers photostats, tear sheets, slides or photographs as samples. Samples not filed are returned. Reports within 8 weeks. Buys first rights and one-time rights. Pays $50-150, b&w, and $100-250, color, inside; on publication.

AUSTRALIAN WOMEN'S WEEKLY, 54 Park St., Sydney Australia 2000. A.C.P. Creative Director: Phil Napper. Readers are average to highly sophisticated women. Monthly. Circ. 1 million +. Original artwork not returned after publication. Art guidelines with SASE (nonresidents include IRC's).
Illustrations: Uses 2 illustrations/issue; buys all from freelancers. Interested in action illustration in traditional style; good anatomy, any medium. Works on assignment only. Provide tear sheets to be filed for possible future assignments. Send samples of style. No samples returned. Reports in 2 weeks. Buys all rights. Pays with Australian dollars; $300-400/color; on acceptance.
Tips: Artists "must be good enough for national publication."

AUTO TRIM NEWS, 1623 Grand Ave., Baldwin NY 11510. Contact: Nat Danas. Query. Does not return original artwork after publication. Pays on publication. Also a need for P-O-P posters "for the small businessman."
Cartoons: Uses 2/issue; buys all from freelancers. Prefers to see roughs; reports in 2 weeks.
Illustrations: Uses 1/issue; buys from freelancers. Works on assignment basis only. Prefers to see roughs and samples of style; samples returned. Reports in 2 weeks. Buys all rights on a work-for-hire basis. Pays $10, spot drawings; $25-50, cover design.
Tips: Artists should "visit a shop" dealing in this field.

AUTOMOBILE QUARTERLY, 221 Nassau St., Princeton NJ 08542. (609)924-7555. Contact: L. Scott Bailey. Concerns autos and auto history. Circ. 30,000. Quarterly. Original artwork returned after publication, by arrangement.
Illustrations: Uses 8 illustrations/issue, all from freelancers. Interested in antique, classic cars and cutaway technical illustrations. Works on assignment only. Provide "sample of rendering" to be kept on file for future assignments. SASE. Reports in 2 weeks. Buys various rights. Negotiates pay (part of payment may be posters of work); pays on publication.

*AUTOMOTIVE AGE, THE DEALER BUSINESS MAGAZINE, 6931 Van Nuys Blvd., Van Nuys CA 91405. (818)997-0644. Art Director: Chris Gallison. Emphasizes car dealership for car and truck dealers. Monthly. Circ. 34,000. Accepts previously published material. Sample copy available.
Illustrations: Buys 2-3 illustrations/issue from freelancers. Prefers realism. Works on assignment only.

Send query letter with samples to be kept on file. Call for appointment to show portfolio. Prefers tear sheets or slides as samples. Samples are returned only if requested. Reports only if interested. Pays $350, b&w and $350-600, color, cover; $150, b&w and $300, color, inside; on publication.

AXIOS, The Orthodox Journal, 800 S. Euclid Ave., Fullerton CA 92632. (714)526-2131. Editor: Daniel Gorham. Estab. 1980. Emphasizes "challenges in ethics and theology, some questions that return to haunt one generation after another, old problems need to be restated with new urgency. *Axios* tries to present the 'unthinkable.' " Works from an Orthodox Catholic viewpoint. Monthly. Circ. 4,798. Accepts previously published material and simultaneous submissions. Original artwork returned after publication. Sample copy $2.

Illustrations: Uses 20-35 illustrations/issue; buys 15-30 illustrations/issue from freelancers. Prefers bold line drawings, seeks ikons, b&w; "no color *ever*; use block prints—do not have to be religious, but must be *bold!*" Send query letter with brochure, resume, business card or samples to be kept on file. Write or call for appointment to show portfolio. Samples are returned by SASE if not kept on file. Reports within 5 weeks. Buys one-time rights. Pays $100, b&w cover and $25-100, b&w inside; on acceptance.

Tips: "Realize that the Orthodox are *not* Roman Catholics, nor Protestants. We do not write from those outlooks. Though we do accept some stories about those religions, be sure *you* know what an Orthodox Catholic is."

BACKPACKER MAGAZINE, 1 Park Ave., New York NY 10016. Art Director: Stan Green. Emphasizes outdoor backpacking; directed to the 25-45 year age group, interested in recreation. Bimonthly. Circ. 175,000. Returns original artwork after publication.

Cartoons: Buys about 1 cartoon/issue from freelancers. Prefers single panel; b&w line drawings, color washes. Send query letter with samples of style to be kept on file; call for appointment to show portfolio. Material not filed is returned by SASE. Reports back only if interested. Buys one-time rights. Pays $100-200, b&w; $200-400, color; on publication.

Illustrations: Buys 1-2 illustrations/issue. Works on assignment only. Call for appointment to show portfolio. Prefers to review photocopies. Reports only if interested. Buys one-time rights or reprint rights. Pays $450, color cover; $100-200, inside b&w and $200-400, inside color; on publication.

*BAJA TIMES, Box 755, San Ysidro CA 92073. (706)612-1244. Editorial Consultant: John W. Utley. Emphasizes Baja California, Mexico for tourists, other prospective visitors and retirees living there. Monthly. Circ. 50,000. Accepts previously published material. Original artwork returned after publication. Sample copy for 9x12 or larger SASE with 85¢ postage.

Cartoons: All must be Baja California-oriented. Prefers single panel with gagline; b&w line drawings. Send query letter with samples of style to be kept on file. Material not filed returned by SASE. Reports within 1 month. Buys one-time rights. Payment not established. Pays on publication.

Illustrations: Theme: Baja California. Send query letter with samples to be kept on file. Prefers tear sheets or photocopies as samples. Samples not filed are returned by SASE. Reports within 1 month. Buys one-time rights. Payment not established. Pays on publication.

Tips: "We have not used art, mostly because it has not been offered to us. If properly oriented to our theme (Baja California), we would consider on an occasional basis."

*BAKERSFIELD LIFESTYLE MAGAZINE, 123 Truxtun Ave., Bakersfield CA 93301. (805)325-7124. Editor: Steve Walsh. City magazine aimed at local lifestyles of college-educated males/females, ages 25-65. Monthly. Circ. 10,000. Accepts previously published material. Original artwork returned after publication. Sample copy $3; art guidelines for SASE.

Cartoons: Buys 4 cartoons/issue from freelancers. No political humor. Prefers single panel with gagline; b&w line drawings or b&w washes. Send finished cartoons to be kept on file. Material not filed is returned by SASE. Reports only if interested. Buys one-time rights or reprints rights. Pays $5, b&w; on publication.

Illustrations: Buys 6 illustrations/issue from freelancers. Send samples to be kept on file; write for appointment to show portfolio. Prefers photostats, tear sheets or photocopies as samples. Samples not filed are returned by SASE. Reports only if interested. Buys one-time rights or reprint rights. Pays $100, b&w and $150, color, cover; $50, b&w and $75, color, inside; on publication.

*BANJO NEWSLETTER, INC., Box 364, Greensboro MD 21639. (301)482-6278. Editor/Publisher: Hub Nitchie. Emphasizes banjo 5-string music for musicians and instrument collectors. Monthly. Circ. 8,000. Accepts previously published material. Original artwork returned after publication. Sample copy $1; deductible on subscription.

Cartoons: Buys 1 cartoon/issue from freelancers. Prefers single panel; b&w line drawings. Send query letter with sample of style to be kept on file Material not filed is returned by SASE. Reports within 2 weeks. Buys one-time rights. Pays $20-25, b&w; on publication.

Illustrations: Buys 1-2 illustrations/issue from freelancers. Send query letter to be kept on file. Samples returned by SASE. Reports within 2 weeks. Buys one-time rights. Pays approximately $50, b&w, cover; $20-30, b&w, inside; on publication.

BANKING TODAY, (formerly *Florida Banker*), Florida Bankers Association, Box 6847, Orlando FL 32853-6847. Vice President and Executive Editor: William P. Seaparke. Communicates educational, legislative and other material relevant to Southeastern US bankers and businesspersons. Published 12 times/year. Circ. 6,500. Original artwork not returned after publication. Sample copy $2.50.
Cartoons: Buys very few cartoons/issue. Interested in banking; single, double and multi-panel with gaglines. Prefers to see roughs. SASE. Reports in 8-12 weeks only if SASE included. "Don't telephone editor." Buys all rights. "Loans rights back to artists on occasion." Pays $15, b&w; on publication.
Illustrations: Buys 1-10 illustrations/issue on business or banking. Works on assignment only. Especially needs "specialized illustrations to accompany stories already prepared for publication. Assignments made only after query. Do not send original art before requested to do so." Provide letter of inquiry to be kept on file for future assignments. No samples returned. Reports in 8-12 weeks. "Don't telephone editor." Buys all rights on a work-for-hire basis. "Loans rights back to artists on occasion." Pays $20-50, b&w illustrations; on publication.
Tips: "We wish to expand our pool of dependable illustrators, but we work better with local artists on-the-spot. Artists are helpful when they send b&w copier sheets of a few of their illustrations. Copier sheets are not returned, but are retained in our files." Especially looks for applicability of art to subject matter of publication and professionalism in presentation. "We have totally redesigned and renamed our major publication (*Banking Today*). Our redesign hopefully, provides for easier, quicker identification of editorial matter through more exploratory headlines, larger type, shorter stories, more photography and illustrations." Also editor of *Cases In Brief* (legal newsletter).

*BASKETBALL DIGEST, 1020 Church St., Evanston IL 60201. (312)491-6440. Art Director: Marcia Kuhr. Emphasizes pro basketball, some college for "the serious sports fan who wants all the scores, stats, and stories behind the action." Monthly. Circ. 130,000. Accepts previously published material. Original artwork returned after publication. Sample copy and art guidelines available.
Cartoons: Basketball themes. Prefers single panel; b&w line drawings. Send query letter. Write for appointment to show portfolio. Material not filed is returned by SASE. Reports only if interested. Pays on publication.
Illustrations: Basketball themes. Works on assignment only. Send query letter. Write for appointment to show portfolio. Samples not filed are returned by SASE. Reports only if interested. Pays on publication.

BAY AND DELTA YACHTSMAN, Recreation Publications, 2019 Clement Ave., Alameda CA 94501. (415)865-7500. Managing Editor: Dave Preston. Art Director: David Hebenstreit. Concerns boating and boat owners in northern California. Monthly. Circ. 20,000. Previously published and simultaneous submissions (if not published in northern California) OK. Original artwork returned after publication if requested. Sample copy $1.50.
Cartoons: Buys 4-5/year on boating. Prefers to see roughs. SASE. Reports in 2 weeks. Buys all rights on a work-for-hire basis. Pays $5 minimum, b&w line drawings; on publication.
Illustrations: Uses 2-3 charts and technical drawings/issue on boating. Prefers to see roughs. SASE. Provide letter of inquiry and resume to be kept on file for future assignments. Reports in 2 weeks. Buys all rights on a work-for-hire basis. Pays $5 minimum, b&w line drawings; on publication.

BEND OF THE RIVER® MAGAZINE, 143 W. Third St., Box 239, Perrysburg OH 43551. Editors-in-Chief: Chris Raizk Alexander and R. Lee Raizk. For local history enthusiasts. Monthly. Circ. 2,500. Previously published and photocopied submissions OK. Original artwork returned after publication. Sample copy $1.
Cartoons: Buys 12 cartoons/issue from freelancers. Interested in early Americana; single panel with gagline. SASE. Buys first North American serial rights or all rights on a work-for-hire basis. Pays $1-3, b&w line drawings.
Illustrations: Buys 20 illustrations/year. Interested in "historic buildings for ads." Works on assignment only. Prefers to see roughs. SASE. No samples returned. Reports in 6 weeks. Buys first North American serial rights or all rights on a work-for-hire basis. Pays $10-15, b&w line drawings, inside.
Tips: "We need more cartoons. Especially looks for "cleverness, i.e., a funny gagline. Artists shouldn't send too many cartoons emphasizing art rather than the gagline."

*BEST WISHES, Box 8, Station C, Toronto, Ontario M6J 3M8 Canada. For new mothers. Quarterly. Mail art. Reports in 1 month. Previously published work OK. Pays on acceptance.
Needs: Buys spot drawings, cartoons and illustrations relating to parenting infants and toddlers. Fees negotiable.

BETTER HOMES & GARDENS, Meredith Corp., 1716 Locust, Des Moines IA 50336. Contact: Cartoon Editor. For "middle-and-up income, homeowning and community-concerned families." Monthly. Circ. 8,000,000. Original artwork not returned after publication. Free artist's guidelines.
Cartoons: Uses 2 cartoons/issue; buys all from freelancers. Receives 50-75 submissions/week from freelancers. Interested in current events, education, environment, family life, humor through youth, politics, religion, retirement, hobbies, sports and businessmen; single panel with gag line. Prefers finished cartoons. SASE. Reports in 2 weeks. Buys all rights. Pays $300 minimum, b&w line drawings; on acceptance.

BEVERAGE WORLD MAGAZINE, 150 Great Neck Rd., Great Neck NY 11021. (516)829-9210. Managing Editor: Jean Lukasick. Emphasizes beverages (beers, wines, spirits, bottled waters, soft drinks, juices) for soft drink bottlers, breweries, bottled water/juice plants, wineries and distilleries. Monthly. Circ. 25,000. Accepts previously published material and simultaneous submissions. Original artwork returned after publication if requested. Sample copy $2.50.
Cartoons: Buys 3 cartoons/issue from freelancers. Prefers caricature/line art styles. Prefers single panel, b&w drawings or color washes. Send query letter with samples of style to be kept on file. Material not kept on file is returned by SASE. Reports only if interested. Buys first rights, one-time rights, reprint rights, all rights. Payment negotiable. Pays on acceptance.
Illustrations: Uses 5 illustrations/issue; buys 3-4 illustrations/issue from freelancers. Works on assignment only. Send query letter with samples to be kept on file. Write for appointment to show portfolio. Prefers photostats, slides or tear sheets as samples. Samples not filed are returned by SASE. Reports only if interested. Negotiates rights purchased. Payment negotiable. Pays on acceptance.

*BICYCLE GUIDE, 128 N. 11th St., Allentown PA 18102. (215)435-7570. Managing Editor: Ted Costantino. Estab. 1984. Magazine. Emphasizes bicycles for bicycle enthusiasts. Published 9 times/year; Sept./Oct., Nov./Dec. and Jan./Feb. are combination issues. Circ. 206,000. Original artwork returned after publication. Sample copy for SASE with $1.37 postage.
Cartoons: Generally doesn't use cartoons, but will consider submissions. Prefers upscale cycling oriented themes. Send query letter with samples of style to be kept on file; write for appointment to show portfolio. Material not filed is returned by SASE. Reports only if interested. Negotiates rights purchased. Payment is negotiable; pays on publication.
Illustrations: Buys 1-10 illustrations/issue from freelancers. Prefers technical themes. Works on assignment only. Send query letter with brochure, resume, business card and samples to be kept on file; write for appointment to show portfolio. Accepts photostats, tear sheets, photocopies, slides, photographs, etc. as samples. Samples not filed are returned by SASE. Reports within 1 month. Negotiates rights purchased. Pays negotiable rate on publication.

BICYCLE USA, Suite 209, 6707 Whitestone Rd., Baltimore MD 21207. (301)944-3399. Editor: Karen Missavage. Readers are members of BICYCLE USA; publication is also sold in bicycle stores. Monthly. Circ. 16,000. Previously published material OK "if not in overlapping market." Original artwork returned after publication. SASE.
Cartoons: Uses 2 cartoons/issue; buys all from freelancers. Interested in recreational or utilitarian use of bicycles, road design, legislation and technical topics; single panel with gagline. Send finished cartoons. Reports in 3 weeks. Buys one-time rights. Pays in copies of magazine; on publication.

BIKEREPORT, Box 8308, Missoula MT 59807. (406)721-1776. Editor: Daniel D'Ambrosio. Magazine. Emphasizes long-distance bicycle touring for bicycle enthusiasts. Circ. 18,000. Accepts previously published material. Original artwork returned after publication. Sample copy and art guidelines free for SASE.
Illustrations: Uses 3-6 illustrations/issue. Themes/styles are open. Works on assignment only. Send query letter with samples to be kept on file; write for appointment to show portfolio. Samples not kept on file are returned. Reports within 1 month. Buys first rights. Pays $40-60, b&w, cover; $15-50, b&w, inside; on publication.

BIRD WATCHER'S DIGEST, Box 110, Marietta OH 45750. (614)373-5285. Editor: Mary B. Bowers. Emphasizes birds and bird watchers for "bird watchers and birders (backyard and field; veteran and novice)." Bimonthly. Circ. 40,000. Previously published material OK. Original work returned after publication. Sample copy $2.
Cartoons: Uses 1-3 cartoons/issue; buys all from freelancers. Interested in themes pertaining to birds and/or bird watchers; single panel with or without gagline, b&w line drawings. Send roughs. Samples returned by SASE. Reports in 1 month. Buys one-time rights and reprint rights. Pays $10, b&w; on publication.
Illustrations: Uses 10 illustrations/issue; buys all from freelancers. Interested in birds. Provide busi-

ness card and tear sheets to be kept on file for possible future assignments. Send samples of style. Samples returned by SASE. Reports in 1 month. Buys one-time rights and reprint rights. Pays $10 minimum inside, b&w line drawings; on publication.

BITTERSWEET, Box 6, Norway ME 04268. (207)625-3975. Editor: Nancy Marcotte. Emphasizes northern New England topics—life, people, literature, the arts—for "well-educated professionals and native residents of Maine, over thirty years old, who have chosen rural living for its pleasures and benefits." Published 12 times a year. Circ. 7,000. Returns original art after publication with SASE. Sample copy free for SASE with $1.50 postage.
Cartoons: Buys 2-5 cartoons/issue from freelancers. Prefers themes "appropriate to the uplands of northern New England. No 'issues,' nothing tasteless." Considers single panel with or without gagline; b&w line drawings, b&w washes or color washes. Send query letter with samples of style or roughs to be kept on file; call for appointment to show portfolio. Material not filed is returned by SASE. Reports within 8 weeks. Buys first rights, one-time rights or reprint rights. Pays $10 maximum for b&w, $25 maximum for color; on publication.
Illustrations: Buys 2-3 illustrations/issue from freelancers. Prefers still lifes, scenics, people appropriate to rural New England. Send query letter with samples to be kept on file; call for appointment to show portfolio. Accepts photostats, tear sheets, photocopies, slides or photographs as samples. Samples not filed are returned by SASE. Reports back within 8 weeks. Buys first rights, one-time rights or reprint rights. Pays $10 for b&w and $25 for color inside illustrations; on acceptance.

BLACK AMERICAN LITERATURE FORUM, Parsons Hall 237, Indiana State University, Terre Haute IN 47809. (812)232-6311, ext 2760. Editor-in-Chief: Joe Weixlmann. Concerns black American writers and their work. Quarterly. Circ. 1,050. Simultaneous submissions OK. Sample copy $4; free artist's guidelines.
Illustrations: Buys 3/issue on black life. Mail art. SASE. Reports in 2 weeks. Buys all rights, but may reassign rights to artist after publication. Cover and inside: Pays $15 maximum, b&w line drawings; on acceptance.
Tips: "We get, and need relatively little work."

THE BLACK COLLEGIAN MAGAZINE, 1240 S. Broad St., New Orleans LA 70125. (504)821-5694. Art Director: Mike Hancock. For black college students and recent graduates with a concentration on career-oriented subjects and job opportunities. Bimonthly. Circ. 171,000. Previously published material and simultaneous submissions accepted. Sample copy available; art guidelines free for SASE.
Illustrations: Uses 6 illustrations/issue; buys 4/issue from freelancers. Send query letter with samples to be kept on file; original work is returned. Call or write for appointment to show portfolio. Prefers photostats or tear sheets as samples. Samples not kept on file are returned by SASE only if requested. Reports within 30 days. Buys one-time rights or reprint rights. Pays $150, b&w and $275, color, for covers; $20 and up for b&w and color, inside. Pays on publication.

THE BLACK WARRIOR REVIEW, University of Alabama, Box 2936, University AL 35486. (205)348-4518. Editor: Gabby Hyman. For general literary audience. Published semiannually. Circ. 2,000. Sample copy $3; "suggest looking at copy of magazine before submitting."
Illustrations: Needs b&w or color illustrations for covers. SASE. Reports in 4 weeks. Buys all rights, but may reassign rights to artist after publication. Pays $25, b&w or color; on publication.

BLUEGRASS UNLIMITED, Box 111, Broad Run VA 22014. Contact: Peter V. Kuykendall. Emphasizes old-time traditional country music for musicians and devotees of bluegrass, ages from teens through the elderly.
Illustrations and Cartoons: Uses 5-6 pen & ink cartoons/year and spot drawings on old-time, traditional or bluegrass country music. Buys all rights, but sometimes reassigns rights to artist after publication. Pays $15-25 plus; on publication.

THE B'NAI B'RITH INTERNATIONAL JEWISH MONTHLY, B'nai B'rith, 1640 Rhode Island Ave. NW, Washington DC 20036. (202)857-6645. Editor: Marc Silver. Emphasizes a variety of articles of interest to the Jewish family. Published 10 times/year. Circ. 200,000. Original artwork returned after publication. Sample copy $1. Also uses artists for "design, lettering, calligraphy on assignment. We call or write the artist, pay on publication."
Illustrations: Buys 2 illustrations/issue from freelancers. Theme and style vary, depending on tone of story illustrated. Works on assignment only. Write or call for appointment to show portfolio. Prefers tear sheets, slides or photographs as samples. Reports within 3 weeks. Samples returned by SASE. Reports in about 1 month. Buys first rights. Pays $150, b&w and $250, color, cover; $100, b&w and $200, color, inside; on publication.

BOATING, 1 Park Ave., New York NY 10016. (212)503-3500. Art Director: Victor Mazurkiewicz. Emphasizes boating for boat owners. Monthly. Circ. 180,000. Accepts simultaneous submissions. Original artwork returned after publication.
Illustrations: Occasionally uses illustrations; buys all from freelancers. Works on assignment only. Send samples and tear sheets to be kept on file. Write or call for appointment to show portfolio. Prefers photostats or photographs as samples. Samples returned only by SASE if not kept on file. Buys first rights. Pays $1,000, color, cover. Pays $100-500, b&w, inside; $1,000, color, 2-page spread, inside. Pays on acceptance.

BOP, #720, 7060 Hollywood Blvd., Hollywood CA 90028. (213)469-3551. Editor/Publisher: Julie Laufer. Estab. 1983. Emphasizes teenage entertainment; directed to 13-year-old girls (average age) interested in movie, TV and music stars. Monthly. Circ. 300,000. Accepts previously published material. Sometimes returns original artwork after publication. Sample copy $2.50.
Cartoons: Prefers teenage entertainment themes. Considers single panel with or without gagline; b&w line drawings. Send query letter with samples of style or finished cartoons to be kept on file. Write for appointment to show portfolio. Material not filed is returned only if requested. Reports within 1 month. Negotiates rights purchased and payment; pays on acceptance.
Illustrations: Buys 4 illustrations/issue from freelancers. Prefers teenage entertainment themes. Send query letter with brochure and samples to be kept on file. Write for appointment to show portfolio. Accepts photostats, tear sheets, photocopies, slides or photographs as samples. Samples not filed are returned by SASE. Reports within 1 month. Negotiates rights purchased and payment; pays on acceptance.

BOW & ARROW MAGAZINE, Box HH, Capistrano Beach CA 92624. (714)493-2101. Managing Editor: Roger Combs. Emphasizes bowhunting and bowhunters. Bimonthly. Original artwork not returned after publication. Art guidelines available.
Cartoons: Uses 2-3 cartoons/issue; buys all from freelancers. Prefers single panel, with gag line; b&w line drawings. Send finished cartoons. Material not kept on file returned by SASE. Reports within 2 months. Buys all rights. Pays $7.50-$10, b&w. Pays on acceptance.
Illustrations: Uses 1-2 illustrations/issue; buys all from freelancers. Prefers live animals/game as themes. Send samples. Prefers photographs or original work as samples. Especially looks for perspective, unique or accurate use of color and shading, and an ability to clearly express a thought, emotion or event. Samples returned by SASE. Reports in 2 months. Buys all rights or negotiates rights purchased. Pays $100-150, color, cover; payment for inside b&w varies. Pays on acceptance.

BOWHUNTER, Editorial Offices, 3150 Mallard Cove Lane, Fort Wayne IN 46804. (219)432-5772. Editor-in-Chief: M.R. James. For "readers of all ages, background and experience. All share two common passions—hunting with the bow and arrow and a love of the great outdoors." Bimonthly. Circ. 170,000.
Cartoons: Uses few cartoons; buys 1/issue from freelancer. Interested in "bowhunting and wildlife. No unsafe hunting conditions; single panel." Prefers to see roughs. SASE. Reports in 4 weeks. Buys all rights on a work-for-hire basis; will reassign rights. Pays $15-25, line drawings; on acceptance.
Illustrations: Uses 1-2 illustrations/issue, all from freelancers. Receives few submissions/week from freelancers. Interested in "wildlife-bowhunting scenes." Prefers to see roughs or sample of style. Provide brochure or flyer to be kept on file for future assignments. SASE. Reports in 4 weeks. Buys all rights on a work-for-hire basis; will reassign rights. Cover: Pays $50-250, color. Inside: Pays $25-150, b&w; on acceptance.
Tips: "We are presently overstocked with cartoons and chances of making a sale aren't good. Wildlife art is always in demand." Especially looks for "a feeling and understanding the artist has for the game represented. Call it atmosphere or mood, or whatever, it's something that is either there or not. The art we select for publication has this extra something the viewer immediately senses. We have started using more color on inside pages. This opens up additional possibilities for freelance artists with good wildlife art. Study the magazine before contacting us. Know what we use before making suggestions or submitting ideas."

BOWLERS JOURNAL, John Hancock Center, 875 N. Michigan Ave., Chicago IL 60611. (312)266-7171. Managing Editor: Jim Dressel. Monthly. Circ. 22,000. Emphasizes bowling. Simultaneous submissions and previously published work OK. Also uses artist for design; specific assignments to suit editorial themes. Query with previously published work.
Cartoons: "We're looking for more cartoons. We buy at least one strip a month—a verticle, single column configuration is ideal; no horizontals. Let us see a sample of your work, and we'll make assignments based on our specific needs."
Illustrations: Needs art to illustrate specific articles. Query with samples or mail finished art. SASE.

"Myron Sahlberg is a highly skilled illustrator who understands what we want," explains Lawrence Libby of **Brigade Leader** *magazine published in Wheaton, Illinois. "This full-page black-and-white illustration enriched the article because it emphasized a subtle aspect of the story. It was not a trite or over-used artistic solution." Sahlberg, of Pennock, Minnesota, received $150 for one-time rights to the artwork. Libby adds, "We also use Sahlberg because his people are natural, and his use of gray, black and white reproduces well in our two-color magazine."*

Reports in 2 months. Buys one-time rights. Pays $10-75, b&w line drawings; $75-150, feature; on acceptance.

Tips: "We've stepped up our use of illustration for our more conceptual articles. We've been bearing down to customize the artwork to the article rather than depend so heavily on our file of stock art. Art or illustration porjects were assigned to a tight coterie of those who have worked with us in the past, but with turnover and increased demands, we would like to see samples or portfolios of those who would like to work in the bowling arena. Humorous and cartoon-style illustrations are assigned on a need basis; usually for an article in the lighter vein."

BOWLING DIGEST, 1020 Church St., Evanston IL 60201. Art Director: Marcia Kuhr. Estab. 1983. Emphasizes pro and amateur bowling. Bimonthly. Circ. 115,000. Original artwork returned after publication. Sample copy and art guidelines available.

Cartoons: Considers sports themes. Prefers single panel; b&w line drawings or color washes. Send query letter. Write for appointment to show portfolio. Material not filed is returned by SASE. Reports only if interested. Pays on publication.

Illustrations: Considers sports—bowling themes. Works on assignment only. Send query letter. Write for appointment to show portfolio. Samples returned by SASE. Reports only if interested. Pays on publication.

BREAD, 6401 The Paseo, Kansas City MO 64131. (816)333-7000. Editor-in-Chief: Gary Sivewright. Christian leisure reading magazine for ages 12-17 with denominational interests. Monthly. Circ. 25,000. Previously published and simultaneous submissions OK. Free sample copy and artist's guidelines *with* SASE.

Cartoons: Buys 10 cartoons/year; buys all from freelancers. Receives 10 submissions/week from freelancers. Interested in humor through youth—teen, school, religious, dating; single panel with gagline. Prefers to see finished cartoons. Reports in 4-6 weeks. Buys first rights. Pays $6-15, b&w line drawings; on acceptance.

Illustrations: Uses 15 illustrations/year. Works on assignment only. Prefers to see samples. Cover: Pays $150-200, color. Inside: Pays $35-80, b&w; on acceptance.

BRIGADE LEADER, Box 150, Wheaton IL 60189. (312)665-0630. For Christian laymen and adult male leaders of boys enrolled in the Brigade man-boy program. Circ. 14,000. Published 4 times/year. Original artwork returned after publication. Sample copy for $1.50 and large SASE; artist's guidelines for SASE.
Cartoons: Contact: Cartoon Editor. Uses 1 cartoon/issue, all from freelancers. Receives 3 submissions/week from freelancers. Interested in sports, nature and youth; single panel with gag line. "Keep it clean." SASE. Buys first rights only. Pays $20, b&w line drawings; on publication.
Illustrations: Art Director: Lawrence Libby. Uses 2 illustrations/issue. Interested in man and boy subjects, sports, camping—out of doors, family. Works on assignment only. Samples returned by SASE. Reports back on future assignment possibilities. Provide resume and flyer to be kept on file for future assignments. Prefers to see portfolio and samples of style. Reports in 2 weeks. Pays $50-85, for inside use of b&w line drawings and washes; on publication.

BROTHERHOOD OF MAINTENANCE OF WAY EMPLOYES JOURNAL, 12050 Woodward Ave., Detroit MI 48203. Associate Editor/Director of Public Relations: R.J. Williamson. For members of international railroad workers' union who build, repair and maintain tracks, buildings and bridges. Monthly. Circ. 120,000. Previously published, photocopied and simultaneous submissions OK. Original artwork returned after publication. Free sample copy available.
Cartoons: Uses 4 cartoons/issue; buys less than 1/issue from freelancers. Receives less than 1 submission/week from freelancers. Interested in railroad/trackwork themes; single panel with gagline, b&w line drawings. Send query letter. Samples returned by SASE. Reports in 1 week. Buys one-time rights. Pays $10, b&w; on acceptance.

***BRUCE JENNER'S BETTER HEALTH & LIVING MAGAZINE**, 800 2nd Ave., New York NY 10017. (212)986-9026. Editorial Director: Julie Davis. Estab. 1985. Emphasizes health, nutrition, exercise, eating, sleeping and living for men and women, business people, ages 25-50. Bimonthly. Circ. 200,000. Does not accept previously published material. Returns original artwork after publication. Sample copy free for SASE.
Illustrations: Uses a varying number/issue. Works on assignment only. Send samples to be kept on file. Prefers tear sheets as samples. Samples not filed are returned by SASE. Does not report back. Negotiates payment and rights purchased. Pays on publication.

BUILDER MAGAZINE, Suite 475, 655 15th St. NW, Washington DC 20005. (202)737-0717. Associate Art Director: Debra A. Burkhead. Emphasizes the housing industry for the National Association of Home Builders members and subscriptions. Monthly. Circ. 185,000. Original artwork not returned after publication unless requested. Sample copy and art guidelines available.
Illustrations: Uses 4-7 illustrations/issue. Prefers b&w line drawings. Works on assignment only. Send query letter with samples to be kept on file. Call for appointment to show portfolio. Prefers tear sheets, photostats or photocopies as samples. Looks for "originality, a distinct style and creativity" when reviewing samples. Reports only if interested. Buys one-time rights. Pays $75-150, b&w; payment negotiable for color, inside. Pays on acceptance.

***BULLETIN OF THE ATOMIC SCIENTISTS**, 5801 S. Kenwood, Chicago IL 60637. (312)363-5225. Production Editor: Lisa Grayson. Emphasizes arms control; science and public affairs for audience of 40% scientists, 40% politicians and policy makers, and 20% interested, educated citizens. Monthly. Circ. 20,000. Original artwork returned after publication. Sample copy $2.50; free artist's guidelines for SASE.
Cartoons: Buys about 5-10 cartoons/issue including humorous illustrations from freelancers. Considers arms control and international relation themes. "We are looking for new ideas. Please, no mushroom clouds or death's heads." Prefers single panel without gagline; b&w line drawings. Send finished cartoons. Cartoon portfolios are not reviewed. Material returned by SASE. Reports within 1 month. Buys first rights. Pays $25, b&w; on acceptance.
Illustrations: Buys 5-8 illustrations/issue from freelancers. Considers serious b&w themes; check 1985 issues for samples. "Do not even consider sending work until you have viewed a few issues. The name of the magazine misleads artists who don't bother to check; they wind up wasting time and postage." Works on assignment only. Send query letter with brochure and samples to be kept on file, except for completely unsuitable work which is returned promptly by SASE. Artist may write or call for appointment to show portfolio but prefers mailed samples. Prefers tear sheets or photostats as samples. Samples not filed are returned by SASE. Reports within 1 month. Buys first world-wide rights. Pays $300, b&w, cover; $75/¼ page, $100/½ page, $200/full page, b&w, inside; on acceptance.

This artwork by Brad Holland, New York City, was published in the Chicago-based Bulletin of the Atomic Scientists. The illustration and a companion piece were used with a series of articles on official secrecy, says Lisa Grayson, production manager. "I admire Mr. Holland's serious, shadowy style—two qualities that seemed ideal for the subject of secrecy." The artist received $75 for first rights only.

BUSINESS & COMMERCIAL AVIATION, Hangar C-1, Westchester City Airport, White Plains NY 10604. Art Director: Mildred Stone. Technical publication for corporate pilots. Monthly. Circ. 55,000.
Illustrations: Especially needs spot art of a business-aviation nature. "We have cut back considerably on use of freelancers in the past year; hope to be able to use more in future. We generally only use artists with a fairly realistic style. This is a serious business publication—graphically conservative. We have begun a bimonthly publication for the commuter industry and another for the helicopter industry. These magazines will have a more consumer-magazine look and will feature more four-color illustration than we've used in the past. Need artists who can work on short deadline time." Query with samples. SASE. Reports in 4 weeks. Photocopies OK. Buys all rights, but may reassign rights to artist after publication.

"Thomas Cheney makes people laugh without trivializing serious subjects," says Lisa Grayson, production editor of the Bulletin of the Atomic Scientists. *"The cartoon falls within a review of a book on 'nuclear winter'; it captures, in an entertaining way, the uncertainty of military testing." Cheney, who lives in Watertown, New York, received $25 for first world rights. Grayson followed the cartoonist's work in* Chicago *magazine and* The New Yorker *prior to his involvement with the* Bulletin.

Pays on acceptance. Cover: Pays $350-1,100, color. Inside: Pays $100-500, color; $50-300, b&w. Pays $5/hour minimum, paste-up/mechanicals; local artists only. Pays $100 minimum, portraits of editors for monthly columns, printed size 2x3".
Tips: "Send or bring samples. I like to buy based more on style than whether an artist has done aircraft drawings before."

BUSINESS: NORTH CAROLINA, Suite 1450, 212 S. Tryon St., Charlotte NC 28281. (704)372-9794. Art Director: Jim Burris. Emphasizes business for businessmen and women in North Carolina with salaries above $30,000 who subscribe to one or more business magazines or tabloids. Monthly. Circ. 24,000. Accepts previously published material. Returns original artwork after publication. Sample copy free for SASE with $1 postage.
Cartoons: Seeks editorial cartoons. Prefers single panel b&w washes. Send query letter with samples of style to be kept on file. Material not filed is returned by SASE. Reports back only if interested. Buys one-time rights. Pays $100, b&w; $150, color; on publication.
Illustrations: Buys 3-4 illustrations/issue from freelancers. Prefers airbrush illustration. Works on assignment only. Send query letter with samples to be kept on file. Prefers tear sheets or slides as samples. Samples not filed are returned by SASE. Reports back only if interested. Buys one-time rights. Pays $500, color, cover; $250 for b&w and $325 for color, inside; on publication.

BUSINESS TODAY, Aaron Burr Hall, Princeton NJ 08540. (609)921-1111. Contact: Graphics Editor. For college undergraduates interested in business, politics and careers in those fields. Published 3 times/academic year. Circ. 205,000. Receives 10 cartoons and 2 illustrations/week from freelance artists. Especially needs illustrations and political cartoons. Query with samples to be kept on file; do not send originals, photocopies only. Will contact artists as needed. Previous work as magazine illustrator preferred. Reports in 2 months. Previously published, photocopied, and simultaneous submissions OK. Buys one-time, reprint or simultaneous rights. Pays on publication. Original artwork returned after publication. Sample copy $2.
Cartoons: Buys 2-3/issue on current events, education, environment, politics, business, college life and careers. "Keep the student readership in mind; *no typical scenes with executives and secretaries.*"
Illustrations: Buys 2-3/issue on current events, education, environment, politics, college life and careers. "We like the style of *The New Yorker* and op-ed cartoons in *The New York Times*." Prefers to have samples of style and topic areas covered. Provide business card and letter of inquiry to be kept on file for future assignments. Cover: Pays $50 minimum, color; $25 minimum, b&w. Inside: Pays $20 minimum, color; $10 minimum, b&w.
Tips: There is a trend toward "more quality, less quantity of artwork; we like to have artwork that says something. We need both concrete and abstract photos, as long as they are quality and in sharp focus."

C.S.P. WORLD NEWS, Box 2608, Station D, Ottawa, Ontario K1P 5W7 Canada. Contact: Guy F. Claude Hamel. Concerns book reviews and poetry. Monthly. Sample copy $2.
Cartoons and Illustrations: Buys 24/year. Needs b&w. Query on cartoons; send samples for illustrations. Reports in 1 week. Negotiates pay; pays on acceptance.

CABLE MARKETING, The Marketing/Management Magazine for Cable TV Executives, 352 Park Ave. S., New York NY 10010. (212)685-4848. Art Director: Ralph Stello. Monthly. Accepts previously published material. Sample copy free for SASE.
Illustrations: Uses 1-2 illustrations/issue; buys all from freelancers. Works on assignment only. Call or write for appointment to show portfolio; send brochure, samples, tear sheets to be kept on file. Samples not filed are returned by SASE. Reports within 4 weeks. Buys all rights. Negotiates payment. Pays on publication.

CALIFORNIA OPTOMETRY, California Optometric Association, Box 2591, Sacramento CA 95812. (916)441-3990. Managing Editor: Lynn Marlowe. Emphasizes optometry and eye care for California doctors of optometry, their staffs and spouses, optometric students. Monthly. Circ. 3,700. Original work returned after publication by request only. Art guidelines available.
Illustrations: Uses approximately 9 illustrations/year, buys all from freelancers. Works on assignment only "as pertains to our feature that month. Due to time factor, we use only local artists for these illustrations." Provide samples to be kept on file for possible future assignments. Samples not kept on file are returned by SASE. Negotiates rights purchased. Negotiates payment; pays on acceptance.

THE CALIFORNIA STATE EMPLOYEE, 1108 O St., Sacramento CA 95814. (916)444-8134. Communications Director: Keith Hearn. Emphasizes public employee labor news for 250,000 civil service and university employees. Semiannual magazine of California State Employees Association. Circ. 131,000. Previously published material OK "depending on where published." Original work not returned after publication. Free sample copy for SASE.
Cartoons: Uses 1 cartoon/issue; buys all from freelancers. Interested in themes related to job or union, any style; single, double or multi-panel with or without gagline, b&w line drawings and washes. Usually buys from work submitted on speculation. Occasionally works on assignment. Send query letter with samples of style. Samples returned by SASE. Reports in 2 weeks. Buys reprint rights. Pays $20 for single panel on spec, $50 on assignment. Negotiates on other sizes. Pays on acceptance.
Illustrations: Uses 1 illustration/issue; buys some from freelancers. Interested in any style, labor theme. Works on assignment only. Send query letter with samples of style. Provide business card, samples and tear sheets to be kept on file. Samples not kept on file are returned by SASE. Reports in 2 weeks. Buys reprint rights. Pays $30-90 inside, b&w line drawings and washes; on acceptance.

CAMPUS LIFE, 465 Gundersen Dr., Carol Stream IL 60188. Senior Editors: Gregg Lewis and Jim Long. For high school and college students. "Though our readership is largely Christian, *Campus Life* reflects the interests of all kids—music, activities, photography, and sports." Monthly. Circ. 175,000. Original artwork returned after publication. "No phone calls, please. Show us what you can do."
Cartoons: Uses 3-5 single-panel cartoons/issue plus cartoon features (assigned). Receives 5 submissions/week from freelancers. Buys 50/year on high school and college education, environment, family life, humor through youth, and politics; apply to 13-23 age groups; prefers single panel, especially vertical format. Prefers to receive finished cartoons. Reports in 4 weeks. Pays $50 minimum, b&w; on acceptance.
Illustrations: Art Director: Jeff Carnehl. Uses 2 illustrations/issue; buys all from freelancers. Receives 5 submissions/week from freelancers. Works on assignment only. Send query letter, brochure, resume and samples; sample transparencies returned by SASE, brochures and tear sheets not returned. Reporting time varies; is at least 2 weeks. Buys first North American serial rights; also considers second rights. Pays $250-400, color; $225-300, b&w; on acceptance.
Tips: "The best way to see what we can use is to ask for several sample copies ($2 each)."

CANADIAN FICTION MAGAZINE, Box 946, Station F, Toronto, Ontario M4Y 2N9 Canada. Editor: Geoffrey Hancock. Anthology devoted exclusively to contemporary Canadian fiction. Quarterly. Canadian artists or residents only. Sample copy $5.50.
Illustrations: Uses 16 pages of art/issue; also cover art. SASE (nonresidents include IRC). Reports in 4-6 weeks. Pays $10/page; $25, cover. Uses b&w line drawings, photographs.
Tips: "Portraits of contemporary Canadian writers in all genres are valuable for archival purposes."

*CANADIAN WEST, Box 3399, Langley, British Columbia V3A 4R7 Canada. Contact: G. Basque. Concerns pioneer history, primarily of Alberta, British Columbia and the Yukon. Quarterly. Circ. 5,000. Original artwork returned after publication with SASE. Sample copy $3.50.

Illustrations: Buys 4 covers/year on Canadian historical scenes. Prefers to see finished art, roughs, portfolio or sample of style. SAE (nonCanadians include International Reply Coupons). Reports in 2 weeks. Buys all rights on a work-for-hire basis. Pays $100 maximum, preferably oils. Query with samples.

CANOE, Canoe America Association, Box 597, Camden ME 04843. Senior Editor: Ginny Hostetter. Art Director: Faith Hague. "Readers are lifestyle canoeists and kayakers; they're interested in touring, camping, sailing, racing and whitewater river running." Bimonthly. Circ. 60,000. Previously published work OK (if published in unrelated or noncompeting magazine). Original artwork usually not returned after publication unless previously arranged. Free sample copy and artist's guidelines with 9x12 SASE.
Cartoons: Uses 1-2 cartoons/issue, all from freelancers. Interested in the environment, everyday canoeing, family canoe life, humor through youth, canoeing, camping, kayaking, fishing and outfitters/retailers; single panel with gagline. Prefers to see finished cartoons. SASE. Reports in 4-5 weeks. Pays $25 minimum, b&w line drawings and washes.
Illustrations: Uses 6 illustrations/issue; buys 1-2/issue from freelancers. Interested in canoeing, kayaking and camping "as fits the subject." Prefers to see finished art. Provide resume, tear sheet and samples to be kept on file for future assignments. SASE. Reports in 3-5 weeks. Buys various rights. Inside: Pays $50 minimum, b&w line drawings and gray opaques; on acceptance.
Tips: "Above all, look at recent back issues for the type of material we're currently using. As for cartoon material, it should fit in with our specialized approach to the sport of paddling . . . aimed at *paddlers*, not just a general audience."

CAR AND DRIVER, CBS Magazines, 2002 Hogback Rd., Ann Arbor MI 48104. (313)994-0055. Editor/Publisher: David E. Davis Jr. Art Director: Linda Moser. For auto enthusiasts; college-educated, professional, median 34 years of age. Monthly. Circ. 900,000 + .
Illustrations: Uses 3 illustrations/issue, all from freelancers. Receives 3 submissions/week from freelancers. Interested in autos. Works on assignment only. Provide business card and samples to be kept on file for future assignments. Samples not kept on file are returned by SASE. Reports in 2 months. Buys first rights. Cover: Pays $475 minimum, b&w; $750 minimum, color; on acceptance.
Tips: "Show inventiveness in concept and media and provide more than a rendering of a subject; we never use art that is just a rendering of a photo."

CAR CRAFT, Petersen Publishing Co., 8490 Sunset Blvd., Los Angeles CA 90069. (213)657-5100. Editor-in-Chief: Jeff Smith. Managing Editor: Tracey Hurst. Art Director: Mike Austin. "We feature articles on automotive modifications and drag racing. Monthly. Circ. 425,000. Original artwork not returned unless prior arrangement is made. Free sample copy and artist's guidelines.
Illustrations: Uses 1 or more illustrations/issue; buys 1/issue from freelancers. Interested in "automotive editorial illustration and design with a more illustrative and less technical look." Works on assignment only. Query with business card, brochure, flyer and tear sheet to be kept on file for future assignments. SASE. Reports in 2 weeks. Buys all rights on a work-for-hire basis.

CARDIOVASCULAR MEDICINE, (formerly *The Journal of Cardiovascular Medicine*), 475 Park Ave. S, New York NY 10016. (212)686-0555. Art Director: Barbara Effron. Audience: physicians. Monthly. Circ. 125,000. Original artwork returned after publication. Sample copy free for SASE.
Illustrations: Uses 2-3 medical illustrations/issue; buys all from freelancers. Works on assignment only. Send query letter with brochure and samples to be kept on file. Call or write for appointment to show portfolio. Proofs, tear sheets or slides as samples. Samples returned by SASE if not kept on file. Reports only if interested. Pays $500 maximum, color, inside; on acceptance.

CAROLINA COOPERATOR, Box 2419, Raleigh NC 27602. (919)828-4411. Managing Editor: Ken Ramey. For farm families in North and South Carolina. Monthly. Circ. 60,000. Previously published work OK. Free sample copy.
Cartoons: Rarely uses cartoons. Prefers themes on farming, outdoor/current events, education and humor through youth; single panel. Query with samples. SASE. Reports in 2 weeks. Pays $5 minimum, line drawings; on acceptance.

CARTOONS, 8490 Sunset Blvd., Los Angeles CA 90069. Contact: Dennis Ellefson. For young males who like cars and bikes. Original artwork returned after publication if requested.
Cartoons: Buys 150 pages of cartoon stories and 60 single-panel cartoons annually. Should be well-drawn, identifiable, detailed cars. Prefers to see roughs. SASE. Reports in 2-4 weeks. Pays $75 minimum/page; $15/single panel; $15, spot drawings.
Tips: "Check out the automotive scene in *Hot Rod* and *Car Craft* magazines. And then look at *Cartoons*."

CASE CURRENTS, Suite 400, 11 Dupont Circle, Washington.DC 20036. (202)328-5944. Art Director: Ellen Cohen. Emphasizes education for professionals at colleges, universities, and independent schools who work in fund raising, alumni relations and educational communications. Monthly. Circ. 12,500. Accepts previously published material. Original artwork returned after publication. Sample copy free for SASE.
Illustrations: Uses 2-3 illustrations/issue; buys all from freelancers. Uses wide variety of themes and styles, "but must be very high quality." Send query letter with brochure, business card and samples to be kept on file. Prefers photocopies only of printed work; "please no slides, photos, stats or originals. Samples not kept on file are returned by SASE. Reports only if interested. Buys first or reprint rights or negotiates. Pays $250, color, cover; $150, b&w, inside; on acceptance.
Tips: Especially seeks "concise conceptualization" in artwork. Current trends include a "simplistic, contemporary look; illustrations which are a bit looser and more 'fun.' "

CAT FANCY, Fancy Publications Inc., Box 6050, Mission Viejo CA 92690. (714)240-6001. Editor: Linda W. Lewis. For cat owners, breeders and fanciers. Readers are men and women of all ages interested in all phases of cat ownership. Monthly. Circ. 130,000. Simultaneous submissions and previously published work OK. Sample copy $3; free artist's guidelines.
Cartoons: Buys 12/year; single, double and multipanel with gagline. "Central character should be a cat." Prefers photostats or photocopies as samples. SASE. Reports in 6 weeks. Query with samples. Pays $20-50, b&w line drawings; on publication. Buys first rights.
Illustrations: Buys 12/year of domestic and wild cats. Query with resume and samples. SASE. Reports in 6 weeks. Inside: Pays $50-125, b&w line drawings; on publication. Buys first rights.
Tips: "We need good cartoons."

*CATHOLIC FORESTER, 425 W. Shuman Blvd., Naperville IL 60566. (312)983-4920. Editor: Barbara Cunningham. Magazine. "We are a fraternal insurance company but use general interest art and photos. Audience is middle-class, many small town as well as big city readers, patriotic, somewhat conservative. We are distributed nationally." Bimonthly. Circ. 150,000. Accepts previously published material. Original artwork returned after publication. Sample copy for SASE with 56¢ postage.
Cartoons: Considers "anything *funny* but it must be clean." Prefers single panel with gagline; b&w line drawings. Send query letter with roughs. Material returned by SASE. Reports within 3 months; "we try to do it sooner." Buys one-time rights or reprint rights. Pays $25, b&w; on acceptance.
Illustrations: Send query letter with samples to be kept on file; write for appointment to show portfolio. Accepts photostats, tear sheets, photocopies, slides, photographs, etc. as samples. Samples not filed are returned by SASE. Reports within 3 months. Buys one-time rights or reprint rights. Payment depends on work and negotiation with artist. "We have large and small needs, so it's impossible to say." Pays on acceptance.

CATS MAGAZINE, Box 37, Port Orange FL 32029. Editor: Linda J. Walton. Emphasizes household pet cats and show cats. Monthly. Circ. 109,000. Returns original artwork after publication on request. Sample copy and art guidelines free for SASE.
Cartoons: Buys 1 cartoon/issue from freelancers. Considers line work suitable for b&w publication with or without gaglines. Send finished cartoons to be kept on file. Material not filed is returned by SASE. Does not report back. Buys first rights. Payment varies; made on publication.
Illustrations: Buys 3-5 illustrations/issue from freelancers. Prefers cats or cat-oriented themes. Send samples; copies are not returned, originals are returned by SASE. Does not report back. Buys first rights. Payment varies; made on publication.

THE CATTLEMAN, 1301 W. Seventh St., Fort Worth TX 76102. (817)332-7155. For Southwestern cattle producers and cattlemen. Monthly. Circ. 22,000. Sample copy $1.50.
Cartoons: Contact Betsy Allen. Uses 3 cartoons/issue. Receives 10 submissions/week from freelancers. Interested in beef cattle raising and the Old West; single panel with gagline. Prefers to see finished cartoons. SASE. Reports in 1 month. Buys first North American serial rights. Pays $10 minimum, b&w line drawings; on acceptance.
Illustrations: Contact Dale Segraves, editor. Interested in beef cattle, raising cattle and horses, western art. Query with resume and samples to be kept on file. Samples not kept on file are returned by SASE. Reports in 2 weeks. Buys first North American serial rights or buys all rights on a work-for-hire basis. Cover: Pays $100 minimum, color washes. Inside: Pays $15-25, color washes and opaque watercolors; $15-20, b&w line drawings, washes and gray opaques; on acceptance.

CAVALIER, Dugent Publishing Corp., 2355 Salzedo St., Coral Gables FL 33134. Contact: Nye Willden. "For young men and college students interested in good fiction, articles and sex." Monthly. Circ. 250,000. Sample copy $2.50; free artist's guidelines. Receives 50-75 cartoons and 3-4 illustra-

tions/week from freelance artists. Original work only; no simultaneous submissions.
Cartoons: Buys 5/issue on erotica; single panel with gagline. Query with samples. SASE. Reports in 2 weeks. Buys first rights. Pays $50-100, b&w line drawings and washes; 30 days before publication.
Illustrations: Buys 3/issue on erotica and assigned themes, including some humorous and cartoon-style illustrations. Bought on assignment only. Query with samples. SASE. Reports in 2 weeks. Buys first rights. **Inside:** Pays $150 minimum, b&w line drawings and washes; $200/page, $300/spread, color washes and full-color work; 30 days before publication.
Tips: "Send 35mm slide samples of your work that art director can *keep* in his file, or tear sheets of published work. We have to have samples to refer to when making assignments. Large portfolios are difficult to handle and return. Also send samples *related* to our publication, i.e., erotica or nude studies. We are an excellent market for unpublished but very talented artists and cartoonists. Many of the top people in both fields — Mort Drucker, Peter Max, Ed Arno, Sid Harris—started with us, and many of them still work for us. Study *our* magazine for samples of acceptable material. *Do not submit* original artwork for our evaluation; slides, photos or stats only."

CHAIN STORE AGE, 425 Park Ave., New York NY 10022. (212)371-9400. Emphasizes retail stores. Readers are buyers, retail executives, merchandise managers, vice presidents of hard lines and store personnel. Monthly. Circ. 30,000.
Cartoons: Occasional use of line art *by assignment only*. Send samples of style to art director. SASE. Keeps file on artists. Pays $50-125 on publication for b&w cartoons. Buys all rights on a work-for-hire basis.
Illustrations: Uses 1-2 illustrations/issue, all from freelancers. We "keep samples on file; must be in NY area. Must see portfolio." Uses inside b&w line drawings and washes, cover color washes and pre-separated art. Send roughs, tear sheets and samples of style, and/or arrange personal appointment to show portfolio to art director. SASE. Reports in 1 week. Pays $50-125 on publication for inside b&w, $300 maximum for color cover, $150-250 for inside color. Buys all rights.

CHANGING TIMES, 1729 H St. NW, Washington DC 20006. Assistant Editor: Susan Sherry. For general, adult audience interested in personal finance, family money management and career advancement. Monthly.
Cartoons: Uses 1 cartoon/issue; buys all from freelancers. Receives 800 submissions/month from freelancers. Interested in financial topics, home budgeting, insurance, stocks, taxes, etc. or of seasonal nature. Uses 1 cartoon/month on letters to editor page. Prefers to see finished drawings. SASE. Reports in 1 month. Pays $250.

*CHAPMAN, 35 E. Claremont St., Edinburgh EH7 4HT Scotland. Editor: Joy Hendry. Emphasizes Scottish literature. Original artwork not returned after publication.
Illustrations: Uses artists for cover illustrations. Send samples. Prefers photostats as samples. Samples not filed are returned by SAE (nonresidents include IRC). Reports in 1 month. Pays by the project, $40 minimum. Considers project's budget when establishing payment. Rights purchased vary according to the project.

*CHARIOT, Ben Hur Life Association, Box 312, Crawfordsville IN 47933. Editor: Loren Harrington. Emphasizes fraternal activities and general interest for members of the Association, a fraternal life insurance benefit society. Quarterly. Circ. 11,000. Accepts previously published material. Original artwork returned after publication if requested. Sample copy free for 9x12 SASE with 88¢ postage; art guidelines for #10 SASE with 22¢ postage.
Cartoons: Rarely buys cartoons from freelancers. Considers humor and some satire. Prefers single panel with gagline; b&w line drawings or washes. Send finished cartoons to be kept on file. Material not filed is returned by SASE. Reports within 1 month. Negotiates rights purchased. Pays $1-20, b&w; on acceptance.
Illustrations: Rarely buys illustrations from freelancers but may work on assignment basis. Prefers line and wash, b&w only. Send query letter with resume and samples to be kept on file. Write for appointment to show portfolio. Accepts any type of sample that portrays quality of work. Reports in 1 month. Negotiates rights purchased and payment. Pays on acceptance.

CHARLOTTE MAGAZINE, Box 221269, Charlotte NC 28222. (704)375-8034. Editor: Terri Bryum. Emphasizes local people and local places. Monthly. Circ. 20,000. Original artwork returned after publication, if requested. Free sample copy and art guidelines.
Illustrations: Usually 3-4/issue; buys all from freelancers. Format: b&w line drawings, and b&w graphic art. Works on assignment only after acceptance of thumbnail or rough. Arrange appointment to show portfolio to editor. Buys first rights. Pays $35-75, b&w; 30 days after publication.

CHESS LIFE, 186 Route 9W, New Windsor NY 12550. (914)562-8350. Art Director: Bruce R. Helm. Official publication of the United States Chess Federation. Contains news of major chess events with special emphasis on American players, plus columns of instruction, general features, historical articles, personality profiles, cartoons, quizzes, humor and short stories. Monthly. Circ. 50,000. Accepts previously published material and simultaneous submissions. Original artwork returned after publication. Sample copy for SASE with $1.07 postage; art guidelines for SASE with 22¢ postage.
Cartoons: Uses 1-3 cartoons/issue; buys all from freelancers. All cartoons must have a chess motif. Prefers single panel, with gagline; b&w line drawings. Send query letter with samples of style or roughs. "We may keep a few cartoons on hand, but most are either bought or returned." Material not kept on file returned by SASE. Reports within 2-4 weeks. Negotiates rights purchased. Pays $10-25, b&w; on acceptance.
Illustrations: Uses 2-4 illustrations/issue; buys 1-2 illustrations/issue from freelancers. All must have a chess motif; uses some humorous and occasionally cartoon-style illustrations. "We use mainly b&w." Works on assignment, but will also consider unsolicited work. Send query letter with samples or tear sheets to be kept on file. Prefers photostats or original work for b&w; slides for color, as samples. Reports within 4 weeks. Negotiates rights purchased. Pays by the project, $25-150 average. Pays on acceptance.
Tips: "I look for work that is clean, well-executed, well thought out and that which will reproduce well in print."

CHIC, Larry Flynt Publications, Suite 3800, 2029 Century Park E., Los Angeles CA 90067. (213)556-9200. Cartoon/Humor Editor: Dwaine Tinsley. For affluent men, 25-30 years of age, college-educated and interested in current affairs, luxuries, investigative reporting, entertainment, sports, sex and fashion. Monthly. Returns original art.
Cartoons: Publishes 20/month; 10 full-page color, 4 color spots and 6 b&w spots. Receives 300-500 cartoons from freelancers. Especially needs "outrageous material. Mainly sexual, but politics, sports OK. Topical humor and seasonal/holiday cartoons good." Mail samples. Prefers 8½x11" size; avoid crayons, chalks or fluorescent colors. Also avoid, if possible, large, heavy illustration board. Samples returned by SASE only. Place name, address and phone number on back of each cartoon. Reports in 3 weeks. Buys first rights with first right to reprint. Pays $150, full page color; $75 spot color; $50 spot b&w. Pays on acceptance.
Tips: Especially needs more cartoons, cartoon breakaways or one-subject series. "Send outrageous humor—work that other magazines would shy away from. Pertinent, political, sexual, whatever. We are constantly looking for new artists to complement our regular contributors and contract artists. An artist's best efforts stand the best chance for acceptance!"

CHICAGO, 3 Illinois Center., Chicago IL 60601. (312)565-5100. Editor-in-Chief: Allen H. Kelson. Editorial Director: Don Gold. Art Director: Bob Post. For active, well-educated, high-income residents of Chicago's metropolitan area concerned with quality of life and seeking insight or guidance into diverse aspects of urban/suburban life. Monthly. Circ. 220,000. Original artwork returned after publication.
Cartoons: Uses 8 cartoons/issue, all from freelancers. Receives 90 submissions/week from freelancers. Interested in "social commentary, urban life, arts and dining." Single panel. Line preferred; halftones and washes OK. Prefers to receive finished cartoons. SASE. Reports in 6 weeks. Buys first North American serial rights. Minimum payment: $100, b&w.
Illustrations: Uses 12-16 illustrations/year. all from freelancers. Interested in "subjective approach often, but depends on subject matter." Works on assignment only. Query with resume, business card, brochure, flyer and samples to be kept on file. Accepts finished art, roughs, transparencies or tear sheets as samples. Samples not filed are returned by SASE. Reports in 4 weeks. Buys first North American serial rights. Negotiates pay for covers, color-separated and reflective art. Inside: Pays $450 minimum, color; $250 minimum, b&w ($75 for spot illustrations); on publication.

CHILD LIFE, 1100 Waterway Blvd., Box 567, Indianapolis IN 46206. (317)636-8881. Art Director: Edward F. Cortese. For children 7-9. Monthly except bimonthly February/March, April/May, June/July and August/September. Receives 3-4 submissions/week from freelance artists. Sample copy 75¢.
Illustrations: Buys 120-180/year on assigned themes. Especially needs health-related (exercise, safety, nutrition, etc.) themes, and stylized and realistic styles of children 7-9 years old. Mail art or query with samples. Especially looks for an artist's ability to draw well consistently. SASE. Reports in 3 weeks. Buys all rights. Cover: pays $175/illustration, color. Inside: pays for illustration by the job, $30-70 (4-color), $30-50 (2-color), $25-35 (b&w); on publication. "All work is considered work for hire."
Tips: Trends in the field include "updates on realistic illustrations of people and stylized illustrations. Changes in our operation include that we have six 4-color pages inside and a 4-color cover, and b&w and 2-color only inside." Artists should "obtain copies of current issues to insure proper submission of art styles needed."

CHILDREN'S DIGEST, Box 567, Indianapolis IN 46206. (317)636-8881. Art Director: Lisa A. Nelson. Special emphasis on health, nutrition, safety and exercise for boys and girls 8-10 years of age. Monthly except bimonthly February/March, April/May, June/July and August/September. Accepts previously published material and simultaneous submissions. Sample copy 75¢; art guidelines free for SASE.
Illustrations: Uses 25-35 illustrations/issue. Works on assignment only. Send query letter with brochure, resume, samples and tear sheets to be kept on file. Write for appointment to show portfolio. Prefers photostats, slides and good photocopies as samples. Samples returned by SASE if not kept on file. Reports within 1 week. Buys all rights. Pays $175, color, cover; $35 b&w; $50 2-color; $70 4-color, inside. Pays on acceptance. "All artwork is considered work for hire."
Tips: Likes to see situation and story-telling illustrations with more than 1 figure. When reviewing samples, especially looks for artists' ability to bring a story to life with their illustrations. "Contemporary artists, by and large, are more experimental in the use of their mediums and are achieving a greater range of creativity. We are aware of this, and welcome the artist who can illustrate a story that will motivate a casual viewer to read."

CHILDREN'S PLAYMATE, Box 567, Indianapolis IN 46206. (317)636-8881. Editorial Director: Beth Wood Thomas. Art Director: Linda Simmons. For ages 5-7; special emphasis on health, nutrition, exercise and safety. Published 8 times/year. Sample copy sent if artist's work might be used.
Illustrations: Uses 25-35 illustrations/issue; buys 10-20 from freelancers. Receives 3-4 submissions/week from freelancers. Interested in "stylized, humorous, realistic themes; also nature and health." Especially needs b&w and 2-color artwork for line or halftone reproduction; text and full-color cover art. Works on assignment only. Prefers to see portfolio and samples of style. SASE. Provide brochure, flyer, tear sheet, stats or good photocopies of sample art to be kept on file. Buys all rights on a work-for-hire basis. Minimum payment: Cover: $175, color. Inside: b&w, $35/page; 2-color, $50/page; full-color, $70/page. Will also consider b&w art, camera-ready for puzzles, such as dot-to-dot, hidden pictures, crosswords, etc. Payment will vary. "All artwork is considered work for hire."
Tips: There is now "a greater concentration on health related subjects" in the magazine. Artists should "take the time to examine our publications."

***CHINA PAINTER**, 3111 N.W. 19th, Oklahoma City OK 73107. (405)943-3841. Founder/Trustee: Pauline Salyer. Emphasizes porcelain china painting for those interested in the fine art. Bimonthly. Circ. 9,000. Original artwork returned after publication. Sample copy $2.75 plus 95¢ postage.
Illustrations: Send query letter. Prefers art designs in color or photographs of hand painted porcelain china art as samples. Samples returned by SASE only if requested.

THE CHRISTIAN CENTURY, 407 S. Dearborn St., Chicago IL 60605. (312)427-5380. Advertising/Production Manager: Kathleen Wind. Emphasizes religion and comments on social, political and religious subjects; includes news of current religious scene, book reviews, humor. Weekly. Circ. 38,000. Original artwork not returned after publication. Sample copy free for SASE.
Cartoons: Occasionally uses cartoons. Prefers social, political, religious issues. Prefers single panel with gagline; b&w line drawings. Send query letter with finished cartoons to be kept on file unless "we can't possibly use them." Material not filed is returned only if requested. Reports only if interested. Buys all rights. Pays $15-20, b&w; on publication.
Illustrations: Uses 4 illustrations/issue; buys 1 from freelancers. Prefers religious and general scenes, people at various activities, books. Send query letter with samples to be kept on file. Prefers photocopies or original work as samples. Samples not filed are returned by SASE. Reports only if interested. Buys all rights. Pays $50, cover and $15, inside b&w; on publication.

CHRISTIAN HERALD, 40 Overlook Dr., Chappaqua NY 10514. (914)769-9000. Associate Editor: Gerald M. Wisz. Emphasizes evangelical Christianity for middle income, theologically conservative readers. Monthly. Circ. 200,000. Original artwork usually returned after publication. Receives 1 cartoon and 3 illustrations/week from freelance artists. Sample copy $2.
Cartoons: Rarely uses cartoons.
Illustrations: Uses 2 illustrations/issue; buys all from freelancers. Prefers pen & ink, airbrush, washes, oils, acrylics; "pencil drawings are unacceptable." Works on assignment only. Send samples of style. Provide samples and tear sheets to be kept on file for possible future assignments. Samples not kept on file are returned by SASE. Reports in 6 weeks. Negotiates rights purchased. Pays $25-150 inside, b&w line drawings or b&w washes; $75-200 inside, color washes; after acceptance.
Tips: "Striving for higher quality in our line art—seeking a more contemporary look. Send samples of published work or slides of original art. Include resume and rates, telling how much lead time needed."

***CHRISTIAN HOME & SCHOOL**, 3350 E. Paris Ave. SE, Grand Rapids MI 49508. (616)957-1070. Assistant Editor: Kimberley D. Paxton. Emhasizes current, crucial issues affecting the Christian

home for parents who support Christian education. Published 8 times/year. Circ. 13,000. Original artwork returned after publication. Sample copy free for SASE with 75¢ postage; art guidelines free for SASE with 22¢ postage.
Illustrations: Buys approximately 2 illustrations/issue from freelancers. Prefers family or school life themes. Works on assignment only. Send query letter with resume and samples. Prefers tear sheets, photocopies or photographs as samples. Samples returned by SASE. Reports only if interested. Buys first rights. Pays on publication.

THE CHRISTIAN MINISTRY, 407 S. Dearborn St., Chicago IL 60605. (312)427-5380. For the professional clergy (primarily liberal Protestant). Bimonthly. Circ. 12,000.
Cartoons: Buys 6 cartoons/issue on religious subjects. Send roughs or finished artwork. SASE. Reports in 1 week. Pays $15 minimum, b&w; on publication.

*THE CHRONICLE OF THE HORSE, Box 46, Middleburg VA 22117. Editor: Peter Winants. Emphasizes horses and English horse sports for dedicated competitors who ride, show and enjoy horses. Weekly. Circ. 21,000. Accepts previously published material. Sample copy available.
Cartoons: Buys 1-2 cartoons/issue from freelancers. Considers anything about English riding and horses. Prefers single panel with or without gagline; b&w line drawings or b&w washes. Send query letter with finished cartoons to be kept on file. Material not filed is returned. Reports within 2 weeks. Buys first rights. Pays $20, b&w; on publication.
Illustrations: "We use a work of art on our cover every week. The work must feature horses, but the medium is unimportant. We do not pay for this art, but we always publish a short blurb on the artist and his or her equestrian involvement, if any." Send query letter with samples to be kept on file. If accepted, insists on high-quality, b&w 8x10 photographs of the original artwork. Samples are returned. Reports within 2 weeks.

CHURCH MANAGEMENT—THE CLERGY JOURNAL, Box 1625, Austin TX 78767. (512)327-8501. Editor: Manfred Holck Jr. For professional clergy and church business administrators. Circ. 20,000. Original artwork returned after publication. Monthly (except June and December).
Cartoons: Uses 4 single panel cartoons/issue on religious themes. SASE. Reports in 2 months. Pays $10, b&w; on publication.

THE CHURCHMAN, 1074 23rd Ave. N., St. Petersburg FL 33704. (813)894-0097. Editor: Edna Ruth Johnson. Published 9 times/year. Circ. 10,000. Original artwork returned after publication. Sample copy available.
Cartoons: Uses 2-3 cartoons/issue. Interested in religious, political and social themes. Prefers to see finished cartoons. SASE. Reports in 1 week. Pays on acceptance.
Illustrations: Uses 2-3 illustrations/issue. Interested in themes with "social implications." Prefers to see finished art. Provide tear sheet to be kept on file for future assignments. SASE. Reports in 1 week. Pays $5, b&w spot drawings; on acceptance.
Tips: "Read current events news so you can apply it humorously."

CINCINNATI MAGAZINE, Suite 300, 35 E. 7th St., Cincinnati OH 45202. (513)421-4300. Editor: Laura Pulfer. Art Director: Kay Ritchie. Emphasizes Cincinnati living. For college-educated, ages 25+ with an excess of $35,000 incomes. Monthly. Circ. 30,000. Previously published and simultaneous submissions OK. Original artwork returned after publication. Buys all rights. Pays on acceptance.
Cartoons: Uses 2 cartoons/issue, all from freelancers. Receives 3 submissions/week from freelancers. Interested in current events, education and politics; single panel. Send finished cartoons. SASE. Reports in 3 weeks. Buys all rights on a work-for-hire basis. Pays $15-25, b&w washes; on acceptance.
Illustrations: Uses 3 illustrations/issue, all from freelancers. Receives 3 illustrations/week from freelance artists. Buys cover art and article illustrations on assigned themes. Works on assignment only. Prefers to see portfolio or samples of style. Samples returned by SASE. Provide resume and brochure to be kept on file. Reports in 3 weeks. Buys all rights on a work-for-hire basis.

CINEFANTASTIQUE, Box 270, Oak Park IL 60303. Editor-in-chief: Frederick S. Clarke. Editor: Michael Kaplan. Emphasizes science fiction, horror and fantasy films for "devotees of 'films of the imagination.' " Bimonthly. Circ. 20,000. Original artwork not returned after publication. Sample copy $6.
Cartoons: Uses 0-1 cartoon/issue; buys all from freelancers. Interested in a variety of themes suited to magazine's subject matter; formats vary. Send query letter with resume and samples of style. Samples not returned. Reports in 3-4 weeks. Buys all rights. Pays $75/page or proportionally for fraction thereof; b&w; on publication.
Illustrations: Uses 1-2 illustrations/issue; buys all from freelancers. Interested in "dynamic, powerful styles, though not limited to a particular look." Works on assignment only. Send query letter with re-

sume, brochure and samples of style to be kept on file. Samples not returned. Reports in 3-4 weeks. Buys all rights. Pays $75 maximum, inside b&w line drawings; $75 maximum, inside b&w washes; $150 maximum, cover color washes; $75 maximum, inside color washes; on publication.

CIRCLE K MAGAZINE, 3636 Woodview Trace, Indianapolis IN 46268. Contact: Production Editor. "Our readership consists almost entirely of college students interested in the concept of voluntary service. They are politically and socially aware and have a wide range of interests." Published 5 times/year. Circ. 12,000.
Cartoons: Buys "minimal" number cartoons/issue on campus, young lifestyle humor. Send finished artwork. SASE. Reports in 2 weeks. Negotiates pay; pays on acceptance.
Illustrations: Buys 1 illustration/issue; assigned according to feature needs. Query with samples. SASE. Reports in 2 weeks. Negotiates pay; pays on acceptance.

CIVIL WAR TIMES ILLUSTRATED, 2245 Kohn Rd., Box 8200, Harrisburg PA 17105. (717)657-9555. Art Director: Geanne Collins. For the general public interested in well-researched historical articles. Monthly except July and August. Circ. 120,000.
Illustrations: Buys American history (1861-1865) themes. Query with samples (photostats of historical illustration work) to be kept on file. Provide rates and deadline requirements with work samples. SASE. Works on assignment only. Reports in 4 weeks. Pays $10-200, b&w or color; on acceptance or publication.
Tips: "Please send photostatic samples of historical illustration work, to be kept on file. We accept no unsolicited submissions. All freelance work is on assignment. All freelancers should provide their rates and deadline requirements with work samples. We use no cartoons."

CLAVIER, 200 Northfield Rd., Northfield IL 60093. Editor: Barbra Barlow Kreader. For teachers and students of keyboard instruments. Published 10 times/year. Buys all rights. Pays on publication for articles. Sample copy available with magazine-sized SASE.
Cartoons: Buys 10-20/year on music, mostly keyboard music. Receives 1 set of cartoons/week from freelance artists. Pays $15 on acceptance.

CLEANING MANAGEMENT, Harris Communications, 17911-C Sky Park Blvd., Irvine CA 92714. (714)261-7192. Editor-in-Chief/Art Director: R.D. Harris, Jr. Managing Editor: Teri Fivecoat-Wilhelm. For managers of in-plant cleaning maintenance crews. Monthly. Circ. 33,000. Query with samples. SASE. Receives 2-3 cartoons and 1-2 illustrations/week from freelance artists. Especially needs cover illustrations. Reports in 3 weeks. Simultaneous submissions OK. Buys first rights. Pays on publication. Free sample copy.
Cartoons: Buys 2-3/issue; single and multipanel with gaglines. Pays $10-15, b&w line drawings.
Illustrations: Just beginning to use illustrations on the custodial field. Pays $25-50, b&w; $20-300, color.
Tips: "Slant cartoons toward our market."

*CLEARWATER NAVIGATOR, 112 Market St., Poughkeepsie NY 12603. (914)454-7673. Graphics Coordinator: Nora Porter. Emphasizes sailing and environmental matters for middle-upper income Easterners with a strong concern for environmental issues. Bimonthly. Circ. 8,000. Accepts previously published material. Original artwork returned after publication. Sample copy free with SASE.
Cartoons: Buys 1 cartoon/issue from freelancers. Prefers editorial lampooning—environmental themes. Prefers single panel with gaglines; b&w line drawings. Send query letter with samples of style to be kept on file. Material not filed is returned only if requested. Reports within 1 month. Buys first rights. Pays negotiable rate, b&w; on publication.

CLEVELAND MAGAZINE, 1621 Euclid Ave., Cleveland OH 44115. (216)771-2833. City magazine emphasizing local news and information. Monthly. Circ. 60,000.
Illustrations: Buys 3-4 editorial or technical illustrations/issue on assigned themes. Especially needs editorial illustrations on assigned themes basically dealing with local politics; sometimes uses humorous or cartoon-style illustrations. Call for appointment. Prefers to see resume. SASE. Reports in 2 weeks. Pays $100/page, b&w; $150/page, color; on publication.
Tips: "Artists used on the basis of talent; no experience criteria. We use many talented college graduates just starting out in the field. We do not publish gag cartoons, but do print editorial illustrations with a humorous twist. Full page editorial illustrations usually deal with local politics and media personalities."

CLIFTON MAGAZINE, 204 Tangeman University Center, University of Cincinnati, Cincinnati OH 45221. (513)475-6379. Editor-in-Chief: David Thiel. General interest publication for the university community and neighborhood. Published 3 times/academic year. Circ. 7,000. Copy available for SASE.

Debora Weber of Narberth, Pennsylvania, created this "drama club in action" cover illustration for Club-house, a magazine for children aged nine to fifteen which is published in Berrien Springs, Michigan. Elaine Meseraull, editor, chose Weber for the assignment because of her "fresh, contemporary style which is highly appealing to children, and the feeling of fun her artwork conveys."

Illustrations: Contact Art Director. Uses illustrations and photography for feature stories; art photos published. Reports in 6-8 weeks. Acquires first serial rights.

*CLUBHOUSE, Box 15, Berrien Springs MI 49103. (616)471-9009. Editor: Elaine Meseraull. Magazine emphasizing stories, puzzles and illustrations for children ages 9-15. Published 10 times/year. Circ. 17,000. Accepts previously published material. Returns original artwork after publication if requested. Sample copy for SASE with 56¢ postage.
Cartoons: Buys 2/issue. Prefers animals, kids and family situation themes; single panel with gagline; b&w line drawings. Accepts previously published material. Pays $10-12 on acceptance.
Illustrations: Buys 19-20/issue on assignment only. Assignments made on basis of samples on file. Send query letter with photocopied samples to be kept on file. Tear sheets or original art will be photocopied and returned by SASE within 1 month. Usually buys one-time rights. Pays according to published size: $30 b&w cover; $25 full page; $18 half page; $15 third page; $12 quarter page; $7.50 spots, b&w inside; on acceptance.

COACHING REVIEW, 333 River Rd., Ottawa, Ontario K1L 8H9 Canada. (613)746-0036. Editor: Vic MacKenzie. Emphasizes volunteer as well as paid sports coaching. Bimonthly. Circ. 15,000. Receives 2-3 cartoons and 2-3 illustrations/week from freelance artists. Especially needs good practical applied information that is original; creative illustration; sport specific and life-like illustration. Original artwork returned after publication. Free sample copy.
Cartoons: Uses 4 cartoons/issue, all from freelancers. Interested in coaching-related situations. Format: single panel b&w line drawings with or without gaglines. Prefers to see roughs and resume. Reports in 2 weeks. Pays on publication. Buys one-time rights.
Illustrations: Uses 6 illustrations/issue, all by freelancers. Illustrations should be in the style of "crea-

tive realism . . . depicting athletes in action." Format: color washes for cover and inside; b&w line drawings for inside. Prefers to see portfolio and samples of style. Provide resume and brochure to be kept on file for future assignments. Reports in 2 weeks. Pays $250-500, color cover; $100-250, inside b&w; on publication.

Tips: There is a trend toward "realistic illustration showing coaching techniques."

COBBLESTONE MAGAZINE, 20 Grove St., Peterborough NH 03458. (603)924-7209. Editor: Carolyn Yoder. Emphasizes American history; features stories, supplemental nonfiction, fiction, biographies, plays, activities, poetry for children between 8 and 14. Monthly. Circ. 45,000. Accepts previously published material and simultaneous submissions. Sample copy $2.95. Material must relate to theme of issue; subjects/topics published in guidelines which are free with SASE.

Illustrations: Uses variable number of illustrations/issue; buys 1-2/issue from freelancers. Prefers historical theme as it pertains to a specific feature. Works on assignment only. Send query letter with brochure, resume, business card, samples or tear sheets to be kept on file. Call or write for appointment to show portfolio. Prefers photocopies as samples. Samples not kept on file are returned by SASE. Buys all rights. Payment varies. Artists should request illustration guidelines. Pays on publication.

Tips: "Study issues of the magazine for style used. Send samples and update samples once or twice a year to help keep your name and work fresh in our minds."

COINS MAGAZINE, 700 E. State St., Iola WI 54990. (715)445-2214. Assistant to the Publisher: Bob Lemke. Emphasizes coin collecting as a hobby or business for collectors of all forms of coins, paper money, medals, etc. Monthly. Circ. 90,000. Previously published material and simultaneous submissions OK. Original artwork not returned after publication. Free sample copy for SASE.

Cartoons: Buys 2-3/issue from freelancers. Prefers b&w line drawings; single panel with gagline. Send roughs with samples of style. Samples returned by SASE. Reports in 2 weeks. Buys first rights and reprint rights. Pays $5, b&w; on acceptance.

Illustrations: Buys 1-2/issue from freelancers. Works on assignment only. Provide brochure and samples to be kept on file. Reports in 2 weeks. Buys first rights and reprint rights. Pays $10-50, inside b&w line drawings; $10-50, inside b&w washes; $75-200, cover color washes; $25-100, inside color washes; on acceptance.

COLLECTIBLE AUTOMOBILE MAGAZINE, 3841 W. Oakton St., Skokie IL 60076. (312)676-3470. Publications Director: Frank E. Peiler. Estab. 1984. Emphasizes collectible cars, 1930-present. Bimonthly. Circ. 100,000. Sometimes returns original artwork after publication. Sample copy $2.10; art guidelines available.

Cartoons: Prefers single panel with or without gagline; color washes. Send samples of styles or roughs to be kept on file. Material not filed is returned only if requested. Reports back only if interested. Buys all rights. Payment varies; pays on acceptance.

Illustrations: Works on assignment only. Send query letter and samples to be kept on file. Write or call for appointment to show portfolio. Prefers slides or photographs as samples. Samples not filed are returned only if requested. Reports back only if interested. Buys all rights. Payment varies; pays on acceptance.

COLLEGIATE MICROCOMPUTER, Rose-Hulman Institute of Technology, Terre Haute IN 47803. (812)877-1511. Managing Editor: Brian J. Winkel. Premier issue 1983. Emphasizes uses of microcomputers in *all* areas of college life, teaching, administration, residence, recreation, etc. for college libraries, college faculty and college students. Quarterly. Circ. 5,000 planned. Original artwork returned after publication. Accepts previously published material and simultaneous submissions.

Cartoons: Plans to use 8-10 cartoons/issue. Prefers activities surrounding microcomputers and the educational environment—spoofs of uses—as themes. Prefers single, double, or multipanel, with or without gagline; b&w line drawings or b&w washes. Query with samples of style, roughs or finished cartoons to be kept on file. Material not kept on file is returned by SASE. Reports within 2 weeks. Negotiates rights purchased and payment. Pays on acceptance.

COLLISION, Box M, Franklin MA 02038. (617)528-6211. Audience is autobody repair, dealers and towing companies for management in small businesses. Published 8 times/year. Circ. 21,000. Accepts previously published material. Sample copy $2 (postage); guidelines free.

Cartoons: Buys 4 cartoons/issue. Prefers themes that are "positive or corrective attitudes." Considers single panel with gagline; b&w line drawings. Send roughs or finished cartoons. Material is returned by SASE. Reports within 2 weeks. Buys first rights and reprint rights. Pays $12.50/cartoon for b&w line art; on acceptance.

Illustrations: Buys 1 illustration/issue from freelancers. Themes and styles depend on editorial content (1 year advance). Send query letter with samples. Prefers originals or photocopies as samples. Samples are returned. Reports within 2 weeks. Buys first rights and reprint rights. Pays $25 and up for b&w inside; on acceptance.

COLUMBIA, Drawer 1670, New Haven CT 06507. (203)772-2130, ext. 263-64. Editor: Elmer Von Feldt. Art Director: John Cummings. Fraternal magazine of the Knights of Columbus; indepth interviews on family life, social problems, education, current events and apostolic activities as seen from the Catholic viewpoint. Monthly. Circ. 1,374,257. Original artwork not returned after publication. Buys all rights. Sample copy available.
Cartoons: Uses 3 cartoons/issue; buys all from freelancers. Interested in pungent, captionless humor. Send roughs or finished cartoons to be kept on file. SASE. Reports in 2 weeks. Buys all rights. Pays $50; on acceptance.
Illustrations: Uses 1 cover illustration/issue; buys all from freelancers. Send query letter with samples to be kept on file for future assignments. Prefers photostats, tear sheets or photographs as samples. SASE. Reports in 4 weeks. Buys all rights. Pays $1,000, full-color cover design; on acceptance.

COLUMBUS MONTHLY, Columbus Monthly Publishing Corp., 171 E. Livingston Ave., Columbus OH 43215. (614)464-4567. Editor: Max S. Brown. Design Director: Sanford Meisel. Regional/city publication. Emphasizes subjects of general interest primarily to Columbus and central Ohio. Circ. 40,000. Sample copy $1.75.
Illustrations: Uses 4-6 illustrations/month; buys most from freelancers. Interested in contemporary editorial illustration. Works on assignment only. Samples not returned. Provide resume, business card, letter of inquiry and brochure to be kept on file for future assignments. Prefers to see portfolio (finished art). SASE. Reports in 6 weeks. Buys all rights on a work-for-hire basis. Cover: Pays $200-350, color washes and full-color art. Inside: Pays $60 minimum, b&w line drawings and washes.

*COMMONWEAL, 232 Madison Ave., New York NY 10016. (212)683-2042. Editor: Peter Steinfels. National journal published by Catholic laypeople emphasizing political, social, cultural and religious issues. Biweekly. Circ. 18,000. Accepts previously published material. Original artwork not returned after publication.
Cartoons: Buys 0-1 cartoon/issue from freelancers. Prefers single panel without gagline; b&w line drawings. Send finished cartoons to be kept on file. Material not filed is not returned. Reports only if interested. Buys one-time rights. Pays $10-15, b&w; on publication.
Illustrations: Buys 0-1 illustration/issue from freelancers. Prefers political/social/religious themes; simple drawings. Send query letter with samples to be kept on file. Prefers tear sheets or photocopies as samples. Samples not filed are not returned. Reports only if interested. Buys one-time rights. Pays $25, cover and $10-15, inside, b&w; on publication.

*COMMUNICATION WORLD, %IABC, Suite 940, 870 Market St., San Francisco CA 94102. (415)433-3400. Managing Editor: Gloria Gordon. Emphasizes communication, public relations (international) for members of International Association of Business Communicators: corporate and nonprofit businesses, hospitals, government communicators, universities, etc. who publish internal and external publications, press releases, annual reports and customer magazines. Monthly. Circ. 17,000. Accepts previously published material. Original artwork returned after publication. Sample copy available.
Cartoons: Buys 1-5 cartoons/issue from freelancers. Considers international communication and publication themes. Prefers single panel with or without gagline; b&w line drawings or washes. Send query letter with samples of style or finished cartoons to be kept on file; write or call for appointment to show portfolio. Material not filed is returned only if requested. Reports only if interested. Buys first rights, one-time rights or reprint rights; negotiates rights purchased. Pays $25-50, b&w; on publication.
Illustrations: Buys 3-10 illustrations/issue from freelancers. Theme and style are compatible to individual article. Send query letter with samples to be kept on file; write or call for appointment to show portfolio. Accepts photostats, tear sheets, photocopies, slides or photographs as samples. Samples not filed are returned only if requested. Reports only if interested. Buys first rights, one-time rights or reprint rights; negotiates rights purchased. Pays $175, b&w and $250, color, cover; $150, b&w and $200, color, inside; on publication.

COMPUTER DECISIONS, 10 Mulholland Dr., Hasbrouck Heights NJ 07604. Art Director: Bonnie Meyer. For computer-involved management in industry, finance, academia, etc.; well-educated, sophisticated and highly paid. Monthly. Circ. 175,000.
Illustrations: Buys 5-8/issue. Assigned to illustrate columns and some feature stories. Works on assignment only. Prefers to see portfolio or samples of style. Provide brochure or sample tear sheet to be kept on file for future assignments. Reports in 1 week. Buys all rights. Negotiates pay.
Tips: "Chartists with good ideas needed. No cartoons—realistic, slick drawings/renderings only."

COMPUTER MERCHANDISING, Eastman Publishing, #222, 15720 Ventura Blvd., Encino CA 91436. (818)995-0436. Creative Director: Judi Slapin. Emphasizes computers; "we publish trade magazines directed to reach retailers of high-technology products." Semimonthly. Circ. 25,000. Accepts previously published material. Does not return original artwork after publication.
Illustrations: Buys 10-15 illustrations/issue from freelancers. Prefers pen & ink, airbrush, watercolor. Works on assignment only. Send brochure and samples to be kept on file. Call for appointment to show portfolio. Prefers tear sheets, photostats or photocopies as samples. Samples not filed are not returned. Reports back only if interested. Buys all rights. Pays $75 for b&w and $125 for color, inside; on publication.

COMPUTERS-R-DIGITAL, Box 8669, Red Bank NJ 07701. (201)291-1208. Publisher: John B. Runyon. Emphasizes Digital Equipment computers for executives, managers, senior technicians. Monthly. Circ. 15,000. Sometimes accepts previously published material. Returns original artwork after publication. Sample copy free for SASE with $5 postage; art guidelines free for SASE with 50¢ postage.
Cartoons: Buys 1 cartoon/issue from freelancers. Seeks themes with appropriate feminine subjects and DEC computers; cartoons and comic strips of hardware, software, etc. Prefers b&w line drawings. Send query letter with samples of style to be kept on file; write for appointment to show portfolio. Material not filed is returned by SASE. Reports within 1 month. Negotiates rights purchased. Artist specifies payment; pays on publication if requested.
Illustrations: Buys 1 illustration/issue from freelancers. Seeks themes with appropriate feminine subjects and DEC computer systems. Send query letter with brochure and samples to be kept on file; write for appointment to show portfolio. Accepts any type of sample. Samples not filed are returned by SASE. Reports within 1 month. Negotiates rights purchased. Artist specifies payment; pays on publication.

CONNECTICUT MAGAZINE, 636 Kings Hwy., Fairfield CT 06430. (203)576-1207. Art Director: Lori Bruzinski Wendin. Emphasizes issues and entertainment in Connecticut for "upscale, 40-50's, Connecticut residents." Monthly. Circ. 66,000. Accepts previously published material. Original artwork returned after publication.
Illustrations: Uses 1-3 illustrations/issue; buys all from freelancers. Works on assignment only. Send query letter with brochure, business card, samples or tear sheets to be kept on file. Call for appointment to show portfolio. Samples not filed are not returned. Pays $75-300, color, cover; $200-600, b&w, $75-300, color, inside; on publication.

CONSERVATIVE DIGEST, 7777 Leesburg Pike, Falls Church VA 22043. (703)893-1411. Publisher: Richard Viguerie. Contact: Marla Mernin. Concerns activities and political issues for "new right" conservatives. Circ. 40,000. Monthly. Simultaneous submissions and previously published work OK. Original artwork returned after publication. Buys one-time and reprint rights. Sample copy $2.25.
Cartoons: Uses 6 cartoons/issue. Receives 80 submissions/week from freelancers and syndicates. Interested in current events and politics (conservative view). Send finished cartoons or veloxes. SASE. Reports in 3 weeks. Buys reprint rights. Pays $15-100, b&w line drawings; on publication.

CONSTRUCTION DIMENSIONS, 25 K St. NE, Washington DC 20002. (202)783-2925. Editor/Publisher: Gerald L. Wykoff. Emphasizes construction for members of the Association of Wall & Ceiling Contractors-International. Monthly. Circ. 10,000. Previously published material and simultaneous submissions OK. Original artwork not returned after publication. Free sample copy for SASE.
Cartoons: Number of cartoons used per issue varies. Interested in themes that pertain to construction business, with emphasis on wall-and-ceiling specialty; also, political, government, small business oriented; single, b&w line drawings. Send photocopies of finished cartoons. Reports in 2 weeks. Negotiates rights purchased. Pays on acceptance.
Tips: "One cartoonist (bless him) has a series of his cartoons printed front and back on an 8½x11 sheet and I can contact him on those I want (thus saving me the trouble of returning, etc.). He says a quick print house costs only a few dollars—and gets him more personal contacts, saves money on SASEs, and assures better payment on the things he wants (plus he saves the original art). Especially valuable idea for small-staff magazines where the administrative manpower is lacking. I'm now using computers to generate graphs (3D) and charts. Because the line is standard, I depend on artists for the personality of the art—India inks, scribble drawings, heavy vs. light lines, etc."

CONSTRUCTION EQUIPMENT OPERATION AND MAINTENANCE, Construction Publications, Inc., Box 1689, Cedar Rapids IA 52406. (319)366-1597. Editor-in-Chief: C.K. Parks. Concerns heavy construction and industrial equipment for contractors, machine operators, mechanics and local government officials involved with construction. Bimonthly. Circ. 67,000. Simultaneous submissions OK. Original artwork not returned after publication. Free sample copy.
Cartoons: Uses 8-10 cartoons/issue, all from freelancers. Interested in themes "related to heavy con-

struction industry" or "cartoons that make contractors and their employees 'look good' and feel good about themselves"; multipanel. Send finished cartoons. SASE. Reports in 2 weeks. Buys all rights, but may reassign rights to artist after publication. Pays $10-15, b&w.
Illustrations: Uses 20 + illustrations/issue; "very few" are from freelancers. Pays $80-125; on acceptance.

THE CONSTRUCTION SPECIFIER, 601 Madison St., Alexandria VA 22314. (703)684-0300. Editor: Kimberly C. Smith. Emphasizes commercial (*not* residential) design and building for architects, engineers and other A/E professionals. Monthly. Circ. 18,000. Returns original artwork after publication if requested. Sample copy free for SASE with $2.07 postage.
Illustrations: Buys 1-2 illustrations/issue from freelancers. Works on assignment only. Send query letter with samples. Accepts photostats, tear sheets, photocopies, slides or photographs as samples. Samples not filed are returned by SASE. Reports back only if interested. Buys one-time rights. Pays on publication.

CONSTRUCTIONEER, 26 Long Hill Rd., Box 362, Guilford CT 06437. (203)453-3717. Features Editor: Carole Guarente. For contractors, public officials, distributors and producers. Biweekly. Previously published work OK. Original artwork not returned after publication.
Cartoons: Buys 4-5 cartoons/year. Interested in heavy construction. Mail art. SASE. Reports in 2 weeks. Pays $5-10; on publication.

*****CONTACT**, Boumain Publishing Co., Box 9248, Berkeley CA 94709. (415)644-0696. Editor: Elliott Leighton. Emphasizes lifestyles and relationships for singles, median age 32. Monthly. Circ. 35,000. Accepts previously published material. Returns original artwork after publication with SASE. Sample copy $3.
Cartoons: Buys 1-3/issue from freelancers. Prefers themes dealing with lifestyles and/or relationships. Prefers single panel with gagline; b&w line drawings. Send query letter with finished cartoons to be kept on file. Write or call for appointment to show portfolio. Material not filed is returned by SASE. Reports only if interested. Buys one-time rights. Pays $5-20, b&w; on publication.
Illustrations: Buys 2-3/issue from freelancers. Prefers themes dealing with lifestyles and/or relationships. Works on assignment only. Send query letter with samples. Accepts any type of sample. Samples not filed are returned by SASE. Reports only if interested. Buys one-time rights. Pays $60, b&w, cover; and $10-30, b&w, inside; on publication.

CONTACTS, Box 407, North Chatham NY 12132. Editor: Joseph Strack. For dental laboratory owners and managers and dental technician staffs. Bimonthly. Circ. 1,000.
Cartoons: Buys 4-5/issue on the dental laboratory industry. Mail art. Reports in 1 week. Buys first serial rights. Pays $25; on acceptance.

CONTRACTORS GUIDE, Century Communications, Inc., 5520G Touhy Ave., Skokie IL 60077. (312)676-4060. Art Director: Judy Krajewski. Magazine for roofing, siding, and insulation contractors. Monthly. Circ. 30,000. Simultaneous submissions and previously published work OK. Sample copy $3.
Illustrations: Cover: buys color and b&w work. Inside: buys b&w line drawings, washes and gray opaques. Arrange interview to show portfolio. SASE. Negotiates pay; pays on publication.

DAVID C. COOK PUBLISHING CO., 850 N. Grove Ave., Elgin IL 60120. (312)741-2400. Director of Design Services: Gregory Eaton Clark. Publishers of magazines, teaching booklets, visual aids and film strips. For Christians, "all age groups."
Illustrations: Buys about 30 illustrations/week from freelancers, b&w line drawings and full-color art. Send tear sheets, slides or photocopies of previously published work; include self-promo pieces. No samples returned unless requested and accompanied by SASE. Reports in 2-4 weeks to personal queries only. Works on assignment only. Pays on acceptance $50 minimum for inside b&w; $275-300 for color cover and $100 minimum for inside color. Considers complexity of project, skill and experience of artist and turnaround time when establishing payment. Buys all rights. Originals can be returned in most cases.
Tips: "We do not buy illustrations or cartoons on speculation. We welcome those just beginning their careers, but it helps if the samples are presented in a neat and professional manner. Our deadlines are generous but must be met. We send out checks as soon as final art is approved, usually within 2 weeks of our receiving the art. We want art radically different from normal Sunday School art. Fresh, dynamic, the highest of quality is our goal; art that appeals to preschoolers to senior citizens; realistic to humorous, all media."

COOKBOOKS, USA, Drawer 5007, Bend OR 97708. (503)382-6878. Contact: Kenneth Asher. Produces cookbooks for fundraisers. Buys 10-15 covers/year. Write for guidelines; submit color photographs of art. Reports in 6 weeks. Negotiates payment. Buys all rights.

COOKING FOR PROFIT, Box 267, Fond du Lac WI 54935. (414)923-3700. Editor: Bill Dittrich. Emphasizes foodservice—restaurants, hotels, hospitals, etc., for smaller foodservice operations in smaller communities. Monthly. Circ. 25,000. Accepts previously published material. Returns original artwork after publication. Sample copies free for SASE with 37¢ postage.
Cartoons: Seeks back-of-the-house (kitchen)-oriented cartoons and humor. Prefers single panel. Send query letter with samples of style to be kept on file. Material not filed is returned by SASE. Reports back only if interested. Buys one-time rights. Pays on publication.
Illustrations: Buys original cover art only. Works on assignment only. Send query letter with brochure and samples to be kept on file. Prefers tear sheets, photocopies or photographs as samples. Samples not filed are returned by SASE. Reports back only if interested. Buys one-time rights. Pays on publication.
Tips: "We chose to go to original art on our cover to separate ourselves from the twenty some other trade journals in foodservice. We want a unique look beyond what type and space could deliver."

CORPORATE FITNESS & RECREATION, 825 S. Barrington Ave., Los Angeles CA 90049. Publishers: Hal Spector and Martin Waldman. Art Director: Tom Medsger. Emphasizes health/fitness corporate programs and professional news.
First Contact & Terms: Submit brochure/flyer to be kept on file for possible future assignment. Reports only when assignment available. Buys all rights. Pays $60-up, spot art; $400, full-color cover; on acceptance.

CORVETTE FEVER MAGAZINE, Box 55532, Fort Washington MD 20744. (301)839-2221. Editor: Patricia Stivers. For "Corvette owners and enthusiasts, average ages: 25-55." Bimonthly. Circ. 35,000. Original artwork not returned after publication. Sample copy $2; general art guidelines for SASE.
Cartoons: Uses 2 cartoons/issue; buys 2-4 from freelancers. Themes "must deal with Corvettes"; single panel with gagline, b&w line drawings. Send roughs. Samples returned by SASE. Reports in 6 weeks. Buys first rights and reprint rights. Pays $15-35, b&w; on publication.
Illustrations: Uses 4-6 illustrations/issue; buys 3-6 from freelancers. Themes "must deal with Corvettes." Provide resume, brochure and tear sheets to be kept on file for possible future assignments. Send roughs with samples of style. Samples returned by SASE. Reports in 6 weeks. Buys first rights and reprint rights. Pays $10-75, inside, b&w line drawings; on publication.

COSMOPOLITAN, 224 W. 57th St., New York NY 10019. Cartoon Editor: Stephen Whitty. For career women, ages 18-34.
Cartoons: Works largely with extensive present list of cartoonists. Receives 200 cartoons/week from freelance artists. Especially looks for "light, sophisticated, female-oriented cartoons."
Tips: "Less and less freelance work is purchased—the competition is tougher. Choose your topics and submissions carefully. We buy only sophisticated cartoons that stress a *positive* view of women—females as the subject of the cartoon but not the butt of the joke. Please read the magazine—there are only about 20 cartoonists who really understand our needs. I can't stress this enough." When reviewing an artist's work, "appropriateness to the magazine comes first. Sense of humor comes next, then quality of art. We like pretty people to be featured in our magazine—even in the cartoons. Be aware of *all* the outlets available to you—papers, ad agencies—then study the market *you're* trying to break into. Every magazine has its own slant. Read half a dozen issues and then ask yourself—can I describe, in two or three sentences, a typical reader's concerns, interests, age and economic background?"

THE COVENANT COMPANION, 5101 N. Francisco Ave., Chicago IL 60625. (312)784-3000. Editor: James R. Hawkinson. Emphasizes Christian life and faith. Monthly. Circ. 27,500. Original artwork returned after publication if requested. Sample copy available for $1.50.
Illustrations: Uses b&w drawings or photos about Easter, Advent, Lent, and Christmas. Works on assignment only. Write or submit art 10 weeks in advance of season. SASE. Reports "within a reasonable time." Buys first North American serial rights. Pays in month after publication.

 The asterisk before a listing indicates that the listing is new in this edition. New markets are often the most receptive to freelance contributions.

CREATIVE CHILD & ADULT QUARTERLY, The National Association for Creative Children and Adults, Teachers College 910, Ball State University, Muncie IN 47306. Editor: Dr. Wallace D. Draper. Emphasizes creativity in *all* its applications for parents, teachers, students, administrators in the professions. Quarterly. Original artwork returned after publication if SASE is enclosed. Sample copy, special price $8; regular price $10.
Cartoons: Uses 1 cartoon/issue. Prefers single panel; b&w line drawings. Send samples of style or finished çartoons to be kept on file. Material not kept on file is returned by SASE. Reports within weeks. Pays in copies of publication.
Illustrations: Uses various number of illustrations/issue, including some humorous and cartoon-style illustrations. Send query letter. Prefers original work as samples. Samples returned by SASE. Reports within weeks. Pays in copies of publication.

*CREATIVE COMPUTING, 39 E. Hanover Ave., Morris Plains NJ 07950. (201)540-0445. Associate Art Director: Peter Kelley. Emphasizes personal and small business computers for mostly male audience who enjoy all aspects of computers. Monthly. Circ. 250,000. Originals returned after publication.
Cartoons: Buys 2-5 cartoons/issue from freelancers. Considers technology and computer themes. Prefers single panel with gagline; b&w line drawings. Send query letter with samples of style. Material returned by SASE. Reports within 1 month. Pays $25, b&w; on acceptance.
Illustrations: Buys 1 illustration/issue from freelancers. Works on assignment only. Send brochure to be kept on file; call for appointment to show portfolio. Prefers tear sheets or slides as samples. Samples not filed are returned by SASE. Reports only if interested. Buys first rights. Pays $500-1,000, color, cover; $150-750, b&w and $250-800, color, inside; on acceptance.

*CREATIVE LIVING, 400 Plaza Dr., Secaucus NJ 07094. (201)865-7500. Art Director: Alice Degenhardt. For "professionals 35-45 with college backgrounds; most have families." Quarterly. Circ. 180,000.
Illustrations: Buys 5-7/issue, all from freelancers. Interested in "very conceptual—fine art quality on family, leadership, health and leisure activities." Works on assignment only. Samples sent through mail are not returned. Provide tear sheets to be kept on file for future assignments. SASE. Reports in 2-3 weeks. Pays $300-600, color; on publication.

CREDITHRIFTALK, 601 NW Second St., Box 59, Evansville IN 47701. (812)464-6638. Editor: Gregory E. Thomas. Emphasizes consumer finance for employees of Credithrift Financial. Monthly. Circ. 4,200+. Free sample copy and art guidelines for SASE (60¢ in stamps).
Cartoons: "We use illustrative cartoons done on an assignment basis only." Send samples of style. Samples not returned. Reports in 2 weeks. Negotiates rights purchased. Pays $25 minimum/cartoon; on acceptance.
Illustrations: Works on assignment only. Send business card, samples or tear sheets, or photocopies of samples or tear sheets to be kept on file for possible future assignments. Likes "variety in samples." Samples not returned. Reports in 2 weeks. Negotiates rights purchased. Pays $50 minimum/b&w illustration.
Tips: "We are using more two-color and more process color. I am looking for sources for airbrush and other types of color illustration."

CROPS & SOILS MAGAZINE, 677 Segoe Rd., Madison WI 53711. Editor: William R. Luellen. Emphasizes practical results of scientific research in agriculture, especially crop and soil science, for the modern farmer and his advisors, seedgrowers, agri-business executives, salesmen, county agents, researchers and vocational-agriculture teachers. Published 9 times/year. Previously published work OK. Original artwork not returned after publication; okay to send clear photocopies and keep your originals.
Cartoons: Uses 6-12 cartoons/issue, all from freelancers. Receives 30-50 submissions/week from freelancers. Prefers finished cartoons; 8½x11" or smaller. SASE. Usually reports in 1 week; "delays generally mean at least one cartoon will be bought from the submission." Buys one-time rights. Pays $10; on acceptance.
Tips: "The first question I ask when evaluating a cartoon is, 'Is it funny?' If not, I go no further. If it makes a statement about human relationships, farm safety or other important topics I look more favorably on it. Remember farmers *do* get off their farms now and then to see a doctor, go to a movie, or a tavern, or take a vacation, and farmers have problems with wives and children as well as with farm prices, suppliers, the government and their cattle."

CROSSCURRENTS, 2200 Glastonbury Rd., Westlake Village CA 91361. Graphic Arts Editor: Michael Hughes. "This is a literary quarterly that uses graphic art as accompaniment to our fiction and poetry. We are aimed at an educated audience interested in reviewing a selection of fiction, poetry and

graphic arts." Circ. 3,000. Original artwork returned after publication. Sample copy $5; art guidelines available for SASE.
Illustrations: Uses 5-7 illustrations/issue; buys 75% from freelancers. Considers "any work of high quality and in good taste that will reproduce b&w, 5x7", with clarity, including but not limited to line drawings, charcoal sketches, etchings, lithographs, engravings; vertical format. No pornography." No simultaneous submissions or previously published material. SASE. Reports in 3 weeks. Buys first rights. Pays $10 minimum cover or inside b&w line drawings and b&w washes; $15 minimum cover, color washes; on acceptance.
Tips: "Study a sample copy of our publication and read our guidelines to understand what it is that we use, and what styles we publish." When reviewing an artist's work, "we look for technical excellence, strength of style, something of worth. A professional, neat submission is a must, of course."

CRUSADER, Box 7244, Grand Rapids MI 49510. (616)241-5616. Editor: G. Richard Broene. For boys ages 9-14. Published 7 times/year by the Calvinist Cadet Corps. Previously published work OK. Sample copy and art guidelines for SASE.
Cartoons: Buys 1/issue. Submit resume. Reports in 6 weeks. Minimum payment: $10, single panel; $20, double panel; $25, full page. "We especially look for originality and quality. If artists care about their work, they send it in clean, neat, appropriate packaging."
Illustrations: Buys 1 story illustration/issue.
Tips: "Too many artists copy existing styles. We are looking for fresh approaches."

CRUSADER, Baptist Brotherhood Commission, 1548 Poplar, Memphis TN 38104. (901)272-2461. Art Director: Herschel Wells. Christian-oriented mission magazine for boys grades 1-6. Monthly. Circ. 100,000. Photocopied and simultaneous submissions OK. Original artwork returned after publication, if requested.
Illustrations: Uses 10 illustrations/issue; buys 2/issue from freelancers. Interested in boys' youth and boys' activities. Works on assignment only. Sample copy provided "if we consider using the artist after we've seen samples." Send roughs or samples of style, which may be returned or duplicated to be kept on file. Samples not filed are returned by SASE. Reports in 3 weeks. Buys first North American serial rights. Cover: Pays $200-250, full color; $100-180, b&w line drawings, washes and gray opaques. Inside: Pays $45-120, b&w line drawings, washes and gray opaques.
Tips: "Please send several samples if you have more than one style. We must see figure work as most of our art requires this."

CRYPTOLOGIA, Rose-Hulman Institute of Technology, Terre Haute IN 47803. (812)877-1511. Managing Editor: Brian J. Winkel. Emphasizes all aspects of cryptology: data (computer) encryption, history, military, science, ancient languages, secret communications for scholars and hobbyists. Quarterly. Circ. 1,000. Accepts previously published material and simultaneous submissions. Original artwork returned after publication.
Cartoons: Uses 2-3 cartoons/issue. Prefers plays on language, communication (secret), ancient language decipherment, computer encryption. Prefers single, double or multipanel, with or without gagline; b&w line drawings or b&w washes. Send query letter with samples of style, roughs, or finished cartoons to be kept on file. Material not kept on file is returned by SASE. Reports within 2 weeks. Negotiates rights purchased. Pays on acceptance.

CURRENT CONSUMER & LIFESTUDIES, 3500 Western Ave., Highland Park IL 60035. (312)432-2700. Photo Editor: Barbara A. Bennett. Emphasizes consumer education and life awareness for seventh- twelfth-grade students. Monthly. Accepts previously published material. Returns original artwork after publication. Sample copy and art guidelines free for 8x11" SASE.
Illustrations: Number purchased/issue varies. Prefers line art. Send samples to be kept on file or returned. Accepts photostats, tear sheets or photocopies as samples. Reports within 2-4 weeks. Buys one-time rights. Negotiates payment; made on publication.

*CURRICULUM INNOVATIONS, INC., 3500 Western Ave., Highland Park IL 60035. (312)432-2700, (800)323-5471. Photo Editor: Barbara A. Bennett. Assistant Photo Editor: Betsy S. Rooth. Produces 10 magazines—*Current Health 1*, *Current Health 2*, *Career World*, *Writing!* and *Current Consumer & Lifestudies* published monthly during the school year and *New Driver* published quarterly. Readership is 7-12th grade students. Remaining four titles are *Your Health & Fitness* and *Your Health & Safety* both bimonthly; *Energy Sense* and *Money Plan* both quarterly. The readership is a general audience. Accepts previously published material. Original artwork returned after publication. Sample copy free for 8x10 SASE; art guidelines also available.
Illustrations: Student publications use a varying number of b&w illustrations/issue. General magazines use 5-10 b&w and color illustrations/issue and work on an assignment basis only. Send query letter with

samples to be filed. Prefers photocopies or slides as samples. Samples are returned only by request with SASE. Reports within 2-4 weeks. Buys one-time rights for student magazines, negotiates payment, pays on publication. Negotiates rights purchased for general magazines; pays $50-300, inside, b&w; $100-500, inside, color; on acceptance.

CURRICULUM REVIEW, 517 S. Jefferson St., Chicago IL 60607. (312)939-3010. Editor-in-Chief: Irene M. Goldman. Emphasizes material of interest to teachers, superintendents, curriculum coordinators, librarians (schools of education and school libraries). Bimonthly. Circ. 10,000. Original artwork returned after publication. Sample copy and art guidelines free for SASE.
Cartoons: Uses variable number of cartoons/issue. Prefers single, double or multipanel with gagline; b&w line drawings. Send query letter with samples of style to be kept on file. Write for appointment to show portfolio. Material not kept on file is returned by SASE. Reports only if interested. Negotiates payment. Pays on publication.
Illustrations: Send query letter with samples and tear sheets to be kept on file. Prefers photostats as samples. Samples not kept on file are returned by SASE. Reports within 1 month only if interested. Buys reprint rights. Negotiates payment. Pays on publication.

CWC/PETERBOROUGH, 80 Pine St., Peterborough NH 03458. (617)924-9471. Creative Director: Christine Destrempes. "We publish 4 microcomputing monthlies and one ham radio monthly: *80 Micro*, *HOT Coco*, *RUN*, *inCider*, and *73*." Circ. 50,000-130,000. Accepts previously published material. Returns original artwork after publication. Sample copy free for SASE; art guidelines available.
Cartoons: Minimal number of cartoons purchased from freelancers. Prefers single panel without gaglines; b&w line drawings, b&w washes or color washes. Send query letter with samples of style or finished cartoons to be kept on file. Material not filed is returned only if requested. Reports within 5 weeks. Rights purchased and payment varies; pays within 30 days.
Illustrations: Number of illustrations purchased from freelancers varies. Works on assignment only. Send query letter with brochure, resume, business card and samples to be kept on file. Prefers tear sheets as samples. Samples not filed are returned only if requested. Reports within 5 weeks. Rights purchased and payments vary; pays within 30 days.

CYCLE WORLD, 1499 Monrovia Ave., Newport Beach CA 92663. (714)720-5300. For active motorcyclists who are "young, affluent, educated, very perceptive." Monthly. Circ. 375,000. "Unless otherwise noted in query letter, we will keep spot drawings in our files for use as future fillers." Previously published work OK. Free sample copy and artist's guidelines.
Cartoons: Uses 6 cartoons/year, all from freelancers. Receives 1 submission/week from freelancers. Interested in motorcycling; single or double panel with gagline. Send roughs or finished art or arrange interview. Buys all rights. Pays $30-250, b&w line drawings, washes and gray opaques; $50-400, color.
Illustrations: Art Director: Elaine Anderson. Uses 7-8 illustrations/issue, all from freelancers. Receives 25-30 submissions/week from freelancers. Interested in motorcycling and assigned themes. Works on assignment only. Prefers to see resume and samples or portfolio. Samples returned, if originals; kept if photocopies. Reports back on future assignment possibilities to artists who phone. Does not report back to artists who contact through mail. Provide brochure, tear sheet, letter of inquiry and business card to be kept on file for future assignments. Buys all rights. Cover: Pays $300-500. Inside: Pays $25-150, b&w; $100-400, color; on publication.
Tips: "We use a lot of spot drawings as fillers."

D.S. MAGAZINES, Sharon Publications, Edrei Communications, 105 Union Ave., Cresskill NJ 07626. (201)569-5055. Art Director in Chief: Paul Castori. Publisher of *Tiger Beat*, *Tiger Beat Star*, *Right On!*, *Focus*, *Class*, *Lovebook*, *Rock!*, *HitMag*, *ZapMag*, *TufMag*, *MaxMag*, *Daytimers*, and more. Also publishes books (see listing under Sharon Publications in Book Publishers section).
Needs: Works with 5 freelance artists/year. Uses artists for magazine layout, illustrations, paste-up and mechanicals.
First Contact & Terms: Send query letter with brochure, resume, business card and samples to be kept on file; call for appointment to show portfolio. Accepts photostats, photographs, photocopies, slides or tear sheets as samples. Samples not filed are returned only if accompanied by SASE. Reports back only if interested. Payment varies according to project; "we have a wide range." Considers the complexity of the project, how the work will be used and the turnaround time. Pays on publication.

*THE DALE CORP., 2684 Industrial Row, Troy MI 48084. (313)288-9540. Contact: Art Director. Publishes law enforcement, corrections and fire fighting publications. Circ. 240,000. Query with previously published work. SASE. Reports in 4 weeks. Buys all rights, but may reassign rights to artist after publication. Pays on acceptance. Free sample copies and artist's guidelines.
Illustrations: Buys 12/year. Cover: Pays $100-200, b&w line drawings; $75-200, color-separated work.

DANCE MAGAZINE, 33 W. 60th St., New York NY 10023. Editor-in-Chief: William Como. Emphasizes performance, education, personalities, books, records, films and lifestyle, all pertaining to the dancer or the dance aficionado. Monthly. Works on assignment only. Original artwork not returned after publication. Sample copy $3.50.
Illustrations: Uses 3-4 illustrations/issue; buys all from freelancers. Interested in dance-related themes (ballet, modern, ethnic, etc.). Provide resume to be kept on file for future assignments. Query. SASE. Reports in 2 weeks. Buys all rights on a work-for-hire basis. Pays on publication.

DASH, Box 150, Wheaton IL 60189. (312)665-0630. Art Director: Lawrence Libby. Senior Graphic Designer: Roy Green. For Christian boys ages 8-11 in the church's Brigade program. Published 6 times/year. Circ. 24,000. Simultaneous submissions and previously published work OK. Original artwork returned after publication. Sample copy for $1.50 and SASE. Free artist's guidelines with SASE.
Cartoons: Send to attention of Cartoon Editor. Uses 1-3 cartoons/issue; buys all from freelancers. Receives 10 submissions/week from freelancers. Interested in family life, humor through youth, nature, school, sports; single panel with gagline. "Keep it clean." Prefers finished cartoons. SASE. Reports in 2-4 weeks. Buys first time rights. Pays $20 minimum, b&w line drawings; on publication.
Illustrations: Contact: Art Director. Uses 3 illustrations/issue; buys 2/issue from freelancers. B&w only; clean/professional look. Works on assignment only. Samples returned by SASE. Reports back on future assignment possibilities. Provide business card or photocopy of samples to be kept on file for future assignments. Prefers to see resume and samples. SASE. Reports in 2 weeks. Buys first time rights. Pays $100-150 for inside use of b&w line drawings and washes; on publication.

DATAMATION MAGAZINE, 12th Floor, 875 Third Ave., New York NY 10022. (212)605-9711. Art Director: Kenneth Surabian. Emphasizes computers for data processing professionals. Bimonthly. Circ. 165,000. Original artwork returned after publication.
Cartoons: Uses 8 cartoons/issue. Prefers computers, business themes in *New Yorker* magazine style. Send query letter with finished cartoons; call for appointment to show portfolio. Material not kept on file is returned by SASE. Reports within 2 weeks. Buys first or one-time rights. Pays $50-75, b&w; on acceptance.
Illustrations: Uses 6 illustrations/issue; buys all from freelancers. Works on assignment only. Send samples and tear sheets to be kept on file; call for appointment to show portfolio. Prefers photostats or promotional cards as samples. Does not report back. Buys first or one-time rights. Pays $500-700, b&w, and $500-1,000, color cover; $400, b&w, $500, color inside; on acceptance.

DECOR, 408 Olive, St. Louis MO 63102. (314)421-5445. Assistant Editor: Sharon Shinn. "Trade publication for retailers of art, picture framing and related wall decor. Subscribers include gallery owners/directors, custom and do-it-yourself picture framers, managers of related departments in department stores, art material store owners and owners of gift/accessory shops." Monthly. Circ. 20,000. Simultaneous submissions and previously published work OK. Original artwork not returned after publication. Sample copy $4.
Cartoons: Uses 6-10 cartoons/year; buys all from freelancers. Receives 5-10 submissions/week from freelancers. Interested in themes of galleries, frame shops, artists and small business problems; single panel with gagline. Especially needs cartoons for January business planning and forecast issue. Using more art-merchandising cartoons than in past. "We need cartoons as a way to 'lighten' our technical and retailing material. Cartoons showing gallery owners' problems with shows, artists and the buying public, inept framing employees, selling custom frames to the buying public and running a small business are most important to us." Send finished cartoons. SASE. Reports in 2 weeks. Buys various rights. Pays $20, b&w line drawings and washes; on acceptance.
Illustrations: Assigns illustration work to local artists.
Tips: "Most of our cartoons fill one-quarter-page spaces. Hence, cartoons that are vertical in design suit our purposes better than those which are horizontal. Send good, clean drawings with return envelopes; no more than 6 cartoons at a time."

DEER & DEER HUNTING, Box 1302, Appleton WI 54912. (414)734-0009. Art Director/Publisher: Jack Brauer. Emphasizes deer, deer hunting, outdoor themes for bow, camera, gun hunters. Bimonthly. Circ. 100,000. Accepts previously published material and simultaneous submissions. Original artwork returned after publication. Sample copy $2.95; art guidelines free for SASE.
Illustrations: Uses 2-3 illustrations/issue; buys some from freelancers. Prefers b&w scenery or hunting-related illustrations; artwork of Whitetail deer. Send resume, business card, samples or tear sheets to be kept on file. Prefers photostats or slides as samples. Samples not filed are returned by SASE. Reports only if interested. Buys one-time rights. Pays $20-50, b&w, and $50-75, color, cover; $20-35, b&w, and $35-50, color, inside; on publication.
Tips: "We prefer vertical work in b&w and especially look for the correct anatomy of deer when reviewing work."

DELAWARE TODAY, 206 E. Ayre St., Wilmington DE 19804 (302)995-7146. Art Director: Ingrid Lynch. Emphasizes the most well-known people, places and events in the area. Monthly. Circ. 17,000. Free sample copy.
Illustrations: Uses 2-3 illustrations/issue; buys all from freelancers. Interested in blackline, ink washes, spots on current events and environment. Works on assignment only. Samples returned by SASE. Provide business card, brochure, flyer and tear sheet to be kept on file for future assignments. Cover: Pays $250, color. Inside: Pays $75-150, b&w; $100-150, color. Pays on publication. Query with resume and samples or arrange interview to show portfolio. SASE. Reports in 1 week. Buys first North American serial rights.
Tips: "I have noticed a lot of illustrators are using flat color and shapes, I would like to find illustrators that do this; also illustrators that draw loosely (not cartoony)."

DELTIOLOGY, Box 456, Tuxedo NC 28784. Contact: Robert C. Quay. For collectors of international antique picture postcards. Bimonthly. Circ. 1,600.
Cartoons: Buys postcard-collector themes. Especially needs cartoons showing postcard collectors in different humorous situations and "material directly related to our field." SASE. Reports in 3 weeks. Pays in copies only; on publication. Sample $1.
Tips: "Since there is little or no profit in submitting cartoons/illustrations for postcard publications, only the newcomers in the field may even want to venture a submission. But it is likely that almost anything submitted will be used, enabling a novice to have his work appear in print for a small readership. That may appeal to someone, somehow, somewhere."

*DERBY, Box 5418, Norman OK 73070. (405)364-9444. Editor: G.D. Hollingsworth. Estab. 1983. Emphasizes thoroughbred horse racing and breeding for owners, breeders and trainers of thoroughbred race horses. Monthly. Circ. 5,000. Accepts previously published material. Original artwork returned after publication. Sample copy $3; art guidelines available.
Illustrations: Buys cover illustration each issue from freelancer. Send query letter with samples to be kept on file. Prefers photos of artwork as samples. Samples not filed are returned. Reports within 2 weeks only if interested. Negotiates rights purchased. Pays $450, color, cover; on publication.

*DETROIT MAGAZINE, 321 W. Lafayette, Detroit MI 48231. (313)222-6446. Art Director: Sheila Young Tomkowiak. Sunday magazine of major metropolitan daily newspaper emphasizing general subjects. Weekly. Circ. 800,000. Original artwork returned after publication. Sample copy available.
Illustrations: Buys 1-2 illustrations/issue from freelancers. Uses a variety of themes and styles, "but we emphasize fine art over cartoons." Works on assignment only. Send query letter with samples to be kept on file unless not considered for assignment. Send "whatever samples best show artwork and can fit into 8½x11" file folder." Samples not filed are not returned. Reports only if interested. Buys first rights. Pays $250-300, color, cover; up to $200, color and up to $175, b&w, inside; on publication.

*DIABETES SELF-MANAGEMENT, 42-15 Crescent St., Long Island City, NY 11101. (718)937-4283. Production Director: Ms Maryanne Schott. Estab. 1983. Magazine. Emphasizes diabetes self-care for diabetics. Quarterly. Circ. 250,000. Original artwork not returned after publication. Sample copy $3.
Cartoons: Buys 6-8 cartoons/issue from freelancers. Themes or styles dependent on editorial content. Prefers single panel or multiple panel; b&w washes, color washes. Send query letter with samples of style to be kept on file. Material not filed is returned by SASE. Reports only if interested. Buys all rights. Pays on publication.
Illustrations: Buys 20-30 illustrations/issue from freelancers. Themes or styles vary from issue to issue based on editorial. Send query letter with samples to be kept on file. Prefers tear sheets, photostats, slides and photos as samples. Samples not filed are returned by SASE. Reports only if interested. Buys all rights. Pays on publication.

THE DISCIPLE, Christian Board of Publication, Box 179, St. Louis MO 63166. Editor: James L. Merrell. For ministers and laypersons. Monthly. Circ. 58,000. Photocopied and simultaneous submissions OK. Original artwork returned after publication, if requested. Sample copy $1.25; free artist's guidelines.
Cartoons: Uses 1 cartoon/issue, all from freelancers. Receives 10 submissions/week from freelancers. Interested in family life and religion; single panel. Church material only. "Originality in content and subject matter stressed. No clergy collars—ties or robes preferred." Especially needs "good religious cartoons along the lines of those which appear in *TV Guide*." Prefers to see finished cartoons. SASE. Reports in 4 weeks. Buys first North American serial rights. Pays $15 minimum, b&w line drawings and washes; on acceptance.
Illustrations: Uses 2 illustrations/issue; buys 1/issue from freelancers. Receives 10 submissions/week

from freelancers. Interested in "seasonal and current religious events/issues." Also uses 4 cartoon-style illustrations/year. Prefers to see resume, roughs and samples of style. SASE. Provide resume to be kept on file for future assignments. Reports in 2 weeks. Buys first North American serial rights. Cover: Pays $60-100, b&w line drawings and washes; on acceptance.

Tips: "We would be very happy to look at samples of artists' work (covers), in case we want to commission. Read the magazine before submitting material. Send seasonal art, especially Easter and Christmas, at least six months in advance."

DISCOVERIES, 6401 The Paseo, Kansas City MO 64131. (816)333-7000. Editor: Elizabeth M. Huffman. Sunday school paper for ages 8-12. Weekly. Circ. 75,000-100,000. Receives 20 cartoons/week from freelance artists. Simultaneous submissions and previously published work OK. Original artwork not returned after publication. Especially needs illustrations of stories about children; realistic art of children in action situations. Free sample copy and artist's guidelines. Receives 20 cartoons and 2-3 illustrations/week from freelance artists.

Cartoons: Buys 1 cartoon/issue, all from freelancers. Interested in "humor that appeals to children: school, animals, children, religion, etc."; single, double or multipanel. Prefers to see finished cartoons. SASE. Reports in 2-4 weeks. Buys first or second rights. Pays $15, b&w line drawings; on acceptance.

Illustrations: Uses 2 illustrations/issue, all from freelancers, on assigned themes. "Illustrations must be realistic and appeal to children 8-12." Prefers to see finished art and samples of style. SASE. Provide resume, letter of inquiry, brochure, flyer or tear sheet to be kept on file for future assignments. Reports in 2-4 weeks. Buys all rights on a work-for-hire basis. Inside: pays $35-40 maximum, b&w only; on acceptance.

Tips: "In the first inquiry send samples of art that suit the purposes and audience of *Discoveries*. This saves a lot of time and money in the long run. It immediately tells us if the artists are prospects or not. We will be shopping for the best artistic value for our art dollars."

DISTRIBUTOR, Box 745, Wheeling IL 60090. (312)537-6460. Editorial Director: Ed Schwenn. Estab. 1983. Emphasizes HVAC/R wholesaling for executives at management level in the wholesale field. Bimonthly. Circ. 10,000. Returns original artwork after publication. Sample copy $4; art guidelines available.

Illustrations: Works on assignment only. Send query letter with brochure and samples to be kept on file. Write for appointment to show portfolio. Accepts photostats, tear sheets, photocopies, slides or photographs as samples; *no* original work. Reports within 2 weeks. Buys first rights. Pays $250 for color cover; on publication.

DIVER MAGAZINE, #210, 1807 Maritime News, Granville Island, Vancouver, British Columbia V6H 3W7 Canada. (604)681-3166. Editor: N. McDaniel. Emphasizes scuba diving, ocean science and technology (commercial and military diving) for a well-educated, outdoor-oriented readership. Published 9 times yearly. Circ. 25,000. Sample copy $2.50; art guidelines for SASE. Nonresidents must include International Reply Coupons.

Cartoons: Uses 1 cartoon/issue; buys from freelancers. Interested in diving-related cartoons only. Prefers single panel b&w line drawings with gagline. Send samples of style. SASE. Reports in 2 weeks. Buys first North American serial rights. Pays $15 for b&w; on publication.

Illustrations: Uses 25 illustrations/issue; buys 20 from freelancers. Interested in diving related illustrations of good quality only. Prefers b&w line drawings for inside. Send samples of style. SASE. Reports in 2 weeks. Buys first North American serial rights. Pays $7 minimum for inside b&w; $60 minimum for color cover and $15 minimum for inside color. Payment four weeks after publication.

DOG FANCY, Box 4030, San Clemente CA 92672. (714)498-1600. Editor: Linda Lewis. For dog owners and breeders of all ages, interested in all phases of dog ownership. Monthly. Circ. 85,000. Simultaneous submissions and previously published work OK. Sample copy $3.; free artist's guidelines.

Cartoons: Buys 12 cartoons/year; single, double or multipanel. "Central character should be a dog." Mail finished art. SASE. Prefers photostats or photocopies as samples. Reports in 6 weeks. Buys first rights. Pays $20-50, b&w line drawings; on publication.

Illustrations: Buys 12 illustrations/year on dogs. Query with resume and samples. SASE. Reports in 6 weeks. Buys first rights. Inside: Pays $50-100, b&w line drawings; on publication.

Tips: Artists should have "originality and intimacy with their subject."

DOLL WORLD, Box 1952, Brooksville FL 33512. Editor: Barbara Hall Pedersen. For doll lovers. Bimonthly. Receives 10 cartoons and 4 illustrations/week from freelance artists. Original artwork returned after publication, if requested. Sample copy with 9x12 SAE and 66¢ postage. Especially needs Christmas line art, crafts and doll making.

Cartoons: Uses 3 cartoons/issue; buys 3/issue from freelancers. Interested in "dolls, but no mean and

sick humor. This magazine is for adults. Gently kid doll collectors." Prefers to see finished cartoons; single panel. SASE. Reports in 2 weeks, if not accepted. "Hold much longer if it's something we can use." Buys all rights on a work-for-hire basis. Pays $15, line drawings; on acceptance.
Illustrations: Uses 2 illustrations/issue; buys 2/issue from freelancers. Interested in "crisp, realistic, b&w line art." Works on assignment only. Provide resume to be kept on file for possible future assignments. Send resume and samples of style. SASE. Reports in 1 week. Buys all rights on a work-for-hire basis.

*THE DOLPHIN LOG, 8440 Santa Monica Blvd., Los Angeles CA 90069. (213)656-4422. Editor: Pamela Stacey. Educational magazine covering "all areas of science, history and the arts related to our global water system to include marine biology, ecology, the environment, and natural history" for children ages 7-15. Quarterly. Circ. 45,000. Accepts previously published material. Original artwork returned after publication. Sample copy for $2 and SASE with 56¢ postage; art guidelines for SASE with 22¢ postage.
Cartoons: Considers themes or styles related to magazine's subject matter. B&w line drawings or b&w or color washes. Send query letter with samples of style to be kept on file; write or call for appointment to show portfolio. Material not filed is returned by SASE. Reports within 1 month. Buys one-time rights and translation rights. Pays $25-200, b&w and color; on publication.
Illustrations: Buys 1-10 illustrations/issue from freelancers. Uses simple, biologically and technically accurate line drawings and scientific illustrations. Subjects should be carefully researched. Send query letter with photocopied samples to be kept on file unless otherwise notified; write or call for appointment to show portfolio. Prefers tear sheets, photocopies, duplicate slides or photographs as samples. "No original artwork, please." Samples not filed are returned by SASE. Reports within 1 month. Buys one-time rights and worldwide translation rights. Pays $100, color, cover; $25-200, b&w and color, inside; on publication.

DOWN EAST, Box 679, Camden ME 04843. (207)594-9544. Art Director: F. Stephen Ward. Concerns Maine's people, places, events and heritage. Monthly. Circ. 75,000. Previously published work OK. Buys first North American serial rights. Sample copy $2.
Illustrations: Buys 50/year on current events, environment, family life and politics. Query with resume and samples or arrange interview to show portfolio. SASE. Reports in 4-6 weeks. Cover: Pays $75, color paintings in any medium; "must have a graphic, poster-like feel and be unmistakably Maine." Inside: Pays $25-200, b&w or color; on publication.
Tips: "Neatness in presentation is as important as the portfolio itself."

DRAGON MAGAZINE, Dragon Publishing, Box 110, Lake Geneva WI 53147. Editor: Kim Mohan. For readers interested in game-playing, particularly fantasy role-playing games. Circ. 120,000. Query with samples. SASE. Usually buys all rights, but may reassign rights to artist after publication, particularly for color covers and full-color pieces used on inside pages. Pays on publication. Sample copy $3 (cover price) plus $1 postage and handling.
Cartoons: Buys 15-20/year on wargaming and fantasy role-playing. Minimum payment: $20, b&w; color cartoons seldom used, but would bring higher price ($50 or more).
Illustrations: Buys at least 100/year on fantasy and science fiction subjects. Minimum payment: cover, $300 (color only); inside: $75/page b&w, $100/page for color.
Tips: "We are interested in top-quality artwork and welcome the opportunity to deal with established professionals in the fantasy/science-fiction genres. Rates of payment may be adjusted upward substantially for artists of evident and proven ability."

DRAMATIKA, 429 Hope St., Tarpon Springs FL 33589. Editor: J. Pyros. For persons interested in the performing arts, avant garde and traditional. Published semiannually. Sample copy $2.
Illustrations: Query first. SASE. Reports in 1 month. Cover: Pays $15, b&w. Inside: Pays $5, b&w line drawings; on acceptance.

*DRAW MAGAZINE, 43 Ankara Ave., Box 98, Brookville OH 45309. (513)833-5677. Publisher/ Editor: Abraham Lincoln. Estab. 1984. Emphasizes good drawing whether in line, pen & ink work, pencil, or watercolors. "Readership is sophisticiated to beginner; college and university drawing instructors and art teachers make up the bulk of our beginning readership. Quarterly, "hoping to go bimonthly." Circ. first issue 10,000. Accepts previously published material. Original artwork returned after publication. Sample copy for $2 postage; art guidelines free for SASE.
Cartoons: Buys approximately 1-2 cartoons/issue from freelancers. Prefers anything related to art, art history, art styles, art trends, and some general interest spots; single panel with gagline; b&w line drawings or b&w or color washes. Send query letter with samples of style or finished cartoons to be kept on

file. Material not filed is returned by SASE. Reports within 2 weeks. Buys first rights. Pays $10, b&w; $25, color; on publication.

Illustrations: Buys 20-50 illustrations/issue from freelancers; many supplied with articles by authors/artists; artwork must be realistic in style; must fit our categories, i.e. technical illustration, medical illustration, portrait (pencil) renderings, pen & ink (detailed) of everything for column; "how-to-do-it." Send query letter with brochure, resume, business card and samples to be kept on file; write for appointment to show portfolio. Prefers photostats, photocopies, photographs, slides "in that order of preference, unless color work is requested by us." Samples returned by SASE. Reports within 2 weeks. Buys first rights. Pays $10-50, b&w and $25-100, color, inside; on publication; assigns covers.

Tips: "Most of our art is with articles supplied to us by artists or authors for specific columns. The Gallery features outstanding artists in any media. There is no pay for this section since the exposure is adequate for these upcoming artists."

DYNAMIC YEARS, 215 Long Beach Blvd., Long Beach CA 90801. Editor: Lorena F. Farrell. For middle-aged career people. Bimonthly. Circ. 250,000. Free sample copy and artist's guidelines.

Cartoons: Uses 4-5 cartoons/issue; buys all from freelancers. Receives 10-30 submissions/week from freelancers. Interested in family life, couples, worklife, travel, preretirement, urban life, health/fitness, seasonal/holidays, and situations pertaining to people in their middle years; single panel with gagline tending toward the sophisticated. Send finished cartoons. SASE. Reports in 4-6 weeks. Buys first North American serial rights. Pays $150 minimum, b&w line drawings.

Illustrations: Uses 15-20 illustrations/issue; buys all from freelancers on assignment only for specific features and layouts. Prefers to see roughs or samples of style. SASE. Provide brochure, flyer or tear sheet to be kept on file for future assignments. Buys first rights. Inside: Pays $150 minimum, b&w line drawings; $200 minimum, color. Pays "competitive rates for full-page illustrations"; on acceptance.

Tips: "Send us a sample of your work so that we can keep it on file for reference when we're looking for a particular style to fit in with a feature article needing illustration."

EARTHWISE: A JOURNAL OF POETRY, Box 680-536, Miami FL 33168. (305)688-8558, 823-5973. Publisher: Barbara Holley. Art Editor: Kathryn L. Vilips. Emphasizes poetry, art and literature for an eclectic group of literate writers, artists and poets, mainly academic, collegiate and aimed at excellence in the field. Quarterly. Circ. 3,000 +. Sometimes accepts previously published material; simultaneous submissions OK. Original artwork returned after publication. Sample copy $4; art guidelines for SASE.

Illustrations: Uses 4-8 illustrations/issue; buys some from freelancers. Provide resume, brochure and samples to be kept on file for possible future assignments. "We especially prefer samples, photocopies or stats which we can purchase and/or keep on file for future publication; our themes occasionally change depending on submissions." Samples returned by SASE "but would like something to keep on file." Reports in 3 months. Buys first rights. Pays $10-50/b&w line drawings, cover; $10-25/b&w line drawings, inside. "Very negotiable depending on size, availability, etc." Pays on publication.

EASY LIVING MAGAZINE, 13279-72 Ave., Surrey, British Columbia V3W 2N5 Canada. Publisher: Roger Sevigny. Contact: Susan Minton-Green, Art Director. Emphasizes community for homeowners, ages 25-45, and children. Monthly. Circ. 350,000. Free sample copy and art guidelines.

Cartoons: Uses themes on homes, children, pets, dining, gardening, cooking, etc. Prefers single or multi-panel with or without gaglines; b&w line drawings and washes. Send roughs and resume with finished cartoons or samples of style. Samples returned by SAE (nonresidents include IRC). Reports in 2 weeks. Buys one-time rights. Pays $30-40, b&w; on publication.

Illustrations: Uses 15 illustrations/issue. Uses full-color art for cover; b&w washes and line drawings inside. Send resume with roughs, finished art or samples of style. Samples returned by SAE (nonresidents include IRC). Reports in 2 weeks. Buys all rights. No set pay rate at present; pays on publication.

Tips: "Currently, we are using local artists bringing our ideas to them. We would like to be presented with ideas from artists."

EASYRIDERS, Box 52, Malibu CA 90265. Contact: Art Director. For adult bikers. Monthly. "Need art and cartoons, scenes with choppers in them, sexy women—in other words, 'bikes, booze and broads,' or scenes depicting the good times derived from owning a Harley-Davidson (if a cycle is illustrated)." Sample copy $2.

Cartoons: Buys 30/month. SASE. Reports in 2 weeks. Buys all rights. Pays $35, small b&w gags; $150, full-page b&w; on acceptance.

Illustrations: "Subject matter is more important than the medium. We use more b&w than color." SASE. Reports in 2 weeks. Buys all rights. Price depends on space and use. A spot drawing pays $25 minimum; a full-page b&w pays $100-200; full-color pays about $350.

EBONY JR!, Johnson Publishing Co., Inc., 820 S. Michigan, Chicago IL 60605. (312)322-9272. Managing Editor: Marcia V. Roebuck-Hoard. Art Director: Herbert Temple. For black children ages 6-12. Published 10 times/year. Circ. 200,000. Original artwork not returned after publication. Sample copy $1; art guidelines for SASE. Also uses artists for "games, especially hidden object games, and out-of-place object games. Freelancers should submit a sketch or photostat of finished art first."
Cartoons: Uses 1 cartoon/issue; buys 1/month from freelancers. Receives 10 submissions/month from freelancers. Interested in education, family life, humor through youth, popular sports and hobbies, varied careers and black children involved in unusual activities; "all from a child's point of view, showing positive, non-sexist characterizations"; single, double and multipanel with gaglines. Send resume with roughs or photostats of art. SASE. Reports in 4-12 weeks. Buys all rights. Pays $15-85, b&w line drawings; $25-125, color-separated work and full-color renderings; on acceptance.
Illustrations: Uses 15 illustrations/issue; buys 15/issue from freelancers. Receives 3-5 submissions/week from freelancers. Interested in humor, sports and hobbies, varied careers, adventure, mystery, wildlife, family life, crafts, recipes, black history, African or Caribbean folklore; all from a child's point of view, showing positive and non-sexist characterizations. Works on assignment only. Provide resume, letter of inquiry, tear sheets to be kept on file for possible future assignments. Send rough sketches or photostats. No samples returned. SASE. Reports in 4-12 weeks. Buys all rights. Cover: Pays $250, color. Inside: Pays $15-85, b&w; $85-125, color.
Tips: "We no longer use 4-color with overlays for illustrations; all color illustrations are now full-color renderings."

*ECLIPSE COMICS, Box 199, Guerneville CA 95446. Editor-in-Chief: Catherine Yronwode. Publishes comic books. "All our comics feature fictional characters in action-adventures. Genres include super-heroes, science fiction, weird horror, western, detective adventure, etc. The emphasis is on drawing the human figure in action. Audience is adolescent to adult. The age varies with each series. (For instance, adolescents prefer *Dnagents*, a teen super-hero team, while adults prefer *Aztec Ace*, a time-travel series with strong romantic and historical overtones.)" Publishes 2 comics/week on average. Most are monthlies, some bi-monthly; others are one-shots or mini-series. Circ. 30,000-80,000, depending on title. Does not accept previously published material except for reprint collections by famous comic book artists. Original artwork returned after publication. Sample copy $1.50; art guidelines for SASE.
Cartoons: "We buy entire illustrated stories, not individual cartoons. We buy approximately 2,900 pages of comic book art by freelancers/year—about 250/month." Interested in realistic illustrative comic book artwork—drawing the human figure in action; good, slick finishes (inking); ability to do righteous 1-, 2- and 3-point perspective required. "We are not currently buying humor style artwork." Only format: b&w line drawings. Send query letter with samples of style to be kept on file. "Send minimum of 4-5 pages of full-size (10x15) photocopies of pencilled *storytelling* (and/or inked too)—no display poses, just typical action layout continuities." Material not filed is returned by SASE. Reports within 2 months by SASE only. Buys first rights and reprint rights. Pays $100-200/page, b&w; "price is for pencils plus inks; many artists only pencil for us, or only ink"; on acceptance (net 30 days).
Illustrations: "We buy 12-15 cover paintings for science fiction and horror books per year." Science fiction paintings: fully rendered science fiction themes (e.g. outer space, aliens); horror paintings: fully rendered horror themes (e.g. vampires, werewolves, etc.). Send query letter with business card and samples to be kept on file. Prefers slides, color photos or tear sheets as samples. Samples not filed are returned by SASE. Reports within 2 months by SASE only. Buys first rights or reprint rights. Pays $200-500, color; on acceptance (net 30 days).

ELECTRIC COMPANY MAGAZINE, 1 Lincoln Plaza, New York NY 10023. (212)595-3456, ext. 512. Art Director: Paul Richer. For ages 6-11.
Illustrations: Buys 60/year. Query with photocopied samples. SASE. Reports in 2 weeks. Buys one-time rights. Pays $150 minimum/page, b&w; $250/page, $450/spread, color; on acceptance.

ELECTRICAL APPARATUS, Barks Publications, Inc., 400 N. Michigan, Chicago IL 60611. Contact: Elsie Dickson. Emphasizes industrial electrical maintenance and repair.
Cartoons: Receives 2-3 cartoons/week from freelance artists. "Always looking for applicable cartoons, as we use a strip (assigned), plus 4-6 individual column-size cartoons in every issue." Query with resume.
Tips: Artists should "know the magazine!"

ELECTRICAL WORLD, McGraw-Hill Inc., 1221 Avenue of the Americas, New York NY 10020. (212)512-2440. Art Director: Kiyo Komoda. Emphasizes operation, maintenance and use of electric utility facilities. For electric utility management and engineers. Monthly. Original artwork returned after publication, on request. Pays on acceptance.

This cover painting by Joseph Chiodo of Los Angeles attracted Dean Mullaney of Eclipse Comics because, explains Mullaney, "it is meticulously rendered in a smooth style which is important for reproduction. The artwork has a good focal point of interest; it features warm hues, which are generally preferred by the comic book-buying public. His female figures, a specialty of sorts, are attractive to our primarily male readership without displaying anatomical distortions or stupidly exploitive posture." Eclipse bought first North American rights to the painting, with reprint rights available for additional payments.

© Joe Chiodo

Cartoons: Uses 1 cartoon/issue; buys all from freelancers, on assignment only. Interested in industry-related situation cartoon, usually related to editorial articles. Buys one-time and reprint rights. Pays on acceptance.

Illustrations: Uses 20 illustrations/issue, buys ⅓ from freelancers. Interested in energy systems; 90% are mechanical line drawings, maps, flow designs, graphs and charts. Works on assignment only. Samples returned by SASE. Provide resume or business card to be kept on file for future assignments. Prefers to see portfolio or finished art. Reports in 1 week. Buys one-time and reprint rights. Cover: Pays $150-350, color. Inside: Pays $30-300, color; $10-200, b&w line drawings. Pays on acceptance.

Tips: "We prefer artists with clean and crisp line work. They should know about color separation and overlays. Young artists welcomed."

ELECTRONICS WEEK, (formerly *Electronics*,) McGraw-Hill Publishing Co., 1221 Avenue of the Americas, New York NY 10020. (212)997-2430. Art Director: Fred Sklenar. For college graduates, electronics engineers, marketing people and executives. Weekly. Circ. 100,000. Also publishes 4 bi-monthly magazines, *Computer Systems Equipment Design, Communications Systems Equipment Design, Military/Space Electronics Design,* and *Industrial Electronics Equipment Design.* Original artwork returned after publication. Photocopied and simultaneous submissions OK.

Illustrations: Uses 30 illustrations/issue; buys all from freelancers. Receives 20-30 illustrations/week from freelance artists. Buys 52 covers/year on assigned themes. Works on assignment only. "Personal interview would be best way to contact." Especially needs engineering drafting, and creative and conceptual illustrations for cover. Samples returned by SASE. Provide tear sheet and sample art to be kept on file for future assignments. Prefers finished art, portfolio, samples of style, or tear sheets as samples.

Buys all first-time world rights. Cover: Pays $600 minimum, color. Inside: Pays $50-500; on acceptance.
Tips: "Prepare portfolio professionally and have samples ready to leave so they may be kept on file."

ELLERY QUEEN'S MYSTERY MAGAZINE, Davis Publications, 380 Lexington Ave., New York NY 10017. (212)557-9100. Editor: Eleanor Sullivan. Emphasizes mystery stories and reviews of mystery books. Reports within 1 month. Pays $25 minimum, line drawings. All other artwork is done in-house. Pays on acceptance.

EMERGENCY MEDICINE MAGAZINE, 475 Park Ave. S, New York NY 10016. (212)686-0555. Art Director: Lois Erlacher. Emphasizes emergency medicine for primary care physicians, emergency room personnel, medical students. Bimonthly. Circ. 139,000. Returns original artwork after publication.
Illustrations: Buys 3-4 illustrations/issue from freelancers. Works on assignment only. Send samples to be kept on file. Write or call for appointment to show portfolio. Accepts tear sheets, transparencies, original art or photostats as samples. Samples not filed are not returned. Reports back only if interested. Buys first rights. Pays $700 for color cover; $300-500 for b&w and $600 for color, inside; on acceptance.

EMPLOYEE SERVICES MANAGEMENT MAGAZINE, NESRA, 2400 S. Downing Ave., Westchester IL 60153. (312)562-8130. Editor: June Cramer. Emphasizes the field of employee services and recreation, which is one aspect of human resources, for human resource professionals, and employee services and recreation managers and leaders within corporations, industries or units of government. Published 10 times/year. Circ. 5,000. Accepts previously published material. Returns original artwork after publication. Sample copy free for SASE with 56¢ postage; art guidelines free for SASE with 22¢ postage.
Illustrations: Buys 0-1 illustration/issue from freelancers. Works on assignment only. Send query letter with resume and samples to be kept on file. Prefers tear sheets or photographs as samples. Samples not filed are returned only if requested. Reports within 1 month. Buys one-time rights. Pays $100-200 for b&w and $300-400 for color covers; on acceptance.
Tips: "We have noticed a change to a simpler, more dramatic style in art and design, one that is not so 'busy.' We have used freelancers who embrace this style."

THE ENSIGN, Official Publication of the United States Power Squadrons, Box 31664, Raleigh NC 27622. (919)821-0892. Editor: Carol Romano. Emphasizes boating safety and education for members of the United States Power Squadrons, a nonprofit organization of boating men and women across the country. Published 11 times each year, monthly with November-December and July-August combined. Circ. approximately 50,000. Does not accept previously published material. Returns original artwork after publication. Sample copy and art guidelines free for SASE.
Cartoons: Prefers single panel, with gagline; b&w line drawings. Send query letter with finished cartoons; "material is reviewed and used or returned by SASE." Reports within 2 weeks. Acquires all rights.
Illustrations: Prefers boating themes. Send query letter with samples; "material is reviewed and used or returned by SASE." Prefers photocopies as samples. Reports within 2 weeks. Acquires all rights.
Tips: "We are happy to accept cartoons and drawings for use in the magazine and provide artists with copies of the magazine at no charge, a letter of appreciation and a certificate of appreciation for their contributions. We provide an opportunity for beginning freelancers to get nationwide exposure, but we have no freelance budget to pay artists at this time."

ENTREPRENEUR MAGAZINE, 2311 Pontius Ave., Los Angeles CA 90064. Editor/Publisher: Ron Smith. Design Director: Richard R. Olson. Emphasizes small business for 90% male audience (35 to 50 years old) with an average income of $65,000. Monthly. Circ. 200,000. Original artwork returned after publication. Sample copy $3; art guidelines for SASE.
Cartoons: Uses various number of cartoons/issue, buys varied number/issue from freelancers. Prefers business oriented themes. Prefers single or double panel with gagline; b&w line drawings. Send query letter with finished cartoons to be kept on file; write for appointment to show portfolio. Material not kept on file is returned by SASE. Reports within 2 months. Buys all rights. Payment varies; on acceptance.
Illustrations: Uses varied number of illustrations/issue; buys varied number/issue from freelancers. Works on assignment only. Send query letter with resume, samples and tear sheets to be kept on file; write for appointment to show portfolio. "Query first about samples." Samples not kept on file are returned by SASE. Reports within 2 months. Buys all rights. Payment varies; on publication.

ENVIRONMENT, 4000 Albemarle St., Washington DC 20016. (202)362-6589. Production Graphics Editor: Ann Rickerich. Emphasizes energy, conservation, pollution, ecology and scientific, technologi-

Freelance art director Victoria Valentine assigned David Povilaitis of Chicago this editorial illustration for Europe magazine. Valentine says, "David interprets article contents well. His work is upbeat, sophisticated, personal and not necessarily realistic. David is really good at off-the-wall imagery of material that doesn't necessarily lend itself to that style." The artist received $150 for one-time use.

cal, and environmental policy issues. Readers are "high school students and college undergrads to scientists and business and government executives." Circ. 12,500. Published 10 times/year. Original artwork returned after publication if requested. Sample copy $4; cartoonist's guidelines available.

Cartoons: Uses 0-1 cartoon/issue; buys all from freelancers. Receives 2 submissions/week from freelancers. Interested in single panel b&w line drawings or b&w washes with or without gagline. Send finished cartoons. SASE. Reports in 2 weeks. Buys first North American serial rights. Pays $35, b&w cartoon; on acceptance.

Tips: "Regarding cartoons, we prefer the witty to the slapstick."

ESQUIRE, 2 Park Ave., New York NY 10016. (212)561-8100. Art Director: April Silver. Emphasizes politics, business, the arts, sports and the family for American men.
Illustrations: Call first; drop-off policy for portfolio. Pays $350 for spot, b&w; $750-1,000 for color.

*ETERNITY MAGAZINE, 1716 Spruce St., Philadelhia PA 19103. (215)546-3696. Design Coordinator: Robin Burnham. Emphasizes cultural analysis from a Christian viewpoint for business people, 30-60 years of age. Monthly. Circ. 45,000. Accepts previously published material. Original artwork returned after publication. Sample copy $2; art guidelines available.
Illustrations: Buys 3-4 illustrations/issue from freelancers. Considers variety of media, serious style—not cartooning. Themes range from war to education to androgeny. Works on assignment only. Send samples to be kept on file; write or call for appointment to show portfolio. Prefers tear sheets, photocopies, photographs as samples. "Please do not send original work." Samples returned by SASE. Reports only if interested. Buys one-time rights. Pays $100-200, b&w, and $150-250, color, cover; $75-150, b&w, inside; on acceptance.

EUROPE, MAGAZINE OF THE EUROPEAN COMMUNITY, #707, 2100 M St. NW, Washington DC 20037. (202)862-9500. Editor: Webster Martin. Emphasizes European affairs, US-European relations—particularly economics, trade and politics. Readers are businessmen, professionals, academics, government officials and consumers. Bimonthly. Circ. 65,000. Free sample copy $2.50.
Cartoons: Occasionally uses cartoons, mostly from a cartoon service. "The magazine publishes arti-

cles on US-European relations in economics, trade, business, industry, politics, energy, inflation, etc."
Considers single panel b&w line drawings or b&w washes with or without gagline. Send resume plus
finished cartoons and/or samples. SASE. Reports in 3-4 weeks. Buys one-time rights. Pays $25; on publication.
Illustrations: Uses 3-5 illustrations/issue. "At present we work exclusively through our designer and
set up charts and graphs to fit our needs. We would be open to commissioning artwork should the need
and opportunity arise. We look for economic graphs, tables, charts and story-related statistical artwork"; b&w line drawings and washes for inside. Send resume and samples of style. SASE. Reports in
3-4 weeks. Buys all rights on a work-for-hire basis. Pays from $25; on publication.

EVANGEL, 901 College Ave., Winona Lake IN 46590. (219)267-7656. Contact: Vera Bethel. Readers
are 65% female, 35% male; ages 25-31; married; city-dwelling; mostly non-professional high school
graduates. Circ. 35,000. Weekly. SASE. Reports in 1 month.
Cartoons: Buys 1/issue on family subjects. Pays $10, b&w; on publication. Mail finished art.
Illustrations: Buys 1/issue on assigned themes. Pays $40, 2-color; on acceptance. Query with samples
or slides.

*THE EVENER, Box 7, Cedar Falls IA 50613. (319)277-3599. Managing Editor: Susan Salterberg.
Magazine. Emphasizes draft horses (*some* mules and oxen). "*The Evener*'s subscribers are primarily
farmers, craftsmen, showmen and women. They are interested in horses, nostalgia—and, oftentimes—
self-sufficiency. Some subscribers work horses, mules or oxen on their farm or ranch and look for features and quality artwork and photographs about people in the industry." Quarterly. Circ. 10,400. Accepts previously published material. Original artwork returned after publication. Sample copy for SASE
with $1.07 postage; art guidelines for SASE with 39¢ postage.
Illustrations: Buys 2 illustrations/issue from freelancers. Usually works on assignment. Send query letter with brochure or samples to be kept on file. Prefers photostats, photographs and slides as samples.
Samples not filed are returned by SASE. Reports within 2 months by SASE only. Negotiates rights purchased; prefers first-time rights. Pays $40-100, b&w, cover; $10-60, b&w, inside; on acceptance.

EVENT, Kwantlen College, Box 9030, Surrey, British Columbia V3T 5H8 Canada. (604)588-4411.
For "those interested in literature and writing." Published semiannually. Circ. 1,000. Original artwork
returned after publication. Sample copy $3.50.
Illustrations: Editor: Ken Hughes. Receives 3 illustrations/week from freelance artists. Uses 16-20 illustrations/issue, buys all from freelancers. Interested in experimental drawings and prints, and thematic or stylistic series of 12-20 works. Mail slides or finished art. SASE (nonresidents include IRC). Reporting time varies; at least 2 weeks. Buys first North American serial rights. Cover and inside: Pays $5
minimum, b&w line drawings, photographs and lithographs; work must reproduce well in one color.
Pays on publication. Payment includes free copy.

EXECUTIVE REPORT, Bigelow Square, Pittsburg PA 15219. (412)471-4585. Editor: Charles W.
Shane. Emphasizes business for middle to top management in western Pennsylvania. Monthly. Circ.
16,000 +. Returns original artwork after publication. Sample copy $2; art guidelines available.
Illustrations: Buys 2-3 illustrations/issue from freelancers. Usually works on assignment. Send query
letter and samples to be kept on file; write for appointment to show portfolio. Prefers photocopies as
samples. Samples not filed are returned only if requested. Reports back only if interested. Negotiates
rights purchased and payment; pays on publication.

EXPECTING MAGAZINE, 685 Third Ave., New York NY 10017. Art Director: Ruth M. Kelly. Emphasizes pregnancy, birth and care of the newborn for pregnant women and new mothers. Quarterly.
Circ. 1.15 million distributed through obstetrician and gynecologist offices nationwide. Original artwork returned after publication.
Illustrations: Buys approximately 5/issue. Color only. Works on assignment only. "We have a drop-off
policy for looking at portfolios; include a card to be kept on file." Buys one-time rights. Pays $250-700;
within 30 days after publication.

FACT MAGAZINE, 305 E. 46th, New York NY 10017. Art Director: Christopher Goldsmith. Estab.
1982. Emphasizes consumer money management and investment. Monthly. Accepts previously
published material. Returns original artwork after publication.
Illustrations: Buys 3-6 illustrations/issue from freelancers. Usually works on assignment. Send business card and samples to be kept on file; then call for appointment to show portfolio. Accepts photostats,
tear sheets, photocopies, slides or photographs as samples. Samples not filed are returned only if requested. Reports back only if interested. Buys first rights or reprint rights. Pays $300-600 for cover;
$75-200 inside.

FAMILY CIRCLE, 488 Madison Ave., New York NY 10022. Art Director: John Bradford. Circ. 7,000,000. Supermarket-distributed publication for women/homemakers covering areas of food, home, beauty, health, child care and careers. 17 issues/year. Does not accept previously published material. Original artwork returned after publication. Sample copy and art guidelines not available.
Cartoons: No unsolicited cartoon submissions accepted. Reviews in office first Wednesday of each month. Uses 1-2 cartoons/issue. Prefers themes related to women's interests, feminist viewpoint. Uses limited seasonal material, primarily Christmas. Prefers single panel with gagline, b&w line drawings or washes. Buys all rights. Pays $325 on acceptance. Contact Sue Oppenheimer, (212)593-7962, for cartoon query only.
Illustrations: Uses 20 illustrations/issue, all from freelancers. Works on assignment only. Reports only if interested. Provide query letter with samples to be kept on file for future assignments. Prefers slides or tear sheets as samples. Samples returned by SASE. Prefers to see portfolio (finished art). Submit portfolio on "portfolio days," every Wednesday. All art is commissioned for specific magazine articles. Reports in 1 week. Buys all rights on a work-for-hire basis. Pays on acceptance.

FAMILY MOTOR COACHING, 8291 Clough Pike, Cincinnati OH 45244. (513)474-3622. Contact: Editor. Emphasizes motorhomes and bus conversions for families who use or own motorhomes. Monthly. Circ. 35,000. Original artwork returned after publication, "if requested." Sample copy $2; art guidelines available with SASE.
Cartoons: Uses 1-5 cartoons/issue; buys all from freelancers. Themes "must pertain to motorhoming, RV lifestyle, travel. No trailers." Prefers single, double, or multipanel with or without gagline, b&w line drawings, b&w washes. Send finished cartoons. Samples returned by SASE. Reports in 2-3 weeks. Buys first rights. Pays $10, b&w; on acceptance.

*FAMILY PLANNING PERSPECTIVES, 111 5th Ave., New York NY 10003. (212)254-5656. Production Manager: Dore Hollander. Magazine. Emphasizes family planning/population for health care providers, educators and policy-makers. Bimonthly. Circ. 15,000. Original artwork returned after publication. Sample copy available.
Cartoons: Buys 0-1 cartoon/issue from freelancers. Prefers political/social aspects of family planning issues as themes. Prefers single panel without gagline; b&w line drawings. Send query letter with samples of style. Material returned by SASE. Replies only if interested. Negotiates rights purchased. Pays on publication.
Illustrations: Buys 0-1 illustration/issue from freelancers. Prefers political/social aspects of family planning issues as themes. Works on assignment only. Send query letter with samples. Samples returned by SASE. Replies only if interested. Negotiates rights purchased. Pays on publication.

FAMILY WEEKLY, C/o Gnotte Co., 1000 Wilson Blvd., 1000 Wilson Blvd., Arlington VA 22209. (703)276-3400. Director of Photography: Jackie Greene. Emphasizes general topics. Weekly. Circ. 13 million. Returns original artwork after publication.
Illustrations: Buys illustrations from freelancers. Considers b&w line drawings and color. Works on assignment only. Send samples to be kept on file; call for appointment to show portfolio. Prefers tear sheets as samples. Samples not filed are returned only by SASE. Buys first rights. Payment negotiable.

*FANTASY BOOK, Box 60126, Pasadena CA 91106. Art Director: Nick Smith. Emphasizes fantasy, horror and science fiction for adult, literate audience interested in both visual and text interpretations in subject areas. Quarterly. Circ. 5,000. Original artwork returned after publication. Sample copy $4; art guidelines for SASE.
Cartoon: Buys 3-4 cartoons/issue from freelancers. Themes are mostly fantasy; horror or science fiction also used. Prefers single panel with gagline; b&w line drawings. Send samples of style or finished cartoons to be kept on file, except for any work the artist wants returned; write for appointment to show portfolio. Material not filed is returned by SASE. Reports within 6 weeks. Buys first rights. Pays $20-40, b&w; on publication.
Illustrations: Buys about 30 illustrations/issue from freelancers. Works on assignment only except for cover art. Send query letter with samples to be kept on file except for any samples artist needs back quickly; write for appointment to show portfolio. Prefers slides of color work, any clear reproduction of b&w as samples. Samples not filed are returned by SASE. Reports within 6 weeks. Buys first rights, or one-time rights (in special cases only). Pays $150-300, color, cover; $20-50, b&w, inside; on publication.

*FANTASY REVIEW, College of Humanities, Florida Atlantic University, Boca Raton FL 33431. (305)393-3839. Editor: Robert A. Collins. Emphasizes fantasy and science fiction for "collectors, book dealers, libraries, academics and fans in general." Monthly. Circ. 3,000. Original artwork returned af-

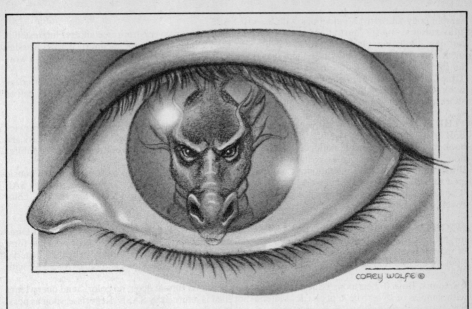

While Corey Wolfe freelances primarily in the video, movie and entertainment fields, he created this editorial illustration to accompany a friend's story which appeared in Fantasy Book. *The artist used black Prismacolor, white chalk pencil and airbrush to create the work. The artist received $37.50 for first North American serial rights. Wolfe lives in Lomita, California.*

ter publication. Sample copy $2.50. Receives very few cartoons ("could use more") and 10 illustrations/week from freelance artists.

Cartoons: Horror, fantasy and science fiction subjects (no space hardware). "Publishing is caught in the Reaganomics squeeze; rates will stay the same or go down."

Illustrations: Uses 5-6 illustrations/issue; buys all from freelancers. Interested in themes pertaining to fantasy and science fiction. "Artists should *not* send originals on speculation—send PMT's, stats, or quality photocopies. Don't send copies larger than 9x12 inches. If we need originals (as for cover illustration), we ask for them. All art is eventually returned, but we assume no responsibility for it." Samples returned "with SASE only." Reports in 4 weeks. Buys one-time publication rights only; all other rights retained by artist. Pays $50-100 cover (b&w with one-color overlays), $10-25 inside (various sizes), all media; pays 3 weeks after acceptance.

Tips: *"Fantasy Review* is now published through the Division of Continuing Education at Florida Atlantic University, a state institution. Payments to artists are slower (red-tape) and nudity is restricted: female, upper body only; no genitalia."

FARM SUPPLIER, Watt Publishing Co., Mount Morris IL 61054. Editor: Beth Miller. For retail farm suppliers and dealers throughout the US. Monthly.

Illustrations: "We use color slides that match editorial material. They should relate to the farm supply retail business, including custom application of chemicals and fertilizers. Query."

FARMFUTURES, Agridata Resources, Inc., 205 W. Highland Ave., Milwaukee WI 53203. (414)273-0873. Art Director: Geri Strigenz. Farm business marketing and managing magazine. Monthly.

Illustrations: Needs 3-4 spot illustrations/issue; all require freelancers. Send samples to be kept on file or request to be returned. Prefers slides or tear sheets as samples. Samples not kept on file are returned by SASE. Works on assignment only. Buys exclusive rights. Originals returned by special arrangement only. Pays $100-300 average for spots.

FARMSTEAD MAGAZINE, Box 111, Freedom ME 04941. (207)382-6200. Publisher: George Frangoulis. Focuses on home gardening and country living. Published 6 times a year. Circ. 175,000. Free sample copy and artist's guidelines with 8½x10 SASE.

Illustrations: Buys 2 illustrations/issue. Receives 5 submissions/week from freelancers. Interested in farming, gardening, plants, livestock, wildlife, etc. (pen & ink, wood block, etching). Works on assignment only. Prefers to review finished art, roughs. SASE. Reports in 8 weeks. Buys all rights on a work-for-hire basis. Pays $25-100, b&w inside; on publication.

Tips: "Send attractive resume that is short and simple, and several samples (photocopies preferred) of work. Creative brochures are eye-catching. Artist should include a telephone number—we often call on short notice. No samples returned without SASE."

*THE FIDDLEHEAD, The Observatory, University of New Brunswick, Fredericton, New Brunswick E3B 5A3 Canada. (506)454-3591. Editor: Roger Ploude. Emphasizes poetry, short stories, essays and book reviews for a general audience. Quarterly. Circ. 1,050. Original artwork returned after publication. Sample copy $4.25 plus postage.

Illustrations: Buys 5-6 illustrations/issue from freelancers. Send samples to be kept on file "if considered suitable." Prefers original work, tear sheets or photographs as samples. Samples returned by SAE (Canadian stamps or IRC). Reports within 6-8 weeks. Buys first rights. Pays $50, b&w and $75, color cover; $20, b&w, inside.

*FIGHTING WOMAN NEWS, Box 1459, Grand Central Station, New York NY 10163. Art Director: Muskat Buckby. Emphasizes women's martial arts for adult women actively practicing some form of martial art; 90% college graduates. Quarterly. Circ. 5,000. Accepts previously published material, "but we must be told about the previous publication." Sample copy $3.50; art guidelines for SASE with 39¢ postage.

Cartoons: Buys 0-2 cartoons/issue from freelancers. Cartoon format open; no color. Send query letter with samples of style to be kept on file. Material not filed is returned by SASE. Reports as soon as possible. Buys one-time rights. Pays in copies.

Illustrations: Buys 0-3 illustrations/issue from freelancers. "No woman black-belt beating up men or 'sexy' themes—done to death!" Send query letter with samples to be kept on file. Prefers tear sheets and photocopies as samples. Samples not filed are returned by SASE. Reports as soon as possible. Buys one-time rights. Pays $10, b&w, cover; in copies, b&w, inside; on publication.

Tips: "We _strongly_ suggest artists examine a sample copy before submitting!"

FIRST HAND LTD., 310 Cedar Ln., Teaneck NJ 07666. (201)836-9177. Art Director: Jeff Madden. Emphasizes homoerotica for a male audience. Monthly. Circ. 60,000. Original artwork can be returned after publication. Sample copy $3; art guidelines available for SASE.

Cartoons: Buys 5 cartoons/issue from freelancers. Prefers single panel with gagline; b&w line drawings. Send finished cartoons to be kept on file. Material not filed is returned by SASE. Reports within 2 weeks. Buys first rights. Pays $15 for b&w; on acceptance.

Illustrations: Buys 20 illustrations/issue from freelancers. Prefers "nude men in a realistic style; very basic, very simple." Send a query letter with samples to be kept on file; call or write for appointment to show portfolio. Prefers photostats or tear sheets as samples. Samples not filed are returned. Reports within 2 weeks. Buys all magazine rights. Pays $25-50 for inside b&w; on acceptance.

Tips: When reviewing a portfolio, looks for "porportion and skill—proof that the artist has seen a human body naked. Don't send artwork that is too large. The closer the art is to the size of the magazine, the better."

FISHING WORLD, 51 Atlantic Ave., New York NY 11001. (516)352-9700. Editor: Keith Gardner. Emphasizes angling. Readers are adult male US sport fishermen. Bimonthly. Circ. 285,000. Original artwork returned after publication. Sample copy $1.

Illustrations: Uses one illustration/issue, buys from freelancers. Interested in realistic illustrations. Uses inside color washes. Works on assignment only. No samples returned. Provide brochure, flyer and tear sheets to be kept on file for future assignments. SASE. Reports in 3 weeks. Buys first North American serial rights. Pays $300 for inside color; on acceptance.

*FLING, Relim Publishing Co., 550 Miller Ave., Mill Valley CA 94941. (415)383-5464. Editor: Arv Miller. Bimonthly. Emphasizes sex, seduction, sports, underworld pieces, success stories, travel, adventure and how-to's for men, 18-34. Sample copy for $4.

Cartoons: Prefers sexual themes. "The female characters must be pretty, sexy and curvy, with extremely big breasts. Sytles should be sophisticated and well-drawn." Pays $30, b&w, $50-100, color; on acceptance.

FLORIST, Florists Transworld Delivery Association, Box 2227, Southfield MI 48037. (313)355-9300. Editor-in-Chief: William Golden. Production Manager: Virginia Alsys. Managing Editor: Susan

Nicholas. Emphasizes information pertaining to the operation of the floral industry. For florists and floriculturists. Monthly. Circ. 24,000. Reports in 1 month. Accepts previously published material. Does not return original artwork after publication.
Cartoons: Uses 5 cartoons/issue, buys all from freelancers. Interested in retail florists and floriculture themes; single panel with gagline. Mail samples or roughs. SASE. Buys one-time rights. Pays $10-50, b&w line drawings; on acceptance.
Illustrations: Works on assignment only. Send query letter with samples. accepts photostats, tear sheets, photocopies, slides or photographs as samples. Samples not filed are returned by SASE. Reports within 3 months. Buys first rights.

FLOWER AND GARDEN, 4251 Pennsylvania, Kansas City MO 64111. (816)531-5730. Emphasizes "gardening for avid home gardeners." Bimonthly. Circ. 500,000. Sample copy $2.
Cartoons: Editor: Rachel Snyder. Uses 1 cartoon/issue. Receives about 10 submissions/week. Needs cartoons related to "indoor or outdoor home gardening." Format: single panel b&w line drawings or washes with gagline. Prefers to see finished cartoons. SASE. Reports in 4 weeks. Buys one-time rights. Pays $20, b&w cartoon; on acceptance.

*FLOWERS & MAGAZINE, Suite 260, Teleflora Plaza, 12233 W. Olympic Blvd., W. Los Angeles CA 90064. (213)826-5253. Art Director: Yukari Lee. Emphasizes flowers/business-related for wholesale/retail floral industry. Monthly. Circ. 26,000. Accepts previously published material. Original artwork returned after publication.
Cartoons: Considers flowers theme. Prefers single panel with gagline; b&w line drawings. Send samples of style to be kept on file. Material not filed is not returned. Reports only if interested. Buys one-time rights or reprint rights. Pays on publication.
Illustrations: Buys 1-5 illustrations/issue from freelancers. Considers all styles. Works on assignment only. Send samples to be kept on file; call for appointment to show portfolio. Prefers tear sheets or photographs as samples. Samples not filed are returned only if requested. Reports only if interested. Buys one-time rights or reprint rights. Pays $500 up, color, cover; $100-700, b&w and $150-800, color, inside; on publication.

FLY FISHERMAN, Editorial Offices, 2245 Kohn Rd., Box 8200, Harrisburg PA 17105. (802)867-5951. Art Director: Jeanne Collins. Emphasizes fly fishing. Readers are 99% male; 79% are college graduates; 79% are married. Published 6 times a year. Circ. 135,000. Original artwork returned after publication. Sample copy $2.95; art guidelines for SASE.
Illustrations: Uses spots, maps, and diagrams. Receives about 10 submissions/week from freelancers. Interested in "saltwater and freshwater fly-fishing or stream-scene in all areas of the country. Scenics including insects, fish—preferably not dead or braces of—and related subjects." Format: b&w line drawings, b&w washes and color washes for inside magazine. Freelancers are selected from "samples and spot-filler-work kept on file." Provide letter of inquiry or a sample of work preferably in the fly-fishing or stream area to be kept on file for future assignments. Prefers to see samples of style or arrange personal appointment to show portfolio. SASE. Reports in 4-6 weeks. Buys one-time North American magazine rights. Pays $25-100 for b&w "depending on size and use inside the magazine"; color payment negotiated; on publication.

THE FLYFISHER, 1387 Cambridge Dr., Idaho Falls ID 83401. (208)523-7300. Editor: Dennis G. Bitton. For members of the Federation of Fly Fishers; concerns fly fishing and conservation. Quarterly. Circ. 10,000. Buys first North American serial rights. Sample copy $3 from Federation of Fly Fishers main office, Box 1088, West Yellowstone, MT 59758.
Illustrations: Interested in fly-fishing themes. Query with resume and samples. Samples returned by SASE. Reports in 2 weeks. Buys first North American serial rights. Inside: Pays $25-150, b&w line drawings and washes; on publication.
Tips: "We always encourage freelancers to submit material. The possibility for a sale is good with good material. We especially look for an artist's ability to illustrate an article by reading the copy. See a current issue of the magazine."

FOOD & WINE, 1120 Avenue of the Americas, New York NY 10036. (212)382-5702. Art Director: Elizabeth Woodson. Emphasizes food and wine for "an upscale audience who cook, entertain and dine out stylishly." Monthly. Circ. 400,000.
Illustrations: Buys all from freelancers. Interested in sophisticated style. Works on assignment only. Send brochure and samples of style to be kept on file; drop portfolio off on third week of the month only. Reports when assignment is available. Buys one-time rights or all rights. Pays $100 minimum, inside, b&w line drawings; on acceptance.

FOOD ENGINEERING MAGAZINE, Chilton Way, Radnor PA 19089. (215)964-4459. Art Director: Scott Stephens. Emphasizes food processing and packaging materials and methods for food processing executives. Monthly. Circ. 50,000. Accepts previously published material. Does not return original artwork after publication. Sample copy available.
Illustrations: Number purchased varies from year to year. Works on assignment only. Send brochure and business card to be kept on file. Call for appointment to show portfolio. Prefers to review slides or photographs. Samples not filed are returned by SASE. Reports back only if interested. Buys all rights. Pays on acceptance.

FOOD PROCESSING, Putman Publishing Co., 301 E. Erie, Chicago IL 60611. Editor/Publisher: Roy Hlavacek. Emphasizes equipment, new developments, laboratory instruments and government regulations of the food processing industry. For executives and managers in food processing industries. Monthly. Circ. 68,000. Photocopied submissions OK. Original artwork not returned after publication. Free sample copy and artist's guidelines.
Cartoons: Uses 1-2 cartoons/issue, all from freelancers. Receives 10-15 submissions/week from freelancers. Interested in "situations in and around the food plant (e.g., mixing, handling, transporting, weighing, analyzing, government inspection, etc.)"; single panel with gagline. Prefers to see finished cartoons. SASE. Reports in 1 week. Buys all rights. Pays $20 minimum, b&w line drawings.
Tips: "Avoid most 'in-the-home' and all retailing cartoon situations. Stick to in-the-food-plant situations—meat packing, vegetable and fruit canning, candymaking, beverage processing, bakery, dairy—including any phase of processing, inspecting, handling, quality control, packaging, storage, shipping, etc."

FORECAST FOR HOME ECONOMICS, 730 Broadway, New York NY 10003. (212)505-3000. Art Editor: Joanne Slattery. Used as a teaching guide for *Choices* magazine. Circ. 78,000. Monthly (September-June). SASE. Pays on publication.
Illustrations: Occasionally needs story illustrations. Pays $50-100, b&w; $50-200, color; varies according to size. Arrange interview to show portfolio.

FOREIGN SERVICE JOURNAL, 2101 E St. NW, Washington DC 20037. (202)338-4045. Contact: Associate Editor. Emphasizes foreign policy for foreign service employees. Monthly. Circ. 9,000. Accepts previously published material. Returns original artwork after publication. Sample copy free for SASE with 87¢ postage.
Cartoons: Write or call for appointment to show portfolio. Buys first rights. Pays on publication.
Illustrations: Buys 1-2 illustrations/issue from freelancers. Works on assignment only. Write or call for appointment to show portfolio. Buys first rights. Pays on publication.

FORMAT: ART AND THE WORLD, Seven Oaks Press, 405 S. 7th St., St. Charles IL 60174. (312)584-0187. Editor: Ms. C.L. Morrison. Emphasizes art, society, artist's lives and social role, criticism and political critiques. Quarterly.
Illustrations: Assigns 3 freelance jobs for covers and 5 for text illustrations/year. "Material accepted must be philosophically or idea-oriented, not slick. May be abstract or accompanied by writing; symbolic, personal sketchbook-type work. Also embarking on a new project in which layouts for a whole issue are given to a single artist who will then do artwork throughout the issue for direct, one-time publication." Send small b&w sketches (photocopies acceptable) with SASE. Do not send slides and do not query. Reports within 8 weeks. Original work returned to artist after job's completion. Considers the project's budget when establishing payment. Pays by the project, $5-15.

FORUM MAGAZINE, 1965 Broadway, New York NY 10023-5965. (212)496-6100. Art Director: John Arocho. Emphasizes medicine/human relations/sexuality. Monthly. Circ. 675,000. Returns original artwork after publication. Art guidelines available.
Illustrations: Buys 6-10 illustrations/issue from freelancers. Prefers graphic b&w, variable subject matter. Works on assignment only. Send query letter with brochure and samples to be kept on file. Call for appointment to show portfolio. Accepts photostats, tear sheets, photocopies, slides or photographs as samples. Samples not filed are returned only if requested. Reports back only if interested. Negotiates rights purchased. Pays $250-800 for b&w and $1,000-1,200 for color, inside; on acceptance.

4-H LEADER-THE NATIONAL MAGAZINE FOR 4-H, (formerly *National 4-H News*), 7100 Connecticut Ave. Chevy Chase MD 20815. (301)656-9000. Editor: Suzanne C. Harting. Emphasizes techniques for working with children, and interests of children, for adults and teenaged 4-H volunteers. Receives few cartoons and 2-3 illustrations/week from freelance artists.
Illustrations: Especially needs themes on families teen interest, and adults interacting with youngsters. Provide tear sheet or photocopies to be kept on file for future assignments. May be any type b&w tech-

nique, watercolor, charcoal sketch, scratchboard, pen & ink or woodcuts. "Art should suggest rather than show literal detail." SASE. Reports in 1 month. Buys one-time rights. Pays $10-50; on acceptance.

THE FRIEND, 50 E. North Temple, Salt Lake City UT 84150. (801)531-2210. Contact: Art Director. Children's publication of the Church of Jesus Christ of Latter-day Saints. Emphasizes the cultures and children of different countries. Original artwork returned after publication, usually after about 1 year. **Illustrations:** Uses 30-35 illustrations/issue; buys about 12/issue from freelancers. Interested in themes mostly specific to individual art assignments from our concepts (child-related, dealing with ages 1-12); excellent, competitive quality. Covers often emphasize seasons and holidays; wide spectrum of styles and ideas. Works with freelancers on assignment basis only except for activity related things. Samples returned if artist requests. Provide printed samples to be kept on file for future assignments. Prefers roughs of ideas before finish art. SASE. Report depends on specific art assignment. Need to retain art for about a year. Pays $100-600, b&w, 2-color and full-color; on acceptance.

FRONT PAGE DETECTIVE, RGH Publications, 20th Floor, 460 W. 34th St., New York NY 10001. Editor: Rose Mandelsberg. For mature adults—law enforcement officials, professional investigators, criminology buffs and interested laymen. Monthly.
Cartoons: Must have crime theme. Submit finished art. SASE. Reports in 10 days. Buys all rights. Pays $25; on acceptance.
Tips: "Make sure the cartoons submitted do not degrade or ridicule law enforcement officials."

FUR-FISH-GAME, A.R. Harding Publishing Co., 2878 E. Main St., Columbus OH 43209. (614)231-9585. Editor/Art Director: Ken Dunwoody. Monthly magazine with circulation of 180,000 for practical outdoorsmen, emphasizing hunting, fishing, trapping and camping. Previously published work OK in some cases. Sample copy $1; free artists' guidelines.
Covers: Uses 12/year, all from freelancers. Receives about 1 submission/week. Interested in game animals, gamebirds, gamefish and furbearers. Prefers to see color photograph of art. SASE. Reports in 4 weeks. Painting must be able to crop into square format for cover. Pays $50-75 for one-time rights for full-color covers; on acceptance.
Illustrations: Uses 20-60 b&w/year, mostly from freelancers responding to assigned work. Interested freelancers should send specific submissions or samples of work. Photostats or other reproductions preferred as submissions. SASE if needed. Pays $15-30 for most, on acceptance.
Tips: "We are seeking quality color paintings for our covers. We work at least 10 weeks in advance with covers and attempt to keep them seasonal. Subjects such as small game, common game fish and furbearers have the best chance of acceptance. Prefer artist's signature on right side of painting. If name is cropped out, credit will be given in table of contents. We are looking for very realistic work that contains a certain freshness and vitality, especially for our covers. The work must not only be visually appealing, but also painstakingly accurate in its detail of wild animals or birds."

FUTURIFIC MAGAZINE, Suite 1210, 280 Madison Ave., New York NY 10016. Publisher: B. Szent-Miklosy. Emphasizes future-related subjects for highly educated, upper income government, corporate leaders of the community. Monthly. Circ. 10,000. Previously published material and simultaneous submissions OK. Original artwork returned after publication. Free sample copy for SASE with 85¢ postage.
Cartoons: Prefers positive, upbeat, futuristic themes; no "doom and gloom." Prefers single, double or multipanel with or without gagline, b&w line drawings. Send finished cartoons. Samples returned by SASE. Reports within 4 weeks. Will negotiate rights and payment. Pays on publication.
Illustrations: Uses 10 illustrations/issue; buys 10 illustrations/issue from freelancers. Prefers postive, upbeat, futuristic themes; no "doom and gloom." Send finished art. Samples returned by SASE. Reports within 4 weeks. Will negotiate rights and payment. Pays on publication.
Tips: "Only optimists need apply." Looking for good, clean art. Interested in furturistic material, but not sci-fi.

THE FUTURIST, 4916 St. Elmo Ave., Bethesda MD 20814. (301)656-8274. Art Director: Cynthia Fowler. Assistant Editor: Tim Willard. Emphasizes all aspects of the future for a well-educated, general audience. Bimonthly. Circ. 30,000. Accepts simultaneous submissions. Return of original artwork following publication depends on individual agreement. Sample copy available.
Illustrations: Buys 3-4 illustrations/issue; buys all from freelancers. Uses a variety of themes and styles "usually line-drawings, often whimsical. We like an artist who can read an article and deal with the concepts and ideas." Works on assignment only. Send query letter with brochure, samples or tear sheets to be kept on file. Call or write for appointment to show portfolio. "Photostats are fine as samples; whatever is easy for the artist." Reports only if interested. Rights purchased negotable. Pays $300-500, color, cover; $100-125, b&w, inside; on acceptance.

GALLERY MAGAZINE, 800 2nd Ave., New York NY 10017. (212)986-9600. Creative Director: Michael Monte. Emphasizes sophisticated men's entertainment for the middle-class, collegiate male. Monthly. Circ. 700,000. No art guidelines, editorial content dictates illustration style.
Cartoons: Uses 5 cartoons/issue; buys all from freelancers. Interested in sexy humor; single, double, or multipanel with or without gag line, color and b&w washes, b&w line drawings. Send finished cartoons. Reports in 1 month. Buys first rights. Pays on publication. Enclose SASE. Contact: J. Linden.
Illustrations: Uses 4 full-page illustrations and 4 spots/issue; buys all from freelancers. Interested in the "highest creative and technical styles." Especially needs slick, high quality, 4-color work. Works on assignment only. Provide flyer, samples and tear sheets to be kept on file for possible future assignments. Send samples of style or submit portfolio. Samples returned by SASE. Reports in several weeks. Negotiates rights purchased. Pays $800 maximum for inside color washes; on publication.

GAMBLING TIMES, 1018 N. Cole Ave., Hollywood CA 90038. (213)463-4833. Editor-in-Chief: Len Miller. Art Director: Carla Schrad. Emphasizes gambling techniques and personalities in gambling. Monthly. Circ. 100,000. Original artwork returned after publication. Sample copy $1; free artist's guidelines.
Cartoons: Buys approximately 20/year on topic directly related to gambling. Prefers finished cartoon, full-page, single panel; b&w line drawings. SASE. Reports in 2 weeks. Buys all rights. Pays $10-35; on publication.
Illustrations: Uses 6-7 illustrations/issue; buys 5/issue from freelancers. Interested in simple and clean b&w line drawings; satirical or humorous visuals used occasionally. Works on assignment only. Samples returned by SASE. Provide business card or tear sheet to be kept on file for future assignments. Prefers to see portfolio. Reports in 1 week. Buys all rights on a work-for-hire basis. Pays on publication.

GAMES, 515 Madison Ave., New York NY 10022. (212)421-5984. Contact: Art Director. Emphasizes games, puzzles, mazes, brain teasers, etc. for teachers, students, computer analysts and mathematicians interested in paper-and-pencil games. Monthly. Circ. 750,000.
Illustrations: Uses 10 illustrations/issue; all supplied by freelancers. Illustrations should be lighthearted but not childish drawings. Anything from Renaissance to cartoons. Format: b&w line drawings and color washes for inside and cover. Contact: art director to arrange personal appointment to show portfolio and/or photocopies of samples with cover letter including experience and turn-around time. Drop off on Wednesday and pick up Thursday. Reports in two weeks or whenever an assignment is available. Pays on acceptance $100-400 b&w/inside; $200-700 color/inside. Buys one-time rights.
Tips: "We encourage artists to create games or puzzles that they can execute in their own style after editorial approval. Illustrations are often required to be lighthearted or humorous but using a unique and sophisticated style."

GARDEN, New York Botanical Garden, Bronx NY 10458. Associate Editor: Anne Schwartz. Emphasizes all aspects of the plant world—botany, horticulture, the environment, etc. for "members of botanical gardens and arboreta—a diverse readership, largely college graduates and professionals, with a common interest in plants." Bimonthly. Circ. 30,000. Accepts previously published material. Original artwork returned after publication. Sample copy $2.50.
Illustrations: Uses 2-3 illustrations/issue; buys 0-1/issue from freelancers. Works on assignment only. Local artists preferred. Send query letter with samples. Prefers photostats, photographs, printed samples or even photocopies as samples. Especially looks for "quality, botanical accuracy and style." Samples not kept on file are returned by SASE. Reports only if interested. Buys one-time rights. Pays $25 minimum, b&w, inside; on publication.

GENESIS, 770 Lexington Ave., New York NY 10021. (212)486-8430. Emphasizes celebrities, current events, issues and personal relationships. For the young male "celebrating all that is in the good life." Monthly. Circ. 300,000.
Cartoons: Contact Cartoon Editor. Uses 2-8 cartoons/issue, all from freelancers. Interested in erotic themes. Prefers finished cartoons. SASE. Reports in 2-4 weeks. Buys first North American serial rights. Pays $75-200, b&w or color; 30 days from acceptance.

GENT, Dugent Publishing Co., 2355 Salzedo St., Coral Gables FL 33134. Publisher: Douglas Allen. Editor: John Fox. Managing Editor: Nye Willden. For men "who like big women."
Cartoons: Buys humor and sexual themes; "major emphasis of magazine is on large D-cup-breasted women." Mail cartoons. Buys first rights. Pays $50, b&w spot drawing; $75/page.
Illustrations: Buys 3-4 illustrations/issue on assigned themes. Submit illustration samples for files. Buys b&w only. Buys first rights. Pays $100-150.
Tips: "Send samples designed especially for our publication. Study our magazine. Be able to draw erotic anatomy. Write for artist's guides and cartoon guides *first*, before submitting samples, since they contain some helpful suggestions."

GENTLEMANS QUARTERLY, 350 Madison Ave., New York NY 10017. (212)880-6691. Art Director: Mary Shanahan. Emphasizes "men's fashions and lifestyles for middle-to upper-income professional males ranging in age from 20 to 40." Monthly. Circ. 650,000. No cartoons.
Illustrations: Uses less than 10 illustrations/issue, all supplied by freelancers. Selection based on review of portfolios ("we have a strict first time drop-off policy") and by reviewing files maintained on freelancers. Send copied samples of b&w and color drawings to art assistant; do not send original work. SASE. Reports in 1 week. Pays 30 days after work is completed. Buys all rights on a work-for-hire basis.

GERIATRICS, 7500 Old Oak Blvd., Middleburg Heights OH 44130. (216)243-8100. Editor: Richard Peck. Emphasizes medical care for the elderly (technical papers on clinical subjects) for primary care physicians in US. Monthly. Circ. 55,000. Original artwork returned after publication. Sample copy and art guidelines free for SASE.
Illustrations: Uses few illustrations/issue, "but growing." Prefers "accurate medical art; artist should be trained medical artist." Especially looks for "accuracy backed by careful research; careful detailing; a clean look; a use of color that is either realistic or quiet enough not to detract from the reader's easy grasp of what is shown. This artwork is more educational than advertising- or commercial-related." Works on assignment only. Send query letter with brochure, resume or samples to be kept on file. Call or write for appointment to show portfolio. Prefers photographs or slides as samples. Pays $800, color, cover; $100-200, b&w, inside; $200-300, color, inside; on acceptance.
Tips: "As we are able to visualize ever smaller and more remote physiological entities, medical art is following suit. However detailed, art still manages to remain clean with imaginative use of color. Artists should study the publication and its particular use of art."

GLAMOUR, 350 Madison Ave., New York NY 10017. (212)880-8800. Art Director: George Hartman. Emphasizes fashion, beauty, travel, lifestyle for women ages 18-35. Query with resume and arrange to show portfolio.
Needs: "All work done here is freelance." Pays $225/page.

***GLASS CRAFT NEWS**, 270 Lafayette St., New York NY 10012. (212)966-6694. Editor: David Ostiller. Estab. 1983. Emphasizes stained glass for hobbyists and professionals. Bimonthly. Circ. 30,000. Accepts previously published material. Original artwork returned after publication. Sample copy free for SASE with 70¢ postage.
Illustrations: Buys 3-5 illustrations/issue from freelancers. Prefers illustrations of techniques. Works on assignment only. Send query letter with samples to be kept on file. Accepts photostats, tear sheets, photocopies, slides, photographs, etc. as samples. Samples not filed are returned by SASE only if requested. Reports within 1 month. Buys reprint rights. Pays $50-100 b&w; on publication.

GLASS DIGEST, 310 Madison Ave., New York NY 10017. Editor: Charles B. Cumpston. For management in the distribution, merchandising, and installation phases of the flat glass, architectural metal, and allied products industry (including stained, art glass and mirrors). Original artwork not returned after publication. Free sample copy.
Cartoons: Uses 0-3 cartoons/issue; buys about 2/issue from freelancers. Receives 5 submissions/week from freelancers. Interested in storefront and curtain wall construction and automotive glass industry. Prefers to see finished cartoons. SASE. Reports in 1 week. Pays $7.50; on acceptance.
Illustrations: Works on assignment only. Prefers to see roughs. Samples returned by SASE. Reports in 1 week. Buys first North American serial rights. Pays on acceptance.
Tips: "Stick to the subject matter."

GOLF JOURNAL, Golf House, Far Hills NJ 07931. (201)234-2300. Managing Editor: George Eberl. Readers are "literate, professional, knowledgeable on the subject of golf." Published 8 times/year. Circ. 140,000. Original artwork not returned after publication. Free sample copy.
Cartoons: Uses several cartoons/issue, all from freelancers. Receives 50 submissions/week from freelancers. "The subject is golf. Golf must be central to the cartoon. Drawings should be professional, and captions sharp, bright and literate, on a par with our generally sophisticated readership." Formats: single or multipanel, b&w line drawings with gagline. Prefers to see finished cartoons. SASE. Reports in 1 month. Buys one-time rights. Pays $25, b&w cartoons; on acceptance.
Illustrations: Uses several illustrations/issue, all from freelancers. "We maintain a file of samples from illustrators. Our needs for illustrations—and we do need talent with an artistic light touch—are based almost solely on assignments, illustrations to accompany specific stories. We would assign a job to an illustrator who is able to capture the feel and mood of a story. Most frequently, it is light-touch golf stories which beg illustrations. A sense of humor is a useful quality in the illustrator; but this sense shouldn't lapse into absurdity." Uses color washes. Provide samples of style to be kept on file for future assignments. SASE. Reports in 1 month. Buys all rights on a work-for-hire basis. Pays on acceptance.

GOLF SHOP OPERATIONS, 495 Westport Ave., Norwalk CT 06856. (203)847-5811. Editor: Nick Romano. Art Director: Karen Polaski. For golf professionals at public and private courses, resorts and driving ranges. Published 6 times/year. Circ. 12,000. Receives 1-6 cartoons/year. Original artwork not returned after publication. Free sample copy.
Illustrations: Uses 4 illustrations/issue. Soft goods oriented. Illustrations often used for conceptual pieces. Works on assignment only. Samples returned by SASE. Reports back on future assignment possibilities. Prefers to see finished art, roughs, portfolio, or samples of style; color or b&w. Reports in 2 weeks. Buys all rights on a work-for-hire basis. Pays $50-350; on publication.

GOOD HOUSEKEEPING, Hearst Corp., 959 8th Ave., New York NY 10019. (212)262-5700. Editor-in-Chief: John Mack Carter. Contact: Art Director. For homemakers. Emphasizes food, fashion, beauty, home decorating, current events, personal relationships and celebrities. Monthly. Circ. 5,000,000.
Cartoons: Buys 150/year on family life, animals and humor through youth; single panel. Arrange an interview to show portfolio. Buys all reproduction rights. Pays $250 maximum, b&w line drawings and washes; on acceptance.
Illustrations: Buys 15 illustrations/issue on romantic themes. "Drop off" policy for portfolios. Reports in 3 weeks. Buys all reproduction rights. Inside: pay for b&w line drawing and washes depends on complexity of job, $1,000-2,000, color washes and full-color renderings; on acceptance.

GOOD NEWS BROADCASTER, Box 82808, Lincoln NE 68501. Managing Editor: Norman Olson. Interdenominational magazine for adults ages 16 and up. Monthly. Circ. 150,000. Previously published work OK. Original artwork returned after publication. Sample copy $1.
Illustrations: Uses at least 2 illustrations/issue. Interested in themes that are "serious, related to the subjects of the articles about the Christian life." Works on assignment only. Query with resume or send samples. Samples returned by SASE. Provide resume, business card, brochure, flyer, tear sheet or "whatever is available" to be kept on file for future assignments. "Helps to know if person is a Christian, too, but not necessary." Reporting time varies. Buys first North American serial rights. Pays on publication.
Tips: Trends in the field today include "more realism, more primary colors and more oil painting than pencil/pen." When reviewing work, "we ask how well does it fit the story and does it have a truly professional look? Artists should think of the publication's needs and pay attention to small, but important, details in artwork that will complement the details in the writing."

GOOD READING MAGAZINE, Box 40, Litchfield IL 62056. (217)324-3425. "Nonfiction magazine which emphasizes travel, business, human interest and novel occupations." Monthly. Circ. 12,000. Original artwork returned after publication, only if requested.
Cartoons: Uses 1 cartoon/issue, all from freelancers. Receives 15 submissions/week from freelancers. Interested in "business, points of interest, people with unusual hobbies and occupations, and wholesome humor." Prefers to see finished cartoons. SASE. Reports in 6-8 weeks. Buys first North American serial rights. Pays on acceptance.

*GOODWIN'S, Box 1043, Station B, Ottawa, Ontario K1P 5R1 Canada. (613)234-8928. Editor: Ron Verzuh. Estab. 1983. Emphasizes social and economic alternatives for audience over 25, with 30,000 annual income, who are politically active and/or aware; parents, homeowners, university educated, city dwellers. Quarterly. Circ. 4,500. Original artwork returned after publication. Sample copy $2.50 plus postage; art guidelines available.
Cartoons: Buys 3 cartoons/issue from freelancers. Considers social issues; "Far Side" (by Gary Larson) type themes. Prefers single panel with gagline; b&w line drawings or b&w washes. Send query letter with samples of style to be kept on file. Material not filed is returned by SASE. Reports within 6 weeks. Buys first rights. Pays $50 maximum, b&w; on publication.
Illustrations: Buys 1 illustration/issue from freelancers. Prefers line drawings; screens and pencil shades acceptable. Usually works on assignment. Send query letter with samples to be kept on file. Prefers photostats as samples. Samples not filed are returned by SASE. Reports within 6 weeks. Buys first rights. Pays $100 maximum, b&w, cover; $50 maximum, b&w, inside; on publication.

GORHAM, 800 S. Euclid Blvd., Fullerton CA 92634. Publisher/Editor: Daniel J. Gorham. Emphasizes genealogy and history for people interested in their family's history. Monthly. Circ. 2,083. Accepts previously published material and simultaneous submissions. Original artwork returned after publication. Sample copy $2.
Illustrations: Uses 15-45 illustrations/issue; buys 20-30/issue from freelancers. Themes and styles are open, but desires "good, serious work." Send query letter with samples to be kept on file; write for appointment to show portfolio. Samples not kept on file are returned by SASE. Reports within 2 months.

Buys first rights. Pays $500-1,000, b&w, cover; $75-500, b&w, inside; on publication.
Tips: Seeks *neat* work, with a "timeless aspect."

GRADUATING ENGINEER, 1221 Ave. of the Americas, New York NY 10020. (212)512-3796. Art Director: Vincent Lomonte. Directed to the young engineer in his last year of school, who is about to enter job market. Quarterly with 3 special issues; computer, women, minority. Circ. 85,000. Returns original artwork after publication. Art guidelines available.
Cartoons: Buys 1-2 cartoons/issue from freelancers. Call for appointment to show portfolio. Pays $135-150, b&w; $300-350, color; on acceptance.
Illustrations: Buys 10-15 illustrations/issue from freelancers. Works on assignment only. Send brochure and business card to be kept on file; call art director for appointment to show portfolio. Will review photostats, tear sheets, photocopies, slides or photographs. Reports back only if interested. Negotiates rights purchased. Pays $200-300 for b&w and $500 for color, cover; $125-225 for b&w inside; on acceptance.

GRAND RAPIDS MAGAZINE, Gemini Communications, Suite 1040, Trust Building, 40 Pearl St. NW, Grand Rapids MI 49503. (616)459-4545. Editor: John Brosky. Managing Editor: William Holm. Staff Artists: Stephen Alley, Kathie L. Manett. For greater Grand Rapids residents. Monthly. Circ. 13,500. Original artwork returned after publication.
Needs: Area artists *only*. Uses 2 cartoons or illustrations/issue. Interested in "Western Michigan, Michigan, Lake Michigan, city, issue or consumer/household themes." Prefers to see finished graphics, illustration or cartoon samples and cover letter. Call for appointment. SASE. Reports within 1 month. Buys all rights. Pays 15th of month of publication.

GRAPHIC ARTS MONTHLY, 875 3rd Ave., New York NY 10022. (212)605-9548. Editor: Roger Ynostroza. Managing Editor: Peter Johnston. For management and production personnel in commercial and specialty printing plants and allied crafts. Monthly. Circ. 90,000. Sample copy $5.
Cartoons: Buys 15 cartoons/year on printing, layout, paste-up, typesetting and proofreading; single panel. Mail art. SASE. Reports in 3 weeks. Buys first rights. Pays on acceptance.

GRAY'S SPORTING JOURNAL, 205 Willow St., So. Hamilton MA 01982. (617)468-4486. Editor-in-Chief: Ed Gray. Art Director: DeCourcy Taylor. Concerns the outdoors, hunting and fishing. Published 4 times/year. Circ. 35,000. Sample copy $6.50; free artist's guidelines. SASE.
Illustrations: Buys 10 illustrations/year on hunting and fishing. Query with samples or previously published work. SASE. Reports in 4 weeks. Buys one-time rights. Inside: Pays $350, full-color art; $50-100, b&w line drawings.

*GREAT LAKE SPORTSMAN GROUP, Box 2266, Oshkosh WI 54903. Contact: Art Director. Publishes four regional outdoor publications: *Michigan Sportsman*, *Minnesota Sportsman*, *Pennsylvania Outdoors*, and *Wisconsin Sportsman*. Bimonthlies. Circ. 200,000. Mail art or query with samples or previously published work. SASE. Material is purchased for use in any or all publications at discretion of editor. Reports in 3 weeks. Photocopied submissions OK. Buys one-time rights. Pays on acceptance. Free sample copy. Especially needs good cover material and multi-media illustrators who can work with one-month deadlines.
Cartoons: Buys 50 cartoons/year on the environment, wildlife, hunting and fishing; single, double and multipanel with or without gaglines. Pays $80-100, b&w and color.
Illustrations: Buys 15-20 illustrations/year on the environment, wildlife and outdoors. "No Disney-type animals. Must be geographically and anatomically correct. No palm trees, snow-capped mountains." Cover: Pays $250 minimum, color. Inside: Pays $50 minimum, b&w; $100 minimum, color.
Tips: "Study the magazines and send SASE with all work."

*GREATER PHOENIX JEWISH NEWS, Suite G, 7220 N. 16th St., Phoenix AZ 85020. (602)870-9470. Production Manager: Mary Gilmore. Tabloid emphasizing topics of interest to Jewish residents of Phoenix and surrounding areas—both local, national and international news. Readers are 35-65; 60% are college graduates. Weekly. Circ. 7,000. Accepts previously published material. Returns original artwork after publication. Sample copy for SASE with $1 postage. Art guidelines available.
Cartoons: Currently buys no cartoons, but will consider. Prefers Jewish issues and family life themes. Prefers single panel with gagline; b&w line drawings. Send query letter with samples of style to be kept on file. Write for appointment to show portfolio. Material not filed is returned by SASE. Reports within 2 weeks. Negotiates rights purchased and payment; pays on acceptance.
Illustrations: Buys 1-3/issue. Works on assignment only. Send query letter with brochure, resume or business card and samples to be kept on file. Write for appointment to show portfolio. Accepts any type sample except slides. Samples not filed are returned by SASE. Reports within 2 weeks. Negotiates rights purchased on any payment; pays on acceptance.

*GREATER PORTLAND MAGAZINE, 142 Free St., Portland ME 04101. (207)772-2811. Editor: Colin Sargent. The city magazine for Portland, Maine. Includes fiction section, interviews, theater and restaurant reviews, and features. "Our contemporary graphics and concept airbrush illustrations aim to please the upscale consumer market—heavy art emphasis." Quarterly. Circ. 10,000. Accepts previously published material if new to this area. Returns original artwork after publication. Sample copy for $1.75.
Cartoons: "I am open to *New Yorkerish* cartoons, but like our stories, they need a local news peg." Also looking for a series with local appeal. Send query letter with samples of style to be kept on file. Write or call for appointment to show portfolio. Materials not kept on file are returned by SASE. Reports within 2 weeks if SASE enclosed. Purchases first rights. Negotiates payment; pays on publication.
Illustrations: Buys 2/issue. Prefers "airbrush for our fiction section, but like a baby *Esquire*, we like any interpretive stuff. Try for the unusual." Works on assignment only "so far, but we'd like to be surprised." Uses humorous and cartoon-style illustrations whenever they fit in with a story already planned. Send query letter with brochure and samples to be kept on file. Write or call for appointment to show portfolio. Prefers tear sheets, slides or photographs as samples. Samples not kept on file are returned by SASE. Reports back within 2 weeks. Pays $150 for color, cover; $100 for b&w, $150 for color, inside; on publication.
Tips: "I'm seeing more interpretive illustrations that disturb rather than coax a reader into reading stories. I'm very interested in seeing conceptual b&w drawings like these. I'd rather be surprised than have my expectations met exactly."

*GREEN FEATHER MAGAZINE, Box 2633, Lakewood OH 44107. Editor: Gary S. Skeens. Emphasizes fiction and poetry for general audience. Annually. Circ. 150-200. Accepts previously published material. Original artwork returned after publication. Sample copy free for SASE with $1 postage; art guidelines free for SASE.
Cartoons: Buys 1 cartoon/issue from freelancers. Prefers single panel with gagline; b&w line drawings. Send query letter with samples of style to be kept on file. Material not filed is returned by SASE. Reports in 1 month. Buys first rights or reprint rights. Negotiates payments. Pays on publication.
Illustrations: Buys 1 illustration/issue from freelancers. Send query letter with resume and samples to be kept on file. Prefers tear sheets or photocopies as samples. Samples not filed are returned by SASE. Reports within 1 month. Buys first rights or reprint rights. Negotiates payment. Pays on publication.

*THE GRENADIER MAGAZINE, 3833 Lake Shore, Oakland CA 94610. (415)763-0928. Senior Editor: S.A. Jefferis-Tibbets. Emphasizes military simulation and its historical context for military professionals, war gamers and game theorists. Bimonthly. Circ. 5,600. Original artwork not returned after publication. Sample copy for 9x12 SASE with $1.25 postage; art guidelines for SASE with 22¢ postage.
Cartoons: Buys 0-1 cartoons/issue from freelancers. Military simulation theme. Prefers single panel with gagline; b&w line drawings or b&w washes. Send query letter with samples of style or finished cartoons to be kept on file; write for appointment to show portfolio. Material not filed is returned by SASE. Reports within 1 month. Buys all rights. Pays $10-5, b&w; open rate, color; on acceptance.
Illustrations: Buys 0-12 illustrations/issue from freelancers. Works on assignment only. Send query letter with brochure and samples to be kept on file; write for appointment to show portfolio. Photocopies OK as samples if they show the artist's style and capability. Samples not filed are returned by SASE. Reports within 1 week. Buys all rights. Pays $250 +, color, cover; $10-25, b&w, inside; on acceptance.

GROUP, Thom Schultz Publications, Inc., Box 481, Loveland CO 80539. (303)669-3836. Editor-in-Chief: Thom Schultz. For adult leaders and high school members of Christian youth groups. Published 8 times/year. Circ. 60,000. Previously published, photocopied and simultaneous submissions OK. Original artwork returned after publication, if requested. Sample copy $1.
Cartoons: Uses 3 cartoons/issue; buys 3/issue from freelancers. Interested in humor through youth and religion. Send finished artwork. Reports in 2 weeks. Buys first, reprint or all rights, but may reassign rights to artist after publication. Pays on acceptance.
Illustrations: Uses 8 illustrations/issue; buys all from freelancers. Query with finished art or roughs. Provide flyer and/or tear sheet to be kept on file for future assignments. Reports in 1 week. Cover: Pays $100 minimum, color. Inside: Pays $25-200, b&w line drawings and washes, color. Buys all rights on a work-for-hire basis.

GUIDEPOSTS, 747 3rd Ave., New York NY 10017. (212)754-2200. Contact: Design Director. "*Guideposts* is an inspirational monthly magazine for all faiths in which men and women from all walks of life tell how they overcame obstacles, rose above failures, not sorrow, learned to master themselves, and became more effective people through the direct application of the religious principles by which they live." Monthly. Original artwork returned after publication. Free sample copy.
Illustrations: Uses 2-3 illustrations/issue; buys 2-3/month from freelancers. Receives 15 samples/

month from freelancers. Works on assignment only. Call Larry Laukhuf for interview; prefers to see portfolio in conjunction with artist. Provide business card, brochure, flyer and tear sheet to be kept on file for future assignments. Buys one-time rights on a work-for-hire basis. Buys full-color illustrations, and washes.

GUN WORLD, Box HH, Capistrano Beach CA 92624. Contact: Managing Editor. For shooters and hunters. Monthly. Circ. 136,000. Mail art. SASE. Reports in 8 weeks. Buys all rights, but may reassign rights to artist after publication. Pays on acceptance.
Cartoons: Buys 3-4 cartoons/issue on shooting and hunting. Pays $7.50-12, halftones.
Illustrations: Buys assigned themes.

HADASSAH MAGAZINE, 50 W. 58th St., New York NY 10019. (212)355-7900. Editor-in-Chief: Alan M. Tigay. Associate Publisher and Advertising Director: Nancy Margolis. Art Director: Meyer Fecher. For American Jewish families; deals with social, economic, political and cultural developments in Israel and Jewish communities in the U.S. and elsewhere. Monthly. Circ. 370,000. Sample copy $1.50. SASE. Reports in 6 weeks. Buys first rights. Pays on acceptance.

HAM RADIO, Greenville NH 03048. (603)878-1441. Editor-in-Chief: Rich Rosen. Assistant Editor: Dorothy Rosa. Art Director: Susan Shorrock. Address inquiries to Dorothy Rosa. For licensed amateur radio operators and electronics experimenters. Monthly. Circ. 50,000.
Cartoons: *Very* limited. Cartoons must pertain to amateur radio. One panel. Pays $15 minimum.
Illustrations: Buys drafting (on assignment), cover art, illustration. Prefers to see photocopied samples; do not send original art unless requested to do so. Reports in 30 days. Minimum payment: cover art, $100; illustration, $20; on publication.
Tips: "On our covers we favor strong graphic interpretations of concepts in electronics. The use of bright, bold colors sets us apart from other publications in our field."

*HAPPY TIMES MAGAZINE, 5600 N. University Ave., Provo UT 84604. (801)225-9000. Art Director: Colleen Hinckley. Associate Art Director: Mark Robison. Estab. 1983. Emphasizes moral values in a non-religious way for children ages 3-7. Publishes 10 times/year. Circ. 85,000. Accepts previously published material. Returns original artwork after publication. Sample copy $1.10.
Illustrations: Buys 10-15/issue. "Artists must be able to draw children well—whether it be a realistic or cartoony style with good use of color. Oil paintings are unacceptable due to color separation problems. We also encourage puzzle and activity artists to submit hidden pictures, dot-to-dots, mazes, and folding activities that reinforce our monthly themes. Theme lists are available on request with SASE." Works on assignment only. Send query letter with samples to be kept on file. Prefers tear sheets and/or slides as samples. "Originals are acceptable only if artist brings a portfolio in person." Samples not filed are returned by SASE. Reports only if interested. Usually buys first North American serial rights. Pays $500 color, cover; and $250, color, inside double spread. Pays 30 days after acceptance.

HARROWSMITH, Camden House Publishing Ltd., Ontario K0K 1J0 Canada. (613)378-6661. Editor-in-Chief: James Lawrence. Graphic Designer: Pamela McDonald. Concerns alternative lifestyles, energy sources and architecture, the environment, country living and gardening. Publishes 6 issues/year. Circ. 154,000. Sample copy $5. Receives 4 cartoons and 6 illustrations/week from freelance artists.
Cartoons: Uses 2-3 cartoons/issue, all from freelancers. Single panel with gagline. Prefers roughs, samples for files and business card; nonresidents include SAE and IRC. Reports in 6 weeks. Pays $25-100 on acceptance.
Illustrations: Uses 12 illustrations/issue, all from freelancers. Interested in "high quality color, drawings and some fine art on country living theme. Many have won awards." Works on assignment only. Likes to have samples on file. Reports back on future assignment possibilities; nonresidents include SAE and IRC. Reports in 6 weeks. Buys first North American serial rights. Cover: Pays $500-1,200, color. Inside: Pays $250-1,000 color; $150-500, b&w; on acceptance.

HEALTH INDUSTRY TODAY, 454 Morris Ave., Springfield NJ 07081. (201)564-9400. Art Director: Janet Fusco. Emphasizes health care supply for hospital, physician, and home health-care supply dealers. Monthly. Circ. 11,000. Accepts previously published material and simultaneous submissions. Original artwork returned after publication if requested. Sample copy free for SASE; artist's guideline available.
Cartoons: Number of cartoons used/issue varies. Prefers single panel with gagline; b&w line drawings and washes. Send finished cartoons to be kept on file; write for appointment to show portfolio. Material not kept on file is returned by SASE only if requested. Reports only if interested. Buys first rights. Payment negotiable; pays on publication.

Illustrations: Number of illustrations used/issue varies. Prefers health care themes. Works on assignment only. Send query letter with brochure to be kept on file; write for appointment to show portfolio. Prefers tear sheets as samples. Samples not kept on file are returned by SASE only if requested. Reports only if interested. Buys first rights. Payment is negotiable; on publication.

HEALTH MAGAZINE, 31st Floor, 3 Park Ave., New York NY 10016. (212)340-9200. Art Director: Reilly Sierra. Circ. 1,000,000. Accepts simultaneous submissions. Original artwork returned after publication. Sample copy available.
Illustrations: Uses 10 illustrations/issue. Works on assignment only. Send samples to be kept on file. Reports within 1 week. Buys first rights. Payment varies; on acceptance.

HEALTHCARE FINANCIAL MANAGEMENT, Suite 500, 1900 Spring Rd., Oak Brook IL 60521. (312)655-4600. National:(800) 252-HEMA; Illinois: (800)821-6459. Editor: Ronald E. Keener, CAE. Managing Editor: Stan Dziedzic. Emphasizes new and existing methods of financial management and accounting. For financial managers of healthcare providers. Monthly. Circ. 25,000. Previously published and simultaneous submissions OK.
Illustrations: Illustrations purchased on a per issue basis. Prefers themes on healthcare financial management, accounting and data processing. Receives 5 illustrations/week from freelance artists. Especially needs preparation of graphs, charts, statistical and tabular material. Query first and submit art, or query with samples. SASE. Reports in 2 weeks. Buys various rights. Minimum payment: Cover: $100, b&w; $150, color. Inside: $75, b&w line drawings; $100, color-separated work; on publication.
Tips: "Realize our needs are very limited. Read the journal well before querying. Theme issues on data processing, space planning, marketing, development and public relations, personnel, tax-exempt financings and construction, risk management, ethics, education—all within the perspective of the financial manager in the healthcare setting."

HIS MAGAZINE, Box 1450, Downers Grove IL 60515. (312)964-5700. Art Director: Kathy Burrows. Emphasizes editing for students on the college campus for Christian college students. Monthly during school year (9 issues—October through June). Accepts simultaneous submissions. Original artwork returned after publication. Sample copy and art guidelines available.
Cartoons: Buys cartoons from freelancers. Send query letter with samples of style. Write for appointment to show portfolio. Material not kept on file is returned. Reports within 1 month. Buys one-time rights. Pays $50-100, b&w; on acceptance.
Illustrations: Buys illustrations from freelancers. Usually works on assignment. Send query letter with samples. Write for appointment to show portfolio. Prefers photostats as samples. Samples not kept on file are returned. Reports within 4 weeks. Buys one-time rights. Pays $250, b&w and color, cover; $150, b&w, inside; on acceptance.

*HOME GYM & FITNESS MAGAZINE, 16200 Ventura Blvd., Encino CA 91436. Art Director; J.R. Martinez. Emphasizes home gym equipment and general fitness. Also has articles directed toward sports, endurance and sports medicine. Monthly. Circ. 80,000. Original art becomes property of publisher. Sample copy and artist guidelines available for SASE.
Illustrations: Full-page, and medium on health, fitness, sport and equipment. Works on assignment only. Send query letter and samples to be kept on file; write or phone for appointment to show portfolio. Samples should be veloxes, tear sheets or slides. Buys all rights. Pays $100-300, b&w; per assignment for 4-color.

HOME HEALTH CARE BUSINESS, 454 Morris Ave., Springfield NJ 07081. (201)564-9400. Art Director: Janet Fusco. For pharmacists with home health care departments. Bimonthly. Circ. 8,000. Accepts previously published material. Returns original artwork after publication. Sample copy and art guidelines free for SASE.
Cartoons: "Always interested" in freelance cartoons. Prefers home health care themes. Considers single panel with gagline; b&w line drawings. Send samples of style to be kept on file. Write for appointment to show portfolio. Material not filed is returned by SASE only if requested. Reports back only if interested. Pays $10 for b&w; on publication.
Illustrations: Send query letter with brochure to be kept on file. Write for appointment to show portfolio. Prefers to review tear sheets. Reports back only if interested. Buys first rights. Pays on publication.

HOME LIFE, 127 9th Ave. N, Nashville TN 37234. Editor: Reuben Herring. Emphasizes Christian family life. For married adults and parents of all ages, but especially newlyweds and middle-aged marrieds. Monthly. Free sample copy and art guidelines.
Cartoons: Buys 2-4 cartoons/issue on family life situations; particularly interested in cartoons on marriage and parenting. Receives 50 cartoons/week from freelance artists. No sex. Submit roughs. Reports

in 45 days. Buys all rights. Pays $30 minimum, line drawings and halftones; on acceptance.
Illustrations: Occasionally buys humorous and cartoon-style illustrations.
Tips: "Submit cartoons to editor; other artwork and illustrations to artist-designer."

*THE HORROR SHOW, Star Rt. 1, Box 151-T, Oak Run CA 96069. (916)472-3540. Editor: David B. Silva. Magazine. Emphasizes short horror fiction for "anyone who enjoys a good chill up their spine." Quarterly. Circ. 2,200. Original artwork not returned after publication. Sample copy $4.95; art guidelines for SASE with 22¢ postage.
Illustrations: Buys 10-15 illustrations/issue from freelancers. Works on assignment only. Send query letter with samples to be kept on file, except for slides, which will be returned. Prefers tear sheets and photocopies as samples. Samples not filed are returned by SASE. Reports within 2 weeks. Buys first rights or reprint rights. Pays $10, color, cover; $5, b&w, inside; on acceptance.

HORSE ILLUSTRATED, Box 6050, Mission Viejo CA 92690. (714)240-6001. Editor: Jill-Marie Jones. For people of all ages who own, show and breed horses, who are interested in all phases of horse ownership. Monthly. Circ. 50,000. Sample copy $3.; free art guidelines.
Cartoons: Buys several cartoons/issue. Prefers single, double or multipanel. "Central character should be a horse." Send finished art. SASE. Reports within 6 weeks. Buys first rights. Pays $10-35, b&w line drawings; on publication.
Illustrations: Buys several illustrations/year on horses. Query with resume and samples. SASE. Reports within 6 weeks. Buys first rights. Inside: pays $20-50, b&w line drawings; on publication.
Tips: When reviewing an illustrator's work, "we look for realism and accurate portrayal of the horse. We don't use 'fantasy' or 'surrealistic' art. For cartoons, we look for drawing ability and humor. We will, however, accept good humor with adequate illustration over good illustration with poor humor. Generally, we use free-standing illustrations as art rather than going to the illustrator and commissioning a work, but this is impossible if the artist sends us poor reproductions. Naturally, this also lessens his chance of our seeking out his services."

HOSPITAL PRACTICE, 575 Lexington Ave., New York NY 10022. (212)421-7320. Design Director: Robert S. Herald. Emphasizes clinical medicine and science for practicing physicians throughout the US. Monthly. Circ. 200,000. Original artwork returned after publication if requested.
Illustrations: Uses 40-50 illustrations/issue; buys 15 illustrations/issue from freelancers. Uses only medical and scientific (conceptual) illustrations. Works on assignment only. Send query letter with resume, samples and tear sheets to be kept on file. Call for appointment to show portfolio. Prefers photostats, photographs, tear sheets as samples. Does not report unless called. Returns material if SASE included. Negotiates rights purchased. Pays $800, color, cover; $150 and up, b&w, inside. Payment on publication.
Tips: "If possible, review the publication before submitting work, to understand specific editorial style."

HOUSE & GARDEN, 350 Madison Ave., New York NY 10017. (212)880-8800. Readers are upper income home owners or renters. Monthly. Circ. 500,000.
Illustrations: Uses minimum number of illustrations/issue; all of which are commissioned by the magazine. Selection based on "previous work, samples on file, and from seeing work in other publications. Illustrations are almost always assigned to fit specific articles." Themes "vary with our current format and with article we want illustrated." Format: b&w line drawings or washes. Portfolios viewed on a drop-off basis or send samples of style to Lloyd Ziff, Editorial Design Director. SASE. Reports "from immediately to 4 weeks." Payment on acceptance "varies depending on artist, size and type of illustration." Buys all rights.

*THE HUMANE SOCIETY (OF THE UNITED STATES) NEWS, 2100 L. Street NW, Washington DC 20037. Editor: Deborah Salem. Emphasizes animal welfare for members of the largest animal-welfare organization in the U.S.A. Quarterly. Circ. 95,000. Original artwork not returned after publication. Sample copy $1.
Illustrations: Buys 1-3 illustrations/issue from freelancers. Works on assignment only. Send brochure and samples to be kept on file. Prefers photostats as samples. Buys all rights. Pays $50, b&w, inside; on acceptance.

HUMPTY DUMPTY'S MAGAZINE, Box 567, Indianapolis IN 46206. (317)636-8881. Editor: Christine French Clark. Art Director: Fred Kreiter. Special emphasis on health, nutrition, safety and exercise for girls and boys, ages 4-6. Monthly except bimonthly February/March, April/May, June/July and August/September. Sample copy 75¢; art guidelines for SASE.
Illustrations: Uses 25-35 illustrations/issue. Works on assignment only. Send query letter with bro-

Close-up

Jean Miller
Medical Illustrator
Richmond Hill, Ontario

Artist: David R. Smiton

Eight years of surgical nursing and a strong interest in painting led Jean Miller into the field of medical illustration. The Canadian chose the University of Toronto to study anatomy, physiology, histology, pathology and neuroanatomy as she worked towards a degree in Art as Applied to Medicine.

From her experiences as a partner in a medical illustration business, Miller is quick to advise artists "until your style is completely established and you feel confident of your business sense, work on your own, not with another artist. Art is an individualistic process and no one should try to influence your work. If you feel you are going to be lonely, then you are entering the wrong line of work."

When the artist began freelancing in 1979, she found rejection to be a "way of life because people either didn't trust my artistic ability or they had never heard of such an animal as a medical illustrator. Art directors seemed to feel that anyone with so much university education could not possibly be creative and would only deliver strict medical textbook illustrations. I proved to them that I could remain accurate medically in my illustrations and still produce an exciting piece of artwork.

"One of the best investments of my career was buying a page in Canada's *Creative Source*. It paid for itself immediately, and I have had at least one inquiry each week from Canadian and American art directors since my work made its first appearance three years ago. I send tear sheets and promotional pieces to current and potential clients who may not receive the *Source*. Other books, like the *Black Book*, the *Medical Illustration Source Book* and the *Graphic Artists Guild Directory* are excellent promotional avenues for the artist. Research which book best suits your purposes and pocketbook."

This illustrator's brochures are another necessary part of her marketing methods. A brochure's effectiveness, according to Miller, is "incredible. You have to have *something*. People want to see your work. They want to see your name next to a piece of art. If the client is interested in hiring you, and your illustrations are good, a well-designed and professionally printed brochure clinches the sale."

Medical illustrators recognize the fact that most art directors do not have much medical knowledge. "For some unknown reason, many art directors on pharmaceutical accounts like to keep the names of the client and the drug a dark mystery. Subsequently you have to be prepared for problems such as when I did an illustration of nasal sinuses for an advertising agency. The art director heard the word sinus at the client's briefing and, having very scant medical knowledge, jumped on the only sinus he was aware of. Later, when I talked with the same client, he complimented me on my nasal sinus illustration. Then he gently explained that he sold cardiac drugs and was a little more interested in the sinuses found in the heart, not in the nose!"

Jean Miller
Medical Illustrator
380 Esna Park Drive,
Markham, Ontario,
L3R 1H5

(416) 883-4114

1. Anaphylaxis
2. Computers in Medicine
3. Editorial on Subacute Sclerosing Panencephalitis
4. Patient teaching aid for Ski Injuries
5. Platelet Transfusions

Photo Credit: Ivor Sharp

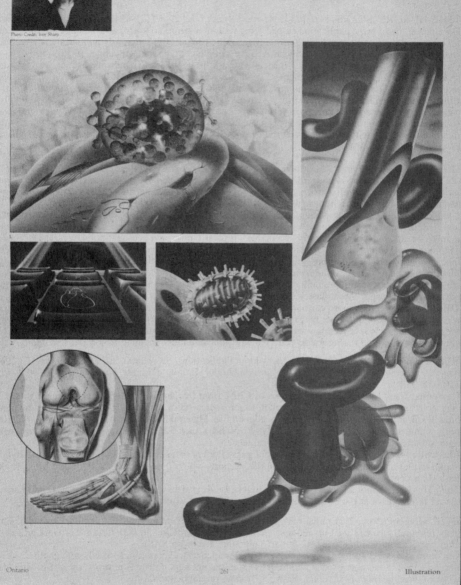

Ontario   261   Illustration

This promotional page from Canada's Creative Source, *a directory of freelance artists, was "one of the best investments of my career," says Miller. "It paid for itself immediately." As part of her payment for the ad, the artist received 500 tear sheets of the page for her own promotional use.*

chure, resume, samples and tear sheets to be kept on file. Write for appointment or mail portfolio. Prefers photostats, slides and good photocopies as samples. Samples returned by SASE if not kept on file. Reports within 1 week. Buys all rights. Pays $175, cover; and $35, b&w; $50, 2-color; $70, 4-color, inside. Pays on publication.
Tips: Illustrations should be figurative and should be composed of story telling situations. Especially looks for "the artist's ability to consistently draw and paint well."

*THE HUNGRY YEARS, Box 7213, Newport Beach CA 92660. (714)548-3324. Editor/Publisher: Les Brown. Small press publication emphasizing fiction, nonfiction, poetry and the work of new talent for creative people of all ages and interests. Biannually. Circ. 1,000. Previously published material OK. Original artwork returned after publication. Free sample copy and art guidelines for SASE.
Cartoons: Uses 2-4 cartoons/issue. "Basically we ask for good taste"; can be in abstract, avant garde style; no pornography or religious themes. Send query letter with roughs or samples of style. Samples returned by SASE. Reports in 6 months. Material not copyrighted. Pays in copies; on publication.
Illustrations: Prefers b&w pen and ink. Artwork is matched with written compositions to mutually complement both works whether poetry, fiction or essays. Will send sample copy to serve as example of styles wanted. Provide samples to be kept on file for possible future assignments. Send query letter with roughs or samples of style. Samples returned by SASE. Reports in 6 months. Material not copyrighted. Pays in copies; on publication.

HUSTLER, Larry Flynt Publications, Suite 3800, 2029 Century Park E., Los Angeles CA 90067. (213)556-9200. Cartoon/Humor Editor: Dwaine Tinsley. For middle income men, 18-35 years of age, interested in current affairs, luxuries, investigative reporting, entertainment, sports, sex and fashion. Monthly. Original artwork returned after publication.
Cartoons: Publishes 23 cartoons/month; 10 full-page color, 4-color spots, 8 b&w and 1 "Most Tasteless." Receives 300-500 cartoons/week from freelance artists. Especially needs "outrageous material, mainly sexual, but politics, sports acceptable. Topical humor and seasonal/holiday cartoons good." Mail samples. Prefers 8½x11" size; avoid crayons, chalks or fluorescent colors. Prefers original art submissions to roughs. Avoid, if possible, large, heavy illustration board. Samples returned by SASE only. Place name, address and phone number on back of each cartoon. Reports in 3 weeks to 1 month. Adheres to Cartoonists Guild guidelines. Pays $300, full page color; $125 ¼-page color; $100 ¼-page b&w; $100, ¼-page "Most Tasteless." Pays on acceptance.
Tips: Especially needs more cartoons, cartoon breakaways or one-subject theme series. "Send outrageous humor—work that other magazines would shy away from. Pertinent, political, sexual, whatever. We are constantly looking for new artists to compliment our regular contributors and contract artists. Let your imagination and daring guide you. We will publish almost anything as long as it is funny."

HUSTLER HUMOR MAGAZINE, Larry Flynt Publications, Suite 3800, 2029 Century Park E., Los Angeles CA 90067. (213)556-9200. Cartoon/Humor Editor: Dwaine Tinsley. Bimonthly. Circ. 150,000.
Cartoons: Uses 150-180 cartoons/issue; buys 30% from freelancers. Prefers "outrageous sexual, social, political" themes. Prefers single panel, multipanel, with or without gag line; b&w line drawings, b&w washes. Send finished cartoons to be kept on file. Material not kept on file returned by SASE. Reports within 1 month. Buys first rights. Pays $7.50 b&w spot, $75 b&w strips/page. Original artwork returned after publication. Payment on acceptance.
Illustrations: Uses 2 covers, full color sight gags. Prefers soft sexual themes; realistic cartoon styles. Send samples and tear sheets to be kept on file. Reports within 2 weeks. Pays $500, front; $200, back. Pays on acceptance.
Tips: This is a "humor magazine consisting of jokes and cartoons exclusively. The material is primarily sexual in nature—but the scope is wide-ranging. We need work *badly* to build our inventory."

IN BUSINESS, Box 323, Emmaus PA 18049. (215)967-4135. Managing Editor: Nora Goldstein. Emphasizes small business start-up and management. Bimonthly. Circ. 50,000. Original artwork returned after publication. Sample copy $2.50; art guidelines free with SASE.
Cartoons: Uses 2-3 cartoons/issue; buys all from freelancers. Prefers single panel, with gagline; b&w line drawings. Send query letter with roughs. Material not kept on file is returned by SASE. Reports within 4 weeks. Buys first rights. Pays $35, b&w; on publication.
Illustrations: Uses 5-6 illustrations/issue; buys all from freelancers. Uses themes related to article subject. Works on assignment only. Send query letter with brochure and tear sheets to be kept on file; call for appointment to show portfolio. Reports within 4 weeks. Buys first rights. Pays $35, b&w, inside; on publication.

INCENTIVE MARKETING/INCORPORATING INCENTIVE TRAVEL, 633 3rd Ave., New York NY 10017. (212)986-4800. Editor: Bruce Bolger. For buyers of merchandise and travel used in motivational sales promotions. Monthly. Circ. 37,000. Original artwork returned after publication. **Cartoons:** Uses 0-2 cartoons/issue; buys all from freelancers. Interested in our topic only, sales contests, bank premium programs, business travel and employee motivation, no general interest. Prefers finished cartoons. SASE. Reports in 2 weeks. Pays $50-75, b&w; on acceptance.

INCENTIVE TRAVEL MANAGER, Brentwood Publishing Corp., 825 S. Barrington Ave., Los Angeles CA 90049. Publishers: Martin H. Waldman and Hal Spector. Art Director: Tom Medsger. **Illustrations:** Submit brochure/flyer to be kept on file for possible future assignment. Reports only when assignment available. Buys all rights. Pays $60 and up, spot art; $400 and up, full-color cover. Pays on acceptance.

INDIANAPOLIS 500 YEARBOOK, Box 24308, Speedway IN 46224. (317)244-4792. Publisher: Carl Hungness. Emphasizes auto racing for auto racing fans. Annually. Circ. 50,000. Previously published material OK. Original artwork returned after publication. Sample copy $12.95. **Illustrations:** Works on assignment only. Provide information to be kept on file for possible future assignments. Send query letter. Samples returned by SASE. Reports in 2 weeks. Buys one-time rights. Pays on publication.

INDIANAPOLIS MAGAZINE, 32 E. Washington St., Indianapolis IN 46204. (317)639-6600. Editor: Nancy Comiskey. Emphasizes any Indianapolis-related problems/features or regionally related topics. Readers have "high income and are highly educated." Monthly. Circ. 20,000. Sample copy $1.75. **Cartoons:** "We are just beginning to accept and publish cartoons and *New Yorker* type illustrations. Will buy all from freelance artists." Needs art related to the "consumer, tourist-business-related or city-related." Receives 5 cartoons/week from freelance artists. Format: single panel b&w line drawings or b&w washes, with or without gagline. Send roughs or photocopied finished cartoons. SASE. Rejects in 2 weeks. "Possibles kept until used which can be a long time. Number published varies." Pays $15 on publication per b&w cartoon. Buys one-time rights. **Illustrations:** Uses 2-5 illustrations/issue, 50% of which are supplied by freelancers. Works on spec or assignment basis. Needs illustrations that are "broad, general interest or Indianapolis-related." Format: b&w line drawings or b&w washes. Send photocopied finished art or roughs. SASE. Reports in 2 weeks, "but depends on production schedule and influx of material." Pays $35 on publication per inside b&w or color illustration. Buys one-time rights. **Tips:** The trend is toward "more sophisticated, mature cartoons. Please, no Farmer Bill cartoons—we're a *city*. Orient cartoons and illustrations to a *professional audience*. Always need food-related, dining cartoons."

INDIANAPOLIS MONTHLY, 701 Broad Ripple Ave., Indianapolis IN 46220. (317)259-8222. Art Director: M.T. Peachey. City magazine. Monthly. Circ. 32,000. Negotiates return of artwork after publication. Sample copy $3 first class; $1.75 second class; art guidelines free for SASE. **Cartoons:** Uses 1 cartoon/issue; buys 1/issue from freelancer. Prefers single panel, with gagline; b&w line drawings. Send query letter with samples of style to be kept on file; write for appointment to show portfolio. Material not kept on file is returned by SASE. Reports only if interested. Negotiates rights purchased and pay. Pays on publication. **Illustrations:** Uses 1 illustration/issue; buys 1/issue from freelancer. Works primarily on assignment. Send query letter with resume, samples and tear sheets to be kept on file; write for appointment to show portfolio. Open to any type of sample. Reports only if interested. Negotiates rights purchased and pay. Pays on publication.

INDUSTRIAL ENGINEERING, 25 Technology Park, Norcross GA 30092. (404)449-0460. Editor/Publisher: E.F. Cudworth. Emphasizes engineering. Monthly. Circ. 47,000. Sample copy $4.50. **Illustrations:** Uses 0-7 illustrations/issue; buys 0-7/issue from freelancers. Prefers airbrush, full color, some b&w line styles. Works on assignment only. Send query letter with brochure and samples to be kept on file. Call for appointment to show portfolio. No preference for samples. Samples not kept on file are returned by SASE. Does not report back. Buys all rights. Pays $400-1,200, color, cover ("we run no b&w on cover"); $50-500, b&w, and $400-1,000, color, inside; on publication.

INDUSTRIAL LAUNDERER, Suite 613, 1730 M St. NW, Washington DC 20036. (202)296-6744. Editor: David A. Ritchey. For decision makers in the industrial laundry business. Monthly. Circ. 3,000. Sample copy $1. **Cartoons:** Submit resume. Reports as soon as possible. Buys first industry rights. Pays on publication. Negotiates pay for b&w line drawings and washes.

INDUSTRIAL MACHINERY NEWS, division of Hearst Business Media Corp., 29516 Southfield Rd., Box 5002, Southfield MI 48086. (313)557-0100. Contact: L.D. Slace. For those in the metalworking industry responsible for manufacturing, purchasing, engineering, metalworking, machinery, equipment and supplies.

Cartoons: Receives 10 cartoons/week from freelance artists. Interested in themes of metalworking or personal relationships. Buys one-time rights. Pays $5 for line ink work; on publication.

Tips: "We have been purchased by the Hearst Corp. If interested in submitting artwork other than cartoons, call or write first. Do not send original art. A photocopy in many cases will do. Think industrial (metalworking) plants, factories, firms and the people who work and manage them."

INDUSTRY WEEK, 1111 Chester Ave., Cleveland OH 44114. (216)696-7000. Editor: Stanley J. Modic. Examines top- and middle-management problems in industry. Biweekly. Circ. 300,000. Simultaneous submissions and previously published work OK. Original artwork returned after publication. Buys first and reprint rights. Sample copy $2.

Cartoons: News Editor: John Carson. Uses 1 cartoon/issue; buys 0-1/issue from freelancers. Receives 10 submissions/week from freelancers. Interested in management themes; single panel. Prefers to see roughs. SASE. Reports in 2 weeks. Buys various rights. Pays $35 minimum, b&w line drawings or washes; pays on acceptance.

Illustrations: Art Director: Nick Dankovich. Uses 2 illustrations/issue. Works on assignment only. Buys various rights. Cover and inside: Buys b&w and color work, all media; pays on acceptance.

Tips: "Read and examine our magazine."

INSIDE, 226 S. 16th St., Philadelphia PA 19102. (215)893-5760. Art Director: Lenore Chorney. Quarterly. Circ. 70,000. Original artwork returned after publication.

Illustrations: Buys 3 or more illustrations/issue from freelancers. Prefers color and b&w drawings. Works on assignment only. Send samples and tear sheets to be kept on file; call for appointment to show portfolio. Samples not kept on file are not returned. Reports only if interested. Buys first rights. Pays from $100, b&w, and from $300 full color, inside; on acceptance. Prefers seeing sketches.

INSIDE DETECTIVE, RGH Publications, 20th Floor, 460 W. 34th St., New York NY 10001. (212)947-6500. Editor: Rose Mandelsberg. For mature adults—law enforcement officials, professional investigators, criminology buffs and interested laymen. Monthly.

Cartoons: Receives approximately 20 cartoons/week from freelance artists. Must have crime theme. Submit finished art. SASE. Reports in 10 days. Buys all rights. Pays $25; on acceptance.

Tips: "Make sure that the humor in the cartoons is *not* at the expense of police officers or law enforcement officials."

*INSIDE SPORTS, 1020 Church St., Evanston IL 60201. Art Director: Marcia Kuhr. Estab. 1983. Emphasizes sports. Monthly. Circ. 325,000. Original artwork returned after publication. Sample copy and art guidelines available.

Cartoons: Considers sports themes. Prefers single panel; b&w line drawings or color washes. Send query letter. Write for appointment to show portfolio. Material not filed is returned by SASE. Reports only if interested. Pays on acceptance.

Illustrations: Considers sports themes. Works on assignment only. Send query letter. Write for appointment to show portfolio. Samples not filed are returned by SASE. Reports only if interested. Pays on acceptance.

*INSIGHT, Box 7244, Grand Rapids MI 49510. Editor: John Knight. For Christians ages 16-21. Monthly (except June and August). Circ. 23,000. Photocopied and simultaneous submissions OK. Free sample copy.

Cartoons: Buys 20 cartoons/year on current events, humor through youth and religion; single panel. "Our favorites are the ones that speak for themselves, no caption." Especially needs continuous cartoon strip, yearly contract. Query. SASE. Reports in 3 weeks. Buys first rights. Minimum payment: $25, b&w; $75, color; on publication.

Illustrations: Uses full-color illustrations. Works on assignment only. Pays $125; on publication.

Tips: There is a trend toward "more color, especially watercolor washes."

INSTANT AND SMALL COMMERCIAL PRINTER, (formerly *Instant Printer*, Box 368, Northbrook IL 60062. Editor: Daniel Witte. Emphasizes the instant/quick and small commercial printing business and successful, profitable, technical and promotional methods for owners and/or managers of print shops, as well as interested employees. Bimonthly. Circ. 25,000. Accepts previously published work and simultaneous submissions "if material is so indicated." Sample copy $3.

Cartoons: Uses 1 cartoon/issue; buys 1/issue from freelancers. Prefers single panel with gagline; b&w line drawings. Send query letter with samples of style, roughs or finished cartoons to be kept on file.

Material not kept on file is returned by SASE only if requested. Reports within 1 month. Buys all rights. Pays $25, b&w; on publication.
Illustrations: Uses 2 illustrations/issue; buys 2/issue from freelancers. Works on assignment only. Send query letter with brochure, resume, business card, samples and tear sheets to be kept on file. Samples not kept on file are returned by SASE only if requested. Reports within 1 month. Buys all rights. Pays $50-150, b&w, and $150-250, color, covers; $50-100, b&w, and $50-200, color, inside; on publication.

THE INSTRUMENTALIST, 200 Northfield Rd., Northfield IL 60093. (312)328-6000. Contact: Jean Oelrich. Emphasizes music education for "school band and orchestra directors and teachers of the instruments in those ensembles." Monthly. Circ. 22,500. Original artwork may be returned after publication. Sample copy $2.
Cartoons: Uses 3 cartoons/issue; buys all from freelancers. Interested in themes stating "music is wonderful." No themes stating "music is a problem"; single panel with gagline, "if needed"; b&w line drawings. Send finished cartoons. Samples not returned. Reports in 1-2 months. Buys all rights. Pay $8-15, b&w; on acceptance.

INSURANCE SALES, Rough Notes Publishing Co. Inc., Box 564, Indianapolis IN 46206. (317)634-1541. Editor: Roy Ragan. For life and health insurance salespeople; "emphasis on sales and marketing methods, and on the uses of life and health insurance to solve personal and business financial situations." Monthly. Circ. 30,000. Sample copy $1. Receives 12-15 cartoons/week from freelance artists.
Cartoons: Uses 40-50 cartoons/year; all from freelancers. Interested in life insurance salesmanship, tax payer and IRS situations, inflation, recession, vagaries of bankers and stock market; single panel. "No cartoons which show salesman holding prospect on ground, twisting arm, knocking doors down, etc." Prefers finished cartoons. SASE. Reports in 1 week. Buys all rights. Pays $15, b&w line drawings; on acceptance.

*INTERNATIONAL WOODWORKING, Suite #6, 35 Main St., Plymouth NH 03264. Executive Director: Peter F. Engel. Estab. 1984. Emphasizes professional and craftsman woodworking for woodworkers of all interests, levels and abilities. Quarterly. Circ. 2,000. Accepts previously published material. Sample copy for magazine-size SASE with 71¢ postage.
Cartoons: Buys 1 cartoon/issue from freelancers on woodworking theme. Prefers multiple panel with gagline. Send query letter with samples of style to be kept on file; write for appointment to show portfolio. Material not filed is returned by SASE. Negotiates rights purchased. Pays negotiable rate, b&w; on publication.
Illustrations: Woodworking theme. Works on assignment only. Send query letter with brochure and samples to be kept on file; write or call for appointment to show portfolio. Prefers tear sheets as samples. Samples not filed are returned by SASE. Reports only if interested. Negotiates rights purchased. Pays negotiable rate for b&w, cover and inside; on publication.

INTERRACIAL BOOKS FOR CHILDREN BULLETIN, 1841 Broadway, New York NY 10023. Managing Editor: Ruth Charnes. Emphasizes "bias-free children's literature and learning materials" for teachers, librarians, parents, authors, and others concerned with children's materials. Published 8 times/year. Circ. 5,000. Accepts previously published material. Original artwork returned after publication. Sample copy $3.50; art guidelines free for SASE.
Cartoons: Rarely uses cartoons. Prefers b&w line drawings. Send query letter with samples of style; material will be kept on file if relevant. Material not kept on file returned by SASE. Reports back within 2 months.
Illustrations: Uses up to 15 illustrations/issue. Send query letter with samples; material will be kept on file if relevant. Prefers photostats and photographs as samples. Samples returned by SASE if not kept on file. Reports back within 4 weeks. Buys one-time rights. Pays $50, b&w, cover; $25, b&w, inside. Pays on publication.

JACK AND JILL, 1100 Waterway Blvd., Box 567, Indianapolis IN 46206. (317)636-8881. Art Director: Edward F. Cortese. Emphasizes entertaining articles written with the purpose of developing the reading skills of the reader. For ages 6-8. Monthly except bimonthly February/March, April/May, June/July and August/September. Buys all rights. Original artwork not returned after publication (except in case where artist wishes to exhibit the art. Art must be available to us on request.) Sample copy 75¢.
Illustrations: Uses 25-35 illustrations/issue; buys 10-15/issue from freelancers. Receives 3-4 submissions/week from freelancers. Interested in "stylized, realistic, humorous, mystery, adventure, science fiction, historical and also nature and health." Works on assignment only. Provide brochure, flyer, tear sheets, stats or good photocopies of artwork to be kept on file for future assignments. Prefers to see portfolio and samples of style. SASE. Reports in 4 weeks. Buys all rights on a work-for-hire basis. Cover:

Pays $175, color. Inside: Pays $30-70, 4-color; $30-50, 2-color, $25-35, b&w; on publication.
Tips: "There is a greater concentration on health-related subjects" in the magazine. Artists should "take the time to examine our publications." Likes to see situation and story telling illustrations with more than 1 figure.

*JAPANOPHILE, Box 223, Okemos MI 48864. (517)349-1795. Editor: Earl R. Snodgrass. Emphasizes cars, bonsai, haiku, sports, etc. for educated audience interested in Japanese culture. Quarterly. Circ. 800. Accepts previously published material. Original artwork not returned after publication. Sample copy $3; art guidelines for SASE.
Cartoons: Buys 1 cartoon/issue from freelancer. Prefers single panel with gagline; b&w line drawings. Send finished cartoons. Material returned only if requested. Reports only if interested. Buys all rights. Pays $5; on publication.
Illustrations: Buys 1-5 illustrations/issue from freelancers. Prefers sumie or line drawings. Send samples to be kept on file if interested. Prefers photostats or tear sheets as samples. Samples returned only if requested. Reports if interested. Buys all rights. Pays $15, cover and $5, inside, b&w; on publication.

*JEMS JOURNAL OF EMERGENCY MEDICAL SERVICES, Box 1026, Solana Beach CA 92075. (619)481-1128. Senior Editor: Rick Minerd. Emphasizes emergency medical services for emergency room physicians, nurses, paramedics, emergency medical technicans and administrators. Monthly. Circ. 30,000. Accepts previously published material. Original artwork returned after publication. Sample copy for SASE with $1.07 postage; art guidelines for SASE with 22¢ postage.
Illustrations: Buys 3-5 illustrations/issue from freelancers. Works on assignment only. Send query letter with samples to be kept on file. Prefers photostats, tear sheets, photocopies, slides or photos as samples. Samples not filed are returned by SASE. Reports within 2 weeks. Buys one-time rights. Pays $150-200, color, cover; $35-50, b&w, and $50-75, color, inside; on publication.

JOURNAL OF THE WEST, 1531 Yuma, Manhattan KS 66502. (913)532-6733. Editor: Robin Higham. Emphasizes the West for readers in public libraries and classrooms. Quarterly. Circ. 4,500 (readership). Original artwork returned after publication. Sample copy and art guidelines available.
Illustrations: Uses cover illustrations only; artist supplies 4-color separation. Send query letter with brochure or samples and/or tear sheets to be kept on file. Prefers either photographs, prints or preferably duplicate slides as samples. Samples not filed are returned only if requested. Reports within 4 days. Negotiates rights purchased. Payment: "We make a trade."
Tips: There is a trend toward "pastels with sometimes interesting and eye-catching results in Western scenes." Looks for work that is "original and not copied from a photograph; and is evidence of artistic talent and ability. Artists send material that is unsuitable to our publication, often because they have never bothered to look at it or to send for a sample copy."

KEYNOTER, Kiwanis International, 3636 Woodview Trace, Indianapolis IN 46268. Executive Editor: Jack Brockley. Art Director: Jim Patterson. Official publication of Key Club International, nonprofit high school service organization. Published 7 times/year. Copyrighted. Circ. 115,000. Previously published, photocopied and simultaneous submissions OK. Original artwork returned after publication. Free sample copy.
Illustrations: Uses 3 illustrations/issue, all from freelancers. Works on assignment only. "We only want to work with illustrators in the Indianapolis area because it is otherwise too inconvenient because of our production schedule. They should call our Production and Art Department for interview." SASE. Reports in 2 weeks. Buys first rights. Pays on publication.

KIWANIS, 3636 Woodview Trace, Indianapolis IN 46268. (317)875-8755. Executive Editor: Chuck Jonak. Art/Director: James Patterson. For business and professional men. Stresses civic and social betterment, business, education, religion and domestic affairs. Uses cartoons, illustrations, and photos from freelancers. Original artwork returned after publication. Published 10 times/year.
Cartoons: Uses 1-2 cartoons/issue, all from freelancers. Interested in "daily life at home or work. Nothing off-color, no silly wife stuff, no blue-collar situations." Prefers finished cartoons. SASE. Reports in 3-4 weeks. Pays $50; on acceptance.
Illustrations: Uses 6-8 illustrations/issue, all from freelancers. Interested in themes that correspond to themes of articles. Works on assignment only. Keeps material on file after in-person contact with artist. Prefers portfolio, "anything and everything." SASE. Reports in 2 weeks. Buys first North American serial rights or negotiates. Cover: Pays $600-900, full-color. Inside: Pays $400-500, full-color; $50-75, spot drawings; on acceptance.

*KONA COMMUNICATIONS, Heavy-Duty Distribution, Renews Magazine, The Successful Dealer, 707 Lake Cook Rd., Deerfield IL 60015. Advertising Production Manager: Theresa L. Vogt.

Emphasizes heavy-duty trucking for fleetowners and rebuilders. Bimonthly. Circ. approximately 17,000 each. Accepts previously published material. Original artwork returned after publication. Sample copy free for SASE; art guidelines free.
Cartoons: Prefers b&w line drawings, b&w washes or color washes. Send query letter with samples of style to be kept on file; write for appointment to show portfolio. Material not filed is returned only if requested. Reports if interested. Buys reprint rights or negotiates rights purchased. Pays on publication.
Illustrations: Send query letter with samples to be kept on file; write for appointment to show portfolio. Prefers photostats, tear sheets or photographs as samples. Samples are returned only if requested. Reports only if interested. Buys reprint rights or negotiates rights purchased. Pays on publication.

LACMA PHYSICIAN, Box 3465, Los Angeles CA 90054. (213)483-1581. Managing Editor: Howard Bender. "Membership publication for physicians who are members of the Los Angeles County Medical Association; covers association news and medical issues." Published 20 times/year, twice monthly except January, July, August and December. Circ. 11,000. Does not accept previously published material. Original artwork returned after publication "if requested." Sample copy for SASE with $1.50 postage.
Illustrations: "Occasionally use illustrations for covers." These are "generally medical, but can relate to a specific feature story topic." Works on assignment only. Send query letter with business card and samples to be filed. Call or write for appointment. Samples not kept on file are returned by SASE. Reports back only if interested. Negotiates pay; pays on acceptance. Buys all rights."

*LADYCOM, The Military Lifestyle Magazine, 1732 Wisconsin Ave. NW, Washington DC 20007. Art Director: Judi Connelly. Emphasizes active-duty military lifestyles for military wives and families. Monthly. Circ. 500,000. Original artwork returned after publication.
Illustrations: Buys 2-6 illustrations/issue from freelancers. Theme/style depends on editorial content. Works on assignment only. Send brochure and business card to be kept on file. Accepts photostats, tear sheets, photocopies, slides, photographs, etc. as samples. Samples returned only if requested. Reports only if interested. Buys first rights. Payment depends on size published, cover and inside; pays on publication.

LANDSCAPE ONTARIO/LANDSCAPE TRADES, 1293 Matheson Blvd., Mississauga, Ontario Canada. (416)629-1184. Jim Bradley. Readers are landscapers, nursery garden centers, grounds maintenance firms, wholesale growers, suppliers of goods to the landscaping industry, parks and recreation officials, horticulturists and others. Monthly. Circ. 2,700. Free sample copy.
Cartoons: Uses 1 cartoon/issue which should relate to the industry and have appeal to readers mentioned above. Prefers single- or multipanel b&w line drawings or washes with or without gag line but will also consider color cartoons. Send finished cartoons or samples of style. Buys one-time rights. Pays $20/b&w on publication.
Illustrations: Uses 1 illustration/issue; buys 0-1 from freelancers. "I'd be happy to keep samples on file and request illustrations when a particular need or idea comes up." Prefers b&w line drawings or washes for inside. Send finished art or samples of style. Pays $20 for inside b&w on publication.

LE BUREAU, Suite 1000, 1001 de Maisonneuve West, Montreal, Quebec H3A 3E1 Canada. (514)845-5141. Editor-in-Chief: Paul Saint-Pierre. For corporate and financial exeuctives, office managers, electronic data processing experts and systems analysts. Bimonthly. Circ. 10,500. Free sample copy if artist sends samples.
Illustrations: Buys 12 illustrations/year on calculators, small computers, in-plant printing and word processing. All covers are freelance illustrations. Especially needs "outstanding drawings illustrating an office situation. We appreciate humor in good taste." Query with samples. SAE (nonresidents include IRC). Reports in 2 weeks. Buys all rights, but may reassign rights to artist after publication. Pays $125-200, color; on acceptance.

THE LEATHERNECK MAGAZINE, Magazine of the Marines, Box 1775, Quantico VA 22134. (703)640-6161. Art Director: John De Grasse. Emphasizes activities of Marines—air, land, sea ships, tanks, aircraft, physical fitness, etc. for Marines, dependents, retired, friends of the Corps, plus former Marines. Monthly. Circ. 95,000. Occasionally accepts previously published material. Only original cover artwork returned after publication. Sample copy available.
Cartoons: Uses 8 cartoons/issue; buys all from freelancers. Prefers Marine-related subjects and "correctly pictured uniforms particularly." Prefers single panel with gagline; b&w line drawings. Send query letter with samples of style. Material not kept on file is returned by SASE. Reports within 30 days. Buys first rights. Pays $25, b&w; on acceptance.
Illustrations: Uses 4 illustrations/issue. Send query letter with samples. Prefers illustrations for covers only. Pays $100-150, b&w, cover; on acceptance.

LEGAL ECONOMICS, Box 11418, Columbia SC 29211. (803)754-3563 or 359-9940. Managing Editor/Art Director: Delmar L. Roberts. For the practicing lawyer. 8 issues (monthly, Jan., Feb., Sept., Oct.; bimonthly Mar./Apr., May/June, Jul./Aug., Nov./Dec.). Circ. 27,000. Previously published work OK. Pays on publication.
Needs: Primarily interested in cartoons "depicting situations inherent in the operation and management of a law office, e.g., operating word processing equipment, computers, interviewing, office meetings, lawyer/office staff situations, and client/lawyer situations. We have rarely used cartoons, primarily because the calibre of the work we have received has not been suitable for our sophisticated audience. We almost never use material relating to trial law." Query with resume. Reports in 90 days. Usually buys all rights. Pays $30-60 for all rights; on publication.
Illustrations: Uses inside illustrations and, infrequently, cover designs. Query with resume. Reports in 90 days. Usually buys all rights. Pays $65-100; more for covers and for 4-color; on publication.
Tips: "There's an increasing need for artwork to illustrate high-tech articles."

LEGION, 359 Kent St., Ottawa, Ontario K2P 0R6 Canada. (613)235-8741. Editor-in-Chief: Jane Dewar. Art Director: Dick Logan. For Royal Canadian Legion members. Monthly. Circ. 558,071. Original artwork returned after publication. Free sample copy.
Illustrations: Uses 6-8 illustrations/issue, all from freelancers. Interested in "various techniques." Works on assignment only. Provide 35mm slides to be kept on file for possible future assignments. Prefers to see portfolio. Reports immediately. Buys various rights. Cover: Pays $450-1,500, color. Inside: Pays $100-1,200, b&w; $100-1,500, color; on acceptance.

*LEISURE WHEELS, Box 7302, Station E, Calgary, Alberta T3C 3M2 Canada. (403)263-2707. Publisher: Murray Gimbel. Emphasizes recreational vehicles, travel and outdoors for upper income ages 30-65. Monthly. Circ. 100,000. Sample copy 50¢; free art guidelines.
Cartoons: Uses 4 cartoons/issue; buys all from freelancers. Receives 1 submission/month from freelancers. Especially needs cartoons. Subject matter should concern traveling and camping as it relates to trailering, motorhoming, fishing or hiking. Prefers b&w line drawings with gag line. Send samples of style. SASE (nonCanadians include International Reply Coupons). Reports in 2 weeks. Cartoons can appear in other publications. Pays $25 for b&w.
Illustrations: Uses 4 illustrations/issue; buys all from freelancers. Receives 1 submission/week from freelancers. Usually works on assignment. Illustration needs identical to cartoons. Prefers b&w line drawings for inside. Send samples of style. SASE (nonCanadians include International Reply Coupons). Reports in 3 weeks. "Prefer illustrations not appear in a similar magazine." Pays $50-100 for inside b&w on publication.
Tips: "We now feature a broader range of editorial content. Basically, any subject that applies to recreational activity outdoors."

*PETER LI, INC./PFLAUM PRESS, 2451 E. River Rd., Dayton OH 45439. (513)294-5785. Art Director: Joe Gast. Publishes three monthly magazines—*The Catechist*, *Classroom Computer Learning* and *Today's Catholic Teacher*.
Illustrations: Works with 20 freelance artists/year. "Local artists are, of course, more preferable but it's not an absolute." Uses artists for 4-color cover illustrations and b&w and 2-color spot illustrations. "We are only interested in *professional* illustrators, especially those with fresh, innovative styles. Experience a plus but not necessary." Works on assignment only. Send query letter with samples. Accepts photostats, photographs, slides or tear sheets as samples. Samples returned by SASE. Reports only if interested. Pays by the project, $100-600 average. Considers complexity of the project when establishing payment. Buys all rights.

*LIFELINES/THE SOFTWARE MAGAZINE, 1651 3rd Ave., New York NY 10128. (212)722-1700. Managing Editor: Brenda Rodriguez. Emphasizes microcomputer software programs for programmers and microcomputer users with advanced knowledge of microcomputers. Monthly. Circ. 5,000. Original artwork not returned after publication. Sample copy available.
Cartoons: Buys 1-2 cartoons/issue from freelancers. Considers computer industry themes. Prefers single, double or multiple panel with gagline; b&w line drawings or washes. Send query letter with samples of style to be kept on file. Material not filed is returned by SASE. Reports within 1 month. Buys reprint rights. Pays $50, b&w; on publication.
Illustrations: Send query letter with samples to be kept on file. Prefers tear sheets, photocopies or photographs as samples. Samples not filed are returned by SASE. Reports within 1 month. Buys reprint rights. Pays negotiable rate, b&w and color, cover; on publication.

LIGHT & LIFE, 901 College Ave., Winona Lake IN 46590. (219)267-7656. Contact: Art Director. "Emphasizes evangelical Christianity with Wesleyan slant for a cross-section readership." Readers are mostly of Free Methodist denomination. Monthly. Circ. 48,000. Original artwork returned after publication, if requested and postage included. Sample copy $1.50.

Cartoons: Rarely used. Interested in religious themes. Format: single panel b&w line drawings with or without gag line. Prefers finished cartoons. SASE. Reports in 4 weeks. Buys all rights. Pays $5 and up; on acceptance.

Illustrations: Uses 2-4 illustrations/issue, all from freelancers. Interested in art that illustrates themes of articles. Works on assignment only. Samples returned by SASE. Provide letter of inquiry and tear sheets to be kept on file for future assignments. Prefers to see portfolio, roughs and samples of style. Reports in 4 weeks. Buys all rights on a work-for-hire basis. Pays $25 and up, inside b&w and 2-color; on publication.

Tips: Especially looks for "warmth and variety in style, and an indication of a willingness to be flexible." Seeks someone "who wants to be a contributor partly because its fun."

LIVING BLUES, Center for the Study of Southern Culture, University of Mississippi, University MS 38677. (601)232-5993. Managing Editor: Frank Childrey. Emphasizes all aspect of blues music and artists; directed to "all manner of blues artists, enthusiasts, record people, researchers, writers and scholars." Bimonthly. Circ. 3,000. Accepts previously published material. Returns original artwork after publication. Sample copy free for SASE with 50¢ postage; art guidelines free for SASE.

Illustrations: Buys 0-10 illustrations/issue from freelancers. Themes must be related to black music and/or culture. Send query letter with brochure, resume and samples to be kept on file. Write or call for appointment to show portfolio. Accepts photostats, tear sheets, photocopies, slides or photographs as samples; prefers color samples of color work. Samples not filed are returned by SASE. Reports within 2 weeks. Negotiates rights purchased. Negotiates payment; pays on publication.

LIVING MAGAZINE, Suite 400, 5757 Alpha Rd., Dallas TX 75240. (214)239-2399. Emphasizes housing and related fields for middle to upper-middle income people interested in buying a home as well as first-time buyers. Limited apartment coverage. Bimonthly. Circ. 530,000. Sample copy and art guidelines available.

Illustrations: Uses 0-2 illustrations/issue. Prefers theme that "pertains to the article/editorial in question." Send query letter. Call for appointment to show portfolio. Reports only if interested. Buys all rights. Payment for cover "depends on the individual situation." Pays on acceptance.

*LOG HOME GUIDE FOR BUILDERS & BUYERS, Exit 447, I-40, Hartford TN 37753. (615)487-2256. Editor: Doris Muir. Emphasizes buying and building log homes; energy-efficiency. Audience: ages 25-60, college educated, middle- upper-middle income; prefer country life. Quarterly. Circ. 125,000. Sometimes accepts previously published material. Original artwork returned after publication. Sample copy $3.50; art guidelines for SASE.

Cartoons: Buys 1-4 cartoons/issue from freelancers. Themes include renderings of log homes; warmth of log home living; amusing aspects of building with logs; and country living. Prefers single panel without gagline; b&w line drawings, b&w and color washes. Send query letter with samples of style or roughs to be kept on file. Material not filed is returned if accompanied by SASE. Reports within 6 weeks. Negotiates rights purchased. Pays $10-25, b&w; $25-50, color; on publication.

Illustrations: Buys 1-4 illustrations/issue from freelancers. Themes include log home renderings; log homes in rural scenes; and beavers and badgers in natural settings. Send query letter with brochure, resume, business card and samples to be kept on file. Prefers tear sheets, slides and photographs as samples. Samples not filed are returned by SASE. Reports within 6 weeks. Negotiates rights purchased. Pays $250, color, cover; $15-35, b&w and $25-50, color, inside; on publication.

THE LOGGER AND LUMBERMAN, 210 N. Main St., Wadley GA 30477. (912)252-5237. For management personnel in the forest products industry. Circ. 23,000. Monthly. Original artwork not returned after publication. Sample copy $1; free artist's guidelines.

Cartoons: Uses 0-1 cartoon/issue, on field of forestry; single panel with gag line. Buys b&w line drawings. Prefers to see finished cartoons. SASE. Reports in 1 week. Buys all rights. Negotiates pay; pays on acceptance.

Illustrations: Uses 0-1 illustration/issue on "things pertaining to loggers, lumber, paper and related fields." Prefers to see finished art. SASE. Reports "as soon as possible." Buys all rights. Pays on acceptance.

*LONE STAR HUMOR DIGEST, Lone Star Publications of Humor, Suite 103, Box 29000, San Antonio TX 78229. Editor/Publisher: Lauren Barnett Scharf. "Book-by-subscription" (magazine-type format). Emphasizes "comedy connoisseurs," and "others who like to laugh." Published about 3 times/year. Circ. 1,200. Sometimes accepts previously published material. Original artwork returned after publication. Sample copy $6; art guidelines for SASE with 22¢ postage.

Cartoons: Buys 20-25 cartoons/issue from freelancers. Prefers single, double or multiple panel with or without gagline; b&w line drawings. Send roughs or finished cartoons. Material returned by SASE. Reports within 3 months. Negotiates rights purchased. Pays $5-20, b&w; on publication ("but we try to pay before").

THE LOOKOUT, 8121 Hamilton Ave., Cincinnati OH 45231. (513)931-4050. Editor-in-Chief: Mark A. Taylor. For conservative Christian adults and young adults. Weekly. Circ. 160,000. Original artwork not returned after publication, unless requested. Sample copy and artists' guidelines available for 50¢.
Cartoons: Uses 1 cartoon/issue; buys 20/year from freelancers. Interested in church, Sunday school and Christian family themes. Send roughs or finished cartoons. SASE. Reports in 2 weeks. Buys one-time rights.
Illustrations: Uses 3-4 illustrations/issue; receives 0 submissions/week from freelancers. Interested in "adults, families, interpersonal relationships; also, graphic treatment of titles." Works on assignment only. Send letter of inquiry, brochure, flyer or tear sheets to be kept on file for future assignments to Frank Sutton art director, at above address. Reporting time varies. Buys all rights, but will reassign. Inside: Pays $100 for b&w, $125 for full-color illustrations, firm; on acceptance. Cover: "Sometimes more for cover work."

LOS ANGELES, 1888 Century Park E, Los Angeles CA 90067. (213)552-1021. Design Director: William Delorme. Emphasizes lifestyles, cultural attractions, pleasures, problems and personalities of Los Angeles and the surrounding area. Monthly. Circ. 160,000. SASE. Reports in 2-3 weeks. Especially needs very localized contributors—custom projects needing person-to-person concepting and implementation. Previously published work OK. Pays on publication. Sample copy $3.
Cartoons: Contact Geoff Miller, editor-in-chief. Buys 3-4/issue on current events, environment, family life, politics, social life and business; single, double or multipanel with gagline. Mail roughs. Pays $25 minimum, b&w line drawings.
Illustrations: Buys 4/issue on assigned themes. Query with resume and samples or submit portfolio for review. Inside: Pays $75 minimum, b&w line drawings.
Tips: "Show work similar to that used in the magazine—a sophisticated style. Study a particular publication's content, style and format. Then proceed accordingly in submitting sample work." There is a trend toward "imaginative imagery and technical brilliance with computer-enhanced art being a factor. Know the stylistic essence of a magazine at a gut level as well as at a perceptive level. Identify with Los Angeles or Southern California."

LOST TREASURE, 15115 S. 76th East Ave., Bixby OK 74008. (918)366-4441. Managing Editor: James D. Watts, Jr. Emphasizes treasure hunting for treasure hunters, coinshooters, metal detector owners. Monthly. Circ. 50,000. Sample copy for 9x12 SASE.
Cartoons: Uses 1-2 cartoons/issue; all from freelancers. Receives 10 cartoons from freelancers/month. Cartoons should pertain to treasure hunting, people using metal detectors, prospecting, etc. Format: Single panel b&w line drawings or b&w washes with gagline. Send finished cartoons. SASE. Reports in 6-8 weeks. Pays $10-15 on publication. Buys first North American serial rights.

LOUISIANA LIFE MAGAZINE, 4200 S. I-10 Service Rd., Metairie LA 70001. (504)456-2220. Art Director: Tessa Tilden-Smith. Emphasizes the lifestyle of Louisiana (food, entertainment, work, etc.) for the upper-income Louisianan, "proud of the state and its diversity." Bimonthly. Circ. 50,000. Accepts previously published material. Original artwork returned after publication. Art guidelines available.
Illustrations: Uses 1-2 illustrations/issue; buys all from freelancers. Prefers watercolor illustrations. Works on assignment only. Send query letter with tear sheets to be kept on file. Prefers to receive tear sheets, but will also review slides. Samples not kept on file are returned by SASE. Reports within 2 weeks. Buys first rights. Pays $150/page, color, inside; on publication.

THE LUTHERAN JOURNAL, 7317 Cahill Rd., Edina MN 55435. Contact: J.W. Leykom. Family magazine for Lutheran Church members, middle aged and older. Previously published work OK. Free sample copy.
Illustrations: Seasonal 1-, 2- or full-color covers. Mail art with price. Buys one-time rights. Pays on publication.

THE LUTHERAN STANDARD, 426 S. 5th St., Box 1209, Minneapolis MN 55440. (612)330-3300. Editor: Lowell G. Almen. Managing Editor: Donn S. McLellan. Emphasizes news in the world of religion, dealing primarily with the Lutheran Church. For members of the American Lutheran Church. Published 20 times/year. Circ. 579,000. Free sample copy.
Cartoons: Uses 1-2 cartoons/issue; buys all from freelancers. Receives 10 submissions/week from free-

lancers. Interested in current events, education, family life, humor through youth and religious themes. Send finished cartoons. SASE. Reports in 3-4 weeks. Buys first or simultaneous rights. Pays $10-25, b&w line drawings and washes; on acceptance.
Illustrations: Buys 4 illustrations/issue; all from freelancers. Assignment only. Send samples (photocopies OK) to be kept on file for future assignments. Send SASE with queries. Reports in 3-4 weeks. Buys all rights on a work-for-hire basis. Inside: Pays $50-150, b&w and 2-color line drawings and washes.

MADE TO MEASURE, 300 W. Adams St., Chicago IL 60606. (312)263-6355. Publisher: William Halper. Emphasizes uniforms, career clothes, men's tailoring and clothing. Magazine distributed to retailers, manufacturers and uniform group purchasers. Semiannually. Circ. 24,000. Art guidelines available.
Cartoons: Buys 15 cartoons/issue from freelancers. Prefers themes relating to subject matter of magazine; also general interest. Prefers single panel with or without gagline; b&w line drawings. Send query letter with samples of style or finished cartoons. Any cartoons not purchased are returned to artist. Reports back. Buys first rights. Pays $20 b&w, on acceptance.

*MAGIC CHANGES, Box 14245, Chicago IL 60614-0245. (312)327-5606. Editor: John Sennett. Emphasizes fantasy and poetry for college students, housewives, teachers, artists and musicians: "People with both interesting and artistic slant." Semiannually. Circ. 500. Accepts previously published material. Original artwork returned after publication. Sample copy $4; art guidelines free for SASE.
Cartoons: Buys 2 cartoons/issue from freelancers. Considers space, art, animals and street activity themes. Single, double, or multiple panel with or without gagline; b&w line drawings. Send query letter with finished cartoons. Material returned by SASE. Reports within 2 weeks. Acquires first rights. Pays in copies.
Illustrations: Buys 15 illustrations/issue from freelancers. Considers city, wilderness, bird, space and fantasy themes. Prefers photocopies as samples. Samples returned by SASE. Reports within 2 weeks. Acquires first rights. Pays in copies.

MAGICAL BLEND, Box 11303, San Francisco CA 94101. Emphasizes the psychic, occult and spiritual. Quarterly. Circ. 12,000. Original artwork returned after publication. Sample copy $4; art guidelines for SASE.
Illustrations: Uses 60 illustrations/issue; buys all from freelancers. Receives 5 submissions/week from freelancers. Interested in fantasy and sorcery. "We keep samples on file and work by assignment according to the artists and our time table and workability. We accept b&w line drawings, also pencil and preseparated color work. We tend towards fantasy and new age styles. We look for pieces with occult, psychic and spiritual subjects with positive, inspiring, uplifting feeling. No dark, bizarre, or negative material will be considered." Especially needs Oriental themes and strong cultural themes, i.e., African, Latin American, Zen brush work, Indian, etc. Provide letter of inquiry, brochure, or flyer to be kept on file for future assignments. Prefers to see portfolio or samples of style. SASE. Reports in 2 months. Buys first North American serial rights. Rights revert to artist. Pays in copies. Also needs "comics and/or comix about occult, sorcery, magic, psychic subjects with positive, uplifting endings."
Tips: "We now are printing color and will consider pre-separated color work. We are getting wider recognition, and thus, more professional. Send good reproductions—not photocopies, not originals. Read the magazines."

MAINE LIFE, Box 111, Freedom ME 04941. (207)382-6200. Publisher: George Frangoulis. Associate Editor: Tim Rice. Emphasizes the State of Maine for the general public. Bimonthly. Circ. 30,000. Previously published material OK. Original artwork returned after publication. Free sample copy for 8½x11 SASE.
Illustrations: Uses 1 illustration/issue. Send query letter. Samples not returned. Reports in 6 weeks. Buys first rights. Pays $25 minimum, inside b&w line drawings; on publication.
Tips: Looking for "illustrations of people in action, wildlife indigenous to Maine, good quality, strong line, well presented package with all components identified and labeled." Color on assignment only.

MANAGEMENT ACCOUNTING, 10 Paragon Dr., Montvale NJ 07645. (201)573-6269. Managing Editor: Robert F. Randall. Emphasizes management accounting for management accountants, controllers, chief accountants, treasurers. Monthly. Circ. 95,000. Accepts simultaneous submissions. Original artwork not returned after publication. Sample copy free for SASE.
Cartoons: Uses 1 cartoon/issue, buys 1/issue from freelancer. Prefers single panel with gagline; b&w line drawings. Send finished cartoons. Material not kept on file is returned by SASE. Reports with 2 weeks. Buys one-time rights. Pays $15-25, b&w; on acceptance.
Illustrations: Uses 1 illustration/issue.

MARRIAGE AND FAMILY LIVING, Abbey Press, St. Meinrad IN 47577. (812)357-8011. Contact: Art Director. For married Christians. Monthly. Circ. 40,000. Buys one-time rights. Pays on publication.
Cartoons: "We try to use one cartoon per month."
Illustrations: Buys 200 illustrations/year.

MARYLAND BUSINESS & LIVING, 1 E. Chase St., Belvedere Hotel, Lower Level, Baltimore MD 21202. (301)234-0990. Managing Editor: Joni Lesage. Emphasizes the personal and work interests of Baltimore and Maryland business people. Monthly. Circ. 25,000. Accepts previously published material. Returns original artwork after publication. Sample copy and art guidelines for SASE with $1.05 postage.
Cartoons: Buys 1-2 cartoons/issue from freelancers. Seeks themes relating to business or a businessperson's personal life. Prefers single panel with gagline; b&w line drawings. Send query letter with samples of style or finished cartoons to be kept on file. Write for appointment to show portfolio. Material not filed is returned by SASE. Reports back only if interested. Buys one-time rights or negotiates rights purchased. Negotiates payment; pays on publication.
Illustrations: Buys 1-2 illustrations/issue from freelancers. Themes or styles depend on story. Works on assignment only. Send query letter with resume and samples to be kept on file. Write for an appointment to show portfolio. Accepts photostats, tear sheets, photocopies, slides or photographs as samples. Samples not filed are returned by SASE. Reports back only if interested. Buys one-time rights. Negotiates payment; pays on publication.

MEDIA & METHODS, 1511 Walnut St., Philadelphia PA 19102. (215)563-3501. Emphasizes the methods and technologies of teaching for all school teachers and administrators. Bimonthly. Circ. 40,000 + . Accepts previously published material. Returns original artwork after publication. Sample copy for SASE.
Cartoons: Buys 0-1 cartoons/issue from freelancers. Prefers education themes. Prefers single panel with gagline; b&w line drawings, b&w washes. Send query letter with samples of style to be kept on file. Material not filed is returned by SASE. Reports back only if interested. Buys first rights or reprint rights; pays on publication.
Illustrations: Buys 1-2 illustrations/issue from freelancers. Send query letter with brochure, business card and samples to be kept on file. Prefers slides, photostats or photographs as samples. Material not filed is returned by SASE. Reports back only if interested. Buys first rights or reprint rights. Pays $175 for b&w and $250 for color, cover; $150 for b&w and $175 for color, inside; on publication.
Tips: "We are willing to work through the mail and look for unique styles."

MEDICAL DETECTIVE, (formerly *Jr. Medical Detective*), 1100 Waterway Blvd., Box 567, Indianapolis IN 46206. (317)636-8881. Art Director: Fred Kreiter. Emphasizes health for teenagers and adults. Quarterly. Circ. 1,300. Original artwork not returned after publication. Sample copy 75¢; art guidelines for SASE with 22¢ postage.
Illustrations: Buys 5/issue. Prefers realistic or humorous styles. Works on assignment only. Send query letter with samples to be kept on file. Write for appointment to show portfolio. Prefers photocopies or slides as samples. Samples not filed are returned by SASE. Buys all rights. Pays $175, color, cover; $35/page, b&w, $50/page, 2-color, and $70/page, 4-color, inside; on publication.

MEDICAL MARKETING & MEDIA, Suite 215, 7200 W. Camino Real, Boca Raton FL 33433. (305)368-9301. Art Director: Barry Moscrop. Emphasizes medical marketing for upper-level marketing executives with health-care firms and ad agencies. Monthly. Circ. 7,000. Original artwork not returned after publication. Sample copy available.
Cartoons: Uses 1 cartoon/issue; buys 1/issue from freelancer. Prefers single panel without gagline; b&w line drawings. Send query letter with samples of style to be kept on file. Call for appointment to show portfolio. Material not kept on file is returned by SASE. Reports only if interested. Buys all rights. Pays $100 (approximately), b&w; on acceptance.
Illustrations: Uses 3 illustrations/issue; buys 3/issue from freelancers. Works on assignment only. Send query letter with samples to be kept on file. Call for appointment to show portfolio. Prefers stats or originals as samples. Samples not kept on file are returned by SASE. Reports only if interested. Buys all rights. Pays $500-600, color, cover; $100-300, b&w, inside; on acceptance.

MEDICAL TIMES, 80 Shore Rd., Port Washington NY 11050. Executive Editor: Susan Carr Jenkins. Emphasizes technical medical articles. Monthly. Circ. 105,000. Sample copy $5.
Cartoons: Buys 5-6 cartoons/year from freelancers. Prefers medical themes, "but nothing insulting to our audience." Accepts single panel with gagline; b&w line drawings. Send query letter with finished cartoons; "we'll either accept and pay or return them within one month." Negotiates rights purchased. Pays $25, b&w; on acceptance.

Illustrations: Buys 5 illustrations/issue from freelancers. Works on assignment only. Send query letter with medical samples only; samples filed if interested. Accepts photostats, tear sheets, photocopies or photographs as samples. Samples not filed are returned. Reports within 1 month. Negotiates rights purchased. Payment varies; pays on acceptance.
Tips: "Send samples. We keep files on artists and photographers, and we assign work to the people we have on file. Samples should be of a medical nature. We only accept material we assign due to the technical nature of our journal."

MEDICINE & COMPUTER, 180 S. Broadway, White Plains NY 10605. (914)681-0040. Art Director: Arline Campbell. Estab. 1983. Magazine and newsletter. Emphasizes the use and current news on computers within the medical profession. Bimonthly. Circ. 50,000. Returns original artwork after publication if requested. Sample copy available.
Cartoons: "Have not met a cartoonist appropriate for this magazine yet. Our audience is sophisticated and *dry*. Considers double panel with gagline; b&w line drawings, color washes. Send query letter with samples of style to be kept on file if appropriate to magazine. Write for appointment to show portfolio. Material not filed is returned by SASE only if requested. Reports within 5 weeks. Negotiates rights purchased. Pays $100, b&w; $150, color; on acceptance.
Illustrations: Buys 10 illustrations/issue from freelancers. Styles should be "conservative with a personal flair. I'm always searching for different ways the computer can be depicted graphically." Works on assignment only. Send query letter with samples to be kept on file. Write for appointment to show portfolio. Prefers tear sheets, photocopies or slides as samples. Samples not filed are returned by SASE only if requested. Reports within 5 weeks. Negotiates rights purchased. Pays $1,000 for b&w cover; $500 for b&w inside; on acceptance.

MEMCO NEWS, Box 1079, Appleton WI 54912. Editor: Richard F. Metko. Emphasizes "welding applications as performed with Miller Electric equipment. Readership ranges from workers in small shops to metallurgical engineers." Quarterly. Circ. 35,000. Previously published material and simultaneous submissions OK. Original artwork not returned after publication.

MENDOCINO REVIEW, Box 888, Mendocino CA 95460. (707)964-3831. Editor: Camille Ranker. Literary journal emphasizing short stories, poetry, photographs and artwork. Annual. Circ. 5,000. Returns original work after publication. Sample copy available when "requested on letterhead or with sample submissions." Art guidelines available.
Cartoons: Have published none to date, but "would love to!" Send query letter with samples of style to be kept on file. Material not filed is returned by SASE. Reports within 1 month. Acquires one-time rights. Prefers single, double or multiple panel with gagline; b&w line drawings or washes. Pays in contributor's copies; on publication.
Illustrations: " We would like to have 'lots' in the magazine, but because we're unable to pay, we've had few. We retain submissions on file and attempt to match the illustrations to stories and poetry as needed." Send query letter and samples; "good quality copies are fine. If accepted we contact for a reproduction or the original as needed." Samples not filed are returned by SASE. Reports within 1 month. Acquires first rights or one-time rights. Pays in contributor's copies; on publication.

*THE MERCEDES-BENZ STAR, 1235 Pierce St., Lakewood CO 80214. (303)235-0116. Editor: Frank Barrett. Emphasizes new and old Mercedes-Benz automobiles for members of the Mercedes-Benz Club of America and other automotive enthusiasts. Bimonthly. Circ. 20,000. Does not usually accept previously published material. Returns original artwork after publication. Sample copy for SASE with $1.75 postage.
Illustrations: Buys 0-1/issue. Prefers Mercedes-Benz related themes. Send query letter with resume and samples to be kept on file except for material requested to be returned. Write for appointment to show portfolio. Prefers slides or photographs as samples. Samples not filed are returned by SASE. Reports within 3 weeks. Buys first rights. Negotiates payment; pays on publication.

MERCURY MAGAZINE, Astronomical Society of the Pacific, 1290 24th Ave., San Francisco CA 94122. (415)661-8660. Editor: Andrew Fraknoi. Emphasizes astronomy for students, teachers, lay people. Bimonthly. Circ. 6,000. Accepts previously published material. Original artwork returned after publication, "but we need to keep photo." Sample copy $2.
Cartoons: Uses 3 cartoons/year. Prefers astronomy theme. Send query letter with a copy of finished cartoons to be kept on file. Material not kept on file is returned by SASE. Buys first rights.
Illustrations: Uses various number of illustrations/issue. Prefers astronomy theme only. Send query letter with samples and tear sheets to be kept on file. Prefers various types of samples. Samples not kept on file are returned by SASE. Buys first rights.

*MESSENGER OF ST. ANTHONY, Basilica del Santo, Via Orto Botanico, 35123 Padua, Italy. Editor: Fr. Livio Poloniato. "Ours is basically a religious, family-oriented magazine." Monthly. Circ. 20,000. Accepts previously published material. Original artwork returned after publication. Sample copy available.
Illustrations: Prefers couples, families, children. Samples returned only if requested. Reports only if interested. Buys one-time rights. Pays $10, b&w and $15, color, inside; on publication.

METAL BUILDING REVIEW, Nickerson and Collins, 1800 Oakton, Des Plaines IL 60018. (312)298-6210. Editor: Gene Adams. Emphasizes constructing and contracting for contractors, dealers, erectors, designers and manufacturers in the metal building industry. Monthly. Circ. 22,000. Accepts previously published material. Does not return orginal artwork after publication. Sample copy and art guidelines available.
Cartoons: Buys 2 cartoons/issue from freelancers. Prefers single panel with gagline; b&w line drawings. Send query letter with samples of style to be kept on file. Material not filed is returned only if requested. Reports within 3 weeks. Buys first rights or all rights. Pays $10-15 for b&w; on acceptance.
Illustrations: Buys 1-2 illustrations/issue from freelancers. Works on assignment only. Send query letter with samples to be kept on file. Accepts photostats, tear sheets, photocopies, slides or photographs as samples. Reports within 3-4 weeks. Rights purchased vary from exclusive to first use. Negotiates pay; on acceptance.

MICHIGAN OUT OF DOORS, Box 30235, Lansing MI 48909. Contact: Kenneth S. Lowe. Emphasizes outdoor recreation, especially hunting and fishing; conservation; and environmental affairs. Sample copy $1.
Illustrations: "Following the various hunting and fishing seasons we have a need for illustration material; we consider submissions 6-8 months in advance." Reports as soon as possible. Pays $15 for pen and ink illustrations in a vertical treatment; on acceptance.
Tips: "Our magazine has shifted from newsprint to enamel stock. We have our own art department and thus do not require a great deal of special material."

*THE MILITARY ENGINEER, 607 Prince St., Box 180, Alexandria VA 22313-0180. (703)549-3800. Editor: John J. Kern. Emphasizes technical and managerial information on government controlled and funded construction and engineerng projects in US and abroad for membership of The Society of American Military Engineers, including engineers, architects, contractors, manufacturers and defense systems suppliers. Bimonthly. Circ. 26,500. Original artwork returned after publication if requested. Sample copy $4.
Cartoons: Buys approximately 2 cartoons/issue from freelancers. Prefers gagline; b&w line drawings. Send query letter with finished cartoons to be kept on file. Material not filed is returned. Reports within several days. Buys first rights or all rights. Pays $25, b&w; on acceptance.

MILITARY MARKET MAGAZINE, Springfield VA 22159-0210. (703)750-8676. Editor: Nancy M. Tucker. Emphasizes "the military's PX and commissary businesses for persons who manage and buy for the military's commissary and post exchange systems; also manufacturers and sales companies who supply them." Monthly. Circ. 11,000. Simultaneous submissions OK. Original artwork not returned after publication.
Cartoons: Uses 2 or 3 cartoons/issue; buys all from freelancers. Interested in themes relating to "retailing/buying of groceries and general merchandise from the point of view of the store managers and workers"; single panel with or without gagline, b&w line drawings. Send finished cartoons. Samples returned by SASE. Reports in 6 months. Buys all rights. Pays $25, b&w; on acceptance.
Tips: "We use freelance cartoonists only—*no* other freelance artwork."

*MILKWEED CHRONICLE, Box 24303, Minneapolis MN 55424. (612)332-3192. Art Director: Randall W. Scholes. Emphasizes poetry, prose and graphics for artists, writers and readers/observers of contemporary thought. Published 3 times/year. Circ. 3,500. Accepts previously published material. Original artwork returned after publication. Sample copy $4; art guidelines for SASE.
Cartoons: Buys 3 cartoons/issue from freelancers. Inquire about themes. All formats acceptable. Send query letter with finished cartoons to be kept on file except for those desiring return. Write or call for appointment to show portfolio. Material not filed is returned by SASE. Reports within 6 months. Buys one-time rights. Pays $5-15, b&w; on publication.
Illustrations: Buys 15 illustrations/issue from freelancers. Works on assignment only for covers. Send query letter with samples to be kept on file except for those wanting returns. Write or call for appointment to show portfolio. Prefers photographs or photostats as samples, but will look at others. Samples returned by SASE. Reports within 6 months. Buys one-time rights. Pays $50-100, b&w, cover; $5-15, b&w, inside; on publication.

MILLER/FREEMAN PUBLICATIONS, 500 Howard St., San Francisco CA 94105. (415)397-1881. Associate Art Director: Janet Duncan. Business magazines on paper and pulp, computers and medical subjects. Monthly. Circ. 100,000 + . Accepts previously published material. Returns original artwork after publication.
Cartoons: Buys 3 cartoons/month from freelancers. Considers single, double or multiple panel without gagline; b&w line drawings, b&w washes, color washes. Send query letter with samples of style to be kept on file. Material not filed is returned by SASE. Reports back only if interested. Negotiates rights purchased. Payment varies; pays on acceptance.
Illustrations: Buys 3 illustrations/month from freelancers. Works on assignment only. Send query letter with samples to be kept on file. Prefers tear sheets as samples. Samples not filed are returned by SASE. Reports back only if interested. Negotiates rights purchased. Payment varies; pays on acceptance.

MPLS. ST. PAUL MAGAZINE, Suite 1030, 12 S. 6th St., Minneapolis MN 55402. (612)339-7571. Contact: Bill Bloedow. City/regional magazine. For "professional people of middle-upper income levels, college educated, interested in the arts, dining and the good life of Minnesota." Monthly. Circ. 48,000. Original artwork returned after publication.
Illustrations: Uses 12 illustrations/issue. Works on assignment only. Arrange interview to show portfolio. Provide business card, flyer or tear sheet to be kept on file for future assignments. Reports in 2 weeks. Buys first North American serial rights, and all rights on a work-for-hire basis. Pays $75-200, b&w; $600 maximum/full-page, color; on acceptance.

*MISSOURI LIFE, 710 N. Tucker, St Louis MO 63101. (314)342-1281. Editor: Debra Gluck. Magazine about Missouri. Readers are people interested in where to go, what to do in the state, and the beauty and fascination of Missouri places and faces. Bimonthly. Circ. 30,000. Original artwork returned after publication. Sample copy $3; art guidelines for SASE.
Cartoons: Used to illustrate some departments and features.
Illustrations: Uses original artwork depicting Missouri places or people. Receives 2 illustrations/week from freelance artists. Especially needs variety of b&w and color line art and other types of art for illustration of specific stories, on assignment; interested in a variety of styles. Format: b&w, color cover washes, inside and cover color washes and original art that will reproduce for offset printing/web. Samples returned by SASE. Provide letter of inquiry, tear sheet, proposal and sample of work to be kept on file for future assignments. Reports in 4 weeks. Buys first North American serial rights. Pays $25-50 for b&w, on publication.
Tips: "Send samples of work that show the styles and media you are experienced and good at. We prefer artists in the mid-Missouri, Kansas City and St. Louis areas."

MISSOURI RURALIST, Suite 600, 2103 Burlington, Columbia MO 65202. (314)474-9557. Contact: Editor. For Missouri farm families. Biweekly (except monthly June, July, December). Circ. 80,000. Previously published material OK. Original artwork not returned after publication.
Cartoons: Uses 0-5 cartoons/issue; buys all from freelancers. Interested in farm and rural themes; single panel with gagline. Send finished cartoons. Samples returned by SASE. Reports in 4 weeks. Negotiates rights purchased. Negotiates pay; pays on publication.
Tips: There is a "definite need for good agricultural cartoonists who understand the agriculture business. They must be able to write as well as draw. Puns on farming and agriculture are taboo. Good agricultural cartoonists are scarce. Most are artists, but not good gag writers."

MODEL RETAILER, Clifton House, Clifton VA 22024. (703)830-1000. Editor: Geoffey A. Wheeler. For hobby store owners. Monthly. Circ. 7,300. Previously published and simultaneous submissions ("must be notified") OK. Original artwork returned after publication. Also interested in art for covers, article illustrations, and headline/blurb blocks.
Cartoons: Uses 3 cartoons/issue, all from freelancers. Receives 10 submissions/month from freelancers. Interested in themes pertaining to hobbies, hobby stores or small businesses; double panel. "Query first, with brief summary of types of work done (ads, covers, headline art, cartoons, etc.); after positive response from us send samples of work (photocopies, etc.) and some references." SASE. Reports in 2 weeks. Buys "first time rights in our field." Pays $25 minimum, line drawings; on publication.
Tips: We are "trying to improve the look of the magazine to gain attention for articles and help emphasize key points through imaginative use of graphics. We want good artwork that could be used to dress up feature articles, especially artwork for the headline/blurb block. Basically, artwork that would look good as line or with color overlays."

MODERN DRUMMER, 870 Pompton Ave., Cedar Grove NJ 07009. (201)239-4140. Editor-in-Chief: Ronald Spagnardi. Art Director: David Creamer. For drummers, all ages and levels of playing

ability with varied interests within the field of drumming. Monthly. Circ. 50,000. Previously published work OK. Original artwork returned after publication. Sample copy $2.50.
Cartoons: Buys 5-10 cartoons/year. Uses 1 cartoon/issue. Interested in drumming; single and double panel. "We want strictly drummer-oriented gags." Prefers finished cartoons or roughs. SASE. Reports in 3 weeks. Buys first North American serial rights. Pays $5-25; on publication.

MODERN MACHINE SHOP, 6600 Clough Pike, Cincinnati OH 45230. (513)231-8020. Editor: Ken M. Gettelman. Emphasizes the metalworking industry for production and engineering management in the metalworking industry. Monthly. Circ. 106,000. Free sample copy.
Cartoons: Uses 1 cartoon/issue; buys 1 from freelancers. Receives 5 cartoons/week from freelance artists. Interested in themes relating to the manufacturing environment; single panel with gag line. A topical cartoon can still be appropriate. Send finished cartoons. Samples returned. Reports in 2 weeks. Buys all rights. Pays $25-35, b&w; on acceptance.
Illustrations: Uses 25 illustrations/issue; buys very few from freelancers. Prefers illustrations with articles; especially needs those relating to the new trends of computer-assisted design and manufacturing. Provide samples and tear sheets to be kept on file for possible future assignments. Call for appointment. Samples returned. Buys all rights. Pays $200-400 for illustrations with articles; on acceptance.
Tips: "We see growth of manufacturing capabilities around the world and growth of computer-assisted manufacturing."

MODERN MATURITY, 215 Long Beach Blvd., Long Beach CA 90801. (213)432-5781. Picture Editor: Ms. M.J. Wadolny. Emphasizes health, lifestyles, travel, sports, finance and contemporary activities for members of American Association of Retired Persons. Bimonthly. Previously published work OK. Original artwork returned after publication. Sample copy available.
Cartoons: Uses 4 cartoons/issue; buys 2/issue from freelancers. Receives 50 submissions/week from freelancers. Interested in general interest themes. Send finished cartoons, color and b&w. SASE. Reports in 1 month. Buys all rights on a work-for-hire basis. Pays $150, 8x10 finished cartoons.

*MODERN SINGLES, Box 213, Station W, Toronto, Ontario M6M 4Z2 Canada. Editor: O. Slembeck. Emphasizes personal finance, short stories, humor, travel, book reviews and features for singles and single parents over age 18. Bimonthly. Circ. 5,000. Does not accept previously published material. Does not return original artwork after publication. Sample copy $3.50. Art guidelines for SASE with 37¢ Canadian postage (nonresidents include IRC).
Cartoons: Buys 2/issue. Prefers gagline; b&w line drawings. Send query letter with finished cartoons to be kept on file. Reports within 2 months. Buys all rights. Pays $10, b&w; on acceptance.
Illustrations: Buys 2/issue. Prefers themes showing couples relaxing, in romantic settings, etc. Send query letter with samples to be kept on file. Write for appointment to show portfolio. Prefers photographs as samples. Samples not filed are not returned. Does not report back to the artist. Buys all rights. Pays up to $100, color, cover; up to $70, color and $30 b&w, inside; on acceptance.

MONTHLY DETROIT MAGAZINE, 1400 Woodbridge, Detroit MI 48207. (313)446-6000. Emphasizes "features on local political, economic, style, cultural, lifestyles, culinary subjects, etc., relating to Detroit and region for middle and upper-middle class, urban and suburban, mostly college-educated professionals." Monthly. Circ. approximately 45,000. "Very rarely" accepts previously published material. Sample copy free for SASE.
Illustrations: Uses 10 illustrations/issue; buys 10/issue from freelancers. Works on assignment only. Send query letter with samples and tear sheets to be kept on file. Call for appointment to show portfolio. Prefers anything *but* original work as samples. Samples not kept on file are returned by SASE. Reports only if interested. Pays $75-300, b&w, and $100-350, color, inside; on publication.

THE MORGAN HORSE, Box 1, Westmoreland NY 13490. (315)735-7522. Assistant Editor/Production: Carol Misiaszek. Emphasizes all aspects of the Morgan horse breed including educating Morgan owners, trainers and enthusiasts on breeding and training programs; the true type of the Morgan breed, techniques on promoting the breed, how-to articles, as well as, preserving the history of the breed. Monthly. Circ. 9,000. Accepts previously published material and simultaneous submissions. Original artwork returned after publication. Sample copy $3; art guidelines free for SASE.
Cartoons: Uses 3-6 cartoons/issue; buys all from freelancers. "Since most of our issues have specific themes, cartoons relating to those themes are most welcome, i.e., our June issue is devoted to youth involved in the breed." Prefers single panel, with gagline; b&w line drawings. Send query letter with finished cartoons to be kept on file "only if purchased and until publication." Material not kept on file is returned by SASE. Reports within 6-8 weeks. Buys one-time rights. Pays $10, b&w; negotiates, color; pays on acceptance.
Illustrations: Uses 2-5 illustrations/issue. "Line drawings are most useful for magazine work. We also

purchase art for promotional projects dealing with the Morgan horse—horses should look like *Morgans.*'' Send query letter with samples and tear sheets; call or write for appointment to show portfolio. Accepts ''anything that clearly shows the artist's style and craftsmanship'' as samples. Samples are returned by SASE. Reports within 6-8 weeks. Buys all rights or negotiates rights purchased. Pays $50 minimum, color cover; $10 minimum, b&w inside; on acceptance.

*MOTOR MAGAZINE, 555 W. 57th St., New York NY 10019. Art Director: Harold A. Perry. Emphasizes automotive technology, repair and maintenance for auto mechanics and technicians. Monthly. Circ. 135,000. Accepts previously published material. Original artwork returned after publication if requested. Never send unsolicited original art.

Illustrations: Buys 5-15 illustrations/issue from freelancers. Prefers realistic/technical line renderings of automotive parts and systems. Works on assignment only. Send query letter with resume and samples to be kept on file. Considers photocopies only as samples. Will call for appointment to see further samples. Samples not filed are not returned. Reports only if interested. Buys one-time rights. Pays negotiable rate for color, cover and inside; $35-150, depending on complexity of illustration, b&w, inside; on acceptance.

Tips: ''*Motor* is an educational, technical magazine and is basiclay immune to illustration trends because our drawings *must* be realistic and technical. As design trends change we try to incorporate these into our magazine (within reason). Though *Motor* is a trade publication, we approach it, design-wise, as if it were a consumer magazine. We make use of white space when possible and use creative abstract and impact photographs and illustration for our opening pages and covers. But we must always retain a 'technical look' to reflect our editorial subject matter.''

MOTOR TREND, 8490 Sunset Blvd., Los Angeles CA 90069. (213)657-5100. Art Director: William Claxton. Emphasizes automobiles, world-wide automotive field. Monthly. Circ. 900,000. Sometimes returns original artwork after publication; depends on agreement with artist. Sample copy available.

Cartoons: Buys 1-2 cartoons/issue from freelancers. Prefers any automotive theme, sophisticated style. Considers single or double panel with gagline; b&w line drawings, b&w washes. Send roughs to be kept on file. Material not filed is returned only if requested. Reports back only if interested. Negotiates rights purchased. Payment varies; pays on acceptance.

Illustrations: Buys 3-4 illustrations/issue from freelancers. Themes are automotive (both technical and general illustrations); personality portraits. Send query letter with samples to be kept on file. Call for appointment to show portfolio. Accepts ''only high-quality samples and examples'' to review. Samples not filed are returned only if requested. Reports back only if interested. Negotiates rights purchased. Payment varies; pays on acceptance.

MUSCLE MAG INTERNATIONAL, Unit 2, 52 Bramsteel Rd., Brampton, Ontario L6W 3M5 Canada. (416)457-3030. Editor-in-Chief: Robert Kennedy. For 16- to 50-year-old men and women interested in physical fitness and overall body improvement. Published 12 times/year. Circ. 210,000. Previously published work OK. Original artwork not returned after publication. Sample copy $3.

Cartoons: Uses 6 cartoons/issue, all from freelancers. Receives 30 submissions/week from freelancers. Interested in weight training and body building; single panel; ''well-drawn work—professional.'' Send finished cartoons. SASE (nonresidents include IRC). Send $3 for return postage. Reports in 3 weeks. Buys all rights on a work-for-hire basis. Pays $15-25, color; $10-20, b&w; on acceptance.

Illustrations: Uses 2 illustrations/issue; buys 1/issue from freelancers. Receives 20 submissions/week from freelancers. Interested in ''professionally drawn exercise art of body builders training with apparatus.'' Prefers to see finished art. SASE (nonresidents include IRC). Send $4 for return postage. Reports in 2 weeks. Buys all rights on a work-for-hire basis. Pays $300, color, cover; $100, color and $80, b&w, inside; on acceptance. ''Pay can be triple for really professional or outstanding artwork.''

Tips: ''We only want to see top line work—we want only the best. Study our publication, then submit material to us.''

*MUSCULAR DEVELOPMENT, Box 1707, York PA 17404. (717)767-6481. Advertising Manager: Philip Redman. Emphasizes body building, powerlifting and strength sports. Bimonthly. Circ. 100,000. Accepts previously published material. Original artwork returned after publication. Sample copy for SASE with $1 postage; art guidelines available.

Illustrations: Buys variable number of illustrations/issue from freelancers. Prefers styles other than line art. Works on assignment only. Send query letter with resume and samples to be kept on file; call for appointment to show portfolio. Prefers photocopies or any other good representation as samples by mail; originals and printed material in person. Samples returned by SASE. Reports only if interested. Buys one-time rights. Pays on publication as determined by artist and negotiations.

MUSIC EDUCATORS JOURNAL, 1902 Association Dr., Reston VA 22091. (703)860-4000. Editor: Rebecca Grier Taylor. Production Manager: Pamela Halonen. For music educators in elementary and secondary schools and universities. Monthly (September-May). Circ. 60,000.

Illustrations: Uses illustrations from freelancers. Interested in collages, drawings, paintings, designs on music education subjects. "Artwork should be geared toward people, faces, etc., in music—not very many abstracts are used. Depictions of instruments must be true to form, correct playing positions." Works on assignment. Provide brochure, flyer or tear sheets to be kept on file for future assignments. Reports in "up to 6 months." Buys one-time rights on a work-for-hire basis. Cover: Pays $100-250, full-color art. Inside: Pays $25-100 per item: b&w line drawings, washes, gray opaques and color-separated work; on acceptance.

Tips: "Contact the production manager (preferrably during April-June). We favor artists from the greater Washington, D.C., area who can come in and show us a portfolio. This market provides opportunities for new artists, but their work must be top-notch. Sometimes we don't have an appropriate subject at the time that an artist sends a sample or brochure. Eventually, though, we find a use for most types of art. Artwork must be clean and appropriate for offset reproduction. Instruments must be accurately drawn and postures and fingerings must be correct. Artwork should show teaching, not just performing." Call for appointment.

*THE NANTUCKET REVIEW, Box 1234, Nantucket MA 02554. Co-Editor: Richard Burns. Emphasizes fiction and poetry for writers, poets, students and academics. Published 3 times/year: spring, summer, fall/winter. Circ. 500. Original artwork returned after publication. Sample copy $2.

Illustrations: Buys 1-5 illustrations/issue from freelancers. "We have used a wide range of themes and styles." Send query letter with samples to be kept on file "except for work we are certain we will not use." Prefers photocopies or slides as samples. Samples not filed are returned by SASE. Reports within 2 months. Buys first rights. Pays $25, b&w, cover; $5, b&w, inside; on acceptance; plus 2 contributor's copies of magazine.

THE NATIONAL FUTURE FARMER, Box 15130, Alexandria VA 22309. (703)360-3600. Editor-in-Chief: Wilson W. Carnes. For members of the Future Farmers of America who are students of vocational agriculture in high school, ages 14-21. Emphasizes careers in agriculture/agribusiness and topics of general interest to youth. Bimonthly. Circ. 500,000. Reports in 3 weeks. Buys all rights. Pays on acceptance. Sample copy available.

Cartoons: Buys 15-20 cartoons/year on Future Farmers of America or assigned themes. Receives 30 cartoons/week from freelance artists. Pays $15, cartoons; more for assignments.

Illustrations: "We are buying more art these days to use as illustration for specific stories; almost always on assignment."

Tips: "We suggest you send samples of work so we can keep your name on file as the need arises. We prefer b&w line art. Please include rates."

NATIONAL GEOGRAPHIC, 17th and M Sts. NW, Washington DC 20036. (202)857-7000. Contact: Art Director. Monthly. Circ. 10,500,000. Original artwork returned after publication, in some cases.

Illustrations: Number of illustrations bought/issue varies. Interested in "full-color, representational renderings of historical and scientific subjects. Nothing that can be photographed is illustrated by artwork. No decorative, design material. We want scientific geological cutaways, maps, historical paintings." Works on assignment only. Prefers to see portfolio and samples of style. Samples are returned by SASE. "The artist should be familiar with the type of painting we use." Provide brochure, flyer or tear sheet to be kept on file for future assignments. Reports in 2 weeks. Minimum payment: Inside: $1,000, color; $200, b&w; on acceptance.

NATIONAL MOTORIST, Suite 300, One Market Plaza, San Francisco CA 94105. (415)777-4000. Editor: Jane Offers. Emphasizes travel on the West Coast for all members of the National Automobile Club in California. Bimonthly. Circ. 205,000. Original artwork returned after publication. Sample copy 50¢.

Cartoons: Uses 1 cartoon/issue; buys 1/issue from freelancer. Prefers auto- or travel-related themes. Prefers b&w line drawings with gaglines. Send query letter with roughs to be kept on file. Material not kept on file is returned. Reports within days. Buys first rights. Pays "on request", b&w and color; on acceptance.

Illustrations: Uses very few illustrations/issue. Prefers auto- or travel-related themes. Send query letter with samples to be kept on file. Prefers original work as samples. Samples not kept on file are returned. Buys first rights. Pays "all on request"; on acceptance.

THE NATIONAL NOTARY, 23012 Ventura Blvd., Box 4625, Woodland Hills CA 91365-4625. (818)347-2035. Contact: Production Editor. Emphasizes "notaries public and notarization—goal is to impart knowledge, understanding, and unity among notaries nationwide and internationally. Readers are notaries of varying primary occupations (legal, government, real estate and financial), as well as state and federal officials and international parties." Bimonthly. Circ. 40,000. Receives 1 cartoon and 2 illustrations/week from freelance artists. Original artwork not returned after publication. Sample copy $4; art guidelines available.

Cartoons: May use. Cartoons "must have a notarial angle"; single or multipanel with gagline, b&w line drawings. Send samples of style; call for appointment. Samples not returned. Reports in 4-6 weeks. Buys all rights. Negotiates pay; on publication.

Illustrations: Uses 5 illustrations/issue; buys all from local freelancers. Themes vary, depending on subjects of articles. Works on assignment only. Send samples of style; call for appointment. Samples not returned. Provide business card, samples and tear sheets to be kept on file for possible future assignments. Reports in 4-6 weeks. Buys all rights. Negotiates pay; on publication.

Tips: "We are very interested in experimenting with various styles of art in illustrating the magazine. Be creative but open to suggestions. Present full-size artwork per request. Be prompt and keep editors aware of progress. Material can be dry at times, needing more thought and creativity on the artist's part to come up with exciting and workable visuals. We will generally work with Southern California artists, as we prefer face-to-face dealings rather than through mail."

*THE NATIONAL REPORTER, Box 647, Ben Franklin Station, Washington DC 20044. (202)328-0178. Editor: John Kelly. Emphasizes CIA, international monetary institutions; U.S. Government policies. Bimonthly. Circ. 10,000. Accepts previously published material. Original artwork returned after publication. Sample copy and art guidelines available.

Cartoons: Buys 2-3 cartoons/issue from freelancers. Prefers gagline; b&w line drawings. Send query letter with samples of style or finished cartoons to be kept on file; write for appointment to show portfolio. Material not filed is returned. Reports within 1-2 weeks. Pays $20-50, b&w; on publication.

Illustrations: Buys 2-3 illustrations/issue from freelancers. Send query letter with samples to be kept on file; write for appointment to show portfolio. Prefers photographs as samples. Samples returned. Reports within 1-2 weeks. Buys first rights. Pays on publication.

NATIONAL REVIEW, 150 E. 35th St., New York NY 10016. Contact: Anna Lieber. Emphasizes world events from a conservative viewpoint. Bimonthly. Original artwork returned after publication.

Cartoons: Uses 15 cartoons/issue; buys all from freelancers. Interested in "political, social commentary." Prefers to receive finished cartoons. SASE. Reports in 2 weeks. Buys first North American serial rights. Pays on publication.

Illustrations: Uses 15 illustrations/issue. Especially needs b&w ink illustration, portraits of political figures and conceptual editorial art (b&w line work). "I look for a strong graphic style; well-developed ideas and well-executed drawings." Works on assignment only. Prefers to see finished art, portfolio, samples of style or "published tear sheets." No samples returned. Reports back on future assignment possibilities. SASE. Also buys small decorative and humorous spot illustrations in advance by mail submission. Buys first North American serial rights. Pays $15, small spots, $35, larger spot, $40, assigned illustration; on publication.

Tips: "Tear sheets and mailers are helpful in remembering an artist's work. Artists ought to make sure their work is professional in quality of idea and execution. Printed samples alongside originals help. Changes in art and design in our field include fine art influence and use of more halftone illustration."

NATIONAL RURAL LETTER CARRIER, Suite 100, 1448 Duke St. Alexandria VA 22314. (703)684-5545. Managing Editor: RuthAnn Saenger. Emphasizes news and analysis of federal law and current events. For rural letter carriers and family-oriented, middle-Americans; many are part-time teachers and businessmen. Weekly. Circ. 65,000. Mail art. SASE. Reports in 4 weeks. Original artwork returned after publication. Previously published, photocopied and simultaneous submissions OK. Buys first rights. Sample copy 24¢. Receives 1 cartoon and 2 illustrations/month from freelance artists.

Illustrations: Buys 12 covers/year on rural scenes, views of rural mailboxes and rural people. Uses 1 illustration/issue; buys from freelancers. Interested in pen & ink or pencil on rural, seasonal and postal matter. Especially needs rural mailboxes and sketches of scenes on rural delivery. Works on assignment only. Samples returned by SASE. Provide resume, samples of work and tear sheet to be kept on file for future assignments. Reports in 1 week, if accepted; 1 month if not accepted. Buys all rights on a work-for-hire basis. Pays $25-50, b&w; on publication.

Tips: "Please send in samples when you inquire about submitting material." Have a definite need for "realistic painting and sketches."

NATIONAL SAFETY AND HEALTH NEWS, (formerly *National Safety News*), National Safety Council, 444 N. Michigan Ave., Chicago IL 60611. (312)527-4800. Editor: Roy Fisher. For those responsible for developing and administering occupational safety and health programs. Monthly. Circ. 56,000. Original artwork returned after publication. Free sample copy and artist's guidelines. Also uses artists for 4-color cover design, publication redesign and layout mock-ups. Contact: Robert Meyer, Periodicals and Technical Publications Director.

Cartoons: Contact: Susan-Marie Kelly. Uses 4-6 cartoons/issue, all from freelancers. Interested in occupational safety and health; single, double or multipanel with gagline. Prefers to see roughs. SASE. Reports in 4 weeks. Buys first North American serial rights or all rights on a work-for-hire basis. Pays $10 minimum, b&w line drawings.

NATIONAL WILDLIFE, INTERNATIONAL WILDLIFE, 8925 Leesburg Pike, Vienna VA 22180. Art Director: Dan Smith. Emphasize wildlife. For those concerned with the future of wildlife and the environment. Bimonthlies. Circ. 800,000.
Illustrations: Assigns art on 1-2 stories/issue. Works on assignment only. Prefers to see samples of style. SASE. Provide flyer, slides or tear sheets to be kept on file. Reports in 3 weeks. Usually buys first, reprint and promotion rights. Pays competitive rates; on acceptance.

NATURAL HISTORY, American Museum of Natural History, Central Park W. and 79th St., New York NY 10024. (212)873-1300. Editor-in-Chief: Alan Ternes. Art Director: Tom Page. Emphasizes social and natural sciences. For well-educated professionals interested in the natural sciences. Monthly. Circ. 500,000. Previously published work OK.
Illustrations: Buys 10-15 illustrations/year; 20-30 maps or diagrams/year. Interested in current events and environment. Works on assignment only. Query with samples. Samples returned by SASE. Provide "any pertinent information" to be kept on file for future assignments. Reports in 1 week. Buys one-time rights. Inside: Pays $100, b&w line drawings and washes; on publication.
Tips: "Be familiar with the publication and the trend toward human ecology."

*NATURE FRIEND MAGAZINE, 22777 State Rd. 119, Goshen IN 46526. (219)534-2245. Editor: Stanley K. Brubaker. Estab. 1983. Emphasizes North American nature and wildlife for children 4-14 + of Christian families who hold a literal view of the Creation. Monthly. Circ. 2,100. Accepts previously published material. Returns original artwork after publication only by SASE. Sample copy for 7x10 SASE with 56¢ postage; art guidelines for 7x10 SASE with 56¢ postage.
Illustrations: Buys up to 5/issue. Prefers "very colorful and accurate closeup scenes of wildlife in action—living nature which is interesting for children, not adult scenery or still life which is too dead." Send business card and samples to be kept on file. Prefers tear sheets as samples. Samples not filed are returned by SASE. Reports only if interested. Buys one-time rights. Pays $20, b&w, inside; $30-35, 2-color or 3-color with overlays, inside; $50 full-color, inside; on publication "unless delayed more than 2 months."

NAVAL INSTITUTE PROCEEDINGS, U.S. Naval Institute, Annapolis MD 21402. (301)268-6110. Editor-in-Chief: Clayton R. Barrow. Emphasizes the Navy, Marine Corps, Coast Guard and related maritime and military topics. Monthly. Circ. 98,000. Returns original artwork after publication. Free sample copy and art guidelines.
Illustrations: Buys about 5 illustrations/issue from freelancers. Themes vary but are mainly military/political. Works on assignment only. Send query letter with samples to be kept on file. Write or call for appointment to show portfolio. Prefers sketches as samples. Samples not filed are returned only if requested. Reports within a few weeks. Negotiates rights purchased and payment. Pays on acceptance.

*NEGATIVE CAPABILITY, 6116 Timberly Rd. N, Mobile AL 36609. Editor: Sue Walker. Journal. Emphasizes fiction, poetry, art, music and essays. Audience is interested in art/literature. Quarterly. Circ. 800. Original artwork returned after publication. Sample copy $3.50.
Cartoons: Buys 3 cartoons/issue from freelancers. Theme or style open. Prefers single or double panel with gagline; b&w line drawings, b&w washes. Send finished cartoons to be kept on file; write for appointment to show portfolio. Material not filed is returned by SASE. Reports within 6 weeks. Acquires one-time rights. Pays in 2 contributor's copies.
Illustrations: Buys 8-10 illustrations/issue from freelancers. Themes or styles open. Send query letter and samples to be kept on file; write for appointment to show portfolio. Samples not filed are returned by SASE. Reports within 6 weeks. Acquires one-time rights. Pays in 2 contributor's copies.

NEW AGE JOURNAL, 342 Western Ave., Brighton MA 02135. (617)787-2005. Art Director: Greg Paul. Emphasizes alternative lifestyles, holistic health, ecology, personal growth, human potential, planetary survival for highly educated young professionals with an interest in their health, personal potential and quality of life. Monthly. Circ. 55,000. Accepts previously published material and simultaneous submissions. Original artwork returned after publication. Sample copy $2.50.
Illustrations: Uses 10-15 illustrations/issue. Illustrations accompany specific manuscripts. Send query letter with samples or tear sheets to be kept on file. Call for appointment to show portfolio. Prefers photostats, photocopies or slides as samples. Samples returned by SASE if not kept on file. Buys one-time rights.

*NEW ENGLAND SAMPLER, R.F.D. #1, Box 2280, Brooks ME 04921. (207)525-3575. Editor/ Publisher: Virginia M. Rimm. Emphasizes New England (rural). Audience is over-30, high school or college level educated, interested in rural New England, traditional family values; large percentage of professionals. "We're an upbeat family-style publication." Published 9 times/year. Circ. 2,000. Accepts previously published material. Original artwork returned after publication. Sample copy $1; art guidelines free for SASE.

Illustrations: Buys 4-5 illustrations/issue from freelancers. Works on assignment only. Send query letter with resume and samples to be kept on file; write for appointment to show portfolio. Prefers tear sheets or photocopies as samples. Samples returned by SASE. Reports within 3 weeks. Acquires one-time rights. Pays in copies only.

NEW HAMPSHIRE PROFILES, 109 W. Main St., Concord NH 03301. (603)224-5193. Editor: Stephen A. Bennett. Emphasizes articles and photographs pertaining to New Hampshire and its residents. Monthly. Circ. 25,000. SASE. Simultaneous submissions OK. Original artwork not returned after publication, unless requested. Sample copy $2; free artist's guidelines.

Cartoons: Seldom uses out-of-state cartoonists, but willing to see samples with New Hampshire themes.

Illustrations: "Varied use of illustrations in every issue. We buy from freelancers and encourage the submission of samples representing an artist's style and range of talents." Works on assignment only. Provide resume and tear sheet to be kept on file for future assignments. Prefers to see resume and samples of style. Samples returned by SASE. Reports in 1 week; 6-8 weeks on unsolicited material. Buys all rights on a work-for-hire basis. Inside: Pays $35-100, b&w line drawings and washes, depending on size and complexity. Does not want to see nature sketches (birds, flowers, etc.).

*NEW JERSEY MONTHLY, 7 Dumont Pl., Morristown NJ 07960. Contact: Art Director. Emphasizes general interest themes dealing with New Jersey. Monthly. Circ. 100,000.

Illustrations: Buys 8 illustrations/issue on assigned themes. Arrange interview to show portfolio. SASE. Reports in 6 weeks. Pays $150/spot, $300/full page, b&w; $300-600, color; on publication.

NEW LETTERS, 5310 Harrison St., Kansas City MO 64110. "Innovative" small magazine with an international scope. Quarterly. Sample copy $4.

Illustrations: Uses camera-ready spot drawings, line drawings and washes; "any medium that will translate well to the 6x9" b&w printed page." Also needs cover designs. Submit art. Reports in 2-8 weeks. Buys all rights. Pays $5-10, pen and inks, line drawings and washes.

Tips: "Fewer pieces of freelance art being accepted; we consider only work of the highest quality. Artwork does not necessarily have to relate to content."

NEW MEXICO MAGAZINE, Bataan Memorial Bldg., Santa Fe NM 87503. (505)827-6180. Art Director: Bonnie Bishop. Emphasizes the state of New Mexico for residents, and visiting vacationers and businesspersons. Monthly. Circ. 100,000. Accepts previously published material and simultaneous submissions. Original artwork returned after publication. No printed artists' guidelines, but may call for information. Also interested in calligraphers.

Cartoons: Uses 12-20 cartoons/year. Prefers single panel; b&w line drawings, b&w washes. Send query letter with samples of style to be kept on file. Material not kept on file is returned only if requested. Reports only if interested. Buys one-time rights. Pays $15-100, b&w; $50-300, color; on acceptance.

Illustrations: Uses 2 illustrations/issue. Works on assignment only. Send query letter with samples to be kept on file. Samples not kept on file are returned only if requested. Reports only if interested. Buys one-time rights. Pays $40 for small illustrations to $300 for 4-color work, usually all inside; on acceptance.

NEW OREGON REVIEW, 537 NE Lincoln St., Hillsboro OR 97123. Editor: Steven Dimeo, Ph.D. For college students, professors and those interested in the humanities. Published semiannually. Circ. 300. Sample copy $3 (mention *Artist's Market*). Receives 1 illustration/month from freelance artists. Would like to receive more freelance submissions.

Illustrations: Buys 2-5 illustrations/year. Primarily purchases photos. "We like drawings that deal uncommonly with the common, surrealistic landscapes of the mind featuring nudes, portraits or nature." Query with samples and 3-5 sentence biographical statement. SASE. Reports in 2-3 months. Buys all rights. Pays $10, b&w line drawings and washes; $25, commissioned work; on publication. Beginning 1985 we will offer $100 prize for best illustration published.

Tips: "A neat presentation of an artist's samplings by means of a flyer or portfolio is almost mandatory."

NEW ORLEANS, ARC Publishing Co., 6666 Morrison Rd., New Orleans LA 70126. (504)246-2700. Art Director: David Maher. Editor: Don Washington. Emphasizes entertainment, travel, sports, news,

business and politics in New Orleans. For readers with high income and education. Monthly. Circ. 200,000. Previously published and photocopied submissions OK. Sample copy $2.50.
Illustrations: Query with samples. SASE. Buys assigned illustrations and cartoons on current events, education and politics. Especially needs assigned feature illustrations "specifically relating to and illustrating a concept in one of our main feature stories." Pays $40-100, spot drawings; $75-200, feature illustrations; on publication.
Tips: "Do not send unassigned, unsolicited work on speculation. It creates a burden for me to sift through work and return it. However, do send nonreturnable photocopies or stats of work so I can keep them on file when work becomes available."

NEW ORLEANS REVIEW, Box 195, Loyola University, New Orleans LA 70118. (504)865-2152. Editor: John Mosier. Journal of literature and culture. Published 4 times/year. Sample copy $7.
Illustrations: Uses 5-10 illustrations/issue. Cover: uses color, all mediums. SASE. Reports in 2-3 weeks. Inside: uses b&w line drawings, photos/slides of all mediums.

NEW REALITIES, Suite 408, 680 Beach St., San Francisco CA 94109. Editor/Publisher: James Bolen. Managing Editor: Shirley Christine. Concerns "holistic health and personal growth." Bimonthly. Pays on publication.
Cartoons: Buys 2 cartoons/issue on assigned themes. Send roughs. Pays $35 minimum, b&w.
Illustrations: Buys 4 illustrations/issue on assigned themes. Arrange interview to show portfolio. Minimum payment: Cover, $150-300, 4/color. Inside: $75-150, b&w and color.

THE NEW REPUBLIC, 1220 19th St. NW, Washington DC 20036. (202)331-7494. Copy Editor: Janey Baylif. Emphasizes politics and culture for a "well-educated, well-off, mostly male audience with a medium age of 40." Weekly. Circ. 100,000. Accepts previously published material and simultaneous submissions. Original artwork returned after publication.
Cartoons: Uses 1 cartoon/issue; buys from freelancers. Prefers single panel, with gagline; b&w line drawings. Send query letter with samples of style and finished cartoons to be kept on file. Write or call for appointment to show portfolio. Material not kept on file returned only if requested. Reports only if samples are accompanied by cover letter or written inquiry. Negotiates rights purchased. Pays $40 b&w; on publication.
Illustrations: Uses 3 illustrations/issue; buys 2/issue from freelancers. Prefers political, literary themes. Works on assignment only. Send query letter with brochure, resume, business card, samples and tear sheets to be kept on file. Call or write for appointment to show portfolio. Prefers "something we can keep that shows artist's abilities in both black and white and color" as samples. Samples returned only if requested. Reports only if samples are accompanied by cover letter or written inquiry. Negotiates rights purchased and payment. Pays on publication.

*NEW WOMAN MAGAZINE**, 215 Lexington Ave., New York NY 10016. (212)685-4790. Art Director: Jane Eldershaw. Magazine emphasizing emotional self-help for women ages 25-34, 66% married. Most have attended college but not graduated. Medium personal income is $14,000. Publishes monthly. Circ. 1 million. Accepts previously published material. Returns original artwork to the artist. Sample copy and art guidelines not available.
Cartoons: Uses approximately 20 freelance cartoons/issue. Prefers single panel, with or without gagline; b&w line drawings. "We have changed quite a bit. We are still pro-women, but not as hard-hitting or as sexist in putting men down. We use cartoons in our sections on food (no gagline), word power, book reviews and letters to the editor. Look at recent issues of the magazine." Contact Rosemarie Lennon, cartoon editor, for more information. Send finished cartoon and SASE. Reports back to the cartoonist. Purchases all serial rights. Pays $225 on acceptance.
Illustrations: Uses 3-4 freelance illustrations/issue. Works on an assignment basis only. Send query letter with samples to be kept on file. Prefers tear sheets and photocpies as samples. Samples not kept on file are not returned. Reports back to the artist only if interested. Payment varies. Pays on acceptance.

NEW YORK MAGAZINE, 755 Second Ave., New York NY 10017. (212)880-0700. Design Director: Robert Best. Art Director: Patricia Bradbury. Emphasizes New York City life; also covers all boroughs for New Yorkers, upper middle income; business people interested in what's happening in the city. Weekly. Original artwork returned after publication.
Illustrations: Works on assignment only. Send query letter with tear sheets to be kept on file. Call or write for appointment to show portfolio (drop-offs). Prefers photostats as samples. Samples returned if requested. Buys first rights. Pays $1,000, b&w and color, cover; $600 for 4-color, $400 b&w full page, inside; $225 for 4-color, $150 b&w spot, inside. Pays on publication.

THE NEW YORKER, 25 W. 43rd St., New York NY 10036. Contact: Art Editor. Emphasizes news analysis and lifestyle features.

Artemas Cole of Alta Loma, California, is a frequent contributor to New Woman magazine in New York City. Cartoon editor Rosemarie Lennon says, "This cartoon was selected because it conformed with the editorial slant of New Woman—a magazine that celebrates the modern, liberated woman." Cole was paid $225 for all magazine and periodical rights.

Needs: Buys cartoons, spots and cover designs. Receives 3,000 cartoons/week. Mail art or deliver sketches on Wednesdays. SASE. "Spots are now purchased every 4 months." Strict standards regarding style, technique, plausibility of drawing. Especially looks for originality. Pays $500 minimum, cartoons; top rates for spots and cover designs.
Tips: "Familiarize yourself with your markets."

THE NEWFOUNDLAND HERALD , (formerly *Newfoundland Herald TV Week*), Box 2015, St. John's, Newfoundland A1C 5R7 Canada. (709)726-7060. Hillier. 130—page informative entertainment magazine with TV listings for the province. Paid circ. 40,000. Weekly. SASE (nonresidents include IRC). Simultaneous submissions and previously published work OK. Not copyrighted. Pays on publication. Free sample copy.
Cartoons: Buys TV, movie, entertainment and Hollywood themes. Send roughs.

THE NEWS CIRCLE, Box 3684, Glendale CA 91201. (818)240-1918. Contact: Laila Haiek. For Arab-Americans. Monthly magazine. Circ. 5,000.
Cartoons: Buys 5-8 cartoons/issue. Needs b&w. Send roughs. Reports in 3 weeks. Negotiates pay; pays on publication.
Illustrations: Buys b&w Arabic and arabesque designs. Query with samples. Reports in 3 weeks. Negotiates pay; pays on publication.

*NEXUS, 1110 N. Fillmore, Amarillo TX 79107. (806)376-6229. Editor: Vance Buck. Emphasizes games for game players. Quarterly. Circ. 10,000. Usually does not accept previously published material. Returns original artwork after publication with SASE. Sample copy for $5; art guidelines for SASE.
Illustrations: Buys 5-20/issue. Prefers themes related to games produced by Task Force Games Company-Star Fleet Battles, StarFire, History of WWII and Battlewagon, etc. Send query letter with samples.

Prefers b&w illustrations in photocopy form. Reports within 3 weeks. Buys one-time rights. Pays $3/column inch; on publication.

NJEA REVIEW, 180 W. State St., Box 1211, Trenton NJ 08607. Editor-in-Chief: Martha O. DeBlieu. Nonprofit, for New Jersey public school employees. Monthly. Circ. 120,000. Previously published work OK. Original artwork not returned after publication. Free sample copy.
Cartoons: Buys 10/year from freelancers. Receives 20 submissions/week from freelancers. Interested in b&w cartoons with an "education theme—do not make fun of school employees or children"; single panel. Prefers to see finished cartoons. Buys all rights on a work-for-hire basis. Pays on acceptance. Limited budget.
Illustrations: Uses 1-2 illustrations/issue, all from freelancers. Receives 1-2 submissions/week from freelancers. Especially needs education-related spot art. Prefers to see samples of style. SASE. Provide resume, tear sheet, and rates to be kept on file for future assignments. Reports as soon as possible. Buys all rights on a work-for-hire basis. Inside: Pays $5-50, b&w; on acceptance.
Tips: "Our lead time is getting shorter and shorter—need people almost overnight. Check out our publication and note what is being used and submit appropriate art work. We prefer bold graphics."

*NORTH AMERICAN HUNTER, Box 35557, Minneapolis MN 55435. (612)941-7654. Editorial Assistant: Valarie Miller. Publishes hunting material only for avid hunters of both small and big game in North America. Bimonthly. Circ. 100,000. Accepts previously published material. Original artwork returned after publication unless all rights are purchased. Free sample copy and art guidelines.
Cartoons: Buys 5 cartoons/issue from freelancers. Considers humorous hunting situations. Prefers single panel with gagline; b&w line drawings or washes. Send samples of style or finished cartoons. Returns unpurchased material immediately. Reports within 5 days. Buys all rights. Pays $15, b&w; on acceptance.
Illustrations: Buys 2-10 illustrations/issue from freelancers; usually includes 1 humorous illustration. Prefers game animal and hunter themes. Send query letter with samples. Prefers tear sheets, slides or photographs as samples. Samples are returned. Reports within 5 days. Buys all rights. Pays $250, color, cover; $75-100, b&w or color, inside; on acceptance.

NORTH AMERICAN MENTOR, Drawer 69, Fennimore WI 53809. (608)822-6237. Editor-in-Chief: John Westburg. Managing Editor: Mildred Westburg. Send art submissions to Martial R. Westburg, art editor, North American Mentor, Box 558, Old Chelsea Station, New York NY 10011. For professional people, half of whom are age 60 or over. Quarterly. Circ. 400. Previously published, photocopied and simultaneous submissions OK. Original artwork not returned after publication. Sample copy $2.
Illustrations: Buys 1 (cover) illustration/issue. Receives less than 10 submissions/year from freelancers. Interested in b&w line drawings only. Send samples of style (nonreturnable). SASE. Provide resume, brochure, flyer and tear sheets to be kept on file for future assignments. Reports in "6 months or more." Buys all rights. Pays $25 minimum, b&w line drawings; on publication.

NORTH LIGHT, 32 Berwick Ct., Fairfield CT 06430. (203)336-4225. Editor: Don Walker. Published monthly for members of North Light Book Club. Most editorial features are book excerpts. Emphasizes art and art instruction for serious amateur artists. Monthly. Circ. 60,000. Will consider how-to articles by professional or experienced amateur artists. Submit only transparencies or prints for review, *not* original artwork. Accepts previously published material. Finished artwork returned to artist after publication. No payment, but artists whose work is published will receive 10 free copies of the issue. Sample copy free for 9x12 SASE with 54¢ postage.

NORTH SHORE MAGAZINE, 874 Green Bay Rd., Winnetka IL 60093. (312)441-7892. Contact: Art Director. City/regional magazine; upscale readership. Monthly. Circ. 37,000 subscribers. Occasionally accepts previously published material. Sometimes returns original artwork after publication. Sample copy free for SASE with $1 postage.
Cartoons: Buys 1-5 cartoons/issue from freelancers. Prefers single panel with gagline; b&w line drawings. Send query letter with samples of style or finished cartoons to be kept on file. Write for appointment to show portfolio. Material not filed is returned by SASE. Reports within 1 week. Buys first rights. Payment varies; pays on publication.
Illustrations: Buys 1-5 illustrations/issue from freelancers. Works on assignment only. Send query letter with resume and samples, if possible. Write for appointment to show portfolio. Accepts "whatever medium best illustrates the artist's work" as samples. Samples not filed are returned by SASE. Reports within 1 week. Buys first rights. Pays on acceptance.

NORTHEAST OUTDOORS, Box 2180, Waterbury CT 06722-2180. (203)755-0158. Editor: Howard Fielding. For camping families in the Northeastern states. Monthly. Circ. 14,000. Original artwork returned after publication, if requested. Previously published material and simultaneous submissions OK if noted in cover letter. Editorial guidelines for SASE with 1 first class stamp; sample copy for 9x12 SASE with 6 first class stamps.

Cartoons: Buys 1 cartoon/issue on camping and recreational vehicle situations. Mail finished art. SASE. Reports in 2 weeks. Pays $10, b&w; on acceptance.

Tips: "Make it neat. Felt-tip pen sketches won't make it in this market any more. Query or send samples for illustration ideas. We occasionally buy or assign to accompany stories. Artists who have accompanying manuscripts have an extra edge, as we rarely buy illustrations alone."

THE NORTHERN LIGHT, Box 519, Lexington MA 02173. (617)862-4410. Editor: Richard H. Curtis. Emphasizes the fraternal order for Scottish Rite Masons and their families. Published 5 times/year. Circ. 475,000. Original artwork returned after publication. Sample copy free.

Cartoons: Number of cartoons used/issue "depends on space and availability." Prefers fraternal themes. Prefers single, double or multipanel with or without gagline; b&w line drawings or b&w washes. Send query letter with samples of style to be kept on file. Write or call for appointment to show portfolio. Material not kept on file is returned only if requested. Reports only if interested. Negotiates rights purchased. Pays on acceptance.

Illustrations: Number of illustrations used/issue "depends on space and availability." Prefers varied styles and themes. Send query letter with samples to be kept on file. Call or write for appointment to show portfolio. Samples not kept on file are returned only if requested. Reports only if interested. Negotiates rights purchased. Pays on acceptance.

THE NORTHERN LOGGER & TIMBER PROCESSOR, Northeastern Loggers Association Inc., Box 69, Old Forge NY 13420. (315)369-3078. Editor: Eric A. Johnson. Emphasizes methods, machinery and manufacturing as related to forestry. "For loggers, timberland managers and processors of primary forest products." Monthly. Circ. 13,000. Previously published material OK. Free sample copy; guidelines sent upon request.

Cartoons: Uses 1 cartoon/issue, all from freelancers. Receives 1 submission/week from freelancers. Interested in "any cartoons involving forest industry situations." Prefers finished cartoons. SASE. Reports in 1 week. Pays $10 minimum, b&w line drawings; on acceptance.

Tips: "Keep it simple and pertinent to the subjects we cover. Also, keep in mind that on-the-job safety is an issue that we like to promote."

NORTHWEST REVIEW, 369 PLC, University of Oregon, Eugene OR 97403. (503)686-3957. Editor: John Witte. Art Editor: Deb Casey. Emphasizes literature. "We publish material of general interest to those who follow American/world poetry and fiction." Original artwork returned after publication. Published 3 times/year. Sample copy $3.

Illustrations: Uses b&w line drawings, graphics and cover designs. Receives 20-30 portfolios/year from freelance artists. Arrange interview or mail slides. SASE. Reports as soon as possible. Acquires one-time rights. Pays in contributor's copies. Especially needs high-quality graphic artwork. "We run a regular art feature of the work of one artist, printed in b&w, 133-line screen on quality coated paper. A statement by the artist often accompanies the feature."

NOTRE DAME, University of Notre Dame, 415 Main Bldg., Box M, Notre Dame IN 46556. Art Director: Don Nelson. For university alumni. Quarterly. Circ. 98,000. Submit samples or brochure; professional artists only. "We don't have time to send sample copies or reply to submissions." Does not accept previously published material. Original artwork returned after publication.

Illustrations: "Not interested in realistic drawings." Seeks " 'graphic' solutions to communication problems." Uses 4 illustrations/issue, all from freelancers. Works on assignment only. Samples returned by SASE. Provide brochure or samples to be kept on file for future assignments. Buys one-time rights. Cover: Pays $800-1000, color. Inside: Pays $150-375, b&w; on acceptance.

NUCLEAR TIMES MAGAZINE, Room 512, 298 5th Ave., New York NY 10001. (212)563-5940. Art Director: Lloyd Dangle. Provides straight news coverage of the anti-nuclear weapons movement. Bimonthly. Circ. 7,000. Accepts previously published material. Returns original artwork after publication. Sample copy $1; art guidelines available.

Cartoons: Buys up to 10 cartoons/issue from freelancers. Accepts single, double or multiple panel with or without gagline; b&w line drawings, b&w washes. Send query letter with photocopies of samples of style, roughs and finished cartoons to be kept on file. Write or call for appointment to show portfolio. Material not kept on file returned by SASE only if requested. Reports within 2 weeks. Buys one-time rights. Pays $25 for b&w; on publication.

Illustrations: Buys 10 + illustrations/issue from freelancers. Only anti-nuclear issues as themes. Primarily works on assignment. Send query letter with brochure, resume, business card and samples to be kept on file. Write or call for appointment to show portfolio. Prefers to review photocopies and tear sheets in mail submissions; originals when shown portfolio at office. Samples not filed are returned only if requested. Reports within 2 weeks. Buys one-time rights. Pays $25-40 for b&w cover; $25 for b&w inside; on publication.

NUGGET, Dugent Publishing Co., 2355 Salzedo St., Coral Gables FL 33134. Editor: John Fox. Illustration Assignments: Nye Willden. For men and women with fetish interests.
Cartoons: Uses 10 cartoons/issue, all from freelancers. Receives 100 submissions/week from freelancers. Interested in "funny fetish themes." B&w only for spots, b&w and color for page. Prefers to see finished cartoons. SASE. Reports in 2 weeks. Buys first North American serial rights. Pays $35, spot drawings; $50, page.
Illustrations: Uses 4 illustrations/issue, all from freelancers. Interested in "erotica, cartoon style, etc." Works on assignment only. Prefers to see samples of style. No samples returned. Reports back on future assignment possibilities. Provide brochure or flyer to be kept on file for future assignments. Buys first North American serial rights. Pays $100-125, b&w.
Tips: Especially interested in "the artist's anatomy skills, professionalism in rendering (whether he's published or not) and drawings which relate to our needs." Current trends include "a return to the 'classical' realistic form of illustration which is fine with us because we prefer realistic and well-rendered illustrations."

OCEANS, Oceanic Society, Fort Mason, San Francisco CA 94123. (415)441-1104. Editor: Jake Widman. Art Director: Dustin Kahn. "For those interested in the beauty, science, adventure and conservation of the oceans and the life forms which live therein." Bimonthly. Circ. 65,000. Original artwork returned after publication. Sample copy $2; free contributor guidelines.
Cartoons: Uses 1 cartoon/issue, all from freelancers. Receives 10 submissions/week from freelancers. Interested in sea-oriented themes. Prefers roughs. SASE. Reports in 1 week. Buys first North American serial rights. Pays $25 minimum, b&w and 2-tone; on publication.
Illustrations: Uses 4 illustrations/issue. Interested in the environment, ocean dwellers and subjects pertaining to oceans. Works on assignment only. Samples returned by SASE. Reports in 1 week. Buys first North American serial rights. Inside: Pays $30-100, b&w and color (including diagrammatic illustrations).

*OFF DUTY, Suite C-2, 3303 Harbor Blvd., Costa Mesa CA 92626. Art Director: John Wong. Three editions: Europe, Pacific and America. Emphasizes general interest topics, e.g. leisure, sports, travel, food, photography, music, finance for military Americans stationed around the world. Combined circ: 683,000. Accepts previously published material and simultaneous submissions if not submitted to other military magazines. Assignment artwork returned after publication. Sample copy $1.
Cartoons: Uses occasional cartoons in two categories. First must relate to military personnel, families and military life. Off-duty situations preferred. Send to Bruce Thorstad, U.S. Editor. Second category relates to hobbies of audio, video, computers or photography. "A military angle in this category is ideal, but not necessary." Send to Mike Michels, Technical Editor. "Keep in mind that all readers are active duty military, not retirees or vets." Pays $40 minimum b&w; more by negotiation.
Illustrations: *Off Duty*'s America edition uses several illustrations per issue, by assignment only. Accepts photocopies or tearsheets of previous work that can be kept on file, but does not want originals or anything that must be returned. Pays $50-150 on acceptance for assignments.

OHIO MAGAZINE, 40 S. Third St., Columbus OH 43215. (614)461-5083. Art Director: Tom Hawley. Managing Editor: Ellen Stein. Emphasizes feature material of Ohio for an educated, urban and urbane readership. Monthly. Circ. 100,000. Previously published work OK. Original artwork returned after publication. Sample copy $2.
Illustrations: Buys 3-4/issue from freelancers. Interested in Ohio scenes and themes. Works on stock and assignment. Query with samples or arrange interview to show portfolio. Provide resume, brochure, duplicate slides or tear sheet to be kept on file for future assignments. SASE. Reports in 2 weeks. Pays $75-150, b&w; $150-350, color; on acceptance. Buys one-time publication rights.
Tips: Magazine is now realizing an "increased use of stock photography and artwork (illustration, paintings, prints). Artwork should exhibit a fine arts 'bent,' but not 'slick.' Uncontrived elegance—rich, noncommercial images which elevate 'real life' in Ohio."

OIL PATCH, Resource Publications, Inc., 3210 Marquart, Houston TX 77027. (713)961-4191. Production Manager/Art Director: Robert Olfe. For executives, managers and engineers in energy-related industries. Monthly. Circ. 18,000. Returns original artwork after publication. Sample copy free for SASE and 80¢ postage.
Illustrations: Buys 0-3 illustrations/issue from freelancers. Prefers oil-related, energy, geology

themes. Works on assignment only. Send query letter with brochure or samples to be kept on file. Write for appointment to show portfolio. Prefers photostats, slides or photographs as samples. Samples not filed are returned by SASE. Reports back only if interested. Buys first rights. Pays $75 for b&w and $150 for color, inside.

OLD BOTTLE MAGAZINE, Box 5007, Bend OR 97708. (503)382-6978. Contact: Kenneth Asher. For collectors of old bottles, insulators, relics. Send art, cartoons, photos. Reports in 6 weeks. Buys all rights. Pays on acceptance.

OLD WEST, Box 2107, Stillwater OK 74076. (405)743-0130. Editor: John Joerschke. Emphasizes American western history from 1830 to 1910 for a primarily rural and suburban audience, middle-age and older, interested in Old West history, horses, cowboys, art, clothing and all things western. Quarterly. Circ. 50,000. Accepts previously published material and considers some simultaneous submissions. Original artwork returned after publication. Sample copy and art guidelines free for SASE.
Illustrations: Uses 5-10 illustrations/issue, including 2 or 3 humorous illustraions; buys all from freelancers. "Inside illustrations are usually, but need not always be, pen and ink line drawings; covers are western paintings." Send query letter with samples to be kept on file; "we return anything on request." Call or write for appointment to show portfolio. "For inside illustrations, we want samples of artist's line drawings. For covers, we need to see full-color transparencies." Reports within 1 month. Buys one-time rights. Pays $100-150 for color transparency for cover; $15-40, b&w, inside; on acceptance.
Tips: "*Old West* has begun moving away from the action-oriented, animated appearance on its cover in recent years. We think the mainstream of interest in Western Americana has moved in the direction of fine art, and we're looking for more material along those lines. A recent cover that we were very pleased with is Summer 1985."

*ONE WORLD, Box 1351, State College PA 16804. (814)238-0793. Secretary: Dana Stuchell. Emphasizes animal rights for "the general public involved in the protection of animals and promotion of animal rights and the philoshical public interested in animal rights as a philosophical/ethical issue." Quarterly. Circ. 1,000. Accepts previously published material. Original artwork returned after publication. Sample copy $1.
Cartoons: Animal rights or environmental issue themes. Send query letter with finished cartoons to be kept on file. Material not filed is returned by SASE. Reports only if interested. Buys reprint rights. Pays negotiable rate, b&w and color; on publication.
Illustrations: Animal rights and environmental issue themes. Send query letter with samples to be kept on file. Samples returned by SASE. Reports only if interested. Buys reprint rights. Pays negotiable rate, b&w and color, cover and inside; on publication.

ONLINE-TODAY MAGAZINE, 5000 Arlington Centre Blvd., Columbus OH 43220. (614)457-8600. Art Director: Thom Misiak. Edited for people and businesses on the leading edge of the personal computing and videotext industries. "*Online-Today* helps people maximize the potential of their personal computing equipment by examining how personal computers can be used to increase productivity, manage financial resources, communicate, inform and educate." Monthly. Circ. 250,000.
Illustrations: Works with 10-20 freelance artists/year. Uses artists for magazine illustration; also for advertising and brochure design, illustration and layout. Works on assignment only. Send query letter with business card and samples to be kept on file. Call for appointment to show portfolio. Prefers tear sheets, photostats or slides as samples. "I look for a professional, clean and organized presentation demonstrating good draughtsmanship and skill in the application of the selected media." Material not filed is returned by SASE. Reports only if interested. Pays by the project, $50-800 average. Considers complexity of the project, available budget, skill and experience of the artist, and turnaround time when establishing payment.
Tips: "The biggest mistake an artist makes is not offering his creative input to the solution of a graphic problem. The artist is not only selling his illustrative talent but also his creative thinking. This should be part of any presentation the artist makes."

OPPORTUNITY MAGAZINE, 6 N. Michigan Ave., Chicago IL 60602. Editor: Jack Weissman. Features articles dealing with direct (door-to-door) selling and on ways to start small businesses. For independent salesmen, agents, jobbers, distributors, sales managers, franchise seekers, route salesmen, wagon jobbers and people seeking an opportunity to make money full- or part-time. Monthly. Original artwork not returned after publication. Sample copy free for SASE with 50¢ postage.
Cartoons: Uses 2-3 cartoons/issue; buys all from freelancers. Interested in themes dealing with humorous sales situations affecting door-to-door salespeople. Considers single panel with gagline; b&w line drawings. Prefers roughs or finished cartoons. SASE. Buys all rights. Pays $5 on publication.
Tips: "Get sample copy beforehand and have an idea of what is appropriate."

OPTICAL INDEX, 633 3rd Ave., New York NY 10017. (212)697-8052. Art Director: Charles Jablonski. Emphasizes eyewear fashion and dispensing for opticians and optometrists. Monthly. Circ. 27,000. Does not return original artwork after publication unless requested. Sample copy for SASE; art guidelines available.
Illustrations: Buys 1-2 illustrations/issue from freelancers. Themes and styles are dependent upon assignment; "usually color, highly stylized." Works on assignment only. Send query letter with brochure and samples to be kept on file. Call for appointment to show portfolio. Accepts photostats, tear sheets, photocopies, slides or photographs as samples. Samples not filed are not returned. Reports back only if interested. Negotiates rights purchased. Pay varies; pays on acceptance.

THE OPTIMIST MAGAZINE, 4494 Lindell Blvd., St. Louis MO 63108. Editor: Dennis R. Osterwisch. Emphasizes activities relating to Optimist clubs in US and Canada (civic-service clubs). "Magazine is mailed to all members of Optimist clubs. Average age is 42, most are management level with some college education." Circ. 152,000. Accepts previously published material. Sample copy free for SASE.
Cartoons: Uses 3 cartoons/issue; buys 2-3 cartoons/issue from freelancers. Prefers themes of general interest; family-oriented, sports, kids, civic clubs. Prefers single panel, with gagline. Send finished cartoons. Submissions returned by SASE. Reports within 1 week. Buys one-time rights. Pays $25/b&w; on acceptance.

ORANGE COAST MAGAZINE, Suite E, 18200 W. McDurmott, Irvine CA 92714. (719)660-8622. Art Director: Suzanne Reid. General interest city magazine. Monthly. Circ. 30,000. Returns original artwork after publication. Sample copy and art guidelines available.
Illustrations: Buys 1 illustration/issue from freelancers. Considers airbrush. Works on assignment only. Send samples to be kept on file. Prefers tear sheets or transparencies as samples. Samples not filed are returned only if requested. Reports back only if interested. Buys one-time rights. Pays on publication.

ORGANIC GARDENING, 33 E. Minor St., Emmaus PA 18049. (215)967-5171. Contact: Art Director. Emphasizes organic gardening and self-sufficiency. Monthly. Circ. 1,400,000.
Cartoons: Interested in gardening, health, wood stove and alternative energy subjects; single panel b&w line drawings and b&w washes. Send resume and samples of style. SASE. Buys all rights. Pays $75-100.
Illustrations: Uses 20 illustrations/issue. Interested in gardening, insects, flowers and vegetables and energy themes. Especially needs line work with very good figure drawings, (people in their gardens). Works on assignment only. Prefers b&w line drawings and washes, some color work for inside. Send resume and business card with samples of style and/or arrange appointment to show portfolio. SASE. Reports in 1 month. Prefers to buy all rights. Pays $55, spot illustrations; larger illustrations priced per job and style.
Tips: "I like to see good figure drawing—if you can handle people realistically, you can handle most anything."

THE ORIGINAL NEW ENGLAND GUIDE, % Historical Times, Inc., 2245 Kohn Rd., Box 8200, Harrisburg PA 17105. Managing Editor: Kathie Kull. Consulting Editor: Mimi E.B. Steadman. Art Director; Jeanne Collins. Emphasizes New England travel of all kinds. Readers are "those planning on going on vacation trips, weekend jaunts, mini-holidays, day trips, conventions, combination business/pleasure trips. For North American and overseas visitors to New England." Annually. Circ. 180,000. Sample copy $5; art guidelines for SASE.
Illustrations: "*The Guide* is almost always able to make its few assignments for artwork locally. However, we are certainly happy to know about freelancers and their special abilities, and welcome letters and/or samples (clips are fine)." Pays $50-150 on publication for inside b&w, depending on use. Send correspondence to Art Director.
Tips: "New ownership, new staff and new concept of magazine including greater use of 4-color pictures, fewer illustrations. Let us know you're available, but don't pin your hopes on an assignment from us, as we are usually able to get what we need from the many talented artists in this area."

ORNAMENT, Box 35029, Los Angeles CA 90035. (213)652-9914. Editor: Robert Liu. Emphasizes jewelry and personal adornment for jewelers, galleries, collectors, designers, craftspeople, schools, universities, museums, manufacturers. Quarterly. Circ. 5,000. Original artwork returned after publication. Sample copy and art guideline available.
Illustrations: Prefers themes on any aspect of body ornamentation; photo illustration. Send query letter with samples. Prefers slides and/or b&w prints as samples. Samples returned by SASE if not kept on file. Reports within 30 days.

THE OTHER SIDE, 300 W. Apsley St., Philadelphia PA 19144. (215)849-2178. Editor: Mark Olson. Art Director: Cathleen Boint. "We are read by Christians with a radical commitment to social justice and a deep allegiance to Biblical faith. We try to help readers put their faith into action." Published 10 times/year. Circ. 15,000. Receives 3 cartoons and 1 illustration/week from freelance artists. Query with samples or previously published work. SASE. Reports in 6 weeks. Photocopied and simultaneous submissions OK. Pays "within 4 weeks of acceptance." Sample copy $2.50.
Cartoons: Buys 2 cartoons/year on current events, environment, economics, politics and religion; single and multi-panel. Pays $10-25, b&w line drawings. "Looking for cartoons with a radical political perspective."
Illustrations: Especially needs b&w line drawings illustrating specific articles. Cover: Pays $125-200, 4-color. Inside: Pays $50-175, b&w line drawings.
Tips: "We're looking for illustrators who share our perspective on social, economic and political issues, and who are willing to work for us on assignment."

OTTAWA MAGAZINE, 340 MacLaren, Ottawa, Ontario K2P 0M6 Canada. (613)234-7751. Art Director: Peter de Gannes. Emphasizes lifestyles for sophisticated, middle and upper income, above average education professionals; most readers are women. Monthly. Circ. 43,650. Accepts previously published material. Sample copy available; include $1.06 Canadian funds to cover postage (nonresidents include 2 IRCs).
Illustrations: Uses 6-8 illustrations/issue; buys all from freelancers. Receives 3-4 submissions/week from freelancers. "Illustrations are geared to editorial copy and run from cartoon sketches to *Esquire*, *New York* and *Psychology Today* styles. Subjects range from fast-food franchising to how civil servants cope with stress. Art usually produced by local artists because of time and communication problems." Open to most styles including b&w line drawings, b&w and color washes, collages, photocopy art, oil and acrylic paintings, airbrush work and paper sculpture for inside. Also uses photographic treatments. Arrange personal appointment to show portfolio or send samples of style. "Do not send original artwork." No samples returned. Reports in 1 month. Buys all rights or by arrangement with artist. Pays $20-100 for inside b&w; and $50-250 for inside color on publication.
Tips: Prefers "work that shows wit, confidence in style and a unique approach to the medium used. Especially in need of artists who can look at a subject from a fresh, unusual perspective. There is a trend toward more exciting illustration, use of unusual techniques like photocopy collages or collages combining photography, pen & ink and watercolor. Freedom given to the artist to develop his treatment. Open to unusual techniques. Have as diversified a portfolio as possible."

***OUI MAGAZINE**, 6th Floor, 300 W. 43rd St., New York NY 10036. (212)397-5889. Executive Editor: Barry Janoff. Men's entertainment magazine: music, movies, erotically-oriented lifestyle for the '80s and '90s, for ages 18-35, "mostly but not all male, high school and/or college educated, upwardly mobile, trendsetters." Monthly. Circ. 500,000. Original artwork returned after publication. Sample copy $5 (check or money order); art guidelines for SASE.
Cartoons: Buys 2-5 cartoons/issue from freelancers. Considers erotically oriented or off-beat themes. Prefers single panel with gagline; b&w line drawings. Send finished cartoons; call for appointment to show portfolio. Material returned by SASE. Reports within 6 weeks. Negotiates rights purchased. Pays $30, b&w; $75, color; on publication.
Illustrations: Buys 0-2 illustrations/issue from freelancers. Theme or style depends on article or fiction. "Artist works with art director and editor to focus on topic being illustrated; 90% of input comes from artist." Works on assignment only. Send query letter with brochure and samples if possible (or copies) to be kept on file; call for appointment to show portfolio. Prefers tear sheets, slides or photostats as samples. Samples not filed are returned by SASE. Reports only if interested. Negotiates rights purchased. Pays $400 + , color, inside; on publication.

OUR FAMILY, Oblate Fathers of St. Mary's Province, Box 249, Battleford, Saskatchewan S0M 0E0 Canada. (306)937-2663. Art Editor: Reb Materi, O.M.I. Inspirational, educational magazine. Monthly. Circ. 17,552. Previously published, photocopied and simultaneous submissions OK. Original artwork not specifically commissioned by *Our Family* returned after publication. Artwork commissioned for *Our Family* is retained by magazine. Sample copy $2 to cover cost of magazine and postage.
Cartoons: Buys 5 cartoons/issue on family situations, especially parent-children relationships; single panel with gagline. Query with finished cartoons. SAE and personal check, postal money order or International Reply Coupon. Reports in 2-4 weeks. Pays $15-20, b&w line drawings and washes; on acceptance.
Illustrations: Buys 1-3 illustrations/issue from freelancers. Receives several submissions/month from freelancers. Subject "depends on the article we want illustrated. We usually commission this work to a specific artist." Works on assignment only. Send samples of work for review. Samples returned by SAE and personal check, postal money order or International Reply Coupon. Provide brochure and tear sheet

to be kept on file for future assignments. Reports in 2-4 weeks. "We will let the artist know what work he can do for us." Buys all rights to commissioned work. Inside: Pays $100 and up for commissioned art.

*OUTDOOR AMERICA MAGAZINE, Suite 1100, 1701 N. Ft. Meyer Dr., Arlington VA 22209. Editor: Carol Dana. Emphasizes conservation and outdoor recreation (fishing, hunting, etc.) for sportsmen and conservationists. Quarterly. Circ. 45,000. Accepts previously published material. Original artwork returned after publication. Sample copy $1.50.
Cartoons: Buys 0-1 cartoon/issue from freelancers. Considers conservation and outdoor recreation themes. Prefers single panel with gagline; b&w line drawings. Send query letter with samples of style to be kept on file. Material not filed is returned by SASE. Buys one-time rights or reprint rights. Pays $25, b&w; on publication.
Illustrations: Buys 1-2 illustrations/issue from freelancers. Send query letter with samples to be kept on file. Prefers tear sheets or photocopies as samples. Samples not filed are returned. Reports within 2 months. Buys one-time rights or reprint rights. Pays on publication. ·

OUTDOOR CANADA MAGAZINE, 953A Eglinton Ave. E, Toronto, Ontario M4G 4B5 Canada. Editor: Sheila Kaighin. Emphasizes "wilderness-oriented Canadian outdoor activities, wildlife, conservation, wild edibles and recreational vehicles. Readers are 81% male, well educated and active; 34.8% are professionals, managers or owners; 26.6% earn from $25,000 to $35,000 annually. Publishes 7 regular issues/year and a fishing edition in April. Circ. 133,000. Original artwork returned after publication if requested. Sample copy $2.
Cartoons: Uses 1 cartoon/issue; buys 1/issue from freelancers. Prefers single panel with gagline; b&w line drawings. Send finished cartoons. Samples returned by SASE if requested (nonresidents include IRC). Reporting time varies considerably. Pays $15; on publication.
Illustrations: Buys approximately 5 paintings/b&w drawings/issue. Pays up to $300, all rights.

OUTDOOR LIFE, 380 Madison Ave., New York NY 10017. (212)687-3000. Art Director: Jim Eckes. Emphasizes hunting, fishing, boating and camping for "male and female, young and old who enjoy the outdoors and what it has to offer." Monthly. Circ. 1.5 million. Original artwork returned after publication "unless we buy all rights." Sample copy available "if work is going to be published."
Cartoons: Very seldom uses cartoons. Send finished cartoons to be kept on file, except for "those we won't ever use." Material not kept on file is returned by SASE. Reports only if interested. Buys first rights. Pays on publication.
Illustrations: Uses 2-3 illustrations/issue. Prefers "realistic themes, realistic humor." Works on assignment only. Send query letter with samples and tear sheets to be kept on file except "those which do not meet our standards." Call for appointment to show portfolio. Prefers slides, tear sheets and originals as samples. Samples not kept on file are returned. Reports only if interested. Negotiates rights purchased. Pays $800, color spread, $1,000, cover; on publication. Payment "depends on size and whether it is a national or regional piece."
Tips: "First of all, we're looking for 'wildlife, realists'—those who know how to illustrate a species realistically and with action."

OUTREACH PUBLICATIONS, INC., Box 1010, Siloam Springs AR 72761. (501)524-9301. Art Director: Darrell Hill. Emphasizes Christian/religious themes. Original artwork not returned after publication. Sample copy and art guidelines available.
Illustrations: Uses 250-350 illustrations/year; buys 150-250 illustrations/year from freelancers. Send query letter with samples to be kept on file. Call or write for appointment to show portfolio. Accepts photostats, photographs, slides, original work as samples. Samples returned only if requested. Reports only if interested. Material not copyrighted. Negotiates payment. Pays within 30 days of receipt.
Tips: Especially looks for "creative concepts and unique style" in artwork.

OUTSIDE, 1165 N. Clark St., Chicago IL 60610. (312)951-0990. Managing Editor: John Rasmus. Design Director: John Askwith. Concerns enjoyment and participation in the great outdoors. Published 12 times/year. Circ. 220,000 + .
Illustrations: Uses 60 illustrations/year; buys 60/year from freelancers. Receives 3-4 submissions/week from freelancers. Ask for artists' guidelines. Especially needs spot (less than ½ page) 4-color art; "contemporary, communicative, powerful illustration. We are also interested in seeing any contemporary stills for assignment purposes." Works on assignment only. Send "good slides" or previously published work as samples. SASE. Reports in 2 weeks. Provide samples or tear sheet to be kept on file for future assignments. Buys one-time rights. Inside: Pays $100-750, b&w line drawings, washes and full-color renderings; on publication.
Tips: "Observe the 'front runners' for style and trends. We presently don't use cartoons."

OVERSEAS!, Bismarckstr 17, 6900 Heidelberg, West Germany. Editorial Director: Charles L. Kaufman. Managing Editor: Greg Ballinger. *"Overseas!* is the leading lifestyle magazine for the U.S. military male stationed throughout Europe. Primary focus is on European travel, with regular features on music, sports, video, audio and photo products, and men's fashion. The average reader is male, age 24." Sample copy for SAE and 4 IRCs; art guidelines for SAE and 1 IRC.
Cartoons: "Always looking for humorous cartoons on travel and being a tourist in Europe. Best bet is to send in a selection of 5-10 for placement of all on one-two pages. Looking for more *National Lampoon* or *Playboy*-style cartoons/humor than a *Saturday Evening Post*-type cartoon. Anything new, different or crazy is given high priority. On cartoons or cartoon features don't query, send nonreturnable photocopies. Pay is negotiable, $25-75/cartoon to start."
Illustrations: Query. Send nonreturnable photocopy samples. "We will assign when needed." Uses 3-5 illustrations/month. Pays $25-75, negotiable.

OZARK MAGAZINE, East-West Network, Inc., Suite 800, 5900 Wilshire Blvd., Los Angeles CA 90036. (213)937-5810. Editor: Laura Dean Bennett. Art Director: Carla Schrad. Emphasizes culture, sports, products and personalities in the Midwest. For the executive. Monthly. Sample copy $2. Accepts previously published material. Originals returned to artists after publication.
Illustrations: Works on assignment only. Query with resume and samples to be filed. Prefers tear sheets, slides and photographs as samples. Samples returned only by request with SASE. Reports only if interested. Buys first rights. Pays $75 minimum, spot art; $450 maximum, full-page illustration; and $800, full-color cover. Pays on acceptance.

PACIFIC COAST JOURNAL, (formerly *The Quarter Horse of the Pacific Coast*), Box 254822, Sacramento CA 95865. Editor-in-Chief: Jill Scopinich. For horse breeders, trainers and owners interested in performance, racing and showing of quarter horses. Monthly. Circ. 7,800. Previously published and simultaneous submissions OK "if we are notified."
Cartoons: Buys 24 cartoons/year on horses; single panel. Query with samples. SASE. Reports in 4 weeks. Buys first, reprint, all or simultaneous rights. Pays $10-20, washes; on acceptance.

PACIFIC DISCOVERY, California Academy of Sciences, San Francisco CA 94118. Editor: Sheridan Warrick. Emphasizes natural history and science research for college educated, amateur naturalists. Quarterly. Circ. 24,000. Returns original artwork after publication. Sample copy free for SASE with $1 postage; art guidelines free for SASE with 22¢ postage.
Illustrations: Buys 2-6 illustrations/issue from freelancers. Usually works on assignment. Send samples to be kept on file. Prefers photocopies as samples. Samples not filed are not returned. Reports back only if interested. Buys one-time rights. Pays $100-200, b&w; $200-400, color inside.

PACIFIC NORTHWEST, 222 Dexter Ave. N, Seattle WA 98109. Editor: Peter Potterfield. Emphasizes regional interests. Published 10 times/year. Circ. 58,000. Previously published material and simultaneous submissions OK if so indicated. Original artwork returned after publication. Free art guidelines for SASE.
Illustrations: Uses 6-10 illustrations/issue; buys 4 from freelancers. Uses illustrations for specific articles. Send query letter, roughs and samples of style. Provide samples to be kept on file for possible future assignments. Samples returned by SASE if not kept on file. Reports in 6 weeks. Buys one-time rights. Pays $100 inside, b&w line drawings or washes; $200 and up for color illustrations; on acceptance.

*THE PACIFIC QUARTERLY, 626 Coate Rd., Orange CA 92669. Editor-in-Chief: Mark D. Stancl. Estab. 1983. Anthology of fiction and nonfiction including book excerpts, prose, poetry, fillers, opinion articles, personal experiences, etc. for "a highly sophisticated, intelligent audience—people who are well versed in academic and world affairs. Quarterly. Circ. 1,400. Accepts previously published material. Original artwork returned after publication. Sample copy for SASE with 85¢ postage; art guidelines for SASE with 22¢ postage.
Cartoons: Buys 5-10 cartoons/issue from freelancers. No specific theme or style preference. Prefers multiple panel with gagline; b&w line drawings, b&w washes. Send query letter with samples of style or roughs to be kept on file; also send finished cartoons. Material not filed is returned by SASE. Reports within 1 month. Buys one-time rights. Payment varies for b&w and color. Pays on acceptance.
Illustrations: Buys 10-15 illustrations/issue from freelancers. No set theme or style. Send query letter with brochure, resume, business card and samples to be kept on file. Any type of sample is acceptable except slides. Samples not filed are returned by SASE. Reports within 1 month. Buys one-time rights. Payment varies for b&w and color, cover and inside. Pays on acceptance.

PAINT HORSE JOURNAL, Box 18519, Fort Worth TX 76118. (817)439-3400. Editor: Bill Shepard. Art Director: Vicki Day. Official publication of breed registry for Paint horses. For people who raise,

breed and show Paint horses. Monthly. Circ. 10,500. Receives 4-5 cartoons and 2-3 illustrations/week from freelance artists. Original artwork returned after publication. Sample copy $1; artist's guidelines free for SASE.
Cartoons: Buys 3-5 cartoons/issue, all from freelancers. Interested in horses; single panel with gagline. Send finished cartoons. Material returned by SASE only if requested. Reports in 1 month. Buys first rights. Pays $10, b&w line drawings; on acceptance.
Illustrations: Uses 2-3 illustrations/issue; buys few/issue from freelancers. Receives few submissions/week from freelancers. Especially needs youth drawings with Paint horses. Send business card and samples to be kept on file. Prefers original art or photostats as samples. Samples returned by SASE if not kept on file. Reports within 1 month. Buys first rights. Pays $7.50, b&w, inside; $50 color.
Tips: "Be sure horses included in artwork are Paint horses! We've lowered the prices we pay for freelance work as we now employ 3 fulltime artists."

PALM BEACH LIFE, 265 Royal Poinciana Way, Palm Beach FL 33480. (305)837-4762. Design Director: Anne Wholf. Emphasizes culture, cuisine, travel, fashion, decorating and Palm Beach County lifestyle. Readers are affluent, educated. Monthly. Circ. 23,000. Sample copy $3.50; art guidelines for SASE.
Illustrations: Uses 3-4 illustrations/issue; all from freelancers. Only assigned work. Uses line drawings to illustrate regular columns on gardening, health and wine, as well as features. Format: color washes for inside and cover; b&w washes and line drawings for inside. "Any technique that can be reproduced is acceptable." Send samples or photocopies and/or arrange appointment to show portfolio. No original artwork returned. SASE. Reports in 4-6 weeks. Buys all rights on a work-for-hire basis. Pays $200-400 on acceptance for color cover; $50-350 for inside color; $30-200 for inside b&w. Top price on covers only paid to established artists; "the exception is that we are looking for super-dramatic covers." Sujects related to Florida and lifestyle of the affluent. Price negotiable. Send slides or prints; do not send original work. *Palm Beach Life* cannot be responsible for unsolicited material.
Tips: "Look at magazines to see what we are like—make an appointment."

*PANDORA, %Empire Books, Box 625, Murray KY 42071-0625. Editor: Jean Lorrah. Emphasizes science fiction and fantasy. Semiannually. Circ. 700. Accepts previously published material. Original artwork returned after publication but prefers photostat. Sample copy $3.50.
Cartoons: Buys 1-2 cartoons/year from freelancers. Considers science fiction themes. Prefers single panel; b&w line drawings. Send query letter with roughs to be kept on file. Material not filed is returned by SASE. Reports within 6 weeks. Buys first North American serial rights. Pays $5, b&w; on acceptance.
Illustrations: Buys 5-7 illustrations/issue from freelancers. Style should suit story. Works on assignment only. Send query letter with samples to be kept on file. Prefers tear sheets or photocopies as samples. Samples not filed are returned by SASE. Reports in 6 weeks. Buys first North American serial rights. Pays $10, b&w, cover and inside; on acceptance. "We pay $15 for a photostat, to avoid the hassles of handling originals."

PARACHUTIST, 1440 Duke St., Alexandria VA 22314. (703)836-3495. Editor: Larry Jaffe. Emphasizes sport parachuting. Monthly. Circ. 18,000. Accepts previously published material. Returns original artwork after publication. Sample copy available.
Cartoons: Prefers skydiving-related themes. Material not filed is returned. Reports within weeks.
Illustrations: Prefers skydiving-related themes. Samples not filed are returned. Reports within weeks.

PARADE MAGAZINE, 750 Third Ave., New York NY 10017. (212)573-7187. Director of Design: Ira Yoffe. Photo Editor: Brent Petersen. Emphasizes general interest subjects. Weekly. Circ. 26 million (readership is 48 million). Original artwork returned after publication. Sample copy and art guidelines available.
Illustrations: Uses varied number of illustrations/issue. Prefers various themes. Works on assignment only. Send query letter with brochure, resume, business card and tear sheets to be kept on file. Call or write for appointment to show portfolio. Reports only if interested. Buys first rights, and occasionally all rights.
Tips: "Provide a good balance of work."

PARENT'S CHOICE, Box 185, Waban MA 02168. (617)332-1298. Editor: Diana Huss Green. Emphasizes review of children's media. Designed to alert parents to trends and events in books, TV, records, movies, music, toys, computer software. Quarterly. Original artwork returned after publication. Sample copy $1.50.
Illustrations: Uses 4 illustrations/issue, 2 from freelancers. Uses "work of exceptional quality." Format: b&w line drawings for inside and cover; no pencil. Works on assignment only. Send samples or ar-

range appointment to show portfolio. Samples returned. Prefers to see portfolio. SASE. Reports in 4-6 weeks. Buys first North American serial rights. Pays on publication.

PARKING, Suite 2000, 1112 16th St. NW, Washington DC 20036. (202)296-4336. Editor: George V. Dragotta. Emphasizes the operation of parking facilities and new developments in and government regulation of the industry. For members of National Parking Association—trade organization of the off-street parking industry—architects, engineers, traffic planners and city officials. Bimonthly. Previously published and simultaneous submissions OK. Original artwork returned after publication.
Cartoons: Uses less than 1 cartoon/issue, all from freelancers. Receives 2 submissions/week from freelancers. Interested in environment, parking, engineering, construction and transportation. Prefers finished cartoons. Reports in 2 weeks. Buys one-time rights. Pays $5 minimum, halftones and washes; on acceptance.
Illustrations: Uses 8 illustrations/issue, all from freelancers. Receives 2 submissions/week from freelancers. Buys parking themes; "would especially like to see a particularly dramatic rendering of attractive parking garage or lot." Prefers roughs. SASE. Reports in 2 weeks. Buys one-time rights. Minimum payment: Cover: $35, color; $20, b&w. Inside: $10, b&w; on acceptance.

*PARTNERSHIP, 465 Gundersen Dr., Carol Stream IL 60188. (312)260-6200. Art Director: Karen Miller. Estab. 1984. Emphasizes a ministry to the wives of men who are pastors. Bimonthly. Circ. 45,000. Accepts previously published material. Original artwork returned after publication only if requested. Sample copy free for SASE.
Cartoons: Buys 6-10 cartoons/issue from freelancers. Prefers inside humor having to do with the parsonage family. Prefers single panel with gagline; b&w line drawings. Send finished cartoons; call for appointment to show portfolio. All cartoons are returned. SASE. Reports within 1 week. Buys first rights. Pays $100, b&w; on acceptance.
Illustrations: Buys 5-6 illustrations/issue from freelancers. Works on assignment only. Send query letter; write for appointment to show portfolio. Accepts photostats, tear sheets, photocopies, slides, photographs, etc. as samples. Samples not filed are returned. Reports within 1 week. Negotiates rights purchased. Pays on acceptance.

*PARTS PUPS, 2999 Circle 75 Parkway, Atlanta GA 30339. Editor: Don Kite. For automotive repairmen. Circ. 258,000. Monthly plus annual publication. Original artwork not returned after publication. Previously published material and simultaneous submissions OK. Free sample copy and artist's guidelines.
Cartoons: Buys 144/year on "girlie" themes, auto repairmen, current events, education, environment, family life, humor through youth, and retirement; single panel with gagline, b&w line drawings and washes. Receives 400 cartoons/week from freelance artists. Mail finished artwork. SASE. Reports in 6 weeks. Pays $30, b&w line drawings and washes; on acceptance.
Tips: "Look over our publication before submitting material."

PASTORAL LIFE, The Magazine for Today's Ministry, Rt. 224, Canfield OH 44406. (216)533-5503. Editor: Rev. Jeffrey Mickler. Emphasizes religion and anything involving pastoral ministers and ministry for Roman Catholic priests (70%); the remainder are sisters, brothers, laity and ministers of other denominations. Monthly. Circ. 7,000. Original artwork returned after publication. Sample copy available.
Illustrations: Prefers religious, pastoral themes. Works on assignment only. Send query letter with brochure, samples and tear sheets to be kept on file. Call or write for appointment to show portfolio. Prefers photostats or photographs as samples. Samples not kept on file are returned by SASE only if requested. Reports within 1 week. Buys first rights. Payment varies; on acceptance.

PB PRESS, 1111 W. Mockingbird Lane, Dallas TX 75247. (214)631-6070. Contact: Editor. Emphasizes safety for salaried and hourly workers for RSR Corporation, a battery recycler. Bimonthly. Circ. 1,500. Previously published material and simultaneous submissions OK. Original artwork returned after publication. Free sample copy for SASE.
Cartoons: Interested in "safety and working people's humor." Send query letter with roughs. Samples returned by SASE if not kept on file. Reports in 1-2 weeks. Buys one-time rights. Pays on acceptance.
Illustrations: Uses 1-2 illustrations/issue; buys all from freelancers. Themes vary, depending on subject of articles. Works on assignment only. Send query letter; call for appointment. Provide business card, brochure, samples and tear sheets to be kept on file for possible future assignments. Samples returned by SASE if not kept on file. Reports in 1-2 weeks. Buys one-time rights. Pays on acceptance.

*PEDIATRIC ANNALS, 6900 Grove Rd., Thorofare NJ 08086. (609)848-1000. Managing Editor: Donna Carpenter. Emphasizes pediatrics for practicing pediatricians. Monthly. Circ. 33,000. Original

artwork returned after publication. Sample copy and art guidelines available.
Illustrations: Buys 4-5 illustrations/issue from freelancers. Send query letter with samples to be kept on file except for those specifically requested back. Prefers tearsheets, slides and photographs as samples. Reports within 2 months. Buys one-time rights or reprint rights. Pays $150, b&w and $200-300, color, cover; $25-30, b&w and $50-100, color, inside; on publication.

PENNSYLVANIA ANGLER, Box 1673, Harrisburg PA 17105-1673. (717)657-4520. Editor: Art Michaels. Emphasizes fishing in Pennsylvania, published by the Pennsylvania Fish Commission. Monthly. Circ. 68,000. Sample copy and art guidelines free for 9x12" SASE with 73¢ postage.
Illustrations: Uses 12 illustrations/issue; buys 4/issue from freelancers. Send query letter with samples and tear sheets to be kept on file; write for appointment to show portfolio. Accepts slides or photocopies as samples. Samples not kept on file are returned by SASE. Reports back. Buys all rights, but rights can be reassigned after publication on written request. Pays $50-300, color, cover; $5-25, b&w, and $25-100, color, inside; on acceptance.

PENNSYLVANIA MAGAZINE, Box 576, Camp Hill PA 17011. (717)761-6620. Editor-in-Chief: Albert Holliday. For college-educated readers, ages 35-60 +, interested in self-improvement, history, and civic and state affairs. Quarterly. Circ. 20,000. Query with samples. SASE. Reports in 3 weeks. Previously published, photocopied and simultaneous submissions OK. Buys first serial rights. Pays on publication. Sample copy $2.50.
Illustrations: Buys 12 illustrations/year on history-related themes. Minimum payment for cover, $70; inside color, $25-50; inside b&w, $5-50.

PENWELL PUBLISHING CO., 1421 S. Sheridan, Tulsa OK 74112. (918)835-3161. Art Director: Mike Reeder. Emphasizes dental economics for practicing dentists; 24-65 years of age. Monthly. Circ. 100,000. Original artwork not returned after publication. Sample copy free for SASE; art guidelines available.
Cartoons: Uses about 1 cartoon/2 issues. Prefers dental related themes. Prefers single panel, with or without gagline; b&w line drawings. Send query letter with samples of style to be kept on file. Material not filed is returned by SASE. Reports only if interested. Negotiates rights purchased and payment. Pays on acceptance.
Illustrations: Currently uses no illustrations/issue. Works on assignment only. Send query letter with brochure to be kept on file. Prefers photostats and photographs as samples. Samples not filed are returned by SASE. Negotiates rights purchased. Pays on acceptance.
Tips: "You can sum up today's trends with two words, fast and exciting, and artists try to capture that feeling in almost everything they do to create the energy and direction of the times." When reviewing samples especially looks for diversification. "For the most part, I like to see a variety of samples to show me that this artist has a firm grasp on the skills needed for this profession!"

PEOPLE IN ACTION, Box 10010, Ogden UT 84409. Editor: Caroll McKanna Halley. Monthly. Distributed to businesses, with appropriate inserts, as house organs; the emphasis is on interesting people nationwide for business owners, families, stockholders, customers and friends. Sample copy $1.
Illustrations: Uses cartoon-style illustrations for occasional humor pieces. Tasteful quality only. Samples returned by SASE. Reports in 2-3 weeks. Pays on acceptance.

*PERSONAL COMPUTING MAGAZINE, 10 Mulholland Dr., Hasbrouck Heights NJ 07604. (201)393-6000. Associate Art Director: Peter Herbert. Emphasizes personal computers for managerial/ professional; upper income audience. Monthly. Circ. 525,000. Original artwork returned after publication. Art guidelines free for SASE.
Illustrations: Buys several illustrations/issue from freelancers. Works on assignment only. Send query letter with samples to be kept on file. Prefers tear sheets or slides as samples. Samples not filed are returned only if requested. Buys first rights. Pays on acceptance.

PERSONNEL JOURNAL, Suite B2, 245 Fischer, Costa Mesa CA 92626. (714)751-1883. Art Director: Susan Overstreet. Emphasizes the hiring, firing, training, recruiting of employees. Directed to directors or managers of corporate personnel departments in organizations with 500 or more employees. Monthly. Circ. 20,000. Original artwork returned after publication. Sample copy and art guidelines free for SASE.
Cartoons: Uses 1 cartoon/issue; buys 1/issue from freelancer. Prefers theme of the world of work, jobs, careers. "Please, no sexist or racist cartoons." Prefers single panel with gagline; b&w line drawings or b&w washes. Send query letter with samples of style to be kept on file. Reports within 3 weeks. Buys one-time rights. Pays $50, b&w; on acceptance.
Illustrations: Uses 3 illustrations/issue; buys all from freelancers. Prefers professional themes such as

Close-up

Kristin Herzog, Design Director
Phi Delta Kappan
Bloomington, Indiana

The graphic art business, like most others, is basically a people business and if you want assignments, you have to learn to deal with art directors on a one-to-one basis. Sometimes examining the other side of a professional relationship gives you insight on how to make sure the relationship proves profitable for both you and your client.

Kristin Herzog, design director for the educational journal, *Phi Delta Kappan*, approaches her dealings with new illustrators in just this manner. Herzog, who has 12 years' experience in publishing, printing and marketing coupled with a master's degree in fine art and extensive freelancing in art, feels that sometimes a little understanding goes a long way in cementing good working relationships.

"Most people are nervous the first time they work with an art director, and I try to recognize this," says Herzog. "Because of their nervousness some artists don't turn in their best work on the first job. But if their portfolio shows potential, and the job is at least appropriate to the editorial copy, I'll go ahead and use it knowing that once the artist gets a little confidence he or she will relax and do something *super*."

At the same time Herzog likes to deal with artists who understand *her* position. "Because I'm the only person here to design, specify type, lay out, paste-up and produce the *Kappan*, I don't have a lot of time to sit around planning and designing. I need artists who can work with very little direction from me. Artists need to be familiar with

Artist: David R. Smiton

our magazine; they need to think; and they need to give me good art that is technically correct for our reproduction process. Even though, ideally, any illustration I buy should be art that I would want to hang on my wall, an artist who consistently delivers technically correct, reasonably good work, on time, will get many more jobs from me than a really great artist who only does *some* of these things."

Herzog applies many guidelines when selecting cartoons for use in the *Kappan*. "I look for a good, well-developed, consistent drawing style. Many cartoonists tend to get sloppy because they think the joke is the most important thing—it is. But if the drawing is really junky it makes my magazine look junky, so I don't want it." Additionally, she advises cartoonists to use a recognizable signature on every cartoon and to keep their addresses updated with both old and new clients. "Cartoonists lose a lot of reprint money because they don't stay in touch," says Herzog.

Herzog sees illustrations in a similar light as she does cartoons. "I want to see good art coupled with good, conceptual thinking."

When you do secure an assignment the design director recommends that you keep a few very important points in mind: "Never accept a job without discussing how you will get paid; get a purchase order to protect yourself; and always be sure you get an actual deadline."

—Rand Ruggeberg

the workplace, office equipment, professionals (line drawings). Works on assignment; will also accept previously published material. Send query letter with resume, business card and samples to be kept on file. Call or write for appointment to show portfolio. Prefers photostats as samples. Samples not kept on file are returned only if requested. Reports only if interested. Negotiates rights purchased. Pays $150-200, b&w, inside; on acceptance.

PET BUSINESS, 5400 N.W. 84th Ave., Miami FL 33166. Editor-in-Chief: Robert Behme. For those in the pet trade: manufacturers, importers, exporters, wholesalers, retailers and livestock breeders. Monthly news magazine. Circ. 14,500. Sample copy $1. Also uses artists for layout and book art.
Cartoons: Buys 2 cartoons/issue on pet-related themes; single panel. Query. SASE. Reports in 3 weeks. Pays $15-25, b&w line drawings and halftones; on acceptance.
Illustrations: Buys 20 illustrations/year on assigned themes. Query. SASE. Reports in 3 weeks. Pays $25-40, b&w; on acceptance.

PETERSENS HUNTING MAGAZINE, Petersen Publishing Co., 8490 Sunset Blvd., Los Angeles CA 90069. (213)657-5100. Editor: Craig Boddington. Art Director: C. A. Yeseta. Emphasizes sport hunting for hunting enthusiasts. Monthly. Circ. 275,000. Sometimes returns originals after publication. Sample copy $1.75. Receives 4-5 cartoons/year and 2-3 illustrations/month from freelance artists. Occasionally uses production paste-up artists on an hourly wage.
Cartoons: Uses 1-2 cartoons/year from freelancers on hunting scenes and wildlife. Prefers to see finished cartoons. Reports in 1 week. Pays on publication.
Illustrations: Buys 8-10 illustrations/year on "very realistic wildlife themes and action hunting scenes"; some "how-to" drawings. Works on assignment only. Prefers to see finished art, roughs, portfolio, samples of style or previously published work. Arrange interview to show portfolio. Samples returned by SASE. Provide resume, business card, letter of inquiry; also brochure or flyer containing examples of work to be kept on file for future assignments. Reports in 4 weeks. Buys various rights. Inside: Pays $75-150, b&w line drawings; on publication.

PHI DELTA KAPPAN, Box 789, Bloomington IN 47402. Editor-in-Chief: Robert W. Cole, Jr. Design Director: Kristin Herzog. Emphasizes issues, policy, research findings and opinions in the field of education. For members of the educational organization Phi Delta Kappa and subscribers. Published 10 times/year. Circ. 135,000. Considers unpublished artists on a speculative basis. SASE. Reports in 2 weeks. Previously published work OK; "specify where item appeared. We return cartoons after publication." Sample copy $2.50—"the journal is available in most public and college libraries."
Cartoons: Uses some cartoons, occasionally from freelancers. Receives 90 submissions/week from freelancers. Interested in themes that "relate to education administration—check our journal and news reports for current topics to use as themes." Considers drawing quality (i.e. line) of vital importance; single panel with gagline. Prefers finished cartoons. SASE. Reporting time varies. Buys one-time rights. Pays $25, occasionally more, b&w line drawings.
Illustrations: Uses 2-5 b&w illustrations/issue, all from freelancers, on education subjects. Occasionally buys humorous illustrations (about 4/year). "Quality of drawing and good concepts most important aspect-i.e., the kind of line, the graphic use of the space. Next is ability to depict appropriate image from editorial content and come up with an interesting concept. Most illustrations depict teachers or principals, theories of learning, testing principles, studies of excellence, international comparisons of education." Samples returned by SASE. Provide business card, tear sheets and photocopies of line drawings to be kept on file for future assignments, samples of style and list of publications. Buys one-time rights on a work-for-hire basis. Cover: Pays $250, color-separated work and full-color renderings. Inside: Pays $40-60 for large, b&w line drawings and washes; pays $25 for spot drawings.
Tips: "I Like best to have some photocopies of your work on file. I can then call you and ask to have you send the original. I very rarely have time to send you an article for you to illustrate. Usually I have to use art that has already been done—so the more photocopies I have of your work—the better. Also, keep your address up to date. We like cartoons which have a positive outlook. We don't like jokes that run people down or jokes that are sexist."

PHILADELPHIA MAGAZINE, 1500 Walnut St., Philadelphia PA 19102. Contact: Art Director. For a professional, upper-middle-income audience. Monthly. Circ. 142,000. Simultaneous submissions OK. Original artwork returned after publication.
Illustrations: Uses 6-15 illustrations/issue; buys all from freelancers. Interested in a variety of themes and styles. Works on assignment only. Provide business card, samples and/or tear sheets to be kept on file for possible future assignments. Send query letter with samples of style, submit portfolio. Samples not returned. Buys one-time rights. Pays on acceptance.
Tips: "Variety is the key word. Personally interested in collage and work crossing over fine line between fine art/commercial illustration. Look at several issues of the magazine in the library. Understand the level of work expected."

PHOENIX HOME/GARDEN, 3136 N. 3rd Ave., Phoenix AZ 85013. (602)234-0840. Editor: Manya Winsted. Managing Editor: Nora Burba. Emphasizes homes, entertainment and gardens for Phoenix area residents interested in better living. Monthly. Circ. 33,000. Original artwork not returned after publication. Sample copy $2.50.
Illustrations: Uses 6-12 illustrations/year; buys 1-5 from freelancers. Interested in botanical illustrations and spot art relevant to topics. Also uses illustrations for promotional material in conjunction with the magazine. Works on assignment only. Send samples of style. Reports in 6 weeks. Provide tear sheets to be kept on file for possible future assignments. Buys all rights on assignments. Pays $30-50 average inside, b&w line drawings. Pays on publication.

PHOTO MARKETING MAGAZINE, 3000 Picture Pl., Jackson MI 49201. (517)788-5980. Executive Editor/Associate Publisher: Bruce Aldrich. Managing Editor: Therese Wood. Emphasizes the photographic industry. Readers are camera store dealers, photofinishers, manufacturers and distributors of photographic equipment. Monthly. Circ. 15,000. Free sample copy; art guidelines for SASE.
Cartoons: Needs vary each issue. Freelancers are selected for particular subject matter or story topic. Format: b&w line drawings without gagline. Send samples of style and resume. SASE. Reports in 1 week. Pays on publication. Buys first North American serial rights.
Illustrations: Runs 2-4 illustrations/issue, all from freelancers. "Selection is made from freelancers on file, per assignment basis only." Uses inside b&w line drawings and color washes. Send resume and samples of style or arrange for a personal appointment to show portfolio. SASE. Reports in 1 week. Pays on publication. Buys first North American serial rights.

PHYSICIAN'S MANAGEMENT, 7500 Old Oak Blvd., Cleveland OH 44130. (216)243-8100, ext. 808. Editor: Robert A. Feigenbaum. Art Director: David Komitau. Published 12 times/year. Circ. 110,000. Emphasizes business, practice management and legal aspects of medical practice for primary care physicians.
Cartoons: Receives 50-70/week from freelancers. Themes typically apply to medical and financial situations although we do publish general humor cartoons. Prefers single and double panel; b&w line drawings with gagline. Uses "only clean-cut line drawings." Send finished cartoons to the editor. SASE. Reports in 2 weeks. Buys one-time rights. Pays $80 for b&w; on acceptance. No previously published material and/or simultaneous submissions.
Illustrations: Accepts b&w and color illustrations. All work done on assignment. Query editor or art director first or send examples of work. Fees negotiable. Buys first rights. No previously published and/or simultaneous submissions.
Tips: "Cartoons should be geared toward the physician—not the patient. No cartoons about drug companies or medicine men. No sexist cartoons. Illustrations should be appropriate for a serious business publication. We do not use cartoonish or comic book styles to illustrate our articles. We work with artists nationwide."

PHYSICS TODAY, 335 E. 45th St., New York NY 10017. (212)661-9404. Senior Art Editor: Elliot Plotkin. Emphasizes educational science for the professional market. Monthly. Original artwork not returned after publication.
Illustrations: Prefers graphs and cartoon style for text illustrations. Send query letter with brochure and samples of style; call for appointment. Provide resume and samples to be kept on file for possible future assignments. Samples not returned. Buys one-time rights, reprint rights or all rights. "All original materials made for publication on assignment are copyrighted for the company."

PIG IRON, Box 237, Youngstown OH 44501. (216)744-2258. Editor-in-Chief: Jim Villani and Rose Sayre. Emphasizes literature/art for writers, artists and intelligent lay audience with emphasis in popular culture. Annually. Circ. 1,000. Previously published and photocopied work OK. Original artwork returned after publication. Sample copy $2.50.
Cartoons: Uses 1-15 cartoons/issue, all from freelancers. Receives 1-3 submissions/week from freelancers. Interested in "the arts, political, science fiction, fantasy, alternative lifestyles, psychology, humor"; multi-panel. Especially needs fine art cartoons. Prefers finished cartoons. SASE. Reports in 1 month. Buys first North American serial rights. Pays $2 minimum, b&w halftones and washes; on acceptance.
Illustrations: Uses 15-30 illustrations/issue, all from freelancers. Receives 1-3 submissions/week from freelancers. Interested in "any media: pen and ink washes, lithographs, silk screen, charcoal, collage, line drawings; any subject matter." B&w only. Prefers finished art or velox. Reports in 2 months. Buys first North American serial rights. Minimum payment: Cover: $4, b&w. Inside: $2; on publication.
Tips: "*Pig Iron* is a publishing opportunity for the fine artist; we publish art in its own right, not as filler or story accompaniment. The artist who is executing black-and-white work for exhibit and gallery presentations can find a publishing outlet with *Pig Iron* that will considerably increase that artist's visibility

James C. Vebeck, editor of **Plan and Print**, Franklin Park, Illinois, needed a slightly humorous touch for a technical article, so he assigned the artwork to John Lambert of Arlington Heights, Illinois. '"John is a fine airbrush artist, particularly in color," says Vebeck. The magazine bought all reproduction rights to the full-page color illustration.

and reputation." Current themes include "humor," and the "wild west." Looking for Third World artists for Third World anthology.

PILLOW TALK, 215 Lexington Ave., New York NY 10016. Editor-in-Chief: I. Catherine Duff. "For people interested in all areas of human relationships: meeting, dating, arguing, making up, sex (in all aspects)." Monthly. Circ. 120,000. Original artwork returned after publication. Buys all rights. Sample copy $1.75; free artist's guidelines with SASE.
Cartoons: "Uses 5-8 cartoons/issue; buys all from freelancers. Receives 100 submissions/week from freelancers. Interested in health, sex, problems and news items"; single panel with gagline. Prefers finished cartoons. SASE. Reports in 2 weeks. Pays $25-35, b&w line drawings, gray opaques, washes and opaque watercolors; on publication. Mail roughs or finished art. No pornography.
Illustrations: Most illustrations are assigned for specific articles. Works on assignment only. Samples returned by SASE. Provide resume and flyers to be kept on file for future assignments. Reports in 2 weeks. Buys first North American serial rights. Inside: Pays $125-150, b&w; on publication.

PITTSBURGH MAGAZINE, 4802 5th Ave., Pittsburgh PA 15213. (412)622-1360. Art Director: Michael Maskarinec. Emphasizes culture, feature stories and material with heavy Pittsburgh city emphasis; public broadcasting television and radio schedule. Monthly. Circ. 58,000. Sample copy $2.
Illustrations: Uses 5-10 illustrations/issue; all from freelancers; inside b&w and 4-color illustrations. Works on assignment only. Prefers to see roughs. SASE. Buys all rights on a work-for-hire basis. Pays on publication.

PLAN AND PRINT, International Reprographic Association, 9931 Franklin Ave., Box 879, Franklin Park IL 60131. Editor: James C. Vebeck. For commercial reproduction company owners and managers and dealers in architects', engineers' and draftsmen's supplies and equipment, in-plant reproduction de-

partment supervisors, in-plant design and drafting specialists, computer aided design users and architects. Monthly. Circ. 23,000. Originals not returned after publication. Free sample copy and artist's guidelines.
Illustrations: Buys 1 spot illustration/issue. Especially needs spots related to the industry. Interested in reprographics and design/drafting. Works on assignment only. Send samples of style. SASE. Keeps files of information on artists for future assignment possibilities. Reports in 1 week. Buys all rights on a work-for-hire basis. Pays $7.50-10, b&w spots. Payment for article illustrations and 4-color cover art varies from $50-450.
Tips: "Heavy use of computer aided design."

PLANE & PILOT MAGAZINE, 16200 Ventura Blvd., Encino CA 91436. Art Director: J.R. Martinez. Emphasizes business and personal aviation for private and small business pilots. Monthly. Circ. 70-100,000. Does not return original artwork after publication. Sample copy available; art guidelines free for SASE.
Illustrations: Buys 1-2 illustrations/issue from freelancers. Prefers business and aircraft oriented work, b&w line, wash or airbrush. Works on assignment only. Send query letter with samples to be kept on file. Write for appointment to show portfolio. Prefers photostats, tear sheets and slides as samples. Reports back. Buys all rights. Pays $100-300 for b&w and per assignment for color, inside; on acceptance.
Tips: "Fewer artists have portfolios oriented toward b&w work. It makes it more difficult to evaluate who would be best for a b&w assignment."

PLANNING, American Planning Association, 1313 E. 60th St., Chicago IL 60637. (312)955-9100. Editor-in-Chief: Sylvia Lewis. Art Director: Richard Sessions. For urban and regional planners interested in land use, housing, transportation and the environment. Monthly. Circ. 25,000. Previously published work OK. Original artwork returned after publication, upon request. Free sample copy and artist's guidelines.
Cartoons: Buys 6 cartoons/year on the environment, city/regional planning, energy, garbage, transportation, housing, power plants, agriculture and land use; single, double and multipanel with gaglines ("provide outside of cartoon body if possible"). SASE. Reports in 2 weeks. Buys all rights. Pays $25 minimum, b&w line drawings; on publication.
Illustrations: Buys 8 illustrations/year on the environment, city/regional planning, energy, garbage, transportation, housing, power plants, agriculture and land use. Prefers to see roughs and samples of style. SASE. Reports in 2 weeks. Buys all rights. Cover: Pays $200 maximum, b&w drawings. Inside: Pays $25 minimum, b&w line drawings; on publication.

PLAYBILL, Suite 320, 71 Vanderbilt Ave., New York NY 10169. (212)557-5757. Editor-in-Chief: Joan Alleman. Concerns theater in New York City. Monthly. Circ. 1,040,000.
Cartoons: Buys b&w line drawings on New York City theater. SASE. Reports in 4 weeks. Buys all rights. Pays on acceptance.
Illustrations: Assigns work on New York City theater. SASE. Reports in 4 weeks. Buys all rights. Pays on acceptance.

PLAYBOY, 919 Michigan Ave., Chicago IL 60611. Executive Art Director: Tom Staebler. Emphasizes celebrities, beautiful women, dining, humor and fiction. For the sophisticated, urban male. All work generally done on assignment. Reports in 3-4 weeks.
Cartoons: Submit roughs with one finished drawing to Michelle Urry, cartoon editor. Buys 40/month on satirical, sophisticated, and other situations. Prefers cartoons that deal with sex and are slanted toward young, urban male market. Also looking for one-line "strips" for Funnies section. "Style and technique very important." Pays $350, b&w; $600, full-page color.
Illustrations: Submit samples to Kerig Pope, managing art director. Pays $1,200/page or $2,000/spread; $200-250, spot drawings.

PLAYGIRL, Suite 3000, 3420 Ocean Park Blvd., Santa Monica CA 90405. (213)450-0900. Assistant Art Director: Scott Rankin. Emphasizes entertainment, fiction, reviews, beauty, fashion, cooking and travel for women ages 18-40. Monthly. Circ. 850,000.
Cartoons: Uses 6-18 cartoons/issue; all by freelancers. Receives 200 + cartoons from freelancers/month. Cartoons should be "slanted towards women's problems, intellectual humor, and topical issues." Format: Single panel b&w washes with gagline. Especially needs 6-inch square, b&w cartoons dealing with women's issues, experiences. Prefers finished cartoons or excellent photocopies. SASE. Reports in 60 days. Pays on publication; $75 for b&w. Buys first North American serial rights. Call Cartoon Editor Mae Bryant for appointment to show a portfolio.
Illustrations: Works on assignment only. Uses 4-12 illustrations/issue; all by freelancers. Artists are selected from "walk-ins" doing editorial artwork to illustrate fiction. "We see portfolios on a walk-in ba-

sis the first Thursday of every month." Format: b&w line drawings and color washes for inside. Especially needs vertical color and b&w. Arrange personal appointment to show portfolio and/or send samples of style and tear sheets. SASE. Reports only if interested. Pays on publication. Buys all rights.
Tips: "There is a trend toward humor with a subliminal sexuality slant. Women are being depicted in a more liberal light, particularly regarding male nudity and in other sexual contexts. We want as strong and contemporary a visual style as possible."

PODIATRY MANAGEMENT MAGAZINE, 401 N. Broad St., Philadelphia PA 19108. (215)925-9744. President: Scott Borowsky. Emphasizes practice management for podiatrists, faculty and students. Published 8 times/year. Circ. 11,000. Original artwork returned after publication. Also uses paste-up artists.
Illustrations: Buys 2-3 b&w illustrations/issue from freelancers. Themes tie in with stories. Works on assignment only. Send query letter with resume to be kept on file; write for appointment to show portfolio. Prefers photostats and tear sheets as samples. Samples returned by SASE. Reports only if interested and if SASE is included. Buys all rights. Pays $100-175, b&w and $250, color, cover; $100, b&w, inside; on publication.

POPULAR COMPUTING, McGraw-Hill Publishing, Inc., Box 372, Hancock NH 03449. (603)924-9281. Art Director: Erik Murphy. Emphasizes personal computers for business applications. Monthly. Circ. 300,000.
Illustrations: Uses 8-15 illustrations/month; buys all from award-winning illustrators. Works on assignment only. Send query letter. Does not return unsolicited material. Provide samples to be kept on file for possible future assignments. Reports in 1 month. Buys first rights. Payment along AIGA guidelines.

POPULAR SCIENCE, Times Mirror Magazines, Inc., 380 Madison Ave., New York NY 10017. Art Director: David Houser. For the well-educated adult male, interested in science, technology, new products. Receives 3 illustrations/week from freelance artists. Original artwork returned after publication.
Illustrations: Uses 30-40 illustrations/issue; buys 30/issue from freelancers. Interested in technical 4-color art and 2-color line art dealing with automotive or architectural subjects. Especially needs science and technological pieces as assigned per layout. Works on assignment only. Samples returned by SASE. Reports back on future assignment possibilities. Provide tear sheet to be kept on file for future assignments. "After seeing portfolios, I photocopy or photostat those samples I feel are indicative of the art we might use." Reports whenever appropriate job is available. Buys first publishing rights.
Tips: "More and more scientific magazines have entered the field. This has provided a larger base of technical artists for us. Be sure your samples relate to our subject matter, i.e., no rose etchings, and be sure to include a tear sheet for our files."

PORTLAND REVIEW, c/o Portland State University, Box 751, Portland OR 97207. (503)229-4468. Editor: Matt Simon. Business Manager: Cyndie Lee. Emphasizes literature and art. Annually. Circ. 2,000. Original artwork returned after publication. Sample copy $2 with SASE; art guidelines free for SASE.
Illustrations: Uses 12-16 illustrations/issue. Prefers b&w graphics of all kinds; "works that stand on their own." Send query letter with samples to be kept on file. Call or write for appointment to show portfolio. Samples returned by SASE if not kept on file. Reports within 6 weeks. Buys one-time rights. Payment almost always in contributor's copies.
Tips: A mistake artists make is "lack of contact. Often the artists will leave their work with us and not check back to see if any decisions have been made, or if we have questions for them."

POWER, McGraw-Hill, Inc., 1221 Avenue of the Americas, New York NY 10020. (212)512-2440. Art Director: Kiyo Komoda. Emphasizes the systems and equipment for the use and conservation of energy. For power generation and plant energy systems. Monthly plus 2 annuals. Original artwork returned after publication, on request only.
Illustrations: Uses 30 illustrations/issue on energy systems. Buys 30%/issue from freelancers; most are graphs, charts and mechanical line drawings. Especially needs "graphs, charts, diagrams with more imagination or creative dramatization of what they represent." Works on assignment only. Samples returned by SASE. Provide resume and business card to be kept on file for future assignments. Arrange interview to show portfolio. Reports in 1 week. Buys one-time and reprint rights. Cover: Pays $150-350, color. Inside: Pays $30-300, color; $10-200, b&w line drawings; on acceptance.
Tips: "We prefer artists with clean and crisp line works. They should know about color separation and the use of Zipatone. Young artists welcomed. Follow the specs—especially those arts with deadlines. I'll never recall any artist if he or she fails to meet specs or deadlines."

*PRAYING, Box 281, Kansas City MO 64141. (816)531-0538. Editor: Arthur N. Winter. Estab. 1983. Emphasizes spirituality for everyday living for lay catholics and members of mainline Protestant

churches; primarily Catholic, non-fundamentalist. "Starting point: The daily world of living, family, job, politics, is the stuff of religious experience and Christian living." Quarterly. Circ. 50,000. Accepts previously published material. Original artwork not returned after publication. Sample copy and art guidelines available.
Cartoons: Buys 1-2 cartoons/issue from freelancers. Especially interested in cartoons that spoof fads and jargon in contemporary spirituality, prayer and religion. Prefers single panel with gagline; b&w line drawings. Send query letter with samples of style to be kept on file. Material not filed is returned. Reports within 2 weeks. Buys one-time rights. Pays $25, b&w; on acceptance.
Illustrations: Buys 2-3 illustrations/issue from freelancers. Prefers contemporary interpretations of traditional Christian symbols to be used as incidental art; also drawings to illustrate articles. Send query letter with samples to be kept on file. Prefers photostats, tear sheets and photocopies as samples. Samples returned if not interested or return requested. Reports within 2 weeks. Buys one-time rights. Pays $25, b&w; on acceptance.

THE PRESBYTERIAN RECORD, 50 Wynford Dr., Don Mills, Ontario M3C 1J7 Canada. (416)441-1111. Production Editor: Mary Visser. Published 11 times/year. Deals with family-oriented religious themes. Circ. 77,320. Original artwork returned after publication. Simultaneous submissions and previously published work OK. Free sample copy and artists' guidelines.
Cartoons: Uses 1 cartoon/issue; buys from freelancers. Interested in some theme or connection to religion. Send roughs. SASE. Reports in 2 weeks. Pays on publication.
Illustrations: Buys 10 illustrations/year on religion. "We use freelance material, and we are interested in excellent color artwork for cover." Any line style acceptable— should reproduce well on newsprint. Works on assignment only. Send roughs. Samples returned by SASE. Provide business card to be kept on file for future assignments. Reports in 2 weeks. Buys all rights on a work-for-hire basis. Cover: Pays $50, color washes and opaque watercolors; inside: pays $5-12, b&w line drawings; on publication. Query with resume and samples.
Tips: "We don't want any 'cute' samples (in cartoons). Prefer some theological insight in cartoons; some comment on religious trends and practices."

PRESBYTERIAN SURVEY, 341 Ponce de Leon Ave. NE, Atlanta GA 30365. (404)873-1549. Art Director: Linda Colgrove. Emphasizes Presbyterian-related features and news, issues facing the church, Christian life. Monthly. Circ. 195,000. Sample copy available.
Cartoons: Runs 1/issue on topics which speak to the issues of the day. Prefers finished cartoons; reports in 6 weeks.
Illustrations: Buys 2/issue. Works on assignment basis only. Prefers to see portfolio or samples of style; samples returned. Reports back if interested; provide letter, brochure, flyer, tear sheets, resume or business card to be kept on file for future assignments. Negotiates rights purchased. Pays $25-100, spot art; $50-250, cover design.

PREVENTION, 33 E. Minor St., Emmaus PA 18049. (215)967-5171. Executive Art Director: Kay Douglas. Emphasizes health, nutrition, fitness, cooking. Monthly. Circ. 3 million. Returns original artwork after publication. Sample copy available.
Cartoons: Buys 2-3 cartoons/issue from freelancers. Prefers themes of health, pets, fitness. Considers single panel with gagline; b&w line drawings, b&w washes. Samples of style are filed; unused roughs or finished cartoons are returned by SASE within 2 weeks. Reports back only if interested. Buys one-time rights. Pays $150, b&w; on acceptance.
Illustrations: Buys about 20 illustrations/issue from freelancers. Themes are assigned on editorial basis. Works on assignment only. Send samples to be kept on file. Prefers tear sheets or slides as samples. Samples not filed are returned by SASE. Reports back only if interested. Buys one-time rights.

***PREVIEWS MAGAZINE**, Suite 245, 919 Santa Monica Blvd., Santa Monica CA 90401. (213)458-3376. Editor: Jan Loomis. Emphasizes community events for upper middle-class, well-educated, sophisticated audience. Monthly. Circ. 37,000. Original artwork returned after publication. Sample copy and art guidelines free for SASE.
Cartoons: Buys 1-2 cartoons/issue from freelancers. Prefers single panel with gagline; b&w line drawings or washes. Send query letter with samples of style or roughs to be kept on file; write for appointment to show portflio. Material not filed is returned by SASE. Reports within 1 month. Negotiates rights purchased. Pays $20, b&w; on publication.
Illustrations: Specific topics illustrated. Works on assignment only. Send query letter with brochure, resume, business card and samples to be kept on file; write or call for appointment to show portfolio. Prefers photocopies as samples. Samples not filed are returned by SASE. Reports within 1 month. Negotiates rights purchased. Pays $100, b&w and $200, color, cover; $50, b&w and $100, color, inside/ page; on publication.

PRIMAVERA, University of Chicago, 1212 E. 59th St., Chicago IL 60637. (312)684-2742. Contact: Editorial Board. Emphasizes art and literature by women for readers interested in contemporary literature and art. Annual. Circ. 800. Original artwork returned after publication. Sample copy $4; art guidelines available for SASE.

Illustrations: Uses 15-20 illustrations/issue; buys all from freelancers. Receives 5 illustrations/week from freelance artists. "We are open to a wide variety of styles and themes. Work must be in b&w with strong contrasts and should not exceed 7" high x 5" wide." Especially needs work with women figures. Send finished art; call for appointment. "If the artist lives in Chicago, she may call us for an appointment." Reports in 1-2 months. Acquires first rights. "We pay in 2 free copies of the issue in which the artwork appears"; on publication.

Tips: "It's a good idea to take a look at a recent issue. Artists often do not investigate the publication and send work which may be totally inappropriate. We publish a wide variety of women artists. We have increased the number of graphics per issue. Send us a *variety* of prints. It is important that the graphics work well with the literature and the other graphics we've accepted. Our decisions are strongly influenced by personal taste and the work we know has already been accepted. Will consider appropriate cartoons and humorous illustrations."

PRIVATE PILOT/AERO/KITPLANES, Box 6050, Mission Viejo CA 92690. (714)240-6001. Contact: Editor. For owners/pilots of private aircraft, student pilots and others aspiring to attain additional ratings and experience. Circ. 80,000. Monthly. Receives 5 cartoons and 3 illustrations/week from freelance artists.

Cartoons: Buys 2-4 cartoons/issue on flying. Send finished artwork. SASE. Reports in 3 months. Pays $35, b&w; on publication.

Illustrations: Query with samples. SASE. Reports in 3 months. Pays $50-100, b&w; $75-150, color. "We also use spot illustrations as column fillers; buys 1-2 spot illustrations/issue. Pays $25/spot."

Tips: "Know the field you wish to represent; we get tired of 'crash' gags submitted to flying publications."

PRIVATE PRACTICE, Suite 470, 3535 NW 58th St., Oklahoma City OK 73112. (405)943-2318. Art Director & Design Director: Rocky C. Hails. Editorial features "maintenance of freedom in all fields of medical practice and the effects of socioeconomic factors on the physician." Monthly. Circ. 180,000. Free sample copy and artists' guidelines. Query with resume and samples or arrange interview to show portfolio. SASE. Reports in 2-3 weeks. Negotiates pay; pays on acceptance.

Cartoons: Buys cartoons regularly.

Illustrations: Buys 1-4 illustrations/issue on politics, medicine, finance and physicians' leisure activities. Also uses artists for 4-color cover illustration. Frequently uses humorous illustrations and occasionally cartoon-style illustrations. Query and arrange interview to show portfolio. SASE. Especially looks for "craftsmanship, combined with an ability to communicate complex concepts." Reports in 2-3 weeks. Buys first and reprint rights. Cover: Pays $200-450, unlimited to media, all forms. Inside: Pays $60-110, color washes and opaque watercolors; $40-100, b&w line drawings and washes; on acceptance.

Tips: "Provide reproductions of several illustrations (that demonstrate the variety of your style) to leave with the art director. It is encouraging to see the wide variety of 'accepted' styles and the design revisions going on in major journals. The trend seems to be less toward 'artsy' selections and more toward constructive communication."

PROBE, Baptist Brotherhood Commission, 1548 Poplar, Memphis TN 38104. (901)272-2461. Art Director: Herschel Wells. Christian-oriented mission magazine for boys grades 7-12. Monthly. Original artwork returned after publication, if requested. Circ. 50,000. Previously published, photocopied and simultaneous submissions OK.

Illustrations: Uses 3 illustrations/issue; buys 1/issue from freelancers. Interested in family life with emphasis on boys and their interests. "Our freelance needs are usually directed toward a specific story; we frequently use humorous illustrations and sometimes use cartoon-style illustrations; we very seldom use art submitted on spec." Send samples of style or roughs with resume. Reports in 3 weeks. Samples returned by SASE. Provide resume or brochure to be kept on file for future assignments. Buys first North American serial rights. Cover: Pays $200-250, full color; $100-180, b&w line drawings, washes and gray opaques. Inside: Pays $45-120, b&w line drawings, washes and gray opaques. Pays on acceptance.

*PROCEEDINGS, U.S. Naval Institute, Annapolis MD 21402. (301)268-6110. Editor-in-Chief: Clayton R. Barrow, Jr. Emphasizes Navy, Marine Corps, Coast Guard, and related maritime and military topics for sea service professionals. Monthly. Circ. 100,000. Original artwork returned after publication. Sample copy and art guidelines available.

Cartoons: Buys a few cartoons/issue on various themes from freelancers. No rigid format guidelines;

prefers b&w line drawings. Send query letter with samples of style to be kept on file, except for rejections. Material not filed is returned only if requested. Reports within a few weeks. Negotiates rights purchased. Pays $25-50, b&w and color; on acceptance.
Illustrations: Buys approximately 5 illustrations/issue on varied themes from freelancers. Works on assignment only. Send query letter with samples. Prefers tear sheets or photocopies as samples. Samples returned only if requested. Reports within a few weeks. Negotiates rights purchased. Pays $200, color, cover; $25-50, b&w and color, inside; on acceptance.

PROFESSIONAL AGENT, 400 N. Washington St., Alexandria VA 22314. (703)836-9340. Editor and Publisher: Janice J. Artandi. For independent insurance agents and other affiliated members of the American Agency System. Monthly. Circ. 40,000. Original artwork returned after publication. Free sample copy.
Illustrations: Buys 3/issue from freelancers. Provide samples to be kept on file for future assignments. Buys first-time North America rights.
Tips: Conceptual approach often required. Local artists preferred. Trends are toward "more realism and fewer cartoons." Looks for "whether an artist's work is reproducible. Editorial experience is helpful."

PROFESSIONAL ELECTRONICS, 2708 W. Berry St., Ft. Worth TX 76109. (817)921-9062. Editor-in-Chief: Wallace S. Harrison. For professionals in electronics, especially owners, technicians and managers of consumer electronics sales and service firms. Bimonthly. Circ. 10,000. Samples of previously published cartoons furnished on request.
Cartoons: Buys themes on electronics sales/service, association management, conventions and directors' meetings; single panel with gagline. Submit art. SASE. Reports in 2 weeks. Buys first rights. Pays $10, b&w line drawings; on acceptance.
Illustrations: Buys assigned themes. Submit art. SASE. Reports in 2 weeks. Buys first rights. Cover: Pays $30-60, b&w line drawings. Inside: Pays $10-15, b&w line drawings; on acceptance.

THE PROGRESSIVE, 409 E. Main St., Madison WI 53703. (608)257-4626. Art Director: Patrick JB Flynn. Monthly. Circ. 50,000. Free sample copy and artists' guidelines.
Illustrations: Uses 15 b&w illustrations/issue; buys all from freelancers. Works on assignment only. Send clips of previously published work. Samples returned by SASE. Provide letter of inquiry and tear sheets or photocopies of work to be kept on file for future assignments. Reports in 2 months. Cover pays $250. Inside pays $75 minimum, b&w line or tone drawings/paintings. Buys first rights. Pays on publication.
Tips: Do not send original art. Send appropriate return postage. "The most obvious trend in editorial work is toward more artistic freedom in idea and individual style. I think the successful art direction of a magazine allows for personal interpretation of an assignment."

PSA, East-West Network, Inc., 5900 Wilshire Blvd., Los Angeles CA 90036. (213)937-5810. Editor: Al Austin. Art Director: George Kenton. Emphasizes events, issues and business in California. For airline passengers. Monthly. Original artwork returned after publication. Sample copy $2.
Illustrations: Works on assignment only. Query with resume. Buys first rights. Pays $125 minimum, spot art; $450 maximum for full-page illustration; other formats negotiable.

*PUBLIC CITIZEN, #605, 2000 P St., Washington DC 20036. (202)293-9142. Editor: Elliott Negin. Emphasizes consumer issues for the membership of Public Citizen, a group founded by Ralph Nader in 1971. Bimonthly. Circ. 50,000. Accepts previously published material. Returns original artwork after publication. Sample copy available.
Cartoons: Buys 1/issue from freelancer. Prefers single panel with gagline; b&w line drawings. Send query letter with samples of style to be kept on file. Call for appointment to show portfolio. Material not filed is returned by SASE. Reports only if interested. Buys first rights or one-time rights. Pays on publication.
Illustrations: Buys up to 10/issue. Send query letter with samples to be kept on file. Write or call for appointment to show portfolio. Prefers tear sheets or photocopies as samples. Samples not filed are returned by SASE. Reports only if interested. Buys first rights or one-time rights. Pays $275, b&w, cover; and $40-150, b&w, inside; on publication.

PUBLIC RELATIONS JOURNAL, 845 3rd Ave., New York NY 10022. (212)826-1757. Art Director: Susan Yip. Emphasizes issues and developments, both theory and practice, for public relations practitioners, educators and their managements. Monthly. Circ. 15,733. Accepts previously published material. Returns original artwork after publication. Art guidelines available.
Cartoons: Buys business cartoons. Send samples of style to be kept on file. Material not kept on file returned only if requested. Reports back only if interested. Negotiates rights purchased. Pays $50, b&w; $75-100, color; on publication.

These two illustrations by Bascove of New York City "work on one level individual-ly," says Patrick Flynn, art director of The Progressive, *Madison, Wisconsin, "and on another level more completely together. Bascove's very heavy black-and-white style has a visual elegance about it. This contrast and its graphic impact are al-most a necessity when reproducing on a ground wood stock." Flynn explains that "when I commission work to an artist half way across the country, I seldom have the time or opportunity to see a sketch. The ideas and composition are usually worked out by phone." Bascove received $150 for one-time rights.*

Illustrations: Buys illustrations from freelancers. Themes and styles vary. Send brochure and samples to be kept on file. Prefers slides or photographs as samples. Samples not filed are returned only if requested. Reports back only if interested. Negotiates rights purchased. Pays $200 for color cover; $75 for b&w and $100 for color inside; on publication.

QUARRY MAGAZINE, Box 1061, Kingston, Ontario K7L 4Y5 Canada. (613)544-5400, ext. 144. Editor: Bob Hilderley. Emphasizes poetry, fiction, short plays, book reviews—Canadian literature. Audience: Canadian writers; libraries (public, high school, college, university); persons interested in current new writing. Quarterly. Circ. 1,000. Original artwork returned after publication. Sample copy $3.
Illustrations: Uses 3-5 illustrations/issue; buys all from freelancers. No set preference on themes or styles; "we need high quality line drawings." Send query letter with samples to be kept on file. Contact only by mail. Prefers originals or good photostats as samples. Reports within 12 weeks. Buys first rights. Pays $25, b&w, cover; $25, b&w, inside. Pays on publication.

QUICK PRINTING, 3255 South US 1, Ft. Pierce FL 33482. (305)465-9450. Publisher: Robert Schweiger. Emphasizes quick printing for owners/managers of quick print, copying and small commercial printshops.. Monthly. Circ. 28,000. Returns original artwork after publication. Sample copy free for SASE with 80¢ postage.
Cartoons: Buys 2 cartoons/issue from freelancers. Prefers themes related to quick printing/copying; b&w line drawings. Send query letter with roughs to be kept on file. Material not filed is returned only if requested. Reports within 1 week. Buys one-time rights. Pays $10 for b&w; on acceptance.
Illustrations: Buys 3 illustrations/issue from freelancers. Works on assignment only. Send query letter to be kept on file. "No samples necessary." Reports within 1 week. Negotiates rights purchased. Pays $100 for b&w and $150 for color, cover; $25 for b&w and $40 for color, inside; on acceptance.

R-A-D-A-R, 8121 Hamilton Ave., Cincinnati OH 45231. Editor: Margaret Williams. For children 3rd-6th grade in Christian Sunday schools. Original artwork not returned after publication.
Cartoons: Buys 1 cartoon/month on animals, school and sports. Prefers to see finished cartoons. Reports in 6 weeks. Pays $10-15; on acceptance.
Illustrations: Uses 5 or more illustrations/issue. "Art that accompanies nature or handicraft articles may be purchased, but almost everything is assigned." Prefers to see samples of style. Samples returned

Freelance artist Robin Morris of Forest Hills, New York, was commissioned to do this cover of Radio City Music Hall by Cliff Sloan, creative director of Rave Communications, New York City. "The Radio City building is world reknowned for its art deco decor, and it was Robin's job to marry that decorative flair with a classy musical atmosphere," says Sloan. "The cover had to appeal to all musical tastes, as the Music Hall hosts a wide variety of performers. It was Robin's ability to create these 'generic' musical personalities, adaptable to a variety of scenarios, that attracted us."

by SASE. Provide tear sheet to be kept on file for future assignments. Reports in 6 weeks. Buys all rights on a work-for-hire basis. Cover: Pays $60, line drawing. Inside: Pays $35-40.

*RANGER RICK, 8925 Leesburg Pike, Vienna VA 22180. Design Director: Donna Miller. Emphasizes wildlife and conservational education for children 6-12 years old. Monthly. Circ. 700,000. Original artwork sometimes returned after publication. Sample copy and art guidelines available.
Illustrations: Buys 3-6 illustrations/issue from freelancers. Works on assignment only. "All assignments involve wildlife, some require ability to draw children." Send query letter with brochure and samples to be kept on file, except for slides that artist needs back. Prefers tear sheets as samples. Samples not filed are returned by SASE. Reports within 2 months. Negotiates rights purchased. Pays $150 minimum, b&w and $250 minimum, color, inside; on acceptance.

RAVE COMMUNICATIONS, 850 7th Ave., New York NY 10019. (212)977-7745. Creative Director: Cliff Sloan. Estab. 1982. Publishes program books: *Rock Bill, Soundcheck, Radio City Music Hall, Miller Time Concerts* and others. Emphasizes music, youth-oriented topics, fashion, film and trends for an audience 18-35 years old, clubgoers, trendsetters with musical interests. Monthly. Circ. 500,000. Returns original artwork after publication. Sample copy free for SASE with 35¢ postage.
Cartoons: Rarely buys cartoons. Prefers youth or musically oriented themes. Accepts single, double or multiple panel with gagline; b&w line drawings, b&w washes, color washes. Send query letter with samples of style to be kept on file. Write for appointment to show portfolio. Material not filed is returned by SASE. Reports back only if interested. Buys first rights. Negotiates payment; pays on publication.

Illustrations: Buys 2 illustrations/issue from freelancers. Themes and styles are geared specifically to articles. Also buys "musical" cover art. Works on assignment only. Send query letter with samples to be kept on file. Write for appointment to show portfolio. Accepts photostats, tear sheets, photocopies, slides or photographs as samples; do not send unsolicited original work. Samples not filed are returned by SASE. Reports back only if interested. Buys first rights. Negotiates payment; pays on publication.

*THE READING TEACHER, International Reading Association, 800 Barksdale Rd., Box 8139, Newark DE 19714-8139. (302)731-1600. Graphic Design Coordinator: Larry F. Husfelt. Journal (6¹⁄₈x9¹⁄₄" perfect bound), emphasizing reading instruction at the elementary level for school reading specialists, classroom teachers, administrators, etc. Monthly (October-May). Circ. 42,000. Original artwork not returned after publication. Sample copy available.
Cartoons: Buys 1 cartoon/issue from freelancers. Considers themes related to reading or school. Prefers single panel with or without gagline; b&w line drawings or b&w washes. Send query letter with roughs or finished cartoons; call for appointment to show portfolio. Material not filed is returned by SASE. Reports within 1 month. Buys one-time rights. Pays $20, b&w; on acceptance.
Illustrations: Buys 1 illustration (cover only)/issue from freelancers. Works on assignment only. Send query letter with samples to be kept on file; call for appointment to show portfolio. Accepts photostats, tear sheets, photocopies, slides, photographs, etc. as samples. Samples returned by SASE. Reports within 1 month. Negotiates rights purchased. Pays $300, b&w, cover; on acceptance.

RELIX MAGAZINE, Box 94, Brooklyn NY 11229. Manager: Toni A. Brown. Emphasizes music—rock, 60's groups, particularly the Grateful Dead for audience 16-39 years of age, 68% male, 32% female. Bimonthly. Circ. 15,000. Sample copy $2. Accepts previously published material. Original artwork not returned after publication. Sample copy for $2; art guidelines free for SASE.
Cartoons: Prefers music-related themes, especially "hippie humor." Prefers multipanel, with gagline; b&w line drawings. Send query letter with samples of style to be kept on file. Material not kept on file is returned by SASE. Reports only if interested. Buys all rights. Pay rate is open; pays on publication.
Illustrations: Uses 3-6 illustrations/issue. Prefers rock and roll themes. Send query letter with samples to be kept on file. Prefers photostats or photographs as samples. Samples not kept on file are returned by SASE. Does not report back. Buys all rights. Pays $150, color, cover; negotiates payment for b&w, inside; pays on publication.
Tips: "We seriously consider anything. We have a lot of opportunities open including t-shirts. We are very accessible."

REPUBLIC, East-West Network, Inc., 5900 Wilshire Blvd., Los Angeles CA 90036. (213)937-5810. Editor: Jerry Lazar. For airline passengers. Monthly. Original artwork not returned after publication. Sample copy $2 for SASE.
Illustrations: Works on assignment only. Query with resume. Reports in 1 month. Buys first rights. Pays $75 minimum, spot art; $350 average, full-page illustrations; and $600, full-color cover.

RESIDENT AND STAFF PHYSICIAN, 80 Shore Rd., Port Washington NY 11050. (516)883-6350. Executive Editor: Anne Mattarella. Emphasizes hospital medical practice from clinical, educational, economic and human standpoints. For hospital physicians, interns and residents. Monthly. Circ. 100,000.
Cartoons: Buys 3-4 cartoons/year. "We occasionally publish sophisticated cartoons in good taste dealing with medical themes." Interested in "inside" medical themes. Submit tear sheets and slides with query letter. SASE. Reports in 2 weeks. Buys all rights. Pays $25; on acceptance. Also buys spots; pays $10-50; on acceptance.
Illustrations: "We commission qualified freelance medical illustrators to do covers and inside material. Artists should send sample work."
Tips: "We like to look at previous work to give us an idea of the artist's style. Since our publication is clinical, we require highly qualified technical artists who are very familiar with medical illustration. We need material from the *doctor's* point of view *not* the patient's"

RESPIRATORY THERAPY, Brentwood Publishing Corp., 825 S. Barrington Ave., Los Angeles CA 90049. Publishers: Hal Spector and Martin Waldman. Art Director: Tom Medsger. Emphasizes technological, medical and professional news. For respiratory and cardiopulmonary therapists.
First Contact & Terms: Submit brochure/flyer to be kept on file for possible future assignment. Reports only when assignment is available. Buys all rights. Pays $60 and up, spot art; $400, full-color cover; on acceptance.

RESTAURANT BUSINESS MAGAZINE, 633 Third Ave., New York NY 10017. (212)986-4800. Art Director: Joan Dworkin. Emphasizes restaurants/hotels for restaurateurs. Monthly. Circ. 110,000.

Original artwork returned after publication. Art guidelines available.

Illustrations: Uses 10 illustrations/issue; buys 6-8/issue from freelancers. Prefers halftones, pencil or wash, and pen & ink line drawings. Works on assignment only. Send query letter with brochure, samples and tear sheets to be kept on file. Write for appointment to show portfolio. No agents. Do not send original work as samples. Reports only if interested. Negotiates rights purchased and payment. Pays within 60 days.

RESTAURANT HOSPITALITY, 1111 Chester Ave., Cleveland OH 44114. (216)696-7000. Associate Editor: David Farkas. Emphasizes the foodservice (restaurant) industry for owners, managers, chefs, etc. (100,000 restaurateurs nationwide). Monthly. Circ. 100,000. Accepts previously published material "if exclusive to foodservice trade press." Original artwork returned after publication. Sample copy $4.

Illustrations: "We want to build a file of freelance illustrators to whom we can assign projects." Works on assignment only. Send query letter with brochure, resume, business card, samples and tear sheets to be kept on file. Prefers photographs as samples, 5x7" or larger, but will accept photostats. Reports back to the artist. Pays $250-400, cover; $100-300, inside; on acceptance.

THE RETIRED OFFICER, 201 N. Washington St., Alexandria VA 22314. (703)549-2311. Art Director: M.L. Woychik. For retired officers of the seven uniformed services; concerns recent military, history, humor, holiday anecdotes, travel, human interest, second career opportunities and current affairs. Monthly. Circ. 350,000.

Illustrations: Buys illustrations on assigned themes. (Generally uses Washington DC area artists.) Query with resume and samples.

REVIEW, East-West Network Inc., 34 E. 51st St., New York NY 10022. (212)888-5900. Art Director: Nina Ovryn. "In-flight Eastern Airlines publication; features fiction and nonfiction articles on art, sports, travel, the media, business, self-improvement and health." Monthly. Simultaneous submissions and previously published work OK. Sample copy $2.

Illustrations: Buys 1-4 illustrations/issue on current events, sports, travel, the media and self-improvement. Call or query with portfolio. Buys first rights. Inside: Pays $450, color; $50-350, b&w; on publication.

THE REVIEW OF THE NEWS, 345 Concord Ave., Belmont MA 02178. (617)489-0605. Editor: Scott Stanley. "News magazine with a conservative and free market orientation for people interested in conservative oriented news in capsulated form." Weekly. Circ. 60,000. Free sample copy (mention *Artist's Market*).

Cartoons: Uses 3 + cartoons/issue, most by freelancers. Receives 1,000 submissions/week from freelancers. Interested in general humor for a conservative family audience. Format: single panel b&w line drawings with gagline. Sizes must be 2x2½ or 4½x2¼. Prefers finished cartoons. SASE. Reports in 8 weeks. Will send tear sheets. Buys all rights. Pays $25; on acceptance.

*RHODE ISLAND REVIEW, Box 3028, Wayland Square Station, Providence RI 02908. Contact: Art Director. "We publish original work by artists in any medium suitable for reproduction on a page." Audience is intelligent, non-academic Southern New Englanders. Quarterly. Circ. 1,000. Original artwork returned after publication. Sample copy $1 and SASE with 96¢ postage.

Cartoons: Buys up to 10 cartoons/issue from freelancers. Cartoons should be intelligent and funny. Considers any format; single or in series. "If it's good, we'll deal with its shape." Send query letter with samples of style, roughs or finished cartoons to be kept on file. Photocopies preferred at first. Material not filed is returned by SASE. Reports within 1 month. Buys first rights. Pays $10, b&w and color; on publication.

Illustrations: Buys approximately 20 illustrations/issue from freelancers. "We are looking for fine, substantial, finished 'art' for a bylined page of its own; illustration of written work, including fiction, and of 3-dimensional art such as sculputre or craft pieces; sketches, fillers, visual ideas; and 3D2D: flat 'patterns' for 3-D objects. Example: We're publishing aerodynamically sound paper airplanes. We're open to imaginative execution in this area." Send query letter with samples to be kept on file. "Good photocopies will give us a good idea if the work interests us." Samples not filed are returned by SASE. Reports within 1 month. Buys first rights. Pays $25, b&w, cover; $10, b&w, inside; on publication.

RISK MANAGEMENT, 205 E. 42nd St., New York NY 10017. (212)286-9292. Production Manager: Edith Reimers. Emphasizes the insurance trade for insurance buyers of *Fortune 500* companies. Monthly. Circ. 10,500. Original artwork returned after publication. Sample copy available.

Illustrations: Uses 3-4 illustrations/issue; buys 2-4 every issue from freelancers. Prefers line illustration or line with color styles; no humorous themes. Works on assignment only. Send samples and tear

sheets to be kept on file; call or write for appointment to show portfolio. Prefers printed pieces as samples; original work will not be kept on file after 1 year. Samples not kept on file are returned only if requested. Buys one-time rights. Pays $200-350, b&w and 4-color, inside; on acceptance.
Tips: When reviewing an artist's work, looks for "neatness, clean pieces and substance, or meaning, within the concept of the illustrations to determine the artist's ability to conceptualize. We have noticed a return to realism and nouveau in our field, and more freelancers feature this in their portfolios."

*RN MAGAZINE, 680 Kinderkamack Rd., Oradell NJ 07649. (201)262-3030. Readers are registered nurses. Monthly. Circ. 330,000. Sample copy $2.
Cartoons: "We are not currently buying cartoons but plan to in the future.
Illustrations: Uses 10 illustrations/issue; buys all from freelancers. Works on assignment only. Provide roughs to be kept on file for future assignments. Samples returned by SASE. Prefers b&w line drawings and washes for inside and color washes, oils, acrylics, etc. for cover. Arrange personal appointment to show portfolio to art director. Buys first World serial rights, reprints and promotional rights. Pays $50-300 for inside b&w, $300-1,000 for color cover and $200-500 for inside color; on publication.
Tips: "The art director sees very little need for outside freelance design help but is willing to accept new ideas and their execution by freelancers if the need arises. Freelance artists should contact the art administrator to schedule an appointment."

ROAD KING MAGAZINE, Box 250, Park Forest IL 60466. (312)481-9240. Editor: George Friend. Emphasizes services for truckers, news of the field, CB radio and fiction; leisure oriented. Readers are over-the-road truckers. Quarterly. Circ. 224,000.
Cartoons: Uses 4 cartoons/issue; buys all from freelancers. Receives 1-2 submissions/week from freelancers. Interested in over-the-road trucking experiences. Prefers single panel b&w line drawings with gagline. Send finished cartoons. SASE. Reports in 2 months. Buys first North American serial rights. Pays $25 for b&w; on acceptance.
Tips: "Stick to our subject matter. No matter how funny the cartoons are, we probably won't buy them unless they are about trucks and trucking."

ROAD RIDER, Box 6050, Mission Viejo CA 92690. Contact: Art Director. Emphasizes motorcycle touring for a primarily male audience. Monthly. Circ. 40,000. Accepts simultaneous submissions. Original artwork returned after publication for SASE. Sample copy $3; art guidelines free for SASE.
Cartoons: Uses 3 cartoons/issue. Prefers motorcycling themes. Prefers single panel with gagline; b&w line drawings. Send query letter with samples of style to be kept on file. Material not kept on file is returned by SASE. Reports within 6 weeks. Buys all rights. Pay varies; on publication.
Illustrations: Uses 2-3 illustrations/issue. Send query letter with samples to be kept on file. Accepts photostats, tearsheets, reprints or photographs (if mailed insured) as samples. Samples not kept on file are returned by SASE. Reports within 6 weeks. Buys all rights. Pay varies; on publication.
Tips: "Artists should submit work that shows they are familiar with reproduction process (printing needs). Present yourself as a business professional and be businesslike in your dealing with clients; i.e., using written agreements for price and deadlines is really a must nowadays."

RODALES NEW SHELTER, 33 E. Minor St., Emmaus PA 18049. (215)967-5171. Art Director: John Pepper. Emphasizes "do-it-yourself energy conservation, home design, repair and management for 30-40-year-old, college-educated males; homeowners, handymen." Published 9 times/year. Circ. 700,000. Receives 1-2 cartoons and 5 illustrations/week from freelance artists. Previously published material OK. Original artwork returned after publication "if requested." Free sample copy for SASE "and samples of artist's work"; art guidelines available for SASE.
Cartoons: Presently uses 1-2/issue—"we're very interested in more. We're open to all styles. We always have an eye open for energy-related cartoons." Prefers single or double panel. Send finished cartoons (or published cartoons as sample of style). Samples returned by SASE. Reports in 2-4 weeks. Buys all rights. Pays up to $40, b&w; on publication.
Illustrations: Uses 15-20 illustrations/issue; buys all from freelancers. Works on assignment only, "although we have used cold submissions in the past." Send business card, brochure, flyer, samples, and tear sheets—"anything to help us decide to use an artist"—to be kept on file for possible future assignments; call or write for appointment to show portfolio. Samples not kept on file are returned by SASE. Reports in 2-4 weeks. Buys all rights. Pays $15-200, inside b&w line drawings; $15-200, inside b&w washes; $50-300, inside color washes; "just prior to publication."
Tips: "Become familiar with the needs and style of publication. Have a unique, innovative style that works with the nature of the magazine."

ROOM OF ONE'S OWN, Box 46160, Station G, Vancouver, British Columbia V6R 4G5 Canada. Contact: Editor. Emphasizes feminist literature for general and academic women, and libraries. Quarterly. Circ. 1,200. Original artwork returned after publication. Sample copy $2.75; art guidelines free for SAE (nonresidents include IRC).

Illustrations: Uses 3-5 illustrations/issue; buys all from freelancers. Prefers good b&w line drawings. Send samples to be kept on file. Accepts photostats, photographs, slides or original work as samples. Samples not kept on file are returned by SAE (nonresidents include IRC). Reports within 1 month. Buys first rights. Pays $50, b&w, cover; $25, b&w, inside; on publication.

*ROSICRUCIAN DIGEST, Rosicrucian Order, AMORC, San Jose CA 95191. (408)287-9171, ext. 213. Editor/Art Director: Mr. Robin M. Thompson. Fraternal magazine featuring articles on science, philosophy, psychology, metaphysics, mysticism, and the arts for men and women of all ages—"inquiring minds seeking answers to some of life's big questions." Monthly. Circ. 70,000. Does not accept previously published material. Returns original artwork to the artist. Sample copy and art guidelines available.

Illustrations: Buys a maximum of 10/year. Send query letter with samples. Prefers photostats, tear sheets and photocopies as samples. Samples returned with SASE. Reports back within 30-60 days. Negotiable payment. Pays on acceptance.

THE ROTARIAN, 1600 Ridge Ave., Evanston IL 60201. Editor: Willmon L. White. Associate Editor: Jo Nugent. Art Director: P. Limbos. Emphasizes general interest and business and management articles. Service organization for business and professional men, their families, and other subscribers. Monthly. Sample copy and editorial fact sheet available. Also uses artists for cover illustration. Most illustrative work, apart from knockout designs that might be considered as covers, is assigned.

Cartoons: Buys 4-5 cartoons/issue. Interested in general themes with emphasis on international business. Avoid topics of sex, national origin, politics." Query. Reports in 2 weeks. Buys all rights. Pays $50 on acceptance.

Illustrations: Buys assigned themes. Most editorial illustrations are commissioned. Buys average 1 illustration/issue; 6 humorous and 2 cartoon-style illustrations/year. Send published samples of work. Reports within 10 working days. Buys all rights. Pays on acceptance.

Tips: "Develop a new boldness and ingenuity in design. More airbrush is being used. Artists should set up appointments with art director to show their portfolios. Preference given to area talent." Current trends include "the invasion of 'punk' style visuals. We use little of this design due to traditional readership and resistance to fads."

ROUGH NOTES, 1200 N. Meridian, Indianapolis IN 46204. Assistant Editor: Beth Dotson. Monthly.

Cartoons: Buys 2-3 cartoons/issue on property and casualty insurance, some life insurance and general humor. No risque material. Receives 30-40 cartoons/week from freelance artists. Submit art the first week of the month. SASE. Reports in 1 month. Buys all rights. Prefers 5x8 or 8x10 finished art. Pays $15, line drawings and halftones; on acceptance.

Tips: "Do not submit sexually discriminating materials. I have a tendency to disregard all of the material if I find any submissions of this type. Send several items for more variety in selection. We would prefer to deal only in finished art, not sketches."

*ROWING USA, Suite 980, 251 N. Illinois St., Indianapolis IN 46204. (317)237-2769. Editor: Kathryn Reith. Emphasizes rowing for U.S. Rowing Association members, both competitive and recreational rowers. Bimonthly. Circ. 12,000. Accepts previously published material. Original artwork returned after publication. Sample copy $3; art guidelines for SASE with 1 first class stamp.

Cartoons: Buys 1-2 cartoons/issue from freelancers. Considers anyting on rowing. Prefers single panel with gagline; b&w line drawings or b&w washes. Send query letter with samples of style to be kept on file. Material not filed is returned. Reports within 1 month. Buys one-time rights. Pays $50, b&w; on publication.

Illustrations: Buys 0-5 (usually 1-2) illustrations/issue from freelancers. Works on assignment only. Send query letter with samples to be kept on file. Prefers tear sheets or photographs as samples. Samples not filed are returned. Reports within 1 month. Buys one-time rights. Pays $125, b&w, cover; $50, b&w, inside; on publication.

*RUN, CW Communications/Peterborough, 80 Pine St., Peterborough NH 03458. Art Director: Glenn Suokko. Estab. 1984. Emphasizes computing for business and families who own and operate a Commodore computer. Monthly. Circ. 225,000. Accepts previously published material. Original artwork returned after publication. Sample copy and art guidelines available.

Illustrations: Buys 5 illustrations/issue from freelancers. Prefers exciting, creative themes or styles. Works on assignment only. Send query letter with brochure, resume, business card and samples to be kept on file. Prefers tear sheets, photographs, or promotional material as samples. Samples not filed are returned by SASE. Reports only if interested. Negotiates rights purchased. Pays $300-600, b&w; $500-1,000, color, cover; $300-600, b&w; $500-1,200, color, inside; on acceptance.

RUNNING TIMES, Suite 20, 14416 Jefferson Davis Hwy., Woodbridge VA 22191. (703)643-1740. Emphasizes distance running. Readers include road runners, cross country and adventure runners; people interested in fitness. Monthly. Sample copy $1.95.
Illustrations: Uses 3-5 illustrations/issue, all from freelancers. Format: b&w line drawings for inside, and color illustrations for inside and cover. Especially needs color illustrations for feature articles and small b&w drawings. Prefers to see finished art, portfolio or sample of style. SASE. Provide tear sheet to be kept on file for future assignments. Reports in 4 weeks. Buys all rights on a work-for-hire basis. Pays $35-200 for inside and $250 minimum for cover; on publication. Buys first North American serial rights.
Tips: "We need more art and would like to see more samples or portfolios!"

RX HOME CARE, Brentwood Publishing Corp., a Prentice-Hall Company, 825 S. Barrington Ave., Los Angeles CA 90049. Publisher: Martin Waldman. Art Director: Tom Medsger. Emphasizes technological, medical and professional news.
First Contact & Terms: Submit brochure/flyer to be kept on file for possible future assignment. Reports only when assignment is available. Buys all rights. Pays $60 and up, spot art; $400, full-color cover; on acceptance.

SACRAMENTO MAGAZINE, Box 2424, Sacramento CA 95811. (916)446-7548. Art Director: Chuck Donald. Emphasizes Sacramento city living for audience 25-54 years old, executives/professionals, married, middle-upper income. Monthly. Circ. 30,000. Accepts previously published material and simultaneous submissions. Sample copy free for SASE.
Illustrations: Uses 3-5 illustrations/issue. Send query letter with samples to be kept on file; appointment necessary to show portfolio. Accepts any type of samples which fairly represent artist's work. Reports only if interested. Negotiates rights purchased. Pays on acceptance.

SAIL, 34 Commercial Wharf, Boston MA 02110. (617)227-0888. Editor: Keith Taylor. Managing Editor: Patience Wales. Design Director: Elizabeth Pollock. For audience of serious-minded sailors. Special issues on cruising (bareboat, crewed boat, bluewater), boat shows, board sailing, America's Cup and more. Monthly. Circ. 179,000. Original artwork returned after publication. Free sample copy.
Illustrations: Uses 3 illustrations/issue; rarely buys from freelancers. Assigned sailing themes. Works on assignment only. Send resume and samples of style. SASE. Provide resume or letter of inquiry to be kept on file for future assignments. Reports in 4 weeks. Buys first North American serial rights. Pays $100-250/page, b&w; $200-400/page, color. Prefers to pay on publication.

SAILING, 125 E. Main St., Port Washington WI 53074. (414)284-3494. Editor: William F. Schanen III. Emphasizes all aspects of sailing (sailboats only). Monthly. Circ. 45,000. Original artwork returned after publication upon special request. Previously published work OK. Sample copy $2.50.
Illustrations: Uses very few illustrations/year. Interested in action sailing only. Works on assignment. Send resume, finished art, or samples of style. Samples returned by SASE, if requested. Provide letter of inquiry to be kept on file for future assignments. Reports in 2-3 weeks. Buys one-time rights.

THE ST. LOUIS JOURNALISM REVIEW, 8606 Olive Blvd., St. Louis MO 63132. (314)991-1699. Contact: Charles L. Klotzer. Features critiques of St. Louis media—print, broadcasting, TV, cable, advertising, public relations and the communication industry. Monthly. Circ. 12,000.
Cartoons: "We have never bought a cartoon, but will consider." Subject should pertain to the news media; preferably local. Query. SASE. Reports in 4-7 weeks. Pays on publication.
Illustrations: Query with samples. SASE. Reports in 4-6 weeks. Pays $15-25 each (negotiable) for b&w and color illustrations pertaining to the news media (preferably local); on publication.

SALES AND MARKETING MANAGEMENT, 633 3rd Ave., New York NY 10017. (212)986-4800. Art Director: Tom Loria. For sales managers. Biweekly. Circ. 50,000. Simultaneous submissions OK. Pays on acceptance.
Cartoons: Buys 36 cartoons/year. Interested in sales management and selling; single panel. Prefers art. SASE. Reports in 1 week. Buys all rights, but may reassign rights to artist after publication. Pays $30-45, b&w; on acceptance.
Illustrations: Buys 2 illustrations/issue. SASE. Reports in 1 week. Buys all rights, but may reassign rights to artist after publication. Pays $30-50, b&w spot line drawings; on acceptance.

SALON TALK, (formerly *The International Designs*), 100 Park Ave., New York NY 10017. (212)532-5588. Editor: Jody Byrne d'Honau. "Elegant publication with emphasis on hair and total beauty in a full service salon, for salon clients and salon professionals. bimonthly. Circ. 15,000. Original artwork returned after publication. Sample copy $7.50.

Illustrations: Uses 1 illustration/issue. Prefers beauty, hair, makeup themes. Send query letter with resume, business card, samples and tear sheets to be kept on file. Call for appointment to show portfolio. Samples not filed are returned by SASE only if requested. Reports only if interested. Buys one-time or all rights.

SALT LICK PRESS, 1804 E. 38½ St., Austin TX 78722. Editor/Publisher: James Haining. Published irregularly. Circ. 1,500. Previously published material and simultaneous submissions OK. Original artwork returned after publication. Sample copy $3.
Illustrations: Uses 12 illustrations/issue; buys 4 from freelancers. Receives 2 illustrations/week from freelance artists. Interested in a variety of themes. Send samples of style. Samples returned by SASE. Reports in 6 weeks. Buys first rights.

SALT WATER SPORTSMAN, 186 Lincoln St., Boston MA 02111. (617)426-4074. Editor-in-Chief/Art Director: Barry Gibson. Emphasizes resorts, areas, techniques, equipment and conservation. For saltwater fishermen, fishing equipment retailers and resort owners. Monthly. Circ. 116,000. Original artwork returned after publication. Free sample copy and artists' guidelines.
Illustrations: Uses 1 illustration/issue; buys from freelancer. Receives 3 submissions/week from freelancers. Interested in themes covering all phases of salt water sport fishing—mood, how-to, etc. Works on assignment only. Reports back on future assignment possibilities. Provide letter of inquiry or brochure to be kept on file for future assignments. Prefers to see finished art or photos of art. SASE. Reports in 4 weeks. Buys first North American serial rights. Cover: Pays $300 minimum, color. Inside: Buys b&w line drawings and washes and color washes; pays on acceptance.
Tips: "Let us see samples of work relevant to our topics/areas. New artists should strive for accuracy in portraying fish, equipment, etc."

SALVAGE SELLER, Suite 201, 6420 Zane Ave. N, Minneapolis MN 55429. (612)535-8383. Publisher: Ron Sauby. Emphasizes salvage. Monthly. Accepts previously published material. Returns original artwork after publication. Sample copy free for SASE; art guidelines available.
Cartoons: Themes, styles and format open. Send query letter with samples of style to be kept on file. Write or call for appointment to show portfolio. Material not filed is returned by SASE. Reports within 30 days. Negotiates rights purchased. Pays on acceptance.
Illustrations: Works on assignment only. Send query letter and samples to be kept on file. Write or call for appointment to show portfolio. Will review photostats, tear sheets, photocopies, slides or photographs. Samples not filed are returned by SASE. Reports within 30 days. Negotiates rights purchased. Pays on acceptance.

SAN FRANCISCO FOCUS MAGAZINE, (formerly *Focus Magazine*), KQED Inc., 500 8th St., San Francisco CA 94103. (415)553-2119. Art Director: Laura Lamar. The city magazine for the San Francisco Bay area including public television station program guide. Audience is 45-year-old average, male/female, professional-managerial, post-graduate, homeowner; average income $70-160,000. Monthly. Circ. 165,000. Sometimes accepts previously published material. Original artwork returned after publication.
Illustrations: Uses 3-6 illustrations/issue; buys 2-4 illustrations/issue from freelancers. Uses a variety of styles according to editorial content; top-level professional artists *only* assignments made on basis of individual style and proficiency. Send resume, business card and samples to be kept on file. No original work—only reproductions (prints, slides, tear sheets, photocopies, stats) as samples. Samples returned by SASE only if requested; prefers to keep on file. No "guidelines" sent. Reports only if interested. Please: no query—only letters. Send samples. Buys one-time rights. Pays $100-400 color, cover; $50-150, b&w and $150-500, color, inside. Pays on publication (30 days after receipt of invoice).
Tips: Do not call to follow up. "We'll call you if and when we have an assignment. We'll keep your work on file."

SAN FRANCISCO MAGAZINE, 950 Battery St., San Francisco CA 94111. (415)956-6262. Design Director: Jim Santore. Emphasizes general interest topics of local or national scope for San Francisco and Northern California Bay area residents. Monthly. Circ. 45,000.
Illustrations: Uses 8-10 spot illustrations, 3-4 illustrations for major pieces; buys all from freelancers. Theme and style depend on the article. Works on assignment only; reports when assignment is available. Send brochure, samples and tear sheets to be kept on file; call for appointment, submit portfolio. Samples not filed are returned by SASE. Buys one-time rights.

SAN JOSE STUDIES, San Jose State University, San Jose CA 95192. (408)277-2841. Editor: Fauneil J. Rinn. Emphasizes the arts, humanities, business, science, social science; scholarly. Published 3 times/year. Circ. 500. Original artwork returned after publication. Sample copy $3.50.

Cartoons: Number of cartoons/issue varies. Interested in "anything that would appeal to the active intellect." Format: single panel b&w line drawings. Prefers to see roughs. SASE. Reports in 2 weeks. Buys first North American serial rights. Pays in 2 copies of publication, plus entry in $100 annual contest.

Illustrations: Number of illustrations/issue varies. Format: b&w line drawings. Prefers to see roughs. SASE. Reports in 2 weeks. Buys first North American serial rights. Pays in 2 copies of publication, plus entry in $100 annual contest.

Tips: "We would be interested in cartoons, and humorous and cartoon-style illustrations especially if accompanied by some description of the artist's techniques, purpose, conception and development of the artwork."

THE SATURDAY EVENING POST, The Saturday Evening Post Society, 1100 Waterway Blvd., Indianapolis IN 46202. (317)636-8881. General interest, family-oriented magazine. Published 9 times/year. Circ. 600,000. Sample copy $1.

Cartoons: Cartoon Editor: Timothy Ehrgott. Buys 20-24 cartoons/issue; single panel with gaglines. Receives 100 batches of cartoons/week from freelance cartoonists. "We look for cartoons with neat line or tone art. The content should be in good taste, suitable for a general-interest, family magazine. It must not be offensive while remaining entertaining. We prefer that artists first send a SASE for guidelines and then review recent issues. Political or violent cartoons are not used." SASE. Reports in 3 weeks. Buys all rights. Pays $125, b&w line drawings and washes, no pre-screened art; on publication.

Illustrations: Consulting Art Director: Don Moldroski. Uses average of 3 illustrations/issue; buys 90% from freelancers. Buys all rights, "generally. All ideas, sketchwork and illustrative art are handled through commissions only and thereby controlled by art direction. Do not send original material (drawings, paintings, etc.) or 'facsimiles of' that you wish returned." Cannot assume any responsibility for loss or damage. "If you wish to show your artistic capabilities, please send nonreturnable, expendable/sampler material (slides, tear sheets, photocopies, etc.)."

SAVINGS INSTITUTIONS, 111 E. Wacker Dr., Chicago IL 60601. (312)644-3100. Art Director: George Glatter. Emphasizes the savings and loan business for people in savings and loan or related businesses. Monthly. Circ. 35,000. Accepts previously published material. Original artwork returned after publication. Sample copy available.

Illustrations: Uses 0-3 illustration/issue; some are humorous or cartoon-style illustrations; buys from freelancer. Works on assignment only. Send samples to be kept on file. Call for appointment to show portfolio. Samples not kept on file returned only if requested. Reports only if interested. Buys first rights, one-time rights, reprint rights or negotiates rights purchased. Negotiates payment. Pays on acceptance.

SCANDINAVIAN REVIEW, 127 E. 73rd St., New York NY 10021. Publisher/Editor: Patricia McFate. Associate Editor: Adrienne Gyongy. For people of Scandinavian descent or interested in contemporary Scandinavia. Quarterly. Circ. 6,000. Accepts previously published material. Original artwork returned after publication. Sample copy and art guidelines available.

Cartoons: Rarely uses cartoons. Should relate to contemporary Scandinavian life, politics, history, economics, culture, or literature. Prefers single panel without gagline; b&w line drawings, b&w or color washes. Send query letter with samples of style to be kept on file. Write for appointment to show portfolio. Material not filed is returned by SASE only if requested. Reports back only if interested. Buys one-time or reprint rights. Pays on publication.

Illustrations: Send query letter with samples to be kept on file; write for appointment to show portfolio. Accepts photostats, photocopies, slides or photographs as samples. Samples not filed are returned by SASE only if requested. Reports back only if interested. Buys one-time rights or reprint rights. Pays on publication.

*SCHOLASTIC INC., 730 Broadway, New York NY 10003. (212)505-3000. Editorial Design Director: Dale E. Moyer. Emphasizes educational classroom supplements dealing with almost all curriculum areas: reading, writing, science, math, social studies, art, computers, home economics for K-12; professional teaching magazine. Weekly, monthly and bimonthly. Circulation varies per publication. Original artwork returned after publication. Sample copy available.

Illustrations: Themes depend on editorial content. Works on assignment only. Send samples to be kept on file; call for appointment to show portfolio. Prefers tear sheets in portfolio. Samples not filed are returned by SASE. Reports only if interested. Buys one-time rights or negotiates rights purchased. Pays $250-300, b&w, and $400, color, cover; $100 minimum, b&w, and $250, color, inside; on acceptance.

SCIENCE AND CHILDREN, National Science Teachers Association, 1742 Connecticut Ave. NW, Washington DC 20009. (202)328-5800. Editor-in-Chief: Phyllis Marcuccio. For elementary and middle

school science teachers, educators, administrators and personnel. Published 8 times/year. Circ. 17,000. Original artwork not returned after publication. Free sample copy.
Cartoons: Uses 1 cartoon/issue; buys all from freelancers. Interested in science-technology and environment; multi-panel with gaglines. Prefers finished cartoons. SASE. Reports in 2 weeks. Buys all rights. Pays $15-25, b&w line drawings and washes; on publication.
Illustrations: Uses 10-15 illustrations/issue; buys all from freelancers. Interested in education and environment; light, stylized, realistic science illustrations (no stock illustrations). Works on assignment only. Samples returned by SASE. Provide resume, brochure, flyer or photocopy of work to be kept on file for future assignments. Prefers to see portfolio with samples of style. Reports in 2 weeks. Buys all rights on a work-for-hire basis. Cover: Pays $50-150, b&w line drawings, washes and color. Inside: Pays $10-100, b&w line drawings and washes; on publication.
Tips: "Looking for new talent. Realistic drawings of children important—scientific renderings secondary."

SCIENCE 86, 10th Floor, 1101 Vermont Ave., Washington DC 20005. (202)842-9581. Emphasizes science-oriented feature articles for a college-educated, lay audience. Published 10 times/year.
Cartoons: Uses 3-4 cartoons/issue; all by freelancers. Buys cartoons with science theme. Format: single b&w line drawings with or without gagline. Send originals to Lynn Crawford, cartoon editor. SASE. Reports in 6 weeks. Pays $300/cartoon; on acceptance.
Illustrations: Uses 15-20 illustrations/issue; all by freelancers. Selects freelancers from "listings, seeing work in other illustrations, reviewing portfolios and samples and through reps." Illustrations should be science related, contemporary themes. Illustrators "must have patience to research subject and offer several sketches." Query about sending portfolio, "if in town, give us a week's notice and we'll see you"; or send samples of style, "we love to receive a transparency or 35mm slide we can keep on file." Especially looks for "clean presentation, strong concepts and mastery of media. I purchase 4-color primarily, so it's important that full-color pieces are presented." SASE. Reports in 3-4 weeks. Pays $750 for full page inside color. Also uses artists gwn, give us a week's notice and we'll see you"; or send samples of style, "we love to receive a transparency or 35mm slide we can keep on file." Especially looks for "clean presentation, strong concepts and mastery of media. I purchase 4-color primarily, so it's important that full-color pieces are presented." SASE. Reports in 3-4 weeks. Pays $750 for full page inside color. Also uses artists on assignment for spot art for departments and possibly promotion. Pays $200 for spot art. Buys "one-time editorial use in the North American and Italian editions of *Science 86.*"

*SCIENCE NEWS, 1719 N St. NW, Washington DC 20036. (202)785-2255. Art Director: Wendy McCarren. Emphasizes all sciences for teachers, students and scientists. Weekly. Circ. 175,000. Accepts previously published material. Original artwork returned after publication. Sample copy free for SASE with 39¢ postage.
Illustrations: Buys 10 illustrations/year from freelancers. Prefers realistic style, scientific themes; uses some cartoon-style illustrations. Works on assignment only. Send query letter with samples to be kept on file. Prefers photostats or photocopies as samples. Samples returned by SASE. Reports only if interested. Buys one-time rights. Pays variable rates; on acceptance.
Tips: Uses some cartoons and cartoon-style illustrations.

SCREEN PRINTING MAGAZINE, 407 Gilbert Ave., Cincinnati OH 45202. (513)421-2050. Art Director: Ann Campbell. Emphasizes screen printing for screen printers, distributors and manufacturers of screen printing equipment and screen printed products. Monthly. Circ. 11,000. Accepts previously published material and simultaneous submissions in noncompeting magazines. Sometimes returns original artwork after publication. Sample copy available.
Cartoons: Call for appointment to show portfolio.
Illustrations: Uses 3 illustrations/issue; buys all from freelancers. Send query letter with samples and tear sheets. Call for appointment to show portfolio. Prefers photostats as samples. Samples returned by SASE if requested. Reports only if interested. Negotiates rights purchased. Payment is open. Pays on acceptance.
Tips: "Ask for sample copy of the magazine."

SEA, 8490 Sunset Blvd., Los Angeles CA 90069. (213)657-5100. Contact: Art Director. Emphasizes recreational boating for owners or users of recreational boats, both power and sail, primarily for cruising and general recreation; some interest in boating competition; regionally oriented to 13 Western states. Monthly. Circ. 50,000. Whether original artwork returned after publication depends upon terms of purchase. Free sample copy for SASE. Samples returned. Reports in 2 months. Negotiates rights purchased and payment. Pays on publication (negotiable).
Illustrations: Uses 6-8 illustrations/issue; buys 90% from freelancers. "I often look for a humorous il-

414 Artist's Market '86

lustration to lighten a technical article." Works on assignment only. Provide business card and tear sheets to be kept on file for possible future assignments. Send query letter. Samples returned. Reports in 6 weeks. Negotiates rights purchased and payment. Pays on publication (negotiable).

Tips: "We will accept students for portfolio review with an eye to obtaining quality art at a reasonable price. We will help start career for illustrators and hope that they will remain loyal to the publication which helped launch their career."

SECURITY MANAGEMENT, c/o ASIS, Suite 1200, 1655 N. Fort Myer Dr., Arlington VA 22209. (703)522-5800. Managing Editor: Pamela James Blumgart. For security managers who protect assets, personnel and information of organizations. Monthly. Circ. 23,000. Previously published and simultaneous submissions acceptable if not submitted to competitors. "Want exclusive in security market. Please state where else work has been submitted." Original artwork not returned after publication. Sample copy $3.

Cartoons: Uses 1 cartoon/issue, all from freelancers. Receives 10-20 submissions/week from freelancers. Interested in "management and protection—avoid emphasizing 'dumb-guard' aspect—our readers are fighting that image and don't appreciate it." Prefers to see roughs. SASE. Reports within 1 month. Negotiates rights purchased. Pays $10-15, b&w; on acceptance.

Illustrations: Uses 1-3 illustrations/issue; buys all from freelancers. Works on assignment only. Send query letter with brochure, business card and samples to be kept on file. Prefers photostats (if work is b&w) as samples. Reports in 1 month. Negotiates rights purchased. Pays $400-500, color, cover; $50-225, b&w and $100-400, color, inside; on publication.

Tips: There is an "increasing use of color in our operation. Artists should get a couple of copies and try to get to know the orientation of the content. We aren't interested in the 'clip art' look or sunset scenes or beautiful women. Send samples of illustrations for other professional/business publications."

SEEK, 8121 Hamilton, Cincinnati OH 45231. (513)931-4050, ext. 365. Emphasizes religion/faith. Readers are middle-aged adults who attend church and Bible classes. Quarterly in weekly issues. Circ. 45,000. Free sample copy and guidelines; SASE appreciated.

Cartoons: Editor: Leah Ann Crussell. Uses 1-2 cartoons/quarter. Buys "church or Bible themes—contemporary situations of applied Christianity." Formats: single panel b&w line drawings with gagline. Send finished cartoons. SASE. Reports in 1 week. Buys first North American serial rights. Pays $10-15 on acceptance.

Illustrations: Art Director: Frank Sutton. Uses 1-2 illustrations/issue. Uses cover & inside b&w line drawings and washes. Works on assignment only; needs vary with articles used. Arrange appointment to show portfolio. Reports in 1 week. Pays $60, cover or full page art; $40, inside pieces; on acceptance. Buys first North American serial rights.

Tips: "We use only 2-color work. The art needs to be attractive as well as realistic. I look for detail, shading and realism."

SELLING DIRECT, 6255 Barfield Rd., Atlanta GA 30328. (404)256-9800. Editor: Robert C. Rawls. Emphasizes selling as a profession and ways for sales persons to improve their techniques and their overall businesses. "For independent businessmen and women who sell door-to-door, by the party-plan method, through direct mail or phone solicitation; products or services are bought directly from manufacturers and sold by our readers." Monthly. Circ. 500,000. Free sample copy and artists' guidelines.

Cartoons: Uses 1-2 cartoons/issue, all from freelancers. Interested in current events, direct selling, salespeople not employed by retailers and self-employed entrepreneurs without employees; single panel. "Cartoons should illustrate the typical door-to-door or office-to-office salesperson, those who sell party-plan, or phone solicitors." SASE. Reports in 6-8 weeks. Buys all rights. Pays $15 minimum, b&w line drawings; on publication.

Tips: "Freelance cartoonists should submit their work along with complete mailing information and a Social Security number. I am interested in cartoons that present a positive aspect of direct selling, and not those whose main purpose is to downgrade salespeople or the industry."

THE SENSIBLE SOUND, 403 Darwin Dr., Snyder NY 14226. Editor: John A. Horan. Emphasizes audio equipment for hobbyists. Quarterly. Circ. 3,800. Accepts previously published material and simultaneous submissions. Original artwork returned after publication. Sample copy $2.

Cartoons: Uses 4 cartoons/year. Prefers single panel, with or without gagline; b&w line drawings. Send samples of style and roughs to be kept on file. Material not kept on file is returned by SASE. Reports within 30 days. Negotiates rights purchased; pay rate varies; on publication.

SERVICE BUSINESS, #345, 1916 Pike Pl., Seattle WA 98101. (206)622-4241. Publisher: Bill Griffin. Managing Editor: Martha M. Ireland. Technical, management and relations emphasis for self-employed cleaning and maintenance service contractors. Quarterly. Circ. 4,500. Prefers first publication material, simultaneous submissions OK. Original artwork returned after publication if requested by SASE. Sample copy $1.

Cartoons: Uses 1-2 cartoons/issue; buys all from freelancers. Must be relevant to magazine's readership. Prefers b&w line drawings.

Illustrations: Uses approximately 12 illustrations/issue including some humorous and cartoon-style illustrations; buys all from freelancers. Send query letters with samples. Samples returned by SASE. Buys first publication rights. Reports only if interested. Payment modest, on publication.

Tips: "Art and design trends include more interest in using graphics."

*SESAME STREET, 1 Lincoln Plaza, New·York NY 10023. (212)595-3456. Art Director: Paul Richer. Emphasizes education for preschool age children. Monthly. Circ. 600,000. Especially needs "people who can draw children well. Also, anyone who thinks they'd like to draw Muppets a lot."

Illustrations: Uses 12-15 illustrations/issue; all supplied by freelancers. Receives 0-4 portfolios from freelancers/week. Selection based on file samples supplied by artist. Artists are usually assigned two-page spreads. Format: any color medium for inside. Drop off portfolio on Wednesday and pick up later the same day. Reports immediately. Pays $250/page, $450/spread after close of issue. Buys one-time rights.

Tips: "Look through the magazine on the newsstand and decide if your work is compatible with the illustrators we use."

7 TRADE PUBLICATIONS, Suite 250, 1700 E. Dyer Rd., Santa Ana CA 92705. (714)250-8060. Vice President Operations: Mike Weldon. Emphasizes motorcycles, spa, waterbed and video for retailers. Monthly. Circ. 15,000. Accepts previously published material. Does not return original artwork after publication. Sample copy free for SASE.

Illustrations: Buys 1 illustration/issue from freelancers. Works on assignment only. Send query letter with resume and business card to be kept on file. Write for appointment to show portfolio. Reviews any type of samples. Reports back only if interested. Buys reprint rights. Payment varies; pays on acceptance.

*SEXTANT, 716 E St. SE, Washington DC 20003. Assistant Publisher: Sharon Conaway. Magazine emphasizing microcomputers made by Zenith Data Systems and the Heath Company. Readers all use Heath/Zenith microcomputers; many are technically sophisticated—30% are engineers/scientists and/or programmers, 15% military, some business users, large hobbyist contingent. Bimonthly. Circ. 15,000. Accepts previously published material. Returns original artwork after publication. Sample copy $3.50.

Cartoons: Buys 1/issue from freelancers. Considers single, double or multipanel with gagline; b&w line drawings. Send query letter with samples of style, roughs and finished cartoons to be kept on file. Material not filed is returned by request. Reports only if interested. Negotiates rights purchased. Pays $75, b&w; on publication.

Illustrations: Buys "very few illustrations up until now but might be interested in the future." Prefers computer industry-related themes. Send query letter with brochure, resume, business card and samples to be kept on file. Accepts any type sample. Samples not filed are returned by request. Reports back only if interested. Negotiates rights purchased. Pays on publication.

SHAPE MAGAZINE, 21100 Erwin St., Woodland Hills CA 91367. (818)884-6800. Creative Director: Nancy Steiny. Emphasizes women's health and fitness. Monthly. Circ. 750,000. Accepts previously published material.

Illustrations: Uses 6 illustrations/issue. Works on assignment only. Send query letter with brochure, samples and tear sheets to be kept on file. Accepts duplicates as samples; *no* originals. Does not report back. Negotiates rights purchased and pay rate. Pays on publication.

THE SHINGLE, 1339 Chestnut St., Philadelphia PA 19107. (215)686-5686. Managing Editor: Nancy L. Hebble. Law-related articles, opinion pieces, news features, book reviews, poetry and fiction for the Philadelphia Bar Association membership (9,100 members). Quarterly. Circ. 10,000. Sample copy free for SASE.

Illustrations: Uses 4 illustrations/issue. Prefers fine line drawings; themes vary with editorial content. Works on assignment only. Send query letter with brochure, resume, business card and samples to be kept on file. Prefers photostats as samples. Samples not kept on file are not returned. Reports only if interested. Buys first or one-time rights. Pay rate varies; pays on acceptance.

SHUTTLE SPINDLE & DYEPOT, 65 LaSalle Rd., West Hartford CT 06117. (203)233-5124. Art Director: Tracy McHugh. Emphasizes weaving and fiber arts for predominantly female weavers and craftspeople, hobbyists and professionals. Quarterly. Circ. 18,500. Accepts simultaneous submissions. Original artwork returned after publication. Sample copy $4.75; art guidelines free for SASE.

Illustrations: Uses 20-30 illustrations/issue; buys "very few" from freelancers. Prefers b&w line drawings. Works on assignment only. Send query letter with resume and samples to be kept on file; write for appointment to show portfolio. Prefers slides as samples. Reports within 6 weeks. Buys first American serial rights. Honorarium only; no payment; on publication. Credit line given.

SIERRA—THE SIERRA CLUB BULLETIN, 530 Bush St., San Francisco CA 94108. (415)981-8634. Art Director: Bill Prochnow. Emphasizes conservation and environmental politics for young adults on up who are well educated, activists, outdoor oriented and politically well informed with a dedication to conservation. Bimonthly. Circ. 310,000. SASE. Reports in 4 weeks.
Illustrations: Uses 1-2 illustrations/issue, all from freelancers. Interested in "pencil, pen/ink, etc.—should show people, usually in outdoor activities (hiking, skiing, etc.)." Works on assignment only. Provide business card, tear sheet and copies of illustrations to be kept on file for future assignments. Prefers to see resume, portfolio and samples of style. SASE if material is to be returned. Buys one-time rights. Pay varies; on publication.

SIGHTLINES, Suite 301, 45 John St., New York NY 10038. (212)227-5599. Publisher: Marilyn Levin. Editor-in-Chief: Judith Trojan. Emphasizes film and video for the non-theatrical film/video world, including librarians in university and public libraries, independent filmmakers, film teachers on the high school and college levels, film programmers in the community, universities, religious organizations and film curators in museums." Quarterly magazine of Educational Film Library Association, Inc. Circ. 3,000. Previously published material OK; simultaneous submissions "OK if not with competitor." Original artwork returned after publication. Sample copy $5 plus $1 shipping.
Cartoons: "We sometimes buy cartoons which deal with library and film/media issues that relate to educational and community use of film"; b&w line drawings. Send query letter with samples of style and resume. Samples returned by SASE. Buys one-time rights. Pays approximately $25 (but negotiable), b&w; on publication.

THE SINGLE PARENT, Suite 1008, 7910 Woodmont Ave., Bethesda MD 20814. (301)654-8850. Editor: Donna Duvall. Assistant Editor: Liz Bostick. Emphasizes family life in all aspects—raising children, psychology, divorce, remarriage, etc.—for all single parents and their children. Bimonthly. Circ. 210,000. Accepts simultaneous submissions and occasionally accepts previously published material. Original artwork returned after publication. Sample copy available.
Cartoons: Uses 1-2 cartoons/issue; buys all from freelancers. Prefers divorce, children, family life topics with single parenthood as the theme. Prefers cartoons with gag line; b&w line drawings, b&w washes. Send finished cartoons to be kept on file. Write or call for appointment to show portfolio. Material not kept on file returned by SASE. Reports within 6 weeks. Negotiates rights purchased. Pays $15, b&w; on publication.
Illustrations: Uses 5-6 illustrations/issue; buys all from freelancers. Works on assignment only for specific stories. Assignments based on artist's style. Send query letter with brochure, resume, samples to be kept on file. Write or call for appointment to show portfolio. Prefers photostats, photographs, tear sheets as samples. Samples returned by SASE if not kept on file. Reports within 6 weeks. Negotiates rights purchased. Pays $75, b&w, cover; $50-75, b&w, inside. Pays on publication.

*SKI, 380 Madison Ave., New York NY 10017. Editor: Richard Needham. Emphasizes instruction, resorts, equipment and personality profiles. For new and expert skiers. Published 8 times/year. Previously published work OK "if we're notified."
Cartoons: Especially needs cartoons of skiers with gagline. "Artist/cartoonist must remember he is reaching experienced skiers who enjoy 'subtle' humor." Mail art. SASE. Reports immediately. Buys first serial rights. Pays $50, b&w skiing themes; on publication.
Illustrations: Mail art. SASE. Reports immediately. Buys one-time rights. Pays $100-300, full-color art; on acceptance.

SKIING, 1 Park Ave., New York NY 10016. (212)503-3900. Art Director: Erin Kenny. Emphasizes skiing, ski areas, ski equipment, instruction for young adults and professionals; good incomes. Published 7 times a year, September-March. Circ. 445,000. Original artwork returned after publication. Sample copy free for SASE.
Cartoons: Uses 1 cartoon/issue. Prefers single panel with or without gagline; b&w line drawings or washes. Send query letter with samples of style to be kept on file. Write or call for appointment. Material returned by SASE if not kept on file. Reports only if interested. Buys first or one-time rights. Pays $35-50; on acceptance.
Illustrations: Uses 2 illustrations/issue on average. Works on assignment basis. Send query letter with samples to be kept on file. Call for appointment to show portfolio. Prefers photostats or photocopies as samples. Samples returned by SASE if not kept on file. Reports only if interested. Buys first or one-time rights. Pays $75-250, b&w, inside; on acceptance.

Tips: "Know the magazine. I find it very annoying when artists come in, never having looked at a copy of *Skiing.*"

SKY AND TELESCOPE, 49 Bay State Rd., Cambridge MA 02238. Editor: L.J. Robinson. Art Director: J. Kelly Beatty. Concerns astronomy, building telescopes and space exploration for enthusiasts and professionals. Monthly. Circ. 75,000. Buys one-time rights. Pays on publication.
Cartoons: Buys 4/year on astronomy, telescopes and space exploration; single panel preferred. Pays $25, b&w line drawings, washes and gray opaques. Query with samples.
Illustrations: Buys assigned themes. Query with previously published work. Pays $50-150.

THE SMALL POND MAGAZINE OF LITERATURE, Box 664, Stratford CT 06497. Emphasizes poetry and short prose. Readers are people who enjoy literature—primarily college educated. Published 3 times/year. Circ. 300. Sample copy $2.50; art guidelines for SASE.
Illustrations: Editor: Napoleon St. Cyr. Uses 1-3 illustrations/issue. Receives 50-75 illustrations/year. Uses "line drawings (inside and on cover) which generally relate to natural settings, but have used abstract work completely unrelated." Especially needs line drawings; "fewer wildlife drawings and more unrelated-to-wildlife material." Send finished art or photocopies. SASE. Reports in 2 weeks. Pays 2 copies of issue in which work appears on publication. Buys copyright in convention countries.
Tips: "Need cover art work, but inquire first or send for sample copy." Especially looks for "smooth clean lines, original movements, an overall impact. In other words, there are two grading systems, technical merit and artistic impression." A developing trend is toward "more use of graphics with a wider scope of artwork considered."

SOAP OPERA DIGEST, 254 W. 31st St., New York NY 10001. Art Director: Andrea Wagner. Emphasizes soap opera and prime-time drama synopses and news. Biweekly. Circ. 825,000. Accepts previously published material. Returns original artwork after publication upon request. Sample copy available.
Cartoons: Seeks humor on soaps, drama or TV. Accepts single or double panel with or without gagline; b&w line drawings, b&w washes. Send query letter with samples of style to be kept on file. Write for appointment to show portfolio. Material not filed is returned only if requested. Reports back only if interested. Pays $35, b&w; $75, color; on acceptance.
Illustrations: Buys 1 illustration/issue from freelancers. Prefers humor, cartoon characters or realistic portraits from a photo. Works on assignment only. Send query letter with samples to be kept on file. Write for appointment to show portfolio. Accepts tear sheets, photocopies, slides or photographs as samples. Samples not filed are returned only if requested. Reports back only if interested. Negotiates rights purchased. Pays $150 for b&w and $250 and higher for color, inside; on acceptance.

SOCIAL POLICY, 33 W. 42nd St., New York NY 10036. (212)840-7619. Managing Editor: Audrey Gartner. Emphasizes the human services—education, health, mental health, self-help, consumer education, neighborhood movement, employment. For social action leaders, academics, social welfare practitioners. Quarterly. Circ. 5,000. Accepts simultaneous submissions. Original artwork returned after publication. Sample copy $2.
Cartoons: Accepts b&w only, "with social consciousness." Sometimes uses humorous illustrations; often uses cartoon-style illustrations. Call or write for appointment to show portfolio. Reports only if interested. Buys one-time rights. Pays on publication.
Illustrations: Uses 6 illustrations/issue; buys all from freelancers. Accepts b&w only, "with social consciousness." Send query letter and tear sheets to be kept on file. Call or write for appointment to show portfolio. Reports only if interested. Buys one-time rights. Pays $100, cover; $25, b&w, inside. Pays on publication.
Tips: When reviewing an artist's work, looks for "sensitivity to the subject matter being illustrated."

SOLAR AGE MAGAZINE, Church Hill, Harrisville NH 03450. (603)827-3347. Art Director: Ed Bonoyer. Emphasizes "alternative energy (not just solar) for builders, homeowners, contractors and architects." Monthly. Circ. 60,000. Receives 2 cartoons and 2 illustrations/month from freelance artists. Previously published material and simultaneous submissions OK. Original artwork returned after publication. Sample copy $3.50.
Cartoons: Occasionally uses cartoons; buys all from freelancers. Interested in energy-related themes; single, double, or multi-panel with or without gagline, color and b&w washes, b&w line drawings. Send query letter with roughs and samples of style. Samples returned by SASE. Reports in 1 week. Buys all rights. Pays approximately $25, b&w or color; on publication.
Illustrations: Uses "numerous" illustrations/issue; buys most from freelancers. Interested in energy-related themes. Especially needs illustration for articles. "Based on samples of artist's work (photocopies) in my files, I'll call and commission a particular concept." Send query letter with resume or brochure

and samples of style to be kept on file. Samples returned by SASE if not kept on file. Reports in 1 week. Buys all rights. Negotiates pay; on acceptance.

SOLAR ENGINEERING & CONTRACTING, Box 3600, Troy MI 48007. (313)362-3700. Editor: Tim Fausch. Emphasizes solar energy for contractors, manufacturers, installers, architects, builders. Bimonthly. Circ. 16,000. Accepts previously published material. Returns original artwork after publication. Sample copy $2.50.
Cartoons: Prefers single panel with gagline; b&w line drawings. Send query letter with samples of style to be kept on file. Material not kept on file returned by SASE. Reports within 6 weeks. Buys first rights. Pays $50 for b&w; on acceptance.
Illustrations: Buys 2 illustrations/issue from freelancers. Send query letter with samples to be kept on file. Reports within 6 weeks. Buys first rights. Pays $250 for color, cover; $50 for b&w and $100 for color, inside.

SOLDIERS MAGAZINE, Cameron Station, Alexandria VA 22304-5050. (202)274-6671. Editor-in-Chief: Lt. Col. Charles G. Cavanaugh, Jr. Lighter Side Compiler: Mr. Steve Hara. Provides "timely and factual information on topics of interest to members of the Active Army, Army National Guard, Army Reserve and Department of Army civilian employees." Monthly. Circ. 207,000. Previously published material and simultaneous submissions OK. Samples available upon request.
Cartoons: Purchases approximately 60 cartoons/year. Should be single panel with gagline. Prefers military and general audience humor. Submit work; reports within 3 weeks. Buys all rights. Pays $25/cartoon on acceptance.
Tips: "We are actively seeking new ideas, fresh humor and looking for new talent—people who haven't been published before. We recommend a review of back issues before making submission. Issues available upon request. Remember that we are an inhouse publication—anti-Army humor, sexist or racist material is totally unacceptable."

SOLIDARITY MAGAZINE, Published by United Auto Workers, 8000 E. Jefferson, Detroit MI 48214. (313)926-5291. Editor: David Elsila. "1.5 million member trade union representing US and Canadian workers in auto, aerospace, agricultural-implement and other industries."
Needs: Works with 10-12 artists/year for illustrations. Uses artists for posters and magazine illustrations. Interested in graphic designs of publications, topical art for magazine covers with liberal-labor political slant. Especially needs illustrations for articles on unemployment, economy.
First Contact & Terms: Prefers Detroit area artists, but not essential. Query by mail, write with resume or samples. Looks for "ability to grasp publication's editorial slant" when reviewing artist's work. Provide resume, flyer and/or tear sheet samples to be kept on file for future assignments. Pays $75/small b&w spot illustration; up to $400 for color covers; $400+/designing small pamphlet.

*SOLO MAGAZINE, Box 1231, Sisters OR 97759. (503)549-0442. Assistant Editor: Ann Staatz. "Our purpose is to encourage, entertain, assist and challenge readers to be all God wants them to be." Audience is primarily Christian single adults (53% never married, 30% divorced), 71% are female; average reader has at least 3 years of college. 85% hold positions of responsibility in their church. Quarterly. Circ. 30,000. Accepts previously published material. Original artwork returned after publication. Sample copy $2 and magazine-size SASE.
Cartoons: Buys 2-3 cartoons/issue from freelancers. Prefers cartoons that relate to single adults and their lifestyle; single panel, with or without gagline; b&w line drawings or b&w washes. Send query letter with samples of style or finished cartoons to be kept on file. Material not filed is returned by SASE. Reports within 1 month. Buys first rights. Pays $15-35, b&w; on publication.
Illustrations: Buys 3-7 illustrations/issue from freelancers. "Usually illustrations are tailored to particular articles, so theme and style varies." Send query letter with samples to be kept on file; write or call for appointment to show portfolio. Prefers photocopies, slides, photographs, tear sheets or actual work as samples. Samples returned by SASE. Reports within 1 month. Buys first rights. Pays $25-90, 2-color, and $15-90, b&w, inside; on publication.

SOUTH CAROLINA WILDLIFE, Box 167, Columbia SC 29202. (803)758-0001. Editor: John Davis. Art Director: Linda Laffitte. Deals with wildlife, outdoor recreation, natural history and environmental concerns. Bimonthly. Circ. 65,000. Previously published work OK. Sample copy and guidelines available.
Illustrations: Uses 10-20 illustrations/issue. Interested in wildlife art; all media; b&w line drawings, washes, full-color illustrations. "Particular need for natural history illustrations of good quality. They must be technically accurate." Subject matter must be appropriate for South Carolina. Prefers to see finished art, portfolio, samples of style, slides, or transparencies. Provide resume, brochure, or flyer to be kept on file. SASE. Reports in 2-8 weeks. Acquires one-time rights. Does not buy art; accepts donations.

Tips: "We are interested in unique illustrations—something that would be impossible to photograph. Make sure proper research has been done and that the art is technically accurate."

SOUTH FLORIDA LIVING MAGAZINE, Bldg. 3, Suite 102, 700 W. Hillsboro Blvd., Deerfield Beach FL 33441. (305)428-5602. Managing Editor: Gene Olazabal. Emphasizes real estate (new developments) and is directed to newcomers to South Florida; homebuyers. Bimonthly. Circ. 80,000. Accepts previously published material. Does not return original artwork after publication. Sample copy available.
Cartoons: Send query letter with samples of style to be kept on file. Write for appointment to show portfolio. Material not filed is returned by SASE. Reports within 1 month. Buys first rights. Negotiates payment; pays on acceptance.
Illustrations: Buys "a few" illustrations/issue from freelancers. Works on assignment only. Send query letter with samples to be kept on file. Write for appointment to show portfolio. Prefers tear sheets or photographs as samples. Samples not filed are returned by SASE. Reports within 1 month. Buys first rights. Negotiates payment; pays on acceptance.

SOUTHERN ANGLER'S & HUNTER'S GUIDE, Box 2188, Hot Springs AR 71913. (501)623-8437. Editor: Don J. Fuelsch. Covers hunting and fishing in southern states. Circ. 125,000. Annual. SASE. Reports in 4 weeks. Pays on acceptance.
Cartoons: Buys 25/issue on fishing and hunting. Mail roughs or finished art.
Illustrations: Buys 300/issue on fish and game. Prefers pen and inks or scratchboards. Query with samples.

SOUTHERN GRAPHICS, 410 W. Verona St., Box 2028, Kissimmee FL 32742. (305)846-2800. Editor: George Meyer. Emphasizes news events and developments in the graphic arts industry. For commercial printing plant management in 14 southern states. Monthly. Circ. 10,000. Previously published work OK. Sample copy $1.25.
Cartoons: Buys 6 cartoons/year on printing industry; single panel with gagline. Mail finished art. SASE. Reports in 4 weeks. Negotiates payment.
Illustrations: Query with previously published work. Uses 4-color cover design. SASE. Reports in 4 weeks.

SOYBEAN DIGEST, 777 Craig Rd., Box 41309, St. Louis MO 63141. (314)432-1600. Editor: Gregg Hillyer. Concerns agricultural and ag-business, specifically soybean production and marketing. Audience: high-acreage soybean growers. Monthly, except combined issues in May/June, July/August and September/October. Circ. 200,000. Previously published work OK. Original artwork returned after publication. Sample copy $2.
Cartoons and Illustrations: Buys maximum 6 cartoons/year and 3 illustrations/year on agriculture, soybean production and marketing. Submit art or query. SASE. Reports in 2-3 weeks. Buys all rights, but may reassign rights to artist after publication.

*SPACE AND TIME, 4B, 138 W. 70th St., New York NY 10023-4432. Editor: Gordon Linzner. Emphasizes fantasy and science fiction stories. "Readers are sf/fantasy fans looking for an alternative to the newsstand magazines." Biannually. Circ. 450. Original artwork returned after publication. Sample copy $4.
Cartoons: Buys 1-2 cartoons/issue from freelancers. Considers sf/fantasy themes—any style. Prefers single panel with or without gagline; b&w line drawings. Send finished cartoons to be kept on file if accepted for publication; write for appointment to show portfolio. Material not filed is returned by SASE. Reports within 3 months. Buys first rights. Pays $2, b&w; on acceptance.
Illustrations: Buys 20-25 illustrations from freelancers. Assigns themes or styles illustrating specific stories. "We use all styles, but could use more representational material." Works on assignment only. Send query letter with samples. Prefers photocopies as samples. Samples not filed are returned by SASE. Reports within 3 months. Buys first rights. Pays $2, b&w, inside; on acceptance.

*SPANISH TODAY Magazine, Box 650909, Miami FL 33265. (305)386-5480. Executive Editor: Andres Rivero. Emphasizes Hispanic concerns and issues for Hispani-American professionals, students and teachers of Spanish language—general public. Bimonthly. Circ. 10,000. Sample copy $3; art guidelines available.
Cartoons: Buys 3 cartoons/issue from freelancers. Considers themes of Hispanic issues and concerns. Prefers single panel with gagline; b&w line drawings. Send query letter to be kept on file. No telephone calls; all business is done by mail only. Material not filed is returned by SASE only if requested. Reports within 6 weeks. Buys first rights. Pays negotiable rate, b&w; on acceptance.
Illustrations: Buys 10 illustrations/issue from freelancers. Prefers themes of Hispanic issues and con-

cerns. Send query letter with business card to be kept on file; write for appointment to show portfolio. Prefers tear sheets as samples. Reports within 6 weeks. Buys first rights. Pays negotiable rate, b&w, cover; on acceptance.

*SPECTRUM STORIES, Box 58367, Louisville KY 40258. Editor: Walter Gammons. Emphasizes short stories, poems of science fiction, fantasy, experimental and horror and suspense; interviews, essays for a mostly well-educated professional adult audience. Quarterly. Circ. 2,500-3,000. Accepts previously published art only. Original artwork returned after publication. Sample copy $5.45; art guidelines for SASE with 44¢ postage.
Cartoons: Buys 4 cartoons/issue from freelancers. Science fiction, science, high tech, writing, publishing (small press angle), fantasy and horror (no gore) themes. Prefers single panel with gagline; b&w line drawings. Send query letter with samples of style or finished cartoons to be kept on file. Material not filed is returned by SASE only if requested. Reports within 2 months. Buys first rights. Pays $5-15, b&w; on publication.
Illustrations: Buys 12 illustrations/issue from freelancers. Prefers science fiction, fantasy, horror and experimental themes. Send query letter with resume and samples to be kept on file. Prefers photostats, slides or photographs as samples. Samples not filed are returned by SASE only if requested. Reports within 2 months. Buys first rights. Pays $50-75, b&w and $75-100, color, cover; $10-25, b&w and $50, color, inside; on publication.

*SPORTS AFIELD MAGAZINE, 250 W. 55th St., New York NY 10019. (212)262-8839. Art Director: Gary Gretter. Magazine emphasizing outdoor activities—fishing, hunting and camping. Monthly. Circ. 600,000. Does not accept previously published material. Returns original artwork after publication.
Illustrations: Buys 2-3/issue. Works on assignment only. Send query letter with samples to be kept on file except for material not of interest. Call for appointment to show portfolio. Prefers slides as samples. Samples not filed are returned by SASE. Buys first rights or negotiates rights purchased. Pays $1,000 spread color.

*SPORTSCAPE, Suite 320, 1415 Beacon St., Brookline MA 02146. (617)277-3823. Art Director; Meg Birnbaum. Magazine, tabloid-size. Emphasizes recreational sports. Monthly. Circ. 70,000. Accepts previously published material. Returns original artwork after publication. Sample copy for SASE with $1.50 postage.
Illustrations: Buys 2/issue. Prefers humor and realism in black, white and grey washes. "Some esoteric only vaguely sports related." Works on assignment only. Send query letter with samples to be kept on file except for "totally inappropriate work." Write for appointment to show portfolio. Accepts any samples. Samples not filed are returned by SASE. Reports within 1 month. Buys one-time rights. Pays $500 for b&w or color, cover; $400 for full-page b&w, inside. Pays on publication.

STARWIND, Box 98, Ripley OH 45167. Contact: Editor. Emphasizes science fiction, fantasy and nonfiction of scientific and technological interest. Quarterly. Circ. 2,500. Sample copy $2.50; art guidelines for SASE.
Cartoons: Uses 5-8 cartoons/issue, buys all from freelancers. Interested in science fiction and fantasy subjects. Format: single and multi-panel b&w line drawings. Prefers finished cartoons. SASE. Reports in 6-8 weeks. Buys first North American serial rights. Pays on publication.
Illustrations: Uses 10-15 illustrations/issue. Sometimes uses humorous and cartoon-style illustrations depending on the type of work being published. Works on assignment only. Samples returned by SASE. Reports back on future assignment possibilities. Provide resume or brochure and samples of style to be kept on file for future assignments. Illustrates stories rather extensively (normally 8x11" and an interior illustration). Format: b&w line drawings (pen & ink and similar media). SASE. Reports in 6-8 weeks. Buys first North American rights. Pays for cover; on publication.
Tips: "We select artists on quality of workmanship and a dependable turnaround time. We also appreciate reasonable rates, as we have a limited budget. We encourage new artists to contact us. Artists are using dry transfer lettering, screens, etc. more to their advantage. This enables them to produce more professional, polished work. They also produce more camera-ready art. We prefer artwork to be camera-ready so we appreciate this trend."

STEREO REVIEW, 1 Park Ave., New York NY 10016. (212)503-4000. Art Director: Sue Llewellyn. Emphasizes stereo equipment, classical and popular music for music enthusiasts. Monthly. Circ. 575,000.
Illustrations: Uses about 6 illustrations/issue; 3 supplied by freelancers. Illustrators "must be local and fast. Our lead time is very short. We are always looking for new talent." Especially interested in artwork and charts to accompany articles on technical subjects. Format: b&w line drawings and color washes for

inside. Send samples of style and photocopies. SASE. Reports in 1 week or when assignment is needed. Payment on acceptance is negotiated. Buys one-time rights plus promotional use.
Tips: "Call for appointment around 20th of month to show portfolio."

STONE COUNTRY, Box 132, Menemsha MA 02552. Editor-in-Chief: Judith Neeld. Art Editor: Pat McCormick. For serious poets and poetry supporters. Published 2 times/year. Circ. 1,000. Previously published artwork OK. Sample copy $3.50; $2.50 for tear sheets and sample covers (postage included).
Illustrations: Uses 2 covers/year and 6-7 illustrations/issue. Receives 1 illustration/week from freelance artists. Must be camera-ready. Cover design can be 8½x5½ or wrap-around 8½x11; inside drawings no larger than 3x4. Interested in b&w drawings only, no washes or pencil shading; to achieve shading, use fine b&w lines. Any style or theme; size is important. "We are interested in abstract as well as representational work. Art students welcome." Good photocopies acceptable. SASE. Provide letter of inquiry, brochure, flyer or tear sheets to be kept on file for future assignments. Reports in 6-8 weeks. Buys first North American serial rights. Cover: Pays $15, b&w; on publication. Inside: Pays 1 contributor's copy, b&w.
Tips: "It is essential to read a copy of the magazine before submitting. Please send all work in sizes shown in listing."

STONE IN AMERICA, 6902 N. High St., Worthington OH 43085. (614)885-2713. Managing Editor: Robert Moon. Journal of the American Monument Association; deals with production, marketing and sales of memorial stones. Circ. 2,600. Monthly. Reports in 4 weeks. Buys first rights. Pays on acceptance. Free sample copy and artist's guidelines.

*THE STUDENT**, 127 9th Ave. N., Nashville TN 37234. (615)251-4580. Photo Librarian: Dot Garner. Magazine emphasizing all facets of college life. Monthly. Circ. 22,000. Accepts previously published material. Returns original artwork after publication. Art guidelines available.
Cartoons: Buys 3/issue. Prefers anything to do with college life. Prefers single panel with gagline; b&w line drawings. Send samples of style. Call for appointment to show portfolio. Material not filed returned by SASE. Reports within 1 month. Buys one-time rights. Pays $15-20, b&w; on acceptance.
Illustrations: Buys 4/issue. Prefers mostly realistic styles with some caricatures. Works on assignment only. Send samples to be kept on file. Call for appointment to show portfolio. Prefers photocopies as samples. Samples not filed are returned. Reports within 1 month. Buys all rights. Pays $125, b&w, cover; and $60-120, b&w, inside; on acceptance.

SUPERMARKET BUSINESS, Suite 707, 25 W. 43rd St., New York NY 10036. (212)354-5169. Editor: Ken Partch. Concerns merchandising methods, industry trends and issues, and surveys of the supermarket industry. Monthly. Circ. 80,000.
Cartoons: "Cartoons are almost never used unless they express a specific idea." Query with samples. SASE. Reports in 1 month. Pays $35 minimum, gray opaques, b&w line drawings and washes; on acceptance.
Illustrations: Buys 12-15/year, usually after working with artist to illustrate a specific story. Query with resume and samples or arrange interview to show portfolio. SASE. Reports in 1 month. Inside: Pays $50 minimum, gray opaques, b&w line drawings and washes; on acceptance.

*SURFER MAGAZINE**, Box 1028, Dana Point CA 92629. Art Director: Jeff Girard. Emphasizes surfing: the sport, the lifestyle. Monthly. Circ. 100,000. Accepts previously published material. Original artwork returned after publication. Free art guidelines.
Cartoons: Buys 1 cartoon/issue from freelancers. Considers surfing and surf lifestyle themes. Reviews all formats. Send query letter with samples of style to be kept on file; write for appointment to show portfolio. Material not filed is not returned. Reports only if interested. Buys one-time rights. Pays $100/page, b&w; $350/page, color; on publication.
Illustrations: Buys 3 illustrations/issue from freelancers. Prefers surfing and surf lifestyle themes; hand lettering or editorial illustrations. Works primarily on assignment. Send query letter with brochure, resume, business card and samples to be kept on file. Prefers tear sheets or 35mm slides as samples for color, photocopies for b&w. "We do not guarantee return of unsolicited material." Samples not filed are not returned. Reports only if intersted. Buys one-time rights. Pays $100/page, b&w, and $350/page, color, inside; on publication.
Tips: "We are doing more feature-type articles, so we may be buying a few more illustrations/year."

*TEACHING AND COMPUTERS, SCHOLASTIC, INC.**, 730 Broadway, New York NY 10003. Art Editor: Shelley Laroche. Emphasizes teaching K-8th grade with computers for teachers and students. Monthly. Circ. 65,000. Accepts previously published material. Original artwork returned after publication. Sample copy and art guidelines available.

Cartoons: Buys 4 cartoons/issue from freelancers. Themes, style and format open. Send query letter with samples of styles to be kept on file; write for appointment to show portfolio or drop off portfolio. Material not filed is returned only if requested. Reports only if interested. Buys first rights or one-time rights depending on job. Payment open; pays on acceptance.

Illustrations: Buys 10-12 illustrations/issue from freelancers. Works on assignment only. Send query letter with brochure, resume, business card and samples to be kept on file; write for appointment to show portfolio. Prefers tear sheets or photographs as samples. Samples not filed are returned only if requested. Reports only if interested. Buys one-time rights. Payment open, b&w and color, inside; pays on acceptance.

TECHNOLOGY REVIEW, Massachusetts Institute of Technology, Cambridge MA 02139. (617)253-8255. Design Director: Nancy L. Cahners. Emphasizes technology and its implications. Published 8 times/year. Circ. 70,000. Accepts previously published material and simultaneous submissions. Original artwork returned after publication. Sample copy $3; art guidelines available.

Illustrations: Uses 10 + illustrations/issue; buys all from freelancers. Works on assignment only. Send query letter with brochure, resume, business card, samples and tear sheets to be kept on file; call or write for appointment to show portfolio. Prefers tear sheets or facsimile as samples. Samples not kept on file are returned by SASE. Reports only if interested. Buys one-time rights. Pays on publication.

'TEEN, Petersen Publishing Co., 8490 Sunset Blvd., Los Angeles CA 90069. (213)657-5100. Art Director: Laurel Watson. Deals with self-development for girls 12-19. Circ. 1,000,000.

Illustrations: Buys 1-4 illustrations/issue for fiction, fashion and beauty sections. Works mostly on assignment basis. Prefers resume and photocopies. "I request photocopies of work for artists from out-of-town, and I look at portfolios of area artists or most who call and make an appointment." SASE. Reports in 4-6 weeks. Buys all rights. Inside: Pays $25 minimum, b&w line drawings, washes, gray opaques and color; on acceptance.

Tips: "Youth today are more involved and the keyword is *active*. Art and photography for our magazine have more movement than in recent years. Keep the young, junior look. We're appealing to an audience that is bright, young and active."

*TELESCOPE, 15201 Wheeler Ln., Sparks MD 21152. (301)771-4544. Editor: Julia Wendell. "A journal of literature and thought for writers, educators and readers of literature." Triannually. Circ. 750. Original artwork returned after publication. Sample copy $2.

Illustrations: Buys 2 illustrations/issue from freelancers. Theme and style are flexible. Send query letter with resume and samples to be kept on file, except for specific request for return by SASE. Prefers tear sheets or photocopies as samples. Reports within 2 months. Buys first rights. Pays negotiable rate, 4-color or b&w, cover and inside; on acceptance.

TENNIS, 495 Westport Ave., Box 5350, Norwalk CT 06856. (203)847-5811. Contact: Art Director. For young, affluent tennis players. Monthly. Circ. 500,000.

Cartoons: Uses 3 cartoons/issue; buys all from freelancers. Receives 6 submissions/week from freelancers on tennis. Prefers finished cartoons, single panel. Reports in 2 weeks. Pays $50 minimum, line drawings.

Illustrations: Uses 10 illustrations/issue; buys 8/issue from freelancers. Works on assignment only. Provide brochure to be kept on file for future assignments. Buys all rights on a work-for-hire basis.

TEXAS ARCHITECT, 1400 Norwood Tower, Austin TX 78701. Associate Editor: Ray Ydoyaga. Emphasizes architecture for architects, urban planners, developers, government officials, libraries. Bimonthly. Circ. 10,000. Returns original artwork after publication. Sample copy $3 plus 50¢ postage.

Illustrations: Works on assignment only. Send query letter with samples to be kept on file. Prefers photostats as samples. Samples not filed are returned. Reports within 2 weeks. Buys first rights. Pays on publication.

TEXAS FOOD & SERVICE NEWS, Box 1429, Austin TX 78767. (512)444-6543. Editor: Kim Goodwin. "As the official trade publication of the Texas Restaurant Association, we are interested in materials which deal with the problems faced by restaurant owners and operators primarily in Texas; some members are managers of clubs, bars and hotels." Published 10 times/year. Circ. 6,000. Simultaneous submissions OK. Original artwork returned after publication. Free sample copy and art guidelines for SASE.

Cartoons: Interested in "cartoons that deal with the problems of restaurant owners or employees. We are not interested in cliched fly-in-soup jokes about food or other digs at restaurants. Humor should be from the point of operators and employees. Understanding of food service is helpful." Prefers single, double or multipanel with or without gagline, b&w line drawings, b&w washes. Send finished cartoons.

Samples returned. Reports in 3 weeks. Negotiates rights purchased. Pays $20, b&w; on acceptance.
Illustrations: "We are not set in style, as long as art is high quality black-and-white or color. However, we would like to see a variety of art styles, including airbrush, watercolor, pastel and pen & ink. We are looking for versatile artists who can illustrate articles about the food service industry in Texas, particularly as it pertains to management. Topics: financing, employee relations, computers, food, decor, etc." Works on assignment only. Send query letter with samples of style; call for appointment. Provide resume, samples and tear sheets to be kept on file for possible future assignments. Samples not kept on file are returned. Reports in 3 weeks. Negotiates rights purchased. Pays $25-50, inside b&w line drawings; $25-50, inside b&w washes; $40-60, cover color washes; $30-50, inside color washes; on acceptance.

THE TEXAS OBSERVER, 600 W. 7th, Austin TX 78701. (512)477-0746. Art Director: Alicia Daniel. Emphasizes Texas political, social and literary topics. Biweekly. Circ. 12,000. Accepts previously published material. Returns original artwork after publication. Sample copy free for SASE with 39¢ postage; art guidelines free for SASE with 22¢ postage.
Cartoons: Buys 2 cartoons/issue from freelancers. Prefers current political and social issues as themes. Considers single or double panel with or without gagline, b&w line drawings, b&w washes. Send samples of style to be kept on file. Write or call for appointment to show portfolio. Material not filed is returned by SASE. Reports within 1 month. Buys one-time rights. Pays $10-50 for b&w; on publication.
Illustrations: Buys 2 illustrations/issue from freelancers. "We only print black and white, so pen & ink is best, washes are fine." Send samples to be kept on file. Write or call for appointment to show portfolio. Accepts photostats, tear sheets, photocopies, slides or photographs as samples. Samples not filed are returned by SASE. Reports within 1 month. Buys one-time rights. Pays $35 for b&w cover; $20, inside; on publication.

*THRUST—Science Fiction in Review, 8217 Langport Terrace, Gaithersburg MD 20877. Publisher/Editor: D. Douglas Fratz. Emphasizes science fiction and fantasy literature for highly knowledgeable science fiction professionals and well-read fans. Biannually. Circ. 1,500. Accepts previously published material. Returns original artwork after pubilcation. Sample copy $2.50. Art guidelines free for SASE with 22¢ postage.
Cartoons: Buys 3-4/issue from freelance artists. Themes must be related to science fiction or fantasy. Prefers single panel; b&w line drawings. Send query letter with samples of style to be kept on file unless SASE included. Reports within 4 weeks. Buys one-time rights. Pays $10/page, b&w; on publication.
Illustrations: Buys 8-12/issue from freelance artists. Science fiction or fantasy themes only. Send query letter with samples to be kept on file unless SASE included. Accepts any style. Samples not filed are returned by SASE. Reports within 4 weeks. Buys one-time rights. Pays $25, b&w, cover; and $10/page, b&w, inside; on publication.

TIC, Box 407, North Chatham NY 12132. Editor: Joseph Strack. For dentists.
Cartoons: "Remember, it's for dentists, not patients—so no pain or open wide cliche gags, please." Reports in 10 days. Buys exclusive dental publication rights; will release reprint rights. Pays $25 for washes, pen and inks and line drawings; on acceptance.

TODAY'S CHRISTIAN PARENT, 8121 Hamilton Ave., Cincinnati OH 45231. Editor: Mildred Mast. Emphasizes the pleasures and problems of parenting from a Christian perspective. Quarterly. Circ. 30,000. No simultaneous submissions. Sample copy available for SASE, 7x9 or larger.
Cartoons: Uses 1 cartoon/issue; from freelancers. Interested in family and seasonal themes. Prefers to see finished cartoons. SASE. Buys all rights on a work-for-hire basis. Negotiates pay; pays on acceptance.
Illustrations: Uses 5-6 illustrations/issue, mostly on assignment, some from freelancers. Interested in "various aspects of family life." Especially needs family activities, including older children and adults. Prefers to see finished art and samples of style, b&w line, wash and halftone. Enclose SASE for return of pieces. Provide brochure and tear sheets to be kept on file for future assignment. Buys all rights on a work-for-hire basis. Negotiates pay; pays on acceptance.

TODAY'S POLICEMAN, Box 594, Kansas City MO 64141. (816)221-7075. Contact: Editor. For persons employed in and interested in police services. Semiannualy. Circ. 10,000.
Cartoons: Buys 6 cartoons/issue dealing with law enforcement and politics. Send finished art. SASE. Pays $2.50 for b&w.

TOURIST ATTRACTIONS AND PARKS, Suite 226, 401 N. Broad St., Philadelphia PA 19108. (215)925-9744. President: Scott Borowsky. Deals with arenas, attractions, fairgrounds, stadiums, concerts, theme and amusement parks. Published 6 times/year. Circ. 20,000. Also uses freelance artists for cover, layout and paste-up.

Illustrations: Buys 6/issue. Query with resume and samples. SASE. Buys all rights. Cover: Pays $50 minimum, gray opaques; on publication. Inside: Buys gray opaques.

TOW-AGE, Box M, Franklin MA 02038. Contact: J. Kruza. For readers who run their own tow service business. Circ. 15,000. Published every 6 weeks.
Cartoons: Pays $12.50 average/cartoon.
Illustrations: $15-60, b&w illustrations preferably in line technique on assigned subjects or themes. Write for lists. Send copies of style. SASE.

TOWN & COUNTRY, 1700 Broadway, New York NY 10019. (212)903-5000. Editor-in-Chief: Frank Zachary. Managing Editor: Jean Cook Barkhorn. Art Director: Melissa Tardiff. For high-income, well-educated adults interested in sophisticated travel, fashion, food, beauty and society. Monthly. Circ. 400,000 + .
Cartoons: Occasionally uses cartoons. Works on assignment only. Buys one-time reproduction rights. Pays on acceptance.
Illustrations: Occasionally uses illustrations. Works on assignment only. Provide business card, flyer and tear sheet to be kept on file for future assignment. Buys first North American serial rights. Pays $100-150 minimum/page; on acceptance. Original artwork returned after publication.

TRADITION, 106 Navajo, Council Bluffs IA 51501. Editor-in-Chief/Art Director: Robert Everhart. "For players and listeners of traditional and country music. We are a small, nonprofit publication and will use whatever is sent to us. A first time gratis use is the best way to establish communication." Monthly. Circ. 2,000. Simultaneous submissions and previously published work OK. Buys one-time rights. Free sample copy.
Cartoons: Buys 1/issue on country music; single panel with gagline. Receives 10-15 cartoons/week from freelance artists. Mail roughs. Pays $5-15, b&w line drawings; on publication.
Illustrations: Buys 1/issue on country music. Query with resume and samples. SASE. Cover: Pays $5-15, b&w line drawings. Inside: Pays $5-15, b&w line drawings; on publication. Reports in 4 weeks.
Tips: "We'd like to see an emphasis on traditional country music."

TRAINING: THE MAGAZINE OF HUMAN RESOURCES DEVELOPMENT, 731 Hennepin Ave., Minneapolis MN 55403. (612)333-0471. Editor: Jack Gordon. Emphasizes "training in business and industry, both theory and practice, for training specialists and managers, personnel directors, sales and marketing managers, general managers, etc." Monthly. Circ. 49,000. Especially needs cartoons about adult education on the job. Original artwork returned after publication "on request." Sample copy $3 plus $1 postage.
Cartoons: Uses 3-8 cartoons/issue; buys 3-6 from freelancers. Prefers a finished illustration style rather than a loose, cartoon style. Considers double panel without gagline; b&w line drawings. Send roughs or finished cartoons. Samples not filed are returned by SASE only if requested. Reports in 4 weeks. Buys reprint rights. Pays $20, b&w; on acceptance.
Illustrations: Buys 2 illustrations/issue from freelancers. Send query letter with samples to be kept on file. Write for appointment to show portfolio, "but we prefer to see samples through the mail." Accepts photostats as samples. Samples not filed are returned only if requested and only by SASE. Reports within 1 month. Buys reprint rights. Pays $250 and up for color cover; $20 and up for b&w inside; on acceptance.

TRANSAMERICA, Transamerica Corp., 600 Montgomery St., San Francisco CA 94111. (415)983-4295. Editor: Beth Quartarolo. For employees. Quarterly. Circ. 42,000. SASE. Previously published work OK. Pays on acceptance.
Illustrations: Buys 3-4/year on assigned themes. Cover: Uses color illustrations. Query with previously published work or arrange interview to show portfolio. Negotiates pay.
Tips: "When trying to sell your work, give some general rates. I need some idea of what the artist is going to charge."

TRANSITIONS GUIDE TO TRAVEL/WORK/ STUDY ABROAD, (formerly *Travel & Study Abroad*), 18 Hulst Rd., Box 344, Amherst MA 01004. Editor: Clayton A. Hubbs. Emphasizes educational low-budget and special interest overseas travel for those who travel to learn. Quarterly. Circ. 13,000. Original artwork returned after publication. Sample copy $3.50; art guidelines for SASE.
Illustrations: Uses 6 illustrations/issue; buys 4 from freelancers. Receives 1 illustration/week from freelance artists. Especially needs illustrations of American travelers in overseas settings; work, travel and study around the world. Works on assignment only. Send roughs to be kept on file. Samples not kept on file are returned by SASE. Reports in 4 weeks. Buys one-time rights. Pays $25-50, cover b&w line drawings; $30-50, cover b&w washes; on publication.

Tips: The trend is toward "more and more interest in budget travel and travel which involves interaction with people in the host country, with a formal or informal educational component. We usually commission graphics to fit specific features. Inclusion of article with graphics vastly increases likelihood of acceptance. Artists should study the publication and determine its needs."

TRAVEL & LEISURE, 1120 6th Ave., New York NY 10036. (212)382-5600. Design/Art Director: Adrian Taylor. Associate Art Directors: Ken Kleppert and Joan Ferrell. Emphasizes travel, resorts, dining and entertainment. Monthly. Circ. 925,000. Original artwork returned after publication. Art guidelines for SASE.
Cartoons: Rarely uses cartoons. Interested in travel or leisure related themes. Format: b&w line drawings and b&w and color washes without gaglines. Prefers to see roughs. SASE. Reports in 1 week. Buys first North American serial rights. Pays $200-800, b&w; on publication.
Illustrations: Uses 1-15 illustrations/issue, all from freelancers. Interested in travel and leisure related themes. "Illustrators are selected by excellence and relevance to the subject." Works on assignment only. Provide business card to be kept on file for future assignment; samples returned by SASE. Reports in 1 week. Buys first North American serial rights. Pays a minimum of $150 inside b&w and $800-1,500 maximum, inside color; on acceptance.

TRI-AD TRUCKING, Suite 201, 6420 Zane Ave. N, Minneapolis MN 55429. (612)535-8383. Publisher: Ron Sauby. Emphasizes trucks. Monthly. Accepts previously published material. Returns original artwork after publication. Sample copy free for SASE; art guidelines available.
Cartoons: Themes, styles and format open. Send query letter with samples of style to be kept on file. Write or call for appointment to show portfolio. Material not filed is returned by SASE. Reports within 30 days. Negotiates rights purchased. Pays on acceptance.
Illustrations: Works on assignment basis only. Send query letter and samples to be kept on file. Write or call for appointment to show portfolio. Will review photostats, tear sheets, photocopies, slides or photographs. Samples not filed are returned by SASE. Reports within 30 days. Negotiates rights purchased. Pays on acceptance.

TRIQUARTERLY, Northwestern University, 1735 Benson Ave., Evanston IL 60201. (312)491-3490. Editor: Reginald Gibbons. Design Director: Gini Kondziolka. Emphasizes "serious contemporary fiction primarily—subject matter varies. Readers are well-read, well-educated and interested in new trends and directions in art, writing, photography, illustration—the arts in general." Published 3 times/year. Circ. 5,000. Original artwork usually returned after publication—"negotiated with the artist." Sample copy $3.
Illustrations: Occasionally uses illustrations from freelancers. "Themes and styles vary according to editorial focus of issue." Works on assignment only. Reports in 6-8 weeks. Buys one-time rights. "Fee negotiated on a per issue basis with artist." Pays on "acceptance of artwork and approval of bill, then it's submitted for payment to Northwestern University."

*TROPIC MAGAZINE, The Miami Herald, 1 Herald Plaza, Miami FL 33101. (305)350-2036. Art Director: Philip Brooker. Emphasizes general (local) interests for Sunday newspaper magazine readers. Weekly. Circ. 55,000. Original artwork returned after publication. Sample copy free with SASE; art guidelines available.
Illustrations: Buys 0-2 illustrations/issue from freelancers. Works on assignment only. Send query letter to be kept on file; call for appointment to show portfolio. Prefers slides as samples. Reports within 2 weeks. Pays $300, b&w and $400-500, color, cover; $75-250, b&w and $300, color, inside; on acceptance.

TRUE WEST/Frontier Times, Box 2107, Stillwater OK 74076. Editor: John Joerschke. Emphasizes American western history from 1830 to 1910 for a primarily rural and suburban audience, middle-age and older, interested in Old West history, horses, cowboys, art, clothing, and all things western. Monthly. Circ. 90,000. Accepts previously published material and considers some simultaneous submissions. Original artwork returned after publication. Sample copy and art guidelines free for SASE.
Illustrations: Uses 5-10 illustrations/issue; buys all from freelancers. "Inside illustrations are usually, but need not always be, pen and ink line drawings; covers are western paintings." Send query letter with samples to be kept on file; "we return anything on request." Call or write for appointment to show portfolio. "For inside illustrations, we want samples of artist's line drawings. For covers, we need to see full color transparencies." Reports within 30 days. Buys one-time rights. Pays $100-150, for color transparency for cover; $15-40, b&w, inside; on acceptance.

TULSA, Townhouse Three, #3, 1612 S. Boston Ct., Tulsa OK 74119. (918)582-5100. Executive Editor: Lynn R. Price. Monthly. Circ. 6,000. Original artwork returned after publication. Sample copy $1.95.

Illustrations: Uses 4-6 illustrations/issue; buys 1-2/issue from freelancers. Works on assignment only. Prefers to see finished art and samples of style. Samples returned by SASE. Provide resume, business card and tear sheet to be kept on file for future assignments. Buys all rights on a work-for-hire basis. Cover: Pays $100-200, full-color. Inside: Pays $50-75, spot drawing.

TURF AND SPORT DIGEST, 511-513 Oakland Ave., Baltimore MD 21212. Publisher: Allen L. Mitzel Jr. Emphasizes thoroughbred racing coverage, personalities, events and handicapping methods for fans of thoroughbred horseracing.
Cartoons: Interested in horse racing themes. Pays $10; on publication.

TURTLE MAGAZINE FOR PRESCHOOL KIDS, 1100 Waterway Blvd., Box 567, Indianapolis IN 46206. (317)636-8881. Art Director: Lawrence Simmons. Emphasizes health, nutrition, exercise and safety for children 2-5 years. Monthly except bimonthly February/March, April/May, June/July and August/September. Accepts previously published material and simultaneous submissions. Original artwork not returned after publication. Sample copy 75¢; art guidelines free for SASE.
Illustrations: Buys 10-20 illustrations/issue from freelancers. Interested in "stylized, humorous, realistic and cartooned themes; also nature and health." Especially needs b&w and 2-color artwork for line or halftone reproduction; full-color text and cover art. Works on assignment only. Send query letter with brochure, samples, tear sheets to be kept on file. Prefers stats or good photocopies, slides as samples. Samples not kept on file returned by SASE. Reports only if interested. Buys all rights. Pays $175, 4-color, cover; $35-50, b&w and 2-color and $70, 4-color, inside. Pays on publication.

TV GUIDE, Radnor PA 19088. Cartoon Editor. M.E. Bilisnansky. Emphasizes news, personalities and programs of television for a general audience. Weekly. Query. Reports in 2 weeks. Buys all rights. Pays on acceptance.
Cartoons: Buys about 35 cartoons/year on TV themes. Pays $200, single cartoon. Also uses cartoons for editorial features. Line drawings and halftones. Buys only single panel cartoons. No cartoon strips.

*UNITED EVANGELICAL ACTION, Box 28, Wheaton IL 60189. (312)665-0500. Executive Editor: Donald R. Brown. Magazine. Emphasizes religious news for leaders, pastors, laypeople in the evangelical church. Bimonthly. Circ. 7,700. Accepts previously published material. Original artwork returned after publication. Sample copy for SASE with 45¢ postage.
Cartoons: Buys 3 cartoons/year from freelancers. Religion-in-the-news themes. Prefers single panel with gagline; b&w line drawings. Send query letter with samples of style to be kept on file; write for appointment to show portfolio. Material not filed is returned by SASE. Reports within 1 month. Buys first rights. Pays $35-50, b&w; on publication.
Illustrations: Buys 1-2 illustrations/year from freelancers. Theme: religion confronting current issues. Send query letter with brochure and samples to be kept on file; write for appointment to show portfolio. Prefers tear sheets as samples. Samples not filed are returned by SASE. Reports within 1 month. Buys first rights. Pays $175, b&w, cover; $75, b&w, inside; on publication.

UNITED MAGAZINE, East-West Network, Inc., 34 E. 51st St., New York NY 10022. (212)888-5900. Editor: Jonathan Black. Art Director: Rick Fiala. Emphasizes prominent Americans, as well as airlines-related items of interest to passengers. Monthly.
Illustrations: Buys 0-2 illustrations/issue. Query with resume. Buys first rights. Pays $75 minimum, spot art; $400, cover; $450 full-page illustration.

*THE UNITED METHODIST PUBLISHING HOUSE, Graded Press Division, 201 Eighth Ave. S, Box 801, Nashville TN 37202. Art Procurement Supervisor: David Dawson. Publishes 60 + magazines, and church and home leaflets for ages 1½ years and up. Uses 30-40 illustrations/publication. Assigns 500-1,000 jobs/year.
First Contact & Terms: Works with 25-50 freelance artists/year. Seeks "artists with editorial and publishing experience. Particularly seeks artists of ethnic background—Korean, Hispanic and black especially." Works on an assignment basis only. Send brochure and samples to be kept on file. Prefers slides, photostats, photographs and tear sheets as samples. Samples not filed are returned only if requested. Reports only if interested. Original work usually not returned to the artist. Considers complexity of the project, skill and experience of artist, project's budget and rights purchased when establishing payment. Buys all rights.
Magazine Covers: Pays by the project, $150-200 for full color.
Magazine Text Illustration: Pays by the project, $5-40 for simple illustrations, $60-125 for full color.
Tips: "The ability to render the human figure is a must. Artists must be able to handle varied and numerous illustrations."

NEW! For the Graphic Arts Professional

The Complete Airbrush & Photoretouching Manual
by Peter Owen & John Sutcliffe

Filled with detailed instruction on how to select, use, and maintain airbrushes for both illustration and photoretouching purposes, plus step-by-step demonstrations of airbrush lettering, illustrations, photoretouching, and color tinting of b&w photos. You'll find information on how to handle every aspect of airbrushing—even for such innovative applications as cake decorating and car customizing. 160 pages/80 color, 80 b&w illus./$19.95

Design Rendering Techniques
by Dick Powell

To communicate good design ideas, you need to present them with maximum clarity and precision. This book presents a variety of design rendering techniques, with: step-by-step drawings showing how to prepare a product visual; a section on automotive design; techniques for rendering cutaways and exploded views; tips on special finishes, backgrounds, and mounting materials—all to help you present your ideas in the most visually exciting way. 160 pages/242 color, 78 one & two color illus./$24.95

(See back for more graphics books)

- -

To order, drop this postpaid card in the mail.

YES! Please send me:

_____ (7326) Complete Airbrush & Photoretouching Manual, $19.95

_____ (7407) Design Rendering Techniques, $24.95

_____ (7666) How to Draw & Sell Cartoons, $14.95

_____ (8240) Print Production Handbook, $14.95

Please include $2.00 postage and handling for one book, 50¢ for each additional book. (Ohio residents add 5½% sales tax.)

☐ Payment enclosed (Slip this card and your payment into an envelope.)

☐ Please charge my: ☐ Visa ☐ MasterCard

Account #_____ Exp. Date _____

Signature_____

Name_____

Address_____

City_____ State_____ Zip_____

Send to: Writer's Digest Books/North Light
9933 Alliance Road
Cincinnati, Ohio 45242

1871

NEW! For the Graphic Arts Professional

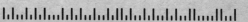

UNMUZZLED OX, 105 Hudson St., New York NY 10013. (212)226-7170. Editor: Michael Andre. Emphasizes poetry, stories, some visual arts (graphics, drawings, photos) for poets, writers, artists, musicians and interested others. Quarterly. Circ. 10,000. Whether original artwork is returned after publication "depends on work—artist should send SASE." Sample copy $4.95 plus $1 postage.
Cartoons: Number used/issue varies. Send query letter. Reports within 10 weeks. No payment for cartoons.
Illustrations: Uses "several" illustrations/issue. Themes vary according to issue. Send query letter and "anything you care to send" to be kept on file for possible future assignments. Send query letter. Reports within 10 weeks.
Tips: Magazine readers and contributors are "highly sophisticated and educated"; artwork should be geared to this market.

THE UNSPEAKABLE VISIONS OF THE INDIVIDUAL, Box 439, California PA 15419. Editors-in-Chief: Arthur and Kit Knight. For people with a better-than-average education interested in "beat" literature. Annually. Circ. 2,000. Sample copy $3.
Illustrations: Uses 3-6 illustrations/issue. Number illustrations/issue bought from freelancers varies. Receives 1 submission/month from freelancers. Interested in "beat" related themes, such as writers Jack Kerouac, William S. Burroughs, Allen Ginsberg, Gary Snyder and Carolyn Cassady. Prefers to see finished art. SASE. "Work without SASE will be destroyed." Reports in 2 weeks-2 months. Buys first North American serial rights. Cover and inside: Pays 2 contributor's copies, minimum; $10 maximum; on publication.
Tips: "See a sample copy."

US MAGAZINE, 745 5th, New York NY 10151. (212)758-3800. Art Director: Robert Priest. Emphasizes Hollywood scene, human interest stories; audience is 60% female. Biweekly. Circ. 1,100,000. Returns original artwork after publication. Sample copy and art guidelines free for SASE.
Cartoons: Send query letter to be kept on file; write for appointment to show portfolio. Reports back only if interested. Negotiates rights purchased. Pays on publication.
Illustrations: Buys 1-2 illustrations/year from freelancers. Works on assignment only. Send query letter to be kept on file. Write for appointment to show portfolio. Prefers to review tear sheets. Reports back only if interested. Negotiates rights purchased. Pays on publication.

USA TODAY, 1860 Broadway, New York NY 10023. (212)265-6680. Contact: Bob Rothenberg. For intellectual college graduates. Monthly. Circ. 170,000. Free sample copy.
Illustrations: Buys 70-80 illustrations/year on assigned themes. Uses only New York artists in the metropolitan area. Query with samples. SASE. Reports in 1 week. Buys all rights. Cover: Pays $125, color. Inside: Pays $15-50, b&w line drawings; on publication.

*VEGETARIAN TIMES, Box 570, Oak Park IL 60303. (312)848-8120. Editor/Publisher: Paul Obis. Consumer food magazine with emphasis on fitness and health for readers 30-50, 75% women. Monthly. Circ. 80,000. Accepts previously published material. Original artwork returned after publication. Sample copy $2.
Cartoons: Buys 2 cartoons/issue from freelancers. Prefers single panel wth gagline. Send samples of style or roughs. Material not filed is returned by SASE. Reports within 30 days. Buys one-time rights, reprint rights or negotiates rights purchased. Negotiates payment, b&w; pays on acceptance.
Illustrations: Buys 5 illustrations/issue from freelancers. Send samples to be kept on file. prefers photocopies as samples. Payment varies.

VENTURE, Box 150, Wheaton IL 60189. (312)665-0630. Art Director: Lawrence Libby. Senior Graphic Designer: Roy Green. For boys 12-18. "We seek to promote consciousness, acceptance of and personal commitment to Jesus Christ." Published 6 times/year. Circ. 13,000. Simultaneous submissions and previously published work OK. Original artwork returned after publication. Sample copy $1.50 with large SASE; artists' guidelines with SASE.
Cartoons: Send to attention of Cartoon Editor. Uses 1-3 cartoons/issue; buys all from freelancers. Receives 2 submissions/week from freelancers, on nature, sports, school, camping, hiking; single panel with gagline. "Keep it clean." Prefers finished cartoon. SASE. Reports in 2-4 weeks. Buys first-time rights. Pays $20 minimum, b&w line drawings; on acceptance.
Illustrations: Contact Art Director. Uses 3 illustrations/issue; buys 2/issue from freelancers, on education, family life and camping. B&w only. Works on assignment only. Samples returned by SASE. Reports back on future assignment possibilities. Provide business card, tear sheet and photocopies of samples to be kept on file for future assignments. Prefers to see samples. SASE. Reports in 2 weeks. Buys first time rights. Pays $100-150 for inside use of b&w line drawings and washes; on publication.

*VERDICT MAGAZINE, 124 Truxtun Ave., Bakersfield CA 93301. (805)325-7124. Editor: Steve Walsh. Emphasizes law for defense lawyers. Circ. 5,000. Accepts previously published material. Original artwork returned after publication. Sample copy for SASE with $3 postage; art guidelines for SASE with 22¢ postage.
Cartoons: Buys 4 cartoons/issue from freelancers. Legal themes. Prefers single panel with gagline; b&w line drawings or b&w washes. Send finished cartoons to be kept on file; write for appointment to show portfolio. Material not filed is returned by SASE. Reports only if interested. Buys one-time rights or reprint rights. Pays $5, b&w; on publication.
Illustrations: Buys 4 illustrations/issue from freelancers. Themes: law, legal. Send samples to be kept on file; write for appointment to show portfolio. Prefers photostats, tear sheets or photocopies as samples. Samples not filed are returned by SASE. Reports only if interested. Buys one-time rights or reprint rights. Pays $10, color, cover; $5, b&w, inside; on publication.

VICTIMOLOGY: AN INTERNATIONAL JOURNAL, Box 39045, Washington DC 20016. (703)528-8872. Editor-in-chief: Emilio Viano. For professionals, lawyers, criminologists, medical personnel and others helping child/spouse abuse programs, hotlines, rape crisis centers and other victim programs. "By 'victim,' we mean not only those victimized by crime, but earthquakes, the environment, accidents, pollution and the state." Quarterly. Circ. 2,500. Query with samples. SASE. Reports in 4 weeks. Buys all rights. Pays on publication. Sample copy $5. Write to be put on mailing list to receive periodical announcements.
Illustrations: Buys several illustrations/year on victimization. "We like to see illustrations on what is done in behalf of the victim." Cover: pays $150, color; $50, b&w. Inside: pays $30, b&w. Brochure: pays $50.

*VICTOR VALLEY MAGAZINE, Box 618, Victorville CA 92392. Publisher/Editor: Grace Hauser. City magazine emphasizing local interest topics. Monthly except February and August. Circ. 5,000. Accepts previously published material. Returns original artwork after publication. Sample copy free for SASE with 22¢ postage.
Illustrations: Buys 1-2/issue from freelancers. Works on assignment only. Send query letter with samples. Prefers tear sheets as samples. Samples are returned by SASE. Reports only if interested. Buys first rights. Pays $40, b&w, and $100, color, cover; $25, b&w and $75, color, inside; on publication.

VIDEO MOVIES™ MAGAZINE, 3841 W. Oakton, Skokie IL 60076. (312)676-3470. Art Director: Jeff Hapner. Estab. 1983. Emphasizes movies available on video tape or disc for home viewing. Monthly. Circ. 200,000. Does not return original artwork after publication. Sample copy $2.95.
Illustrations: Works on assignment only. Send samples to be kept on file. Write for appointment to show portfolio. "Photocopies are fine as samples, whatever the artist usually sends." Samples not filed are returned only if requested. Reports back only if interested. Buys all rights. Payment varies according to project; pays on acceptance.

VIDEO REVIEW, 902 Broadway, New York NY 10010. (212)477-2200. Art Director: Orit. Emphasizes home video for owners and prospective owners of home video equipment. Monthly. Circ. 375,000. Original artwork returned after publication.
Cartoons: Uses 1-2 cartoons/issue; buys all from freelancers. Accepts "anything humorous" concerning home video use; single panel. Send photocopies of finished cartoons. Samples not returned. Reports in 1 month if requested. Buys first reproduction rights. Pays $35-100, b&w. Pays 4-6 weeks after publication.
Illustrations: Uses 3-5 illustrations/issue; buys all from freelancers. Prefers air brush, line drawings, sculpture and color for cover. Works on assignment only. Provide resume and samples to be kept on file for possible future assignments. Send samples of style; call or write for appointment. Samples not returned. Reports when an assignment is available. Negotiates rights purchased. Pays $250-950; 6-8 weeks after publication.

VIDEOGRAPHY, 50 W. 23rd St., New York NY 10010. (212)645-1000. Art Director: Jean Fujisaki. Audience is video professionals. Monthly. Circ. 100,000. Original artwork returned after publication. Art guidelines free for SASE.
Cartoons: Number of cartoons used/issue varies. Themes vary; artist "must be able to draw technical equipment." Prefers single panel with gagline; b&w line drawings. Send query letter with samples of style to be kept on file; call for appointment to show portfolio. Material not kept on file is returned by SASE only if requested. Reports within 1 day. Buys one-time rights or negotiates. Pay rate varies; pays on publication.
Illustrations: Number of illustrations used/issue varies. Works on assignment only. Send query letter with samples to be kept on file; call for appointment to show portfolio. Samples not kept on file are re-

turned by SASE. Reports within 1 day. Buys one-time rights or negotiates. Pay rate varies; pays on publication.

*VISIONS, THE INTERNATIONAL MAGAZINE OF ILLUSTRATED POETRY, Black Buzzard Press, 4705 S. 8th Rd., Arlington VA 22204. Editors: Bradley R. Strahan, Ursula Gill and Shirley Sullivan. Emphasizes literature and the illustrative arts for "well educated, very literate audience, very much into art and poetry." Published 3 times/year. Circ. 650. Sometimes accepts previously published material under special circumstances. Original artwork returned after publication. Sample copy $2.50 (latest issue $3); art guidelines free for SASE.
Illustrations: Buys approximately 50 illustrations/year from freelancers. Representational to surrealistic and some cubism style. Works on assignment only. Send query letter with SASE and samples to be kept on file. Samples should clearly show artist's style and capability; no slides or originals. Samples not filed are returned by SASE. Reports within 2 months. Buys first rights. "For information on releases on artwork, please contact the editors at the above address." Payment varies.

VOGUE, 350 Madison Ave., New York NY 10017. Art Director: Roger Schoening. Emphasizes fashion, health, beauty, culture and decorating for women. Write and send resume; will then review portfolio; works primarily with New York area artists. Leave photocopies for referral.

VOLKSWAGEN'S WORLD, (formerly *Small World*), Volkswagen of America, Troy MI 48099. (313)362-6770. Editor: Ed Rabinowitz. For Volkswagen owners. Quarterly. Circ. 250,000. Receives 2-3 cartoons and 2-3 illustrations/week from freelance artists. Previously published and photocopied submissions OK. Free sample copy.
Cartoons: Buys 10/year on Volkswagens and their owners. Query with samples. SASE. Reports in 6 weeks. Buys all rights. Pays $15 minimum, halftones and washes; on acceptance.
Illustrations: Buys 12/year on assigned themes. Query with samples. SASE. Reports in 6 weeks. Buys all rights. Cover: Pays $250 minimum, color. Inside: Pays $15 minimum, b&w and color; on acceptance.
Tips: "We're happy to send sample issues to prospective contributors. It's the best way of seeing what our needs are."

WASHINGTON FOOD DEALER MAGAZINE,8288 Lake City Way NE, Seattle WA 98115. Managing Editor/Advertising Director: T.J. Robison. Emphasizes the food industry, particularly retail grocers (independents). Monthly. Circ. 3,800. Accepts previously published material. Does not return original artwork after publication. Sample copy $1; art guidelines available.
Cartoons: Interested in cartoons on food industry trends with an editorial message. Prefers single panel with b&w line drawings. Send query letter with samples of style to be kept on file. Write for appointment to show portfolio. Material not filed is returned only if requested. Reports back only if interested. Negotiates rights purchased. Negotiates pay; pays on publication.
Illustrations: Buys 1-2 illustrations/issue from freelance. Prefers food industry themes. Works on assignment only. Send query letter with resume and samples to be kept on file. Write for appointment to show portfolio. Prefers tear sheets as samples. Samples not filed are returned by SASE. Reports back only if interested. Negotiates rights purchased and payment. Pays on publication.

THE WASHINGTON MONTHLY, 1711 Connecticut Ave. NW, Washington DC 20009. (202)462-0128. Art Director: Bevi Chagnon. For journalists, government officials and general public interested in public affairs. "We examine government's failures and suggest solutions." Monthly. Circ. 39,000. Previously published and photocopied submissions OK.
Illustrations: Buys 20-40 illustrations/year on politics and government. Query with samples or arrange interview to show portfolio; local artists preferred. SASE. Reports in 2 weeks. Buys one-time rights. Inside: Pays $50-125, b&w line drawings and washes. Cover: Pay is negotiable for color-separated work; $100 minimum, b&w; on publication.
Tips: "We need fast turn-around; artist should read articles before attempting work."

THE WASHINGTONIAN MAGAZINE, Suite 200, 1828 L St. NW, Washington DC 20036. (202)296-3600. Emphasizes politics, cultural events, personalities, entertainment and dining. About Washington, for Washingtonians. Monthly. Circ. 135,000. Simultaneous submissions and previously published work OK. Original artwork returned after publication if requested. No artists' guidelines available.
Cartoons: Cartoon Editor: Randy Rieland. Uses 5 cartoons/issue; buys 5/issue from freelancers, on "sophisticated topics, urban life"; single and double panel with gagline. Uses b&w line drawings, gray opaques, b&w washes, and opaque watercolors. Prefers finished cartoons. Reports in 4-6 weeks. Buys one-time rights. Pays $50, b&w; on publication.

Illustrations: Design Director: Linda Otto. Uses 5 illustrations/issue; buys 3/issue from freelancers, on a variety of subjects. Uses b&w line drawings, gray opaques, b&w washes, color washes and opaque watercolor. Works on assignment only. Returns samples if requested. Does not report back on future assignment possibilities. Provide resume, business card and tear sheets to be kept on file for future assignments. Prefers to see portfolio and samples of style. SASE. Reports in 1 week. Buys one-time rights. Pay is negotiable; on publication. Also uses freelance pasteup artists.

WATER SKI MAGAZINE, (formerly *World Water Skiing*), Box 2456, Winter Park Fl 32790. (305)628-4802. Publisher: Terry Snow. Send query letter to: Terry Temple, editor. Emphasizes water skiing for an audience generally 18-34 years old, 80% male, active, educated, affluent. Published 8 times/year. Circ. 56,000. Accepts previously published material and simultaneous submissions. Original artwork returned after publication. Query for guidelines.
Cartoons: Uses 1-4 cartoons/issue, buys all from freelancers. 90% assigned. Prefers single panel with gagline, color or b&w washes or b&w line drawings. Prefers to receive query letter with samples or roughs first, but will review finished work. Samples returned. Reports within 3 weeks. Negotiates rights purchased. Negotiates payment, usually $15-30, b&w; up to $300, color, depending on topic. Pays 30 days after publication.
Illustrations: Uses 10 illustrations/issue; buys 5 illustrations/issue from freelancers. Prefers strong lines in a realistic style. Works on assignment "most of the time." Send query letter with resume, samples and tear sheets to be kept on file; may also submit portfolio. Samples returned by SASE if not kept on file. Reports within 3 weeks. Negotiates payment and rights purchased. Pays on publication.

*WAVES, (Fine Canadian Writing), 79 Denham Dr., Richmond Hill, Ontario L4C 6H9 Canada. (416)889-6703. Editor: Bernice Lever. Emphasizes literature for readers of contemporary poetry and fiction. Published triannually. Circ. 1,100. Returns original artwork after publication. Sample copy for SASE (nonresidents include IRC). Art guidelines available.
Illustrations: Uses 3-15/issue. Themes and styles are open. "Art does not relate to the literature printed. It can contrast or harmonize." Send query letter with samples to be kept on file for 6 months. Write for appointment to show portfolio. Prefers photostats or tear sheets as samples—high contrast line drawings. Samples not filed are returned by SASE (nonresidents include IRC). Reports within 1 month. Buys one-time North American rights. Pays $6.50, b&w, inside; and $25, b&w, cover; on publication.

WEEDS TREES & TURF, 7500 Old Oak Blvd., Cleveland OH 44130. Executive Editor: Bruce Shank. Emphasizes landscape management, i.e., golf courses, estates, parks, schools, and private landscape contractors for golf course superintendents, landscape contractors, park supervisors, athletic field directors, estate managers, staff groundskeepers. Monthly. Circ. 46,000. Accepts previously published material. Sample copy and art guidelines free for SASE.
Illustrations: Uses 2 illustrations/issue; buys all from freelancers. Prefers line art and color art. Works on assignment basis only. Send query letter with samples to be kept on file; write for appointment to show portfolio. Accepts photostats, photographs, slides or original work as samples. Samples not kept on file are returned. Reports within 30 days. Negotiates rights purchased. Pays $300-500, color, cover; $50, b&w, $200, color, inside; on publication.

WEIGHT WATCHERS MAGAZINE, 360 Lexington Ave., New York NY 10017. (212)370-0644. Art Director: Joy Toltzis Makon. Emphasizes food, health, fashion, beauty for the weight and beauty conscious, 25-45 years old. Monthly. Circ. 850,000. Original artwork returned after publication.
Illustrations: Uses 6 illustrations/issue. Works on assignment only. Send query letter with brochure to be kept on file. Portfolios seen by drop-off only. Reports only if interested. Buys one-time rights. Pays on acceptance.

THE WEIRDBOOK SAMPLER, (formerly *Eerie Country*), Box 149, Amherst Branch, Buffalo NY 14226. Editor-in-Chief: W. Paul Ganley. An irregular companion publication to *Weirdbook* for those interested in fantasy, adventure and horror. Irregular publications. Circ. 200. Buys first or all rights. Sample copy $2.75.
Illustrations: Buys 10-20 illustrations/year. Interested in weird, macabre, supernatural and fantastic themes. "Illustrate scenes from famous weird writers like Bradbury, Lovecraft, Poe, etc." Mail art. Photocopies OK. Must be suited to photocopy. SASE. Reports within 3 months. Cover: Pays $10, b&w; Inside: Pays $5/page; on publication. *Currently overstocked.*
Tips: "Plan to reduce art to 85% of actual size; column width of 4" or double column width of 8 ¼" 'intermediate sizes can be used.' Art that does not require half-toning preferred, particularly on interiors. Leave at least ¼" around interiors for cropping (⅜" on full page sizes). No pencil drawings or slides. Copies OK if suitable for reproduction. All due care will be used in handling, but send a reminder letter when you want them back (about 6 weeks after publication). B&w artwork only, no color."

WEST, 750 Ridder Park Dr., San Jose CA 95190. (408)920-5602. Editor: Jeffrey Klein. Art Director: Bambi Nicklen. General interest magazine for subscribers of the *San Jose Mercury News*. Circ. 307,000. Weekly. Free sample copy.
Illustrations: Buys 2-3/issue on all themes except erotica. Query with resume and samples or previously published work, or arrange interview to show portfolio. Cover: Pays up to $500, opaque watercolors, oils, acrylics or mixed media. Inside: Pays $125-400, b&w line drawings, washes and gray opaques; $150-400, color washes, opaque watercolors, oils, acrylics or mixed media. Pays on acceptance.

WESTERN HUMANITIES REVIEW, University of Utah, Salt Lake City UT 84112. (801)581-7438. Literary magazine. Readers are "highly educated and interested in all aspects of the humanities. Most of our subscribers are libraries." Quarterly. Circ. 1,100. Original artwork returned after publication. Sample copy $4. "We also need covers, for which we pay $150 each. Artists should look at past issues to see the sort of things we use."
Cartoons: Uses 4 cartoons/issue; buys all from freelancers. Receives 4 submissions/week from freelancers. Format: b&w line drawings with a touch of wit preferred. Single panel *without gagline*. "Artists should look at some of the recent issues." Send finished cartoons to Jack Garlington, editor. SASE. Reports in 1 week if "uninterested; longer if interested." Pays $50 on acceptance. Buys first North American serial rights.
Illustrations: Uses 4 illustrations/issue; buys all from freelancers. Receives 4 submissions/week from freelancers. Prefers to see finished art. SASE. Reports in 1 week if "uninterested; longer if interested." Buys first North American serial rights. Pays on acceptance.

WESTERN OUTDOORS,3197-E Airport Loop Dr., Costa Mesa CA 92626. (714)546-4370. Art Director: Gayle Radestock. Emphasizes hunting and fishing and related activities in the western states; directed to men and women interested in pursuing these activities in the 11 contiguous western states plus Alaska, Hawaii, British Columbia and western Mexico. Published 10 times/year. Circ. 150,000. Returns original artwork after publication.
Illustrations: Works on assignment only. Send query letter with samples to be kept on file; write for appointment to show portfolio. Accepts photocopies as samples. Samples not filed are returned by SASE. Reports within 30 days. Buys first rights. Pays on acceptance.

THE WESTERN PRODUCER, Box 2500, Saskatoon, Saskatchewan S7K 2C4 Canada. (306)665-3500. For farm families in western Canada. Weekly. Circ. 140,000.
Cartoons: Receives 12/week from freelance artists. Uses only cartoons about rural life. SASE (nonresidents include IRC). Reports in 3 weeks. Buys first Canadian rights. Pays $15, b&w line drawings; on acceptance. No illustrations.

WESTERN SPORTSMAN, Nimrod Publications Ltd., Box 737, Regina, Saskatchewan S4P 3A8 Canada. (306)352-8384. Editor-in-Chief: Red Wilkinson. For fishermen, hunters, campers and outdoorsmen. Bimonthly. Circ. 28,000. Previously published and simultaneous submissions OK "as long as they're not in our market area of Alberta and Saskatchewan". Original artwork not returned after publication. Sample copy $3; artist's guidelines for SASE (nonresidents include IRC).
Cartoons: Buys 90 cartoons/year on the outdoors; single, double and multi-panel with gaglines. Mail art or query with samples. SASE (nonresidents include IRC). Reports in 3 weeks. Buys first, reprint, simultaneous or first North American serial rights. Pays $20, b&w line drawings; on acceptance.
Illustrations: Buys 8 illustrations/year on the outdoors. Mail art or query with samples. SASE (nonresidents include IRC). Reports in 3 weeks. Buys first, reprint, simultaneous or first North American serial rights. Inside: Pays $50-200, b&w line drawings; on acceptance.

WESTERN'S WORLD, East-West Network, Inc., Suite 800, 5900 Wilshire Blvd., Los Angeles CA 90036. (213)937-5810. Editor: Ed Dwyer. Art Director: Claire Kleffel. For airline passengers. Monthly. Original work returned after publication. Sample copy $2.
Illustrations: Works on assignment only. Query with resume. Reports in 1 month. Buys first rights. Pays $75 minimum/spot art; $450 maximum, full-page illustration; and $800, full-color cover.

WESTWAYS, Terminal Annex, Box 2890, Los Angeles CA 90051. (213)741-4760. Editor: Mary Ann Fisher. Production Manager: Vincent J. Corso. For the people of the Western US. Emphasizes current and historical events, culture, art, travel and recreation. Monthly. Circ. 478,000.
Illustrations: Buys assigned themes on travel, history, and arts in the West. Send resume to be kept on file. Do not call. Buys first rights, based on decision of the editor. Cover: Pays $400. Inside: Pays $50-150, drawings; $150, 4-color illustrations; on publication.

WHISKEY ISLAND MAGAZINE, University Center 7, Cleveland State University, Cleveland OH 44115. Editor: Leah Borovich. For all writers; poetry, short fiction and drama. Published 2-3 times an-

nually. Circ. 2,000. Photocopied and simultaneous submissions OK.
Illustrations: All photos and other graphics accepted; no limitation by theme; b&w. Mail art. SASE. Reports in 12 weeks.

WHISPERS, 70 Highland Ave., Binghamton NY 13905. Editor-in-Chief/Art Director: Stuart David Schiff. For college-educated adults interested in literate fantasy, horror, art and fiction. Published 1-2 times/year. Circ. 3,000. Original artwork returned after publication. Sample copy $3.50.
Illustrations: Uses 10-20 illustrations/issue; buys 2-3/issue from freelancers. Receives 5-10 submissions/week from freelancers. Interested in fantasy and horror. Send photocopied samples of finished art. SASE. Provide flyer and tear sheets to be kept on file for future assignments. Reports in 30-60 days. Buys first North American serial rights. Cover: Pays $100-200, color. Inside: Pays $10-25, b&w. Pays by arrangement to retain artwork after use.
Tips: Especially looks for "clean lines, originality and non-comic book appearance of human" in artwork.

WILSON LIBRARY BULLETIN, 950 University Ave., Bronx NY 10452. (212)588-8400. Editor: Milo Nelson. Emphasizes the issues and the practice of library science. Published 10 times/year. Circ. 25,000. Free sample copy.
Cartoons: Buys 2-3 cartoons/issue on education and library science; single panel with gagline. Mail finished art. SASE. Reports back only if interested. Buys first rights. Pays $100, b&w line drawings and washes; on acceptance.
Illustrations: Uses 1-2 illustrations/issue; buys all from freelancers. Works on assignment only. Send query letter, business card and samples to be kept on file. Call for appointment to show portfolio. Reports back only if interested. Buys first rights. Cover: Pays $300, color washes. Inside: Pays $100-200, b&w line drawings and washes; $20, spot drawings; on publication.

WINDSOR THIS MONTH MAGAZINE, Box 1029, Station A, Windsor, Ontario N9A 6P4 Canada. (519)966-7411. Publisher: J.S. Woloschuk. Editor: Laura Rosenthal. Features Windsor-oriented issues, interviews, opinion, answers. Published 12 times/year. Circ. 22,000.
Illustrations: Buys 3/issue on assigned themes. Query with samples. Include SASE (nonresidents include IRC). Reports in 1 week. Buys first North American serial rights. Negotiates pay, color and b&w; on publication.
Tips: "Send sample of published work."

WINES & VINES, 1800 Lincoln Ave., San Rafael CA 94901. (415)453-9700. Editor: Philip E. Hiaring. Emphasizes the grape and wine industry in North America for the trade—growers, winemakers, merchants. Monthly. Circ. 5,800. Accepts previously published material. Original artwork not returned after publication.
Cartoons: Buys approximately 3 cartoons/year. Prefers single panel with gagline; b&w line drawings. Send query letter with roughs to be kept on file. Material not kept on file is not returned. Reports within 1 month. Buys first rights. Pays $10.
Illustrations: Send query letter to be kept on file. Reports within 1 month. Buys first rights. Pays $50-100, color, cover; $15, b&w, inside. Pays on acceptance.

WIRE JOURNAL INTERNATIONAL, 1570 Boston Post Rd., Guilford CT 06437. (203)453-2777. Contact: Art Director. Emphasizes the wire industry worldwide, members of Wire Association International, industry suppliers, manufacturers, research/developers, engineers, etc. Monthly. Circ. 12,500. Original artwork not returned after publication. Free sample copy and art guidelines.
Illustrations: Uses "no set number" of illustrations/issue; illustrations are "used infrequently." Works on assignment only. Provide samples, business card and tear sheets to be kept on file for possible future assignments. Call for appointment or submit portfolio. Reports "as soon as possible." Buys all rights. Pay is negotiable; on publication.
Tips: "Show practical artwork that relates to industrial needs and avoid bringing samples of surrealism art, for example. Also, show a better variety of techniques—and know something about who we are and the industry we serve."

WISCONSIN RESTAURATEUR, 122 W. Washington, Madison WI 53703. (608)251-3663. Editor: Jan LaRue. Emphasizes the restaurant industry. Readers are "restaurateurs, hospitals, schools, institutions, cafeterias, food service students, chefs, etc." Monthly. Circ. 3,600, except convention issue (March), 13,000. Original artwork returned after publication. Free sample copy; art guidelines for SASE. Especially needs cover material.
Cartoons: Uses 1 cartoon/issue; buys from freelancer. Receives 5 cartoons/week from freelancers. "Uses much material pertaining to conventions, food shows, etc. Sanitation issue good. Cartoons about

employees. No off-color material." Format: b&w line drawings with gaglines. Send finished cartoons. SASE. Reports in 2 weeks. Buys first North American serial rights. Pays $8 on publication.
Illustrations: Uses 5 illustrations/issue; buys 1/issue from freelancer. Receives 1 illustration/week from freelance artists. Freelancers chosen "at random, depending on theme and articles featured for the month." Looks for "the unusual, pertaining to the food service industry. No offbeat or questionable material." Format: b&w line drawings and washes for covers. Send samples of style to be kept on file for future assignments. Buys first North American serial rights. Pays $10-50 on acceptance for b&w cover and $5-20 for inside b&w.
Tips: Trends within the field include "smaller portions, lighter quality, more variety and more convenience foods." Changes within the magazine include "new cover design, and the use of more freelance material—pictures and illustrations."

*WISCONSIN REVIEW, Box 276, Dempsey Hall, University of Wisconsin-Oshkosh, Oshkosh WI 54901. (414)424-2267. Editor: Patricia Haebig. Emphasizes literature (poetry, short fiction, reviews) and the arts. Tri-annual. Circ. 2,000. Original artwork returned after publication "if requested." Sample copy $1.50; art guidelines available for SASE.
Illustrations: Uses 5-10 illustrations/issue. "We are primarily interested in material that in one way or another attempts to elucidate, explain, discover or otherwise untangle the manifestly complex circumstances in which we find ourselves in the 1980's." Provide samples and tear sheets with "updated address and phone number" to be kept on file for possible future assignments. Send query letter with roughs, finished art or samples of style. Samples returned by SASE. Reports in 5 months. Pays in contributor's copies/cover, 2 copies/inside; on publication.

WISCONSIN TRAILS, Box 5650, Madison WI 53705. (608)231-2444. Production Manager: Nancy Mead. Concerns travel, recreation, history, industry and personalities in Wisconsin. Published 6 times/year. Circ. 25,000. Previously published and photocopied submissions OK. Artists' guidelines for SASE.
Illustrations: Uses 6 illustrations/issue, all from freelancers. Receives less than 1 submission/week from freelancers. "Art work is done on assignment, to illustrate specific articles. All articles deal with Wisconsin. We allow artists considerable stylistic latitude." Provide samples (photocopies OK) of style; indication of artist's favorite topics; name, address and phone number to be kept on file for future assignments. SASE. Reporting time varies. Buys one-time rights on a work-for-hire basis. Inside: Pays $25-100 on publication.

THE WITTENBURG DOOR, 1224 Greenfield Dr., El Cajon CA 92021. (619)440-2333, (916)842-1301. Editor: Mike Yaconelli. For men and women, usually connected with the church. Bimonthly. Circ. 20,000. Reports in 3 months.
Cartoons: Buys 2-4 cartoons/issue on assignment. Receives 2 cartoons/month from freelance artists. "Very selective." Uses satire/humor on religious themes geared to evangelicals. Mail finished art or roughs, b&w. SASE. Reports in 3 months. Pays $20-150; on publication.

WOMAN BEAUTIFUL, Drawer 189, Palm Beach FL 33480. (305)833-4583. Editor: Mark Adams. For students at beauty schools and people who patronize beauty salons. Bimonthly. Circ. 12,000.
Cartoons: Buys 2 cartoons/issue on any subject. Send finished art. SASE. Reports in 2 months. Pays $10 for b&w; on publication.

WOMEN IN BUSINESS, Box 8728, Kansas City MO 64114. (816)361-6621. Art Director: Melissa Kirby. For businesswomen, all levels in all fields. Published 6 times/year. Circ. 110,000.
Illustrations: Buys 10-12 illustrations/year, mostly b&w. Assigns themes; usually "business related illustrations with women." Send samples or photocopies. Returns samples if requested. Provide copies of samples and resumes to be kept on file for future assignments. Reports in 4 weeks. Buys all rights, but may reassign rights to artist after publication. Negotiates pay.
Tips: "Buying more freelance art, but the art is done to specifications of the art director."

*WONDER TIME, 6401 The Paseo, Kansas City MO 64131. (816)333-7000. Editor: Evelyn Beals. "Story paper" emphasizing inspiration and character building material for first and second graders, 6-8 years old. Weekly. Circ. 40,000. Does not accept previously published material. Original artwork not returned to the artist after publication. Sample copy free for SASE with 44¢ postage. Art guidelines available.
Illustrations: Buys 1/issue. Works on assignment only. Send query letter with samples to be kept on file. Prefers tear sheets or photocopies as samples. Reports only if interested. Buys all rights. Pays $30-40, b&w, cover; on acceptance.

WOODENBOAT, Box 78, Brooklin ME 04616. Editor: Jonathan A. Wilson. Executive Editor: Peter H. Spectre. Managing Editor: Jennifer Buckley. Concerns designing, building, repairing, using and maintaining wooden boats. Bimonthly. Circ. 100,000. Previously published work OK. Sample copy $3.50.
Illustrations: Buys 48/year on wooden boats or related items. Query with samples. SASE for return of material. Reports in 1-2 months. "We are always in need of high quality technical drawings. Rates vary, but usually $25-300. Buys first North American serial rights. Pays on publication.
Tips: "We work with several professionals on an assignment basis, but most of the illustrative material that we use in the magazine is submitted with a feature article. When we no need additional material, however, we will try to contact a good freelancer in the appropriate geographic area."

WOODMEN OF THE WORLD, 1700 Farnam St., Omaha NE 68102. (402)342-1890. Editor-in-Chief: Leland A. Larson. For members of the Woodmen of the World Life Insurance Society and their families. Emphasizes Society activities, children's and women's interests and humor. Monthly. Circ. 470,000. Previously published work OK. Original artwork returned after publication, if arrangements are made. Free sample copy.
Cartoons: Uses 1-6 cartoons/issue; buys all from freelancers. Receives 10-50 submissions/week from freelancers. Especially needs cartoons. Interested in general interest subjects; single panel. Send finished cartoons. SASE. Reports in 2 weeks. Buys various rights. Pays $10, b&w line drawings, washes and halftones; on acceptance.
Illustrations: Uses 5-10 illustrations/year; buys 3-4/year from freelancers. Interested in lodge activities, seasonal, humorous and human interest themes. Works on assignment only. Prefers to see finished art. SASE. Reports in 2 weeks. Provide brochure or flyers to be kept on file for future assignments. Buys one-time rights. Payment varies according to job.
Tips: Especially looks for creative thinking, technique and quality when reviewing samples. Artists should avoid "one-track stylization; vary the media used and techniques, if possible."

WORDS, 1015 N. York Rd, Willow Grove PA 19090. (215)657-3220. Art Director: Judy L. Clark. Emphasizes information systems and word processing for word processing professionals, consultants, educators and manufacturers; male and female; 20-50 years of age. Bimonthly. Circ. over 18,000. Original artwork returned after publication. Free sample copy for SASE.
Illustrations: Uses 4-5 illustrations/issue; buys 4-5 from freelancers. Interested in "all styles" and "themes on editorial features of office automation." Works on assignment only. Send brochure with samples of style; call for appointment. Samples returned by SASE. Provide resume, business card and/or brochure to be kept on file for possible future assignments. Reports in 3 weeks. Pays $50-300 inside, b&w line or wash; $300-500 for 4-color cover art; on publication.
Tips: "We're interested in a variety of styles and treatments. We're looking for clean, competent, modern and hi-tech looking graphics; simple, yet sophisticated. Present what you feel represents your best work (quality vs. quantity)."

WORKBENCH, Modern Handcraft, Inc., 4251 Pennsylvania, Kansas City MO 64111. Editor-in-Chief: Jay W. Hedden. For woodworkers and do-it-yourself persons. Bimonthly. Circ. 870,000. "Art accepted only as part of a package of copy, photos and drawings." Free sample copy and artists' guidelines.
Cartoons: Buys 15 cartoons/year. Interested in woodworking and do-it-yourself themes; single panel with gagline. Submit art. SASE. Reports in 1 month. Buys all rights, but may reassign rights to artist after publication. Pays on acceptance. Pays $20 minimum, b&w line drawings.

WORKING MOTHER MAGAZINE, 230 Park Ave., New York NY 10169. (212)551-9533. Art Director: Nina Scerbo. For the working mothers in the US whose problems and concerns are determined by the fact that they have children under 18 living at home. Monthly. Circ. 500,000. Receives 5-10 illustrations/week from freelance artists. Occasionally accepts previously published material. Original artwork is returned to the artist.
Cartoons: Send all cartoon inquiries to Katherine Minton. Uses 1-2 cartoons/issue; all from freelancers.
Illustrations: Uses 10-15 illustrations/issue; all from freelancers. 4-color double- and single-page illustration, 4-color and b&w spots. "I keep all samples from portfolios that I review on file; also refer frequently to books such as *The Black Book* and *American Showcase*, and the *Illustrators Annual*. For editorial work I use artists on assignment only. However, I do buy b&w filler art from material that is submitted by artists. I look for artists who can handle women and children in an interesting and believable way; I will consider all styles—realistic, representational, humorous, highly stylized—and am interested in all media and techniques." Drop off portfolio or send nonreturnable samples of style. Reports immediately on commissioned work. Pays $150-250 on acceptance for inside b&w (spot illustration) and $150-500 for inside color. Buys one time rights with the right to determine additional usage.

WRITER'S DIGEST, 9933 Alliance Rd., Cincinnati OH 45242. Art Director: Carol Buchanan. Assistant Editor: Sharon Rudd (for cartoons). Emphasizes freelance writing for freelance writers. Monthly. Circ. 200,000. Original artwork returned after publication. Sample copy $2.
Cartoons: Buys 3 cartoons/issue from freelancers. Theme: the writing life—cartoons that deal with writers and the trials of writing and selling their work. Also, writing from a historical standpoint (past works), language use and other literary themes. Prefers single panel with or without gagline. Send finished cartoons. Material returned by SASE. Reports within 1 month. Buys first rights or one-time rights. Pays $50-85, b&w; on acceptance.
Illustrations: Buys 4 illustrations/month from freelancers. Theme: the writing life (b&w line art primarily). Works on assignment only. Send brochure and samples to be kept on file; slides will be returned; write for appointment to show portfolio. Accepts photocopies as samples. Samples returned by SASE. Reports only if interested. Buys one-time rights. Pays $400, color, cover; $50-200, inside, b&w. Pays on acceptance.

WRITER'S YEARBOOK, 9933 Alliance Rd., Cincinnati OH 45242. Submissions Editor: Sharon Rudd. Emphasizes writing and marketing techniques, business topics for writers and writing opportunities for freelance writers and people trying to get started in writing. Annually. Original artwork returned with one copy of the issue in which it appears. Sample copy $3.95.
Cartoons: Uses 6-10 freelance cartoons/issue. "All cartoons must pertain to writing—its joys, agonies, quirks. All styles accepted, but high-quality art is a must." Prefers single panel, with or without gagline, b&w line drawings or washes. "Verticals are always considered, but horizontals—especially severe horizontals—are hard to come by." Send finished cartoons. Samples returned by SASE. Reports within 3 weeks. Buys first North American serial rights, one-time use. Pays $50 minimum, b&w. Pays on acceptance.
Tips: "A cluttery style does not appeal to us. Send finished, not rough art, with clearly typed gaglines. Cartoons without gaglines must be particularly well executed."

***X-IT MAGAZINE**, Box 102, Station C, St. John's, Newfoundland A1C 5H5 Canada. (709)753-8802. Editor: Ken J. Harvey. Emphasizes arts and entertainment for those interested in the visual and literary arts. Triannually. Circ. 3,000. Accepts previously published material. Original artwork returned after publication. Sample copy $3.
Cartoons: Buys 3-6 cartoons/issue from freelancers. Prefers contemporary, but open to wide area of styles. Accepts single, double or multiple panel with or without gagline; b&w line drawings or washes. Send b&w samples of style or finished cartoons; write for appointment to show portfolio. Material returned by SASE (nonresidents include IRCs) only if requested. Reports within 3 weeks. Buys first rights or one-time rights. Pays $15-150, b&w; on publication.
Illustrations: Buys 7-12 illustrations/issue from freelancers. Prefers contemporary, but open to many styles. Send query letter with brochure and samples; write for appointment to show portfolio. Prefers tear sheets or photocopies as samples. Samples returned by SASE (nonresidents include IRCs) only if requested. Reports within 3 weeks. Buys first rights or one-time rights. Pays $15-150, b&w, inside; on publication.

***YACHT RACING & CRUISING**, 23 Leroy Ave., Box 1700, Darien CT 06820. (203)655-2531. Managing Editor: Kristan Meyer. Emphasizes performance sailboat events and instructional articles for "performance-oriented sailors." Published 12 times/year. Circ. 45,000. Original artwork returned after publication. Sample copy $2.50.
Illustrations: Works on assignment only. Send query letter with roughs. Samples returned by SASE. Buys first rights. Pays on publication.

YACHTING, 5 River Rd., Box 1200, Cos Cob CT 06807. (203)629-8300. Associate Editor: Deborah Meisels. For top-level participants in boating in all its forms, power and sail. Monthly. Circ. 150,000. Art guidelines for SASE.
Illustrations: Buys 10 spot illustrations/year. Query. SASE. Reports in 2-3 weeks. Buys all rights. Pays $25, b&w, inside.

YANKEE MAGAZINE, Main St., Dublin NH 03444. (603)563-8111. Creative Director: J. Porter. Regional magazine about New England. Monthly. Circ. 1 million. Accepts previously published material. Returns original artwork after publication. Sample copy $1.50.
Cartoons: Buys 4 cartoons/issue from freelancers. Cartoons must be "very funny and relative to New England lifestyle." Send query letter with samples of style to be kept on file. Material not filed is returned by SASE. Reports only if interested. Buys one-time rights. Pays $25-100, b&w; $35-125, color.
Illustrations: Buys 30 illustrations/issue from freelancers. Send query letter with samples to be kept on file. Prefers tear sheets, slides or photographs as samples. Samples not filed are returned by SASE. Re-

ports only if interested. Buys one-time rights. Pays $200-750 for color cover; $100-550 for b&w and $150-750 for color, inside; on acceptance.

*YELLOW SILK: Journal of Erotic Arts, Box 6374, Albany CA 94706. (415)841-6500 (out of state calls returned collect). Publisher: Lily Pond. Emphasizes erotic literature and arts for well educated, highly literate readership, generally personally involved in arts field. Quarterly. Circ. 4,500. Does not accept previously published material. Returns original artwork after publication. Sample copy $3.
Cartoons: Uses 0-3/issue. Prefers themes involving sexuality and/or human relationships. " 'All persuasions, no brutality' is editoral policy. Nothing tasteless." Accepts any cartoon format except color. Send query letter with finished cartoons to be kept on file. Include phone number, name and address on each sample. Material not filed is returned by SASE with correct stamps, no meters. Reports only if SASE included. Buys first rights or reprint rights. Pays $1/panel plus 3 copies; on publication.
Illustrations: Uses 9-12/issue by one artist if possible. Considers "anything in the widest definitions of eroticism except brutality, bondage or S&M. Nothing tasteless. No pornography. All sexual persuasions represented." Send query letter with samples to be kept on file. Prefers photocopies, slides, photostats, photographs or originals, "all sent at artist's risk." Include name, address and telephone number on all samples. Samples not filed returned by SASE. Reports within weeks. Buys first rights or reprint rights. Pays $1/illustration plus 50 copies of issue; on publication.

YOUNG AMBASSADOR, Box 82808, Lincoln NE 68501. (402)474-4567. Art Director: Win Mumma. "Our purpose is to help Christian teens live consistently for Christ, and to help them grow in their knowledge of the Bible and its principles for living." Monthly. Circ. 80,000. Original artwork not returned after publication. Free sample copy.
Cartoons: Managing Editor: David W. Lambert. Uses 2-3 cartoons/issue; buys 2-3/issue from freelancers. Receives 4 submissions/week from freelancers. Interested in wholesome humor for teens; single panel. Prefers to see finished cartoons. Reports in 3 weeks. Buys all rights on a work-for-hire basis.
Illustrations: Some illustrations purchased on assignment only. Submit slides or tear sheets with query letter. Humorous and cartoon-style illustrations mostly done in-house; a few assigned. Pays $50 b&w, $100, color.

YOUR HOME, Meridian Publishing, Box 10010, Ogden UT 84409. Editor: Peggie Bingham. Monthly. Circ. 90,000. Distributed to businesses with their inserts, as their house organ. "We are a pictorial magazine." Emphasis is on home and garden decorating and improvement.
Needs: "We use illustrations and 3-4 cartoons per year. There is a 1-year lead time." Payment on acceptance; $20/cartoon. Send SASE for guidelines. Sample copy $1. "We would like simple, well-defined cartoons that would aid the message of the article."

*ZOOBOOKS, Suite #14, 930 W. Washington St., San Diego CA 92103. (619)488-1755. Art Director: Walter Stuart. Magazine featuring wildlife for grades kindergarten and up. Publishes 12 issues/year.
First Contact & Terms: Works with 20 freelance artists/year. Artists must be able to render animals in color with a high degree of accuracy and technical excellence. Works on assignment basis only. Send query letter with resume and samples to be kept on file. Call or write for appointment to show portfolio. Write for artists' guidelines. Prefers color slides and printed pieces as samples. Samples not filed are returned if accompanied by an SASE. Reports back to the artist within 4 weeks. Original work is returned to the artist. Considers complexity of the project, skill and experience of artist, turnaround time and rights purchased when establishing payment. Buys all rights.
Text Illustration: Prefers highly real gouache or acrylic work. Pays by the project, $5,000-7,000.

Newspapers & Newsletters ——————

This section is similar to the Magazines section because of the diversity, but it is unique because even the diversity is diverse! Not only do you have publications whose *contents* vary dramatically, as do magazines, but there is also a variance among the newspapers and newsletters themselves. They can be daily, weekly, quarterly or semiannual, published only on Sundays or just for a particular company or organization. They can be consumer or trade, general or limited interest, large or small. Medicine, psychology, softball, running, art and skydiving are a few of the specialty areas in this section which seek freelance graphic artists. Alaska; Nevada; Milwaukee; Kutztown, Pennsylvania; and dozens of other regions offer markets to artists and are listed here. In simple terms, the Newspapers/Newsletters section offers something for everyone.

Since many of these publications have specialized audiences, either by area of interest or geographic region, your ability to understand the slant of a publication will be a great asset in making sales here.

The major needs of these publications are cartoons and illustrations, but if you reside nearby, don't overlook those that indicate they use freelance artists for advertising, layout, production work and other services. Strong black-and-white artwork is most desirable here since few of these publications work in color, although more and more major newspapers are changing that. An artist's understanding of size reduction and the absorption quality of newsprint can help him to produce work that will be more acceptable to some of these markets.

Read past copies of the publication you're interested in approaching (many libraries carry out-of-town papers or write to the paper and request a sample copy); research the newspaper/newsletter field in general to improve your understanding of the mechanics of publishing.

For further information and other names and addresses, consult *Writer's Market 1986, The Newspaper Directory, Ayer Directory of Publications* and *Editor & Publisher* magazine.

Mike Peters © Dayton Daily News—United Feature Syndicate

NOW I'LL NEVER GET BACK TO KANSAS ...

This effective editorial cartoon epitomizes Close-up Mike Peter's ability to humorously illustrate the topic of nuclear war. The artist's editorial cartoons, originated for the **Dayton Daily News,** *are syndicated to over 270 newspapers.*

AMERICAN MEDICAL NEWS, 535 N. Dearborn St., Chicago IL 60610. (312)751-6633. Editor: Dick Walt. Emphasizes news and opinions on developments, legislation and business in medicine. For physicians. Weekly newspaper. Circ. 315,000. Photocopied and simultaneous submissions OK. Original artwork not returned after publication. Free sample copy.
Cartoons: Contact: Sher Watts, senior editor. Uses 1 cartoon/issue, all from freelancers. Receives "dozens of submissions/week from freelancers. Interested in medical themes; single panel. Prefers to see finished cartoons. SASE. Reports in 4 weeks. Usually buys first North American rights. Pays up to $100, b&w; on acceptance.
Illustrations: Contact: Barbara Bolsen, executive editor. Number illustrations used/issue varies; number bought/issue from freelancers varies. Works on assignment only. Samples returned by SASE. Provide resume, letter of inquiry, brochure and flyer to be kept on file for future assignments. Usually buys first North American rights. Payment negotiable. Pays on acceptance.
Tips: "We work mostly with Chicago area illustrators."

*THE AMERICAN NEWSPAPER CARRIER, Box 15300, Winston-Salem NC 27113. Editor: Marilyn H. Rollins. A monthly inspirational newsletter for pre-teen and teenage newspaper carriers. Original artwork not returned after publication. Sample copy and art guidelines free for SASE.
Cartoons: Uses freelance and staff cartoons. Publishes 2-3 single-panel and 1 multi-panel per issue. Prefers original b&w line drawings. Usually buys all rights. Pays $10-30 on acceptance.
Illustrations: Buys 1-2 per issue, all freelance. Works on assignment only. Send query letter with samples to be kept on file. Prefers photocopies as samples. Samples not returned. Usually buys all rights; pays $10-30 on acceptance.

ANCHOR BAY BEACON, 51170 Washington, New Baltimore MI 48047. (313)725-4531. Executive Editor: Michael Eckert. Newspaper emphasizing local news for paid readership in one city, one village and three townships. Weekly. Circ. 8,000. Accepts previously published material. Original work returned after publication. Sample copy free for large manilla SASE with 50¢ postage.
Cartoons: Number of cartoons purchased/issue from freelancers is open. No color. Send query letter with samples of style to be kept on file. Material filed returned only if requested. Reports only if interested. Buys reprint rights. Negotiates pay rate; pays on publication.
Illustrations: Works on assignment only. Send query letter to be kept on file. Write for appointment to show portfolio. Reports only if interested. Buys reprint rights. Negotiates pay rate; pays on publication.

ANDERSON VALLEY ADVERTISER, Box 459, Boonville CA 95415. (707)895-3536. Editor: Bruce Anderson. Newspaper emphasizing left/liberal rural themes for a sophisticated/rural audience. Weekly. Circ. 1600. Accepts previously published material. Returns original artwork after publication. Sample copy available.
Cartoons: Buys 1 cartoon/issue from freelance artists. Prefers single panel with or without gagline. Send finished cartoons to be kept on file. Material not filed returned only if requested. Reports within 5 days. Buys one-time rights. Pays $10 for b&w; on acceptance.
Illustrations: Buys 1-2 illustrations/issue from freelance artists. Prefers sophisticated, *Lampoon/New Yorker* quality. Send samples to be kept on file; write for appointment to show portfolio. Prefers tear sheets as samples. Samples not filed are returned. Reports within 5 days. Buys one-time rights. Pays $10 for b&w; on acceptance.

APA MONITOR, American Psychological Association, 1200 17th St. NW, Washington DC 20036. (202)955-7690. Editor: Jeffrey Mervis. Associate Editor: Kathleen Fisher. Monthly tabloid newspaper for psychologists and other behavioral scientists. 64-72 pages. Circ. 70,000.
Illustrations: Uses 30 illustrations/year on current events and feature articles in behavioral sciences/mental health area. Works on assignment only; reports back on future assignment possibilities. Washington area artists preferred. Query with samples or arrange interview to show portfolio. Sample copy $2.50. SASE. Original artwork returned after publication, if requested. Buys first North American serial rights. Pays $40-250, b&w; on publication.
Tips: "Good ideas are hard to come by. Being able to translate abstract concepts into strong, graphic presentation is essential for use in our paper."

ARIZONA MAGAZINE, 120 E. Van Buren, Phoenix AZ 85001. (602)271-8291. Art Director: Ron Schwartz. Sunday magazine. General audience. Weekly. Circ. 400,000. Accepts previously published material. Original artwork returned after publication.
Cartoons: Uses 4 cartoons/issue; buys all from freelancers. Prefers single panel, with or without gagline; b&w line drawings, b&w washes. Send query letter with finished cartoons to be kept on file. Material not kept on file is returned by SASE. Reports only if interested. Buys first-rights or one-time rights; pays on publication.

Illustrations: Works on assignment with local artists. Send query letter with brochure, business card and samples to be kept on file; call for appointment to show portfolio. Prefers photostats, photographs or slides as samples. Samples not kept on file are returned by SASE. Reports within 2 weeks. Buys first rights or one-time rights; pays on publication.

BALLS AND STRIKES NEWSPAPER, 2801 N.E. 50th St., Oklahoma City OK 73111. (405)424-5266. Communications Director: Bill Plummer III. Official publication of the amateur softball association. Emphasizes amateur softball for "the more than 30 million people who play amateur softball; they come from all walks of life and hold varied jobs." Published 8 times/year. Circ. 250,000. Previously published material OK. Original work returned after publication. Free sample copy available.
Cartoons: Buys all from freelancers. Interested in b&w line drawings. Send query letter with samples of style. Samples returned. Reports in 3 days. Buys all rights. Pays $35-50, b&w; $100, color; on acceptance.
Illustrations: Uses 2-4 illustrations/issue. No drug or alcohol themes. Works on assignment only. Send query letter with samples of style. Samples returned. Reports in 3 days. Provide resume and business card to be kept on file for possible future assignments. Buys all rights.

BALTIMORE SUN MAGAZINE, Calvert and Centre Sts., Baltimore MD 21278. (301)332-6600. Editor: Susan Baer. Emphasizes general interest topics to the Maryland area; audience is families, educated. Weekly. Circ. 400,000. Accepts previously published material. Returns original art after publication. Sample copy free for SASE.
Illustrations: Uses 2 illustrations/issue; buys both from freelancers. Considers all styles. Works on assignment only. Send query letter with samples to be kept on file. Call or write for appointment to show portfolio. Prefers slides or tear sheets as samples. Material not filed is returned. Reports in 2-3 weeks. Negotiates rights purchased. Pays $200-300, color cover; $100, b&w, and $200, color, inside; on publication.

BARTER COMMUNIQUE, Box 2527, Sarasota FL 33578. (813)349-3300. Art Director: Robert J. Murley. Concerns bartering; for radio, TV stations, newspapers, magazines, travel and ad agencies. Quarterly tabloid. Circ. 50,000.
Cartoons: Buys 5/issue on barter situations. Send roughs. Pays $5, b&w; on publication.
Illustrations: Query with samples. SASE. Reports in 2 weeks. Pays $5, b&w; on publication.
Tips: Looks for "uniqueness" in reviewing samples.

BERKSHIRE COURIER, 268 Main St., Great Barrington MA 01230. (413)528-3024. Production/Art Director: James DelGrande. Newspaper emphasizing features, area history, local news and art/theatre for an intelligent, well-bred second-home area and local small town country. Weekly. Circ. 5,500. Accepts previously published material. Original work returned after publication. Sample copy 40¢.
Cartoons: Buys 1 cartoon/issue from freelancers. Prefers local country and high social themes. Prefers single or double panel; b&w line drawings, b&w washes. Send finished cartoons to be kept on file. Material not filed is returned by SASE. Reports back only if interested. Negotiates rights purchased. Varying pay rate; pays on publication.
Illustrations: Buys 1 illustration/issue from freelancers. Prefers local country and high social themes. Works on assignment only. Send query letter with samples to be kept on file. Prefers photostats, tear sheets and photographs as samples. Samples not filed are returned by SASE. Reports back only if interested. Negotiates rights purchased. Varying pay rate; pays on publication.

BLACK VOICE NEWS, Box 1581, Riverside CA 92502. (714)824-8884 or 682-6070. Contact: Hardy Brown, Jr. Newspaper emphasizing general topics for "the black community with various backgrounds, and Hispanics and whites who are in tune with that community." Weekly. Circ. 5,000. Sample copy free for SASE.
Cartoons: Prefers political, historic and topical themes. Accepts single, double or multiple panel with or without gagline; b&w line drawings. Send query letter with samples of style to be kept on file; write for appointment to show portfolio. Material not filed is returned by SASE. Reports back only if interested. Buys one-time or reprint rights; pays on publication.
Illustrations: Send query letter with samples to be kept on file; write for appointment to show portfolio. Samples not filed are returned by SASE. Reports back only if interested. Buys one-time or reprint rights; pays on publication.

BOOKPLATES IN THE NEWS, Apt.#F, 605 N. Stoneman Ave., Alhambra CA 91801. (213)283-1936 (evenings and weekends). Director: Audrey Spencer Arellanes. Emphasizes bookplates for those who use bookplates whether individuals or institutions, those who collect them, artists who design them, art historians, genealogists, historians, antiquarian booktrade and others for tracing provenance

of a volume; also publishes yearbook annually. Quarterly. Circ. 200. Original work returned after publication. Previously published material OK "on occasion, usually from foreign publications." Sample copy $4; art guidelines for SASE.
Illustrations: Illustrations are bookplates. "Appearance of work in our publications should produce requests for bookplate commissions." Send query letter and finished art. Reports in 3 weeks. No payment.

*THE BOSTON PHOENIX, 100 Massachusetts Ave., Boston MA 02115. (617)536-5390. Design Director: Cleo Leontis. Weekly. Circ. 150,000. Original work returned after publication by SASE. Sample copy $3.50.
Illustrations: Uses 2-8 b&w illustrations/issue, occasional color; buys all from freelancers. Uses 1-2 humorous and cartoon-style illustrations/week on assignment. Send samples of style (no originals) and resume to be kept on file for possible future assignments. Call for appointment. Reports in 6 weeks. Buys one-time rights. Pays on publication.

THE BOSTON REVIEW, 33 Harrison Ave., Boston MA 02111. (617)350-5353. Editor: Mark Silk. Tabloid. Emphasizes arts and culture for persons of college age and older interested/involved in the arts, literature and related cultural and political topics. Bimonthly. Circ. 10,000. Accepts simultaneous submissions. Original artwork returned after publication. Sample copy $3.
Cartoons: Has not previously used cartoons, but will consider. "Must be b&w work, anything original, creative, inspiring." Prefers single panel, b&w line drawings. Material not kept on file is returned by SASE. Reports only if interested. Negotiates rights purchased. Negotiates payment. Pays on publication.
Illustrations: Uses 4-10 illustrations/issue; buys all from freelancers. Themes and styles are open; b&w work only. Send query letter with resume and samples to be kept on file; call for appointment to show portfolio. Open to any type of sample. Samples not kept on file are returned by SASE. Reports only if interested. Negotiates rights purchased. Negotiates pay for inside art. Pays on publication.

THE BREAD RAPPER, 2103 Noyes, Evanston IL 60201. Editor-in-Chief: Laurie Lawlor. Concerns banking services and involvement of bank with community; received with checking account statement. Photocopied submissions OK. Sample copy and artist's guidelines with SASE.
Cartoons: Buys 1 cartoon/issue on banking; single panel with gagline. No negative bank slants (bank robberies, etc.), please. Mail art. SASE. Reports within 8 weeks. Buys all rights. Pays $20 minimum, b&w line drawings and washes; on publication.

BUILDING BRIEFS, Dan Burch Associates, 2338 Frankfort Ave., Louisville KY 40206. (502)895-4881. Program Manager: Leslie Auberry. Newsletter. Emphasizes design/build and conventional methods of construction for commercial and industrial buildings, plus other topics such as landscaping, security, energy-saving ideas. Directed to potential clients of a building contractor in the nonresidential market, company presidents, board members and managerial personnel who will construct or renovate their buildings. Bimonthly. Circ. 25,000 + . Original artwork returned after publication. Sample copy available.
Cartoons: Uses 1 cartoon/issue; buys 1/issue from freelancers. Prefers themes related to construction; light humor, simple line art. Prefers single panel with gagline; b&w line drawings. Send query letter with finished cartoons to be kept on file. Material not kept on file is returned. Reports only if interested. Buys one-time rights. Pays $50, b&w; on publication.
Tips: "Spend a little time researching the design/build industry. Talk to a design/build contractor to learn the basics—what the concept of design/build is. Two industry publications where more can be learned are *Metal Construction News* and *Metal Building Review*."

THE BURLINGTON LOOK, Burlington Industries, Box 21207, Greensboro NC 27420. (919)379-2339. Publications Editor: Melissa Staples. Tabloid. Emphasizes textiles and home furnishings for all domestic employees of Burlington Industries plus opinion leaders in the plant communities. Published 8 times/year. Circ. 62,000. Accepts previously published material and simultaneous submissions. Original artwork not returned after publication unless requested. Sample copy free for SASE.
Cartoons: Uses 1-2 cartoons/issue; buys all from freelancers. Prefers single, double or multipanel without gagline; b&w line drawings. Send query letter with samples of style to be kept on file. Call for appointment to show portfolio; "if local artists are interested, we will view portfolios." Material not kept on file is returned only if requested. Reports within 10 days. Negotiates rights purchased and payment; pays on acceptance.
Illustrations: Currently uses 1-2 illustrations/issue—"would like more"; buys all from freelancers. Themes/styles vary depending on subject matter. Works on assignment only. Send query letter with resume, business card, samples and tear sheets to be kept on file. Prefers photostats or photographs as

samples; "I'd rather not have original work for fear it may be damaged or get lost." Samples not kept on file are returned only if requested. Reports within 2 weeks. Negotiates rights purchased. Payment varies according to size and complexity; pays on acceptance.
Tips: "Looking for illustrators with the creativity to be able to illustrate and visually communicate various story concepts."

BY-LINES, Box 48, Ft. Smith AR 72902. Director Public Relations & Advertising: John T. Greer. Tabloid. Emphasizes business (trucking related) for employees of ABF Freight System, Inc. Monthly. Circ. 7,000. Accepts previously published material and simultaneous submissions. Original artwork returned after publication. Sends art guidelines only if specifically interested in artist's work.
Cartoons: Uses 1-2 cartoons/issue. Prefers single panel; b&w line drawings, b&w washes. Send query letter with samples of style to be kept on file; write for appointment to show portfolio. Material not kept on file is returned only if requested. Reports only if interested. Buys reprint rights. Payment varies; pays on acceptance.
Illustrations: Number of illustrations used/issue varies. Works on assignment only. Send query letter with samples to be kept on file; write for appointment to show portfolio. Samples not kept on file are returned only if requested. Reports only if interested. Buys reprint rights. Payment varies; pays on acceptance.

CALIFORNIA APPAREL NEWS, 945 S. Wall St., Los Angeles CA 90015. (213)626-0411. Art Director: John Miller. Emphasizes fashion for the trade. Weekly. Circ. 25,000. Returns originals after publication.
Illustrations: Buys 10 illustrations/issue from freelancers. Considers fashion illustration. Works on assignment only. Send query letter with brochure, resume, business card and samples to be kept on file. Call for appointment to show portfolio. Accepts photostats, tear sheets, photocopies, slides or photographs as samples. Samples not filed returned only if requested. Reports only if interested. Negotiates rights purchased. Pays on publication.

CENTRAL MASS MEDIA INC., Worcester Magazine, Business Worcester, Ocean State Business, Centrumguide, Box 1000, Worcester MA 01614. (617)799-0511. Art Director: Mark Minter. Concerns central Massachusetts. Weekly and monthly newspapers. Circ. 50,000.
Illustrations: Buys on assigned themes. Query with resume and samples or arrange interview to show portfolio. Buys one-time rights. Cover: Pays $75-100, gray opaques, b&w line drawings and washes; $100, color. Inside: Pays $10-50, gray opaques, b&w line drawings and washes; on acceptance.

THE CHARLOTTE OBSERVER/THE CHARLOTTE NEWS, 600 S. Tryon St., Charlotte NC 28202. Promotion Manager: Coco Killian. Art Director for Advertising: Chuck Cole. Daily newspapers; "largest in the Carolinas." Circ. 250,000 + .
Illustrations: Call for appointment to show portfolio. Especially looks for "quality, neatness, creativity and imagination. It doesn't have to bowl me over—sometimes it can be just a spark."

CHICAGO READER, Box 11101, Chicago IL 60611. (312)828-0350. Editor-in-Chief: Robert A. Roth. Cartoon/Illustration Editor: Robert E. McCamant. For young adults in lakefront neighborhoods interested in things to do in Chicago and feature stories on city life. Weekly. Circ. 120,000. Sample copy $2.
Cartoons: Buys 9 cartoons/issue on any topic; single, double and multi-panel. Pays $10 and up. "At present, we carry eight regular cartoon features, plus one or more irregularly-appearing ones. While we are not actively looking for more, we will consider anything, and find the space if the material warrants it." Send photocopies (no originals). Buys one-time rights; pays by 15th of month following publication
Illustrations: Buys 3 illustrations/issue on assigned themes. Send photocopies or arrange interview to show portfolio. SASE. Buys one-time rights. Pays by 15th of month following publication. Cover and inside: Pays $100-180, b&w line drawings and washes.

*THE CHRISTIAN SCIENCE MONITOR, 1 Norway St., Boston MA 02130. (617)262-2300. Design Director: Robin Jareaux. Newspaper emphasizing analytical reporting of current events; diverse features and news features for well-educated, well-informed readers in all fields—specifically politicians, educators, business people. Daily. Circ. 160,000. Original artwork returned after publication. Sample copy and art guidelines available.
Illustrations: Buys 1-2 illustrations/issue from freelancers. Prefers editorial ("op-ed') conceptual themes; line, wash or scratchboard. Works on assignment only. Send samples to be filed. Samples should be 8½x11" photocopies; no originals. Samples not returned. Reports only if interested. Buys first rights. Pays $80-150, b&w, inside; on publication.

Artist: Bob Dahm

This illustration accompanied an article on UAW negotiations in The Christian Science Monitor. *Robin Jareaux, design director, telephoned freelance illustrator Bob Dahm of Cranston, Rhode Island, and gave him the needed dimensions and discussed possible ideas. Since the newspaper's articles are usually on short lead time, Jareaux says, "I'll usually call the illustrator and read the article over the phone. I try to communicate our approach in dealing with articles." The final artwork was delivered in four days; Dahm was paid $120 for first rights.*

THE CHRONICLE OF HIGHER EDUCATION, Suite 700, 1255 23rd St. NW, Washington DC 20037. (202)466-1035. Art Director: Peter Stafford. Emphasizes all aspects of higher education for college and university administrators, professors, students and staff. Weekly. Circ. 70,000. Sample copy available.

Cartoons: Uses approximately 3 cartoons/year. Will accept previously published material. Prefers higher education related themes, i.e., sports, high cost of tuition, student loans, energy conservation on campus. Prefers single panel, with gagline; b&w line drawings or b&w washes. Send query letter with samples of style to be kept on file. Material not kept on file is returned only if requested. Reports only if interested. Buys one-time rights. Pays on publication.

Illustrations: Uses 1 illustration/issue; buys all from freelancers. Uses a variety of styles, depending on the tone of the story. Works on assignment only. Send query letter with resume, business card, samples and tear sheets to be kept on file. Prefers photostats or good quality photocopy for line work; photographs or slides for halftone work as samples. Samples are returned only if requested. Reports only if interested. Buys one-time rights. Pays $100 and up depending on size, b&w, inside. Pays on publication.

CINCINNATI ENQUIRER SUNDAY MAGAZINE, 617 Vine St., Cincinnati OH 45202. (513)721-2700. Editor: Betsa Marsh. Art Director: Marty Eggerding. Weekly. Circ. 300,000.

Illustrations: Uses 1-2 illustrations/issue on assigned themes. "We rarely, if ever, use unsolicited freelance art. The usual procedure is for the artist to show a portfolio. If we like the work, we'll give the artist a manuscript to illustrate." Works on assignment only. Samples returned by SASE. Reports back on future assignment possibilities. Provide business card to be kept on file for future assignments. Prefers to see portfolio. SASE. Reporting time varies. Buys all rights on a work-for-hire basis. Pays $50-200, b&w line drawings and washes; $150-350, color illustrations and cover.

*CLEVELAND PLAIN DEALER, 1801 Superior Ave., Cleveland OH 44114. (216)344-4447. Graphics Editor: Chris Pett-Ridge. Newspaper. Emphasizes current events, features for metropolitan

daily readership. Circ. 500,000. Accepts previously published material. Original artwork returned after publication if requested. Sample copy available.
Illustrations: Buys 6 illustrations/week from freelancers. Preferred themes are any dealing with current affairs. Works on assignment only. Send query letter with samples to be kept on file. Prefers photostats as samples. Samples not filed are returned only if requested. Reports only interested. Buys one-time rights. Pays $130, b&w, cover; $50, b&w, inside; on acceptance.

COMPUTERWORLD, 375 Cochituate Rd., Framingham MA 01701. Graphic Director: Kristie Van Valkinburgh. Emphasizes news and products relating to the computer field. Weekly. Returns original artwork after publication. Sample copy free for SASE.
Illustrations: Number purchased/issue varies. Themes depend on the storyline. Works on assignment only. Send query letter with brochure and samples to be kept on file. Write for appointment to show portfolio. Prefers photocopies as samples. Reports back only if interested. Buys first rights. Pays $175-200 for b&w and $225-400 for color, inside; on acceptance.

COMPUTERWORLD FOCUS, (formerly *Computerworld on Office Automation*), 375 Cochituate Rd., Framingham MA 01701. Art Director: Tom Monahan. Tabloid. Emphasizes news and products relating to the computer field. Monthly. Returns original artwork after publication. Sample copy free for SASE.
Cartoons: Cartoons must be computer related. Considers horizontal single panel with or without gagline (preferred), b&w line drawings. Send query letter with samples of style to be kept on file. Write for appointment to show portfolio. Material not filed is returned only if requested. Reports within 1 month only if interested. Buys first rights. Pays $25, b&w; on publication.
Illustrations: Number purchased/issue varies. Themes depend on the storyline. Works on assignment only. Send query letter with brochure and samples to be kept on file. Write for appointment to show portfolio. Prefers photocopies as samples. Reports back only if interested. Buys first rights. Pays $175-200 for b&w and $225-400 for color, inside; on acceptance.

COMPUTERWORLD ON COMMUNICATIONS, 375 Cochituate Rd., Framingham MA 01701. (617)879-0700. Art Designer: Diane Gronberg. Tabloid. Emphasizes news and products relating to the computer field. Bimonthly. Returns original artwork after publication. Sample copy free for SASE.
Illustrations: Number purchased/issue varies. Themes depend on the storyline. Works on assignment only. Send query letter with brochure and samples to be kept on file. Write for appointment to show portfolio. Prefers photocopies as samples. Reports only if interested. Buys first rights. Pays $175-200 for b&w and $225-400 for color, inside; on acceptance.

CONNECTICUT TRAVELER, 2276 Whitney Ave., Hamden CT 06518. (213)288-7441. Managing Director of Publications: Elke P. Martin. Newspaper. Estab. 1983. Emphasizes automobile travel, safety and maintenance, national and international travel and regional events (New England) for AAA members. Monthly. Circ. 155,000. Accepts previously published material. Returns original artwork after publication. Sample copy free for SASE; art guidelines available.
Cartoons: Buys 1 cartoon/issue from freelancers. Prefers single panel with gagline; b&w line drawings; b&w washes. Send query letter with samples of style to be kept on file. Reports within 2 weeks. Buys reprint rights or negotiates rights purchased. Pays on publication.

THE CONSTANTIAN, 123 Orr Rd., Pittsburgh PA 15241. (412)831-8750. Editor: Randall J. Dicks. "We (Constantian Society) are monarchists and royalists, interested in monarchy as a political system and royalty as persons and personalities." Bimonthly newsletter. Circ. 400. Previously published work OK. Sample copy for SASE; free artist's guidelines.
Cartoons: "We have used a cartoon only once, but would certainly consider using them. It is best to write us about the idea first and send samples." SASE. Reports within 1 week. Buys various rights. Pays $5-10, b&w line drawings; on acceptance or publication.
Illustrations: "We use a lot of decorative drawings and work which relate to our subject matter (heraldic items of different nationalities, coats of arms, monograms, etc.)." SASE. Reports within 1 week. Buys various rights. Pays $5 minimum, b&w line drawings; on acceptance or publication.

CONSTRUCTION SUPERVISION & SAFETY LETTER, 24 Rope Ferry Rd., Waterford CT 06386. (203)442-4365. Editor: DeLoris Lidestri. Emphasizes construction supervision for supervisors who work with their crews. Covers bricklayers, carpenters, electricians, painters, plasterers, plumbers and building laborers. Semimonthly. Circ. 3,700. Original artwork not returned after publication. Free sample copy.
Cartoons: Uses 1 cartoon/issue which is done by a freelancer. Receives 5-7 submissions/week from freelancers. Uses "situations that deal with supervision in construction. Cartoons that depict both men

and women as workers and/or supervisors needed. No sexist material, please." Format: single panel, b&w line drawings with gagline. Prefers to see finished cartoons. SASE. Reports in 2 weeks. Buys all rights. Pays $10 on acceptance.

THE CRANSTON MIRROR, 250 Auburn St., Cranston RI 02910. Contact: Malcolm L. Daniels. Weekly newspaper. Circ. 10,000. Original artwork returned after publication. Prefers local artists. Also uses artists for layout, illustration, technical art, paste-up, lettering and retouching. Pays $175, booklet; $15-75, illustrations.
Cartoons: Uses 2 cartoons/issue; buys 1 or none/issue from freelancers. Receives 3-4 submissions/week from freelancers. Interested in local editorial subjects. Call for interview to show portfolio (except July and August). Prefers to see finished cartoons. Reports in 1 week.
Illustrations: Uses 2-4 illustrations/issue; buys 1-2/issue from freelancers. Call for interview to show portfolio (except July and August). Provide resume to be kept on file for future assignments. Reports in 1 week.
Tips: Especially looks for "unique idea, quality workmanship and regard to detail. Ideas, however, are paramount."

CYCLE NEWS, Box 498, Long Beach CA 90801. (213)427-7433. Editor: John Ulrich. For the motor-cycle enthusiast. Weekly newspaper. Circ. 88,000. Previously published work OK. Returns originals to artist after publication. Sample copy available. Art guidelines not available.
Cartoons: Buys 0-2 cartoons/issue. Send query letter with finished cartoons and SASE. Reports back only if interested. Negotiates payment and rights purchased. Pays on publication.
Illustrations: Buys varying number of illustrations/issue. Works on assignment only. Send query letter with samples and SASE. Prefers photocopies as samples. Reports only if interested. Negotiates payment and rights purchased. Pays on publication.

DOLLARS & SENSE, 325 Pennsylvania Ave. SE, Washington DC 20003. (202)543-1300. Editor: Tom Palmer. For people interested in reducing taxes and government spending. 10 issues/year. Circ. 140,000. Previously published material and simultaneous submissions OK. Especially needs federal budget information. Original work not returned after publication. Free sample copy for SASE.
Cartoons: Uses 3 cartoons/issue; number bought from freelancers varies. Interested in political/taxa-tion themes. Send finished cartoons. Samples returned by SASE. Reports within 2 weeks. Negotiates one-time and first rights. Payment varies; on publication.
Illustrations: Uses 4 illustrations/issue. Interested in political themes. Send finished art or samples of style. Samples returned by SASE. Reports within 2 weeks. Negotiates rights. Pays $60-150 cover, color washes; inside, payment varies; on publication.
Tips: "Either make the graphics very general in nature or send in very specific cartoons."

*THE EVENING SUN, 501 N. Calvert St., Baltimore MD 21278. (301)332-6529. Art Director: Chuck Lankford. Daily newspaper for general audience. Circ. 145,000. Accepts previously published material. Original artwork sometimes returned after publication. Art guidelines available.
Cartoons: Buys 2-3 cartoons/issue from freelancers. Theme and style vary according to story content. Prefers multiple panel without gagline; b&w line drawings or color washes. Send samples of style to be kept on file; write for appointment to show portfolio. Material not filed is returned by SASE only if re-quested. Reports only if interested. Buys all rights or negotiates rights purchased. Pays variable rate, b&w and color, on publication.
Illustrations: Theme and style vary according to story content. Send query letter with samples to be kept on file; write for appointment to show portfolio. Photocopies acceptable as samples. Samples not filed are returned only if requested. Reports only if interested. Negotiates rights purchased. Pays varia-ble rate, b&w and color; on publcation.

THE FAYETTEVILLE OBSERVER, Box 849, Fayetteville NC 28302. (919)323-4848. City Editor: Jim Kyle. Daily. Circ. 46,000 daily; 74,000 Sunday. Accepts previously published material and simul-taneous submissions. Original artwork not returned after publication. Sample copy and art guidelines for SASE.
Illustrations: Uses 3 illustrations/issue. Interested in general illustrations to accompany wire or local copy. Send query letter with samples to be kept on file. Write for appointment to show portfolio. Prefers photostats as samples. Samples not kept on file are returned by SASE. Reports only if interested. Nego-tiates rights purchased. Pays on publication.

*FOR YOUR EYES ONLY, Box 8759, Amarillo TX 79114. (806)655-2009. Editor: Stephen V. Cole. Newsletter emphasizing military affairs after 1980 for military contractors, officers and interested par-ties. Bi-weekly. Circ. 1,000. Accepts previously published material. Returns original artwork after pub-lication with SASE. Sample copy for $2.

Illustrations: Buys 1-2/issue. Prefers modern military themes in realistic styles. Send query letter with samples to be kept on file. Prefers photocopies as samples. Reports within 2 weeks. Negotiates rights purchased. Pays $5-20, b&w, cover; on publication.

FRUITION, Box 872-am, Santa Cruz CA 95061. (408)425-1708. Editor: C.L. Olson. Newsletter. Emphasizes planting of public access food trees; establishing community food tree nurseries; achieving superior health through simple natural means. Biannually. Circ. 310. Accepts previously published material and simultaneous submissions. Originals returned to artist after publication if stamped, artist-supplied packaging is provided. Sample copy for $2; art guidelines free for SASE.
Cartoons: Uses 1 cartoon/issue. Prefers single panel; b&w line drawings, b&w washes. Send query letter with finished cartoons. Material is returned by SASE. Reports within 3 weeks if interested. Negotiates rights purchased and pay rate; pays on acceptance.
Illustrations: Uses 4 illustrations/issue; buys 1/issue from freelancers. Send query letter with samples. Prefers photostats, photographs or original work as samples. Samples not kept on file are returned by SASE. Reports within 3 weeks. Negotiates pay rate; pays on acceptance.
Tips: Especially looks for "good line work and overall balance relating to fruit and nut trees."

GAY NEWS, 254 S. 11th St., Philadelphia PA 19107. (215)625-8501. Design Director: Gary L. Day. Newspaper. Emphasizes news and feature articles for gay men and lesbians. Weekly. Readership estimate, 45-50,000. Accepts previously published material and simultaneous submissions. Original artwork returned after publication. Sample copy and art guidelines free for SASE.
Cartoons: Uses 1 cartoon/issue; buys from freelancer. Editorial cartoons only. Prefers single panel, with gagline; b&w line drawings. Send query letter with samples of style to be kept on file; write for appointment to show portfolio. Material not kept on file returned by SASE. Reports within 2 weeks. Negotiates rights purchased and pay rate; pays on publication.
Illustrations: Uses 3 illustrations/issue; buys all from freelancers. Themes and styles depend on accompanying article. Works on assignment only. Send query letter with business card, samples and tear sheets to be kept on file; write for appointment to show portfolio. Prefers photostats or photographs as samples; "we prefer not to be sent original art as a sample." Samples not kept on file returned by SASE. Reports within 2 weeks. Negotiates rights purchased and pay rate; pays on publication.

THE GERMANTOWN COURIER, 156 W. Chelten Ave., Philadelphia PA 19144. (215)848-4300. Editor: Debbie Flood. Newspaper emphasizing neighborhood news in northwest Philadelphia; low to middle income. Weekly. Circ. 25,000. Original work returned after publication. Sample copy and art guidelines available.
Cartoons: Prefers themes on Philadelphia news/general news and events; political-cultural relevance. Single, double or multi-panel with gagline OK; b&w line drawings. Send query letter with finished cartoons to be kept on file. Material not filed returned only if requested. Reports only if interested. Buys first rights or reprint rights. Pays $5, b&w; on publication.
Illustrations: Occasionally buys illustrations from freelancers. Uses illustrations to accompany news stories. Works on assignment only. Send query letter with resume and samples to be kept on file. Prefers good quality photocopies as samples. Samples not filed returned by SASE only if requested. Reports only if interested. Buys first rights or reprint rights. Pays $5 on publication.

THE GOODY MIRROR, 1000 W. Main St., Manchester GA 31816. (404)846-8481. Contact: Editor. Emphasizes employee communications for employees, production, supervision, management, stock holders. Quarterly. Circ. 5,000. Accepts previously published material and simultaneous submissions. Original artwork returned after publication. Sample copy for SASE.
Cartoons: Uses 1-2 cartoons/issue; buys all from freelancers. Prefers single panel with gagline; b&w line drawings. Send query letter with samples of style and roughs to be kept on file. Material not kept on file is returned only if requested. Reports within 3 weeks. Buys one-time rights. Pays $10, b&w. Pays on acceptance.
Illustrations: Uses 2 illustrations/issue; buys all from freelancers. Prefers themes illustrative of editorial thrusts—dollar breakdown, specific situations. Works on assignment only. Send query letter with samples to be kept on file. Prefers photostats as samples. Samples are returned by SASE if not kept on file. Reports within 3 weeks. Buys one-time rights. Payment depends on assignment. Pays on acceptance.

GOUSHA/CHEK-CHART SERVICE BULLETIN, Box 6227, San Jose CA 95150. (408)296-1060. Editor: Jo L. Phelps. Emphasizes automotives—cars, light trucks, engines, new technology for mechanics, service station managers and dealers. Monthly. Circ. 25,000. Original work not returned after publication. Free sample copy and art guidelines for SASE.
Illustrations: Uses 10-12 illustrations/issue; number bought from freelancers varies. Interested in ink

line drawings. Send query letter. Provide business card and samples to be kept on file for possible future assignments. Samples not kept on file are returned by SASE. Reports in 3 weeks. Buys first rights. Pays on acceptance.

*GUARDIAN,33 W. 17th ST., New York NY 10011. Photo/Graphics Editor: Michael Kaufman. Independent radical newspaper with national and international news and cultural reviews for nonsectarian leftists and activists. Weekly. Circ. 20,000. Accepts previously published material. Original artwork returned by SASE after publication. Sample copy available; art guidelines free for SASE.
Cartoons: Buys 7 cartoons/issue from freelancers. Prefers b&w, pen & ink, scratch board; progressive themes. Prefers single, double or multi-panel; b&w, pen & ink, scratch board; progressive style not larger than 8½x11" to be kept on file; write for appointment to show portfolio. Material not filed is returned by SASE. Reports only if interested. Negotiates rights purchased. Pays $15, b&w; on publication.
Illustrations: Buys 3 illustrations/issue from freelancers. Themes: progressive politics, issues. Send query letter and samples not larger than 8½x11" to be kept on file; write for appointment to show portfolio. Prefers photocopies as samples. Samples not filed are returned by SASE. Reports only if interested. Negotiates rights purchased. Pays $15, b&w, cover, inside; on publication.

HARRISON COUNTY PRESS, Box 98, Corydon IN 47112. (502)384-2176. Editor: Richard Martin. Newspaper emphasizing rural, small town local news. Weekly. Circ. 2,900. Accepts previously published material. Sample copy free for SASE with 55¢ postage.
Illustrations: Prefers conservative style. Send query letter with samples to be kept on file. Write for appointment to show portfolio. Samples not filed returned by SASE. Reports only if interested.

HIGH COUNTRY NEWS, Box 1090, Paonia CO 81428. (303)527-4898. Emphasizes energy, economic and environmental issues, Rocky Mountain regional pieces for national audience, all ages, occupation. Biweekly. Circ. 4,200. Accepts previously published material and simultaneous submissions. Original artwork returned after publication if accompanied by postage.
Illustrations: Uses 5 illustrations/issue; buys 3 illustrations/issue from freelancers. Send query letter with samples and/or tear sheets to be kept on file. Prefers photocopies as samples. Samples not kept on file are returned by SASE. Reports within 1 month. Negotiates rights purchased. Pays after publication.

HIGH-TECH MANAGER'S BULLETIN, 24 Rope Ferry Rd., Waterford CT 06386. (203)442-4365. Contact: Editor. Emphasis is on the supervision of technicians in high technology industry. Semimonthly. Free sample copy.
Cartoons: Uses 1 cartoon/issue; buys from freelancer. Interested in non-sexist material which pokes fun at aspects of high technology production and supervision. Prefers single panel b&w line drawings with or without the gagline. Send roughs. SASE. Reports in 3-6 weeks. Buys all rights. Pays $10 for b&w acceptances.

HOSPITAL SUPERVISOR'S BULLETIN, 24 Rope Ferry Rd., Waterford CT 06386. (203)442-4365. Editor: Jill Wasserman. Emphasizes management methods for hospital supervisors of nonmedical departments. Bimonthly newsletter. Circ. 7,000. Original artwork not returned after publication. Free sample copy and artist's guidelines.
Cartoons: Buys 1/issue on any aspect of hospital environment; single panel with gagline. "We prefer cartoons that emphasize the natural humor in life, life's foibles, rather than humor at the expense of others." Pays $10, b&w line drawings. Mail roughs. SASE. Reports within 2 weeks. Pays on acceptance. Buys all rights.
Tips: "We see more professionalism and more dignity in our field. Stay away from sexist humor and demoralizing humor—poking fun at people. Laugh with them not at them."

JEWISH TIMES, 2104 N. Charles St., Baltimore MD 21218. (301)752-3504. Art Director: Kim Muller-Thym. Tabloid. Emphasizes Jewish editorial content: lifestyle, politics, trends, "runs the gamut of subject matter"; averages 160 pages; "lots of ads." Weekly. Circ. 20,000 (estimated 100,000 readers). Accepts previously published material and simultaneous submissions. Original artwork returned after publication. Sample copy free for SASE.
Illustrations: Uses 2 illustrations/issue; buys all from freelancers. Works on assignment only. Send query letter with samples to be kept on file; call or write for appointment to show portfolio. Prefers photostats as samples. Samples not kept on file are returned by SASE. Reports only if interested. Buys first rights. Pays $150, color and $100, b&w, cover; $40-80, b&w, inside; on publication.

THE JOURNAL, Addiction Research Foundation, 33 Russell St., Toronto, Ontario M5S 2S1 Canada. (416)595-6053. Editor: Anne MacLennan. Concerns drug and alcohol research, treatment, prevention

and education. Monthly. Circ. 26,000. Free sample copy and guidelines.
Cartoons: Uses 1-2 cartoons/issue; buys 1/issue from freelancers. Receives 1 submission/month from freelancers. Interested in "themes relating to alcohol and other drug use." Prefers finished cartoons. Pays from $35, 3x5 minimum cartoons; on publication.

THE JOURNAL, INC., 106 W. Main St., Box 369, Williamston SC 29697. (803)847-7361. Publisher: William C. Meade. Newspaper. Audience is rural and urban—mill town, agricultural and industrial. Weekly. Circ. 5,700. Accepts previously published material. Sample copy available.
Cartoons: Prefers political, humorous and family themes. Prefers double-panel with gagline; b&w line drawings. Send finished cartoons to be kept on file. Material not filed not returned. Reports only if interested. Pays on publication.

JOURNAL PUBLISHING CO. INC., 7 Main St., Box 68, Adams NY 13605. (315)232-2141. Editor: Robert S. Rhodes. Newspapers for farm and recreation audience. *North County Farm*; bimonthly; circ. 9,000; and *Jefferson County Journal*; weekly; circ. 3,500. Accepts previously published material. Original work returned after publication. Sample copy free for SASE. Art guidelines available.
Cartoons: Buys 2-3 cartoons/issue from freelancers. Prefers single panel with or without gagline; b&w line drawings. Send query letter with samples of style or finished cartoons to be kept on file. Material not filed returned by SASE. Pays on acceptance.
Illustrations: Send query letter with samples to be kept on file. Prefers tear sheets as samples.

KEEPERS VOICE, 2309 State St., Saginaw MI 48602. (517)799-8208. Editor: Bob Barrington. Professional association publication emphasizing law enforcement and corrections for correctional officers and police officers. Bimonthly. Circ. 9,000. Previously published material and simultaneous submissions OK. Original work returned after publication. Sample copy and art guidelines available.
Cartoons: Uses 2-4 cartoons/issue. Prefers themes related to corrections (jails and prisons); single panel with gagline. Send roughs and resume. Samples returned by SASE. Reports in 1 week. Buys all rights. Pays $50-150/b&w or color; on publication.
Illustrations: Uses 1 illustration/issue. Interested in anything related to corrections (jails and prisons). Provide resume and samples to be kept on file for possible future assignments. Send resume and samples of style. Samples returned. Reports in 1 week. Buys all rights. Pays $50-150 cover, $30-100 inside, b&w line drawings and b&w or color washes; on publication.

THE KERSHAW NEWS-ERA, 110 S. Hart St., Box 398, Kershaw SC 29067. (803)475-6095. Co-owner/Editor: Jim McKeown Jr. Newspaper emphasizing general news including textile industry and agriculture; music, theatre and drama; hunting; and creative crafts. Weekly. Circ. 2,000. Accepts previously published material. Original work returned after publication. Sample copy free for SASE with 50¢ postage. Art guidelines free for SASE with 50¢ postage or postage required for return mailing.
Cartoons: Buys 2 cartoons/issue from freelancers. Prefers political and humorous themes appropriate for small town. Prefers multi-panel with gagline; b&w line drawings. Send query letter with samples of style to be kept on file. Material not filed returned by SASE. Reports only if interested. Buys reprint rights. Negotiates payment. Pays on publication.

KEY, Voice Publications, 1016 S. Fly Ave., Goreville IL 62939-9720. (618)995-2027. Editor: Bernard Lyons. For direct marketing/mail order people and firms which use mail order/classified media. Quarterly newsletter. Sample copy $2.
Cartoons: Buys 3 cartoons/issue on direct marketing/mail order themes—especially from the business point of view, e.g., selling by mail; single panel. "We seldom use cartoons because we can't get what we want." Favors wordless humor. Mail art. SASE. Reports in 1 week. Buys all rights. Pays 25-35, b&w line drawings; on acceptance. Pays $10 first printing, and $5 for each reprint. We usually reprint 1-3 times!
Tips: There is a trend toward "dramatic growth—mail order is increasing in size, volume, dollars faster than any other business. We doubled the size of the newsletter to 16 pages—and now publish quarterly. See a sample copy. We help our readers make money. We're not interested in 'knocking' the post office, etc." Artists need to "take some time to learn a field or publication before sending work." Unfortunately, some "seem to turn out work and sell it on a production line basis, rather than establish an ongoing relationship with an editor or publication."

LAS CRUCES BULLETIN, Box 637, Las Cruces NM 88004. (505)524-8061. Publisher: Steve Klinger. Newspaper emphasizing local news and some national politics for college students and adults, most residing within the Las Cruces area. Weekly. Circ. 20,000. Accepts previously published material. Returns original artwork after publication. Sample copy and art guidelines free for SASE with $1 postage.

Close-up

Mike Peters
Cartoonist
Dayton, Ohio

Artist: David R. Smiton

"I was lucky because I knew what I wanted to do when I was five years old—I've *always* wanted to be a cartoonist." The same hobby Mike Peters enjoyed and developed throughout his youth sustains him today professionally as a Pulitzer Prize-winning editorial cartoonist with the *Dayton Daily News*, and creator of the comic strip "Mother Goose and Grimm," syndicated by Tribune Media Services.

Peters was only 13 when his first editorial cartoons were published. "Small local papers do not have enough money to hire their own editorial cartoonists, so they run national [syndicated] cartoons. I discovered that editors are *dying* for local editorial work, so I would constantly turn in cartoons to our local newspaper. I advise cartoonists all the time to use the same method. If the local newspapers are writing about potholes in the roads being too deep in your city, then do cartoons about potholes in *specific* roads in your community. Develop and refine your work, and keep submitting new ideas to get a foot in the door."

Peters found that being published is not the only obstacle facing a cartoonist. After he was hired as an editorial cartoonist with the *Daily News*, Peters began to feel the pressure of being the new kid in the cartooning world. In the company of so many established and influential cartoonists nationwide, he had a difficult time understanding and developing his *own* style. "All the people I've revered professionally are

strong cartoonists like Paul Conrad of the *Los Angeles Times*, and Paul Szep of the *Boston Globe*, who say things very simply and strongly, and 'have fire in their bellies' as Conrad would say.

"I was trying to be all those other people, and my style and approach to cartooning were constantly changing—I was just wandering. So I gathered up what I considered my best cartoons and laid them out. I discovered what I have that makes me different is my humorous approach to my subjects. Once I recognized and began to accentuate my own style, my work came very easily."

After 15 years of drawing editorial cartoons, Peters decided to capitalize on his sense of humor and make the transition to comic strips, with "Mother Goose and Grimm."

"I didn't know how I could stretch my time to add a daily strip to my routine without sacrificing my family, but I realized I had been spending up to 12 hours some days creating the same editorial cartoons that I could actually do in an hour when I was *really* under pressure.

"I just began moving my deadline back and planning my time better to do both my editorial work and the strip. I'm absolutely regimented now—I have to do five editorial cartoons and seven strips a week, generally working three months ahead on the strip."

"Mother Goose and Grimm" has been published in almost 200 newspapers nationwide since its fall of 1984 syndication. Peters has negotiated the printing of his comic strip characters on notebooks and other paper products, and his first book on the strip appears in February 1986 through Dell Publishing. Peters is also a moderator for the Public Broadcasting System's "The World of Cartooning," a television program focusing on the creators behind some of today's most popular cartoons.

The business side of comic strips differs greatly from editorial cartooning and has forced Peters to make some adjustments. Peters says, "There are some 200 editorial cartoonists nationwide, but only about 20 are syndicated. You don't have new editorial cartoons being syndicated each week, but you do get new strips each week. Because of the competition and the small number of spaces available on the comic pages, strips must be constantly marketed to new papers by syndicate salespeople, who are trying to sell your work along with that of 50 other people. I have to be in constant communication with these salespeople so they have ammunition to sell my strip to the newspaper editors."

In order to inspire editors to run "Mother Goose and Grimm," Peters has created a newsletter that includes positive letters from his readers, lists of newspapers that carry the strip, and general public relations-type information. Peters has learned that "a comic strip is about two-thirds creativity—the other third is marketing and moving the product."

—*Lisa S. Hulse*

Mike Peters © Tribune Media Services

Originally torn between developing a comic strip around Mother Goose or a beer can crunching, loveable but dumb dog, Peters decided to combine both ideas. "Mother Goose and Grimm" was born!

Of the approximately 200 editorial cartoonists across the country, Mike Peters is one of only 20 whose work is syndicated. A 1985 Publishers Weekly *syndicate survey ranked Peters fourth in the number of newspapers carrying his cartoons.*

Mike Peters © *Dayton Daily News*—United Feature Syndicate

Cartoons: Buys 1-2 cartoons/issue from freelance artists. Prefers political satire and contemporary issues. Accepts single, double or multiple panel with or without gaglines; b&w line drawings. Send query letter with samples of style to be kept on file. Material not filed is returned by SASE. Reports back only if interested. Negotiates rights purchased. Pays on publication.

Illustrations: Number of illustrations purchased from freelance artists varies/issue. Prefers topical or political themes. Works on assignment only. Send query letter with samples to be kept on file. Prefers tear sheets or photocopies as samples. Samples not filed are returned by SASE. Reports back only if interested. Negotiates rights purchased. Pays on publication.

LAURENS COUNTY ADVERTISER, Box 490, Laurens SC 29360. (803)984-2586. Managing Editor: Ken Garfield. Newspaper emphasizing local news for a "strictly county audience looking for strictly county news." Biweekly. Circ. 9,000. Accepts previously published material. Sample copy available.

Cartoons: "We may need cartoons on occasion to accompany specific stories." Send query letter with samples of style. Reports within 1 week. Pay rate negotiable on publication.

Illustrations: "We need illustrations on occasion with specific stories." Works on assignment only. Send query letter with samples. Reports within 1 week. Negotiates payment.

LIGHTWAVE, the Journal of Fiber Optics, 1345 Main St., Waltham MA 02154. (617)899-8030. Editor: John Ryan. Estab. 1984. Newspaper. Emphasizes fiber optics for communication and sensing for engineers. Monthly. Circ. 10,000. Sometimes accepts previously published material. Returns original artwork after publication on request. Sample copy free for SASE with postage.

Cartoons: Considers b&w line drawings with or without gaglines. Send query letter with samples of style or roughs to be kept on file. Write for appointment to show portfolio. Material not filed returned by SASE. Reports only if interested. Buys first rights. Pays $100 for b&w; on acceptance.

Illustrations: Buys 2 illustrations/issue from freelancers. Prefers sketches of real people or objects. Send query letter with samples to be kept on file. Write for appointment to show portfolio. Prefers tear sheets or photocopies as samples. Samples not filed returned by SASE. Reports only if interested. Buys first rights. Pays $50-100 for b&w; on acceptance.

*THE LOCAL NEWS, Box 466, Windermere FL 32786. (305)298-2401. Associate Editor: Darrell R. Julian. News magazine with emphasis on local events; general interest. Audience: 60% ages 25-40 years, upper middle-class, educated and sophisticated; 40% ages over 55, middle-class retirees reflecting all areas of US. Prefers original material, but previously published material considered if publications disclosed. Sample copy $1.40.

Cartoons: Buys 1-2 cartoons/issue from freelancers. Interested in "witty and comic development that reveals the absurdities of everyday life; off-the-wall styles in the Gary Larson "The Far Side" vein; and political cartoons tailored for a very conservative (poltically) audience." Prefers single, double or multiple panel with or without gagline; b&w line drawings or washes. Send finished cartoons to be kept on file. Material not filed returned by SASE if requested. Reports within 2 months. Buys first rights, one-time rights or reprint rights. Pays $10-20, b&w; on accpetance.

Illustrations: Theme and style depend on requirements of piece. Works on assignment only. Send query letter with samples to be kept on file; write for appointment to show portfolio. Accepts photostats, tear sheets, photocopies or photographs as samples "whatever best suits the work submitted." Samples returned by SASE if requested. Buys first rights, one-time or reprint rights. Pays $10, b&w, inside.

THE MANITOBA TEACHER, 191 Harcourt St., Winnipeg, Manitoba R3J 3H2 Canada. (204)888-7961. Editor: Mrs. Miep van Raalte. Emphasizes education for teachers and others in Manitoba. 4 issues/year between September and June. Circ. 16,300. Free sample copy and art guidelines.

Cartoons: Uses less than 2 cartoons/year relating to education in Manitoba. Prefers single panel b&w line drawings with gagline. Send roughs and samples of style. SAE (nonresidents include IRC). Reports in 1 month.

Illustrations: Interested in b&w line drawings for inside. Send roughs and samples of style. SAE (nonresidents include IRC). Reports in 1 month.

Tips: Especially needs cartoons and illustrations related directly to the Manitoba scene. "Inquire before sending work."

MASS HIGH TECH, 755 Mt. Auburn St., Watertown MA 02172. (617)924-2422. Editor-in-Chief: Alan R. Earls. Newspaper. Emphasizes high technology businesses, schools, etc., in greater Boston (Eastern Massachusetts) and New England area for programmers, engineers, managers and other technical professionals. Bimonthly. Circ. 36,000. Original artwork returned after publication. Sample copy with $1 postage or money order.

Cartoons: Uses 1-2 cartoons/issue; buys all from freelancers. Prefers single panel. Send actual work or

samples. Reports in 1 month. Buys first North American serial rights. Pays $25 + on publication.
Illustrations: Works on assignment only. Send query letter with brochure to be kept on file. Prefers photostats as samples. Samples not kept on file are returned only if requested. Reports only if interested. Material not copyrighted. Pays $25 + on publication.

MEDICAL ADVERTISING NEWS, 505 8th Ave., New York NY 10018. (212)736-6000. Publisher: Karl Engel. Tabloid. Emphasizes pharmaceutical advertising for marketing and product managers, account executives, creative directors. Semi-monthly. Circ. 9,000. Accepts previously published material. Returns original artwork after publication. Sample copy and art guidelines available.
Cartoons: Seeks medical, advertising themes. Prefers b&w line drawings. Send query letter with samples of style to be kept on file. Material not filed is returned by SASE. Reports back only if interested. Buys one-time rights. Pays on publication.
Illustrations: Send query letter with resume to be kept on file. Prefers to review tear sheets. Reports back only if interested. Pays on publication.

MICRO MARKETWORLD, 375 Cochituate Rd., Framingham MA 01701. Art Director: Ann Bartolotti. Emphasizes news and products relating to the computer field. Biweekly. Returns original artwork after publication.
Illustrations: Buys 1-2/issue. Themes depend on the storyline. "I use all types of illustration; *does not* have to be computer-related or technical." Local New England illustrators only. Works on assignment only. Send query letter with brochure and samples to be kept on file. Prefers photocopies as samples. Reports back only if interested. Buys first rights. Pays $150-250 for b&w and $225-350 for color, inside; on acceptance.

THE MILLINGTON HERALD AND LAKEVILLE AERIAL, 4724 E. Main St., Millington MI 48746. Editor: Lucy M. Decker. Tabloid emphasizing general and farm news for farmers and factory workers. Weekly. Circ. 6,000. Accepts previously published material. Original work returned after publication. Sample copy $1.
Cartoons: Prefers single panel with gagline; b&w line drawings. Send query letter with samples of style. Material not filed is returned by SASE only if requested. Reports back only if interested. Negotiates rights purchased.
Illustrations: Send query letter with samples to be kept on file. Write for appointment to show portfolio. Prefers tear sheets as samples. Samples not filed are returned by SASE. Negotiates rights purchased. Pays on publication.

MILWAUKEE JOURNAL, Box 661, Milwaukee WI 53201. Managing Editor/News: Joseph W. Shoquist. Daily. Circ. 310,000.
Cartoons: Managing Editor/Features: George Lockwood. Buys themes acceptable to family readership; single panel. Query with samples. SASE. Reports in 2 weeks. Buys one-time rights. Pays $15 minimum, washes.
Illustrations: Art Director: Vincent Catteruccia. Buys themes acceptable to family readership. Query with samples. SASE. Reports in 2 weeks. Buys all rights. Inside: Pays $10 minimum.
Tips: There is a trend toward "more graphics to accompany news stories."

NATIONAL ENQUIRER, Lantana FL 33464. Cartoon Editor: Michele L. Cooke. Weekly tabloid. Circ. 6,000,000. Previously published work OK if cartoonist owns rights.
Cartoons: Buys 450 cartoons/year on "all subjects the family reader can relate to, especially animal and husband-wife situations. Captionless cartoons have a better chance of selling here." Receives 2,000 cartoons/week from freelance artists. Especially needs Christmas cartoon spread (submit by August). Mail 8½x11" art. SASE. Reports in 2 weeks. Buys first rights. Pays $300 maximum, b&w single panel; $40 every panel thereafter. Pays on acceptance.
Tips: "Study 5-6 issues before submitting. Check captions for spelling. New submitters should send introductory letter. All cartoonists should include phone and social security number. Know your market. We have no use for political or off-color gags. Neatness counts and sloppy, stained artwork registers a negative reaction. Besides neatness, we also look for "correct spelling and punctuation on captions and in the body of the cartoon, accurate rendering of the subject (if the subject is a duck, make it look like a duck and not a goose, swan or chicken), and *most important* is visual impact! Prefers 8½x11" instead of 'halfs.' If submitting reprints, know *who* owns the rights."

*THE NATIONAL LAW JOURNAL, Suite 900, 111 8th Ave., New York NY 10011. (212)741-8300. Art Director: Cynthia Currie. Tabloid emphasizing law for attorneys. Weekly. Circ. 38,000. Original artwork returned after publication. Sample copy $2.
Cartoons: Buys 1 cartoon/issue from freelancers. Prefers single panel; b&w line drawings. Send query

letter with samples of style or finished cartoons. Material not filed is returned. Reports within 2 weeks. Buys all rights. Pays $100, b&w; on acceptance.
Illustrations: Buys 2 illustrations/issue from freelancers. Works on assignment only. Send query letter with brochure to be kept on file. Samples returned only if requested. Reports within 2 weeks. Buys all rights. Pays $100, b&w, cover, inside; on acceptance.

NETWORK, The Paper for Parents, 410 Wilde Lake Village Green, Columbia MD 21044. (301)997-9300. Editor: Chrissie Bamber. Tabloid. Emphasizes parent/citizen involvement in public schools. Published 8 times during school year. Circ. 6,000. Original artwork not returned after publication. Sample copy and art guidelines free for SASE.
Cartoons: Uses 1-2 cartoons/issue; buys all from freelancers. Prefers single-panel, without gagline; b&w line drawings, b&w washes. Send query letter with samples of style to be kept on file; write for appointment to show portfolio. Material not kept on file returned only if requested. Reports within 2 weeks. Negotiates rights purchased. Pays 50¢, b&w; on publication.
Illustrations: Uses 1-2 illustrations/issue; buys all from freelancers. Works on assignment only. Send query letter with tear sheets to be kept on file. Samples not kept on file returned only if requested. Reports within 2 weeks. Negotiates rights purchased. Pays $50, b&w, cover; $50, b&w, inside; on publication.

THE NEVADAN, Box 70, Las Vegas NV 89101. Editor: A. D. Hopkins. Deals with history, outdoor and small-town life in Nevada. Weekly newspaper. Circ. 109,000. Previously published work OK. Free sample copy. Receives "about 10 submissions/year, never anything we can use."
Illustrations: Buys art *only* with accompanying mss. "Material must be from our region: Nevada and the adjacent areas of Northern Arizona, Southern Utah and Southeastern California. Emphasis on good research in historical writing and illustration." Query with resume and samples. SASE. Reports in 3 weeks. Pays $10, b&w line drawings and gray opaques in addition to $60 and up for the manuscript; on publication.
Tips: "Our particular magazine has always been history oriented. A lot of good history pieces must be rejected because there is no art or photography with them. An artist who could also write could sell history pieces to us. We do not buy art for art's sake. We might buy a series of illustrations about a particular town or subject we would normally treat in print, doing a picture story with drawn art rather than photos. We have a 3,000 word limit but would take a much shorter piece with several illustrations suitable for a two-page tabloid layout. Whatever supporting text was submitted would count as manuscript for pay."

NEW ALASKAN, Rt. 1, Box 677, Ketchikan AK 99901. (907)247-2490. Editor: Bob Pickrell. Emphasizes Southeastern Alaska lifestyle, history and politics for general public in this area. Monthly. Circ. 6,000. Previously published material and simultaneous submissions OK. Original work returned after publication by SASE. Sample copy $1.50; art guidelines for SASE.
Cartoons: Uses 1 cartoon/issue; buys 1 from freelancers. Interested only in art with a Southeastern Alaska tie-in; single panel with or without gagline, b&w line drawings. Send roughs or samples of style. Samples returned by SASE. Reports in 3 months. Negotiates rights purchased. Pays $25 up, b&w; on publication.
Illustrations: Uses 2 illustrations/issue; buys 1 from freelancers. Interested only in art with a Southeastern tie-in. "We prefer mss with illustrations except for cover art which can stand by itself." Works on assignment only. Provide business card and samples to be kept on file for possible future assignments. Samples returned by SASE. Reports in 3 months. Negotiates rights purchased and payment; on publication.

NEW ENGLAND RUNNING, Box 658, Brattleboro VT 05301. Contact: Editorial Department. Tabloid. Emphasizes New England running, primarily competitive. Monthly. Circ. 4,000. Accepts previously published material and simultaneous submissions. Original artwork returned after publication. Sample copy $2.
Cartoons: Uses 1 cartoon/issue; buys from freelancer. Prefers single panel, with gagline; b&w line drawings. Send query letter with samples of style to be kept on file. Material not kept on file is returned by SASE. Reports in 1 month. Buys one-time rights. Pays $10, b&w; on publication.
Illustrations: Uses 2 illustrations/issue; buys all from freelancers. Send query letter with samples and tear sheets to be kept on file. Prefers clippings or photocopies as samples. Samples not kept on file are returned by SASE. Reports within 1 month. Buys one-time rights. Pays $10-20, b&w; on publication.

*THE NEW SOUTHERN LITERARY MESSENGER, 400 S. Laurel St., Richmond VA 23220. (804)780-1244. Editor: Charles Lohmann. Tabloid. Emphasizes poetry and short stories. Quarterly. Circ. 400. Accepts previously published material. Returns original artwork after publication. Sample copy $1. Art guidelines free for SASE with 32¢ postage.

Cartoons: Buys 3 or 4/issue. Prefers single, double or multiple panel with or without gagline; b&w line drawings. Send query letter to be kept on file. Write for appointment to show portfolio. Reports within 3 weeks. Purchases reprint rights. Pays $5; on publication.

NEW YORK ANTIQUE ALMANAC, Box 335, Lawrence NY 11559. (516)371-3300. Editor: Carol Nadel. For art, antiques and nostalgia collectors/investors. Monthly tabloid. Circ. 52,000. Reports within 4-6 weeks. Previously published work OK. Original artwork returned after publication, if requested. Free sample copy.
Cartoons: Uses 1 cartoon/issue; buys 1/issue from freelancers. Receives 1 submission/week from freelancers. Interested in antiques, nostalgia and money. Prefers finished cartoons. SASE. Reports within 4 weeks. Buys all rights, but may reassign rights to artist after publication. Pays $5-20, b&w; on publication.
Illustrations: Buys 24/year on collecting and investing. Buys all rights, but may reassign rights to artist after publication. Pays $5 minimum, b&w; on publication.

THE NEWS OF SOUTHERN BERKS, 124 N. Chestnut St., Boyertown PA 19512. (215)689-9558. General Manager, Editor: Joseph Reedy. Weekly family newspaper (weddings, births, editorials, sports, school coverage, local government) for all ages and income. Circ. 4,000. Accepts previously published material. Original work returned after publication with SASE. Sample copy free for SASE with 75¢ postage.
Cartoons: Prefers local themes (Southeastern Berks County, Pennsylvania). Send samples of style. Write for appointment to show portfolio. Material not filed returned by SASE. Negotiates rights purchased. Pays on acceptance.
Illustrations: Send samples. Write for appointment to show portfolio. Prefers photocopies as samples. Samples not filed returned by SASE. Negotiates rights purchased. Pays on acceptance.

NORTH MYRTLE BEACH TIMES, Box 725, North Myrtle Beach SC 29597. (803)249-1122 or 249-3525. Managing Editor: Elbert Marshall. Biweekly. Circ. 9,500. Simultaneous submissions OK. Original work returned after publication if requested. Free sample copy and art guidelines.
Cartoons: Uses 2 cartoons/issue. Interested in editorial themes; double panel b&w line drawings with gagline. Send query letter with resume and samples of style. Samples returned by SASE. Reports in 2 weeks. Material not copyrighted. Pays on publication.
Illustrations: Uses editorial themes. Send query letter with samples of style. Samples returned by SASE. Reports in 2 weeks. Material not copyrighted. Pays on publication.
Tips: "Be original and able to express ideas well."

NORTHEAST MAGAZINE, THE HARTFORD COURANT, Suite 411, 179 Allyn St., Hartford CT 06103. (203)241-3701. Design Director: Riki Allred. Weekly newspaper magazine. General audience. Circ. 300,000. Original artwork returned after publication. Sample copy available.
Illustrations: Uses 3 illustrations/issue; buys all from freelancers. Styles vary. Works on assignment only. Send query letter with brochure and samples; call for appointment to show portfolio. Desires whatever samples best represent work. Samples returned by SASE. Reports only if interested. Buys one-time rights. Pays $400, color, cover; $100-300, b&w, and $300, color, inside; on acceptance; send invoice.

NORTHEAST OUTDOORS, Box 2180, Waterbury CT 06722-2180. (203)755-0158. Editor: Howard Fielding. Emphasizes all facets of camping and hiking, with articles on camping areas, equipment and individual accounts of trips. For campers living in the Northeastern states. Monthly. Circ. 14,000. Free sample copy and editorial guidelines, including photos and art.
Cartoons: Uses 1 cartoon/issue. Interested in family camping and recreational vehicles, all in Northeastern states setting; single panel with gagline. Send finished cartoons. SASE. Reports in 2-4 weeks. Buys one-time rights. Pays $10 minimum, b&w line drawings; on acceptance.
Illustrations: "We rarely use illustrations unless accompanying a story; drawings to accompany a ms would be a welcome change (rarely do we find writer/artists submitting). Although we've never done it, I'd consider a cover illustration if it dealt directly with camping and RVs. In terms of marketing, an artist could send a few samples along with a query letter to find out if any upcoming stories need illustrations. It would help jog my memory to think about unillustrated stories, instead of overlooking them."

NURSINGWORLD JOURNAL, 470 Boston Post Rd., Weston MA 02193. (617)899-2702. Editor: Bernard Smith. Readers are "student and experienced nurses interested in keeping their skills current and seeking employment, trends in nursing, relocation or area hiring trends in nursing, reviews of nursing articles, feature stories." Monthly. Circ. 40,000. Sample copy $2.
Cartoons: Uses 1-3 cartoons/issue. Receives 25 submissions/month from freelancers. Interested in hospital or nursing themes. Prefers b&w line drawing with gagline. Send finished cartoons. SASE. Reports

within 6 months. Buys one-time rights. Pays $5-10 for b&w, on publication.
Illustrations: Uses 3 illustrations/issue. Receives 10 submissions/month from freelancers. Interested in general illustrations that go along with editorial; usually people or nature. Works on assignment. "Freelancers call, send us samples, and we make a decision at that time if their style fits our paper. If it does, we keep their names on file, then contact them for assignments." Send roughs. SASE. Reports within 6 months. Prefers b&w line drawings. Buys all rights on a work-for-hire basis. Pays $50-100 for b&w or color cover, $50 for inside b&w. Pays on publication.

NUTRITION HEALTH REVIEW, 171 Madison Ave., New York NY 10016. Features Editor: F.R. Rifkin. Tabloid. Emphasizes physical health, mental health, nutrition, food preparation and medicine. For a general audience. Quarterly. Circ. 165,000 paid. Accepts simultaneous submissions. Sample copy $1.25.
Cartoons: Uses 10 cartoons/issue. Prefers single panel with or without gagline; b&w line drawings. Send finished cartoons to be kept on file; samples returned by SASE if not purchased. Reports within 30 days. Buys first rights or all rights. Pays $15 + , b&w; on acceptance.
Illustrations: Number illustrations varies/issue. Send samples to be kept on file; write for appointment to show portfolio. If samples are requested, prefers to see photostats. Samples returned by SASE. Reports back. Buys first rights or all rights. Pays $150, b&w, cover and $25 for b&w inside; on acceptance.

*THE OFFICIAL COMDEX SHOW DAILY, 300 1st Ave., Needham MA 02194. (617)449-6600. Production Manager/Art Director: Linda Peterson. Estab. 1983. Tabloid. Emphasizes computers and computer-related products for attendees and exhibitors at the U.S. Comdex Shows. Seasonal: Fall, Winter, Spring. Circ. 35,000. Accepts previously published material. Original artwork returned after publication if requested. Sample copy free for SASE; art guidelines available.
Cartoons: Buys 50-100 cartoons/issue from freelancers. "Computer grahics used in cartoon illustration. Application ties in well as our newspaper is read by people in the computer industry." Wants anything related to computers, trade shows, Las Vegas, Los Angeles or Atlanta. Prefers single panel with or without gagline; b&w line drawings. Send query letter with roughs or finished cartoons to be kept on file. Material not filed is returned by SASE only if requested. Reports within several weeks. Buys one-time rights. Pays $18; on acceptance.
Illustrations: Themes: computers/trade shows/computer related products. Humorous and cartoon-style illustrations used once a year. Works on assignment only. Send query letter with samples to be kept on fiel. Prefers photocopies as samples. Samples returned by SASE only if requested. Reports within several weeks only if interested. Buys one-time rights. Pays $50-100, b&w; on acceptance.

*OFFSHORE, New England's Boating Magazine, 1981 Chestnut St., Newton MA 02164. (617)244-7520. Art Director: Bianca Leonardi. Tabloid emphasizing boating for New England boat owners. Monthly. Circ. 18,000. Accepts previously published material. Original artwork returned after publication. Sample copy for SASE with $1.15 postage.
Cartoons: Buys 2 cartoons/issue from freelancers. Prefers single panel; b&w line drawings. Send query letter with samples of style to be kept on file. Material not filed is returned by SASE. Reports within 1 week. Buys first rights. Pays $10-25, b&w; on acceptance.
Illustrations: Buys 2 illustrations/issue from freelancers. Prefers hard line. Works on assignment only. Send samples to be kept on file. Prefers photostats or tear sheets as samples. Samples not filed are returned by SASE. Reports within 1 week. Buys first rights. Pays $100-175, color, cover; $20-50, b&w, inside; on acceptance.

OHIO MOTORIST, AAA-Ohio Motorists Association, Box 6150, Cleveland OH 44101. Editor-in-Chief: F. Jerome Turk. For automobile club members. Published 12 times/year. Circ. 286,000. Previously published and simultaneous submissions OK. Free sample copy.
Cartoons: Receives 35 cartoons/week from freelance artists. Buys 50 cartoons/year on current events, driving and travel; single panel with gagline. Submit art. SASE. Reports in 2 weeks. Pays $10-15, b&w line drawings; $25-75, editorial page cartoons on travel and automobiles; on acceptance.

OUR GANG, One Children's Plaza, Dayton OH 45404. (513)226-8332. Editor/Communications Specialist: Susan A. Brockman. Magapaper. Emphasizes hospital (CMC) programs, employees, volunteers, health topics. Monthly. Circ. 2,200. Accepts previously published material and simultaneous submissions. Original artwork returned after publication. Sample copy and art guidelines free for SASE.
Cartoons: Uses cartoons 6 times/year; buys all from freelancers. Prefers offbeat, funny-looking people (i.e., Phil Frank). Prefers single panel, without gagline; b&w line drawings. Send query letter with samples of style to be kept on file; write for appointment to show portfolio. Material not kept on file is returned by SASE if requested. Reports only if interested. Negotiates rights purchased and pay rate; pays on publication.

Illustrations: Uses illustrations 12 times/year; buys all from freelancers. Prefers "cartoonish" style. Works on assignment only. Send query letter with tear sheets to be kept on file; call or write for appointment to show portfolio. Prefers photostats as samples. Samples not kept on file are returned by SASE if requested. Reports only if interested. Negotiates rights purchased and pay rate; pays on publication.

*THE PAPERWORKER, Box 1475, Nashville TN 37202. (615)834-8590. Editor/Director of Publications: Monte L. Byers. Emphasizes labor subjects for membership of industrial union. Monthly tabloid. Circ. 250,000. Accepts previously published material. Original artwork not returned after publication. Sample copy free for SASE with 20¢ postage.
Cartoons: Buys 1-5 cartoons/issue from freelancers. Considers labor and national issue themes. Prefers single panel with gagline; b&w line drawings. Send query letter with finished cartoons to be kept on file. Material not filed is returned by SASE only if requested. Reports within several weeks. Buys one-time rights. Pays variable rates for b&w and color; on publication.
Illustrations: Buys 1-3 illustrations/issue from freelancers. Themes/styles vary to accompany text. Works on assignment only. Send query letter with samples to be kept on file. Prefers tear sheets as samples. Samples returned only if requested. Reports within several weeks. Buys one-time rights. Pays variable rates for b&w and color, inside; on publication.

THE PATRIOT, Box 346, Kutztown PA 19530. (215)683-7343. Editor: Stephen Fellman. For general audience. Weekly newspaper. Circ. 4,000. Originals returned to artist after publication.
Illustrations: Buys newspaper ad layouts and sales promotion art. Works on assignment only. Samples returned by SASE; reports back on future assignment possibilities. Provide business card to be kept on file for future assignments. Prefers portfolio (roughs). Pays $5-10/sketch.

*PAWPRINTS, FONZ Publications, National Zoological Park, Washington DC 20008. (202)673-4993. Publications Director: Bettina Conner. Newsletter emphasing zoo animals, conservation and preservation of endangered species for children, 6-16. Bimonthly. Circ. 8,000. Accepts previously published material. Returns original artwork after publication. Sample copy for $1.
Illustrations: Buys 1-2/issue from freelance artists. Prefers educational games and puzzles depicting exotic animals. Send samples. Prefers photocopies or tear sheets as samples. Samples are returned by SASE. Reports within 6 weeks. Buys first rights. Pays $50-100, per game; on publication.

PERSONNEL ADVISORY BULLETIN, Bureau of Business Practice, 24 Rope Ferry Rd., Waterford CT 06386. Editor: John Fuller. For personnel managers and practitioners in smaller companies—white collar and industrial. Features interviewing and hiring, training, benefits, career development, promotion practices, counseling, record keeping, etc. Bimonthly newsletter. Original artwork not returned after publication. No previously published material or simultaneous submissions. Free sample copy.
Cartoons: Uses 1 cartoon/issue; buys 1/issue from freelancers. Receives 15-20 submissions/week from freelancers. Buys 30/year on "personnel-oriented situations. Please, no sexist situations and male boss/dumb female secretary jokes." Single panel. Mail finished art. SASE. Reports in 2 weeks. Buys all rights. Pays $10 for b&w line drawings. Pays on acceptance.
Tips: "We're trying to be more selective in choosing strictly personnel-oriented subject matter. Avoid anything smacking of sexism or other discriminatory attitudes. Don't overdo hiring-firing situations. Make captions *literate* and *funny*."

THE PLAIN DEALER MAGAZINE, 1801 Superior Ave., Cleveland OH 44114. (216)344-4578. Design Director: Gerard Sealy. Sunday color roto magazine supplement to *The Plain Dealer* newspaper. Broad-based, general audience. Weekly. Circ. 500,000. Original artwork returned after publication. Sample copy free for SASE.
Cartoons: Uses 2-3 cartoons/issue; buys 1-2/issue from freelancers. Prefers single panel with or without gagline; b&w line drawings. Send finished cartoons. Material is returned by SASE. Reports only if interested. Buys one-time rights. Pays $50, b&w; on publication.
Illustrations: Buys 4-5 illustrations/issue; buys all from freelancers. All styles considered. Works on assignment basis only. Send query letter with brochure, business card and samples to be kept on file; call for appointment to show portfolio. No original art; all other types of samples considered. Reports only if interested. Buys first rights. Pays $400 maximum, color, cover; $300 maximum, b&w, and $400 maximum, color, inside; on publication.

*PRESS-ENTERPRISE, Box 792, Riverside CA 92502. (714)684-1200. Features Editor: Sally Ann Maas. Daily newspaper in Southern California emphasizing general subjects. Circ. 130,000. Original artwork returned after publication. Sample copy and art guidelines available.
Illustrations: Buys 1 editorial illustration/week from freelancers. Uses various themes and styles. Works on assignment only. Send query letter with resume and samples to be kept on file; write for ap-

A portfolio review led Joel Smitherman, then a recent art school graduate, to illustrate a story on entertaining vegetarians for the food section of the Press-Enterprise, Riverside, California. The newspaper's editorial artist Gary Aagaard gave Smitherman the concept "to see what the artist could do." Smitherman now works regularly for the daily, usually doing the complete conceptualization and illustration of assignments. The Sunnymead, California, freelancer was paid $50 for one-time use of this graphite piece.

pointment to show portfolio. Samples not filed are returned only if requested. Reports within 2 weeks. Negotiates rights purchased. Pays variable rates; on publication.

PUBLISHING CONCEPTS CORPORATION, Main St., Luttrell TN 37779. For a general audience with middle to upper incomes. Weekly. Circ. 60,190. Previously published material OK. Original artwork returned after publication. Free sample copy for SASE; art guidelines available. Receives 8 cartoons and 3 illustrations/week from freelance artists.
Cartoons: Uses 10 cartoons/issue; buys all from freelancers. Interested in general, national themes; single panel, b&w line drawings. Send finished cartoons. Samples returned by SASE. Reports in 1 week. Negotiates rights purchased. Pays $10-50, b&w; on acceptance.
Illustrations: Number of illustrations/issue varies. Will review all themes and styles for interest. Provide business card and samples to be kept on file for possible future assignments. Send samples of style. Samples returned by SASE. Reports in 1 week. Buys one-time rights. Pays $10-40 cover, b&w line drawings; on acceptance.
Tips: "We publish several publications and work submitted on a freelance basis may be considered for any one of several publications. Prices paid vary with quality of work, degree of interest at the time received or readership interest for the next two weeks."

ROLLING STONE, 745 5th Ave., New York NY 10151. (212)758-3800. Art Director: Derek W. Ungless. Coverage includes music, film, social issues, investigative reporting, books and new life styles. Biweekly tabloid. Original artwork returned after publication.
Illustrations: Buys 1-2 illustrations/issue. Illustrations are assigned to particular editorial needs. Works on assignment only. Samples returned by SASE. Provide business card to be kept on file for future assignments. Submit samples of style or portfolio. Reports as soon as possible. Buys one-time publication rights.

SALESMANSHIP AND FOREMANSHIP AND EFFECTIVE EXECUTIVE, Dartnell Corporation, 4660 N. Ravenswood Ave., Chicago IL 60640. Art Director: G.C. Gormaly, Jr. Emphasizes salesmanship. Monthly. Previously published material OK.
Cartoons: Uses 1 cartoon/issue. Prefers single panel with or without gagline, b&w line drawings or b&w washes. Send query letter and samples of style. Samples returned. Reports in 1 month. Negotiates rights purchased. Pays $20-50, b&w; on acceptance.

Illustrations: Uses illustrations occasionally; seldom buys from freelancers. Send query letter and samples of style to be kept on file for possible future assignments. Samples not kept on file are returned. Reports in 2 months. Buys reprint rights. Pays $50-250 cover, $40-100 inside, b&w line or tone drawings; on acceptance.

SAN FRANCISCO BAY GUARDIAN, 2700 19th St., San Francisco CA 94110. (415)824-7660. Art Director: Kim Gale. For "a young liberal, well-educated audience." Circ. 105,000. Weekly newspaper. SASE. Pays on publication. Reviews portfolios on Friday. Sets up appointment by phone.
Cartoons: "Almost all illustrations are assigned; we are, however, always looking for cartoons and strips that have a Bay Area theme. We pay, on the average, $35 per cartoon, which can be a one-shot deal or continuing." Query.
Illustrations: Buys assigned themes. Pays $75-100. Arrange interview to show portfolio.
Tips: "I am always looking for artwork for our cover done by *Bay Area* artists. Current trends include "the New Wave look which has affected all phases of graphics, type and design. The most sweeping change is in the use of type—faces are mixed with absolute abandon and freedom. It's great!"

*SHOW BUSINESS, 29th Fl., 1501 Broadway, New York NY 10036. (212)354-7600, ext. 81. Assistant Publisher: Phillip Anderson. Casting newspaper for investors, producers, directors, press people, agents, photographers, peforming artists and models. Weekly. Circ. 36,000. Accepts previously published material. Original artwork returned after publication. Art guidelines free for SASE with $1.37 postage.
Cartoons: Considers theatre or film themes. Prefers double panel. Send samples of style. Call for appointment to show portfolio. Material returned by SASE. Reports within 2 weeks. Negotiates rights purchased. Pays on publication.
Illustrations: Buys 4 illustrations/issue from freelancers. Prefers theatre or film themes. Send query letter with samples. Call for appointment to show portfolio. Prefers photostats as samples. Samples are returned by SASE. Reports within 2 weeks. Negotiates rights purchased. Pays on publication.

SHUTTERBUG ADS, 407 S. Washington Ave., Box F, Titusville FL 32780. Contact: Linda Rew. Photography and computer newspapers. Published monthly. Nationwide distribution. Previously published work OK. Original artwork not returned after publication.
Cartoons: Uses 1 or 2 cartoons/issue, all from freelancers. Interested in "photography related and computer related themes." Prefers finished cartoons. SASE. Reports "when cartoons are published." Pays $10-25 spot drawing or full cartoon; on publication.
Tips: Artwork "must be reproducible at reductions from original size."

SKYDIVING, Box 1520, Deland FL 32721. (904)736-9779. Editor: Michael Truffer. Emphasizes skydiving for sport parachutists, worldwide dealers and equipment manufacturers. Monthly. Circ. 7,200.
Cartoons: Uses 1-2 cartoons/issue; buys 0-1 from freelancers. Receives 1-2 submissions/week from freelancers. Interested in themes relating to skydiving or aviation. Prefers single panel b&w line drawings with gagline. Send finished cartoons or samples of style. SASE. Reports in 1 week. Buys one-time rights. Pays $10 minimum for b&w; on publication.
Tips: Artists "must *know* parachuting; cartoons must be funny."

SOUTHERN JEWISH WEEKLY, Box 3297, Jacksonville FL 32206. (904)355-3459. Editor: I. Moscovitz. Emphasizes human interest material and short stories. "The only Jewish newspaper covering all of Florida and the Southeast." Weekly. Circ. 28,500.
Illustrations: Buys 2 illustrations/year on Jewish themes that pertain to newspaper's articles. Pays $10 minimum, b&w; on acceptance. Query with samples. Seasonal themes must arrive 2 weeks in advance of holiday. SASE. Reports in 1 week.

SOUTHWEST DIGEST, 510 E. 23rd St., Lubbock TX 79404. (806)762-3612. Co-Publisher-Managing Editor: Eddie P. Richardson. Newspaper emphasizing positive black images, and community building and rebuilding "primarily oriented to the black community and basically reflective of the black community, but serving all people." Weekly. Accepts previously published material. Original work returned after publication.
Cartoons: Number of cartoons purchased/issue from freelancers varies. Prefers economic development, community development, community pride and awareness, and black uplifting themes. Single, double or multi-panel with gagline; b&w line drawings. Send query letter with samples of style, roughs or finished cartoons to be kept on file. Write or call for appointment to show portfolio. Material not filed returned by SASE only if requested. Buys first, one-time, reprint, or all rights; or negotiates rights purchased. Pays on publication.
Illustrations: Send query letter with brochure or samples to be kept on file. Write or call for appoint-

ment to show portfolio. Prefers photostats, tear sheets, photocopies, photographs, etc. as samples. Samples not filed returned by SASE only if requested. Reports only if interested. Negotiates rights purchased. Pays on publication.

THE STATE JOURNAL-REGISTER, 1 Copley Plaza, Box 219, Springfield IL 62705. (217)788-1475. Photography Editor: Barry Locher. Emphasizes news and features for the town and surrounding area. Daily. Circ. 75,000. Accepts previously published material and simultaneous submissions. Original artwork returned after publication. Sample copy and art guidelines free for SASE.
Illustrations: Uses 4 illustrations/issue; buys all from freelancers. Works on assignment only. Send query letter with samples to be kept on file. Samples are returned if not kept on file. Negotiates rights purchased. Pays $100-200, b&w and color, cover. Pays $50-150, b&w and color, inside. Pays on publication.

THE SUPERVISOR, Kemper Group, Long Grove IL 60049. (312)540-2094. Editor: Mary Puccinelli. Newsletter. Emphasizes industrial and fleet safety for supervisors responsible for industrial safety and/or fleet safety. Bimonthly. Circ. 50,000. Accepts simultaneous submissions. Original artwork not returned after publication. Sample copy free for SASE.
Cartoons: Uses 2 cartoons/issue; buys all from freelancers. Seeks "very funny cartoons;" can be "offbeat" but not offensive. Topics for the year are sent to prospective artists in June. Prefers single panel, with gagline; b&w line drawings. Send query letter with samples of style to be kept on file. Material not kept on file is returned by SASE. Reports within 1 month. Buys all rights. Payment varies; on acceptance.

SUPERVISOR'S BULLETIN, 24 Rope Ferry Rd., Waterford CT 06386. (203)739-0286. Editor: Winifred Bonney. Emphasizes "manufacturing supervision for front-line supervision in the shop. Not office and non-union." Semimonthly. Free sample copy.
Cartoons: Uses 1-2 cartoons/issue; buys all from freelancers. Receives "a dozen or so/month." Interested in nonsexist material that represents the real world, women and minorities, and pokes fun at aspects of shop supervision: safety, productivity, motivation, discipline, etc. Prefers single panel b&w line drawings with or without gagline. Send roughs. SASE. Reports in 2 weeks. Buys all rights. Pays $10 for b&w; on acceptance.

SWCP CATALYST, (Self Winding Clock Publications Catalyst), Box 7704, Long Beach CA 90807. (213)427-4202. Publisher: Dr. Bengt E. Honning. Emphasizes horology/clocks, the self winding clock and other antique battery clocks for time standards department—USL, NASA, etc., Western Union, collectors, antique battery clock service. Bimonthly. Circ. 450. Accepts previously published material and simultaneous submissions. Original artwork returned after publication. Sample copy and art guidelines free for SASE.
Illustrations: Uses 3-4 illustrations/issue. Prefers horology themes. Send query letter with business card and samples. Prefers photocopies as samples; "dimensions of original if otherwise." Samples returned by SASE. Reports within 2 weeks. Material not copyrighted.

TELEBRIEFS, Illinois Bell Telephone Co., 225 W. Randolph, Chicago IL 60606. Contact: Editor. Monthly newsletter for telephone customers. Circ. 3,500,000. Mail art. SASE. Reports in 2 weeks. Photocopies OK. Original artwork not returned after publication. Free sample copy.
Cartoons: Uses 1 cartoon/issue, all from freelancers. Receives 8 submissions/month from freelancers. Cartoons "must be telephone, telephone company or communications related." Single panel. "No ethnic humor. We reduce cartoons to 1¾x1¾ so we need few elements, drawn very boldly. Prefer strong visual with captions of 10 or fewer words." Prefers finished cartoons. SASE. Reports in 2 weeks. Buys all rights on a work-for-hire basis. Pays $40, line drawings with shading; on acceptance.

*THE TIMES-PICAYUNE/THE STATES-ITEM, 3800 Howard Ave., New Orleans LA 70140. (504)586-3454. Art Director: George Berke. Daily newspaper with general features, anusements, political subjects for wide cross-section of readers. Circ. 300,000. Accepts previously published material. Original artwork returned after publication. Sample copy and art guidelines available.
Illustrations: Buys 1 illustration/issue from freelancers. Works on assignment only. Send query letter with resume and samples to be kept on file; write or call for appointment to show portfolio. Accepts photostats, tear sheets, photocopies, slides or photographs as samples. Samples returned by SASE. Reports only if interested. Buys one-time rights. Pays variable rates; on acceptance.

TOWERS CLUB, USA, Box 2038, Vancouver WA 98668. (206)699-4428. Chief Executive Officer: Jerry Buchanan. Emphasizes "anything that offers a new entrepreneurial opportunity, especially through mail order. The newsletter for 'Find a Need and Fill It' people." Readers are 80% male with average age of 48 and income of $35,000. Monthly except August and December. Circ. 4,000. Previously published material and simultaneous submissions OK. Original work returned after publication by SASE. Sample copy $3. Receives 1-2 submissions/year.

Cartoons: Uses 1 cartoon/issue; buys all from freelancers. Interested in themes of selling how-to-do-it information, showing it as a profitable and honorable profession; single panel with gagline, b&w line drawings. Send finished cartoons. Samples returned by SASE. Reports in 1 week. Buys one-time rights. Pays $15, b&w; on publication.

Illustrations: Uses 5-7 illustrations/issue. Interested in realistic illustrative art of typists, computers, small print shop operations, mail order, etc.; no comical themes. Especially needs line drawings of typists/writers/office workers, money, mail delivery, affluent people, intelligent and successful faces, etc. Send finished art. Provide samples to be kept on file for possible future assignments. Samples not kept on file are returned by SASE. Reports in 1 week. Buys one-time rights. Makes some permanent purchases. Negotiates payment depending on rights purchased; on acceptance.

Tips: "Newsletters are going more to using typesetting and artwork to brighten pages. Subscribe to our *Towers Club, USA* newsletter and study content and artwork used. Normally $46 per year, we will give discount to artists who show us a portfolio of their work. Our theme will lead them to much other business, as we are about creative self-publishing/marketing exclusively."

TUNDRA DRUMS, Box 868, Bethel AK 99559. (907)543-3500. Publisher/Editor: Rosie Porter. Newspaper emphasizing local area news, views and interests. Audience is "20,000 people in 69,000 sq. miles of rural (to the extreme) Western Alaska (60% Eskimo)." Weekly. Circ. 6,000. Accepts previously published material. Returns original art after publication.

Cartoons: Buys cartoons from freelancers infrequently. Seeks national/international political cartoons; local themes done inhouse. Prefers single or multiple panel with gagline; b&w line drawings, b&w washes. Send query letter with samples of style to be kept on file. Material not filed is returned by SASE only if requested. Reports within weeks. Negotiates rights purchased. Pay is "low, naturally;" on publication.

Illustrations: Buys a few illustrations from freelancers. Send query letter with samples to be kept on file. Prefers photostats as samples. Samples not filed are returned by SASE. Reports within weeks. Negotiates rights purchased. Pay is "low"; on publication.

UTILITY SUPERVISION, (formerly *Utility Supervisions and Safety Letter*), 24 Rope Ferry Rd., Waterford CT 06386. (203)442-4365. Editor: DeLoris Lidestri. Emphasizes utility system installation, maintenance and repair for front-line supervisors in the field (not plant or office). Semimonthly. Circ. 4,000. Free sample copy.

Cartoons: Uses 1 cartoon/issue; buys all from freelancers. Interested in non-sexist material which pokes fun at some of the problems of utility supervision and/or utility field work. Prefers single panel b&w line drawings with or without gagline. Send finished cartoons. SASE. Reports in 2 weeks. Buys all rights. Pays $10 for b&w on acceptance.

VELO-NEWS, Box 1257, Brattleboro VT 05301. Editor: Barbara George. Tabloid. Emphasizes bicycle racing for competitors, coaches, officials, enthusiasts. Published 18 times/year. Circ. 15,000. Accepts previously published material and simultaneous submissions. Original artwork returned after publication. Sample copy $2.

Cartoons: Uses 1 cartoon/issue; buys from freelancer. Prefers single panel, with gagline; b&w line drawings. Send query letter with samples of style to be kept on file. Material not kept on file is returned by SASE. Reports within 2 weeks. Buys one-time rights. Pays $15, b&w; on publication.

WAREHOUSING SUPERVISOR'S BULLETIN, 24 Rope Ferry Rd., Waterford CT 06386. (203)442-4365. Contact: Editor. Emphasizes warehouse, shipping, traffic, material handling for front-line supervision. Semimonthly. Free sample copy.

Cartoons: Uses 1 cartoon/issue; buys from freelancer. Interested in non-sexist material which pokes fun at aspects of warehouse operations and supervision. Prefers single panel b&w line drawings with or without gagline. Send roughs. SASE. Reports in 3-6 weeks. Buys all rights. Pays $10 for b&w on acceptance.

WDS FORUM, 9933 Alliance Rd., Cincinnati OH 45242. (513)984-0717. Editor: Ms. Kirk Polking. Emphasizes writing techniques and marketing for Writer's Digest School students. Monthly. Circ. 10,000.

Cartoons: Needs work on "the joys and griefs of freelancing, that first check/rejection slip, trying to find time to write, postal problems, editor/author relations, etc." Send either finished art or roughs. SASE. Reports in 3 weeks. Pays $10, b&w.

Illustrations: "We might buy a few spot drawings, as fillers, of writer-related subject matter." SASE.

Reports in 3 weeks. Query with samples. Pays $5, each drawing; on acceptance. "Sorry our rates are so low but we carry no advertising and our newletter is primarily a service to our students."

WESTART, Box 6868, Auburn CA 95604. Editor: Martha Garcia. Emphasizes art for practicing artists, teachers, students, craftsmen, collectors and art patrons. Biweekly. Circ. 6,500. Previously published material OK. Original work returned after publication; SASE required. Free sample copy for SASE; art guidelines available. Photographs, cartoons and illustrations used as works of art in connection with current West Coast exhibition.

*WESTERN CANADA OUTDOORS, Box 430, North Battleford, Saskatchewan S9A 2Y5 Canada. (306)445-4401. Publisher: S. Nowakowski. For hunting, fishing and outdoor families. Bimonthly newspaper. Circ. 42,000. Previously published work OK. Free sample copy.
Cartoons: Uses 3 cartoons/issue, all by freelancers. Receives 0-1 submission/week from freelancer. Interested in "an outdoor, conserving environment theme"; single panel. Prefers to see finished cartoons. SASE (nonresidents include SAE and International Reply Coupons). Reports in 1 month. Buys "once-rental" rights. Pays $5-10, halftones; on acceptance.
Illustrations: Uses 0-1 illustrations/issue, all from freelancer. Receives no submissions/week from freelancers. Interested in wildlife. Especially needs hunting and fishing related artwork; must have some interest for Western Canada. Prefers to see finished art. SASE (nonresidents include SAE and International Reply Coupons). Reports in 1 month. Buys "once-rental" rights. Pays on acceptance.

THE WETUMPKA HERALD, 300 Green St., Box 29, Wetumpka AL 36092. (205)567-7811. Editor & Publisher: Ellen T. Harris. Newspaper emphasizing local news, sports, etc. (small town) for family audience. Weekly. Circ. 3,000. Accepts previously published material. Sample copy free for SASE with 25¢ postage. Art guidelines free for SASE with 50¢ postage.
Cartoons: Single-panel with gagline; b&w line drawings. Send samples of style to be kept on file "except for material we do not consider using in the future." Write for appointment to show portfolio. Material not filed not returned. Reports only if interested.
Illustrations: Buys 1 illustration/issue from freelancers. Send query letter with samples to be kept on file "except for material we do not consider using in future." Write for appointment to show portfolio. Prefers photocopies or tearsheets as samples. Samples not filed not returned. Reports only if interested. Pays on publication.

*THE WINE SPECTATOR, Suite 2040, 601 Van Ness, San Francisco CA 94102. (415)673-2040. Production Manager: Karen Magnuson. Tabloid emphasizing wine for wine lovers—consumer and trade. Bimonthly. Circ. 45,000. Original artwork not returned after publication.
Cartoons: Buys 1/issue from freelance artists. Send samples of style to be kept on file. Write or call for appointment to show portfolio. Material not filed is not returned. Reports only if interested. Buys all rights. Pays $50-100, b&w.
Illustrations: Buys 2-3/issue from freelance artists. Works on assignment only. Send samples to be kept on file. Call for appointment to show portfolio. Prefers photostats or tear sheets as samples. Does not report back. Buys all rights. Pays $100-200, b&w, or $200, color cover; and $50-150, b&w or $100-175, color, inside; on publication.

*YOUNG AMERICAN, Box 12409, Portland OR 97212. (503)230-1895. Design Director: Richard Ferguson. Tabloid emphasizing fiction, fantasy, science, news and specialty subjects for children, 4-16 and family members. Monthly. Circ. 100,000. Accepts previously published material. Returns originals after publication. Sample copy free for SASE.
Cartoons: Buys 3-4/issue. "Themes should be relatable to children. We prefer realistic styles over free-style cartoons." Prefers single or multi-panel with gagline; b&w line drawings or b&w washes. Send finished cartoons to be kept on file. Material not filed returned by SASE. Reports only if interested. Buys reprint rights. Pays $5-10, b&w; on publication.
Illustrations: Buys 3-4/issue. Works on assignment only. Send brochure, business card and samples to be kept on file. Call for appointment to show portfolio. Prefers photostats or tear sheets for b&w samples; color slides or printed material for color samples. Samples not filed are returned by SASE. Reports only if interested. Buys one-time rights. Pays $20-50, b&w, inside; $100 maximum, color, inside; on publication.

Performing Arts

Music, theatre, dance and opera—the performing arts areas found in this section—seek artists capable of communicating information through original, dynamic design and strong imagery.

For many groups, specifically symphonies and operas, design work is becoming bolder in order to compete with television, movies and other forms of entertainment. These former bastions of conservatism are employing lighter, less stuffy images in an attempt to appeal to younger or cross-over audiences.

The graphic artist providing art and design to a performing arts group is often faced with three tasks. First, he must communicate to the public what the group offers—song, dance or drama—with information on when this offering occurs—time, place and date. Second, he must keep in mind that the artwork will most likely be used on different printed materials so as to carry the same theme throughout a pro-

"Will Sherwood has a fresh new outlook on the subject of orchestras," says Hannelore N. Rogers, marketing/statewide director of the New Mexico Symphony Orchestra. The Los Angeles artist received $5,000 for the design and illustration of the orchestra's eight-page 1984-85 season program shown here.

motional, marketing and advertising campaign. Finally, the artist is often expected to produce at a very reasonable price, especially if he's working for a nonprofit organization.

As with any market area, research a performing arts group as much as possible before approaching them with your work. If you feel an empathy for one area over another, perhaps a preference for dance rather than theatre, then focus your efforts in that area. You needn't be an expert in a particular performing arts area, but a familiarity and a "feel" will certainly help you visually translate the unique qualities into print.

The listings provide descriptions of a variety of groups. Some have only seasonal needs such as summer theatres; we've tried to indicate when a group's needs are heaviest. Many of the organizations seek set and costume designers, and residencies in different areas are also available, usually on a short-term basis.

For further names and information regarding the performing arts, consult the *American Dance Directory, Dance Magazine, Summer Theatre Directory, American Theatre Association Directory, Theatre Profiles* and the *Music Industry Directory.* Your Yellow Pages list local performing arts groups and theatres.

AFRICA I DANCE THEATRE, 1194 Nostrand Ave., Brooklyn NY 11225. (212)493-4500. Administrator: Roger Francis. African dance company and theatre, repertory, 23 members.
Needs: Works with 5-10 freelance artists/year. Uses artists for advertising and brochure design and illustration; program and set design, posters, lighting and scenery.
First Contact & Terms: Prefers local artists with performing arts experience. Send query letter with brochure, resume, business card, samples and tear sheets to be kept on file. Prefers photostats, photographs, etc. as samples. Reports within 2 weeks. Payment dependent upon extensiveness of project. Considers complexity of project, available budget, skill and experience of artist, how work will be used, turnaround time and rights purchased when establishing payment.

*ALABAMA SHAKESPEARE FESTIVAL, The State Theatre, Suite 20, Building A, 2820 Fairlane Dr., Montgomery AL 36116. Director of Marketing: Jay Drury. LORT classical theatre company.
Needs: Works with 3 freelance artists/year. Uses artists for advertising and brochure design illustration layout; poster and program design and illustration.
First Contact & Terms: Prefers experienced area artists. Works on assignment only. Send query letter with resume and samples (very important) to be kept on file; write for appointment to show portfolio. Reports only if interested. Pays by the project; fees differ widely.

*ALLENBERRY PLAYHOUSE, Boiling Springs PA 17007. (717)258-3211. Managing Director: Nelson Sheeley. 400 seat Equity summer stock theatre offering 10-12 productions, 2 of which are musicals; shows run 3-4 weeks.
Needs: Number of freelance artists used/year varies; needs heaviest during season, April-November. Uses artists for set and costume design, lighting and scenery. Especially needs scenic designer and costume designer.
First Contact & Terms: Send query letter with resume. Prefers slides as samples. Samples returned by SASE. Reports within 3 weeks. Provide material to be kept on file for possible future assignments. Pays scenic designers $200/week plus room; costumers $200/week plus room; assistant costumer $100/week plus room. Considers available budget when establishing payment.
Tips: "Be prepared to stay for entire season. Apply shortly after January 1."

AMAS REPERTORY THEATRE, INC., 1 E. 104th St., New York NY 10029. (212)369-8000. Founder and Artistic Director: Rosetta LeNoire. Administrators: Gary Halcott and Jerry Lapidus. A professional, nonprofit, off-Broadway performing arts organization. Programs include the creation of original musical theatre, classes for young people and adults, a senior citizens tour, etc.
Needs: Works with 8-12 freelance artists/year. Needs heaviest in fall, winter and spring. Uses artists for brochure design, illustration and layout; poster design and illustration; program, set and costume design; lighting; and scenery.
First Contact & Terms: Works on assignment only. Send query letter with brochure, resume and samples to be kept on file. Prefers tear sheets, originals or photocopies as samples. Reports back within 1 month. Pays for design by the project, $50-350 average. Considers how work will be used when establishing payment.

ARIZONA OPERA COMPANY, 3501 N. Mountain Ave., Tucson AZ 85719. (602)293-4336. General Director: Glynn Ross. "The only state-wide opera company in the United States, and the only opera company in Arizona, performing in both Tucson and Phoenix. It presents Grand Opera with professional artists, nationally recognized directors, full staging with elaborate costumes, lighting and so forth."
Needs: Works with 3-4 freelance artists/year. Needs heaviest October-May. Uses artists for advertising design, illustration and layout; poster design and illustration; brochure, set and costume design; lighting and scenery.
First Contact & Terms: Local artists are preferred for convenience; experience is required. Works on assignment only. Send query letter with resume to be kept on file. Material not filed returned by SASE. Considers complexity of project and how work will be used when establishing payment.

BALLETACOMA, 508 6th Ave., Tacoma WA 98402. (206)272-9631. Administrative Director: Carlene Garner. Nonprofit regional ballet company composed of 30 dancers; performance season includes "The Nutcracker Ballet" and two other major productions.
Needs: Works with 3 freelance artists/year; needs heaviest in August-September, January, March. Uses artists for advertising, brochure and program design, illustration and layout; set and costume design; posters, lighting and scenery.
First Contact & Terms: Send query letter with resume and samples to be kept on file. Call for appointment to show portfolio. Prefers photostats and photographs as samples. Reports within 2 weeks. Pays for design and illustration by the project, $25-500 average. Considers complexity of project, available budget, skill and experience of artist and how work will be used when establishing payment.

BALTIMORE OPERA COMPANY, 40 W. Chase St., Baltimore MD 21201. (301)727-0592. Public Relations Director: Kathleen Laughery. Producer of grand opera and a touring opera company presenting 3 main productions annually.
Needs: Uses artists for advertising and catalog layout; brochure design and layout; poster design and illustration; program and set design; scenery.
First Contact & Terms: Works on assignment only. Send query letter with resume and samples to be kept on file. Write for appointment to show portfolio. Reports back only if interested. Considers project's budget, and skill and experience of the artist when establishing payment.

THE BATON ROUGE SYMPHONY ORCHESTRA, Box 103, Baton Rouge LA 70821. (504)387-6166. Publicist: John Cade. Eighty-member professional symphony orchestra with fulltime resident music director/conductor. Fourteen regular-season concerts/year (October-May), an outdoor concert series, ensemble appearances, etc.; 2,500 subscribers.
Needs: Works with 1-2 freelance artists/year; needs heaviest in spring: design and produce brochure promoting fall season - 25,000 copies. Summer: design and produce 2 season program covers. Uses artists for advertising, brochure and program design, illustration and layout; posters, t-shirt and billboard design. "We look for extremely high quality, a certain level of sophistication, dramatic impact and an artist who can work well with our staff and who can project the image we want."
First Contact & Terms: Send query letter with brochure, resume, business card, samples and tear sheets to be kept on file. Call for appointment to show portfolio. Prefers copies of actual produced work, such as brochures, if possible; otherwise, photostats. Reports only if interested. Considers complexity of project, available budget, skill and experience of artist, how work will be used, turnaround time and rights purchased when establishing payment. "We prefer to establish a fee for the project at hand. Our status as a nonprofit institution means we have a rather small budget, but we are willing to pay competitive prices for good work."
Tips: "We look for originality in design and concept and require technical accuracy. When submitting, submit treatments only and research thoroughly before including designs depicting musical instruments, instrumentation, period, etc."

BERKSHIRE PUBLIC THEATRE, INC., Box 860, Pittsfield MA 01202. (413)445-4631. Director: Frank Bessell. Regional repertory theatre with an artistic and technical company of 200, an administrative staff of 10 and an audience of 30,000 yearly.
Needs: Works with 10 freelance artists/year. Uses artists for advertising, brochure, poster and program design; set and costume design; lighting and scenery.
First Contact & Terms: Send query letter. Provide resume and samples to be kept on file for possible future assignments. Pays by the project for design and illustration; negotiates payment. "Sometimes barters exchanges in lieu of dollars."
Tips: There is a "need for great flexibility—a broad range of skills and willingness to create design work outside a specific narrow field."

BINGHAMTON SYMPHONY ORCHESTRA, 334 N Press Bldg., 19 Chenango St., Binghamton NY 13901. (607)723-8242. Contact: Publicity Director or Executive Director. Classical and popular orchestral music entertainment; also, chamber music.
Needs: Works with 2-4 freelance artists/year. Needs are seasonal. Uses artists for advertising and brochure design, illustration and layout; poster and program design and illustration.
First Contact & Terms: Interested in quality, inexpensive work. Send query letter with brochure, resume and samples to be kept on file. Samples not filed are returned only if requested. Pays $50-500 average.

BROOKLYN CENTER FOR THE PERFORMING ARTS AT BROOKLYN COLLEGE (BCBC), Box 163, Brooklyn NY 11210. (212)780-5291. Director of Public Relations and Promotion: Marian Skokan. Two auditoriums used for music, dance and theatre. Assigns 20 jobs/year; local artists only. Query with samples. No work returned. Reports in 1 month.
Needs: Uses artists for illustration, design, layout and production of advertising, direct mail brochures, flyers and graphics. Pay determined by job.

*PAUL BUNYAN PLAYHOUSE, Box 752, Bemidji MN 56601. (218)751-7270 (season); (218)829-4345 (off-season). Professional summer theatre with a 10-week season; "the oldest continuous running summer theatre in Minnesota."
Needs: Works with 16 freelance artists/year; needs heaviest in June-August. Uses artists for set and costume design, lighting and scenery.
First Contact & Terms: Artists must be in-residence during season. Artists are company members, hiring is done in March. Send query letter with brochure/flyer and resume. Samples returned by SASE.

Reports in 4 weeks. Provide brochure/flyer, resume and business card to be kept on file for possible future assignments. Pays a salary for the season.

CASA MANANA MUSICALS INC., Box 9054, Ft. Worth TX 76107. (817)332-9319. General Manager/Producer: Bud Franks. Director of Playhouse/Assistant Manager: Charles Ballinger. Dance troupe performing summer stock, children's theatre and classics.
Needs: Assigns 8 jobs/year. Uses artists for costumes, promotional materials, sets and theatrical lighting.
First Contact & Terms: Query with resume. SASE. Reports within 2 weeks. Pay varies.

*CENTRAL CITY OPERA HOUSE ASSOCIATION, #614, 1615 California St., Denver CO 80212. (303)623-7167. Artistic Director: John Moriarty. Produces opera and music theatre and related performance events in a 100-year-old opera house, preserving historic properties related to the functioning of the opera house and the production of opera in Denver; 756 seats, principal patronage from Denver metro area.
Needs: Works with varied number of freelance artists/year; needs heaviest in spring and early summer. Uses artists for advertising, brochure, poster, program, set and costume design; brochure, poster and program illustration; brochure layout, lighting and scenery. Also uses artists for occasional reports. "The art must attract and project contemporary thrust of historic non-profit organization."
First Contact & Terms: Send brochure/flyer or resume with actual work; if possible, write for appointment, submit portfolio for review. Samples not returned. Reporting time varies with season. Provide brochure/flyer, resume and samples to be kept on file for possible future assignments. Pays $25-50/hour average for design and illustration.

THE CHARLESTON SYMPHONY ORCHESTRA, Box 2292, Charleston WV 25328. (304)342-0151. Director of Communications: Michael Fanning. Symphony orchestra "whose patrons represent a broad socio-economic spectrum of music lovers—from classical to pops."
Needs: Works with 1-2 freelance artists/year. Needs heaviest in January-February. Uses artists for advertising and brochure design and illustration; and poster illustration. Prefers "clean, contemporary lines with slight feel of elegance; however, not overstated."
First Contact & Terms: Works on assignment only. Send query letter with brochure, resume, business card and samples to be kept on file. Call for appointment to show portfolio. Samples not filed are returned. Reports only if interested. Payment negotiated; usually on a bidding process. Considers project's budget, skill and experience of the artist, and turnaround time when establishing payment.

CHARLOTTE OPERA ASSOCIATION, INC., 110 E. 7th St., Charlotte NC 28202. Public Relations Director: Leslie Paliyenko. Presents 3 fully-staged operas/season, a 3-state tour of a fully-staged opera, 2 educational operas and an Opera Extravaganza.
Needs: Works with 3 freelance artists/year; needs heaviest in late summer and fall. Uses artists for advertising design, illustration and layout; other jobs as they occur.
First Contact & Terms: Local artists only with 3 years' experience. Send query letter with brochure, samples, resume and business card to be kept on file. "We like to know how other organizations felt about the artist's work." Write for appointment to show portfolio. Prefers original work as samples; samples returned only if requested. Reports within 3 months. Negotiates payment. Considers complexity of project, available budget, and skill and experience of artist when establishing payment.
Tips: "We would encourage any artists with unique artistic creativity to contact us. We seek design that is classic, above average and outstanding."

*CHEN & DANCERS/HTDC, 2nd Fl., 70 Mulberry St., New York NY 10013. (212)349-0126. Artistic Director: Chen Hsueh-Tung. Chen & dancers is a modern dance company performing theatrical, humorous and poetic works rooted in Asian themes. The company presents regular NY seasons and tours the U.S. and abroad.
Needs: Works with 10 freelance artists/year. Needs heaviest in fall and spring. Uses freelance artists for advertising, brochure, catalog, poster, program, set and costume design; lighting and scenery. "As an Asian-American modern dance company, we need designs that are contemporary expressions of our traditional heritage."
First Contact & Terms: "Artists must be able to produce theatrical designs with an oriental aesthetic

Market conditions are constantly changing! If this is 1987 or later, buy the newest edition of Artist's Market at your favorite bookstore or order directly from Writer's Digest Books.

sensibility—simple, not ornate or garish. Send query letter with brochure, resume, business card and samples to be kept on file. Call or write for appointment to show portfolio. Accepts photostats, slides, photographs, photocopies or tear sheets as samples. Reports back only if interested. Pays by the project up to $500 for design. Considers complexity of project, project's budget, skill and experience of the artist and how work will be used when estabiliting payment.

CHICAGO CITY THEATRE COMPANY, 3340 N. Clark St., Chicago IL 60657. (312)880-1002. Co-director: Joseph Ehrenberg. Performing arts organization including dance, theatre and music training.
Needs: Works with 4-6 freelance artists/year; needs heaviest in late summer through spring. Uses artists for advertising, brochure and program design; set and costume design; posters and lighting. "We have logo and basic approach to advertising designs."
First Contact & Terms: Send brochure, resume and samples usually to be kept on file. "Samples might be thrown after observing" or returned by SASE if requested. Call or write for appointment to show portfolio. Accepts any type of samples. Reports only if interested. Pays for design by the project, $50-500 average. Considers complexity of project, available budget and rights purchased when establishing payment.

THE CLEVELAND INSTITUTE OF MUSIC, 11021 East Blvd., Cleveland OH 44106. (216)791-5165. Public Relations Director: Jean Caldwell. Performing arts center and conservatory of music.
Needs: Assigns 15 jobs and buys 20 illustrations/year. Uses artists for illustration, layout and graphics for advertising, annual reports, bumper stickers, costumes, direct mail brochures, exhibits, flyers, graphics, posters, programs, stages, record jackets and catalogs.
First Contact & Terms: Local artists only. Query with samples or arrange interview. SASE. Reports within 1 day.

*COCTEAU REPERTORY CO., 330 Bowery, New York NY 10012. (212)677-0060. Artistic Director: Eve Adamson. Performs 6 plays in rotating repertory with a resident company each year.
Needs: Works with 6-10 freelance artists/year. Needs heaviest August-March. Uses artists for brochure, set and costume design; and lighting and scenery. "We prefer non-realistic designs, strong, central concepts."
First Contact & Terms: "We prefer classical repertory and/or European experience." Works on assignment only. Send query letter with resume to be kept on file for 1 season. "We encourage artists to see our work before application." Samples accepted at interview only. Samples not filed are returned by SASE. Reports back only if interested. Pays for design by the project, $200-300 average. Pays for illustration by the project, $150-650 average. Considers project's budget when establishing payment.

CONNECTICUT OPERA, 15 Lewis St., Hartford CT 06103. (203)241-0251. Director of Communications: Ginny Ludwig. Sixth oldest professional opera company in the US. Main season is 2 performances each of 4 major productions in the original language and one performance in English performed in Bushnell Hall. Also operates a resident touring company, which performs fully staged and costumed productions throughout New England and the East Coast.
Needs: Works with 2 freelance artists/year. "We use freelance artists when we design our season brochure in the late winter and when we design brochures for single productions, etc. Probably our heaviest needs are in late winter/early spring." Uses artists for advertising and brochure design, illustration and layout; program, set and costume design; and scenery.
First Contact & Terms: Send query letter with brochure and tear sheets to be kept on file. Call or write for appointment to show portfolio. Samples not kept on file are returned by SASE only if requested. Reports only if interested. The fee depends on the project.
Tips: When reviewing an artist's work, looks for "originality and strong imagery whether it be graphic or illustrative; dynamic design rather than obscure. We are interested in strong graphic design that will help to market the product. Good design that doesn't translate into black-and-white newspaper ads is valueless."

CORTLAND REPERTORY THEATRE INC., Box 783, Cortland NY 13045. Resident summer theatre which produces 5 shows in summer. Assigns 5 jobs/summer.
Needs: Works with 5 designers/year; summers only. Uses designers for properties, sets, costume and lighting. Also uses artists for brochures (donation drive, subscription series) and flyer (early bird renewal).
First Contact & Terms: Query with resume in early winter. Works on assignment only. Pays $1,000-1,700 for 2 months work. Pays for design and illustrations by the project, $50-200 average. Considers available budget, skill and experience of artist and rights purchased when establishing payment.
Tips: "Do volunteer work in the area of your interest. This way you keep your skills sharp, you learn,

and it places you in front of people who may someday be able to hire you. I also find trading services an excellent means to opening job situations. More and more industries and businesses are turning to professional artists for help in packaging, displays and advertising. This is very evident in the theatrical field."

*DALLAS THEATER CENTER, 3636 Turtle Creek Blvd., Dallas TX 75219. Contact: Public Relations Director. A professional resident theatre with 3 performing spaces—Frank LW Theater, Arts District Theatre and In The Basement (experimental theater). Performs variety of plays from classic to contemporary. Yearly attendance of 100,000.
Needs: Uses a varying number of freelance artists/year. Needs are heaviest in spring and fall although possibilities exist year-round for program and poster work. Uses freelance artists for advertising and brochure design, illustration and layout; poster and program design and illustration.
First Contact & Terms: Prefers local artists as "we often need work rather quickly." Works on assignment basis only. Send query letter with business card and samples to be kept on file. Write for appointment to show portfolio. Prefers photocopies as samples. Samples not kept on file are returned only with an SASE. Reports only if interested. Pays by the project for design; by the hour or by the project, for illustration. Considers complexity of project, project's budget, skill and experience of the artist, how work will be used, turnaround time and rights purchased when establishing payment.

DANCE GALLERY, 242 E. 14th St., New York NY 10003. (212)685-5972. Administrative Director: J. Antony Siciliano. Dance troupe and theatre.
Needs: Works with 2 illustrators and 2 designers/year. Uses artists for direct mail brochures, posters, programs, flyers and newspaper ads.
First Contact & Terms: Query with resume or arrange interview to show portfolio. SASE. Reports within 2 weeks. Works on assignment only. Provide resume and brochure to be kept on file for future assignments. Negotiates pay by the project for design and illustration.

DANCE KALEIDOSCOPE, 429 E. Vermont, Indianapolis IN 46202. (317)634-8484. Artistic Director: Cherri Jaffee. Professional modern dance repertory company which tours Indiana. The repertory comes largely from guest choreographers out of New York City.
Needs: Works with several freelance artists/year; needs heaviest in October, March and May. Uses artists for advertising, brochure, program, set and costume design; advertising, brochure and program layout; advertising illustration, posters, lighting and scenery. Prefers clean, bold style "that sells the product, not the graphics."
First Contact & Terms: Local artists only with previous experience in the arts "who enjoy the challenge of working within a limited budget. Artist must be willing to take direction from the board of directors." Send query letter with brochure, resume, business card, samples and tear sheets to be kept on file. Call for appointment to show portfolio. Samples not returned. Reports only if interested. Pays for design by the hour, $10-30 average; by the project, $50-100 average. Considers complexity of project, available budget, turnaround time and rights purchased when establishing payment.
Tips: "Artist must respect the company's need to use 'words' in some publications and not expect the art to carry the entire message."

*DANCE PLANT, INC., Box 66, W. Medford MA 02156; Box 861, Miami FL 33233. (617)395-2199. Director: Diane Pariser. Public relations, management and booking services provided to folk/ethnic/jazz dance and music groups and individual choreographers, instrumentalists, theater artists, etc.
Needs: Works with 3 freelance artists/year. Uses artists for advertising, and catalog design, illustration and layout; poster and program design; and lighting. Style varies according to group/artist's needs.
First Contact & Terms; Works on assignment only. Send samples to be kept on file. Samples should be accurate and easy to look at or read. Samples not filed are returned only if requested. Reports only if interested. Pays for design by the project, $75-500 average. Pays for illustration by the the project, $35 minimum. Considers complexity of project, how work will be used, turnaround time and rights purchased when establishing payment.

*DANCE 10, 334 Lakeview Ave., Clifton NJ 07011. (201)772-2120. Also: 2-4 Franklin Ave., Rutherford NJ 07070. (201)438-3628. Manager: Carl L. Presto. Service-related dance/theatre company providing jazz dance performances, lectures and demonstrations.
Needs: Works with 20 freelance artists/year. Uses artists for advertising, brochure, catalog and program design, illustration and layout; set and costume design, posters, lighting and scenery.
First Contact & Terms: Send query letter with resume and samples to be kept on file. Write for appointment to show portfolio. Prefers photographs as samples. Reports within 1 week. Pays for design by the project. Considers complexity of project, available budget, how work will be used and rights purchased when establishing payment.

DAYTON BALLET, 140 N. Main St., Dayton OH 45402. (513)222-3661. Director: Stuart Sebastian. Ballet company of 15 professional dancers with a 12-member nonprofessional training company, board of trustees and friends organization.
Needs: Works with 2-3 freelance artists/year. Uses artists for advertising, brochure, set and costume design; lighting and scenery.
First Contact & Terms: Send query letter with resume and samples. Samples returned. Reports within 3 weeks. Works on assignment only. Provide brochure/flyer and resume to be kept on file for possible future assignments. Pays by the project; negotiable.
Tips: "Line drawings are comic, romantic and flowing."

*DEL LA CROIX PRODUCTIONS INTERNATIONAL INC., 3843 Massachusetts Ave. NW, Washington DC 20016. (202)364-0718. Executive Producer: Maximilien De Lafayette. Estab. 1983. Produces shows, plays, music, and various artistic projects; recruits, trains, promotes and manages artists, actors, actresses, choreographers, designers, dancers, singers and stage directors as well as freelance painters and illustrators.
Needs: Works with 110 freelance artists/year. Uses artists for advertising, brochure, catalog, and magazine/newspaper design, illustration and layout; AV presentations; exhibits; displays; signage; posters and design for plays and artistic productions.
First Contact & Terms: Send resume, at least 2 letters of reference and samples to be kept on file; write for appointment to show portfolio. Prefers photostats as samples. Reports within 2 weeks. Works on assignment only. Pays by the project. Considers skill and experience of artist when establishing payment.
Tips: Looks for "originality, new style, creativity, ability to meet work schedule, precision and flexibility when considering freelance artists."

DENVER SYMPHONY ORCHESTRA, Suite 330, 910 Fifteenth St., Denver CO 80202.(303)572-1151. Marketing & Public Relations Director: Al Kosmal. Professional 88-member symphony orchestra performing classical and pops concerts.
Needs: Works with "numerous" freelance artists/year. Uses artists for advertising, brochure and catalog design, illustration and layout; poster and program design and illustration.
First Contact & Terms: Works on assignment only. Send query letter with brochure, resume, samples to be kept on file. Call or write for appointment to show portfolio. Accepts photostats, slides, photographs, photocopies or tear sheets as samples. Samples not filed are returned only if requested. Reports within 3 weeks. Payment varies. Considers complexity of project, project's budget, skill and experience of the artist, how work will be used and turnaround time when establishing payment.

DIABLO VALLEY PHILHARMONIC, 321 Golf Club Rd., Pleasant Hill CA 94523. (415)685-1230. Conductor: Fredric Johnson. Symphony orchestra.
Needs: Works with 1 freelance artist/year. Needs heaviest May-July. Uses artists for advertising and brochure design, illustration and layout; and program design and illustration. Prefers an "eloquent, classy" style.
First Contact & Terms: Send query letter with brochure and samples to be kept on file. Write for appointment to show portfolio. Samples not filed are not returned. Reports back only if interested. Pays for design and illustration by the project, $200 average. Considers complexity of project, project's budget and turnaround time when establishing payment.

*EL TEATRO CAMPESINO, Box 1240, San Juan Bautista CA 95045. Publicist: Andres Gutierrez. Creates and produces original theater productions, some combining drama, music and dance. Productions include social, political and Hispanic themes.
Needs: Works with 4 freelance artists/year. Uses artists for poster and program design and illustration; set and costume design; lighting, sound and scenery.
First Contact & Terms: Works on assignment only. Send query letter with resume and samples to be kept on file. "If interested we will write artist for appointment to see a portfolio. Prefers slides and photos as samples. Pays by the project, $100-350, for design and illustration. Considers project's budget and turnaround time when establishing payment.

*EMPIRE STATE INSTITUTE FOR THE PERFORMING ARTS (ESIPA), Empire State Plaza, Albany NY 12223. (518)474-1199. Producing Director: Patricia B. Snyder. Professional resident theatre and performing arts center; 2 theatres 900, 450; usually 8 productions requiring designers each season.
Needs: Works with 30-40 artists/year. Uses artists for poster illustration, set and costume design, lighting and scenery.
First Contact & Terms: Works on assignment only. Send query letter and resume to be kept on file; do not send samples with first contact. Reports back only if interested. Pays for design; usually by the pro-

ject, $1,000 average. Pays for illustration usually by the project, $500 average. Considers complexity of project, project's budget, skill and experience of the artist, and rights purchased when establishing payment.

*FIRST ALL CHILREN'S THEATRE, 37 W. 65th St., New York NY 10023. (212)873-6400. Production Manager: Eric Vennerbeck. A repertory company for young people now in its 16th season. "Our goal is to create a national center for children in the performing arts."
Needs: Works with 4-6 freelance artists/year. Needs heaviest September-May. Uses artists for set and costume design, lighting and scenery.
First Contact & Terms: Works on assignment only. Send query letter with resume to be kept on file. Reports back only if interested. Negotiates payment by project. Considers complexity of project, project's budget and skill and experience of the artist when establishing payment.

FLAGSTAFF SYMPHONY ASSOCIATION, Box 122, Flagstaff AZ 86002. (602)774-4231. Manager: Harold Weller. The FSA is the "major musical arts organization in Northern Arizona, operating the Flagstaff Symphony Orchestra and sponsoring programs and concerts in addition to the orchestra's 15 concerts."
Needs: Works with 6 freelance artists/year. Needs heaviest in March and April. Uses artists for advertising, brochure and program design; newsletter layout and design (published quarterly).
First Contact & Terms: Local artists only. Works on assignment only. Send query letter with samples to be kept on file. Prefers photocopies as samples. Samples not filed are returned only if requested. Reports only if interested. Pays by individual arrangement. Considers project's budget when establishing payment.

FLINT BALLET THEATRE, 6255 Torrey Rd., Flint MI 48507. (313)655-4960. Treasurer: Dixie Gean Nelson. Dance company of 31 adult dancers, 33 apprentice dancers, 32 children's group. Performs mostly full length classical ballets. Nonprofit organization; self-supporting with fund raising drives and selling of candy, etc.
Needs: Works with 3 freelance artists/year. Uses artists for set design, costume design, posters, lighting, scenery.
First Contact & Terms: Send resume to be kept on file. Write for appointment to show portfolio. Reports only if interested. Negotiates payment. Considers available budget, and skill and experience of artist when establishing payment.

*GEVA THEATRE, 168 S. Clinton Ave., Rochester NY 14604. (716)232-1366. Director Marketing/Public Relations: Adele Fico-McCarthy. LORT C resident professional theatre with 6 plays/season, fall and winter; varied repetoire: classic, contemporary, premieres.
Needs: Works with 6 freelance artists/year. Needs heaviest September-June. Uses artists for advertising, and brochure and catalog design, illustration and layout; and poster design and illustration. Prefers "crisp, clean, slick" style.
First Contact & Terms: Local artists only. Works on assignment only. Send query letter with brochure, resume, business card and samples to be kept on file; call or write for appointment to show portfolio. Prefers slides, photographs or photocopies as samples. Samples not filed are returned by SASE only if requested. Reports only if interested. Pays for design and illustration by the project, $50-500 average; separate payment for layout and mechanicals. Considers complexity of the project, project's budget, skill and experience of the artist, how work will be used, turnaround time and rights purchased when establishing payment.

GUS GIORDANO JAZZ DANCE CHICAGO, 614 Davis St., Evanston IL 60201. (312)866-9442. Coordinator: Mrs. Gus Giordano. Jazz dance company consisting of 10 members.
Needs: Works with 4 freelance artists/year. Uses artists for advertising and costume design, lighting and scenery.
First Contact & Terms: Chicago area artists only. Call for appointment. Samples returned by SASE. Reports within weeks. Works on assignment only. Provide resume to be kept on file for possible future assignments. Negotiates payment.

GLEN ECHO DANCE THEATER, INC., Glen Echo Park, MacArthur Blvd., Glen Echo MD 20812. (301)229-6022. Artistic Director: Jan Tievsky. Nonprofit organization including a professional modern dance company, an apprentice program, a dance studio offering a variety of dance techniques and the site of a 3½ month Summer Dance Festival. Program sponsored by the National Park Service.
Needs: Works with 10-15 freelance artists/year. Uses artists for advertising, brochure and program design, illustration and layout; set and costume design, posters, lighting, photography and video; occasional collaboratives with visual artists.

First Contact & Terms: Send query letter with brochure, resume, samples and tear sheets to be kept on file. Accepts any type of samples; original work returned. Reports only if interested. Pays for design by the hour, project or day depending on the nature of work. Considers complexity and nature of project, available budget, skill and experience of artist, how work will be used and quality of work when establishing payment.

*GROUP MOTION MULTI-MEDIA DANCE THEATER, 624 S. 4th St., Philadelphia PA 19147. (215)928-1495. Co-Directors: Brigitta Herrmann, Manfred Fishbeck. Group motion multi-media dance theatre specializing in modern and innovative dance. "We have a local audience and offer performances, a variety of classes for children and adults, and workshops."
Needs: Works with 12 freelance artists/year. Needs heaviest fall through spring. Uses artists for advertising, brochure and poster design; and lighting.
First Contact & Terms: Works on assignment only. Send query letter with samples to be kept on file; call or write for appointment to show portfolio. Reports only if interested. Pays for design and illustration by the project, $25 minimum. Considers complexity of the project, project's budget, skill and experience of the artist and how work will be used when establishing payment.

*HARLEQUIN DINNER THEATRE, 1330 Gude Dr., Rockville MD 20850. (301)340-6813. Assistant Producer: Bradford Watkins. Non-equity dinner theatre producing 6 shows a season plus mounting numerous original and touring productions.
Needs: Works with 20 freelance artists/year. Uses artists for set and costume design; lighting and scenery.
First Contact & Terms: East coast artists only; must be available for personal interview. Send resume and submit portfolio for review. Samples not returned. Reporting time "depends on current openings." Works on assignment only. Provide resume to be kept on file for possible future assignments. Negotiates payment by the project.

HARRISBURG SYMPHONY ASSOCIATION, Suite 403, Keystone Bldg., 22 S. 3rd St., Harrisburg PA 17101. (717)232-8751. Marketing Director: Cynthia Baka. An 80-member, fully professional orchestra and a 70-member youth symphony.
Needs: Works with 2 freelance artists/year. Needs heaviest in December-March, August-October. Uses artists for brochure design, illustration and layout; and poster design and illustration.
First Contact & Terms: "We need someone close enough to Harrisburg to meet in person with the executive director during the length of job." Works on assignment only. Send query letter with brochure and samples to be kept on file. Prefers photographs, tear sheets and brochures as samples. Reports back within 2 weeks. Pays for design and illustration by the project, on bid. Considers complexity of the project, project's budget, and skill and experience of the artist when establishing payment.
Tips: "Considering the high labor cost of quality artists, our organization frequently utilizes the donated services of area artists and printers. Thus we usually do not actively seek freelance artists. However, we do consider commissioning particular designers when planning special brochures and projects."

HARTFORD BALLET, 15 Lewis St., Hartford CT 06103. (203)549-0466. Director of Communications: Ginny Ludwig. Nationally recognized company under the artistic direction of Michael Uthoff, with a repertory in classical and contemporary ballet; mainstage performances include twelve performances of the annual holiday "Nutcracker" and other repertory productions featuring world premieres and revivals.
Needs: Freelance artists needed for brochure and advertising design, particularly in the spring and fall. Designers also needed for costume and scenic design, depending upon the needs of the current production.
First Contact & Terms: Forward query letter and samples of work to be kept on file. Call or write for an appointment to show portfolio. If return of samples is requested, send SASE. Terms discussed before any work is contracted. Fees based upon project needs.

HARTFORD SYMPHONY ORCHESTRA, 609 Farmington Ave., Hartford CT 06105. (203)236-6101. Acting Director of Promotion: James Galvic. Full symphony orchestra averaging 40-50 concerts annually: outdoor summer concerts, presentation of chamber concerts, special festivals.
Needs: Works with 2-3 freelance artists/year; needs heaviest in January-April. Uses artists for advertising, brochure and program illustration; and posters. Style of artwork depends specifically on event to be promoted.
First Contact & Terms: Only concerned with quality of work, willingness to be flexible and overall cost. Send query letter with resume, business card and samples to be kept on file. Call for appointment to show portfolio. Prefers samples of original work if possible, e.g., the printed piece for which work was done; slides also accepted. Samples returned by SASE if not kept on file. Reports within 1 month. Pays

for design by the project, $200-700 average. Pays for illustration by the project, $50-500 average. "We primarily work by project only; price agreed upon prior to any finished work commissioned/submitted." Considers available budget, skill and experience of artist, how work will be used and turnaround time when establishing payment.

*HONOLULU SYMPHONY, Suite 901, 1000 Bishop St., Honolulu HI 96813. (808)537-6171. Director of Communications and Marketing: Henry Adams.
Needs: Assigns 30 jobs/year. Uses artists for direct mail, brochures, posters, programs, annual reports, newspaper ads and season promotions. "Graphic design should be bold, clean and careful."
First Contact & Terms: Local artists only. Query with previously published work. SASE. Reports within 2 weeks. Pays for design or illustration by the hour, $15-30 average; by the project, $100-250 average. Considers available budget, how work will be used and turnaround time when establishing payment.
Tips: "A local advertising agency has taken the Honolulu Symphony on as a public service account; therefore, freelance needs have been reduced."

INTAR-INTERNATIONAL ARTS RELATIONS, Box 788, New York NY 10108. (212)695-6134. Artistic Director: Max Ferra. Produces 3 theatrical performances and 3 workshops/year.
Needs: Assigns 12-20 jobs/year; local artists only. Query with samples. Uses artists for set, costumes, light design. Also flyers and posters. Pays for design by the project, $100-500 average. Pays for illustrations by the project, $100-300. Considers complexity of project, available budget, skill and experience of artist, how work will be used and turnaround time when establishing payment.
Tips: "We prefer designers of Hispanic background or empathy with our culture, but it's not a prerequisite. We are trying to produce only new works, not the classics. Hispanic-Americans are our number one consideration."

ROBERT IVEY BALLET COMPANY, 1632 Ashley Hall Rd., Charleston SC 29407. (803)556-1343. Artistic Director: Robert C. Ivey. Consists of two companies: The Senior Company—classically trained men and women chosen in open auditions providing educational outreach in schools, lecture-demonstrations for community organizations and joint performances with area arts groups; and The Charleston Youth Ballet, offering training to dancers age 9-13.
Needs: Works with 12 freelance artists/year; needs heaviest in spring and fall. Uses artists for advertising, brochure, program, set and costume design; posters, lighting and scenery.
First Contact & Terms: Send query letter with resume and samples to be kept on file. Write for appointment to show portfolio. Prefers slides and photographs as samples. Pays for design by the project, $300-500 average. Pays for illustration by the project, $500-800 average. "Poster illustrations and ad layouts change with each performance. Costume and set design pays considerably more." Considers complexity of project and available budget when establishing payment.
Tips: Artists fail to consider "the budget of the organization when presenting specs. Also that total budget must cover many phases. Artwork should be able to be recycled for several ventures."

JAZZ TAP ENSEMBLE, 1426 Spruce St., Berkeley CA 94709. (415)524-1203. Contact: Company Manager. Company of three jazz tap dancers and three jazz musicians performing original works created by its members. It tours the US and extensively within California and hopes to begin touring internationally.
Needs: Works with 1 freelance artist/year; needs heaviest preceding the company's fall and spring tours (September and March). Uses artists for brochure design illustration and layout; and posters.
First Contact & Terms: Prefers California (either LA or the Bay Area) artists. Send query letter with resume and samples to be kept on file. Call for appointment to show portfolio. Prefers photostats or photographs as samples; no slides. Reports within 1 month. Pays for design by the hour, $5-10 average; by the project, $100-250 average. Considers complexity of project, available budget, skill and experience of artist and how work will be used when establishing payment.

JOHNSTOWN SYMPHONY ORCHESTRA, 230 Walnut St., Johnstown PA 15901. General Manager: Jeanne Gleason. Assigns 2-5 jobs/year.
Needs: Works with 1-2 illustrators/year in February. Needs design work in December and February. Uses artists for bumper stickers, direct mail brochures, flyers, graphics, posters, programs and record jackets. Pays $25-200/job for design.
First Contact & Terms: Query with samples and resume. SASE. Reports within 1 week. Provide resume, brochure and flyer to be kept on file for future assignments.

MATTI LASCOE DANCE THEATRE CO., 1012-D Cabrillo Park Dr., Santa Ana CA 92701. (714)542-1463. Artistic Director: Matti Lascoe. Sixteen member Caribbean dance and music ensemble

with drummers and the Trinidad Steel Drum Band. Concert is called "Caribbean Spi...
Needs: Works with 2 freelance artists/year; needs heaviest in September-November, January-M...
artists for advertising, brochure, set and costume design; lighting and scenery.
First Contact & Terms: Experienced artists only. Send resume and tear sheets to be kept on file. Write
for artists' guidelines. Prefers photographs as samples. Samples returned by SASE only if requested.
Reports only if interested. Pays for design and illustration by the project. Considers available budget
when establishing payment.

LE GROUPE DE LA PLACE ROYALE, 130 Sparks St., Ottawa, Ontario K1P 5B6 Canada.
(613)235-1493. "Innovative, professional modern dance company with a 48-week season, seven dancers, artistic director, voice coach and an assistant artistic director. All choreography is original and there
is voice and live musical accompaniment used in performance by the dancers. Use of original set and
costume design by visual artists since 1966."
Needs: Works with 2-3 freelance artists/year. Uses artists for advertising, brochure and program design,
illustration and layout; posters, lighting, holography, experimental film, photography and slide montage. "Company normally has a very good idea of what it wants. It is then up to the artist to produce at
least three variations on a given theme."
First Contact & Terms: Prefers to work with artists with at least a minimum exposure to modern dance.
Send query letter with brochure, resume and samples to be kept on file. "A letter will be sent if company
is interested in artist's work. Will then ask about availability and request that an appointment be scheduled for an exchange with the artistic director and public relations officer." Prefers photographs, posters, flyers or slides if artwork is set or costume design, as samples. Samples returned by SASE only if requested. Reports within 2 weeks. Pays for design by the hour, $5-20 average; by the project, $750-2,500
average; by the day, $50-200 average. "Maximum payment varies with scope of project and/or avail-
ability of funds." Considers complexity of project, available budget, skill and experience of artist, how
work will be used and rights purchased when establishing payment.
Tips: "Approach should focus on movement and its visual expression."

*LOOKING GLASS THEATRE, 175 Mathewson St., Providence RI 02903. (401)331-9080. Producing Director: Pamela Messore. A touring children's theatre company of five professional actors that
tours throughout New England performing for school-age children.
Needs: Works with 6 freelance artists/year. Needs heaviest in September to June. Uses freelance artists
for advertising, set and costume design; also scenery.
First Contact & Terms: Works on an assignment basis only. Send query letter with samples to be kept
on file. Write for appointment to show portfolio. Prefers slides and photographs as samples. Samples not
kept on file are returned if accompanied by SASE. Reports back within 6 weeks. Payment is negotiated
depending upon project's budget and turnaround time.

*LOST SILVER MINE OUTDOOR DRAMA, Box 2057, Lakeview MO 65737. (417)272-8100.
Manager: Artie Ayrres. "The play, performed 3-4 nights a week during the summer, is about the history
of Missouri and the first white settlers in the 1800's."
Needs: Works with 3 freelance artists/year. Needs heaviest in summer. Uses artists for advertising design, illustration and layout; poster design and illustration; set and costume design; and lighting.
First Contact & Terms: Works with local artists only. Send query letter with resume and samples to be
kept on file. Prefers photographs as samples. Samples not filed are returned by SASE. Reports back only if interested. Pays for design by the hour, approximately $10 average. Pays for illustration by the hour,
approxiamtely $10 average. Considers how work will be used when establishing payment.

LYRIC THEATRE OF OKLAHOMA, INC., 2501 N. Blackwelder, Oklahoma City OK 73106.
(405)528-3636. General Manager: Clyde Rader. A non-equity, not-for-profit summer musical company
producing full-scale Broadway-type musicals each summer; housed on the Oklahoma City University
campus in Oklahoma City.
Needs: Works with 2-3 freelance artists/year. Needs are seasonal. Uses artists for brochure design, illustration and layout; poster and program design and illustration.
First Contact & Terms: Prefers local artists. Works on assignment only. Send query letter with resume
and samples to be kept on file. Prefers photographs and tear sheets as samples. Samples not filed returned by SASE. Reports only if interested. Pays for design by the hour, $6-10 average. Pays for illustra-
tion by the project, $50-400 average. Considers complexity of project, project's budget, and skill and
experience of the artist when establishing payment.

MARYLAND DANCE THEATER, Dance Dept., University of Maryland, College Park MD 20742.
(301)454-3399. Artistic Director: Larry Warren. Incorporated, nonprofit, modern dance repertory company in residence at the University of Maryland consisting of approximately 15 students, faculty and ar-

ea artists. Performances are given in the Washington/Baltimore area and throughout the mid-Atlantic states.
Needs: Works with 3-4 freelance artists/year; needs heaviest in November-May. Uses artists for advertising, brochure and program design and layout; costume design, posters and lighting.
First Contact & Terms: Works primarily with local artists. Send query letter with description of past work. Call or write for appointment to show portfolio. Pays for design by the project, $25-400 average, maybe higher depending on project. Considers complexity of project, available budget, skill and experience of artist, how work will be used and turnaround time when establishing payment.

MICHIGAN OPERA THEATRE, 350 Madison Ave., Detroit MI 48226. (313)963-3717. Director of Public Relations/Marketing: John Finck. Assigns 7-8 jobs/year.
Needs: Uses artists for ads, billboards, bumper stickers, direct mail pieces, brochures, flyers, posters, program books, costumes, set and theatrical lighting.
First Contact & Terms: Local artists only. Query with samples or portfolio. SASE. Reports within 1 month. Works on assignment only. Samples returned by SASE. Reports on future assignment possibilities. Provide resume and brochure to be kept on file for future assignments. Pays by the project. Considers complexity of project, available budget, skill and experience of artist, how work will be used and turnaround time when establishing payment.

MID-WILLAMETTE BALLET ENSEMBLE, Box 55, Salem OR 97308. (503)363-1403. Director, Salem Ballet School: Elfie Stevenin, DMA-DEA. Dance company of 8-12 senior students performing locally for community events and traditional concerts.
Needs: Works with 3 artists for poster designs, photography, brochure design; all fund-raising through parent organization only; needs heaviest in fall and spring. Uses artists for brochure design, posters and photography.
First Contact & Terms: Local artists only—"for the most part, they are artists who have children enrolled in classes." Send business card to be kept on file. Pays for design by the project. Considers available budget when establishing payment.

MILWAUKEE SYMPHONY ORCHESTRA, 212 W. Wisconsin Ave., Milwaukee WI 53203. (414)291-6010. Public Relations: Jane Keegan. Query or arrange interview; local artists only. SASE. Reports in 2 weeks.
Needs: Uses artists for advertising, flyers, graphics and posters. Pays by the project according to complexity of project, available budget and turnaround time. Also considers trade of symphony tickets for artwork.

*MINNESOTA DANCE THEATRE AND SCHOOL, 528 Hennepin Ave., Minneapolis MN 55403. (612)339-9150. General Manager: John M. Coughlin. Classical ballet and contemporary dance company and school. Assigns 5 jobs/year; local artists primarily. Query with samples.
Needs: Uses artists for flyers and graphics. Pays $50 minimum/job for design and illustration; $25 minimum/job for layout.

MINNESOTA JAZZ DANCE COMPANY, Zoe Sealy Dance Center, 1815 E. 38th St., Minneapolis MN 55407. (612)721-3031. Company Manager: Tim Conkright. Dance company which "creates and presents jazz dance in its concert art form; collaborates with visual artists; educates audiences through lecture demonstrations and workshops throughout the US."
Needs: Works with 6 freelance artists/year. Uses artists for advertising, brochure and program design, illustration and layout; set and costume design, posters and lighting.
First Contact & Terms: Send query letter with brochure, resume, business card, samples and tear sheets to be kept on file. Call or write for appointment to show portfolio. Prefers original work as samples. Samples returned by SASE only if requested. Reports within 6 weeks. Pays for design and illustration by the hour, $5-40 average; by the project, $50-100 average; by the day, $25-50 average. Considers available budget, and skill and experience of artist when establishing payment.

THE MISSISSAUGA SYMPHONY ORCHESTRA, 161 Lakeshore Rd. W, Mississauga, Ontario Canada L5H 1G3. (416)274-1571. Executive Director: Colleen Goulet. A 95-member community orchestra, a nonprofit organization.
Needs: Works with 1 freelance artist/year. Needs heaviest June through January. Uses artists for brochure design, illustration and layout; and poster and program design and illustration. Prefers "a classy, bold, yet not overpowering look that follows similar prior guidelines (i.e. more conservative than modern)".
First Contact & Terms: "Artist should have examples of fine workmanship, helpful and flexible personality, and be willing to *negotiate* and work closely with executive director." Works on assignment

only. Send query letter with business card and samples to be kept on file. Prefers photostats and photocopies as samples. Samples not filed returned only if requested. Reports only if interested. "Design and illustration have previously been donated. If not possible, a minimum payment would be arranged due to lack of funds." Would consider complexity of project, project's budget (due to nonprofit status) and turnaround time when establishing payment.

MJT DANCE CO., Box 108, Watertown MA 02172. (617)482-0351. Director: Margie J. Topf. Modern dance troupe.
Needs: Assigns 2-10 jobs/year. Uses artists for advertising, bumper stickers, direct mail brochures, flyers, graphics, posters, programs, tickets, exhibits and lighting. Especially needs brochure design, layout, paste-up.
First Contact & Terms: Local artists only. Query with resume or arrange interview. SASE. Reports within 2 weeks. Pays $5-10/hour.
Tips: "Video is becoming a major consideration in the performing arts. Be well-versed in many different art forms."

MME. CADILLAC DANCERS & MUSICIANS-Dances of 17th Century French Settlers, Apt. 903, 15 E. Kirby, Detroit MI 48202. (313)967-4030 or 864-9067. Artistic Director: Harriet Berg. Performs 16th century dance in costume.
Needs: Assigns 4 jobs/year. Uses artists for flyers, programs, announcements and ads.
First Contact & Terms: Query. SASE. Negotiates pay.

MUSIC SOCIETY OF THE MIDLAND CENTER FOR THE ARTS, 1801 W. St. Andrews, Midland MI 48640. (517)631-1072. Public Relations Coordinator: Sally Goggin. A not-for-profit dance, theatre and music organization. "We produce our own events during the fall and winter season (mostly musical comedy and choral/dance concerts), and are presenters during our Summer Festival (June-August)."
Needs: Works with 3 freelance artists/year. Needs heaviest in spring and summer. Uses artists for advertising and brochure design and layout. "We are open to any style—as long as it looks like fun."
First Contact & Terms: Works on assignment only. Send query letter with brochure, resume, business card and samples to be kept on file. Samples not filed are returned by SASE only if requested. Reports back only if interested. Payment varies greatly. Considers project's budget, skill and experience of the artist and turnaround time when establishing payment.

NASHVILLE SYMPHONY ORCHESTRA, 208 23rd Ave. N., Nashville TN 37203. (615)329-3033. Marketing and Public Relations Director: Debra Campagna. Regional symphony.
Needs: Works with 4 freelance artists/year. Uses artists for advertising and brochure design, illustration, and layout; poster and program design and illustration.
First Contact & Terms: Works on assignment only. Send query letter with brochure, business card and samples to be kept on file. Call for appointment to show portfolio. Prefers brochures and tear sheets as samples. Reports back only if interested. "We determine a project estimate." Considers complexity of project, project's budget, how work will be used and turnaround time when establishing payment. Looks for a "clean, simple design that makes an immediate visual statement—copy aside."

NEW JERSEY SHAKESPEARE FESTIVAL, Drew University, Madison NJ 07940. Artistic Director: Paul Barry. Contemporary and classical theatrical troupe. Assigns 3-6 jobs/year.
Needs: Works with 1 or 2 illustrators and 3 designers/year. Design work for costumes, sets, props and lighting is seasonal, May-December. Uses artists for advertising, costumes, designer-in-residence, direct mail brochures, exhibits, flyers, graphics, posters, programs, sets and theatrical lighting.
First Contact & Terms: Query with resume or arrange interview to show portfolio. SASE. Reports within 1 week. Interviews for designers are held in March and April. Provide resume to be kept on file for future assignments. Pays $800-1,000/show for set and costume design (large shows).
Tips: "Our season has expanded to 27 playing weeks." An artist's work should display an "understanding of historical period, good use of color, practicality and fit of costumes. Sets should show an ease to build, and to change from one show to another."

NEW MEXICO SYMPHONY ORCHESTRA, Box 769, Albuquerque NM 87103. (505)843-7657. Executive Administrator: William Weinrod. Regional orchestra based in Albuquerque but serving state of New Mexico. Performs 50-60 concerts/year and 150 school programs. Basic concert series currently consists of 18 subscription concerts. In addition there are pops concerts and "specials" which require graphic promotional materials.
Needs: Works with 3-4 freelance artists/year; needs heaviest in spring/fall. Uses artists for advertising, brochure and program design, illustration and layout; and posters.

Cyd Riley's illustration and the "Marketing with Music" slogan were used on a promotional piece/mailer sent out to prospective program advertisers by the New Mexico Symphony Orchestra. The artist lives in Albuquerque, which is also the home base for the orchestra. This performing arts organization is a frequent user of contemporary design, illustration and graphics in its printed materials.

First Contact & Terms: Prefers local artists with performing arts art experience especially for layouts of ads and brochures. Send query letter with samples to be kept on file. Write for appointment to show portfolio. Prefers actual print samples. Samples returned only by request. Pays for design by the project, $100-2,500 average. Considers complexity of project and available budget when establishing payment.

*NEW PLAYWRIGHTS' THEATRE, 1742 Church St. NW, Washington DC 20036. (202)232-4527. Director of Marketing: Shelly Clark. New Playwrights' is an alternative theatre dedicated to the development of new American playwriting talent. It is an intimate theatre, seating only 125 people with over 1,000 season subscribers.
Needs: Works with 12 freelance artists/year. Needs heaviest September through June. Uses artists for brochure design, illustration and layout; poster design and illustration; set and costume design; lighting and scenery.
First Contact & Terms: Works on assignment only. Send query letter with samples to be kept on file. Call or write for appointment to show portfolio. Prefers slides, photographs, photocopies or tear sheets as samples. Samples are not returned. Reports back only if interested. Pays by the project, $200-1,000 for design; $50-300 for illustration. Considers complexity of project, project's budget, skill and experience of the artist, how work will be used and turnaround time when establishing payment.

NEW YORK CITY OPERA NATIONAL COMPANY, NY State Theater, Lincoln Center, New York NY 10023. (212)870-5635. Administrative Director: Nancy Kelly. Opera company founded in 1979 by

Use an up-to-date Market Directory!

Don't let your <u>Artist's Market</u> turn old on you.

You may be reluctant to give up this copy of <u>Artist's Market</u>. After all, you would never discard an old friend.

But resist the urge to hold onto an old <u>Artist's Market</u>! Like your first portfolio or your favorite pair of jeans, the time will come when this copy of <u>Artist's Market</u> will have to be replaced.

In fact, if you're still using this <u>1986 Artist's Market</u> when the calendar reads 1987, your old friend isn't your best friend anymore. Many of the buyers listed here have moved or been promoted. Many of the addresses are now incorrect. Rates of pay have certainly changed, and even each buyer's art needs are changed from last year.

You can't afford to use an out-of-date book to plan your marketing efforts. But there's an easy way for you to stay current—order the <u>1987 Artist's Market</u>. All you have to do is complete the attached post card and return it with your payment or charge card information. Best of all, we'll send you the 1987 edition at the 1986 price—just $16.95. The <u>1987 Artist's Market</u> will be published and ready for shipment in October 1986.

Make sure you have the most current marketing information—order the new edition of <u>Artist's Market</u> now.

To order, drop this postpaid card in the mail.

☐ YES! I want the most current edition of <u>Artist's Market</u>. Please send me the <u>1987 Artist's Market</u> at the 1986 price—$16.95. I have included $2.00 for postage and handling. (Ohio residents add 5½% sales tax.)

☐ Payment enclosed (Slip this card and your payment into an envelope.)

☐ Charge my: ☐ Visa   ☐ MasterCard

Account #_____ Exp. Date_____

Signature_____

Name_____

Address_____

City_____ State_____ Zip_____

(This offer expires August 1, 1987. Please allow 30 days for delivery.)
NOTE: <u>1987 Artist's Market</u> will be ready for shipment in October 1986.

Writer's Digest Books

9933 Alliance Road
Cincinnati, Ohio 45242

1861

Make sure you have a current edition of Artist's Market

rtist's Market
as been the artist's
ble for many years.
ach edition contains
undreds of changes
o give you the most
urrent information to
ork with. Make sure your
opy is the latest edition.

his card will get you he 1987 edition... at 1986 prices! ⬇

Beverly Sills as a national touring company with the purpose of bringing opera to areas of the country without resident opera associations. Its primary function is to provide young singers an opportunity to gain performing experience; veteran singers use the tours to try new roles before singing them in New York.

Needs: Needs for freelance artists heaviest prior to tours in fall and winter. Uses artists for set and costume design. "Scenic and costume designers should be aware of the rigors of traveling productions and should think about portability and economics." Artists also used for graphics for marketing the current production.

First Contact & Terms: Previous experience is advisable; union memberships are required for set and costume design. Send query letter with resume to be kept on file. Reports only if interested. Pays for design by the project; "varies according to design; follows union rates." Considers complexity of project and available budget when establishing payment.

Tips: "The use of artists is tied specifically to whatever opera we may be performing in a given year. We generally tour in the January-April time period and hire artists one year ahead of each tour."

NEW YORK HARP ENSEMBLE, 140 W. End Ave., New York NY 10023. Director: Dr. Aristid von Wurtzler. Concert group which tours the U.S., Europe, Africa, South America, Australia and the Near and Far East.

Needs: Works with 1 designer/year, summer only. Uses artists for direct mail brochures, posters, programs and record cover layouts. Especially needs work for brochures, posters and record cover.

First Contact & Terms: Local artists only. Submit samples (brochures, posters and record covers). Works on assignment only. Samples returned by SASE. Reports back on future assignment possibilities. Provide flyer to be kept on file for future assignments. Pays by the project for design and illustration. Considers available budget, and skill and experience of artist when establishing payment.

ODYSSEY THEATRE ENSEMBLE, 12111 Ohio Ave., West Los Angeles CA 90025. (213)826-1626. Production Manager: Lucy Pollak. Experimental theater troupe.

Needs: Uses artists for set and costume design, lighting and scenery.

First Contact & Terms: Works with 20 artists. Query letter with resume and samples. Prefers photographs or slides as samples. SASE. Reports within 1 month. Pays $25-300 for design and illustration; negotiates payment. Considers complexity of project, budget, skill and experience of the artist, and previous work done on a volunteer basis for the theatre.

Tips: "We have expanded our facility to three 99-seat Equity-waiver performing spaces."

*OLYMPIC BALLET THEATRE, Anderson Cultural Center, 700 Main St., Edmonds WA 98020. (206)774-7570. Director: John and Helen Wilkins. Ballet company with 20 dancers, approximately 100 members and a Board of Trustees of 20 which does a full-length "Nutcracker" Spring Showcase and tour, lecture-demo's and mini-performances.

Needs: Works with 2 freelance artists/year. Needs heaviest in fall, winter and spring. Uses freelance artists for advertising, brochure, catalog, poster and program design and illustration, set and costume design.

First Contact & Terms: Works on assignment only. Call or write for appointment to show portfolio. Pays by the project, $25-500 for design; $25-100 for illustration. Considers complexity of project and project's budget when establishing payment.

ONE PLUS ONE . . .QUARTET, Box 1705, Champaign IL 61820. (217)367-9126. Artistic Director: Patricia Hruby. Dance-music theater with 4 performers: 2 dancers; 1 trombonist; 1 trumpeter.

Needs: Works with 6 freelance artists/year. Uses artists for advertising, brochure and poster design; advertising and brochure layout; brochure illustration; and lighting.

First Contact & Terms: Prefers artists "who want experience and love dance and music." Send samples. Samples returned by SASE. Reports "as soon as possible." Works on assignment only. Provide brochure/flyer and samples to be kept on file for possible future assignments. Negotiates payment by the project for design and illustration.

OPERA/COLUMBUS, 50 W. Broad St. Mezz., Columbus OH 43215. (614)461-8101. Audience Development Director: Richard Wickersham. Opera company with 5 full-time staff members, 42-member board of trustees and 2,300 series ticket subscribers.

Needs: Works primarily with advertising and graphic design agency. Occasional needs include brochure illustration and layout, poster design, advertising design.

First Contact & Terms: Prefers local experienced artists. Works on assignment only. Send query letter with brochure, resume and samples to be kept on file; write for appointment to show portfolio. Prefers slides, photos, renderings or tear sheets as samples; slides are not filed. Samples not filed are returned only if requested. Reports back only if interested. Pays by the project. Considers complexity of project, project's budget and turnaround time when establishing payment.

Callboard *art director, Laura Tylersmith, assigned Kathleen Volp of Somerville, Massachusetts, to do the cover of the Pennsylvania Stage Company's program/magazine because of her "unique ability to execute the concept of an illustration without a loss in translation." Lisa K. Higgins, editor of* Callboard, *adds, "Ms. Volp truly listens to the art director and delivers illustrations that capture the mood and purpose of the assignment. Also, her ability for a 'quick turnaround' is commendable." The artist received $125 for one-time rights to the artwork.*

ORCHESTRA LONDON CANADA, 520 Wellington St., London, Ontario Canada. (519)679-8558. Marketing and Communications Coordinator: A. de Peralta, Jr. A professional symphony orchestra whose programs include chamber music, pops presentations and internationally acclaimed guest artists.
Needs: Works with 3 freelance artists/year. Needs heaviest between May and September. Uses artists for advertising, poster, and program design and illustration.
First Contact & Terms: "Artists should have 3 years' experience including prior symphony work." Works on assignment only. Send query letter with business card and samples to be kept on file. Call for appointment to show portfolio. Prefers photocopies and tear sheets as samples. Samples not filed are not returned. Reports back only if interested. Pays for illustration by the hour, $4-20 average; by the project, $40-350 average. Considers complexity of project and project's budget when establishing payment.

PARADISE SYMPHONY ORCHESTRA, 6686 Brook Way, Paradise CA 95969. (916)877-8360. Conductor: Thomas E. Wilson. Query with resume; prefers local artists. SASE. Reports within 1 month.
Needs: Uses artists for logos and direct mail brochures. "The use of the material would determine its value."
Tips: "First class promotional materials are necessary."

PASADENA DANCE CENTER, 25 S. Sierra Madre Blvd., Pasadena CA 91107. (213)792-0873. Director: Elly Van Dijk. Offers classes in classical ballet, modern, jazz, creative dance, tap, musical comedy—all ages, all levels.
Needs: Works with about 15 freelance artists/year. Uses artists for brochure and program design, and posters.
First Contact & Terms: Los Angeles area artists only; performing arts art experience necessary. Send query letter with resume to be kept on file. Reports only if interested and needed. Pays percentage basis with minimum guarantee. Considers skill and experience of artist when establishing payment.

PENNSYLVANIA STAGE COMPANY, 837 Linden St., Allentown PA 18101. (215)434-6110. Producing Director: Gregory S. Hurst. "We are a LORT theatre, located 2 hours from New York City devoted to a diverse repertory of new and old works from Shakespeare to the world premiere production of a new musical. Our house seats 274 people, and we currently have 6,000 subscribers."
Needs: Works with 10 freelance artists/year; "We need freelance designers for our season which runs from October-July." Uses artists for set and costume design, lighting and scenery. "As a growing professional regional theatre, we have increased needs for graphic artists and photography for print materials (brochures, flyers), and particularly for our program magazine, *Callboard*, which is published eight times a year. "We would also be interested in theatre cartoons."
First Contact & Terms: "Artists must be able to come to Allentown for design consultation and construction." Send query letter with resume; write for appointment. Prefers photostats, slides, b&w photos, color washes, roughs as samples. Samples returned by SASE. Works on assignment only; reports back whether to expect possible future assignments. Provide resume to be kept on file for possible future assignments. Pays by the project, $500-1,500 average, for design; $25-125 for print material. Considers complexity of project, available budget, and skill and experience of artist when establishing payment.
Tips: "We prefer that designers have extensive experience designing for professional theater."

RUDY PEREZ PERFORMANCE ENSEMBLE, Box 36614, Los Angeles CA 90036. (213)931-3604. Artistic Director: Rudy Perez. Performance art and experimental dance company, also known as the Rudy Perez Dance Theater, is a nonprofit organization dependent on funding from National Endowment for the Arts and the California Arts Council; box office and bookings currently in the LA area.
Needs: "The work is mainly collaborations with visual artists and composers." Uses artists for publicity before performances and updating press kits, brochures, etc.
First Contact & Terms: Send query letter with brochure and resume to be kept on file. Reports within 1 week. "Since we are a nonprofit organization we depend on in-kind services and/or negotiable fees."
Tips: Artists should have "an awareness of dance and theatre."

PICCOLO OPERA COMPANY, Lee Jon Associates, 18662 Fairfield Ave., Detroit MI 48221. (313)861-6930. Contact: Lee Jon Associates. SASE. Reports in 3-4 weeks.
Needs: Uses artists for design of flyers for individual productions and general brochures. Pays by the project, $25-300; negotiable. Considers available budget, skill and experience of artist and creative talent of artist when establishing payment.
Tips: Prefers artists with layout experience. When reviewing work, especially looks for "the impact of subject matter. Artists shouldn't overemphasize the design at the expense of the information; consider color in relation to legibility. We deal in emotions and the nostalgia aroused by music, so look for more 'romantic' design." Also interested in cartoon-style illustrations.

PIONEER PLAYHOUSE OF KENTUCKY, Danville KY 40422. (606)236-2747. Contact: Eben Henson. Regular summer stock theatre.
Needs: Works with 10 freelance artists/year; needs heaviest in summer. Uses artists for advertising, poster, set and costume design; lighting and scenery.
First Contact & Terms: Prefers artists willing to work in the nature of apprenticeship. Send query letter. Reports within 4 weeks. Provide material to be kept on file for possible future assignments. No payment of salary; apprenticeships provide room and board.
Tips: "For persons breaking into any form of the theatre, apprenticeship is necessary. First one must establish himself with a reputable theatre in order to advance in the theatrical profession."

POSEY SCHOOL OF DANCE, INC., Box 254, Northport NY 11768. (516)757-2700. President: Elsa Posey. Private school/professional training in performing arts.
Needs: Works with 4 or more freelance artists/year; needs heaviest in spring and fall. Uses artists for advertising and brochure design, illustration and layout; poster and program design and illustration, set and costume design, lighting and scenery. Also uses artists for a newsletter and for advertising copy. Interested in *appropriate* cartoons.
First Contact & Terms: Prefers regional artists willing to work within nonprofit performing arts budget. Send query letter with resume. Samples returned by SASE. Reports within 4 weeks. Works on assignment only. Provide resume to be kept on file for possible future assignments. Pays for design, $10-200 average; for illustration, $10-50 average. Negotiates payment. Considers complexity of project, available budget, skill and experience of artist, how work will be used and rights purchased when establishing payment.
Tips: Artist must have "illustrative ability with understanding of dance, dancer's body and movement."

PROJECT OPERA, INC., 160 Main St., Northampton MA 01060. (413)584-8811. Artistic Director: Richard R. Rescia. Stated productions of opera.

Needs: Needs heaviest in fall and spring. Uses artists for set and costume design, and scenery.
First Contact & Terms: "We use local artists where possible." Send query letter with resume and samples to be kept on file. Prefers photocopies as samples. Samples not filed are returned by SASE. Pays for design by the project. Considers complexity of project and project's budget when establishing payment.

THE REPERTORY DANCE THEATRE (RDT), Box 8088, Salt Lake City UT 84108. General Manager: Douglas C. Sonntag. Ten-member modern dance company with national touring, home seasons in Salt Lake City and summer workshops.
Needs: Works with 2-3 freelance artists/year; needs heaviest in summer/fall. Uses artists for advertising and brochure design, illustration and layout; poster design and illustration.
First Contact & Terms: Prefers local artists. Send query letter with resume, brochure, tear sheets and samples to be kept on file. Prefers "any samples which best represent work;" samples should be dance or movement related. Samples returned by SASE if not kept on file. Reports within 2 weeks. Works on assignment only. Pays for design by the project, $50-500 average. Negotiates payment according to complexity of project and available budget.

ROCHESTER PHILHARMONIC ORCHESTRA, 108 East Ave., Rochester NY 14604. (716)454-2620. Promotion Manager: Nancy Calocerinos. Major orchestra performing 48 weeks/year, winter and summer seasons.
Needs: Works with 2 freelance artists/year. Needs heaviest between January and April. Uses artists for brochure, poster and program design.
First Contact & Terms: Local artists only, with at least three years' experience and a working knowledge of music. Works on assignment only. Send query letter with samples to be kept on file. Prefers photocopies or tear sheets as samples. Samples not filed are returned. Reports back only if interested. Pays for design by the project. Considers project's budget when establishing payment.

ROOSEVELT PARK AMPHITHEATRE, Middlesex County Department of Parks and Recreation, Box 661, New Brunswick NJ 08903. (201)548-2884. Producing Director: Ernest Albrecht. Musical theatre.
Needs: Works with 5 freelance artists/year; needs heaviest in late fall through mid-winter. Uses artists for set and costume design, lighting and scenery.
First Contact & Terms: Send query letter. Prefers samples to be brought in person. Reports within 3 weeks. Works on assignment only. Provide resume to be kept on file for possible future assignments. Pays $400-500 average for design; salary.

SALT LAKE SYMPHONIC CHOIR, Box 45, Salt Lake City UT 84110. (801)466-8701. Contact: Manager. Assigns 5 jobs/year.
Needs: Works with 5 illustrators and 2 designers/year; fall only. Uses artists for advertising, billboards, costumes, direct mail brochures, flyers, posters, programs, theatrical lighting and record jackets.
First Contact & Terms: Mail art. SASE. Works on assignment. Provide resume, brochure and flyer to be kept on file for future assignments. Negotiates pay by the project.

SAN DIEGO OPERA, Box 988, San Diego CA 92112. (619)232-7636. Director of Marketing and Public Relations: Rosella Stern. Professional opera company presenting 24 major performances of 6 grand operas/year.
Needs: Works with 2-3 freelance artists/year; needs heaviest when major campaigns are organized and designed in November, December and January. Uses artists for advertising and brochure design; program illustration and posters. "Extensive advertising via direct mail; membership programs and educational programs auxiliary to the opera production company also require advertising and printed material support."
First Contact & Terms: Send query letter with brochure and samples to be kept on file. Call or write for appointment to show portfolio. "Interested predominantly in printed piece samples; *do not send slides, photographs, or original work*—these are seen only at portfolio appointments." Samples returned only by request. Reports within 2 weeks. Pays for design by the project, $200-5,000 average. Considers complexity of project and how work will be used when establishing payment.

SAN FRANCISCO OPERA CENTER, War Memorial Opera House, San Francisco Opera, San Francisco CA 94102. (415)565-6435. Manager: Christine Bullin. Assistant to the Manager: Susan Lamb. SFOC is the umbrella organization for the affiliates of the San Francisco Opera.
Needs: Works with 3-4 freelance artists/year; needs heaviest in summer preparing for fall and spring seasons. Uses artists for advertising, brochure and program design, illustration and layout; set and costume design, posters, lighting, scenery, and PR and educational packets.

First Contact & Terms: Send query letter with brochure, resume and business card to be kept on file. Write for appointment to show portfolio. Prefers photostats, slides and photographs as samples. Reports only if interested. Pays for design and illustration by the project, $50-300 average. Considers available budget, how work will be used and rights purchased when establishing payment.

SAN JOSE SYMPHONY, Suite 200, 476 Park Ave., San Jose CA 95110. (408)287-7383. Contact: Public Relations Director.
Needs: Assigns 10-15 jobs/year. Uses artists for advertising, direct mail/developmental brochures, ticket sales material, flyers, posters, programs and educational materials.
First Contact & Terms: Local artists only. Query with resume and samples. SASE. Reports within 1 month. Pays for design or illustration by the hour, $25 minimum; by the project, $275-500 average. Considers complexity of project, available budget and how work will be used when establishing payment.

THE SAVANNAH BALLET, INC., 2212 Lincoln St., Savannah GA 31401. (912)233-8492. Cultural and educational performing arts organization.
Needs: Works with 3 freelance artists/year; needs heaviest in September-April. Uses artists for advertising and brochure design, illustration and layout; poster and program design and illustration; set and costume design; lighting and scenery.
First Contact & Terms: Send query letter with resume and samples (tear sheets) to be kept on file for possible future assignments. Works on assignment only. Pays by the project for design and illustration.

SEATTLE OPERA ASSOCIATION, 305 Harrison, Seattle WA 98109. (206)443-4700. Press and Public Relations Director: Ernesto Alorda. Opera company.
Needs: Works with 5-7 freelance artists/year; needs heaviest in winter and spring. Uses artists for flyer/brochure design and layout, and season/festival posters.
First Contact & Terms: Send query letter with brochure, business card and samples to be kept on file. Call for appointment to show portfolio. Prefers photostats and photographs as samples. Samples returned by SASE if not kept on file. Pays $350/poster. Considers complexity of project, available budget and how work will be used when establishing payment.

SEATTLE SYMPHONY ORCHESTRA, 305 Harrison St., Seattle WA 98109. (206)447-4740. Director of Public Relations and Marketing: Marianne Lewis. Assigns approximately 4 jobs/year.
Needs: Works with 4 illustrators/year; September-June, only. Uses artists for advertising, direct mail brochures, flyers, graphics and posters. Especially needs design of season flyer, special flyers and posters.
First Contact & Terms: Local artists only. Query with samples. SASE. Reports within 2 weeks. Works on assignment only. No samples returned. Reports back on future assignment possibilities. Provide resume, brochure and flyer to be kept on file for future assignments. Pays market rate for design and illustration.
Tips: The trend is toward "excellent graphic design work—greater emphasis on business solicitation and businesslike look."

SHAWNEE SUMMER THEATRE OF GREENE COUNTY, INC., Box 22, Bloomfield IN 47424. Producer: Frank Hayashida. Resident production company offering 7 plays a year: serious, a musical, a mystery, comedies and 1 children's play.
Needs: Works with 25 freelance artists/year; only in late spring and summer. Uses artists for set and costume design, lighting and scenery.
First Contact & Terms: "Ours is a production company and all work is done by that company while in residence. All applicants must be willing to fill in as actors in large cast plays or musicals." Send query letter with resume and color photos or slides of sample works; "We also insist on some kind of photograph of the applicant, even if only a Polaroid." Samples returned by SASE. Pays by the week.
Tips: "The theatre manages an art gallery and artist's work could be hung for one of the weeks during productions. Also, photos of work, articles concerning work and exhibits, and a good strong resume are helpful."

*SINGING BOYS OF PENNSYLVANIA, Box 110, State College, East Stroudsburg PA 18301, or Box 206, Wind Gap PA 18091. (717)421-6137 (business office). Director: K. Bernard Schade.
Needs: Uses artists for direct mail brochures, flyers, posters and record jackets.
First Contact & Terms: Local artists only. Query.

*SOUTH STREET DANCE COMPANY, 759 S. 6th St., Philadelphia PA 19147. Director: Ellen Forman. Modern dance theatre repertory company performing experimental, "avant-garde" (usually) original dance. 10 performers; young, educated audience.

Needs: Works with 3-5 freelance artists/year. Needs heaviest in early fall and early spring. Uses artists for advertising, brochure, and catalog design, illustration and layout; poster and program design and illustration; set and costume design; and lighting and scenery. Prefers "nontraditional, bold" style.

First Contact & Terms: Freelance artists must be experienced. Works on assignment only. Send query letter with resume, business card and samples to be kept on file. Prefers actual printed piece or good copy of work done in the performing arts field. No slides. Samples not filed are returned only if requested. Reports back only if interested. Pays for design by the project, $150-500 average. Pays for illustration by the project, $500 average. Considers project's budget and skill and experience of the artist when establishing payment.

SOUTHWEST JAZZ BALLET COMPANY, Box 38233, Houston TX 77088. (713)686-6299. Contact: President. Dance company; producers of "America in Concert."

Needs: Works with 5 freelance artists/year. Uses artists for brochure design, illustration and layout; set design, posters and scenery.

First Contact & Terms: Send query letter with samples to be kept on file. Prefers to see "end product" as samples. Reports within 1 month. Considers complexity of project when establishing payment.

*SPRINGFIELD SYMPHONY ORCHESTRA, Box 5191, Springfield IL 62705. (217)522-2838. General Manager: Catherine Wichterman. Metropolitan symphony orchestra performing 20 concerts.

Needs: Works with 1 freelance artist/year. Uses artist for brochure and program design. Contact in April.

First Contact & Terms: Send samples and cost estimate to be kept on file. Prefers "original brochure work and program cover for symphony concerts" as samples. Reports only if interested. Pays by the project. Considers available budget when establishing payment.

*EDITH STEPHEN DANCE CONNECTION, Studio 630A, 55 Bethume St., New York NY 10014. (212)989-2250. Administrator: E. Kapel. A dance/theatre company performing unique multi-media productions connecting dance, theatre, music, poetry, art, visuals and environmental sculpture.

Needs: Works with a varying number of freelance artists/year. Uses freelance artists for advertising, brochure, poster, program, and costume design; also lighting. Prefers avant-garde style art.

First Contact & Terms: Works on assignment only. Send query letter with resume to be kept on file. Prefers photographs and tear sheets as samples. Samples not kept on file are returned if accompanied by SASE. Reports back to the artist within a short time. Pays by the hour. Considers project's budget when establishing payment.

Tips: "There is more free-form art and design in our field."

*THE STEPPENWOLF THEATRE COMPANY, 2851 N. Halsted St., Chicago IL 60675. (312)472-4515. Managing Director: Stephen B. Eich. "We are a fifteen-member ensemble theatre company based upon a subscription of 3,500 patrons. Our productions are as exciting and varied as our recent *Fool For Love* and *Tracers* in Chicago, and our other smash hit *Balm in Gilead* in New York."

Needs: Works with 10 freelance artists/year. Needs heaviest September-May. Uses artists for advertising, and brochure design, illustration and layout; poster and program design and illustration; set and costume design; and lighting and scenery.

First Contact & Terms: Send query letter with resume and samples to be kept on file, or write for appointment to show portfolio. Prefers photographs or photocopies as samples. Samples not filed are returned by SASE. Reports back only if interested. Method and amount of payment varies. Considers complexity of the project, project's budget, skill and experience of the artist, and how work will be used when establishing payment.

"STRIKE AT THE WIND!" OUTDOOR DRAMA, Box 1059, Pembroke NC 28372. (919)521-2480 or 521-3112. General Manager: Carnell Locklear. Outdoor drama about Henry B. Lowery and the Indians of Robeson County during the Civil War. The company consists of 75 persons. Assigns 1 job/year.

Needs: Uses artists for billboards, bumper stickers, poster, animated TV spots, souvenir program cover, brochure illustration, poster illustrations and inside ads and editorials. Needs art that is "dramatic, historically accurate, entertainment-oriented with concepts illustrating Civil War era characters, places and things in southeastern North Carolina."

First Contact & Terms: Prefers local artists. Mail brochure or resume with photographs. Call for an appointment to show a portfolio. Reports in 4 weeks. Works on assignment only. Material is kept on file. Provide resume, calling card, brochure, flyer and tear sheets to be kept on file for future assignments. Pays by the project. Considers complexity of the project when establishing payment.

*SYRACUSE OPERA COMPANY, INC., Opera Center, 410 E. Willow St., Syracuse NY 13203. Managing Director: Christine J. Day.
Needs: Uses artists for direct mail brochures, posters, newspaper/trade magazine ads, bumper stickers and programs. Especially needs season brochures; fund raising flyers; opera posters, 500 bumper stickers, 500 T-shirts, and display ads, Pays by the project.
Tips: "Create the cleanest, most appealing materials for the least amount of printing requirements. We like good, attractive art, but we cannot afford multiple color separations and expensive paper stock. Short and simple."

THEATRE CONCORD, 1950 Parkside Dr., Concord CA 94519. (415)671-3065. Contact: Jim Jester. Produces musicals, comedy, drama and ballet year round. Assigns 3-10 jobs/year.
Needs: Works with up to 4 illustrators and 4 designers/year. Uses artists for costume design, flyers, graphic/set design, posters, programs and theatrical lighting.
First Contact & Terms: Query, then mail slides or photos. Works on assignment only. Samples returned by SASE; reports back on future assignment possibilities. Provide resume to be kept on file for future assignments.

THEATRE OF YOUTH (TOY) CO. INC., Center Theatre, 681 Main St., Buffalo NY 14203. (716)856-4410. Artistic Director: Rosalind Cramer. "Buffalo's only professional resident theatre company, performing a full season of children and adult plays at their residence; while also touring schools with productions and workshops." Assigns 5 full-time and 4-10 professional service jobs per year. Write.
Needs: Professional actors, set and costume designers, and graphic artists. Uses artists for brochure designs, flyers, marquees, posters. Pays $250-500 costume and set designs and per show publicity design.
Tips: "Small companies such as TOY are seeking well-rounded practitioners, as opposed to rigid specialists, with an emphasis on ensemble. Submit inquiries early in the year, January through March, so we can arrange personal interviews."

THEATRE UNDER THE STARS, 4235 San Felipe, Houston TX 77027. (713)622-1626. Public Relations Director: Tammy Gilbert. Musical theatre production company producing 5 shows a year, one in Houston's outdoor theatre and 4 in the downtown music hall.
Needs: Works with 5-10 freelance artists/year. Uses artists for advertising and brochure design, illustration, and layout; and poster design and illustration.
First Contact & Terms: Works on assignment only. Send query letter with samples to be kept on file. Call for appointment to show portfolio. Samples not filed are returned by SASE. Reports back within 2 weeks. Pays by the project; design, $50-5,000 average; illustration, $50-4,500 average. Considers complexity of the project, project's budget, skill and experience of the artist, how work will be used, turn-around time and rights purchased when establishing payment.

*UNIVERSITY OF ROCHESTER SUMMER THEATER, River Station, Box 30185, Rochester NY 14627. (716)275-4088 (Monday-Wednesday-Friday). Managing Director: David Runzo. Semi-professional company offering 3 productions of classical and contemporary theatre each summer and a 4-hour college credit program.
Needs: Works with 6 freelance artists/year; needs heaviest in June, July, August. Uses artists for set and costume design, lighting, scenery, as technical directors and stage manager. Also for brochures, programs and ads.
First Contact & Terms: Artists must be able to teach area of concentration. Send query letter with resume to be kept on file; call or write for appointment. Prefers slides and b&w photos as samples. Samples returned by SASE. Reports within 3 weeks. Works on assignment only. Pays salary of $1,500-1,800 average for 11 weeks for design plus train transportation and half room—"paid through our budget of $2,500 by university artists."

VALOIS COMPANY OF DANCERS, HEC 214, University of Toledo, Toledo OH 43606. (419)537-2741. Art Director: Elaine Valois. Resident modern dance company active in public schools, workshops and mini-concerts plus an annual May show.
Needs: Works with 6 freelance artist/year. Heaviest needs in spring. Uses artists for brochure and program design, costume design, and posters. "Student artists often help us, and we continue to support them and purchase from them when they go professional."
First Contact & Terms: Prefers local artists. Send query letter with brochure, business card and samples to be kept on file. Prefers photostats as samples. Samples not kept on file are returned only if requested. Reports within 2 weeks. Pays by the project, $50-200 average, for design and illustration. Considers complexity of project, available budget and how work will be used when establishing payment.
Tips: "We have noticed more inventive use of photographic material blended in with graphics."

*VICTORY GARDENS THEATER, 2257 N. Lincoln Ave., Chicago IL 60614. (312)549-5788. General Manager: Marcelle McVay. "Subscriber-based not-for-profit professional theatre, dedicated to the development of new works, and using Chicago talent."
Needs: Works with 10-20 freelance artists/year. Uses artists for advertising, brochure, catalog and poster design and illustration; set, lighting and costume design.
First Contact & Terms: Works with developing or experienced, local artists on assignment only. Send query letter with resume and samples to be kept on file. Prefers tear sheets as samples. Samples not filed are returned by SASE. Reports back only if interested. Pays for poster design by the project, $100-300 average; pays set, lighting and costume design according to U.S.A.A. Considers complexity of project, project's budget, skill and experience of the artist, and turnaround time when establishing payment.

THE VIRGINIA SYMPHONY, (formerly *The Virginia Orchestra Group*), Box 26, Norfolk VA 23501. (804)623-8590. Director of Marketing: Harriet Ervin. Manages The Virginia Symphony and Virginia Symphony Pops. The Symphony and Pops perform about 75 concerts/season.
Needs: Works with 1-2 freelance artists/year; needs heaviest in September-June. Uses artists for advertising, brochure and program design; brochure layout and posters.
First Contact & Terms: Send query letter with resume, business card and samples to be kept on file. Write for appointment to show portfolio. Prefers photostats and original work on brochures as samples. Samples not kept on file are returned only if requested. Reports only if interested. Considers available budget and turnaround time when establishing payment.

*RUSS WALTON AGENCY, 183 Galewood Circle, San Francisco CA 94131-1131. Manager: Russ Walton. Theatre/music talent and production agency representing San Francisco musical performers and variety artists, and producing San Francisco concert and theatre presentations.
Needs: Works with 3-4 freelance artists/year. Uses artists for advertising design and layout; set and costume design; posters, lighting and scenery.
First Contact & Terms: Prefers local artists, previous experience in producing commercial arts is required. Send query letter with resume, business card and samples to be kept on file. Prefers photographs and photostats as samples. Reports only if interested. Pays for design and ilustration by the project, $25-50 average. Considers complexity of project, available budget, skill and experience of artist, how work will be used and turnaround time when establishing payment.

*JENNY WILEY THEATRE, Box 22, Prestonsburg KY 41653. (606)886-9274. Managing Director: Keith Stevens. An outdoor summer musical theatre with 50 company members performing 3 Broadway musicals in repertory. Average yearly attendance is 18,000.
Needs: Works with 1 freelance artist/year. Needs heaviest in fall and winter. Uses artists for brochure design, illustration and layout; poster design and illustration.
First Contact & Terms: Send query letter with resume and samples. Prefers photostats and tear sheets as samples. Samples returned if accompanied by SASE. Reports within 1 month. Pays by the project, $500-1,000, for design. Considers complexity of the project, project's budget and turnaround time when establishing payment.

ANNA WYMAN DANCE THEATRE, 1705 Marine Dr., West Vancouver, British Columbia V7V 1J5 Canada. (604)926-6041. General Manager: Peter Kaiser. Dance company.
Needs: Works with several freelance artists/year. Uses artists for advertising, brochure and program design, illustration and layout; set and costume design; and posters.
First Contact & Terms: All commercial artists are subject to portfolio review and recommendation/approval by Artistic Director Anna Wyman. Send query letter with brochure, resume, business card, samples and tear sheets to be kept on file; call or write for appointment to show portfolio. Prefers copies as samples to be kept on file. Samples not kept on file are returned only if requested. Reports within weeks. Pays by the project. Considers complexity of project and available budget when establishing payment.

*ZIVILI/TO LIFE! Celebrating Yugoslavia in Dance and Song, 12 Clover Ct., Granville OH 43023. (614)855-7805. Managing Director: Melissa Pintar Obenauf. Professional dance company performing exclusively the dances and songs of Yugoslavia. Consists of 40 dancers, singers and musicians.
Needs: Works with 10 freelance artists/year; needs heaviest in fall and spring. Uses artists for advertising, brochure, program design, illustration and layout; posters and lighting.
First Contact & Terms: Send query letter with resume, business card and samples to be kept on file. Accepts "any type" of samples. Reports within 2 weeks. Negotiates pay. Considers complexity of project, available budget, skill and experience of artist and how work will be used when establishing payment.

Record Companies

For the freelance graphic artist, art and music are two very compatible art forms. They frequently embrace one another in art exhibits with specially-selected music; on videocassettes, where the music and lyrics come to life; and most commonly for freelance artists, on album covers.

Recording industry art directors have recognized the value of combining the *right* album cover art style with the right musical style. Not only are the results more aesthetic, the financial rewards for the record company are generally greater. The bottom line is that album cover artwork must fit the concept of the record and the mood of the music.

While record cover artists should be well-rounded artistically—capable of doing layouts, paste-up and basic art production—they must also have a distinctive style. Originality and provocativeness are musts. Remember, album cover artwork is being used to *sell* records, not just look good.

Cover illustration and design are the primary, but not the only, uses for artwork in this section. Don't overlook the peripheral materials for assignments—P-O-P displays, blow-ups, posters and mobiles are promotional tools used to guarantee the financial success of the musical product.

To learn what art styles are used by record companies on both covers and promotional materials study those already in the marketplace; spend time in your local record shop or library studying styles and deciding which are most effective.

Computer-manipulated art is increasingly prevalent on record album covers, but it is still most widely used in music video productions. As music videos continue to grow in popularity, artists will be needed for many facets of art direction in their production.

For additional names and addresses of hundreds of record companies and affiliated services for the music industry (such as design, artwork, promotions and public relations firms) see *Songwriter's Market 1986, Billboard International Buyer's Guide* and *Music Industry Directory.*

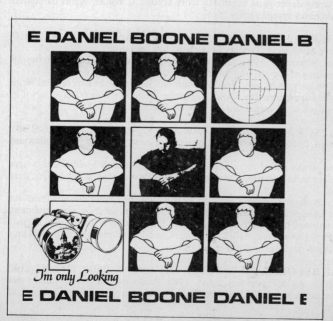

Ron Lee, manager of Lematt Music Ltd./Swoop Records in England, assigned this cover design and illustration of a Daniel Boone single to local artist Philip Dunn. Lee selected Dunn because of the artist's wide range of art skills.

© Swoop Records

*AIRWAVE INTERNATIONAL RECORDS & PUBLISHING, 5th Floor, 6381 Hollywood Blvd., Hollywood CA 90028. President: Terry M. Brown. Produces rock and roll, disco/dance, soul, pop, and rhythm and blues; group and solo artists. Recent releases: "Love Transfusion," by Cindi Todd; "Dr. Sey," by Pleasure & The Beast; and "Stupid Cupid," by Linda Kendrick.
Needs: Produces 24 records/year; works with 12-24 recording artists/year. Works with 2 visual artists/year. Uses artists for album cover and advertising design and illustration, advertising layout and posters.
First Contact & Terms: "I would be willing to look at any work submitted for consideration." Send query letter with brochure, resume and samples to be kept on file; call or write for appointment to show portfolio. Prefers photostats, photographs, photocopies or tear sheets as samples. Samples not filed are returned by SASE only if requested. Reports within 3 weeks. Original artwork sometimes returned to artist. Pays by the project, $100-3,000 average. Considers complexity of project, available budget, turnaround time and rights purchased when establishing payment. "I negotiate the entire contract before deposit is made."

*AMAZING RECORDS, Box 26265, Fort Worth TX 76116. Owner: Jim Yanaway. Produces rock and roll, country/western, jazz, folk, and rhythm and blues. Recent releases: "Rock-It To Stardom," by The Legendary Stardust Cowboy; "Check This Action," by The LeRoi Brothers; and "The Joints Jumpin'," by The Juke Jumpers.
Needs: Produces 6-8 records/year; 6-8 recording artists/year. Works with 11 visual artists/year. Uses artists for album cover design and illustration, brochure layout, and catalog and advertising illustration and layout.
First Contact & Terms: Send query letter with brochure and samples to be kept on file; write for appointment to show portfolio. Prefers photographs as samples. Samples not filed are returned by SASE only if requested. Reports only if interested. Original artwork not returned to artist. Pays by the project, $50-1,500 average. Considers complexity of project, skill and experience of commercial artist, how work will be used and turnaround time when establishing payment. Negotiates rights purchased.

*AMERICAN HARMONY ARTIST, Box 55224, Station B, Omaha NE 68155. (402)345-6619. Director of Marketing/Sales: Thomas L. Encepretson. Produces rock and roll, classical, disco, soul, country/western, jazz, folk, pop, and rhythm and blues; group and solo artists. Recent releases: "My Melody Heart," and "Love Me Hon," by Wihh (Whip) Cord.
Needs: Produces 3 single records and 3 albums/year. Uses artists for album cover and catalog design and illustration; catalog layout; advertising design, illustration and layout; direct mail packages; and posters.
First Contact & Terms: Send business card and samples; call or write for appointment to show portfolio. Prefers tear sheets as samples. Samples returned by SASE only if requested. Original artwork returned to artist if requested. Payment depends on volume of work needed. Considers rights purchased when establishing payment. Purchases reprint rights.

APON RECORD COMPANY, INC., Steinway Station, Box 3082, Long Island City NY 11103. (212)721-8599. President: Andre M. Poncic. Produces classical, folk and pop.
Needs: Produces 20 records/year. Works with 10 visual artists/year. Uses artists for album cover design and illustration, catalog illustration and layout, and posters.
First Contact & Terms: Works on assignment only. Send brochure and samples to be kept on file. Write for art guidelines. Samples not filed are returned by SASE. Reports to the artist within 60 days only if interested. Considers available budget when establishing payment. Purchases all rights.

*ART ATTACK RECORDS, INC., Box 31475, Fort Lowell Station, Tucson AZ 85751. (602)881-1212. President: William Cashman. Produces rock and roll, country/western, jazz, pop, and rhythm and blues, and solo artists.
Needs: Produces 4 records/year; works with 4 recording artists/year. Works with 5 visual artists/year. Uses artists for album cover design and illustration; catalog design and layout; advertising design, illustration and layout; and posters.
First Contact & Terms: Works on assignment only. Send query letter with brochure, business card and samples to be kept on file; write for appointment to show portfolio. Prefers tear sheets or photographs as samples. Samples not filed are returned by SASE only if requested. Reports only if interested. Original artwork not returned to artist. Pays by the hour, $10-25 average. Considers complexity of project and available budget when establishing payment. Purchases all rights.

*ARTIST INTERNATIONAL RECORDS, 221 W. 57th St., New York NY 10019. (212)582-2190. Contact: Managing Director/Marketing & Promotion. Estab. 1983. Produces rock and roll, disco and pop; group and solo artists. Recent releases: "Stage Struck" and 'Babylon," by Justine Johns; and "Love Magazine," by Sylvahn.
Needs: Produces 12 records/year. Works with 5 visual artists/year. Uses artists for album cover design

and illustration; catalog design; advertising design, illustration and layout; direct mail packages; and posters.

First Contact & Terms: Works on assignment only. Send brochure, resume and samples to be kept on file; write for appointment to show portfolio. Prefers photographs, photocopies and tear sheets as samples. Samples not filed are returned by SASE. Reports within 30 days. Original artwork returned to artist. Negotiates payment. Considers complexity of project, skill and experience of commercial artist, turnaround time and rights purchased when establishing payment. Negotiates rights purchased.

ARZEE RECORD COMPANY and ARCADE RECORD COMPANY, 3010 N. Front St., Philadelphia Pa 19133. (215)426-5682. President: Rex Zario. Produces rock and roll, country/western, and rhythm and blues. Recent releases: "Rock Around the Clock," by James E. Myers; "World Apart," by Ray Whitley; "Why Do I Cry Over You," by Bill Haley.
Needs: Produces 25 records/year. Works with 150 visual artists/year. Uses artists for brochure and catalog design; posters. ·
First Contact & Terms: Send query letter with brochure and tear sheets to be kept on file. Call for appointment to show portfolio. Samples not kept on file are returned by SASE if requested. Reports within 6 weeks. Originals not returned after job's completion. Buys all rights.

ATTIC RECORDS LIMITED, 624 King St. W, Toronto, Ontario M5V 1M7 Canada. (416)862-0352. Director of Sales/Marketing: Lindsay Gillespie. Produces rock and roll, disco, jazz, pop, and rhythm and blues; group and solo artists. Recent releases: "Electric Splash," by Belinda Metz, Katrina and The Waves; "Metal Queen," by Lee Aaron; and "Seamless," by The Nylons.
Needs: Produces 25 records/year; works with 15 recording artists/year. Works with 6 visual artists/year. Uses artists for album cover design and illustration, catalog design, advertising design, illustration and layout, and posters.
First Contact & Terms: Works on assignment only. Send query letter with brochure to be kept on file. Call or write for appointment to show portfolio. Samples required only with appointment. Samples not filed are returned only if requested. Reports to the artist only if interested. Original art sometimes returned to the artist. Pays by the hour, $15 minimum; by the project, $500 minimum. Considers complexity of project, available budget, how work will be used and rights purchased when considering payment. Purchases all rights.
Tips: "We see increased use of computer graphics in our field."

*AUDIOFIDELITY ENTERPRISES, INC., 519 Capobianco Plaza, Rahway NJ 07065. (201)388-5000. Art Director: Ron Warwell. Produces rock and roll, classical, disco, soul, country western, jazz, folk, pop, educational, rhythm and blues, salsa, ethnic, and specialty, plus more. Recent releases: Ahmad Jamal Live in Concert, John Coltrain, Fats Domino, Jim Messina.
Needs: Produces 100 records and cassettes/year. Works with 10 freelance artists/year. Uses artists for album cover, catalog and advertising illustration, and posters.
First Contact & Terms: "Super pros" only. Send query letter with brochure and samples to be kept on file. Prefers c-prints as samples. Samples not kept on file returned by SASE if requested. Reports only if interested. Pays by the project, $500 maximum. Considers complexity of project, available budget, skill and experience of artist, how work will be used and rights purchased when establishing payment. Negotiates rights purchased.

*AWARD RECORDS, Suite 108, 3701 Twin Lakes Ct., Baltimore MD 21207. (301)922-6585. Vice President: Bobby Astri. Produces rock and roll, disco, country/western, pop, and rhythm and blues; group and solo artists. Recent releases: "Love Is on the Menu," by Shirley Graff; "In a Country State of Mind," by John Fitzwater; and "Loving You Once," by Toni Bellin.
Needs: Produces 20 records/year; works with 10 recording artists/year. Works with 4 visual artists/year. Uses artists for album cover design and illustration, and posters.
First Contact & Terms: Works on assignment only. Send query letter with brochure and samples to be kept on file. Write for appointment to show portfolio. Accepts photostats, photographs or tear sheets as samples. Samples not filed returned by SASE, only if requested. Reports within 30 days. Pay is negotiable. Considers complexity of project, available budget, how work will be used and turnaround time when establishing payment. Negotiates rights purchased.

*CLIFF AYERS PRODUCTIONS, 62 Music Sq. W., Nashville TN 37203. (615)361-7902. Producer: Chris Ostermeyer. Produces rock and roll, country/western and pop; group and solo artists. Recent releases: "Talk Back Tremblin' Lips," by Ernie Ashworth; "As Long As We're Together," by John Melnick; and "Nobody's Perfect," by Marilyn Jeffries.
Needs: Produces 75 records/year. Works with 40 visual artists/year. Uses artists for album cover design and illustration, brochure design and layout and direct mail packages.

First Contact & Terms: Works on assignment only. Send resume to be kept on file; write for appointment to show portfolio. Prefers tear sheets as samples. Samples are not returned. Reports only if interested. Original art returned at job's completion. Pays by the project. Considers available budget when establishing payment. Buys first rights.

B.G.S. PRODUCTIONS LTD., Newtown St., Kilsyth, Glasgow G65 0JX Scotland. 0236-821081. Director: Dougie Stevenson. Produces rock and roll, country/western, jazz and folk; solo artists. Recent releases: "From Scotland With Love," by Sydney Devine; "The Pipes and Strings of Scotland," instrumental; and "Lena Martell Today."
Needs: Produces 20 records/year. Works with 2 visual artists/year. Uses artists for album cover design and illustration; brochure design, illustration and layout; catalog design, illustration and layout; advertising design, illustration and layout; posters.
First Contact & Terms: Send brochure, resume and samples to be kept on file. Call or write for appointment to show portfolio. Accepts photostats, photographs, photocopies or tear sheets as samples. Samples not filed are returned only if requested. Reports only if interested. Pays by the hour, $20 average. Considers available budget when establishing payment. Purchases all rights.

BIG BEAR RECORDS, 190 Monument Rd., Birmingham B16 8UU England. (021)454-7020. Managing Director: Jim Simpson. Produces soul, jazz, and rhythm and blues; group artists. Recent releases: "American Blues Legends '84," by Homesick James, Snooky Prior and others; "Kansas City Giants," by Claude 'The Fiddler' Williams; and "Shake Your Boogie," by Snooky Prior.
Needs: Produces 25 records/year; works with 20-25 groups or soloists. Works with 3-4 visual artists/year. Uses artists for album cover design and illustration.
First Contact & Terms: Works on assignment only. Send query letter with samples to be kept on file. Prefers photographs or photocopies as samples. Samples not filed are returned only by SAE (nonresidents include IRC). Negotiates payment. Considers complexity of project and how work will be used when establishing payment. Purchases all rights.

*BIOGRAPH RECORDS, INC., 16 River St., Chatham NY 12029. President: Arnold S. Caplin. Produces jazz, folk, blues, rhythm and blues, and nostalgia. Recent releases: "American Dreamer," by Oscar Brand; "How High The Moon," by Randy Weston; "Big Stampede," by Zoot Sims; and "Tenors Anyone," by Stan Getz.
Needs: Number of records produced/year varies. 25% of the album covers have been assigned to freelance designers and illustrators. Uses artists for album and catalog design; album illustration; and direct mail packages.
First Contact & Terms: Send query letter with resume and samples; write for appointment to show portfolio. Prefers photostats and slides as samples. Samples returned by SASE. Reports within 6 weeks. Works on assignment only. Provide business card, resume and samples to be kept on file for possible future assignments. Original work not returned after job's completion. Negotiates payment and rights purchased.

BLUE ISLAND GRAPHICS, Box 171265, San Diego CA 92117-0975. (619)477-4442. President: Bob Gilbert. Produces rock and roll, country/western and pop. "We are a new company and will be signing new artists this year. Even though we are new, we always are looking for talent."
Needs: Produces 10-15 records/year. Uses 3 visual artists/year. Uses artists for album cover, brochure and advertising illustration; brochure, catalog and advertising layout; brochure and advertising design.
First Contact & Terms: No restrictions, but must submit resume and/or sample materials with return postage. Send query letter with resume, samples and tear sheets to be kept on file. Write for appointment to show portfolio. Prefers photostats or original work as samples. Samples not kept on file are returned by SASE if requested. Reports within 1 month. Works on assignment only. Originals not returned after job's completion. Pays by the hour, $10-15 average. Considers skill and experience of artist when establishing payment. Buys all rights.

BOLIVIA RECORDS CO., 1219 Kerlin Ave., Brewton AL 36426. (205)867-2228. Manager: Roy Edwards. Produces soul, country/western, pop, and rhythm and blues. Recent releases: "Was Young Love Born to Die," by Bobbie Roberson.
Needs: Produces 20 records/year; 40% of the album covers assigned to freelance designers and illustrators. Assigns 25 freelance jobs/year. Uses artists for album cover, brochure, poster, catalog and advertising design; album cover and catalog illustration; brochure and catalog layout; and direct mail packages. Prefers western scenes and color washes of landscapes as themes.
First Contact & Terms: Experienced artists only. Send query letter with brochure/flyer and samples or actual work. Prefers original work as samples. Samples returned by SASE. Works on assignment only. Reports back. Provide brochure/flyer, business card and samples to be kept on file for possible future as-

signments. Negotiates payment by the project. Buys all rights.
Tips: "Do good work and be dependable."

BOUQUET-ORCHID ENTERPRISES, Box 18284, Shreveport LA 71138. (318)686-7362. President: Bill Bohannon. Produces country, pop and contemporary gospel.
Needs: Produces 10 records/year; 5 of which have cover/jackets designed and illustrated by freelance artists. Uses artists for record album and brochure design.
First Contact & Terms: Query with resume and samples. "I prefer a brief but concise overview of an artist's background and works showing the range of his talents." SASE. Reports within 2 weeks. Provide resume, letter of inquiry and brochure to be kept on file for future assignments. Negotiates pay.

*BOYD RECORDS, 2609 NW 36th St., Oklahoma City OK 73112. (405)942-0462. President: Bobby Boyd. Produces rock and roll, country/western and pop.
Needs: Produces 20 records/year. Works with 2-4 visual artists/year. Uses artists for album cover design and illustrations.
First Contact & Terms: Works on assignment only. Send query letter; write for appointment to show portfolio. Prefers tear sheets as samples. Original artwork returned to artist. Pays by the project. Considers how work will be used when establishing payment. Purchases all rights.

*BRANCH INTERNATIONAL RECORDS, Box 31819, Dallas TX 75231. (214)750-0720. Promotion Director: Rusti James. Produces country/western and folk. Recent releases: "No Satin Sheets to Cry On," by Janet Cave; "Old Man on the Square," by Charlie Seybert.
Needs: Produces 10 records/year. Uses artists for album cover and brochure design, direct mail packages, posters.
First Contact & Terms: Send query letter with samples to be kept on file. Prefers photographs as samples. Samples not kept on file returned by SASE. Reports only if interested. Works on assignment only. Originals not returned after job's completion. Considers complexity of project, skill and experience of artist, how work will be used and rights purchased when establishing payment. Buys all rights.

CACTUS MUSIC & GIDGET PUBLISHING, 5 Aldom Cr., W. Caldwell NJ 07006. (201)226-0035. Contact: Jim Hall or Gidget Starr. Recent releases: "I'm Still in Love With You," by Charlie Bailey; and "Truck Driving Man," by Sal Franco.
Needs: Produces 3-4 records/year; works with 3-4 recording artists/year. Uses artists for advertising layout and posters.
First Contact & Terms: Send query letter with resume and samples to be kept on file. Write for art guidelines. Prefers photographs or tear sheets as samples. Samples not filed are not returned. Reports only if interested. Considers available budget when establishing payment. Purchases all rights.

*CALIFORNIA INTERNATIONAL RECORDS & VIDEO, Box 2818, Newport Beach CA 92663. Vice President: Cheryl Gammon-Nicoletti. Produces rock and roll, and pop; solo artists. Recent releases: "Lets Put the Fun Back in Rock n' Roll," by Freddie Cannon & the Belmonts; "Child of Technology" and "Children Are the Future," by Joseph Nicoletti.
Needs: Produces 2-3 records/year; works with 1-2 recording artists/year. Uses artists for album cover design and illustration, catalog design, illustration and layout, advertising design and illustration, direct mail packages and posters.
First Contact & Terms: Works on assignment only. Send brochure, resume, business card and samples to be kept on file. Samples not filed are not returned. Reports only if interested. Original art sometimes returned. Pays by the project. Considers complexity of project, available budget, skill and experience of commercial artist, how work will be used, turnaround time and rights purchased when establishing payment. Negotiates rights purchased.

*CARROLL ENTERPRISES, 1818 E. Ardmore, Phoenix AZ 85040. (602)276-2039. President: Lawrence Carroll. Produces soul, and rhythm and blues. Recent releases: "Crossroads," by Bobby Barnes and "DJ Rap," by Poor Boy Rappers.
Needs: Produces 10 records/year. Works with 5 visual artists/year. Uses artists for cover design and illustration.
First Contact & Terms: Contact only through artist's representative with brochure, resume and samples to be kept on file. Prefers photographs and albums as samples. Samples not filed are returned by SASE. Original artwork returned to artist. Pays by the project or percentage basis. Considers available budget and skill and experience of commercial artist when establishing payment. Purchases one-time rights.

CASTLE RECORDS, Box 1338, Merchantville NY 08109. President: Rob Russen. Produces rock and roll, disco, soul, country/western, and rhythm and blues. Recent releases: "Ain't No Thing" and

"Be Happy," by Phoenix; "Luscious," by Heavy Weather.
Needs: Produces 6-12 records/year. Works with 3-6 freelance commercial artists/year. Uses artists for album cover design and posters.
First Contact & Terms: Send query letter with resume, business card and samples to be kept on file. Prefers photographs as samples. Samples not kept on file are returned by SASE if requested. Reports within 10 days. Originals not returned to artist after job's completion. Pay varies. Considers available budget, how work will be used and rights purchased when establishing payment. Buys all rights.

*CDE, Box 41551, Atlanta GA 30331. President: Charles Edwards. Produces disco, soul, jazz, and rhythm and blues.
Needs: Produces 6-10 records/year; 100% of the album covers assigned to freelance designers, 100% to freelance illustrators. Assigns varying number of freelance jobs/year. Uses artists for album cover, poster, brochure and advertising design; album cover, poster and brochure illustration; and direct mail packages. No set style, "we are open-minded to any style."
First Contact & Terms: Send query letter and samples. Prefers photostats and original work as samples. Samples not returned. Reports within 2 months. Works on assignment only. Provide brochure/flyer, business card and samples to be kept on file for possible future assignments. Original work returned after job's completion "by request." Negotiates payment. Buys first rights or negotiates rights purchased.
Tips: "The business needs new and creative people."

CELESTIAL SOUND PRODUCTIONS, 28 South Villas, London NW1 England. 41-01-405-9883. Managing Director: Ron Warren Ganderton. Produces rock and roll, classical, soul, country/western, jazz, pop, educational, and rhythm and blues. Recent releases: "Starforce One," "Red Door," and "Once Bitten."
Needs: Works with "many" visual artists/year. Uses artists for album cover design and illustration; advertising design, illustration and layout; and posters.
First Contact & Terms: Send query letter with resume, business card and samples to be kept on file "for a reasonable time." Call or write for appointment to show portfolio. Samples not filed are returned by SASE only if requested. Reports within 5 days. Original artwork returned after job's completion. Pays by the project. Considers available budget, how work will be used and rights purchased when establishing payment. Buys all rights, reprint rights or negotiates rights purchased.

*CLARUS MUSIC LTD., 340 Bellevue Ave., Yonkers NY 10703. (914)591-7715. President: Selma Fass. Music publisher and children's record company. Assigns 2-3 jobs/year.
Needs: Produces 2-3 records/year; all of which have cover/jackets designed and illustrated by freelance artists. Uses artists for record covers, lettering and catalog design.
First Contact & Terms: Query with resume and samples. SASE. Prefers slides or photos of work as samples. Reports within 2-4 weeks. Works on assignment only. Provide resume, letter of inquiry, brochure, flyer and tear sheet to be kept on file for future assignments. Pays $250-450; negotiates pay by the project. Buys all rights.

*CLAY PIGEON INTERNATIONAL RECORDS, Box 20346, Chicago IL 60620. (312)778-8760. Contact: Vito Beleska or Rudy Markus. Prodoces rock and roll, pop, New Wave and avant-garde. Recent releases: "Tribe of Dolls," by The Band That Never Made It.
Needs: Produces 5 records/year; 3 of which have cover/jackets designed and illustrated by freelance artists. Uses artists for design and illustrations for LP jackets, brochures, 45 RPM picture sleeves and advertising. Interested in "anything good, especially newer concepts, unusually creative approaches, art that does more with less."
First Contact & Terms: Send query (do not phone) with resume or brochure and materials that can be kept on file for future reference. Prefers "whatever shows artist's work best" as samples; "simple, inexpensive presentation OK." Samples not returned except by special arrangement. Reports within 1 month or when assignment is available. Negotiates pay based on amount of creativity required and artist's previous experience/reputation.

*CODEX INTERNATIONAL RECORDS, Box 37156, Cincinnati OH 45222. (513)891-2366. Contact: Saul Halper. Produces soul, country/western, and rhythm and blues.
Needs: Uses artists for album cover and advertising illustration.
First Contact & Terms: Works on assignment only. Send query letter with resume; write for appointment to show portfolio. Samples not filed are returned by SASE. Reports only if interested.

*CONCORD JAZZ, INC., Box 845, Concord CA 94522. (415)682-6770. Promotion Director: Ellen Findlay. Produces classical, jazz and Latin. Recent releases: "An Evening at Charlie's," by Mel Torme;

"You're Looking at Me," by Carmen McRae; "Bien Sabroso!" by Poncho Sanchez; and "World Class," by Woody Herman.

Needs: Produces 30 records/year; works with numerous recording groups and artists/year. Works with 5 visual artists/year. Uses artists for album cover design and illustration and posters.

First Contact & Terms: Looks for quality work. "Artist must meet strict deadlines, accept little pay but *great* exposure." Works on assignment only. Send query letter with brochure, resume and samples to be kept on file; write for appointment to show portfolio. Samples not filed are returned by SASE only if requested. Reports only if interested. Original artwork not returned. Pays by individual quotes. Considers available budget and how work will be used when establishing payment.

THE COVER STORY, 3836 Austin Ave. Waco TX 76710. Art Director: Joan Tankersley. Produces rock and roll, classical and pop.

Needs: Produces 20 covers/year. Works with 10 visual artists/year. Uses artists for album cover design and illustration, advertising design and layout.

First Contact & Terms: Artists with at least 2 years' experience only. Will consider out-of-town illustrators. Send query letter with resume and samples to be kept on file. Prefers slides or tear sheets as samples. Reports within 2 weeks. Works on assignment only. No originals returned to artist after job's completion. Pays by the project, $500 minimum. Considers complexity of project, available budget, skill and experience of artist and how work will be used when establishing payment. Buys all rights.

Tips: Especially seeks artists who display non-commissioned work. "I desire to see more self-motivated material. I have noticed more freedom in conceptualizing in art and design in our field. Basically anything goes. I can experiment with a broad variety of illustration styles."

*COZGEM RECORDS, Box 324 Northgate Station, Seattle WA 98125. (206)821-6137. Vice President: Bob Cozzetti. Produces rock and roll and jazz. Recent release: "Concerto for Padre," by Cozzetti and Gemmill.

Needs: Works with 2 visual artists/year. Uses artists for album cover design and illustration; brochure, catalog and advertising design, illustration and layout; direct mail packages; and posters.

First Contact & Terms: Works with local artists with 2-3 years experience or out-of-town artists with a good track record. Works on assignment only. Send query letter with brochure, resume and samples to be kept on file; call or write for appointment to show portfolio; write for art guidelines.

Editor's Note: As this edition was going to the press it was learned that Cozgem Records no longer seeks freelance submissions.

THE CREATION CO., Skylight Records Division, 939 Felix Ave. Lwr., Windsor, Ontario N9C 3L2 Canada. (519)256-6604. President: Jim Thomson II. Produces rock and roll, classical, jazz, folk, pop, and rhythm and blues. Recent releases: "Old Gypsy Moon," by Jim Thomson II; and "Raw," by Preflyte.

Needs: Produces 1 album, 2 single records/year; works with 2 recording artists/year. Works with 1 visual artist/year. Uses artists for album cover design and illustration, and posters.

First Contact & Terms: Prefers artists with "personal moral standards as well as artistic standards and convictions." Send query letter with brochure, resume, business card and samples to be kept on file. Prefers photographs as samples. Call or write for appointment to show portfolio. Samples not kept on file are not returned. Reports only if interested. Originals sometimes returned to artist after job's completion. Pays by the project, $30-900 average; "depends on source and scope of job; usually on percentage sold." Considers complexity of project, available budget, how work will be used, turnover time and rights purchased when establishing payment. Negotiates rights purchased.

*CRIMSON DYNASTY RECORD CORP., B-271, Cedar and West Aves., Jenkintown PA 19046. Vice President: Frank Mulvenna. Produces country/western, rhythm and blues, and novelty. Recent releases: "I'm the Greatest," by MuHammad Ali; and "Restless," by Summerfield.

Needs: Produces 6 albums/year. Works with 4-5 visual artists/year. Uses artists for album cover design and illustration; brochure design, illustration and layout; catalog design, illustration and layout; advertising design, illustration and layout; direct mail packages; and posters.

First Contact & Terms: Send resume and samples to be kept on file. Prefers color photostats, photographs, photocopies or tear sheets as samples. Samples not filed are not returned; "sample artwork is kept in our files for future consideration. We need the samples for our reference." Original art not returned to the artist. Pays by the hour, $15 minimum, plus possible royalty arrangement; or by the project, $250, minimum. Considers complexity of project, how work will be used and rights purchased when establishing payment. Purchases all rights.

CRYIN' IN THE STREETS RECORDS CORPORATION & AFFILIATES, Box 2544, Baton Rouge LA 70821. (504)924-6865. Director: Jimmy Angel/Ebb-Tide. Produces soul, country/western,

jazz, pop, and rhythm and blues; group and solo artists. Recent releases: "Let 'Jesus' In," by The Mighty Serenades; "One More Lie," by Betsy Davidson; and "Ease My Mind," by George Perkins.
Needs: Produces fifteen 45's and 6 albums/year; works with 21-25 recording artists/year. Works with 100+ visual artists/year; averages 12 album covers/year. Uses artists for album cover design and illustration, brochure design and illustration, catalog layout, advertising illustration, direct mail packages, posters, video backdrops and production layouts. Acceptable art styles include cartoons and humorous and cartoon-style illustrations.
First Contact & Terms: Works with "professionals" only. Works on assignment only. Send query letter with resume and business card to be kept on file only if accepted. Write for appointment to show portfolio. Prefers photocopies, photographs or tear sheets only when requested. Samples not filed are returned only by SASE. Reports within 30 days. Original art returned to the artist. Pays by the project, $100-1,000 average. Considers complexity of project, available budget, skill and experience of commercial artist, how work will be used, turnaround time and rights purchased when establishing payment. Purchases all rights.

*CUMMINGS PRODUCTIONS, Suite 303, 14045 S. Main, Houston TX 77035. (713)870-8422, 641-0793. Vice President/A&R: Robert Jackson and Linda Harris. Produces rock and roll, disco, soul, country/western, jazz, pop, educational, and rhythm and blues; group and solo artists. Recent releases: "Gimme The Chance," by Chance; and "I Would Like To Know You," by Carl Stewart.
Needs: Produces 20 records/year; by 3 soloists and 4 groups. Works with 2 visual artists/year. Uses artists for album cover design and illustration, advertising design and illustration, direct mail packages and posters.
First Contact & Terms: Experienced artists only. Send query letter with brochure to be kept on file. Write for appointment to show portfolio. Reports within 1 month. Original art returned to the artist. Pay is negotiable. Considers available budget and how work will be used when establishing payment. Negotiates rights purchased.

CURTISS UNIVERSAL RECORD MASTERS, Box 4740, Nashville TN 37216. (615)865-4740. Manager: S.D. Neal. Produces soul, country, jazz, folk, pop, rock and roll, and rhythm and blues. Recent releases by Dixie Dee & The Rhythm Rockers, and Ben Williams.
Needs: Produces 6 records/year; some of which have cover/jackets designed and illustrated by freelance artists. Uses artists for album cover and poster design.
First Contact & Terms: Send samples; submit portfolio for review. SASE. Reports within 3 weeks. Works on assignment only. Provide business card and samples to be kept on file for possible future assignments. Originals returned to artist after job's completion. Negotiates pay based on artist involved. Negotiates rights purchased.

DANCE-A-THON RECORDS, 26 17th St., Box 13584, Atlanta GA 30324. (404)872-6000. Director of Creative Services: O.P Cooper. Produces rock, disco, bluegrass, country and spoken-word comedy records.
Needs: Buys 5 illustrations/year. Uses artists for designing album jackets and accompanying advertising logos for labels and artists.
First Contact & Terms: Prefers artists with previous experience in the advertising/record medium. Query with resume and samples or previously published work. SASE. Reports within 6-8 weeks. Pays $100-350.

DAWN PRODUCTIONS, Joey Welz Music Complex, 2338 Fruitville Pike, Lancaster PA 17601. President: Joey Welz. Produces country/western, New Wave, rock and pop music albums. Recent releases: "American Made Country Roll" (LP) and "No More Nightmares" (single), by Joey Welz (Caprice Records).
Needs: Produces 2 LPs and five 45s/year. Works with 2 visual artists/ year. Buys 1-3 illustrations/year. Uses artists for album cover designs. Especially needs stock jackets. No rock music art.
First Contact & Terms: "Artists must be ready to go." Send samples and tear sheets. SASE. Reports only if interested. Considers available budget, rights purchased and how work will be used when establishing payment; "percentage paid by label releasing product."
Tips: "We are now using stock jackets and want to see simplicity of design. Have sample of finished stock jackets." There is a trend toward "more picture discs and more elaborate jackets."

DELMARK RECORDS, 4243 N. Lincoln, Chicago IL 60618. (312)528-8834. Art Director: Bob Koester. Produces blues and jazz. Recent releases: "The Blues World of Little Walter";"North South" by Jimmy Johnson; and "Reality," by Frank Walton.
Needs: Chicago area artists only. Produces 5-10 records/year; all of which have cover/jackets designed and illustrated by freelance artists. "Our records do not sell like hits, but remain in our catalog and active

in the market for many years. We are therefore more interested in clean designs that do not date rather than in flashy covers. Most of the artists who work for us are interested in the music we issue: jazz and blues. We are especially interested in artists who can arrive at interesting multi-color designs based on black and white photographs."
First Contact & Terms: Arrange interview to show portfolio (mixture of original and printed art). Works on assignment only. Samples returned by SASE. Reports back on future assignment possibilities. Provide resume, tear sheet and samples to be kept on file for future assignments. Pays $50-250.

DESTINY RECORDS, Destiny Recording Studio, 31 Nassau Ave., Wilmington MA 01887. Contact: Larry Feeney. Produces rock and roll, classical, disco, soul, country/western, jazz, folk, pop, and rhythm and blues; group and solo artists. Recent releases: "Decision," by Rude Awakening; "Prisoners," by Tinted Glass; and "When You Thought I Had It," by True Desire.
Needs: Produces 6 records/year. Works with 3 visual artists/year. Uses artists for album cover design and illustration, and brochure illustration. "We're interested in futuoristic forms."
First Contact & Terms: Send query letter with brochure and samples to be kept on file. Write for appointment to show portfolio; do not call. Prefers photographs as samples. Samples not filed are not returned. Original art sometimes returned to the artist. Payment varies.

*DYNACOM COMMUNICATIONS, INC., Box 702, Snowdon Station, Montreal, Quebec H3X 3X8 Canada. General Manager: D. Leonard. Produces rock and roll, disco, soul, country/western, jazz, folk, pop, educational, and rhythm and blues.
Needs: Produces 10 records/year. Uses artists for album cover design and illustration; brochure, catalog and advertising design, illustration and layout; direct mail packages and posters.
First Contact & Terms: Send query letter with brochure, resume, business card, samples and tear sheets. Prefers photostats, slides or photographs as samples. Samples not returned. Works on assignment only. Considers complexity of project, available budget, skill and experience of artist, how work will be used, turnaround time and rights purchased when establishing payment. Negotiates rights purchased.

*E.L.J. RECORD CO., 1344 Waldron, St. Louis MO 63130. (314)863-3605. President: Eddie Johnson. Produces rhythm and blues, rock and roll, jazz and pop music. Recent releases: "Morning Star," by Jimmy Jones; "Rock House Annie," by Ann Richardson; "Strange Feeling," by Eddie Johnson Trio; and "Wish I Was an Itty Bitty Girl," by the M&M Girls.
Needs: Produces 12 records/year; all of which have cover/jackets designed by freelance artists.
First Contact & Terms: Send query and samples. SASE. Reports within 6 weeks. Negotiates pay based on amount of creativity required and rights purchased.
Tips: "Send prices and sample designs of some of my material."

*ENCHANTED DOOR, INC., Box 1235, New Rochelle NY 10802. Vice President/Promotion: Joe Messina. Produces rock and roll, and pop; group and solo artists. Recent releases: "Struck by Lightnin'," by Rat Race Choir (Crescent Records); "Forever," by Wowii (Cartoon Records); and "Since I Don't Have You," by Spyder Turner (Cap-orion Records).
Needs: Produces 6 records/year; works with 3 recording artists/year. Works with 2 visual artists/year. Uses artists for album cover design, brochure design, advertising layout, direct mail packages and posters.
First Contact & Terms: Works on assignment only. Send query letter with brochure and samples to be kept on file. Samples not filed returned by SASE. Reports only if interested. Original art sometimes returned. Pays by the project, $250-2,500 average. Considers complexity of project, available budget and rights purchased when establishing payment. Negotiates rights purchased.

*ENERGY RECORDS, Suite 1301, 50 E. 42nd St., New York NY 10017. (212)687-2299. Contact in writing only: Howard Kruger, Vice President Creative Affairs. Produces rock and roll, classical, disco, soul, country/western, jazz, pop, and rhythm and blues. Recent releases: David Soul, John Travolta, Lady Love, Glen Campbell and Valentine Bros.
Needs: Produces 10 records/year; 100% of the album covers were assigned to freelance designers. Assigns 10 freelance jobs/year. Uses artists for album cover, poster, catalog and advertising design. Themes vary per album subject matter.
First Contact & Terms: Prefers artists with experience. Send resume and samples. Prefers photostats and slides as samples. Samples not returned. Reports within 2 weeks. Works on assignment only. Provide business card, resume and samples to be kept on file for possible future assignments. Original work not returned after job's completion. Negotiates payment by the project. Negotiates rights purchased.

EPOCH UNIVERSAL PUBLICATIONS/NORTH AMERICAN LITURGY RESOURCES, 10802 N. 23rd Ave., Phoenix AZ 85029. (602)864-1980. Vice President: David Serey. Produces contemporary Christian inspirational, liturgical music. Recent releases: "Lord of Light," by St. Louis Jesuits; "Awaken, My Heart," by Fri Lucien Deiss.

Needs: Produces 10-20 records/year; 100% of the album covers were assigned to freelance designers. Works with 2-3 artist/year. Uses artists for album cover design and illustration; brochure, catalog and advertising design, illustration and layout; direct mail packages and posters. Prefers inspirational, symbolic themes, "in any medium that works."

First Contact & Terms: Prefers local artists with 3 or more years' experience, capable of quality work and willing to negotiate. Send query letter with brochure/flyer or resume and samples to be kept on file for possible future assignments. Write for appointment to show portfolio. Prefers 10 photostats or slides as samples. Samples not kept on file are returned by SASE. Reports only if interested. Original work not returned to artist after job's completion. Negotiates payment by the project, $10-2,000 average. Rights purchased vary, depending on project; "we like to buy all rights."

Tips: "Phone calls are of little value. However, all mail is answered and all submissions are screened very carefully. Untried artists/designers or just beginning artists must be willing to do some work for the promotional aspect—giving exposure to their work."

*ESQUIRE RECORDS, 185A Newmarket Rd., Norwich, Norfolk NR4 6AP England. 44-06-035-1139. Producer: Peter Newbrook. Produces jazz. Recent releases: "A Lover and His Lass," by Cleo Laine and John Dankworth; "Tenor Contrasts," by Stan Getz and James Moody; and "The Heat's On," by Roy Eldridge and Howard McGhee.

Needs: Produces 4-6 records/year. Works with 2 freelance artists/year. Uses artists for album cover design and illustration.

First Contact & Terms: Send query letter with samples to be kept on file. Prefers photostats or photographs as samples. Reports only if interested. Works on assignment only. Originals returned to artist after job's completion. Negotiates pay rate. Considers available budget when establishing payment. Buys all rights.

*EXECUTIVE RECORDS, 11 Shady Oak Trail, Charlotte NC 28210. (704)554-1162. Executive Director: Butch Kelly. Produces rock and roll, disco, soul, country/western, jazz, pop, and rhythm and blues; group and solo artists. Recent releases include "Fantasy," by Wylie; "13 Years," by L.A. Stars; and "Fantasy II," by Melisa Kelly.

Needs: Produces 6 records/year. Works with 3 groups and 3 solo recording artists/year. Works with 2 visual artists/year. Uses artists for album cover design, advertising design and layout, and direct mail packages.

First Contact & Terms: Seeks artists with 3 years' experience. Works on assignment only. Send query letter with brochure, resume and samples to be kept on file. Write for appointment to show portfolio. Prefers photographs or photocopies as samples. Samples not filed returned by SASE. Reports back only if interested. Original art sometimes returned to the artist. Pays by the project, $25-100 average. Considers available budget, and skill and experience of commercial artist when establishing payment. Buys all rights.

FACTORY BEAT RECORDS, INC., 521 5th Ave., New York NY 10175. Produces disco, pop, contemporary, and rhythm and blues. Recent releases: "Dance It Off" and "I Love Your Beat," by Rena; "Let's Slip Away" and "Everybody's Doin' It," by Charles T. Hudson.

Needs: Produces 2 albums/year.

First Contact & Terms: Send query letter with brochure and samples to be kept on file. Prefers original work as samples. Samples not kept on file returned by SASE. Reports only if interested. Originals not returned to artist after job's completion. Considers available budget when establishing payment. Negotiates rights purchased.

FALCON PRODUCTIONS, 3080 Lenworth Ave., Mississauga, Ontario L4X 2G1 Canada. (416)625-3865. Art Director: Nick Kosonic, W.A.N.K. Design. Produces rock and roll, pop, and rhythm and blues. Recent releases: "The Lydia Taylor Band" and "Bitch," by The Lydia Taylor Band; "I'm Worried about the Boys," by Zon; "Affairs in Babylon" by Refugee; and "Call Billy" by Billy Durst.

Needs: Produces 4-5 records/year; works with 5-6 freelance artists/year. Uses artists and photographers for album cover design and illustration, advertising illustration and layout, and posters.

First Contact & Terms: Works on assignment only. Send resume, business card and samples; call or write for appointment to show portfolio. Prefers photostats, slides or photographs (of any 3-dimensional work) as samples. Samples not filed are returned by SAE (nonresidents include IRC) only if requested. Reports within 30 days. Original work not returned after job's completion. Pays by the hour, $15-30 average. Considers complexity of project, available budget, how work will be used and rights purchased when establishing payment. Negotiates rights purchased.

Tips: Looks for artists who do not follow trends. "Originality is so difficult to achieve but so important to maintain."

FAMOUS DOOR RECORDS, 141-10 Holly Ave., Flushing NY 11355. (718)463-6281. Contact: Harry Lim. Produces jazz. Recent releases: "Stardust," by The Glenn Zottola Quartet & Quintet; "Symphony," by Ross Tompkins Trio & Quartet; "Hail to the Chief: Butch Miles salutes Count Basie," by The Butch Miles Octet.
Needs: Produces 8 records/year. Works with freelancers "only when regular artist is not available." Uses artists for album cover design.
First Contact & Terms: Prefers local artists. Send business card to be kept on file. Reports within 2 weeks. Works on assignment only. Originals not returned to artist after job's completion. Pays by the project, $150 minimum. Considers available budget when establishing payment. Buys all rights.

FARR MUSIC AND RECORDS, Box 1098, Somerville NJ 08876. Contact: Candace Campbell. Produces rock and roll, disco, soul, country/western, folk and pop; group and solo artists.
Needs: Produces 15 records/year. Works with 40 visual artists/year. Uses artists for album cover design, brochure design and illustration, and posters.
First Contact & Terms: Send query letter with brochure, resume and samples to be kept on file. Prefers photographs as samples. Samples not filed are returned by SASE. Reports within 3 weeks. Original art returned to the artist. Purchases first rights or all rights.

FISCHER & LUCUS, INC., Suite 902, 50 Music Sq. W, Nashville TN 37203. Director of Merchandising: Gayle Baldwin. Produces country/western.
Needs: Produces 25 records/year.
First Contact & Terms: Send brochure/flyer. Samples not returned. Provide material to be kept on file for possible future assignments. Original work not returned to artist after job's completion. Negotiates payment.

FRECKLE RECORDS, Pioneer Square, Box 4005, Seattle WA 98104. (206)682-3200. General Manager: Jack Burg. Produces folk and pop; group and solo artists. Recent release: "A Lonely Grain of Corn," by Uncle Bonsai.
Needs: Produces 3 records/year. Uses artists for album cover design and illustration, brochure design and layout, advertising design and layout, and posters.
First Contact & Terms: Prefers local experienced artists. Works on assignment only. Send query letter with brochure, resume, business card and samples to be kept on file. Call or write for appointment to show portfolio. Samples not filed are returned by SASE. Reports only if interested. Pays by the project. Considers complexity of project, available budget, skill and experience of commercial artist, how work will be used, turnaround time and rights purchased when establishing payment. Negotiates rights purchased.

***G & P RECORDS, INC.**, 539 W. 25th St., New York NY 10001. (212)675-6060. Vice President: George Hornfeck. Produces rock and roll, and pop. Recent release: "Front Page News," by Thrills.
Needs: Produces 3 records/year. Works with 3 freelance artists/year. Uses artists for album cover design, and advertising design and layout.
First Contact & Terms: Send samples to be kept on file. Call or write for appointment to show portfolio. Samples not kept on file are returned. Reports within 3 weeks. Works on assignment only. Original art not returned at job's completion. Buys all rights.

GCS RECORDS, Suite 206, 1508 Harlem, Memphis TN 38114. (901)274-2726. Art Director: Reggie Ekridge. Produces disco, soul, pop, gospel, and rhythm and blues; group artists. Recent releases: "Early Morning Man," by Cheryl Fox; and "Keep On Dancing," by Roy Malone.
Needs: Produces 20 records/year. Works with 3 visual artists/year. Uses artists for album cover design and illustration; brochure design and layout; catalog design and illustration; advertising design, illustration and layout; direct mail packages, posters, artist logos and more.
First Contact & Terms: Prefers local artists. Send query letter with brochure, resume and samples to be kept on file. Call or write for appointment to show portfolio. Accepts any samples. Samples not filed are returned by SASE only if requested. Reports only if interested. Payment negotiated/job. Considers complexity of project, available budget, how work will be used and rights purchased when establishing payment. Negotiates rights purchased.

***GEMCOM INC.**, 4375 S.W. 60th Ave., Ft. Lauderdale FL 33314. (305)581-9050. President: Robert W. Schachner. Produces jazz and educational. Recent releases: "Aerobic Dancing," B.B. King, Pat Metheny, Dave Brubeck; and "Dr. Who Photo Album."
Needs: Produces 25 records/year. Works with 5 visual artists/year. Uses artists for album cover, brochure and catalog design and illustration; brochure layout; and direct mail packages.
First Contact & Terms: Works on assignment only. Send query letter with brochure, resume and sam-

ples to be kept on file. Prefers photographs and tear sheets as samples. Samples not filed are not returned. Original artwork not returned to artist. Considers complexity of project and available budget when establishing payment. Purchases all rights.

*GLOBAL RECORDS, Bakersfield Records, Chris Music Publishing, Sara Lee Music Publishing, 133 Arbutus Ave., Box 396, Mantistique MI 49854. Contact: Art Department. Produces soul, country/western, folk, rhythm and blues, and contemporary gospel; group artists. Recent release "Diamonds & Pearls," by Paradons; Milestone Records and Tapes, K-Tel Albums and casettes.
Needs: Produces 11 records/year. Works with 2 visual artists/year. Uses artists for advertising design, illustration and layout; also advertising design for other businesses.
First Contact & Terms: Prefers amateur artists. Works on assignment only. Send query letter with brochure to be kept on file. Prefers photographs or tear sheets as samples. Samples returned by SASE. Reports within 3 months. Original artwork not returned to artist. Negotiates payment by the project. Considers available budget when establishing payment. Purchases all rights.

HARD HAT RECORDS AND CASSETTE TAPES, 519 N. Halifax Ave., Daytona Beach FL 32018. (904)252-0381. Vice President, Sales/Promotion: Bobby Lee. Produces rock and roll, country/western, folk and educational; group and solo artists. Publishes high school/college marching band arrangements. Recent releases: "Our Bed of Roses," "Worried, Worried Man," and "Heard You Married Him Today," by Blue Bandana Country Band.
Needs: Produces 12-30 records/year. Works with 2-3 visual artists/year. Uses artists for album cover design and illustration, advertising design and sheet music covers.
First Contact & Terms: Works on assignment only. Send query letter with brochure to be kept on file one year. Write for appointment to show portfolio. Samples not filed are returned by SASE. Reports within 2 weeks. Pays by the project. Considers complexity of project, available budget, skill and experience of commercial artist, how work will be used, turnaround time and rights purchased when establishing payment. Purchases all rights.
Tips: "Video is playing a bigger part in the art market for record and tape companies. The market for this medium of musical entertainment has its own styles and needs."

HOLLYROCK RECORDS, Suite 170, 14116 E. Whittier Blvd., Whither CA 90602. A&R Directors: Dave Paton, Bob Brown. Produces country/western, rock, progressive rock, folk, pop, and rhythm and blues; group and solo artists, also comedy acts.
Needs: Produces 10 records/year. Works with 4 visual artists/year.
First Contact & Terms: Send samples to be kept on file. Write for appointment to show portfolio. Accepts slides, photostats, photographs, photocopies or tear sheets as samples. Reports within 4 weeks. Original art sometimes returned to the artist. Pay is negotiable. Considers complexity of project, available budget, skill and experience of commercial artist, how work will be used, turnaround time and rights purchased when establishing payment. Purchases first rights or all rights.

JAY JAY, 35 62nd St. NE, Miami FL 33138. (305)758-0000. President: Walter Jagiello. Produces country/western, jazz and polkas. Recent releases: "Polish Feelings" and "God Bless Our Polish Pope," by Li'l Wally; and "Back to the Beat of the Polka," by Eddie & the Slovenes.
Needs: Produces 6 albums/year. Uses artists for album cover design and illustration, brochure design, catalog layout, advertising design, illustration and layout, and posters.
First Contact & Terms: Works on assignment only. Send brochure and samples to be kept on file. Call or write for appointment to show portfolio. Prefers tear sheets as samples. Samples not filed are returned by SASE. Reports within 2 months. Pays by the project. Considers skill and experience of commercial artist when establishing payment. Purchases all rights.

JEWEL RECORD CORP., 728 Texas St., Box 1125, Shreveport LA 71163. (318)222-7182. Director of Sales & Marketing: Ms. Donnis Lewis. Produces disco, soul, country/western, pop, rhythm and blues, and black gospel. Recent releases: "Blues Boy," by Artie White; "Just In Time," by Ernie Johnson; and "Cool Out" by Magnum Force.
Needs: Uses artists for album cover design and illustration; brochure design and layout; catalog design, illustration and layout; advertising design, illustration and layout; and direct mail packages.
First Contact & Terms: Send query letter with resume and samples to be kept on file. Write for appointment to show portfolio. Accepts photographs, photocopies or tear sheets as samples. Samples not filed are returned by SASE. Reports within 3 weeks. Original art returned to the artist. Pay is negotiable. Considers complexity of project, available budget, how work will be used and rights purchased when establishing payment. Negotiates rights purchased.

JODY RECORDS, 2226 McDonald Ave., Brooklyn NY 11223. General Manager: Tom Busco. Promotion: Tom Pedi. Public Relations: Gloria Black. Musical Director: Mickey Marlett. Produces rock

and roll, disco, soul, country/western, jazz, and rhythm and blues. Recent releases: "Rosalita" and "Rabbit on the Run," by Ron King; "This is the Day," by Eddie Hailey.
Needs: Produces 50 records/year. Works with 4 visual artists/year. Uses artists for album cover design, advertising illustration and posters.
First Contact & Terms: Send query letter with resume and samples to be kept on file. Prefers photostats as samples. Samples not kept on file returned by SASE. Works on assignment only. Originals returned to artist after job's completion. Pays by the project, $150-500 average. Considers how work will be used when establishing payment. Negotiates rights purchased.

*KENYON ENTERTAINMENT CORP., A#1, 8191 N.W. 91st. Terrace, Miami FL 33166. Contact: Joseph Stanzione. Produces soul, jazz and Caribbean (reggae). Recent releases: "Missin' Mr. Marley," by Sue Chalonex; "Conquerer," by Derrick Morgan; and "Reggae USA," by Althea Ranks.
Needs: Produces 5-10 records/year. Works with 2 visual artists/year.
First Contact & Terms: Works on assignment only. Send query letter with brochure and samples to be kept on file. Samples not filed are returned by SASE. Reports only if interested. Original art not returned to artist. Pays by the project. Considers how work will be used when establishing payment. Purchases all rights.

*KICKING MULE RECORDS, Box 158, Alderpoint CA 95411. Manager: Ed Denson. Produces guitar, banjo and dulcimer records. Catalog 25¢. Recent releases: "Elizabethians Dulcimer," by Randy Wilkinson; "Runoff," by Chris Proctor; and "Snapping the Strings," by Bob Brozman.
Needs: Buys 10-20 designs/year. Especially needs book design and layout, cover art and book graphics.
First Contact & Terms: Query with full-size covers or layouts; local artists only. Does not wish to see illustrations. SASE. Reports in 4 weeks. Buys all rights. Pays $2.50/page, layout of tab books; $300, album cover design; $100, album liner design.
Tips: "Get to know the performers—they often pick their own designers."

KIDERIAN RECORDS PRODUCTS, 4926 W. Gunnison, Chicago IL 60630. (312)399-5535. President: Raymond Peck. Produces rock and roll, classical, disco, soul, country/western, jazz, folk, pop, educational, rhythm and blues, and New Wave; group and solo artists. Recent releases: "Boyz," by Boy; "Creme Soda," by Creme Soda; and "Kiderian Sampler 2."
Needs: Produces 35-40 records/year; 100% of the album covers were assigned to freelance designers, 100% to freelance illustrators. Works with 8-14 visual artists/year. Half of all jobs/year require freelance artists. Uses artists for album cover design and illustration; posters; brochure design, illustration and layout; catalog design, illustration and layout; advertising design, illustration and layout; and direct mail packages. Accepts all styles.
First Contact & Terms: Works on assignment only. Send query letter, resume and samples to be kept on file. Prefers photographs and slides as samples. Samples not filed are returned by SASE. Original work returned to artist after job's completion. Pays by the project, $200-$450 average. Purchases all rights.

*KIMBO EDUCATIONAL, 10 N. 3rd Ave., Long Branch NJ 07740. Production Coordinators: Amy Laufer and James Kimble. Educational record/cassette company. Produces 8 records and cassettes/year for schools, teacher supply stores and parents. Contents primarily early childhood physical fitness although other materials are produced for all ages.
Needs: Works with 3 freelance artists/year. Uses artists for ads, catalog design, album covers and flyer designs. Artist must have experience in the preparation of album jackets.
First Contact & Terms: Local artists only. "It is very hard to do this type of material via mail." Works on assignment only. Write for appointment to show portfolio. Prefers photographs or actual samples of past work. Reports only if interested. Pays by the project. Album cover minimum $100; flyers, etc. lower minimum. Considers complexity of project and budget when establishing payment. Buys all rights.
Tips: "The jobs at Kimbo vary tremendously. We are an educational record company that produces material from infant level to senior citizen level. Sometimes we need cute 'kid-like' illustrations and sometimes graphic design will suffice. A person expereinced in preparing an album cover would certainly have an edge."

SID KLEINER MUSIC ENTERPRISES, 3701 25th Ave. SW, Naples FL 33964. Managing Director: Sid Kleiner. Produces folk, rock, jazz, middle of the road and country recordings, and nutritional, organic gardening and health audiovisuals. Recent releases: "A Simple Life," by Dave Kleiner. Query. SASE. Reports within 4 weeks. Material copyrighted.
Needs: Uses artists for album design, type specifying and audiovisuals. Pays $50 minimum/job.

L & R PRODUCTIONS, 16 E. Broad St., Mt. Vernon NY 10552. (914)668-4488. President: Richard Rashbaum. Produces rhythm and blues, and disco records. Recent releases: "Everybody Get Off," and

Local artist William R. Laird of Oakhurst, New Jersey, received the assignment for this album cover for a children's recording from Amy Laufer, production coordinator at Kimbo Educational in Long Branch, New Jersey. This company produces educational records and cassettes, and uses artists for the illustration of ads and album covers, and the design of catalogs and flyers.

"Romance at a Disco," by Daybreak. Assigns 3 jobs/year.

Needs: Produces 2 records/year; both have cover/jackets designed and illustrated by freelance artists. Uses artists primarily for record album design, also for jacket design, and album and ad illustrations. Especially needs album design and posters.

First Contact & Terms: Local artists only. Query with resume and samples. Reports within 2 weeks. Works on assignment only. Provide resume, brochure and flyer to be kept on file for future assignments. Samples returned by SASE.

Tips: "We are presently developing a group concept for artists."

*LEMATT MUSIC LTD./Pogo Records Ltd./Swoop Records/Grenouille Records/Check Records/Lee Music Ltd., % Steward House, Hill Bottom Rd., Sands, IND, EST, Highwycombe, Buckinghamshire England. 0494-36301/36401. Manager: Ron Lee. Produces rock and roll, disco, country/western, pop, and rhythm and blues; and solo artists. Recent releases: "I'm Only Looking," by Daniel Boone; "New York Jets," by Emmitt Till and "I'm a Rep," by The Chromatics.

Needs: Produces 25 records/year; works with 6 groups or soloists/year. Works with 1-2 visual artists/year. Uses artists for album cover design and illustration; advertising design, illustration and layout; and posters.

First Contact & Terms: Works on assignment only; uses a few cartoons and humorous and cartoon-style illustrations where applicable. Send query letter with brochure, resume, business card and samples to be kept on file. Prefers slides, photographs and videos as samples. Samples not filed are returned by SASE (nonresidents send IRCs). Reports within 3 weeks. Original artwork sometimes returned to artist. Considers complexity of project, available budget, skill and experience of commercial artist, how work will be used and turnaround time when establishing payment.

LEMON SQUARE PRODUCTIONS, Box 31819, Dallas TX 75231. (214)750-0720. A&R Director: Mike Anthony. Produces country and gospel music. Recent releases: "Glen Bailey" and "Audie Henry."
Needs: Plans on having cover/jackets designed and illustrated by freelance artists. Will use artists for record album, jacket and brochure design; album and print ad illustrations; posters; and artist promos.
First Contact & Terms: Send business card, samples and tear sheets to be kept on file for future reference. Prefers photos as samples. SASE. Reports only when assignment available. Negotiates pay based on complexity of project, available budget, how work will be used and amount of creativity required.

LOADSTONE, LOCK & OPEN RECORD MUSIC COMPANY, 163 Orizaba Ave., San Francisco CA 94132. (415)334-2247. President: W.C. Stone. Produces rock and roll, disco, soul, jazz and religious.
Needs: Produces 4-10 records/year. Uses artists for poster and brochure design.
First Contact & Terms: Send query letter with brochure/flyer. Samples not returned. Reports within 2 weeks. Provide material to be kept on file for possible future assignments. Original work not returned after job's completion. Buys all rights.

LOCK RECORD CO., A subsidiary of Loadstone & Open Record Co., 163 Orizaba Ave., San Francisco CA 94132. (415)334-2247. Director: W.C. Stone. Recent releases: "Headed for the Streets," by Herman H. Harper III; "You Touched The Inner Part of Me," by Celest Hardie; and "Love Bandit," by Lee Rogers.
Needs: Produces 2-6 records/year. Uses artists for direct mail packages and posters.
First Contact & Terms: Send samples to be kept on file. Call or write for appointment to show portfolio. Prefers photocopies as samples. Samples not filed returned by SASE. Reports only if interested. Pays by the project. Considers complexity of project when establishing payment. Purchases all rights.

*LOCONTO PRODUCTIONS, 7766 N.W. 44th St., Sunrise FL 33321. (305)741-7766. Executive Vice President: Phyllis Finney Loconto. Produces rock and roll, classical, disco, soul, country/western, jazz, folk, pop, educational, and rhythm and blues; group and solo artists. Recent releases: "Barber Shop Quartet," by Suntones; "Drama/Keyboard," by Irving Fields; and "Jamming-Country," by Basoom "Bill" Dillon.
Needs: Works with 10 visual artists/year. Uses artists for album cover design and illustration; brochure, catalog and advertising design, illustration and layout; direct mail packages; and posters.
First Contact & Terms: Works on assignment only. Send business card. Pays by the project. Considers available budget when establishing payment. Negotiates rights purchased.

L'ORIENT PRODUCTIONS/WOULDN SHOE RECORDS, Box H, Harvard MA 01451. (617)456-8111. Art Director: Anne-Marie Alden. Chief Executive Officer: Stephen Bond Garvan. Produces rock and roll, soul, country/western and pop. Recent releases: "Time For Us," by Dean Adrien; "Inside the Storm," by New Moon; and "Your Time Too," by Linda Blaze.
Needs: Produces 3-6 records/year; works with 3-6 recording artists/year. Works with 3-4 visual artists/year. Uses artists for album cover design and illustration, advertising design and illustration, and posters.
First Contact & Terms: Works on assignment only. Send query letter with brochure, resume and samples. Accepts slides, photostats, photographs or tear sheets as samples. Samples not filed are returned by SASE. Reports only if interested. Original art sometimes returned to artist. Pays by the project, $50 minimum. Considers complexity of project, available budget, how work will be used, turnaround time and rights purchased when establishing payment. Purchases all rights.

LUCIFER RECORDS, INC., Box 263, Brigantine NJ 08203. (609)266-2623. President: Ron Luciano. Produces pop, disco, and rock and roll.
Needs: Produces 2-12 records/year. Uses artists for album cover design and illustration; brochure design, illustration and layout; advertising layout; and posters.
First Contact & Terms: Experienced artists only. Works on assignment only. Send query letter with brochure, resume, business card and samples to be kept on file. Prefers slides or photos as samples; SASE. Reports only if interested. Original art sometimes returned to artist. Considers budget, how work

will be used, rights purchased and the assignment when establishing payment. Negotiates pay and rights purchased.

LEE MAGID c/o GRASS ROOTS PRODUCTIONS, Box 532, Malibu CA 90265. (213)858-7282. President: Lee Magid. Produces jazz, rock, country, blues, instrumental, gospel, classical, disco, folk, educational, pop and reggae; group and solo artists. Recent releases: "Hear Me Now," and "Again," by Ernie Andrews; "On The Streets Again," and "Live," by Rags Waldorf; and "Have Horns, Will Travel," by Russ Gary Big Band Express. Assigns 15 jobs/year.
Needs: Produces 15-20 records/year; works with 5 artists/year. Uses artists for album design and illustration; brochure design, illustration and layout; and advertising illustration. Sometimes uses cartoons and humorous and cartoon-style illustrations depending on project.
First Contact & Terms: Local artists only. Works on assignment only. Send query letter with resume and samples to be kept on file. SASE. Write for appointment to show portfolio. Accepts slides, photostats, photographs, photocopies or tear sheets as samples. Samples not filed are returned by SASE. Reports only if interested. Pays by the project. Considers available budget when establishing payment. Purchases all rights.
Tips: "It's important for the artist to work closely with the producer, to coincide the feeling of the album, rather than throwing a piece of art against the wrong sound." Artists shouldn't "get too progressive. 'Commercial' is the name of the game."

MAJEGA RECORDS/PRODUCTIONS, 240 E. Radcliffe Dr., Claremont CA 91711. (714)624-0677. President: Gary K. Buckley. Produces gospel, country and pop records, audiovisual presentations; i.e., filmstrips, slide/sound sync and multimedia programs. Recent releases: "Country Love," by Jerry Roark; "Steppin Out," by The Gospelmen; and "Sending a Copy Home," by Jody Barry.
Needs: Produces about 6 records/year; 4 of which have cover/jackets designed and illustrated by freelance artists. Uses artists for album covers, ad illustrations, logo designs, cartoons, charts & graphs and other promotional materials.
First Contact & Terms: Query by letter with resume, brochure, flyer and samples (2-3 tear sheets of varied styles if possible) to be kept on file for future assignments. "Samples provided should be relevant to type of work requested." Works on assignment only. Samples returned by SASE. Reports back on future assignment possibilities. Negotiates pay according to complexity of project and available budget.
Tips: "Look at existing covers and be conscious of the style of music inside. This will illustrate what the industry is accepting and give the artist a solid base to start creating from."

MAJOR RECORDING STUDIOS, Box 2072, Waynesboro VA 22980. (703)949-0106. Contact: John H. Major. Produces rock and roll, soul, country/western, folk, bluegrass and gospel by various recording artists.
Needs: Produces 100 records/year. Uses artists for album cover design.
First Contact & Terms: Send query letter with samples to be kept on file. Write for appointment to show portfolio. Prefers original work as samples. Samples not kept on file returned by SASE. Reports within 30 days. Works on assignment only. Originals not returned to artist after job's completion. Pays by the project, $150 minimum. Considers skill and experience of artist when establishing payment. Negotiates rights purchased.

MASTER-TRAK ENTERPRISES, 413 N. Parkerson Ave., Crowley LA 70526. (318)783-1601. General Manager: Mark Miller. Produces rock and roll, disco, soul, country/western, rhythm and blues, and Cajun French. Recent releases: "Ils Sont Partis" and "Buckwheat II," by Buckwheat; "25 Years of the Blues," by Tabby Thomas; and "Cruisin' On," by Sam Brothers.
Needs: Produces 15-20 records/year; 75% of the album covers were assigned to freelance designers, 25% to freelance illustrators. Uses artists for album cover design and illustration. Accepts various themes and styles.
First Contact & Terms: Send samples to be kept on file for possible future assignment; submit portfolio for review. Prefers variety of samples. Samples not returned. Reports within 5 weeks. Negotiates payment by the project. Considers available budget, and skill and experience of commercial artist when establishing payment. Buys one-time rights or negotiates.
Tips: There is a "present increase in use of artists. Would like to see sketchings of phonographs. Submit work related to country, blues, rock and Cajun music."

MELODEE RECORDS, Box 1010, Hendersonville TN 37077-1010. (615)451-3920. President: Dee Mullins. Produces country/western.
Needs: Uses artists for album cover design and illustration; brochure design, illustration and layout; catalog design, illustration and layout; advertising design, illustration and layout; direct mail packages; and posters.

First Contact & Terms: Experienced artists only. Works on assignment only. Write for appointment to show portfolio. Samples not filed are returned by SASE.

*MESA RECORDS, 1204 Elmwood, Nashville TN 37212. (615)269-0593. General Manager: Taylor Sparks. Produces country/western. Recent releases: "Handsome Man," and "We Just Gotta Dance," by Karen Taylor-Good.
Needs: Produces 1 album/year. Works with 1 visual artist/year. Uses artists for album cover design and illustration.
First Contact & Terms: Send query letter with resume to be kept on file. Reports only if interested. Original art not returned to artist. Negotiates payment. Considers complexity of project, available budget and rights purchased when establishing payment. Negotiates rights purchased.

MILLENNIUM RECORDS, 1697 Broadway, New York NY 10019. (212)974-0200. Director: Andrew Frances. Produces rock and roll. Recent releases: "Believers," by Don McLean; "Makin' the Point," by Franke & the Knockouts; "So Easy to Love," by Tommy James; and "Inner City Front," by Bruce Cockburn.
Needs: Produces 6 records/year. Works with varying number of freelance artists/year. Uses artists for album cover design and illustration; posters and publicity items.
First Contact & Terms: Send query letter with business card, samples and tear sheets to be kept on file. Write for appointment to show portfolio. Prefers photos and slides as samples. "Uninteresting or wrong material" returned by SASE. Reports only if interested. Originals returned after job's completion. Pays by the project. Considers complexity of project, available budget, skill and experience of artist, how work will be used, turnaround time and rights purchased when establishing payment. Negotiates rights purchased.

MIRROR RECORDS INC; HOUSE OF GUITARS BLVD., 645 Titus Ave., Rochester NY 14617. (716)544-3500. Art Director: Armand Schaubroeck. Produces rock and roll, Heavy Metal, middle of the road and New Wave music. Recent releases: "Over the Rainbow," by Don Potter; "Here are the Chesterfield Kings" and "I Shot My Guardian Angel," by Armand Schaubroeck Steals; and "The Village Churchmice."
Needs: Produces 4 records/year; all of which have cover/jackets designed and illustrated by freelance artists. Uses artists for catalogs, album covers, inner sleeves and advertising designs. "Always looking for new talent."
First Contact & Terms: Send query and samples. SASE. Reports within 1 month. Or send brochure or materials that can be kept on file for future reference. Negotiates pay based on amount of creativity required, artist's previous experience, amount of time and artist expense.

MONTAGE RECORDS INC., 1221 Bainbridge St., Philadelphia PA 19147. (215)567-1697. Creative Director: Nancy Becker. Produces disco, soul, and rhythm and blues; group and solo artists. Recent releases: "Magic Touch," by Rose Royce; and "For You," by L.T.D.
Needs: Produces 30 records/year; works with 20 recording artists/year. Works with 3-4 visual artists/year. Uses artists for album cover design and illustration, advertising illustration and posters.
First Contact & Terms: Works on assignment only. Send query letter with brochure, business card and samples to be kept on file. Write for appointment to show portfolio. Prefers photographs or photocopies as samples. Samples not filed returned by SASE. Reports only if interested. Originals sometimes returned. Pays by the project, $100-1,000. Considers available budget, skill and experience of commercial artist and rights purchased when establishing payment. Negotiates rights purchased.

MOTOWN RECORD CORP., Graphics Dept., 16th Floor, 6255 Sunset Blvd., Los Angeles CA 90028. (213)468-3500. Art Director: Johnny Lee. Produces rock and roll, soul, pop, and rhythm and blues. Recent releases: "Lionel Richie," by Lionel Richie; "Touch the Sky," by Smokey Robinson; and "Throwin' Down," by Rick James.
Needs: Produces 50 records/year. Works with 30 freelance artists/year. Uses artists for album cover, catalog and advertising design and illustration; catalog and advertising layout and posters.
First Contact & Terms: Send brochure, samples and tear sheets to be kept on file; write for appointment to show portfolio. Prefers slides or photographs as samples. Samples not kept on file returned by SASE. Reports only if interested. Works on assignment. Originals returned after job's completion. Pay depends on the project. Considers complexity of project, available budget and how work will be used when establishing payment. Buys one-time rights.

MOUNTAIN RAILROAD RECORDS, INC., Box 1681, Madison WI 53701. (608)256-6000. President/Production Manager: Stephen Powers. Produces rock and roll, country/western, folk and pop. Recent releases: "The Paxton Report," by Tom Paxton; "Last Night In Town," by Betsy Kaske; and "Roy

Rogers Meets Albert Einstein,'' by Snopek.
Needs: Produces 10 records/year; 100% of the album covers were assigned to freelance designers, 20% to freelance illustrators. Assigns 10 freelance jobs/year. Uses artists for album cover and poster design and illustration. "No continuous theme, each cover relates to the specific group and album."
First Contact & Terms: "We tend to work more with artists in our area." Send query letter with brochure/flyer and samples. Samples returned by SASE. Reports within 1 month. Works on assignment only. Provide brochure/flyer, business card and samples to be kept on file for possible future assignments. Original work may be returned after job's completion. Negotiates payment by the project, $50-500 average. Considers complexity of project, available budget and rights purchased when establishing payment. Buys one-time rights or all rights.
Tips: Needs "art that sells the product. Think 'marketing.' Trend is toward more art, fewer photos."

MUSI-MATION, 135 E. Muller Rd., East Peoria IL 61611. (309)699-4000. General Manager: Martin Mitchell. Produces country/western and religious; solo artists. Recent releases: "Why Not Ask Jesus," by Joann Standridge; and "Follow Me," by Frank Radley.
Needs: Produces 20-30 records/year; works with 20-30 recording artists/year. Works with 2 visual artists/year. Uses artists for album cover design and illustration, brochure design and layout, advertising layout and direct mail packages.
First Contact & Terms: Send query letter with samples to be kept on file. Accepts any samples "which the artist feels displays his work best." Prefers to keep all samples. Reports within 2 weeks. Original art returned to artist. Pay is negotiable. Artist submits proposal stating how he wants to work. Negotiates rights purchased.

MYSTIC OAK RECORDS, 1727 Elm St., Bethlehem PA 18017. (215)865-1083. Project Coordinator: Bill Byron. Produces rock and roll, classical, new wave and experimental. Recent releases: "Dreams," by Office Toys; "I Don't Lie," by the Polygraphs; and "Believe It Or Not," by the Trendsetters.
Needs: Produces 4-16 records/year. Works with 6-12 freelance artists/year. Uses artists for album cover, brochure, and advertising design and illustration; and posters.
First Contact & Terms: Send query letter with brochure, resume, business card, samples and tear sheets to be kept on file. Prefers original work as samples. Samples not kept on file are returned by SASE. Reports only if interested. Returns original artwork after job's completion if requested. Pays by the project, $100-1,200 average. Considers complexity of project, available budget and how work will be used when establishing payment. Negotiates rights purchased.
Tips: Especially looks for a "developed style that can be used throughout an artist's career to identify and separate his work from others."

NEAT RECORDS (D.W.E. LTD.), 71 High St. E, Wallsend NE28 7RJ England. A&R Director: Diane Davison. Produces rock and roll, and pop. Recent releases: "All For One," by Raven; and "At War with Satan," by Venom.
Needs: Produces 10 records/year. Works with 2-3 visual artists/year. Uses artists for album cover design and illustration, and posters.
First Contact & Terms: Send query letter with samples to be kept on file. Prefers examples of printed sleeves, not originals, as samples. Samples not kept on file are not returned. Reports only if interested. No originals returned to artist after job's completion. Negotiates fees. Considers complexity of project when establishing payment. Negotiates rights purchased.

NERVOUS RECORDS, 4/36 Dabbs Hill Ln., Northolt, Middlesex England. 44-01-422-3462. Contact: R. Williams. Produces rock and roll, and rockabilly. Recent releases: "Roll Over," by Ronnie & the Jitters; "At My Front Door," by Freddy Frogs; and "Do You Feel Restless," by Restless.
Needs: Produces 7 albums/year; works with 7 groups and soloists/year. Works with 3-4 visual artists/year. Uses artists for album cover design, brochure design, catalog design and advertising design.
First Contact & Terms: Send query letter with samples; material may be kept on file. Write for appointment to show portfolio. Prefers tear sheets as samples. Samples not filed are returned by SAE (nonresidents include IRC). Reports only if interested. Original art returned to the artist. Pays by the project, $50-200 average. Considers available budget and how work will be used when establishing payment. Purchases first rights.
Tips: "We have noticed more use of imagery and caricatures in our field so fewer actual photographs used."

NEW ENGLAND ("HANK THE DRIFTER") HITS, Drawer 520, Stafford TX 77477. Produces country and western cassettes, albums, 45s and 8-track tapes.
Needs: Uses artists for record album and jacket design. Considers skill and experience of commercial artist when establishing payment. Send postage for reply and return of material.

NUCLEUS RECORDS, Box 111, Sea Bright NJ 07760. President: Robert Bowden. Produces country/western and pop. Recent release: "Pressure Cooker," by Jean Schweitzer.
Needs: Produces 1 record/year. Currently works with no freelance artists. Uses artists for advertising design.
First Contact & Terms: Artists with 3 years' experience only. Send query letter. Write for appointment to show portfolio. Prefers original work and photographs as samples. Samples are returned. Reports within 1 month. Originals returned to artist after job's completion. Considers skill and experience of artist when establishing payment. Buys all rights.

O.T.L. PRODUCTIONS, Suite 5, 74 Main St., Maynard MA 01754. (617)897-8459. Producer-In-Chief: David 'db' Butler. Produces rock and roll, soul, jazz, pop, rhythm and blues, and dance-oriented music. Recent releases: "Tina's Song," by Limbo Race; "Face in the Photograph," by TRAGUS; and "Suzanne," by Midnight Traveler.
Needs: Produces 6-9 records/year; works with 2-3 freelance artists/year. Uses artists for album cover design and illustration, advertising design, and posters.
First Contact & Terms: Artists capable of producing "excellent, totally professional quality" work only. Send query letter with brochure and samples to be kept on file. Prefers photographs as samples. Samples not filed are not returned. Reports only if interested. Sometimes returns original work after job's completion; "varies with agreement." Pays by the project, $150 minimum. Considers available budget, skill and experience of artist, turnaround time and rights purchased when establishing payment. Negotiates rights purchased.

OHIO RECORDS, Box 655, Hudson OH 44236. (216)650-1330. A&R Director: Russ Delaney. Produces country/western; group and solo artists. Recent releases: "Taste of the Blues," (single) and "Heeere's Ethel," by Ethel Delaney.
Needs: Produces 1 album, 2 singles/year. Uses artists for album cover design, brochure design and posters.
First Contact & Terms: Send samples to be kept on file. Accepts any samples. Samples not filed are returned by SASE. Reports only if interested. Pay is negotiable. Considers available budget when establishing payment.

P.M. RECORDS, INC., 20 Martha St., Woodcliff Lake NJ 07675. (201)391-2486. President: G. Perla. Produces jazz, pop, latin and funk. Recent releases: "A Very Rare Evening," by Nina Simone; and "Heads Up," by Stone Alliance.
Needs: Produces 2 records/year; 100% of the album covers were assigned to freelance designers and illustrators. Assigns 2 freelance jobs/year. Uses artists for album cover, poster, brochure, catalog and advertising design and illustration; and brochure, catalog and advertising layout.
First Contact & Terms: Prefers artists capable of "capturing the mood." Send brochure/flyer and samples; submit portfolio for review. Samples returned by SASE. Works on assignment only. Provide business card and samples to be kept on file for possible future assignments. Pays by the project.

*PETER PAN INDUSTRIES, 145 Komorn St., Newark NJ 07105. (201)344-4214. Creative director (A&R/Art): Rob Lavery. Produces rock and roll, disco, soul, pop, educational, rhythm and blues, aerobics and self-help; group and solo artists. Recent releases: "Total Shape Up," by Joanie Greggins; and "30 Minutes to Better Jogging," by Alberto Salazer (Olympic Champ).
Needs: Produces 15 records/year. Works with many visual artists each year. Uses artists for album cover design and illustration; brochure, catalog and advertising design, illustration and layout; direct mail packages; poster; and packaging.
First Contact & Terms: Works on assignment only. Send query letter with samples to be kept on file; call or write for appointment to show portfolio. Prefers photocopies or tear sheets as samples. Samples not filed are returned only if requested. Reports only if interested. Original artwork returned to artist. Payment open. Considers complexity of project and turnaround time when establishing payment. Purchases all rights.

POLKA TOWNE, 211 Post Ave., Westbury NY 11590. President: Teresa Zapolska. Produces polka records. Recent releases: "Dances of Poland," by Ted Maksymowicz Orchestra; "Jedzie Boat," by Frank Wojnarowski Orchestra; "Merry Christmas—Polish Carols," by Aria Choir; "I'm Proud To Be Polish" and "We're The Girls" by Teresa Zapolska Orchestra.
Needs: Uses freelance artists for album cover design and illustration; uses 4-color covers.
First Contact & Terms: Send tear sheets and samples to be kept on file for possible future assignments.; "no photostats." Samples must apply to the polka area only. Reply and samples returned by SASE. Reports within 6 weeks. Works on assignment only. Original work not returned to artist after job's completion. Negotiates flat fee. Buys all rights.

THE PRESCRIPTION CO., 70 Murray Ave., Port Washington NY 11050. (516)767-1929. President: David F. Gasman. Produces rock and roll, disco, soul, country/western, jazz, folk, pop, and rhythm and blues. Recent releases: "You Came In," by Medicine Mike (single).
Needs: Presently uses artists for album cover and advertising design and illustration; advertising layout; and direct mail packages. Future uses for poster, brochure, and catalog design and illustration; and catalog layout.
First Contact & Terms: Local artists considered first because of convenience. Send query letter and flyer or sample c/o Mitch Vidur (general manager). Prefers prints, posters, covers and brochures as samples. Samples not returned. "We contact artists when we need them." Works on assignment only. Original work not returned to artist after job's completion "unless by prior agreement." Negotiates payment by the project; considers complexity of project, available budget, how work will be used and rights purchased when establishing payment.
Tips: "What we need depends on the individual projects we take up." Sees trend towards work of a "higher quality—more sophisticated technique."

RANDALL PRODUCTIONS, Box 11960, Chicago IL 60611. (312)561-0027. President/Director: Mary Freeman. Produces rock and roll, disco, soul, country/western, jazz, pop, gospel, and rhythm and blues. Recent releases: "I Wanna Be With You," by Mickey Dee; "Power Funk" and "Everynite," by Power; and "Why Do You Do Me Like You Do", by Emmett Beard (single).
Needs: Produces 10-12 records/year. Works with 5 freelance artists/year. Uses artists for album cover, brochure, catalog and advertising design; photography; video; and posters.
First Contact & Terms: Send query letter with brochure and samples to be kept on file. Prefers original work and photographs as samples. Samples not kept on file returned by SASE if requested. Reports within 2 weeks. Pays by the project, $5-200 average. Considers complexity of project and available budget when establishing payment.
Tips: "We live in an age of identity, where the most liked are the least conservative."

*RARE RHYTHM RECORDS, 1 and 3 Lucy St., Manchester M15 4BX England. 44-061-872-3995. Managing Director: Kevin Kinsella. Produces rock and roll, country/western, folk, and rhythm and blues. Recent releases: "Rock Me," by Sham Lee Parker; "First Offence," by Steve McGarry; and "Hazard," by Blue Birds.
Needs: Produces 60 records/year. Works with 4-5 freelance artists/year. Uses artists for brochure and advertising design, illustration and layout; and album cover design and illustration.
First Contact & Terms: Send query letter with brochure, resume and business card to be kept on file; call or write for appointment to show portfolio. Prefers artists' working papers as samples. Reports within 6 weeks. Works on assignment only. Originals returned to artist after job's completion. Pay determined by arrangement. Negotiates rights purchased.

RAVEN RECORDS, 1918 Wise Dr., Dothan AL 36303. (205)793-1329. President: Jerry Wise. Vice President: Steve Clayton. Produces rock and roll, soul, country/western, pop, and rhythm and blues. Recent releases: "Runner in the Night," by Frontrunner; and "Tell Me That You Love Me," by Heart to Heart.
Needs: Produces 5-10 records/year. Works with 2 freelance artists/year. Uses artists for album cover and brochure design.
First Contact & Terms: "Most of our artists work on a speculation basis." Send query letter with brochure and samples to be kept on file. Call for appointment to show portfolio. Prefers "a combination of original work and photographs" as samples. Samples not kept on file returned by SASE. Reports within 30 days. Originals not returned to artist after job's completion. Pays by the project, $25-500 average. Considers available budget, turnaround time and rights purchased when establishing payment. Buys all rights.

*RCI RECORDS, INC., Box 126, Elmsford NY 10523. (914)592-7983. Contact: Art Director. Produces rock and roll, country/western, jazz and pop. Recent releases: "Tenamock Georgia," by Charlie Bandy; "Love You Right Of My Mind," by Charlie Bandy; and "I Aint Playin," by Fights.
Needs: Produces 15 records/year. Works with 4 freelance artists/year. Uses artists for album cover design and illustration.
First Contact & Terms: Send query letter with samples to be kept on file; call or write for appointment to show portfolio. Prefers photocopies or photographs as samples. Samples not kept on file are returned by SASE. Reports only if interested. Works on assignment only. Originals returned to artist after job's completion. Pays by the project, $100 average minimim. Considers complexity of project, available budget and turnaround time when establishing payment. Negotiates rights purchased.

RECORD COMPANY OF THE SOUTH, 5220 Essen Ln., Baton Rouge LA 70808. (504)766-3233. Art Director: Ed Lakin. Produces rock and roll, and rhythm and blues. Recent releases: "Don't Take It

Out On The Dog," by Butch Hornsby; "World Class," by Luther Kent; "Off My Leg," by Terry Burhans.
Needs: Produces 5 records/year; 20% of the album covers were assigned to freelance illustrators. Assigns 1 job/year. Uses artists for album cover and poster illustration, and direct mail packages.
First Contact & Terms: Prefers artists from the South. Make contact through agent; send query letter with brochure/flyer and samples. Prefers photostats and slides as samples. Samples returned by SASE. Reports within 3 weeks. Works on assignment only; reports back whether to expect possible future assignments. Provide brochure/flyer to be kept on file for possible future assignments. Original work returned to artist after job's completion. Pays by the project, $500-1,000 average; by the hour, $40-70 average; or a flat fee of $1,000 for covers. Considers complexity of project and available budget when establishing payment. "We generally buy first rights and reprint rights."
Tips: "Illustrators need to stay on the cutting edge of design." Make personal contact before sending samples. "Pastels—'Post Modern' colors are Hot."

*RED BUD RECORDS, A Division of CAE Inc., 611 Empire Mill Rd., Bloomington IN 47401. (812)824-2400. General Manager: Rick Heinsohn. Produces classical, country/western, jazz, folk, pop; group and solo artists. Recent releases: "Who Dunnit?" by Dave Porter; "Seventy-Five," by Josef Gingold; and "Guesswork," by Joel Erwin.
Needs: Produces 6 records/year; works with 6 recording artists/year. Works with 3 visual artists/year. Uses artists for album cover, brochure, catalog and advertising design, illustration and layout; direct mail packages; and posters.
First Contact & Terms: Works with professionals only; prefers local artists. Works on assignment only. Send query letter with business card and samples to be kept on file; write for appointment to show portfolio. Prefers tear sheets as samples. Samples not filed returned by SASE. Reports only if interested. Original artwork sometimes returned to artist. Pays by the project, $50-500 average. Considers complexity of project, available budgt and how work will be used when establishing payment. Negotiates rights purchased.

REVONAH RECORDS, Box 217, Ferndale NY 12734. (914)292-5965. Contact: Paul Gerry. Produces country/western and bluegrass.
Needs: Produces 6-10 records/year. Works with 3-4 freelance artists/year. Uses artists for album cover design.
First Contact & Terms: "Work must be of a professional grade." Works on assignment only. Send query letter with samples to be kept on file. Call or write for appointment to show portfolio. Prefers slides or actual work as samples. Samples not filed returned by SASE. Reports within 1 month. Works on assignment only. Return of original artwork after job's completion "can be negotiated." Pays by the project, $75-250 average. Considers complexity of project, available budget, skill and experience of artist, how work will be used, turnaround time and rights purchased when establishing payment. Buys all rights.

RHYTHMS PRODUCTIONS, Whitney Bldg., Box 34485, Los Angeles CA 90034. (213)836-4678. President: R.S. White. Record and book publisher for children's market.
Needs: Works on assignment only. Prefers California artists. Produces 12 records and cassettes/year; all of which have cover/jackets designed and illustrated by freelance artists. Works with 3 visual artists/year. Uses artists for catalog covers/illustrations, direct mail brochures, layout, magazine ads, multimedia kits, paste-up, album design and book illustration. Artists must have a style that appeals to children.
First Contact & Terms: Buys 3-4 designs/year. Send query letter, brochure, resume and samples. Accepts any type sample. SASE. Reports within 3 weeks. Buys all rights on a work-for-hire basis.

RMS TRIAD PRODUCTIONS, 6267 Potomac Cr., West Bloomfield MI 48033. (313)661-5167. Contact: Bob Szajner. Produces jazz records. Recent releases: "Jazz Opus 20/40," "Sound Ideas," and "Afterthoughts," all by the Bob Szajner Triad.
Needs: Produces 3 records/year; 100% of the album covers assigned to freelance designers/illustrators. Assigns 3 freelance jobs/year. Uses artists for album cover, brochure and advertising design and illustration; and brochure and advertising layout. Especially wants "anything innovative."
First Contact & Terms: Send query letter with brochure/flyer and samples or actual work to be kept on file for possible future assignments. Prefers original work as samples. Samples not returned. Reports within 2 weeks. Works on assignment only. Original work not returned after job's completion. Negotiates payment. Buys all rights.

ROBBINS RECORDS, HC80, Box 5B, Leesville LA 71446. National Representative: Sherree Stephens. Produces country/western and religious. Recent releases: "Jesus Amazes Me," "Wait till you See My Miracle Home," and "Since I've Had a Change of Heart," all by Sherrie Stephens.
Needs: Produces various number of records/year. Works with various number of freelance artists/year.

Uses artists for album cover design and posters.
First Contact and Terms: Send brochure to be kept on file. Write for appointment to show portfolio. Reports only if interested. Works on assignment only. Originals not returned to artist after job's completion. Pays by the project. Considers skill and experience of commercial artist, how work will be used and rights purchased when establishing payment. Buys all rights.

ROB-LEE MUSIC/ALL STAR PROMOTIONS, Box 1338, Merchantville NJ 08109. (215)561-5822. President: Rob Russen. Produces rock and roll, disco, soul and country/western. Recent releases: "I Came to Dance (I Came to Boogie)," by Phoenix; "Slow Down," by Philly Cream; and "Country Showdown," by Cross Country.
Needs: Produces 6 records/year. Works with 6 freelance artists/year. Uses artists for album cover, brochure and catalog design, and direct mail packages.
First Contact & Terms: Send query letter with brochure, resume, business card, samples and tear sheets to be kept on file. Prefers slides or photographs as samples. Reports only if interested. Originals returned after job's completion. Pay varies. Considers complexity of project, available budget, how work will be used and rights purchased when establishing payment. Buy first, reprint or all rights; negotiates rights purchased.

ROOFTOP RECORDS, INC., Box 669, Wilderville OR 97543. (503)474-1987. Coordinator: Laura Gattoni. Produces rock and roll, classical, pop, and rhythm and blues; group and solo artists. Recent releases: "Caught in the Act of Loving Him," by Servant; "Simple Direction," by Loyd Thogmartin; and "Prophets and Clowns," by Shelter.
Needs: Produces 4 records/year; works with 2 groups and 2 soloists. Works with 3 visual artists/year. Uses artists for album cover design and illustration.
First Contact & Terms: Send query letter with brochure, resume, business card and samples to be kept on file. Accepts photographs, tear sheets or copies as samples. Samples not filed returned only if requested. Reports only if interested. Original art sometimes returned. Pays by the project, $1,000 average minimum. Considers available budget when establishing payment. Purchases all rights.

ROSE HILL GROUP, 1326 Midland Ave., Syracuse NY 13205. (315)475-2936. Managing Director: Vincent Taft. Produces rock and roll, disco, pop and more. Recent releases: "Ocean Algae," by Taksim; "Lucky At Cards," by Kentucky; and "Skytrain," by Zarm.
Needs: Produces 5-10 records/year. Works with 5-10 freelance artists/year. Uses artists for album cover and advertising design, and posters.
First Contact & Terms: Send samples to be kept on file; write for appointment to show portfolio. Accepts "any legible format" as samples. Samples not filed returned by SASE. Reports only if interested. Works on assignment only. No originals returned after job's completion. Pays by the project, $50-500 average. Considers complexity of project and available budget when establishing payment. Negotiates rights purchased.

RUMBLE RECORDS INC., Box 202, Urbana IL 61801. (217)384-8258. Art Director: Beverly Dempsey. Produces rock and roll, pop, rhythm and blues, and dance music. Recent releases: "Power Wire Blues," by Luther Allison; "Jimmy & Hip Live," by Jimmy Dawkins and Hip Linkchain; and "Lovers End," by the Rave.
Needs: Produces 3 records/year. Works with 1-2 freelance artists/year. Uses artists for album cover and advertising design, and posters.
First Contact & Terms: Artists must be "imaginative and open-minded." Send query letter with resume to be kept on file; write for appointment to show portfolio. Reports within 1 month. Works on assignment only. Original art returned after job's completion "unless we purchase all of the rights." Pays by the hour, $5-40 average. Considers complexity of project, how work will be used and rights purchased when establishing payment. Negotiates rights purchased.
Tips: "Try to free yourself from personal preferences and approach the project from the consumer's point of view."

*S.O.S. RECORDS & TAPES, Box 1663, Warren MI 48090. (313)365-7294. President: Jeff Stirnweis. Produces rock and roll, and pop. Recent releases: "On the Move," by Nichel Romeo; "Street Life," by L.P.J.; and "Private Life," by Private Life.
Needs: Produces 3-4 records/year; works with 3-4 recording artists/year. Works with 2-3 visual artists/year. Uses artists for album cover, brochure and advertising design; brochure and advertising illustration and layout; and posters.
First Contact & Terms: Works with experienced artists on assignment only. Send query letter with brochure, resume, business card and samples to be kept on file. Prefers photostats and photocopies as samples. Samples not filed are returned. Reports within 3-4 weeks. Original artwork sometimes returned to

artist. Pays by the project, $150 minimum. Considers complexity of project, available budget, skill and experience of commercial artist and rights purchased when establishing payment. Purchases first rights or reprint rights or negotiates rights purchased.
Tips: "There are more available artists with newer and fresher designs. Being a new music agency working with the very newest talent has helped in keeping current."

*SAIN (RECORDIAU) CYF, Llandwrog, Caernarfon, Gwynedd, Cymru, U.K. 0286-831-111. Director: Dafydd Iwan. Produces rock and roll, classical, disco, country/western, folk, pop, educaional, ballad and traditional Welsh; groups, solo artists and choral. Recent releases: "Ave Maria," by Aled Jones; "Cerddi Fy Nawlad," by Stuart Burrows; and "Best of Welsh Folk," by various folk groups.
Needs: Produces 45 records/year; works with 40 recording artists/year. Works with 8 visual artist/year. Uses artists for album cover design and illustration, catalog and advertising design and layout, posters, and casette inlay design.
First Contact & Terms: Works mostly with local artists. Works on assignment only. Send query letter with samples to be kept on file; write for appointment to show portfolio. Prefers slides or photos as samples. Samples not filed are returned by SASE (nonresident use IRCs). Reports within 2 weeks. Original artwork sometimes returned to artist. Pays by the project, $100-400 average. Considers available budget, skill and experience of commercial artist, Welsh background and turnaround time when establishing payment. Purchases one-time rights.

SCARAMOUCHE RECORDS, Drawer 1967, Warner Robins GA 31099. (912)953-2800. President: Robert R. Kovach. Produces rock and roll, soul, country/western and pop.
Needs: Produces 6 records/year; 50% of the album covers assigned to freelance designers. Works with 3 recording artists/year. Works with 2 visual artists/year. Assigns 5 freelance jobs/year. Uses artists for album cover design and illustration; brochure design, illustration and layout; advertising design, illustration and layout; and posters.
First Contact & Terms: Send query letter with samples, brochure and resume to be kept on file. Prefers photocopies or tear sheets as samples. Samples returned by SASE. Reports within 3 months only if interested. Works on assignment only. Original art sometimes returned. Pays by the project, $25-300 average. Considers complexity of project, available budget, skill and experience of artist and rights purchased when establishing payment. Negotiates rights purchased.

SHANACHIE RECORDS CORP., Dalebrook Park, Ho-Ho-Kus NJ 07423. (201)445-5561. Art Director: Richard Nevins. Produces rock and roll, folk, pop, reggae and Irish music.
Needs: Produces 40 records/year. Works with 10 freelance artists/year. Uses artists for album cover design and illustration.
First Contact & Terms: Send query letter with samples and tear sheets to be kept on file; call or write for appointment to show portfolio. Prefers to review photographs and printed samples. Reports within 21 days. Artwork sometimes returned after job's completion. Pays by the project, $500 minimum. Considers complexity of project and available budget when establishing payment. Negotiates rights purchased.

SILVER BLUE PRODUCTIONS LTD., 220 Central Park S., New York NY 10019. (212)586-3535. President: Joel Diamond. Produces rock and roll, disco, country/western and pop. Recent releases: albums by Englebert Humperdinck, Helen Reddy, Sister Sledge, Gloria Gaynor.
Needs: Produces 20 records/year. All artwork is freelanced. Uses artists for album cover design and illustration, direct mail packages and posters.
First Contact & Terms: Send query letter with brochure, resume, business card, samples and tear sheets to be kept on file. Prefers original work or photographs as samples. Works on assignment only. Originals returned after job's completion. Negotiates pay. Considers complexity of project, available budget, skill and experience of artist, how work will be used, turnaround time and rights purchased when establishing payment. Negotiates rights purchased.

SINGSPIRATION MUSIC/RECORDS, Division of Zondervan Corp., 1415 Lake Dr. SE, Grand Rapids MI 49506. (616)698-6900. Contact: Phil Brower. Produces religious records.
Needs: Produces 20 records/year; all have cover/jackets designed and illustrated by freelance artists. Uses artists for design and illustration of albums and jackets.

The asterisk before a listing indicates that the listing is new in this edition. New markets are often the most receptive to freelance contributions.

First Contact & Terms: Query with photocopied samples of previous art to be kept on file for future assignments. Works on assignment only. Reports within 2 weeks. SASE. Negotiates pay.

Tips: There is a trend toward "computer art and more airbrush; also more emphasis on lettering and type." When reviewing work looks for technique, style and up-to-date material—"no school assignment work if possible."

SONIC WAVE RECORDS, c/o Kiderian Records, 4926 W. Gunnison, Chicago IL 60630. (312)399-5535. President: Tom Petreli. Produces rock and roll, rhythm and blues, and new wave. Recent releases: "New Wave Sampler," by Tom Petreli.

Needs: Produces 5-10 records/year. Assigns all jobs/year to freelance artists. Uses artists for album cover, poster, brochure, catalog and advertising design; and direct mail packages. Prefers "outrageous" covers.

First Contact & Terms: Send resume and samples. Prefers photostats and slides as samples. Reports within 1 month. Provide tear sheets, business card, resume and samples to be kept on file for possible future assignments. Samples not kept on file returned by SASE. Original work returned to artist after job's completion. Negotiates payment. Buys reprint rights.

SOUND SOUTH RECORDS, CAROLINA ATTRACTIONS & SOUND SOUTH TALENT, 203 Culver Ave., Charleston SC 29407. (803)766-2500. Assistant Manager: Chris Gabrielli. Produces rock and roll, soul, rhythm and blues, and beach music. Recent releases by Tams, Drifters, and Cornelius Brothers & Sister Rose.

Needs: Produces 6 albums/year. Works with 12 freelance artists/year. Uses artists for album cover design and direct mail packages.

First Contact & Terms: Send samples to be kept on file. Samples not kept on file are returned. Reports within 60 days. Works on assignment only. Originals returned after job's completion. Considers rights purchased when establishing payment. Buys all rights.

SOUNDS OF WINCHESTER, Box 574, Winchester VA 22601. (703)667-9379. Contact: Jim McCoy. Produces rock and roll, country/western and gospel. Recent releases: "Mr. Blue Grass," by Carroll County Ramblers; "Thank You Jesus," by Jubilee Travelers; "Going With Jesus," by Middleburg Harmonizers; and "The Outlaw," by Alvin Kesner.

Needs: Produces 18 records/year; 40% of the album covers were assigned to freelance designers. Assigns 3-4 freelance jobs/year. Uses artists for album cover and brochure design, and direct mail packages. Accepts "all types of scenes."

First Contact & Terms: Send material to be kept on file. Prefers original work as samples. Reports only if interested. Works on assignment only; reports back whether to expect possible future assignments. Provide brochure/flyer and samples to be kept on file for possible future assignments. Original work not returned to artist after job's completion. Pays by the project. Buys one-time rights.

STARBORN RECORDS INTERNATIONAL/A Division of Brian Ross Productions, Box 2950, Hollywood CA 90078. Chairman/President: Brian Ross. Full service record firm producing all categories of music including new wave/techno-pop. Recent album releases by Robert Jason, Music Machine and Didi Anthony, also Jamtrak from Chicago and Lance Powers Group.

Needs: Produces 25-50 records/year. Works with 5-10 freelance artists/year. Uses artists for brochure, catalog and advertising design, illustration and layout; album cover design and illustration; direct mail packages, posters, and corporate logos. "We are especially interested in logo designs. We need logos for album covers, artist names, corporate identity. Please send photocopies of your current logos for our examination."

First Contact & Terms: No experience necessary. "We don't buy what you have done in the past—we want to know what you can do for us. We advertise in over 50 publications world-wide." Send query letter with brochure, resume, business card, samples and tear sheets to be kept on file; write for appointment to show portfolio. Prefers to see comprehensives rather than pencil sketches. "The best presentations will be considered first. Show us examples of your artistic style please." Samples not kept on file are returned by SASE. Reports the same day. Works on assignment only. Originals returned to artist after job's completion. Pays "by the project as agreed upon by our firm and the artist. We show our appreciation by overpaying artists who work hard, are creative and whose work we are thrilled with. Those who turn in sloppy work are never used again." Buys all rights. "Our corporate brochures that are distributed world-wide are indigenous to our firm, and would have no relevance to an artist; therefore we request all rights to art work and logos used for business. We do pay a royalty."

STARTIME RECORDS, Fred Rice Productions, Inc., 48-780 Eisenhower Rd., Box 643, La Quinta CA 92253. President: Fred Rice. Produces rock and roll, country/western and educational. Recent releases: "Train of Life," by Rob Carter; "Johnny B. Bad," by Rockenstein; and "Quarterhorse," by Dale Robertson.

Needs: Produces 4 records/year; works with 4 recording artists/year. Works with 2-3 visual artists/year. Uses artists for album cover design and illustration, and liner art.
First Contact & Terms: Works on assignment only. Send query letter with samples to be kept on file. Write for appointment to show portfolio. Prefers photographs, photocopies or tear sheets as samples. Samples not filed returned by SASE. Reports within 1 month. Pays by the project, $250 minimum. Considers available budget when establishing payment. Purchases all rights. Original art is not returned to the artist.
Tips: Especially seeks "art with a new look, and exciting, provocative concepts to match music."

SUSAN RECORDS, Box 4740, Nashville TN 37216. (615)865-4740. Manager: Susan Neal. Produces rock and roll, disco, soul, country/western, rock-a-billy, jazz, pop, and rhythm and blues; group and solo artists. Recent release: "That's It Baby," by Dixie Dee.
Needs: Produces 15 records/year. Uses artists for album cover design and illustration; brochure design, illustration and layout; catalog design, illustration and layout; advertising design and layout.
First Contact & Terms: Send brochure, business card, SASE and samples to be kept on file unless return requested. Write for appointment to show portfolio. Prefers photographs as samples. Samples not filed returned by SASE. Reports within 15 days. Original art returned to the artist. Considers available budget and rights purchased when establishing payment. Negotiates rights purchased.

*3 G'S INDUSTRIES INC., 5500 Troost, Kansas City MO 64110. (816)361-8455. General Manager: Eugene Gold. Produces disco, soul, country/western, and rhythm and blues; group and solo artists. Recent releases: "Magic," and "Doin' It After Hours," by Suspension; and "Bootie Cutie," by Robert Newsome.
Needs: Produces 4 records/year. Works with 5 visual artists/year. Uses artists for album cover and advertising design, illustration and layout; and direct mail packages.
First Contact & Terms: Works on assignment only. Send samples to be kept on file; call for appointment to show portfolio. Prefers photographs as samples. Samples not filed returned by SASE. Reports only if interested. Original artwork not returned to artist. Negotiates payment by the project. Considers skill and experience of commercial artist when establishing payment. Negotiates rights purchased.

TMC PRODUCTIONS, Box 12353, San Antonio TX 78212. (512)735-3322. Business Manager: Joe Scates. Produces country/western, folk and comedy; group and solo artists. Recent releases: "Heartache County," by Ray Sanders; "High Heel Sneakers," by Carroll Gilley; and "Once More With Felling," by Carla Neet and Jerry Blanton.
Needs: Produces 15-20 records/year. Works with 2-3 artists/year. Uses artists for album cover design and illustration, and advertising illustration; occasionally uses humorous illustrations for album covers.
First Contact & Terms: Send query letter with samples to be kept on file. Prefers photostats or photocopies as samples. Samples not filed returned only if requested by artist. Reports only if interested. Pay is negotiable. Considers complexity of project, available budget, skill and experience of commercial artist and rights purchased when establishing payment. Negotiates rights purchased.
Tips: "I think much art work has become too animated or cartoon-orientated. I like good pen and ink drawings showing character and detail. Andrew Wyeth represents what I like in art."

TOTAL SOUND RECORDS, Box 741, Lake Charles LA 70602. Branch offices: Box 1659, Beverly Hills CA 90213 and Box 1003, Milford PA 18337. Contact: Dr. Lawrence Herbst. (Beverly Hills Music, K-Larr Broadcasting Network, Larr Computer Corp., Lawrence Herbst Investment Trust, Inc., Lawrence Herbst Records.) Produces all types of record products.
Needs: Uses artists for album design and illustration, poster design, ad design and layout, brochure and catalog design, illustration and layout, and direct mail packages. Sometimes buys cartoons and humorous and cartoon-style illustrations.
First Contact & Terms: Query with resume or brochure, business card and samples to be kept on file for possible future assignments; submit portfolio for review. Prefers photostats, slides or original work as samples. Samples returned by SASE only. Works an assignment only. Originals returned to artist at job's completion. Reports within 8 weeks. Pays $25 minimum; offers 14-20% royalties and advances. Buys all rights.

TUTCH MUSIC/RED HORSE RECORDS, Box 163, W. Redding CT 06896. Art Director: R. Kidd. Produces rock and roll, country/western and pop; solo artists. Recent releases: "Love You So Well," by Maureen Hutchinson; "Rest of Your Love," by Patty Terry; and "Memory of You," by Ken Scott.
Needs: Produces 10 records/year. Works with 3-5 visual artists/year. Uses artists for album cover design and illustration, and posters.
First Contact & Terms: Send samples to be kept on file if interested. Original art returned to the artist. Pays by the project. Considers available budget and how work will be used when establishing payment.

TYSCOT AND CIRCLE CITY RECORDS, 3403 N. Ralston Ave., Indianapolis IN 46218. (317)926-6271. Vice President, General Manager: Rick Clark. Produces disco, soul, rhythm and blues, traditional and contemporary gospel. Recent releases: "All Power," by Laura Lee; "Something Old, Something New," by Reverend Bill Sawyer. and "We're On Our Way," by Pentecostal Ambassadors.
Needs: Produces 20-25 records/year. Works with 4 freelance artists/year. Uses artists for album cover, brochure, catalog and advertising design; catalog and advertising illustration; advertising layout and posters. Artists are used primarily for album cover design.
First Contact & Terms: Send query letter with brochure, resume and samples to be kept on file; call for appointment to show portfolio. Accepts photostats, slides, original work or photographs as samples. Samples not kept on file returned by SASE. Reports only if interested. Works on assignment only. Originals returned to artist after job's completion. Pays by the project. Considers available budget when establishing payment. Negotiates rights purchased.
Tips: "We are open to all artists. We look for uniqueness and quality in an artist's work, whether the art portrays what is currently in the marketplace—whether the art is marketable," says president Leonard Scott.

VOICE BOX RECORDS, 5180-B Park Ave., Memphis TN 38119. (901)761-5074. President: Mark Blackwood. General Manager: Jerry Goin. Produces Christian music. Recent releases: "That Brighter Day," by the Blackwood Brothers; "We're In This Together," by Sparrow; and "Livin' For The Light," by Tony Pilcher.
Needs: Produces 5 records/year. Works with 3 visual artists/year. Uses artists for album cover, brochure, catalog and advertising design and illustration, and posters.
First Contact & Terms: Experienced artists only who can show a resume and examples of artwork done for other clients. Send query letter with resume, business card and samples to be kept on file; write for appointment to show portfolio. Prefers prints or photographs "so we can keep them for reference if we are looking for a certain style." Samples not kept on file returned by SASE. Reports within 1-2 weeks. Works on assignment only. No originals returned to artist after job's completion. Pays flat rate for each product according to time, effort and difficulty. Considers complexity of project, available budget, skill and experience of artist, how work will be used, turnaround time and rights purchased when establishing payment. Buys all rights.

WILCOX ORGANIZATION LTD (ZODIAC RECORDS), Zodiac House, 1099A Finchley Rd., London NW11 England. 01-455-6620. Executive Director: Herb W. Wilcox. Produces rock and roll, soul, country/western, jazz, folk, and rhythm and blues. Recent releases: "Blues and All That Jazz," by Jeannie Lambe and U.K. All Stars; "Store It Up Til' Morning," by Kim Lesley & All Star U.K. Bands; and "After You've Gone," by Earl Hines-Mussy Spainer All Stars.
Needs: Produces 6 albums/year. Works with 50 freelance artists/year. Uses artists for album cover, catalog and advertising design; catalog and advertising layout; catalog illustration; direct mail packages and posters.
First Contact & Terms: Send query letter with brochure, resume, business card, samples and tear sheets to be kept on file; write for appointment to show portfolio. Contact only through artist's agent. Prefers photostats or photographs as samples. Samples not kept on file returned by SAE (nonresidents include IRC). Reports within 7 days. Originals returned to artist after job's completion. Negotiates pay. Considers complexity of project and available budget when establishing payment. Negotiates rights purchased.

YAZOO RECORDS, INC., 245 Waverly Pl., New York NY 10014. (212)255-3698. Contact: Nick Perls. Produces jazz, folk, blues and ragtime. Recent releases: "Memphis Jug Band," by Memphis Jug Band; "Yazoo's History of Jazz," by various artists; and "Mississippi John Hurt," by M. John Hurt.
Needs: Works with 10 freelance artists/year. Uses artists for album cover design and illustration.
First Contact & Terms: Desires "only artists who have good technique and can do portraiture if asked. Oil, gouache or watercolor OK. No colored pencils." Send query letter with samples to be kept on file; call or write for appointment to show portfolio. Open to any form of sample. Samples not kept on file returned by SASE only if requested. Reports only if interested. Works on assignment only. Originals returned to artist after job's completion. Pays by the project. Considers complexity of project and rights purchased when establishing payment. Negotiates rights purchased.

Syndicates & Clip Art Firms ————

This clip artwork by Lynne Srba of Research Triangle Park, North Carolina, was reproduced as part of a series designed for use in pediatric department promotion, brochures and folders. Srba was paid $40 for all reproduction rights to the artwork. "The artist is excellent at rendering children and people in general," says William A. Ries, publisher of Hospital PR Graphics.

The two areas listed in this section, syndicates and clip art firms, play a common role in the freelance art market—both serve as the middleman between the artist and the art buyer. To the graphic artist, syndicates are synonymous with cartoon panels, editorial cartoons and comic strips, although they also provide editorial columns, puzzles and games to their newspaper clients. Clip art firms provide their clients—individuals and businesses—with camera-ready illustrations, cartoons, spot drawings and decorative art in various sizes for use in newsletters, brochures, advertisements and more.

Artists interested in approaching clip art firms with their work should keep in mind that most firms are looking for work that appeals to a mass audience. A variety of styles might be accepted, but the overwhelming priority is that the artwork reproduce well in black and white.

Clip art is becoming more and more imaginative and sophisticated in its subject matter, style and technique. Areas illustrated for today's market are diverse, ranging from animals and food to medicine and child abuse.

In the syndicate market, artwork must be original, timely and of universal interest in its direction and contents. Cliché humor no longer sells. Jeff MacNelly's syndicated strip, "Shoe," is popular not only because it is funny, but because its characters are atypically birds who do human things—like play tennis—and do them in unusual places—atop trees. Many syndicates see a continuing trend towards more sophisticated humor, such as Gary Larsen's "The Far Side," as more and more artists and readers are college-educated.

Selling your ideas and work to a syndicate isn't easy. The best approach is to have distinct characters—well-developed personalities—revolving around a central theme that carries through your work. Create several weeks' worth of work drawn in a size two to three times larger than the standard size of a daily strip. Keep story lines, illustration quality, ruling, spelling and lettering in mind while preparing your strip—lettering must be readable and illustration lines clear when the strip is reduced. Send quality photocopies or photostats. If a syndicate wishes to see originals, it will contact you.

For additional information on syndication read the Close-up in this section on Pulitzer Prize-winning cartoonist Mike Peters and the upfront article "Cartooning—Today's Marketplace." Both pieces offer advice on what it takes to get into the syndication market and what happens once you're there.

Names and addresses of other syndicates are available in *Editor & Publisher Directory of Syndicated Services.*

ADVENTURE FEATURE SYNDICATE, Suite 400, 329 Harvey Dr., Glendale CA 91206. (213)247-1721. Executive Editor: Orpha Harryman Barry. Syndicates to 200 newspaper and book publishers.
Needs: Buys from 20 freelance artists/year. Considers single, double and multi-panel cartoons. Prefers mystery, adventure and drama as themes. Also needs comic strips, and comic book and panel cartoonists.
First Contact & Terms: Works on assignment only. Send query letter with resume, samples and tear sheets to be kept on file; write for appointment to show portfolio. Prefers photostats as samples. Samples not kept on file are returned by SASE. Reports within 30 days. Pays 50% of gross income; on publication. Considers salability of artwork when establishing payment. Buys reprint rights; negotiates rights purchased.
Tips: "Comic strips need a four-week presentation package reduced to newspaper size."

CELEBRATION: A CREATIVE WORSHIP SERVICE, Box 281, Kansas City MO 64141. (816)531-0538. Editorial Office, 11211 Monticello Ave., Silver Spring MD 20902. (301)649-4937. Editor: Bill Freburger. Clients: Churches, clergy and worship committees.
Needs: Assigns 60/year. Uses artists for spot and line drawings on religious themes.
First Contact & Terms: Query; out-of-town artists only. Reports within 1 week. No originals returned to artist at job's completion. Pays $35/illustration.

*CLASSIFIED INTERNATIONAL ADVERTISING SERVICES INC., 3211 N. 74th Ave., Hollywood FL 33024. Contact: Art & Research Director: Clip art service. Clients: auto dealers, real estate agencies and newspapers.
Needs: B&w line drawings, cartoons and limited photography.
First Contact & Terms: Mail samples only please. Samples returned by SASE. Reports only if interested. Works on assignment only. Pays by the project. Considers complexity of project, and skill and experience of artist when establishing payment.
Tips: "We provide work for classifieds departments of newspaper firms. We have three sections to our service: automotive, real estate and self-promotion. Our company provides our service to all parts of the country, so our needs range so as to provide for the variety of tastes in the field of art. We provide cartoons, illustrations and realism, depending on the particular idea we're trying to convey."

COLLEGE PRESS SERVICE, 2629 18th St., Denver CO 80211. (303)458-7216. Art Director: Ed Stein. Syndicates to 600 college newspapers.
Needs: Buys 6 cartoons/week. "Looking primarily for single-panel cartoons dealing with campus and educational themes. No comic strips." Humorous and cartoon-style illustrations by commission only.
First Contact & Terms: Send query letter with samples. Prefers photostats as samples. Samples returned by SASE. Reports within 1 month. Returns original art after reproduction by arrangement with artist. Rights purchased vary. Negotiates payment according to project. Pays on publication.
Tips: Especially seeks "clean, professional display, strong and technically sound drawings and original, offbeat ideas. Like all publications, we are looking for cartoons aimed at our market: college students and faculty."

COMMUNITY AND SUBURBAN PRESS SERVICE, Box 639, Frankfort KY 40602. (502)223-1736. Editor/Publisher: Kennison Keene. Syndicates to 300 weekly, small daily and shopper publications throughout the USA, and 1,500 or more yearly.
Needs: Buys from 10 or more freelance artists/year. Considers double panel cartoons; illustrations and line drawings; b&w. Prefers humorous themes. Also uses artists for graduation and Christmas ads.
First Contact & Terms: Send samples; write for appointment to show portfolio. Write for artists' guidelines. "Usually cartoon artists will submit 8 or 9 cartoons at a time, together with SASE." Samples not kept on file returned by SASE. Reports within 1 week. Works on assignment only. "We pay $15/cartoon, if work is acceptable to us. Price to be negotiated on holiday greeting ads and graduation greeting ads." Pays on acceptance. Considers salability of artwork. Buys first rights.

COMMUNITY FEATURES, Dept. C, Box 1062, Berkeley CA 94701. Art Editor: B. Miller. Syndicates to 250 daily and weekly newspapers, shoppers, consumer magazines. Mails brochure of new syndicated offerings to 500+ newspapers. Guidelines $1 and #10 SASE. Specify artists' guidelines.
Needs: Interested in professional quality b&w illustrations, spot drawings, line art, square single, double and multi-panel cartoons; comic strips, illustrated educational panels, how-to, etc. Does not seek color. Looking for illustrators for regular weekly assignments, editorial cartoonists.
First Contact & Terms: Send samples (published and unpublished). Prefers tear sheets, veloxes, PMTs or excellent photocopies of art-boards. Reports within 2-6 weeks. Buys various rights. Purchases some one-shot. Will consider line-art on all topics listed in guidelines. Pays flat rate for one-shot and occasional work; 50% commission for regularly appearing features. Pays on publication.

Tips: "We look for a bold, modern look. Submit very clear copies with SASE if return is desired. We keep samples on file of illustrators' work and will contact as the need arises."

*COWLES SYNDICATE, INC., (formerly *The Register and Tribune Syndicate, Inc.*), Box 4994, Des Moines IA 50304. President: Dennis R. Allen. Submission Editor: Tom Norquist. Syndicates to 1,700 newspapers.
Needs: Buys several regular comic strips or panels/year. "We are looking for well-drawn, amusing/humorous comic strips (2 and 3 panel) to consider. Must have contemporary theme and apply to newspaper market; necessary to be consistently humorous. Continuity strips not marketable at this time. Submit strong representatives of versatility, art style, writing and humor abilities and background information of the concept as well as the background of creators of the comic."
First Contact & Terms: Submit work. SASE. Reports within 8 weeks. Buys all rights. Pays on publication.
Tips: "Three areas of importance I consider when evaluating a comic are: 1) topic; 2) artwork; 3) humor and storyline. Each area can be off slightly, as a syndicate can work with a creator, but copies of work submitted should best address those areas."

*CRONIN FEATURE SYNDICATING INC., 7688 S.W. 105th Place, Miami FL 33173. (305)595-6050. Director of Marketing: Henry Carlton. Syndicate serving 400 newspapers, magazines and television.
Needs: Buys form a varying number of freelance artists/year.
First Contact & Terms: Send query letter with samples. Prefers photocopies as samples. Samples returned only if accompanied by an SASE. Payment is open and negotiable; on publication. Considers client's preferences when establishing payment. Negotiates rights purchased.
Tips: "Be as brief as possible with letters and samples."

DYNAMIC GRAPHICS INC., 6000 N. Forest Park Dr., Peoria IL 61614. (309)688-8800. Art Director: Frank Antal. Distributes to thousands of magazines, newspapers, agencies, industries and educational institutions.
Needs: Works with 15-20 artists/year. Illustrations, graphic design and elements; primarily b&w, but will consider some 2- and full-color. "We are currently seeking to contact established illustrators capable of handling b&w highly realistic illustration of contemporary people and situations."
First Contact & Terms: Submit portfolio. SASE. Reports within 1 month. Buys all rights. Pays on acceptance. Negotiates payment.
Tips: "Concentrate on mastering the basics in anatomy and figure illustration before settling into a 'personal' or 'interpretive' style!"

PAULA ROYCE GRAHAM, 2770 W. 5th St., Brooklyn NY 11224. (212)372-1920. Contact: Paula Royce Graham. Syndicates to newspapers and magazines.
Needs: Considers illustrations; b&w. Also uses artists for advertising and graphics.
First Contact & Terms: Send business card and tear sheets to be kept on file; write for appointment to show portfolio. Write for artists' guidelines. Samples not filed returned by SASE. Reports within days. Pay is negotiable; on publication. Considers skill and experience of artist, client's preferences and rights purchased when establishing payment. Buys all rights.

GRAPHIC ARTS COMMUNICATIONS, Box 421, Farrell PA 16121. (412)962-2522. President: Bill Murray. Syndicates to 200 newspapers and magazines. Buys 400 pieces/year.
Needs: Humor through youth and family themes for single panel, strips and multi-panel cartoons. Needs ideas for anagrams, editorial cartoons and puzzles, and for new comic panel "Sugar & Spike."
First Contact & Terms: Query for guidelines. SASE. Reports within 4-6 weeks. No originals returned. Buys all rights. Pays 40% commission on acceptance.

GRAPHIC NEWS BUREAU, gabriel graphics inc, Box 38, Madison Square Station, New York NY 10010. (212)254-8863. Cable: NOLNOEL. Director: J.G. Bumberg. Custom syndications and promotions to customized lists, small dailies and selected weeklies.
Needs: Buys from 4-6 freelance artists/year. No dogmatic, regional or pornographic themes. Uses single panel cartoons, illustration, halftones in line conversions and line drawings.
First Contact & Terms: Prefers artists within easy access. Send query letter only. Reports within 4-6 weeks. Returns original art after reproduction on request. Provide 3x5 card to be kept on file for possible future assignments. Negotiates rights purchased and payment; on publication.

*HARRIS & ASSOCIATES PUBLISHING DIVISION, 615 Carla Way, LaJolla CA 92037-8002. (619)488-3851. Contact: Dick Harris. Syndicates to 200 newspapers.

"The artist's sensitivity in handling pathos and his ability to capture this in litho pencil on RossBoard made us select him for the assignment," says William A. Ries of Hospital PR Graphics in Kitty Hawk, North Carolina. This clip artwork by Joseph Stein of Bismarck, North Dakota, was "reproduced in our monthly subscription service, for hospitals as one of a series of illustrations on the subject of child abuse." Stein received $30 for all reproduction rights to the artwork.

Needs: Buys 10-12 cartoons/year on golf, tennis and families.

First Contact & Terms: Query with photocopies or roughs. SASE. Reports within 2 weeks. Buys all rights. Pays $5-25, b&w; on acceptance.

HISPANIC LINK NEWS SERVICE, 1420 N St. NW, Washington DC 20005. (202)234-0737. General Manager: Hector Ericksen-Mendoza. Syndicated column service to 200 newspapers and a newsletter serving 750 private subscribers, "movers and shakers in the Hispanic community in U.S., plus others interested in Hispanics."

Needs: Buys from 20 freelance artists/year. Considers single-panel cartoons; b&w pen & ink line drawings. Work should have a Hispanic angle; "most are editorial cartoons, some straight humor."

First Contact & Terms: Send query letter with resume and samples to be kept on file. Call for appointment to show portfolio or contact through artist's agent. Accepts photocopies as samples. Samples not filed returned by SASE. Reports within 3 weeks. Pays flat fee of $25 average; on acceptance. Considers clients' preferences when establishing payment. Buys reprint rights and negotiates rights purchased; "while we ask for reprint rights, we also allow the artist to sell later."

Tips: "While we accept work from all artists, we are particularly interested in helping Hispanic artists showcase their work. Cartoons should offer a Hispanic perspective on current events or a Hispanic view of life."

HOSPITAL PR GRAPHICS, Box 529, Kitty Hawk NC 27949. (919)441-3141. President: William A. Ries. Clip art firm. Distributes monthly to hospitals and other health care organizations.

Needs: Works wih 4-5 freelance artists/year (at present). Uses illustrations, line drawings, spot drawings and graphic symbols related to health care for use in brochures, folders, newsletters, etc. Prefers sensitive line illustrations, spot drawings and graphics related to hospitals, nurses, doctors, patients, technicians, medical apparatus. Also buys 12 cartoons/year maximum.

First Contact & Terms: Experienced illustrators only, preferably having hospital exposure or access to resource material. Works on assignment only. Send query letter, resume and samples to be kept on file. Prefers photostats or photocopies as samples. Samples returned by SASE if not kept on file. Reports within 1 month. Original art not returned at job's completion. Buys all rights. Pays flat rate of $20-60 for

illustrations; negotiates payment, varies according to project. Pays on acceptance.
Tips: "We are looking to establish a continuing relationship with at least 5-6 freelance graphic designers and illustrators. Illustration style should be serious, sensitive and somewhat idealized. Send enough samples to show the variety (if any) of styles you're capable of handling. Indicate the length of time it took to complete each illustration or graphic."

INTERNATIONAL ECO FEATURES SYNDICATE, Box 69193, West Hollywood CA 90069. (213)274-0954. Chief of Operations: Patrick C. Wall. Syndicate serving 100 daily newspapers, alternative newspapers, animal rights publications and alternative consciousness magazines.
Needs: Buys from 5-10 freelance artists/year. Considers single, double and multi-panel cartoons and illustrations; b&w pen & ink drawings. Prefers ecology, the environment and animal rights as themes. Also uses artists for "possible work on behalf of environmental groups with which we are associated."
First Contact & Terms: Send query letter with samples to be kept on file unless not appropriate for stated themes. Write for appointment to show portfolio "if you are in Los Angeles area; don't make a special trip." Prefers photocopies as samples. Samples not filed returned by SASE. Reports back only if interested. Pays 50% of gross income; on publication "when we receive client's check." Considers salability of artwork when establishing payment. Buys one-time rights.
Tips: "If your artwork does not concern the environment, ecology or animal rights, don't bother to submit to us."

INTERPRESS OF LONDON AND NEW YORK, 400 Madison Ave., New York NY 10017. (212)832-2839. Editor/Publisher: Jeffrey Blyth. Syndicates to several dozen European magazines and newspapers.
Needs: Buys from 4-5 freelance artists/year. Prefers material which is universal in appeal; no "American only" material. Uses single and multi-panel cartoons.
First Contact & Terms: Send query letter; write for artists' guidelines. Prefers to see photographs as samples. Samples not kept on file returned by SASE. Reports within 3 weeks. Purchases European rights. Pays 60% of net proceeds on publication.

KING FEATURES SYNDICATE, 235 E. 45th St., New York NY 10017. (212)682-5600. Contact: Bob Schroeter. Buys 300 cartoons/year for syndicated panel feature Laff-a-day.
First Contact & Terms: Submit roughs. SASE. Reports within 2 weeks. Buys all rights. Pays $50, cartoon panels, on acceptance.

*LOS ANGELES TIMES SYNDICATE, 218 S. Spring St., Los Angeles CA 90012. (213)972-5198. Comics Editor: David Seidman.
Needs: Comic strips, panel cartoons and editorial cartoons. "We prefer humor to dramatic continuity (although humorous continuity is certainly acceptable). We need cartoons that run daily only—that is, Monday through Saturday—or daily-and-Sunday. We don't plan to buy cartoons that run on Sunday alone." Cartoons may be of any size as long as they're to scale with cartoons running in newspapers. (Strips usually run approximately 6^{7}/16x2", panel cartoons 3^{1}/8x4"; editorial cartoons vary.)
First Contact & Terms: "Submit photocopies or photostats of 24 dailies. Submitting Sunday cartoons is optional; if you choose to submit them, send at least four of them. Coloring them is optional." Reports within 2 months. SASE. "We sign contracts with cartoonists to produce a set number of cartoons week after week. We send out about four contracts a year." Syndicate buys all rights. "We sell the cartoons to newspapers (if possible, we also sell merchandising rights) and split the net profit with cartoonists."
Tips: "Don't imitate cartoons that are already in the paper. We prefer original features rather than strips that copy 'Garfield' or 'Doonesbury,' or editorial cartoonists who emulate Conrad or MacNelly. Since newspapers print cartoons very small and on newsprint, be careful with clutter, pattern screens or fine details. Avoid items that might bleed together, fade out or reproduce too small to see clearly. Keep sex, alcohol, violence and other potentially offensive subjects to a minimum. Politics is OK if you avoid being strident. (Mind you, don't censor yourself too much or become bland. We'd rather you be too wild than too boring.) We're very open to hearing from cartoonists. To confer with the comics editor, telephone between 8 a.m. and 6 p.m. Pacific time and ask for David Seidman (pronounced Seedman). We hardly ever match artists with writers or vice versa. Whether you yourself write or you work with a writer, we prefer people or teams who can do the entire job of creating a feature."

METRO ADVERTISING & MARKETING SERVICES, 33 W. 34th St., New York NY 10011. (800)223-1600. Contact: Andrew Shapiro. Clip art firm. Distributes to 4,200 daily and weekly paid and free circulation newspapers, schools and ad agencies and retail chains.
Needs: Buys from 50 freelance artists/year. Considers single panel cartoons; illustrations and line and spot drawings; b&w and color. Prefers all categories of themes associated with retail, classified, promotion and advertising. Also needs artists for special-interest tabloid section covers.

First Contact & Terms: Send query letter with brochure, resume, business card, samples and tear sheets to be kept on file; call or write for appointment to show portfolio. Prefers photostats and slides as samples. Samples not kept on file returned by SASE. Reports only if interested. Works on assignment only. Pays flat fee of $50-500 average; on acceptance. Considers skill and experience of artist, salability of artwork and clients' preferences when establishing payment. Buys all rights.

Tips: "Metro provides steady work, lead time and prompt payment. All applicants are seriously considered. Don't rely on 1-2 samples to create interest. Show a variety of styles and special ability to draw people in realistic situations. If specialty is graphic design, think how you would use samples in advertising."

*MILLER SERVICES LIMITED, 45 Charles St. E, Toronto, Ontario M47 1S6 Canada. (416)925-4323. Features Editor: Valerie Carter. Syndicate serving approximately 200 daily and weekly newspapers.

Needs: Buys from 10 freelance artists/year. Considers single and multi-panel cartoons, editorial cartoons; b&w.

First Contact & Terms: Send query letter with resume and samples; call or write for appointment to show portfolio. Prefers photocopies as samples. Samples returned only by SASE. Reports within a few weeks. Artist receives 50% of gross income on publication. Cnsiders skill and experience of artist, salability of artwork and clients' preferences when establishing payment. Negotiates rights purchased.

MINORITY FEATURES SYNDICATE, Box 421, Farrell PA 16121. (412)962-2522. Chairman of the Board: Bill Murray. Clip art firm serving approximately 500 outlets.

Needs: Buys from 600 freelance artists/year. Considers single, double and multi-panel cartoons; illustrations and spot drawings. Prefers b&w pen & ink line drawings with family themes. Also uses artists for advertising art.

First Contact & Terms: Published artists only. Works on assignment only. Send query letter to be kept on file; write for artists' guidelines. Prefers photocopies as samples. Samples returned by SASE. Reports only if interested. Pay to artist is 50%; on acceptance. Considers rights purchased when establishing payment. Buys all rights.

Tips: "Submit only your best efforts."

NATIONAL CATHOLIC NEWS SERVICE, 1312 Massachusetts Ave. NW, Washington DC 20005. Picture Editor: Bob Strawn. Syndicates to Catholic religious press. Buys one-time rights. Pays on acceptance.

Needs: Religious or moral commentary 8x10" ink drawings/cartoons. Buys 4 cartoons/month; some humorous and cartoon-style illustrations. Pays $15-75 original illustration for religious education series; $15 gag cartoons. Especially looks for "simplicity, ability to capture an idea graphically and communicate it to a mass audience."

Tips: "This year we are looking for artists who can do simple line drawings of Catholic symbols and rituals. We will buy some on submission, others by assignment, but we will need to see samples before any assignments can be made. We also are looking for someone who can do maps and charts."

NATIONAL NEWS BUREAU, 2019 Chancellor St., Philadelphia PA 19103. (215)569-0700. Editor: Harry Jay Katz. Syndicates to 1,000 outlets and publishes entertainment newspapers on a contract basis.

Needs: Buys from 500 freelance artists/year. Prefers entertainment themes. Uses single, double and multi-panel cartoons, illustrations, line and spot drawings.

First Contact & Terms: Send samples and resume. Samples returned by SASE. Reports within 2 weeks. Returns original art after reproduction. Provide resume and samples to be kept on file for future assignments. Negotiates purchase rights. Pays flat rate; $5-100 for each piece on publication.

NEWS AMERICA SYNDICATE, (formerly Field Newspaper Syndicate), 1703 Kaiser Ave., Irvine CA 92714. President/CEO: Rick Newcombe. Syndicates to 2,500 newspapers. Titles include "Andy Capp," "Mary Worth" and "Dennis the Menace."

Needs: Considers cartoon strips; single, double and multi-panel; must have strong main characters and theme.

First Contact & Terms: Submit work (6-12 unpublished items) with cover letter. SASE. Reports within 2 months. Buys various rights. Pays royalties on publication. Free artists' guidelines.

NEWSPAPER ENTERPRISE ASSOCIATION INC./UNITED FEATURE SYNDICATE, 200 Park Ave., New York NY 10166. Editorial Director: David Hendin. Syndicates to more than 1,000 newspapers and periodicals.

Needs: Comic strip ideas, editorial cartoons and comic panels. Contact via mail. Send copies, not originals, and SASE for return. All submissions answered. If used in NEA Daily Service, pays flat fee. If used in syndicate division, 50% commission.

Tips: "We are looking for innovative comic features with interesting characters. There should be an idea behind your feature that allows it to be open-ended. Whatever the "staging," you need an on-going narrative structure."

OCEANIC PRESS SERVICE, Box 6538, Buena Park CA 90622-6538. (714)527-5651. Manager: Nat Carlton. Syndicates to 300 magazines, newspapers and subscribers in 30 countries. Titles include "What Every Woman Should Know About Men" and "How to Avoid Pressure."

Needs: Buys several hundred pieces/year. Considers cartoon strips (single, double and multi-panel) and illustrations. Themes include published sex cartoons, family cartoons, inflation, juvenile activities and jacket covers for paperbacks (color transparencies). Especially needs juvenile activity drawings and unusual sports cartoons; also sex cartoons. "God, sex and action is still a good formula. Poke fun at established TV shows. Bad economy means people must do their own home, car and other repairs. How-to articles with b&w line drawings are needed. Magazines will buy less and have more features staff-written. Quality is needed. People like to read more about celebrities but it has to have a special angle, not the usual biographic run-of-the-mill profile. Much will be TV related. I'd like to see a good cartoon book on Sherlock Holmes, on Hollywood, on leading TV shows."

First Contact & Terms: Query with work. Accepts tear sheets and clippings. SASE. Reports within 4 weeks. Buys all rights. Pays on publication. Originals returned to artist, or put on auction. Guidelines $1 with SASE.

Tips: "The trend is definitely toward women's market: money saving topics, service features—how to do home repair—anything to fight inflation; also unusual cartoons about unusual happenings; unusual sports; and cartoons with sophisticated international settings, credit cards, air travel. We would like to receive more clippings for foreign reprints. Competition is keen—artists should strive for better quality submissions."

PRESS ASSOCIATES INC., 806 15th St. NW, Washington DC 20005. (202)638-0444. Contact: Art Editor. News service serving "hundreds" of trade union newspapers and magazines.

Needs: Buys from 10-15 freelance artists/year. Considers single-panel cartoons; line drawings; b&w. Prefers humor, political and workplace themes—manufacturing, office, retail, etc.

First Contact & Terms: Send query letter with samples. Prefers original cartoons as samples. Samples not kept on file returned by SASE only if requested. Pays flat rate of $7.50; on acceptance. Considers clients' preferences when establishing payment. Buys first or reprint rights.

PROFESSIONAL ADVISORY COUNSEL, INC., Suite A-10, 7701 Broadway, Oklahoma City OK 73116. President: Larry W. Beavers. Syndicate serving approximately 1,000 international outlets.

Needs: Buys from over 30 freelance artists/year. Considers illustrations and spot drawings, b&w and color. Prefers camera-ready artwork. Also uses artists for advertising. Considers any media.

First Contact & Terms: Works on assignment only. Send query letter with brochure, resume, business card and samples to be kept on file if interested. Write for appointment to show portfolio and for artists' guidelines. Accepts any type of sample. Samples returned only by SASE. Especially looks for "simplicity and fast-relating/assimilating potential." Reports only if interested. Pays flat fee, $10-100 average; on acceptance. Buys all rights.

Tips: "We supply a 'phrase'—ten words or less—and the artist creates artwork based on the phrase. Make your contact quick, concise and to-the-point."

*PUBLICATIONS CO., 1220 Maple Ave., Los Angeles CA 90015. Contact: George Dubow. Distributes to inhouse publications.

Needs: Buys 8-10/month on general themes. Considers line drawings and pen & inks.

First Contact & Terms: Send art. Reports within 2 weeks. Previously published work OK. Buys all rights. Originals returned to artist only upon request. Pays $7.50-10; on acceptance.

SAWYER PRESS, Newspaper Feature Syndicate Dept., Box 46-578, Los Angeles CA 90046. President: E. Matlen. Syndicate and clip art to 100 national adult magazines, college newspapers, computer and electronics magazines, regional periodicals and book companies.

Needs: Buys from 50 freelance artists/year. Considers single, double and multi-panel cartoons; illustrations and line and spot drawings; b&w and color. Prefers pen & ink, line or washes, but considers all media. Emphasis on sexy, satirical, off-beat and pin-up themes. Generally works on assignment only, but open to unsolicited submissions. Send query letter with samples and tear sheets (if available); write for appointment to show portfolio. "We do not review portfolios without first seeing samples." Samples returned by SASE. Reports within 2-3 weeks. Pays flat fee of $10-25/illustration; payment varies for one-show versus a continuing feature/strip. Usually pays on acceptance; occasionally on publication. Con-

siders skill and experience of artist, salability of artwork, clients' preferences and rights purchased when establishing payment. Buys all rights.
Tips: "No nature/greeting card material please! Keep work very tight and professional and enclose SASE."

SINGER COMMUNICATIONS, INC., 3164 Tyler Ave., Anaheim CA 92801. (714)527-5650. Acting President: Natalie Carlton. Syndicates to 300 magazines, newspapers, book publishers and poster firms; strips include *They Changed History*, and *How It Began*. Artists' guidelines $1.
Needs: Buys several thousand pieces/year. Considers cartoon strips; single, double and multi-panel; family, children, sex, juvenile activities and games themes; universal material on current topics. Especially needs business, outerspace and credit card cartoons of 3-4 panels. Prefers to buy reprints or clips of previously published material.
First Contact & Terms: Send clips. "Prefer to see tear sheets or photocopies of published work." SASE. Reports within 2-3 weeks. Returns originals to artist at job's completion if requested at time of submission with SASE. Buys reprint or all rights; prefers foreign reprint rights. Pays 50% commission.
Tips: "Send us cartoons on subjects like inflation, taxes, sports or Christmas; we get thousands on sex. Everyone wants new ideas—not the same old characters, same old humor at the doctor or psychiatrist or at the bar. More sophistication is needed. Background is also needed—not just 2 people talking."

TEENAGE CORNER INC., 70-540 Gardenia Ct., Rancho Mirage CA 92270. President: David J. Lavin. Syndicates rights. Negotiates pay.
Needs: Spot drawings and illustrations.
First Contact & Terms: Query. SASE. Reports within 1 week. Buys one-time and reprint rights. Negotiates commission. Pays on publication.

TRIBUNE MEDIA SERVICES, INC., 720 N. Orange Ave., Orlando FL 32801. (305)422-8181. Editor: Mike Argirion. Syndicate serving daily and Sunday newspapers.
Needs: Seeks comic strips and newspaper panels.
First Contact & Terms: Send query letter with resume and samples. Prefers photocopies as samples. Samples not filed are returned. Reports back within 2-4 weeks.

UNITED MEDIA, 200 Park Ave., New York NY 10166. (212)557-2333. Art Director: Donald C. Demaio. Multimedia—United Feature Syndicate, NEA Feature Service, World Almanac, World Almanac Book Division for 800-1,000 newspapers and bookstores.
Needs: Buys from 25-50 freelance artists/year. Themes vary according to assignment. Uses illustrations, line and spot drawings, book jacket and brochure designs.
First Contact & Terms: Send samples and resume or write for appointment. Prefers 6-12 tear sheets or photostats as samples. Samples returned by SASE. Reports within 3 weeks. Return of originals after reproduction is negotiable. Provide resume and tear sheets to be kept on file for future assignments. Negotiates rights purchased and payment. Pays on acceptance.

UNIVERSAL PRESS SYNDICATE, 4400 Johnson Dr., Fairway KS 66205. Editorial Director: Lee Salem.
Needs: Comic strips and panels; text features.
First Contact & Terms: Include return postage with submission. Reports within 4 weeks. Buys syndication rights.
Tips: "A well-conceived comic strip with strong characters, good humor and a contemporary feel will almost always get a good response."

WEEKLY FEATURES SYNDICATE, (formerly *Dickson-Bennett International Features*), 126 S. 8th St., St. Joseph MO 64501. (816)364-2920. President: Gerald Bennett. Syndicates to 200 daily newspapers; titles include *Button's Bunch, Zany Cross-Word Puzzles and Tex Benson*.
Needs: "Seeks specialized material, drawn by top-quality artists with proven sales ability. We are getting more requests for speciality-type artwork, from cartoons to illustrations, also requests for color separation and art with text. This is highly specialized artwork and requires a very professional artist skilled in this field. We also buy crossword puzzles, 15x 15 squares with approximately 60 words across and down. Cartoons must be from professionals with the ability to do not only b&w work but also color." May use cartoon-style illustrations; depends upon the material needed for publication.
First Contact & Terms: "Write to Comic Art Editor; send samples of work and ask for type of work needed." Submit camera-ready (reduced to correct size—strips 2¼x7; single panel 3½x3½). First showing can be photocopy. "We need to see 8-10 sample pieces to determine style and acceptability." SASE. Reports within 6 weeks. Originals only returned upon request. Pays 50% commission. Artists' guidelines for SASE.

Tips: "Daily newspapers are asking more for special features, such as crossword puzzles on sports, general subjects or celebrity stars. Puzzles must be camera-ready. (We do not finish artist's work, such as typesetting of puzzles). The dailies also want kid features and new ideas for their Sunday sections. Show your feature to many newspaper editors in your locale before sending it off to a syndicate for consideration. An artist must be willing and able to furnish us with at least one complete year's material upon acceptance of his new feature (52 drawings). Be sure in your mind that a cartoon strip or panel is what you really want in life and then give 100% to it. Do not expect to become rich over night. Be prepared to work with your syndicate at least 5 years if need be. The small syndicates need your co-operation and help in any way you can. Try to see how you can help them sell your feature. We now have sales agents in 48 countries overseas."

WIDEWORLD ART STUDIOS, Box 20056, St. Louis MO 63144. Director: John Ford. Syndicates to 30 regional magazines.
Needs: Buys from 12 freelance artists/year. Uses illustrations, line and spot drawings.
First Contact & Terms: Send samples or submit portfolio for review. Prefers photostats as samples. Samples returned by SASE. Reports within 2 weeks. Returns original art after reproduction. Provide tear sheets to be kept on file for future assignments. Buys one-time rights. Negotiates payment. Pays on acceptance.

WRITERS CLEARINGHOUSE, Fabyan Rd., Box 118, Fabyan CT 06245. (203)923-9925. Managing Director: Richard D. Carreno.
Needs: Buys from 5 freelance artists/year. Considers illustrations, line and spot drawings; b&w. Uses artists for advertising, publicity, promotion, brochure and marketing.
First Contact & Terms: Prefers regional artists because of convenience. Do not need to have been published before, but work must be of professional quality. Send query letter with brochure, resume, business card, samples and tear sheets to be kept on file. "Telephone for appointment. We don't encourage prospecting." Prefers photocopies as samples. Samples not kept on file returned by SASE. Reports within 3 weeks (send SASE). Works on assignment only. Pay is a flat fee per job; on acceptance. Considers skill and experience of artist, salability of artwork and clients' preferences when establishing payment. Buys all rights or negotiates rights purchased. "Material copyrighted at times."
Tips: "Keep trying. I will assist qualified artists in placing work elsewhere if their work doesn't meet my needs, but only after I've established a relationship with the artists."

Art Publishers/Distributors

This section, listing art publishers and distributors, is included in this directory to allow graphic designers, illustrators, and those artists who frequently cross the line between graphic and fine art, the opportunity to have their artwork reproduced and distributed.

During the past two years the art buyers in this market have witnessed an increase in the popularity and sales of offset reproductions (posters and limited edition prints) and hand-pulled original prints. To satisfy the market's demand, publishers and distributors continue to work with an increasing number of freelance artists. For the fine or graphic artist, this strengthening—evidenced by 38 new listings this year—translates into an immediate opportunity to promote your artwork on a large scale and to give your freelance career a hardy push.

Before entering this market, you need to understand the three possible roles you could play as a freelancer. The first is to work with a publisher who both prints and distributes your artwork. Secondly, you can find a company to distribute your *already* printed posters or prints. Finally you can work exclusively with a publisher/distributor as a printmaker and produce your own handpulled print editions.

Before contacting an art publisher, study the information in his listing

This Samuel Beckett linocut by Rachael Romero of New York City was reproduced on a postcard as part of a series "Innovators in the Arts," published by Leon Klayman Publishing, New York City. Klayman, publisher, liked Romero's "bold, clear, strong, human and dramatic style. The work has been well received," he adds. "The artist has a clear understanding of how her work translates into print."

to determine the art styles and media he seeks. Study the advertisements and the articles in *Decor* and *Art Business News* to keep up on current themes, styles and trends.

If your artwork is accepted by an art publisher/distributor, don't expect overnight success. It takes time to market fine art posters and prints, and if your work is unknown it takes time to build a following. Payment methods vary throughout this market. You can be paid a flat fee for all or partial reproduction rights, a royalty on prints sold or a combination of these two methods.

Read the upfront article "Breaking into Specialty Art Markets" for more information on payment methods, reproduction rights, how to contact publishers and how to stay on top of trends and changes in the field. Also, in this section is the Close-up with Kelly Omana, president of Art Beats Inc., a small but successful art publisher/distributor in Salt Lake City. Omana offers artists the publisher's perspective of the industry—what she looks for in artwork, how she pays and more.

AARDVARK ART, INC., 1100 Bryn Mawr, Bensenville IL 60106. (312)766-0400. President: Gerald McGlothlin. Produces limited and unlimited edition art reproductions for galleries. Publishes 10 artists/year. Negotiates ownership of original art. Send letter of inquiry and photos of art. SASE.
Acceptable Work: High-tech artwork. Must be very graphic and reflect a lifestyle of high status and elegance. Photography and artwork of all kinds considered. Size to be proportional to 12x16", 18x24", or 24x36".

AARON ASHLEY INC., Room 1905, 230 5th Ave., New York NY 10001. (212)532-9227. Contact: Philip D. Ginsburg. Produces unlimited edition fine quality 4-color offset and hand colored reproductions for distributors, manufacturers, jobbers, museums, schools and galleries. Publishes "many" new artists/year. Pays royalties or fee. Offers advance. Exclusive representation for unlimited editions. Written contract. Query, arrange interview or submit slides or photos. SASE. Reports immediately.
Needs: Unframed realistic and impressionistic paintings, especially marine, landscapes, sportings, florals, botanicals and Americana.

*ALJON INTERNATIONAL, 1481 SW 32 Ave., Pompano Beach FL 33069. (305)971-0070. President: Ronald Dvoretz. Art distributor of watercolors, acrylic and oil paintings, enamels on copper and collages. Clients: galleries, furniture stores, home show people, interior designers and other wholesalers and jobbers. Distributes work for 18 domestic artists/year. Pays flat fee. Negotiates payment method; very often pays on weekly basis. Negotiates rights purchased. Required exclusive representation. Provides insurance while work is at distributor, promotion and shipping to and from distributor. Send query letter with brochure and samples. Call or write for appointment to show portfolio. Prefers slides or photos or originals as samples. Samples returned only if requested. Reports only if interested.
Acceptable Work: Considers oil and acrylic paintings, watercolors, mixed media and enamels on copper. Especially likes large (4'x5' or larger) acrylic abstracts—can be college work.
Tips: "Disregard retail pricing and come equipped with adequate samples. We must know colors. Subject matter is not of utmost importance."

APPLE ARTS, LTD., Industrial Complex, Rt. 33 E, Freehold NJ 07728. (201)462-8686. President: M. Lav. Produces limited edition hand-pulled originals, positones and aluminum plate lithographs for own publishing and distribution, and custom work for the trade. Publishes 40-80 artists/year. Pays flat fee. Offers advance. Buys all rights. Provides promotion and shipping. Artist owns original art. Arrange interview. SASE. Reports in 2 weeks. Needs unframed woodcuts, etchings and lithographs.

*HERBERT ARNOT, INC., 250 W. 57th St., New York NY 10019. (212)245-8287. President: Peter Arnot. Art distributor of original oil paintings. Clients: galleries. Distributes work for 250 artists/year. Pays flat fee, $100-1,000 average. Provides promotion and shipping to and from distributor. Send query letter with brochure, resume, business card and samples to be kept on file. Call or write for appointment to show portfolio. Prefers slides, photographs or original work as samples. Samples not filed are returned. Reports within 1 month.
Acceptable Work: Considers oil and acrylic paintings. Has wide range of themes and styles—"mostly traditional/impressionistic, not modern."
Tips: "Professional quality, please."

*ART BEATS, INC., 2435 S. Highland Dr., Salt Lake City UT 84106. (801)487-1588. President: Kelly Omana. Vice President: Jill Gerrard. Art publisher and distributor of limited and unlimited editions and offset reproductions. Clients: gift shops, frame stores, department stores and galleries. Publishes 8 freelance artists/year. Distributes work for 20 or more artists/year. Pays royalty of 10%; negotiates payment method. Prefers to buy all rights, but will make exclusions. Provides promotion and written contract. Send query letter with or without samples to be kept on file; or call or write for appointment to show portfolio. Accepts slides, photographs, tear sheets, original work or photostats as samples. Samples not filed returned only if requested. Reports within 1 month.
Acceptable Work: Considers oil and acrylic paintings, pastels, watercolors and mixed media; no b&w. Especially likes children's, country and floral themes, "but always interested in new things."

ART IMAGE INC., 1577 Barry Ave., Los Angeles CA 90025. (213)826-9000. President: Allan Fierstein. Publishes and produces limited editions that are pencil signed and numbered by the artist. Also distributes etchings, serigraphs, lithographs and water color paintings. All work sold to galleries, frame shops, framed picture manufacturers, interior decorators and auctioneers. Publishes 12-16 artists per year. Negotiates payment, provides promotion. Query to arrange interview or send photos or slides. SASE. Reports within 1 week.
Acceptable Work: "All subject matter and all media in pairs or series of companion pieces."
Tips: "We are publishing and distributing more and more subject matter from offset limited editions to etchings, serigraphs, lithographs and original water color paintings."

Close-up

Kelly Omana, President
Art Beats, Inc.
Salt Lake City, Utah

Artist: David R. Smiton

Opportunities abound within the graphic arts industry for artists and nonartists alike to learn, grow and find new directions. Several years' experience as a framer/co-manager for a successful frame shop enabled Kelly Omana to gain insight into the fine art poster industry. Her awareness included knowledge of interior design color and style trends, and the most salable subject matter. Armed with this inside information, Omana joined forces with artist/framer Jill Gerrard in 1982 to establish Art Beats—a new career direction for both women.

Omana and Gerrard find today's poster industry to be highly competitive because of the burgeoning of poster publishers throughout the country. The key to Art Beats' success is its fresh image. "We have our own unique look, something a little different from what everyone else offers," explains Omana. "We aren't interested in going the way of the traditional poster company by large expansion."

Omana and Gerrard are open-minded regarding the art styles, media and themes they consider. "We found a void in the juvenile art market when we began. We plan to continue expanding our children's line, but don't want to limit ourselves exclusively to that. We constantly try to broaden our line into new areas."

The freelance artist finds advantages to working with this Utah art publisher. The artist's name is incorporated into the poster, and Omana sees this as the artist's greatest advantage because of the advertisement and promotion. "Most artists have a fairly limited following and marketing area. We open this up completely. If a poster is good, the financial rewards go without saying. A good poster will sell no matter what the reputation of the artist. But do not expect overnight success; it usually takes several months to build the channels through which the poster is marketed."

What determines the marketability of a particular work of art? "I don't think there is a set formula to determine this," says Omana. "If there were, publishing would be easy and all the risks for a publisher would be gone. Jill and I usually have an emotional response to a piece of artwork. By emotional I don't mean sentimental, but the kind of response any good art evokes. Even with that, there are some wonderful pieces of art that simply won't work as posters."

A positive artist-publisher relationship is important to these businesswomen. "We like to work with someone who is excited about working with us. It's really a symbiotic relationship, and each party must understand and respect the service which the other provides. An artist who is overly arrogant is often not worth the trouble. An artist must be professional, consistent in his work quality, able to accept criticism and direction, and willing to meet deadlines."

Omana offers additional advice for artists interested in approaching an art publisher. "Too many times artists bring in portfolios with unfinished pieces or send unprofessional, out-of-focus snapshots to represent their work. We like to see samples of finished products suitable for production into poster format. Your images should be drawn well with good composition and a sense of design. Color is critical. Be aware of what colors are currently popular for home interiors. Fashion magazines give previews of upcoming colors a year or more in advance. Develop your own style. A successful poster is unique due to its freshness and originality."

Dawna Barton Watercolors
art beats editions

"This unlimited edition fine art poster by local artist Dawna Barton is one of our top sellers," explains Gerrard. "We were attracted to the fresh, natural style of the artist and thought the piece had a nice feeling with mass appeal."

side-car

"We were attracted to the clean, simple style and strong design element in this piece. We felt that it was contemporary yet had an almost nostalgic feeling," says Gerrard. The artwork by David R. Johnsen was reproduced as a fine art poster.

*ART 101 LTD., 1401 Chattahoochee Ave. NW, Atlanta GA 30318. (404)351-9146. Creative Director: Kenneth Grooms. Art publisher of unlimited editions. Clients: gift and card shops. Pays flat fee of $500-1,500 average. All work as "work for hire," fees negotiated. Offers advance. Buys all rights. Provides shipping to firm and written contract. Send query letter with brochure, resume and samples to be kept o file; or call or write for appointment to show portfolio. Prefers original work as samples. Samples not filed are returned. Reports within 10 days.
Acceptable Work: Posters combine extensive copy and specially selected type with strong graphic design. Illustrations are secondary to the copy and design.

ART RESOURCES INTERNATIONAL, LTD., (formerly RR Art Resources International, Ltd.), 7 Depinedo Ave., Stamford CT 06902. (203)967-4545, (800)228-2989. Vice President: Robin E. Bonnist. Art publisher. Publishes unlimited edition offset lithographs. Clients: galleries, department stores, distributors, framers throughout the world. Publishes 30 freelance artists/year. Also uses artists for advertising layout and brochure illustration. Pays by royalty. Offers advance in some cases. Negotiates rights purchased. Requires exclusive representation of the artist for prints/posters during period of contract. Provides in-transit insurance, insurance while work is at publisher, promotion and a written contract. Artist owns original work. Send query letter with brochure, resume and samples to be kept on file or returned if requested; call or write for appointment to show portfolio. Prefers to see slides initially as samples, then reviews originals. Samples not kept on file returned by SASE. Reports within 1 month.
Acceptable Work: Considers oil and acrylic paintings, pastels, watercolors and mixed media. Prefers pairs or series.

ART SOURCE, Unit 10, 70 Gibson Dr., Markham, Toronto, Ontario L3R 4C2 Canada. (416)475-8181. Art publisher and distributor. Produces posters, offset reproductions, handpulled originals; and prints using offset, lithograph, screen and etching for galleries and department stores. Publishes 20 freelance artists/year. Negotiates payment method. Possibly offers advance. Negotiates rights purchased. Provides insurance while work is at publisher, promotion and a written contract. Negotiates ownership of original art. Send query letter with brochure, resume, business card, samples and tear sheets to be kept on file. Call or write for appointment to show portfolio. Samples not kept on file returned by SASE if requested. Reports within 14 days.
Acceptable Work: Considers oil and acrylic paintings, pastels, watercolors, mixed media and photographs. Themes and styles open. Prefers pairs and series; unframed.
Tips: "Show us your work in its best possible way. We see you through what you show us." One of today's most popular mediums is the poster—"we publish many of them." Artists should be very sensitive to the needs of the markets where they are trying to sell their work.

ART SPECTRUM, division of Mitch Morse Gallery, Inc., 305 E. 63rd St., New York NY 10021. (212)593-1812. President: Mitch Morse. Art publisher. Produces limited editions (maximum of 250 prints) and handpulled originals—all 'multi-original' editions of lithographs, etchings, collographs, serigraphs. Serves galleries, frame shops, interior designers, architects hotels and corporate art specifiers. Publishes 8-10 freelance artists/year. Negotiates payment method. Offers advance. Negotiates rights purchased. Artist owns original art. Send query letter with samples to be kept on file. Call for appointment to show portfolio. Prefers original work and slides as samples. Samples not kept on file are returned. Reports within 1 week.
Acceptable Work: Considers original fine art prints only. Offers "subjects primarily suitable for corporate offices. Not too literal; not too avant-garde." Prefers series; unframed (framed unacceptable); 30x40"maximum.
Tips: "Do not stop by without appointment. Do not come to an appointment with slides only—examples of actual work must be seen. No interest in reproductive (photo-mechanical) prints—originals only. Submit work that is "an improved version of an existing 'look' or something completely innovative." Trends show that the "current demand for contemporary has not yet peaked in many parts of the country. The leading indicators in the New York City design market point to a strong resurgence of Old English."

ART VENTURES, LTD., (formerly Northern Lights Press), 315 West 9th St., Bottineau ND 58318. (701)228-3855. President: Mike Haberman. Art publisher/distributor/gallery. Produces limited and unlimited editions of offset reproductions using a 4-color process—"Up to 15 colors as needed by print." Clients: galleries. Publishes 4-5 freelance artists/year. Also uses artists for advertising layout and brochure illustration. Negotiates payment method. Offers advance. Buys all rights. Provides in-transit insurance, insurance while work is at publisher, promotion, shipping to publisher, shipping from publisher and a written contract. Negotiates ownership of original art. Send query with brochure, resume, business card and tear sheets to be kept on file; also send samples; call or write for appointment to show portfolio. Accepts photostats, slides or photographs as samples; original work if possible. Samples not kept on file returned only if requested. Reports within 3 weeks.

An invitation

to all artists: beginners . . . serious amateurs . . . professionals . . . art educators . . . art students . . .

to accept an examination copy of America's newest, most exciting how-to magazine for artists

with our compliments and without obligation.

See for yourself how THE ARTIST'S MAGAZINE can make you a better artist. Return the postage-paid card below and get a free introductory issue to read and use in your work.

With your free-examination copy we'll enter a 100% NO RISK Introductory Subscription for you . . . at a $9.00 savings off the regular price. If THE ARTIST'S MAGAZINE doesn't help you improve your skills, simply write "cancel" on our invoice, return it and keep the sample issue *with our compliments.*

In your introductory issue you'll see:

- Colorful, step-by-step instruction from America's top art professionals.
- Practical information on how and where to exhibit and sell your artwork.

- Regular columns on technique, questions and answers, new products and issues of interest both to amateurs and professionals
- The latest updates on books, seminars, tools and competitions for artists.

To accept this invitation

just phone our TOLL FREE number and charge your subscription to your credit card. Or tear off and mail this card today — no postage is needed.

1-800-341-1522
(in Maine call collect 236-2896)

Free Issue Offer

YES! Send me a free-examination copy of THE ARTIST'S MAGAZINE. If the magazine doesn't help me improve my skills and show me how and where to exhibit and sell my work, I'll return your invoice marked "cancel" and owe nothing . . . or I'll honor it and pay just $15* for the next 11 issues (12 in all). That's a $9.00 savings off the regular subscription price!

Initial here: _____

NAME

ADDRESS

CITY   STATE   ZIP

Watch for your first issue to arrive in five weeks!

*Additional $4 postage billed for Canadian and foreign subscriptions.

VAM86-1

America's top artists show you how they create their work in practical step-by-step instruction

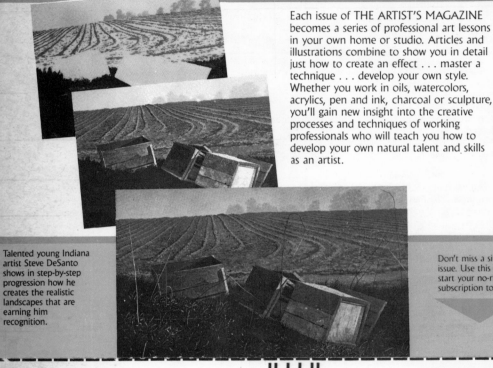

Each issue of THE ARTIST'S MAGAZINE becomes a series of professional art lessons in your own home or studio. Articles and illustrations combine to show you in detail just how to create an effect . . . master a technique . . . develop your own style. Whether you work in oils, watercolors, acrylics, pen and ink, charcoal or sculpture, you'll gain new insight into the creative processes and techniques of working professionals who will teach you how to develop your own natural talent and skills as an artist.

Talented young Indiana artist Steve DeSanto shows in step-by-step progression how he creates the realistic landscapes that are earning him recognition.

Don't miss a single issue. Use this card to start your no-risk subscription today.

Acceptable Work: Considers pen & ink line drawings, oil and acrylic paintings, pastels, watercolor and mixed media. Prefers Western, wildlife, landscape, modern themes. Prefers individual works of art or series.

*ARTAFAX SYSTEMS LTD. INC., Box 568, N. Commercial St., Manchester NH 03105. (603)669-3162. President: Robert Arens. Contract art publisher. Publishes hand-painted and hand-screened originals for architects, interior designers and specifiers for the contract furnishings market. Query with contact sheets, slides or photos of art; prefers out-of-town artists and photographers. Reports within weeks. Provides promotion, shipping from publisher and written agreement. Also needs "nostalgia photos—old trains, airplanes, automobiles and city scenes."
Acceptable Work: Line drawings and photos, primarily nature-oriented. "Our present line is primarily hard-edge geometric in nature (hand-painted by our own people in various sizes as specified by the purchaser). We plan to increase our screen printing department to include other 'themes' and styles as required by the contract art market." Especially needs items that we can screen-print on fabric, one or two colors, large sizes. Negotiates pay.
Tips: "When designing for two or three colors, registration is key concern since most items are in the 2x4' to 4x8' range."

*ARTHUR'S INTERNATIONAL, Box 10599, Honolulu HI 96816. President: Marvin C. Arthur. Art distributor handling original oil paintings primarily and also limited edition prints. Clients: galleries, collectors, etc. "Normally we purchase and pay for all art works handled. Exceptions have been made, though rarely, for other forms of representations." Negotiates payment determined by the talents of artist and his wants. "Artists may be represented on an exclusive basis for the Hawaiian Islands and to our own international gallery customers. May be on a selective per picture arrangement or encompass the taking on of all works produced." Provides agreement or contract. "We promote items purchased." Send brochure and samples to be kept on file if interested. Send slides or photographs as samples; no originals. Samples not filed returned by SASE. Reports back normally within 1 week.
Acceptable Work: Considers oil paintings; serigraphs, stone ithographs, plate lithographs, and gravures. "All paintings should be photographic in texture or have an eye appeal of the subject matter that is not a modern art puzzle."
Tips: "We are interested in fine quality work. Be realistic in compensation desired. Include information on artist's background, manner of painting and reason for art work subject matter selection; also any track record on sales, wholesale or retail prices, type of outlets where sales made and what type of promotional work has been done. If you have no track record, that is fine also. Some of the highest paid started out with us when they were unknowns but they were very talented."

*ARTISTWORKS, INC., 1337 Beacon St., Box 9, Brookline MA 02146. (617)738-0602. Contact: Michael Markowicz. Art publisher and art distributor of offset reproductions and handpulled originals. Clinets: distributors, galleries, decorators and other retailers. Works with 10-20 freelance artists/year. Negotiates payment method. Advance depends on payment method. Negotiates rights purchased. Requires exclusive representation. Provides in-transit insurance, insurance while work is at firm, promotion, shipping to and from firm and written contract. Send query letter with resume and samples to be kept on file. Prefers slides as samples, photographic prints are acceptable. "We only review original work after first seeing slides." Samples not filed returned by SASE.
Acceptable Work: Considers oil and acrylic paintings, pastels and watercolors; serigraphs. Especially likes still life/landscapes.
Tips: "We only consider work of extremely high quality. Please do not submit work unless you are a serious professional artist with a track record of sales and exhibitions, or you feel that your work is comparable with that of other established artists."

ATLANTIC GALLERY, 1055 Thomas Jefferson St. NW, Washington DC 20007. (202)337-2299. Director: Virginia Smith. Art publisher/distributor. Publishes signed prints using offset lithography and hand-colored, handpulled restrike engravings. Clients: retail galleries, department stores, decorators, large commercial accounts. Publishes 3 freelance artists/year. Pays flat fee, $250-1,000 average. Offers advance. Buys one-time rights. Provides in-transit insurance, insurance while work is at publisher, promotion, shipping to and from publisher and a written contract. Negotiates ownership of original art. Send query letter with brochure, resume, samples and tear sheets to be kept on file; call or write for appointment to show portfolio. Prefers slides or photographs as samples. Samples not kept on file returned by SASE. Reports within 3 weeks.
Acceptable Work: Considers oil and acrylic paintings, pastels and watercolors. Prefers traditional art.

KATHLEEN BEHBEHANI FINE ART, INC., 5614 Royalton, Houston TX 77081. (713)661-8003. President: Kathleen Behbehani. Art publisher/distributor/artists' agent. Handles limited edition hand-

pulled original graphics, fiber art, works on paper, pastels, watercolors, canvases, sculpture. Clients: galleries, design trade, art consultants. Represents approximately 75 artists. Negotiates payment method; sometimes offers advance. Requires exclusive representation. Provides some insurance while work is at firm, promotion, shipping to and from firm. Written contract available. Work is given "full-time quality representation." Send query letter with resume and samples to be kept on file unless return is requested. Contact Kathleen Behbehani or Melissa Markley by phone or mail for appointment to show portfolio. Prefers slides or photographs by mail and original work in person. Samples not filed returned only if requested. Reports within 30 days.
Acceptable Work: Considers pen & ink line drawings, oils, acrylics, pastels, watercolors and mixed media; serigraphs, linocuts and stone or plate lithographs, woodcuts, etchings, sculptured work, handmade/cast paper.

LORENZO BERGEN GRAPHICS, 1519 Esplanade Ave., New Orleans LA 70116. Art publisher/distributor/gallery. Publishes limited and unlimited editions; offset reproductions and handpulled silkscreens. Clients: galleries. Especially needs fresh new poster images. Negotiates payment method, advance and rights purchased. Provides promotion and a written contract. Send query letter with brochure, samples and tear sheets to be kept on file; write for appointment to show portfolio. Prefers to see original work; will accept photographs as samples. Samples not kept on file returned by SASE if requested. Reports only if interested.
Acceptable Work: Considers pen & ink drawings, oil and acrylic paintings, pastels, watercolors and mixed media.

BERNARD PICTURE CO. INC., Box 4744, Stamford CT 06907. (203)357-7600. Vice President: Michael Katz. Designer: Rosemary Pellicone. Art publisher. Produces offset reproductions using offset lithography for "manufacturers of product world-wide, i.e., framed pictures, plaques, etc." Publishes 300 freelance artists/year. Pays royalties to artist of 10%. Offers advance "depending on artist." Buys reprint rights. "Sometimes" requires exclusive representation of the artist. Provides in-transit insurance and insurance while work is at publisher. Artist owns original art. Send query letter with samples. Call or write for appointment to show portfolio. Prefers slides, photos as samples—"then original work." Samples returned. Reports within 2 weeks.
Acceptable Work: Considers all media, including, photograpy. Prefers series and sets; unframed.

C.R. FINE ARTS LTD., 249 A St., Boston MA 02210. (617)236-4225. President: Carol Robinson. Art publisher/distributor/gallery handling limited and unlimited editions, offset reproductions and posters. Clients: galleries, poster stores, department stores, decorators, art consultants. Publishes 5-6 artists/year; distributes work of 30 artists/year. Pays royalty (20%) or works on consignment (40% commission); payment method is negotiated. Offers advance. Negotiates rights purchased. Provides in-transit insurance, insurance while work is at firm, promotion, shipping to and from firm and a written contract. Send query letter with resume and samples to be kept on file; write for appointment to show portfolio. Prefers slides as samples. Samples not filed returned by SASE only if requested. Reports within 3 weeks.
Acceptable Work: Considers pastels, watercolors and mixed media; serigraphs, and stone or plate lithographs. Especially likes flowers, seascapes, contemporary themes,' beach scenes, animals, music themes, abstracts.

CANADIAN ART PRINTS INC., 736 Richards St., Vancouver, British Columbia V6B 3A4 Canada. (604)681-3485. President: J.H. Krieger. Publishes limited edition handpulled originals and offset reproductions for galleries, card and gift shops, department stores, framers and museum shops. Publishes 40-50 artists/year. Send slides or photos. Reports within 5 weeks. Provides promotion, shipping from publisher and written contract. Pays royalties.
Acceptable Work: Considers paintings, pastels, watercolors, intaglio, stone lithographs and serigraphs by Canadian artists; series.

*CHINA ARTS INTERNATIONAL TRADING CO., INC., 54 Mott St., New York NY 10013. (212)226-5094. Assistant Manager: Hall P. Tam. Art distributor and gallery handling unlimited editions. Clients: galleries and wholesale distributors. Works with 20 freelance artists/year. Negotiates payment method. Buys reprint rights or negotiates rights purchased. Provides promotion and shipping from firm. Send brochure and business card to be kept on file; or write for appointment to show portfolio. Prefers original work as samples. Samples not filed returned by SASE. Reports within 1 month.
Acceptable Work: Considers watercolors. Especially likes lady, flower and bird, and landscape themes. Handles oriental paintings only.
Tips: Low prices are an important consideration.

*CIRRUS EDITIONS, 542 S. Alameda St., Los Angeles CA 90013. President: Jean R. Milant. Produces limited edition hand-pulled originals for museums, galleries and private collectors. Publishes 3-4 artists/year. Send samples of work. Prefers slides as samples. Samples returned by SASE.
Acceptable Work: Contemporary paintings and sculpture.

COLLECTIVE IMPRESSIONS LTD., Suite 121, 1700 Reisterstown Rd., Baltimore MD 21208. (301)486-0040, 828-5525. President: D.H. Isennock. Produces limited edition handpulled originals for graphics retailers, investors and corporate sales. Primarily interested in publishing original lithos, silk-screens, etchings. Also interested in purchasing quantities of hand-printed original graphics from the artist. (Prefers to see a sample of the graphic rather than a slide or photo for artist-printed graphics.) Publishes 2-5 artists/year. Provides insurance, promotion, shipping and written contract. Artist owns original art (subject to purchase by publisher). Query and submit slides or photos. SASE. Reports within 2 weeks.
Acceptable Work: Unframed abstract and impressionistic paintings and etchings; individual works. Original graphics primarily.
Tips: Artists should show "professionalism."

CONTEMPLATIVE INVESTMENTS, INC., 2067 Range Rd., Clearwater FL 33575. (813)441-2821. President: Joseph F. Boiros. Art publisher/distributor. Publishes offset reproductions; posters and serigraphs; "we look for a certain theme and publish a series on that theme." Clients: galleries, department stores, furniture stores. Publishes 4-6 freelance artists/year. Also needs original oil paintings. Negotiates payment method. Negotiates rights purchased. Provides insurance while work is at publisher, promotion and a written contract. Send query letter with brochure, resume, business card, samples and tear sheets to be kept on file; call or write for appointment to show portfolio. Considers "what artist has available" to review as samples. Samples not kept on file returned by SASE. Reports within 7 days.
Acceptable Work: Considers oil and acrylic paintings, watercolors and mixed media.
Tips: "Offer something different and interesting."

*GREG COPELAND INC., 10-14 Courtland St., Paterson NJ 07503. (201)279-6166. President: Greg Copeland. Art publisher and distributor of limited editions, handpulled originals, editions of sculpture, cast paper, paintings and dimensional sculpture. Clients: designers, architects, galleries, commercial designers, department store galleries and designer showrooms. Publishes 10-15 freelance artists/year. Works with 25-40 artists/year. Pays in royalties of 5% or negotiates payment method. Negotiates rights purchased. Provides shipping to firm. Send query letter with samples; or call or write for appointment to show portfolio. Prefers original work as samples. Samples are returned. Reports within 10 days.
Acceptable Work: Considers pen & ink line drawings, acrylic paintings, pastels, watercolors, mixed media, dimentional sculpture and scultpure; serigraphs. Looks for "beauty-excitement." Especially likes still lifes; modern style.

DAVIS BLUE ARTWORK, 3820 Hoke Ave., Culver City CA 90230. (213)202-1550. Art Director: Robert Blue. Art publisher/distributor. Produces posters and limited edition prints for wide ranging distribution. Publishes 25 + freelance artists/year. Pays flat fee or royalty; negotiates payment method and right purchased. Provides promotion and international distribution. Send query letter with duplicate set of slides; slides returned if SASE provided. Reports within 2 weeks.
Acceptable Work: Considers paintings, pastels, watercolors, photography, silkscreens, lithographs, most any limited edition method.

DISCOVERY GALLERIES, 1260 Santa Monica Mall, Santa Monica CA 90401. (213)450-8989. Contact: Monroe Mendelsohn. Art publisher of gallery posters. Clients: frame shops and poster distributors, national and international. "We have five artists on our roster and are interested in adding 3 or 4 more in the next 12 months." Pays royalty and/or flat fees; offers advance. Buys all poster rights. Requires exclusive representation for posters. Provides insurance while work is at firm, promotion and a written contract. Send query letter with brochure and printed samples or slides; call or write for appointment to show portfolio. "Never send us original artwork unsolicited." Material is filed only at artist's request; "if artist is local, we like to look at portfolio." Prefers slides or color photographs as samples. Samples not filed returned by SASE only. Reports within a week if interested; "otherwise, we simply mail back the samples within a couple of days after we receive them."
Acceptable Work: Considers acrylics and airbrush; offset and silkscreen posters.
Tips: "We are interested in publishing only 'decorative' work with a contemporary look aimed at a middle-brow audience; florals, still lifes and highly stylized landscapes. We look upon ourselves as publishers of wall decor. Colors are important and subject matter should be up-tempo and pleasant to look at. Remember, someone is choosing the work to decorate his living quarters. For hints and suggestions about color and moods, an artist does well to study some good contemporary wallpaper catalogs."

DODO GRAPHICS, INC., 119 Cornelia St., Box 585, Plattsburgh NY 12901. (518)561-7294. President: Frank How. Art publisher. Produces offset reproductions, art posters and handpulled originals for galleries, frame stores, manufacturers and distributors of prints and framed prints. Publishes 3-4 freelance artists/year. Buys copyright outright; also negotiates. Requires exclusive representation. Provides promotion, shipping to publisher and a written contract. Negotiates ownership of original art. Send brochure/flyer and samples of work; write for appointment. Prefers slides or photographs as samples. Samples returned. Reports within 3 months.
Acceptable Work: Considers pastels, watercolors and mixed media with floral, landscapes, still life in a contemporary style. Prefers unframed series; maximum size 28x22".
Tips: "Never send any original work. Slides or photographs, as many as possible, should be submitted." Sees a trend toward "more florals in the form of posters."

DONALD ART CO. INC., and division Impress-Graphics®, 30 Commerce Rd., Stamford CT 06904-2102. (203)348-9494. Art Coordinator: Bob Roberts. Produces unlimited edition offset reproductions for wholesale picture frame manufacturers, and manufacturers using art in their end products, for premiums and promotions. Send query letter with resume and photos or slides. Write for appointment to show a portfolio. Reports within 4 weeks. Works with approximately 20 freelance artists/year. Exclusive area representation required. Provides in-transit insurance, insurance while work is at publisher, shipping, promotion and written contract. Samples returned by SASE. Pays advance (sometimes) against 10% royalties. Negotiates rights purchased.
Acceptable Work: Publishes 150 artists/year. Considers all types of paintings; oil, acrylic, watercolor, pastels, mixed media. Also needs work suitable for gallery posters.
Tips: "We have developed our division, Impress Graphics, for the publication and distribution of gallery posters. We will also be entering into the limited edition field, with some limited edition subjects already available. Look at the market to see what type of artwork is selling."

DRUCKER/VINCENT, INC., 45 Sheridan St., San Francisco CA 94103. (415)626-8610. Art Director: Richard Whittaker. Produces limited and unlimited editions, offset reproductions; fine art posters. Uses both offset lithography and silkscreen. Negotiates payment and rights purchased. Send query letter with samples and tear sheets to be kept on file. Call or write for appointment to show portfolio. Prefers slides and photographs as samples. *No original work.* Samples returned by SASE if not kept on file.
Acceptable Work: All types of flat art, photographs, mechanicals, etc. Prefers work contemporary in style.

*EDELMAN FINE ARTS, LTD., Suite 1503, 1140 Broadway, New York NY 10001. (212)683-4266. Vice President: H. Heather Edelman. Art distributor of original oil paintings. Clients: galleries, interior designers and furniture stores. Distributes work for 150 artists/year. Negotiates payment method. Buys all rights. Provides in-transit insurance, insurance while work is at firm, promotion, shipping from firm and written contract. Send query letter with brochure and samples to be kept on file; or call or write for appointment to show portfolio. Prefers slides, photographs or original paintings as samples. Reports within 1 week.
Acceptable Work: Considers oil and acrylic paintings, watercolors and mixed media. Especially likes Old World and Impressionist themes or styles.
Tips: Portfolio should include originals and only best work.

EMROSE ART CORPORATION OF FLORIDA, 5181 NE 12th Ave., Ft. Lauderdale FL 33334. (305)772-1386. President: Marvin Rosenbaum. Art publisher and dealer. Produces limited edition original lithographs for galleries, auctioneers and furniture stories. Pays flat fee. Negotiates rights purchased and ownership of original art. Send query letter. Prefers photos as samples. Samples not returned. Reports within 1 week. Provide material to be kept on file for possible future assignments.
Acceptable Work: Considers pen & ink line drawings, oil and acrylic paintings and watercolors. Accepts assorted styles and themes; prefers design oriented art. Prefers framed or unframed individual works of art.

*EXACTLY MY THOUGHTS, INC., 1909 Charlotte Dr., Charlotte NC 28203. (704)372-2747. President: Ronald D. Unger. Art publisher and distributor of limited and unlimited editions, offset reproductions and handpulled originals. Clients: galleries, specialty shops and hotel gift shops. Publishes 4 freelance artists/year. Distributes work for 8 artists/year. Pays in royalty of 25%. Buys first rights or reprint rights. Requires exclusive representation. Provides promotion and written contract. Send query letter with brochure, resume and samples to be kept on file. Prefers slides or photographs as samples. Samples not filed are returned. Reports within 1 month.
Acceptable Work: Considers pastels and watercolors; serigraphs, linocuts and woodcuts. Especially likes fantasy and dream-like themes or styles.

FAIRFAX PRINTS LTD., Box 230, E. Lansing MI 48823. President: Gary Fairfax. Publishes limited and inexpensive unlimited edition offset reproductions for bookstores, record stores, galleries and department stores. Publishes 1-2 artists/year. Send slides, SASE. Reports within 4-6 weeks. Provides insurance while work is at publisher, promotion, shipping from publisher and written contract. Buys poster rights only; sometimes negotiates rights; may also purchase originals.
Acceptable Work: Subjects: wildlife and fantasy *only*. Realistic paintings (*no* photograpic work) and sculpture on wildlife (primarily "big cats" and predatory birds), or fantasy/science fiction themes (though work can be quite stylized); series. Pays advance against 5-10% royalties.

FELIX ROSENSTIEL'S WIDOW & SON LTD., 33-35 Markham St., London SW3 England. 44-1-352-3551. Also New York office. Director: David A. Roe. Art publisher/distributor/gallery handling limited and unlimited editions, offset reproductions and handpulled originals. Clients: "all facets of the trade." Works with 130 artists/year. Negotiates payment method. Offers advance. Buys all rights or negotiates rights purchased. Provides in-transit insurance, insurance while work is at firm, promotion, shipping from firm and a written contract. Send query letter with brochure and samples; call or write for appointment to show portfolio. Prefers slides or photographs as samples. Samples returned by SAE (nonresidents include IRC). Reports within 30 days.
Acceptable Work: Considers pen & ink line drawings, oils, acrylics, pastels, watercolors and mixed media; serigraphs and stone or plate lithographs, woodcuts, linocuts, etchings and engravings.
Tips: "Posters are declining."

FINE ART RESOURCES, INC., 2179 Queensburg Lane, Palatine IL 60074. President: Gerard V. Perez. Art publisher. Publishes limited editions of handpulled original prints for galleries. *Does not* publish reproductions. Publishes 80 freelance artists/year. Pays flat fee, $500-5,000 average. Offers advance. Negotiates rights purchased. Requires exclusive representation of the artist. Provides insurance while work is at publisher, promotion and a written contract. Plates or screens destroyed after printing. Send query letter with samples and tear sheets. Prefers original work, slides and photographs as samples. Samples returned by SASE. Reports within 10 days.
Acceptable Work: Considers "strictly original prints." Publishes representational style. Prefers individual works of art; unframed; 30x40" maximum.

FINE LINE POSTERS INC., Box 475, Sunderland MA 01375. (413)665-4898. President: Susan Friedman. Art publisher/distributor of unlimited editions. Clients: art retailers and wholesale distributors. Works with 10-20 artists/year. Pays royalties on posters sold. Requires exclusive representation in poster format of specific image contracted. Provides promotion and a written contract. Send query letter with samples. Prefers slides or 4x5's (maximum of 10); do *not* send originals. Samples not filed returned *only* by SASE. Reports within 1 month.
Acceptable Work: Considers oils, acrylics, pastels, watercolors and mixed media; serigraphs and stone or plate lithographs. Especially likes contemporary imagery/impressionist and expressionistic.
Tips: Artists who are "well represented by other poster publishers need not apply."

RUSSELL A. FINK GALLERY, 9843 Gunston Rd., Box 250, Lorton VA 22079. (703)550-9699. Contact: Russell A. Fink. Art publisher/dealer. Publishes offset reproductions using five-color offset lithography for galleries, individuals, framers. Publishes 3 freelance artists/year. Pays royalties to artist or negotiates payment method. Negotiates rights purchased. Provides insurance while work is at publisher, promotion and shipping from publisher. Negotiates ownership of original art. Send query letter with samples to be kept on file. Call or write for appointment to show portfolio. Prefers slides or photographs as samples. Samples returned if not kept on file.
Acceptable Work: Considers oil and acrylic paintings and watercolors. Prefers wildlife and sporting themes. Prefers individual works of art; unframed. "Submit photos or slides of at least near professional quality. Include size, price, media and other pertinent data regarding the artwork. Also send personal resume and be courteous enough to include SASE for return of any material sent to me."
Tips: Looks for composition, style and technique in samples. Also "how the artist views his own art." Mistakes artists make are arrogance, overpricing, explaining their art and underrating the dealer."

FIRST IMPRESSIONS, 3373 Wrightwood Dr., Studio City CA 91604. (213)656-1797. Marketing Director: Dana Axelrod. Art consultant and dealer. Original graphics for galleries, designers and corporate clients. Work accepted on consignment basis only. Drawings, paintings, sculptures and tapestries accepted. Send resume and slides of artwork and net price. Slides returned by SASE. Reports within 1-2 weeks. Accepted slides kept on file for client presentation. Acceptance of work based on review of slides and resume. No personal interview without slide review.
Acceptable Work: Considers all themes and styles of artwork. Prefers large individual works, series or pairs. Professional quality only.

Tips: Colors and images today tend to be influenced by the interior design colors and styles. Large format 30x40 unique works on paper, contemporary imagery.

*GALAXY OF GRAPHICS, LTD., 460 W. 34th St., New York NY 10001. (212)947-8989. Sales Manager: George F. Barnes. Art publisher of unlimited editions and offset reproductions. Clients: galleries and picture frame manufacturers. Publishes 25-50 freelance artists/year. Works with several hundred artists/year. Pays flat or royalty of 10% depending on work. Offers advance. Buys all rights. Prefers exclusive representation. Provides insurance while work is at firm, promotion, shipping from firm and written contract. Send photos or color slides for consideration; or call or write for appointment to show portfolio. Samples are returned. Reports within a few days.
Acceptable Work: Considers pen & ink line drawings, oil and acrylic paintings, pastels, watercolors and mixed media; "any currently popular and generally accepted theme."
Tips: "Send us some samples of exciting, new subject matter, finely painted which we can successfully market. Pastels are starting to wane—we feel the market is slowly beginning to return to the primary colors for images."

GALLERY ENTERPRISES, 1881 Abington Rd. or 310 Bethlehem Plaza Mall, Bethlehem PA 18018. (215)868-1139. Contact: David Michael Donnangelo. Art publisher/distributor/gallery agents. Publishes limited and unlimited edition offset reproductions and handpulled originals using etching; lithography and offset methods. Clients: galleries and volume art buyers. Publishes 2 freelance artists/ year. Negotiates payment method. Buys all rights. Provides a written contract. Publishes own original art. Send resume and samples to be kept on file; write for appointment to show portfolio. Prefers actual sample print as a representation. Samples are kept on file. Reports within 3 months.
Acceptable Work: Considers pen & ink drawings and etchings. All works considered but prefers traditional and wildlife themes. Prefers series; 20x30" maximum.
Tips: Artists "must be able to produce original images in volume. Only interested in commercially-minded artists."

GALLERY PRINTS, INC., 3719 Magazine St., New Orleans LA 70115. (504)891-6376. Marketing Director: Dan Resnic. Art publisher/distributor of limited edition, handpulled original and offset reproductions. Clients: galleries, frame shops, bookstores and retail customers. Publishes 10 artists/year; distributes 40 artists/year. Pays on a consignment basis (50% commission) or payment method is negotiated. Offers advance. Negotiates rights purchased. Sometimes requires exclusive representation. Provides promotion, shipping from firm and a written contract. Send query letter with samples. Prefers photographs or original work as samples. Samples are not filed and are returned only if requested with an SASE. Reports back within 1 week.
Acceptable Work: Considers acrylics, pastels, watercolors and mixed media; serigraphs, etchings, cast paper and lithographs.
Tips: "Send all information with samples and follow up with a phone call after 10-14 working days."

GEME ART INC., 209 W. 6th St., Vancouver WA 98660. (206)693-7772. Art Director: Merilee Will. Publishes fine art prints and reproductions in unlimited editions. Clients: galleries, department stores—the general art market. Works with 40-80 artists/year. Publishes the works of 15-20 artists; distributes 23-40. Payment is negotiated on a royalty basis. Normally purchases all rights. Provides promotion, shipping from publisher and a contract. Query with color slides or photos. SASE. Reports only if interested. Call or write for appointment to show portfolio. Simultaneous submissions OK.
Acceptable Work: Considers oils, acrylics, pastels, watercolor and mixed media. Themework is open.

GESTATION PERIOD, 1946 N. Fourth St., Columbus OH 43201. Operations Manager: Charles Butts. Art distributor of offset reproductions. Clients: galleries, framers, college stores, gift stores. Payment method is negotiated. Sometimes requires exclusive representation of the artist. Provides promotion and shipping from firm. Send query letter with brochure and/or samples to be kept on file. Prefers photographs as samples. Samples not filed returned only if requested. Reports within 1 month.
Acceptable Work: Considers any medium including photography. Especially likes fine art/exhibition posters and humor.

GOURMENT GRAFIKS, INC., 300 Montgomery St., Alexandria VA 22314. (703)683-4686. President: Mary Nokes Berry. Art publisher of offset reproductions. Clients: galleries, department stores, interior designers and independent stores. Publishes 2 freelance artists/year. Negotiates payment method and rights purchased. Provides promotion and written contract. Send query letter with brochure, resume, business card and samples to be kept on file; write for appointment to show portfolio. Prefers slides as samples. Samples not filed returned only if requested. Reports within 1 month.
Acceptable Work: Considers pen & ink line drawings, oils, acrylics, pastels, watercolors, mixed me-

dia and photography for publication and distribution.

Tips: Especially looks for timely pieces—new graphic approaches, current subjects, colors and themes. And, of course, the rare "timeless'" art that is acceptable always. A mistake artists make is "ignoring the trends of the times and the suggestions which will make their work reflect what people want in their homes. There's a balance between accepting an artist's work exactly as is and using modifications (interpretation) to make the work timely."

*GRAPHIC ORIGINALS INC., 153 W. 27th St., New York NY 10001. (212)807-6180. President: Martin Levine. Art publisher and dealer. Produces limited editions of etchings and silkscreens for galleries. Negotiates payment and rights purchased. Publisher owns original art. Call for appointment. Prefers photos or originals as samples. Samples returned by SASE. Reports within 3 weeks. Provide resume to be kept on file for possible future assignments.
Acceptable Work: Considers contemporary, traditional and realistic themes. Prefers unframed works; 24x30" maximum.

GRAPHICS INTERNATIONAL, Station E, Box 13292, Oakland CA 94661. (415)339-9310. Vice President: Rob R. Kral. Art publisher/distributor of limited and unlimited edition handpulled originals. Clients: galleries, frame shops, distributors and department stores. Number of artists worked with per year varies. Negotiates payment method. Buys all rights. Requires exclusive representation. Provides shipping from firm and a written contract. Send query letter with brochure, resume and samples to be kept on file. Accepts slides, photographs or original work as samples. Reports only if interested.
Acceptable Work: Considers pen & ink line drawings, watercolors and etchings. Especially likes traditional style.

GRAPHIQUE DE FRANCE, 46 Waltham St., Boston MA 02118. (617)482-5066. Contact: Scott Slater or Jean-Jacques Toulotte. Art publisher/distributor of offset reproduction posters. Clients: art galleries, designers, architects, department stores and art consultants. Publishes 10 freelance artists/year; distributes work for more than 100. Pays royalty, 8-10% of wholesale selling price. Occasionally offers advance. Buys reprint rights; "we retain the right to reproduce the artwork in poster form." Send query letter and samples to be kept on file; call or write for appointment to show portfolio. Accepts "anything that is pictorial" as samples. Samples not filed are returned. Reports within 2-3 weeks.
Acceptable Work: Considers pen & ink line drawings, oils, acrylics, pastels, watercolors and mixed media. Especially likes realistic and decorate images.

GREAT CANADIAN PRINT COMPANY LTD, 404-63 Albert St., Winnipeg, Manitoba R3B 1G4 Canada. (204)942-7961. Officers: Gary Nerman and Allan Kiesler. Art publisher. Produces limited edition silkscreens for galleries, native craft stores. Publishes 15 freelance artists/year. "We publish only native (Indian) art with preference towards Canadian or Woodland. We will not look at queries from other sources and recommend that non-native artists not submit to us." Pays by royalty. Buys all rights. Requires exclusive representation of the artist. Provides a written contract. Send query letter with resume to be kept on file. If samples are requested, prefers to see original works, slides or photographs. Samples not kept on file returned only if requested. Reports within 4 weeks.
Acceptable Work: Prefers works on paper, any medium. Looks for "a unique style that still conforms to the parameters that make up native (Indian) art."

GREEN RIVER TRADING CO., Boston Corners Rd., RD2, Box 130, Millerton NY 12546. (518)789-3311. President: Art Kerber. Art publisher. Produces limited edition, signed and numbered prints of Western and wildlife art for galleries, wholesale and retail. Works with 3 freelance artists/year. Also uses artists for advertising, brochure and catalog design, illustration and layout.
First Contact & Terms: Send query letter with brochure, resume, business card, samples and tear sheets to be kept on file; write for appointment to show portfolio. Prefers slides and photographs as samples. Samples not kept on file returned only if requested. Reports within 2 weeks. Works on assignment only. Pays by the hour, $65 maximum; by the project, $200-2,000 average. Considers complexity of project, skill and experience of artist, turnaround time and rights purchased when establishing payment.
Tips: Artists must be willing "to take advice."

Market conditions are constantly changing! If this is 1987 or later, buy the newest edition of *Artist's Market* at your favorite bookstore or order directly from Writer's Digest Books.

HADDAD'S FINE ARTS INC., Box 3016 C, Anaheim CA 92803. President: James Haddad. Produces limited and unlimited edition originals and offset reproductions for galleries, art stores, schools and libraries. Publishes 40-70 artists/year. Buys reproduction rights. Provides insurance while work is at publisher, shipping from publisher and written contract. Submit slides. SASE. Reports within 60 days.
Acceptable Work: Unframed individual works and pairs; all media.

HANG-UPS, 1319 W. Katella, Orange CA 92667. (714)997-9999. Sales Manager: Michael Tienhaara. Art publisher/distributor/gallery handling limited and unlimited editions, offset reproductions and handpulled originals. Clients: galleries, department stores, hotels, designers, architects and distributors. Works with more than 100 artists/year. Negotiates payment method and rights purchased; sometimes offers advance. Provides insurance while work is at firm, promotion, shipping from firm and a written contract. Send query letter with brochure, resume, business card and samples to be kept on file; call for appointment to show portfolio. Prefers slides as samples, followed by original work. Samples not filed are returned. Reports within 10 days.
Acceptable Work: Considers pen & ink line drawings, oils, acrylics, pastels, watercolors and mixed media; serigraphs, stone or plate lithographs, woodcuts, linocuts and etchings.
Tips: "Artists must exhibit a professional and flexible attitude that demonstrates their awareness that art distribution is a *business*."

HEDGEROW HOUSE PUBLISHING CO. INC., 230 5th Ave., New York NY 10001. (212)679-2532. Publisher/President: Robert A. Hill. Clients: national framing companies, designers, dealers and framers, galleries. Artist *must* send slides or some illustration of work *before* calling for an appointment. "If we feel the material is of interest we will contact you for an appointment." All material will be returned promptly. Do *not* forward any original art.
Acceptable Work: Art decorative and suitable for the home furnishing industry. Prefers oils, watercolors for reproduction in offset lithography. Do not submit abstract or b&w art.

HOW & PEYER, LTD., Box 506, Laprairie, Quebec J5R 4X2 Canada. (514)843-4491. President: Frank How. Art publisher. Produces offset reproductions, art posters and handpulled originals for frame shops, art galleries, wholesale framers, department stores and distributors in over 20 countries. Publishes 2-4 freelance artists/year. Negotiates payment. Buys all rights. Requires exclusive representation. Provides promotion and a written contract. Negotiates ownership of original art. Send resume and samples of work. Prefers photographs or slides, brochure, if available, as samples. Samples returned. Reports within 3 months. Provide resume, business card and brochure/flyer to be kept on file for possible future assignments.
Acceptable Work: Considers oil and acrylic paintings, pastels, watercolors and mixed media. Contemporary realistic styles and themes with broad appeal (no local scenes); landscapes, still-lifes, etc. Prefers unframed series; maximum 20x30" either horizontal or vertical.
Tips: "When submitting photographs, send as many different ones as possible. The artist should not make selection but should leave it up to the publisher. The more we can see, the better the chance that we are interested."

ICART VENDOR GRAPHICS, 8568 Pico Blvd., Los Angeles CA 90035. (213)653-3190. Director: Sandy Verin. Art publisher/distributor/gallery. Produces limited and unlimited editions of offset reproductions and handpulled original prints for galleries, decorators, corporations, collectors. Publishes 3-5 freelance artists/year. Distributes 15-25 artists/year. Pays flat fee, $250-1,000; royalties (5-10%) or negotiates payment method. "We also distribute." Offers advance. Buys all rights. Usually requires exclusive representation of the artist. Provides insurance while work is at publisher. Negotiates ownership of original art. Send brochure and samples. Prefers photographs as samples. Samples returned by SASE. Reports within 2 weeks.
Acceptable Work: Considers oils, acrylics, watercolors and mixed media, also serigraphy and lithography. Likes airbrush. Prefers "turn-of-the-century through Art Deco period (1900s-1930s) styles." Prefers individual works of art, pairs, series; 30x40" maximum.
Tips: "Please send samples of work via photo including phone number and address for further contact if indicated. Work should be done in the Art Deco style or Art Nouveau. Art Deco is preferred. Work should be clean and not sloppy or dirty. All errors become magnified in the printing process."
Tips: Posters are a very popular trend in today's market.

*****INTERNATIONAL EDITIONS, INC.**, 1642 Westwood Blvd., Los Angeles CA 90024. (213)475-1233. Marketing Director: Sam Kasoff. Art publisher and distributor of limited editions and handpulled originals. Clients: galleries. Works with 3-4 artists/year. Negotiates payment method. Buys all rights. Provides insurance while work is at firm, promotion and a written contract. Send query letter with bro-

"We published this beautiful watercolor by Muramasa Kudo as a fine art poster," explains Sandy Verin, owner of Icart Vendor Graphics in Los Angeles. "We have published six of his posters and all have been accepted favorably by galleries and the public." The artist received a deposit guarantee against royalties plus artist copies of the poster. "He is very creative, with new ideas that are well presented."

chure, resume and business card. Prefers photographs as samples. Samples are returned. Reports within 1 month.

Acceptable Work: Considers oil and acrylic paintings, pastels, watercolors and mixed media; serigraphs and stone lithographs.

ARTHUR A. KAPLAN CO. INC.,, 460 W. 34th St., New York NY 10001. (212)947-8989. National Sales Manager: Reid Fader. Art publisher of offset reproduction prints and posters. Clients: galleries, department stores and picture frame manufacturers. Publishes approximately 30 freelance artists/year. Pays a flat fee or a royalty of 5-10%. Offers advance. Buys all rights. Requires exclusive representation. Provides insurance while work is at firm, promotion, shipping from firm and a written contract. Send query letter to be kept on file; write for appointment to show portfolio. Prefers to review slides or photographs. Material not filed is returned. Reports within 2-3 weeks.

Acceptable Work: Considers pen & ink line drawings, oils, acrylics, pastels, watercolors and mixed media.

Tips: "We cater to a mass market and require fine quality art with decorative and appealing subject matter."

*LEON KLAYMAN PUBLISHING, Prince Station, Box 281, New York NY 10012. Publisher: Leon Klayman. Art publisher and gallery handling postcard reproductions. Clients: museum shops, galleries, bookshops and quality postcard shops around the world. Publishes 6 freelance artists/year. Negotiates payment method. Does not offer an advance. Negotiates rights purchased. Does not require exclusive representation. Provides promotion and written contract. Send query letter with samples. Prefers slides and high quality photostats. Samples returned only by SASE. Reports within 1 month.

Acceptable Work: Considers pen & ink line drawings, oil paintings, acrylic paintings, pastels, watercolors, mixed media, collages, wood and linoleum cuts.
Tips: "We select new high quality fine art with integrity that expresses human concerns and excites the human spirit."

MURRAY KLEIN ASSOCIATES INC., Box 741, 1983 Ladenburg Dr., Westbury NY 11590. (516)333-0516. President: Murray Klein. Publishes unlimited edition offset reproductions for art galleries, museums, colleges, and book and department stores. Publishes 4 artists/year. Query or arrange interview. Reports within 2-3 weeks. Provides promotion, shipping to publisher and written contract.
Acceptable Work: Impressionistic drawings, cartoons, paintings and watercolors including wildlife and flowers; series. Maximum size: 22x28". Pays $200 mimimum against 5-15% royalties. Also will work on consignment with commission arrangement. Offers advance.

DAVID LAWRENCE EDITIONS, Suite 38, 22541A Pacific Coast Hwy., Malibu CA 90265. (818)343-2293. President: David Lawrence. Art publisher/distributor handling limited and unlimited editions of offset reproductions. Clients: galleries and frame shops. Publishes 5-10 freelance artists and distributes work for 25 artists/year. Negotiates payment method and rights purchased. Requires exclusive representation. Provides promotion, shipping from firm and a written contract. Send a resume and samples to be kept on file; call or write for appointment to show portfolio. Accepts "anything that gives a good representation of work" as samples. Reports back only if interested.
Acceptable Work: Considers all media for publication and distribution.

*MARTIN LAWRENCE LIMITED EDITIONS, 7011 Hayvenhurst Ave., Van Nuys CA 91406. (818)988-0630. Art publisher. Publishes limited edition graphics, unlimited edition posters and originals by internationally known, up-an-coming and new artists.
First Contact & Terms: Contact by mail only. Send good quality slides or photographs, pertinent biographical information and SASE. Exclusive representation required.
Acceptable Work: Prefers oils, acrylics, watercolors, serigraphs, lithographs and etchings.

LAWRENCE UNLIMITED, 8721 Darby Ave., Box 611, Northridge CA 91328. (213)349-4120. Contact: Lawrence A. Anenberg. Art publisher. Produces limited editions, handpulled original etchings, watercolors, oils and serigraphs for national galleries, department stores, designers and corporations. Publishes 8 freelance artists/year. Also uses artists for new original designs and works. Negotiates payment method "on individual terms." Offers advance "when applicable." Negotiates rights purchased. Requires exclusive representation of the artist "for specified times." Provides in-transit insurance, insurance while work is at publisher, promotion and shipping from publisher. Negotiates ownership of original art. Send query letter with brochure, samples and tear sheets to be kept on file. Material "returned at once if not applicable for our needs." Call or write for appointment to show portfolio. Prefers original work; will accept photographs. Samples returned. Reports within 1 week.
Acceptable Work: Considers oil paintings, watercolors and etchings. Prefers contemporary or Old World; no hard edge styles. Prefers pairs and series; unframed. No size restrictions.
Tips: "Be prepared to price for quantity and for promotion and distribution."

LIPMAN PUBLISHING INC., 8336 West 3rd St., Los Angeles CA 90048. (213)653-6512. Director: Louise Lipman. Art publisher. Produces fine art posters using offset lithography, 5-color for retail poster shops. Publishes 10-12 freelance artists/year. Also uses artists for occasional design requirements for poster design. Pays royalties. Offers advance. Pays first rights, reprint rights or negotiates rights purchased. Sometimes requires exclusive representation of the artist. Provides insurance while work is at publisher, promotion and a written contract. Artist owns original art. Send query letter with samples to be kept on file. Prefers photostats, slides and photographs as samples. Samples returned only if requested.
Acceptable Work: Considers oil and acrylic paintings, pastels, watercolors and photographs. Prefers decorative, colorful themes and styles, graphically presented.
Tips: "It's best to send slides or photos with a letter; do not expect them returned unless specified. Look at posters on the market to see what is being published these days."

*LITHOS' Publishers and Distributors of Collector Prints, Box 4591, St. Louis MO 63108. (314)367-2177. Publisher: Linda Thomas. Estab. 1983. Handles limited edition prints (maximum 1,000/edition). Clients: framers, galleries, interior designs and art collectors. Publishes 4-6 freelance artists/year; 6-10 artists/year; 8 artists/year. Pays negotiable royalty. Negotiates rights purchased. Provides insurance while work is at firm, promotion, shipping from your firm and a written contract. Send query letter with resume, business card and samples to be kept on file; write for appointment to show portfolio; or write for artists' guidelines. Prefers slides and photographs as samples. Reports back within 1 month.

Acceptable Work: Oil paintings, acrylic paintings, pastels and watercolors. Especially likes contemporary themes or styles.
Tips: "We are interested in never before published images only. Artist should be prepared to give Lithos' exclusive publication rights for at least twenty-four months. Broad name recognition is not a prerequistion; good work is!"

*LUBLIN GRAPHICS, INC., 95 East Putnam Ave., Greenwich CT 06830. (203)622-8777. Art Director: Nadya Lublin Beck. Art publisher. Publishes limited edition handpulled prints. Publishes 15 artists/year. Pays flat fee. Exclusive representation required. Send query letter with resume, slides, photographs and SASE. Resume only is filed.
Acceptable Work: Considers oils, acrylics, watercolors, pastels, serigraphs and lithographs.

*MARCO DISTRIBUTORS, 1412 S. Laredo, Aurora CO 80017. (303)752-4819. President: Mark Woodmansee. Art publisher and distributor of limited editions, handpulled originals, oil washes and oil on canvas. Clients: corporations, galleries and interior designers. Publishes 2 freelance artists/year. Distributes work for 10 artists/year. Pays in royalty of 10-20%; on consignment basis; or negotiates payment method. Buys all rights or reprint rights or negotiates rights purchased. Requires exclusive representation. Provides promotion, shipping to and from firm and written contract. Send brochure and samples to be kept on file; call or write for appointment to show portfolio; or contact through artist's agent. Prefers photographs, tear sheets or original work as samples. Samples not filed are not returned. Reports back to artist.
Acceptable work: Considers oil and acrylic paintings, pastels, watercolors and mixed media; serigraphs, stone lithographs, plate lithographs and woodcuts. Especially likes landscapes, some unique figures and impressionist style.
Tips: "Send photos of your work; follow with a call."

*MIGNECO & SMITH, Via Delle Oche 11/R, Florence 50122 Italy. (055)263.390. Director: Philippa Sutcliffe-Smith. Art publisher, distributor and gallery handling fine art posters. Clients: galleries, framers, bookshops, museums, quality, department stores, interior decorators, architects, etc. Publishes 10-30 freelance artists/year. Distributes work for 400-500 artists/year. Pays in royalty of 10% distribution price; or negotiates payment method. Sometimes offers advance. Usually requires exclusive representation. Provides promotion, shipping to and from firm, written contract and free accomodation in Florence during proofing. Send query letter with brochure and samples to be kept on file. Prefers slides, color photographs or reproductions as samples. Samples not filed returned only if requested. Reports only if interested.
Acceptable Work: Considers pen & ink line drawings, oil and acrylic paintings, pastels, watercolors, mixed media and printing (lithography, serigraphy, etc.). Especially likes landscapes, florals, figurative, abstracts, architecture, photographic subjects, music themes, still lifes, animals, fashion, interiors and surrealism; "anything different especially considered."
Tips: "Work should be professionally executed. Artists could take a guideline from the many successful posters on the market although plagiarism of any form would not be acceptable to us."

MINOTAUR, 34 Bridgman Ave., Toronto, Ontario M54 1X3 Canada. (416)530-1454. Contact: J. Kevin Kelleher. Art publisher/distributor of fine art and photography posters. Clients: galleries, framers, wholesale framers and gift shops. Works with 18 artists/year. Pays flat fee, royalty or negotiates method; "a combination of purchase of rights plus royalty." Offers advance. Buys first rights. Provides a written contract. Send query letter with business card to be kept on file; write for appointment to show portfolio. Prefers to review slides, photographs or tear sheets. Material not filed is returned. Reports within days.
Acceptable Work: Considers pen & ink line drawings, oils, acrylics, pastels and watercolors; serigraphs and stone or plate lithographs. Accepts "almost any contemporary theme."

MODERNART EDITIONS, INC., 80 5th Ave., New York NY 10011. (212)675-8505. Vice President: Elaine Lingwood. Art publisher. Publishes art posters using stone or plate lithography, silkscreen, lithographic offset. Publishes 15 freelance artists/year. Negotiates payment method. Negotiates rights purchased. Provides insurance while work is at publisher. Artist owns original art. Send slides. Call or write for appointment to show portfolio. Samples not returned.
Acceptable Work: Considers oil and acrylic paintings, pastels, watercolors and mixed media. Prefers representational and graphic styles; interiors with flowers, land and cityscapes, beach scenes or gardens as themes. Prefers artwork unframed.

MITCH MORSE GALLERY INC., 305 E. 63rd St., New York NY 10021. (212)593-1812. President: Mitch Morse. Produces limited edition handpulled originals for framers, galleries, interior design-

ers, architects, hotels and better furniture stores. Publishes 15 artists/year. Negotiates payment. Offers advance. Arrange interview or submit slides or photos. SASE. Reports within 1 week.
Acceptable Work: Unframed realistic, impressionistic and romantic paintings, lithographs, serigraphs and etchings; individual works; 4x6' maximum.
Tips: "There is continued emphasis on color as a major ingredient in the selection of art and greater interest in more traditional subject matter.

NEW DECO, INC. (formerly Deco Arts Ltd.), 9328-D Sable Ridge Ct., Boca Raton FL 33428. (305)482-6295. President: Brad Morris. Art publisher/distributor/gallery. Produces limited editions using offset lithography for galleries. Publishes 1 freelance artist/year. Needs new designs for reproduction. Pays flat fee. Offers advance. Negotiates rights purchased. Provides promotion and a written contract. Negotiates ownership of original art. Send brochure, resume, business card, samples and tear sheets to be kept on file; call or write for appointment to show portflio. Prefers photostats or photographs as samples. Samples not kept on file are returned. Reports only if interested.
Acceptable Work: Prefers Art Deco, Art Nouveau themes and styles. Prefers individual works of art, pairs or series.

*****NEW YORK GRAPHIC SOCIETY**, Box 1469, Greenwich CT 06836. (203)661-2400. Art & Production Manager: Caron Caswell. Art publisher/art distributor of limited editions, offset reproductions and handpulled originals. Clients: galleries, frame shops, museums and foreign trade. Publishes 10 new freelance artists/year while publishing a total of 110 artists. Pays flat fee or royalty of 1.2%. Offers advance. Buys all print reproduction rights. Provides in-transit insurance from firm to artist, insurance while work is at firm, promotion, shipping from firm and a written contract; provide insurance for art requested. Send query letter with samples; write for artist's guidelines. Prefers slides or photographs as samples. All submissions returned to artist by SASE after review. Reports within 2 months.
Acceptable Work: Considers oils, acrylics, pastels, watercolors and mixed media; pencil drawings (colored). Distributes posters only. Publishes/distributes serigraphs, stone lithographs, plate lithographs and woodcuts.
Tips: "We publish a broad variety of styles and themes. However, we do not publish experimental, hard-edge, sexually explicit or suggestive material. work that is by definition fine art and easy to live with, that is, which would be decorative, is what we seek whether it be abstract or representational."

*****NORTH BEACH STUDIOS, INC.**, 2565 Blackburn St., Clearwater FL 33575. President: James Cournoyer. Art publisher/art distributor/gallery handling limited editions of handpulled originals. Clients: galleries, architects, interior designers and art consultants. Negotiates payment method and rights purchased. Provides promotion, written contract and internationally distributed Fine Art catalogue (3 ring binder) containing expressly-selecte original hand-made editions of a small number of contemporary artists. Send query letter with brochure, resume, business card and samples to be kept on file; or write for appointment to show portfolio. Accepts any sample showing reasonable reproduction. Samples returned by SASE only if requested. Reports within 1 month.
Acceptable Work: Considers pen & ink line drawings and mixed media; serigraphs, stone lithographs, plate lithographs, woodcuts and linocuts. Especially likes contemporary, unusual and original themes or styles.
Tips: "Send as many details as possible, i.e., title, medium, size, price (retail), edition remaining etc."

PAPER LIONS INC., #A, 6307 Desoto Ave., Woodland Hills CA 91367. (213)999-4100. President: Gordon Brown. Art publisher of unlimited editions. Clients: galleries, framers, department stores, craft stores, mass market and auto specialty. Publishes 3-5 freelance artists/year. Payment method is negotiated. Buys all rights. Requires exclusive representation of artist. Provides a written contract. Send query letter with brochure, resume and samples to be kept on file. Call for appointment to show portfolio. Reports within 3 weeks.
Acceptable Work: "Any medium from which fine art posters can be made." Specializing in automotive art.

PARK SOUTH PRESENTATIONS LTD., 147 24th St., New York NY 10011. (212)807-8989. Vice President: Arline Cummings. Publishes limited and unlimited edition reproductions and handpulled originals using genuine lithography (lithoverite), offset lithography, and silkscreen (seriography). Clients: retail, galleries, distributors, exporters, importers, collectors. Publishes 2 freelance artists/year. Negotiates payment method. Buys first rights, reprint rights or negotiates. Provides in-transit insurance, insurance while work is at publisher, promotion, shipping to and from publisher and written contract. Send query letter with samples to be kept on file; write for appointment to show portfolio. Prefers slides as samples. Samples not kept on file returned by SASE. Reports within a few weeks.
Acceptable Work: Considers oils, pen & ink drawings, acrylic paintings, pastels and watercolors.

*PHILLIPS GALLERY, #151 7026 Old Katy Rd, Houston TX 77024. (713)664-7819. Contact: Janice Phillips. Hand pulled original, lithographs etchings and silk screens for galleries, designers, sells to the trade only; also buys some already completed works from freelance artists. Publishes 8-12 freelance artists/year. Negotiates payment and rights purchased. Provides in-transit insurance, shipping to and from publisher, distribution and sometimes advertisement. Negotiates ownership of original art. Send samples of work. Prefers studio and artist proofs, and slides as samples. Samples returned. Reports within 3 weeks. Provide resume and tear sheets to be kept on file for possible future assignments.
Acceptable Work: Considers watercolors and mixed media, landscape and wildlife themes in traditional and contemporary styles. Prefers unframed series. Also seeking art glass and sculptures (wood and stone both).
Tips:"The market seems to be moving more to the traditional."

JUDITH L. POSNER & ASSOCIATES, INC., 207 N. Milwaukee St., Milwaukee WI 53202. (414)352-3097. President: Judith L. Posner. Art publisher/distributor/gallery. Produces limited and unlimited editions of offset reproductions and original serigraphs and lithographs. Publishes 100 freelance artists/year. Pays royalty or works on consignment (50% commission). Buys one-time rights. Sometimes requires exclusive representation of artist. Provides a written contract. Send resume and samples. Prefers photographs, slides or transparencies as samples. Samples not kept on file are returned. Reports within 10 days.
Acceptable Work: Considers all media. Prefers series. Specializes in contemporary.
Tips: "Have something very exciting and unusual to show."

POSTERS INTERNATIONAL, 508 Eglinton Ave. W, Toronto, Ontario M5N 1A5 Canada. (416)481-5127. Art publisher/distributor/gallery handling limited and unlimited editions of offset reproduction and handpulled original prints. Clients: international poster distributors (Canadian and US), wholesalers and retail galleries. Send query letter; write for appointment to show portfolio. Material not filed returned only if requested by SAE (nonresidents include IRC).
Acceptable Work: Oils, acrylics, pastels, watercolors and mixed media; serigraphs, stone or plate lithographs, photography. Especially interested in "strong graphic images that relate to today's art poster market as seen advertised in the trade magazines."

PRESTIGE ART GALLERIES, INC., 3909 W. Howard, Skokie IL 60076. (312)679-2555. President: Louis Schutz. Art publisher/dealer/gallery. Publishes limited editions and offset reproductions for retail professionals and galleries. Publishes 4 freelance artists/year. Works on consignment basis; firm charges 33% commission. Buys allright or negotiates rights purchased. Provides insurance while work is at publisher, promotion and a written contract. Publisher owns original art. Send query letter with brochure, resume and samples to be kept on file. Prefers slides as samples. Samples returned by SASE. Reports only if interested.
Acceptable Work: Considers oil and acrylic paintings. Prefers realism, and mother and child themes. Prefers individual works of art; unframed; 30x40" maximum.
Tips: "Be professional."

PRIMROSE PRESS, Box 302, New Hope PA 18938. (215)862-5518. President: George Knight. Art publisher. Publishes limited edition collotype reproductions for galleries. Publishes 3-5 freelance artists/year. Pays royalties to artist of 10-20%. Buys one-time rights. Provides in-transit insurance, insurance while work is at publisher, shipping from publisher and a written contract. Artist owns original art. Send query letter with tear sheets to be kept on file. Prefers slides as samples. Samples returned by SASE if not kept on file. Reports within 10 days.
Acceptable Work: Considers pen & ink line drawings, oil and acrylic paintings, watercolors and mixed media. Publishes representational themes. Prefers individual works of art; 40x30" maximum.

THE PRINTMAKERS, 3373 Wrightwood Dr., Studio City CA 91604. (213)656-1797. President: Marcia Isaacs. Fine Art Publishers. Handpulled original graphics for galleries, designers and corporate clients. Publishes 10 new artists/year. Send slides or photos and resume. SASE. No personal interviews without staff slide review. Reports within 1-2 weeks. Provides printing and distribution.
Acceptable Work: Publishes etchings, purchases original lithographs and serigraphs. Prefers representational and contemporary styles; "the artist must be able to produce the *original plate* from which the prints are pulled in our studio." Interested in landscape, still life, abstract, etc. Subjects must be suitable for gallery sales and office interiors. Minimum sizes: 18x24, 30x40". Written contract upon acceptance. Royalties paid quarterly or purchase.
Tips: To meet our requirements, artists need "good technical printmaking skill. We prefer B.A. degree and/or art school background. Professional artists/printmakers only."

PROCREATIONS PUBLISHING COMPANY, 8129 Earhart Blvd., New Orleans LA 70118. (504)486-7787. Art Director: Bud Brimberg. Art publisher/dealer. Publishes limited and unlimited editions and handpulled original serigraphs and lithographs. "We distribute to over 2,000 galleries and via direct retail mail order and sales at festivals." Publishes 6 freelance artists/year. Pays flat fee, $1,000-3,500 average or royalties to artist of 5-10%; negotiates payment method. Offers advance. Buys all or reprint rights; negotiates rights purchased. Requires exclusive representation of the artist. Provides promotion (catalogs, announcements, publicity), shipping to publisher, shipping from publisher and a written contract. Negotiates ownership of original art. Send query letter with brochure, samples, tear sheets and transparencies to be kept on file. Call or write for appointment to show portfolio. Prefers direct contact including non-returnable transparencies. Prefers slides as samples. Samples not kept on file returned only if requested. Reports within 30 days.
Acceptable Work: Considers "all media, but preferably those easily translated as serigraphs or lithographs. We publish limited edition posters for pre-eminent events around the world including jazz festivals, the Boston Marathon, Mardi Gras, State Fair of Texas, etc." Prefers individual works of art, pairs or series; unframed; 32x22" maximum.
Tips: "Artists should have a working knowledge of silkscreen and lithographic processes, be able to work under an art director on deadline, have a strong graphic style and good color sense, understand the unique communicative nature of posters and the history of poster art. Since these are decorative art objects, artists should have a feel for interior design. Be professional in your presentation. Let the work speak for itself—don't explain what you *attempted* to do. Listen *carefully* to what the person says about the work and to what he says his needs are."

*RED LION FINE ARTS INC., 200 Red Lion Rd., Vincentown NJ 08088. (609)859-9696. President: Jung Park. Art publisher of limited and unlimited editions, offset reproductions and handpulled originals. Clients: galleries and furniture stores. Pubishes 2 freelance artists/year. Negotiates payment method. Negotiates rights purchased. Provides shipping from firm. Send brochure and samples. Prefers photostats as samples. Samples not returned. Reports only if interested.
Acceptable Work: Considers acrylic paintings, pastels, watercolors and mixed media; serigraphs.
Tips: Send "something unusual."

ROSEART/ROSENBAUM FINE ART INC., 5181 NE 12th Ave., Ft. Lauderdale FL 33334. (305)772-1387. President: Howard Rosenbaum. Produces limited edition handpulled originals lithographs, etchings, monoprints and silkscreens for museums, auctioneers, designers and architects. Publishes 75 artists/year. Send slides or photos. SASE. Reports within 2 weeks. Provides insurance, promotion and written contract.
Acceptable Work: Drawings, paintings, pastels and watercolors; all styles and subjects; series. Maximum size: 30x40". Payment is negotiable.

ROSELAND PUBLISHING CO., 1423 Armour Blvd., Mundelein IL 60060. President: Mark Rowland. Art publisher of limited edition handpulled original serigraphs. Clients: galleries, decorators and a distributor of wall accessories. Publishes 6 freelance artists/year. Pays royalty of 10% or negotiates payment method. Negotiates rights purchased. Provides promotion and shipping from firm. Send query letter and samples to be kept on file unless requested otherwise. Write for appointment to show portfolio. Prefers slides or photographs as samples. Samples not filed returned by SASE. Reports only if interested.
Acceptable Work: Considers pen & ink drawings, oils, acrylics, pastels, mixed media and serigraphs.
Tips: "Submit work that lends itself well to serigraphic reproduction. It should incorporate current decor color schemes and a clear, crisp, professional look."

*ROSENBAUM FINE ART CORP., 5171 NE 12th Ave., Ft. Lauderdale FL 33334. (305)772-1386. Chairman: Marvin Rosenbaum. Art publisher of limited editions. Clients: galleries. Publishes 20 freelance artists/year. Distributes work for 50 artists/year. Pays flat fee. Buys all rights. Provides shipping to firm and written contract. Send query letter with samples to be kept on file; write for appointment to show portfolio. Prefers slides as samples. Samples returned.
Acceptable Work: Considers pen & ink line drawings, oil and acrylic paintings, watercolors and mixed media; serigraphs and stone lithographs. Especially likes contemporary graphics.

*SPORTSMAN'S COLLECTION, INC., Box 23, Grafton OH 44044. (216)458-8498. Vice President Sales: Bill Kaatz. Art publisher and art distributor. Clients: galleries and corporations. Publishes 1 freelance artist/year. Works with 3-4 artists/year. Negotiates payment method. Sometimes offers advance. Negotiates rights purchased. Sometimes requires exclusive representation. Provides in-transit insurance, insurance while work is at firm, promotion, shipping from firm and written contract. Send query letter with brochure and samples to be kept on file; or write for appointment to show portfolio.

Prefers slides or photographs as samples. Samples not filed returned by SASE only if requested. Reports within 2 weeks.
Acceptable Work: Considers oil and acrylic paintings and watercolors. Especially likes wildlife themes.
Tips: "There is a demand for high quality wildlife posters and limited edition prints—landscape with wildlife."

*STERLING PORTFOLIO, INC., Box 236, Camstadt NJ 07072. (800)221-2119. Publisher: Lois Wagner. Art publisher of limited editions and offset reproductions. Clients: galleries, museums and individuals. Publishes 3 freelance artists/year. Negotiates payment method. Buys reprint rights. Provides promotion and shipping to and from firm. Send query letter with brochure, resume and samples to be kept on file; or write for appointment to show portfolio. Prefers slides or tear sheets as samples. Reports within several weeks.
Acceptable Work: Considers oil paintings and watercolors. Wants only representational subjects— landscapes or figurative work.

*STUDIO HOUSE EDITONS, 415 W. Superior, Chicago IL 60610. (312)751-0974. Director: Bill Sosin. Art publisher of offset reproductions. Clients: galleries. Publishes 7 freelance artists/year. Distributes 15 artists/year. Negotiates payment method and rights purchased. Provides promotion. Send query letter with brochure and samples to be kept on file. Prefers slides as samples. Samples not filed returned only if requested. Reports only if interested.
Acceptable Work: Photographs; stone lithographs and plate lithographs. Especially likes decor themes or styles.
Tips: "Send only high quality transparent duplicates of best work."

*JOHN SZOKE GRAPHICS INC., 164 Mercer St., New York NY 10012. Director: John Szoke. Produces limited edition handpulled originals for galleries, museums and private collectors. Publishes 10-25 artists/year. Charges commission or negotiates royalties. Offers advance. Provides promotion and written contract. Publisher owns original art. Arrange interview or submit slides. SASE. Reports within 1 week.

TRIG GRAPHICS, 145 Palisade St., Dobbs Ferry NY 10522. (914)693-6700. Contact: Laura Gardner. Art publisher/dealer. Publishes art exhibition posters using offset lithography and silkscreen for galleries, museum shops, bookstores and interior designers. Pays flat fee or negotiates payment. Offers advance. Buys reprint rights. Provides in-transit insurance, promotion and written contract. Artist owns original art. Send query letter with samples to be kept on file. Call or write for appointment to show portfolio. Send slides first, then originals. Samples returned by SASE if requested. Reports only if interested.
Acceptable Work: Considers oil and acrylic paintings, pastels, watercolors and photography. Prefers individual works of art, pairs or series. No maximum required.
Tips: We see a current trend toward "more decorative images." Artists should have a definite "grasp of the marketplace" before they try to sell their work.

TRITON PRESS, 263 Ninth Ave., New York NY 10001. (212)255-3703. President: Derek Limbocker. Director: Rosina Lardieri. Art publishers, fine art printers. Publishes and prints limited editions by collotype (continuous tone direct printing process) and collolith (combination of collotype and offset lithography) for galleries. Publishes 5 freelance artists/year. Negotiates royalties. Buys reprint rights. Provides written contract. Artist owns original art. Send query letter with brochure, resume and tear sheets to be kept on file; also send samples. Write for appointment to show portfolio. Prefers slides as samples. Samples returned. Reports within "a few" weeks.
Acceptable Work: Considers oil and acrylic paintings and watercolors. Prefers landscapes without recognizable figures; Western subjects; Oriental subjects. Prefers individual works of art.
Tips: "Send slides and resumes first."

VALLEY COTTAGE GRAPHICS, Box 564, Valley Cottage NY 10989. (914)358-7605 or 358-7606; or (800)431-2902. Contact: Ms. Claire Scafa or Ms. Sheila Berkowitz. Publishes "top of the line" unlimited edition posters and prints. Clients: galleries and custom frame shops nationwide. Buys reproduction rights (exclusively) and/or negotiates exclusive distribution rights to "special, innovative, existing fine art publications." Query first; submit slides, photographs of unpublished originals, or samples of published pieces available for exclusive distribution. Reports within 2-3 weeks.
Acceptable Work: Prefers large, contemporary pieces; 18x24'', 22x28'', 24x36''.

VERKERKE REPRODUCTIONS USA., INC., Walnut St., Norwood NJ 07648. (201)768-0601 or (800)526-0300. Assistant to the President: Diana E. Scheele. Art publisher/distributor of limited and

unlimited editions. Clients: galleries, department stores, gift stores. Works with 300 artists/year. Payment method is negotiated. Offers advance. Negotiates rights purchased. Provides insurance while work is at firm, promotion, shipping to and from firm and a written contract. Send query with brochure and samples to be kept on file. Call for appointment to show portfolio. Prefers photographs, tear sheets or original work as samples. Samples not filed returned only if requested. Reports within 2 months.
Acceptable Work: Considers mixed media.
Tips: "Please do *not* submit unsolicited work without contacting us beforehand."

*VIVA GRAPHICS, 10612 Culver Blvd., Culver City CA 90232. (213)202-1336. President: Janet Ames. Art publisher of offset reproductions and handpulled originals. Clients: galleries, frame shops, designers and department stores. Publishes at least 1 freelance artist/year. Negotiates payment method, advance and rights purchased. Provides insurance while work is at firm, promotion, shipping from firm and written contract. "We provide our full resources and energy to make the venture successful for all." Send resume and photogrpahs; or call or write for appointment to show portfolio. "Samples of original work are always best but not always feasible so photos on slides will help to determine if there is initial interest on our part." Samples not filed are returned by SASE. Reports within 1 month.
Acceptable Work: Considers oil and acrylic paintings, pastels, watercolors and mixed media. "We are looking for the new and different that will work decoratively in today's market."
Tips: "Please, please do not waste our time and yours with submissions of religious art, nudes or portraiture."

VOYAGEUR ART, 2828 Anthony Ln. S, Minneapolis MN 55418. (612)788-2253. Contact: Lowell Thompson and James Knuckey. Art publisher. Produces limited and unlimited edition offset lithograph reproductions for galleries, frameshops, corporations and retail outlets. Payment method is negotiated. Buys one-time rights "with certain restrictions." Provides in-transit insurance, insurance while work is at publisher, promotion, shipping to and from publisher and a written contract. Send query letter with brochure, resume, samples and tear sheets to be kept on file unless return of samples or originals is requested. Write for appointment to show portfolio. Prefers original work, slides or colored prints as samples; "before final publishing agreement, original art must be seen."
Acceptable Work: Considers oil and acrylic paintings, pastels, watercolors and mixed media. Prefers wildlife, Western, landscape, human interest subjects, flowers as themes; "generally all subject matter," limited edition, open edition and posters.
Tips: "Be professional in your approach and send samples of only your very best work. Your letter should include your goals as an artist. We see continued growth and broadening of the market as more people begin to buy art. Proliferation of prints is subsiding as people become more selective. This is good in the long run for the market and art business."

*EDWARD WESTON EDITIONS, 19355 Business Center Dr., Northridge CA 91324. (818)885-1044. Vice President/Secretary: Ann Weston. Art publisher, distributor and gallery handling limited and unlimited editions, offset reproductions and handpulled originals. Publishes 6 freelance artists/year. Distributes work for 30 artists/year. Pays flat fee; in royalty of 10% of lowest selling price; or negotiates payment method. Sometimes offers advance. Buys first rights, all rights, reprint rights or negotiates rights purchased. Requires exclusive representation. Provides promotion and written contract. Send brochure and samples to be kept on file; or write for appointment to show portfolio. Prefers original work as samples. Samples not filed returned by SASE. Reports within 2 months.
Acceptable Work: Considers all media. Especially likes "new, different, unusual techniques and style."

*THE WINN CORPORATION, Box 80096, Seattle WA 98108. (206)763-9544. President: Larry Winn. Art publisher and distributor of limited editions, offset reproductions and handpulled originals. Clients: interior designers, art galleries, frame shops, architects, art consultants, corporations, hotels, etc. Publishes 10 freelance artists/year (prints). Distributes work for 120 artists/year (posters). Negotiates payment method. Offers advance. Negotiates rights purchased. Requires exclusive representation. Provides in-transit insurance, insurance while work is at firm, promotion, shipping from firm and written contract. Send query letter with resume and slides. Slides returned by SASE. Reports within 1 month.
Acceptable Work: Considers pen & ink line drawings, oil and acrylic paintings, pastels, watercolors and mixed media; serigraphs, stone lithographs, plate lithographs, woodcuts and linocuts. Especially interested in "good design and contemporary imagery."

Appendix

The Business of Freelancing

For most artists striving to get ahead in the freelance graphic art market, desire—while necessary—is not enough. Talent and good art skills are requisites, as are consistency and flexibility in completing the various assignments you receive. Of almost equal importance to all these qualities combined is a sense of professionalism and knowledge of the business aspect of freelancing. The information that follows provides general guidelines covering basic areas of business. Use this Appendix to approach a market, submit work and handle your freelance business knowledgeably and professionally.

The Sample Package

Your sample package, whether offered through the mail or at an inperson review, is the silent salesman for your talent and skills and must be compiled with conscientious planning, research, a monetary and time commitment, and consideration for the art director's role.

For peak effectiveness, keep in mind first, the editing of your samples to apply to the market area and specific firm you're approaching. Research done ahead of time communicates to an art director that you're sincerely interested in selling to his firm and are businesslike in marketing your work. Second, when considering the number of samples, go for quality not quantity. Weak samples dilute the overall impression of a package. Third, an art director's time is precious to him, so your package must have an immediate and positive visual impact (cleanliness, neatness, legibility), be convenient to open and to review, and contain information to facilitate his contacting you.

Mailed submissions are absentee presentations and thus must be the most critically compiled. A typical mailed sample package contains a cover letter, business card, samples and a self-addressed, stamped envelope (SASE). Optional materials are a brochure that contains examples of your work (especially if samples are to be returned), a self-addressed, stamped reply card (with check-off responses to prompt action), a resume (often not necessary unless specifically requested by an *Artist's Market* listing) and a client list (especially if past experience increases assignment possibilities).

A cover letter should be typed on your letterhead, never longer than one page, and concisely state who you are, what you do, what services you can provide and what follow-up (if any) you plan to make. Indicate whether samples are to be returned or filed; if they are to be returned, be sure your SASE contains sufficient postage. (Enclose International Reply Coupons, not domestic stamps, for return of samples from foreign countries.) If they are to be filed and you have not included a reply card, your SASE may be a #10 legal size envelope for a letter response.

Your samples shouldn't scatter when removed from the envelope. An acetate cover with a plastic spine holds samples together and keeps them free of fingerprints. The book-like quality of the the presentation allows a quick, simple and manageable review. Folders with pockets or paper clips can be used, but each of these necessitates separating the samples for review. All samples should be no larger than 8½x11'' so that they fit easily into a standard file.

If you're putting together a portfolio of original artwork, the case should be serviceable and easy to carry, with or without a ring binder. If you plan to mail your portfolio, purchase a case that has puncture-proof sides.

Most likely you will not leave these samples for an art director's file, so time and money should be invested to have them mounted and acetate covered. Tear sheets accompanying the originals can be mounted and laminated or simply laminated. Apply information regarding each piece to the back or include a separate reference sheet. Firms frequently need to know an artist's ability for problem solving (particularly in design), depth of involvement in a project and time needed for completion.

Always leave behind printed material for the art director's file to keep his memory fresh regarding your style and the services you provide.

Types of Samples/Labeling

The types of samples most commonly requested by art buyers are slides or transparencies, photographs, photostats, photocopies, tear sheets and original work. With the first four types you are submitting a copy of your artwork, so your goal is to have as accurate a reproduction as possible within the limitations of the process. Original artwork should be submitted *only* if mandatory. It is too valuable to treat carelessly and casually, and even with an SASE the return of your work is *not* guaranteed.

When considering what type of samples to submit, take these factors into consideration: 1) whether the art buyer has requested a specific type of sample; 2) the amount you have to invest financially; 3) whether your original is color or black-and-white; 4) the number of duplicates you are having made; 5) whether the samples are to be returned or kept on file; and 6) your marketing area.

Color work will most accurately be depicted by either photographs or transparencies (a transparency is a positive image on a translucent film base; a slide is a 35mm transparency in a mount.) Transparencies reproduce a greater range of tones than any method of printing and can be made in varying sizes, even as large as 8x10''.

Always check your original slides and photographs, whether taken by you or a professional photographer, to be sure that: 1) the background is of a neutral color and not distracting to the work; 2) there is nothing in the film's frame but the artwork and a small amount of background; 3) the colors are as close as possible to the original work; 4) the work is in focus; 5) light areas have a little texture and dark areas are distinct and rich; 6) it is the best possible reproduction of your work. Request cardboard mounts for slides. Plastic has been known to melt in projectors and glass breaks too easily.

If working with a professional photographer, find out before he begins what his policy is if you want work reshot to meet your criteria. Some photographers will reshoot until you are pleased; some charge a reduced fee for the extra work, while others demand full payment as if the work had never been done.

If you are having duplicates made of your prints or transparencies, get to know a reliable camera store or processing lab. Check with other artists in your area and see where they have had good results. Try just one of your shots and judge its duplicates—check that the color accuracy holds up through each copy. If there are problems, see if they can be worked out and listen to any suggestions offered.

Black-and-white artwork lends itself readily to photocopies and photostats at less cost than prints and transparencies. A photostat is obtained by a special machine which uses a camera and inexpensive, high contrast, opaque paper on a roll. Original work can be reduced or enlarged, and glossy paper gives a sharp, crisp reproduction. Photocopying is the reproduction method most readily available and gives a black-and-white copy on regular paper stock, seldom with the same "snap" of a photostat. Some machines now offer reduction and enlargement within limitations. Although cheapest, photocopies must have a dark, consistent black, no blurred edges and no superfluous scratches on the paper to be considered appropriate for samples.

Color work can be photostated and photocopied, but on these black-and-white machines colors reproduce as various shades of gray. Color photocopiers will render the various colors of your original work, but the accuracy depends on how well the machine is adjusted. Photostating is more expensive than photocopying; color photocopies more expensive than black-and-white. Photostatic copying and photocopying service firms can be found in the Yellow Pages.

If samples are to be kept on file or are being used only to show examples of your style, you may want to invest in some of the less expensive forms of reproduction, but only if you feel they accurately convey your product to the art buyer. If not, then you're better off to invest in the more expensive methods to land the assignments you want. The price often goes down the more duplicates you have made of prints and transparencies. You may not get these price breaks on photostating or photocopying.

Remember your market—if you are approaching a slick, top-notch ad agency or magazine complete with viewing rooms and several art directors, you will want your sample package to reflect not only your talent but your understanding of what will be expected of you as a competing professional. If your chosen market is smaller or more laid-back, your samples might receive more attention if they are good quality photostats that can be viewed quickly by one person, not requiring inaccessible (or perhaps nonexistent) equipment.

Original work seldom should be sent unsolicited through the mail. In black-and-white work, art buyers often can work with a photostat or *very* good quality photocopy and may never need the original.

Label everything! With photographs, photostats and photocopies, use the back to list your name, address and phone number (a pre-printed label hurries this process); arrows indicating which way is up; the size of the original; and, if submitting several, mark each "1 of 5 photostats (photographs, photocopies)," "2 of 5 photostats," etc. These numbers may also refer to a separate information sheet. If you send one, add "see info sheet" under the number.

Slides are labeled in similar fashion. On the "front" (image is correct when held up to a light), list your last name, size of original work, medium, number, "see info sheet" (if applicable) and arrows indicating the top. Your full name, address and phone number may be printed on the reverse side.

Plastic sleeves are available in photography, art supply and stationery stores for holding photographs and slides. If sending only a few samples, cut the plastic sleeve to correctly accommodate them.

Packaging

Your primary goal in packaging is to have your work or samples arrive undamaged. Before packaging original work make sure you have a copy (photograph, photostat, photocopy, slide or transparency) in your file at home. If changes are necessary on an assigned job, you can then see on your copy what the art director is discussing over the phone. Most important, if your work is lost you can make a duplicate.

If working on an assignment, allow mailing time in your production schedule.

With today's overnight services, this will not necessarily have to be a great consideration, but one which must be kept in mind.

Flat work can be packaged between heavy cardboard or styrofoam. Cut the material slightly larger than the piece of flatwork and tape it closed. It is wise to include your business card or a piece of paper with your name and address on it on the outside of this packaging material in case the outer wrapper becomes separated from the inner packing. The work at least can then be returned to you.

The outer wrapping, depending on package size and quality of inner wrapping, may be a manila envelope, a foam padded envelope, a "bubble" envelope (one with plastic "bubbles" lining the inside), or brown wrapping paper. Use reinforced tape for closures. Make sure *one* side is clearly addressed.

Check the various types of envelopes and packaging material available at your local art supply, photography or stationery stores. Don't miss the opportunity to buy in bulk quantities if you are going to be doing a lot of mailing. The price is always lower.

Mailing

Become familiar with the types of mailing available. Your local post office has an information number for your questions and will be glad to provide you the information you need.

The U.S. Post Office mail classifications with which you will be most concerned are First Class and Fourth Class, more commonly called parcel post.

First Class mail is the type used every day for letters, etc. If the piece you are mailing is not the usual letter size, make sure to mark it First Class. Fourth Class is used for packages weighing 1-40 pounds and not more than 84 inches in length and girth combined.

The greatest disadvantage to using these classes of mail is that you cannot be guaranteed when the package/letter will arrive. If time is important to you, consider the special services the post office offers, such as, Priority Mail, Express Mail Next Day Service, and Special Delivery.

Certified mail includes a mailing receipt and provides a record of delivery at the addressee's post office. This type of mail is handled like ordinary mail, but you can request a return receipt on certain types of mail as your proof of delivery.

The post office offers insurance for a nominal cost.

United Parcel Service (UPS) will accept packages up to 50 pounds in weight and 108" length and girth combined. Cost is determined by weight, size and destination of the package and automatically includes insurance up to $100. You can purchase additional insurance.

UPS does have wrapping restrictions. Packages must be in heavy corrugated cardboard, with no string or paper on the outside, and be sealed with reinforced tape. UPS cannot guarantee how long it will take a package to arrive at its destination, but will track lost packages. It also offers Two-Day Blue Label Air Service to any destination in the U.S., and Next Day Service in specific zip code zones. Check locally to see if Next Day Service is available for your package. There is an additional charge for these services and for package pickup.

Today there is a growing number of airfreight services which make overnight delivery common. Check to see which ones are available in your area, but some of the more familiar names are Emery, Purolator and Federal Express. These firms offer varying rates according to weight of the package and urgency.

If you will be airfreighting large numbers of works or portfolios, it is advisable to set up an account. Most have priority service which offers overnight delivery direct to the client, or regular service which is delivery within two days. Some companies offer both an airfreight service and a ground courier service. The advantages of airfreight are the guaranteed delivery time and efficiency in tracking missing packages. The cost reflects these added services.

Greyhound Bus Lines and some commerical airlines also offer same-day or overnight package delivery. Check locally for rates and restrictions.

Pricing and Negotiation

Pricing can be a stumbling block for a freelancer and each job will present the artist with a new and different pricing situation. However, some basic considerations for establishing a price are: the rights sold; complexity of the project; the turnaround time or time needed for completion; how widely the project is being used (local, national or worldwide); the client's project budget; the ownership of the original art; use of an expense account; the going rate in that market area for similar projects; and the artist's reputation, skill and experience.

Negotiation is the art of reaching a mutual agreement so that both parties feel satisfied with the outcome. When a client details a project to you, you are hearing the client's needs and wants. He will never know (nor is it his responsibility to know) *your* needs and wants unless *you* speak up.

Experience is often the best teacher, but even in the beginning there are a few rules you can follow. First and foremost, *relax*. You're not out to win at all costs, but rather to work cooperatively *with* your client toward a common solution. Convey a positive attitude and listen carefully. Try to put yourself in your client's place so you "hear" what he is really saying. When you speak, do it slowly and distinctly which will force a rushed art buyer to slow down and listen to *you*. Most important, know your artist's rights and industry ethics thoroughly so you're a knowledgeable negotiator.

Contracts

In simplest terms, a contract is an agreement between two or more persons containing an offer, acceptance and consideration (each party giving something of value). Contracts may be written, oral or tacit, but to protect yourself most from misunderstanding and faulty memories, make it a practice to have a *written* contract *signed* and *dated* by you and the party you are dealing with.

Written contracts need not be extremely complicated forms—they can be as simple as a letter or note from you to your client listing the terms you have agreed upon verbally. The wisest move is to ask your client to sign the letter and return it to you; however, action taken on his part that is in accordance with the conditions of the agreement, such as sending you written instructions, etc., may also be interpreted as acceptance.

Read carefully any contract or purchase order you are asked to sign. If the terms are very complex or if you do not understand them, seek professional advice *before* signing. If it is a pre-printed or "standard" contract look for terms within the copy which may not be agreeable to you such as "work-for-hire."

The items you want specified in your contract will vary according to the assignment and complexity of the project, but some basics are: your fee (basic fee and possibly kill fees, payment schedule, advances, expense compensation, etc.); service (an exact and specific description of what you are providing for the fee); usage (an exact and specific description of how the work may be used); and return of the original art. You may also wish to specify deadlines, how changes will be handled and/or compensated, etc.

Further information on contracts can be obtained from *Selling Your Graphic Design & Illustration* by Tad Crawford and Arie Kopelman.

Record Keeping

All your talent and art skills will mean nothing when it comes time to give an accounting of your business' profitability or when the IRS demands tax returns, if you haven't kept good business records.

It is usually the part least liked by artists, yet you have to realize that the free-lancer is an independent businessperson and is held accountable as such.

The record keeping of daily expenses and income does not have to be an elabo-rate setup of ledgers. You can accomplish a satisfactory record by having two note-books—one marked *accounts receivable* or money paid or owed you for work you have created, and the other marked *accounts payable*, or money you have spent on supplies, studio rent, fuel, etc.

The accounts receivable book should have areas for listing each project com-pleted, the date it was completed, to whom it was delivered, the delivery date, the price of the job, the amount you received, the date you received it and any further re-marks you think are necessary, such as rights sold.

The accounts payable book should include entries for work supplies pur-chased, the quantity, the cost, the date of the bill, the amount you paid, the date you paid it and any further remarks necessary. Save all bills and receipts.

This simple method of keeping track of your business will enable you to know how much you are bringing in versus your expenses. The most important thing is not to let a month's worth of statements and bills pile up—you will find yourself hope-lessly lost and forgetting to enter information.

Begin to develop standard business practices. Ask for a receipt with every pur-chase. If possible, keep a separate checking account for business expenses alone. Cancelled checks not only help keep accurate records, but serve as evidence if a payment is challenged.

Don't forget to record driving expenses. A diary in the car helps you keep an ac-curate log of mileage, especially when on a local trip for supplies, etc. As long as your drive was business-related, you have a legitimate expenditure and tax deduc-tion.

Are you entertaining a client at a business dinner? Keep a record of the date, place, cost, business relationship and the purpose of the meeting. Use your car diary to record these transactions immediately. Don't hesitate to ask the waiter or cashier for a receipt—it's a common business practice.

Even if you are not sure in some cases if a particular expense qualifies as a busi-ness-related tax deduction, obtain a receipt or bill. A tax advisor can clarify it for you later and it is always better to be safe than sorry.

If your business is very complex, you can have books set up for you by an ac-countant and continue the record keeping yourself. Retain your business records for at least four years.

Developing a file for each job is a good way to keep track of expenses. Drop in all related receipts and you can then determine if your fee was sufficient to cover these expenses and give you a profit. When preparing an invoice, you will have all perti-nent material in one place. Place a copy of the invoice in the job file as well as re-cords of payments and you can keep track of billing.

Taxes

First you must convince the Internal Revenue Service (IRS) that you are con-ducting a business and not a hobby. This can be helped by keeping a separate busi-ness checking account, letterhead stationery and accurate bookkeeping. Then as a self-employed person, you are allowed business-related deductions which reduce the amount of taxable income you have to report, such as mileage for business trips, overnight lodging, depreciation on equipment, etc. You will be filing Schedule C of Form 1040, Profit (or Loss) from Business or Profession.

Depending on the complexity of your business and tax expertise, you may want to have a professional tax advisor to consult with or to complete your tax form. Skill levels vary among tax consultants so whom you choose depends on the amount of help you need and what you can afford. Those with the most training and skills will generally command the highest fees.

Most IRS offices have walk-in centers open year-round and offer over 90 free IRS publications containing tax information to help in preparation of your return. Be aware, however, that no matter what information you are given at an IRS office, it is still your responsibility to see that your return is correct.

The booklet that comes with your tax return forms contains names and addresses of Forms Distribution Centers by region where you can write for further information. Some post offices also carry a limited supply of forms.

The U.S. Small Business Administration can offer some assistance in supplying information on taxes. Contact your nearest SBA District Office. Many workshops are held by arts organizations around the country covering business management, often including detailed tax information. Inquire at your arts council, local arts organizations or a nearby college/university to see if a workshop is scheduled.

You will be asked to provide your Social Security number or your Employer Identification number (if you are a business) to the person/firm for whom you are doing a freelance project. This information is now necessary in order for payment to be made.

As this publication is going to press major tax reforms are being discussed. Anticipated changes will take effect sometime in 1986.

Home Office Deduction

The Tax Reform Act of 1976 narrowed the opportunities for a taxpayer to be eligible for the home office deduction, restricting it to where the home office was the principal site of business and used on a regular, exclusive basis for the business. A taxpayer could claim only one principal place of business; thus anyone with a full-time job, plus operating an art business out of his home, could not claim both as a principal place of business.

The rule has now been liberalized somewhat to permit taxpayers to claim the deduction if the space is used *exclusively* and *regularly* as a principal place of business "including a secondary trade or business." Thus, the taxpayer with more than one business can claim a principal place of business for each and claim a deduction for the studio at home. The factors taken into consideration by the IRS are the amount of income produced, the amount of time spent there and the nature of the facility. In some areas of the country, a studio can even share the same space with a nonbusiness use as long as a clearly defined area is used exclusively for business.

When a studio is a part of the principal residence, deductions are possible on an appropriate portion of mortgage interest, property taxes, rent, repair and utility bills, and depreciation.

When a studio is in a structure separate from the principal residence, requirements to obtain the deduction are less stringent.

However, check into the rule carefully to see if you *qualify* for the deduction. Consult a tax advisor to be certain you meet all of the requirements before attempting to take this deduction since its requirements and interpretations frequently change.

Copyright

Copyright protection for works of art has been made less confusing by the copyright law of 1978. With this law, the copyright to a piece of art is automatic from the moment of creation—it belongs to the artist immediately.

Copyright protection prevents unauthorized copying, selling or other infringements on your work of art. You do not have to register your work with the U.S. Copyright Office until an infringement takes place. However, if you want to collect damages and attorney's fees, you have to register it within 3 months of publication. To protect yourself as much as possible and to avoid the risk of losing your copyright after publication, place a copyright notice on your work as soon as it is created.

The copyright notice is a c with a circle around it ©, followed by the year date and your name or an abbreviation by which your name can be recognized—You can place the copyright notice on any accessible place, such as the back of a framed piece, but the front is preferable for commercial art. Definitely have your copyright notice on any work you are submitting to a noncopyrighted publication.

Your copyright can only be transferred in writing and you or someone acting on your behalf must sign the transfer.

There are two exceptions to owning the copyright to a work from the moment of its creation. They are when you create work as part of your fulltime employment for someone else or when you agree to "work-for-hire," i.e., you're working for a client *as if* you are a fulltime employee. Then you own neither the copyright nor any of the reproduction rights to your work. Opposition by artists to work-for-hire is growing nationwide. Contact your state art council, national art organizations, and state and federal legislators to determine what legislation is being considered to change work-for-hire.

It is not difficult to register your work. Write to the U.S. Copyright Office, Library of Congress, Washington, DC 20559. You will be asked to complete the appropriate forms and send them with the required fee ($10 per individual published piece or for a group of unpublished pieces) and copies or photos of your work. You will receive a certificate of registration which offers you more indepth protection if you anticipate legal problems than the copyright notice alone. You can also write and request the Copyright Information Kit, which explains copyright in more detail.

To receive a free guideline on copyright regulations and procedures for cartoons and comic strips, write for Circular R44, Information & Publication Section LM-455, U.S. Copyright Office, Library of Congress, Washington DC 20559.

An Artist's Handbook on Copyright is available for $6.95 (price includes postage and handling) from the Georgia Volunteer Lawyers for the Arts, Inc., Suite 521, 32 Peachtree St. NW, Atlanta GA 30303.

Reproduction Rights

When you sell "rights" to your work, you are selling the reproduction rights inherent in your ownership of the copyright. You are telling the art buyer how he can use your work, thus maintaining control over where and how it appears. The more rights you sell to one client, the more money you should receive. Negotiate this upfront with the art buyer *before* an agreement is signed.

If you sell first reproduction rights, you are giving the art buyer the right to reproduce your work once and to be the first to use it. You cannot sell first rights to two buyers—each cannot be "first." This differs from one-time rights, which mean the art buyer has the right to reproduce your work once, but he does not have to be first. Once the buyer has used the rights he purchased, he has no further claim to your work. If he wants to use it a second or third time, he must pay additional fees for that privilege.

Try to ascertain the use the buyer wishes to make of the artwork so that the rights sold can be worded accordingly. A publisher, for example, may ask for all rights but may actually only *need* first North American serial rights. Your immediate compensation may be less, but once he has published it you can sell the use of the artwork to other buyers which you could not do if the publisher owned all rights.

When you sell all reproduction rights, you are essentially allowing the buyer to reproduce the artwork as many times and in any way he wishes. You may still possess the original work, but the art buyer owns the reproduction rights to it and the financial compensation to you should reflect what you have sold.

Always know what rights you are selling. Contact and become involved in the Graphic Artists Guild (30 E. 20th St., New York NY 10003), which now includes the Cartoonists Guild, or other professional organizations for guidance in the areas of copyright and contracts. For further information consult *Legal Guide for the Visual Artist*, by Tad Crawford, *Selling Your Graphic Design & Illustration*, and *Pricing and Ethical Guidelines*, available from the Graphic Artists Guild.

Artist's Resource List ⸺⸺

The following list is a veritable goldmine for the freelance graphic artist. These publications—directories, magazines, books and tabloids—offer thousands of listings of art buyers. Read the section introductions in this directory to find out which art market is served by which publication. The bullets by the directories indicate that they are available in business or reference libraries. The remaining publications are available either from the publisher or in a bookstore. To insure accurate names and addresses, use copies of these resources that are no older than three years.

- **AIA Journal**, The American Institute of Architects, 457 Madison Ave., New York NY 10022

  Advertising Age, 740 Rush St., Chicago IL 60611

  Adweek, A/S/M Communications, Inc., 820 Second Ave., New York NY 10017
- **American Theatre Association Directory**, 6th floor, 1010 Wisconsin Ave. NW, Washington DC 20007

  Architectural Digest, Knapp Communications Corp., 5900 Wilshire Blvd., Los Angeles CA 90036

  Architectural Record, McGraw-Hill Inc., 1221 Avenue of the Americas, New York NY 10020

  The Art and Craft of Greeting Cards by Susan Evarts, North Light Publishing, 9933 Alliance Rd., Cincinnati OH 45242

  Art Business News, Myers Publishing Co., 2135 Summer St., Stamford CT 06905
- **Audio Video Market Place**, R.R. Bowker Company, 205 E. 42nd St., New York NY 10017
- **Ayer Directory of Publications**, IMS Press, 426 Pennsylvania Ave., Ft. Washington PA 19034
- **Barron's Profiles of American Colleges**, Barron's Educational Series, Inc., 113 Crossways Park Dr., Woodbury NY 11797

  Better Homes & Gardens, Meredith Corporation, Locust at 17th, Des Moines IA 50336

  Billboard International Buyer's Guide, Billboard Publications, 1515 Broadway, New York NY 10035
- **Books In Print**, vol. 4, R.R. Bowker Company, 205 E. 42nd St., New York NY 10017

  Collector's Mart, WEB Publications, Inc., 15100 W. Kellogg, Wichita KS 67235
- **Comparative Guide to American Colleges**, Harper & Row, 10 E. 53rd St., New York NY 10022

  Dancemagazine, Dance Magazine Inc., 33 W. 60th St., New York NY 10036

  Decor Source List, Commerce Publishing Co., 408 Olive St., St. Louis MO 63102
- **The Design Directory**, Wefler & Associates, Inc., Box 1591, Evanston IL 60204

  Designing Greeting Cards and Paper Products by Ron Lister, Prentice-Hall, Inc., Englewood Cliffs NJ 07632
- **Directory of Directories**, Gale Research Co., Book Tower, Detroit MI 48226

  Editor & Publisher, The Editor & Publisher Co. Inc., 575 Lexington Ave., New York NY 10022

  Editor & Publisher's Syndicate Directory, The Editor & Publisher Co. Inc., 575 Lexington Ave., New York NY 10022
- **Encyclopedia of Associations**, Gale Research Co., Book Tower, Detroit MI 48226

  Figurine Magazine, Collectors Media Inc., Box 1729, San Marcos TX 78667-1729
- **Gebbie Press All-In-One-Directory**, Gebbie Press, Box 1000, New Paltz NY 12561

  Gifts and Decorative Accessories, Geyer-McAllister Publications, 51 Madison Ave., New York NY 10010. Buyer's guide and December issue.

  Greetings Magazine, MacKay Publishing Corp., 309 Fifth Ave., New York NY 10016

Homesewing Trade News, E-Z Maid Inc., 330 Sunrise Hwy., Box 286, Rockville Centre NY 11571

House and Garden, The Conde Nast Publications, Inc., Conde Nast Bldg., 350 Madison Ave., New York NY 10017

House Beautiful, Hearst Corporation, 1700 Broadway, New York NY 10019

Interior Design, Whitney Communications Corp., 850 Third Ave., New York NY 10017

● **Internal Publications Directory**, National Research Bureau, Suite 1150, 310 S. Michigan Ave., Chicago IL 60604

● **International Directory of Little Magazines and Small Presses**, Dustbooks, Box 100, Paradise CA 95969

Legal Guide for the Visual Artist, E.P. Dutton, Two Park Ave., New York NY 10016

● **Literary Market Place**, R.R. Bowker Company, 205 E. 42nd St., New York NY 10017

● **The Magazine Directory**, National Research Bureau, Suite 1150, 310 S. Michigan Ave., Chicago IL 60604

● **Magazine Industry Market Place**, R.R. Bowker Company, 205 E. 42nd St., New York NY 10017

Medical Marketing & Media, CPS Communications, Inc., Box 3011, Boca Raton FL 33431. December issue.

● **Music Industry Directory**, Marquis Professional Publications, 200 E. Ohio St., Chicago IL 60611

● **Musical America Directory**, ABC Leisure Magazines Inc., 825 Seventh Ave., New York NY 10019

● **The Newspaper Directory**, National Research Bureau, Suite 1150, 310 S. Michigan Ave., Chicago IL 60604

● **O'Dwyer's Directory of Public Relations Firms**, J.R. O'Dwyer Company, Inc., 271 Madison Ave., New York NY 10016

Plate World, Plate World Inc., 6054 W. Touhy Ave., Chicago IL 60648

Publishers Weekly, 1180 Avenue of the Americas, New York NY 10036

Selling Your Graphic Design & Illustration, St. Martin's Press, 175 Fifth Ave., New York NY 10010

Songwriter's Market 1986, Writer's Digest Books, 9933 Alliance Rd., Cincinnati OH 45242

● **Standard Directory of Advertising Agencies**, National Register Publishing Co., Inc., 5201 Old Orchard Rd., Skokie IL 60077

● **Standard Rate and Data Service**, 3004 Glenview Rd., Wilmette IL 60091. Consumer magazine volume.

● **Summer Theatre Directory**, Leo Shull Publications, 1501 Broadway, New York NY 10036

Theatre Profiles, Theatre Communications Group, Inc., 355 Lexington Ave., New York NY 10017

● **Thomas Register of Manufacturers**, Thomas Publishing Co., 1 Penn Plaza, New York NY 10001

● **Ulrich's International Periodicals Directory**, R.R. Bowker Company, 205 E. 42nd St., New York NY 10017

Visual Merchandising & Store Design, Signs of the Times Publishing Company, 407 Gilbert Ave., Cincinnati OH 45202

W, Fairchild Publications, 7 E. 12th St., New York NY 10003

Women's Wear Daily, Fairchild Publications, 7 E. 12th St., New York NY 10003

Writer's Market 1986, Writer's Digest Books, 9933 Alliance Rd., Cincinnati OH 45242

Glossary

Acceptance (payment on). The artist is paid for his work as soon as the buyer decides to use it.

Airbrush. Small pencil-shaped pressure gun used to spray ink, paint or dyes to obtain graduated tonal effects.

ASAP. Abbreviation for as soon as possible.

Ben-day. An artificial process of shading line illustrations, named after its inventor.

Biennially. Once every two years.

Bimonthly. Once every two months.

Biweekly. Once every two weeks.

Buy-out. The sale of all reproduction rights, and sometimes the original work, by the artist.

Calligraphy. The art of fine handwriting.

Camera-ready. Art that is completely prepared for copy camera platemaking.

Cel art. Artwork applied to plastic film, especially used in animation; also an abbreviation for artwork on celluoid.

Cibachrome. Trade name for a full color positive print made from a transparency.

Collaterals. Accompanying or auxiliary pieces, especially in advertising.

Collotype. A screenless, flat, printing process in which plates are coated with gelatin, exposed to continuous-tone negatives and printed on lithographic presses.

Color separation. Process of preparing artwork for the printer by separating one color from another by using overlays of transparent or translucent material for each color.

Commission. 1. Percentage of retail price taken by a sponsor/salesman on artwork sold. 2. Assignment given to an artist.

Comprehensive. Complete sketch of layout showing how a finished illustration will look when printed; also called a comp.

Direct-mail package. Sales or promotional material that is distributed by mail. Usually consists of an outer envelope, a cover letter, brochure or flyer, SASE, and postpaid reply card, or order form with business reply envelope.

Edition. The total number of prints published of one piece of art.

Elhi. Abbreviation for elementary/high school.

Gagline. The words usually printed directly beneath a cartoon; also called a caption.

Gouache. Opaque watercolor with definite, appreciable film thickness and an actual paint layer.

Halftone. Reproduction of a continuous tone illustration with the image formed by dots produced by a camera lens screen.

IRC. International Reply Coupon; purchased at the post office to enclose with artwork sent to a foreign buyer to cover his postage cost when replying.

Keyline. Identification, through signs and symbols, of the positions of illustrations and copy for the printer.

Kill fee. Portion of the agreed-upon price the artist receives for a job that was assigned, started, but then canceled.

Layout. Arrangement of photographs, illustrations, text and headlines for printed material.

Light table. Table with a light source beneath a glass top; especially useful in transferring art by tracing.

Line drawing. Illustration done with pencil or ink using no wash or other shading.

Lithography. Printing process based on a design made with a greasy substance on a limestone slab or metal plate and chemically treated so image areas take ink and non-image areas repel ink; during printing, non-image areas are kept wet with water.

Logotype.   Name or design of a company or product used as a trademark on letterheads, direct mail packages, in advertising, etc., to establish visual identity; also called logo.

Mechanicals.   Paste-up or preparation of work for printing.

Ms, mss.   Abbreviation for manuscript(s).

Offset.   Printing process in which a flat printing plate is treated to be ink-receptive in image areas and ink-repellent in non-image areas. Ink is transferred from the printing plate to a rubber plate, and then to the paper.

Overlay.   Transparent cover over copy, where instructions, corrections or color location directions are given.

Panel.   In cartooning, refers to the number of boxed-in illustrations, i.e. single panel, double panel or multi-panel.

Paste-up.   Procedure involving coating the backside of art, type, photostats, etc., with rubber cement or wax and adhering them in their proper positions to the mechanical board. The boards are then used as finished art by the printer.

Perspective.   The ability to see objects in relation to their relative positions and distance, and depict the volume and spatial relationships on paper.

Photostat.   Black-and-white copies produced by an inexpensive photographic process using paper negatives; only line values are held with accuracy. Also called stat.

Pin registration.   The use of highly accurate holes and special pins on copy, film, plates and presses to insure proper positioning and alignment of colors.

P-O-P.   Point-of-purchase; a display device or structure located with the product in or at the retail outlet to advertise or hold the product to increase sales.

Publication (payment on).   The artist is paid for his work when it is published.

Query.   Letter of inquiry to an editor or buyer eliciting his interest in a work you want to do or sell.

Rendering.   A drawn representation of a building, interior, etc., in perspective.

Roughs.   Preliminary sketches or drawings.

Royalty.   An agreed percentage paid by the publisher to the artist for each copy of his work sold.

SASE.   Abbreviation for self-addressed, stamped envelope.

Semiannual.   Once every six months.

Semimonthly.   Once every two weeks.

Semiweekly.   Twice a week.

Serigraph.   Silkscreen; stencil method of printing involving a stencil adhered to a fine mesh cloth and stretched tightly over a wooden frame. Paint is forced through the holes of the screen not blocked by the stencil.

Simultaneous submissions.   Submission of the same artwork to more than one potential buyer at the same time.

Speculation.   Creating artwork with no assurance that the buyer will purchase it or reimburse expenses in any way, as opposed to creating artwork on assignment.

Spot drawing.   Small illustration used to decorate or enhance a page of type, or to serve as a column ending.

Storyboard.   Series of panels which illustrates a progressive sequence of graphics and story copy for a TV commercial, film or filmstrip. Serves as a guide for the eventual finished product.

Tabloid.   Publication where an ordinary newspaper page is turned sideways.

Tear sheet.   Published page containing an artist's illustration, cartoon, design or photograph.

Template.   Plastic stencil containing various sizes of commonly used shapes, symbols or letters which can be traced one at a time.

Type spec.   Type specification; determination of the size and style of type to be used in a layout.

Velox.   Photoprint of a continuous tone subject that has been transformed into line art by means of a halftone screen.

Video.   General category comprised of videocassettes and videotapes.

Wash.   Thin application of transparent color, or watercolor black, for a pastel or gray tonal effect.

Index

Other Books of Interest

Graphic Arts

The Art & Craft of Greeting Cards, by Susan Evarts, $13.95 (paper)
The Complete Airbrush & Photoretouching Manual, by Peter Owen & John Sutcliffe, $19.95 (cloth)
Graphics Handbook, by Howard Munce, $11.95 (paper)
How to Draw & Sell Cartoons, by Ross Thomson & Bill Hewison, $14.95 (cloth)
The Print Production Handbook, by David Bann, $14.95 (cloth)

The Business of Art/Art Reference

Living By Your Brush Alone, by Edna W. Piersol, $9.95 (paper)
North Light Dictionary of Art Terms, by Margy Lee Elspass, $10.95 (paper)

Drawing

Drawing By Sea & River, by John Croney, $14.95 (cloth)
Drawing for Pleasure, edited by Peter D. Johnson, $15.95 (cloth)
Encyclopaedia of Drawing, by Clive Ashwin, $22.50 (cloth)
The Figure, edited by Walt Reed, $14.95 (paper)
Keys to Drawing, by Bert Dodson, $19.95 (cloth)
The Pencil, by Paul Calle, $15.95 (paper)
Perspective in Art, by Michael Woods, $12.95 (cloth)

Watercolor

Basic Watercolor Painting, by Judith Campbell-Reed, $14.95 (paper)
Painting Flowers in Watercolor, by Ethel Todd George, $16.95 (paper)
Painting in Watercolors, edited by Yvonne Deutsch, $18.95 (cloth)
Transparent Watercolor, by Edward D. Walker, $24.95 (cloth)
Watercolor Energies, by Frank Webb, $16.95 (paper)
Watercolor—The Creative Experience, by Barbara Nechis, $14.95 (paper)

Mixed Media

Basic Course in Design, by Ray Prohaska, $12.95 (paper)
The Basis of Successful Art: Concept & Composition, by Fritz Henning, $16.95 (paper)
Catching Light in Your Paintings, by Charles Sovek, $22.50 (cloth)
Drawing and Painting Animals, by Fritz Henning, $14.95 (paper)
Drawing and Painting Buildings, by Reggie Stanton, $19.95 (cloth)
Exploring Color, by Nita Leland, $26.95 (cloth)
The Eye of the Artist, by Jack Clifton, $14.95 (paper)
Painting & Drawing Boats, by Moira Huntley, $16.95 (paper)
Painting a Likeness, by Douglas Graves, $19.95 (cloth)
Painting Floral Still Lifes, by Joyce Pike, $19.95 (cloth)
Painting Nature, by Franklin Jones, $17.95 (paper)
Painting with Pastels, edited by Peter D. Johnson, $16.95 (cloth)
The Roller Art Book, by Sig Purwin, $11.95 (paper)
The Techniques of Wood Sculpture, by David Orchard, $12.95 (cloth)

Oils

Controlled Painting, by Frank Covino, $14.95 (paper)
Encyclopaedia of Oil Painting, by Frederick Palmer, $22.50 (cloth)
Painting in Oils, edited by Michael Bowers, $18.95 (cloth)

To order directly from the publisher, include $2.00 postage and handling for one book and 50¢ for each additional book. Allow 30 days for delivery.

Writer's Digest Books
9933 Alliance Road
Cincinnati, OH 45242

Prices subject to change without notice.